Southwest USA

**Las Vegas
& Nevada**
p58

Utah
p351

Arizona
p111

New Mexico
p234

Hugh McNaughtan, Carolyn McCarthy,
Christopher Pitts, Benedict Walker

GOLDEN EAGLE P503

SANTA FE P254

Contents

TUCSON P208

PHOTO BY MIRKO LIU / GETTY IMAGES / MOMENT RF ©

ARCHES NATIONAL PAR
P379

Contents

BRYCE CANYON NATIONAL PARK P399

UNDERSTAND

SURVIVAL GUIDE

SPECIAL FEATURES

Welcome to Southwest USA

The Southwest is America's untamed playground, luring adventurous travelers with thrilling red-rock landscapes, the legends of shoot-'em-up cowboys and the kicky delights of green-chile stew.

Nature's Glory

Beauty and adventure are a fun-loving team in the Southwest. They crank up the rapids, unleash the singletrack, add blooms to the trail and drape a sunset across red rocks. This captivating mix of scenery and possibility lures travelers who want to rejuvenate physically, mentally and spiritually. The big draw is the Grand Canyon, a two-billion-year-old wonder that shares its geologic treasures with a healthy dose of fun. Next door in Utah and Nevada, the red rocks will nourish your soul while thrashing your bike. In New Mexico, skiing the steeps and climbing peaks never looked so good.

History You Can Touch

The Southwest wears its history on its big, sandy sleeve. A decade before the Pilgrims even landed at Plymouth Rock, Santa Fe was already a capital city – albeit in what was then another country. Dig quite a bit deeper and you'll find the oldest ruins north of Mexico: the great houses in Chaco Canyon, the cliff houses at Mesa Verde and numerous others sites scattered throughout the Four Corners. The descendants of these early cultures now live in Pueblo villages at Hopi, Acoma, Taos and elsewhere, the oldest continuously inhabited homes in the United States.

A Multicultural Mash-Up

The arrival of the Spanish missionaries and settlers – and their subsequent interactions and conflicts over the centuries with the Pueblos, Navajo, Apache and, eventually, the Americans – laid the foundations for the unique multicultural mix that defines the Southwest today. Tribal traditions and imagery influence art across the region. Cowboys still roam the landscape, and their cultural legacy remains apparent in fashion, festivals and local attitudes. And Hispanic and Mexican cultures, of course, remain an integral part of daily life, from the place names, language and food to headlines about immigration.

Savouring the Southwest

Green-chile cheeseburgers and red-chile posole in New Mexico. Sonoran dogs and huevos rancheros in Tucson. Regional specialties are pleasingly diverse in the Southwest and sampling homegrown fare is a big reason to get excited about an upcoming trip. Top restaurants are increasingly focused on fresh and locally grown fare – and providing a solid selection of craft brews. The ever-expanding crop of small batch breweries, distilleries and vineyards that have taken the region by storm provide the perfect accompaniment to those smothered blue-corn enchiladas or the gastronomic excesses of Vegas.

Why I Love Southwest USA

By Christopher Pitts, Writer

In this part of the world, it's easy to tap into that sense that we're all a part of something bigger: the expansive vistas from atop a mesa that stretch to the edge of a curving Earth, the transcendent arc of the Milky Way spanning the night sky. The hundreds of millions of geological years that unfold as your eye follows a canyon wall downwards, and the howls of coyotes that send a shiver down your spine as you soak in a hot spring. Adventure, beauty and hardscrabble life – they're all reasons I love the Southwest, and why you will too.

For more about our writers, see p544

Above: Grand Canyon National Park (p160)

Southwest USA

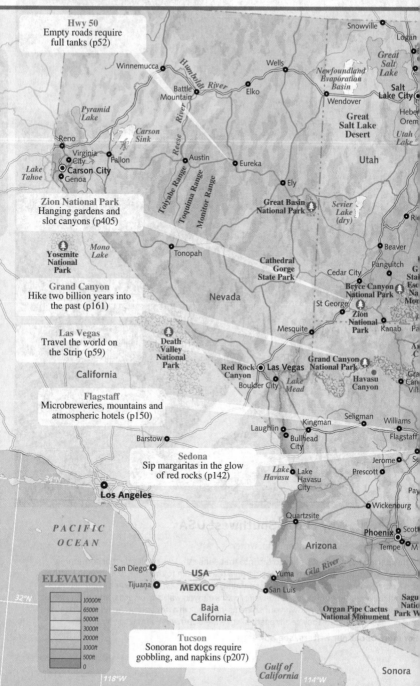

Hwy 50
Empty roads require full tanks (p52)

Zion National Park
Hanging gardens and slot canyons (p405)

Grand Canyon
Hike two billion years into the past (p161)

Las Vegas
Travel the world on the Strip (p59)

Flagstaff
Microbreweries, mountains and atmospheric hotels (p150)

Sedona
Sip margaritas in the glow of red rocks (p142)

Tucson
Sonoran hot dogs require gobbling, and napkins (p207)

ELEVATION

10000ft
6500ft
5000ft
3000ft
2000ft
1000ft
500ft
0

Snowville
Logan
Great Salt Lake
Newfoundland Evaporation Basin
Salt Lake City
Heber
Orem
Utah Lake
Great Salt Lake Desert
Wells
Winnemucca
Humboldt River
Battle Mountain
Elko
Wendover
Pyramid Lake
Reno
Carson Sink
Reese River
Austin
Eureka
Virginia City
Fallon
Utah
Ri
Lake Tahoe
Genoa
Carson City
Ely
Sevier Lake (dry)
Great Basin National Park
Toiyabe Range
Toquima Range
Monitor Range
Beaver
Yosemite National Park
Mono Lake
Tonopah
Cathedral Gorge State Park
Cedar City
Panguitch
G Sta Esc Na Mon
Bryce Canyon National Park
Nevada
St George
Zion National Park
Kanab
Pa
Mesquite
Ar C
California
Death Valley National Park
Red Rock Canyon
Las Vegas
Grand Canyon National Park
Gra Can Vill
Boulder City
Lake Mead
Havasu Canyon
Seligman
Williams
Kingman
Laughlin
Flagstaff
Barstow
Bullhead City
Jerome
Se
Lake Havasu
Lake Havasu City
Prescott
Los Angeles
Pay
Wickenburg
PACIFIC OCEAN
Quartzsite
Phoenix
Scot
Arizona
Tempe
M
San Diego
USA
Yuma
Gila River
Tijuana
MEXICO
San Luis
Baja California
Sagu Natio Park W
Organ Pipe Cactus National Monument
Tucson
Sonoran hot dogs require gobbling, and napkins (p207)
Gulf of California
Sonora
34°N
32°N
118°W
114°W

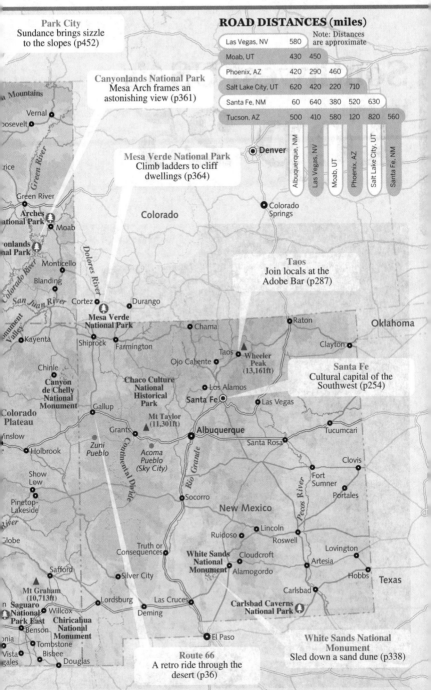

Park City
Sundance brings sizzle to the slopes (p452)

Canyonlands National Park
Mesa Arch frames an astonishing view (p361)

Mesa Verde National Park
Climb ladders to cliff dwellings (p364)

Taos
Join locals at the Adobe Bar (p287)

Santa Fe
Cultural capital of the Southwest (p254)

Route 66
A retro ride through the desert (p36)

White Sands National Monument
Sled down a sand dune (p338)

ROAD DISTANCES (miles)

Note: Distances are approximate

	Albuquerque, NM	Las Vegas, NV	Moab, UT	Phoenix, AZ	Salt Lake City, UT	Santa Fe, NM
Las Vegas, NV	580					
Moab, UT	430	450				
Phoenix, AZ	420	290	460			
Salt Lake City, UT	620	420	220	710		
Santa Fe, NM	60	640	380	520	630	
Tucson, AZ	500	410	580	120	820	560

Vernal
osevelt

a Mountains

rice

Green River

Arches
ational Park

Moab

onlands
nal Park

Monticello

Blanding

Cortez

Durango

Mesa Verde
National Park

ument
ley

Kayenta

Shiprock   Farmington

Chinle

Canyon
de Chelly
National
Monument

Gallup

Colorado
Plateau

inslow

Holbrook

Show
Low

Pinetop-
Lakeside

iver

lobe

Safford

Mt Graham
(10,713ft)

n
National
Park East

Saguaro

Willcox

Benson

onia

Vista
gales

Tombstone

Bisbee

Douglas

Chiricahua
National
Monument

Lordsburg

Deming

Silver City

Las Cruces

El Paso

Denver

Colorado

Colorado
Springs

Raton   Oklahoma

Chama

Clayton

Ojo Caliente   Taos   Wheeler
Peak
(13,161ft)

Chaco Culture
National
Historical
Park

Los Alamos

Santa Fe

Las Vegas

Mt Taylor
(11,301ft)

Grants

Albuquerque

Tucumcari

Zuni
Pueblo

Acoma
Pueblo
(Sky City)

Santa Rosa

Clovis

Fort
Sumner

Portales

Socorro

New Mexico

Ruidoso   Lincoln

Roswell

Truth or
Consequences

White Sands
National
Monument

Cloudcroft

Alamogordo

Lovington

Artesia

Hobbs   Texas

Carlsbad

Carlsbad Caverns
National Park

Green River

Dolores River

Colorado River

San Juan River

Rio Grande

Pecos River

Continental Divide

Southwest USA's
Top 25

Grand Canyon National Park

1 The sheer immensity of the Grand Canyon (p160) is what grabs you first: it's a two-billion-year-old rip across the landscape that reveals the Earth's geologic secrets with commanding authority. But it's Mother Nature's artistic touches – from sun-dappled ridges and striated cliffs to lush oases and a ribbon-like river – that hold your attention and demand your return. Whether you're peering over the edge from the North Rim or backpacking to Phantom Ranch, you'll likely agree with Theodore Roosevelt: this is a natural wonder 'unparalleled throughout the rest of the world.'

Route 66

2 As you step up to the counter at the Snow Cap Drive-In in Seligman, AZ, you know a prank is coming – a squirt of fake mustard or ridiculously incorrect change. And though it's all a bit hokey, you'd be disappointed if the owner forgot to 'get you'. It's these kitschy, down-home touches that make the Mother Road (p36) so memorable. Begging burros, the Wigwam Motel, the neon of Tucumcari – you gotta have something to break up the scrubby Southwest plains. We'll take a squirt of fake mustard over a mass-consumption McBurger every time.

Bottom right: Santa Rosa, NM (p348)

ILEXIMAGE / GETTY IMAGES ©

ALAN COPSON / GETTY IMAGES ©

Santa Fe

3 Although Santa Fe (p254) is more than 400 years old, its sense of style remains timeless. On Friday nights, art lovers flock to Canyon Rd to gab with artists, sip wine and explore more than 100 galleries and shops. Art and history partner up within the city's consortium of museums, with international crafts, American Indian art, Modernist collections and a history museum competing for attention. With that turquoise sky overhead and the Sangre de Cristos as a backdrop, dining and shopping by the Plaza isn't just satisfying, it's sublime.

Angels Landing (Zion)

4 The climb to Angels Landing (p412) i among the most memorable day hike in the Southwest, if not North America. T 5-mile trail hugs the face of a towering cli snakes through a cool canyon and climbs up Walter's Wiggles (a series of 21 sharp switchbacks) before finally ascending a narrow, exposed ridge – where steel chair and the encouraging words of strangers a your only friends. Your reward after the fir scramble to the 5790ft summit? A lofty vi of Zion Canyon and some unreal photos o your vertigo-defying adventure.

WHIT RICHARDSON / GETTY IMAGES ©

TYPHOONSKI / GETTY IMAGES ©

as Vegas

5 Just as you awaken from your in-flight [na]p – rested, content, [re]ady for red-rock inspira[ti]on – here comes Vegas [(p](59) on the horizon, like [a]showgirl looking for [tr]ouble. As you leave the [air]port and glide beneath [th]e neon of the Strip, she [pu]ts on a dazzling show: [da]ncing fountains, a spew[in]g volcano, the Eiffel [To]wer. But she saves her [m]ost dangerous charms [fo]r the gambling dens – [se]ductive lairs where [th]e fresh-pumped air [an]d hypnotic swirl share [th]e goal: separating you [fr]om your money. Step [a]way if you can for fine [re]staurants and dazzling [e]ntertainment.

Moab

6 Moab (p368) is the mountain-biking capital of the world, where the desert slickrock surrounding the town makes a perfect 'sticky' surface for knobbly tires. Challenging trails ascend steep bluffs, twist through forests and slam over 4WD roads into the wilds of canyon country. And you'll surely redefine adventure after treading the roller-coaster rock face of the 12.7-mile Slickrock Bike Trail. There's a reason why some Moab hotels have showers for bikes. One trip and you'll be hooked.

Arizona's Old-West Towns

7 If you judge an Old West town by the quality of its nickname, then Jerome (p138), once known as the Wickedest Town in the West, and Tombstone, the Town too Tough to Die, are the most fascinating spots in Arizona. While Bisbee's moniker – Queen of the Copper Camps – isn't quite as intriguing, the town shares key traits with the others: a rough-and-tumble mining past, a remote location capping a scenic drive, and a quirky cast of entrepreneurial citizens putting their spin on galleries, B&Bs and restaurants. Pardner, they're truly the best of the West.

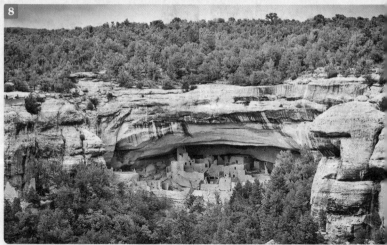

Mesa Verde National Park

8 You don't just walk into the past at Mesa Verde (p364), the site of 600 ancient cliff dwellings. You scramble up 10ft ladders, scale a 60ft rock face, and crawl 12ft through a tunnel. Yes, it's interactive exploring at its most low tech, but it's also one of the most exhilarating adventures in the Southwest. It's also a place to puzzle out the clues left by its former inhabitants – Ancestral Puebloans vacated the site in AD 1300 for reasons still not fully understood.

Monument Valley & Navajo Nation

9 'May I walk in beauty' is the final line of a famous Navajo prayer. Beauty comes in many forms on the Navajo's vas reservation, making a famous appearance at Monument Valley (p191), a majestic cluster of buttes and spires. Beauty swoops in on the wings of birds at Canyo de Chelly, a sandstone valley where farm ers till the land near age-old cliff dwelling Elsewhere, beauty is in the connections, from the docent explaining Navajo clans the waiter offering a welcoming smile.

...eblos

10 Nineteen Indian Pueblos are scattered across New Mexico. These ...obe villages – sometimes rising several ...ries above the ground – offer a glimpse ... the distinct cultures of some of ...erica's oldest communities. Not all are ...rist attractions, but several offer unique ...eriences that may be among your most ...morable in the Southwest. Marvel at the ...sa-top views at Acoma, shop for jewelry ...Zuni and immerse yourself in history at ... Taos Pueblo (p298; pictured) – where ... fry bread makes a tasty distraction.

Rafting

11 Rafting the Colorado River (p168) through the Grand Canyon is a once-in-a-lifetime journey, but rafting in the Southwest isn't limited to bucket-list expeditions that last for a week or more. For a mellow float, take a relaxing ride on the Green River outside Moab, or look for wildlife alongside the Colorado River in Utah's Westwater Canyon. For an adrenaline rush, smash through Class V rapids on the Rio Grande through the Taos Box. Low-key, scenic or wild – the rafts and rivers here are worth a ride.

Arches & Canyonlands National Parks

12 More than 2000 sandstone formations cluster at Arches (p379), a cauldron of geologic wonders that includes a balanced rock, a swath of giant fins and one span that's so iconic it's on Utah license plates. Just south is equally stunning Canyonlands, a maze of plateaus, mesas and canyons as forbidding as it is beautiful. How best to understand the subtle power of the landscape? As ecowarrior Edward Abbey said, you won't see anything looking out of a car window. So get out, breathe in and walk.

Sedona

13 The beauty of the red rocks hits you on an elemental level. Yes, the jeep tours, crystal shops and chichi galleries add to the fun, but it's the crimson buttes – strange yet familiar – that make Sedona (p142) unique. Soak up th beauty by hiking to Airport Mesa, cyclin beneath Bell Rock or sliding across Oak Creek. New Agers might tell you to seek out the vortexes, which allegedly radiate the Earth's power, but even non-believer can appreciate the sacred nature of this breathtaking tableau. Bottom: West Fork Tra Oak Creek Canyon (p143)

ucson

14 Tucson (p208) may sprawl, yet it ll manages to feel like a hesive whole that's won-rfully eclectic. From the destrian-friendly anchor 4th Ave, you can walk st indie clothing bou-ues and live-music clubs at balance cowboy rock th East Coast punk. You n stop to eat at the place ere the chimichanga ginated, and then see a ow at a gothy burlesque b. With wheels, you can low the saguaros to their mesake park. Conclude th a Sonoran hot dog, a ste of delicious excess at epitomizes the city's lticultural heritage. ove left: Saguaro National rk (p210)

Taos

15 With its snowy peaks, crisp blue skies and steep-walled gorge, Taos (p287) makes a dazzling first impression. But the city is more than just a pretty face. Its rebellious, slightly groovy temperament springs from a long line of local artists, writers and innovators. See for yourself on a tour of the eye-catching Earth-ships or with a drink at the quirky Adobe Bar. Ski slopes, hiking trails and white-water rapids lure outdoor adventurers, while Taos Pueblo and diverse museums offer cultural distraction. One guaran-tee? You'll never get bored in Taos. Top right: Earthship dwelling (p289)

Bryce Canyon National Park

16 At sunrise and sun-set, the golden-red spires of Utah's smallest national park (p399) shim-mer like trees in a magical stone forest – a hypnotic, Tolkien-esque place that is surely inhabited by nimble elves and mischievous sprites. The otherworldly feeling continues as you navigate the maze of crum-bly hoodoos beside the 1.4-mile Navajo Loop trail, which drops 521ft from Sunset Point. Geologically, the park is magical too; the spires are the limestone edges of the Paunsaugunt Plateau – eroded by rain, shaped by freezing water.

LIYINUO / GETTY IMAGES ©

Hwy 50: America's Loneliest Road

17 You say you want to drop off the grid? Are you sure? Test your resolve on this desolate strip of pavement that stretches across the white-hot belly of Nevada. The highway (p92) passes through a poetic assort-ment of tumbleweed towns following the route of the Overland Stagecoach, the Pony Express and the first transcontinental telephone line. Today, it looks like the backdrop for a David Lynch film, with scrappy ghost towns, hardscrab-ble saloons, singing sand dunes and ancient petro-glyphs – keeping things more than a little off-kilter.

American Indian Art

18 American Indian art continues to thrive in the Southwest. While designs often have a ceremonial purpose or religious significance, the baskets, rugs and jewelry that are crafted today often put a fresh spin on the ancient traditions – in Phoenix's Heard Museum (p115), dedicated to South-west cultures, you'll even see pottery emblazed with a Harry Potter theme. From Hopi kachina dolls and Navajo rugs to Zuni jewelry and the baskets of the White Mountain Apaches, art is a window into the heart of the native South-west peoples.

Carlsbad Cavern National Park

19 As the elevator drops, it's hard to comprehend the ranger's words. Wait, what? We're plunging the length of the Empire State Building? I'm not sure that's such a great idea. But then the doors open, and look, there's a subterranean village down here (p347): a snack bar, water fountains, restroom and, most impressive, the 255ft-high Big Room where geologic wonders line a 1.25-mile path. But you're not the only one thinking it's cool – 400,000 Mexi-can free-tailed bats roost here from April to October, swooping out to feed at sunset.

ark City

20 Park City (p452), how'd you get be so cool? Sure, you sted events in the 2002 nter Olympics, and u're home to the US Ski am, but it's not just the w sports. There's the ndance Film Festival, ich draws enough glitati to keep the world uzz. We're also digging stylish restaurants; y serve fine cuisine but er take themselves too iously. Maybe that's key – it's a world-class stination comfortable h its small-town roots. nt: Park City Mountain Resort 53)

ERIK ISAISON / GETTY IMAGES / TETRA IMAGES RF ©

RICHARD CUMMINS / GETTY IMAGES ©

Phoenix

21 Sometimes you just have to ask: what about me? Phoenix (p114) answers that question with a stylish grin. Golfers have their pick of more than 200 courses. Posh resorts cater to families, honeymooners and even dear old Fido. The spas are just as decadent, offering aquatic massages, citrusy facials and healing desert-clay wraps. Add in world-class museums, patio-dining extraordinaire, chichi shopping, five professional sports teams, a surreal desert landscape and more than 300 days of sunshine, and it's easy to condone a little selfishness. Above left: Civic Space Park, Downtown Phoenix

White Sands National Monument

22 Frisbee on the dunes, colorful umbrellas in the sand, kids riding wind-blown swells – the only thing missing at this beach (p339) is the water. But you don't really mind its absence, not with 275 sq miles of gypsum draping the landscape with a hypnotic whiteness that rolls and rises across the New Mexico horizon. A 16-mile scenic drive loops past one-of-a-kind views, but to best get a handle on the place, full immersion is key: buy a sled at the gift store, trudge to the top of a dune, run a few steps and ... wheee!

Microbreweries

23 Outdoor towns and microbreweries – it's hard to imagine one without the other these days. Flagstaff. Moab. Bisbee. In all of these outposts the local breweries (p497) are the center of the action. And though they are spread far and wide across the region, these watering holes share a few commonalities: convivial beer drinkers, flavorful craft brews and cavernous drinking rooms that sme of malt and adventure. A when it comes to memor ble beer names, Wasatc Brew Pub & Brewery in Park City earns kudos fo its Polygamy Porter tagline: Why Have Just One

alt Lake City

24 Big city fun. Small town charm. Proximity to outdoor adventure. oking for a city with all three? To echo y founder Brigham Young: 'This is the ace.' Tourists and new residents are ooping in for epic hiking, climbing and ing. In the process they're infusing this rmon enclave with rebel spirit. For cades the populace was like its streets: derly and square, with the LDS influ- ce keeping change at bay. But no more. day the city (p430) hums with bustling ewpubs, eclectic restaurants and a urishing arts scene.

Flagstaff

25 Flagstaff (p150) is finally the per- fect Southwest town. For years this outdoorsy mecca – there's hiking, biking, skiing and stargazing – fell short of perfection due to the persistent blare of passing trains, up to 125 daily. Today, the horns have been silenced and Grand Canyon travelers can finally enjoy a decent night's sleep. Well rested? Stay longer to walk the vibrant downtown, loaded with ecofriendly restaurants, indie coffee shops, genial breweries and atmospheric hotels. It's a liberal-minded, energetic place fueled by students at North Arizona University – and it's ready to share the fun.

Need to Know

For more information, see Survival Guide (p511)

Currency
US dollar ($)

Languages
English, Spanish

Visas
Generally not required for stays of up to 90 days for countries in the Visa Waiver Program. ESTA required (apply online in advance).

Money
ATMs widely available in cities and towns, but less prevalent on American Indian land. Credit cards accepted in most hotels and restaurants.

Cell Phones
Cell-phone reception can be nonexistent in remote or mountainous areas and map apps can lead you astray.

Time
Arizona, Colorado, New Mexico and Utah are on Mountain Time (GMT/UTC minus seven hours). Nevada is on Pacific Time (GMT/UTC minus eight hours). Arizona does not observe Daylight Savings Time (DST).

When to Go

Salt Lake City
GO year-round

Las Vegas
GO year-round

Grand Canyon
GO Apr–May & Sep–Oct

Santa Fe
GO May–Oct

Phoenix
GO Oct–May

Desert, dry climate
Mild to hot summers, cold winters
Warm to hot summers, mild winters

High Season
➡ Summer temperatures (Jun–Aug) soar well above 100°F and national parks are at max capacity; higher elevations bring cool relief.

➡ In winter (Dec–Mar), hit the slopes in Utah and New Mexico; giddy-up at southern Arizona dude ranches.

Shoulder Season
➡ Fall (Sep–Nov) is the best season; check out colorful aspens in northern New Mexico.

➡ Cooler temperatures and lighter crowds (Apr–May, Sep–Nov) on the Grand Canyon South Rim.

Low Season
➡ National parks in Utah and northern Arizona clear out as the snow arrives (Dec–Mar).

➡ In summer (Jun–Aug), locals flee the heat in southern Arizona. Rates plummet at top resorts in Phoenix and Tucson.

Useful Websites

National Park Service (www.nps.gov) Current information about national parks.

Lonely Planet (www.lonelyplanet.com/usa/southwest) Destination information, hotel bookings, traveler forum and more.

Recreation.gov (www.recreation.gov) Camping and tour reservations on federally managed lands.

Grand Canyon Association (www.grandcanyon.org) Online bookstore with helpful links.

Important Numbers

If you need any kind of emergency assistance, call ☑911. Some rural phones might not have this service, in which case dial ☑0 for the operator and ask for emergency assistance.

Country code	☑1
International access code	☑011
Emergency	☑911
National sexual assault hotline	☑800-656-4673
Statewide road conditions	☑511

Exchange Rates

Australia	A$1	$0.78
Canada	C$1	$0.80
Europe	€1	$1.18
Japan	¥100	$0.90
Mexico	10 pesos	$0.53
New Zealand	NZ$1	$0.71
UK	£1	$1.33

For current exchange rates see www.xe.com.

Daily Costs

Budget: Less than $100

➡ Campgrounds and hostels: $10–45

➡ Food at markets, taquerias, sidewalk vendors: $7–12

➡ Economy car rental: $20 per day

Midrange: $100–250

➡ Mom-and-pop motels, low-priced chains: $50–100

➡ Diners, good local restaurants: $10–30

➡ Museums, national and state parks: $5–25

➡ Midsize car rental: $30 per day

Top End: More than $250

➡ Boutique hotels, B&Bs, resorts, park lodges: from $150

➡ Upscale restaurants: $30–75 plus drinks

➡ Guided adventures, top shows: from $100

➡ SUV or convertible rental: from $60 per day

Opening Hours

Opening hours vary throughout the year. Many attractions open longer in high season. We've provided high-season hours.

Banks 8:30am to 4:30pm Monday to Thursday, to 5:30pm Friday; some open 9am to 12:30pm Saturday

Bars 5pm to midnight, to 2am Friday and Saturday

Restaurants breakfast 7am to 10:30am Monday to Friday, brunch 9am to 2pm Saturday and Sunday, lunch 11:30am to 2:30pm Monday to Friday, dinner 5pm to 9:30pm, later Friday and Saturday

Stores 10am to 6pm Monday to Saturday, noon to 5pm Sunday

Arriving in Southwest USA

McCarran International Airport (Las Vegas, NV) Shuttles cost $11 to the Strip (35 to 40 minutes), and are available at exits 7 to 13 by the baggage claim in Terminal 1, and on Level Zero in Terminal 3. Taxis cost $23 to $28 to the Strip (30 minutes in heavy traffic).

Sky Harbor International Airport (Phoenix, AZ) Shuttles cost $18 to downtown (20 minutes), $21 to Old Town Scottsdale (30 minutes). Taxis are slightly faster and cost $23 to $30 to downtown, $30 to Old Town Scottsdale.

Getting Around

Car This is the best option for travelers who want to leave urban areas to explore national parks and more remote areas. Drive on the right.

Train Amtrak can be slow due to frequent delays. Travel by train can be a scenic way to travel between Los Angeles and a few tourist-track cities in Arizona and New Mexico.

Bus Cheaper and slower than trains; can be a good option for travel to cities not serviced by Amtrak.

Shuttle Commercial outfitters provide guided tours and van transportation to many national parks and scenic areas from nearby cities.

Helicopter Fly round-trip between Las Vegas and Hualapai Reservation and Skywalk.

For much more on **getting around**, see p522

If You Like...

Geology

The Southwest's geologic story starts with oceans, sediment and uplift, followed by millions of years of erosion – and it's all visible.

Grand Canyon A 277-mile river cuts through two-billion-year-old rock with geologic secrets that are layered and revealed within a mile-high stack. (p160)

Arches National Park Sweeping arcs of sandstone create windows on the snowy peaks and desert landscapes. (p379)

Chiricahua National Monument A rugged wonderland of rock chiseled by rain and wind into pinnacles, bridges and balanced rocks. (p230)

Bryce Canyon Pastel daggers, sorbet hoodoos and a maze of fins make up this geological wonderland. (p399)

Carlsbad Caverns An 800ft plunge to a subterranean wonderland. (p347)

Paria Canyon Slot canyons and rippling waves of desert slickrock. (p421)

White Sands National Monument The white and chalky gypsum sand dunes are, simply put, mesmerizing. (p339)

Hiking

As you descend the South Kaibab Trail past two billion years of geologic history, it's very easy to feel insignificant. The Southwest is a rambler's paradise, with scenery to satisfy every type of craving: mountain, riparian, desert and red rock.

Grand Canyon Trails The Rim Trail offers inspiring views, but hike into its depths to really appreciate the age and immensity of the canyon. (p165)

Zion National Park Slot canyons, hanging gardens and lofty scrambles make this stunner Utah's top national park for hiking. (p405)

Canyonlands Go off trail in the otherworldly Needles or get lost altogether in the Maze. (p361)

Sedona Hike to energy vortexes and red rocks at this breathtaking town and New Age pilgrimage site. (p142)

Sangre de Cristos Explore the New Mexico wilderness outside Santa Fe and Taos. (p263)

Piestewa Peak Stroll past saguaros and scale a 2608ft peak in the scrubby heart of Phoenix. (p122)

Art

The Southwest has inspired self-expression in all its forms. Today, former mining towns have re-emerged as artists' communities, and you'll find galleries and studios lining 1800s-era main streets.

Santa Fe Sidewalk artisans, chichi galleries and fabulous museums are framed by crisp skies and the Sangre de Cristos. (p254)

Heard Museum The art, craftsmanship and culture of Southwestern tribes earn the spotlight at this engaging Phoenix museum. (p115)

Ghost Ranch Captivating red-rock landscapes that Georgia O'Keeffe claimed as her own, near the town of Abiquiú. (p281)

Bellagio Gallery of Fine Art Art? On the Las Vegas Strip? You betcha, and the exhibits here draw from top museums and collections. (p62)

Jerome This former mining town lures weekend warriors with artist cooperatives, an art walk and one-of-a-kind gift shops. (p138)

Taos Contemporary artists at the Pueblo, fabulous historic museums in town. (p287)

Regional Cuisine

Up for a bit of culinary adventuring? Try some of the dishes associated with various cities, cultures and climates. Most of them are utterly delicious.

Green Chile Roasted and sold throughout New Mexico in fall. Hatch is the epicenter of all things chile. (p333)

Red Chile New Mexican specialty best enjoyed with a smothered enchilada or as a simple stew. (p266)

Sonoran Dog This Tucson specialty is a bacon-wrapped hot dog with cheese, pinto beans, salsa and more. (p218)

Prickly-Pear Margarita Bright pink elixir infused with syrup from the prickly-pear cactus. Enjoy one with a view at El Tovar. (p173)

Posole Hearty New Mexican stew made with hulled corn, red chile and pork. (p269)

Navajo Taco Topped fry bread served at Navajo restaurants and trading posts. (p160)

Wildlife

You'd be surprised how much wildlife you can see from your car – roadrunners, coyotes, elk and maybe a condor too.

Birdwatching Southern Arizona is the place to be in April, May and September. Migrating birds are attracted to its riparian forests. (p233)

Valles Caldera National Preserve Dormant crater of a supervolcano is home to New Mexico's largest elk herd. (p278)

Top: Hiker inside the Grand Canyon (p165)

Bottom: Zuni Pueblo dancers in traditional dress (p318)

Gila Wilderness Javelina, bear and trout live in this remote and rugged corner of New Mexico. (p328)

California Condors This prehistoric bird, recently on the verge of extinction, is making a comeback near the Vermilion Cliffs and in Zion. (p405)

Arizona-Sonora Desert Museum Education-minded wildlife repository spotlights desert creatures. (p212)

Snow Canyon State Park Gila monsters, roadrunners, desert tortoises and rattlesnakes – a perfect assembly of desert wildlife in Utah. (p427)

Historic Sights

Across the Southwest, dinosaurs left footprints, ancient civilizations left cliff dwellings and Apache warriors left lasting legacies. Many sights have barely changed over the centuries, making it easy to visualize how history unfolded.

Dinosaur National Monument Touch a 150-million-year-old fossil at one of the largest fossil beds in North America, discovered in 1909. (p424)

Mesa Verde Climb up to cliff dwellings that housed Ancestral Puebloans more than 700 years ago. (p364)

Fort Bowie Hike 1.5 miles into the past on your way to the fort at the center of the Apache Wars. (p232)

Picacho Peak State Park On April 15, 1862, this desolate place witnessed the westernmost battle of the Civil War. (p221)

Golden Spike National Historic Site Union Pacific Railroad and Central Pacific Railroad met here on May 10, 1869, completing the transcontinental railroad. (p444)

Bosque Redondo Memorial at Fort Sumner A tragic reminder of what was once a prison to some 9500 Navajo and Apache. (p350)

Kit Carson Home & Museum The iconic American mountain man, Carson's legacy is both complex and consuming. (p290)

Waterborne Adventure

Thank the big dams – Hoover, Glen Canyon and Parker – for the region's big lakes and their splashy activities. Paddle through white water, float on a plastic tube or chill by the pool – there's something here to fit your speed.

Grand Canyon Rafting the Colorado through the Big Ditch is the Southwest's most thrilling, iconic expedition. (p160)

Pools & Theme Parks Las Vegas pools are playgrounds for adults; Phoenix water parks are ideal splash grounds for kids. (p121)

Moab Rivers The Colorado and Green Rivers offer rafting, canoeing and kayaking. (p369)

Big Lakes Water-skiers zip across Lake Mead and houseboaters putter below crimson rocks on Lake Powell. (p89)

Navajo Dam Fabulous year-round fly fishing on the San Juan River in northwestern New Mexico. (p311)

The Old West

The legend of the Wild West has captured the imagination of writers, singers, filmmakers and travelers around the world.

Lincoln Billy the Kid's old stomping – and shooting – ground during the Lincoln County War. (p341)

Tombstone Famous for the Gunfight at the OK Corral, this dusty town is also home to Boothill Graveyard and the Bird Cage Theater. (p226)

Whiskey Row This block of Victorian-era saloons has survived fires and filmmakers. (p135)

Virginia City Sip beer in the Bucket of Blood Saloon then stroll the streets of this national historic landmark. (p106)

Mesilla Stop for a margarita or a wander around the historic adobe buildings outside Las Cruces. (p331)

Skiing

Skiing, snowboarding, snowshoeing, cross-country, backcountry snow-cat tours and ski mountaineering competitions: the Southwest has some of the best snow – and most fun – in the world.

Park City Park City and Canyons combine for more than 7000 acres of bliss and light, fluffy powder. (p453)

Salt Lake City Does Utah have the best skiing? Brighton, Alta, Solitude, Snowbird and 500in of powder annually say yes. (p447)

Taos New ownership and expansions on- and off-mountain are keeping the Taos steeps in the mix. (p299)

Lake Tahoe Has a dozen resorts, including Heavenly and Squaw Valley. (p109)

Cowboys on horseback in Tombstone (p226)

Wine & Craft Beers

Celebrate your adventures with a post-workout toast at brewpubs, microbreweries and wineries scattered across the region.

Marble Brewery A home away from home for New Mexico's beer nerds. (p248)

Alpine Pedaler Hop on this 14-passenger bicycle and pedal to breweries in Flagstaff. (p153)

Verde Valley Wine Country Home to an inviting Arizona wine trail that winds past wineries and vineyards in Cottonwood, Jerome and Cornville. (p134)

Spotted Dog Chill with a cold one in blistering hot Las Cruces. (p334)

Shopping

High-quality American Indian jewelry and crafts make shopping in the Southwest unique, plus there are many first-rate art galleries in New Mexico and Arizona.

Pueblos & Reservations Places such as the Taos Pueblo or Navajo Reservation are top spots to buy jewellery and crafts direct from artists. (p298)

Santa Fe Boutiques Eclectic specialty stores and 100-plus galleries dot the town. (p271)

Scottsdale Manolo up: we don't have *malls* in Scottsdale, we have promenades, commons and fashion squares. (p131)

The Strip Over-the-top goes over-the-top at Vegas' designer-label malls: Crystals at City Center and the Shoppes at Palazzo. (p59)

Singing Wind Bookshop Indie bookstore has everything you'll ever want to read about the Southwest, and a whole lot more. (p232)

Film Locations

From glowing red buttes to scrubby desert plains to the twinkling lights of Vegas, the landscape glows with cinematic appeal. It's simultaneously a place of refuge, unknown dangers and breathtaking beauty.

Monument Valley Stride John Wayne–tall beneath the iconic red monoliths that starred in seven of the Duke's beloved Westerns. (p191)

Las Vegas Bad boys and their high-jinks brought Sin City back to the big screen in *Oceans Eleven* and *The Hangover*. (p59)

Moab & Around Directors of *Thelma & Louise* and *127 Hours* shot their most dramatic scenes in nearby parks. (p368)

Kanab From *Stagecoach* to *Planet of the Apes*, Kanab has been a Hollywood favorite since the 1930s. (p417)

Very Large Array Twenty-seven giant antenna dishes look to the stars in extraterrestrial-themed movies such as *Contact* and *Cocoon*. (p322)

Cultural Diversity

American Indians and the descendants of Hispanic settlers and Mormon pioneers still live in the region, giving the Southwest a multicultural flair evident in its art, food and festivals.

Pueblos New Mexico's multilevel adobe villages, some up to 1000 years old, are home to a diverse array of American Indian peoples. (p240)

National Hispanic Cultural Center Galleries and a stage spotlight Hispanic arts. (p242)

Canyon de Chelly Learn about the history and traditions of the Navajo on a hike into this remote but stunning canyon. (p192)

Hopi Reservation The past and present merge atop the Hopi's long-inhabited mesas, the center of their spiritual world. (p194)

Mora Valley Off-the-beaten-track agricultural region in New Mexico, home to Hispanic farmers since the late 18th century. (p307)

Temple Square Trace the history of Mormon pioneers and their leaders on a 10-acre block in Salt Lake City. (p430)

The Kitsch & Kooky

There's a lot of empty space in the Southwest, and it draws the weird out of people: dinosaur sculptures, museums of the bizarre, and festivals that spotlight cannibals and desert creativity.

Route 66 This two-lane ode to Americana is dotted with wacky roadside attractions, especially in western Arizona. (p36)

Burning Man A temporary city in the Nevada desert attracts 61,000 for a week of self-expression and blowing sand. (p108)

Roswell, NM Did a UFO really crash outside Roswell in 1947? Explore whether the truth is out there. (p342)

Ogden Eccles Dinosaur Park Roadside dinosaurs at their kitschy, animatronic best. (p462)

Wacky museums View the death mask of John Dillinger in Bisbee, a prostitute's 'crib' in Tombstone and towering neon signs in Las Vegas. (p228)

Classical Gas Ancient gas pumps and neon signs make up this junkyard ode to Route 66. (p285)

Small-Town USA

The small towns of the Southwest may have been settled by ornery miners, greedy cattle barons and single-minded Mormon refugees, but today you'll find artist communities, outdoorsy outposts and a warm hello.

Bisbee One-time mining town merges artsy, grungy and quirky with thoroughly engaging flair. (p228)

Torrey Mecca for outdoor-lovers headed into Capital Reef National Park and home to pioneer buildings. (p388)

Billy the Kid National Scenic Byway Named for the outlaw, this scenic byway swoops past shoot-'em-up Lincoln, Smokey Bear's Capitan and woodsy Ruidoso. (p38)

Wickenburg Channels the 1890s with an ice-cream parlor, Old West museum and several dude ranches on the range. (p133)

Silver City Quirky, Old West town on the border of the Gila National Forest. (p326)

Month by Month

January

Artsy events such as film festivals and poetry readings will turn your mind from the cold, while snowbirds keep warm in Phoenix and Yuma. Ski season is kicking into gear.

☆ Cowboy Poetry

Wranglers and ropers gather in Elko, NV, for a week of poetry readings and folklore performances. Started in 1985, this event has inspired cowboy poetry gatherings across the region. (p99)

🎿 Sundance Film Festival

Hollywood moves to Park City in late January when aspiring filmmakers, actors and industry buffs gather for a week of cutting-edge films. (p457)

🏃 Fiesta Bowl

This college football bowl game is played at the University of Phoenix Stadium in Glendale, and usually takes place on either January 1 or December 31. It is part of the College Football Playoff and is accompanied by one of the largest parades in the Southwest. (p123)

February

It's all about playing in the snow in February, but if winter sports aren't your thing, head south for surreal cacti, pool lounging and warmer weather.

🔒 Tucson Gem Show

The largest mineral and gem show in the US is held over the second full weekend in February. More than 250 dealers sell jewelry, fossils, crafts and lots and lots of rocks. Lectures, seminars and a silent auction round out the weekend. (p214)

March

March is spring-break season in the US. Hordes of rowdy college students descend on Arizona's lakes while families head to the region's national parks and ski slopes. Lodging prices may jump in response.

◉ Wildflower Season

Depending on rainfall and elevation, spring (March through May) is wildflower season in the desert. Check www.desertusa.com for wildflower bloom reports at your favorite national and state parks.

🏃 Cactus League

Major league baseball fans have it good in March. Arizona hosts the preseason Cactus League (www.cactusleague.com), when some of the best pro teams play ball in Phoenix and Tucson.

☆ Mountain Music Festival

This nonprofit Phoenix music fest pulls in big names – think Beck, the Avett Brothers and Trombone Shorty – and donates the proceeds to local charities. Also a good spot to check out up-and-coming local bands. (p123)

April

Nature preserves lure birders, who scan for migrating favorites. Spring is also the season for outdoor art and music festivals. Runners might consider the Salt Lake City marathon.

🎿 Gathering of the Nations

More than 3000 American Indian dancers and singers from the US and Canada come together at the Gathering of Nations Powwow to compete in late April in Albuquerque, NM. There's also an Indian market with more than 800 artists and craftsmen. (p244)

May

May is a good time to enjoy pleasant weather and lighter crowds at many national parks. Southern Arizona starts to heat up. Memorial Day weekend marks the start of summer fun.

🏃 Route 66 Fun Run

Classic cars, not joggers, 'run' down Route 66 between Seligman and Golden Shores in early May. Roadster enthusiasts can check out the cars, vans and buses at the Powerhouse Visitor Center parking lot in Kingman on Saturday afternoon. (p201)

✨ Cinco de Mayo

Mexico's 1862 victory over the French in the Battle of Puebla is celebrated on May 5 with parades, dances, music, arts and crafts, and street fairs. And lots of Mexican beer.

June

School is out! High season begins across most of the Southwest. Look for rodeos and food and music festivals. Inner-tubers can now get their float on.

☆ Electric Daisy Carnival

The world's largest EDM (electronic dance music) fest, the Electric Daisy Carnival, is a nonstop three-night party with DJs, carnival rides, art installations and performers at the Las Vegas Motor Speedway. (p71)

☆ Utah Shakespeare Festival

The play's the thing in Cedar City, where visitors can enjoy a dramatic 'Shakesperience' with performances, literary seminars and educational backstage tours from mid-June to mid-October. (p422)

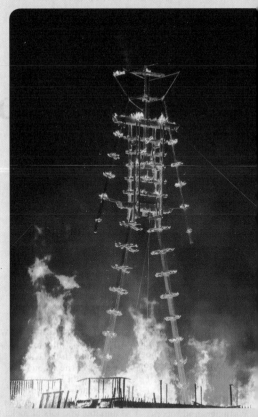

Top: Burning Man

Bottom: Balloon Fiesta

July

Summer is in full swing, with annual 4th of July celebrations across the country. It's hot enough to melt eyeballs in the desert, but the mountains offer cool respite – now's the time to hike the high country.

Independence Day

Cities and towns everywhere celebrate America's birth with music, parades and fireworks on the 4th of July. For something different, drive Route 66 to Oatman for the 4th of July sidewalk egg fry.

UFO Festival

Held over the 4th of July weekend, this festival beams down on Roswell, NM, with an otherworldly costume parade, extra-terrestrial speakers and workshops. (p343)

Poker World Series

Everyone from Hollywood celebs and European soccer players to professional gamblers and maybe even your next-door neighbor vie for millions from June through mid-July, with the main championship event taking place in mid-July.

August

This is the month to check out American Indian culture, with art fairs, markets and ceremonial gatherings in several cities and towns. Popular national parks are still booked up, but you can always find a place to pitch your tent.

Navajo Festival

Artists, dancers and storytellers share the customs and history of the Diné in Flagstaff in early August.

Santa Fe Indian Market

Only the best get approved to show their work at this top Santa Fe festival, held the third week of August on the historic plaza. Wander past exhibits by more than 1100 artists from 220-plus tribes and Pueblos. (p264)

September

It's back to school for the kiddies, which means lighter crowds at the national parks. Temperatures are becoming bearable again, making fall a particularly nice time for an overnight hike to the bottom of the Grand Canyon.

Burning Man

In 2016 some 70,000 people attended this outdoor celebration of self-expression known for its elaborate art displays, barter system, blowing sand and final burning of the man (www.burningman.org).

October

Shimmering aspens bring road-trippers to northern New Mexico for the annual fall show. Keep an eye out for goblins, ghouls and ghost tours as Halloween makes its annual peek-a-boo appearance.

Sedona Arts Festival

This fine-art show overflows with jewelry, ceramics, glass and sculptures in mid-October. One hundred and twenty-five artists exhibit their art at Sedona's Red Rock High School. (p146)

Balloon Fiesta

Albuquerque hosts the world's biggest gathering of hot-air balloons. The daily mass lift-offs inspire childlike awe. (p244)

November

Early-season ski deals abound, though you won't find any bargains around Thanksgiving weekend.

Dia de los Muertos

Mexican communities honor dead ancestors on November 2 with costumed parades, sugar skulls, graveyard picnics, candlelight processions and fabulous altars.

Festival of the Cranes

The Rocky Mountain Sandhill Crane spends the winter at Bosque del Apache National Wildlife Refuge. Mark the return of this red-crested bird with tours and workshops the weekend before Thanksgiving. (p322)

December

It's Christmas season in the Southwest, which means nativity pageants and holiday lights displays. It's also high season at resorts across the region, from Phoenix to ski towns.

Festival of Lights

Some 6000 luminaries twinkle in Tlaquepaque Arts & Crafts Village in mid-December in Sedona, with Santa Claus and live music.

Shalako

The most famous ceremony at the Zuni Pueblo, the all-night Shalako ceremonial dance welcomes the messengers of the rain gods. It's held around the first weekend in December.

Itineraries

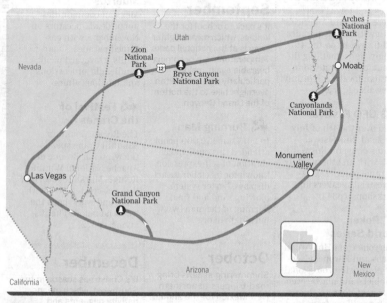

 Vegas, Grand Canyon & Southern Utah Loop

Want the biggest bang for your buck, and for your two-week vacation? Drive this scenic loop, which swings past the Southwest's most famous city, canyon and scenery.

Start in **Las Vegas** and dedicate two days to traveling the world on the Strip. When you've soaked up enough decadence, head east to canyon country – **Grand Canyon** country, that is. Spend a couple of days exploring America's most famous park. For a once-in-a-lifetime experience, descend into the South Rim on a mule and spend the night at Phantom Ranch on the canyon floor.

From the Grand Canyon head northeast through **Monument Valley**, with scenery straight out of a Hollywood Western, to the national parks in Utah's southeast corner – they're some of the most visually stunning in the country. Hike the shape-shifting slot canyons of **Canyonlands National Park**, watch the sun set in **Arches National Park**, or mountain-bike sick slickrock outside **Moab**. Then drive Hwy 12, a spectacular stretch of pavement sweeping in **Bryce Canyon National Park**, followed by **Zion National Park** on Hwy 9. Continue west to I-15 and follow it south to Las Vegas.

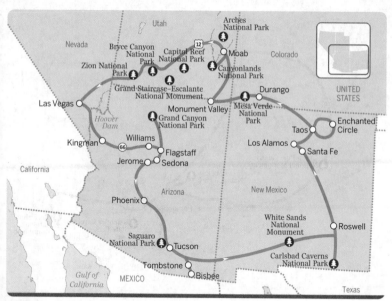

Grand Tour

Grab cowboy boots or walking shoes and get ready to ride. This trip covers geographic, historic and scenic highlights. If you're curious and outdoorsy, this trip is for you.

Roll the dice for two days on the **Las Vegas Strip** then cross the Mike O'Callaghan–Pat Tillman Memorial Bridge, 900ft above the Colorado River and the second-highest bridge in the US. Be sure to ogle **Hoover Dam** as you swoop into Arizona. Next is Route 66, which chases trains and Burma-Shave signs as it unfurls between the historic highway towns of **Kingman** and **Williams**. Regroup in funky **Flagstaff** before venturing into **Grand Canyon National Park**, where a hike is a must-do. After three days, end the week among the red rocks of **Sedona**.

Head south for shabby-chic in **Jerome**. Drive to **Phoenix** for two days of shopping and museums. Next mellow out on 4th Ave, **Tucson**, study cacti at **Saguaro National Park** and fancy yourself a gunslinger in **Tombstone**. End the week in charming **Bisbee**.

Next is New Mexico: sled down sand dunes in **White Sands National Monument**, spend a day exploring caves at **Carlsbad Caverns National Park**, then head to **Roswell** to ponder its UFO mysteries. Spend two days in **Santa Fe**, a foodie haven and art-fiend magnet. Atomic-age secrets are revealed at **Los Alamos**, followed by laid-back musings of hippies and ski bums just north in **Taos**. Drive the luscious **Enchanted Circle** then duck into Colorado to chill with a microbrew and bike ride in **Durango**. Ponder the past inside cliff dwellings at **Mesa Verde National Park**, then be equally amazed by the towering red buttes at **Monument Valley**.

For the most stunning wilderness in the US, spend your last week in Utah's national parks. Use **Moab** as a base to visit the desert backcountry of **Canyonlands National Park** and **Arches National Park**. From Moab follow Hwy 12 back to Las Vegas, stopping at the petroglyphs and rifts of **Capitol Reef National Park**, the spooky, serpentine slot canyons of **Grand Staircase–Escalante National Monument**, the pastel-colored spires of **Bryce Canyon National Park** and the sheer, red-rock walls at **Zion National Park**.

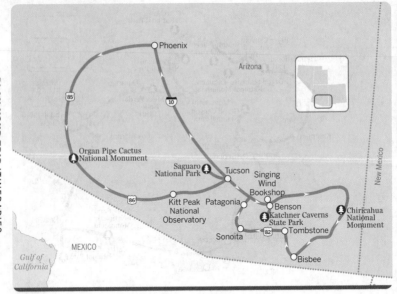

12 DAYS Southern Arizona

Explore the Old West and the New West on this crazy-eight loop that swings past legendary mining towns, art galleries and pretty wineries. There's plenty of desert scenery too, and opportunities to get out of the car for a taste of this unique American landscape.

This adventure starts in **Phoenix**, where a multitude of posh spas, top museums and upscale dining and shopping options will have you primed for exploring. Escape the urban crush with a long drive south on Hwy 85 to the lonely but rejuvenating **Organ Pipe Cactus National Monument**, the only place in the US to see the senita cactus. Hike, explore and relax for two days. From there, take Hwy 85 north to Hwy 86. Follow this lonely two-lane road east to lofty **Kitt Peak National Observatory**, site of 24 optical telescopes – the largest collection in the world. Take a tour or reserve a spot for nighttime stargazing.

Just northeast, laid-back **Tucson** is Arizona's second-largest city and a pleasant place to chill out for a day or two. Indie shops line 4th Ave, and Congress St is the place to catch live music. Stop and smell the cacti in **Saguaro National Park** – the inimitable saguaro blossom is Arizona's state flower – before spending the night in **Benson**, a good launchpad for the pristine **Kartchner Caverns** and home of the gloriously eclectic **Singing Wind Bookshop**. Wander the odd rock formations made up of volcanic ash at **Chiricahua National Monument** then loop south on Hwys 191 and 181 for eye-catching galleries, great restaurants and an interesting mine tour in **Bisbee**. And you can't drive this far south without swinging by **Tombstone** for a reenactment of the shootout at the OK Corral. From Tombstone, Hwy 82 unfurls across sweeping grasslands, the horizon interrupted by scenic mountain ranges (known in these parts as sky islands).

Enjoy a day of wine-tasting in the villages of Elgin and **Sonoita**, capped off with a slice of Elvis-inspired pizza in **Patagonia**. Close the loop with a drive west on I-10, swinging back through Tucson to grab a Sonoran dog before the return to Phoenix.

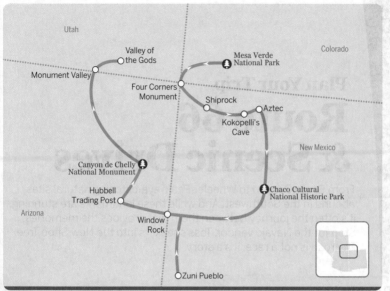

8 DAYS **Four Corners – An American Indian Journey**

American Indian culture and history are in the spotlight on this trip though the Four Corners region, where Colorado, New Mexico, Arizona and Utah meet. Climb into cliff dwellings, buy a dreamcatcher and drive through the sunset glory of Monument Valley.

Start at the **Four Corners Monument** itself, and don't forget to snap a cheesy picture with your hands and feet in four different states. Next, duck into Colorado to visit the enigmatic ruins at **Mesa Verde National Park** before heading south on Hwy 491.

As you head into New Mexico, ogle **Shiprock**, a stunning 1700ft-high volcanic plug known to the Navajo as 'the rock with wings.' Spend the night at a motel in nearby **Aztec** or enjoy a snooze inside **Kokopelli's Cave**, a B&B room 70ft underground – complete with hot tub.

A dusty, rutted drive leads to the isolated **Chaco Culture National Historical Park**, a one-time cultural hub and one of the oldest ruins in the US. Marvel at the engineering prowess of this ancient culture and then spend the night camped out in the canyon. Pass through **Window Rock**, the capital of the Navajo Reservation, and be sure to check out the namesake rock. The old-world **Hubbell Trading Post** was the reservation's lifeline when it was established in the 1870s. Along the way, consider a detour through the **Zuni Pueblo**, renowned for its carved animal fetishes.

Next up? The relatively verdant **Canyon de Chelly National Monument**, an inhabited, cultivated canyon with hogans (traditional home of the Navajo) and sheep herds. Remember to breathe as you approach the otherworldly **Monument Valley**. Drive the 17-mile loop around the towering buttes then spend the night at the View Hotel or camping in the sand; you'll want to spend time – a lot of time – gaping at the sunrise. Finish the trip with a drive north through the otherworldly (and unpaved) **Valley of the Gods** in southern Utah.

Plan Your Trip
Route 66 & Scenic Drives

From Bryce Canyon to Wheeler Peak, eye-catching natural sites abound in the Southwest. And while these landmarks are stunning, it's often the journey between them that provides the memories. Stop for the Navajo vendor. Toss sneakers into the New Shoe Tree. The road is not a race, it's a story.

Buckle Up

Route 66
A classic journey through small-town America; 758 to 882 miles depending on segments driven.

Hwys 89 & 89A: Wickenburg to Sedona
Old West meets New West on this drive past dude ranches, mining towns, art galleries and stylish wineries; 120 miles.

Billy the Kid National Scenic Byway
This outlaw loop shoots through Billy the Kid's old stomping grounds; 84 miles.

Hwy 12
See cinematic rock formations in the southern wilds of Utah, with delicious dining along the way; 124 miles.

Hwy 50: The Loneliest Road
This off-the-grid ramble mixes quirky, historic and lonesome in tumbleweed Nevada; 320 miles.

High Road to Taos
A picturesque cruise between Santa Fe and Taos; 85 miles.

Route 66

'Get your kitsch on Route 66' might be a better slogan for the scrubby stretch of Mother Road running through Arizona and New Mexico. Begging burros. Lumbering dinosaurs. A wigwam motel. It's a bit offbeat, but the folks along the way sure seem glad that you're stopping by.

Why Go?

History, scenery and the open road. This alluring combination is what makes a road trip on Route 66 so fun. From Topock, AZ, heading east, highlights include the begging burros of Oatman, the Route 66 Museum in Kingman and an eclectic general store in tiny Hackberry. Kitsch roars its dinosaury head at Grand Canyon Caverns (p204), luring you 21 stories underground for a tour and even an overnight stay. Burma-Shave signs spout amusing advice on the way to Seligman, a funny little village that greets travelers with retro motels, a roadkill cafe and a squirt of fake mustard at the Snow Cap Drive-In.

Next up is Williams, a railroad town lined with courtyard motels and brimming with small-town charm. Route 66 runs parallel to the train tracks through Flagstaff, passing the wonderful Mu-

HISTORY OF ROUTE 66

Launched in 1926, Route 66 stretched from Chicago to Los Angeles, linking a ribbon of small towns and country byways as it rolled across eight states. The road gained notoriety during the Great Depression, when migrant farmers followed it west from the Dust Bowl across the Great Plains. Its nickname, 'Mother Road,' first appeared in John Steinbeck's novel about the era, *The Grapes of Wrath*. Things got a bit more fun after WWII, when newfound prosperity prompted Americans to get behind the wheel and explore. Sadly, just as things got going, the Feds rolled out the interstate system, which eventually caused the Mother Road's demise. The very last town on Route 66 to be bypassed by an interstate was Arizona's very own Williams, in 1984.

seum Club (p157), a cabin-like roadhouse where everyone's having fun. From here, must-sees include Meteor Crater and the 'Take it Easy' town of Winslow where there's a girl, my Lord, in a flatbed Ford, commemorating the Eagles song. Snap a photo of the famous corner then savor a spectacular dinner in the Turquoise Room (p198) at La Posada hotel. Finish Arizona in kitschy style with a snooze in a concrete teepee in Holbrook.

In New Mexico, Route 66 runs uninterrupted through Gallup, passing near the restored 1926 Spanish Colonial El Morro Theatre (p317) and right by the 1937 El Rancho hotel (p317; John Wayne slept here!). Next up? Albuquerque, where a stop by Frontier for green-chile stew is a delicious pit stop. Then it's on to Santa Rosa's scuba-ready Blue Hole (p348) followed by the neon signs of Tucumcari, comforting reminders of civilization as dusk falls over the lonesome plains.

When to Go?

The best time to travel Route 66 is from May to September, when the weather is warm and you'll be able to take advantage of more outdoor activities.

The Route (882 miles)

This journey starts in Topock, AZ, then continues northeast to Kingman. After crossing I-40, Route 66 travels east and cuts through Flagstaff, Winslow and Holbrook. In New Mexico, it passes through Gallup and Grants before entering Albuquerque, Santa Rosa and Tucumcari.

Time

Even if you're racing down the Mother Road, this trip will still take about two days because the route is primarily two-lane and there are lots of stoplights in the cities. If you have some time, it's best explored over the course of a week.

Highways 89 & 89A: Wickenburg to Sedona

Hwy 89 and its sidekick Hwy 89A are familiar to Arizona road-trippers because they cross some of the most scenic and distinct regions in the center of the state. This section travels from Wickenburg over the Weaver and Mingus Mountains before rolling into Sedona.

Why Go?

This is our favorite drive in Arizona. It may not be the prettiest or the wildest, but the trip is infused with a palpable sense of the Old West, like you've slipped through the swinging doors of history. But the route's not stuck in the 19th century. Weekend art walks, a burgeoning wine trail, stylish indie shops and top-notch restaurants all add 21st-century spark. For those interested in cowboy history, Wickenburg and its dude ranches are a good place to spend some time. Hwy 89 leaves town via Hwy 93 and soon tackles the Weaver Mountains, climbing 2500ft in 4 miles. The road levels out at mountain-topping Yarnell, then swoops easily past grassy buttes and grazing cattle in the Peeples Valley. From here, highlights include Prescott's Whiskey Row, towering Thumb Butte and the unusual boulders at Granite Dells.

Follow Hwy 89A and hold on tight. This serpentine section of road brooks no distraction, clinging tight to the side of

Route 66 & Scenic Drives

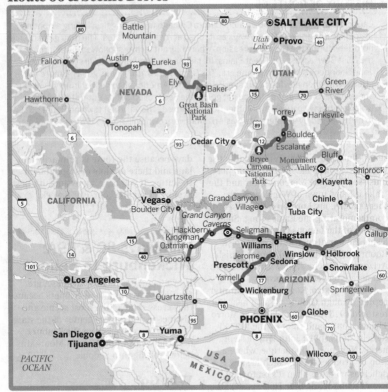

Mingus Mountain. If you dare, glance east for stunning views of the Verde Valley. The zigzagging road reaches epic proportions in Jerome, a former mining town cleaved into the side of Cleopatra Hill. Pull over for art galleries, tasting rooms, quirky inns and an unusually high number of ghosts. Hwy 89A then drops into Clarkdale, Tuzigoot National Monument (p141) and Old Town Cottonwood. On the way to the red rocks of Sedona and Oak Creek Canyon, detour to wineries on Page Springs Rd or loop into town via the Red Rock Loop Rd past Cathedral Rock.

When to Go

This route is best traveled in spring, summer and fall to avoid winter snow – although you might see a few flakes in the mountains in April. In the dead of summer, you won't want to linger in low-lying, toasty Wickenburg.

The Route (120 miles)

From Wickenburg, follow Hwy 93 to Hwy 89 then drive north to Prescott. North of town pick up Hwy 89A, following it to Sedona.

Time

This trip takes about a half-day to drive without stopping, assuming you don't get stuck behind a slow-moving recreational vehicle. To fully enjoy the scenery and towns, give yourself four to five days.

Billy the Kid National Scenic Byway

Named for the controversial outlaw famous for his role in the Lincoln County War, the Billy the Kid National Scenic

Routes
- Route 66
- Hwy 89/89A: Wickenburg to Sedona
- Billy the Kid National Scenic Byway
- Hwy 12
- Hwy 50: The Loneliest Road
- High Road to Taos

itan, hike up Sierra Blanca Peak, or take in a bit of horse racing at Ruidoso Downs.

When to Go

Although there's skiing in the area in winter, the best time for a scenic drive is summer, when average temperatures hover between 77°F (25°C) and 82°F (28°C). It's also a pleasant time to enjoy hiking and fly-fishing in the surrounding national forest.

The Route (84 miles)

From Roswell, follow Hwy 70 west to Hwy 380, following it through Hondo, Lincoln and Capitan before looping south on Hwy 48 to Ruidoso. Then take Hwy 70 east to close the loop at Hondo.

Detour

From Ruidoso, a spectacular 40-mile drive south travels through the **Mescalero Apache Indian Reservation** (mescaleroapachetribe.com), where you're still likely to see American Indian cowboys riding the range, and on to Cloudcroft, home to a historic hilltop hotel and great hiking.

Time

If you're not stopping, this route should take about half a day. To see the sights, including Cloudcroft, allow three days.

Byway loops around his old stomping grounds in the rugged mountains of Lincoln National Forest in southeastern New Mexico.

Why Go?

This mountain-hugging loop provides a cool respite from the heat and hustle-bustle of Roswell and Alamogordo. For a primer on Billy the Kid, also known as William Bonney, head to Lincoln, population 50. This one-road hamlet was the focal point of the Lincoln County War, a bloody rivalry between two competing merchants and their gangs in the late 1870s. Billy took an active role in the conflict and evidence of his involvement can be seen today at the courthouse: a bullet hole left in the wall after he shot his way to freedom during a jailbreak. From here, you can visit Smokey Bear's grave in Cap-

Highway 12

Arguably Utah's most diverse and stunning drive, Hwy 12 winds through remote and rugged canyon land, linking several national and state parks – and destination restaurants – in the state's red-rock center.

Why Go?

With its mesmerizing mix of crimson canyons, sprawling deserts, thick forests and lofty peaks, Hwy 12 works well for adventurous explorers. The trip kicks off at Bryce Canyon National Park, where gold-and-crimson spires set the stage for the color-infused journey to come.

Traveling east, the first highlight is Kodachrome Basin State Park, home to

DRIVING IN THE SOUTHWEST

The interstate system is thriving in the Southwest, but smaller state roads and fine scenic byways offer unparalleled opportunities for exploration.

➡ I-10 runs east–west through southern Arizona.

➡ I-40 runs east–west through Arizona and central New Mexico.

➡ I-70 runs east–west through central Utah.

➡ I-80 runs east–west through northern Utah.

➡ I-15 links Las Vegas to Salt Lake City.

➡ I-25 runs through central New Mexico to Denver, CO.

➡ Route 66 more or less follows the modern-day I-40 through Arizona and New Mexico.

On scenic drives in the Southwest, don't be surprised if you glance in your rearview mirror and see a pack of motorcycles roaring up behind you. Arizona's backroads are popular with motorcycle riders, and Harleys and other bikes are often lined up like horses in front of watering holes on lonely highways.

Long-distance motorcycle driving can be dangerous because of the fatigue factor. Use caution during long hauls.

petrified geysers and red, pink and white sandstone chimneys. Pass through tiny Escalante then pull over for Head of the Rocks Overlook atop Aquarius Plateau. From here, giant mesas, towering domes, deep canyons and undulating slickrock unfurl in an explosion of color.

The adjacent Grand Staircase-Escalante National Monument is the largest park in the Southwest at nearly 1.9 million acres. At the Lower Calf Creek Recreation Area, stretch your legs on the 6-mile round-trip hike to the impressive 126ft Lower Calf Creek Falls. The razor-thin Hogback Ridge, between Escalante and Boulder, is stunning too.

The best section of the drive? Many consider it to be the switchbacks and petrified sand dunes between Boulder and Torrey. But it's not just about the views. In Boulder enjoy a locally sourced meal at Hell's Backbone Grill (p393) followed by homemade dessert at the Burr Trail Grill & Outpost (p393), or enjoy a flavor-packed Southwestern dish at Cafe Diablo (p391) further north in Torrey.

When to Go

For the best weather and driving conditions – especially over 11,000ft Boulder Mountain – drive Hwy 12 between May and October.

The Route (124 miles)

From US Hwy 89 in Utah, follow Hwy 12 east to Bryce Canyon National Park. The road takes a northerly turn at Kodachrome Basin State Park then continues to Torrey.

Time

Although the route could be driven in a few hours, two to three days will allow for a bit of exploration.

Highway 50: The Loneliest Road

Stretching east from Fallon, NV, to Great Basin National Park and the Nevada state line, remote Hwy 50 follows some of America's most iconic routes – the Pony Express, the Overland Stagecoach and the Lincoln Hwy – across the heart of the state.

Why Go?

Why would you drive the Loneliest Road in America? As mountaineer George Mallory said about Everest: 'Because it's there.' And yes, Mallory disappeared while attempting the feat, but the lesson still applies. You drive Hwy 50 because something might just ... happen. So point your ride toward Fallon, a former pioneer town now home to the US Navy's Top Gun fighter-pilot school. From here, listen for the singing dunes at **Sand Mountain Recreation Area** (☎775-885-6000; www.blm.gov/nv; 7-day permit $40, entry free Tue & Wed; ⏰24hr; 🅿), then pull over and hike to the ruins of a Pony Express station.

Just east of Austin (population 192) look for petroglyphs, then yell 'Eureka!' for the tiny town that coughed up $40 million in silver in the 1800s. Next, check out the beehive-shaped buildings at Ward Charcoal Ovens State Historic Park (p96) near Ely, where charcoal was created to use in the silver smelters. End this trip with a 12-mile scenic drive up Wheeler Peak inside Great Basin National Park. After ascending 4000ft, the end-of-trip reward is an expansive view of the Great Basin Desert.

When to Go?

Your best bet is summer. Sections of the road get hit with snow and rain in winter and early spring; in a few towns the road requires 4WD and chains during the worst conditions. Spring can be nice driving east, for views of snowcapped peaks.

The Route (320 miles)

From Fallon, NV – about 75 miles east of Lake Tahoe – follow Hwy 50 east to Austin, Eureka, Ely and then Great Basin National National Park, bordering Utah.

Time

The Loneliest Road can be driven in less than a day, but to check out a few sites and the national park, allow for two or three.

High Road to Taos

This picturesque byway in northern New Mexico links Santa Fe and Taos, rippling through a series of adobe villages and mountain-flanked vistas in and around the Truchas Peaks.

Why Go?

Santa Fe and Taos are well-known artists' communities, lovely places brimming with galleries, studios and museums that are framed by turquoise skies and lofty mountains. These two stunning cities are linked by an artistically pleasing byway: the High Road to Taos, a wandering route that climbs into the mountains.

In Nambé, hike to waterfalls or simply meditate at Lake Nambé. From here, the road leads north to picturesque Chimayo. Ponder the crutches left in the El Santuario de Chimayó (p283) or admire fine weaving and wood carving in family-run galleries. Near Truchas, a village of galleries and century-old adobes, you'll find the High Road Marketplace (p284). This cooperative sells a variety of artwork by area artists.

Further up Hwy 76, original paintings and carvings remain in good condition

---

ROADSIDE ODDITIES: ROUTE 66

Grand Canyon Caverns (p203) A guided tour 21 stories below the Earth's surface loops past mummified bobcats, civil-defense supplies and an $800 motel room.

Burma-Shave signs Red-and-white ads from a bygone era line the roadside, offering tongue-in-cheek advice for life.

Snow Cap Drive-In (p203) Juan Delgadillo opened this prankish burger joint and ice-cream shop in 1953.

Meteor Crater (p197) A fiery rock slammed into the Earth 50,000 years ago, leaving a 550ft-deep pockmark that's nearly 1 mile across.

Wigwam Motel (p198) Concrete wigwams will flash you back to the 1950s with retro hickory log-pole furniture.

US BORDER PATROL

Officers of the United States Border Patrol (USBP) are ubiquitous in southern Arizona and New Mexico. Border patrol officers are law enforcement personnel who have the ability to pull you over, ask for ID and search your car if they have reasonable cause. There's a good chance they'll flash you to the side of the road if you're driving down back roads in a rental or out-of-state car. These roads have been used to smuggle both people and drugs north from Mexico.

➡ Always carry ID, including a valid tourist visa if you're a foreign citizen, and car registration (if it's a rental car, your rental contract should suffice).

➡ Be polite and they should be polite to you.

➡ If they ask, it's best to allow the agents to see inside your trunk (boot) and backseat.

It's almost guaranteed that you'll drive through checkpoints down here. If you've never done so before, the 'stop side' of the checkpoints is the route going from south (Mexico) to north (USA).

You may just be waved through the checkpoint; otherwise slow down, stop, answer a few questions (regarding your citizenship and the nature of your visit) and possibly pop your trunk and roll down your windows so officers can peek inside your car. Visitors may consider the above intrusive, but grin and bear it. For better or worse, this is a reality of traveling on the border.

---

inside the Church of San José de Gracia (p278), considered one of the finest surviving 18th-century churches in the USA. The ride swoops through Peñasco, a gateway to the Pecos Wilderness and also home of the engagingly experimental Peñasco Theatre (p285). From here, follow Hwy 75 and 518 to Taos.

When to Go

The high season is summer, but you can catch blooms in spring and see changing leaves in the fall. Winter is not the best time to visit as there may be snowfall.

The Route (85 miles)

From Santa Fe, take 84/285 north to Pojoaque and turn right on Hwy 503, toward Nambé. From Hwy 503, turn left onto Juan Medina Rd. Continue to Chimayo then drive north on Hwy 76. Turn right onto Hwy 75. At Hwy 518 turn left towards Taos.

Time

You can spend half a day enjoying just the scenery, or two days checking out the history and galleries as well.

Plan Your Trip

Southwest USA Outdoors

The Southwest earns its reputation as the USA's land of adventure with a dizzying array of outdoor landscapes. Plunging canyons, snowcapped peaks, prickly deserts and red-rock formations galore. Where to start? Pick an outdoor town – Moab, Flagstaff, Durango – in a multisport region and launch yourself into the wild.

Hiking

Hiking is the main and most accessible activity in the national parks and can be done at any time of year. Walks can be as short or as long as you like, but remember this when planning: you need to be prepared. The wild desert may be unlike anything you have ever experienced, and designating certain parcels as 'national parks' has not tamed it. Bringing a map and a compass is always a good idea.

Planning

It's always hiking season somewhere in the Southwest. When temperatures in Phoenix hit the 100s (about 40°C), cooler mountain trails beckon in the high country. When highland paths are blanketed in snow, southern Arizona provides balmy weather. Parks near St George in southwestern Utah offer pleasant hiking possibilities well into midwinter. Of course, hardy and experienced backpackers can always don cross-country skis or snowshoes and head out for beautiful wintertime mountain treks.

More and more people venture further from their cars and into the wilds these days, so logistics isn't the only reason for careful planning. Some places cap the number of backpackers due to ecological

Best Experiences

Best Short Hikes to Big Views

➡ South Kaibab Trail to Cedar Ridge (South Rim, Grand Canyon National Park)

➡ Bright Angel Point Trail (North Rim, Grand Canyon National Park)

➡ Angels Landing (Zion National Park)

➡ Mesa Arch Trail (Canyonlands National Park)

➡ Spider Rock Overlook (Canyon de Chelly National Monument)

Best Wildlife-Watching

➡ Birds (Patagonia-Sonoita Creek Preserve and Ramsey Canyon Preserve, AZ)

➡ Elk (Jemez Trail, Valles Caldera, NM)

➡ Eagles (Mesa Canyon near Durango, CO)

➡ California condors (Zion National Park; Vermilion Cliffs, AZ)

Best Water Activities

➡ One-day rafting trip (Rio Grande near Taos; the Colorado and Green Rivers in Moab)

➡ Multiday rafting trip (Colorado River through the Canyonlands or Grand Canyon)

➡ Canyoneering (The Narrows or Subway, Zion)

➡ Fly fishing (Dolores, CO)

sensitivity or limited facilities. Permits are essential for backcountry travel in highly visited areas such as the Grand Canyon and Zion and during the busy spring and fall months in more seasonal areas such as Canyonlands National Park. Consider going to the less heavily visited Bryce Canyon National Park or Bureau of Land Management (BLM) lands and state parks for a backpacking trip during busy months. Not only are they less restrictive than the national parks, but usually you can just show up and head out.

Backcountry areas are fragile and cannot support an inundation of human activity, especially when the activity is insensitive or careless. The key is to minimize your impact, leaving no trace of your visit and taking nothing but photographs and memories. To avoid erosion and damage, stay on main trails.

Safety

The climate is partly responsible for the epic nature of the Southwestern landscape. The weather is extraordinary in its unpredictability and sheer, pummeling force – from blazing sun to blinding blizzards and deadly flash floods. When there's too much water – the kind of amounts necessary to scour a slot canyon smooth – drowning can occur. Too little water combined with unforgiving heat leads to crippling dehydration. A gallon (3.8L) of water per person per day is the recommended minimum in hot weather. Sun protection (brimmed hats, sunglasses and sunblock) is vital to a desert hiker. Know your limitations, pace yourself accordingly and be realistic about your abilities and interests.

Solo travelers should always let someone know where they are going and how long they plan to be gone. At the very least, use sign-in boards at trailheads

or ranger stations. Travelers looking for hiking companions can inquire or post notices at ranger stations, outdoors stores, campgrounds and hostels.

Mountain Biking & Cycling

The Southwest kills it when it comes to mountain biking: from Moab's world-famous slickrock to the prickly-pedal 800-mile Arizona Trail and ponderosa-scented alpine climbs outside Durango, you can find all sorts of fat-tire fun in every state.

If you're not hauling a bike with you, you can usually find a rental shop in major hubs. Sometimes you'll need to rent a bike rack to get to the good stuff, other times you can pedal straight out of the shop. Check www.mtbproject.com for trail descriptions and maps.

Road cycling is also a good option in many places, depending upon the season. Tucson and Albuquerque are both bicycle-friendly with many bike lanes and parks. The area around St George, UT, is another good location with miles of bike lanes.

Cycling on the South Rim of the Grand Canyon is a fun way to explore the park. The development of the cyclist-friendly Greenway Trail and a bike-rental shop at the visitor center make this easier than ever.

Black Canyon, Gunnison National Park

A dark, narrow gash above the Gunnison River leads down a 2000ft-deep chasm that's as eerie as it is spectacular. Head to the 6-mile-long South Rim Rd, which takes you to 11 overlooks. To challenge your senses, cycle along the smooth pavement running parallel to the rim.

The nearest town to this area is Montrose. For more information contact **Black Canyon of the Gunnison National Park** (☑970-641-2337; www.nps.gov/blca; 7-day admission per vehicle/pedestrians & cyclists $15/7)

Carson National Forest

Carson contains an enormous network of mountain-bike and multiuse trails between Taos, Angel Fire and Picuris Peak. The nearest town is Taos, where you can rent

---

ACCESSIBLE ADVENTURES

If you're disabled but want to run white water, canoe, rock climb or Nordic ski, head to Salt Lake City–based Splore (p433), which runs outdoor trips in the area. **Disabled Sports USA** (☑301-217-0960; www.disabledsportsusa.org) also organizes outdoor activities in the area.

Top: Canyoneering near Moab, Utah (p373)

Bottom: Skiing the Wasatch Mountains (p445)

ERIK ISAKSON / GETTY IMAGES / TETRA IMAGES RF ©

NATIONAL PARKS & MONUMENTS

PARK	FEATURES	ACTIVITIES
Arches NP	sandstone arches, diverse geologic formations	hiking, camping, scenic drives
Bandelier NM	Ancestral Puebloan sites	hiking, camping
Black Canyon of the Gunnison NP	rugged deep canyon, ancient rocks	rock climbing, rafting, hiking, horseback riding
Bosque del Apache NWR	Rio Grande wetlands, cranes & geese in winter	birding
Bryce Canyon NP	red & orange hoodoos & pillars	camping, hiking, scenic drives, stargazing, cross-country skiing
Canyon de Chelly NM	ancient cliff dwellings, canyons, cliffs	guided hiking, horseback riding, scenic overlooks
Canyonlands NP	desert wilderness at confluence of Green & Colorado Rivers	rafting, camping, mountain biking, backpacking
Capitol Reef NP	buckled sandstone cliffs along the Waterpocket Fold	mountain biking, hiking, camping, wilderness, solitude
Carlsbad Caverns NP	enormous underground caves, bat flight in evening	ranger-led walks, spelunking (experienced only), backpacking
Chaco Canyon NP	Ancestral Puebloan sites	hiking, camping, solitude
Dinosaur NM	fossil beds along Yampa & Green Rivers, dinosaur fossils & exhibits	hiking, scenic drives, camping, rafting
Grand Canyon NP	canyon scenery, geologic record, remote wilderness, condors	rafting, hiking, camping, mountain biking, road cycling
Grand Staircase–Escalante NM	desert wilderness, mountains, slot canyons	mountain biking, hiking, camping, canyoning
Great Basin NP	desert mountains, canyons, wildlife, fall colors	hiking, camping
Mesa Verde NP	Ancestral Puebloan sites	hiking, camping
Monument Valley Navajo Tribal Park	desert basin with sandstone pillars & buttes	scenic drive, guided tours, horseback riding, camping
Natural Bridges NM	premier examples of stone arches	hiking, camping, sightseeing
Organ Pipe Cactus NM	Sonoran Desert, cactus bloom May & Jun	cactus viewing, scenic drives, mountain biking
Petrified Forest NP	Painted Desert, fossilized logs	scenic drives, backcountry hiking
Red Rock Canyon NCA	unique geologic features close to Las Vegas, waterfalls	scenic drives, hiking, rock climbing
Saguaro NP	desert slopes, giant saguaro, wildflowers, Gila woodpeckers, wildlife	cactus viewing, hiking, camping
San Pedro Riparian NCA	40 miles of protected river habitats	birding, picnicking, fishing, horseback riding
Sunset Crater Volcano NM	dramatic volcanic landscape	hiking, sightseeing
White Sands NM	white sand dunes, specially adapted plants & animals	scenic drives, hiking, moonlight bicycle tours, sledding
Zion NP	sandstone canyons, high mesas	hiking, canyoning, camping, scenic drives, rock climbing

NP – National Park; NM – National Monument; NCA – National Conservation Area; NWR – National Wildlife Refuge

bikes from Gearing Up Bicycle Shop (p290). For more information contact **Carson National Forest** (www.fs.usda.gov/carson).

Kaibab National Forest

One of the premier mountain-biking destinations in Arizona is the 800-plus-mile Arizona Trail. A popular section that's great for families is the Tusayan Bike Trail System, east of the town of Tusayan. It's a pretty easy ride mostly on an old logging road that cuts through the Kaibab National Forest to the South Rim of the Grand Canyon. If you ride or walk the trail into the park, you have to pay the $12 entrance fee that's good for seven days. For more information contact the Tusayan Ranger Station. (p176)

Moab

Bikers from around the world come to pedal the steep slickrock trails and challenging 4WD roads winding through woods and into canyon country around Moab. The legendary Slickrock Trail is for experts only, while intermediate riders can learn to ride slickrock on Klondike Bluffs Trail, a 15.6-mile round-trip that passes dinosaur tracks. For a family-friendly ride, try the 8-mile Bar-M Loop.

Full-suspension bikes can be rented at Rim Cyclery (p368) – check out its museum. Visit www.go-utah.com/Moab/Biking and www.discovermoab.com/biking.htm for excellent Moab biking information. Both have loads of easy-to-access pictures, ratings and descriptions about specific trails.

Snow Sports

All five states offer snow sports on some level. Yes, you can even ski in Arizona. Southwestern Colorado is riddled with fabulous ski resorts, while the Lake Tahoe area reigns in Nevada. In New Mexico head to the steeps at Taos and in Utah the resorts outside Salt Lake City – the host of the Winter Olympic Games.

Downhill Skiing & Snowboarding

Endless vistas, blood-curdling chutes, sweet glades and ricocheting half-pipes: downhill skiing and boarding are epic,

whether you're hitting fancy resorts or local haunts. The season lasts from late November to mid-April, depending on where you are.

Salt Lake City and nearby towns hosted the 2002 Winter Olympics, and have rip-roaring routes to test your edges. Slopes are not crowded at Snowbasin, where the Olympic downhill races were held. The terrain here is, in turns, gentle and ultra-yikes. Nearby Alta is the quintessential Utah ski experience: unpretentious and packed with powder fields, gullies, chutes and glades. Meanwhile Park City, when combined with neighboring Canyons, is the second-largest resort in the US.

New Mexico's Taos Ski Valley is easily one of the most challenging mountains in the US, while Ski Santa Fe, just 15 miles outside town, allows you the chance to ski in the morning and shop Canyon Rd galleries come afternoon.

In Colorado you'll want to head to Telluride or Crested Butte. For extreme skiing, try Silverton. All three are wonderfully laid-back, old mining-turned-ski towns, offering the opportunity to ride some of the best powder in the state by day, then chill in some of the coolest old saloons at night. For something completely local and low-key, check out family-run Wolf Creek. For more details visit www.coloradoski.com. The website lists 'ski and stay' specials and provides resort details and snow reports.

The Lake Tahoe area, straddling the Nevada–California border, is home to nearly a dozen ski and snowboard resorts.

And then there's Arizona. Yes, you can ski. The snow isn't anything to write home about, but the novelty value may be. Head to the Arizona Snowbowl outside Flagstaff.

Ski areas generally have full resort amenities, including lessons and equipment rentals (although renting in nearby towns can be cheaper). Got kids? Don't leave them at home when you can stash them at ski school for a day. For 'ski, fly and stay' deals check out web consolidators and the ski areas' own websites.

Cross-country & Backcountry Skiing

Backcountry and cross-country skiing and snowshoeing are increasingly popular ways to explore the untamed Southwestern terrain.

A must-ski for cross-country aficionados? Utah's serene Soldier Hollow, which was the Nordic course used in the 2002 Winter Olympics. It's accessible to all skill levels.

The North and South Rims of the Grand Canyon both have cross-country trails. The North Rim is much more remote. On the south side, you'll find several trails of easy to medium difficulty groomed and signed within the Kaibab National Forest. Bryce Canyon also has cross-country trails.

The San Juan Hut System is legendary: a great series of shelters along a 60-mile route in Colorado from Telluride to Ouray – the scenery is fantastic.

Rock Climbing

Tolkien meets Dr Seuss in the Southwest, a surreal landscape filled with enormous blobs, spires, blobs on spires and soaring cliffs. While southern Utah seems to have the market cornered on rock climbing, the rest of the region isn't too shabby when it comes to the vertical scene. Just keep an eye on the thermometer – those rocks can really sizzle during summer. Help keep climbing spaces open by respecting access restrictions, whether they are set by landowners or because of endangered, cliff-dwelling birds that need space and silence during nesting season.

Southwestern Utah's Snow Canyon State Park offers more than 150 bolted and sport routes. Zion Canyon has some of the most famous big-wall climbs in the country, including Moonlight Buttress, Prodigal Sun, Touchstone and Space Shot. In southeastern Utah, awesome destinations include Moab, Indian Creek and the Castleton desert towers. Outdoor outfitters in Moab and Springdale offer classes for beginners and sell gear.

Otherwise, make a swift approach to central Arizona's Granite Mountain Wilderness, which attracts rock climbers in warmer months. Pack your rack for the rocky reaches of Taos Ski Valley or your picks for the Ouray Ice Park, where a 2-mile stretch of the Uncompahgre Gorge has become world renowned for its sublime ice formations.

Chicks Climbing & Skiing (☎970-325-3858; www.chickswithpicks.net) empowers more women to take up rock, ice and alpine climbing.

Canyoneering

Canyons can be secret, mystical destinations, with an eerie, unsettling beauty that sometimes gives the feeling that you're wandering the sacred ruins of an ancient civilization – although the smooth, scalloped walls and strange,

---

FLASH FLOODS: A DEADLY DESERT DANGER

Flash floods are an ever-present danger in the Southwest, as the floods that swept away seven victims in Zion's Keyhole Canyon in September 2015 sadly demonstrated. These floods, which occur when large amounts of rain fall suddenly and quickly, are most common during the 'monsoon' months from July to early September. They occur with little warning and reach a raging peak in minutes. Even when it's sunny overhead, rainfall miles away can be funneled from the surrounding mountains into a normally dry wash or canyon, with rushing water appearing seemingly out of nowhere. If you see a flash flood coming, the only recommendation is to reach higher ground as quickly as possible.

Floods carry a battering mixture of rocks and trees and can be extremely dangerous. The swiftly moving water is much stronger than it appears; at only a foot high, it will easily knock over a strong adult. A 2ft-high flood sweeps away vehicles.

Heed local warnings and weather forecasts, especially during the monsoon season. Canyoneers are at the most risk – be sure to check in with the local ranger station for the day's flash-flood warnings. Avoid camping in sandy washes and canyon bottoms, which are the likeliest spots for flash floods. Campers and hikers are not the only potential victims; every year foolhardy drivers crossing flooded roads are swept away. Flash floods usually subside fairly quickly. A road that is closed will often be passable later on the same day.

HORSEBACK RIDING

WHERE	WHAT	INFORMATION
Southern Arizona dude ranches	cowboy up in Old West country; most ranches close in summer due to the heat	www.azdra.com
Grand Canyon South Rim, AZ	low-key trips through Kaibab National Forest; campfire ride	www.apachestables.com
Santa Fe, NM	themed trail rides; sunsets	www.bishopslodge.com
Telluride, CO	all-season rides in the hills	www.ridewithroudy.com

sculpted dimples and pockmarks aren't the creations of any human culture, but the echoes of a much older visitor: water.

This is, perhaps, the ultimate Southwest outdoors adventure, where you can experience the thrill of squeezing yourself into a dark narrow slot, rappelling over the lip of a 70ft chute or swimming across a cold subterranean pool. For many people, a nontechnical hike or a guided canyoneering trip or intro course is the best solution. For others, nothing short of full-on immersion will do.

Zion is the premier destination for canyoneers, with dozens of routes in the surrounding area, though Escalante National Monument and the San Rafael Swell (all in Utah) also have some legendary routes. The Paria Canyon on the Arizona-Utah border includes Buckskin Gulch, a 12-mile-long canyon 400ft deep that's only 15ft wide for most of the way. Perhaps the best known – and most highly commercialized – nontechnical slot is Antelope Canyon, near Lake Powell.

Canyoneers must also be especially mindful of flash floods and high water levels (wetsuits are required for some routes, regardless of the season). Being inside the cogs and wheels of Earth's geological machinery is very cool – until they switch on. Always check the day's flash flood forecast before you go out. If you're attempting a serious route, a solid understanding of technical skills – how to tie knots, set up an anchor, use a rappelling device, unsnag a stuck rope and so on – is required. And always remember: rappelling into a canyon is a particularly easy way to put yourself into situations you may not be able to get out of, especially if you get hurt.

Golfing

With more than 300 golf courses, Arizona is ranked the number-one golf destination in North America by the International Association of Golf Tour Operators. The state has some of the top golf resorts in the country, with the best ones designed by famous pros. Just about every sizable town in Arizona has a course and the bigger cities have dozens. The Phoenix area alone has about 200.

In many desert areas, golf courses are viewed as welcome grassy amenities that also bring in tourist dollars, but this comes at a high price – the courses need lots of water, and conservationists decry the use of this most precious of desert resources for entertainment. In 2010 about 15% of the state's courses were considered at-risk because of a dip in tourism, increased competition and higher costs for water and labor.

Golf is also expensive for players. Some courses don't allow golfers to walk from hole to hole. A round of 18 holes on the best courses, often in upscale resorts that specialize in golf vacations, can cost hundreds of dollars (including use of a golf cart) during the balmy days of a southern Arizona winter. In the heat of summer, rates can drop to less than $100 for the same resort. If you don't have that kind of

> **TOP SPOTS FOR WHITE-WATER RAFTING**
>
> **Grand Canyon National Park** AZ
>
> **Cataract Canyon** Moab, UT
>
> **Westwater Canyon** Moab, UT
>
> **Taos Box** Pilar, NM
>
> **Animas River** Durango, CO

RANKING RAPIDS

White-water rapids are rated on a class scale of I to V, with Class V being the wildest and Class I being nearly flat water. Most beginner trips take rafters on Class III rivers, which means you'll experience big rolling waves and some bumps along the way, but nothing super-technical. In Class IV water you can expect to find short drops, big holes (meaning giant waves) and stronger undertows, making it a bit rougher if you get thrown off the boat. Class V rapids are the baddest of all and should only be attempted by strong swimmers with previous white-water experience – if you get thrown out of a boat and sucked under you'll need to know what to do.

If you do get thrown, float through the rapid, lying on your back – your life vest will keep you afloat. Point your feet downriver and keep your toes up. Protect your head and neck with your arms (don't leave them loose or they can get caught in rocks).

The I to V class system applies to all Southwestern rivers except for the section of the Colorado River running through the Grand Canyon. This portion is just too wild to play by traditional rules and requires its own scale system – from Class I to Class X – to rank its 160-plus rapids. Many of the Grand's rapids are ranked Class V or higher; two merit a perfect 10.

money, try the public city courses where rounds are more reasonable. Several Phoenix city courses charge less than $50 for 18 holes in winter.

Water Sports

Water in the desert? You betcha. In fact, few places in the US offer as much watery diversity as the Southwest. Bronco-busting rivers share the territory with enormous lakes and sweet trickles that open into great escapes. If you're into diving, check out Blue Hole (p348) near Santa Rosa, NM. It has a 70ft-deep natural well.

Boating

Near the California-Arizona state line, a series of dammed lakes on the lower Colorado River is thronged with boaters year-round. Area marinas rent canoes, fishing boats, speedboats, water-skiing boats, jet skis and windsurfers. On the biggest lakes – especially Arizona's Lake Powell in the Glen Canyon National Recreation Area near the Grand Canyon and Lake Mead in the Lake Mead National Recreation Area near Las Vegas – houseboat rentals sleep six to 12 people and allow exploration of remote areas difficult to reach on foot.

The thrill of speed mixed with alcohol makes popular houseboat areas dangerous for kayakers and canoeists. If you're renting a big rig, take the same care with alcohol as you would when driving a car. Travel at a speed that is safe based on the conditions, which include the amount of traffic on the water and the likelihood of underwater hazards (more common when water levels drop). Carbon monoxide emitted by houseboat engines is a recently recognized threat. Colorless and odorless, the deadly gas is heavier than air and gathers at water level, creating dangerous conditions for swimmers and boaters. In recent years, several swimmers have drowned after being overcome by carbon monoxide.

Swimming & Tubing

Most lakes and many reservoirs in the Southwest allow swimmers. The exception will be high-traffic areas of the bigger lakes, where swimming is very dangerous due to the number of motorboats. It's not unusual to see locals swimming in rivers during the hot summer months, and tubing on creeks throughout the Southwest is popular. If you happen to see a bunch of people riding down a creek, and wish to join, just ask where they go for their tires – where there's tubing in this region there is usually an entrepreneur renting tubes from a van in the nearest parking lot. Swimming in lakes and rivers is generally free but if you are in a state or national park, or on a reservoir, you may have to pay an entrance fee to enter the property itself.

Plan Your Trip
Travel with Children

The Southwest is a blast for families, with entertaining attractions for all ages: national parks, aquariums, zoos, science museums, theme parks, lively campgrounds, and hiking and biking in outrageously scenic places. Geology, history and wildlife are accessible in concrete ways at every turn, making the Southwest as educational as it is fun.

Southwest USA for Kids

Why visit the Southwest with your family? Because it's fun. Yes, the long drives, harsh desert landscape and oppressive summer heat can be daunting, but the rewards for families far outweigh the challenges. These rewards can be found in the most mundane of activities – splashing in the creek in New Mexico's Jemez Mountains, picnicking on the edge of the Grand Canyon in Arizona or watching an old Western on the big screen at Parry Lodge's Old Barn playhouse in Kanab, UT.

Education comes easy too, with docents at museums, rangers in the parks and interpretative signage along numerous trails. Most national parks in the Southwest have a free Junior Ranger Program, with activities geared to children. Ask for details at the visitor center or check the park website before your trip for details.

Lodging

Hotels and motels typically offer rooms with two beds, which are ideal for families. Some have cribs and rollaway beds, sometimes for a minimal fee (these are usually portable cribs which may not work for all children). Ask about suites, adjoining rooms and rooms with microwaves or refrigerators. Some hotels offer 'kids stay

Best Regions for Kids

Arizona

Outdoorsy families can cycle the Greenway near Grand Canyon Village and study saguaros outside Tucson. Water parks lure kids to Phoenix, while dude ranches, ghost towns and cliff dwellings are only a scenic drive away.

New Mexico

Swoop up a mountain on the Sandia Peak Tramway, drop into Carlsbad Caverns or scramble to the Gila Cliff Dwellings.

Utah

National parks sprawl across swaths of red-rock country, offering fantastic hiking, cycling and rafting. In the mountains, skis, alpine slides or snow tubes are equally fun.

Nevada

Children are not allowed in the gaming areas of casinos, but roller coasters and animal exhibits cater to the kiddies in Las Vegas. For outdoor adventure, head to Great Basin National Park or Valley of Fire State Park.

free' programs for children up to 12, and sometimes up to 18 years old. Many B&Bs don't allow children, so ask before booking.

Full-scale resorts with kids' programs, lovely grounds, full service and in-house babysitting can be found throughout the region, but particularly in Phoenix and, to a lesser degree, Tucson. For the real Western-immersion cowboy experience, complete with trail rides through the chamisa, cattle wrangling and beans 'n' corn bread 'round the fire, stay at a dude ranch, such as the Flying E Ranch (p133) in Wickenburg, AZ.

If it's late and you don't want surprises, head to a chain motel or hotel. Hilton perches at the high end of the scale, while Motel 6 and Super 8, usually the least expensive, offer minimal services. Best Western is notoriously inconsistent. Your best bets are Holiday Inn Express, Fairfield Inn & Suites and Drury Inn & Suites, which usually offers free popcorn and soda in the evening.

Beautiful campsites perfect for car-camping are easily found in national and state forests, and parks throughout the region. You can't beat the flexibility and price, and kids love it.

Dining

While the Southwest offers the usual fast-food suspects, you may find yourself driving mile after mile without a neon-lit fast-food joint anywhere. Be prepared with snacks and a cooler packed with picnic items. Many lodgings offer free breakfast.

Don't sacrifice a good meal or attractive ambience because you have kids. All but a handful of upscale restaurants welcome families and many provide crayons and children's menus. To avoid the dilemma of yet another fried meal, ubiquitous on kids' menus, simply ask for small adaptations to the standard menu, such as grilled chicken with no sauce, a side of steamed vegetables or rice with soy sauce.

HELPFUL RESOURCES FOR FAMILIES

For all-around information and advice, check out Lonely Planet's *Travel with Children*. For outdoor advice, read *Kids in the Wild: A Family Guide to Outdoor Recreation* by Cindy Ross and Todd Gladfelter, and Alice Cary's *Parents' Guide to Hiking & Camping*.

Children's Highlights

Outdoor Adventures

Grand Canyon National Park, AZ Explore the canyon trails. (p160)

Oak Creek Canyon, AZ Swoosh down a red-rock waterslide at Red Rock State Park. (p142)

Ghost Ranch, NM Ride horses on the former property of Georgia O'Keeffe. (p281)

Nordic Valley, UT Ski the powdery slopes. (p463)

Theme Parks & Museums

Arizona-Sonora Desert Museum, Tucson, AZ Take in coyotes, cacti and demos. (p212)

Museum of Natural History & Science, Albuquerque, NM Check out the Seismosaurus in the Age of Super Giants Hall. (p238)

Santa Fe Children's Museum, NM Visit with local artists and scientists. (p259)

Rawhide Western Town & Steakhouse, Mesa, AZ Relive the rootin', tootin' Old West with gold panning, burro rides and shoot-outs. (p120)

Thanksgiving Point, Salt Lake City, UT Enjoy 55 acres of gardens, a petting farm, a movie theater and golf. (p433)

Wacky Attractions

Oatman, AZ Take a photo of the burros that loiter in the middle of downtown. (p202)

Grand Canyon Caverns, AZ Marvel at the fake dinosaurs and mummified bobcats. (p203)

Rattlesnake Museum, Albuquerque, NM Gaze at the world's most comprehensive collection of rattlesnake species. (p239)

International UFO Museum & Research Center, Roswell, NM Discover the truth, and lots of wild theories. (p342)

Mexican Hat, UT Hey, that rock looks like a sombrero! (p358)

American Indian Sites

Bandelier National Monument, NM Climb four ladders to a ceremonial cave that combines education with adventure. (p280)

Taos Pueblo, NM Explore ancient living history inside a multistory pueblo village dating to the 1400s. (p298)

Top: International UFO
Museum & Research
Center (p342)

Bottom: Outdoor
adventures in Utah

KENNAN HARVEY / GETTY IMAGES ©

Acoma Pueblo, NM Discover this spot, aka Sky City, which sits atop a mesa 7000ft above sea level. (p321)

Mesa Verde National Park, CO Climb into cliff dwellings for hands-on learning at its best. (p364)

Monument Valley Navajo Tribal Park, AZ Match the names to the butte – Mittens, Eagle Rock. (p191)

Planning

Planning Ahead

Perhaps the most difficult part of a family trip to this region will be deciding where to go and avoiding the temptation to squeeze in too much. Distances are deceptive and any one state could easily fill a two-week family vacation. Choose a handful of primary destinations, such as major cities and national parks, to serve as the backbone. Then sit down with the map and connect these dots with a flexible driving plan.

Book rooms at the major destinations and make advance reservations for horseback rides, rafting trips, scenic train rides and educational programs or camps, but allow a couple of days between each to follow your fancy.

What to Bring

If you plan on hiking, you'll want a front baby carrier or a backpack with a built-in shade top. These can be purchased or rented from outfitters throughout the region. Older kids need sturdy shoes and, for playing in streams, water sandals.

Other things you'll want to include are towels, rain gear, a snuggly fleece or heavy sweater (even in summer, desert nights can be cold – if you're camping, bring hats) and bug repellent. To avoid children's angst at sleeping in new places and to minimize concerns about bed configurations, bring a travel playpen/bed for infants and sleeping bags for older children.

Transportation

Car-Seat Laws

Child restraint laws vary by state and are subject to change. The requirements listed here should be verified before departure.

Arizona law states that children under the age of five must be properly secured in a child-restraint device. Children five to seven years must use a booster seat unless they are 4ft 9in or taller. Children aged between eight and 15 years must wear a seat belt.

In Colorado, infants under the age of one year and weighing less than 20lb must be in a rear-facing infant seat in the back seat. Children aged one to three years and between 20lb and 40lb must be in a car seat. Four- to seven-year-olds must use a booster. Seat belts are required for children aged eight to 15, in both the front and back seats. Anyone 16 or older who is driving a car or is a passenger in the front seat must wear a seat belt.

Nevada requires children aged five and under, and those weighing less than 60lb, to use a child seat. In New Mexico, infants under one year must be restrained in a rear-facing infant seat in the back seat, children aged one to four or weighing less than 40lb must use a child safety seat, and five- and six-year-olds and kids weighing less than 60lb must use a booster seat.

Utah law requires children under eight years old or shorter than 4ft 9in to sit in a car seat; children who are not yet eight but who are 4ft 9in or taller can use the car seat belt alone.

Most car-rental agencies rent rear-facing car seats (for infants under one), forward-facing seats (for one to four years old or up to a certain height/weight) and boosters for around $15 per day, reserved in advance. Clarify the type of seat when you make the reservation as each is suitable for specified ages and weights only.

Flying

Children under two can fly free on most airlines when sitting on a parent's lap. Remember to bring a copy of your child's birth certificate – if the airline asks for it and you don't have it, you won't be able to board. Ask about children's fares and reserve seats together in advance. Other passengers have no obligation to switch seats. Southwest Airlines' open seating policy helps avoid this.

Regions at a Glance

Las Vegas works best for travelers seeking urban adventures, from fine dining to late-night club-hopping. Head to Nevada's mountains and deserts for outdoor thrills. Arizona offers nightlife and culture in Phoenix and Tucson, but the state earns bragging rights at the Grand Canyon. Its mining towns and American Indian sites are also a draw, attracting cultural explorers to the deserts and mountains. New Mexico is a top spot for artists, but its chile-infused cuisine and Pueblo culture lure crowds too. Peak baggers and cyclists love Colorado's lofty San Juan Mountains, while Mesa Verde wins praise from history buffs. And potheads love, well, all of it, man. Utah draws hikers and cyclists with red-rock parks, slot canyons, sandstone trails and delicate natural grace.

Las Vegas & Nevada

Nightlife
Dining
Offbeat

Casinos

The flashy casinos on the Las Vegas Strip are self-contained party caves where you can hold 'em, fold 'em, sip cocktails, shake your booty and watch contortionists and comedians.

Cornucopias

In Vegas, food is about both quantity and quality. Stretch your budget and your waistline at the ubiquitous buffets or dine like royalty at a chef-driven sanctuary.

Out There

From Hwy 50 (the Loneliest Road) to Hwy 375 (the Extraterrestrial Hwy), Nevada is wild and wacky. Caravan to the Black Rock Desert in September for Burning Man, a conflagration of self-expression.

p58

Arizona

Culture
Adventure
Scenery

American Indian Culture

From craftwork to cliff dwellings to sprawling reservations, tribal traditions flourish across the state. Tribal history and art are also unique.

Hiking & Rafting

Want to take it easy? Hike a desert interpretative trail or kayak a human-made lake. To ramp it up, head to canyon country to clamber over red rocks or bounce over white-capped rapids.

Canyons & Arches

After the continents collided, Mother Nature got involved with the decorating. Crumbly hoodoos, graceful spans, glowing buttes and crimson ridges – do you have batteries for the camera?

p111

New Mexico

Art
Culture
Food

Santa Fe

Vendors on the Plaza. Galleries on Canyon Rd and at the Railyard. The Georgia O'Keeffe Museum. Art is all around us. The city itself is a living work of art, framed by mountains and crisp blue skies.

Pueblos

Nineteen American Indian Pueblos are clustered in the north-central and western regions of the state. They share similarities, but their histories, customs and craftwork are distinctly fascinating.

Red & Green

New Mexican food comes with a chile-infused twist. Red or green – chiles are not just for salsas but are an integral part of the whole. Stuffed *sopaipillas*. Posole. *Carne adovada* (marinated pork). Isn't this why you're here?

p234

Utah

Outdoors
Ancient Sites
History

Room to Roam

When it comes to large, all-natural playgrounds, Utah takes the lead. From sprawling national parks to empty Bureau of Land Management (BLM) expanses, the place is ready-made for big adventures – often with a sandstone backdrop.

Rock On

Dinosaurs roamed the Earth and trilobites swam the seas, leaving footprints and fossils as calling cards. Elsewhere, cliff dwellings and rock art remind us we weren't the first inhabitants.

The Land of Mormon

The Mormons arrived in the 1840s, building temples, streets, farms and communities. Get some background at Temple Sq in Salt Lake City, then explore downtown.

p351

On the Road

Las Vegas & Nevada

Includes →

Best Places to Eat

→ Morimoto (p76)
→ Andiamo Steakhouse (p77)
→ eat. (p76)
→ Wild River Grille (p103)
→ Star Hotel (p100)

Best Places to Sleep

→ Cosmopolitan (p73)
→ Encore (p62)
→ Red Rock Casino Resort & Spa (p75)
→ Whitney Peak (p103)
→ El Cortez (p74)

Why Go?

Nevada is defined by contrasts and contradictions, juxtaposing arid plains with skyward, snowcapped mountains, while stilettos demand equal suitcase space with ski boots. Many visitors come only for the main event: Las Vegas. Nevada's twinkling desert jewel is a mecca for pleasure-seekers, and where privilege and poverty collide and three-quarters of the state's population resides.

In this libertarian state, rural brothels coexist with Mormon churches, casinos and cowboys. Isolated ghost towns recall a pioneering past and the promise of a better life – just as Vegas riches lure punters today. But Nevada's rightful drawcard is nature, with Reno's rushing Truckee River, Lake Tahoe's crystal waters and forested peaks, the playas of the Black Rock Desert and the expanses of the Great Basin and the 'Loneliest Road in America.'

A place of discovery, Nevada is full of firsts, where there's something for daredevils and dreamers alike.

When to Go
Las Vegas

Apr–May Southern Nevada is balmy by day and pleasantly cool at night.

Jun–Aug While temps soar, low season in Las Vegas means great hotel deals.

Dec Sin City deals in excess, yet it's never more buck wild than at Christmas.

History

You ask, what history? It's true that, unlike the rest of the ruin-laden Southwest, traces of early history are scarce in the Silver State.

Contrary to Hollywood legend, there was much more at the dusty crossroads than a gambling parlor and some tumbleweeds the day mobster Ben 'Bugsy' Siegel rolled in and erected a glamorous tropical-themed casino, the Flamingo, under the searing sun.

In 1855, Mormon missionaries built and then abandoned a fort in the Las Vegas valley, where a natural-springs oasis flowed. In 1859, the richest vein of silver ever discovered in the USA, the Comstock Lode, was struck at Virginia City, which became the most notorious boomtown in the West. President Abraham Lincoln ratified Nevada as a state in 1864.

After the completion of the railroad, Las Vegas finally boomed in the 1920s. Gambling dens, brothels and saloons soon sprang up beside the tracks, especially in Las Vegas' infamous Block 16 red-light district, which survived Nevada's bans on gambling and the supposedly 'dry' years of Prohibition.

The legalization of gambling in 1931, and the sudden lessening of the divorce residency requirement to six weeks, guaranteed an influx of jet-setting divorcées and taxable tourist dollars that carried Vegas through the Great Depression. WWII brought a huge air-force base and big aerospace bucks, plus a paved highway to Los Angeles. Soon after, the Cold War justified the Nevada Test Site. Monthly aboveground atomic blasts shattered casino windows in Las Vegas, while the city's official 'Miss Atomic Bomb' beauty queen graced tourism campaigns.

A building spree sparked by the Flamingo in 1946 led to mob-backed tycoons upping the glitz ante at every turn. Big-name entertainers, like Frank Sinatra, Liberace and Sammy Davis Jr, arrived on stage at the same time as topless French showgirls in the 'Fabulous Fifties.'

Since then, driven by a belief that sex, money and fame equate to power and success, Sin City continues to exist chiefly to satisfy the desires of visitors, and those who live here to serve them compete with each other to reach the top of a ladder that most will never see. The pinnacle of success in money-hungry Vegas is never attainable ... someone always has 'more.'

When the US housing bubble burst, Las Vegas, once North America's fastest-growing metropolitan area, and Nevada in general, were hit especially hard. Even today, among the glittering lights of the Strip you'll spot unlit, vacant condominium towers that speak to a need for economic revival. In 2012 the CEO of online shoe company Zappos announced he was injecting $350 million into revitalizing the downtown neighborhood, using a model based on the tenets of Burning Man, and that he would do it in five years. Now, more than five years later, the project has stalled somewhat, although there has been some improvement to what was once a very sketchy place indeed. Now it's just sketchy in parts.

The revival of the Arts District will be the one to watch, and the City of Las Vegas' official master plan for the future (www.visionlv.com) is currently in development and one in which you can get involved.

LAS VEGAS

♪ 702, 725 / POP 594,294 / ELEV 2000FT

An oasis of indulgence dazzling in the desert, Vegas' seduction is unrivaled. The Strip shimmers hypnotically, promising excitement, entertainment, fortune and fame. Seeing is believing.

⊙ Sights

◉ The Strip

Vegas is famous for its shameless recreations of famous sights: Egyptian pyramids, the Eiffel Tower, Venetian canals. Jet from Europe to Polynesia and back without changing time zones – or even leaving the Strip.

★**Cosmopolitan**   CASINO
(Map p64; ♪ 702-698-7000; www.cosmopolitanlasvegas.com; 3708 S Las Vegas Blvd; ⊙24hr; P) Hipsters who thought they were too cool for Vegas finally have a place to go where they don't need irony to endure – or enjoy – the aesthetics of the Strip. Like the new Hollywood 'It' girl, the Cosmopolitan casino looks absolutely fabulous at all times. A steady stream of ingenues and entourages parade through the lobby (with some of the coolest design elements we've seen) along with anyone else who adores contemporary art and design.

Las Vegas & Nevada Highlights

1 Being mesmerized by the twinkling lights and the possibility that anything is possible in **Las Vegas** (p59).

2 Recognizing beauty in the isolation and desolation of the ancient desert at **Valley of Fire State Park** (p86).

3 Getting to know yourself against the backdrop of Hwy 50's jaw-dropping vistas, the **Loneliest Road in America** (p92).

4 Building a community, expressing yourself freely at **Burning Man** (p108), then 'leaving no trace.'

5 Skiing in the morning, having an alfresco patio lunch, then sunning yourself by **South Lake Tahoe** (p110).

Map labels

319

Pioche

Cathedral Gorge State Park **8**

Panaca

Caliente

Rachel

517

Extraterrestrial Hwy

Nellis Air Force Range

6

Tonopah

95

Goldfield

265

264

266

Basalt

Humboldt-Toiyabe National Forest

Yosemite Village

Yosemite National Park

120

120

49

140

41

180

99

Madera

Fresno

CALIFORNIA

41

65

180

Kettleman City

99

33

5

Coast Range

166

58

Santa Barbara

Mesquite

15

Overton

Valley of Fire State Park **2**

Pahranagat National Wildlife Refuge **4**

93

93

168

Desert National Wildlife Range

93

167

Colorado River

Hoover Dam

Las Vegas **1**

Boulder City

Goodsprings

Jean

Primm

164

Willow Beach

93

95

Searchlight

Lake Mohave

Laughlin

68

Needles

95

40

95

Christmas Tree Pass

ARIZONA

Hualapai Reservation

66

50 miles

100 km

N

Mt Charleston

95

Humboldt-Toiyabe National Forest

Pahrump

Red Rock Canyon **6**

572

Mercury

Amargosa Valley

Nevada Test Site

Area 51

373

Beatty

Rhyolite

267

190

190

178

Fort Irwin Military Reservation

127

15

15

China Lake Naval Weapons Center

China Lake Naval Weapons Center

178

395

58

Palmdale

138

Valencia

5

Los Angeles Aqueduct

Death Valley National Park **4**

Bishop

395

168

Owens River

Mammoth Lakes

203

6

Kings Canyon National Park

Sequoia National Park

Sequoia National Forest

Bakersfield

58

99

33

5

CALIFORNIA

Sierra Nevada

San Joaquin River

Stanislaus River

Legend items

6 Soaking your troubles away in the **Spencer Hot Springs** (p94) while the sun sets on the sierra.

7 Hiking by waterfalls and meadows of wildflowers in **Lamoille Recreation Area** (p99).

8 Paying your respects in nature's cathedral, the **Cathedral Gorge State Park** (p95).

9 Floating down a lazy Reno river with a beer in hand in **Truckee River Whitewater Park** (p102).

10 Marveling at the history of Nevada – a unique, liberal state – at the **Nevada State Museum** (p105) in Carson City.

★**Mandalay Bay** CASINO
(Map p64; ☎702-632-7700; www.mandalaybay.
com; 3950 S Las Vegas Blvd; ⏰24hr; P⏾) Since
opening in 1999, in place of the former '50s-
era Hacienda, Mandalay Bay has anchored
the southern Strip. Its theme may be tropical, but it sure ain't tacky, nor is its 135,000-
sq-ft casino. Well-dressed sports fans find
their way to the upscale race and sports
book near the high-stakes poker room.
Refusing to be pigeonholed, the Bay's standout attractions are many and include the
multilevel **Shark Reef Aquarium** (☎702-
632-4555; www.sharkreef.com; adult/child $25/19;
⏰10am-8pm Sun-Thu, to 10pm Fri & Sat; P⏾),
decadent day spas, oodles of signature
dining and the unrivaled **Mandalay Bay
Beach** (☎877-632-7800; www.mandalaybay.
com/en/amenities/beach.html; ⏰pool 8am-5pm,
Moorea Beach Club 11am-6pm; ⏾).

★**Bellagio** CASINO
(Map p64; ☎888-987-6667; www.bellagio.com;
3600 S Las Vegas Blvd; ⏰24hr; P⏾) The Bellagio experience transcends its decadent
casino floor of high-limit gaming tables
and in excess of 2300 slot machines; locals
say odds here are less than favorable. A
stop on the World Poker Tour, Bellagio's
tournament-worthy poker room offers
kitchen-to-gaming-table delivery around-
the-clock. Most, however, come for the
property's stunning architecture, interiors
and amenities, including the **Conservatory & Botanical Gardens** (⏰24hr; P⏾)
FREE, **Gallery of Fine Art** (☎702-693-7871;
adult/child under 12yr $18/free; ⏰10am-8pm,
last entry 7:30pm; P⏾), unmissable **Fountains of Bellagio** (⏰shows every 30min
3-8pm Mon-Fri, noon-8pm Sat, 11am-7pm Sun,
every 15min 8pm-midnight Mon-Sat, from 7pm
Sun; P⏾) FREE and the 2000-plus hand-
blown glass flowers embellishing the **hotel**
lobby (weekday/weekend r from $179/249;
P⏾@⏾⏾⏾).

★**LINQ Casino** CASINO
(Map p64; ☎800-634-6441; www.caesars.com/
linq; 3535 S Las Vegas Blvd; ⏰24hr; P) With a
fresh, young and funky vibe, one of Vegas'
newest casinos benefits from also being one
of its smallest with just over 60 tables and
around 750 slot machines. There's an airy,
spacious feel to the place, tables feature
high-backed, ruby-red, patent-vinyl chairs,
and when you need to escape, the fun and
frivolity of **LINQ Promenade** (Map p64; www.

caesars.com/linq; ⏰24hr; P⏾) is just outside
the door.

★**Wynn & Encore Casinos** CASINO
(Map p64; ☎702-770-0000; www.wynnlasvegas.
com; 3131 S Las Vegas Blvd; ⏰24hr; P⏾@⏾⏾)
Steve Wynn's signature casino hotel
(literally – his name is emblazoned across
the top) **Wynn** (weekday/weekend r from
$199/259) and its younger sibling **Encore**
(☎702-770-7100; r/ste from $199/259) are a pair
of curvaceous, copper-toned twin towers,
whose entrances are obscured by high fences
and lush greenery. Each hotel is unique, but
their sprawling subterranean casinos converge to form the Strip's second-largest and
arguably most elegant gaming floor, whose
popular poker rooms lure pros around the
clock and labyrinth of slot machines range
from a penny to $5000 per pull!

★**Stratosphere** CASINO
(Map p64; ☎702-380-7777; www.stratosphere
hotel.com; 2000 S Las Vegas Blvd; tower adult/child
$20/10, all-day pass incl unlimited thrill rides $40;
⏰casino 24hr, tower & thrill rides 10am-1am Sun-
Thu, to 2am Fri & Sat, weather permitting; P⏾)
Vegas has many buildings over 20 stories
tall, but only Stratosphere exceeds 100 and
boasts the nation's highest thrill rides. Atop
the 1149ft-high tapered tripod tower, vertiginous indoor and outdoor viewing decks
afford Vegas' best 360-degree panoramas.
There you'll also find **Top of the World**
(☎702-380-7711; www.topoftheworldlv.com; mains
lunch $25-34, dinner $40-79; ⏰11am-11pm), a
revolving restaurant, and the jazzy 107 Sky-
Lounge (p78) cocktail bar. To get to the top
of Vegas' lucky landmark, ride one of America's fastest elevators, lifting you 108 floors in
a mere 37 ear-popping seconds.

★**MGM Grand** CASINO
(Map p64; ☎877-880-0880; www.mgmgrand.
com; 3799 S Las Vegas Blvd; ⏰24hr; P⏾)
Owned by the eponymous Hollywood studio, the Grand liberally borrows Hollywood themes. Flashing LED screens and
computerized fountains add extra theat-
rics to the 100,000lb, 45ft-tall bronze lion
statue at the casino's entrance. Inside the
labyrinthine casino bedecked with giant
screens, you can get table-side massages
or take free Texas hold'em lessons in the
poker room. Top billing attractions include
Hakkasan (p78) nightclub, one-time center
of the electronic dance-music universe,
Cirque du Soleil's martial-arts-inspired **Kà**

([📞]702-531-3826; www.cirquedusoleil.com; adult $69-150, child 5-12yr $35-75; [⏱]7pm & 9:30pm Sat-Wed; [♿]) and the massive **MGM Grand Garden Arena** ([📞]877-880-0880; www.mgmgrand.com/entertainment; ticket prices vary; [⏱]box office 9am-8:30pm).

★**Caesars Palace**   CASINO
(Map p64; [📞]866-227-5938; www.caesarspalace.com; 3570 S Las Vegas Blvd; [⏱]24hr; [P]) Caesars Palace claims that its smartly renovated casino floor has more million-dollar slots than anywhere in the world, but its claims to fame are far more numerous than that. Entertainment's heavyweights Celine Dion and Elton John 'own' its custom-built **Colosseum** (www.thecolosseum.com; Caesars Palace; tickets $55-500) theater, fashionistas saunter around the **Shops at Forum** (www.simon.com/mall/the-forum-shops-at-caesars-palace/stores; [⏱]10am-11pm Sun-Thu, to midnight Fri & Sat), while Caesars group hotel guests quaff cocktails in the **Garden of the Gods Pool Oasis**. By night, megaclub Omnia (p78) is the only place to get off your face this side of Ibiza.

★**CityCenter**   LANDMARK
(Map p64; www.citycenter.com; 3780 S Las Vegas Blvd; [P]) We've seen this symbiotic relationship before (think giant hotel anchored by a mall 'concept'), but the way that this futuristic-feeling complex places a small galaxy of hypermodern, chichi hotels in orbit around the glitzy Shops at Crystals (p81) is a first. The uber-upscale spread includes the subdued, stylish **Vdara** ([📞]702-590-2111; www.vdara.com; 2600 W Harmon Ave, weekday/weekend ste from $129/189; [P][♿][❄][@][📶][🏊][🐾]) ✎, the hush-hush opulent Mandarin Oriental (p74) and the dramatic architectural showpiece **Aria** ([📞]702-590-7111; www.aria.com; 3730 S Las Vegas Blvd, [⏱]24hr; [P]), whose sophisticated casino provides a fitting backdrop to its many drop-dead-gorgeous restaurants. CityCenter's hotels have in excess of 6700 rooms!

★**Venetian**   CASINO
(Map p64; [📞]702-414-1000; www.venetian.com; 3355 S Las Vegas Blvd; [⏱]24hr; [P]) The Venetian's regal 120,000-sq-ft casino has marble floors, hand-painted ceiling frescoes and 120 table games, including a high-limit lounge and an elegant nonsmoking poker room, where women are especially welcome (unlike at many other poker rooms in town). When combined with its younger,

VINTAGE VEGAS

As if Vegas was ashamed of its sordid but fascinating history, old-school casinos are being demolished at a frenetic pace and the heyday of outrageous theme hotels is almost over. This is precisely why a trip to a hold-out like **Circus Circus** (Map p64; [📞]702-734-0410; www.circuscircus.com; 2880 S Las Vegas Blvd; [⏱]24hr; [P][♿]) is so satisfying. One million vintage bulbs illuminate the entry to this campy casino with low-roller tables, a classic steakhouse, carnival and arcade games, and free circus acts suspended high above the casino floor. Scout out more vintage Vegas gems Downtown, but oh, the times, they are a-changin'…

neighboring sibling **Palazzo** ([📞]702-607-7777; www.palazzo.com; 3325 S Las Vegas Blvd; [⏱]24hr; [P]), the properties claim the largest casino space in Las Vegas. Unmissable on the Strip, a highlight of this miniature replica of Venice is to take a **gondola ride** ([📞]702-414-4300; www.venetian.com/resort/attractions/gondola-rides.html; shared ride per person $29, child under 3yr free, private 2-passenger ride $116; [⏱]indoor 10am-11pm Sun-Thu, to midnight Fri & Sat, outdoor rides 11am-10pm, weather permitting; [♿]) down its Grand Canal.

★**New York–New York**   CASINO
(Map p64; [📞]800-689-1797; www.newyorknewyork.com; 3790 S Las Vegas Blvd; [⏱]24hr; [P]) Opened in 1997, the mini-megalopolis of New York–New York remains a perennial hit with spring breakers. Tables in the casino's 'Party Pit' are set against a backdrop of go-go dancers and occasional live entertainers, while out front, perspective-warping replicas of the Statue of Liberty, Brooklyn Bridge, and Chrysler and Empire State buildings delight visitors from abroad. Tying it all together, the **Big Apple Arcade** ([⏱]8am-midnight; [P][♿]) and **Roller Coaster** ([📞]702-740-6616; single ride/day pass $15/26; [⏱]11am-11pm Sun-Thu, 10:30am-midnight Fri & Sat; [P][♿]) are timeless hits with kids and big kids alike.

★**Paris Las Vegas**   CASINO
(Map p64; [📞]877-603-4386; www.parislasvegas.com; 3655 S Las Vegas Blvd; [⏱]24hr; [P]) This mini-version of the French capital might lack the charm of the City of Light,

The Strip

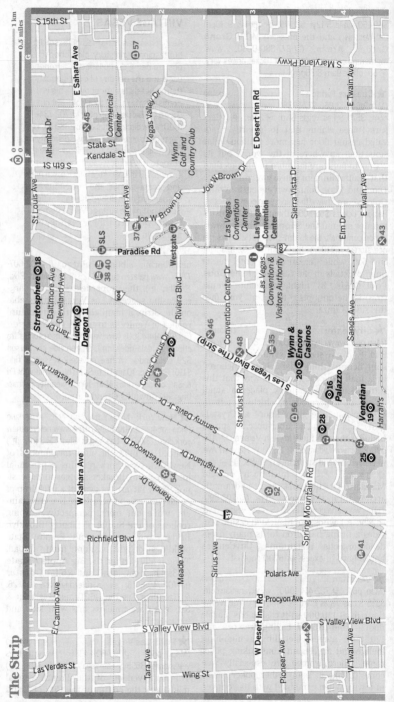

LAS VEGAS & NEVADA

1 km
0.5 miles

S 15th St
E Sahara Ave
S 6th St
Alhambra Dr
St Louis Ave
Baltimore Ave
Cleveland Ave
Tam Dr
Western Ave

S 57

X 45
Commercial Center
State St
Kendale St

Vegas Valley Dr
Wynn Golf and Country Club
Joe W Brown Dr
Karen Ave
Joe W Brown Dr

S Maryland Pkwy
E Desert Inn Rd
Sierra Vista Dr
Elm Dr
E Twain Ave
S Maryland Pkwy

X 43

Stratosphere ⊙ 18
Lucky ⊙
Dragon 11

37
SLS ⊙
Paradise Rd
Westgate
38 40

Las Vegas Convention Center
Las Vegas Convention Center

605
Las Vegas Convention & Visitors Authority

Riviera Blvd
Convention Center Dr

X 46
X 48
35

22 ⊙
29
Circus Circus Dr
Stardust Rd
S Highland Dr
Sammy Davis Jr Dr

Las Vegas Blvd (The Strip)

Wynn & ⊙
20 ⊙ Encore Casinos
⊙ 16 Palazzo

56
28
25
Venetian
19 ⊙
Harrah's

Sands Ave

W Sahara Ave
Rancho Dr
Westwood Dr
54
52
15
Spring Mountain Rd

Richfield Blvd
Meade Ave
Sirius Ave
Polaris Ave
S Valley View Blvd

41

El Camino Ave
Tara Ave
Wing St
Pioneer Ave
S Valley View Blvd
Procyon Ave
W Desert Inn Rd
Las Verdes St

44
W Twain Ave

604

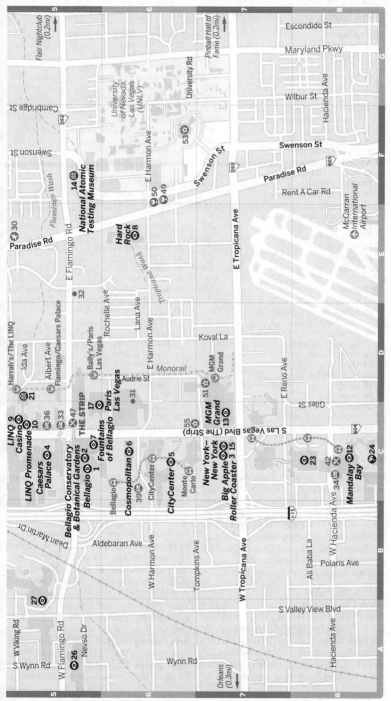

Escondido St

Maryland Pkwy

Wilbur St

Hacienda Ave

University Rd

University of Nevada, Las Vegas (UNLV)

Swenson St

Cambridge St

Swenson St

53

Paradise Rd

Rent A Car Rd

E Harmon Ave

Flamingo Wash

National Atomic Testing Museum 14

50
49

E Flamingo Rd

Flamingo/Caesars Palace

Paradise Rd

30

McCarran International Airport

Hard Rock 8

Tropicana Wash

E Tropicana Ave

Ida Ave

Albert Ave

32

Rochelle Ave

Lana Ave

Koval La

Harrah's/The LINQ

Bally's/Paris Las Vegas

E Harmon Ave

Monorail

MGM Grand

E Reno Ave

21

17

Audrie St

31

Paris Las Vegas

51

MGM Grand 13

Giles St

LINQ 9
Casino

10

36
33

47

THE STRIP

7

1

2

Fountains of Bellagio

55

MGM Grand

New York–
New York

E Reno Ave

S Las Vegas Blvd (The Strip)

LINQ Promenade

Caesars Palace 4

Bellagio Conservatory & Botanical Gardens

Bellagio 1

Cosmopolitan 6

5

CityCenter

Monte Carlo

New York–
New York 3 15

Big Apple Roller Coaster 3 15

23

Bellagio

39

CityCenter

42

Mandalay Ave 34

24

Dean Martin Dr

Aldebaran Ave

W Harmon Ave

Tompkins Ave

W Tropicana Ave

Ali Baba La

Mandalay Bay 12

W Hacienda Ave

I-15

604

27

26

W Flamingo Rd

W Viking Rd

S Wynn Rd

Nevso Dr

Orleans
(0.3mi)

Wynn Rd

Polaris Ave

S Valley View Blvd

Hacienda Ave

Flair Nightclub (0.2mi)

Pinball Hall of Fame (0.2mi)

The Strip

but its efforts to emulate Paris' landmarks, including a 34-story Hotel de Ville and facades from the Opera House and Louvre, make it a fun stop for families and anyone yet to see the real thing. Its vaulted casino ceilings simulate sunny skies above myriad tables and slots, while its high-limit authentic French roulette wheels, sans 0 and 00, slightly improve your odds.

Auto Collections
Vegas Car Museum   MUSEUM
(Map p64; ☎702-794-3174; LINQ; adult/child $13/8; ☺10am-5pm Mon-Sat) Located on the 5th floor of the LINQ parking facility, this fascinating car museum has more than 250 antique, hot-rod and historically significant cars on display. Everything you can see is for

sale – that is, if you can afford the average asking price of around $1 million!

◎ Downtown

For tourists, the five-block **Fremont Street Experience** (Map p68; ☎702-678-5600; www. vegasexperience.com; Fremont St Mall; ☺shows hourly dusk-midnight or 1am; ☐Deuce, SDX) **FREE** is the focal point of Downtown, with its wealth of vintage casinos, where today's Vegas was born – and fear not, they're still going strong. Further south, the **18b Arts District** (www.18b.org) revolves around the **Arts Factory** (Map p68; ☎702-383-9907; www. theartsfactory.com; 107 E Charleston Blvd; ☺9am-6pm; ☐Deuce, SDX), while heading east on Fremont St will take you to the sweetest little hodgepodge of hip bars and happening restaurants that you could possibly imagine.

★ **Mob Museum**   MUSEUM
(Map p68; ☎702-229-2734; www.themob museum.org; 300 Stewart Ave; adult/child $24/14; ◎9am-9pm; P; ⊒Deuce) It's hard to say what's more impressive: the museum's physical location in a historic federal courthouse where mobsters sat for federal hearings in 1950–51, the fact that the board of directors is headed up by a former FBI Special Agent, or the thoughtfully curated exhibits telling the story of organized crime in America. In addition to hands-on FBI equipment and mob-related artifacts, the museum boasts a series of multimedia exhibits featuring interviews with real-life Tony Sopranos.

★ **Container Park**   CULTURAL CENTER
(Map p68; ☎702-359-9982; downtowncontainer park.com; 707 Fremont St E; ◎11am-9pm Mon-Thu, 10am-10pm Fri & Sat, to 8pm Sun) An incubator for up-and-coming fashion designers and local artisans, the edgy Container Park stacks pop-up shops on top of one another. Wander along the sidewalks and catwalks while searching out handmade jewelry, contemporary art and clothing at a dozen or so specialty boutiques, eateries and art installations. When the sun sets, the container bars come to life and host regular themed events and movie nights. It's adults only (21-plus) after 9pm.

★ **Golden Nugget**   CASINO
(Map p68; ☎702-385-7111; www.goldennugget.com; 129 Fremont St E; ◎24hr; P⚕; ⊒Deuce, SDX)

Downtown Las Vegas

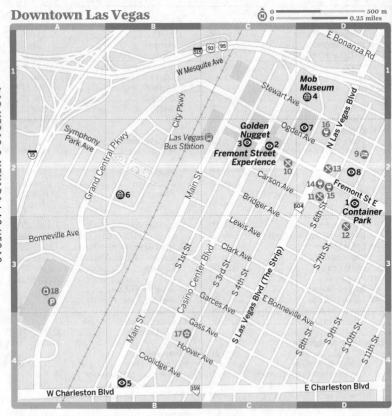

Check out the polished brass and white-leather seats in the casino: day or night, the Golden Nugget is downtown's poshest address. With classy eateries and a swimming pool famous for its shark tank, the Golden Nugget outshines its competition. This swank carpet joint rakes in a moneyed crowd with a 38,000-sq-ft casino populated by table games and slot machines with the same odds as at Strip megaresorts. The nonsmoking poker room hosts daily tournaments.

Downtown Grand   CASINO
(Map p68; ☑702-953-4343; www.downtown grand.com; 206 N 3rd St; ⊙24hr; ☑Deuce, SDX) Reborn from the shell of the Lady Luck casino, the Downtown Grand is a shiny new player on the Downtown gambling scene. Just north of Fremont St, the urban-chic casino combines chandeliers with 'street dice' gamblers placing bets outdoors, weather permitting. The diminutive casino holds about 600 slot machines and 30 table games. A quirky

bunch of bars and restaurants includes a roof-top pool bar serving food in picnic baskets.

Discovery Children's Museum   MUSEUM
(Map p68; ☑702-382-3445; www.discovery kidslv.org; 360 Promenade Pl, Symphony Park; $14.50; ⊙10am-5pm Mon-Sat, noon-5pm Sun Jun-early Sep, 9am-4pm Tue-Fri, noon-5pm Sat & Sun rest of year; ⊞; ☑SDX) Designed for toddlers to pre-teens, the Discovery Children's Museum has undergone a major overhaul and reopened in a state-of-the-art building in Symphony Park. Highlights include 'The Summit,' a 12-story tower of interactive activities and play space, plus themed educational and entertaining exhibits such as Eco City, Water World, Toddler Town, Fantasy Festival, Patents Pending and Young at Art.

◉ East of the Strip

This is locals' Vegas, home for many of the folks whose hard work makes the Strip tick.

Downtown Las Vegas

Wander with awareness around these grassroots, culturally diverse neighborhoods: the insatiability that passes on the Strip isn't kosher here.

★ **Pinball Hall of Fame** MUSEUM
(☎702-597-2627; www.pinballmuseum.org; 1610 E Tropicana Ave; per game 25¢-$1; ⊙11am-11pm Sun-Thu, to midnight Fri & Sat; ⍟; ☐201) You may have more fun at this no-frills arcade than playing slot machines back on the Strip. Tim Arnold shares his collection of 200-plus vintage pinball and video games with the public. Take time to read the handwritten curatorial cards explaining the unusual history behind these restored machines.

★ **Hard Rock** CASINO
(Map p64; ☎702-693-5000; www.hardrock hotel.com; 4455 Paradise Rd; ⊙24hr; ☐108) The world's original rock-and-roll casino houses what may be the most impressive collection of rock-star memorabilia ever assembled under one roof. Priceless items being watched over by security guards suited up like bouncers are concert attire worn by Elvis, Britney Spears and Prince; a display case filled with Beatles mementos; Jim Morrison's handwritten lyrics to one of the Doors' greatest hits; and dozens of leather jackets and guitars formerly owned by everyone from the Ramones to U2.

★ **National Atomic
Testing Museum** MUSEUM
(Map p64; ☎702-794-5151; www.nationalatomic testingmuseum.org; 755 Flamingo Rd E, Desert Research Institute; adult/child $22/16; ⊙10am-5pm Mon-Sat, noon-5pm Sun; ☐202) Fascinating multimedia exhibits focus on science, technology and the social history of the 'Atomic Age,' which lasted from WWII until atmospheric bomb testing was driven underground in 1961 and a worldwide ban on nuclear testing was declared in 1992. View footage of atomic testing and examine southern Nevada's nuclear past, present and future, from American Indian ways of life to the environmental legacy of atomic testing. Don't miss the ticket booth (how could you?); it's a Nevada Test Site guard-station replica.

◎ West of the Strip

It's not so much about what's to see west of the Strip, but what's to do, from zip-lining off the top of a skyscraper, to exploring the breadth of Asian cuisine at **Lucky Dragon** (Map p64; ☎702-889-8018; www.luckydragonlv. com; 300 W Sahara Ave; ⊙24hr) casino and **Chinatown Plaza**, and checking out the suburbs where the locals live, eat, sleep and play.

★ **Springs Preserve** NATURE RESERVE
(☎702-822-7700; www.springspreserve.org; 333 S Valley View Blvd; adult/child $19/11; ⊙9am-5pm; ⍟; ☐104) ⌀ On the site of the natural springs (which ran dry in 1962) that fed *las vegas* ('the meadows'), where southern Paiutes and Spanish Trail traders camped, and later Mormon missionaries and Western pioneers settled the valley, this educational complex is an incredible trip through historical, cultural and biological time. The touchstone is the **Desert Living Center**, demonstrating sustainable architectural design and everyday ecoconscious living.

★ **Nevada State Museum**   MUSEUM
(✍ 702-486-5205; nvdtca.org/museums; 309 S Valley View Blvd; adult/child $20/12; ⏰ 9am-5pm Tue-Sun; ♿) If you've got a hankering to see a stuffed Columbian mammoth or the Nevada state fossil (psst, it's an ichthyosaur) you've come to the right place. However, the most interesting exhibit at this modern, updated center is the 'Viva Las Vegas' display on the modern history of Vegas, replete with casino memorabilia and exhibits about the Hoover Dam project and 1950s atomic testing.

🏃 Activities

★ **Stratosphere Thrill Rides**   AMUSEMENT PARK
(Map p64; ✍ 702-383-5210; www.stratosphere hotel.com/Attractions/Thrill-Rides; Stratosphere; elevator adult $20, incl 3 thrill rides $35, all-day pass $40; ⏰ 10am-1am Sun-Thu, to 2am Fri & Sat; 🚌 Sahara) The world's highest thrill rides await, a whopping 110 stories above the Strip. Big Shot straps riders into completely exposed seats that zip up the tower's pinnacle, while Insanity spins riders out over the tower's edge. X-Scream leaves you hanging 27ft over the edge, 866ft above ground. For a real adrenaline rush, save your dough for SkyJump (✍ 702-380-7777; www.skyjumplasvegas.com; per jump $120; ⏰ 10am-1am Sun-Thu, to 2am Fri & Sat).

★ **Dream Racing**   ADVENTURE SPORTS
(✍ 702-605-3000; www.dreamracing.com; 7000 N Las Vegas Blvd, Las Vegas Motor Speedway; 5-lap experiences $199-599; ⏰ by appointment; 🅿) Ever wanted to get behind the wheel of a Porsche 911, Lamborghini, Lotus, AMG Mercedes or McLaren and really let fly? Of course you have. Well, now you can choose from the largest selection of insured supercars in the world, without having to buy one.

GAMBLING

You're on your third martini. You just won the last three hands. Adrenaline pumping, you double down and lose the down payment on your next car. For every game except poker, the house has a statistical winning edge over the gambler and for nearly every payout, the house 'holds' a small portion of the winnings. Have fun, but understand the games you're playing and stop when you're ahead.

Papillon Grand Canyon Helicopters   SCENIC FLIGHTS
(Map p64; ✍ 702-736-7243; www.papillon.com; 3900 Paradise Rd #233; ground tours from $149, air tours from $229) This flightseeing tour operator offers luxury Grand Canyon tours. Its 10-minute 'Neon Nights Express' jetcopter flyover of the Strip (adult/child from $69/49) is popular.

VooDoo ZipLine   ADVENTURE SPORTS
(Map p64; ✍ 702-388-0477; voodoozipline.com; Rio; $27; ⏰ 11am-midnight) How does 'flying' between Rio's two hotel towers sound? The ride starts with you strapped into a seat on a 50-story tower. Four hundred feet below is the expansive pool area, and beyond is the cityscape. Once the operator sets you free, you'll whiz down metal lines to a lower tower, taking in the 800ft-long rush ... then get pulled back!

★ **Spa at Encore**   SPA
(Map p64; ✍ 702-770-3900; Encore; spa & fitness center day pass $40; ⏰ 7am-8pm) Newer than the spa at Wynn (p62), Encore's luxurious spa is splurge-worthy. Stroll down exotic, tranquil passageways lined with flickering Middle Eastern lamps and golden Buddha statues, then sink into hot or cold plunge pools under glowing Swarovski crystal chandeliers or recline on a heated chaise longue before trying a Thai oil fusion massage or the Moroccan mud wrap.

★ **Sahra Spa & Hammam**   SPA
(Map p64; ✍ 702-698-7171; www.cosmopolitan lasvegas.com/spa; Cosmopolitan; day pass fitness center $20, spa $35-45; ⏰ 7am-8pm) The Cosmopolitan's (p59) spa specializes in extravagant rituals and 'transformations' inspired by Middle Eastern traditions of bathing and detoxification – just the ticket after a wild night of clubbing. Rent the heated-stone hammam for just yourself or with a few friends, followed by a clay wrap scented with cardamom, a full-body scrub or a rub-down massage. Book appointments in advance.

★ **Qua Baths & Spa**   SPA
(Map p64; ✍ 866-782-0655; Caesars Palace; fitness center day pass $25, incl spa facilities $50; ⏰ 6am-8pm) Qua evokes the ancient Roman rituals of indulgent bathing. Try a signature 'bath liqueur,' a personalized potion of herbs and oils poured into your own private tub. The women's side includes a tea lounge, a herbal steam room and an Arctic ice room where

artificial snow falls. On the men's side, there's a barber spa and big-screen sports TVs.

🎓 Courses

Stripper 101 DANCING
(Map p64; ☑866-932-1818; www.stripper101.com; 3663 S Las Vegas Blvd, Miracle Mile Shops, V Theater; classes from $40; ⊙hours vary) In a cabaret setting complete with strobe lights, cocktails and feather boas, these (non-nude) pole-dancing classes are popular with bachelorettes.

👉 Tours

Big Bus Las Vegas BUS
(☑702-685-6578; www.bigbustours.com/en/las-vegas; 3201 Builders Ave; tours adult/child from $41/26) Operates hop-on, hop-off tours of Las Vegas, following two routes, and three-hour nightly tours of Vegas' shining lights.

Vegas Mob Tour BUS
(Map p64; ☑702-677-9015; www.vegasmobtour. com; 255 E Flamingo Rd, Tuscany Suites; 3hr tour $90) Created with input from real-life mobsters and historians, this bus tour delves into the Mafia underworld of Sin City's past, including celebrity scandals, mobster assassinations and other dirty laundry. Tickets include pizza and admission to Downtown's Mob Museum (p67). By reservation only.

🎊 Festivals & Events

Electric Daisy Carnival MUSIC
(www.electricdaisycarnival.com; ⊙Jun) The largest of its kind in the world, the Electric Daisy Carnival brings huge crowds of EDM (electronic dance music) fans to the Las Vegas Motor Speedway (p81) for three nights of DJs and live acts and a series of parties from dusk till dawn.

First Friday ART
(www.ffflv.org; ⊙5-11pm 1st Friday every month) A carnival of 10,000 art lovers, hipsters, indie musicians and sundry hangers-on wander around the Downtown arts and antiques district for First Friday evenings. These giant block parties come alive with gallery openings accompanied by performance art, music, fortune tellers and tattoo artists.

Vegas Uncork'd WINE
(www.vegasuncorked.com; ⊙Apr; 🎫) 🍷 Four days of fabulous wine and food in the city known for its fabulous food, including sessions with celebrity chefs such as Gordon Ramsay and Giada De Laurentiis famed for heading the restaurants that create said

DESERT NATIONAL WILDLIFE REFUGE

While Las Vegas has 2.3 million residents, it's next to this immense region with zero human inhabitants, but home to bighorn sheep, mountain lions, eagles, foxes, lizards and more. Lovers of science and nature will be thrilled by the **wildlife refuge** (☑702-879-6110; www.fws.gov/refuge/desert; 16001 Corn Creek Rd; ⊙24hr) FREE and its expansive vistas, found just 25 miles northwest of Summerlin and 32 miles from Downtown Las Vegas. Most of the park occupies harsh, rugged terrain that is difficult to reach. Begin your visit at the Desert NWR Visitor Center.

fabulous food. Uncork'd is as good a reason as any to justify a trip to Vegas.

Rise Festival CULTURAL
(risefestival.com; ⊙Jun & Jul; 🎫) 🍷 Rise is everything that's good about the world: a celebration of light, music, the earth and its people. This unique community gathering south of Las Vegas, outside the town of Jean, which culminates with each attendee releasing a floating lantern into the dark desert sky as a symbolic beacon of light, is a treat for the senses.

Viva Las Vegas MUSIC
(www.vivalasvegas.net; ⊙mid-Apr) The ultimate celebration of 1950s rockabilly music and culture is held over one jam-packed weekend at the **Orleans** (☑702-365-7111; www.orleanscasino.com; 4500 W Tropicana Ave; ⊙24hr; 🎫; 🚌 free Strip shuttle) hotel and casino.

🛏️ Sleeping

With more than 150,000 hotel rooms and consistently high occupancy rates, prices in Vegas fluctuate constantly. Sometimes the best deals are found in advance, other times, at the last minute.

🛏️ The Strip

SLS HOTEL $
(Map p64; ☑702-761-7000; www.slslasvegas.com; 2535 S Las Vegas Blvd; d from $79; P❄🕸🛜🏊) You can nab a room at Vegas' SLS (the Starwood Hotel Group's boutique brand) on the north Strip at a crazy rate compared to same-branded properties in other cities. The

DON'T MISS

Even if late nights, gambling and neon aren't your style, cut loose and cruise Las Vegas' infamous Strip (p59) for at least a day or two: chill out poolside at a four-star resort, hit the clubs, and splurge on steak and martinis in Rat Pack style. While you're there, don't miss a Cirque du Soleil show.

In a state known for lovably bizarre small towns, the prize for the most unique is a toss-up between Virginia City (p107), where the gold rush and the Wild West live on, or spirited Elko (p98), with its Basque restaurants and cowboy poetry festival.

For incomparable outdoor bliss, Lake Tahoe offers fairy-tale winter ski slopes and pristine summer beaches. If untamed wilderness strikes your fancy, you'll want to get lost in the vast **Great Basin National Park** (☎775-234-7331; www.nps.gov/grba; ⌚24hr) FREE or brave the eerily deserted US Hwy 50 (p92), nicknamed the 'Loneliest Road in America.'

Finally, the hottest place in Nevada is also home to one of the Southwest's most unique annual events: the **Burning Man festival** (p108), where iconoclasts, rebels, artists, soul-seekers and the irrepressibly curious celebrate and create in the shimmering heat of the Black Rock Desert.

hotel's quirky style is infectious: you'll have fun with the acronym within minutes.

Flamingo CASINO HOTEL $
(Map p64; ☎702-733-3111; www.flamingolasvegas.com; 3555 S Las Vegas Blvd; weekday/weekend r from $49/99; P ❄ @ ☕ ≋ 🐾) Recent updates have stolen some of this legendary gangster-era casino's retro charm, and service levels fail to wow, but its down-to-earth, live-it-up vibe and prime center Strip location opening on to lively LINQ Promenade (p62) might be just the ticket for some, especially when rates are low.

Treasure Island CASINO HOTEL $
(Map p64; ☎702-894-7111; www.treasureisland.com; 3300 S Las Vegas Blvd; weekday/weekend r from $59/109; P ❄ @ ☕ ≋) Breezy, recently renovated rooms are stylish and comfortable enough, although on-site dining and amenities are only so-so. Treasure Island offers good value in terms of the quality, size and condition of said rooms and its don't-go-too-much-further-north location.

New York–New York CASINO HOTEL $
(Map p64; ☎702-740-6969; www.newyorknewyork.com; 3790 S Las Vegas Blvd; weekday/weekend r from $49/89; P ❄ @ ☕ ≋) A favorite of college students, these digs are decent but a little on the smaller side – just as you'd expect if you were up-and-coming in New York City.

★**Cromwell Las Vegas** BOUTIQUE HOTEL $$
(Map p64; ☎702-777-3777; www.caesars.com/cromwell; 3595 S Las Vegas Blvd; r/ste from $199/399; P ❄ ☕ ≋ 🐾) If you're 20- to 30-something, can hold your own with the cool kids, or you're just effortlessly stylish whatever your demographic, there are a few good reasons to choose Cromwell, the best being its location and frequently excellent rates on sassy, entry-level rooms. The others? You've got your sites set on partying at Drai's (p79) or dining downstairs at **Giada** (☎855-442-3271; mains $25-58; ⌚8am-11pm).

★**W Las Vegas** BOUTIQUE HOTEL $$
(Map p64; ☎702-761-8700; www.wlasvegas.com; 2535 S Las Vegas Blvd; r from $109; P ❄ ☕ ≋ 🐾) At the time of writing, the new W Las Vegas, occupying what was one of two towers belonging to sister property SLS (p71), was the hottest ticket on the north Strip, offering excellent rates for a stylish brand-new product by this exciting world-recognized brand. If you like design and a cooler crowd, head north and hang here.

★**NOBU Hotel** HOTEL $$
(Map p64; ☎800-727-4923; www.nobucaesarspalace.com; 3570 S Las Vegas Blvd, Caesars Palace; d from $159) This exclusive boutique hotel within Caesars Palace (p63) is one for lovers of Japanese design from the traditional to the modern. Rooms are in high demand and suites are often the domain of celebrities.

★**Aria Las Vegas Resort** CASINO HOTEL $$
(Map p64; ☎702-590-7111; www.aria.com; 3730 S Las Vegas Blvd, CityCenter; r weekday/weekend from $129/189; P ❄ @ ☕ ≋) Aria's sleek resort hotel at CityCenter (p63) has no theme, unlike the Strip's other mega-properties. Instead, its 4000-plus deluxe rooms (520 sq ft) and 560 tower suites (920-plus sq ft) are all about soothing design, spaciousness and luxury, and every room has a corner view. If

you've cash to burn, **Aria Sky Suites & Villas** (ste/villa from $340/3000), a hotel-within-a-hotel, might be for you.

★ Mandalay Bay
CASINO HOTEL $$

(Map p64; ☑ 702-632-7700; www.mandalaybay. com; 3950 S Las Vegas Blvd; weekday/weekend r from $119/229; P✷@🛜⛱) Anchoring the south Strip, upscale Mandalay Bay's (p62) same-named hotel has a cache of classy rooms worthy of your attention in their own right, not to mention the exclusive **Four Seasons Hotel** (☑ 702-632-5000; www.fourseasons.com/lasvegas; weekday/weekend r from $229/289; P✷@🛜⛱🛁) and boutique Delano within its bounds and a diverse range of noteworthy attractions and amenities, not least of which is Mandalay Bay Beach (p62).

★ LINQ Hotel
CASINO HOTEL $$

(Map p64; ☑ 800-634-6441; www.caesars.com/ linq; 3535 S Las Vegas Blvd; d/ste from $109/209; P✷🛜⛱🛁) Launching onto the Las Vegas Strip in late 2014, LINQ, formerly the Quad, has cemented its position as a solid all-rounder. Its fresh, white rooms have fun splashes of color and sleek Euro-styled furniture, there's a wealth of available amenities (this being part of the Caesars group) and it has an enviable location at the center of its eponymous promenade (p62).

Venetian
CASINO HOTEL $$

(Map p64; ☑ 702-414-1000; www.venetian.com; 3355 S Las Vegas Blvd; weekday/weekend ste from $169/299; P✷@🛜⛱) Vegas' own 'Most Serene Republic', the Venetian features huge suites with sunken living rooms and countless luxuries from deep soaking tubs to pillow menus, and a general overall shared experience with its younger sister, **Palazzo** (Map p64; ☑ 702-607-7777; www. palazzo.com; 3325 S Las Vegas Blvd; weekday/ weekend ste from $199/369; P✷@🛜⛱).

Delano
HOTEL $$

(Map p64; ☑ 877-632-7800; www.delano lasvegas.com; Mandalay Bay; r/ste from $69/129; P✷@🛜⛱🛁) One of Mandalay Bay's two hotels-within-a-hotel, Delano is its boutique offering. Its light-filled guest rooms have fresh, clean lines, softened by downy fabrics, mosaic wallpapers and pastel flourishes that speak to a discerning crowd old enough to have refined their tastes and who enjoy life's finer details. Excellent rates can be found due to the south-Strip location.

Caesars Palace
CASINO HOTEL $$

(Map p64; ☑ 866-227-5938; www.caesarspalace. com; 3570 S Las Vegas Blvd; weekday/weekend r from $109/149; P✷@🛜⛱🛁) In 2016, Caesars celebrated turning 50 by (how else?) throwing a bunch of money into shaking off some gaudy and making itself look fabulous. Almost 600 rooms in its Roman Tower got a lavish makeover and the tower, a new name: Julius, of course! Augustus' guest rooms got some style too: think grey, white-gold and royal blue.

★ Cosmopolitan
CASINO HOTEL $$$

(Map p64; ☑ 702-698-7575, 702-698-7000; www. cosmopolitanlasvegas.com; 3708 S Las Vegas Blvd; r/ste from $250/300; P✷@🛜⛱🛁; 🚍 Deuce) With at least eight distinctively different and equally stylish room types to choose from, Cosmo's digs are the hippest on the Strip. Ranging from oversized to decadent, about 2200 of its 2900 or so rooms have balconies (all but the entry-level category), many sport sunken Japanese tubs and all feature plush furnishings and design quirks you'll delight in uncovering.

★ Villas at the Mirage
VILLA $$$

(Map p64; ☑ 800-374-9000; www.mgmresorts. com/mirage/villas; Mirage; villas from $2400; P✷🛜⛱🛁) Formerly the domain of 'whales' – the highest echelon of casino hotshot who'd be enticed to the property with complimentary stays – these secluded,

---

LAS VEGAS FOR KIDS

If you look past the smoke and glitter – which is hard to do in this town – you'll notice a range of family-friendly attractions and activities. Most casinos have virtual-reality and video-game arcades. At New York–New York, a roller coaster (p63) shoots out of a fake Big Apple skyline, while Circus Circus has the **Adventuredome** (Map p64; ☑ 702-794-3939; www.adventuredome.com; day pass over/under 48in tall $32/18; ⊙ 10am-6pm daily, later on weekends & May-Sep; 👶) theme park and free acrobat shows. Teens will get a thrill from the Stratosphere (p62) tower and its adrenaline-pumping rides. Cirque du Soleil's show Mystère welcomes all ages, while Kà, Michael Jackson ONE and Beatles LOVE can be fun for children aged five and up.

unique self-contained oases with private pools were completely renovated by Mirage, which decided to reintroduce them into the paid luxury and celebrity market. If you can afford one, you probably know about this hush-hush release already.

★ Mandarin Oriental
HOTEL $$$

(Map p64; 702-590-8888; www.mandarin oriental.com; 3752 S Las Vegas Blvd, CityCenter; r/ste from $239/469; ❄ 🛜 🛒) Part of the CityCenter (p63) complex, luscious oriental flavors meet the latest technology in Mandarin Oriental's 392 slick, state-of-the-art yet effortlessly elegant guest rooms and suites, undoubtedly some of the finest to be found on a Strip dripping with gold and shimmering with shiny things. Add a high ratio of courteous, attentive staff to each guest and you're on a winning streak.

★ Skylofts
HOTEL $$$

(Map p64; 877-646-5638; www.skyloftsmgm grand.com; MGM Grand; ste from $1000; P ❄ @ 🛜 🛒) Glamorous, one-of-a-kind apartments designed by innovative architect Tony Chi have loft bedrooms and two-story windows. They're also outfitted with almost every imaginable indulgence, from spa tubs and steamy 'immersion' showers to gourmet kitchens and top-flight entertainment centers. A 24-hour butler and personal concierge are included, of course.

🛌 Downtown

★ El Cortez
CASINO HOTEL $

(Map p68; 702-385-5200; www.elcortezhotel casino.com; 651 E Ogden Ave; weekday/weekend r from $40/80; P ❄ @ 🛜) A wide range of rooms with all kinds of vibes are available at this fun, retro property close to all the action on Fremont St. Rooms are in the 1980s tower addition to the heritage-listed 1941 El Cortez (600 Fremont St E; ⏱ 24hr; 🚌 Deuce) casino and the modern, flashier El Cortez Suites, across

---

RESERVATIONS

Las Vegas has more hotel rooms than any other city in the world (around 150,000)! Despite this, it is almost always busy. Don't show up during the 'March Madness' conference season (all of March) or Spring Break (April to May) without a reservation. At other times, you could wing it and show up for last-minute bargains, but why take the gamble? Ooohh...

---

the street. Rates offered are generally great value, though don't expect the Earth.

★ Golden Nugget
CASINO HOTEL $

(Map p68; 702-385-7111; www.goldennugget. com; 129 Fremont St E; weekday/weekend r from $45/85; P ❄ @ 🛜 🛒) Pretend to relive the fabulous heyday of Vegas in the 1950s at this swank Fremont St address. Rooms in the Rush Tower are the best in the house.

🛌 East of the Strip

★ Hilton Grand Vacations on Paradise
HOTEL $

(Map p64; 702-946-9210; www.hiltongrand vacations.com/nevada/hgvc-paradise; 455 Karen Ave; ste from $79; P ❄ 🛜 🛒) The spacious studio suites and one- and two-bedroom apartments of this well-maintained resort-style facility, less than a mile from the center Strip, offer excellent value, especially for traveling families.

★ Hard Rock
CASINO HOTEL $

(Map p64; 702-693-5000; www.hardrock hotel.com; 4455 Paradise Rd; weekday/weekend r from $45/89; P ❄ @ 🛜 🛒) Sexy, oversized rooms and HRH suites underwent a bunch of refurbishments in 2016 and 2017, making this party palace for music lovers a great alternative to staying on the Strip – there's even a free shuttle to take you there and bring you back.

🛌 West of the Strip

Rio
CASINO HOTEL $

(Map p64; 866-746-7671; www.riolasvegas. com; 3700 W Flamingo Rd; weekday/weekend ste from $30/80; P ❄ 🛜 🛒 🏊) This Carnaval-themed hotel just off the Strip attracts families, poker players and bachelor/ette parties. Free, frequent Strip shuttles and a rooftop zip line (p70) are bonuses, but the exterior of the hotel and the rooms themselves could really do with some love.

Wyndham Desert Blue
RESORT $$

(Map p64; 702-691-2600; www.clubwyndham. com; 3200 W Twain Ave; ste from $157; P ❄ 🛜 🛒) There's a two-night minimum stay at this sleek, new-in-2015, condo-style timeshare resort, with ubercool decor and bargain rates to be found through online booking engines. Family-friendly, its fully equipped one- and two-bedroom suites make it easy to create a home base in Vegas that's not too far from the excitement of the Strip.

Greater Las Vegas

★ Red Rock Casino Resort & Spa
CASINO HOTEL $$
(☎702-797-7777; www.redrock.sclv.com; 11011 Charleston Blvd; d from $179; P ❄ 🛜 🏊) Located 6 miles east of the Red Rock Canyon Visitor Center (p85) and a world away from the Strip, this luxe resort boasts dining, services and entertainment on par with the city's top casinos. Centered on a sumptuous pool, a wide range of gorgeous rooms, suites and villas, all with great views, awaits. Worth considering if you prefer nature over neon.

Element Las Vegas Summerlin
BOUTIQUE HOTEL $$
(☎702-589-2000; www.elementlasvegassummerlin. com; 10555 Discovery Dr; d/ste from $139/150; P 🛜 🏊) 🍴 Westin's foray into the niche fitness-and-lifestyle market has come to Summerlin. Enjoy Element's complimentary healthy breakfast options, evening receptions, full gym and ecoconscious hotel policies. Stylish accommodations are decorated in neutral grays with sleek lines and bright-green accents, and range in size from standard hotel rooms to studio and one-bedroom suites with kitchen facilities.

Eating

The Strip

It's impossible to cover even a fraction of the dining options along the Strip, but it should be noted that anywhere you dine, you'll be paying more for the privilege, just because it's Vegas.

★ Umami Burger
BURGERS $
(Map p64; ☎702-761-7614; www.slslasvegas.com/ dining/umami-burger; SLS, 2535 S Las Vegas Blvd; burgers $12-15; ⏰11am-10pm; P) SLS' (p71) burger offering is one of the best on the Strip, with its outdoor beer garden, extensive craft-beer selection and juicy boutique burgers made by the chain that won *GQ* magazine's prestigious 'burger of the year' crown.

★ Tacos El Gordo
MEXICAN $
(Map p64; ☎702-251-8226; www.tacoselgordo bc.com; 3049 S Las Vegas Blvd; small plates $3-12; ⏰10am-2am Sun-Thu, to 4am Fri & Sat; P 🍴 🎮; 🚊Deuce, SDX) This Tijuana-style taco shop from SoCal is just the ticket when it's way late, you've got almost no money left and you're desperately craving *carne asada* (beef) or *adobada* (chile-marinated pork) tacos in hot, handmade tortillas. Adventurous eaters order the authentic *sesos* (beef brains), *cabeza* (roasted cow's head) or tripe (intestines) variations.

★ Ramen-ya Katana
RAMEN $
(Map p64; ☎702-586-6889; www.ramen-katanaya. com; 3615 S Las Vegas Blvd, Grand Bazaar Shops; meals $9-14; ⏰9:30am-1am; ❄) Granted, purists who follow the Japanese religion of ramen might get picky, but we won't. In a sea of complicated, overpriced and prohibitive dining, Katana offers humble bowls of hot broth swimming with hearty noodles at *almost* normal prices, on the center Strip. In true San Franciscan fashion, they've even thrown sushi burritos on the menu. Winning!

★ Guy Fieri's Vegas Kitchen & Bar
AMERICAN $$
(Map p64; ☎702-794-3139; www.caesars.com; LINQ Casino; mains $12-28; ⏰9am-midnight) *Diners, Drive-ins and Dives* celebrity chef Guy Fieri has opened his first restaurant on the Strip at LINQ Casino (p62), dishing out an eclectic menu of his own design, inspired by many years journeying America's back roads for the best and fairest down-home cooking.

★ Grand Wok
CHINESE $$
(Map p64; ☎702-891-7879; www.mgmgrand.com/ en/restaurants.html; MGM Grand; mains $12-28; ⏰11am-10pm Sun-Thu, to 11pm Fri & Sat) Come to Grand Wok, in business for more than 25 years serving some of the best pan-Asian dishes you'll find this side of the Far East. Try the garlic-shrimp fried rice with dried scallops. Sensational.

★ Burger Bar
AMERICAN $$
(Map p64; ☎702-632-9364; www.burger-bar. com; Shoppes at Mandalay Place; mains $10-60; ⏰11am-11pm Sun-Thu, to 1am Fri & Sat; P ❄ 🎮) Since when can a hamburger be worth $60? When it's built with Kobe beef, sautéed foie gras and truffle sauce: it's the Rossini burger, the signature sandwich of chef Hubert Keller. Most menu options are more down-to-earth – diners select their own gourmet burger toppings and pair them with skinny fries and a liquor-spiked milkshake or beer float.

★ Eiffel Tower Restaurant
FRENCH $$$
(Map p64; ☎702-948-6937; www.eiffeltower restaurant.com; Paris Las Vegas; mains lunch $14-32, dinner $32-89, tasting menu without/with

wine pairings $125/205; ⊙11:30am-10pm Mon-Fri, 11am-11pm Sat & Sun) At this haute eatery midway up its namesake tower, the Franco-phile wine list is vast, the chocolate soufflé is unforgettable, and views of the Strip and Bellagio's fountains are breathtaking. Contemporary renditions of French classics are generally well executed. Lunch is your best bet, but it's more popular to come for sunset. Reservations essential.

★Morimoto   FUSION $$$
(Map p64; ☑702-891-1111; www.mgmgrand.com; MGM Grand; mains $24-75; ⊙5-10pm) Iron Chef Masaharu Morimoto's latest Vegas incarnation is in his eponymous showcase restaurant, which pays homage to his Japanese roots and the cuisine of this city that has propelled him to legend status around the world. Dining here is an experience in every possible way and, we think, worth every penny.

★Joël Robuchon   FRENCH $$$
(Map p64; ☑702-891-7925; www.joel-robuchon.com/en; MGM Grand; tasting menus $120-425; ⊙5-10pm) The acclaimed 'Chef of the Century' leads the pack in the French culinary invasion of the Strip. Adjacent to the MGM Grand's (p62) high-rollers' gaming area, Robuchon's plush dining rooms, done up in leather and velvet, feel like a dinner party at a 1930s Paris mansion. Complex seasonal tasting menus promise the meal of a lifetime – and they often deliver.

Reservations are essential for dinner here, as well as at the slightly less-expensive **L'Atelier de Joël Robuchon** (Map p64; ☑702-891-7358; MGM Grand; mains $41-97, tasting menu without/with wine pairings $159/265; ⊙5-10:30pm; ☑) next door, where bar seats front an exhibition kitchen.

★Momofuku   ASIAN $$$
(Map p64; ☑702-698-2663; www.vegas.momofuku.com; Cosmopolitan; mains $33-115; ⊙11am-2am; ☑) This is a place to show others who know about David Chang's global sensation that you're a trendsetting jet-setter too... Cosmopolitan (p59) is the perfect place for Momofuku to find a Vegas home for its mouthwatering pan-Asian menu, featuring the likes of the humble pork bun, chicken *katsu* and not-so-ordinary salt-and-pepper lobster.

★Border Grill   MEXICAN $$$
(Map p64; ☑702-632-7403; www.bordergrill.com; Mandalay Bay; mains $17-36; ⊙11am-10pm Mon-Fri, from 10am Sat & Sun; ℗☑🍴) ✈ With colorful modern murals and views over Mandalay Bay Beach (p62), this festive eatery dishes up modern Mexican fare designed by chefs from Bravo's *Top Chef Masters* and the Food Network's *Too Hot Tamales.* Come for the weekend brunch of unlimited Latin-inspired tapas ($35) and bottomless mimosas (extra $15). Border Grill uses only hormone-free meat and sustainably caught seafood. Reservations helpful.

★Bouchon   FRENCH $$$
(Map p64; ☑702-414-6200; www.thomaskeller.com/bouchonlasvegas; Venetian; mains breakfast & brunch $12-26, dinner $19-51; ⊙7am-1pm & 5-10pm Mon-Fri, 7am-2pm & 5-10pm Sat & Sun; ℗☑) ✈ Napa Valley wunderkind Thomas Keller's rendition of a Lyonnaise bistro features a seasonal menu of French classics. The poolside setting complements the oyster bar (open 3pm to 10pm daily) and an extensive raw seafood selection. Decadent breakfasts and brunches, imported cheeses, caviar, foie gras and a superb French and Californian wine list all make appearances. Reservations recommended.

★Costa di Mare   SEAFOOD $$$
(Map p64; ☑702-770-3305; www.wynnlasvegas.com; Wynn; mains $30-60, tasting menus $150-180; ⊙5:30-10pm; ℗✱☑) Even in Vegas it doesn't get much posher than Costa di Mare, where you can book a private cabana beside Wynn's (p62) Lake of Dreams and dine on fresh Mediterranean blue rock lobster under a fluttering white canopy. The upscale Italian-style seafood restaurant has a short, highly specialized menu – the whole fish served are indigenous to Italy, and simply prepared. Reservations essential.

✕ Downtown

Downtown's dining scene is evolving: in addition to a few worthy restaurants inside casinos, trendy eateries are popping up in the city's historic core.

★eat.   BREAKFAST $
(Map p68; ☑702-534-1515; eatdtlv.com; 707 Carson Ave; mains $7-14; ⊙8am-3pm Mon-Fri, to 2pm Sat & Sun; ☑) ✈ Community spirit and creative cooking provide reason enough to venture off Fremont St to find this cafe. With a concrete floor and spare decor, it can get loud as folks chow down

on truffled egg sandwiches, cinnamon biscuits with strawberry compote, shrimp po'boy sandwiches and bowls of New Mexican green-chile chicken posole. Metered parking is available on the street, or take the Deuce bus to the Fremont Street Experience (p66), then walk two blocks east on Fremont and one block south on 7th, to Carson Ave.

★**Park on Fremont**   GASTROPUB **$**
(Map p68; ☑702-834-3160; www.parkon fremont.com; 506 Fremont St E; light meals $9-14; ⊘11am-3am) The best thing about this gorgeous little oasis away from the Fremont St frenzy are its outdoor patio and courtyard areas. OK, the burgers are great too, but not as exciting as the crispy brussels sprouts and cheesy garbage fries. It's a great place to just sit and sip a margarita and watch the crowds go by.

★**Carson Kitchen**   AMERICAN **$$**
(Map p68; ☑702-473-9523; www.carson kitchen.com; 124 S 6th St; tapas & mains $8-22; ⊘11:30am-11pm Thu-Sat, to 10pm Sun-Wed; ☒Deuce) This tiny eatery with an industrial theme of exposed beams, bare bulbs and chunky share tables hops with downtowners looking to escape the mayhem of Fremont St or the Strip's high prices. Excellent shared plates include rainbow cauliflower, watermelon and feta salad and decadent mac 'n' cheese, and there's a creative 'libations' menu.

★**Andiamo Steakhouse**   STEAK **$$$**
(Map p68; ☑702-388-2220; www.thed.com; 301 Fremont St E, The D; mains $24-79; ⊘5-11pm; ☒Deuce, SDX) Of all the old-school steakhouses inside Downtown's carpet joints, the current front-runner is Joe Vicari's Andiamo Steakhouse. Upstairs from the casino, richly upholstered half-moon booths and impeccably polite waiters set the tone for a classic Italian steakhouse feast of surf-and-turf platters and housemade pasta, followed by a rolling dessert cart. Extensive Californian and European wine list. Reservations recommended.

✕ **East & West of the Strip**

Most of the culinary action east of the Strip is found along Paradise Rd; there are only a few reasons to venture west of the Strip just to dine.

★**Go Vegan Cafe**   VEGAN **$**
(☑702-405-8550; www.govegan.cafe; 5875 S Rainbow Blvd #104; light meals $6-14; ⊘9am-8pm Mon-Sat, to 5pm Sun; ℗❋☎🅿) Vegetarians and vegans alike go west for this popular, healthy cafe serving sandwiches, smoothies, salads and baked treats.

★**Firefly**   TAPAS **$$**
(Map p64; ☑702-369-3971; www.fireflylv.com; 3824 Paradise Rd; shared plates $5-12, mains $15-20; ⊘11:30am-1am Mon-Thu, to 2am Fri & Sat, 10am-1am Sun; ☒108) Firefly is always packed with a fashionable local crowd, who come for well-prepared Spanish and Latin American tapas, such as *patatas bravas,* chorizo-stuffed empanadas and vegetarian bites like garbanzo beans seasoned with chili, lime and sea salt. A backlit bar dispenses the house-specialty, sangria – red, white or sparkling – and fruity mojitos. Reservations strongly recommended.

★**Lotus of Siam**   THAI **$$**
(Map p64; ☑702-735-3033; www.lotusofsiamlv. com; 953 E Sahara Ave; mains $9-30; ⊘11am-2:30pm Mon-Fri, 5:30-10pm daily; 🅿; ☒SDX) Saipin Chutima's authentic northern Thai cooking has won almost as many awards as her distinguished European and New World wine cellar. Critics have suggested this might be America's best Thai restaurant and we're sure it's up there with the best. Although the strip-mall hole-in-the-wall may not look like much, foodies flock here. Reservations essential.

★**Hot n Juicy Crawfish**   SEAFOOD **$$**
(Map p64; ☑702-891-8889; www.hotnjuicy crawfish.com; 4810 Spring Mountain Rd; baskets $12-20; ⊘noon-10pm Sun-Thu, to 11pm Fri & Sat; ℗🅿♿) The name says it all: spicy, hot and juicy crawfish served by the pound or in baskets and a wide range of other seafood treats. Ridiculously popular.

★**Alizé**   FRENCH **$$$**
(Map p64; ☑702-951-7000; www.alizelv.com; 4321 W Flamingo Rd, Palms; mains $46-68, tasting menu without/with wine pairings $155/245; ⊘6-10pm; ☒202) Las Vegas chef André Rochat's top-drawer gourmet room is named after a gentle Mediterranean trade wind. Enjoyed by nearly every table, panoramic floor-to-ceiling views of the glittering Strip are even more stunning than the haute French cuisine and remarkably deep wine cellar. Reservations essential; upscale dress code.

Drinking & Nightlife

The Strip

The Strip is ground zero for some of the country's hottest clubs and most happening bars, where you never know who you'll be rubbing shoulders with.

★Omnia
CLUB

(Map p64; www.omnianightclub.com; Caesars Palace; cover female/male $20/40; ⊙10pm-4am Tue & Thu-Sun) Hakkasan group's new Caesars megaclub offers Top 40/hip-hop DJs, plus bottle service and Strip views with a Miami Beach vibe. Residencies by Calvin Harris, Steve Aoki and Martin Garrix.

★Hakkasan
CLUB

(Map p64; ☎702-891-3838; www.hakkasanlv.com; MGM Grand; cover $20-75; ⊙10pm-4am Wed-Sun) At this lavish Asian-inspired nightclub, international jet-set DJs like Tiësto and Steve Aoki rule the jam-packed main dance floor bordered by VIP booths and floor-to-ceiling LED screens. More offbeat sounds spin in the intimate Ling Ling Club, revealing leather sofas and backlit amber glass. Bouncers enforce the dress code: upscale nightlife attire (no athletic wear, collared shirts required for men).

★Marquee
CLUB

(Map p64; ☎702-333-9000; www.marquee lasvegas.com; Cosmopolitan; ⊙10pm-5am Mon, Fri & Sat) The Cosmopolitan's (p59) glam nightclub cashes in on its multimillion-dollar sound system and a happening dance floor surrounded by towering LED screens displaying light projections that complement EDM tracks hand-picked by famous DJs. From late spring through early fall, Marquee's mega-popular daytime pool club heads outside to a lively party deck overlooking the Strip, with VIP cabanas and bungalows.

★Skyfall Lounge
BAR

(Map p64; ☎702-632-7575; www.delanolasvegas. com; Delano; ⊙5pm-midnight Sun-Thu, to 1:30am Fri & Sat) Enjoy unparalleled views of the southern Strip from this rooftop bar atop Mandalay Bay's Delano (p73) hotel. Sit and sip cocktails as the sun sets over the Spring Mountains to the west, then dance the night away to mellow DJ beats, spun from 9pm.

★Jewel
CLUB

(Map p64; ☎702-590-8000; www.jewelnight club.com; Aria; cover female/male from $20/30;

⊙10:30am-4am Fri, Sat & Mon) From the creators of Hakkasan, long-awaited Jewel replaces its predecessor Haze, which failed to dazzle. Boasting five VIP suites (because it's all about being seen) and over 1400 sq ft of shimmering LED ribbon lighting, Jewel, despite accommodating up to 2000 revelers, is pitched as an 'intimate' alternative to the Strip's megaclubs. Monday nights offer locals free admission.

★Chateau Nightclub & Gardens
BAR

(Map p64; ☎702-776-7770; www.chateau nights.com; Paris Las Vegas; ⊙10pm-4am Wed, Fri & Sat) Hip-hop prevails at this rooftop venue landscaped to look like Parisian gardens. Views over the Strip are divine from tiered outdoor terraces while, back inside, go-go dancers do their thing above a small dance floor, which can be half empty even on weekends. Sometimes on summer days, the lounge space on the open-air deck doubles as a beer garden.

★Wet Republic
CLUB

(Map p64; ☎702-891-3563; www.wetrepublic.com; MGM Grand; cover $20-40; ⊙11am-5pm Mon & Thu-Sun) Think of Wet Republic, the city's biggest 'ultra pool,' as a nightclub brought out into the sunlight. The mostly 20- and 30-something crowd in stylish swimwear show up for EDM tunes spun by megawatt DJs like Calvin Harris, fruity cocktails and bobbing oh-so-coolly around saltwater pools while checking out the bikini-clad scenery. Book ahead for VIP bungalows, daybeds and cabanas.

★107 SkyLounge
LOUNGE

(Map p64; ☎702-380-7711; www.topoftheworld lv.com/level107.php; 2000 S Las Vegas Blvd, 107th fl, Stratosphere Tower; ⊙4pm-4am) There's just no place to get any higher in Las Vegas – without the approval of an air traffic controller – than the lounge overlooking the revolving Top of the World (p62) restaurant. Come during happy hour (4pm to 7pm daily) for two-for-one cocktails, half-price appetizers and striking sunset views.

★Encore Beach Club
CLUB

(Map p64; ☎702-770-7300; www.encorebeach club.com; cover $30-40; ⊙10pm-4am Thu, 11am-7pm Fri & Sun, from 10am Sat) Soak up sunshine on a larger-than-life 'lilypad,' bob around the pool to DJ-spun tunes, play high-stakes blackjack by the pool or kick back in a private bungalow or a cabana with its own hot tub. The club features three tiered pools (one with an island platform for dancing), plus a gaming pavilion and top international DJs.

★ **Surrender** CLUB
(Map p64; ☎ 702-770-7300; www.surrender nightclub.com; Encore; cover $20-40; ⊙ 10:30pm-4am Wed, Fri & Sat) Even the club-averse admit that this is an audaciously gorgeous place to hang out, with its saffron-colored silk walls, mustard banquettes, bright yellow patent leather entrance and a shimmering wall-art snake coiled behind the bar. Play blackjack or just hang out by the pool after dark during summer. EDM and hip-hop DJs and musicians pull huge crowds.

★ **Chandelier Lounge** COCKTAIL BAR
(Map p64; ☎ 702-698-7979; www.cosmopolitan lasvegas.com/lounges-bars/chandelier; Cosmopolitan; ⊙ 24hr; 🚌 Deuce) Towering high in the center of Cosmopolitan (p59), this ethereal cocktail bar is inventive yet beautifully simple, with three levels connected by romantic curved staircases, all draped with glowing strands of glass beads. The second level is headquarters for molecular mixology (order a martini made with liquid nitrogen), while the third specializes in floral and fruit infusions.

★ **Fireside Lounge** LOUNGE
(Map p64; ☎ 702-735-7635; www.peppermill lasvegas.com; 2985 S Las Vegas Blvd, Peppermill; ⊙ 24hr; 🚌 Deuce) Don't be blinded by the outlandishly bright neon outside. The Strip's most spellbinding retro hideaway awaits at the pint-sized **Peppermill** (☎ 702-735-4177; mains $8-32; ⊙ 24hr) casino. Courting couples adore the sunken fire pit, fake tropical foliage and 64oz goblet-sized 'Scorpion' cocktails served by waiters in black evening gowns.

★ **XS** CLUB
(Map p64; ☎ 702-770-0097; www.xslasvegas.com; Encore; cover $20-50; ⊙ 10pm-4am Fri & Sat, from 9:30pm Sun, from 10:30pm Mon) XS is the hottest nightclub in Vegas – at least for now. Its extravagantly gold-drenched decor and over-the-top design mean you'll be waiting in line for cocktails at a bar towered over by ultra-curvaceous, larger-than-life golden statues of female torsos. Big-name electronica DJs make the dance floor writhe, while high rollers opt for VIP bottle service at private poolside cabanas.

★ **Nine Fine Irishmen** PUB
(Map p64; ☎ 702-740-6463; www.ninefineirish men.com; New York–New York; ⊙ 11am-11pm, live music from 9pm; 🛜) Built in Ireland and shipped piece by piece to America, this pub has cavernous interior booths and outdoor patio tables beside NYNY's Brooklyn Bridge. Genuine stouts, ales, ciders and Irish whiskeys are always stocked at the bar. Live entertainment is a mix of Celtic rock and traditional Irish country tunes, occasionally with sing-alongs and a champion Irish dancer.

★ **Drai's Beachclub & Nightclub** CLUB
(Map p64; ☎ 702-777-3800; www.draislv.com; Cromwell Las Vegas; nightclub cover $20-50; ⊙ nightclub 10pm-5am Thu-Sun, beach club 11am-6pm Fri-Sun) Feel ready for an after-hours party scene straight outta Hollywood? Or maybe you just wanna hang out all day poolside, then shake your booty on the petite dance floor while DJs spin hip-hop, mash-ups and electronica? This multivenue club has you covered pretty much all day and night. Dress to kill: no sneakers, tank tops or baggy jeans.

🍴 Downtown

Locals and in-the-know tourists make a beeline for the Fremont East Entertainment Precinct (www.fremonteast.com) for the city's best grassroots nightlife.

★ **Gold Spike** BAR
(Map p68; ☎ 702-476-1082; www.goldspike.com; 217 N Las Vegas Blvd; ⊙ 24hr) Gold Spike, with its playroom, living room and backyard, is many things: bar, nightclub, performance space, work space; sometime host of roller derbies, discos, live bands or dance parties; or just somewhere to soak up the sun with a relaxed crew and escape mainstream Vegas. Australians will think it's very Melburnian and feel right at home.

★ **Commonwealth** BAR
(Map p68; ☎ 702-445-6400; www.common wealthlv.com; 525 Fremont St E; ⊙ 7pm-late Tue-Sat; 🚌 Deuce) It might be a little too cool for school but, whoa, that Prohibition-era interior is worth a look: plush booths, softly glowing chandeliers, Victorian-era bric-a-brac and a saloon bar. Imbibe your old-fashioned cocktails on the rooftop patio overlooking the Fremont East scene. They say there's a secret cocktail bar within the bar, but you didn't hear that from us.

★ **Beauty Bar** BAR

(Map p68; ☑ 702-598-3757; www.thebeautybar.com; 517 Fremont St E; cover free-$10; ⊙9pm-4am; ☐Deuce) Swill a cocktail or just chill with the cool kids inside the salvaged innards of a 1950s New Jersey beauty salon. DJs and live bands rotate nightly, spinning everything from tiki lounge tunes, disco and '80s hits to punk, metal, glam and indie rock. Check the website for special events like 'Karate Karaoke.' There's often no cover charge.

Off the Strip

South of the Hard Rock along Paradise Rd is the 'Fruit Loop,' Vegas' loose-knit lesbigay community's equivalent of a 'village.' We think the moniker is disempowering in the context of Las Vegas' patriarchal attitudes toward women and sex. Time for a rebrand? Why not head to a bar and have a chat about it?

★ **Double Down Saloon** BAR

(Map p64; ☑ 702-791-5775; www.doubledownsaloon.com; 4640 Paradise Rd; ⊙24hr; ☐108) This dark, psychedelic gin joint appeals to the lunatic fringe. It never closes, there's never a cover charge, the house drink is called 'ass juice' and it claims to be the birthplace of the bacon martini. When live bands aren't terrorizing the crowd, the jukebox vibrates with New Orleans jazz, British punk, Chicago blues and surf-guitar king Dick Dale.

★ **Hofbräuhaus** BAR

(Map p64; ☑ 702-853-2337; www.hofbrauhauslasvegas.com; 4510 Paradise Rd; ⊙11am-11pm Sun-Thu, to midnight Fri & Sat) This Bavarian beer hall and garden is a replica of the original in Munich. Celebrate Oktoberfest year-round with premium imported suds, fair *Fräuleins* and live oompah bands nightly.

★ **Ghostbar** LOUNGE

(Map p64; ☑ 702-942-6832; www.palms.com; 4321 W Flamingo Rd, Palms; cover $10-25; ⊙8pm-4am; ☐202) A clubby crowd, often thick with pop-culture celebs and pro athletes, packs this sky-high watering hole at **Palms** (☑ 702-942-7770; ⊙24hr). DJs spin hip-hop and house while wannabe gangsters and Jersey girls sip pricey cocktails. The plush mansion decor and 360-degree panoramas are to die for. Dress to kill. Happy hour goes until 10pm nightly.

Flair Nightclub GAY & LESBIAN

(☑702-733-8787; www.flairvegas.com; 1700 E Flamingo Rd; ⊙10pm-4am Thu-Sun) Vegas' premier LGBT venue has three bars and an outdoor patio.

☆ Entertainment

That sensory overload of blindingly bright neon lights means you've finally landed on Las Vegas Blvd. The infamous Strip has the lion's share of gigantic casino hotels, all flashily competing to lure you (and your wallet) inside, with larger-than-life production shows, celebrity-filled nightclubs and burlesque cabarets. Head off-Strip to find jukebox dive bars, arty cocktail lounges, strip clubs and more.

Live Music

House of Blues LIVE MUSIC

(Map p64; ☑702-632-7600; www.houseofblues.com; Mandalay Bay; ⊙box office 9am-9pm) The blues is definitely not the only game at this imitation Mississippi Delta juke joint. Big-name touring acts entertain the standing-room-only audiences with soul, pop, rock, metal, country, jazz and even burlesque. For some shows, you can skip the long lines to get in by eating dinner in the restaurant beforehand, then showing your same-day receipt.

Legends in Concert LIVE MUSIC

(Map p64; ☑702-777-2782; www.legendsinconcert.com; Flamingo; adult/child from $58/36; ⊙shows 4pm, 7:30pm & 9:30pm) Vegas' top pop-star impersonator show features real singing and dancing talent mimicking famous performers such as the Beatles, Elvis, Madonna, James Brown, Britney Spears, Shania Twain and many more.

★ **Don't Tell Mama** LIVE MUSIC

(Map p68; ☑702-207-0788; www.donttellmama.com; 517 Fremont St E; ⊙8pm-3am Tue-Sun; ☐Deuce) This friendly Fremont East piano bar is a hit with locals, who crowd the place on weekends to hear their favorite 'singing bartenders' belting out requests. Free-flowing cocktails keep the scene thumping into the wee hours. It only takes reservations if you plan to arrive before 9pm. No cover charge.

Production Shows & Comedy

★ **Le Rêve the Dream** THEATER

(Map p64; ☑702-770-9966; boxoffice.wynnlasvegas.com; Wynn; tickets $105-205; ⊙shows 7pm & 9:30pm Fri-Tue) Underwater acrobatic feats by scuba-certified performers are the centerpiece of this intimate 'aqua-in-the-round' theater, which holds a one-million-gallon swimming pool. Critics call it a less-inspiring version of Cirque's *O,* while devoted fans find the romantic underwater tango, thrilling high dives and visually spectacular adventures to be superior. Beware: the cheapest seats are in the 'splash zone.'

★ **O** THEATER

(Map p64; ☑ 888-488-7111; www.cirquedusoleil.com; Bellagio; tickets $99-185; ☺ 7pm & 9:30pm Wed-Sun) Phonetically speaking, it's the French word for water *(eau).* With a lithe international cast performing in, on and above water, Cirque du Soleil's *O* tells the tale of theater through the ages. It's a spectacular feat of imagination and engineering, and you'll pay dearly to see it – it's one of the Strip's few shows that rarely sells discounted tickets.

★ **Aces of Comedy** COMEDY

(Map p64; ☑ 702-792-7777; www.mirage.com; Mirage; tickets $40-100; ☺ schedules vary, box office 10am-10pm Thu-Mon, to 8pm Tue & Wed) You'd be hard pressed to find a better A-list collection of famous stand-up comedians than this year-round series of appearances at the **Mirage** (☑ 702-791-7111; ☺ 24hr; P), which delivers the likes of Jay Leno, Kathy Griffin and Lewis Black to the Strip. Buy tickets in advance online or by phone, or go in person to the Mirage's **Cirque du Soleil** (☑ 877-924-7783; www.cirquedusoleil.com/las-vegas; discount tickets from $49, full price from $69) box office.

★ **Blue Man Group** LIVE PERFORMANCE

(Map p64; ☑ 702-262-4400; www.blueman.com; Luxor; tickets $80-190; ☺ shows at 7pm & 9:30pm; ♿) Art, music and technology combine with a dash of comedy in one of Vegas' most popular, family-friendly shows at **Luxor** (☑ 702-262-4000; www.luxor.com; 3900 S Las Vegas Blvd; ☺ 24hr; P).

★ **Michael Jackson ONE** THEATER

(Map p64; ☑ 702-632-7580; www.cirquedusoleil.com; Mandalay Bay; tickets from $69; ☺ 7pm & 9:30pm Fri-Tue) Cirque du Soleil's musical tribute to the King of Pop blasts onto Mandalay Bay's (p62) stage with showstopping dancers and lissome acrobats and aerialists all moving to a soundtrack of MJ's hits, moon walking all the way back to his break-out platinum album *Thriller.* No children under five years old allowed.

Cinema

★ **Eclipse Theaters** CINEMA

(Map p68; ☑ 702-816-4300; eclipsetheaters.com; 814 S 3rd St; prices vary; ☺ show times vary) Opened in late 2016, this is *the* place to catch a movie Downtown, with its plush seating, luxe atmosphere and fancy menu of strong cocktails and chef-prepared eats delivered to your seat. Because of the liquor license, children are not permitted in any of the cinema's theaters.

United Artists Showcase Theatre 8 CINEMA

(Map p64; ☑ 844-462-7342; www.regmovies.com; 3769 S Las Vegas Blvd, Showcase Mall; adult/child 3-11yr $12/9; ♿) This is the only place to see first-run movies on the Strip, which means it's always packed. Although it's not the city's most modern cinema, stadium seating and digital sound bring it up to date. Afternoon matinee shows are discounted for adults.

Sports

Las Vegas Motor Speedway SPECTATOR SPORT

(☑ 800-644-4444; www.lvms.com; 7000 N Las Vegas Blvd) For adrenaline-pumped Nascar, Indy, and dirt-track and drag races, drive out to this $200-million facility featuring a 1.5-mile superspeedway, a state-of-the-art dragway, a paved oval short track called 'The Bullring' and a racing school (for ride-alongs). Show up early for autograph sessions at the track before start time. In March, **Nascar Weekend** (www.nascar.com; ♿) draws more than 300,000 spectators.

Thomas & Mack Center SPECTATOR SPORT

(Map p64; ☑ 702-739-3267; www.unlvtickets.com; S Swenson St at Tropicana Ave, UNLV campus) Wrestling, boxing and pro rodeo events; 18,000 seats.

🔒 Shopping

Surprisingly, Vegas has evolved into a sophisticated shopping destination.

🏛 The Strip

★ **Shops at Crystals** MALL

(Map p64; www.crystalsatcitycenter.com; 3720 S Las Vegas Blvd, CityCenter; ☺ 10am-11pm Sun-Thu, to midnight Fri & Sat) Design-conscious Crystals is the most striking shopping center on the Strip. Win big at blackjack? Waltz inside Christian Dior, Dolce & Gabbana, Prada, Hermès, Harry Winston, Paul Smith or Stella McCartney showrooms at CityCenter's (p63) shrine to haute couture.

For sexy couples with unlimited cash to burn, Kiki de Montparnasse is a one-stop shop for lingerie and bedroom toys.

Wynn & Encore Esplanades MALL
(Map p64; ☏702-770-7000; www.wynnlasvegas. com; Wynn & Encore; ◷10am-11pm) Steve Wynn's blockbuster resort has lured top-of-the-line retailers such as Chanel, Cartier, Dior, Oscar de la Renta, Manolo Blahnik and Louis Vuitton to the twin shopping arcades at Wynn & Encore (p62).

Via Bellagio MALL
(Map p64; Bellagio; ◷10am-midnight) Bellagio's swish indoor promenade, Via Bellagio, is home to a who's who of fashion-plate designers: Bottega Veneta, Chanel, Dior, Fendi, Giorgio Armani, Gucci, Hermès, Prada, Louis Vuitton and Tiffany & Co. If you've been bewitched by Dale Chihuly's colorful blown-glass sculptures, drop by his signature gallery shop on the Via Fiore, a much shorter shopping promenade.

Fashion Show MALL
(Map p64; ☏702-369-8382; www.thefashion show.com; 3200 S Las Vegas Blvd; ◷10am-9pm Mon-Sat, 11am-7pm Sun; 🚇) Nevada's largest shopping mall is an eye-catcher: topped off by 'the Cloud,' a silver multimedia canopy resembling a flamenco hat, Fashion Show harbors more than 250 chain shops and department stores. Hot European additions to the mainstream lineup include British clothier Topshop (and Topman for men). Live runway shows happen hourly from noon to 5pm on Friday, Saturday and Sunday.

**Grand Canal Shoppes
at the Palazzo** MALL
(Map p64; ☏702-414-4525; www.grandcanal shoppes.com; 3377 S Las Vegas Blvd, Palazzo; ◷10am-11pm Sun-Thu, to midnight Fri & Sat) Don't be surprised to find Hollywood celebrities inside this high-design shopping mall. Anchored by the three-story department store Barneys New York, the Palazzo's shops are dazzling: Canali for tailor-made Italian apparel, London fashion imports Chloe and Thomas Pink and luxury US trendsetters such as Diane von Furstenberg. Bauman Rare Books carries rare, signed editions and antiquarian titles.

Town Square MALL
(☏702-269-5001; www.mytownsquarelasvegas. com; 6605 S Las Vegas Blvd; ◷10am-9pm Mon-Thu, to 10pm Fri & Sat, 11am-8pm Sun; 🚇; ▯SDX) South of the Strip, this village-style shopping center is geared more to locals than to tourists, with a range of mainstream and upscale chain shops, restaurants, happy-hour bars like Blue Martini and a Whole Foods supermarket. It may be worth the trip if you're traveling with kids just for the playground park, toy train and outdoor films in summer.

🔒 Downtown

★ Las Vegas
Premium Outlets North MALL
(Map p68; ☏702-474-7500; www.premium outlets.com/vegasnorth; 875 S Grand Central Pkwy; ◷9am-9pm Mon-Sat, to 8pm Sun; 🚇; ▯SDX) Vegas' biggest-ticket outlet mall features 120 mostly high-end names such as Armani, Brooks Brothers, Diane von Furstenberg, Elle Tahari, Kate Spade, Michael Kors, Theory and Tory Burch, alongside casual brands like Banana Republic and Diesel.

🔒 East of the Strip

★ Inyo Fine Cannabis
Dispensary DISPENSARY
(Map p64; ☏702-707-8888; www.inyolasvegas. com; 2520 Maryland Pkwy #2; ◷10am-8pm) One of the first medical marijuana dispensaries in Las Vegas is all set for the burgeoning legal recreational market.

ℹ Information

EMERGENCY

US country code	☏1
International access code	☏011
Ambulance	☏911
Fire	☏911
Police	☏911

INTERNET ACCESS
Most casino hotels charge a fee of up to $15 per 24 hours (sometimes only wired access is available). Free wi-fi hot spots are more common off-Strip. Cheap internet cafes hide inside souvenir shops on the Strip and along Maryland Pkwy opposite the UNLV campus.

MEDIA
Newspapers & magazines Las Vegas Review Journal (www.reviewjournal.com), Las Vegas Weekly (www.lasvegasweekly.com), Las Vegas Life (www.lvlife.com).

Radio National Public Radio (NPR), lower end of FM dial.

TV PBS (public broadcasting); cable: CNN (news), ESPN (sports), HBO (movies), Weather Channel.

DVDs Coded for region 1 (USA and Canada) only.

MEDICAL SERVICES

Sunrise Hospital & Medical Center (☑702-731-8000; sunrisehospital.com; 3186 S Maryland Pkwy; ⊙24hr) Specialized children's trauma services available at a 24-hour emergency room.

University Medical Center (UMC; ☑702-383-2000; www.umcsn.com; 1800 W Charleston Blvd; ⊙24hr) Southern Nevada's most advanced trauma center has a 24-hour ER.

Walgreens (☑702-739-9645; 3765 S Las Vegas Blvd; ⊙ store 24hr, pharmacy 8am-10pm, clinic 9am-5:30pm) Has an in-store healthcare walk-in clinic.

MONEY

ATM transaction fees inside casino gaming areas are high. Credit cards are widely accepted.

Casinos charge ridiculous rates for currency exchange. Try **Travelex** (☑702-369-2219; www.travelex.com; 3200 S Las Vegas Blvd, Fashion Show; ⊙10am-9pm Mon-Sat, 11am-7pm Sun) kiosks at the Fashion Show mall and inside McCarran International Airport to change your money at more competitive rates.

Tipping

Keep small bills on hand. Leave a poor tip for remarkably lousy service, or in exceptionally bad (rare) cases, none at all. Reward exceptional service. Minimum tipping standards:

Hotels Porters: $1 to $2 per bag; housekeeping $1 to $2 per night; valet $2 to $5 (paid when keys returned)

Restaurants 15% to 25% of total bill

Bars/casinos $1 per drink or 15% per round

Taxis/limos 15% of fare, at your discretion

TOURIST INFORMATION

The **Las Vegas Convention & Visitors Authority** (LVCVA; Map p64; ☑702-892-7575; www.lasvegas.com; 3150 Paradise Rd; ⊙8am-5:30pm Mon-Fri; ⊕Las Vegas Convention Center) also has a hotline providing up-to-date information about shows, attractions, activities and more.

USEFUL WEBSITES

Eater Vegas (vegas.eater.com) Has the scene covered: restaurant openings (and closings), chef interviews, gossipy rumors and 'heat maps' of where to eat right now.

Las Vegas Review-Journal (www.lvrj.com) Runs thoughtful restaurant reviews.

Las Vegas Weekly (www.lasvegasweekly.com) Digs up more budget-friendly and unusual finds, especially off-Strip.

Restaurant.com (www.restaurant.com) Good for discount dining certificates.

❶ Getting There & Away

AIR

McCarran International Airport (LAS; Map p64; ☑702-261-5211; www.mccarran.com; 5757 Wayne Newton Blvd; ☎) ranks among the USA's 10 busiest airports. Security lines are notoriously slow, but self-service check-in and luggage drop-off kiosks at the airport and other locations, including the **McCarran Rent-a-Car Center** (☑702-261-6001; www.mccarran.com/Go/RentalCars.aspx; 7135 Gillespie St; ⊙24hr), the Las Vegas Convention Center and some Strip casino hotels, can ease headaches. For arriving passengers, the airport has advance check-in kiosks for a few Strip casino hotels, but skip them if lines are long.

Most domestic flights use Terminal 1 (A, B, C and satellite concourse D gates); international, charter and some domestic flights use Terminal 3 (E gates and satellite concourse D gates). A free, wheelchair-accessible tram links outlying gates, while free shuttle buses link Terminals 1 and 3.

BUS

Greyhound (☑800-231-2222; www.greyhound.com) runs long-distance buses connecting Las Vegas with Reno ($81, 9½ hours) and Salt Lake City (from $48, eight hours), as well as regular discounted services to/from Los Angeles (from $11, five to eight hours). Book in advance for the cheapest fares.

Located off Fremont St in the old Las Vegas Station, the **Las Vegas Bus Station** (Map p68; ☑702-384-9561; www.greyhound.com; 200 S Main St; ⊙24hr; ☐SDX) is a short walk from Downtown casino hotels and the Deuce and SDX express bus lines south to the Strip.

CAR & MOTORCYCLE

The main roads into and out of Las Vegas are the I-15 Fwy and US Hwy 95. US Hwy 93 connects downtown with Hoover Dam. I-215 goes by McCarran International Airport. Freeway traffic often crawls along, particularly during morning and afternoon rush hours and on weekend nights, especially near the Strip (Las Vegas Blvd).

❶ Getting Around

TO/FROM THE AIRPORT

The easiest and cheapest way to get to your hotel is by airport shuttle (one-way to Strip/downtown hotels from $7/9) or a ride-share service (from $10). As you exit baggage claim, look for shuttle-bus kiosks lining the curb; prices and destinations are clearly marked.

CAR & MOTORCYCLE

The only document that international short-term visitors legally need to rent or drive a car or motorcycle is a license from their home country. You may be required to show an international driving permit (IDP) if your license isn't written in English. Driving on the Strip can be stressful. Locals are known for driving carelessly and crashes on interstate approaches are commonplace, as are drunk drivers. Keep your wits about you.

Parking

As of April 2017, the golden days of free self-parking (and sometimes even valet parking) at Strip casino hotels and shopping malls are over. For an up-to-date list of the latest rates, go to www.vegas.com/transportation/parking-garages.

PUBLIC TRANSPORTATION

RTC (Regional Transportation Commission of Southern Nevada; ☑ 702-228-7433, 800-228-3911; www.rtcsnv.com/transit; single ride $2, 2/24/72hr bus pass $6/8/20, child under 5yr free) buses operate from 5am to 2am daily, with popular Strip and downtown routes running 24/7 every 15 to 20 minutes. Double-decker Deuce buses to/from downtown stop every block or two along the Strip. Quicker SDX express buses stop outside some Strip casino hotels and at the Fashion Show (p82), the city's convention center and a few off-Strip shopping malls. Have exact change or bills ready when boarding or buy a pass before boarding from ticket vending machines at bus stops.

Many off-Strip casino hotels offer limited shuttle buses to/from the Strip, usually reserved for hotel guests (sometimes free, but a surcharge may apply).

Free air-conditioned trams that anyone can ride shuttle between some Strip casino hotels. One connects the Bellagio, CityCenter and the Monte Carlo. Another links Treasure Island and the Mirage. A third zips between Excalibur, Luxor and Mandalay Bay. Trams run all day and into the evening, usually stopping late-night until the early morning hours.

The **Las Vegas Monorail** (☑ 702-699-8299; www.lvmonorail.com; single ride $5, 24/72hr pass $12/28; ⊙ 7am-midnight Mon, to 2am Tue-Thu, to 3am Fri-Sun) links some Strip casino-resorts, zipping between MGM Grand, Bally's/Paris, Flamingo/Caesars, Harrah's/LINQ, Las Vegas Convention Center, Westgate and SLS/W. Although service is frequent (every four to 12 minutes), stations are only on the east side of the Strip, set back from Las Vegas Blvd at the rear of the casinos served. On the plus side, air-conditioned trains are stroller- and wheelchair-friendly, and it takes just 13 minutes to travel the entire route.

TAXI

It's illegal to hail a cab on the street. Instead taxi stands are found at almost every casino hotel and shopping mall. By law, the maximum number of passengers is five. All companies must have at least one wheelchair-accessible van, but you'll usually have to call ahead and then wait.

AROUND LAS VEGAS

Red Rock Canyon

There's a stark contrast between this magnificent canyon, with its steep, 3000ft-high, rugged, red-rock escarpment, formed naturally and abruptly some 65 million years ago, and the deliberate, artificial beauty of the Strip, born of ongoing human toil, less than 20 miles to its east. A 13-mile, one-way **scenic loop drive** (☑ 702-515-5350; www.redrockcanyonlv.org; 1000 Scenic Loop Dr; car/bicycle $7/3; ⊙ scenic loop 6am-8pm Apr-Sep, to 7pm Mar & Oct, to 5pm Nov-Feb; ♿) passes some of the canyon's most striking features, evidence of dramatic tectonic-plate collisions. Opportunities for hiking and rock climbing abound, or just be mesmerized by the vistas – as long as you're not the driver.

South of the loop, a side road leaves Hwy 159 and enters the petite **Spring Mountain Ranch State Park** (☑ 702-875-4141; parks.nv.gov/parks/spring-mountain-ranch; 6375 Hwy 159, Blue Diamond; $9; ⊙ 8am-dusk), abutting the cliffs of the Wilson Range.

🏃 Activities & Tours

★ **Scoot City Tours**   TOURS
(☑ 702-699-5700; www.scootcitytours.com; 200 Polaris Ave #42; per 2 people $250; ⊙ 8am & 1pm daily Apr-Oct, 1pm Nov-Mar) An alternative to ho-hum bus and van tours, drive your own three-wheeled scooter-car around Red Rock Canyon's scenic loop drive on a semi-guided group tour. It can be very cold in winter. Drivers must be at least 21 years old; no passengers under eight years old allowed (sorry kids, we know you try to!).

Las Vegas Cyclery   CYCLING
(☑ 702-596-2953; lasvegascyclery.com; 10575 Discovery Dr; bicycle rental per day $40-150; ⊙ 10am-7pm Mon-Fri, 9am-6pm Sat, 10am-4pm Sun) Rent high-quality road and mountain bikes in suburban Summerlin, 10 miles west

of the Strip. Ask about guided cycling and mountain-biking tours of Red Rock Canyon.

Cowboy Trail Rides HORSEBACK RIDING
(☏ 702-387-2457; www.cowboytrailrides.com; 4053 Fossil Ridge Rd; tours $69-329; ☑) To ride 'em cowboy, make reservations for a good ol' Western horseback ride along Fossil Ridge on the canyon rim or a sunset trip on the canyon floor followed by a BBQ cookout.

🍴 Sleeping & Eating

Accommodations here are limited to camping under the stars or the nearby Red Rock Casino, whose upmarket rooms and wonderful position make it a worthy alternative to the Strip's mega-hotels. Bring your own food for a picnic, or dine at the nearby casino's numerous offerings. Alternatively, head back to Vegas for dinner.

ℹ Information

Stop at the **Red Rock Canyon Visitor Center** (☏ 702-515-5350; www.redrockcanyonlv.org; ⊙ 8:30am-4:30pm; ☑) for its natural-history exhibits and information on hiking trails, rock-climbing areas and 4WD routes. The **Red Rock Canyon Interpretive Association** (☏ 702-515-5367; www.redrockcanyonlv.org; 1000 Scenic Loop Dr) operates the nonprofit bookstore there and organizes activities, including birding and wildflower walks (advance reservations may be required).

Mt Charleston

The source of much confusion among visitors, the Spring Mountains National Recreation Area, part of the Humboldt-Toiyabe National Forest and referred to most commonly as Mt Charleston (and/or Lee Canyon), forms the western boundary of the Las Vegas Valley, with higher rainfall, lower temperatures and fragrant pine, juniper and mountain mahogany forests.

The name Mt Charleston correctly refers to the eponymous peak and the little village of Mt Charleston tucked away in the center of the park. From here, you can embark upon several hikes, including the demanding 16.6-mile round-trip South Loop Trail ascent of Charleston Peak (elevation 11,918ft), starting from Cathedral Rock picnic area. The easier, 2.8-mile round-trip Cathedral Rock Trail offers canyon views.

Deeper within the park, Lee Canyon is a popular ski resort. Open almost year-round, Lee Canyon's 'green season' draws folks for biking, hiking, concerts and weddings.

◎ Sights & Activities

**Spring Mountains
Visitor Gateway** NATURE CENTER
(☏ 702-872-5486; www.facebook.com/smvgw; 2525 Kyle Canyon Rd; ⊙ 9am-4pm) **FREE** Just west of Las Vegas, the limestone cliffs and alpine forested peaks of the lofty Spring Mountains rise unmistakably above the Mojave Desert. This modern, state-of-the-art interpretive center featuring educational dioramas, exhibits and artworks should be your first port of call for explorations into the Spring Mountains National Recreation Area section of the Humboldt-Toiyabe National Forest. Rangers are on hand to steer you toward your ideal forest experience.

Lee Canyon SNOW SPORTS
(☏ 702-385-2754, snow report 702-593-9500; www.leecanyonlv.com; 6725 Lee Canyon Rd; half-day pass adult/child $60/30; ⊙ green season Jun-Sep, snow season mid-Nov–Apr; ☑) Lee Canyon has three lifts, 30 serviced snow trails (longest run 3000ft), a snowboarding half-pipe and terrain park, and a private VIP snow cabana (very Vegas ...)! Surprised? Don't be. 'Nevada' is derived from the Spanish word for snow, and over 120in of the powdery stuff falls on these slopes each year. Equipment and clothing rentals are first-come, first-served.

🍴 Sleeping & Eating

Camping is king in the Spring Mountains National Recreation Area, with numerous campsites available throughout the park. Dining on the mountain is limited to its two accommodation options, or bringing in your own food for a fabulous picnic in the area's many picnic spots.

Resort on Mt Charleston HOTEL **$**
(☏ 702-872-5500; www.mtcharlestonresort.com; 2275 Kyle Canyon Rd; r from $59; P ❄ 🛜) Terming this large private mountain hotel a resort is a little misleading, as it lacks most of the facilities commonly associated with a resort. That said, it does have the best, most modern rooms of Mt Charleston's two main lodgings, although they've not been updated in a few years. The property is located 4 miles east of Mt Charleston village.

WORTH A TRIP

VALLEY OF FIRE STATE PARK

It's about 50 miles from the Fremont Street Experience (p66) to the visitor center at **Valley of Fire State Park** (☑ 702-397-2088; www.parks.nv.gov/parks/valley-of-fire; 29450 Valley of Fire Hwy, Overton; per vehicle $10; ☉ visitor center 8:30am-4:30pm, park 7am-7pm). Make this your first port of call to find out how best to tackle this masterpiece of south-west desert scenery containing 40,000 acres of red Aztec sandstone, petrified trees and ancient American Indian petroglyphs (at Atlatl Rock). Dedicated in 1935, the park was Nevada's first designated state park. Its psychedelic landscape has been carved by wind and water over thousands of years.

Must-see spots within the valley include **White Domes**, **Rainbow Vista**, **Fire Canyon** and **Silica Dome**: each is as magnificent as it sounds. For more information on the unique geological features of the park, the visitor center also sells books and maps and takes reservations for guided hikes and ranger-led stargazing expeditions. Here, you can also try your luck for one of the 72 extremely popular, first-come, first-served primitive campsites ($20 per night).

Spring Mountains Campgrounds
CAMPGROUND **$**

(☑ 518-885-3639; www.fs.usda.gov/activity/htnf/recreation/camping-cabins; tent & RV sites $15-25; ☉ mid-May–Oct, some year-round) There are five designated campgrounds on Mt Charleston, outside of special group camping areas. Check in at the Spring Mountains Visitor Gateway (p85) to pay your fees and chat with a ranger about which campground is best for you.

Mesquite

☑ 702 / POP 16,439 / ELEV 1600FT

Just over an hour's drive northeast of Las Vegas, Mesquite straddles the Nevada–Arizona state line although its closest neighbor is the city of St George in Utah, 49 miles northeast. It's stuffed full of casino hotels cashing in on slot-starved visitors from its sister states and has no less than six pristine golf courses for those who fancy a round.

🛏 Sleeping & Eating

Mesquite has plenty of chain motels and casino hotels offering decent rooms at reasonable prices.

Dining in Mesquite is unremarkable, but you won't starve: franchise restaurants, fast-food joints and all-day casino dining denote the mainstay of culinary options.

Henderson

☑ 702 / POP 257,729 / ELEV 1765FT

Technically a city in itself, the area known as Henderson, around 15 miles east of Las Vegas, makes a pleasant alternative base away from the hustle and bustle of the Strip and Downtown, especially if you're traveling with kids. The Strip's obsession with shiny things, human pleasures and earthly delights takes much more of a back seat out here, with nature stepping in to take center stage.

With its own lake, water park and wetlands, and proximity to the Hoover Dam (p89), Lake Mead National Recreation Area (p89) and Valley of Fire State Park, Henderson is a go-to spot for cooling off, coming down and getting back to basics. Combine this change of pace with a selection of good-value accommodations, a pleasant setting and accessible, low-cost dining, in comparison to the Strip, and you can see why the locals are that much more mellow than their Vegas neighbors.

👁 Sights

⭐ **Cowabunga Bay** AMUSEMENT PARK
(☑ 702-850-9000; www.cowabungabayvegas.com; 900 Galleria Dr; day pass adult/child $40/30; ☉ Apr-Sep; 👪) Kids go crazy for this massive, seasonal water park with slides, surfing, swimming, a lazy river, and cabanas for the big kids who paid for the tickets. Opening hours vary greatly from week to week as the calendar progresses: check the website for details.

Clark County Museum MUSEUM
(☑ 702-455-7955; www.clarkcountynv.gov/parks/Pages/clark-county-museum; 1830 S Boulder Hwy; adult/child $2/1; ☉ 9am-4:30pm; 🅿 👪) Amble among recreations of what the Las Vegas region looked like decades and even centuries before the modern neon-lit era

of casinos and hotels. From dioramas of prehistoric ecology and later local American Indian heritage to displays of steamships that plied the mighty Colorado River nearby in the 19th and early 20th centuries, this is an unexpected treasure. 'Heritage Street' recreates a small town scene of the area's early modern days. It's perfect for families with kids.

El Dorado Canyon   GHOST TOWN
(☏ 702-291-0026; eldoradocanyonminetours. com; 16880 NV Hwy 165, Searchlight; ⊗ hours vary) If you're looking for a ghost-town experience filled with weather-beaten buildings, derelict automobiles and vintage signs, El Dorado Canyon, 30 miles southeast of Henderson, is a picturesque mother lode. Easily accessed by car, the canyon's bonanza is the **Techatticup Mine** district, which is set in a vista of towering rocks with the Colorado River and Arizona on the horizon. A small store offers tours, kayak rentals and cold drinks; it's funky and filled with old-timey knickknacks and taxidermy, too.

🏃 Activities

Because of Henderson's mountains, lake and parklands, folks here seem to get out and do more than the more jaded locals living closer to the Strip.

★Sky Combat Ace   SCENIC FLIGHTS
(☏ 888-494-5850; www.skycombatace.com; 1420 Jet Stream Dr #100; experiences $249-1995) You really need to visit this truly unique attraction's homepage to get a full understanding of what you're getting yourself in for. In short, you'll be at the controls of a stunt plane, in the air, with varying levels of control. If those kids at Stratosphere (p70) think they're daredevils, they haven't seen 'nuthin' yet!

★Speedvegas   ADVENTURE SPORTS
(☏ 702-874-8888; www.speedvegas.com; 14200 S Las Vegas Blvd; laps $39-99, experiences $395-995; ⊗ 10am-4:30pm) Fabulously cool and fun, Speedvegas differs from other driving attractions in Vegas, as it's the only one operating from a private 1.5-mile-long track and offers fully insured single-lap high-octane drives (making it accessible to those who *don't* have cash to burn) through to packaged experiences. It's as simple as 'here are the keys to a Ferrari, here's an open racetrack ... GO!'

🛌 Sleeping & Eating

Henderson has a handful of good accommodations and its share of upscale casinos offering the same steak/buffet/burger dining formula as casinos the city over.

East Side Cannery   CASINO HOTEL $
(☏ 702-856-5300; www.eastsidecannery.com; 5255 Boulder Hwy; r from $69; P ❄ 🛜 ≋) Light-filled rooms at this modern casino hotel midway between Henderson and the center Strip are good value for money if you don't mind being a little away from the action.

★M Resort   CASINO HOTEL $$
(☏ 702-797-1000; www.themresort.com; 12300 S Las Vegas Blvd; r from $110; P ❄ @ 🛜 ≋) Elegant, earth-toned pads with marble baths beckon at this off-the-beaten-path casino resort offering free airport and Strip shuttles.

★Bootlegger Bistro   BISTRO $$
(☏ 702-736-4939; bootleggerlasvegas.com; 7700 S Las Vegas Blvd; mains $12-28; ⊗ 24hr; P 🅿 ♿) This family friendly Italian bistro has been serving the people of Vegas since 1949. It's open around the clock, so you'll always be able to get a hearty lasagna like mama used to make.

🍸 Drinking & Nightlife

The **Henderson Booze District** (www.face book.com/BoozeDistrict; 7330 Eastgate Rd; ⊗ hours vary) should be your port of call if you're a lover of the microbrew phenomenon and want to check out what's going on. Otherwise, local casinos or heading back to the Strip are your best bets for a good night out.

ℹ Getting There & Away

RTC (p84) operates regular scheduled buses and express services between Henderson and Downtown/the Strip.

Boulder City

The planned community of Boulder City was built in the 1930s to house the workers who built the Hoover Dam – the massive structure that tamed the Colorado River – and to power Sin City's glittering lights. Casinos were outlawed here at the time, to prevent distractions from the workers' monumental task, and to this day, remain absent: Boulder City is the only Nevada town sans casino. If you simply can't stand the serenity, it's only a few miles to Henderson for a gambling fix.

The city's charming historic downtown is replete with antique shops, sellers of Southwestern kitsch and grassy, tree-lined parks, which frequently host weekend art festivals, fetes and even classic car jamborees.

Lovers of art-deco architecture will also feel right at home here: Boulder is the best small-town Americana section of the greater Las Vegas region by far.

◉ Sights

Nevada State Railroad Museum　MUSEUM
(☑702-486-5933; www.nevadasouthern.com; 601 Yucca St; adult/child $10/5; ☉9am-1pm Mon & Tue, 10am-3:30pm Sat & Sun) Before highways streamed with vacation-minded drivers and airliners landed at McCarran International Airport, the most reliable way to travel to Las Vegas was by train. Massive displays of old-school engine cars thrill 'iron horse' enthusiasts and families looking for a retro experience.

⭐ Activities & Tours

★Flightlinez Bootleg Canyon　OUTDOORS
(☑702-293-6885; www.flightlinezbootleg.com; 1644 Nevada Hwy; 2½hr tour $159) This thrilling aerial adventure is like zip lining, but with a paragliding harness. Morning tours see the coolest temps, while late afternoon tours may catch sunset over the desert. Riders must weigh between 75lb and 250lb (fully dressed) and wear close-toed shoes.

Historic Railroad Tunnel Trail　HIKING
(www.nps.gov/lake/planyourvisit/hikerr.htm; Lake Mead National Recreation Area) One of the most popular and picturesque hiking trails near Las Vegas, the Historic Railroad Tunnel Trail is a wide and level causeway that wends through a series of passageways cut into hard-rock outcroppings during the construction of the Hoover Dam in the early 1930s. It offers great vistas for photography overlooking Lake Mead and its sere desert surroundings.

Desert Adventures　KAYAKING
(☑702-293-5026; www.kayaklasvegas.com; 1647a Nevada Hwy; full-day Colorado River kayak $179; ☉9am-6pm Apr-Oct, 10am-4pm Nov-Mar) Would-be river rats should check in here for guided kayaking and stand up paddle surfing (SUP) tours on Lake Mead and the Colorado River. Experienced paddlers can rent canoes and kayaks for DIY trips.

🛏 Sleeping

Boulder City has the unique and historic Boulder Dam Hotel, but you'll find more lodgings in nearby Henderson and the mother lode of tourist beds back in Las Vegas.

Boulder Dam Hotel　HISTORIC HOTEL $
(☑702-293-3510; www.boulderdamhotel.com; 1305 Arizona St; r from $89; ❋@🛜) For a peaceful night's sleep worlds away from the madding crowds and neon of Vegas, head to this gracious Dutch Colonial–style hotel (listed on the National Register of Historic Places), which has welcomed illustrious guests since 1933. Relax with a cocktail at the art-deco jazz lounge on-site.

NPS Campgrounds　CAMPGROUND $
(☑702-293-8906; www.nps.gov/lake/planyourvisit/campgrounds.htm; tent/RV sites from $20/30) Check the website for a full listing of Lake Mead National Recreation Area campgrounds. Ten are located around Lake Mead at Boulder Beach, Callville Bay, Echo Bay and Las Vegas Bay, and there are five campgrounds at Lake Mohave. It's first-come, first-served.

🍴 Eating & Drinking

Boulder City has some charming art-deco cafes and diners. If you can't find what you're looking for, Las Vegas, 27 miles down the road, always has something special to savor. And likewise, while there are some quaint local haunts for a nightcap after dark, make your way back to Sin City if you're looking for something a little wilder.

Milo's Cellar　AMERICAN $
(☑702-293-9540; www.milosbouldercity.com; 534 Nevada Hwy; mains $9-14; ☉11am-10pm Sun-Thu, to 11pm Fri & Sat) The unassuming Milo's Cellar just down the street from the Boulder Dam Hotel makes a relaxing spot for tasty sandwiches, salads, soups, gourmet cheese plates and wine flights. There's sidewalk seating and a small wine shop.

ℹ Information

Nevada Welcome Center (☑702-294-1252; www.visitbouldercity.com; 100 Nevada Hwy; ☉8am-4:30pm) Near Hoover Dam .

DON'T MISS

HOOVER DAM & LAKE MEAD

Even those who question the USA's commitment to damming the great rivers of the West have to marvel at the engineering and architecture of the **Hoover Dam** (☎702-494-2517, 866-730-9097; www.usbr.gov/lc/hooverdam; off Hwy 93; ☉9am-6pm Apr-Oct, to 5pm Nov-Mar; 🚻) over the Colorado River. Completed in 1936, the dam, towering over Black Canyon in the bone-dry Mohave Desert, created the enormous Lake Mead, with its 759 miles of shoreline. Fifteen years later, its sibling, the Davis Dam, 70 miles south, created smaller **Lake Mohave** (www.nps.gov/lake/nature/overview-of-lake-mohave.htm). Both dams are dissected by the Nevada–Arizona state line. The dams, both lakes and this stretch of the Colorado River are contained within the popular **Lake Mead National Recreation Area** (☎702-293-8906, www.nps.gov/lake; 7-day entry per vehicle $10; ☉24hr; 🚻), created in 1964.

Built by thousands of men who migrated to the area at the height of the Depression, the art-deco styled, graceful curve of the 726ft-high Hoover Dam contrasts superbly with the stark landscape that surrounds it. For the best views, take a walk across the Mike O'Callaghan–Pat Tillman Memorial Bridge…unless you suffer from vertigo. As you contemplate this gargantuan pre-WWII structure, spare a thought for the 96 men who died in industrial accidents during its construction.

Guided tours of the dam depart from the **Hoover Dam Parking Garage & Visitor Center** (☎702-494-2517; 81 Hoover Dam Access Rd; incl parking $10; ☉9am-5pm). Packaged tours to Hoover Dam from Vegas can save ticketing and transportation hassles, with many operators including pick-ups and drop-offs from Las Vegas hotels. The ubiquitous Las Vegas listings guides always include advertisements for packaged day trips to the dam.

If you're going it alone, the excellent **Lake Mead Visitor Center** (☎702-293-8990; Lakeshore Scenic Dr, off US Hwy 93; ☉9am-4:30pm), halfway between Boulder City and Hoover Dam, off Hwy 93, is a great place to start your explorations of the area. From here, North Shore Rd winds around Lake Mead and makes a great scenic drive.

ⓘ Getting There & Away

From the Strip, take I-15 south to I-215 east to I-515/US 93 and 95 and continue over Railroad Pass, staying on US Hwy 93 to Boulder City.

RTC (p84) operates regular scheduled bus services between Boulder City and Downtown Las Vegas (single trip adult/child $2/1). A Residential Routes day pass gets you multiple trips between Las Vegas and Boulder City (adult/child $5/2.50), while an All-Access day pass ($6/3) adds the benefit and value of being able to ride the 24-hour Deuce and SDX (Strip and Downtown Express) services as well.

GREAT BASIN

Anchored by the population centers of the Reno-Tahoe area to the west, and Las Vegas to the southeast, the vast area referred to as Northern Nevada (or the Great Basin) holds most of Nevada's landmass but relatively few residents. It's a high desert of vast, empty valleys stretching out in all directions until they collide with range after range of great, craggy mountains, draped white in winter, dusted white in early spring and late fall, and desert brown in the summer sun.

Along Highway 95

Running vaguely north–south through western Nevada, Hwy 95 is hardly a direct route, but is the fastest way to get from Las Vegas to Reno. Still, it's a long and uninspiring full day's high-speed drive of 450 miles. The highway zigzags to avoid mountain ranges and passes through old mining centers that are not much more than ghost towns today. There's little to excite travelers, except perhaps those with an interest in Nevada's alleged connection to UFOs, conspiracy theories and the top-secret Area 51 USAF military facility at Groom Lake.

Beatty

☎775 / POP 1010 / ELEV 3300FT

From Las Vegas, it's one hour and 45 minutes to quirky, small-town Beatty, the northeastern gateway to **Death Valley National Park**, the hottest, driest and lowest national park in the land. While most of the park is located in California, its northern extent forms part of the California–Nevada state line. The popular park is notoriously short on places to sleep for the visitor numbers it attracts, making Beatty an excellent alternative base from which to explore.

Otherwise, there's a few humble but worthwhile things to see and do in and around the town, and if conditions come together, from March to May, the surrounding desert is daubed yellow with a carpet of wildflowers: magical.

Don't be shocked if you run into any of Beatty's local 'cowboys' (www.beatty cowboys.com) dressed in period garb and getting up to general mischief in the streets: they're harmless enough!

◎ Sights & Activities

Beatty Museum   MUSEUM
(☑775-553-2303; www.beattymuseum.org; 417 Main St; ⊙10am-3pm; P) FREE What first began in 1995 as the dream of three local women who realized they needed to preserve the history of the town that raised them, has outgrown the original cottage that housed it and now occupies a historic church in the center of town with a custom-built additional wing. Come to browse the fascinating collection of memorabilia from Beatty's past and to chat with the friendly volunteers.

Rhyolite   GHOST TOWN
(off Hwy 374; P●) FREE The best thing about what was once the mining township of Rhyolite, when compared to other of Nevada's many ghost towns, is its accessibility. Four miles west of Beatty, off NV Hwy 374, the State of Nevada Historic Townsite features crumbling stone buildings, including the skeletal remains of a three-story bank, the 1906 Tom Kelly Bottle House and the handsome Las Vegas–Tonopah railroad station. Bring your camera.

Goldwell Open Air Museum   MUSEUM
(☑702-870-9946; www.goldwellmuseum.org; off Hwy 374; ⊙24hr; P●) FREE Off Hwy 374, a few miles southwest of Beatty, and a few hundred yards south of Rhyolite, the Goldwell Open Air Museum is a rather mysterious 8-acre outdoor sculpture site surrounded by desert, begun by Belgian artist Albert Szukalski in 1984.

Bailey's Hot Springs   HOT SPRINGS
(☑775-553-2395; www.baileyshotsprings.com; Hwy 95; hot springs $8, tent/RV sites $15/25; ⊙8am-8pm) Five miles north of Beatty, Bailey's Hot Springs, a 1906 former railroad depot, has two private hot-spring baths in antique bathhouses. Overnight guests get complimentary usage, and day-trippers pay $8 per person for a 40-minute soak.

⌂ Sleeping

Small-town Beatty has more than 340 rooms across five basic, independent motels and one franchise offering, in addition to more than 100 RV sites.

Atomic Inn   MOTEL $
(☑775-553-2250; www.atomicinnbeatty.com; 350 S 1st St; r from $62; ❄☏) 🗲 At this nicely updated, mid-century motel, get a deluxe room to enjoy (somewhat) more contemporary design, flat-screen TVs and DVD players (there's a movie library). Classic movies play in the lobby nightly. Kudos for the solar water-heating system, xeriscaped grounds and little green men out front.

Stagecoach Hotel & Casino   MOTEL $
(☑775-553-2419; 900 E Hwy 95 N; r from $96; P❄☏☲☺) This small, smoky, thoroughly rural Nevadan casino at the edge of town has its own hotel with large, comfortable enough, though unremarkable rooms. The pool is a nice place to lounge away a dusty day in Death Valley, especially if you're traveling with kids, who'll also appreciate the casino's games 'arcade.'

✖ Eating & Drinking

If you're a fan of diners and home-style cooking, you'll be well fed. There are also at least two drinking holes in Beatty for a cleansing ale after a hot day in the desert.

Mel's Diner   DINER $
(☑775-553-9003; 600 Hwy 95; breakfast $5-12; ⊙6am-3pm; 🗲●) Mel's is the go-to place in town for hearty, non-greasy (well, not too greasy) breakfasts, as well as heavier home-style cookin' like meatloaf and country fried steak for lunch. Salads too!

Happy Burro Chili & Beer   BAR
(☑775-553-9099; 100 W Main St; ⊙noon-10pm) There's a fabulously friendly vibe going on at this creaky antique-y bar straight out of the Wild West, but without the wild bit. Dishing out tasty, cheap chili and chilled beer served in preserve jars, it's a great spot

for a sit and ponder, whether inside or on the lazy patio.

ℹ️ Information

Beatty Chamber of Commerce (📞 775-553-2424; www.beattynevada.org; 119 Main St; ⏰ 9:30am-2:30pm Tue-Sat) Tourist information.

ℹ️ Getting There & Away

Greyhound (p83) operates one bus per day from Las Vegas ($31, 2½ hours) continuing on to Reno ($62, seven hours).

Tonopah

📞 775 / POP 2478 / ELEV 6047FT

Huge mine-head frames loom above this historic silver- and gold-mining town, which, had it not been for the devotion of its townsfolk who've clung to their pioneering past and lovingly preserved the history of their town, might have seen a similar fate to that of Goldfield, 27 miles to the south, one of Nevada's many ghost towns.

In recent years, but for very different reasons, Tonopah has once more come into the spotlight, thanks to the construction of the planet's first 24/7 solar power plant, the Crescent Dunes Solar Thermal Energy Project (www.solarreserve.com), just outside town. The plant generates enough green energy to power 75,000 homes and receives plenty of interest from around the world – good news for this little desert economy.

Hundreds of miles from any significant light pollution, the night skies here are breathtaking: consider spending an evening if you're making the drive between Nevada's two largest cities.

◎ Sights

Goldfield   GHOST TOWN
(www.goldfieldnevada.org) FREE Goldfield became Nevada's biggest boomtown after gold was struck here in 1902. Much of the town was destroyed by a fire in 1923, but a few precious historic structures survive today, including the **Goldfield Hotel**, a restored firehouse (now a museum), the county courthouse, with its Tiffany lamps, and the rough-and-tumble **Santa Fe Saloon** (📞 775-485-3431; 925 N 5th Ave, Goldfield; ⏰ 2-9pm). Although there's a resident population of 268, some days you wouldn't know it.

Central Nevada Museum   MUSEUM
(📞 775-482-9676; www.tonopahnevada.com/CentralNevadaMuseum.html; 1900 Logan Field Rd; ⏰ 9am-5pm Tue-Fri, from 1pm Sat; 🅿️) FREE
The Central Nevada Museum has a good collection of Shoshone baskets, early photographs, mining relics and morticians' instruments housed in a variety of interesting and historic buildings.

🛏️ Sleeping & Eating

There are six motels in town, including one heritage gem. Perhaps unexpectedly, there's also a small selection of above-average restaurants to augment Tonopah's predictable selection of down-country American fare.

⭐ **Mizpah Hotel**   BOUTIQUE HOTEL $$
(📞 775-482-3030; www.themizpahhotel.com; 100 N Main St; r $102-159; 🅿️❄️🛜) Once the height of opulence when it was built in 1907 – as Tonopah approached the peak of its heady, strike-it-rich era – the Mizpah has been returned to its former glory. Rooms at this country-luxury, 52-suite boutique hotel feature quality bedding and linens and decadent period decor that belies the high-speed wi-fi and flat-screen TVs within.

El Marques Restaurant   MEXICAN $
(📞 775-482-3885; 348 N Main St; mains $7-18; ⏰ 11am-9pm) Icy cold margaritas are a great way to cool down after a day in the desert sun. Follow them with old-school Mexican favorites (tacos, enchiladas, fajitas, chimichangas, burritos) accompanied by homemade guacamole, salsa and corn chips, and you have a winning combination.

🍺 Drinking & Nightlife

It gets hot out here in the desert, so you'll be relieved to know Tonopah has a handful of places where you can down a cold amber ale, including its very own brewery!

⭐ **Tonopah Brewing Company**   BREWERY
(📞 775-482-2000; www.tonopahbrewing.com; 315 S Main St; ⏰ 11am-9pm) If this smart craft brewery is an indicator of things to come, we predict the future is looking bright for tourism in Tonopah. Be sure to stop in for a pint of local brew and some kick-ass country barbecue in a modern tap room, whose gorgeous bar pays homage to its historic roots.

🛈 Information

Check out the town of Tonopah's excellent website at www.tonopahnevada.com.

🛈 Getting There & Away

Greyhound (p83) operates one bus service per day from Las Vegas ($45, four hours), continuing on to Reno ($48, 5¼ hours).

Along Highway 93

This is the oft-deserted route from Las Vegas to Great Basin National Park, a 300-mile trip taking over five hours. Expect to pass by mining ghost towns, wide-open ranges populated by more cattle than humans...and not much else.

Caliente

✒ 775 / POP 1169 / ELEV 4400FT

Heading north from Las Vegas, past Alamo and Ash Springs, US Hwy 93 leads to a junction, where you turn east through some desolate countryside to Caliente, a former railroad town with a Mission-style 1923 railway depot that makes for a cool photo op.

The main reason you'll be passing through is en route to the spectacular Cathedral Gorge State Park (p95), 15 miles to the north. Visits here can be tied in with journeys along SR-375, 'The Extraterrestrial Highway,' which begins at Crystal Springs, what is now little more than a ghost town, some 44 miles west of Caliente.

◉ Sights

Spring Valley State Park　　　　PARK
(✒775-962-5102; parks.nv.gov/parks/spring-valley; Eagle Valley Rd, Pioche; $7, tent sites $17; ⊘24hr; P🚸) With exposed faults of pinky-gray rock, historic ranch houses and an artificial reservoir where you can swim, fish and frolic, it's easy to see why this state park has its admirers, despite its distance from civilization – although that's half the charm. Primitive camping is available.

**Pahranagat National
Wildlife Refuge**　　　　　　　　PARK
(✒775-725-3417; www.fws.gov/refuge/Pahranagat; ⊘24hr; P) FREE US Hwy 93 parallels the eastern edge of the Desert National Wildlife Range (where bighorn sheep can be spotted) and runs by this wildlife sanctuary where spring-fed lakes surrounded by cottonwoods are a major stopover for migratory

birds. Free undeveloped campsites line the east shore of **Upper Lake**, 4 miles south of Alamo. The park entrance is approximately 90 miles north of Las Vegas and 63 miles southwest of Caliente.

🛏 Sleeping & Eating

Little Caliente has three basic, but pleasant, independent motels and five American and fast-food joints.

Cathedral Gorge Campground　CAMPGROUND $
(✒775-728-4460; parks.nv.gov/parks/cathedral-gorge; Hwy 93; tent/RV sites $17/27; P) Within the grounds of the stunning Cathedral Gorge State Park (p95), there are 22 basic campsites here, each with a table, grill and shade sail.

Along Highway 50

The nickname says it all: on the 'Loneliest Road in America' barren, brown desert hills collide with big blue skies. The highway goes on forever, crossing solitary terrain, with towns few and far between, and the only sounds being the whisper of wind or the rattle-and-hum of a truck engine. Once part of the coast-to-coast Lincoln Hwy, Hwy 50 follows the route of the Overland Stagecoach, the Pony Express and the first transcontinental telegraph line.

Fallon

✒ 775 / POP 8390 / ELEV 3960FT

The main reason you'll come through Fallon is if you're driving Hwy 50. The Top Gun fighter-pilot training base is just outside town: don't be alarmed if you see F-16s darting overhead or hear them breaking the sound barrier.

Hwy 50 goes right through town, which is itself unremarkable, but you'll find some nice state parks and recreation areas and interesting geological formations all short drives from town.

◉ Sights & Entertainment

**Walker Lake State
Recreation Area**　　　　　　STATE PARK
(✒775-867-3001; www.parks.travelnevada.com; P) FREE North of the town of Hawthorne, Hwy 95 traces the shrinking shoreline of this popular picnicking, swimming, boating and fishing spot.

WORTH A TRIP

THE EXTRATERRESTRIAL HIGHWAY

Die-hard ufologists won't want to miss the way-out-there trip toward **Area 51**, a detachment of the Edwards Air Force Base, and a mecca for conspiracy theorists the world over. While it's not our general practice to list maximum-security military installations (authorized to shoot trespassers), we've made an exception in this instance because this mysterious, top-secret compound has such interesting extraterrestrial links. Some believe the base, located on the shores of Groom Lake, a dry salt lake roughly 30 miles from Hwy 95 and 130 miles north of Las Vegas, is where government research into reverse-engineering alien technology, and testing of said technology, takes place.

Coming from Las Vegas, you'll head west on Hwy 375, now officially named 'The Extraterrestrial Highway,' from its junction with Hwy 93 at Crystal Springs. Less than a mile down the road, you'll spot the **Alien Research Center** (☑ 775-725-3750; www. alienresearchcenter.com; 100 SR-375, Hiko; ⊘ 11am-7pm), a glorified souvenir shop where you can chat about your ambitions to approach Area 51. Locals might give you the lowdown on how to get right up to the perimeter of the compound, but make no mistake, you will be watched – very closely. You are strongly advised to take all warnings about prosecution and/or the military's constitutional right to shoot trespassers without questions, seriously.

Continuing on, you're likely to find a small horde of sky-watchers (or nobody at all) gathering between the 29- and 30-mile markers on the south side of the highway, where there used to be a black mailbox belonging to a local rancher, Steve Medlin, which Area 51 'pilgrims' began flooding with letters to 'aliens.' The mailbox has since been removed but its location remains an unofficial meeting point along the highway.

If you're determined to see what the fuss out here is all about, your best bet is **Rachel**, the closest occupied township to the base, itself about 83 miles west of Caliente along Hwy 375. Here you can have burgers and beer, snap selfies and spend what could be quite the spooky night at the **Little A'le' Inn** (☑ 775-729-2515; www.littlealeinn.com; 9631 Old Mill St, Rachel; RV sites with hookups $15, r $50-165; ⊘ restaurant 8am-10pm; ❄ 🛜 🐾).

If in the morning you decide you want to get the hell outta here, it's another 109 miles to Tonopah.

Stillwater National Wildlife Refuge   PARK
(☑ 775-428-6452; www.fws.gov/refuge/Stillwater; Hunter Rd, Stillwater; ⊘ 24hr; **P**) **FREE** A bird-watcher's delight, northeast of Fallon off Stillwater Rd (NV Hwy 166), Stillwater National Wildlife Refuge is a haven for over 280 species of birds, at their most active in mid-May. Free primitive campsites are available.

Top Gun Raceway   SPECTATOR SPORT
(☑ 775-423-0223; www.topgunraceway.com; 15550 Schurz Hwy; adult/child 6-12yr $10/5) Overhead you might spot an F-16 flying over Fallon, home of the US Navy's Top Gun fighter-pilot school, but on the ground, dragsters and classic hot rods compete at the Top Gun Raceway between March and November. High-octane action.

🛏 Sleeping & Eating

Fallon is a logical overnight stop if you're heading between Carson City and Ely.

You'll find plenty of dining options, mostly fast food, but with a handful of pleasant surprises.

Comfort Inn   MOTEL **$**
(☑ 775-423-5554; www.choicehotels.com/nevada/fallon/comfort-inn-hotels/nv021; 1830 W Williams Ave; r from $69; **P** ❄ 🛜 🐾) This simple chain motel has Fallon's freshest (newest) and best-value rooms, in a good location near a bunch of shops and restaurants.

★ Middlegate Station   BURGERS **$**
(☑ 775-423-7134; www.facebook.com/middlegate. station; 42500 Austin Hwy, cnr Hwys 50 & 361; mains $6-17; ⊘ 6am-2am) A legendary pit stop on the 'Loneliest Road in America,' 47 miles from Fallon, this quirky, ramshackle ranch-style saloon is famous for its Middlegate Monster Burger and general Wild West vibe. While burgers are king here, there's plenty of other high-calorie, high-cholesterol delights to dismantle and devour. Dr Atkins would be so proud!

★ **Slanted Porch** AMERICAN $$
(☑775-423-4489; www.slantedporch.com; 310 S Taylor St; lunch $9-12; ⊙11am-3pm Mon-Sat; 🛜🍴🐾) Fresh salads, hot sandwiches and burgers fill the lunch menu of this gorgeous little bar-restaurant in a converted old home, with, of course, a slanted porch, which feels slightly out of place in no-frills Fallon. Phone ahead to see if they're offering a dinner service (mains $12 to $26) when you're in town.

❶ Getting There & Away

Greyhound (p83) operates one coach per day from Fallon to Reno (from $25, 1¼ hours) and Las Vegas (from $69, 7½ hours).

Austin

☑775 / POP 200 / ELEV 6605FT

Little Austin is an essential stop after hours of uninterrupted basin-and-range driving on Hwy 50, the 'Loneliest Road in America'. There's not a lot here, just a few frontier churches and atmospherically decrepit buildings along the short main street. Most folks will stop here for lunch and a stroll, but if the weather is fine and you're into outdoor activities, there are some special spots for mountain biking and hot-spring soaking just a little off the beaten track outside town.

◉ Sights & Activities

★ **Spencer Hot Springs** HOT SPRINGS
(☑775-964-2200; Spencer Hot Springs Rd; ⊙24hr) FREE One of the best reasons to visit Austin is for these outdoor hot-spring pools in the middle of nowhere, with breathtaking vistas over the Big Smoky Valley to the majestic mountains beyond. On public land, these three (sometimes four) natural geothermal hot spots have been 'improved' by locals with baths made from cattle troughs. Access is by well-maintained dirt road.

Toquima Caves CAVE
(Pete's Summit, Toiyabe National Forest; ⊙24hr; 🅿) Inquire at the USDA Forest Service Austin Ranger District Office if you're interested in visiting these remote and sacred caves. They feature red, yellow, black and white pictographs painted by the Western Shoshones that are dated at between 1500 and 3000 years old. Access is by dirt road only.

Austin Historical Museum MUSEUM
(☑775-238-4150; austinnevada.com/austin-nevada-rich-history/austin-museum; 180 Main St (Hwy 50); ⊙9am-5pm or by appointment) FREE

Housed within the former US Forest Service building, this quaint local history museum, inaugurated in 1992, has olde-worlde displays about mining, ranching, the railroad and local indigenous and pioneering history.

Hickison Petroglyph Recreation Area PARK
(☑775-635-4000; www.blm.gov/nv; ⊙24hr; 🅿) FREE North of Hwy 50 at Hickison Summit, about 24 miles east of Austin, Hickison Petroglyph Recreation Area has panoramic lookout points, a self-guided tour, an ADA-accessible trail for viewing the petroglyphs, and a primitive campground (vault toilets, no toilet paper, and no running or drinking water).

🛏 Sleeping & Eating

There are just a handful of basic motels on Austin's main street, and the two places to eat are closed of an evening during the off-season.

Cozy Mountain Motel MOTEL $
(☑775-964-2471; 40 Main St (Hwy 50); d&tw from $60; 🅿😷❄) The name fits: this is a cozy, clean and tastefully refurbished 12-room motel on Austin's Main St, which is effectively in the mountains. There's a friendly host-owner and it's meticulously maintained – the neat-as-a-pin rooms are on the smaller side, but make for a comfortable place to rest and rejuvenate after all that driving, and have quality beds and linens, hot showers and satellite TV.

Toiyabe Cafe CAFE $
(☑775-964-2301; 150 Main St (Hwy 50); mains $6-12; ⊙6am-2pm Oct-Apr, 6am-9pm May-Sep) This down-to-earth cafe is the go-to for daily breakfasts and basic comfort food like grilled cheese, burgers, meatloaf and milkshakes. Less touristy than the International Cafe & Saloon, it's also a fun spot to meet or observe the locals at their friendly best.

❶ Information

The friendly folk at the **Austin Chamber of Commerce** (☑775-964-2200; www.austinnevada.com; 122 Main St (Hwy 50); ⊙9am-noon Mon-Thu) and the **USDA Forest Service Austin Ranger District Office** (☑775-964-2671; www.fs.fed.us/htnf; 100 Midas Canyon Rd, off US Hwy 50; ⊙7:30am-4:30pm Mon-Fri) can help you out with maps and local information, including directions to the best spots, most of which are word-of-mouth (the locals like to keep things unspoiled... who can blame them?).

🛈 Getting There & Away

Austin is located on Hwy 50, 70 miles west of Eureka and 111 miles east of Fallon, with virtually no services in between, in either direction.

The only way to get here is by road and there are no scheduled transportation services, so you'll need wheels if you plan to visit.

Eureka

📞 775 / POP 610 / ELEV 6500FT

An essential stop along the 'Loneliest Road in America', Eureka was so named during the late 19th century, when $40 million worth of silver was extracted from the surrounding hills, although you'd hardly realize that today.

Many of the historic buildings along the main street (also Hwy 50) have been lovingly preserved and include a handsome courthouse, an interesting local history museum and a beautifully restored opera house.

Many folks will visit as a stop along the route, then be on their way to Austin or Ely: there's no compelling reason to linger here, despite the quaintness of the town.

🔾 Sights

Opera House   HISTORIC BUILDING
(📞 775-237-6006; 31 S Main St; ⊘ 8am-noon & 1-5pm Mon-Fri) Dating from 1880, the interior of Eureka's original opera house (oh, how times have changed!) has been beautifully restored, although its facade is a little bland. The building houses an art gallery and hosts folk-music concerts in summer.

Eureka Sentinel Museum   MUSEUM
(📞 775-237-5010; 10 N Monroe St; ⊘ 10am-6pm Tue-Sat Nov-Apr, daily May-Oct) FREE The Eureka Sentinel Museum displays yesteryear newspaper technology and some colorful examples of period reportage, housed in a cute-as-a-button freestanding terrace.

🛏 Sleeping & Eating

Eureka has two basic motels and two quaint heritage B&Bs. Dining options are limited: there's a diner, a steakhouse and a bar and grill.

🛈 Getting There & Away

Eureka is 70 miles east of Austin, along Hwy 50. It's 180 miles east of Fallon, the nearest city. There's practically nothing in between but spectacular vistas.

OFF THE BEATEN TRACK

CATHEDRAL GORGE STATE PARK

Fifteen miles north of Caliente, just past the turn-off to Panaca, **Cathedral Gorge State Park** (📞 775-728-4460; parks.nv.gov/parks/cathedral-gorge; Hwy 93, Pioche; $7; ⊘ visitor center 9am-4:30pm, park 24hr; 🅿 ♿) is one of those magical out-of-the-way places that you never regret traveling all that way for. Wandering among its wind- and water-eroded shapes, you get the feeling that you've stepped into a magnificent, many-spired cathedral, albeit one whose dome is the blue sky above. Head to the Miller Point Overlook for sweeping views and easy hikes into narrow side canyons.

Sleep beneath a blanket of stars amid badlands-style cliffs at the popular, first-come, first-served campground.

Ely

📞 775 / POP 4260 / ELEV 6440FT

The biggest town for miles around, Ely is the logical eastern terminus for drives along the Nevada stretch of Hwy 50, the 'Loneliest Road in America.' It's about as remote a town of any size that you'll find in Nevada, and you'll most likely want to overnight once you get here. A good thing then that it's a pretty little town with some worthwhile attractions and a photogenic old-Nevada downtown comprising a nice park, vibrant regional history murals and plenty of original vintage neon signage to keep the shutterbugs and Instagrammers busy.

🔾 Sights & Activities

Nevada Northern Railway Museum   MUSEUM
(📞 775-289-2085; www.nvdtca.org/eastelyrailroaddepotmuseum; 1100 Ave A; adult/child under 18yr $8/4; ⊘ 8am-4:30pm Mon-Fri) Ely was established as a mining town in the 1860s, but the railroad didn't arrive until 1907. This rail museum inhabits the historic East Ely Depot, which is the departure point for the Nevada Northern Railway. (p96)

Ely Renaissance Village   HISTORIC SITE
(📞 800-496-9350; 400 Ely St; ⊘ 10am-4pm Sat Jul-Sep) If you're in town on a Saturday in season, drop in to see this fabulous little collection of 12 'shotgun houses,' built by

GREAT BASIN NATIONAL PARK

Near the Nevada–Utah border, 67 miles east of Ely, this uncrowded national park encompasses the 13,063ft Wheeler Peak, rising abruptly from the desert and creating an awesome range of life zones and landscapes within a compact area, including the richly decorated Lehman Caves (book guided tours through the Lehman Caves Visitor Center).

The peak's narrow, twisting scenic drive is open only during summer, usually from June through October. Hiking trails near the summit take in superb country made up of glacial lakes, groves of ancient bristlecone pines (some more tha 5000 years old) and even a permanent ice field. The summit trail is an 8.2-mile round-trip trek, with a vertical ascent of nearly 3000ft.

The park's four developed campgrounds are open during summer; only Lower Lehman Creek is available year-round. Primitive camping is free; tent and RV sites cost between $6 and $25.

settlers from France, Slovakia, China, Italy, Greece and other nations in 1908. Each house is now a small museum dedicated to the home country of the settler who built it.

Ward Charcoal Ovens State Historic Park
PARK

(☑ 775-728-4460; parks.nv.gov/parks/ward-charcoal-ovens; entry $7) Ward Charcoal Ovens State Historic Park sits off Hwy 93 south of Ely via signposted, well-maintained dirt roads. Perched in the Egan Mountain Range, it protects a half-dozen beehive-shaped structures dating from 1876 that were once used to make charcoal to supply the silver smelters.

★Nevada Northern Railway
RAIL

(☑ 775-289-2085; www.nnry.com; 1100 Ave A; adult/child 4-12yr from $37/27; ☺ Apr-Dec) Departing from the Nevada Northern Railway Museum (p95), which occupies the former East Ely Depot, the Nevada Northern Railway offers a variety of themed, scheduled rail excursions on trains pulled by historic steam engines, plus the chance to sleep overnight in the railyard bunkhouse ($139)...spooky! A must for trainspotters.

🍴 Sleeping & Eating

Almost all Ely's accommodations are roadside motels, ranging from dingy to above average. There is a handful of original restaurants and franchise fast-food eateries in town.

Bristlecone Motel
MOTEL $

(☑ 800-497-7404; www.bristleconemotelelynv.com; 700 Avenue I; r from $69; P ☻ ☎) We love the old-style charm and welcome of the Bristlecone Motel, with staff who go the extra mile and simple, sparkling rooms.

Hotel Nevada
HOTEL $

(☑ 775-289-6665; www.hotelnevada.com; 501 Aultman St; r from $79; P ✳ @ ☎) Ely's most famous building, the historic Hotel Nevada, which opened with 100 guest rooms in 1929, is both hotel and casino. Despite the smoky casino on the ground floors and the compact size of the rooms, the hotel is at least worth a look for its iconic appeal, if not charm.

Silver State Restaurant
AMERICAN $$

(☑ 775-289-8866; 1204 Aultman St; mains $6-18; ☺ 6am-9pm) Reopened in 2017 under new management, Ely's favourite old-school diner is the kind where waitresses call you 'hun' and comfort food is the only thing on the menu. They do a mean chicken fried steak, and don't go past the Piccadillies (a kind of fried potato) or fresh, home-baked pies.

🍷 Drinking & Nightlife

Ely has its share of casinos where you can whittle away your hard-earned cash. Fortunately for non-gamblers there are some regular bars in town, but you can count their number on the digits of one hand.

ℹ️ Information

Lehman Caves Visitor Center (☑ 775-234-7331, tour reservations 775-234-7517; www.nps.gov/grba; 5500 NV-488, Baker; adult $8-10, child $4-5; ☺ 8am-4:30pm, tours 8:30am-4pm) Sells tickets for guided tours (one to 1½ hours) of Lehman Caves, which are brimming with limestone formations. Note that the temperature inside the caves is a constant 50°F (10°C): bring a sweater.

White Pine County Tourism & Recreation Board (☑ 775-289-3720; www.elynevada.

net; 150 Sixth St; ⊘ 8am-5pm Mon-Fri)
Inquire here for information on local events
like Cocktails and Cannons and the annual
Bathtub Races.

ℹ Getting There & Away

Ely is 139 miles south of Wells on a particularly
pretty, though sparsely populated, stretch of
National Hwy 93, here known as the Great Basin
Highway, which continues south for 243 miles
to Las Vegas.

Along I-80

The I-80 loosely follows an original fur
trappers' route snaking along the Humboldt River from northeast Nevada to Lovelock, near Reno. It's also one of the earliest
emigrant trails to California. Transcontinental railroad tracks reached Reno in 1868
and crossed the state within a year. By the
1920s, the Victory Hwy traveled the same
route, which later became the interstate.
Although not always the most direct route
across Nevada, the I-80 skirts many of the
Great Basin's steep mountain ranges. Overnight stops in the Basque-flavored country
around Elko or Winnemucca will give you a
true taste of cowboy life.

Lovelock

☑ 775 / POP 1958 / ELEV 3980FT

Cashing in on a name, Lovelock historically
lured couples wanting to leave a piece of
their romance in Nevada by symbolically
locking their passion to a monument behind
the courthouse. That ruse doesn't seem to
be attracting too many lovers today: parts of
town have seen better days. If you're trying
to wow your partner and thought Lovelock
would be the place to do it, you'll probably
get a warmer reception from the apple of
your eye in Tahoe or Vegas. There ain't much
romance here.

Located 90 minutes' drive northeast of
Reno on the I-80, Lovelock is timed right for
a pit stop to support the local economy. Why
not check out the few sites while you're here.

◉ Sights

**Pershing County
Courthouse** HISTORIC BUILDING
(☑ 775-273-7213; 400 S Main St; ⊘ 8am-5pm
Mon-Fri) Lovelock's courthouse was inspired
by Rome's Pantheon. On its grounds you
can symbolically lock your passion on a
chain for all eternity in **Lover's Lock Plaza**

(www.loverslock.com), which is actually nothing like it sounds.

Rye Patch State Recreation Area PARK
(☑ 775-538-7321; www.parks.nv.gov; entry $7)
Almost exactly 25 miles north of Lovelock,
just off the I-80, this little patch is a sum-
mery oasis amid the vast plains, where you
can camp (tent/RV sites $14/27), swim, fish
or go boating.

🛏 Sleeping & Eating

If you need to overnight here, there are
some basic to rundown motels as you enter
and exit town. There are a handful of simple
eateries, fast-food franchises and one standout local cafe to choose from.

Cowpoke Cafe CAFE $
(☑ 775-273-2444; 995 Cornell Ave; meals $6-14;
⊘ 6am-9pm Mon-Fri, to 3pm Sat; ✑) Get yerself
some buffalo burgers, brisket sandwiches
and homemade desserts like red velvet
cake, all made from scratch, in this popular
local diner.

Winnemucca

☑ 775 / POP 8000 / ELEV 4300FT

Winnemucca has been a travelers' stop
since the days of the emigrant trail – even
Butch Cassidy dropped in once to rob a
bank. Named after a Paiute chief, the biggest town on this stretch of the I-80 is also
a center for the state's Basque community,
descended from 19th-century immigrant
shepherds. Although Winnemucca isn't an
attractive town, it's worth a look if you'd
like to sample Basque cooking, shop for
antiques or get into the great outdoors.

◉ Sights & Activities

Humboldt County Museum MUSEUM
(☑ 775-623-2912; www.humboldtmuseum.org; 175
Museum Lane; ⊘ 9am-4pm Wed-Fri, 1-4pm Sat) FREE
North of the river in Winnemucca in a former church, the Humboldt County Museum
shows off antique cars, farming implements
and beautiful Paiute baskets, among its eclectic collection of artifacts recounting life in
Winnemucca through the ages.

Bloody Shins Trails MOUNTAIN BIKING
(Highland Dr) Drop in to the **BLM Winnemucca Field Office** (☑ 775-623-1500; www.
blm.nv.gov; 5100 E Winnemucca Blvd; ⊘ 7:30am-
4:30pm Mon-Fri) for the lowdown on the town's
burgeoning mountain-biking trail system:
this Bloody Shins Trail section, which begins

off Highland Dr at the end of Kluncy Canyon Rd, is one of the more challenging.

Festivals & Events

Winnemucca Basque Festival CULTURAL
(Jun) FREE For one day every June for more than three decades, the Basque communities of Winnemucca and beyond come together at the Winnemucca Convention Center to celebrate their unique heritage: expect lots of food, booze, dancing, fun and games, and even a parade.

Sleeping

Winnemucca's main drag has abundant motels and a few casino hotels with 24-hour restaurants.

Winnemucca Inn HOTEL $$
(775-623-2565; www.winnemuccainn.com; 741 W Winnemucca Blvd; r from $119) It's hard to believe this low-profile casino hotel has 105 rooms. All are spacious, tastefully furnished and well equipped, but it's the bustling casino, 24-hour restaurant and children's arcade that most guests come for.

Eating

There are some surprisingly rewarding and unique dining experiences here including the opportunity to sample Basque cuisine, and a fabulous family-run diner from the '50s. Otherwise, there are lots of franchised food outlets.

★**Griddle** CAFE $
(www.thegriddle.com; 460 W Winnemucca Blvd; mains $6-16; 7am-2pm) Don't miss a stop at the Griddle, one of Nevada's best retro cafe-diners, serving up fantastic breakfasts, diner classics and homemade desserts since 1948.

Martin Hotel BASQUE $$
(775-623-3197; www.themartinhotel.com; 94 W Railroad St; dinner $18-36; 11:30am-2pm Mon-Fri, 4-9pm nightly;) Those overnighting should plan their evening around dinner at the Martin Hotel, where ranchers, locals and weary travelers have come since 1898 to enjoy family-style Basque meals under pressed-tin ceilings.

Drinking & Nightlife

Winnemucca has its fair share of casinos, bars and brothels for a town of its size. This is Nevada, after all.

Delizioso Global Coffee CAFE
(775-625-1000; 508a W Winnemucca Blvd; 5am-5pm Mon-Fri, 6am-1pm Sat;) For fueling up for what will likely be a long drive in any direction out of Winnemucca, delightful Delizioso Global Coffee offers creative espresso drinks like the 'Winnemocha' and fresh scones amid a fanciful forest-like interior.

Information

Winnemucca Visitors Center & Chamber of Commerce (775-623-5071; www.winnemucca.com; 50 W Winnemucca Blvd; 9am-5pm Mon-Fri, 9am-noon Sat, 11am-4pm Sun) Inside you'll find the Buckaroo Hall of Fame, full of cowboy art and folklore, and can inquire about self-guided walking tours, horseback riding at local ranches, and what's happening when and where.

Getting There & Away

Winnemucca is 166 miles northeast of Reno on the I-80 (and 124 miles west of Elko).

Greyhound (800-231-2222; www.greyhound.com) operates one coach per day from Reno to Winnemucca (from $22, 2¾ hours), onwards to Elko (from $20, 2½ hours) and Salt Lake City (from $41, 6¾ hours).

The **Amtrak** (800-872-7245; www.amtrak.com) *California Zephyr* train connects Winnemucca to Reno (from $22, 2¾ hours), heading west, and Elko (from $16, 2½ hours), heading east onwards to Chicago.

Elko

775 / POP 20,074 / ELEV 5070FT
Elko is the largest town in rural Nevada, a center of cowboy culture with a calendar of Western-themed cultural events and a museum big on buckaroos, stagecoaches and the Pony Express. The other cultural influence is Basque; in fact, Basque shepherds and Old West cattlemen had some violent conflicts over grazing rights in the late 19th century.

South of Elko, the Ruby Mountains are a superbly rugged range, nicknamed 'Nevada's alps' for their prominent peaks, glacial lakes and alpine vegetation. The village of **Lamoille** has basic food and lodging, and one of the most photographed rural churches in the US. Just before the village, Lamoille Canyon Rd branches south, following a forested canyon for 12 miles past cliffs and waterfalls to the Ruby Crest trailhead at 8800ft.

⊙ Sights & Activities

Lamoille Recreation Area NATURE RESERVE
(☑775-738-5171; www.fs.usda.gov/recarea/htnf/recarea/?recid=75383) The Lamoille Recreation Area is part of the Ruby Mountains section of the multilocation Humboldt-Toiyabe National Forest. It comprises the spectacular Lamoille Canyon Scenic Byway, which twists and climbs through the glacial-carved canyon to 8800ft, and is one of Nevada's most beautiful sections of national park. Receiving the state's highest annual average rainfall, the canyon, unlike anywhere else in predominantly arid Nevada, is lush with meadows, bursting with wildflowers and waterfalls and home to an abundance of wildlife. There are many hiking opportunities; bring your camera.

California Trail Interpretive Center MUSEUM
(☑775-738-1849; www.californiatrailcenter.org; 1 Trail Center Way, I-80, Exit 292; ⊙9am-4.30pm Wed-Sun; P) FREE If you're driving the I-80, which follows, in parts, the route of the original California Trail that pioneers trod when opening up the West, a stop at this fascinating and informative center with interactive exhibits and historical demonstrations is a must. The center, 8 miles west of Elko, highlights just how remarkable a task it was for these men, women and children to have forged their way across the country by wagon and foot.

Western Folklife Center ARTS CENTER
(☑775-738-7508; www.westernfolklife.org; 501 Railroad St; adult/child 6-18yr $5/1; ⊙10am-5:30pm Mon-Fri, 10am-5pm Sat) To get a taste of life in the Wild West, aspiring cowboys and cowgirls should visit this cultural center, incorporating the Wiegand Gallery's impressive collection of interactive multimedia works, housed in the former Pioneer Hotel. The center hosts the remarkably popular National Cowboy Poetry Gathering in January/February, as well as visiting exhibitions and special events year-round.

Northeastern Nevada Museum MUSEUM
(☑775-738-3418, reservations 775-778-4068; www.museumelko.org; 1515 Idaho St; adult/youth 13-18yr/child 3-12yr $5/3/1; ⊙9am-5pm Mon-Sat, 1-5pm Sun; P) The Northeastern Nevada Museum has excellent displays on pioneer life, Pony Express riders, Basque settlers and modern mining techniques. Free monthly tours of the nearby Newmont gold mine usually start here; call for reservations.

✯ Festivals & Events

National Cowboy Poetry Gathering LITERATURE
(www.nationalcowboypoetrygathering.org; ⊙late Jan-early Feb) You can't get more authentic than this celebration of the written and spoken word, sharing the stories of the men and women who work the land. Held over six days, the festival features readings, workshops, dinners, dancing, and a cast of characters as unique and engaging as Nevada itself.

🛏 Sleeping & Eating

A popular overnight stop for truckers and travelers, Elko has more than 2000 rooms that fill up fast, especially on weekends. Chain motels and hotels line Idaho St, particularly east of downtown, but you won't find any five-star lodgings here.

Thunderbird Motel MOTEL $
(☑775-738-7115; www.thunderbirdmotelelko.com; 345 Idaho St; d from $59; P✳🐾❄🐕) This centrally located pet-friendly motel has all the standard inclusions for its low rates. Although a little dated, the decor of its comfortable, spotlessly clean rooms won't have you calling the style police, and the friendly, helpful staff do their best to make you feel at home. There's even an outdoor swimming pool.

Red Lion Hotel & Casino HOTEL $$
(☑775-738-2111; www.redlionhotelelko.com; 2065 Idaho St; d/ste from $89/138; P✳🛜❄) Elko's plushest oversized rooms, featuring chunky dark woods, plump armchairs and luxurious bed linens, are found at its most popular casino, which also has a bar, Starbucks and two restaurants on-site. Most rooms have floor-to-ceiling sliding glass doors opening on to a large balcony, and there's an outdoor pool for those warmer months.

Hilton Garden Inn HOTEL $$
(☑775-777-1200; www.hiltongardeninn.com; 3650 E Idaho St; d/tw/ste from $129; P✳@🛜❄) Elko's Garden Inn is not dissimilar to any other Garden Inn the nation over: a comfy, chain option with above-average king-sized bedding, neutral decor and service the Hilton brand is known for. Six oversized suites with separate sitting room and Jacuzzi are available.

Cowboy Joe CAFE $
(☑775-753-5612; www.cowboyjoecoffee.com; 376 5th St; dishes $3-7; ⊙5:30am-4:30pm Mon-Fri, 6am-5:30pm Sat, 7am-noon Sun; 🛜) A great

small-town coffeehouse with cute namesake paraphernalia for sale, friendly service and an eponymous signature drink that will keep you going till Reno...or Salt Lake City.

★ **Star Hotel** BASQUE $$
(☑ 775-753-8696; www.eatdrinkandbebasque.com; 246 Silver St; lunch $8-14, dinner $16-38; ☺11am-2pm & 5-9pm Mon-Fri, 4:30-9:30pm Sat) If you've never sampled Basque food, the best place in town for your inaugural experience is the Star Hotel, a family-style supper club located in a 1910 boarding house for Basque sheepherders. Offerings include steak, trout and lobster grilled over hot coals, lamb stews, bean dishes and decadent desserts.

Machi's Saloon & Grill AMERICAN $$
(☑ 775-738-9772; www.machissaloon.com; 450 Commercial St; mains $12-24; ☺11am-9pm Mon-Fri; ☑) This tiny local favorite is almost always buzzing due to its Modern American cuisine, which is a cut above the offerings of your typical Nevadan grill or bar. Menu items range from sandwiches, steak and salads to fancier choices such as oven-roasted prime rib and Alaskan king crab. Yum!

🍷 Drinking & Nightlife

There are a few bars in the downtown area centered around 5th and Idaho Sts, and of course, being Nevada, some casino action and a small and somewhat dingy red-light district.

Stray Dog Pub & Café PUB
(☑ 775-753-4888; 374 5th St; ☺3pm-2am Mon-Sat) This friendly pub, decked out with old bikes and surfboards, is popular with locals and visitors alike, and serves local Nevadan beer, tasty pizzas and pub-style comfort food.

🛍 Shopping

JM Capriola Co. CLOTHING
(☑ 775-738-5816; www.capriolas.com; 500 Commercial St; ☺9am-5pm Mon-Sat) If you fancy yourself to be a bit of a cowboy or cowgirl, kit yourself up at this Elko family business, in operation since 1929, selling custom saddles, boots and jeans galore, and all manner of cowboy-type garb that city-slickers have no clue about.

❶ Information

Sherman Station Visitors Center (☑ 800-248-3556; www.elkocva.com; 1405 Idaho St;

☺9am-5pm) Situated in the historic Sherman Station ranch house. You'll also find an 1860s Pony Express station, relocated here in 1960, next door. For information on summer art walks and wine walks, see www.elkodowntown.com.

❶ Getting There & Away

Elko is serviced by Hwy I-80. It's 108 miles from West Wendover and the Utah border to the east, and 124 miles from Winnemucca to the west.

Greyhound (p98) operates one coach per day from Elko to Reno (from $34, 5½ hours) and Salt Lake City (from $29, 4¼ hours).

The **Amtrak** (p98) *California Zephyr* train connects Elko to Winnemucca (from $16, 2¼ hours), onwards to Reno (from $35, 5½ hours) and San Francisco/Emeryville.

The tiny **Elko Regional Airport** (☑ 775-777-7190; www.flyelkonevada.com; 975 Terminal Way) has at least two direct services per day to Salt Lake City, connecting on to 42 domestic destinations.

Wells

☑ 775 / POP 1320 / ELEV 5630FT

In 2008 the historic, far-flung town of Wells was rocked by a shallow 6.0-magnitude earthquake that destroyed many of the town's heritage buildings. Sadly, it's never really recovered, and today feels a bit like a ghost town that people still inhabit.

Locals would want you to know that heavyweight boxing champ Jack Dempsey started his career here, as a bouncer in the local bars. After strolling around what's left of the **Front Street historic district**, its hard to imagine that there ever were any.

Southwest of town, scenic Hwy 231 heads into the mountains, climbing alongside sagebrush and aspen trees toward cobalt-blue **Angel Lake** (8378ft), a glacial cirque beautifully embedded in the East Humboldt Range.

◉ Sights

Trail of the '49ers Interpretive Center MUSEUM
(☑ 775-752-3540; www.wellsnevada.com; 436 S 6th St; ☺hours vary) **FREE** The Trail of the '49ers Interpretive Center is a sweet little local history museum that tells the story of mid-19th-century pioneers on the emigrant trail to California. By the time you leave you'll be an expert on the California Trail and the Pony Express.

🛏 Sleeping & Eating

Wells has some rough-and-tumble residential motels downtown and a handful of the big chain offerings out by the interstate. Dining options other than the ubiquitous highway-side chains are limited to say the least.

Angel Lake Campgrounds　CAMPGROUND $
(☎775-752-3357; www.recreation.gov; Angel Lake Rd; tent & RV sites $16-32; ⊙ Jun-Oct) Southwest of Wells, scenic byway NV Hwy 231 heads into the mountains. The road stops at Angel Lake, where you'll find these campgrounds, part of the multisite Humboldt-Toiyabe National Forest.

West Wendover

☑775 / POP 4498 / ELEV 4460FT

If you can't quite make it to Salt Lake City before dark, stop in West Wendover, where ginormous casino hotels with 24-hour restaurants line Wendover Blvd. For the lowdown, check out www.wendoverfun.com.

Just across the state line, in Utah, the nearby Bonneville Salt Flats are a spectacular sight. Since 1935 daredevils have been coming here to try and break the world land-speed records. 'Speed Week' time trials in August and the 'World of Speed' event in September draw huge crowds each year.

◉ Sights

Bonneville Speed Museum　MUSEUM
(☎775-664-4400; www.bonnevillespeedmuseum. com; 1000 E Wendover Blvd, Wendover; adult/child $2/1; ⊙10am-6pm Jun-Nov) This museum documents attempts to set land-speed records on the nearby Bonneville Salt Flats.

🛏 Sleeping & Eating

Most of the big chain-motel brands are represented here, and there are some relatively luxurious options in the town's higher-end casinos. Also head to the big casinos for decent dining with 24-hour options.

ℹ Getting There & Away

The I-80 runs through West Wendover, which abuts the Utah state line. It's 58 miles east of Wells and 123 miles west of Salt Lake City, in Utah.

Greyhound (p98) operates one coach per day connecting West Wendover with Elko (from $18, two hours) and Salt Lake City (also from $18, two hours).

RENO-TAHOE AREA

The state's western corner, carved by the Nevada sierra dense with conifers, drops off near Genoa. It's a vast treeless steppe of sagebrush, unfurling itself like a plush green-gray carpet laid out on the plains of the Great Basin. In this transitional place, where pine-covered mountains fade into an arid sea of lowland shrubs, rogue Nevada reveals its gentler side.

It's here that pioneers of the California Trail established trade, and it's where the earth gave up its precious silver: a gift that sustained the Union through the Civil War, funded the rise of Virginia City and earned Nevada statehood.

From Lake Tahoe's sandy shores, the historic hamlet of Virginia City and the enduring gentility of Carson City, to little Reno, Burning Man, Black Rock and beyond – it's Nevada's softness that will steal your heart, not its screaming inner-teen.

Reno

☑775 / POP 233,294 / ELEV 4505FT

Reno has a compact clutch of big casinos in the shadow of the Sierra Nevada. It has a reputation for being a 'poor man's Vegas,' but while in some ways that cap fits, we're here to set the record straight: Reno is oh, so much more. Beyond the garish downtown, with its photoworthy mid-century modern architecture, neon signs and Truckee River, sprawls a city of parks and pretty houses inhabited by a friendly bunch eager to welcome you.

Stealing a piece of California's tech-pie, the gargantuan Tesla Gigafactory will open its doors here in 2020, bringing plenty of cashed-up youngsters to town, and Reno is ready: the transformation of the formerly gritty Midtown District continues, injecting a dose of funky new bars, top-notch restaurants and vibrant arts spaces into Reno's already unique and eclectic mix.

◉ Sights

★National Automobile Museum　MUSEUM
(☎775-333-9300; www.automuseum.org; 10 S Lake St; adult/child 6-18yr $10/4; ⊙9:30am-5:30pm Mon-Sat, 10am-4pm Sun) Stylized street scenes illustrate a century's worth of automobile history at this engaging car museum. The collection is enormous and impressive, with one-of-a-kind vehicles – including James Dean's 1949 Mercury from *Rebel*

Without a Cause, a 1938 Phantom Corsair and a 24-karat gold-plated DeLorean – and rotating exhibits with all kinds of souped-up and fabulously retro rides.

★ **The Discovery** MUSEUM
(Terry Lee Wells Nevada Discovery Museum; ☑ 775-786-1000; www.nvdm.org; 490 S Center St; entry $10, after 4pm Wed $5; ⊙ 10am-5pm Tue, Thu-Sat, to 8pm Wed, noon-5pm Sun; P ♿) Since opening its doors in 2011 as a children's museum, the Discovery rapidly grew in popularity and expanded its focus to become a world-class, hands-on center for 'science, technology, engineering, art and math' (STEAM) learning, with 11 permanent, participatory exhibitions designed to inspire kids and young adults to have fun and develop an interest in these disciplines.

Nevada Museum of Art MUSEUM
(☑ 775-329-3333; www.nevadaart.org; 160 W Liberty St; adult/child 6-12yr $10/1; ⊙ 10am-5pm Wed & Fri-Sun, to 8pm Thu) In a sparkling building inspired by the geological formations of the Black Rock Desert north of town, a floating staircase leads to galleries showcasing temporary exhibits and eclectic collections on the American West, labor and contemporary landscape photography. In 2016 the museum opened its $6.2-million Sky Room function area. Visitors are free to explore and enjoy the space – a rooftop penthouse and patio with killer views – providing it's not in use.

Nevada Historical Society Museum MUSEUM
(☑ 775-688-1190; www.nvdtca.org/historicalsociety; 1650 N Virginia St; adult/child under 17yr $5/free; ⊙ 10am-4:30pm Tue-Sat) Within the main campus of the University of Nevada, the state's oldest museum includes permanent exhibits on neon signs, local American Indian culture and the presence of the federal government.

◉ **Virginia St**

Wedged between the I-80 and the Truckee River, downtown's N Virginia St is casino central.

★ **Atlantis** CASINO
(☑ 775-825-4700; www.atlantiscasino.com; 3800 S Virginia St; ⊙ 24hr) Looking like it's straight out of a 1970s B-grade flick on the outside, Atlantis is all fun on the inside, modeled on the legendary underwater city, with a mirrored ceiling and tropical flourishes like indoor waterfalls and palm trees. It's one of Reno's most popular offerings, though not downtown.

Silver Legacy CASINO
(☑ 775-329-4777; www.silverlegacyreno.com; 407 N Virginia St; ⊙ 24hr) A Victorian-themed place, the Silver Legacy is easily recognized by its white landmark dome, where a giant mock mining rig periodically erupts into a fairly tame sound-and-light spectacle.

Eldorado CASINO
(☑ 775-786-5700; www.eldoradoreno.com; 345 N Virginia St; ⊙ 24hr) Right downtown, near the Reno Arch, the Eldorado has a kitschy Fountain of Fortune that probably has Italian sculptor Bernini spinning in his grave.

Peppermill CASINO
(☑ 775-826-2121; www.peppermillreno.com; 2707 S Virginia St; ⊙ 24hr) About 2 miles south of downtown, the Peppermill, one of the newer and more stylish casinos in town, dazzles with a 17-story Tuscan-style tower and a killer pool.

🏃 **Activities**

Historic Reno Preservation Society WALKING
(☑ 775-747-4478; www.historicreno.org; suggested donation $10) Dig deeper with a walking or biking tour of Reno that highlights subjects including architecture, politics and literary history. Check the website for the exhaustive list of tours available.

Sierra Adventures OUTDOORS
(☑ 866-323-8928, 775-323-8928; www.wildsierra.com; Truckee River Lane; kayak rental from $22) This affable outfitter offers tons of adventure: kayaking, tubing, mountain biking, skiing, horseback riding and snowmobiling.

Truckee River Whitewater Park OUTDOORS
(www.reno.gov; Wingfield Park) Mere steps from the casinos, the park's class II and III rapids are gentle enough for kids riding inner tubes, yet sufficiently challenging for professional freestyle kayakers. Two courses wrap around Wingfield Park, a small river island that hosts free concerts in summertime.

🎊 **Festivals & Events**

Hot August Nights CULTURAL
(www.hotaugustnights.net; ⊙ Aug) Catch the *American Graffiti* vibe during this celebration of hot rods and rock and roll in early August held over separate dates and various locations around Reno and Virginia City. Hotel rates skyrocket.

🛏 Sleeping

Reno has a wide range of accommodations, from budget motels to boutique hotels and decadent casino suites. Room rates in smoky casino towers can sometimes seem ridiculously inexpensive – this is to get as many people through the doors as possible. Many casinos also whack on a resort fee to your bill. Reno's prices are generally higher than in other parts of the state, especially on weekends.

Mt Rose Campground   CAMPGROUND $
(📞877-444-6777; www.recreation.gov; Mt Rose Hwy/Hwy 431; RV & tent sites $20-50; ⏰mid-Jun–Sep; 🅿🏊) Reserve your spot a minimum of four days in advance for this gorgeous and popular high-altitude (9300ft!) campsite overlooking Lake Tahoe. It's located within the Humboldt-Toiyabe National Forest, 28 miles from downtown Reno. Reservations can be made via the website.

Sands Regency   HOTEL $
(📞775-348-2200; www.sandsregency.com; 345 N Arlington Ave; r Sun-Thu from $49, Fri & Sat from $89; 🅿🌀🛜🏊🐾) The Sands Regency has some of the largest standard digs in town. Its rooms are decked out in a cheerful tropical palette of upbeat blues, reds and greens – a visual relief from typical motel decor. Empress Tower rooms are best. The 17th-floor gym and Jacuzzi are perfectly positioned to capture the drop-dead panoramic mountain views, and an outdoor pool opens in summer.

★**Whitney Peak**   DESIGN HOTEL $$
(📞775-398-5400; www.whitneypeakhotel.com; 255 N Virginia St; d from $129; 🅿🌀🛜) 🏄 What's not to love about this independent, inventive, funky, friendly, nonsmoking, non-gambling downtown hotel? Spacious guest rooms have a youthful, fun vibe celebrating the great outdoors and don't skimp on designer creature comforts. With an executive-level concierge lounge, free use of the external climbing wall (if you're game), a noteworthy on-site restaurant and friendly, professional staff, Whitney Peak is hard to beat.

🍴 Eating

Reno's dining scene is coming of age, finally going beyond the cheap casino buffets and ubiquitous old-school diners. Many downtown restaurants are open around the clock, or at least until the wee hours. The Midtown

GALENA CREEK

Just 19 miles from downtown Reno is **Galena Creek** (📞775-849-4948; www.galenacreekvisitorcenter.org/trail-map.html; 18250 Mt Rose Hwy), a complex network of scenic hiking trails that gets you right into the heart of the wilderness of the Humboldt-Toiyabe National Forest. Check in with the visitor center (⏰9am-6pm Tue-Sun) when you arrive for the latest conditions and friendly advice.

District has an impressive selection of new restaurants across a wide genre of cuisine.

★**Gold 'n Silver Inn**   DINER $
(📞775-323-2696; www.goldnsilverreno.com; 790 W 4th St; mains $6-20; ⏰24hr) A Reno institution for over 50 years, this slightly divey but superfriendly 24-hour diner has a huge menu of home-style American favorites such as meatloaf, plated dinners, all-day breakfasts and burgers, not to mention seriously incredible caramel milkshakes.

Peg's Glorified Ham & Eggs   DINER $
(www.eatatpegs.com; 420 S Sierra St; mains $7-16; ⏰6:30am-2pm; 👶) Locally regarded as having the best breakfast in town, Peg's offers tasty grill food that's not too greasy.

★**Old Granite Street Eatery**   AMERICAN $$
(📞775-622-3222; www.oldgranitestreeteatery.com; 243 S Sierra St; dinner mains $12-29; ⏰11am-10pm Mon-Thu, to 11pm Fri, 10am-11pm Sat, to 3pm Sun; 🍴) A lovely well-lit place for organic and local comfort food, old-school artisanal cocktails and craft beers, this antique-strewn hot spot enchants diners with its stately wooden bar, water served in old liquor bottles and lengthy seasonal menu. Forgot to make a reservation? Check out the iconic rooster and pig murals and wait at a communal table fashioned from a barn door.

★**Wild River Grille**   GRILL $$
(📞775-847-455; www.wildrivergrille.com; 17 S Virginia St; mains lunch $11-16, dinner $21-37; ⏰11am-9pm; 🍴) At the Wild River Grille you'll love the smart-casual dining and the varied menu of creative cuisine, from the Gruyère croquettes to the lobster ravioli, but most of all the wonderful patio overlooking the lovely Truckee River: it's also the best spot in town for a drink on a balmy summer's evening and a great place to take a date.

THE RENO ARCH

Be sure to check out the iconic **Reno Arch** (cnr Virginia St & Commercial Row), a fabulously retro neon sign spanning Virginia St at the intersection of Commercial Row, denoting the epicenter of 'casino central' and proclaiming Reno to be 'The Biggest Little City in the World'. First built in 1926, the arch has had a number of incarnations in different locations downtown. Its slogan was chosen by competition in 1929, and has held tight, despite attempts to change it: proud locals love that Reno remains the 'biggest little city'.

Louis' Basque Corner   BASQUE $$
(☑ 775-323-7203; www.louisbasquecorner.com; 301 E 4th St; dinner menu $12-29; ⊘ 11am-9:30pm Tue-Sat, 4-9:30pm Sun & Mon) Get ready to dine on lamb, rabbit, sweetbreads and more lamb at a big table full of people you've never met before. A different set-course menu is offered every day and posted in the window.

🍸 Drinking & Nightlife

Reno is a fun place with plenty going on, including regular monthly pub crawls, the only gay bars outside Las Vegas and an emerging arts scene. The free weekly *Reno News & Review* (www.newsreview.com/reno/home) is your best source for listings.

★ Pignic   BAR
(☑ 775-376-1948; www.renoriver.org/pignic-pub-patio; 235 Flint St; ⊘ 3-11pm) This awesome little place gets points for originality: occupying what was formerly a private home, the concept is simple. You bring your own food and barbecue it here, and buy drinks at the bar. It's participatory, friendly and speaks to the importance of friends, family and community.

★ Imperial Bar & Lounge   BAR
(☑ 775-324-6399; www.imperialbarandlounge.com; 150 N Arlington Ave; ⊘ 11am-2am Fri & Sat, to 10pm Sun-Thu) A classy bar inhabiting a relic of the past – this building was once an old bank, and in the middle of the wood floor you can see cement where the vault once stood. Sandwiches and pizzas go with 16 beers on tap and a buzzing weekend scene.

Chapel Tavern   COCKTAIL BAR
(☑ 775-324-2244; www.chapeltavern.com; 1099 S Virginia St; ⊘ 2pm-2am Mon-Wed, to 4am Thu-Sun) Midtown's cocktail mecca makes its own infusions – try the bourbon with fig – and a seasonal drinks menu attracts year-round interest to its antler-adorned bar and outdoor patio. DJs keep it jamming on Friday and Saturday, patrons comprise a diverse age mix.

St James Infirmary   BAR
(☑ 775-657-8484; www.saintjamesinfirmaryreno.com; 445 California Ave; ⊘ 4pm-midnight) With an eclectic menu of 120 bottled varieties and 18 on tap here, beer aficionados will short-circuit with delight. The bar hosts sporadic events, including jazz and bluegrass performances.

Patio   GAY & LESBIAN
(☑ 775-323-6565; 600 W 5th St; ⊘ 11am-2am) This compact offering is the best (mellowest) of Reno's two downtown gay bars, with friendly staff and good live karaoke: it's a thing here.

☆ Entertainment

Knitting Factory   LIVE MUSIC
(☑ 775-323-5648; re.knittingfactory.com; 211 N Virginia St) This midsized music venue books mainstream and indie favorites.

ⓘ Information

Reno-Sparks Convention & Visitors Authority Visitor Center (☑ 775-682-3800; www.visitrenotahoe.com; 135 N Sierra St; ⊘ 9am-6pm) Drop in for the latest on what's on, where and when. There's also a desk at the airport.

ⓘ Getting There & Away

About 5 miles southeast of downtown, the **Reno-Tahoe International Airport** (RNO; www.renoairport.com; 🛜) is served by most major airlines, with connections throughout the US to international routes.

The **North Lake Tahoe Express** (☑ 866-216-5222; www.northlaketahoeexpress.com; one-way $49) operates a shuttle (six to eight daily, 3:30am to midnight) to and from the airport to multiple North Shore Lake Tahoe locations including Truckee, Squaw Valley and Incline Village. Reserve in advance.

The **South Tahoe Airporter** (☑ 866-898-2463; www.southtahoeairporter.com; adult/child one-way $29.75/16.75, round-trip $53/30.25) operates several daily shuttle buses from the airport to Stateline casinos; the journey takes from 75 minutes to two hours.

RTC Washoe (☑ 775-348-0400; www.rtc washoe.com) operates six wi-fi-equipped RTC Intercity buses per day from Monday to Friday to Carson City ($5, one hour), which loosely connect to BlueGo buses – operated by **Tahoe Transportation District** (☑ 775-589-5500; www.tahoetransportation.org) – to the Stateline Transit Center in South Lake Tahoe (adult/child $4/2 with RTC Intercity transfer, one hour).

Greyhound (p98) offers up to five direct buses a day to Reno from San Francisco (from $8, from five hours): book in advance for the lowest fares.

Discount bus company **Megabus** (www.mega bus.com) has two daily departures to San Francisco (from $15, 4½ hours) via Sacramento.

The Amtrak (p98) *California Zephyr* train makes one daily departure from Emeryville/San Francisco ($52, 6¾ hours) to Reno, onwards to Chicago (from $122, 44¾ hours): a shared sleeper berth will set you back $467. Up to three other daily services depart Emeryville/San Francisco for Sacramento, connecting with a bus service to Reno ($60, from 6½ hours).

❶ Getting Around

It's easy to get around Reno on foot, but parts of downtown beyond the 24-hour casino area can be sketchy after dark. Exercise caution when walking along Ralston St, between W 4th and 5th Sts, especially at night.

Casino hotels usually offer frequent free airport shuttles for their guests (and generally don't ask to see reservations – just saying …).

The local RTC Washoe Ride buses blanket the city, and most routes converge at the RTC 4th St station downtown (between Lake St and Evans Ave). Useful routes include the RTC Rapid line for S Virginia St, 11 for Sparks and 19 for the airport.

The Sierra Spirit bus (50¢) loops around all major downtown landmarks – including the casinos and the university – every 15 minutes from 7am to 7pm.

Carson City

☑ 775 / POP 54,080 / ELEV 4800FT

While nearby gateway city Reno garners plenty of attention with its glut of casinos and promises of excitement, Carson City, surrounded by majestic mountains and with a distinctly more mellow vibe, might just be Nevada's best-kept secret. If you agree with the locals, it's also a great place to raise a family.

With excellent road connections to Reno, Lake Tahoe, Genoa and Virginia City, some attractive heritage architecture beyond the main drag, tree-lined streets and a handful of interesting attractions, the state capital is worth considering as a base from which to explore the region, especially if you're traveling with kids.

⊙ Sights & Activities

★ Bower's Mansion

Regional Park   HISTORIC BUILDING, PARK
(☑ 775-849-1825; www.washoecounty.us/parks; 4005 Bower's Mansion Rd; house tours by appointment $8, pool adult/child $5/4; ⊙ house 10am-4pm Sat & Sun, pool noon-5pm, Jun-Nov) Just 12 miles north of Carson City off Hwy I-580, almost halfway to Reno, you'll find this fabulous regional park with manicured gardens perfect for picnicking, the stunning former 1864 residence of Comstock millionaire Sandy Bowers and his psychic wife Eilley (now fully restored and a fascinating museum), as well as a Z-shaped, 44m outdoor pool heated by a hot spring. Taste the good life!

★ Nevada State Museum   MUSEUM
(☑ 775-687-4810; nvdtca.org/nevadastatemuseum carsoncity; 600 N Carson St; adult/child under 18yr $8/free; ⊙ 8:30am-4:30pm Tue-Sun) Housed inside the 1869 US Mint building, the Nevada State Museum generally hosts one visiting exhibition to complement its four excellent permanent exhibitions: *Carson City Mint, Nevada's Changing Earth, Nevada: A People & Place Through Time,* and *Under One Sky,* to tell the story of what is one of America's most unique and liberal states.

Nevada State Railroad Museum   MUSEUM
(☑ 775-687-6953; nvdtca.org/nevadastaterailroad museumcarsoncity; 2180 S Carson St; adult/child under 18 yr $6/free; ⊙ 9am-5pm Thu-Mon) Loved by adults and kids alike, the hugely popular Nevada State Railroad Museum is worth a visit, even if you're not a rail buff, for its impressive collection of over 60 train cars and locomotives from the 1800s to the early 1900s. Train rides are available every weekend from June to November: check the website for schedules.

Nevada State Capitol   HISTORIC BUILDING
(☑ 775-684-5670; 101 North Carson St; ⊙ 8am-5pm Mon-Fri) FREE Built in 1870, the handsome, robust Nevada State Capitol is complete with a silver-covered dome symbolizing its 'Silver State' status. The original senate chamber now houses a museum of statehood paraphernalia. They say the governor's door is always open, but you'll have to charm your way past the assistant.

★ Carson Hot Springs   HOT SPRINGS
(☑ 775-885-8844; www.carsonhotsprings.com; 1500 Old Hot Springs Rd; general entry $12, private spa $20; ⊙ 7am-10pm) There's something

OLD-TIME SALOONS

Palace Restaurant & Saloon (www.palacerestaurant1875.com; 54 S C St; mains $7-14; ☺ hours vary) More about the setting than the food, the Palace Restaurant & Saloon, which is full of town memorabilia, serves up good renditions of traditional American breakfasts and lunches: fry ups, sandwiches, soups and salads.

Bucket of Blood Saloon (www.bucketofbloodsaloonvc.com; 1 S C St; ☺ 10am-7pm) The longtime family-run Bucket of Blood Saloon serves up beer and other booze at its antique wooden bar with expansive views out the huge back window, and features live Western bands on Saturday and Sunday afternoons.

truly unique and wonderful about this unfussy complex of hot-spring pools, first established here in 1849. Opt for a private spa room (first-come, first-served) where you can soak alone, or with a friend, as nature intended it: nude (optional), for up to two hours. Private baths include entry to the main outdoor pools – bathing suits required... this isn't Japan.

🛏 Sleeping

Carson City has a good selection of midrange tourist and business hotels including offerings from most of the big chains. For more luxurious digs, you'll need to head to Lake Tahoe or Reno.

Holiday Inn Express HOTEL $
(☎ 775-283-4055; www.ihg.com/holidayinnexpress/hotels/us/en/carson-city/csncn/hoteldetail; 4055 N Carson St; d from $99; P ☺ ☻ ☎ ☒) Fresh from a complete refurbishment in 2016, Carson's Holiday Inn Express has helpful, professional staff and contemporary, well-designed rooms with great views of the nearby mountains, plus easy access to Hwy I-580.

Carson Tahoe Hotel HOTEL $
(☎ 800-338-7760; carsontahoehotel.com; 800 N Carson St; d from $79; P ☀ ☎) Newly rebranded and remodeled, this central hotel has the city's freshest rooms, with plush bedding, plump fluffy pillows and lots of space to unwind.

🍴 Eating & Drinking

You'll find some neat eats in Carson, with plenty of ethnic flavours to savour compared to the rest of Nevada, as well as family restaurants, franchises and fast food galore. While not the party towns Reno and Lake Tahoe have become, Carson has a handful of good bars and a small selection of casinos.

★ Sassafras AMERICAN $
(☎ 775-884-4471; www.sassafrascarsoncity.com; 1500 Old Hot Springs Rd; mains $8-20; ☺ 11am-9pm; ☒) What's not to love about this brilliant food joint, with an inventive menu of original burgers, pizzas and salads and dreamy daily specials, featuring flavours from abroad? With starters like black-and-blue shrimp fondue, killer cocktails, nightly live music and the best servers in the biz, it could be a long night...

★ Basil THAI $
(☎ 775-841-6100; www.thebasilrestaurant.com; 311 N Carson St; mains $12-26; ☺ 11am-9pm; ☒) Who would have thought some of the best (seriously) Thai cuisine outside Thailand would be found in downtown Carson City in this spotless restaurant? All the food looks and tastes as appealing as the decor is stylish and the service impeccable.

Kim Lee's Sushi & Teriyaki SUSHI $$
(☎ 775-883-2372; www.kimleesushi.com; 319 N Carson St; all-you-can-eat lunch/dinner $18/23; ☺ 11am-9pm Sun-Thu, 11am-10pm Fri & Sat; ☒) Did you know Nevada is one of the only states in the US to offer all-you-can-eat (AYCE) sushi, ubiquitous in Canada? Well now you do, and award-winning Kim Lee's is Carson's best, with a huge menu to gorge yourself on in a pleasant setting showcasing the works of local artists for you to enjoy as you dine.

Firkin & Fox PUB
(☎ 775-883-1369; www.foxbrewpub.com; 310 S Carson St; ☺ 11am-midnight Sun-Thu, to 2am Fri & Sat) Sink into a well-worn red-velvet booth to down pints and satisfy your hunger on tasty pub grub at this downtown institution in the historic St Charles Hotel.

ℹ Information

Carson City being the state capital, there are plenty of helpful resources here at your disposal, covering all things Nevada:

Carson City Visitors Bureau (☑775-687-7410; www.visitcarsoncity.com; 716 N Carson St; ⊙9am-5pm Mon-Sat) A treasure trove of information on Carson City, Lake Tahoe, Reno and beyond, including hiking and biking trails and walking tours with downloadable podcasts.

Nevada Department of Transportation (☑877-687-6237, in-state 511; www.nvroads.com) For up-to-date road conditions.

Nevada Division of State Parks (☑775-684-2770; www.parks.nv.gov; 901 S Stewart St, 5th fl; ⊙8am-5pm Mon-Fri) For info on camping and access.

Nevada Tourism Commission (☑775-687-4322; www.travelnevada.com; 401 N Carson St; ⊙9am-5pm Mon-Fri) Sends free books, maps and information on accommodations, campgrounds and events.

❶ Getting There & Away

Carson City is a zippy, 35-minute drive from Reno (32 miles) along Hwy I-580/395, and 40 minutes (28 miles) from South Lake Tahoe, across the California border, on Hwy 50.

Tahoe Transportation District (p105) runs up to six daily BlueGo bus services between Carson City (at Washington and Plaza Sts) and Stateline, at the California border with South Lake Tahoe ($4, 1¾ hours).

RTC Washoe (p104) operates six RTC Intercity buses per day from Monday to Friday between Carson City and Reno ($5, one hour).

Virginia City
☑775 / POP 855 / ELEV 6150FT

Twenty-five miles south of Reno, this national landmark is the site where the legendary Comstock Lode was struck, sparking a silver bonanza that began in 1859 and stands as one of the world's richest strikes. Some of Virginia City's silver barons went on to become major players in California history, among them Leland Stanford of university fame and Bank of California founder William Ralston. Much of San Francisco was built with the treasure dug up from the soil beneath the town.

At its peak during the 1860s gold rush, Virginia City was a high-flying, rip-roaring Wild West boomtown with 30,000 residents. Today, with fewer than 1000 residents and a main street of wooden sidewalks and historic saloons in restored grand Victorians, it can sometimes feel like a frontier theme park. Even so, it's still a fun and photogenic place to while away a few hours.

◉ Sights & Activities

Mackay Mansion HISTORIC BUILDING
(☑775-847-0373; www.uniquitiesmackaymansion.com; 291 S D St; adult/child $5/free; ⊙10am-6pm) Built by George Hearst in 1859, the allegedly haunted Mackay Mansion was purchased by miner John Mackay, who amassed a fortune of more than $130 million. Guided tours available.

The Way It Was Museum MUSEUM
(☑775-847-0766; 113 N C St; adult/child under 11yr $3/free; ⊙10am-6pm) One of the town's star attractions, this quirky museum is a fun, old-fashioned place offering good background information on mining the lode.

★**Virginia & Truckee Railroad** RAIL
(☑775-847-0380; www.virginiatruckee.com; F & Washington Sts) From May through October, train buffs can ride the historic route of the Virginia & Truckee Railroad to nearby Gold Hill ($10 to $12, 35 minutes, seven daily) or take the round-trip from Carson City ($32 to $48, three hours, one departure on Friday, Saturday and Sunday).

🛏 Sleeping

Virginia City has a handful of options, but you'd need to really be in love with the place to want to overnight here. More choice and better lodgings can be found in nearby Reno or Carson City.

★**Gold Hill Hotel & Saloon** HOTEL $
(☑775-847-0111; www.goldhillhotel.net; 1540 S Main St; r from $55; P❋⑨) A mile south of town via NV Hwy 342, the cool Gold Hill Hotel & Saloon claims to be Nevada's oldest hotel, and feels like it, with a breezy, old-fashioned charm and atmospheric bar boasting a great wine and spirits selection. Some rooms have fireplaces, original tubs and views of the Sierras.

Silverland Inn & Suites HOTEL $$
(☑775-847-4484; www.silverlandusa.com; 100 N E St; r from $108; P❋⑨⊛❋) The renovated rooms at Silverland Inn & Suites will appeal to those who prefer modern (if nondescript) digs. There's a sunny pool and hot-tub area with mountain views.

🍴 Eating & Drinking

Dining in Virginia City caters to the tourist dollar, but you'll have no problem finding hearty comfort food in the town's 'saloons.'

WORTH A TRIP

BURNING MAN

About two hours' drive north of Reno, along SR 447, the dusty, former railway town of Gerlach, with its gas station, motel, cafe and handful of watering holes, hovers for most of the year in a state of limbo on the edge of the **Black Rock Desert**, on whose dry, mud-cracked playas, world land-speed records have been set and broken. Although this vast wilderness is primed for outdoor adventures year-round, most will only visit over one week in August, when **Burning Man** (www.burningman.com; $425; ☉Aug) rouses the residents of sleepy Gerlach as it explodes onto the sunbaked desert to build the impermanent Black Rock City. Temporary home to as many as 70,000 'Burners,' it becomes Nevada's third-largest populace for the duration.

What began as a small gathering on a San Francisco beach in 1986 is now one of the most talked about festivals in the world. To many, Burning Man is an alternative universe, a whirlwind of outlandish theme camps, a community of sharing and bartering, costume-enhanced nudity and a general relinquishment of inhibitions that climaxes in the ritual and symbolic immolation of a towering stick figure, the Burning Man.

Much more than just a festival, Burning Man is for many a way of life and a vision for the future. Its founding principles have been taken up by countless other organizations around the globe. For a better understanding of what all the fuss is about, check out burningman.org/culture/philosophical-center/10-principles.

Firehouse Saloon & Grill BARBECUE $
(☎775-847-4774; 171 S C St; mains $8-17; ☉11am-10pm) For gorgeous 100-mile views of the surrounding valleys, have an ice-cream cone on the back porch of the Firehouse Saloon & Grill, where the friendly owners serve up burgers and pulled-pork sandwiches.

Roasting House CAFE
(☎775-847-0708; www.theroastinghouse.com; 55 N C St; ☉7am-4pm Mon-Fri, 9:30am-5pm Sat, noon-4pm Sun) Get your caffeine fix at the Roasting House, a micro-roaster on the main strip.

ⓘ Information

Virginia City Visitor Center (☎775-847-7500, 800-718-7587; www.visitvirginiacitynv.com; 86 S C St; ☉9am-5pm Mon-Sat, 10am-4pm Sun) The visitor center is on the town's main drag, inside the historic Crystal Bar.

Genoa

☎775 / POP 940 / ELEV 4800FT

This pretty little village at the edge of Carson Valley, at the foothills of the Sierra Nevada mountains, was the first European settlement at the western edge of the former Utah Territory. Its beautifully preserved colonial buildings are worth taking a look at when driving between Lake Tahoe and Carson City – it'll only add a few extra minutes of driving time.

◉ Sights & Activities

Genoa Courthouse Museum MUSEUM
(☎775-782-4325; www.genoanevada.org/genoa museum.htm; 2304 Main St; adult/child $3/2; ☉10am-4:30pm May-Oct) The Genoa Courthouse Museum contains the original jail and a collection of woven Washoe baskets, along with exhibits on the famous Pony Express, which had a stop in town.

**1862 David Walley's
Hot Springs & Spa** HOT SPRINGS
(☎775-782-8155; www.1862hotsprings.com; 2001 Foothill Rd; entry $50; ☉7am-9:30pm) About 2 miles south of Genoa, off NV Hwy 206, this sprawling facility in an idyllic location cashes in on a local bore that was discovered in 1862. There are five tantalizing outdoor pools in which to soak, but it'll cost you the princely sum of $50 for the pleasure! If money is no obstacle, dive, well, step right in.

✕ Eating & Drinking

There are a handful of quaint eateries in the little village, making it a lovely place to stop for lunch. For a wider selection, head to Lake Tahoe or Carson City.

Pink House CHEESE $
(☎775-392-4279; www.thepinkhousegenoa.com; 193 Genoa Lane; light meals $8-18; ☉11am-8pm Tue-Sat, to 5pm Sun) You can't miss this pink heritage-listed home, restored in 2015 and

furnished in the style of the 1850s. Inside you'll find a cheese shop and charcuterie, which also offers light lunches of soup, salad and sandwiches and a token dinner menu served after 5pm.

★ **Genoa Bar & Saloon**   PUB
(🖉 775-782-3870; www.genoabarandsaloon.com; 2282 Main St; ⊙ 10am-10pm) The oldest drinking parlor, as they were once known, in Nevada (dating to 1853) oozes charm and begs to be photographed: beer is the bonus, as are weekend bands and weekly drink specials. Don't get too cozy or you might not want to leave.

Pyramid Lake

A piercingly blue expanse in an otherwise barren landscape, Pyramid Lake lies 25 miles north of Reno on the Paiute Indian Reservation. Nearer its east side, iconic pyramid-like Anaho Island is a bird sanctuary for American white pelicans. You'll pass by Pyramid Lake if you're taking SR 447 to Gerlach and the Black Rock Desert, home of the Burning Man festival.

◉ Sights

★ **Pyramid Lake**   LAKE
Pyramid Lake is a stunning standalone sight, with shores lined with beaches and eye-catching tufa (a kind of limestone) formations.

Black Rock Desert   DESERT
(🖉 775-557-2900;   www.blackrockfriends.org) Outside Gerlach, which is itself 60 miles north of the southern shore of Pyramid Lake, world land-speed records have been set on these dry, mud-cracked playas. Although most people only visit during Burning Man, this vast wilderness is primed for outdoor adventures year-round. Drop by Gerlach's small museum for information and advice before heading out.

✖ Eating & Sleeping

Sutcliffe, on the lake's western shore, is about the only place you'll be able to grab a bite, with only a handful of options. Be sure to bring your own munchies or a backup packed lunch if you're visiting on a day trip from Reno. Popular for camping and fishing, the area offers permits for both at outdoor

suppliers and CVS drugstore locations in Reno, as well as at the **Pyramid Lake Ranger Station** (🖉 775-476-1155; plpt.nsn.us/ rangers; 2500 Lakeview Dr, Sutcliffe; ⊙ 9am-1pm & 2-6pm Thu-Mon) in Sutcliffe, where you'll also find a basic motel. There are no other accommodations around the lake.

Bruno's Country Club   AMERICAN $
(🖉 775-557-2220; 445 Main St, Gerlach; meals $8-20; ⊙ 10am-8pm Tue-Sun) In Gerlach, on the fringe of the Black Rock Desert, some 60 miles north of Pyramid Lake's southern shore, friendly, family-owned Bruno's (famous for meaty ravioli in cheese sauce) lost a little of its rustic charm when it gained a shiny new makeover.

Lake Tahoe

Shimmering in myriad shades of blue and green, Lake Tahoe is the USA's second-deepest lake and, at 6255ft high, it is also one of the highest-elevation lakes in the country. Driving around the spellbinding 72-mile scenic shoreline will give you quite a workout behind the wheel. Generally, the north shore is quiet and upscale; the west shore, rugged and old-timey; the east shore, undeveloped; the south shore, busy and tacky, with aging motels and flashy casinos; and nearby Reno, the biggest little city in the region.

The horned peaks surrounding the lake, which straddles the California–Nevada state line, are year-round destinations. The sun shines on Tahoe three out of every four days. Swimming, boating, kayaking, windsurfing, stand up paddle-boarding (SUP) and other water sports take over in summer, as do hiking, camping and wilderness backpacking adventures. Winter brings bundles of snow, perfect for hitting Tahoe's top-tier ski and snowboard resorts.

Tahoe gets packed in summer, on winter weekends and holidays, when reservations are essential. **Lake Tahoe Visitors Authority** (🖉 800-288-2463; www.tahoesouth.com; 169 Hwy 50, Stateline, NV; ⊙ 9am-5pm Mon-Fri) and **North Lake Tahoe Visitors' Bureaus** (🖉 800-468-2463; www.gotahoenorth.com) can help with accommodations and tourist information. There's camping in **state parks** (🖉 800-444-7275; www.reserveamerica.com) and on **USFS lands** (🖉 518-885-3639; www.recreation.gov; campsites $17-48; 🐾).

Lake Tahoe Eastern Shore

Lake Tahoe's eastern shore lies entirely within Nevada. Much of it is relatively undeveloped thanks to George Whittell Jr, an eccentric San Franciscan playboy who once owned a lot of this land, including 27 miles of shoreline. Upon his death in 1969, it was sold off to a private investor, who later wheeled and dealed most of it to the US Forest Service and Nevada State Parks. And lucky it was, because today the eastern shore offers some of Tahoe's best scenery and outdoor diversion.

◉ Sights & Activities

Lake Tahoe-Nevada State Park   STATE PARK
(☑ 775-831-0494; www.parks.nv.gov; per car $7-12; Ⓟ 👪) Lake Tahoe-Nevada State Park is the east shore's biggest draw with beaches and hiking for all. Summer crowds splash in the turquoise waters of **Sand Harbor** (☑ 775-831-0494; www.parks.nv.gov/parks/sand-harbor; 2005 Hwy 28; per car $7-12). The **Flume Trail**, a mountain biker's holy grail, starts further south at **Spooner Lake** (☑ 775-749-5980; www.parks.nv.gov; per car $7-10).

Lake Tahoe Shakespeare Festival   THEATER
(☑ 800-747-4697; www.laketahoeshakespeare.com; ☉ Jul & Aug) A lively festival incorporating works by the Bard and new pieces, performed outdoors by the lake.

🍴 Eating & Sleeping

Secluded resorts and campgrounds are scattered on the eastern shore; the density of accommodations is much less than further south. Incline Village features some good diner options.

Zephyr Cove Resort   CABIN, CAMPGROUND $$
(☑ 775-589-4907; www.zephyrcove.com; 760 Hwy 50, NV; tent & RV sites with/without hookups from $75/45, cabins $165-394; ☉ camping May-Sep, cabins year-round; 🤶🐾) In Nevada, about 4 miles north of Stateline, this family oriented lakeside resort has historic cabins scattered among the pines and good facilities, including hot showers, barbecue grills and fire rings. Take your pick of 93 paved

RV or 10 drive-in tent sites (some with lake views), or 47 walk-in tent sites tucked deeper into the shady forest.

Austin's   AMERICAN $
(www.austinstahoe.com; 120 Country Club Dr; mains $9-17; ☉ 11am-9pm; 🚗 👪) A hearty welcome for the whole family is what you'll find at this wood-cabin diner with an outdoor deck. Buttermilk fries with jalapeño dipping sauce, chicken-fried steak, classic meatloaf, burgers, huge salad bowls and sandwiches will fill you up – and so will mountain-sized martinis.

Lake Tahoe Northern Shore

Northeast of Tahoe City, Hwy 28 cruises through a string of cute, low-key towns, many fronting superb sandy beaches, with reasonably priced roadside motels and hotels all crowded together along the lakeshore. Oozing old-fashioned charm, the north shore is a blissful escape from the teeming crowds of South Lake Tahoe, Tahoe City and Truckee, but still puts you within easy reach of winter ski resorts and snow parks, and summertime swimming, kayaking, hiking trails and more.

The North Lake Tahoe Visitors' Bureaus (p109) can help get you oriented, although the closest walk-in office is at Incline Village, NV.

South Lake Tahoe & Stateline

Highly congested and arguably overdeveloped, South Lake Tahoe is a chockablock commercial strip bordering the lake and framed by picture-perfect alpine mountains. At the foot of the world-class **Heavenly** (☑ 775-586-7000; www.skiheavenly.com; 4080 Lake Tahoe Blvd; adult/child 5-12yr/youth 13-18yr $135/79/113; ☉ 9am-4pm Mon-Fri, from 8:30am Sat, Sun & holidays; 👪) mountain resort, and buzzing from the gambling tables in the casinos in Stateline, Lake Tahoe's south shore draws visitors with a cornucopia of activities, lodging and restaurant options, especially for summer beach access and tons of powdery winter snow.

Arizona

Best Places to Eat

➜ Kai Restaurant (p128)

➜ Elote Cafe (p148)

➜ Cafe Poca Cosa (p217)

➜ Brix Restaurant & Wine Bar (p157)

Best Places to Sleep

➜ El Tovar (p172)

➜ Grand Canyon Lodge (p183)

➜ Arizona Biltmore Resort & Spa (p124)

➜ Enchantment Resort (p147)

Why Go?

Arizona is made for road trips. Yes, the state has its show-stoppers – Monument Valley, the Grand Canyon, Cathedral Rock – but you'll remember the long, romantic miles under endless skies for as long as you do the icons in between. Each drive reveals a little more of the state's soul: for a dose of mom-and-pop friendliness, follow Route 66 into Flagstaff; to understand the sheer will of Arizona's mining barons, take a twisting drive through rugged Jerome; and American Indian history becomes contemporary as you drive past mesa-top Hopi villages dating back 1000 years.

Controversies about hot-button issues – immigration, gay rights – have grabbed headlines recently. But these can't cancel out the Southwestern warmth and historical depth you'll find. And Arizona's ancient beauty reminds you that human affairs are short-lived. The majestic Grand Canyon, the saguaro-dotted deserts of Tucson, and the red rocks of Sedona...they're here for the long-term.

When to Go
Phoenix

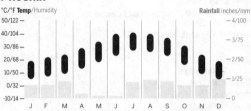

Jan–Mar Visit dude ranches in southern Arizona. Ski in Kaibab National Forest.

Jun–Aug High season for the Grand Canyon, Monument Valley and Sedona.

Sep & Oct Hike down to Phantom Ranch from the Grand Canyon's South Rim.

Arizona Highlights

1 Trying to find unused superlatives to do justice to **Grand Canyon National Park** (p160), a wonder of the natural world.

2 Dropping your jaw at the surreal buttes and mesas of the desert wonderland that is **Monument Valley Navajo Tribal Park** (p191).

3 Drinking in the lonely beauty of **Chiricahua National Monument** (p230).

4 Tracing the Earth's vortexes in **Sedona** (p142), a stunning town of crimson canyons.

5 Watching migrating birds and tasting Arizona's best wines in **Patagonia** (p224), a slice of Argentina by the Mexican border.

6 Dipping into all the world's musical traditions at **Musical Instrument Museum** (p115) in Phoenix, a paean to marvelous music makers.

7 Seeing prehistoric pueblos set into the cliffs in the ancestral home of the Navajos at **Canyon de Chelly National Monument** (p192).

8 Getting your kitsch on in **Seligman** (p203), a town that embraces its Route 66 heritage.

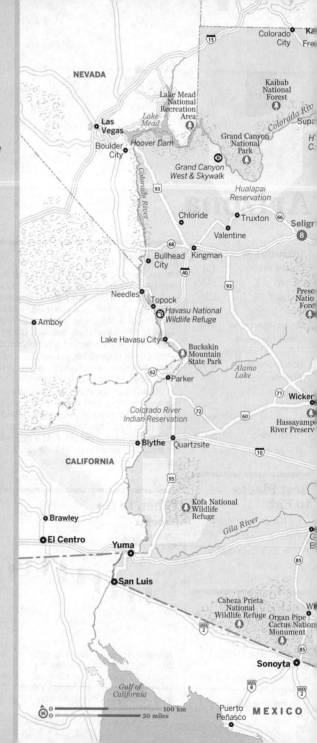

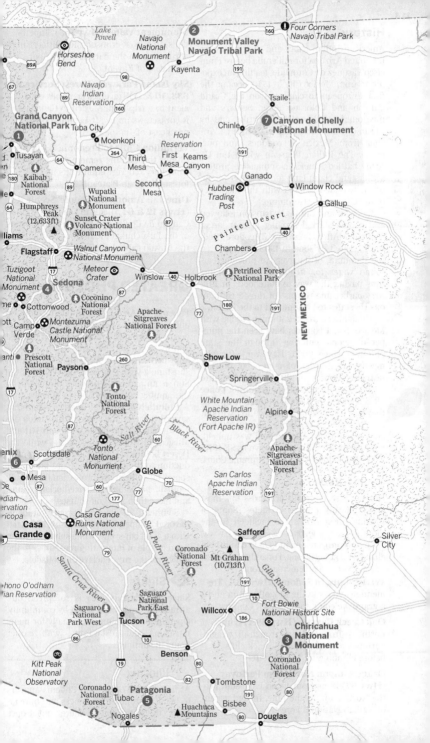

History

American Indian tribes and their ancestors inhabited Arizona for millennia before Francisco Vásquez de Coronado, leading an expedition from Mexico City in 1540, became the first European to clap eyes on the Grand Canyon and Colorado River. Settlers and missionaries followed in his wake, and by the mid-19th century the US acquired Arizona from Mexico by conquest and purchase. The Indian Wars, in which the US Army battled American Indians to protect settlers and claim land for the government, officially ended in 1886 with the surrender of Apache warrior Geronimo.

Railroad and mining expansion followed and people started arriving in ever larger numbers. After President Theodore Roosevelt visited Arizona in 1903 he supported the damming of its rivers to provide year-round water for irrigation and drinking, thus paving the way to statehood: in 1912 Arizona became the last of the 48 contiguous US states to be admitted to the Union.

The state shares a 250-mile border with Mexico. Strict controls have seen the number of people entering through the state plummet since 2005. However, after the mysterious murder of a popular rancher near the border in 2010, the legislature passed a controversial law requiring police officers to ask for identification from anyone they suspect of being in the country without immigration papers. While the constitutionality of the request for papers was upheld, key provisions of the law, known as SB 1070, were struck down by the US Supreme Court.

Scenic Routes

Dozens of scenic roads crisscross this most geographically diverse of states. Some of Arizona's best drives are included in the monthly magazine *Arizona Highways* (www.arizhwys.com), created in 1925 to cover them all and still going strong. For additional ideas visit www.arizonascenicroads.com.

Wickenburg to Sedona (Hwy 89A) Tremendous views of the Mogollon Rim and a grand welcome to Red Rock Country.

Oak Creek Canyon (Hwy 89A) Winds northeast from Sedona through dizzyingly narrow walls and dramatic rock cliffs before climbing up to Flagstaff.

Grand Canyon North Rim Parkway (Hwy 67) Runs from Jacob Lake south to the North Rim via the pine, fir and aspen of Kaibab National Forest.

Monument Valley (Hwy 163) Stupendous drive past crimson monoliths rising abruptly from the barren desert floor northeast of Kayenta.

Sky Island Parkway (Forest Service Rds 833, 10 & 11) Traverses ecozones equivalent to a trip from Mexico to Canada as it corkscrews up to Mt Lemmon (9157ft), northeast of Tucson.

Vermilion Cliffs to Fredonia (Hwy 89A) Climbs through the remote Arizona Strip from fiery red Vermilion Cliffs up the forested Kaibab Plateau.

Diné Tah 'Among the People' Scenic Rd (Hwys 12 & 64) Takes in the north rim of Canyon de Chelly and the lakes and forests of the Lukachukai Mountains, en route to the Navajo capital of Window Rock.

GREATER PHOENIX

POP 1,563,025 / ELEV 1124FT

Phoenix is Arizona's indubitable cultural and economic powerhouse, a thriving desert metropolis boasting some of the best Southwestern and Mexican food you'll find anywhere. And with more than 300 days of sunshine a year, exploring the 'Valley of the Sun' is an agreeable proposition (except in the sapping heat from June to August).

Culturally, it offers an opera, a symphony, several theaters and three of the state's finest museums – the Heard, Phoenix Art and Musical Instrument Museums – while the Desert Botanical Garden is a stunning introduction to the region's flora and fauna. For sports fans, there are professional baseball, football, basketball and ice-hockey teams, and more than 200 golf courses.

Southeast of Phoenix proper, student-flavored Tempe (*tem*-pee) is a lively district with a good bar scene, while suburban Mesa has a couple of interesting museums. To the north lies the ritzy enclave of Scottsdale.

◎ Sights

Since the Phoenix area is so spread out, attractions are broken down by community. Opening hours change seasonally for many museums and restaurants, with earlier hours in summer.

◉ Phoenix

At first glance, downtown Phoenix appears to be all buttoned-up business and bureaucracy (the state capitol is here), but it does have a spring in its step. The new downtown dining and entertainment district Cityscape (www.cityscapephoenix.com) is welcoming guests, and, as the site of Super Bowl XLIX in 2015, the city has once again been in the national spotlight.

★ **Musical Instrument Museum**   MUSEUM
(Map p116; ☑ 480-478-6000; www.themim. org; 4725 E Mayo Blvd; adult/teen/child 4-12yr $20/15/10; ☺9am-5pm; ℗) From Uganda thumb pianos to Hawaiian ukuleles to Indonesian boat lutes, the ears have it at this lively museum that celebrates the world's musical instruments. More than 200 countries and territories are represented within five regional galleries, with wireless recordings bringing many to life as you get within 'earshot' (headsets are provided). You can also bang a drum in the Experiences Gallery and listen to Taylor Swift or Elvis Presley rock out in the Artist Gallery.

★ **Heard Museum**   MUSEUM
(Map p122; ☑602-252-8848; www.heard.org; 2301 N Central Ave; adult $18, child 6-17yr & student $7.50, senior $13.50; ☺9:30am-5pm Mon-Sat, 11am-5pm Sun; ℗⛄) This extraordinary museum spotlights the history, life, arts and culture of American Indian tribes in the Southwest. Visitors will find art galleries, ethnographic displays, films, a get-creative kids' exhibit and an unrivaled collection of Hopi kachinas (elaborate spirit dolls, many gifted by Presidential nominee Barry Goldwater). The Heard emphasizes quality over quantity and is one of the best museums of its kind in America.

★ **Desert Botanical Garden**   GARDENS
(Map p118; ☑480-941-1225; www.dbg.org; 1201 N Galvin Pkwy; adult/senior/student 13-18yr/ child 3-12yr $22/20/12/10; ☺8am-8pm Oct-Apr, 7am-8pm May-Sep) Blue bells and Mexican gold poppies are just two of the colorful showstoppers blooming from March to May along the Desert Wildflower Loop Trail at this well-nurtured botanical garden, a lovely place to reconnect with nature while learning about desert plant life. Looping trails lead past a profusion of desert denizens, arranged by theme (including a Sonoran Desert nature loop and an edible desert garden). It's pretty dazzling year-round, but the flowering spring season is the busiest and most colorful.

Children's Museum of Phoenix   MUSEUM
(Map p122; ☑602-253-0501; childrensmuseum ofphoenix.org; 215 N 7th St; $11; ☺9am-4pm Tue-Sun; ⛄) Designed to encourage active involvement rather than passive contemplation (text-heavy signs are ditched in favor of interactive exhibits and invitations to paint, climb, play and even ride tricycles), this three-story juvenile Jurassic park is an ideal way to beguile the kids, from babies to under-10s, for a few hours. Free entry 5pm to 9pm the first Friday of each month.

Pueblo Grande Museum   MUSEUM
(Map p118; ☑602-495-0901; www.pueblogrande. com; 4619 E Washington St; adult/senior/child 6-17yr $6/5/3; ☺9am-4:45pm Mon-Sat, 1-4:45pm Sun) The O'odham Indians use the word 'Hohokam' ('all used up') for the ancestors who mysteriously abandoned this adobe city and the intricate irrigation system that sustained it. Despite the proximity of busy highways it remains impressive, with a central platform, dwellings, ceremonial ball court and hints of a surrounding 1000-mile canal network that was one of precontact America's greatest engineering feats. An interpretive trail and small museum take you deeper inside a culture that flourished here until the 15th century.

Phoenix Art Museum   MUSEUM
(Map p122; ☑602-257-1880; www.phxart.org; 1625 N Central Ave; adult/senior/student/child 6-17yr $18/15/13/9; ☺10am-5pm Tue & Thu-Sat, 10am-9pm Wed, noon-5pm Sun; ℗⛄) Arizona's premier repository of fine art includes works by Claude Monet, Diego Rivera and Georgia O'Keeffe. Make a beeline for the Western Gallery, to see how the astonishing Arizona landscape has inspired everyone from the early pioneers to modernists. Got kids? Pick up a Kidpack at Visitor Services, examine the ingeniously crafted miniature period Thorne Rooms or visit the PhxArtKids Gallery.

Arizona Science Center   MUSEUM
(Map p122; ☑602-716-2000; www.azscience.org; 600 E Washington St; adult/child $18/13; ☺10am-5pm; ⛄) At the popular Arizona Science Center, play with 300-odd hands-on exhibits, watch live demonstrations or take in the mysteries of the universe at the planetarium. If you have the fortitude, you can even walk through a working model of the stomach.

Heritage Square   PARK
(Map p122; ☑park office 602-262-5070, recording 602-262-5029; www.phoenix.gov; 115 N 6th St) This cluster of late-Victorian and early 20th-century homes stands in stark contrast to the soaring modernity of downtown Phoenix. With the buildings now sensitively repurposed (the Stevens-Hautsgen house

Greater Phoenix

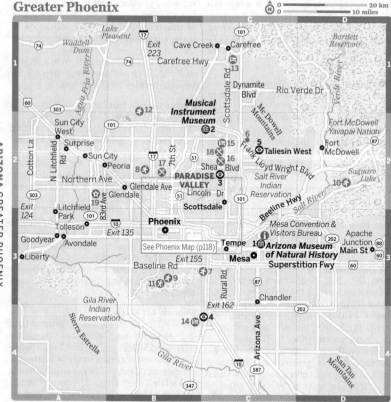

contains a gallery, while others serve as bars, restaurants and the ticket office), it's possible to see inside many, including the fully restored, stately **Rosson House** (☑602-262-5070; www.rossonhousemuseum.org; 115 N 6th St; tours adult/senior/6-12yr $9/8/4; ⊙10am-4pm Wed-Sat, noon-4pm Sun, last tour at 3pm).

◎ Scottsdale

Scottsdale sparkles with self-confidence, her glossy allure fueled by good looks, charm and money. Distractions include a pedestrian-friendly downtown, chic hotels and a vibrant food and nightlife scene. For a list of permanent and temporary public art displays, which are often quite intriguing, visit www.scottsdalepublicart.org.

The free **Scottsdale Trolley** (☑480-317-7250; www.scottsdaleaz.gov/trolley; ⊙10am-9pm) links Old Town Scottsdale with Fashion Square Mall via the new Scottsdale Waterfront, a retail and office complex on the Arizona Canal, every 10 minutes from 10am to 9pm. At the eastern end of the pedestrian walkway along the waterfront, look for the 100ft-long **Soleri Bridge**, a stainless-steel wonder by artist and architect Paoli Soleri. The bridge is also a solar calendar.

Old Town Scottsdale AREA
(Map p124; downtownscottsdale.com) Tucked among Scottsdale's malls and bistros is its Old Town, a Wild West–themed enclave filled with cutesy buildings, covered sidewalks and stores hawking mass-produced 'Indian' artifacts. There's also a museum, public sculptures, saloons, a few galleries, and horse-drawn buggies and singing cowboys in the cooler months.

Cosanti ARCHITECTURE
(Map p116; ☑480-948-6145; www.arcosanti.org/cosanti; 6433 E Doubletree Ranch Rd; donations appreciated; ⊙9am-5pm Mon-Sat, 11am-5pm Sun) The home and studio of Frank Lloyd Wright student Paolo Soleri, who died in 2013, this

Greater Phoenix

unusual complex of cast-concrete structures was a stepping stone for Soleri's experimental Arcosanti village, 65 miles north. Cosanti is also where Soleri's signature bronze and ceramic bells are crafted. You're free to walk around, see the bells poured (usually between 9am and 11am weekdays, but call to confirm), and browse the gift shop.

Taliesin West   ARCHITECTURE
(Map p116; ☑ 480-860-2700; www.franklloyd wright.org; 12621 N Frank Lloyd Wright Blvd; tours from $26; ☺8:30am-6pm Oct-May, shorter hours Jun-Sep, closed Tue & Wed Jun-Aug) Taliesin West was the desert home and studio of Frank Lloyd Wright, one of America's greatest 20th-century architects. A prime example of organic architecture, with buildings incorporating elements and structures found in surrounding nature, it was built between 1938 and 1940, and is still home to an architecture school. It's now a National Historical Monument, open to the public for informative guided tours.

**Scottsdale Museum of
Contemporary Art**   MUSEUM
(Map p124; ☑ 480-874-4666; www.smoca.org; 7374 E 2nd St; adult/student/child 15yr & under $10/5/free, free Thu & after 5pm Fri & Sat; ☺noon-5pm Sun, Tue & Wed, noon-9pm Thu-Sat) Complementing the adjacent Scottsdale Center for the Performing Arts, SMoCA's five galleries, housed in a cleverly adapted old movie theater, showcase global art, architecture and design, including James Turrell's otherworldly Knight Rise skyspace in the sculpture garden. The museum anchors an area sprinkled with public art and eateries.

Scottsdale Historical Museum   MUSEUM
(Map p124; ☑ 480-945-4499; www.scottsdale museum.org; 7333 E Scottsdale Mall; ☺10am-5pm Wed-Sun Oct-May, to 2pm Wed-Sun Jun & Sep) **FREE** One of the buildings with genuine history in Old Town Scottsdale is the Little Red School House, now home to the Scottsdale Historical Museum, where low-key exhibits highlight Scottsdale's origins and early history, showing the radical change in the cityscape since the mid-20th century. Kids may enjoy ringing the old school bell.

Tempe

Sandwiched between downtown Phoenix and Mesa, just south of Scottsdale, Tempe is a fun and energetic district enlivened by the 50,000 students of **Arizona State University** (ASU; Map p118; ☑ 480-965-2100; www. asu.edu). Founded in 1885, the vast campus is home to Sun Devil Stadium, performance venues, galleries and museums.

ASU Art Museum   MUSEUM
(Map p118; ☑ 480-965-2787; asuartmuseum.asu. edu; 51 E 10th St; ☺11am-5pm Tue, Wed, Fri, Sat, to 8pm Thu) **FREE** This airy, contemporary gallery space has permanent collections of contemporary, Southwestern, North and Latin American art, hosts regular temporary shows, and houses international artists-in-residence. It's the anchor of an impressive arts precinct that includes the adjacent Gammage Auditorium, designed by Frank Lloyd Wright.

Gammage Auditorium   ARCHITECTURE
(Map p118; ☑ box office 480-965-3434, tours 480-965-6912; www.asugammage.com; 1200 S Forest Ave, cnr Mill Ave & Apache Blvd; entry free, performances from $20; ☺box office 10am-5pm Mon-Thu in summer, 10am-6pm Mon-Fri rest of year) Architecture fans will appreciate the fanciful colosseum-style Gammage Auditorium,

ARIZONA GREATER PHOENIX

Phoenix

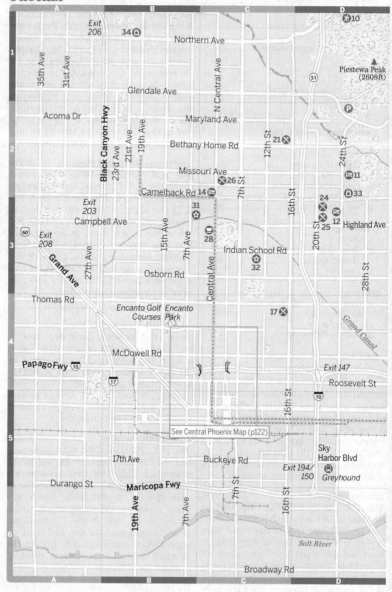

notable as Frank Lloyd Wright's last major public commission, and based on unrealized designs for an opera house in Baghdad. A popular performance venue, it stages primarily Broadway-style musicals and shows. Call ahead to arrange a tour.

Tempe Center for the Arts   ARTS CENTER
(Map p118; ☑ box office 480-350-2822; www.tempe.gov/tca; 700 W Rio Salado Pkwy; ☺ box office 10am-6pm Mon-Fri & 2hr before performances; ⓟ) On the Tempe Town Lake, this shiny arts center has a 600-seat auditorium, a 200-seat studio theater, a 3500-sq-ft

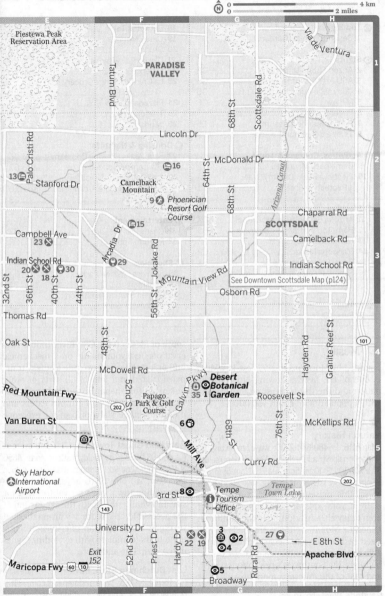

gallery and an exterior sculpture garden. Comedy, symphonic performance, dance and other arts find a common home here.

Mill Ave STREET
(Map p118) Along the western edge of Arizona State University, Mill Ave is Tempe's main drag and is lined with restaurants, bars and a mix of national chains and indie boutiques. The free Orbit bus runs along Mill Ave and around the university every 15 minutes from Monday to Saturday and every 30 minutes on Sunday.

Phoenix

⊙ Mesa

Founded by Mormons in 1877, low-key Mesa is one of the fastest-growing cities in the nation and the third-largest city in Arizona with a population of about 450,0000.

★Arizona Museum of
Natural History   MUSEUM
(Map p116; ☎480-644-2230; www.azmnh.org; 53 N MacDonald St; adult/child 3-12yr/student/senior $12/7/8/10; ⊙10am-5pm Tue-Fri, 11am-5pm Sat, 1-5pm Sun; ⌖) Even if you're not staying in Mesa, this museum is worth a trip, especially if your kids are into dinosaurs (and aren't they all?). In addition to the multilevel Dinosaur Mountain, there are loads of life-sized casts of the giant beasts plus a touchable apatosaurus thighbone. Other exhibits highlight the Southwest's pre-conquest past, and that of the Americas more broadly.

Rawhide Western Town
& Steakhouse   AMUSEMENT PARK
(Map p116; ☎480-502-5600; www.rawhide.com; 5700 W N Loop Rd, Chandler; entry free, per attraction/show $5, unlimited day pass $15; ⊙5-10pm Fri, noon-10pm Sat, noon-8pm Sun; ᴾ⌖) Every 'howdy' sounds sincere at this recreated 1880s frontier town located about 20 miles

south of Mesa on the Gila River Indian Reservation. Test your mettle on a mechanical bull or a stubborn burro, ride a cutesy train, pan for gold and join in all sorts of other hokey-but-fun shenanigans. The steakhouse has rattlesnake for adventurous eaters and mesquite-grilled slabs of beef for everyone else. Parking costs $5.

Goldfield Ghost Town   GHOST TOWN
(☎480-983-0333; goldfieldghosttown.com; 4650 N Mammoth Mine Rd; ⊙shops 10am-5pm, saloon 11am-9pm; ⌖) The 1890s heyday of this former mining town, once a rival to Mesa for size and vitality, died with the exhaustion of the accessible ore. Today it's an unabashed yet enjoyable tourist trap, offering gunfights, mine tours (complete with exploding 'dynamite'), a zip line and more.

Lost Dutchman State Park   STATE PARK
(☎480-982-4485; www.azstateparks.com; 6109 N Apache Trail, Apache Junction; per vehicle/bicycle $7/3; ⊙sunrise-10pm; ⌖) Located 40 miles east of Phoenix, leading into the snaggle-toothed Superstition Mountains, this 320-acre state park is popular with day-trippers and campers alike. RV and tent sites are available for $20, plus a $5 reservation fee: call ☎520-586-2283. The park's name comes from a legendary 'lost'

gold mine, actually founded by a German, somewhere in the area.

Activities

In Phoenix, it's actually pretty easy to take a walk on the wild side and escape the urban jungle. Find maps and trail descriptions for Camelback Mountain, Piestewa Peak and South Mountain Park at www.phoenix.gov.

Salt River Recreation WATER SPORTS
(Map p116; ☎ 480-984-3305; www.saltriver tubing.com; 9200 N Bush Hwy; tubes & shuttle $17; ☺ 8:30am-6pm May-late Sep, hours vary after Labor Day; ☛) With Salt River Recreation you can float in an inner tube on the Lower Salt River through the stark Tonto National Forest. The launch is in northeast Mesa, about 15 miles north of Hwy 60 on Power Rd. Floats are two, three or five hours long, including the shuttle-bus ride back. Cash only.

Camelback Mountain HIKING
(Map p118; ☎ 602-261-8318; www.phoenix.gov; ☺ sunrise-sunset) This 2704ft twin-humped mountain sits smack in the center of the Phoenix action. Two trails, the Cholla Trail (6131 E Cholla Lane) and the Echo Canyon Trail (4925 E McDonald Dr), climb about 1200ft to the summit. The newly renovated Echo Canyon Trail is extremely popular in spring and winter – the car park fills very early, even with 135 spots.

Art Walk CULTURAL
(Map p124; www.scottsdalegalleries.com; ☺ 7-9pm) Phoenix has worked its way up the ladder of art cities that matter. In particular, Scottsdale has galleries laden with everything from epic Western oil paintings to cutting-edge sculpture and moody Southwestern landscapes. Around 100 of these galleries stay open every Thursday from 7pm to 9pm for Art Walk, which centers on Marshall Way and Main St.

South Mountain Park HIKING
(Map p116; ☎ 602-262-7393; www.phoenix.gov; 10211 S Central Ave; ☺ 5am-11pm, last entry 7pm) At more than 25 sq miles (larger than Manhattan), this local favorite is great for hiking and trail riding. The 51-mile network (leashed dogs allowed) dips through canyons, over grassy hills and past granite walls, offering city views and access to Indian petroglyphs. The main entrance is at 10211 S Central Ave, and the Pima Canyon entrance is at 4771 E Pima Canyon Rd.

Cactus Adventures MOUNTAIN BIKING
(Map p116; ☎ 480-688-4743; www.cactus adventures.com; 8000 S Arizona Grand Pkwy; half-day rental $60; ☺ phone line 8am-8pm) Based at Arizona Grand Resort, Cactus Adventures rents bikes for use at South Mountain and offers guided hiking and biking tours at various parks. For rentals, they will meet you at the trailhead; guided tours start from $155 per person (minimum two people).

ARIZONA GREATER PHOENIX

PHOENIX FOR CHILDREN

Phoenix Zoo (Map p118; ☎ 602-286-3800; www.phoenixzoo.org; 455 N Galvin Pkwy; adult/child 3-13yr $25/15; ☺ 9am-5pm, shorter hours summer & winter; ☊ ☛) Home to more than 1400 animals, including local natives such as the bald eagle and bighorn sheep, Phoenix Zoo houses species rare and common in several distinct and natural-looking environments. If you plan to make a day of it with the kids, the 'Total Experience' ticket (adult/child $40/30) is also good for the immersive '4-D Theater,' riding the Safari Train and unlimited carousel rides, among other activities.

Wet 'n' Wild Phoenix (Map p116; ☎ 623-201-2000; www.wetnwildphoenix.com; 4243 W Pinnacle Peak Rd, Glendale; over/under 42in tall $43/33, senior $33; ☺ 10am-8pm Sun-Thu, to 10pm Fri & Sat Jun & Jul, shorter hours & weeks Mar-May & Aug-Oct; ☛) Cool off in summer with pools, tube slides, wave pools, waterfalls, floating rivers and thrill rides. Wet 'n' Wild is located in Glendale, 2 miles west of I-17 at exit 217, about 30 miles north of downtown Phoenix. Parking is $8 and adult tickets are cheaper online or on weekdays.

Castles-n-Coasters (Map p116; ☎ 602-997-7575; www.castlesncoasters.com; 9445 E N Metro Pkwy; unlimited rides from $30; ☺ 10am-midnight Fri & Sat peak season, shorter hours other days & months; ☛) Fans of mini golf, fairgrounds and roller coasters will enjoy Castles-n-Coasters, a big amusement park by the Metrocenter Mall about 20 miles northwest of downtown, near exit 207 off I-17. Kids that are 44 inches and shorter can get a bronze pass for just $12.50 (although they'll be too small for the more adrenaline-soaked rides).

Central Phoenix

ARIZONA GREATER PHOENIX

Piestewa Peak/Dreamy Draw
Recreation Area HIKING
(Map p118; ☎602-261-8318; www.phoenix.gov; 2701 Squaw Peak Dr; ☺trails 5am-7pm) Dotted with saguaros, ocotillos and other local cacti, this convenient summit was previously known as Squaw Peak. Be forewarned: the trek to the 2608ft summit is hugely popular and the park can get jammed on winter weekends.

Ponderosa Stables HORSEBACK RIDING
(Map p116; ☎602-268-1261; www.arizona-horses.com; 10215 S Central Ave; 1/2/3hr rides $40/60/80, minimum 2 riders for 3hr rides; ☺9am-8pm Mon-Sat; ☒) This outfitter leads

breakfast, lunch, dinner and sunset rides through South Mountain Park. Reservations are required for most trips. The stables are around 7 miles south of downtown Phoenix, directly down Central Ave.

☞ Tours

Arizona Outback
Adventures HIKING
(Map p116; ☎480-945-2881; www.aoa -adventures.com; 16447 N 91st St, Suite 101, Scottsdale; ☺office 8am-5pm) This gung-ho outfit offers day trips to go hiking (from $95, minimum two people) and mountain biking (from $140, minimum two people), and

Central Phoenix

plenty of other active outings in Phoenix, the surrounding desert and mountains, and even interstate.

✦ Festivals & Events

McDowell Mountain
Music Festival   MUSIC
(🏷 602-343-0453; mmmf.com; 1202 N 3rd St, Margaret T Hance Park; 1-/3-day entry $60/105; 🕙 early Mar; 🚼) Attracting headliners of the caliber of Beck and The Shins, 'M3F' is unique in that 100% of its profits go to two local charities: the Phoenix Children's Hospital Foundation and UMOM New Day Center, the city's largest homeless shelter. Held over three days in early March, it's also a great showcase for local talent. Children under 10 attend for free.

First Fridays   ART
(www.artlinkphoenix.com; 🕙 6-10pm 1st Fri of month) Up to 20,000 people hit the streets of downtown Phoenix on the first Friday of every month for this self-guided 'art walk', held across more than 70 galleries and performance spaces. Free shuttles radiating out from the Phoenix Art Museum ferry the cognoscenti from venue to venue.

Fiesta Bowl   SPORTS
(🏷 480-350-0911; www.fiestabowl.org; 1 Cardinals Dr, Glendale; 🕙 late Dec/early Jan) The most popular event in Phoenix is the Fiesta Bowl college football game, held around late December or early January at the University of Phoenix Stadium. It's accompanied by pregame parties and one of the largest parades in the Southwest.

Arizona State Fair   FAIR
(🏷 602-252-6771; www.azstatefair.com; 1826 W McDowell Rd; adult/child 5-13yr $10/5; 🕙 Oct) This fair lures more than a million folks to the Arizona State Fairgrounds every October, with a rodeo, rides and amusements, livestock displays, a pie-eating contest and plenty of live performances.

🛏 Sleeping

Greater Phoenix is well stocked with hotels and resorts, but you won't find many B&Bs, cozy inns or low-cost mom-and-pop motels. Overall, the lowest rates can be found at national chain hotels. Prices plummet in summer, and you'll see plenty of Valley residents taking advantage of super-low prices at their favorite resorts when the mercury rises.

🛏 Phoenix

HI Phoenix Hostel   HOSTEL $
(Map p122; 🏷 602-254-9803; www.phxhostel.org; 1026 N 9th St; dm/r from $24/37; ❄ @ 🛜) Fall in love with backpacking again at this small hostel with fun owners who know Phoenix and want to enjoy it with you. The 22-bed hostel sits in an up-and-coming working-class neighborhood and has relaxing garden nooks. The 'talking table' – at which laptops and other devices are banned from 8am to 10am and 5pm to 10pm each day – is a very sociable innovation. Check-in is also from 8am to 10am and 5pm to 10pm.

Hampton Inn Phoenix-Biltmore   HOTEL $$
(Map p118; 🏷 602-956-5221; www.hamptoninn. com; 2310 E Highland Ave; r from $229; 🅿 🐾 ❄ @ 🛜 ♒) Adopting the Biltmore name that

Downtown Scottsdale

ARIZONA GREATER PHOENIX

graces so many (unconnected) businesses in this part of town, this Hampton Inn doesn't break the template: hearty free breakfasts, freshly washed duvets and an efficient front desk. But it is close to the Biltmore Fashion Park and some of Phoenix's new restaurants. The free hotel shuttle runs within a 3-mile radius.

Maricopa Manor   BOUTIQUE HOTEL $$
(Map p118; ☎602-264-9200, 800-292-6403; www.maricopamanor.com; 15 W Pasadena Ave; ste from $149; P🐾🛜🏊) This small, Spanish-ranch-style place right near busy Central Ave has six individually appointed suites, many with French doors onto a deck overlooking the pool, garden and fountain areas. Although Maricopa Manor is central, it's well supplied with shady garden nooks, and privacy is easily achieved.

⭐ **Arizona Biltmore Resort & Spa**   RESORT $$$
(Map p118; ☎800-950-0086, 602-955-6600; www.arizonabiltmore.com; 2400 E Missouri Ave; d from $480; P🐾@🛜🏊🐾) With architecture inspired by Frank Lloyd Wright and past guests including Irving Berlin, Marilyn Monroe and many presidents, the Biltmore is perfect for connecting to the magic of yesterday. A landmark, lending its name to much in the surrounding area, it boasts over 700 beautifully appointed units, two golf courses, several pools and endless luxe touches. The daily resort fee is $28; self-parking is $12 per night. Pets require a $100 deposit per stay, with $50 refundable.

Palomar Phoenix   HOTEL $$$
(Map p122; ☎602-253-6633, reservations 877-488-1908; www.hotelpalomar-phoenix.com; 2 E Jefferson St; r/ste from $449/509; P🐾🛜🏊🐾) Shaggy pillows, antler-shaped lamps and portraits of blue cows. Yep, the 242 rooms

Downtown Scottsdale

of the Palomar are whimsical, and we like it. Larger than average and popping with fresh, modern style, the rooms come with yoga mats and Italian Frette linens. There's a nightly wine reception, and Phoenix's major baseball and basketball stadiums are just around the corner.

Hermosa Inn BOUTIQUE HOTEL $$$
(Map p118; ☑ 602-955-8614; www.hermosainn. com; 5532 N Palo Cristi Rd; r & casitas from $440; P ✳ 🛜 ⊠ 🐾) The signage is discreet but the flowers are not at this gorgeous retreat. The 43 rooms and casitas of this 1930s dwelling give off soothing vibes, thanks to Spanish Colonial decor chosen by the original owner, artist 'Lon' Megargee. The resort fee is $25 per day, there's an excellent restaurant on-site and pets can stay for $75.

Royal Palms Resort & Spa RESORT $$$
(Map p118; ☑ 602-840-3610; www.royalpalms hotel.com; 5200 E Camelback Rd; r/ste from $499/519; P ✳ 🛜 ⊠ 🐾) Camelback Mountain is the photogenic backdrop for this posh and intimate resort, built in 1929. Today, it's a hushed and elegant place, dotted with Spanish Colonial villas, flower-lined walkways and palms imported from Egypt. Pets can go Pavlovian for soft beds, personalized biscuits and walking services.

Scottsdale

★ **Hotel Valley Ho** BOUTIQUE HOTEL $$$
(Map p124; ☑ 480-376-2600; www.hotelvalleyho. com; 6850 E Main St; r/ste $409/532; P ✳ @ 🛜 ⊠ 🐾) Everything's swell at the Valley Ho, where midcentury modern gets a 21st-century twist. This jazzy joint once bedded Bing Crosby, Natalie Wood and Janet Leigh, and today it's a top pick for movie stars filming on location in Phoenix. Bebop music, upbeat staff and eye magnets like the 'ice fireplace' recapture the Rat Pack vibe, and the theme travels well to the balconied rooms.

★ **Bespoke Inn, Cafe & Bicycles** B&B $$$
(Map p124; ☑ 480-664-0730; www.bespokeinn. com; 3701 N Marshall Way; d incl brunch from $349; P ✳ 🛜 ⊠ 🐾) A small slice of 'European' hospitality in downtown Scottsdale, this breezy B&B offers guests chocolate scones to nibble in the chic cafe, an infinity pool to loll in and Pashley city bikes to roam the neighborhood on. Rooms are plush, with handsome touches like handcrafted furniture and nickel bath fixtures. Gourmet brunch is served at the on-site restaurant Virtu. Book early.

Sanctuary on Camelback Mountain RESORT $$$
(Map p118; ☑ 480-948-2100; www.sanctuaryon camelback.com; 5700 E McDonald Dr; casita/ ste/house from $716/909/2000; P ✳ 🛜 ⊠ 🐾) Draped across the northern slopes of Camelback Mountain, this luxe resort and spa feels like a hideaway of the gods. Mountain suites, spa casitas, private homes – no matter your choice, you will feel pampered, protected and deserving. Lodgings are decorated in slick modern tones that contrast with the ochres of the desert.

Boulders RESORT $$$
(Map p116; ☑ 480-488-9009; www.theboulders. com; 34631 N Tom Darlington Dr, Scottsdale; casitas/villas from $239/391; P ✳ @ 🛜 ⊠ 🐾) Tensions evaporate upon arrival at this desert oasis that blends into a landscape of natural rock formations – and that's before you've put in a session at the on-site spa or settled in at one of the four pools. Basically, everything here is calculated to make life better.

Saguaro HOTEL $$$
(Map p124; ☑ 480-308-1100, 877-808-2440; thesaguaro.com/scottsdale; 4000 N Drinkwater Blvd; r/ste from $399/499; P ✳ 🛜 ⊠ 🐾) This candy-bright collection of rooms doesn't exactly fit thematically with Old Town Scottsdale, but the look is fresh, the service

generally good, and the vibe young. There's a palm-dotted pool and the well-located Saguaro's rates are lower than many neighborhood competitors.

Sleep Inn HOTEL **$$$**
(Map p116; ☑866-477-6424; www.sleepinn scottsdale.com; 16630 N Scottsdale Rd; r $309; P ✳ ☏) It's part of a national chain, but this Sleep Inn wins points for its extensive complimentary breakfast, afternoon cookies, friendly staff and proximity to Taliesin West (p117). There's also a laundry, free fitness passes and a 24-hour hotel shuttle that runs within 5 miles of the hotel.

Tempe & Mesa

Lost Dutchman State Park
Campground CAMPGROUND **$**
(☑reservations 520-586-2283; www.azstateparks. com; 6109 N Apache Trail, Apache Junction; tent/ hookup from $15/25; ⊙reservations 8am-5pm; P) With saguaros up close and a craggy offshoot of the Superstition Mountains as a backdrop, this is one of the prettiest campgrounds in eastern Arizona. It has 134 campsites, 68 powered, and 24/7 online booking is available all year.

Sheraton Wild Horse Pass
Resort & Spa RESORT **$$$**
(Map p116; ☑602-225-0100; www.wildhorse passresort.com; 5594 W Wild Horse Pass Blvd, Chandler; r/ste from $339/534; P ✳ ☏ ☁) At sunset, scan the lonely horizon for the eponymous wild horses silhouetted against the South Mountains. Owned by the Gila River tribe and nestled on their sweeping reservation south of Tempe, this 500-room resort is a stunning alchemy of modern luxury and American Indian tradition. The domed lobby is a mural-festooned roundhouse, and rooms reflect the traditions of local tribes.

✖ Eating

Phoenix has the biggest selection of restaurants in the Southwest. Reservations are recommended at the more fashionable places.

✖ Phoenix

★Desoto Central Market MARKET **$**
(Map p122; ☑602-680-7747; desotocentral market.com; 915 N Central Ave; mains $11-15; ⊙7am-10pm Mon-Wed, 7am-midnight Thu-Sat, 8am-9pm Sun) Making great use of a sensitively restored 1920s DeSoto dealership, this indoor 'market' is really a collective

of inventive kitchens, slinging their goods together under the one roof. Special mention goes to New Southern affair the Larder and the Delta, whose shrimp 'n' grits (with smoked andouille sausage and hot sauce) or chili-garlic glazed baby back ribs will leave you gasping.

★Phoenix Public Market CAFE **$**
(Map p122; ☑602-253-2700; www.phxpublic market.com; 14 E Pierce St; mains $9-10; ⊙7am-10pm; ☏☱) This buzzing barn of a place – the on-site cafe for Arizona's largest farmers market – attracts a dedicated clientele of Arizona State University (ASU) students, local professionals at lunch, vegetarians and food lovers of all stripes. The housemade bagels and flame-roasted chicken are fantastic, while inventive daily specials, community dinners and happy hours keep the cognoscenti coming at all hours.

Phoenix Streetfood
Coalition STREET FOOD **$**
(Map p122; ☑480-620-8479; www.phxstreet food.org; cnr S 5th Ave & W Madison St, Maricopa County Sherriff's Office; mains $8-12; ⊙11am-1pm Mon, Wed & Fri) One of the Coalition's larger regular gatherings sees a gourmand's galaxy of food trucks gather outside the County Sherriff's office three times a week, to sling American Indian frybread, tacos, outrageously good BBQ brisket, poutine with duck confit and any number of other delicacies.

La 15 y Salsas MEXICAN **$**
(Map p116; ☑602-870-2056; 15ysalsas.com; 1507 W Hatcher Rd; mains $8-13; ⊙9am-8pm Mon-Sat, to 6:30pm Sun) La 15 y Salsas brings the unapologetic flavors of Mexico's Oaxaca province to northern Phoenix, with hand-ground mole pastes (such as the mole negro, made with chocolate and a complex blend of spices, nuts and chilis), moreish tamales and spicy amarillo chicken soup. After dinner, browse the shelves for Oaxacan groceries to go.

La Grande Orange
Grocery & Pizzeria CAFE **$**
(Map p118; ☑602-840-7777; www.lagrande orangegrocery.com; 4410 N 40th St; breakfast $6-8, lunch $7-10, pizza $12-15; ⊙6:30am-10pm; ☏☱) Buzzing from daybreak until well after sundown, this bustling gourmet market, bakery, cafe and pizzeria is good for a muffin and coffee at breakfast, a guacamole BLT at lunch, or a margherita pizza and a glass of something sympathetic at dinner.

In a hurry? Check the online menu then call ahead for curbside service.

Crudo
ITALIAN $$

(Map p118; 602-358-8666; www.crudoaz.com; 3603 E Indian School Rd, Gaslight Sq; mains $14-18; 5-10pm Tue-Sat;) In the unlikely setting of a nondescript mall (that's Phoenix for you), Crudo is dishing out some seriously good Italian food, and mixing up some stunnng cocktails. Your choices might include albacore tuna cured in citrus and dill as antipasti, a market fish Livorne se stew for secondi, and a pasta of lamb-neck ragu with semolina gnocchi. Cocktails lure the work crowd to the chatty bar

Barrio Café
MEXICAN $$

(Map p118; 602-636-0240; www.barriocafe.com; 2814 N 16th St; mains $12-29; 11am-10pm Tue-Sat, to 9pm Sun;) Barrio's staff wear T-shirts emblazoned with *comida chingona*, which translates as 'fucking good food,' and they don't lie. This is Mexican food at its most creative: how many menus have you seen featuring guacamole spiked with pomegranate seeds, buttered corn with chipotle, aged cheese, cilantro and lime or goat's-milk-caramel-filled churros? Drinks are half-price from 2pm to 5pm daily.

Pizzeria Bianco
PIZZA $$

(Map p118; 602-368-3273; www.pizzeriabianco.com; 4743 N 20th St; pizza $15-18; 11am-9pm Sun-Thu, to 10pm Fri & Sat;) This second location of the famous downtown **pizza joint** (Map p122; 602-258-8300; 623 E Adams St, Heritage Sq; 11am-9pm Mon-Wed, 11am-10pm Thu-Sat, noon-7pm Sun) is in the Town & Country Shopping Center, near Biltmore Fashion Park. It also serves pasta, salad and sandwiches.

Beckett's Table
AMERICAN $$

(Map p118; 602-954-1700; www.beckettstable.com; 3717 E Indian School Rd; mains $21-26; 5-10pm Tue-Sat, to 9pm Sun;) It's country supper in the village's most stylish barn, complete with concrete floor, trussed beams, a walnut communal table and other wooden accents. But the urban farm concept really shines as you savor Justin Beckett's locally sourced dishes, from tender pork *osso bucco* to short ribs with mashed potatoes. Inventive salads such as heirloom tomato with lemon ricotta keep vegetarians happy.

★ Dick's Hideaway
NEW MEXICAN $$$

(Map p118; 602-265-5886; richardsonsnm.com; 6008 N 16th St; breakfast $15-16, mains $25-27; 8am-11pm Sun-Wed, to midnight Thu-Sat) At this pocket-sized ode to New Mexican cuisine, grab a small table beside the bar or settle in at the communal table in the side room and prepare for hearty servings of savory, chile-slathered New Mexican fare, from enchiladas to tamales to rellenos. We especially like the Hideaway for breakfast, when the Bloody Marys arrive with a shot of beer.

Tratto
TRATTORIA $$$

(Map p118; 602-296-7761; www.trattophx.com; 4743 N 20th St, Town & Country Shopping Center; mains $32-36; 5-9pm Mon-Thu, to 10pm Fri & Sat) Tratto is the place to head for handmade pasta and expertly cooked poultry, fish and meat. The weekly menu focuses on depth, not breadth, with only a few pastas, main dishes and vegetable *contorni* on offer at any one time.

✕ Scottsdale

Fresh Mint
VIETNAMESE $

(Map p116; 480-443-2556; www.freshmint.us.com; 13802 N Scottsdale Rd; lunch $8, mains $11-12; 11am-9pm Mon-Sat;) What? Never had kosher Vietnamese vegan? Well, there's always a first time – and if it tastes anything like the food at Fresh Mint, you'll want to get more. If you're skeptical of soy chicken and tofu (served many ways), we understand, but we respectfully submit that this stuff is as tasty as any bacon cheeseburger.

★ The Mission
MEXICAN $$

(Map p124; 480-636-5005; www.themissionaz.com; 3815 N Brown Ave; lunch $14-18, dinner $14-30; 11am-3pm & 5-10pm) With its dark interior and glowing votives, we'll call this *nuevo* Latin spot sexy – although our exclamations about the food's deliciousness may ruin the sultry vibe. The Tecate-marinated steak taco with lime and avocado is superb and makes for a satisfying light lunch. The guacamole is made table-side, and wins raves. Margaritas and mojitos round out the fun.

Mastro's Ocean Club
SEAFOOD $$$

(Map p116; 480-443-8555; www.mastrosrestaurants.com; 15045 N Kierland Blvd; mains $40-60; 5-10pm Sun-Thu, to 11pm Fri & Sat;) Mastro's is gunning for the title of best seafood in the Valley of the Sun, and we think it may deserve the crown. Part of an upscale chain linking major cities across the US, it makes up for Arizona's lack of ocean by freighting in sea bass from Chile, salmon from Scotland and tuna from Hawaii.

Tempe

Essence
CAFE $

(Map p118; ☑ 480-966-2745; www.essence bakery.com; 825 W University Dr; breakfast $7-9, lunch $8-9; ☉7am-3pm Tue-Sat; ⊘) Look for French toast and egg dishes at breakfast, and salads, gourmet sandwiches and a few Mediterranean specialties at lunch. The eco-minded cafe strives to serve organic, locally grown fare. The popular macaroons are mighty fine.

Casey Moore's
PUB FOOD $$

(Map p118; ☑ 480-968-9935; www.casey moores.com; 850 S Ash Ave; mains $22-26; ☉11am-2am; ☏) Did somebody say oysters? Oh yes they did. And Casey Moore's is the place to slurp them. Part Irish pub, part seafood restaurant, part Tempe institution, Casey's is a fun and friendly place to hang out on a Saturday afternoon. The patio is dog-friendly until 5pm; things may get more rambunctious at night.

★Kai Restaurant
AMERICAN INDIAN $$$

(Map p116; ☑ 602-225-0100; www.wildhorsepass resort.com; 5594 W Wild Horse Pass Blvd, Chandler; mains $48-54, tasting menus $145-$245; ☉5:30-9pm Tue-Sat) American Indian cuisine – based on traditional crops grown along the Gila River – soars to new heights at Kai ('seed'). Expect creations such as grilled buffalo tenderloin with smoked corn puree and cholla buds, or wild scallops with mesquite-smoked caviar and tepary-bean crackling. The unobtrusive service is flawless, the wine list expertly curated and the room decorated with American Indian art.

🍷 Drinking & Nightlife

Posh watering holes are found in the most unlikely of spots in the Phoenix area, even amid chain stores in strip malls. Scottsdale has the greatest concentration of trendy bars and clubs as well as a convivial lineup of patios on Scottsdale Rd in Old Town; Tempe attracts the student crowd.

🍷 Phoenix

★Bitter & Twisted
COCKTAIL BAR

(Map p122; ☑ 602-340-1924; bitterandtwisted az.com; 1 W Jefferson St; ☉4pm-2am Tue-Sat) Housed in the former Arizona Prohibition Headquarters, this stylish seating-only cocktail bar shakes up some serious mixes and slings some delicious food to keep drinkers upright. Particularly lip-smacking is the

dragon dumpling burger – pork and beef with Sichuan pickle and dumpling sauce.

Lux Central Coffeebar
CAFE

(Map p118; ☑ 602-327-1396; www.luxcoffee.com; 4402 N Central Ave; ☉6am-midnight Sun-Thu, to 2am Fri & Sat; ☏) MacBooks, tatts and hipster looks are de rigueur at this cafe-bar. The staff are adept and welcoming, the coffee is hand-roasted and the vibe is lively – everything you need to while away an hour over mid-morning coffee, dinner or a cocktail.

Cobra Arcade Bar
BAR

(Map p122; ☑ 602-595-5873; cobraarcadebar.com; 801 N 2nd St, Ste 100; ☉4pm-2am; ☏) Nostalgia overload for Gen X and its predecessors, this slinky downtown bar has 40 vintage arcade games to accompany 14 different draft beers and game-themed cocktails (try the Crazy Kong: Irish whiskey, banana liqueur, lemon and ginger beer). Settle in and see if you can clock Galaga. At 25¢ per game, the prices are vintage, too.

Postino Winecafé Arcadia
WINE BAR

(Map p118; ☑ 602-852-3939; www.postino winecafe.com; 3939 E Campbell Ave, cnr 40th St; ☉11am-11pm Mon-Thu, 11am-midnight Fri, 9am-midnight Sat, 9am-10pm Sun; ☏) This convivial, indoor-outdoor wine bar in the former Arcadia Post Office is a perfect gathering spot for friends ready to enjoy the good life – but solos will do fine too. Highlights include the misting patio, inventive bruschetta (try the burrata with bacon, arugula and tomato) and more than 20 wines by the glass for $5 between 11am and 5pm.

OHSO Brewery & Distillery
BREWERY

(Map p118; ☑ 602-955-0358; www.ohsobrewery. com; 4900 E Indian School Rd; ☉11am-midnight Mon-Thu, 11am-1:30am Fri, 9am-1:30am Sat, 9am-midnight Sun; ☏) With a distillery and two new locations added to the Arcadia original, the 'Outrageous Homebrewer's Social Outpost' is clearly doing something the locals like. Small batch brews and Arizona beers are the stars, the atmosphere is usually boisterous and welcoming, and the food (perhaps a skillet of green chilis, pulled pork, roasted corn and poblano aioli) is perfect with beer.

Vig Arcadia
BAR

(Map p118; ☑ 602-553-7227; www.thevig.us; 4041 N 40th St; ☉11am-2am Mon-Fri, 10am-2am Sat & Sun; ☏) Ignore the imposing Soviet-style exterior and step inside. The Vig is where the smart set – stylish, well-scrubbed, happy – come to knock back a few cocktails. Sleek booths, a dark bar and a bustling patio complete with a bocce court, an upbeat vibe and complimentary valet parking: be careful or you might find yourself spending half a day here. There's a new uptown outpost, too.

Alice Cooperstown SPORTS BAR
(Map p122; ☑ 602-253-7337; www.alicecoopers town.com; 101 E Jackson St; ⊙ 11am-9pm Mon-Thu, to 10pm Fri & Sat) This beer hall is an unusual amalgam of sports bar and rock dive, a place where gothed-up waitresses coexist with the Baseball Hall of Fame. On game days it floods with giddy sports lovers toasting their teams. For music fans, rock-and-roll memorabilia and the ghoulish visage of A Cooper himself are ubiquitous.

Scottsdale

BS West GAY
(Map p122; ☑ 480-945-9028; www.bswest.com; 7125 E 5th Ave; ⊙ 2pm-2am) Most agree that when it comes to the Valley's gay clubs, this high-energy video bar and dance club in Scottsdale is the place to be: the boys are hot, the music is loud and straight interlopers, while present, haven't overwhelmed the dance floor. There are pool tables, drag shows and 'drunk karaoke' on Sunday nights.

Rusty Spur Saloon BAR
(Map p124; ☑ 480-425-7787; www.rusty spursaloon.com; 7245 E Main St; ⊙ 10am-1am Sun-Thu, to 2am Fri & Sat) Nobody's putting on airs at this fun-lovin', pack-'em-in-tight country bar where the grizzled Budweiser crowd gathers for cheap drinks and twangy bands. It's in an old bank building that closed during the Depression; the vault now holds liquor instead of greenbacks – except for the dollar bills hanging from the ceiling. We kinda like this place, pardner.

Tempe

Four Peaks Brewing Company BREWERY
(Map p118; ☑ 480-303-9967; www.fourpeaks. com; 1340 E 8th St; ⊙ 11am-midnight Mon-Wed, 11am-1am Thu & Fri, 9am-midnight Sat & Sun; 🛜) Hipsters, families, craft-beer obsessives and the plain thirsty congregate happily in this 1890s brick brewhouse, filling growlers of Kilt Lifter or Pitchfork Pale from the tap, or just chatting over a pint or two. There's also toothsome pub grub, tasting tours ($10 per head), a gift shop, and further locations in Tempe, Scottsdale and Phoenix Sky Harbor.

 **Entertainment**

The entertainment scene in Phoenix is lively and multifaceted, if not particularly edgy. Spectator sports are huge. The Thursday edition of the **Arizona Republic Calendar** (www.azcentral.com/thingstodo/events) includes a special section with entertainment listings. **Phoenix New Times** (www.phoenixnew times.com), a free, alternative weekly that is plugged into the local scene, is published on Thursday and available citywide.

Performing Arts

Phoenix Symphony CLASSICAL MUSIC
(Map p122; ☑ administration 602-495-1117, box office 602-495-1999; www.phoenixsymphony.org; 75 N 2nd St) Arizona's only full-time professional orchestra plays classics and pops, mostly at **Symphony Hall** (Map p122; ☑ 602-262-6225; www.phoenixconventioncenter.com) and sometimes at other regional venues, from September to early June. Minor series and special performances take place at other times of the year. There are two box offices: at Symphony Hall (open two hours prior to performances) and at 1 N 1st St, Suite 200 (9am to 5pm Monday to Friday).

Crescent Ballroom LIVE MUSIC
(Map p122; ☑ 602-716-2222; www.crescentphx. com; 308 N 2nd Ave; bar free, shows ticketed; ⊙ 11am-midnight Mon-Wed, 11am-2am Thu & Fri, 5pm-2am Sat, 10am-midnight Sun; 🛜) A 1917 brick garage beside the historic Dixie Overland Hwy is now home to one of Phoenix's most diverse live venues, hosting everything from indie to hip-hop and *lucha libre* Mexican wrestling. Even when shows aren't on, you can always cozy up at the bar, or dive into the 'Mexican-accented road food' served at the house restaurant, Cocina 10.

Arizona Opera OPERA
(Map p122; ☑ 602-266-7464; www.azopera. com; 75 N 2nd St) Housed in the 2300-seat Symphony Hall (also home to the Phoenix Symphony and Ballet Arizona), the state ensemble produces five operas per season, usually big-ticket favorites such as *Madama Butterfly* and *Tosca*. Smaller-scale vocal recitals are held between the principal productions.

Phoenix Theatre PERFORMING ARTS
(Map p122; ☑ 602-254-2151; www.phoenix theatre.com; 100 E McDowell Rd) The city's main dramatic group puts on a good mix of mainstream and edgier performances. The attached Cookie Company does children's shows.

Sports

Phoenix Suns
BASKETBALL

(Map p122; ☑ 602-379-7900; www.nba.com/suns; 201 E Jefferson St) The Suns, twice champions of the NBA Western Conference, play regular-season games at downtown's Talking Stick Resort Arena from October to April.

Arizona Cardinals
FOOTBALL

(Map p116; ☑ 602-379-0101; www.azcardinals.com; 1 Cardinals Dr, Glendale) Between September and December/January the Cardinals play at the architecturally distinguished University of Phoenix Stadium in Glendale, which boasts a roll-out natural grass field and retractable roof. Check the stadium website (www.universityofphoenixstadium.com) for information about 75-minute stadium tours (adult/child $9/7).

Arizona Diamondbacks
BASEBALL

(Map p122; ☑ 602-462-6500; arizona.diamond backs.mlb.com; 401 E Jefferson St) The Diamondbacks, who last won the MLB World Series in 2001, play at downtown Chase Field, which features a retractable domed roof to help keep temperatures cool.

Phoenix Mercury
BASKETBALL

(Map p122; ☑ 602-252-9622; www.wnba.com/mercury; 201 E Jefferson St) Phoenix's WNBA team plays at the downtown Talking Stick Resort Arena from May to September; they won the national championship in 2007, 2009 and 2014.

Live Music

Rhythm Room
LIVE MUSIC

(Map p118; ☑ 602-265-4842; www.rhythmroom.com; 1019 E Indian School Rd; ⊗doors usually open 7:30pm) Some of the Valley's best live acts take the stage at this small venue, an unpromising aqua cube on a busy stretch of road. It tends to attract more local and regional talent than big names, and it's easy to feel like you're in the front row of every gig. Check the calendar for show times.

Char's Has the Blues
BLUES

(Map p118; ☑ 602-230-0205; www.charshas theblues.com; 4631 N 7th Ave; cover Thu-Sun $3; ⊗8pm-1am) Dark and intimate – but very welcoming – this shabby-fronted blues and R&B shack packs 'em in with solid acts most nights of the week, but somehow still manages to feel like a well-kept secret.

🔒 Shopping

The Valley of the Sun is also the Valley of the consumer. From Western wear to arts and crafts and American Indian items, it's easy to find a souvenir. Mall culture is also huge. Old Town Scottsdale (p116) is known for its art galleries and Southwestern crafts shops. Mill Ave (p119) in Tempe has a mix of indie and chain boutiques.

🔒 Phoenix

Phoenix Public Market
MARKET

(Map p122; ☑ 602-625-6736; phxpublicmarket. com; 721 N Central Ave; ⊗8am-1pm Sat Oct-Apr, 8am-noon Sat May-Sep) The largest farmers market in Arizona brings the state's best produce, both fresh and pre-made, together in one open-air jamboree of good tastes. Alongside spanking-fresh fruit and veg, you can find indigenous foods, wonderful bread, spices, pastes and salsas, organic meat, BBQ trucks and plenty more to eat on the spot. Jewelry, textiles and body products also make appearances.

Heard Museum Shop & Bookstore
ARTS & CRAFTS

(Map p122; ☑ 602-252-8344; www.heardmuseum shop.com; 2301 N Central Ave; ⊗9:30am-5pm Mon-Sat, 11am-5pm Sun; 🐾) This museum store has a top-notch collection of American Indian original arts and crafts; the variety and quality of kachina dolls alone is mind-boggling. Jewelry, pottery, American Indian books and a broad selection of fine arts can also be found, while the bookstore sells a wide array of books about the American Indian cultures of the Southwest.

Bookmans
BOOKS

(Map p118; ☑ 602-433-0255; www.bookmans.com; 8034 N 19th Ave; ⊗9am-10pm; 🐾) Originating in Tucson, this bibliophile's indie mecca offers aisle after aisle of new and used books, mags and music, a neighborhood vibe, various events and free wi-fi.

Garden Shop at the Desert Botanical Garden
GIFTS & SOUVENIRS

(Map p118; ☑ 480-526-8890; gardenshop.dbg.org; 1201 N Galvin Pkwy; ⊗8am-8pm; 🐾) Plant your own desert garden with a starter cactus from this indoor-outdoor gift shop. Southwestern cards, cactus jellies and desert-focused gardening books are also on sale.

Biltmore Fashion Park
MALL

(Map p118; ☑ 602-955-8400; www.shopbiltmore. com; 2502 E Camelback Rd; ⊗10am-8pm Mon-Sat, noon-6pm Sun) Packed with high-end fashion retailers, this exclusive mall preens from its perch on Camelback just south of the

Arizona Biltmore Resort. Parking for under two hours is free, with validation.

Scottsdale

Scottsdale Fashion Square MALL (Map p124; www.fashionsquare.com; 7014 E Camelback Rd; 10am-9pm Mon-Sat, 11am-6pm Sun;) This upscale mall has over 200 fashion retailers, department stores and restaurants, including Abercrombie & Fitch, Nordstrom and Z'Tejas Grill.

Information

EMERGENCY

Police (emergency 911, non-emergency 602-262-6151; phoenix.gov/police; 620 W Washington St)

INTERNET ACCESS

Burton Barr Central Library (602-262-4636; www.phoenixpubliclibrary.org; 1221 N Central Ave; 9am-5pm Mon, Fri & Sat, 9am-9pm Tue-Thu, 1-5pm Sun;) Free internet; see the website for additional locations.

MEDICAL SERVICES

Both hospitals have 24-hour emergency rooms.

Banner – University Medical Center Phoenix (602-839-2000; www.bannerhealth.com; 1111 E McDowell Rd)

St Joseph's Hospital & Medical Center (602-406-3000; www.stjosephs-phx.org; 350 W Thomas Rd)

POST

Downtown Post Office (Map p122; 602-253-9648; www.usps.com; 522 N Central Ave; 9am-5pm Mon-Fri) Housed in a beautiful 1930s federal building.

TELEPHONE

Greater Phoenix has three telephone area codes: 480, 602 and 623. You always need to dial the area code, regardless of where you are.

TOURIST INFORMATION

Downtown Phoenix Visitor Information Center (Map p122; 877-225-5749; www.visitphoenix.com; 125 N 2nd St, Suite 120; 8am-5pm Mon-Fri) The Valley's most complete source of tourist information. Located across from the Hyatt Regency.

Experience Scottsdale (Map p124; 480-421-1004, 800-782-1117; www.experiencescottsdale.com; 7014 E Camelback Rd; 9am-6pm Mon-Sat, 10am-5pm Sun) In the Food Court of Scottsdale Fashion Square.

Mesa Convention & Visitors Bureau (Map p116; 480-827-4700, 800-283-6372; www.

visitmesa.com; 120 N Center St; 8am-5pm Mon-Fri)

Tempe Tourism Office (Map p118; 800-283-6734, 480-894-8158; www.tempetourism.com; 222 S Mill Ave, Suite 120; 8:30am-5pm Mon-Fri)

Getting There & Away

Sky Harbor International Airport (Map p118; 602-273-3300; skyharbor.com; 3400 E Sky Harbor Blvd;) is 3 miles southeast of downtown Phoenix and served by airlines including United, American, Delta and British Airways. Its three terminals (Terminals 2, 3 and 4; Terminal 1 was demolished in 1990) and the parking lots are linked by free shuttles and the Phoenix Sky Train.

Greyhound (Map p118; 602-389-4200; www.greyhound.com; 2115 E Buckeye Rd) runs buses to Tucson ($18, two hours, six daily), Flagstaff ($25, three hours, five daily), Albuquerque ($70 to $87, 9½ hours, three daily) and Los Angeles ($46, 7½ hours, seven daily). Valley Metro's No 13 bus links the airport and the Greyhound station; tell the driver your destination is the Greyhound station.

Getting Around

TO/FROM THE AIRPORT

For shared rides from the airport, the citywide door-to-door shuttle service provided by **Super Shuttle** (602-244-9000, 800-258-3826; www.supershuttle.com) costs about $13 to downtown Phoenix, $15 to Tempe, $17 to Old Town Scottsdale and $21 to Mesa.

AAA Yellow Cab (480-888-8888; www.yellowcabaz.com) and **Apache** (480-804-1000; www.apachetaxi.com) are taxi companies serving the airport. The charge is $5 for the first mile and $2.30 for each additional mile; from the airport there's a $1 surcharge and $15 is the minimum fare. Expect to pay $16 to $19 to downtown.

The new **Phoenix Sky Train** (www.skyharbor.com/phxskytrain) runs through Terminals 3 and 4 to the Metro light-rail station at 44th St and E Washington St, via the airport's east economy parking area. Bus 13 also connects the airport to town ($2 per ride).

CAR & MOTORCYCLE

The network of freeways here is starting to rival Los Angeles and so is the intensity of traffic. Always allow for traffic jams in your sightseeing schedule. The I-10 and US 60 are the main east–west thoroughfares, while the I-17 and SR 51 are the major north–south arteries. Loops 101 and 202 link most of the suburbs. Parking is plentiful outside of the downtown area.

All international car-rental companies have offices at the airport. Rent motorcyles with **Arizona Funtime Rentals** (☑ 480-968-2522; www.azfuntimerentals.com).

PUBLIC TRANSPORTATION

Valley Metro (☑ 602-253-5000; www.valleymetro.org) operates buses all over the Valley and a 20-mile light-rail line linking north Phoenix with downtown Phoenix, Tempe/ASU and downtown Mesa. Fares for both light-rail and bus are $2 per ride (no transfers) or $4 for a day pass. Buses run daily at intermittent times.

The free **Orbit Bus** (www.tempe.gov/orbit; ☉ 6am-10pm) loops around downtown Tempe, along Mill Ave and University Dr. The downtown Scottsdale Trolley (p116) loops past Old Town, the Main Street Arts District, and Scottsdale Fashion Square, also at no charge.

CENTRAL ARIZONA

Much of the area north of Phoenix lies on the Colorado Plateau and is cool, wooded and mountainous. It's also blessed with the state's most diverse and scenic array of sites and attractions. You can clamber the cinder-strewn flanks of a volcano, sip wine in a cliff-hugging former mining town, hike through juniper-scented canyons, schuss down alpine slopes, admire the 1000-year-old dwellings of the ancestral Puebloans and get the dust of the Old West on your boots. The main hub, Flagstaff, is a lively and delightful college town and gateway to the Grand Canyon South Rim. Summer, spring and fall are the best times to visit.

Verde Valley

Arizona's leading viticultural area rubs shoulders with ancient cliff dwellings and experiments in 'arcology' (architecture and ecology), either side of the I-17 running north of Phoenix.

◉ Sights

Arcosanti   ARCHITECTURE
(☑ 928-632-7135; www.arcosanti.org; 13555 S Cross L Rd, Mayer; suggested donation for tours $10; ☉ tours 10am-4pm) Two miles east of I-17 exit 262 (at Cordes Junction, 65 miles north of Phoenix), Arcosanti is an architectural experiment in urban living that's been a work in progress since 1970. The brainchild of the late, groundbreaking architect and urban planner Paolo Soleri, it's based on his concept of 'arcology,', which seeks to create communities in harmony with their natural surroundings, minimizing the use of energy, raw materials and land.

Montezuma Castle National Monument   RUINS
(☑ 928-567-3322; www.nps.gov/moca; Montezuma Castle Rd, Camp Verde; combination pass with Tuzigoot National Monument adult/child 15yr & under $10/free; ☉ 8am-5pm; P ♿) Like nearby Tuzigoot National Monument (p141), Montezuma Castle is a stunningly well-preserved, 1000-year-old Sinagua cliff dwelling: early explorers thought the five-story-high pueblo was Aztec and hence dubbed it Montezuma. A **museum** interprets the archaeology of the site, which can be seen from a short, self-guiding, wheelchair-accessible trail. Entrance into the 'castle' itself is prohibited, but nearby vantage points and an audiovisual diorama give you a good idea of what you're looking at. Take exit 289 from I-17, then Montezuma Castle Rd.

Fort Verde State Historic Park   STATE PARK
(☑ 928-567-3275; azstateparks.com/fort-verde; 125 E Hollamon St, Camp Verde; adult/child 7-13yr $7/4; ☉ 9am-5pm) Founded by the US Army in 1871 on the site of a farming settlement, Fort Verde was designed to prevent Indian raids on Anglo settlers. Tonto Apache chief Chalipun surrendered here in April 1873. Today, the town's Fort Verde State Historic Park offers an authentic snapshot of frontier life in the 1880s. To get here, take exit 287 off I-17, then Hwy 260 south, turn left at Finnie Flat Rd and again at Hollamon St.

V-Bar-V Heritage Site   HISTORIC SITE
(☑ 928-203-2900; www.redrockcountry.org/recreation/cultural/v-v; 6750 N Forest Ranger Rd, Rimrock; ☉ 9:30am-3pm Fri-Mon) More than 1000 petrolgyphs have been identified at this well-protected Forest Service site, for which you'll need a Red Rock or Federal Interagency Pass. Many appear unique to the Southern Sinaguan who lived here between AD 1150 and 1400; the site was probably used by shamans, in part as a solar calendar. And the embracing stick-figure couple? Not dancing. Take Exit 298 from I-17, follow FR 618 east about 2.5 miles to the entrance, on your right beyond Beaver Creek Campground.

Montezuma Well   RUINS
(☑ 928-567-4521; www.nps.gov/moca; ☉ 8am-5pm) FREE An outlying site of Montezuma Castle National Monument, Montezuma Well is a natural limestone sinkhole 470ft

wide, surrounded by both Sinaguan and Hohokam dwellings dating back to AD 1050. Water from the well was used for irrigation by the American Indians and is still used today by residents of nearby Rimrock. Access is from I-17 exit 293, 4 miles north of the Montezuma Castle exit. Follow the signs for another 4 miles through McGuireville and Rimrock.

🛏 Sleeping & Eating

Motels are thickest on the ground in and around Cottonwood. Many tasting rooms have interesting menus of wine-friendly food.

Rock Springs Café   AMERICAN $
(☎623-374-5794; www.rockspringscafe.com; 35769 S Old Black Canyon Hwy; breakfast $10-12, lunch & dinner $13-15; ☺7am-9pm Sun-Thu, to 10pm Fri & Sat) A pit stop for pie? You betcha. Especially if it's a slice of fresh pie ($4.50) at Rock Springs Café in Black Canyon City. Only problem? This Old West eatery, just off I-17 at exit 242, will drive you crazy with choices – apple crumble, blueberry, rhubarb, chocolate – all sitting pretty in a cooler in the dining room.

Wickenburg

📞 928 / POP 6806 / ELEV 2100FT

Wickenburg looks like it fell out of the sky – directly from the 1890s. Downtown streets are flanked by Old West storefronts, historic buildings and several life-sized statues of the prospectors and cowboys who brought this place to life in the 1800s. In later years, once the mining and ranching played out, guest ranches began to flourish, drawing people in search of the romance of the open range. Today, the one-time 'dude ranch capital of the world' still hosts weekend wranglers, but it has also evolved (quietly and discreetly) into a 'rehab capital' for A-listers. The town, located 60 miles northwest of Phoenix via Hwy 60, is pleasant at anytime but summer, when temperatures can top 110°F (43°C).

⊙ Sights

The small downtown is dotted with statues of the town's founders and a few colorful characters. One of the latter was George Sayers, a 'bibulous reprobate' who was once chained to the town's **Jail Tree** on Tegner St in the late 1800s.

Desert Caballeros Western Museum   MUSEUM
(☎928-684-2272; www.westernmuseum.org; 21 N Frontier St; adult/senior/child 17yr & under $12/10/ free; ☺10am-5pm Mon-Sat, noon-4pm Sun, closed Mon Jun-Aug) Take a stroll into the early 1900s at the Desert Caballeros Western Museum, where recreated street scenes lead to an old-time saloon, the post office and the general store. Hopi kachina dolls, colorful Arizona minerals and eye-catching art are also highlights. The annual Cowgirl Up! exhibit and sale in March/April is a terrific tribute to an eclectic array of Western women artists; we bet you won't leave empty-handed.

Vulture Mine   MINE
(www.vultureminetours.com; 36610 N 355 Ave, off Vulture Mine Rd; donation $10; ☺tours 8:30am Sat early May–mid-Oct, 10am Sat mid-Oct–early May) Town founder Henry Wickenburg discovered gold nuggets here in 1863. The mine spat out gold until 1942, then petered out along with surrounding Vulture City, which decayed into an atmospheric ghost town. Vulture Peak Gold, the company that purchased the property in 2011, offers two-hour guided tours on Saturday mornings (cash only; bring water and ID). Visit the website for more details. Head west on Hwy 60, turn left onto Vulture Mine Rd and follow it for 12 miles.

Hassayampa River Preserve   NATURE RESERVE
(☎928-684-2772; www.nature.org/hassayampa; 49614 Hwy 60; adult/child 12yr & under $5/free; ☺7-11am Fri-Sun mid-May–mid-Sep, 8am-5pm Wed-Sun mid-Sep–mid-May) The Hassayampa River normally runs underground, but just outside downtown it shows off its crystalline shimmer. Currently managed by Parks and Recreation, it's one of the few riparian habitats remaining in Arizona and a great place for birders to look for the 280 or so resident and migrating species, or to spot javelinas, lizards and mule deer. The 770-acre preserve is on the west side of Hwy 60, 3 miles south of town. Trails shut 30 minutes before closing time.

🛏 Sleeping

Dude ranches like those in Wickenburg typically close for the summer in southern Arizona.

★ Flying E Ranch   RANCH $$$
(☎928-684-2690; www.flyingeranch.com; 2801 W Wickenburg Way; s/d/house from $205/280/330; ☺Nov-Apr; 🛜🐾) The coolest place at this down-home working cattle ranch is the boot room, which is lined with scuffed-up cowboy boots and hats that guests can borrow on their rides. Sitting on 20,000 acres in the Hassayampa Valley, the ranch is a big hit

VERDE VALLEY WINE TRAIL

Vineyards, wineries and tasting rooms are increasingly thick on the ground in the well-watered valley of the Verde River. Bringing star power is Maynard James Keenan, lead singer of the band Tool and owner of Caduceus Cellars and Merkin Vineyards. His 2010 documentary *Blood into Vine* takes a no-holds-barred look at the wine industry.

In Cottonwood, drive or float to **Alcantara Vineyards** (☑928-649-8463; www.alcantaravineyard.com; 3445 S Grapevine Rd, Cottonwood; wine tasting $10-15; ☉11am-5pm) on the Verde River, then stroll through Old Town where **Arizona Stronghold** (☑928-639-2789; www.azstronghold.com; 1023 N Main St; wine tasting $9; ☉noon-7pm Sun-Thu, to 9pm Fri & Sat), **Merkin Vineyards Osteria** (p142) and **Pillsbury Wine Company** (☑928-639-0646; www.pillsburywine.com; 1012 N Main St; wine tasting $10-12; ☉11am-6pm Sun-Thu, to 9pm Fri & Sat) are three of the best wine-tasting rooms on oenophile-friendly Main St.

In Jerome, start at **Cellar 433** (p140) near the visitor center. From there, stroll up to Keenan's **Caduceus Cellars** (p140), near the Connor Hotel.

Three wineries with tasting rooms hug a scrubby stretch of Page Springs Rd east of Cornville: bistro-housing **Page Springs Cellars** (☑928-639-3004; pagespringscellars.com; 1500 Page Springs Rd, Cornville; tours $10; ☉11am-7pm Sun-Wed, to 9pm Thu-Sat), the welcoming **Oak Creek Vineyards** (☑928-649-0290; www.oakcreekvineyards.net; 1555 N Page Springs Rd, Cornville; wine tasting $10; ☉10am-6pm) and the mellow-rock-playing **Javelina Leap Vineyard** (☑928-649-2681; www.javelinaleapwinery.com; 1565 Page Springs Rd, Cornville; tasting per wine $2-3; ☉11am-5pm Sun-Thu, to 6pm Fri & Sat).

For a wine-trail map and more details about the wineries, visit www.vvwinetrail.com.

with families and also works well for groups. Two-hour horseback rides cost $50 (or $80 for two).

Rancho de los Caballeros RANCH $$$
(☑800-684-5030, 928-684-5484; www.ranchodeloscaballeros.com; 1551 S Vulture Mine Rd; r/ste from $295/445; ☉Oct–mid-May; ❋☒) With an 18-hole golf course, spa, kids' program and fine dining, this sprawling ranch feels more *Dallas* than *Bonanza*. The lovely main lodge – with flagstone floor, brightly painted furniture and copper fireplace – leads to cozy rooms decked out stylishly with American Indian rugs and handcrafted furniture. Dinner is a dress-up affair; cut loose afterwards with nightly cowboy music in the saloon.

Eating

Honest diner fare and Americanized Mexican food are the most common offerings in Wickenburg.

Horseshoe Cafe DINER $
(☑928-684-7377; 207 E Wickenburg Way; mains $8-10; ☉5am-2pm Sep-May, shorter hours Jun-Aug) If you judge the quality of a restaurant by the number of guests wearing cowboy hats, then this charming place has got to be the best eatery in town. It's gussied up with chaps, a saddle or two and, of course, some horseshoes. Service is super-welcoming, and the biscuit with a side of gravy is lick-the-platter good.

Nana's Sandwich Shoppe SANDWICHES $
(☑928-684-5539; nanassandwichsaloon.com; 48 N Tegner St; sandwiches $7-9; ☉7:30am-3pm Mon-Sat; ☏) Order at the counter of this busy sandwich shop in the heart of Wickenburg. The God-fearing folks here load 'em up right, from the Mustang (hot pastrami, swiss cheese, house dressing, lettuce, tomato and red onion) to the Cowboy (roast beef, swiss cheese and horseradish).

❶ Information

Chamber of Commerce (☑928-684-5479; www.wickenburgchamber.com; 216 N Frontier St; ☉9am-5pm Mon-Fri, 10am-2pm Sat & Sun) Inside an 1895 Santa Fe Railroad depot; offers local info and a walking tour of downtown.

Prescott

☑928 / POP 41,899 / ELEV 5374FT
Fire raged through Whiskey Row in downtown Prescott (*press*-kit) on July 14, 1900. Quick-thinking locals managed to save the town's most prized possession: the 24ft-long Brunswick Bar that anchored the Palace Saloon. After lugging the solid oak bar across the street onto Courthouse Plaza, they grabbed their drinks and continued the party.

Prescott's cooperative spirit lives on, infusing the historic downtown and mountain-flanked surroundings with a welcoming vibe. This easy-to-explore city, which served as Arizona's first territorial capital and celebrated its 150th birthday in 2014, also charms visitors with its eye-catching Victorian buildings, breezy sidewalk cafes, tree-lined central plaza and burgeoning arts scene. But it's not all artsy gentility and Victorian airs. Whiskey Row hasn't changed much from the 1800s, and there's always a party within its scrappy saloons.

○ Sights

Historic Downtown AREA
Montezuma St west of Courthouse Plaza was once the infamous **Whiskey Row**, where 40 drinking establishments supplied suds to rough-hewn cowboys, miners and wastrels. In 1900 a devastating fire destroyed 25 saloons, five hotels and the red-light district, although several early buildings remain. Many are still bars to this day, mixed in with boutiques, galleries and restaurants.

In the infamous Palace Saloon (p137), rebuilt in 1901, a museum's worth of photographs and artifacts (including the Brunswick Bar, which survived the 1900 fire) are scattered throughout the bar and restaurant. A scene from the 1972 Steve McQueen movie *Junior Bonner* was filmed here, and a mural honoring the film covers an inside wall.

Whiskey Row also has a second identity as Gallery Row. Standout galleries here include **Arts Prescott Gallery** (☑928-776-7717; www.artsprescott.com; 134 S Montezuma St; ⊙10am-6pm), a collective of 24 local artists working in all media, and Van Gogh's Ear (p137), with metal art, fine woodwork and handmade leather shoes by nationally known artists for sale. On the last Friday evening of each month you can sample Prescott's gallery scene during the 4th Friday Art Walk (p136).

Dating from 1916 and anchoring the elm-shaded plaza, the columned **County Courthouse** is particularly pretty when sporting its lavish Christmas decorations. **Cortez St** runs along the east side of the plaza and is a hive of antique and collectible stores; visit **Ogg's Hogan** (☑928-443-9856; 111 N Cortez St), with its excellent selection of American Indian crafts and jewelry, mostly from Arizona tribes.

Buildings east and south of the plaza escaped the 1900 fire. Some are Victorian houses built by East Coast settlers and are markedly different from Southwestern adobe buildings. Look for the fanciest digs on Union St; **No 217** is the ancestral Goldwater family mansion (of Senator Barry Goldwater fame).

★**Sharlot Hall Museum** MUSEUM
(☑928-445-3122; www.sharlot.org; 415 W Gurley St; adult/child 13-17yr $9/5; ⊙10am-5pm Mon-Sat, noon-4pm Sun May-Sep, shorter hours Oct-Apr) Prescott's chief museum highlights the town's period as territorial capital (1863–67). The museum is named for its 1928 founder, pioneer woman Sharlot Hall (1870–1943). A small exhibit in the lobby commemorates her legacy. The most interesting of the nine buildings here is the 1864 **Governor's Mansion**, a log cabin where Hall lived in the attic until her death. It's filled with memorabilia, from guns and opium pipes to letters. The **Sharlot Hall Building** next door is the main exhibit hall.

Smoki Museum MUSEUM
(☑928-445-1230; www.smokimuseum.org; 147 N Arizona Ave; adult/senior/student/child $7/6/5/free; ⊙10am-4pm Mon-Sat, 1-4pm Sun) This pueblo-style museum displays Southwestern Indian objects – baskets, pottery, kachina dolls – dating from prehistoric times to the present. The museum works with area tribes to instill understanding and respect for the region's indigenous cultures, and Hopi, Apache, Yavapai, Paiute, Papago, Hualapai and other cultures are represented. Surprisingly, the 'Smoki Tribe' (pronounced 'smoke-eye') is a fiction – a philanthropic society created by white Prescottonians to raise money for the city's rodeo.

Phippen Museum MUSEUM
(☑928-778-1385; www.phippenartmuseum.org; 4701 Hwy 89 N; adult/student/child 12yr & under $7/5/free; ⊙10am-4pm Tue-Sat, 1-4pm Sun) The Phippen, located 7 miles north of Prescott en route to Jerome, is named after cowboy artist George Phippen. The museum hosts changing exhibits of celebrated Western artists, along with a permanent collection of painting, sculpture, photography and other media depicting the American West. On Memorial Day weekend the museum hosts the Western Art Show & Sale at Courthouse Plaza, which typically features more than 100 artists.

☆ Activities

The Prescott National Forest Office (p137) has information about local hikes, picnic areas and campgrounds. A day-use fee of $5 per vehicle is required – and payable – at many 'standard amenity sites' (picnic areas, trails and the like). Federal Interagency Passes, including the America the Beautiful pass, are also valid, and can be bought at the Forest Service office.

4th Friday Art Walk
WALKING

(✆928-237-9402; www.artthe4th.com; ⊙5-8pm spring & summer, 5-7pm fall & winter) Join this tour of 18 of Prescott's downtown galleries, on the last Friday evening of each month. Food, music and sociability make the aesthetic experience all the sweeter.

⚔ Festivals & Events

Prescott has a packed year-round events calendar. See www.visit-prescott.com for the full scoop.

★ World's Oldest Rodeo
RODEO

(✆928-445-3103; www.worldsoldestrodeo.com; 840 Rodeo Dr; tickets $12-25; ⊙Jul) While Payson to the east holds the title for having the world's longest continuously run rodeo, most acknowledge Prescott's event was the first professional rodeo. Busting broncos since 1888, it also involves a parade and an arts and crafts fair, and fills the week leading up to July 4.

🛏 Sleeping

Don't expect many lodging bargains in Prescott. Check out www.prescottbb.com for links to B&Bs and inns. Free dispersed camping is permitted in parts of the Bradshaw, Chino Valley and Verde Ranger Districts of Prescott National Forest. The Forest Service also manages nine campgrounds (sites free or $10 to $18). Two cabins are also available ($100 to $125). See www.fs.usda.gov/prescott.

The City of Prescott also manages 19 bookable **summer tent camping sites** (✆928-777-1122; www.cityofprescott.net/services/parks/rentals; Watson Lake Park Rd; camping incl parking fee $15; ⊙Thu-Mon Apr-early Oct) at Watson Lake Park.

Apache Lodge
MOTEL $

(✆928-445-1422; www.apachelodge.com; 1130 E Gurley St; d from $75; ❋🛜🐾) The well-worn Apache, around since 1946, won't impress domestic divas, but for everyone else the accommodating service and wallet-friendly price should be enough of a draw (although prices rise by as much as $70 on Friday and Saturday). The striking white exterior is pretty cool too. The pet fee is $20 per day.

★ Motor Lodge
BUNGALOW $$

(✆928-717-0157; www.themotorlodge.com; 503 S Montezuma St; r/ste/apt from $109/129/139; ❋🛜) Set three blocks south of Courthouse Plaza, the 12 snazzy bungalows here form a bright and welcoming horseshoe around a central driveway. Inside, the rooms, whimsical prints and comfy bedding add to the overall appeal, making the Motor Lodge a top choice. Rooms and bathrooms, built in 1936, can be snug, but many have kitchens and porches.

Grand Highland Hotel
BOUTIQUE HOTEL $$

(✆928-776-9963; www.grandhighlandhotel.com; 154 S Montezuma St; r/ste from $159/219; ❋🛜) The pedigree of this 12-room hotel in the heart of Whiskey Row stretches back to 1903, although the present, gracefully decorated manifestation emerged from the ashes of a 2012 fire. Themed rooms, from the 'Rodeo' to the 'Speak Easy,' spotlight regional history; while some are quite snug, the art-deco and art-nouveau decor is always inviting.

Hotel Vendome
BOUTIQUE HOTEL $$

(✆928-776-0900; www.vendomehotel.com; 230 S Cortez St; r from $129; ❋🛜) This dapper inn, dating from 1917, blends up-to-date style with period touches such as claw-foot tubs. The small Fremont Bar, beside the lobby, is a fun place to sip a mulled wine in winter, a sangria in summer, or an interesting draft beer anytime.

Hassayampa Inn
HISTORIC HOTEL $$

(✆928-778-9434; www.hassayampainn.com; 122 E Gurley St; d from $219; ❋🛜🐾) One of Arizona's most elegant hotels when it opened in 1927, the restored Hassayampa retains original furnishings, hand-painted wall decorations and the handsome on-site restaurant, the **Peacock Room & Bar** (✆928-777-9563; breakfast $10-11, lunch $13-15, dinner $24-32; ⊙7am-2pm & 4:30-9pm). The 67 rooms vary, but all boast quality linens and sturdy dark-wood furniture. Pets under 45lbs are no extra charge, and breakfast is included.

🍴 Eating

Hearty breakfast joints and hotel-restaurants are rounded out with some excellent Southwestern fare.

★ Raven Café
CAFE $

(✆928-717-0009; www.ravencafe.com; 142 N Cortez St; breakfast $9-10, lunch & dinner $11-13; ⊙7:30am-11pm Mon-Wed, 7:30am-midnight Thu-Sat, 8am-3pm Sun; 🛜🍽) This laid-back cafe-bar, Prescott's closest thing to a bohemian hot spot, changes its stripes from daytime coffee hangout to after-dark pub with live music and an overwhelming choice of 46 beers on tap. The mostly organic menu offers a mix of sandwiches, burgers, salads and a few 'big plates' – plus lots of vegetarian options, too.

The Local ✈   CAFE $

(☑928-237-4724; 520 W Sheldon St; mains $11-12; ☺7am-2.30pm; 🛜) Southwestern fare is the focus at this easy-to-miss daytime cafe in a nondescript side street. Their fantastic breakfasts are served all day – try the tamales with *pico de gallo*, eggs and avocado, and rest assured that nearly all the produce is organic, ethical and locally sourced. Baked treats – made fresh in-house each day – are also excellent.

★ Iron Springs Cafe   AMERICAN, CAJUN $$

(☑928-443-8800; www.ironspringscafe.com; 1501 Iron Springs Rd; brunch & lunch $11-13, dinner $16-20; ☺11am-8pm Wed-Sat, 9am-2pm Sun) Cajun and Southwestern specialties mingle delightfully inside this former train station – from the N'awlins muffuletta with sliced ham, salami and mortadella to the crab cakes and thick, spicy sausage and okra gumbo, it's all delicious, and served with real warmth. Train decor, colorful blankets and easy-bantering waitstaff enliven three tiny rooms. It's open for brunch on Sundays only.

🍷 Drinking & Nightlife

Prescott likes to have a good time. Live music can be enjoyed at clubs downtown on the weekends, while it's always fun on Whiskey Row. St Patrick's Day sees a corporate-sponsored pub crawl through downtown.

Palace Saloon   BAR

(☑928-541-1996; www.historicpalace.com; 120 S Montezuma St; ☺11am-10pm Sun-Thu, to 11pm Fri & Sat) Push open the swinging doors and time-warp to 19th-century Whiskey Row days, back when the Earp brothers would knock 'em back with Doc Holliday at the huge Brunswick Bar. A scene from the 1972 Steve McQueen movie *Junior Bonner* was filmed here, and a mural honoring the film covers an inside wall. Dinner shows include tribute bands and historical plays.

Matt's Saloon   BAR

(☑928-778-9914; www.mattssaloon.com; 112 S Montezuma St; ☺11am-2am Mon-Sat, to midnight Sun) This dark beer barn occupies a 1901 store that became a Prohibition speakeasy in the 1920s, a legitimate saloon in 1934, and the honky-tonk palace it is today in the early '60s. Buck Owens and Waylon Jennings used to perform live back then; today it's still Prescott's kickiest two-stepping place. Come for live music on Friday and Saturday nights.

Bird Cage Saloon   BAR

(☑928-778-9921; www.birdcagesaloon.com; 160 S Montezuma St; ☺9am-2am) The original Bird Cage Saloon – famous for its collection of taxidermied birds – burned down in 2012, but came back bigger and better a year later, just south of its old location. A few of the old birds survived, and you'll find them, together with the surviving back bar, ready for business. There's live rock and blues on Friday and Saturday.

🛍 Shopping

Van Gogh's Ear   ARTS & CRAFTS

(☑928-776-1080; www.vgegallery.com; 156B S Montezuma St; ☺10am-6pm) Deep pockets are required at Van Gogh's Ear, where you can snap up John Lutes' ethereal glass bowls, Dale O'Dell's stunning photographs, or works by three dozen other nationally known artists, many making their home in the Prescott area.

ⓘ Information

Visitor Center (☑800-266-7534, 928-445-2000; prescott.org; 117 W Goodwin St; ☺9am-5pm Mon-Fri, 10am-2pm Sat & Sun) Information and brochures galore, including a handy walking-tour pamphlet of Prescott.

Prescott National Forest Office (☑928-443-8000; www.fs.usda.gov/prescott; 344 S Cortez St; ☺8am-4:30pm Mon-Fri) Info on camping, hiking and more in the surrounding national forest.

Post Office (☑928-778-7411; 101 W Goodwin St; ☺9:30am-12:30pm & 1-4pm Mon-Fri) There's another **branch** (☑800-275-8777; 442 Miller Valley Rd; ☺8:30am-5pm Mon-Fri, 10am-2pm Sat).

Police (☑928-777-1900, emergency 911; 222 S Marina St)

Yavapai Regional Medical Center West (☑928-445-2700; www.yrmc.org; 1003 Willow Creek Rd; ☺24hr emergency room)

ⓘ Getting There & Away

The tiny **Prescott Municipal Airport** (☑928-777-1114; www.prcairport.com; 6500 Mac Curdy Dr) is about 9 miles north of town on Hwy 89; Great Lakes Airlines offers daily connections with Los Angeles, and less regular ones with Denver.

It's 100 miles south on AZ 69 and I-17 to Phoenix, and 96 miles north on the AZ 69, AZ 169 and I-17 to Flagstaff.

Jerome

📞 928 / POP 456 / ELEV 5000FT

This stubborn hamlet, which enjoys one of the most spectacular views in Arizona, is wedged into steep Cleopatra Hill. Once home to the fertile United Verde Mine, and the copper-rich Little Daisy Mine, the 'Wickedest Town in the West' once teemed with brothels, saloons and opium dens.

When the mines petered out in 1953, Jerome's population plummeted from 15,000 to just 50 stalwarts, practically overnight. Then came the '60s, and scores of hippies with an eye for the town's latent charm. They snapped up crumbling buildings for pennies, more or less restored them and, along the way, injected a dose of artistic spirit that survives to this day inside the numerous galleries scattered across town. A bohemian *joie de vivre* permeates the place, and at times it seems like every shop is peddling wine, art and good times.

◉ Sights

If you're interested in Jerome's unique history, take an hour to stroll past some of its most historic buildings. Start at the corner of Main St and Jerome Ave at the Connor Hotel, the town's first solid-stone lodging. From there, a leg-stretching climb leads to the Jerome Grand Hotel, the one-time home of the United Verde Hospital, which served miners and the community between 1927 and 1951. Known for its ghosts, it's actually a relaxing place to enjoy expansive views of the crimson-gold rocks of Sedona and the Verde Valley.

Heading back downhill, consider the fact that there are 88 miles of tunnel under your feet. Combine these tunnels with steep hills and periodic dynamiting, and it's easy to see why buildings in Jerome regularly collapsed, caught fire or migrated downhill. The **Sliding Jail**, southeast of the Chamber of Commerce visitor center (p140), has moved 225ft from its original 1927 location.

The most memorable aspect of Jerome is its panoramic views of the Verde Valley, embracing the fiery red rocks of Sedona and culminating in the snowy San Francisco Peaks. Sunsets? Ridiculously romantic, trust us.

Jerome State Historic Park   MUSEUM
(📞928-634-5381; www.azstateparks.com; 100 Douglas Rd; adult/child 7-13yr $7/4; ⊙8:30am-5pm) This state park preserves the 1916 mansion of eccentric mining mogul Jimmy 'Rawhide' Douglas, who developed the Little Daisy Mine. An interesting variety of exhibits offers insight into the town's mining heyday. Don't miss the cool 3D model of Jerome and the mining tunnels running below it. The folksy video is also worth watching before you explore the museum.

Audrey Headframe Park   MINE
(www.jeromehistoricalsociety.com; 55 Douglas Rd; ⊙8am-5pm) FREE At this small park, run by the Jerome Historical Society, bold travelers can stand on a glass platform under Arizona's largest wooden headframe, and overlooking a 1918 mining shaft. The inky black tunnel drops 1900ft, which is longer than the Empire State Building by 650ft!

Mine Museum   MUSEUM
(📞928-634-5477; www.jeromehistoricalsociety.com; 200 Main St; adult/senior/child 12yr & under $2/1/free; ⊙9am-6pm, shorter hours in winter) Two halves of a 4-ton flywheel mark the entry to this small but informative museum that highlights Jerome's hardscrabble past. Displays include a claustrophobic mining cage, a Chinese laundry machine, a story about a beloved prostitute (worth a read!) and a wall dedicated to an old-school sheriff who gunned down three vigilantes on Main St, then went home and ate lunch – without mentioning to his wife what had happened. The pistol used to mete out justice is proudly displayed.

🏃 Activities

Jerome Art Walk   CULTURAL
(www.jeromeartwalk.com; ⊙5-8pm 1st Sat of month) During this 26-gallery art walk, a free shuttle runs between the high school, downtown galleries and the Jerome Grand Hotel. Some galleries have openings, live music and refreshments.

🛏 Sleeping

Historic hotels, cozy inns and a few B&Bs are your choices in Jerome, and you won't find a single national chain. In fact, most accommodations are as charmingly eccentric as the town itself. (And many are home to a ghost or two.)

Mile High Inn   INN $
(📞928-634-5094; www.jeromemilehighinn.com; 309 Main St; r from $85; ❊🛜) Rooms are dapper and a bit pert at this snug B&B, which once had a stint as a bordello. The seven remodeled rooms have unusual furnishings, and supposedly the ghost of the former madam haunts the room dubbed Lariat &

Jerome

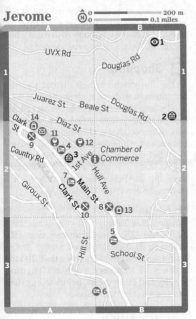

Lace – which is also home to a climb-up lodgepole bed. A full breakfast is served at the downstairs restaurant. Four rooms have shared bathrooms.

Jerome Grand Hotel　　　　　HOTEL **$$**
(☑928-634-8200;　　www.jeromegrandhotel.com; 200 Hill St; r/ste $225/325; ✳🗢) This former hospital looks like the perfect setting for a sequel to *The Shining*. Built in 1926 for the mining community, the sturdy fortress plays up its unusual history. The halls are filled with relics of the past, from incinerator chutes to patient call lights. There's even a key-operated Otis elevator. Victorian-style rooms are more traditionally furnished.

Ghost City B&B　　　　　B&B **$$**
(☑888-634-4678; www.ghostcityinn.com; 541 Main St; r from $105; ✳🗢) This 1885 timber boarding house, badly damaged after an illicit still on the 2nd floor exploded in the 1930s, is now a quirky and delightful B&B. Each room has a different theme, from the cowboy-inspired Western room to the Victorian-era Verde View (with killer views, naturally), and a grinning skeleton greets guests from the front porch.

Connor Hotel　　　　　HISTORIC HOTEL **$$**
(☑800-523-3554, 928-634-5006; www.connorhotel.com; 160 Main St; r from $105; ✳🗢) The 12 restored rooms convincingly capture the Victorian period, with such touches as pedestal sinks, flowery wallpaper and pressed-tin ceilings. It's above the popular Spirit Room (p140), which has live music on weekends; rooms 1 to 4 get most of the bar noise.

🍴 Eating

Jerome is a gourmand's delight, and you'll probably be happy at any of the restaurants in town. Enjoy!

Flatiron Café　　　　　CAFE **$**
(☑928-634-2733;　　www.theflatironjerome.com; 416 Main St; breakfast $8-10, lunch $11-13; ⊙8:30am-3:30pm Wed-Mon) This tiny cafe packs a big, delicious punch. Savor a scrambled-egg quesadilla with hatch chiles, beans and *pico de gallo* at breakfast, or a vegan sandwich with lemon-cumin chickpeas, fennel, sprouts and other goodies at lunch. Grab one of three inside tables, or head across the street to the small patio. It also has excellent coffee.

Grapes　　　　　AMERICAN **$$**
(☑928-639-8477; www.grapesjerome.com; 111 Main St; lunch & dinner $11-17; ⊙11am-8pm Sun-Thu, to 9pm Fri & Sat) Wine newbies and grape connoisseurs are equally happy at this breezy, brick-walled bistro that serves ahi tuna burgers and 10 different gourmet

pizzas. Wine selections come with a bin number, helpfully paired with food on the menu, and from 5pm to 9pm on weekdays all wines by the glass are $5.

Haunted Hamburger
BURGERS **$$**

(☑928-634-0554; www.thehauntedhamburger. com; 410 Clark St; mains $5-22; ◷11am-9pm; 🕸) This beloved hamburger joint, perched high on a hill and often packed, has only grown in popularity since opening in 1994. Come here for awesome views, solid burgers and your choice of local draft beers and cocktails, but be prepared to wait when Jerome is busy. Is it haunted? They say the the spirit here likes hammers.

★ Asylum Restaurant
AMERICAN **$$$**

(☑928-639-3197; www.asylumrestaurant.com; 200 Hill St; lunch $12-14, dinner $26-28; ◷11am-3pm & 5-9pm; 🕸) Deep-red walls, lazily twirling fans, gilded artwork and captivating views make the venerable dining room at the Jerome Grand Hotel (p139) one of the state's top fine diners. The wine list has won awards, and we've heard Senator John McCain loves it here.

🍷 Drinking & Nightlife

New wine-tasting rooms have opened in and around Jerome, adding another level of fun.

Cellar 433
WINE BAR

(☑928-634-7033; www.cellar433.com; 240 Hull Ave; ◷11am-6pm Thu-Sun, to 5pm Mon-Wed) Showcasing wines from Willcox, southeast of Tucson and now a designated American Viticultural Area, Cellar 433 is a split-level tasting room (wine tastings $10 to $12) with arresting Verde Valley views and a convivial vibe. If you've settled in to taste a dozen, you may need to whistle up a cheese plate to sustain you.

Spirit Room
BAR

(☑928-634-8809; www.spiritroom.com; 166 Main St; ◷11am-1am) If you want to let your hair down in Jerome, the Spirit Room – the in-house bar of the historic Connor Hotel (p139) – is the place. Whether you sip a pint at the bar, shoot pool, strike up a conversation with (friendly) Harley riders or study the bordello-scene mural, you'll have a fine time at this dark, old-time saloon.

Caduceus Cellars
WINE BAR

(☑928-639-9463; www.caduceus.org; 158 Main St; ◷11am-6pm Sun-Thu, to 8pm Sat) The public outlet for the winery owned by Maynard James Keenan, lead singer of Tool, Caduceus

makes for a nice, vinous reward after struggling up Cleopatra Hill (wine tastings $9 to $13). It also makes one of Jerome's best espressos, from 8am to noon every day.

🛍 Shopping

In the downtown business district, galleries are mixed in with souvenir shops.

The handsome **New State Motors Building** (Main St; ◷11am-5pm) houses a quirky mix of music shops, glass-blowers and fortune tellers, while downhill, the **Old Jerome High School** harbors artist studios and galleries. Many are open to the public most days, but the best time to visit them all is during the Jerome Art Walk (p138).

★ Jerome Artists Cooperative Gallery
ARTS & CRAFTS

(☑928-639-4276; www.jeromecoop.com; 502 N Main St; ◷10am-6pm) Need a gift? At this bright and scenic gallery more than 30 local artists work in pottery, woodwork, painting, jewelry and other media, before selling their creations at very fair prices.

ℹ Information

Chamber of Commerce (☑928-634-2900; www.jeromechamber.com; 310 Hull Ave; ◷11am-3pm Thu-Mon) Offers tourist information.

Police (☑928-634-8992, emergency 911; 305 Main St)

Post Office (☑928-634-8241; 120 Main St; ◷8:15am-noon & 12:30-2:45pm Mon-Fri)

Cottonwood

☑928 / POP 11,818 / ELEV 3300-3900FT

Founded in 1879 and booming by the 1920s, Cottonwood is now enjoying something of a renaissance. For decades the city was one of the less interesting communities in central Arizona – simply a good place to find budget lodging near Sedona. But today? Cottonwood, particularly its walkable Old Town district, is buzzing with new restaurants, stylish wine-tasting rooms and an eclectic array of indie shops. And, so far, it remains a cheap and convenient base for regional exploring. Located in the Verde Valley, it's only 16 miles from Sedona and 9 miles from Jerome.

The old mining town of **Clarkdale** sits just off Hwy 89A between Jerome and Cottonwood. Clarkdale was a company town built in 1914 to process ore from the mines in nearby Jerome.

⊙ Sights & Activities

Tuzigoot National Monument RUINS
(☎928-634-5564; www.nps.gov/tuzi; adult/child 15yr & under $10/free; ⊙8am-5pm; P⛟) Atop a ridge due east of Clarkdale, Tuzigoot National Monument – a Sinaguan pueblo like nearby Montezuma Castle (p132) – is believed to have been inhabited from AD 1000 to 1400. At its peak as many as 225 people lived in its 110 rooms. Stop by the visitor center to examine tools, pottery and other artifacts dug up from the ruin, then trudge up a short, steep trail (not suitable for wheelchairs) for memorable views of the Verde River Valley. The entry fee, good for a seven-day period, also gets you entry to Montezuma Castle.

Dead Horse Ranch State Park STATE PARK
(☎928-634-5283; www.azstateparks.com; 675 Dead Horse Ranch Rd; day use per vehicle/bicycle or pedestrian $7/3; ⊙visitors center 8am-5pm; P⛟) The Verde River runs past this 423-acre park, which offers picnicking, fishing, 20-plus miles of multi-use trails (for bikes, horses and hikers) and a playground. Bird-watchers will want to make the short trek to the bird-watching stand at **Tavasci Marsh** in hopes of a sighting of the least bittern, the Yuma clapper rail or the belted kingfisher.

Verde Canyon Railroad RAIL
(☎928-639-0010,800-293-7245; www.verdecanyonrr.com; 300 N Broadway, Clarkdale; coach adult/senior/child $65/60/45, 1st class all passengers $90) From Clarkdale, 4 miles northwest of Cottonwood, vintage FP7 engines pull climate-controlled cabooses on leisurely four-hour narrated round-trips into the splendid canyon north of Cottonwood Pass. Trains leave at 1pm (and sometimes 9am and 2:30pm), but days of the week vary. Check the schedule online and make reservations.

Trail Horse Adventures HORSEBACK RIDING
(☎866-958-7245; www.trailhorseadventures.com; rides $65-129; ⛟) In Dead Horse Ranch State Park, Trail Horse Adventures offers rides lasting one to 2½ hours. There's also an option for a three-hour lunch ride ($129).

🛏 Sleeping

Cottonwood's sprawling new town is a land of motels, mostly of the chain variety, but prices are as low as you'll find in the area.

Dead Horse Ranch State Park Campground CAMPGROUND $
(☎520-586-2283; www.azstateparks.com; 675 Dead Horse Ranch Rd; tent/RV/cabin from $20/30/60; ⊙reservations 8am-5pm)

Overnighters to Dead Horse Ranch State Park can choose between cabins or campsites, some with hookups, and enjoy hot showers. Camping reservations are available online, as well as by phone ($5 reservation fee per site).

Pines Motel MOTEL $
(☎928-634-9975; www.azpinesmotel.com; 920 S Camino Real; r/ste from $90/100; ❄️🛜🛗🐾) This two-story motel, on a hill with nice views, offers minisuites with kitchenettes, in addition to standard king and queen units. Pets are an additional $20 the first night, then $5 each night after that. Guest laundry and electric-car charging are available.

View Motel MOTEL $
(☎928-634-7581; www.theviewmotel.com; 818 S Main St; r from $65; ❄️🛜🛗🐾) Set uphill from the main drag, this professionally run motel delivers the views its name promises. It's an older property, but the refurbished and renovated rooms are very clean and come with a refrigerator and microwave. A few have kitchenettes, dogs are $10 extra per night and it offers smoking and nonsmoking rooms.

🍴 Eating

Bocce Pizzeria PIZZA $
(☎928-202-3597; www.boccecottonwood.com; 1060 N Main St; pizza $13-14; ⊙4-10pm Mon-Fri, noon-10pm Sat, noon-4pm Sun; 🛜) This hip gourmet pizzeria goes the extra mile to ensure authenticity: the chef earned her dough-stretching stripes in Naples, the oven burns wood, the mozzarella's stretched in-house and even the flour is imported. Craft beers, Verde Valley wines, a tasteful soundtrack and a sleek tile-and-timber interior round out a very appealing package.

Crema Craft Kitchen & Bar AMERICAN $
(☎928-649-5785; www.cremacafe89a.com; 917 N Main St; breakfast $10-11, lunch $13-15; ⊙7am-2pm; 🛜) In recent years Crema has morphed from a low-key coffee shop with pastries, sandwiches and gelato to a full-on 'craft kitchen' with an impressive line-up of gourmet breakfast and lunch sandwiches, fancy burritos, ingredient-packed salads and a full license. Decor is sleek olive, the staff are upbeat and the small-batch gelato is still as delicious as ever.

Blazin' M Ranch AMERICAN $$
(☎800-937-8643, 928-634-0334; www.blazinm.com; 1875 Mabery Ranch Rd; dinner & show adult/senior/child 3-12yr $40/35/20; ⊙site opens from 5pm Wed-Sat Feb-Dec; ⛟) Near Dead Horse

Ranch State Park, here you can yee-haw with the rest of them at chuckwagon suppers – in the dinner barn – paired with rootin' tootin' cowboy entertainment. Opening times may vary seasonally, but generally dinner is 6:30pm, and the show an hour later.

Drinking & Nightlife

The Verde Valley's burgeoning wine scene is the impetus behind a cluster of tasting rooms strung along the Old Town's main drag.

Merkin Vineyards Osteria　　WINE BAR
(☑928-639-1001; merkinvineyardsosteria.com; 1001 N Main St; ⊙11am-9pm; 🐾) Complementing 100% Arizona wines with top-notch Arizona produce (the eponymous winery's high-elevation varietals come largely from fruit grown in Wilcox, AZ, while local suppliers provide the basis of the Italian menu), this excellent osteria is further distinguished by its owner, Maynard James Keenan, Tool lead singer and winemaker.

Burning Tree Cellars　　WINE BAR
(☑928-649-8733; burningtreecellars.com; 1040 N Main St; ⊙noon-7pm Sun-Thu, to 10pm Fri & Sat) Boutique, small-batch Arizona wines are the focus of this stylish, welcoming tasting room. Come on Friday or Saturday for live music.

❶ Information

Chamber of Commerce (☑928-634-7593; www.cottonwoodchamberaz.com; 1010 S Main St; ⊙9am-5pm Mon-Fri) Information on Cottonwood, Clarkdale and the Verde Valley.

Sedona

☑928 / POP 10.388 / ELEV 4500FT

Nestled amid striking red sandstone formations at the south end of the 16-mile Oak Creek Canyon, Sedona attracts spiritual seekers, artists and healers, as well as day-trippers from Phoenix trying to escape the oppressive heat. Many New Age types believe that this area is the center of vortexes (not 'vortices' here in Sedona) that radiate the Earth's power, and you'll find all sorts of alternative medicines and practices on display. More tangibly, the surrounding canyons offer outstanding hiking, biking, swimming and camping.

The town itself bustles with art galleries and expensive gourmet restaurants. In summer the traffic and the crowds can be heavy. Regionally, Oak Creek Canyon begins north of Uptown Sedona; the Village of Oak Creek, however, is south of the city.

◉ Sights

Several vortexes (swirling energy centers where the Earth's power is said to be strongly felt) are located in Sedona's Red Rock Mountains. The best-known are **Bell Rock**, Cathedral Rock, Airport Mesa and Boynton Canyon (p144).

★**Red Rock State Park**　　PARK
(☑928-282-6907; azstateparks.com/red-rock; 4050 Red Rock Loop Rd; adult $7, child 7-13yr $4, 6yr & under free; ⊙8am-5pm, visitor center 9am-4:30pm; 🚻) Not to be confused with Slide Rock State Park, this 286-acre park includes an environmental education center, picnic areas and 5 miles of well-marked, interconnecting trails in a riparian environment amid gorgeous red-rock country. Trails range from flat creekside saunters to moderate climbs to scenic ridges. Ranger-led activities include nature and bird walks. Swimming in the creek is prohibited. It's 9 miles west of downtown Sedona off Hwy 89A, on the eastern edge of the 15-mile Lime Kiln Trail.

★**Chapel of the Holy Cross**　　CHURCH
(☑928-282-4069, 888-242-7359; www.chapeloftheholycross.com; 780 Chapel Rd; ⊙9am-5pm Dec-Feb, to 6pm Mar-Nov) **FREE** Situated between spectacular, statuesque natural stone columns 3 miles south of Sedona, this 1956 Roman Catholic chapel soars from the rock like a slice of the land itself. Creator Marguerite Brunswig Staude followed the tradition of Frank Lloyd Wright – its wall of glass and the perch it occupies offer a dramatic perspective on the landscape, and the architecture is stunning. Though there are no traditional services, the church offers a 'Taize prayer service' on Mondays at 5pm.

Palatki Heritage Site　　ARCHAEOLOGICAL SITE
(☑reservations 928-282-3854; www.fs.usda.gov; Red Rock or Federal Interagency Pass $5; ⊙9:30am-3pm) **FREE** Thousand-year-old Sinagua cliff dwellings and rock art are good-enough reasons to brave the seven or so miles of dirt road leading to this enchantingly located archaeological site on the edge of the wilderness. There's a small visitor center and three easy trails suitable for strollers, but not wheelchairs. Parties taking the trail up to the dwellings themselves are limited to 10 at a time; phone to reserve in advance. The Honanki Heritage Site, also Sinaguan, lies a further 3 miles north.

Honanki Heritage Site　　ARCHAEOLOGICAL SITE
(www.fs.usda.gov; Red Rock Pass $5; ⊙9:30am-3pm) Honanki is another impressive

vestige of the Sinaguan culture, responsible for the construction of this pueblo, as well as Montezuma Castle (p132), Tuzigoot (p141) and other sites in the years between AD 1000 and 1400. This site includes significant cliff dwellings and petroglyphs, and was subsequently inhabited by Yavapai and Apache people.

Sedona Arts Center   ARTS CENTER
(☑ 928-282-3809, 888-954-4442; www.sedonaarts center.com; 15 Art Barn Rd; ⊙ 10am-5pm) Founded in the 1950s in a former apple-packing barn, this arts center features changing exhibits of local and regional artists, a gift shop and classes in performing and visual arts. It also stages a variety of cultural events like the Sedona Plein Air Festival – featuring local artists in an outdoor festival.

Amitabha Stupa & Peace Park   BUDDHIST SITE
(☑ 877-788-7229; www.stupas.org; 2650 Pueblo Dr; donations accepted; ⊙ sunrise-sunset) This consecrated Buddhist shrine and park is set quite stunningly in West Sedona amid piñon and juniper pine and the ubiquitous rocks. A few steps below the 36ft Amitabha Stupa look for the 6ft White Tara Stupa. Heading along Hwy 89A west from the Y, turn right on Andante Dr, left on Pueblo Dr, then head up the gated trail on your right.

 Activities

Scenic Drives
The easiest scenic drive is also one of the best: the **Red Rock Scenic Byway** (red-rockscenicbyway.com). This National Scenic Byway and All-American Road tracks Hwy 179 from I-17 (exit 298) for 7.5 miles, ending just north of the Village of Oak Creek in a smash-bang, pull-over, grab-your-camera explosion of red-rock impressiveness.

In Sedona, the short drive up paved **Airport Rd** opens up to panoramic views of the valley. At sunset, the rocks blaze a psychedelic red and orange. **Airport Mesa** (Airport Rd) is the closest vortex to town.

Any time is a good time to drive the winding 7-mile **Red Rock Loop Rd**, which is all paved except for one short section and gives access to Red Rock State Park as well as **Red Rock Crossing/Crescent Moon Recreation Area** (Upper Red Rock Loop Rd; day-use per vehicle $10, cash only; ⊕). A small army of photographers usually gathers at the crossing at sunset to record the dramatic light show unfolding on iconic **Cathedral Rock**, another vortex. There's also swimming in

Oak Creek. Access is via Upper Red Rock Loop Rd off Hwy 89A, 4 miles west of the Y.

For a breathtaking loop, follow Dry Creek Rd to **Boynton Pass Rd**, turn left, then left again at Forest Rd 525. It's mostly paved but there are lumpy, unpaved sections. The route passes two of the most memorable rock formations, Vultee Arch and Devil's Bridge. Extend this trip by turning right on FR 525 and taking in the Palatki Heritage Site.

Hiking & Cycling
Hiking and **mountain-biking** trails criss-cross the red-rock country surrounding Sedona and the woods and meadows of green Oak Creek Canyon. The free and very helpful *Recreation Guide to Your National Forest* is available online from the US Forest Service (www.fs.fed.us) and at visitor centers and ranger stations. It describes hiking and biking trails for all skill levels and includes a summary of scenic drives. One deservedly popular hiking trail in Oak Creek Canyon is the 3.4-mile one-way **West Fork Trail** (☑ 928-527-3600; Hwy 89A, Oak Creek Canyon; day-use $10), which follows the creek – the canyon walls rise more than 200ft in places. Wander up as far as you want, splash around at the numerous creek crossings and turn back when you've had enough. A sign notes the trail's official end. The trailhead lies about 3 miles north of Slide Rock, in the Call of the Canyon Recreation Area.

Rent bikes and buy coffee at **Bike & Bean** (☑ 928-284-0210; www.bike-bean.com; 30 Bell Rock Plaza, Village of Oak Creek; bike rental per hr/day from $19/55; ⊙ 8am-5pm) in the Village of Oak Creek, not far from the bike-friendly **Bell Rock Pathway**.

Oak Creek holds several good swimming holes. If Slide Rock is too crowded, check out Grasshopper Point (p149) a few miles south. Southwest of Sedona you can splash around and enjoy splendid views of Cathedral Rock at Red Rock Crossing/Crescent Moon Recreation Area.

For an easy hike that leads almost immediately to gorgeous views, check out Airport Mesa. From Hwy 89A, follow Airport Dr about half a mile up the side of the mesa to a small parking turnout on your left. From here, the short **Sedona View Trail** leads to an awe-inspiring view of Courthouse Butte and, after a brief scramble, a sweeping 360-degree panorama of the city and its flanking red rocks. This is one of Sedona's vortex sites. If you can, start this hike before 8:30am, when the parking lot starts to fill up. The Sedona View Trail links onto the longer **Airport Loop Trail**.

Sedona

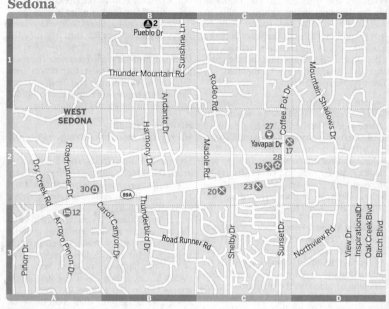

Sedona

Another stunningly beautiful place to hike is through the red rock of **Boynton Canyon**, where some have reported experiencing the antics of energetic spirits (who may not necessarily want them trekking through)! For additional details see www. redrockcountry.org.

Hi Line Trail   MOUNTAIN BIKING
(Hwy 179, off Yavapai Vista parking lot) This black-diamond, single-track, mountain-bike trail runs along the ridge to a great view of Cathedral Rock. It also makes a beautiful hike; 3 miles one-way.

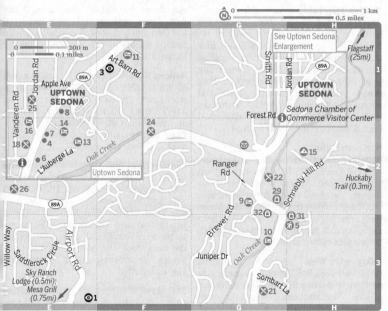

Hike House
HIKING

(📞928-282-5820; www.thehikehouse.com; 431 Hwy 179, Suite B-1; ⏱9am-6pm Mon-Sat, to 5pm Sun) This forward-thinking hiking store offers an 'energy cafe,' online resources such as a trail finder and 'Grand Canyon Planning Station,' gear and maps. You'll also find experienced staff who have tackled all of Sedona's trails and detailed guides, and are happy to pass on their knowledge.

Huckaby Trail
HIKING

Just north of town on Hwy 89, from the signed trailhead a few miles up from the roundabout on Schnebley Rd to Midgley Bridge, this trail cuts across the desert scrub, along a ridge with panoramic views of Sedona, and down to Oak Creek. It's a great one-way hike if you can arrange a pick-up at Midgley Bridge.

Horseback Riding

M Diamond Ranch
HORSEBACK RIDING

(📞928-300-6466; www.sedonahorsebackrides. com; 3255 FR 618; 1hr trail ride adult/child $75/55, ride & cookout adult/child $120/105; ⏱Mon-Sat; 👫) This working cattle ranch takes small groups of people on trail rides through eye-catching countryside. Staff will pick you up and drop you off from your Sedona hotel, and for $275, you can stay overnight in the six-person lodge.

🕝 Tours

Sedona's scenery is the backdrop for many a rugged adventure, and numerous tour operators stand by to take you into the heart of it. Bumpy off-road jeep tours are popular, but it can be confusing distinguishing one company from the next. One thing to check is backcountry accessibility, as the companies have permits for different routes and sites. If there's a specific rock formation or region you'd like to explore, be sure to ask. Some companies expect a minimum of four participants and charge more per person for smaller groups. Many offer discounted tour prices if you reserve online.

Two trolley companies, both with offices in Uptown, provide narrated tours of Sedona. The **Sedona Trolley** (📞928-282-4211; www.sedonatrolley.com; 276 N Hwy 89A, Suite B; adult/child $15/10; ⏱9am-6pm) runs two different 55-minute tours. Tour A stops at Tlaquepaque Village and the Chapel of the Holy Cross and Tour B heads west to Boynton and Long Canyons. The **Red Rock Magic Trolley** (📞928-821-6706; www.redrockmagictrolley.com; 252 N Hwy 89A; adult $15-25, child $8-12) offers tours from 55 to 85 minutes, one heading to Boynton Canyon, one to the Chapel of the Holy Cross and another to Bell Rock.

★**Pink Jeep Tours** DRIVING
(☎800-873-3662, 928-282-5000; www.pinkjeep
tours.com; 204 N Hwy 89A; ☺6am-10pm; ♿)
It seems like this veteran of Sedona's tour
industry has jeeps everywhere, buzzing
around like pink flies. But once you join a
tour, you'll see why they're so popular. Pink
runs 15 thrilling, bone-rattling off-road and
adventure tours around Sedona, with most
lasting from about two hours (adult/child
from $59/54) to four hours (from $154/139).

Northern Light
Balloon Expeditions BALLOONING
(☎800-230-6222, 928-282-2274; www.northern
lightballoon.com) Spend about one hour
floating above red-rock country at sunrise
($220 per person) then enjoy a champagne
picnic back on solid ground. Northern
Light can pick you up at your Sedona hotel,
30 minutes before sunrise.

A Day in the West TOURS
(☎800-973-3662, 928-282-4320; www.adayinthe
west.com; 252 N Hwy 89A; ♿) The 'pardners'
of this Western-themed jeep tour company offer a combo jeep tour and horseback ride with a Western-style dinner and
show (adult/child $190/170); a jeep and
winery trip ($129/45); and several back-
country-only trips (from $59/47). Online
reservations can attract a 20% discount.

Sedona Star Gazing TOURS
(☎928-853-9778; www.eveningskytours.com;
Verde Valley School Rd, Village of Oak Creek;
☺closed mid-Jul–mid-Aug, start times vary seasonally) Sedona is an International Dark
Sky City: take advantage of its annual average of 300 dry, clear nights to view planets,
stars, galaxies and nebulae with the naked
eye and through large telescopes. Tours (90
minutes) cost adult/child $60/35.

✯ Festivals & Events

Sedona International Film Festival FILM
(☎928-282-1177; www.sedonafilmfestival.org;
☺Feb/Mar) The Sedona International Film
Festival features art and documentary
films and film-inspired special events.

Sedona Arts Festival ART
(☎928-282-1177; www.sedonaartsfestival.org;
☺Oct) Fine arts, crafts and nonstop entertainment in early October.

🛏 Sleeping

Sedona is rich with beautiful B&Bs, creekside cabins and full-service resorts. Rates
at chain motels range from $100 to $150,
reasonable by Sedona standards. Apart
from these options and some beautiful
but ferociously contested campsites, chichi
Sedona doesn't have many choices for the
budget traveler.

Rancho Sedona RV Park CAMPGROUND $
(☎928-282-7255, 888-641-4261; www.rancho
sedona.com; 135 Bear Wallow Lane; RV sites
$37-77; 🛜🐾) Offers a laundry, showers
and more than 60 RV sites under cottonwood and sycamore trees, most with full
hookups. No tent camping.

Lantern Light Inn INN $$
(☎928-282-3419; www.lanternlightinn.com;
3085 W Hwy 89A; r/guesthouse $159/309; 🛜)
Kris and Ed, the lovely couple running
this small inn in West Sedona, will put
you right at ease. The antique-filled rooms
range from small and cozy, overlooking
the back deck and garden, to the huge
guesthouse out back, and all feel comfort-
ably overstuffed.

Star Motel MOTEL $$
(☎928-282-3641; www.starmotelsedona.com;
295 Jordan Rd; r/ste from $110/180; 🛜) This
10-room, 1950s-era motel in Uptown is one
of Sedona's best deals. Rooms are simple,
with a few artsy touches, but what we like
most is the hospitality. Plus the beds are
comfortable, the showers strong and the
refrigerators handy for chilling those sunset beers. Shops, eateries and the visitor
center are just outside your door.

Inn Above Oak Creek B&B $$
(☎928-282-7896; www.innaboveoakcreek.
com; 556 Hwy 179; d/ste from $150/350; ❄🛜)
Though this bright and immaculate place
sits on Hwy 179, it backs onto Oak Creek,
and the Pottery Barn–styled rooms are
peaceful and lovely. Some face the water
and have fireplaces and Jacuzzis, while the
tiny 'Bonus Room' ($85) is excellent value.

Cozy Cactus B&B $$
(☎800-788-2082, 928-284-0082; www.cozy
cactus.com; 80 Canyon Circle Dr, Village of Oak
Creek; d from $210; ❄🛜) This five-room
B&B, run by Carrie and Mark, works
well for adventure-loving types – the
Southwest-style house bumps up against
Agave Trail, and is just around the bend
from cyclist-friendly Bell Rock Pathway.
Post-adventuring, get comfy beside the
firepit on the back patio, perfect for wildlife-watching and stargazing, and enjoy
the three-course breakfast that awaits you
the next morning.

Sky Ranch Lodge   MOTEL $$

(📞888-708-6400, 928-282-6400; www.skyranch
lodge.com; 1105 Airport Rd; d from $218;
❄🛜♨🐾) At the top of winding Airport Rd,
Sky Ranch boasts spectacular views of the
town and surrounding red-rock country. It's
a quiet respite from Sedona's peak-season
hubbub, with spacious motel rooms scattered among six landscaped acres. It's free
from fancy frills, with a pleasantly low-key
wine bar off the lobby.

La Petite Sedona   MOTEL $$

(📞928-282-7301; www.lapetitesedona.com; 500
N Hwy 89A; r/ste $159/219; ❄🛜) Right on the
side of the highway leading into Oak Creek
Canyon, this basic, family-run motel has
clean rooms in a variety of configurations,
plus one suite. Some rooms are decked out
with porches, tile floors, microwaves, sofas,
refrigerators and bathtubs.

★Enchantment Resort   RESORT $$$

(📞888-250-1699; www.enchantmentresort.com;
525 Boynton Canyon Rd; r/studio from $695/740;
🕙11am-11pm; ❄🛜♨) Chic, exclusive and
tucked into beautiful Boynton Canyon, this
country-club-style resort lives up to
its name. Stylish, spacious rooms with private patios and big views sprawl across the
expansive grounds. Guests can hike in the
canyon, splash in the pool, play tennis or
golf, or utterly unwind in Mii Amo Spa. The
daily resort fee is $34.

★El Portal   B&B $$$

(📞928-203-9405, 800-313-0017; www.elportal
sedona.com; 95 Portal Lane; d from $300; 🛜♨)
🐾 This discreet little inn is a beautiful blend
of Southwestern and Craftsman style. It's a
pocket of relaxed luxury tucked away in a corner across from the galleries and restaurants
of Tlaquepaque, and marvelously removed
from the chaos of Sedona's tourist-heavy
downtown. The look is rustic but sophisticated, incorporating reclaimed wood, Navajo
rugs, river rock and thick adobe walls.

Orchards Inn of Sedona   INN $$$

(📞928-282-2405; www.orchardsinn.com; 254 N
Hwy 89A; r/ste from $339/374; 🛜♨♨) Smack
in the middle of Uptown, set back from
the main strip, this multi-level motel is a
charmer. From your private patio, enjoy
views of Cleopatra Hill and the 'Snoopy'
formation. A 2016 renovation saw the
installation of HD LCD TVs, crisp white
bedding and granite bathroom counters in
all rooms, plus fireplaces in the suites and
deluxe rooms.

L'Auberge de Sedona   BOUTIQUE HOTEL $$$

(📞928-282-1661; www.lauberge.com; 301 L'Au-
berge Lane; lodge/cottage from $625/745;
❄🛜♨) With luxurious cottages amid shady
green lawns, immaculate public spaces, an
intimate spa and easy access to sparkling
Oak Creek, this hotel is one of red-rock
country's swankiest (the least expensive
rooms are in the lodge rather than individual cottages). Dogs are welcome, while
human activities include creekside yoga,
morning duck feeding and stargazing.

🍴 Eating

Sedona's restaurants are clustered around
Uptown and strung along Highways 89A
and 179. Pick up groceries and picnic ingredients at **Whole Foods** (📞928-282-6311; 1420
W Hwy 89A; 🕙8am-9pm Mon-Sat, to 8pm Sun; 🌱)
or **Bashas'** (📞928-282-5351; 160 Coffee Pot Dr;
🕙6am-11pm).

Sedona Memories   DELI $

(📞928-282-0032; 321 Jordan Rd; sandwiches
$8.50; 🕙10am-2pm Mon-Fri) This tiny local spot
assembles gigantic sandwiches on slabs of
homemade bread. A great choice for a picnic,
as they pack 'em tight to-go, so there's less
mess. If you call in your order, they'll toss in a
free cookie. Cash only.

Java Love   CAFE $

(📞928-204-1500; www.javalovesedona.com; 2155
Hwy 89A; snacks $6-8; 🕙8am-2pm) The best
coffee shop in town, this local hangout has
an earthy, eclectic feel, with ready-made
breakfast burritos, baked French toast oat-
meal, sandwiches and wraps, and made-to-
order items as well.

Black Cow Café   ICE CREAM $

(📞928-203-9868; 229 N Hwy 89A; medium ice
cream $5; 🕙10:30am-9pm) Many claim the
Black Cow's homemade ice cream is the best
in town: try the prickly pear.

Coffee Pot Restaurant   BREAKFAST $

(📞928-282-6626; www.coffeepotsedona.com;
2050 W Hwy 89A; breakfast $8-9, lunch $9-10;
🕙6am-2pm; 🚸) A go-to breakfast and lunch
joint since the 1950s, the Pot is nothing
fancy but gets the refueling job done, with
massive plates of reasonably priced fare and
a huge selection. There are a bewildering 101
types of omelet available.

Red Rock Cafe   AMERICAN $

(📞928-284-1441; redrockcafeaz.com; 100 Verde
Valley School Rd, Village of Oak Creek; breakfast
$9-10, lunch $9-12; 🕙7am-2pm) Look for the

kokopelli on the window then step inside and nab a seat – quickly if it's Sunday morning (the place bustles with locals squeezing in breakfast before church). Come here for blue-corn huevos rancheros, or a Wild West Reuben before hitting Bell Rock Pathway.

Mesa Grill AMERICAN $$
(☑928-282-2400; www.mesagrillsedona.com; 1185 Airport Rd; mains $13-18; ⊘7am-9pm; 🛜) Yes, it's a bit odd to choose to eat at an airport, on a patio next to airplanes, but 'airport' is a misnomer – it's really more of a landing strip for scenic flights. Mesa does interesting Southwestern fare, such as gulf shrimp with crispy pork belly and cheesy grits, offered in contemporary surrounds.

Hideaway House ITALIAN $$
(☑928-202-4082; www.sedonahideawayhouse.com; 231 Hwy 179; mains $19-21; ⊘11am-9pm Sun-Thu, to 10pm Fri & Sat) The best reason for coming to the Hideaway is to dine on the deck at sunset, when gorgeous red-rock views serve as the appetizer. As the name suggests, this hidden-away spot is easy to miss, although easy to get to. Retreat from the Uptown madness and enjoy a glass of wine with American-style Italian food and specialty pizzas.

★Elote Cafe MEXICAN $$$
(☑928-203-0105; www.elotecafe.com; Arabella Hotel, 771 Hwy 179; mains $22-28; ⊘5-10pm Tue-Sat) Come here for some of the best, most authentic Mexican food in the region. Elote Cafe serves unusual and traditional dishes you won't find elsewhere, like the namesake *elote* (fire-roasted corn with spicy mayo, lime and cotija cheese) or smoked chicken in guajillo chiles. Reservations are not accepted and the line can be off-putting: come early, bring a book, order a margarita.

Mariposa LATIN AMERICAN $$$
(☑928-862-4444; www.mariposasedona.com; 700 W Hwy 89A; mains $30-38; ⊘11:30am-9pm Sun-Thu, to 10pm Fri & Sat) Stunning mountain views and divine (if steeply priced) Latin-inspired food from the grill are the hallmarks of this upmarket eatery from local celebrity chef Lisa Dahl. You don't need to drop $125 on the prime rib eye – the poke of sushi-grade yellowfin tuna or the skirt steak with chimichurri and black beans deliver just as much pleasure.

Dahl & DiLuca Ristorante ITALIAN $$$
(☑928-282-5219; www.dahlanddiluca.com; 2321 Hwy 89A; mains $27-38; ⊘5-10pm) Though

this lovely Italian place fits perfectly into the groove and color scheme of Sedona, at the same time it feels like the kind of place you'd find in a small Italian seaside town. It's a bustling, welcoming spot serving excellent, authentic Italian food. Try the pork chop and asparagus from the grill or the four-cheese ravioli in truffle cream.

Rene at Tlaquepaque INTERNATIONAL $$$
(☑928-282-9225; www.renerestaurantsedona.com; Hwy 179, Tlaquepaque Village; lunch $12-14, dinner $32-45; ⊘11:30am-8:30pm; 🛜) Specializing in French cuisine with Southwestern touches, Rene does meat best (lamb is a specialty), but even lunches go well beyond the sandwich/burger/salad routine with such selections as scallops with cilantro pesto or a BLT with a side of tomato bisque. Rene is a sentimental favorite, and the patio is an inviting spot for a respite after a morning of shopping.

⬤ Drinking & Nightlife

For a tourist town, Sedona is surprisingly low on pubs and breweries.

View 180 BAR
(☑928-282-2900; www.enchantmentresort.com; 525 Boynton Canyon Rd; ⊘2pm-midnight) Head to this bar and bistro in the Enchantment Resort (p147) in stunning Boynton Canyon for sunset cocktails.

Oak Creek Brewing Company BREWERY
(☑928-204-1300; www.oakcreekbrew.com; 2050 Yavapai Dr; ⊘noon-10pm Sun-Thu, to midnight Fri & Sat) In West Sedona, this spare brewery and taproom has a bit of indoor seating and a patio. Inside you'll also find the Sedona BBQ Co, slinging smokin' pork, brisket and hot dogs ($5 to $8), and there's live music most weekends.

☆ Entertainment

Mary D Fisher Theatre CINEMA
(☑928-282-1177; www.sedonafilmfestival.org; 2030 Hwy 89A) A Sedona International Film Festival venue in February, this movie theater also screens documentaries and arthouse films year-round.

🔒 Shopping

Shopping is a big draw in Sedona, and visitors will find everything from expensive boutiques to T-shirt stores. Uptown along Hwy 89A is the place to go souvenir hunting.

For New Age shops, try **Crystal Magic** (☑928-282-1622; www.crystalmagic.com; 2978

Hwy 89A; ⊙9am-9pm Mon-Sat, to 8pm Sun) or **Center for the New Age** (☑928-282-7220; www.sedonanewagestore.com; 341 Hwy 179; ⊙8:30am-8pm).

Garland's Navajo Rugs   ARTS & CRAFTS
(☑928-282-4070; www.garlandsrugs.com; 411 Hwy 179; ⊙10am-5pm) Founded in 1976, this Sedona institution offers the area's best selection of rugs, and sells other American Indian crafts, both current and vintage. It's an interesting store to visit, displaying naturally dyed yarns with their botanical sources of color, as well as descriptions of how many hours it takes to create a handwoven rug.

Tlaquepaque Village   MALL
(☑928-282-4838; www.tlaq.com; 336 Hwy 179; ⊙10am-5pm) Just south of Hwy 89A on Hwy 179, Tlaquepaque is a series of Mexican-style interconnected plazas home to dozens of high-end art galleries, shops and restaurants. Founded by Nevada businessman and Sedona-lover Abe Miller in the 1970s and constructed of stucco walls, wrought iron, stone and patterned tiles, it has the organic feel of an old Mexican village.

ℹ Information

Sedona Chamber of Commerce Visitor Center (☑928-282-7722, 800-288-7336; www.visitsedona.com; 331 Forest Rd; ⊙8:30am-5pm) Located in the pedestrian center of Uptown Sedona; pick up free maps and buy a Red Rock Pass here.

Red Rock Country Visitor Center (☑928-203-2900; www.redrockcountry.org; 8375 Hwy 179; ⊙9am-4:30pm) Get a Red Rock Pass here, as well as hiking guides, maps and local national forest information.

Verde Valley Medical Center (☑928-204-3000; nahealth.com; 3700 W Hwy 89A; ⊙24hr emergency) On Hwy 89A, west of Uptown Sedona.

Police Station (☑emergency 911, non-emergency ☑928-282-3100; 100 Roadrunner Dr)

Post Office (☑928-282-3511; 190 W Hwy 89A; ⊙9am-4:30pm Mon-Fri, 9am-1pm Sat)

ℹ Getting There & Around

While scenic flights depart from Sedona, the closest commercial airports are Phoenix (two hours' drive) or Flagstaff (30 minutes' drive). **Ace Xpress** (☑800-336-2239, 928-649-2720; www.acexshuttle.com; one-way/round-trip adult $68/109, child $35/55; ⊙office 7am-8pm Mon-Fri, 8am-8pm Sat & Sun) and **Arizona Shuttle** (☑800-888-2749, 928-282-2066; www.arizonashuttle.com) run shuttle services between Sedona and Phoenix's Sky Harbor International Airport.

Amtrak (☑800-872-7245; www.amtrak.com) and **Greyhound** (☑800-231-2222; www.greyhound.com) both stop in nearby Flagstaff.

Barlow Jeep Rentals (☑928-282-8700, 800-928-5337; www.barlows.us; 3009 W Hwy 89A; half-/1-/3-day jeep rental $250/350/576; ⊙8am-6pm) is great for rough-road exploring. Free maps and trail information are provided. **Bob's Taxi** (☑982-282-1234; www.bobstaxisedona.com) is a good local operator, while rental cars are available at **Enterprise** (☑928-282-2052; www.enterprise.com; 2090 W Hwy 89A; per day from $50; ⊙8am-6pm Mon-Fri, 9am-2pm Sat & Sun).

Oak Creek Canyon

Hwy 89A from Sedona into Oak Creek Canyon is a surreally scenic drive that you won't soon forget. The canyon is at its narrowest and most dramatic here, with russet and vermilion cliffs carpeted in pine and sycamore rising up from the chuckling waterway at its base. Giant cottonwoods clump along the creek, providing a scenic, shady backdrop for trout fishing and swimming, and turn a dramatic golden in fall. A small **visitor center** (☑928-203-0624; www.fs.usda.gov; Hwy 89A, Indian Gardens; ⊙9am-4pm Apr-Oct) is open seasonally, and there's a year-round American Indian arts and crafts market. Unfortunately, traffic can be brutal in summer.

🏃 Activities

About 2 miles north of Sedona, **Grasshopper Point** (☑928-203-2900; www.fs.usda.gov; vehicle/pedestrian $8/3; ⊙9am-6pm Mon-Thu, 8am-6pm Fri-Sun) is a great swimming hole. Another hugely popular splash zone awaits a further 5 miles north at **Slide Rock State Park** (☑928-282-3034; information line 602-542-0202; www.azstateparks.com/parks/slro; 6871 N Hwy 89A, Oak Creek Canyon; per car Jun-Sep $20, Oct-May $10; ⊙8am-7pm Jun-Aug, shorter hours rest of the year; ♿).

About 13 miles into the canyon, the road zigzags dramatically, climbing 700ft in 2.3 miles. Pull into **Oak Creek Vista** for a bird's-eye perspective.

🛏 Sleeping

Oak Creek Canyon's exceptional beauty is the *raison d'être* for an excellent selection of cabins and other lodgings, many screened behind cottonwoods on the verge of the creek itself.

Camping

Dispersed camping is not permitted in the area of Red Rock District that includes Oak Creek Canyon. However, the USFS runs three campgrounds along the 15-mile stretch of Hwy 89A, none with hookups. All are nestled in the woods just off the road, offering great access to the trout-filled stream and various hiking trails, and you won't need a Red Rock Pass. Reservations are accepted for some sites at all three: try www.recreation.gov if you can't get through by phone. It's cash only for first-come, first-served sites, except at Cave Springs.

Manzanita (✓ international reservations 518-885-3639, reservations 877-444-6777; www.fs.usda.gov/coconino; 5900 Hwy 89A; campsites $22) has 18 sites; open year-round; 6 miles north of Sedona.

Cave Springs (✓ international reservations 518-885-3639, reservations 877-444-6777; www.fs.usda.gov/coconino; 11345 Hwy 89A; camping $22; ☉ 24 Mar-early Nov) has 82 sites; showers ($4); 11.5 miles north of Sedona.

Pine Flat (✓ international reservations 518-885-3639, ✓ reservations 877-444-6777; www.fs.usda.gov/coconino; 12240 Hwy 89A; camping $22; ☉ Apr-Oct; 🐾) has 56 sites; 12.5 miles north of Sedona.

Lodging

Butterfly Garden Inn CABIN $$
(✓ 855-255-8244; www.thebutterflygardeninn.com; 9440 N Hwy 89A; 2 nights from $330; 🛜🐾) Tucked amid the pine trees 10 miles north of Sedona, this low-key, welcoming place is well-suited for relaxation. The 18 log cabins hit the sweet spot between rustic and stylish, while the breakfast basket starts each day perfectly. Delivered early, this basket of deliciousness comes with bread, scones, fruit, granola-topped yogurt and orange juice.

★**Briar Patch Inn** CABIN $$$
(✓ 928-282-2342; www.briarpatchinn.com; 3190 N Hwy 89A; cabins from $265; 🛜) Nestled in nine wooded and grassy acres above Oak Creek, this bucolic and peaceful B&B hideaway offers 19 handsome cabins with Southwestern decor and American Indian art. All include patios and kitchens, many have fireplaces and several sit just above the gurgling waters. The buffet breakfast, served on the creekside patio, includes fruit, quiche, eggs, muffins and yogurt.

Junipine Resort LODGE $$$
(✓ 928-282-3375; www.junipine.com; 8351 N Hwy 89A; creekhouses from $266; @🛜) In Oak Creek Canyon 8 miles north of Sedona, this resort offers lovely, spacious one- and two-bedroom 'creekhouses.' All have kitchens, living/dining rooms, wood-burning stoves and decks. Some have lofts, and the largest are 1400 sq ft. The Table on-site restaurant serves lunch and dinner Wednesday through Sunday and breakfast on weekends. Discounts are offered on 30-day advance bookings.

Orchard Canyon on Oak Creek CABIN $$$
(✓ 928-890-4023; enjoyorchardcanyon.com; 8067 Hwy 89A; cabins from $275; ☉ closed for arrivals Sun; 🛜) 🍴 Set back from Oak Creek on 10 secluded and verdant acres with broad lawns, woods and an apple orchard, this friendly lodge 8 miles north of Sedona offers deliciously cozy Western log cabins, many with fireplaces. Rates include a full hot breakfast, 4pm tea and a four-course dinner (worth visiting for even if you're not staying).

🍴 Eating

There are several very good restaurants, both in hotels and stand-alone, strung at regular intervals along the canyon, plus Sedona is only ever a short drive away.

★**Indian Gardens Cafe & Market** CAFE $
(✓ 928-282-7702; www.indiangardens.com; 3951 N Hwy 89A; breakfast $8-9, lunch $9-11; ☉ 7:30am-5pm Mon-Thu, to 6pm Fri-Sun; 🅿) Grab a breakfast sandwich here before heading north to the West Fork Trail or stop by for lunch (until 4pm each day). Lunch choices include a butternut squash and kale salad, a turkey and avocado sandwich, and a bacon and brie melt. Coffee and craft beer are also available, and there's a lovely back garden to enjoy the fruits of your foraging.

Flagstaff

✓ 928 / POP 70,320 / ELEV 7000FT

Flagstaff's laid-back charms are many, from a pedestrian-friendly historic downtown crammed with eclectic vernacular architecture and vintage neon, to hiking and skiing in the country's largest ponderosa pine forest. And the locals are a happy, athletic bunch, skewing more toward granola than gunslinger: buskers play bluegrass on street corners while cycling culture flourishes. Northern Arizona University (NAU) gives Flag its college-town flavor, while its railroad history still figures firmly in the town's identity. Throw in a healthy appreciation for craft beer, freshly roasted coffee beans and an all-around good time and you have the makings of the perfect northern Arizonan escape.

⊙ Sights

With its wonderful mix of cultural sites, historic downtown and access to outdoorsy pursuits, it's hard not to fall for Flagstaff.

★ **Museum of Northern Arizona**　MUSEUM
(☑928-774-5213; musnaz.org; 3101 N Fort Valley Rd; adult/senior/child 10-17yr $12/10/8; ☺10am-5pm Mon-Sat, noon-5pm Sun; ⊕) Housed in an attractive Craftsman-style stone building amid a pine grove, this small but excellent museum spotlights local American Indian archaeology, history and culture, as well as geology, biology and the arts. Intriguing permanent collections are augmented by exhibitions on subjects such as John James Audubon's paintings of North American mammals. On the way to the Grand Canyon it makes a wonderful introduction to the human and natural history of the region.

★ **Lowell Observatory**　OBSERVATORY
(Map p152; ☑928-774-3358, recorded information 928-233-3211; www.lowell.edu; 1400 W Mars Hill Rd; adult/senior/child 5-17yr $15/14/8; ☺10am-10pm Mon-Sat, to 5pm Sun; ⊕) Sitting atop a hill just west of downtown, this national historic landmark was built by Percival Lowell in 1894. Weather permitting, visitors can stargaze through on-site telescopes, including the famed 1896 Clark Telescope, the impetus behind the now-accepted theory of an expanding universe. Kids will love the paved Pluto Walk, which meanders through a scale model of our solar system.

Riordan Mansion
State Historic Park　HISTORIC SITE
(Map p152; ☑928-779-4395; azstateparks.com/riordan-mansion; 409 W Riordan Rd; tour adult/child 7-13yr $10/5; ☺9:30am-5pm May-Oct, 10:30am-5pm Thu-Mon Nov-Apr) Having made a fortune from their Arizona Lumber Company, brothers Michael and Timothy Riordan built this sprawling duplex in 1904. The Craftsman-style design was the brainchild of architect Charles Whittlesey, who also designed El Tovar in Grand Canyon Village. The exterior features hand-split wooden shingles, log-slab siding and rustic stone. Filled with Edison, Stickley, Tiffany and Steinway furniture, the interior is a shrine to arts and crafts.

Arboretum　GARDENS
(☑928-774-1442; www.thearb.org; 4001 S Woody Mountain Rd; adult/child $10/5; ☺9am-5pm Wed-Mon May-Oct) This 200-acre arboretum is a lovely spot to take a break and rejuvenate your spirits. Two short trails hug a meadow

WORTH A TRIP

WALNUT CANYON

The Sinagua cliff dwellings at **Walnut Canyon** (☑928-526-3367; www.nps.gov/waca; I-40 exit 204; adult/child under 16yr $8/free; ☺8am-5pm Jun-Oct, 9am-5pm Nov-May, trails close 1hr earlier; ℗) are set in the nearly vertical walls of a small limestone butte amid this stunning forested canyon. The mile-long **Island Trail** steeply descends 185ft (more than 200 stairs), passing 25 rooms built under the natural overhangs of the curvaceous butte. A shorter, wheelchair-accessible Rim Trail affords several views of the cliff dwelling from across the canyon.

Even if you're not all that interested in the history of the Sinagua people, who abandoned the site about 700 years ago, Walnut Canyon itself is a beautiful place to visit, 8 miles east of Flagstaff.

and wind beneath ponderosa pines, passing a herb garden, native plants and wildflowers, and a longer loop makes an easy amble through the woods. There are also tours, summer concerts and soirees, and even wine and theater in the woods. Follow Woody Mountain Rd 3.8 miles south from Route 66 – it's unpaved, but feasible for most cars.

🏃 Activities

Flagstaff is full of active citizens, so there's no shortage of outdoor stores and places to buy or rent camping, cycling and skiing equipment. For ski rentals, swing by Peace Surplus (p159).

Hiking & Biking
Scores of hiking and mountain-biking trails are easily accessed in and around Flagstaff. Fifty-six miles of trails crisscross the city as part of the **Flagstaff Urban Trail System**; maps are available online (www.flagstaff.az.gov/futs) or at the Visitor Center (p159).

Stop by the USFS Flagstaff Ranger Station (p159) for information about trails in the surrounding national forest or check www.fs.fed.us. The steep 3-mile hike (one-way) up 9299ft **Mt Elden** leads to a lookout at the top of the peak's tower. If it's locked when you get there, knock and if someone is there, you may be able to climb the stairs to the lookout.

Arizona Snowbowl offers several trails, including the strenuous 4.5-mile one-way hike up 12,633ft **Humphreys Peak**, the highest point in Arizona; wear decent boots

ARIZONA FLAGSTAFF

Flagstaff

2 km
1 mile

Ñ N

USFS Flagstaff
Ranger Station
Flagstaff
KOA (0.2mi)

Rio de Flag

Exit
201

Elden Hills
Golf Course

Country Club Dr

Mt Pleasant Dr

Lake
Elaine

Skyview St

Kaspar Dr

Foxglenn
Park

EAST
FLAGSTAFF

Industrial Dr

5

9

Bushmaster
Park

Lewis Dr

Lockett Rd

Butler Ave

Cedar Ave

7th Ave

3

4th Ave

4th St

2nd Ave

4th St

Maple Av

Huntington Dr

10

Lucky Ln

4

Exit 198

Santa Fe Ave (Rte 66)

McMillan Mesa

Switzer
Mesa

Forest Ave

Turquoise Dr

Switzer Canyon Dr

E Sawmill Rd

McPherson
Park

Switzer
Canyon

Butler Ave

Buffalo Park

Beaver St

N San Francisco St

Cherry Ave

Greyhound

8

Lone Tree Rd

Southside
Park

Columbus Ave

Leroux St

See Central Flagstaff Map (p156)

7

Fort Valley Rd

Thorpe
Park

Clay Ave

Aspen Ave

Northern
Arizona
University
(NAU)

Riordan Ranch St

University Dr

Observatory
Mesa

Lowell
Observatory

1

W Mars Hill Rd

Riordan Rd

2

6

S Milton Rd

University Ave

Plaza Way

Bashas
(0.6mi)

W Old Rte 66 Bus

Museum of
Northern Arizona
(0.5mi)

Flagstaff

as sections of the trail cross crumbly volcanic rock. In summer you can ride the **chairlift** (📞928-779-1951; www.arizonasnowbowl.com; 9300 N Snowbowl Rd; adult $19, senior & child 8-12yr $13; ⊙10am-4pm Fri-Sun late May–mid-Oct; 🚻) to 11,500ft, where you can hike, attend ranger talks and take in the desert and mountain views. Children under eight ride for free.

For the inside track on the local mountain-biking scene, visit the super-friendly gearheads at **Absolute Bikes** (Map p156; 📞928-779-5969; www.absolutebikes.net; 202 E Rte 66; bike rentals per day from $39; ⊙9am-7pm Mon-Fri, 9am-6pm Sat, 10am-4pm Sun Apr-Thanksgiving, shorter hours Dec-Mar).

Humphreys Peak   HIKING
(www.fs.usda.gov) The state's highest mountain (12,633ft) is a reasonably straightforward, though strenuous, hike in summer. The trail, which begins north of the Arizona Snowbowl parking lot, winds through forest, eventually coming out above the beautifully barren tree line. It's a little over 5 miles one-way; allow six to eight hours for the round-trip.

Kachina Trail   HIKING
(Snowbowl Rd) A gentle 5-mile one-way hike through ponderosa forest and meadows offering lovely views. The trail begins at 9500ft and descends 700ft.

Horseback Riding
The forest around Flagstaff offers delightful trail-riding. **Hitchin' Post** (📞928-774-1719; historichitchinpoststables.com; 4848 Lake Mary Rd; 1/2hr ride $55/100; 🚻) and **MCS** (📞928-774-5835; www.mcsstables.com; 8301 S Highway 89A; per night from $25) are two of the best stables to try.

Snow Sports

Flagstaff Nordic Center   SKIING
(📞928-220-0550; www.flagstaffnordiccenter.com; 16848 Hwy 180; weekend/weekday trail pass $20/12; ⊙9am-4pm Dec-Mar) 🌿 Fifteen miles north of Flagstaff, the Nordic Center offers 25 miles of groomed trails for cross-country skiing, as well as lessons and rentals (skis are $20 on weekends). It also has snowshoe and multi-use trails, and nearby you can ski – no permit required – across Forest Service land. The parking lot is at Mile 232 on Hwy 180.

Arizona Snowbowl   SKIING
(📞928-779-1951; www.arizonasnowbowl.com; 9300 N Snowbowl Rd; lift ticket adult $75, youth 13-17yr $64, child 8-12yr $42; ⊙9am-4pm mid-Nov–mid-Apr; 🚻) About 14 miles north of downtown Flagstaff, Arizona Snowbowl is small but lofty, with eight lifts that service 40 ski runs between 9200ft and 11,500ft. The season normally runs from November to April.

🔾 Tours

All-Star Grand Canyon Tours   HIKING
(Map p152; 📞800-940-0445; www.allstargrandcanyontours.com; 2420 N 3rd, Suite D; day hike per person incl lunch beginner/advanced $200/300) This well-regarded ecofriendly outfit runs private tours, backpacking treks and day hikes to the Canyon, with pick-ups in Flagstaff, Sedona, Las Vegas and Phoenix. The sightseeing trips are good for the less mobile, while longer treks (up to four nights) require a decent standard of fitness.

Alpine Pedaler   TOURS
(📞928-213-9233; www.alpinepedaler.com; seats from $17; ⊙11am-11pm) Hop on the 14-passenger trolley (or is it a bicycle?) to pedal on a tour of downtown bars. Tours are two hours, you can BYOB (in cans or boxes), and there's also a smaller (six-seat) 'CRAB.'

🛏 Sleeping

Unlike in southern Arizona, summer is high season here.

Camping
Free dispersed camping is permitted in the Coconino National Forest surrounding Flagstaff. There are also campgrounds in Oak Creek Canyon to the south of town and Sunset Crater to the north.

Flagstaff KOA CAMPGROUND $
(928-526-9926, reservations 800-562-3524; www.flagstaffkoa.com; 5803 N Hwy 89; tent/RV site $33/38, cabins & tipis from $65; ⓟ 🛜 🐕) This big ponderosa-shaded campground lies a mile north of I-40 off exit 201, 5 miles northeast of downtown Flagstaff. A path leads from the campground to trails at Mt Elden, and it's family-friendly, with banana-bike rentals, summer barrel-train rides, weekend movies and a splash park. The four one-room cabins sleep four, but bedding isn't supplied.

Little Elden Springs Horse Camp CAMPGROUND $
(877-444-6777, condition updates 928-226-0493; www.recreation.gov; Elden Springs Rd; sites $22; ⊙ late Mar-late Sep) In the Coconino National Forest just outside of Flagstaff, Little Elden Springs Horse Camp is a campground designated only for people with horses. It offers 15 horse-friendly campsites with hitching posts but no corrals. From here, riders can access more than 30 miles of equestrian trails through the pines, ranging from easy to challenging Heart Trail.

Lodging

★**Motel Dubeau** HOSTEL $
(Map p156; 928-774-6731; www.modubeau.com; 19 W Phoenix Ave; dm/r from $27/53; ⓟ❄@🛜) Built in 1929 as Flagstaff's first motel, this independent hostel offers the same friendly service and clean, well-run accommodations as its sister property, Grand Canyon International Hostel. The private rooms are similar to basic but handsome hotel rooms, with refrigerators, cable TV and private bathrooms. On-site Nomads serves beer, wine and light snacks. There are also kitchen and laundry facilities.

Grand Canyon International Hostel HOSTEL $
(Map p156; 928-779-9421; www.grandcanyon hostel.com; 19 S San Francisco St; dm/r from $24/56; ❄@🛜) Housed in a historic building with hardwood floors and Southwestern decor, this bright, homey and immaculate hostel offers eight private rooms and dorms with a four-person maximum. There's also a kitchen and laundry, plus complimentary coffee, pastries and instant oatmeal.

★**Hotel Monte Vista** HISTORIC HOTEL $$
(Map p156; 928-779-6971; www.hotelmonte vista.com; 100 N San Francisco St; r/ste from $115/145; ❄🛜) A huge, old-fashioned neon sign towers over this 1926 landmark hotel, hinting at what's inside: feather lampshades, vintage furniture, bold colors and eclectic decor. Rooms are named for the movie stars who stayed here, including the 'Humphrey Bogart,' with dramatic black walls, yellow ceiling and gold-satin bedding. Several resident ghosts supposedly make regular appearances.

★**Inn at 410** B&B $$
(Map p156; 928-774-0088; www.inn410.com; 410 N Leroux St; r from $185; ⓟ❄🛜) This fully renovated 1894 house offers 10 spacious, beautifully decorated and themed bedrooms, each with a fridge and bathroom, and many with four-poster beds and delightful views. A short stroll from downtown, the inn has a shady orchard-garden and a cozy dining room, where a full gourmet breakfast and afternoon snacks are served.

Little America Hotel HOTEL $$
(Map p152; 928-779-7900; flagstaff.little america.com; 2515 E Butler Ave; d from $149; ❄🛜🏊) When you reach the Sinclair truck stop just off I-40, don't drive away thinking you have the wrong place. A little further down the side driveway behind an unassuming exterior and hugging 500 acres of ponderosa forest you'll find this sprawling two-story hotel. Little America has spacious French Provincial–styled rooms, upscale bedding with goose-down pillows and large retro-tiled bathrooms.

Starlight Pines B&B $$
(Map p152; 928-527-1912; www.starlight pinesbb.com; 3380 E Lockett Rd; r from $159; ❄🛜) Low-key and friendly Starlight Pines is located in a Victorian-style home and offers four spacious, homey rooms, each with Tiffany-style lamps, antique claw-foot tubs and other lovely touches. The Lily Room makes great use of Mt Elden views, with a telescope on its private balcony.

Weatherford Hotel HISTORIC HOTEL $$
(Map p156; 928-779-1919; www.weatherford hotel.com; 23 N Leroux St; s/d from $115/155; ❄🛜) This charming historic hotel in downtown Flagstaff opened its doors in 1900, and the rooms maintain a pared-down-turn-of-the-20th-century authenticity, while many of them incorporate modern amenities such as TVs and air-conditioning. There's a lovely wraparound porch on the 3rd floor.

Comfi Cottages COTTAGE $$
(928-774-0731, 888-774-0731; www.comfi cottages.com; cottages from $150; 🛜🐕) All but one of the these well-kept bungalows are within a mile of Flagstaff's historic district.

WORTH A TRIP

WUPATKI NATIONAL MONUMENT

The first eruptions of Sunset Crater (AD 1040–1100) enriched the surrounding soil, luring the ancestors of today's Hopi, Zuni and Navajo to the rich agriculture land. By AD 1180, it was home to roughly 100 people, and 2000 more peppered the immediate area. By 1250, however, their pueblos stood abandoned. About 2700 of these structures lie within **Wupatki National Monument** (928-679-2365; www.nps.gov/wupa; Park Loop Rd 545; car/motorcycle/bicycle or pedestrian $20/15/10; visitor center 9am-5pm, trails sunrise-sunset;), though only a few are open to the public. Entry is also valid for nearby **Sunset Crater Volcano National Monument** (928-526-0502; www.nps.gov/sucr; Park Loop Rd 545; car/motorcycle/bicycle or pedestrian $20/15/10; 9am-5pm Nov-May, from 8am Jun-Oct).

A short self-guided tour of the largest dwelling, **Wupatki Pueblo**, begins behind the visitor center. **Lomaki**, **Citadel** and **Nalakihu Pueblos** sit within a half-mile of the loop road just north of the visitor center, and a 2.5-mile road veers west from the center to Wukoki Pueblo, the best preserved of the buildings.

On weekends in April and October rangers lead visitors on a 25-mile, round-trip, overnight backpacking tour ($75; supply your own food and gear) of **Crack-in-Rock Pueblo** and nearby petroglyphs, normally off-limits to the public. Chosen by lottery, only 12 people may join each tour; call the visitor center for applications, which can be submitted up to August 31 (for October trips) or February 28 (for April trips).

Most were built in the 1920s and have a comfortable homey feel, with wood floors, Craftsman-style kitchens, board games and little lawns. The friendly owners have lived in Flagstaff for many years, and they're a wonderful source of tourist information.

✖ Eating

Flagstaff's college population and general dedication to living well translate into one of the best dining scenes in the state. Self-caterers can try **Bashas'** (928-774-3882; www.bashas. com; 2700 S Woodlands Village Blvd; 6am-11pm), a local chain supermarket with a respectable selection of organic foods. For healthy food, there's **Whole Foods Market** (Map p152; 928-774-5747; www.wholefoodsmarket.com; 320 S Cambridge Lane; 7am-9pm;).

★ **Proper Meats + Provisions** DELI $
(Map p156; 928-774-9001; www.propermeats. com; 110 S San Francisco St; sandwiches $12-13; 10am-7pm) Come here for house-made salami and pancetta, local grass-fed beef for the barbecue and other meat-lover delights. There's also wine, an eclectic selection of non-alcoholic drinks, cheese and fresh-baked rustic bread. And don't miss the sensational sandwiches – perhaps the perenially popular seven-day pastrami with Aleppo pepper and cactus cream cheese, or the Vietnamese *banh mi* with confit pork shoulder.

★ **Tourist Home Urban Market** CAFE $
(Map p156; 928-779-2811; www.touristhome urbanmarket.com; 52 S San Francisco St; mains $10-12; 6am-8pm;) Housed in a beautifully renovated 1926 house that was originally home to Basque sheepherder immigrants, this upscale market cafe serves up the best breakfast in a town full of excellent morning vittles. Try the Hash Bowl: eggs any style served on breakfast potatoes and accompanied by chorizo, spiced beets and a cilantro pesto.

★ **Pizzicletta** PIZZA $
(Map p156; 928-774-3242; www.pizzicletta. com; 203 W Phoenix Ave; pizzas $11-15; 5-9pm Sun-Thu, to 10pm Fri & Sat) Tiny Pizzicletta, where the excellent thin-crusted wood-fired pizzas are loaded with gourmet toppings like arugula and aged prosciutto, is housed in a sliver of a white-brick building. Inside there's an open kitchen, one long table with iron chairs, Edison bulbs and industrial surrounds. You can order in while you enjoy some suds at Mother Road Brewing Company (p158) next door.

★ **Macy's** CAFE $
(Map p156; 928-774-2243; www.macyscoffee. net; 14 S Beaver St; breakfast/lunch $6/7; 6am-6pm;) The delicious coffee at this Flagstaff institution – house roasted in the original, handsome, fire-engine-red roaster in the corner – has kept local students and caffeine devotees buzzing since the 1980s. The vegetarian menu includes many vegan choices, along with traditional cafe grub like pastries, steamed eggs, waffles, yogurt and granola, salads and veggie sandwiches.

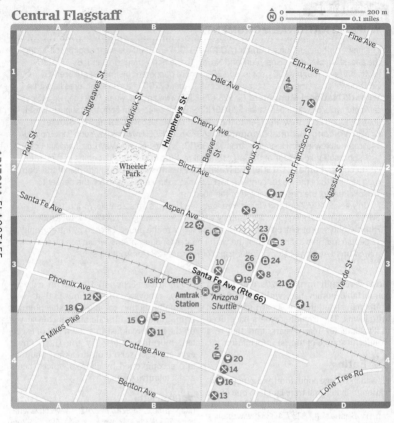

Central Flagstaff

Karma Sushi Bar   JAPANESE $
(Map p156; ☑928-774-6100; www.karmaflagstaff.
com; 6 E Rte 66; mains $11-13, sushi $6-7; ⊙11am-
10pm Mon-Sat, 4:30-10pm Sun) A slick sushi bar
with low lights and black lacquer, Karma
is known for its tasty, reasonably priced
rolls – try the Lucy, a signature concoction
of salmon, avocado and roasted red pepper,
with 10% of its proceeds donated to animal
shelters. And the ramen is right on point, too.

Diablo Burger   BURGERS $
(Map p156; ☑928-774-3274; www.diabloburger.
com; 120 N Leroux St; mains $11-14; ⊙11am-9pm
Sun-Wed, 11am-10pm Thu-Sat; ☎) This locally
focused gourmet-burger joint slings hefty
burgers on English-muffin buns and delicious Herbes de Provence seasoned fries. The
cheddar-topped Blake gives a nod to New
Mexico with Hatch-chile mayo and roasted
green chiles. The place is tiny, so come early
or sit outside and people-watch. Beer and
wine are also served.

★Criollo Latin Kitchen   FUSION $$
(Map p156; ☑928-774-0541; www.criollolatin
kitchen.com; 16 N San Francisco St; mains $17-20;
⊙11am-9pm Mon-Fri, 9am-9pm Sat & Sun) ✐ Sis-
ter to Brix Restaurant & Wine Bar and Proper
Meats + Provisions (p155), this on-trend
Latin-fusion restaurant gives similar encour-
agement to local producers, sourcing ingre-
dients from Arizona wherever possible. Set
up your day with the Haitian brunch of slow-
roasted pork with over-easy eggs, pinto beans
and Ti-Malice hot sauce, or come back at
happy hour (3pm to 6pm Monday to Friday)
for fish tacos and $4 margaritas.

★Coppa Cafe   CAFE $$$
(Map p152; ☑928-637-6813; www.coppacafe.net;
1300 S Milton Rd; lunch & brunch $11-15, mains
$28-31; ⊙3-9pm Wed-Fri, 11am-3pm & 5-9pm Sat,
10am-3pm Sun; ☎) Brian Konefal and Paola
Fioravanti, who met at an Italian culinary
school, are the husband-and-wife team
behind this friendly, art-strewn bistro with
egg-yolk-yellow walls. Expect ingredients
foraged from nearby woods (and further
afield in Arizona) in dishes such as slow-
roasted top loin with wildflower butter, or
clay-baked duck's egg with a 'risotto' of Sonoran wheat and wild herbs.

**★Brix Restaurant
& Wine Bar**   INTERNATIONAL $$$
(Map p156; ☑928-213-1021; www.brixflagstaff.com;
413 N San Francisco St; mains $30-32; ⊙5-9pm
Sun & Tue-Thu, to 10pm Fri & Sat; ✐) Brix offers
seasonal, locally sourced and generally

top-notch fare in a handsome room with
exposed brick walls and an intimate copper
bar. Sister business Proper Meats + Pro-
visions (p155), on S San Francisco St, sup-
plies charcuterie, free-range pork and other
fundamentals of lip-smacking dishes that
include cavatelli with Calabrese sausage, kale
and preserved lemon. The wine list is well
curated, and reservations are recommended.

Josephine's   AMERICAN $$$
(Map p152; ☑928-779-3400; www.josephines
restaurant.com; 503 N Humphreys St; mains
$23-30; ⊙10am-2pm Fri-Sun & 5-9pm Mon-Sat)
Occupying a 1911 Craftsman-style bungalow,
Josephine's feels more like someone's home
than a restaurant. There's pleasant patio
dining, a great old stone bar, a fireplace
and Craftsman light fixtures. Consider stopping for lunch – the salad of crab cakes and
jicama slaw and 'BLT' of Scottish salmon are
welcome changes from typical lunch fare.

🍷 **Drinking & Nightlife**

For details about festivals and music programs, call the Visitor Center (p159) or
check www.flagstaff365.com. On Friday and
Saturday nights in summer, people gather
on blankets for free music and family movies at Heritage Sq. The fun starts at 5pm.
    On Thursdays pick up a free copy of *Flag-
staff Live!* (www.flaglive.com) for current
shows and happenings around town.

★Tinderbox Kitchen & Annex   COCKTAIL BAR
(Map p156; ☑928-226-8440; www.tinderbox
kitchen.com; 34 S San Francisco St; ⊙4-11pm Sun-
Thu, 3pm-midnight Fri & Sat) This slinky cocktail
bar mixes up great originals and classics: the
Moscow Mule with mint and cucumber might
just be the best cocktail in Flagstaff. The outdoor patio, actually a handball court built by
Basque immigrants in 1926, attracts a low-key
local crowd. Annexed to the wonderful **Tin-
derbox Kitchen** (5-10pm) it also does poutine
and other top-notch drinking food.

★Hops on Birch   PUB
(Map p156; ☑928-774-4011; www.hopsonbirch.com;
22 E Birch Ave; ⊙1:30pm-12:30am Mon-Thu, to 2am
Fri, noon-2am Sat, noon-12.30am Sun) Simple and
handsome, Hops on Birch has 34 rotating
beers on tap, live music five nights a week and
a friendly local-crowd vibe. In classic Flagstaff
style, dogs are as welcome as humans.

★Museum Club   BAR
(Map p152; ☑928-526-9434; www.themuseum
club.com; 3404 E Rte 66; ⊙11am-2am) This

honky-tonk roadhouse on Route 66 has been kicking up its heels since 1936. Inside what looks like a huge log cabin you'll find a large wooden dance floor, animal mounts and a sumptuous elixir-filled mahogany bar. The origins of the name? In 1931 it housed a taxidermy museum.

Historic Brewing Co Barrel & Bottle House
MICROBREWERY

(Map p156; 928-774-0454; www.historicbrewingcompany.com; 110 S San Francisco St; 11am-10pm Sun-Thu, to midnight Fri & Sat;) The taproom for the Historic Brewing Co, Flagstaff's local microbrew, has 26 craft-beer taps, wine flights and bottles produced by the local Grand Canyon Winery. There's also a massive wall-refrigerator lined with a dizzying selection of beer by the bottle or can.

State Bar
BAR

(Map p156; 928-266-1282; thestatebararizona.com; 10 E Rte 66; 3pm-midnight Mon-Thu, noon-2am Fri & Sat, noon-midnight Sun) Dedicated exclusively to Arizona's ever-growing selection of state-produced beer and wine, this welcoming little spot in a copper-ceilinged Victorian building on Route 66 has live music on weekends. The only problem you may face is options paralysis, staring at 36 taps of beer, cider and even mead.

Mother Road Brewing Company
BREWERY

(Map p156; 928-774-9139; www.motherroadbeer.com; 7 S Mikes Pike; 2-9pm Mon-Thu, 2-10pm Fri, noon-10pm Sat, noon-9pm Sun) Chill out with a hoppy Tower Station IPA and a wood-fired pizza from nearby Pizzicletta (p155) at this popular, stripped-back taproom beside the old Route 66. There are usually 10 beers on tap (growlers are available for takeout) while board games, toys and a relaxing patio add to the kid- and dog-friendly bonhomie.

Monte Vista Cocktail Lounge
BAR

(Map p156; 928-779-6971; www.hotelmontevista.com; 100 N San Francisco St, Hotel Monte Vista; 4pm-2am Mon-Sat) With a prime corner spot in downtown Flagstaff, complete with broad windows for people-watching, this former speakeasy in the historic Hotel Monte Vista (p154) has a pressed-tin ceiling, pool table, live music three nights a week, plus a Sunday quiz, karaoke and all-day 'happy hour' on Mondays.

Beaver Street Brewery
BREWERY

(Map p156; 928-779-0079; www.beaverstreetbrewery.com; 11 S Beaver St; 11am-11pm Sun-Thu, to midnight Fri & Sat;) Families, river guides, ski bums and businesspeople – everybody is here or on the way. The menu is typical brewpub fare, with pizzas, burgers and salads whipped up in the open kitchen. Relax with a season brew on the small outdoor terrace, or head to the cozy old-fashioned-feeling Brews & Cues (21 years and older) for a round of pool.

☆ Entertainment

Orpheum Theater
THEATER

(Map p156; 928-556-1580; www.orpheumflagstaff.com; 15 W Aspen Ave; tickets from $15) A grand old-style movie house from 1911, the Orpheum Theater is now a fine-looking music venue – complete with balcony, seating, bar and lounge – that hosts top regional and national bands and the occasional movie night. It has seen some troubles (heavy snowfall collapsed the roof in 1915, and it closed between 1999 and 2002), but has come back better than ever.

Green Room
LIVE MUSIC

(Map p156; 928-266-8669; flagstaffgreenroom.com; 15 N Aggasiz St; 5pm-2am Mon-Thu, 3pm-2am Fri-Sun) Grungy, cavernous and welcoming, the Green Room is Flag's best place to catch indie, punk, electronic and other acts. There are plenty of DJ nights too (reggae and electro are popular), some of which are free.

🔒 Shopping

Babbitt's Backcountry Outfitters
SPORTS & OUTDOORS

(Map p156; 928-774-4775; www.babbittsbackcountry.com; 12 E Aspen Ave; 9am-8pm Mon-Sat, 10am-6pm Sun) Named for a pair of rancher brothers who arrived from Ohio in 1886, Babbitt's rents backpacks, tents, boots, poles, snowshoes and other outdoor gear, and sells books and USGS maps.

The Artists' Gallery
ARTS & CRAFTS

(Map p156; 928-773-0958; www.flagstaffartistsgallery.com; 17 N San Francisco St; 9:30am-7:30pm Mon-Sat, to 5:30pm Sun) This art co-op, locally owned and operated since 1992, carries the work of over 30 northern Arizona artists, including two-dimensional art, jewelry, ceramics and glasswork.

Painted Desert Trading Co
ARTS & CRAFTS

(Map p156; 928-226-8313; www.painteddeserttrading.com; 18 N San Francisco St; 10am-6pm) Carries fine wares and art created by the Navajo, Hopi, Zuni and other American Indian nations, plus an excellent selection of books on regional topics.

Peace Surplus   SPORTS & OUTDOORS
(Map p156; ☑928-779-4521; www.peacesurplus.
com; 14 W Rte 66; ☺8am-9pm) Sells and rents
a huge array of outdoor clothing and equipment, including downhill and cross-country
skis and snowboards.

❶ Information

Visitor Center (Map p156; ☑800-842-7293,
928-213-2951; www.flagstaffarizona.org; 1 E
Rte 66; ☺8am-5pm Mon-Sat, 9am-4pm Sun)
Located inside the Amtrak station, the visitor
center has a great Flagstaff Discovery map and
tons of information on things to do.

USFS Flagstaff Ranger Station (Map p152;
☑928-526-0866; www.fs.usda.gov; 5075 N
Hwy 89; ☺8am-4pm Mon-Fri) Provides information on the Mt Elden, Humphreys Peak and
O'Leary Peak areas north of Flagstaff.

Police Station (☑emergency 911, general
information 928-779-3646, non-emergency
dispatch 928-774-1414; 911 E Sawmill Rd;
☺emergency 24hr)

Post Office (Map p156; ☑928-779-2371; 104 N
Agassiz St; ☺10am-4pm Mon-Fri, 9am-1pm Sat)

Flagstaff Medical Center (☑928-779-3366;
nahealth.com; 1200 N Beaver St; ☺emergency
24hr) One of the nearest hospitals to the Grand
Canyon South Rim.

**Flagstaff City-Coconino County Public Li-
brary** (☑928-779-7670; flagstaffpubliclibrary.
org; 300 W Aspen Ave; ☺10am-9pm Mon-Thu,
to 7pm Fri, to 6pm Sat, to 2pm Sun; ☎) Free
internet and wi-fi.

❶ Getting There & Away

Greyhound (Map p152; ☑928-774-4573,
800-231-2222; www.greyhound.com; 880 E
Butler Ave; ☺10am-6.30am) stops in Flagstaff
en route to/from Albuquerque, Las Vegas, Los
Angeles and Phoenix.

    Arizona Shuttle (Map p156; ☑928-226-
8060, 800-888-2749; www.arizonashuttle.com)
and **Flagstaff Shuttle & Charter** (☑888-215-
3105; www.flagshuttle.com) have shuttles that
run between Flagstaff, Grand Canyon National
Park, Williams, Sedona and Phoenix's Sky Harbor International Airport.

    Operated by **Amtrak** (☑800-872-7245,
928-774-8679; www.amtrak.com; 1 E Rte 66;
☺3:30am-10:30pm), the *Southwest Chief* stops
at Flagstaff on its daily run between Chicago and
Los Angeles.

❶ Getting Around

Mountain Line Transit (☑928-779-6624;
www.mountainline.az.gov; one-way adult/child
$1.25/0.60) has several fixed bus routes daily;
pick up a user-friendly map at the visitor center.

Buses are equipped with ramps for passengers
in wheelchairs.

    If you need a taxi, call **Action Cab** (☑928-
774-4427) or **Sun Taxi** (☑928-774-7400; www.
suntaxiandtours.com). Several major car-rental
agencies operate from the airport and downtown.

Payson & Mogollon Rim

If you're traveling between Phoenix and Flagstaff and have extra time, consider a detour
to Payson and the Mogollon (pronounced
'muggy-own') Rim. This splendid country,
the southern lip of the vast Colorado Plateau,
is an often-overlooked paradise of ruddy rock
towers and deep whispering pine forests.

    Payson was founded by gold miners in
1882, although its real riches turned out to be
above ground. Vast pine forests fed a booming timber industry, ranchers ran cattle along
the Mogollon Rim and down to the Tonto
Basin, and wild game was plentiful. Frontier
life here captivated Western author Zane
Grey, who kept a cabin outside town. Prime
activities are hunting and fishing in the forests, lakes and streams around the Rim. The
World's Oldest Continuous Rodeo has
been held in Payson every August since 1884.

❂ Sights

The natural travertine bridge at **Tonto Natural Bridge State Park** (☑928-476-4202;
www.azstateparks.com/tonto; off Hwy 87; adult/
child 7-13yr $7/4; ☺8am-6pm Jun-Aug, 9am-5pm
Sep-May) is thought to be the world's largest. For more natural beauty, drive east
from Payson on Hwy 260 through **Tonto
National Forest**.

Rim Country Museum   MUSEUM
(☑928-474-3483; www.rimcountrymuseums.com;
700 S Green Valley Pkwy; adult/senior/student/
child under 12yr $5/4/3/free; ☺10am-4pm Mon &
Wed-Sat, 1-4pm Sun; ℗) This lakeside museum
is the only real sight in Payson, with exhibits that illustrate the native, pioneer and
resource-extraction history of the region.
Highlights include a replica of a blacksmith
shop and a walk-through of the Zane Grey
Cabin, faithfully rebuilt after the author's
original homestead burned in the 1990 Dude
Fire. You can only check out the museum on
a guided tour, which, at about 1½ hours,
seems a bit long, especially for kids.

▭ Sleeping

Payson is surrounded by Tonto National
Forest, which offers a mix of campsites and
(free) dispersed-camping areas. Check the

US Forest Service website (www.fs.usda.gov) for details. Hotel rates in Payson vary depending on demand, so you might find yourself paying $20 more or less depending on the day or the season. Chain motels are scattered along Beeline Hwy and Hwy 260.

Majestic Mountain Inn MOTEL $
(☑928-474-0185; www.majesticmountaininn.com; 602 E Hwy 260; d from $69; P❄🐾🛎) Set among landscaped pines and grassy lawns, this is easily the nicest lodging in Payson – and a good value one, too. The two-story property is more of a motel than a lodge-like inn, but the luxury rooms have double-sided gas fireplaces, sloped wooden ceilings and spa tubs.

Ponderosa Campground CAMPGROUND $
(☑877-444-6777; www.recreation.gov; Hwy 260; campsites $18; ☺Apr-Oct) This USFS spot is 12 miles northeast of Payson on Hwy 260 and has 48 single sites and two group sites as well as drinking water and toilets, but no showers. Inquire at the ranger station for other campgrounds in the Tonto National Forest.

✖ Eating

Fine dining isn't the draw in this rugged, woodsy part of the state, but you will find perfectly good diners and other options in Payson.

Beeline Cafe DINER $
(☑928-474-9960; 815 S Beeline Hwy; mains $8-12; ☺5am-9pm) This home-style diner, with its padded stools and booths, could be called the bee*hive*, so busy are its mornings, with locals swarming in for massive breakfasts. Cash only.

❶ Information

Rim Country Regional Chamber of Commerce (☑928-474-4515; www.rimcountrychamber.com; 100 W Main St, cnr Hwy 87, Payson; ☺9am-5pm Mon-Fri, 10am-2pm Sat) Stocks plenty of brochures about local activities and events.

Cameron

☑928 / POP 978
A tiny, windswept community 32 miles east of the Grand Canyon's East Entrance and 54 miles north of Flagstaff, Cameron sits on the western edge of the Navajo Reservation. There's not much to it; in fact, the town basically comprises just the Cameron Trading Postand the attached motel and restaurant. In the early 1900s Hopis and Navajos came

to the trading post to barter wool, blankets and livestock for flour, sugar and other goods. Today visitors can browse a large selection of quality American Indian crafts, including Navajo rugs, basketry, jewelry and pottery, and plenty of kitschy knickknacks.

🛏 Sleeping

Grand Canyon Hotel Lodge MOTEL $$
(☑800-338-7385; www.camerontradingpost.com; Hwy 89; r/ste $129/169; P❄🛎) Attached to the historic Cameron Trading Post, this motel offers spacious rooms with hand-carved furniture and a Southwestern motif spread out in three two-story, adobe-style buildings. The nicest is the Hopi, set around a lovely, lush garden with fountains and benches. Ask for a room with a garden view or a view of the Little Colorado River Gorge.

✖ Eating

Cameron Trading Post Dining Room AMERICAN INDIAN $
(☑928-679-2231; www.camerontradingpost.com; breakfast $9-11, lunch $10-13, dinner $14-16; ☺6am-9:30pm, shorter hours in winter) A good place to try the Navajo taco (Indian frybread topped with whole beans, ground beef, green chile and cheese), the Cameron Trading Post Dining Room also does steak, fried chicken and other staples.

🛍 Shopping

Cameron Trading Post ARTS & CRAFTS
(☑928-679-2231; www.camerontradingpost.com; 466 Hwy 89; ☺6am-9:30pm, shorter hours in winter) Selling everything from wonderfully intricate Navajo rugs, antique textiles and fine ceramics to plush buffalo toys and T-shirts, this historic trading post has been running since 1916, just after the first swayback bridge across the Little Colorado River was built here.

GRAND CANYON REGION

No matter how much you read about the Grand Canyon or how many photographs you've seen, nothing really prepares you for the sight of it. One of the world's seven natural wonders, it's so startlingly familiar and iconic you can't take your eyes off it. The canyon's immensity, the sheer intensity of light and shadow at sunrise or sunset, even its very age, scream for superlatives.

At about two billion years old – half of the Earth's total life span – the layer of Vishnu Schist at the bottom of the canyon is some

Grand Canyon Region

0 ——— 25 miles
0 ——— 50 km

UTAH
NEVADA
ARIZONA

Navajo Mtn (10,388ft)

Rainbow Bridge National Monument

Glen Canyon National Recreation Area

Navajo Creek

Hopi Reservation

264

Navajo Reservation

Page

Marble Canyon

Antelope Canyon

98

89T

Tuba City

160

Moenkopi

Cameron

Little Colorado River Gorge

89

Gray Mountain

Bitter Springs

89

Navajo Bridge

Paria Canyon-Vermilion Cliffs Wilderness

Lees Ferry

89 Alt

Lodge

Interpretive Center

Point Imperial (8803ft)

Bright Angel Point

Cape Royal (7876ft)

East Entrance Station

Kanab

Fredonia

Kaibab Paiute Reservation

Paria Plateau

Jacob Lake

67

Kaibab Plateau

North Rim Entrance Station

North Rim

South Rim

Grand Canyon National Park

Grand Canyon Village

Grandview Lookout Tower

Kaibab National Forest

180

Valle

Arizona Strip

Kaibab National Forest

South Entrance Station

Tusayan

64

Pipe Spring National Monument

389

Colorado City

Hurricane Cliffs

Kanab Creek

Supai

Hilltop

Hualapai

Havasu Canyon

Coconino Plateau

Grand Canyon Railway

Toroweap

Toroweap Overlook

Hualapai Reservation

18

Grand Canyon Caverns

66

Peach Springs

Lake Mead National Recreation Area

Pearce Ferry

Grand Canyon West & Skywalk

Diamond Bar Rd

Music Mountains

Truxton

15

Dolan Springs

Pierce Ferry Rd

Stockton Hill Rd

Red Lake (dry)

Colorado River

Hualapai Reservation

of the oldest exposed rock on the planet. And the means by which it was exposed is, of course, the living, mighty Colorado River, which continues to carve its way 277 miles through the canyon as it has for the past six million years.

South Rim

ELEV 7000FT

Grand Canyon National Park – South Rim

If you don't mind bumping elbows with other travelers, you'll be fine on the accessible and (comparatively) developed Grand Canyon South Rim (www.nps.gov/grca). This is particularly true in summer when camera-toting day-trippers converge en masse, clogging its roads and easiest trails. Infrastrucure is abundant: you'll find an entire village worth of lodgings, restaurants, bookstores, libraries, a supermarket and a deli. Shuttles ply two scenic drives, and the flat and paved Rim Trail allows the mobility-impaired and stroller-pushing parents to take in the dramatic, sweeping canyon views.

Though the accessibility of the South Rim means sharing your experience with many others, there are numerous ways to commune with the canyon and its wildlife, and enjoy its sublime beauty, one on one. Escaping the crowds can be as easy as taking a day hike below the rim or merely tramping a hundred yards away from a scenic overlook.

Most visitors arrive via the South Entrance, 80 miles northwest of Flagstaff on Hwy 64/180. Avoid summer wait times of 30 minutes or more by prepaying for your park ticket at the National Geographic Visitor Center & IMAX Theater (Map p164; ☑928-638-2203; www.explorethecanyon.com; 450 Hwy 64; adult/child $14/11; ⊙visitor center 8am-10pm Mar-Oct, 10am-8pm Nov-Feb; ☒Tusayan) in Tusayan, which allows you to cruise through in a special lane. Or arrive at the East Entrance instead. In summer, if you've bought your ticket or have a park pass, you can now hop on the park's shuttle at the IMAX Theater in Tusayan and disembark at the Grand Canyon Visitor Center (p174).

A few miles north of the South Entrance, Grand Canyon Village (or simply the Village) is the primary hub of activity. Here you'll find lodges, restaurants, two of the three developed campgrounds, a backcountry office, visitor center, medical clinic, bank, grocery store, shuttles and other services. Coin-operated showers and laundry facilities are located next to Mather Campground.

West of the Village, Hermit Rd follows the rim for 7 miles, ending at Hermits Rest. Seven pullouts along the way offer spectacular views; from those at Mohave and Hopi Points you can spot three Colorado River rapids. Interpretive signs explain the canyon's features and geology. From March to November the road is closed to private vehicles and accessible only by tour or the free shuttle bus.

In the opposite direction, Desert View Dr meanders 25 miles to the East Entrance on Hwy 64, passing some of the park's finest viewpoints, picnic areas, the Tusayan Museum & Ruins (p165) and the Desert View Watchtower (Map p164; Desert View, East Entrance; ⊙8am-sunset mid-May–Aug, 9am-6pm Sep–mid-Oct, 9am-5pm mid-Oct–Feb, 8am-6pm Mar–mid-May). A campground, snack bar, small information center and general store are in Desert View, right by the entrance. Also here is the park's only gas station, which offers 24-hour, pay-at-the-pump service from April to September. Gas stations in Tusayan are closer to the Village and open year-round.

Limited hours are in effect between October and March. If you have questions, NPS rangers and the people who staff the hotels, restaurants and services here are typically helpful and friendly.

Climate

On average, temperatures are 20°F (about 11°C) cooler on the South Rim than at the bottom of the Grand Canyon. In summer, expect highs in the 80s°F and lows of around 50°F (highs in the 20s/30s°C and lows around 10°C). Weather is cooler and more changeable in fall, and snow and freezing overnight temperatures are likely by November. January has average overnight lows in the teens °F (-10°C to -7°C) and daytime highs of around 40°F (4°C). Winter weather can be beautifully clear, but be prepared for snowstorms that can cause havoc.

The inner canyon is much drier, with about 8in of rain annually, around half that of the South Rim. During summer, temperatures inside the canyon soar above 100°F (38°C) almost daily, often accompanied by strong hot winds. Even in midwinter, the mercury rarely drops to freezing, with average temperatures hovering between 37°F and 58°F (3°C and 14°C).

◉ Sights

The Grand Canyon's natural splendor is the prime draw, but to enrich your trip it pays to visit the park's cultural and architectural sites. Several museums and historic stone buildings illuminate the park's human history, and rangers lead a host of daily programs on subjects from geology to resurgent condors. Some of the most important buildings were designed by noted architect Mary Jane Colter to complement the landscape and reflect the local culture.

Travelers can take a **cell-phone audio tour** at 30 sites across the North and South Rims. These ranger-narrated tours last two minutes and can be accessed, at no extra charge, by dialing ☏ 928-225-2907 and pressing the designated stop number.

Mather Point   VIEWPOINT
(Map p168; Visitor Center Plaza, Grand Canyon Village; ☐ Kaibab/Rim) The busiest and most popular overlook at the Grand Canyon, due in part to its proximity to the visitor center. It's named after Stephen Mather, the first director of the National Park Service.

Yavapai Geology Museum   MUSEUM
(Map p168; ☏ 928-638-7890; Grand Canyon Village; ⊘ 8am-7pm Mar-May & Sep-Nov, to 6pm Dec-Feb, to 8pm Jun-Aug; ♿; ☐ Kaibab/Rim) FREE Views don't get much better than those unfolding behind the plate-glass windows of this little stone building at Yavapai Point. Handy panels identify and explain the various formations before you, and displays (including a scale model) highlight the canyon's multilayered geologic history.

★ Trail of Time   MUSEUM
(Map p168; tot.unm.edu; Grand Canyon Village; ♿; ☐ Village) This interpretative display traces the history of the canyon's formation – each meter equals one million years of geologic history. From the trail's start you pass 2.1 billion years in around a mile. Rock samples from within the canyon line the trail – look through specially positioned metal cylinders to view these rocks on the far canyon wall. Brass placards continue beyond Verkamp's. It's located on the Rim Trail, west from Yavapai Geology Museum.

Kolb Studio   HISTORIC BUILDING
(Map p168; ☏ 928-638-2771; National Historic Landmark District; ⊘ 8am-7pm Mar-May & Sep-Nov, to 6pm Dec-Feb, to 8pm Jun-Aug; ☐ Village) FREE In 1905 Ellsworth and Emery Kolb built a small photography studio on

TOP FIVE OVERLOOKS
➡ **Mohave Point** (Map p164; Hermit Rd; ☐ Hermits Rest)

➡ **Hopi Point** (Map p164; Hermit Rd; ☐ Hermits Rest)

➡ **Lipan Point** (Map p164; Desert View Dr)

➡ **Desert View Watchtower** (p162)

➡ **Yaki Point** (Map p164; Yaki Point Rd, off Desert View Dr; ☐ Kaibab/Rim)

the edge of the rim, which has since been expanded and now holds a bookstore and museum. Today, an original Kolb brothers 1911 silent film runs continuously, offering incredible footage of their early explorations of the Colorado River, and a museum displays mementos and photographs from their careers. In January and February, the NPS offers tours of their original Craftsman home, in a lower level of the studio.

El Tovar   HISTORIC BUILDING
(Map p168; Village Loop Dr; ☐ Village) Built in 1905 as a railroad hotel, El Tovar was designed by architect Charles Whittlesey as a blend between a Swiss chalet and the more rustic style that would come to define national park lodges in the 1920s. With its unusual spires and dark-wood beams rising behind the Rim Trail, elegant El Tovar remains a grande dame of national park lodges.

The public spaces look much as they did when the lodge opened, and wide, inviting porches with rocking chairs offer travelers a comfortable and elegant place to relax after a long journey to the park. Moose and elk trophy heads, reproduction Remington bronzes and Craftsman-style furniture lend the interior a classic Western feel. The lodge sits about 100 yards from the rim, and though it's thronged with tourists by day, the scene mellows considerably in the evening. The bench swing on the side porch is the best spot on the South Rim to relax with a cocktail and watch the comings and goings along the canyon rim.

Hopi House   HISTORIC BUILDING
(Map p168; Grand Canyon Village; ⊘ 8am-8pm mid-May–Aug, 9am-6pm Sep–mid-Oct, 9am-5pm mid-Oct–mid-May; ☐ Village) A beautiful Mary Colter–designed stone building, Hopi House has been offering high-quality American Indian jewelry, basketwork, pottery

Grand Canyon (South Rim)

0 ——— 5 km
0 ——— 2.5 miles

Grand Canyon (South Rim)

and other crafts since its 1905 opening. The structure was built by the Hopi from native stone and wood, inspired by traditional dwellings on their reservation.

Tusayan Museum & Ruins   MUSEUM, RUIN
(Map p164; Desert View Dr; ⊙9am-5pm) Just west of Desert View and 22 miles east of Grand Canyon Village, these small ruins and museum examine the culture and lives of the Ancestral Puebloan people who lived here 800 years ago. Only partially excavated to minimize erosion damage, it's less impressive than other such ruins in the Southwest but still well worth a look. Pottery, jewelry and split-twig animal figurines on display date back 2000 to 4000 years, and there are ranger-led tours at 11am and 1.30pm daily.

Verkamp's Visitor Center   HISTORIC BUILDING
(Map p168; National Historic Landmark District, Grand Canyon Village; ⊙8am-7pm; ♿; ☐ Village) **FREE** In 1898 John G Verkamp sold souvenirs from a tent outside Bright Angel Lodge to persevering travelers arriving after long, arduous stagecoach rides. He was a little before his time, however, as there weren't yet enough customers to make a living, and he closed down his operation after only a few weeks. The arrival of the railroad in 1901 opened up the canyon to more and more tourists, and in 1905 Verkamp returned to build the modified Mission-style Verkamp's Curios.

After running the shop for more than 100 years, Verkamp's descendants closed down the business, and the NPS revamped the building as a small visitor center (p174) in 2008. It maintains an old-fashioned, dusty feel, and the tiny museum gives a timeline of Grand Canyon pioneer history in the context of other national events.

🏃 Activities

Hiking
To experience the full majesty of the canyon, hit the trail. It may look daunting, but there are options for all levels of skill and fitness. Though summer is the most popular season for day hikes – despite oppressively hot temperatures of over 100°F (38°C) below the rim – experienced canyon hikers know that it's much more pleasant to hike in the spring and fall, when there are also significantly fewer visitors. For short, easy-to-print trail descriptions (with mileages, turnaround points and basic maps) check out the Plan Your Visit section of the park website (www.nps.gov/grca); click through to backcountry hiking.

The easiest and most popular is the **Rim Trail** (Map p168; ♿; ☐Hermits Rest, ☐Village, ☐Kaibab/Rim), which is quite literally a walk in the park. It connects a series of scenic points and historical sights stretching 13 miles from the South Kaibab trailhead west to **Hermits Rest** (Map p164; Hermit

Rd; Hermits Rest). The section of the Rim Trail between the South Kaibab Trailhead to **Lookout Studio** (Map p168; 8am-sunset mid-May–Aug, 9am-5pm Sep–mid-May; Village) **FREE** is paved, and mostly wheelchair accessible. It's possible to catch a shuttle bus to a viewpoint, walk a stretch, then catch the next shuttle back or onward. The 3 miles or so winding through the Village are usually packed, but crowds thin out further west.

If you want to venture into the inner gorge you'll have several trails to choose from, but be aware: heading down into the canyon means negotiating supersteep switchbacks. The most popular is the **Bright Angel Trail** (Map p168), which is wide, well graded and easy to follow. Starting in the Village, just west of Kolb Studio (p163), it's a heavily trafficked route that's equally attractive to first-time canyon hikers, seasoned pros and mule trains. The trailhead was revamped in 2013 and is now surrounded by a small plaza with seating and restrooms. The popularity of the trail doesn't lessen the sheer beauty. The steep and scenic 7.8-mile descent to the Colorado River is punctuated with four logical turnaround spots, including two resthouses offering shade and water. The first resthouse is about 1.5 miles down the trail, the second is 3 miles. Day hikers and first-timers should strongly consider turning around at one of them or otherwise hitting the trail at dawn to safely make the longer hikes to Indian Garden or **Plateau Point** (Map p164; 9.2 and 12.2 miles round-trip, respectively). Hiking to the Colorado River for the day is not an option.

One of the park's prettiest trails, the **South Kaibab Trail** (Map p164; Yaki Point Rd, off Desert View Dr; Kaibab/Rim) combines stunning scenery and adventurous hiking with every step. The only corridor trail to follow a ridgeline, the red-dirt path allows for unobstructed 360-degree views. It's steep, rough and wholly exposed, which is why rangers discourage all but the shortest of day hikes during summer. A good place to turn around is **Cedar Ridge** (Map p164), reached after about an hour. It's a dazzling spot, particularly at sunrise, when the deep ruddy umbers and reds of each canyon fold seem to glow from within. During the rest of the year, the trek to Skeleton Point, 1.5 miles beyond Cedar Ridge, makes for a fine hike – though the climb back up is a beast in any season. The South Kaibab Trailhead is 4.5 miles east of the Village on Yaki Point Rd and can only be reached by shuttle or the Hikers' Express Bus leaving from Bright Angel Lodge around dawn (stopping at the Backcountry Information Center).

One of the steepest trails in the park, dropping 1200ft in the first 0.75 miles, **Grandview Trail** is also one of the finest and most popular hikes. The payoff is an up-close look at one of the inner canyon's sagebrush-tufted mesas and a spectacular sense of solitude. While rangers don't recommend the trek to **Horseshoe Mesa** (3 miles, four to six hours) in summer – there's no water on the very exposed trail, and the climb out is a doozy – it's not overly long and certainly doable for strong hikers strapped with a hydration system and hiking early or late in the day. For a shorter but still rewarding option, hike as far as **Coconino Saddle**. Though it's only about 2 miles round-trip, it packs a quick and precipitous punch as you plunge 1600ft in less than a mile. With the exception of a few short level sections, the Grandview is a rugged, narrow and rocky trail. The trailhead is at **Grandview Point** (Map p164; Desert View Dr;), 12 miles east of the Village on Desert View Dr.

The wild **Hermit Trail** (Map p164) descends into pretty Hermit Canyon via a cool spring. It's a rocky trip down, but if you set out early and take it slow, it offers a wonderfully serene hike and glimpses into secluded corners. Day hikers should steer toward **Santa Maria Spring** (5 miles round-trip) or to **Dripping Springs** via a spur trail (7 miles round-trip). The upper section of the Hermit is well shaded in the morning, making it a cool option in summer. The trailhead is at the end of its namesake road, 8 miles west of the Village. Although the road is only accessible via shuttle bus during the summer peak season, overnight backpackers with a Hermit Trail backcountry permit are allowed to park near the trailhead year-round.

Biking

Cyclists have limited options inside the park, as bicycles are only allowed on paved roads, dirt roads that are open to the public and the **Greenway Trail** (Map p168). This multi-use trail, open to cyclists, pedestrians and wheelchairs, stretches about 13 miles from Hermit's Rest all the way to the South Kaibab Trailhead.

Hermit Rd offers a scenic ride west to Hermits Rest (p165), about 8 miles from the Village. Shuttles ply this road every 15 minutes between March and November (the rest of the year, traffic is minimal). They are not permitted to pass cyclists, so for the first 4 miles you'll have to pull over each time one drives by. However, starting from **Monument Creek Vista** (Map p164; Hermit Rd; 🚌 Hermits Rest), a completed section of the Greenway Trail diverges from the road and continues separately all the way to Hermits Rest.

Alternatively, you could ride out to the East Entrance along Desert View Dr, a 50-mile round-trip from the Village. The route is largely shuttle-free but sees a lot of car traffic in summer. Just off Desert View Dr, the 1-mile dirt road to **Shoshone Point** (Map p164) is an easy, nearly level ride that ends at this secluded panoramic vista, one of the few places to escape South Rim crowds.

Bright Angel Bicycles & Cafe at Mather Point
CYCLING

(Map p168; ☎ 928-814-8704, 928-638-3055; www.bikegrandcanyon.com; 10 S Entrance Rd, Visitor Center Plaza; 24hr rental adult/child 16yr & under $40/30, 5hr rental $30/20, wheelchair $10, s/d stroller up to 8hr $18/27; ⏰ 7am-5pm Mar-Oct; 🚌 Village, 🚌 Kaibab/Rim) Half- or full-day bicycle rentals, with helmets and an add-on pull-along trailer option, can be reserved in advance online or by phone. With the exception of the peak stretch from July through mid-August, however, walk-ins can usually be accommodated. Hermit Rd bicycle-shuttle packages allow you to ride past overlooks going one way, and hop on one of their private shuttles the other.

On the one-way package (adult/child $37/25, 10.5 miles, five to seven hours), you ride from the rental shop west through busy Grand Canyon Village, on Hermit Rd to Monument Creek Vista, and finally along the multi-use Greenway Trail to Hermits Rest. From there, a shuttle returns you to the visitor center complex. The round-trip package (adult/child $34/23, 5.5 miles, two hours) includes a shuttle from the shop straight to Hopi Point, allowing you to focus your time and energy on the most beautiful stretch and to avoid cycling through the Village and the uphill leg.

For folks with limited time or small children, the **Orange Route** is a moderate ride that heads east on a 7-mile round-trip from Bright Angel Bicycles to the South Kaibab Trailhead and Yaki Point. It's a lovely winding cruise through the piñon, past some canyon-view picnic spots and spectacular overlooks. The only traffic is the short stretch with Yaki Point Rd shuttles.

Guided tours of Yaki Point (adult/child $52/42) or Hermit Rd (adult/child $62/47) are offered multiple times daily.

Mule Rides

Visitors who want to view the canyon by mule have two choices: a three-hour day trip along the rim or a two-day trip to the bottom of canyon, which includes a night at Phantom Ranch. Due to erosion concerns, the National Park Service (NPS) no longer allows one-day mule rides into the canyon. Both trips are run by Canyon Vistas Mule Rides.

The three-hour Canyon Vistas Ride ($135) meets at the livery barn in Grand Canyon Village then travels by bus to the South Kaibab Trailhead, where the mules await. Guests enjoy an interpretative ride along a newly constructed 4-mile trail beside the east rim.

Overnight Phantom Ranch trips (one/two people $552/961) and two-night trips (one/two people $788/1292) still follow the Bright Angel Trail to the river, travel east on the River Trail and cross the river on the Kaibab Suspension Bridge. Riders spend the night at Phantom Ranch. It's a 5½-hour, 10.5-mile trip to Phantom Ranch, but the return trip up the 7.8-mile South Kaibab Trail is a half-hour shorter. Overnight trips include cabin accommodations and all meals at Phantom.

Riders must be at least 4ft 7in tall, speak and understand fluent English and weigh no more than 225lb (Canyon Vistas) or 200lb (Phantom Ranch) fully clothed. Personal backpacks, waist packs and purses are not allowed on the mules. Anything that could possibly fall off and injure someone in the canyon below will be kept for you until you return. For complete regulations and more information, consult their website.

Mule trips are popular and fill up quickly; call ahead to book a trip more than 24 hours and up to 13 months in advance. If you arrive at the park and want to join a mule trip the following day, ask about availability at the transportation desk at Bright Angel Lodge (your chances are much better during the off-season). If the trips are booked, join a waiting list, cross your fingers and show up at the lodge at 6:15am on the day of the trip and hope there's been a cancellation. Or make tracks to the other side of the canyon: mule rides on the North Rim are usually available the day before the trip.

★ Canyon Vistas Mule Rides
TOURS

(Map p168; ☎ 888-297-2757, same day & next day reservations 928-638-3283; www.grandcanyonlodges.com; Bright Angel Lodge; 3hr mule ride $135, 1-/2-night mule ride incl meals & accommodation $552/788; ⏰ rides available year-round, hours vary) This outfit takes groups of up to 20 mules 4 miles along the East Rim Trail.

Grand Canyon Village

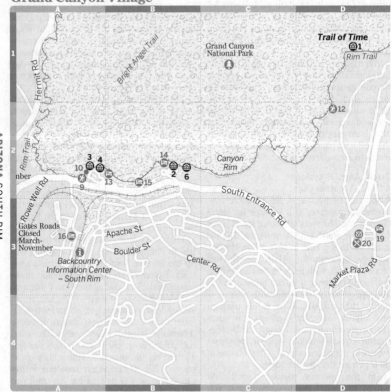

If you want to descend into the canyon, the only option is an overnight trip to Phantom Ranch. These trips follow the Bright Angel Trail 10.5 miles (5½ hours) down, spend one or two nights at Phantom Ranch, and return 7.8 miles (five hours) along the South Kaibab Trail.

Reservations can be made up to 13 months in advance. If rides are booked, and they often fill up within weeks of availability, call or show up at the Bright Angel Transportation Desk (p174) no earlier than 5am on the day before you want to ride and put your name on a waiting list. On the day of the ride, you must show up at the transportation desk at 7am, and if there are any no-shows they will accept those on the waiting list. Check the website for age and weight restrictions.

White-Water Rafting

Rafting the Colorado – the King Kong of North American rivers – is an epic, adrenaline-pumping adventure. The biggest single drop at Lava Falls plummets 37 stomach-churning feet in just 300yd. But roller-coaster thrills are only the beginning. The canyon's true grandeur is best grasped looking up from the river, not down from the rim. Its human history comes alive in ruins, wrecks and rock art. You can hike to mystical grottoes and waterfalls, explore ethereally lit slot canyons and view wildlife.

Commercial trips vary in length from three days to three weeks and in the type of watercraft used. Motorized pontoon rafts are the most stable and generally the least scary option. The huge inflatable boats seat eight to 16 passengers and go twice as fast as oar or paddle boats. Oar boats are more common, and more exciting. Rowed by an experienced guide, they provide good stability but feel more like a raft.

A fun and intimate alternative is to float in a river dory, a small, elegant hard-shelled rowboat for four passengers that's a lot speedier than a raft. Still, if it's thrills you're

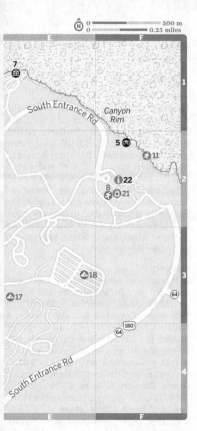

after, book a trip in an inflatable raft, which has you, your raft-mates and a guide paddling all at once.

At night you'll be camping under stars on sandy beaches (gear provided). It's not as primitive as it sounds – guides are legendary not only for their white-water acumen but also for their culinary skills.

It takes about two or three weeks to run the entire 279 miles of river through the canyon. Shorter sections of around 100 miles take four to nine days.

Arizona Raft Adventures   RAFTING
(☎800-786-7238, 928-526-8200; www.azraft.com; 6-day Upper Canyon hybrid/paddle trips $2097/2197, 10-day Full Canyon motor trips $3160) ✐ This multigenerational-family-run outfit offers motor, paddle, oar and hybrid (with opportunities for both paddling and floating) trips. Music fans can join one of the folk and bluegrass trips, with professional pickers and banjo players providing background music.

Wilderness River Adventures RAFTING
(✆ 800-992-8022, 928-645-3296; www.river
adventures.com; 6-day full-Canyon motor trips
$2525, 12-day full-Canyon oar trips $3900) ✐ Wilderness River Adventures' hybrid trips give
rafters the chance to be active and relaxed,
combining hands-on paddling with floating.
The company partners with Green Thread,
an environmental organization operating in
national parks. Check the website: you can
save hundreds of dollars on the quoted rates
by choosing the 'Pay Now' option online.

OARS RAFTING
(✆ 800-346-6277, 209-736-4677; www.oars.com;
1-week Upper Canyon oar trip from $2658, 2-we
Full Canyon dory trips from $5661) ✐ One of the
best outfitters working in the canyon, OARS
boasts the best guide-to-guest ratio in the
business (1:4). With oar, paddle and dory
trips, and the option of carbon offsetting
your trip, OARS offers extra elegance than
the standard – they claim you'll eat better
with them than you do at home – and partners with local artisans.

Ranger-led Activities
Rangers are fonts of information, which
they happily share in free programs on both
rims. Their talks cover everything from condors to fire ecology, American Indian history
to constellations, while their hikes deepen
your understanding of the canyon's fossils,
geology and history. Check the *Guide,* given
to every vehicle at the park entrance, or
check park visitor centers for subjects and
times of the latest offerings.

Rim View Walk HIKING
(Map p168; Grand Canyon Village; ⊙8.30am Mon,
Wed & Fri Jun-Aug) This two-hour ranger-led
walk along a paved 2-mile section of the Rim
Trail examines natural history and contemporary Grand Canyon issues.

Fossil Discovery Walk ECOTOUR
(Map p168; Bright Angel Trailhead; ⊙9.30am Jun-
Aug; 🚸) An easy half-mile, one-way, ranger-
led walk to exposed fossil beds along the
rim, a particularly nice activity if you plan
on hiking into the canyon from Hermits
Rest, and great for kids. If you attend the
ranger talk, you'll be able to recognize fossils
that lie about 10 minutes down the trail. The
tour begins at the Bright Angel Trailhead
restrooms.

A Walk Through History WALKING
(Map p168; Grand Canyon Village) Leaving from
Verkamp's Visitor Center at 1pm every day
in summer, this 45-minute walking tour of
historical buildings in Grand Canyon Village
offers loads of stories about the human history of the park.

☞ Tours
Coach Tours
First-time visitors can keep the overwhelm
factor at bay by joining one of several narrated bus tours, run by **Xanterra** (✆888-
297-2757, 303-297-2757, 928-638-3283; www.
grandcanyonlodges.com). Tours travel west to
Hermits Rest (two hours, $36) and east to
Desert View (about four hours, $65, combination tour $80), stopping at key viewpoints.
Sunrise and sunset tours are also available.
Stop by the transportation desk at any lodge,
or ask the concierge at El Tovar (p174) for
the latest schedule and tickets. Kids aged 16
and under ride for free.

Flyovers
Helicopter and airplane flights have been
restricted in number, altitude and routes
to reduce noise pollution affecting the
experience of other visitors and wildlife. A
National Park Service proposal to further
protect the Grand Canyon's soundscape,
by capping the number of annual flights at
65,000, was quashed by Congress in 2012.

Companies offering scenic flyovers include
Grand Canyon Airlines (✆866-235-9422,
702-835-8484; www.grandcanyonairlines.com),
Grand Canyon Helicopters (✆702-835-
8477, 928-638-2764; www.grandcanyonhelicopter.
com), **Maverick Helicopters** (✆888-261-
4414, 702-261-0007; www.maverickhelicopter.
com), **Papillon Grand Canyon Helicopters**
(✆702-736-7243, 888-635-7272; www.papillon.
com) and **Scenic Airlines** (✆800-634-6801,
702-638-3300; www.scenic.com). Contact them
for specific rates, as each offers several
options. Most flights leave from Tusayan and
Las Vegas but check itinerary and departure
points carefully; Grand Canyon West is not
part of Grand Canyon National Park.

🛏 Sleeping
Pitch a tent in one of three campgrounds or
enjoy a solid roof in one of the six hotels,
ranging from no-frill motels to luxurious
lodges. Xanterra operates all park lodges,
as well as Trailer Village. Reservations
are accepted up to 13 months in advance
and should be made as early as possible.
For same-day bookings call the South Rim
Switchboard (✆928-638-2631). Children
under 16 stay free; cribs/cots are $10 per day.

GETTING STARTED

Admission to the Grand Canyon National Park is valid for seven days at both rims. Bus and train passengers may pay a lesser fee or have it included in the tour price. Upon entering, you'll be given a map and the *Guide*, an incredibly useful newspaper thick with additional maps, the latest park news and information about ranger programs, hikes and park services. It also lists opening hours of restaurants and businesses.

On the South Rim, the Grand Canyon Visitor Center (p174) should be your first stop. Helpfully staffed, it offers a number of new interpretive exhibits plus, in the attached theater, the film Grand Canyon: A Journey of Wonder, a 20-minute introduction to the park's geology, history and plant and animal life. If you plan to hike, look for helpful trail summaries displayed on the adjacent plaza.

If you haven't been to the park in a few years, note that you can no longer pull over on the side of the road after entering and dash to Mather Point (p163). Traffic is now directed away from the rim, passing several new parking lots on the way into Grand Canyon Village. Instead, follow the visitor center plaza out to Mather Point – where the views are still just as amazing.

For more information, head to **Lonely Planet** (www.lonelyplanet.com/usa/grand-canyon-national-park) for planning advice, writer recommendations, traveler reviews and insider tips.

Camping

The **National Park Service** (☑877-444-6777, international 518-885-3639; www.recreation.gov) operates Mather and Desert View Campgrounds. Reservations for Mather are accepted up to six months in advance, up until the day before your arrival.

Stays at any of the three campgrounds below the rim require a backcountry overnight permit. **Indian Garden Campground** (Map p164; ☑Backcountry Information Center 928-638-7875; Bright Angel Trail; backcountry permit $10, plus per person per night $8; ☉year-round) has 15 sites and is 4.6 miles down the Bright Angel Trail, while **Bright Angel Campground** (Map p164; ☑Backcountry Information Center 928-638-7875; backcountry permit $10, plus per person per night $8; ☉year-round) is on the canyon floor near Phantom Ranch, some 9.3 miles via the Bright Angel Trail. Both are ranger-staffed and have water and toilets. **Cottonwood Campground** (☑928-638-7888; www.nps.gov; backcountry permit $10) is halfway up the North Kaibab Trail to the North Rim, about 16.6 miles from the South Rim.

Desert View Campground   CAMPGROUND $
(Map p164; Desert View; campsites $12; ☉mid-Apr–mid-Oct) In a piñon-juniper forest near the East Entrance, this first-come, first-served 50-site NPS campground is quieter than campgrounds in the Village, with a spread-out design that ensures a bit of privacy. The best time to secure a spot is mid-morning, when people are breaking camp. It usually fills by mid-afternoon.

Facilities include toilets and drinking water, but no showers or hookups.

Mather Campground   CAMPGROUND $
(Map p168; ☑877-444-6777, late arrival 928-638-7851; www.recreation.gov; 1 Mather Campground Rd; campsites $18; ☉year-round; ☎; ☐Village) South Rim's primary campground has shaded and fairly well-dispersed sites set in ponderosa forest, 1 mile from the canyon rim. There are pay showers and laundry facilities in the Camper Services building (open 8am to 6pm), drinking water, toilets, grills and a small general store. Reservations are accepted from March through mid-November; the rest of the year it's first-come, first-served. No hookups.

Trailer Village   CARAVAN PARK $
(Map p168; ☑877-404-4611, same-day booking 928-638-1006; www.visitgrandcanyon.com; Trailer Village Rd; hookups $45; ☉year-round; ☐Village) A trailer park with RVs lined up tightly at paved pull-through sites on a rather barren patch of ground. You'll find picnic tables, barbecue grills and full hookups, but coin-operated showers and laundry are a quarter-mile away at Mather Campground. It's about a mile walk along the bicycle-friendly Greenway Trail to the canyon rim.

Lodges

Phantom Ranch sits on the canyon floor, but the other lodges are in Grand Canyon Village. All lodges are booked through Xanterra. Advance reservations are highly recommended. For same-day reservations or to reach any lodge, call the **South Rim Switchboard** (☑928-638-2631). Pets are not allowed in any of the lodges, but there is a kennel in the Village.

Phantom Ranch   CABIN $

(Map p164; ☑888-297-2757, same day or next-day reservations 928-638-3283; www.grandcanyon lodges.com; dm $49, cabin d $142; ❄) Bunks at this camp-like complex on the canyon floor are spread across cozy private cabins sleeping up to four people and single-sex dorms for 10 people. Rates include bedding, liquid soap and towels, but meals are extra and must be reserved when booking your bunk. Phantom is only accessible by mule trip, on foot or via raft on the Colorado River.

Snacks, pack lunches, limited supplies, and beer and wine are sold at the canteen. You're free to bring your own food and stove. Without a reservation, put yourself on the waiting list at the Bright Angel Transportation Desk (p174) the day before you want to go (starting at 5am) then show up again at 6.15am the next morning and hope to snag a canceled bed. You can also check with Xanterra (p170) the day before about cancellations. Note that the ranch's 10-person cabins are usually booked by mule trips.

★ Bright Angel Lodge   LODGE $$

(Map p168; ☑888-297-2757, ext 6285, front desk & reservations within 48hr 928-638-2631; www.grand canyonlodges.com; Village Loop Dr; r with/without bath $110/89, cabins/ste $197/426; 🅿 🐾 ; 🖵 Village) This 1935 log-and-stone lodge on the canyon ledge delivers simple historic charm by the bucketload. Small public spaces bustle with activity, and the transportation desk (p174) in the lobby is the central contact for hiking services, mule rides and guided trips. Though the lodges are an excellent economy option, historic cabins are brighter, airier and have tasteful Western character.

Most options are scattered in the piñon behind the main building, but Rim Cabins and the two suites are some of the best accommodations in the South Rim and well worth the extra bucks. Cabins 6157 and 6158 offer the quietest views and a gas fireplace. Only the Red Horse Suite has air-conditioning.

Maswik Lodge   MOTEL $$

(Map p168; ☑888-297-2757, ext 6784, front desk & reservations within 48hr 928-638-2631; www.grandcanyonlodges.com; Grand Canyon Village; r South/North $107/205; 🅿 ❄ @ 🐾 ; 🖵 Village) The Maswik Lodge includes 18 modern two-story buildings set in the woods a quarter-mile from the canyon rim. Standard motel rooms at Maswik North feature private patios, air-conditioning, cable TV, high ceilings and forest views. Those at Maswik South are smaller, with fewer amenities, no air-conditioning and more forgettable views.

The Maswik lodging complex includes the **Maswik Food Court** and **Pizza Pub** (Map p168; ☑928-638-4044, 928-638-2631; www.grandcanyonlodges.com; Maswik Lodge; pizzas $18-19; ⊙11am-11pm; 🖺 ; 🖵 Village).

Kachina & Thunderbird Lodges   LODGE $$

(Map p168; ☑888-297-2757, reservations within 48hr 928-638-2631; www.grandcanyonlodges.com; National Historic Landmark District, Grand Canyon Village; r streetside/canyonside $225/243; 🅿 ❄ 🐾 ; 🖵 Village) These institutional-looking lodges, built in the late 1960s, offer standard motel-style rooms with two queen beds or one king, and full bath, flat-screen TV and refrigerator. Though amazingly ugly on the outside, inside the rooms are bright and comfortable, and you're steps away from the historic charms of El Tovar and the canyon rim. Location, location, location.

If staying at Kachina, check-in at El Tovar; if staying at Thunderbird, check in at Bright Angel Lodge.

Yavapai Lodge   MOTEL $$

(Map p168; ☑877-404-4611, reservations within 48hr 928-638-6421; www.visitgrandcanyon.com; 11 Yavapai Lodge Rd; r from $153; ⊙year-round; 🅿 ❄ @ 🐾 🐾 ; 🖵 Village) Basic one- and two-story, motel-style lodgings cluster in the piñon and juniper forest about a mile from the rim. Air-conditioned rooms at Yavapai East sleep four to six, and offer two queen beds or a king and bunk beds. Rooms in Yavapai West sleep up to four and do not have air-conditioning.

Note that Yavapai Lodge and Trailer Village are the only South Rim accommodations that are not run by Xanterra, and Yavapai West is the only South Rim option that allows pets.

★ El Tovar   LODGE $$$

(Map p168; ☑888-297-2757, ext 6380, front desk & reservations within 48hr 928-638-2631; www.grandcanyonlodges.com; Village Loop Dr; r/ste from $187/381; ⊙year-round; 🅿 ❄ 🐾 ; 🖵 Village) Stuffed mounts. Thick pine walls. Sturdy fireplaces. Is this the fanciest hotel on the South Rim or a backcountry hunting lodge? Despite renovations, this rambling 1905 wooden lodge hasn't lost a lick of its genteel historic patina, or its charm.

✖ Eating & Drinking

Grand Canyon Village has all the eating options you need, whether it's picking up picnic sandwiches at **Canyon Village Market** (Map p168; ☎928-638-2262; Market Plaza, Grand Canyon Village; ⊙6:30am-9pm May 19-Sep 13, shorter hours rest of year; 🖵Village), an après-hike ice-cream cone at **Bright Angel Ice-Cream Fountain** (Map p168; ☎928-638-2631; www.grandcanyonlodges.com; Bright Angel Lodge; mains $4-6; ⊙11am-6pm May-Sep, shorter hours rest of year; 🖈; 🖵Village) or a sit-down celebratory dinner at El Tovar Dining Room. All South Rim bars close at 11pm, and drinks are prohibited along the rim itself.

Canyon Village Deli
CAFETERIA $
(Map p168; ☎928-638-2262; Canyon Village Market, Market Plaza; mains $6-8; ⊙6:30am-8pm May 19-Sep 3, shorter hours of year; 🖵Village) Fresh-made sandwiches, hot dogs and grab-and-go meals are available inside the grocery store.

Desert View Market
SUPERMARKET $
(Map p164; ☎928-638-2393; Desert View; ⊙8am-8pm Mar-Sep, shorter hours rest of year; 🖵Village) A general store with simple groceries, beer, wine, souvenirs and an ATM.

Maswik Food Court
CAFETERIA $
(Map p168; ☎928-638-2631; www.grandcanyon lodges.com; Maswik Lodge; mains $8-13; ⊙6am-10pm May-Aug, hour vary rest of year; 🖈; 🖵Village) Though fairly predictable, the food here encompasses a nice variety and is filling after a day's hiking. The various food stations serve burgers, pasta, Mexican food, chili bowls and comfort food. There's a deli, and grab-and-go sandwiches, beer and wine are available.

Bright Angel Restaurant
AMERICAN $$
(Map p168; ☎928-638-2631; www.grandcanyon lodges.com; Bright Angel Lodge; mains $13-21; ⊙6am-10pm; 🖈; 🖵Village) In unfortunately windowless surrounds, Bright Angel offers a standard menu of burgers, fajitas, salads and pastas. The interesting original graphic from Bright Angel's 1920s menu, also shown on the back of the modern menu, is available on notecards in the gift shop.

★ El Tovar Dining Room & Lounge
AMERICAN $$$
(Map p168; ☎928-638-2631; www.grandcanyon lodges.com; National Historic Landmark District; mains $20-30; ⊙restaurant 6-10:30am, 11am-2pm & 4:30-10pm, lounge 11am-11pm; 🖈; 🖵Village) Dark-wood tables are set with china and white linen, eye-catching murals spotlight American Indian tribes and huge windows frame views of the Rim Trail and canyon beyond. Breakfast options include El Tovar's pancake trio (buttermilk, blue cornmeal and buckwheat pancakes with pine-nut butter and prickly-pear syrup), and blackened trout with two eggs.

Reservations are required for dinner. To avoid lunchtime crowds, eat before the Grand Canyon Railway train arrives at 11:45am. The adjacent cocktail lounge is busy for afternoon cocktails and after-dinner drinks. Parties of six or more can request the intimate Teddy Roosevelt Room across from the hostess desk – pop your head in to check out the mustache motif carved into the wood paneling.

Phantom Ranch Canteen
AMERICAN $$$
(Map p164; www.grandcanyonlodges.com; Phantom Ranch; mains $21-46; ⊙breakfast 5am & 6:30am Apr-Oct, 5:30am & 7am Nov-Mar, dinner 5pm & 6:30pm) The communal meals at Phantom Ranch are fun – but not for the faint of heart. The hikers here are a hungry bunch, and they tend to eat fast. Grab the bacon when you can! Filling breakfasts and dinners are served, and sack lunches ($13) are prepared for the trail. You must make meal reservations before your descent, ideally when you reserve your accommodations.

The set dinner menu, served family-style, offers three choices: steaks, hearty stew and vegetarian chili, plus sides. The canteen is open to the public for cold lemonade and packaged snacks between 8am and 4pm (from 8:30am November to March), and for beer, wine and hot drinks from 8pm to 10pm.

Arizona Room
AMERICAN $$$
(Map p168; ☎928-638-2631; www.grandcanyon lodges.com; 9 Village Loop Dr, Bright Angel Lodge; lunch $13-16, dinner $22-28; ⊙11:30am-3pm & 4:30-10pm Jan-Oct; 🖈; 🖵Village) Antler chandeliers hang from the ceiling and picture windows overlook the Rim Trail and canyon beyond. Try to get on the waitlist when the doors open at 4:30pm, because by 4:40pm you may have an hour's wait – reservations are not accepted. Agave and citrus-marinated chicken, oven-roasted squash and ribs with chipotle barbecue give a Western vibe.

You can pick up a drink from the bar and take it outside to the small, informal deck and watch passersby on the Rim Trail while you wait, and you'll be buzzed when your table is ready.

ARIZONA SOUTH RIM

Yavapai Tavern BAR
(Map p168; ☑928-638-6421; www.visitgrand canyon.com; 11 Yavapai Lodge Rd, Yavapai Lodge; ☉11am-11pm May-Sep, shorter hours rest of year; 🖵Village) The tavern at Yavapai Lodge, 1 mile from the canyon rim, has specialty cocktails and a bar menu.

Bright Angel Lounge BAR
(Map p168; www.grandcanyonlodges.com; Bright Angel Lodge; ☉11am-11pm; 🖵Village) The dark, windowless bar inside Bright Angel Lodge doesn't offer much character, but it's a cozy and friendly spot for a beer and occasionally live music. It serves coffee, yogurt and pastries in the morning.

🛍 Shopping

Visitor Center Plaza Park Store BOOKS
(Map p168; ☑800-858-2808; www.grandcanyon. org; Visitor Center Plaza; ☉8am-8pm Jun-Aug, shorter hours rest of year; 🖵Village, Kaibab/ Rim) An extensive collection of adult and children's books about the canyon, as well as canyon prints and T-shirts. The store is run by the Grand Canyon Association, which supports education and research at the park.

ⓘ Information

INTERNET ACCESS

Grand Canyon Community Library (Navajo St; ☉10:30am-5pm Mon-Sat; 🕾; 🖵Village) Free wi-fi and and several terminals with free internet access.

Grand Canyon National Park Library (☑928-638-7768; www.nps.gov; S Entrance Rd, Park Headquarters; ☉8am-4:30pm Mon-Thu & every 2nd Fri; 🕾; 🖵Village) At the back of the courtyard at Park Headquarters, this small library offers free internet access and free wi-fi.

MONEY

Chase Bank (☑928-638-2437; Market Plaza, Grand Canyon Village; ☉9am-5pm Mon-Thu, 9am-6pm Fri; 🖵Village) Currency exchange for Chase Bank customers only, and a 24-hour ATM.

POST

Post Office (Map p168; ☑928-638-2512; Market Plaza; ☉8:30am-3:30pm Mon-Fri) Stamps are available via a vending machine from 5am to 10pm. There's a walk-up window and pay phones ($1 for four minutes).

TOURIST INFORMATION

Grand Canyon Village has abundant sources of tourist information. Information regarding each of the centers is available at: www.nps.gov/grca/planyourvisit/visitorcenters.htm

Backcountry Information Center – South Rim (Map p168; ☑928-638-7875; Grand Canyon Village; ☉8am-noon & 1-5pm, phone staffed 8am-5pm Mon-Fri; 🖵Village)

Bright Angel Transportation Desk (Map p168; ☑928-638-3283; Bright Angel Lodge; ☉5am-8pm summer; 🖵Village)

Canyon View Information Plaza (Map p168; ☑928-638-7644; ☉8am-5pm)

East Entrance Ranger Station (Map p164; ☑928-638-7893; ☉8am-5pm Jun-Aug, 9am-5pm rest of year)

El Tovar Concierge (Map p168; www.grand canyonlodges.com; El Tovar, Village Loop Dr; ☉8am-5pm; 🖵Village)

Grand Canyon Association (www.grand canyon.org)

Grand Canyon Visitor Center (Map p168; ☑928-638-7888; Visitor Center Plaza, Grand Canyon Village; ☉9am-5pm; 🖵Village, 🖵Kaibab/Rim) (Also includes **Lost & Found** ☑928-638-7798, 928-638-2631)

South Entrance Ranger Station (Map p164; ☑928-638-7888)

Verkamp's Visitor Center (Map p168; ☑928-638-7888; Rim Trail; ☉8am-8pm Jun-Aug, shorter hours rest of year; 🖵Village)

ⓘ Getting There & Away

The South Rim is the more accessible of the Grand Canyon's two mighty brinks. Located at its heart, the Grand Canyon Village is accessed via Hwy 64, south to Flagstaff (79 miles, partly on Hwy 180) and east to Hwy 89. You can take a scheduled bus service or bookable shuttle along this route if you don't have your own vehicle, or there's the tourist train from Williams. Grand Canyon National Park Airport, in Tusayan just south of the park's south entrance, handles charter flights, scenic flights and helicopters, and can get you to Boulder City or Las Vegas.

ⓘ Getting Around

Though the park can seem overwhelming when you first arrive, it's actually quite easy to navigate, especially when you leave it to shuttle drivers. The *Guide* contains a color-coded shuttle-route map in the centerfold.

CAR

Grand Canyon Village is very congested in summer. Day-trippers should park in one of the four lots at the Grand Canyon Visitor Center, or ride the shuttle from Tusayan to the visitor center, then catch a shuttle into the Village. If you do drive into the Village and can't find parking near the rim, try the lot beside the Backcountry Information Center. Note that from March through November, cars are not allowed on Hermit Rd, which heads west from the Village to Hermits Rest.

There is a **garage** (📞 928-638-2631; S Entrance Rd; ⊗ 8am-noon & 1-5pm) with emergency repair and tow services. The **Desert View Service Station** (Desert View Dr, East Entrance; ⊗ 9am-5pm Mar-Oct, 24hr for credit-card service) is the only gas station on the South Rim.

SHUTTLE

Free shuttle buses ply three routes along the South Rim. In the pre-dawn hours, shuttles run every half-hour or so and typically begin running about an hour before sunrise; check the *Guide* for current sunrise and sunset information. From early morning until after sunset, buses run every 15 minutes.

Hermits Rest Route Shuttle (Red) (⊗ Mar-Nov)

Hikers' Express Bus (Grand Canyon Village; ⊗ 5am, 6am & 7am May & Sep, 4am, 5am & 6am Jun-Aug, 6am, 7am & 8am Apr & Oct, 8am, 9am & 10am Nov-Mar)

Kaibab/Rim Route Shuttle (Orange) (Visitor Center Plaza, Grand Canyon Village)

Tusayan Route Shuttle (Purple) (⊗ 8am-9:30pm mid-May–early Sep)

Village Route Shuttle (Blue) (Grand Canyon Village)

TAXI

Grand Canyon South Rim Taxi Service (📞 928-638-2822; Tusayan & Grand Canyon South Rim; ⊗ 24hr) offers taxi service to and from Tusayan and within the park.

Tusayan

The little town of Tusayan, situated 1 mile south of the Grand Canyon National Park's South Entrance along Hwy 64, is basically a half-mile strip of hotels and restaurants. The National Geographic Visitor Center & IMAX Theater (p162) is a good place to regroup – and buy your park tickets – before arriving at the South Entrance. In summer, to avoid traffic jams and parking hassles inside the park, you can catch the Tusayan shuttle from here into the park.

🏃 Activities & Tours

Tusayan Bike Trail   CYCLING
(Map p164) A popular, moderate ride is along the Tusayan Bike Trail, actually an old logging road. The trailhead is 0.3 miles north of Tusayan on the west side of Hwy 64/180 (Fire Rd 605). It's 16 miles from the trailhead to the Grandview Lookout Tower (p176), just off the South Rim's Desert View Dr.

Apache Stables   HORSEBACK RIDING
(Map p164; 📞 928-638-2891; www.apachestables. com; Moqui Dr/Forest Service Rd 328; 1/2hr ride $53/93; ⊗ vary seasonally) Trail rides (and sometimes wagon rides) through the forest, with no canyon views but plenty of serenity. You can also take a one-hour evening pony trek to a campfire and return by wagon or go both ways by wagon. The stables are about 1 mile north of Tusayan on Moqui Dr (Forest Service Rd 328) off Hwy 64/180.

🛏️ Sleeping & Eating

Ten-X Campground   CAMPGROUND $
(Map p164; 📞 877-444-6777, 928-638-2443; www.recreation.gov; Hwy 64; RV & tent sites $10; ⊗ May-Sep) Woodsy and peaceful, this USFS campground, 2 miles south of Tusayan, has 70 sites and can fill up early in the summer. You'll find large sites, picnic tables, fire rings and barbecue grills (the campground host sells firewood), cold water and toilets, but no showers. Fifteen sites are reservable up to six months in advance; the rest are first-come, first-served. No hookups.

Seven Mile Lodge   MOTEL $
(Map p164; 📞 928-638-2291; Hwy 64; r $99; ❄ 🛜) Friendly and basic motel accommodations that don't take reservations; rooms here are usually filled by early afternoon in the summer.

Best Western Grand Canyon Squire Inn   HOTEL $$$
(Map p164; 📞 928-638-2681; www.grandcanyon squire.com; 74 Hwy 64; d/ste $244/477; ❄ @ 🛜 ⊡; 🚍 Tusayan) Spread over three buildings, this swanky modern hotel offers 318 rooms ranging from standard doubles in a two-story 1973 annex (sans elevator) to a spacious interior and rooms in the main hotel (with elevator). Amenities include the most upscale dining in town, a bowling alley, pool tables, game room, coin laundry and seasonal outdoor pool. The shuttle here runs only from mid-May through to mid-September.

RP's Stage Stop   CAFE $
(Map p164; www.rpsstagestop.com; 400 Hwy 64; breakfast under $6, lunch $7; ⊗ 7am-5pm; 🛜 ♿) The only place in Tusayan to grab an espresso and pick up a sack lunch ($10.50); it also offers wi-fi.

Plaza Bonita   MEXICAN $$
(Map p164; 📞 928-638-8900; www.casabonitaaz. com; 352 Hwy 64; mains $17-21; ⊗ 7am-11pm) Part

of a (small) chain it may be, but this colorful spot serves up thoroughly satisfying plates of Mexican food, with burritos, enchiladas and combo platters all hitting the mark. Mole is here, too, for the more adventurous.

Coronado Room AMERICAN $$$
(Map p164; 928-638-2681; 74 Hwy 64, Best Western Grand Canyon Squire Inn; mains $31-36; 4-9pm;) This restaurant at the Best Western Grand Canyon Squire Inn serves the most upscale cuisine in town, offering bison, elk and boar as well as salmon and steak.

ⓘ Information

Tusayan Ranger Station (Map p164; 928-638-2443; www.fs.usda.gov/kaibab) This ranger station has trail maps and directions.

ⓘ Getting There & Around

Arizona Shuttle (800-888-2749; www.arizonashuttle.com) Can get you from Flagstaff to Tusayan, via Williams, for $32 one-way. You'll most likely have to drive yourself here, however, via Hwy 64 from Williams, or 180 and 64, from Flagstaff.

Grand Canyon National Park Airport (Map p164; 928-638-2446; 871 Liberator Dr) Scenic flights over the canyon take off from here.

Valle

928 / POP 832

About 25 miles south of Grand Canyon National Park, Valle marks the intersection of Hwy 64 (to Williams) and Hwy 180 (to Flagstaff). There isn't much to it apart from a couple of curiosities, as well as a gas station, minimart and rooms at the Grand Canyon Inn & Motel.

⊙ Sights

Planes of Fame Air Museum MUSEUM
(928-635-1000; www.planesoffame.org; 755 Mustang Way, cnr Hwys 64 & 180; adult $7, child 5-12yr $2; 9am-5pm) This little air museum has a collection of about 40 vintage airplanes on display, most fully functional and in immaculate condition.

Flintstones Bedrock City AMUSEMENT PARK
(928-635-2600; www.bedrockaz.com; 101 S Hwy 180, junction with Hwy 64; adult $5, child under 5yr free; 6am-8:30pm May-Oct, 7am-5pm Nov-Apr;) Little kids, Flintstones fans and devotees of kitsch will get a kick out of this very bizarre and well-worn 1972 roadside attraction. Walk through the handful of Bedrock-style buildings, including the hair

salon and dentist, and take photos next to cardboard cut-outs of Fred and Barney. Finish with a Bronto Burger and Gravelberry Pie in Fred's Diner.

🛏 Sleeping

Grand Canyon Inn & Motel HOTEL $$
(928-635-9203, 800-635-9203; www.grandcanyoninn.com; 317 S Hwy 64; r $180;) It's nothing fancy, but the family-owned Grand Canyon Inn gets the job done, with standard rooms, basic, older furnishing – except for flat-screen TVs – and a heated outdoor pool for summertime plunging and a restaurant. Bunkhouse rooms sleep two and are the least expensive; rates for the motel and inn are for up to five people.

Kaibab National Forest

No canyon views, but no crowds either. Divided by the Grand Canyon into two distinct ecosystems, this 1.6-million-acre forest offers a peaceful escape from the park madness. Thick stands of ponderosa dominate the higher elevations, while piñon and juniper create a fragrant backdrop further down. Sightings of elk, mule, deer, turkeys, coyotes (and even mountain lions and black bears) are all possible.

🏃 Activities

Hiking & Cycling

There are literally hundreds of miles of hiking trails to explore, and dogs are allowed off-leash as long as they don't bother anyone. Mountain biking is also possible after the snowmelt, roughly between April and November. A popular, moderate ride is along the Tusayan Bike Trail (p175), actually an old logging road. The trailhead is 0.3 miles north of Tusayan on the west side of Hwy 64/180 (Fire Rd 605). It's 16 miles from the trailhead to the **Grandview Lookout Tower** (Map p164), an 80ft-high fire tower with fabulous views. If you don't want to ride all that way, three interconnected loops offer round-trips of 3, 8 and 9 miles. The trailhead of the Tusayan Bike Trail (p175) and the Grandview Lookout Tower are also access points for cycling on the Arizona Trail (www.aztrail.org), which connects the two points.

From the lookout you can hike or ride part or all of the still-evolving Arizona Trail, a 24-mile one-way ride to the south boundary of the Tusayan Ranger District. This is an excellent and relatively easy ride.

The northern segment of the trail unfolds beneath ponderosa pines and gambel oaks; further south, the trail passes piñon-juniper stands, sage and grasslands. Bring plenty of water, as there are no dependable sources along the trail. Ask at the ranger station about other hikes.

Horseriding
Apache Stables (p175) offers horseback rides through the forest. There are no canyon views, but there is plenty of serenity.

Williams
📞928 / POP 3122 / ELEV 6780FT

A pretty slow spot by day, Williams comes to life in the evening when the Grand Canyon Railway train returns with passengers from the South Rim...and then closes down again on the early side. It's a friendly town, with history up its sleeve, and an openness to Grand Canyon tourists. Route 66 passes through the main historic district as a one-way street headed east; Railroad Ave parallels the tracks and Route 66, and heads one-way west.

◉ Sights & Activities
There are plenty of opportunities for hiking and biking in nearby Kaibab, Coconino and Prescott National Forests.

Bearizona   ZOO
(📞928-635-2289; www.bearizona.com; 1500 E Route 66; adult/child 4-12yr $22/11; ⊙8am-6pm Jun-Aug, reduced hours rest of year; [P][👪]) The ostensible main attraction here is the wildlife park – where visitors drive themselves slowly along a road that winds through 160 acres inhabited by roaming gray wolves, bison, bighorn sheep and black bears – but the real draw is the small zoo dubbed Fort Bearizona. Here, under ponderosa shade, you can see tiny baby bears sidle up the trees and playful otter brothers slide and bob through the water, plus porcupines, badgers and a handful of other small animals indigenous to the area.

Grand Canyon Railway   RAIL
(📞reservations 800-843-8724; www.thetrain.com; 233 N Grand Canyon Bvd, Railway Depot; round-trip adult/child from $79/47) Following a 9am Wild West show by the tracks, this historic train departs for its 2¼-hour ride to the South Rim. If you're only visiting the rim for the day, this is a fun and hassle-free way to travel. Once there, you can explore by foot,

shuttle or tour bus, and arrive back in Williams at 5:45pm.

Route 66 Zipline   ADVENTURE SPORTS
(📞928-635-5358; www.ziplineroute66.com; 200 North Grand Canyon Bvd; $12-15; ⊙hours vary, Mar 15-Oct 31 & select days Nov & Dec) Only 1400ft as a round-trip, this kitschy Route 66–inspired ride zips over the parking lot in downtown Williams. More like a carnival attraction than a zip line, it can be a very fun distraction on a lazy Williams summer evening.

🛌 Sleeping
Camping
Free dispersed camping is allowed in the national forest provided you refrain from camping in meadows, within a quarter-mile of the highway or any surface water, or within a half-mile of any developed campground.

Dogtown Lake (📞928-699-1239; www.recreation.gov; tent & RV sites $20; ⊙May-Oct), **Kaibab Lake** (📞928-699-1239, reservations 877-444-6777; www.recreation.gov; tent & RV sites $20-32; ⊙Apr–mid-Oct; ✪) and **White Horse Lake** (📞928-699-1239; www.recreation.gov; FR 109; tent & RV sites $24; ⊙May-Sep; ✪) are three pleasant USFS campgrounds near Williams that offer seasonal camping without hookups. Swimming isn't allowed in any of the lakes. Contact the Visitor Center (p179) or the Williams Ranger Station (p179) for information.

Circle Pines KOA   CAMPGROUND $
(📞928-635-2626, 800-562-9379; www.koa.com/campgrounds/williams; 1000 Circle Pines Rd; powered tent & RV site from $50, cabin from $223; ⊙mid-Mar–Oct; 🛜✪✪) Amid 27 acres of ponderosa pine forest, a half-mile north of I-40 (take exit 167), Circle Pines offers plenty of activities for children and adults alike, including bikes, a pool, sauna and even mini golf.

Lodging
Canyon Country Inn   MOTEL $
(📞928-635-2349; 422 W Rte 66; r $90; ✳🛜) Rooms at this small family-run motel are a step up from typical motel rooms and give you more of a B&B feel. The country-style

decor includes frilly curtains, floral bed-spreads and a teddy bear on the bed.

Canyon Motel & RV Park
MOTEL $

(☑ 928-635-9371, 800-482-3955; www.the canyonmotel.com; 1900 E Rodeo Rd; tent/RV sites from $31/44, cottages/cabooses from $90/180; ❋ 🛜 🐾 🏊) Stone cottages (c 1940s) and rooms in two 1929 railroad cabooses and a former Grand Canyon Railway coach-car offer a quirky alternative to a standard motel. Kids will especially love the cozy caboose rooms, with bunks and modern conveniences; the larger one can include up to six guests, while five people can fit into the smaller one.

Red Garter Inn
B&B $$

(☑ 928-635-1484; www.redgarter.com; 137 W Railroad Ave; d from $170; ❋ 🛜) Up until the 1940s, gambling and girls were the draw at this 1897 bordello-turned-B&B across from the tracks. Nowadays the place trades on its historic charm and reputation for hauntings. Of the four restored rooms, the suite was once reserved for the house's 'best gals,' who would lean out the window to flag down customers.

Grand Canyon Railway Hotel
HOTEL $$

(☑ 928-635-4010; www.thetrain.com; 235 N Grand Canyon Blvd; r/ste $180/249; ❋ 🛜 🏊) This sprawling 297-room hotel caters primarily to Grand Canyon Railway passengers. An elegant lobby with chandelier, stone fireplace and plush leather chairs are designed to take travelers back to the romance of train travel, but rooms are the basic upscale roadside hotel variety. It's spacious, comfortable and centrally located, with a glass-enclosed indoor pool.

Packages that include one night's accommodation and the round-trip train to the South Rim start at $210. Other packages include accommodation at the South Rim's Maswik Lodge. Pets are not allowed, but the hotel operates the modern Railway Pet Resort.

✖ Eating

Williams boasts some lovely old-fashioned diners, alongside a smattering of more cosmopolitan food offerings.

Dara Thai Cafe
THAI $

(☑ 928-635-2201; 145 W Route 66, Suite C; mains $10-14; ⊙ 11am-2pm & 5-9pm Mon-Sat; 🍴) An unassuming spot tucked down a quiet side street, this is your only option for a lighter alternative to meat-heavy menus elsewhere

in town. Despite its address, look for the front door along S 2nd St.

Grand Canyon Coffee & Café
DINER $

(☑ 928-635-4907; www.grandcanyoncoffeeand cafe.com; 137 W Railroad Ave; breakfast $7-8, mains $8-9; ⊙ 6am-2pm Sun-Thu, to 7pm Fri & Sat) Inside the Red Garter Inn, this cafe (aka Anna's) slings classic breakfasts, sandwiches and a smattering of Mexican and Asian dishes. The canyon burrito includes scrambled eggs and pork green chile, and there's a lovely brick patio. You may stumble in to find locals tuning their fiddles over afternoon coffee, and it's popular with Grand Canyon Railway passengers.

Station 66 Italian Bistro
ITALIAN $$

(☑ 928-635-3992; www.thestation66.com; 144 W Route 66; mains $8-18; ⊙ 11am-10pm) Housed in an old Route 66 gas station, with live music in the sidewalk cafe and rooftop dining. Wood-fire-pizza toppings include fresh mozzarella, artichoke and prosciutto, and the $20 Butcher's Board appetizer is big enough for a meal. Owned by the same folk who run neighboring Grand Canyon Winery, Station 66 serves locally produced wine and beer.

Rod's Steak House
STEAK $$

(☑ 928-635-2671; www.rods-steakhouse.com; 301 E Route 66; mains $17-23; ⊙ 11am-9:30pm Mon-Sat) The cow-shaped sign and menus spell things out – if you want steak and potatoes, this has been the place to come since 1946. A dark and old-school Route 66 classic with iceberg wedge salad and prime rib.

Red Raven Restaurant
AMERICAN $$

(☑ 928-635-4980; www.redravenrestaurant.com; 135 W Route 66; mains $22-25; ⊙ 11am-2pm & 5-9pm, hours vary seasonally) The most upscale dining experience you'll find in Williams. There's a fair amount of meat on the menu (the lamb brochette with chimichurri and broiled rib eye are good) but pastas, salads and seafood also get a look-in.

🍷 Drinking & Nightlife

Rusted-on dive bars rub shoulders with newer wine-tasting rooms.

World Famous Sultana Bar
BAR

(☑ 928-635-2021; 301 W Route 66; ⊙ 10am-2am, shorter hours in winter) A slightly daunting local hangout, this 100-year-old bar is pretty darn cool, especially if you like the sort of place that's kitted out with deer skulls, stuffed mountain lions and crusty locals. It was a speakeasy during Prohibition. No food, and no doors on the male toilet stalls.

Grand Canyon Winery   WINERY
(☎855-598-0999; www.thegrandcanyonwinery.com; 138 W Route 66; ⊗noon-9pm) Grand Canyon Winery has excellent wines, produced with local grapes, and craft beer from their sister Historic Brewing Co, served by the mason glass or hefty portioned flight. It's a friendly low-key spot, with a handful of stools along the tiny bar and a few tables.

❶ Information

Police Station (☎928-635-4461, emergency 911; 501 W Route 66)

Post Office (☎928-635-4572; 120 S 1st St; ⊗8:30am-3.30pm Mon-Fri)

North Country HealthCare (☎928-635-4441; www.northcountryhealthcare.org/williams.htm; 301 S 7th St; ⊗8am-8pm urgent care)

Visitor Center (☎928-635-4061, 800-863-0546; www.experiencewilliams.com; 200 Railroad Ave; ⊗8am-6pm summer) Inside the 1901 train depot, with a small but interesting museum on Williams' history, and a bookstore selling titles on the Grand Canyon, Kaibab National Forest and other areas of interest. You can purchase Grand Canyon entrance passes here.

Williams Ranger Station (☎928-635-5600; www.fs.usda.gov/kaibab; 742 S Clover Rd; ⊗8am-4:30pm Mon-Fri) Maps and details for hiking, biking, fishing and camping in the surrounding national forest. It sits just off I-40, west of downtown.

❶ Getting There & Away

Williams is 35 miles west of Flagstaff on I-40 and 55 miles south of the Grand Canyon National Park, via Hwy 64.

Amtrak (☎800-872-7245; www.amtrak.com; 233 N Grand Canyon Blvd) has trains stopping at the Grand Canyon Railway Depot.

Arizona Shuttle (☎800-563-1980, 928-225-2290; www.arizonashuttle.com) offers three daily shuttles between Flagstaff and the Grand Canyon's South Rim (per person $32) and between Williams and the Grand Canyon (per person $24).

Havasupai Reservation

The blue-green waterfalls of Havasu Canyon are among the Grand Canyon region's greatest treasures. Tucked in a hidden valley, the five stunning, spring-fed waterfalls – and their inviting azure swimming holes – sit in the heart of the 185,000-acre Havasupai Reservation. Parts of the canyon floor, as well as the rock underneath the waterfalls and pools, are made up of limestone deposited by flowing water. Known as travertine, these limestone deposits give the famous blue-green water its otherworldly hue.

The Havasupai Reservation lies south of the Colorado River and west of the Grand Canyon National Park's South Rim – a three- to four-hour drive. Supai, the only village within the Grand Canyon, is situated 8 miles below the rim. From Hualapai Hilltop, a well-maintained trail leads to Supai, the waterfalls and the Colorado River.

About a mile beyond Supai are the newly formed (and unofficially named) New Navajo Falls and Rock Falls and their blue pools below. These new falls developed above the original Navajo Falls, which were lost after a major flash flood in 2008 rerouted the water. After crossing two bridges, you will reach beautiful Havasu Falls; this waterfall drops 100ft into a sparkling blue pool surrounded by cottonwoods and is a popular swimming hole. Havasu Campground sits a quarter-mile beyond Havasu Falls. Just beyond the campground, the trail passes Mooney Falls, which tumble 200ft down into another blue-green swimming hole. To get to the swimming hole, you must climb through two tunnels and descend a very steep trail – chains provide welcome handholds, but this trail is not for the faint of heart. Carefully pick your way down, keeping in mind that these falls were named for prospector DW James Mooney, who fell to his death here. After a picnic and a swim, continue about 2 miles to Beaver Falls. The Colorado River is 5 miles beyond. It's generally recommended that you don't attempt to hike to the river and, in fact, the reservation actively discourages this.

❶ Fees & Reservations

Because the falls lie 10 miles below the rim, most trips are combined with a stay at either Havasupai Lodge in Supai or at the nearby campground. Before heading down to Supai, you must have reservations to camp or stay in the lodge. Do not try to hike down and back in one day – not only is it dangerous, but it doesn't allow enough time to see the waterfalls.

Entry requires payment of a $50 fee. A $10 environmental care fee is also assessed.

Liquor, recreational drugs, pets and nude swimming are not allowed, nor are trail bikes allowed below Hualapai Hilltop.

For detailed information on traveling into Havasu Canyon, see www.havasupai-nsn.gov.

🛏 Sleeping & Eating

It is essential that you make reservations in advance; if you hike in without a reservation, you will not be allowed to stay in Supai and will have to hike 8 miles back up to your vehicle at Hualapai Hilltop.

In Supai, the **Supai Cafe** (☎928-448-2981; Supai; mains $9-13; ⊙7am-6:15pm) serves breakfast, lunch and dinner daily; **Sinyella Store** (☎928-448-2343; Supai; ⊙7am-7pm) sells good homemade tamales, plus basic groceries, as does the **Havasupai Trading Post** (☎928-448-2951; Supai; ⊙8am-5pm).

★**Havasu Campground**   CAMPGROUND $
(☎928-448-2180, 928-448-2141, 928-448-2121, 928-448-2137; www.havasuwaterfalls.net; Havasu Canyon; campsites per person per night $25) Two miles past Supai, the campground stretches 0.75 miles along Havasu Creek between Havasu and Mooney Falls. Sites have picnic tables and the campground features several composting toilets and spring water (treat before drinking). Fires are not permitted but gas stoves are allowed. Reservations required, but sites are first-come, first-served.

Getting a permit to camp is the main and maddeningly near-impossible thing. Be prepared to spend a long time on the phone, and hope. You'll need to add the $50 entrance fee and $10 environmental care fee to the cost of your stay.

Supai Lodge   LODGE $$
(☎928-448-2201, 928-448-2111; www.havasuwaterfalls.net; Supai; r for up to 4 people $145; ❄) The only lodging in Supai offers bare-bone white-walled motel rooms, each with two double beds and private showers. Reservations are accepted by phone only, but this is a good fallback if camping permits are impossible to secure.

ℹ Information

The local **post office** (Supai; ⊙8-11am & 1:30-4:30pm Mon-Fri) is the only one in the country still delivering its mail by mule, and mail sent from here bears a special postmark to prove it.
Havasupai Tourist Enterprise (☎928-448-2180; 160 Main St, Supai; ⊙9am-3pm Mon-Fri) You can pay the relevant permits here.
Emergency Clinic (☎928-448-2641; Supai; ⊙8am-noon & 1-5pm Mon-Fri)

ℹ Getting There & Around

Seven miles east of Peach Springs on historic Route 66, a signed turnoff leads to the 62-mile paved road ending at Hualapai Hilltop. Here you'll find the parking area, stables and the trailhead into the canyon – but no services.

Don't let place names confuse you: Hualapai Hilltop is on the Havasupai Reservation, not the Hualapai Reservation, as one might think.

HELICOPTER

On Monday, Thursday and Friday and Sunday from late March through mid-October, **Airwest Helicopters** (☎623-516-2790; www.havasuwaterfalls.net; Hualapai Hilltop & Supai; one-way $85) flies between Hualapai Hilltop and Supai. It operates Sundays and Fridays the rest of the year (and is closed for federal and tribal holidays). Advance reservations are not accepted; show up at the parking lot and sign up. However, service is prioritized for tribal members and those offering services and deliveries to the reservation. Call Havasupai Tourist Enterprise before you arrive to be sure the helicopter is running.

HORSE & MULE

If you don't want to hike to Supai, you can ride a horse (one-way/round-trip to the Supai Lodge $121/242). You can also arrange for a packhorse or mule, for the same price, to carry your pack into and out of the canyon.

Horses and mules depart from Hualapai Hilltop. Call the Supai Lodge or Havasu Campground (wherever you'll be staying) to arrange a ride and set a time.

Hualapai Reservation & Skywalk

Home to the much-hyped Skywalk, the Hualapai Reservation borders many miles of the Colorado River northeast of Kingman, covering the southwest rim of the Grand Canyon and bordering the Havasupai Reservation to the east and Lake Mead National Recreation Area to the west.

In 1988 the Hualapai Nation opened Grand Canyon West, which is *not* part of Grand Canyon National Park. Though the views here are lovely, they're not as sublime as those on the South Rim – but the unveiling of the glass bridge known as the Grand Canyon Skywalk in 2007 added a novel way to view the canyon, vertigo permitting.

Grand Canyon West

The only way to visit **Grand Canyon West** (☎888-868-9378, 928-769-2636; www.grandcanyonwest.com; Hualapai Reservation; per person \$44-81; ⊘7am-7pm Apr-Sep, 8am-5pm Oct-Mar), the section of the West Rim overseen by the Hualapai Nation, is to purchase a package tour. These tours include a hop-on, hop-off shuttle ride, which loops to scenic points along the rim. Tours can include lunch, cowboy activities at an ersatz Western town and informal American Indian performances.

Included in all but the cheapest packages is entry the **Grand Canyon Skywalk**. This horseshoe-shaped glass bridge is cantilevered 4000ft above the canyon floor and juts out almost 70ft over the canyon, allowing visitors to see the canyon through the glass walkway. Another stop, the unfortunately named **Guano Point**, is good for lunch, shopping and a bit of exploring, with fantastic canyon and river views.

Since would-be visitors to the Skywalk are required to purchase a package tour – and the extra-cost Skywalk is the primary draw – the experience can be a pricey prospect.

Peach Springs

The tribal capital of the Hualapai Reservation is tiny Peach Springs, also a jumping-off point for the only one-day rafting excursions on the Colorado River. Grand Canyon West is about 55 miles northwest of here via what locals have dubbed 'Buck-and-Doe-Rd.' It's beautiful, but don't even think about taking it without a 4WD.

If you plan to travel off Route 66 on the Hualapai Reservation, you need to buy a permit at the desk of Hualapai Tourism at the Hualapai Lodge. This is also where you arrange raft trips operated by **Hualapai River Runners** (☑928-769-2636, tourism office 928-769-2219; www.grandcanyonwest.com; 1-/2-day rafting trip \$451/740; ⊘mid-Mar–Oct). Packages include transportation from the lodge to the river at Diamond Creek via a bone-jarring 22-mile track (the only road anywhere to the bottom of the canyon), the 40-mile motorized raft trip to Pierce Ferry landing, a helicopter ride out of the canyon, and the bus ride back to Peach Springs.

Hualapai Lodge HOTEL **$$**
(☑928-769-2230; www.goroute66.us; 900 Route 66; r from \$109; ❄ 🛜 ☀) The modern Hualapai Lodge is the only place to stay in Peach Springs and, quite oddly, has a saltwater swimming pool and hot tub. The attached Diamond Creek Restaurant serves American standards. Lodging/rafting packages are available.

Diamond Creek Restaurant AMERICAN, AMERICAN INDIAN **$$**
(☑928-769-2800; 900 Route 66, Hualapai Lodge; mains \$12-20; ⊘6:30am-9pm) The in-house restaurant of the Hualapai Lodge serves American standards alongside frybread and other American Indian fare.

ℹ️ Information

Hualapai Tourism (☑928-769-2636; www.grandcanyonwest.com; 900 Route 66, Hualapai Lodge; ⊘variable) Has a desk at Hualapai Lodge in the microscopic town of Peach Springs and is the contact for scenic overlooks, flights and accommodations at Grand Canyon West, and day-trip white-water or smooth-water rafting trips on the Colorado River.

North Rim

Grand Canyon National Park North Rim

Solitude reigns supreme on the **Grand Canyon National Park North Rim** (www.nps.gov/grca; per vehicle \$30, per motorcycle \$25, per bicycle, pedestrian or shuttle-bus passenger \$15; ⊘mid-May–mid-Oct). All you'll find here are a classic rimside lodge, campground, motel and general store, plus miles of trails carving through meadows thick with wildflowers, willowy aspen and towering ponderosa pines. You'll also find peace, room to breathe and a less fettered Grand Canyon experience.

At 8000ft, the North Rim is about 10°F (6°C) cooler than the South – even on summer evenings you'll need a sweater. All services are closed from mid-October through mid-May, although the road usually stays open through November. Outdoor types can cross-country ski in and stay at the campground.

Park admission is valid for seven days at both rims. Upon entering, you'll be given a map and *The North Rim Pocket Map and Services Guide*. It's 24 miles from Jacob Lake to the North Rim, on Hwy 67, and another 20 miles to the Grand Canyon Lodge.

◉ Sights & Activities

Hiking & Backpacking

Your first hike? The short and easy paved trail to **Bright Angel Point** (www.nps.gov; half-mile round-trip) provides an impressive introduction to the region. Beginning from the back porch of the Grand Canyon Lodge, it leads to a narrow finger of an overlook with unfettered views of the mesas, buttes, spires and temples of Bright Angel Canyon.

That's the South Rim, 11 miles away, and beyond it the San Francisco Peaks, near Flagstaff.

The 3-mile round-trip **Transept Trail**, a rocky dirt path with moderate inclines, meanders north from the lodge through aspens to the North Rim Campground. The winding **Widforss Trail** follows the rim for 5 miles with views of canyon, meadows and woods, finishing at Widforss Point. To get to the trailhead, drive a quarter-mile south of Cape Royal Rd on Hwy 67, then turn west onto the dirt road and drive 1 mile to the trailhead, where you can obtain a self-guiding brochure. The 4-mile round-trip **Cape Final Trail** begins in a healthy grove of ponderosa pines and ends with incredible views of the canyon.

The steep and difficult **North Kaibab Trail** drops 6000ft over 14 miles to the river and is the only maintained rim-to-river trail on the North Rim. It connects with trails to the South Rim near Phantom Ranch (p172). The trailhead is 2 miles north of Grand Canyon Lodge. There's a parking lot, but it's often full soon after daylight. A Hikers' Shuttle (p184) departs from outside the lodge at 5:45am and 7:10am – sign up 24 hours in advance at the front desk of the lodge.

If you just want to get a taste of inner-canyon hiking, walk 0.75 miles from the North Kaibab trailhead down to **Coconino Overlook** or 2 miles to the **Supai Tunnel**. More ambitious day-hikers can continue another 2 miles or so to the waterfall at **Roaring Springs** to complete a strenuous 9.4-mile round-trip day hike. At the Springs, take the short detour to the left, where you'll find picnic tables and a pool to cool your feet. Seasonal water is available mid-May to mid-October.

If you wish to continue to the river, plan on camping overnight (backcountry permit required) at Cottonwood Campground (p171), some 2 miles beyond Roaring Springs.

From the campground, it's a gentle downhill walk along Bright Angel Creek to the Colorado River. Phantom Ranch (p172) and the Bright Angel Campground (p171) are 7 and 7.5 miles respectively below Cottonwood.

Rangers suggest three nights as a minimum to enjoy a rim-to-river-to-rim hike, staying at Cottonwood on the first and third nights and Bright Angel on the second. Faster trips would be an endurance slog and not much fun.

Hiking from the North Rim to the South Rim requires a ride on the Trans-Canyon Shuttle (p184) to get you back.

Mule Rides

See **Canyon Trail Rides** (☎ 435-679-8665; www.canyonrides.com; North Rim; 1hr/half-day mule ride $45/90; ⊙ schedules vary mid-May–mid-Oct) for details and bookings.

One Hour Rim of the Grand Canyon
(minimum 7 years old; 225lb weight limit; $45; departures between 8:30am and 1:30pm) Wooded ride to an overlook.

Half-Day Trip to Uncle Jim's Point
(minimum 10 years old; 225lb weight limit; $90; 7:30am & 12:30pm) Follow the Ken Patrick Trail through the woods.

Half-Day Canyon Mule Trip to Supai Tunnel (minimum 10 years old; 200lb weight limit; $90; 7:30am & 12:30pm) Descend 2300ft into the canyon along the North Kaibab Trail.

Cross-Country Skiing

Once the first heavy snowfall closes Hwy 67 into the park (as early as late October or as late as January), you can cross-country ski the 45 miles to the rim. A backcountry permit ($10) is required for an overnight stay; request the permit at least two weeks in advance if you want to receive it by mail. For last-minute trips, to avoid driving to the Backcountry Information Center on the South Rim for a permit, you may be able to pick one up at Pipe Spring National Monument (p187).

In the park, you can camp at the campground (no water; pit toilets) or spend the night in the six-person **North Rim Yurt** (☎ 928-638-7888; www.nps.gov; permit $10, per group $8; ⊙ Dec 2-Apr 14). You can ski any of the rim trails, though none are groomed. For more information call the Backcountry Information Center – South Rim (p174) between 1pm and 5pm. The closest ski rental is in Flagstaff.

Scenic Drives

Driving on the North Rim involves miles of slow, twisty roads through dense stands of evergreens and aspen to get to the most spectacular overlooks. From Grand Canyon Lodge, drive north for about 3 miles, then take the signed turn east to Cape Royal and Point Imperial and continue for 5 miles to a fork in the road called the Y.

From the Y it's another 15 miles south to **Cape Royal** (7876ft) past overlooks, picnic tables and an Ancestral Puebloan site. A 0.6-mile paved path, lined with piñon, cliffrose and interpretive signs, leads from the parking lot to a natural arch and **Cape Royal Point**, arguably the best view from this side of the canyon.

Point Imperial, the park's highest overlook at 8803ft, is reached by following Point Imperial Rd from the Y for an easy 3 miles. Expansive views include Nankoweap Creek, the Vermilion Cliffs, the Painted Desert and the Little Colorado River.

The dirt roads to **Point Sublime** (34 miles round-trip; an appropriately named 270-degree overlook) and **Toroweap/Tuweep** (122 miles round-trip; a sheer-drop view of the Colorado River 3000ft below) are rough, require high-clearance vehicles and are not recommended for 2WDs. While they certainly offer amazing views, they require navigating treacherous roads and if your goal is absolute solitude, you might be disappointed. Camping at Tuweep now requires a backcountry permit. The dirt road to Point Sublime starts about 1 mile west of Hwy 67, 2.7 miles north of Grand Canyon Lodge (look for the Widforss Trail sign). It should take about two hours to drive the 17 miles each way. Toroweap is reached via BLM Rd 109, a rough dirt road heading south off Hwy 389, 8 miles west of Fredonia. The one-way trip is 61 miles and should take at least two hours. Reportedly, one-quarter of all visitors get a flat tire!

🛏 Sleeping

Accommodations on the North Rim are limited to one lodge and one campground.

If these two options are fully booked, try snagging a cabin at the **Kaibab Lodge** (☎928-638-2389; www.kaibablodge.com; Hwy 67; cabin from $90; ☉May 15-Oct 20; 🐾), or a site at the nearby **DeMotte Campground** (☎877-444-6777, visitor center 928-643-7298; www.recreation.gov; FR 616A, off Hwy 67; campsite $18; ☉May 14-Oct 15; 🐾).

There's also free dispersed camping in the surrounding Kaibab National Forest. Otherwise, you'll find more options another 60 miles north in Kanab, Utah.

North Rim Campground CAMPGROUND $
(☎877-444-6777, 928-638-7814; www.recreation.gov; tent sites $18, RV sites $18-25; ☉by reservation May 15-Oct 15, first-come, first-served Oct 16-31; 🐾) Operated by the National Park Service, this campground, 1.5 miles north of the Grand Canyon Lodge, offers shaded sites on level ground blanketed in pine needles. Sites 11, 14, 15, 16 and 18 overlook

the Transept (a side canyon) and cost $25. There's water, a store, a snack bar, coin-operated showers and laundry facilities, but no hookups. Make reservations online.

⭐**Grand Canyon Lodge** HISTORIC HOTEL $$
(☎advance reservations 877-386-4383, reservations outside USA 480-337-1320, same-day reservations 928-638-2611; www.grandcanyonlodgenorth.com; r/cabins from $130/143; ☉May 15-Oct 15) 🍃 Walk through the front door of the lodge, and here, framed by picture windows, is the canyon in all its glory. Built in 1937 with wood, Kaibab limestone and glass, the lodge features a spacious rimside dining room and sun porches lined with Adirondack chairs. Guest rooms are not in the lodge itself – most accommodations are cozy log cabins nearby.

🍴 Eating & Drinking

North Rim General Store SUPERMARKET $
(☎928-638-2611; ☉7am-8pm mid-May–mid-Oct; 🛜) Pick up basic groceries and supplies at the General Store, adjacent to the North Rim Campground and just over a mile from the Grand Canyon Lodge. This is also the only place around the North Rim with a wi-fi signal: grab a coffee from the small cafe kiosk and take a seat to use it.

Deli in the Pines CAFETERIA $
(☎928-638-2611; lunch & dinner $7-15; ☉10:30am-9pm mid-May–mid-Oct) The name is a bit misleading: this isn't a deli, but a small cafeteria adjacent to the Grand Canyon Lodge serving takeaway salads and sandwiches to pack for a hike or picnic. There's also pizza, soft-serve ice cream, and a handful of daily specials like chili and pulled pork.

⭐**Grand Canyon Lodge Dining Room** AMERICAN $$
(☎May-Oct 928-638-2611, Nov-Apr 928-645-6865; www.grandcanyonforever.com; breakfast $8-11, lunch $10-13, dinner $18-28; ☉6:30-10:30am, 11:30am-2:30pm & 4:30-9:30pm May 15-Oct 15; 🚹♿) Although seats beside the window are wonderful, views from the dining room are so huge it really doesn't matter where you sit. While the solid dinner menu includes buffalo steak, western trout and several vegetarian options, don't expect great culinary memories – the view is the thing. Make reservations in advance of your arrival to guarantee a spot for dinner.

Grand Canyon Cookout Experience AMERICAN $$$
(☎928-638-2611; Grand Canyon Lodge; adult/child 6-15yr $30/$15; ☉5:45-9pm Jun 1-Sep 30; ♿)

ARIZONA NORTH RIM

Feast on smoked beef brisket, roasted chicken, skillet cornbread and all the fixings – served with a side of Western songs and jokes. It's cheesy, but it's a lot of fun, old-school National Park–style, and it's great for kids. Take the Bridle Trail from the Grand Canyon Lodge to the cookout site, or catch the complimentary train or shuttle van.

Coffee Shop
& Rough Rider Saloon   COFFEE, BAR

(www.grandcanyonforever.com; Grand Canyon Lodge; ⊙ 5:30-10:30am & 11:30am-10:30pm) If you're up for an early morning hike, stop for coffee or a quick breakfast at the cozy Coffee Shop – a space that morphs back into a saloon by noon, serving beer, wine and mixed drinks, plus sandwiches, wraps and pizza. Teddy Roosevelt memorabilia lines the walls (and inspires the cocktails), honoring his role in the history of the park. This is the only bar in the lodge, so if you want to enjoy a cocktail on the sun porch or in your room, pick it up here.

ℹ Information

ATMs can be found in the North Rim General Store (p183) and the Coffee Shop & Rough Rider Saloon.
Post Office (☏ 928-643-7122; ⊙ 8am-noon & 1-5pm Mon-Fri May 15-Oct 15) Offers post and parcel services from a window next to the Coffee Shop & Rough Rider Saloon.
North Rim Backcountry Information Center (☏ 928-638-7875; www.nps.gov/grca/planyourvisit/backcountry-permit.htm; Administrative Bldg; ⊙ 8am-noon & 1-5pm May 15-Oct 15) Backcountry permits for overnight camping on and below the rim, at Tuweep Campground, or camping anytime between November 1 and May 14.
North Rim Visitor Center (☏ 928-638-7888; www.nps.gov/grca/planyourvisit/visitorcenters.htm; ⊙ 8am-6pm May 15-Oct 15) Beside Grand Canyon Lodge, this is the place to get information on the park, and the starting point for ranger-led nature walks.

ℹ Getting There & Around

The only access road to the Grand Canyon North Rim is Hwy 67, which closes with the first snowfall and reopens in spring after the snowmelt (exact dates vary).

Although only 11 miles from the South Rim as the crow flies, it's a grueling 215-mile, four-to five-hour drive on winding desert roads between here and Grand Canyon Village. You can drive yourself or take the **Trans-Canyon Shuttle** (☏ 928-638-2820, 877-638-2820; www.trans-canyonshuttle.com; one-way rim to rim $90, one-way South Rim to Marble Canyon $80). Reserve at least two weeks in advance.

The complimentary **Hikers' Shuttle** (⊙ 5:45am & 7:10am) takes hikers from the Grand Canyon Lodge to the North Kaibab Trailhead twice daily. Sign up 24 hours in advance. Note that there's no service from North Kaibab Trailhead back to the lodge, but it's only a couple of miles down the road.

Arizona Strip

Wedged between the Grand Canyon and Utah, the vast Arizona Strip is one of the state's most remote and sparsely populated regions. Only about 6000 people live here, in relative isolation, many of them members of the Fundamentalist Church of Latter-Day Saints (FLDS), who defy US law by practicing polygamy.

Larger than Vermont, this 14,000-sq-mile region is traversed by only one major road – Hwy 89A. It crosses the Colorado River at Marble Canyon before getting sandwiched by the crimson-hued Vermilion Cliffs to the north and House Rock Valley to the south. Desert scrub gives way to piñon and juniper as the highway climbs up the Kaibab Plateau to enter the Kaibab National Forest. At Jacob Lake, it meets with Hwy 67 to the Grand Canyon North Rim. Past Jacob Lake, as the road drops, you get stupendous views across southern Utah.

Marble Canyon & Lees Ferry

About 14 miles past the Hwy 89/89A fork, Hwy 89A crosses the Navajo Bridge over the Colorado River at Marble Canyon. Actually, there are two bridges: one built in 1995 and a historical one from 1929. Walking across the latter, you'll enjoy fabulous views down Marble Canyon to the northeast lip of the Grand Canyon. The Navajo Bridge Interpretive Center (p189) on the west bank has info about the bridges, as well as the area's natural wonders. Keep an eye out for California condors!

Just past the bridge, a stunning 6-mile drive leads to the fly-fishing mecca of Lees Ferry. Sitting on a sweeping bend of the Colorado River, it's in the far southwestern corner of Glen Canyon National Recreation Area and a premier put-in spot for Grand Canyon rafters. Fishing here requires an Arizona fishing license, available at local fly shops and outfitters such as Marble Canyon Lodge.

◉ Sights & Activities

Historic Lees Ferry & Lonely Dell Ranch
HISTORIC SITE

(☎928-608-6200; www.nps.gov/glca/planyour visit/lees-ferry.htm; Glen Canyon National Recreation Area; 7-day Glen Canyon Pass, per vehicle/motorcycle/person $25/15/10) Lees Ferry was the site of the region's original ferry crossing, and of Charles Spencer's 1910 effort to extract gold from the surrounding hills. Today it's the launching area for rafting trips down the Colorado through the Grand Canyon. Nearby, Lonely Dell Ranch provided for families who worked at the crossing in the 1880s and '90s. Their log cabins and a pioneer cemetery remain, as well an an idyllic orchard where visitors are welcome to pick (and eat) the fruit.

Marble Canyon Outfitters
FISHING

(☎800-533-7339, 928-645-2781; www.leesferry flyfishing.com) This outfit takes anglers fly-fishing on the broad shallows of the Colorado River at Lees Ferry. Guided trips are $400 for one, $500 for two and $600 for three people. Anglers meet at Marble Canyon Lodge.

🛏 Sleeping

Lees Ferry Campground
CAMPGROUND $

(☎928-608-6200; www.nps.gov/glca; Lees Ferry, Glen Canyon National Recreation Area; tent & RV sites $20) On a small hill, Lees Ferry Campground has 54 river-view sites along with drinking water and toilets, but no hookups. With views of towering red rocks and the river, it's a strikingly pretty spot to camp. Public coin showers and a laundry are available at Marble Canyon Lodge.

Cliff Dwellers Lodge & Restaurant
LODGE $

(☎928-355-2261, 800-962-9755; www.cliffdwellers lodge.com; Hwy 89, Marble Canyon; d/house from $90/250; ⊙6am-9pm; ☎) This roadside lodge, charmingly set at the base of enormous cliffs 10 miles west of Navajo Bridge, is ground zero for fly-fishing enthusiasts, popular for its excellent restaurant, with breezy porch seating. Opt for a room with knotty pine walls and a recently remodeled bathroom. The owners run on-site **Lees Ferry Anglers** (☎800-962-9755, 928-355-2261; www.leesferry.com; Hwy 89A, Cliff Dwellers Lodge; ⊙6am-9pm): ask about guided trips and local hikes.

Lees Ferry Lodge
LODGE $

(☎928-355-2231; www.vermilioncliffs.com; Hwy 89A, Vermilion Cliffs; r/apt $74/125; P❄☎) Rustic,

OFF THE BEATEN TRACK

VERMILION CLIFFS CONDOR RELEASE SITE

The largest population of wild California condors anywhere calls these spectacular cliffs home, giving you your best shot at catching a glimpse of these massive birds. Coming from Vermilion Cliffs or Navajo Bridge, the site is located on Hwy 89A, on the way to Jacob Lake. Turn right on House Rock Rd – the release site is located 2 miles north.

comfortable, but not actually in Lees Ferry (it's 3 miles west of Marble Canyon), this lodge has 10 rooms, plus a restaurant/bar with a huge array of international beers. The bar is the kind where you're never quite sure who's going to roar off the highway and stomp through the door – but they'll surely have an interesting story.

Marble Canyon Lodge
LODGE $

(☎928-355-2225; www.marblecanyoncompany. com; Hwy 89, Marble Canyon; s/d/apt $82/94/187; P) The closest accommodations to Navajo Bridge (and nearby Lees Ferry) are at this friendly lodge, with 60 rooms, eight suites and apartments for up to six people. There's also a mini market, where you can buy a fishing permit, and a basic restaurant.

Jacob Lake

From Marble Canyon, Hwy 89A climbs 5000ft over 40 miles to the Kaibab National Forest and the oddly lakeless outpost of Jacob Lake. All you'll find is a motel with a restaurant, a gas station and the USFS **Kaibab Plateau Visitor Center** (☎928-643-7298; www.fs.usda.gov; cnr Hwys 89A & 67; ⊙8am-5pm May 15-Oct 15). From here Hwy 67 runs south for 44 miles past meadows, aspen and ponderosa pine to the Grand Canyon North Rim. The only facilities between Jacob Lake and the rim are the Kaibab Lodge Camper Village, **North Rim Country Store** (☎928-638-2383; www.northrimcountrystore.com; Hwy 67; ⊙7:30am-7pm May 14-Oct 27) and DeMotte Campground (p183).

🛏 Sleeping & Eating

Kaibab Lodge Camper Village
CAMPGROUND $

(☎928-643-7804; www.kaibabcampervillage.com; tent/RV site $18/37, cabin $50-85; ⊙mid-May–mid-Oct) Open during the Grand Canyon

ⓘ NEED A LIFT?

The main town in the Arizona Strip is postage-stamp-sized Fredonia, some 30 miles northwest of Jacob Lake. Here you'll find the **North Kaibab Ranger District Office** (☏928-635-8200; www.fs.usda.gov; 430 S Main St, Fredonia; ⊙8am-4:30pm Mon-Fri), where you can pick up info on hiking and camping in the forest. There's also a service station, **Judd Auto Service** (☏928-643-7107; 623 S Main St, Fredonia; ⊙7am-7pm), in case you need mechanical help.

North Rim's annual season (May 15 to October 15), this pine-shaded campground a mile south of Jacob Lake has more than 100 bookable sites for tents and RVs. There are also one- and two-person cabins available; you need to bring your own bedding for the economy ones.

Jacob Lake Inn　　　　　　MOTEL $$
(☏928-643-7232; www.jacoblake.com; cnr Hwys 89A & 67; r/cabin from $128/96; ⊙6:30am-9pm mid-May–mid-Oct, 8am-8pm mid-Oct–mid-May; P🐾) Nearly everyone stops at this minor landmark on their way to the Grand Canyon North Rim entrance, 44 miles south. There's year-round lodging of various types – no-frills cabins with tiny bathrooms (summer only), and well-worn motel rooms and spacious doubles in the modern hotel-style building. The Inn is also famous for its cookies, milkshakes and American Indian–themed gift shop.

Jacob Lake Inn Restaurant　　AMERICAN $$
(☏928-643-7232; www.jacoblake.com; cnr Hwys 89A & 67; mains $19-22; ⊙6:30am-9pm mid-May–mid-Oct, 8am-8pm mid-Oct–mid-May; P) Be surprised by dishes as adventurous as mountain trout almondine, or pork schnitzel in 'Kaibab hunter's sauce.' There's also an ice-cream counter and a great bakery, famed for its cookies. Try the Cookie in a Cloud, a cakey cookie topped with marshmallow and chocolate. During winter, dining is only available at the counter and the kitchen closes a half-hour earlier.

Page & Glen Canyon National Recreation Area

An enormous lake tucked into a landlocked swath of desert? You can guess how popular it is to play in the spangly waters of Lake Powell. Part of the **Glen Canyon National Recreation Area** (Map p386; ☏928-608-6200; www.nps.gov/glca; 7-day pass per vehicle $25, per pedestrian or cyclist $12), the country's second-largest artificial reservoir was created by the construction of Glen Canyon Dam in 1963. To house the scores of workers an entire town, Page, was built from scratch near the dam.

Straddling the Utah–Arizona border, the 186-mile-long lake has 1960 miles of empty shoreline set amid striking red-rock formations, sharply cut canyons and dramatic desert scenery. Lake Powell is famous for its houseboating, which appeals to families and college students alike.

The gateway to Lake Powell is the small town of Page, which sits right next to Glen Canyon Dam in the far southwest corner of the recreation area. Hwy 89 (called N Lake Powell Blvd in town) forms the main strip.

⊙ Sights

★**Horseshoe Bend**　　　　　CANYON
(Hwy 89; P) Calling the view at Horseshoe Bend 'dramatic' is an understatement – the overlook sits on sheer cliffs that drop 1000ft to the river below, as it carves a perfect horseshoe through the Navajo sandstone. Toddlers should be kept safely away from the edge at all times, as there are no guardrails and the rim of the canyon can be treacherous. The trailhead is south of Page off Hwy 89, just past Mile 545.

Glen Canyon Dam　　　　　DAM
(☏928-608-6072; www.glencanyonnha.org; Hwy 89; tour adult/child 7-16yr $5/2.50; ⊙tours 8am-6pm Mon, Tue, Thu, Sun, to 5pm Fri & Sat, to 4pm Wed) At 710ft tall, Glen Canyon Dam is the nation's highest concrete arch dam (the Hoover Dam, 16ft taller, is a different kind of structure). It was constructed between 1956 and 1966. From April through October, 45-minute guided tours depart from the Carl Hayden Visitor Center (p189) and descend deep inside the dam via elevators. Exhibits tell the story of the dam's construction, complete with all kinds of astounding technical facts. Three different videos spotlight various aspects of the region.

John Wesley Powell Museum　　MUSEUM
(☏928-645-9496; www.powellmuseum.org; 61 N Lake Powell Blvd; adult/senior/child 5-15yr $3/2/1; ⊙9am-5pm Apr-Dec, 10am-3pm Jan-Mar) In 1869, one-armed John Wesley Powell led the first Colorado River expedition through the Grand Canyon. This small museum displays

memorabilia of early river runners, including a model of Powell's boat, with photos and illustrations of his excursions. It also has exhibits on geology, paleontology and the history of Page, and houses the regional visitor center.

🏃 Activities

Colorado River Discovery   BOATING
(☑928-645-9175, 888-522-6644; www.raftthe canyon.com; 130 6th Ave; half-day adult/child $93/83, full day $113/103, raft & helicopter tour $299/269; ☺Mar-Nov) Offers smooth-water float trips down the Colorado from Glen Canyon Dam. Boats stop at petroglyphs, where you can also splash and cool off in the frigid water, and guides explain the natural and human history along the way. It's a beautiful trip through the deep, sheer redrock sides of Glen Canyon.

Lake Powell Resorts & Marinas   BOATING
(☑888-896-3829; www.lakepowell.com; 100 Lakeshore Dr) Popular trips include the Rainbow Bridge cruise (adult/child $122/77, seven hours), the Canyon Adventure cruise (adult/child $75/49, three hours) and the Canyon Princess Dinner Cruise (adult/child $80/35, two hours, Tuesday and Saturday only). They also do half-day trips to Navajo Tapestry, and 1½-hour rides to Antelope Canyon.

Slot Canyon Hummer
Adventures   DRIVING
(☑928-645-2266; www.hummeradventures.net; 12 N Lake Powell Bvd; 1hr tour adult/child $90/65) Runs 4WD tours to several slot canyons on Navajo land. With only six people to a vehicle, and no crowds vying for the perfect angle to shoot a photo, it's an excellent alternative to Antelope Canyon's mayhem.

Boating & Cruises
At Wahweap and Bullfrog Marinas you can rent kayaks ($50 per day), 19ft powerboats ($550), personal watercraft ($450) and other toys. Stand up paddleboards are available at Wahweap for $90 per day. From Wahweap Marina, Aramark runs boat cruises to Rainbow Bridge National Monument (p383). Canyon cruises and a dinner cruise are also offered.

🛏 Sleeping

You can camp anywhere along the Lake Powell shoreline for free, as long as you have a portable toilet or toilet facilities on your boat. There are several good mom-and-pop

PIPE SPRING NATIONAL MONUMENT
....
Fourteen miles southwest of Fredonia on Hwy 389, **Pipe Spring** (☑928-643-7105; www.nps.gov/pisp; 406 N Pipe Spring Rd; adult/child $7/free; ☺visitor center 8:30am-4:30pm) is a literal oasis in the desert. For thousands of years a vital source of water for American Indians, Mormons and pioneers, it's now a National Monument, preserving the remains of 19th-century survival in this starkly beautiful and unforgiving setting. Tours (on the hour and half-hour) let you peek inside the stone **Winsor Castle**, and there's also a small **museum**.

motels along the 'Avenue of Little Motels' in downtown Page.

Best Western View of
Lake Powell Hotel   HOTEL $$
(☑800-780-7234, 928-645-8868; www.book. bestwestern.com; 716 Rimview Dr; d from $243; ❄🛜🐕) Possibly the nicest Best Western you'll stay in. Perched on the edge of a hill overlooking Glen Canyon Dam, this smartly updated chain has surprisingly modern guest rooms, a swimming pool with a spectacular view, and a complimentary breakfast buffet with a yogurt bar and make-it-yourself waffles.

Lake Powell Motel   MOTEL $$
(☑480-452-9895; www.lakepowellmotel.net; 750 S Navajo Dr; ste from $99, r with kitchen from $139; ☺Apr-Oct; ❄🛜) Formerly Bashful Bob's, this revamped motel was originally constructed to house Glen Canyon Dam builders. Four units have kitchens and book up quickly. A fifth smaller room is typically held for walkups, unless specifically requested.

Lake Powell Resort   RESORT $$$
(☑888-528-6154; www.lakepowell.com; 100 Lakeshore Dr; r/ste from $199/344, child under 18yr free; ❄🛜🐕🐾) This bustling resort on the shores of Lake Powell offers beautiful views and a lovely little pool perched in the rocks above the lake, but it is impersonal and frenetic. Rates for lake-view rooms with tiny patios are well worth the extra money. In the lobby you can book boat tours. Wi-fi is available in the lobby and lounge only. Pets require a $20 non-refundable deposit.

DON'T MISS

ANTELOPE CANYON

Many visitors plans trips to Page just to experience the oft-photographed **Antelope Canyon**, a surreal landscape you'll have to see to believe. It's divided into two sections, Upper and Lower. The Navajo names for both sides hint at what to expect: the Upper Canyon is *Tsé bighánílíní* ('The place where water runs through rocks') and the Lower Canyon is known as *Hasdestwazi* ('Spiral rock arches').

Managed by the Lake Powell Navajo Tribal Park, the canyon can only be visited by tour. The Upper Canyon is more accessible and appropriate for small children, while the Lower Canyon involves steep staircases and is considered more beautiful. The tours are through one of several local outfitters, such as **Ken's Tours** (☑928-606-2168; www.lowerantelope.com; guided tour adult/child $25/17; ☉8am-5pm early Mar-early Nov, 9am-4pm early Nov-early Mar) or **Roger Ekis' Antelope Canyon Tours** (☑928-645-9102; www.antelopecanyon.com; 22 S Lake Powell Blvd; adult/child 5-12yr from $45/35). Reservations are recommended if you'd like to secure a particular tour time (noon tours receive the best light); otherwise, walk-ins are served on a first-come, first-served basis.

✖ Eating & Drinking

★ River's End Cafe
CAFE **$**

(☑928-645-9175; www.raftthecanyon.com/rivers-end-cafe; 130 6th Ave; mains $9-12; ☉8am-3pm) Tucked away inside Colorado River Discovery's headquarters, this espresso bar and cafe may be the best place in town for a light lunch: have a cappuccino and an egg-white omelet in the morning, or a Thai chicken wrap and cranberry feta salad later in the day. River's End also does takeout bistro bags ($11.50 to $14) for hikers and rafters.

Big John's Texas BBQ
BARBECUE **$**

(☑928-645-3300; www.bigjohnstexasbbq.com; 153 S Lake Powell Blvd; mains $13-18; ☉11am-10pm; ⬛) Cheerfully occupying a partially open-air space that was once a gas station, this barbecue joint is a friendly place to feast on pulled-pork sandwiches and ribs. Pull up a seat at one of the casual picnic tables, and look for live folk and bluegrass music several evenings of the week.

Latitude 37
AMERICAN **$$**

(www.lakepowell.com; 100 Lakeshore Dr, Lake Powell Resort; mains $12-25; ☉11am-9pm Fri-Sun Jun-Oct) Lake Powell Resort's floating restaurant is only open in high season, when boaters pull straight up to table-side slips. The Southwest-inspired menu includes smoked ribs and burgers, while the vistas of Castle Rock and Navajo Mountain provide an excellent cocktail-sipping backdrop.

Blue Buddha Sushi Lounge
SUSHI **$$**

(☑648-645-0007; bluebuddhasushilounge.com; 644 N Navajo Dr; sushi $8-11, mains $20-29; ☉5-9pm Tue-Sat) Darn good sushi for the desert we say, and the food and drinks at this blue-hued, ultra-cool hideaway hit the spot after a hot and dusty day of exploring. Beyond sushi, there's teppanyaki, steak and seafood.

Rainbow Room
BAR

(☑928-645-2433; www.lakepowell.com; 100 Lakeshore Dr, Lake Powell Resort; ☉6-10am & 5-9pm) The Rainbow Room is perched above Lake Powell, with picture windows framing dramatic red-rock formations against blue water. Your best bet is to eat elsewhere and come to the bar here for a beautiful sunset drink.

ⓘ Information

The Glen Canyon National Recreation Area entrance fees, good for up to seven days, are $25 per vehicle or $12 per individual entering on foot or bicycle. Boat entry is $30.

EMERGENCY

For the National Park Service 24-Hour Dispatch Center, call ☑800-582-4351 or 928-608-6300.

On the water, use Marine Band Channel 16.

Police Station (☑928-645-2462, emergency 911; 808 Coppermine Rd)

MARINAS

All the marinas except Antelope Point have rangers stations, and **Wahweap** (☑928-645-2433; www.nps.gov/glca) and Bullfrog Marinas rent boats. Check the Glen Canyon National Recreation Area newspaper for additional services at each marina.

MEDICAL SERVICES

Page Hospital (☑928-645-2424; www.banner health.com; 501 N Navajo Dr) Has 24-hour emergency services.

Pharmacy (☑928-645-5714; 650 Elm St; ☉9am-8pm Mon-Fri, 9am-6pm Sat, 10am-4pm Sun) Inside the Safeway.

POST

Post Office (☑ 928-645-2571; 101 W Glenn St; ◷7:30am-4pm Mon-Fri)

TOURIST INFORMATION

For regional information, stop by the **John Wesley Powell Museum** (p186). In addition to the **Carl Hayden Visitor Center** (☑ store 928-608-6068, tours 928-608-6072; www.nps.gov/glca; Hwy 89; ◷8am-4pm mid-May–mid-Sep, shorter hours mid-Sep–mid-May), there is a third GCN-RA Visitor Center 39 miles southwest of Page at **Navajo Bridge** (☑ 928-355-2319; www.nps.gov/glca; Hwy 89A; ◷9am-5pm Wed-Sun Mar-early Nov; P) in Marble Canyon.

❶ Getting There & Away

Great Lakes Airlines (☑ 928-645-1355, 800-554-5111; www.flygreatlakes.com) offers flights between **Page Municipal Airport** (☑ 928-645-4240; www.cityofpage.org/departments/airport; 238 N 10th Ave) and Phoenix. Page sits 125 miles northwest of the North Rim.

Car rental is available at the airport through **Avis** (☑ 928-645-2024, 800-331-1212; www.avis.com; 238 N 10th Ave, Page Municipal Airport; ◷8am-5:30pm Mon-Sat).

NAVAJO RESERVATION

A famous Diné (Navajo) poem ends with the phrase 'May I walk in beauty.' This request is easily granted at many spots on the Navajo Reservation in northeastern Arizona. At 27,000 sq miles the reservation is the country's largest, spilling over into the neighboring states of Utah, Colorado and New Mexico. Most of this land is as flat as a calm sea and just as barren, until – all of a sudden – Monument Valley's crimson red buttes rise before you, or you come face-to-face with ancient history at the cliff dwellings at Canyon de Chelly and Navajo National Monuments. Elsewhere, you can walk in dinosaur tracks or gaze at the shifting light of hauntingly beautiful Antelope Canyon.

Many Navajo rely on the tourist economy for survival. You can help keep their heritage alive by staying on the reservation, purchasing their crafts and trying their foods, such as the ubiquitous Navajo taco.

❶ Information

Unlike Arizona, the Navajo Reservation observes daylight saving time.

The single best source of information for the entire reservation is the Navajo Nation Tourism Department (p194).

Contact the **Navajo Parks & Recreation Department** (☑ Central Office 928-871-6647, Lake Powell 928-698-2808; www.navajonationparks.org; hiking & backcountry permit $12; ◷8am-5pm) for general information about the required permits for hiking and camping ($5 to $12 per person per night). For a list of park offices selling permits, visit www.navajonationparks.org/permits.htm.

Pick up a copy of the *Navajo Times* (www.navajotimes.com) for the latest Navajo news. Tune your radio to AM 660 KTNN for a mix of Navajo- and English-language news and music.

Keep in mind that alcohol is not permitted in the Navajo Nation.

❶ Getting There & Around

You really need your own wheels to properly explore this sprawling land. Gas stations are scarce and fuel prices are higher than outside the reservation.

The only public transportation is provided by the **Navajo Transit System** (☑ 866-243-6260, 928-729-4002; www.navajotransit.com; fare $2), but this bus service is geared toward local, not tourist, needs. There are currently 18 listed routes, with destinations within and outside the reservations, but not all of them are daily and some are not always in service. Rte 1 currently runs one service per day in each direction, Monday through Thursday, from Tuba City to Window Rock and Fort Defiance via the Hopi Reservation.

Tuba City & Moenkopi

☑ 928 / POP 9575 / ELEV 4936FT

Hwy 160 splits these contiguous towns in two: to the northwest, Tuba City is the largest single community in the Navajo Nation; to the southeast is the village of Moenkopi, a small Hopi island surrounded by Navajo land. Moenkopi has a gas station, a new 24-hour Denny's and one of the best hotels on either reservation – but not much else.

Tuba City is named for 19th-century Hopi chief Tuve (or Toova), who converted to Mormonism, then welcomed a group of Utah Mormons to build a village of their own, next to Moenkopi. The best reason to stop on this side of Hwy 160 is the Explore Navajo Interactive Museum.

◉ Sights

Explore Navajo Interactive Museum MUSEUM
(☑ 928-640-0684; www.explorenavajo.com; 10 N Main St; adult/senior/child 7-12yr $4.50/3.50/3; ◷8am-6pm Mon-Sat, noon-6pm Sun) A perfect precursor to exploring the Navajo Reservation, this museum will deepen your

understanding of the land, its people and their traditions. You'll learn why the Navajo call themselves the 'People of the Fourth World,' details about the Long Walk and aspects of contemporary life. Included in your entry fee is next door's small exhibition about the Navajo Code Talkers (open 8am to 5pm Monday to Friday, to 4pm Saturday and Sunday), with a display explaining how the famously uncrackable code was designed.

Tuba City Trading Post ARTS & CRAFTS
(☑928-283-5441; 10 Main St; ☺8am-5pm Mon-Fri, to 4pm Sat & Sun) Open since 1870, this hogan-shaped (octagonal) trading post sells mainly Navajo-made clothing, jewelry, dolls, paintings and other art and crafts.

🍴 Sleeping & Eating

Tuba City/Moenkopi is a convenient place to stay before or after a trip through the Hopi Reservation to the east.

Moenkopi Legacy Inn & Suites HOTEL $$
(☑928-283-4500; www.experiencehopi.com; cnr Hwys 160 & 264; r/ste from $160/171; ❉☎❊) Unquestionably the most luxurious digs in Moenkopi, the Legacy Inn is built in a stylized version of traditional Hopi village architecture – the lobby, with its soaring ceiling supported by pine pillars, is particularly effective. Rooms have marble and granite baths and reproductions of historical photographs from the Hopi archives at Northern Arizona University.

Quality Inn HOTEL $$
(☑928-283-4545; www.choicehotels.com; 10 N Main St; r/ste $190/200; ❉@☎❊) Comfortable, modern and well maintained, the Quality Inn has been a longtime standby, and it still holds up. Room rates include breakfast at the popular **Hogan Family Restaurant** (☑928-283-5260; 10 N Main St; mains $12-16; ☺6am-9pm; ⓟ) next door. Smoking rooms are available, there's a small fitness center and pets are $10 per night.

Hogan Espresso & More COFFEE
(☑928-283-4545; 10 N Main St; ☺8am-7pm; ☎) For your cappuccino fix or web-surfing session, swing by Hogan Espresso & More.

Navajo National Monument

The sublimely well-preserved Ancestral Puebloan cliff dwellings of Betatakin and Keet Seel are protected within the Navajo National Monument (☑928-672-2700; www.nps.gov/nava; Hwy 564; ☺visitor center 8am-5:30pm Jun-early Sep, 9am-5pm early Sep-May) FREE and can only be reached on foot. This walk in the park is no walk in the park, but there's truly something magical about approaching these ancient stone villages in relative solitude, among the piñon and juniper. The National Park Service controls access to the site and maintains the visitor center, which is informative and has excellent staff.

During summer months the park observes daylight saving time.

Betatakin, which translates as 'ledge house,' is reached on one of two ranger-led hikes that run between Memorial Day and Labor Day: a strenuous 5-mile round-trip departing from the visitor center daily at 8:15am or a 3-mile round-trip on a shorter (but even more tiring) trail at 10am. Carry plenty of water; it's a tough slog back up to the canyon rim. For a distant glimpse of Betatakin, follow the easy Sandal Trail about half a mile from the visitor center.

The 17-mile round-trip to the astonishingly beautiful **Keet Seel** is steep and strenuous and involves crossing sand gullies and shallow streams, but it's well worth the effort. The trail is open from Memorial Day to Labor Day and requires a free backcountry permit, reservable from early February. Call early, as daily access is limited to 20 people; alternatively show up early on the day and hope for cancellations. You hike on your own but are met at the pueblo by a ranger who will take you on a tour. Because the hike is demanding, most visitors stay at the primitive campground down in the canyon, which has composting toilets but no drinking water. Check the park website (www.nps.gov/nava) for more details.

Kayenta

☑928 / POP 5189 / ELEV 5641FT

A dispersed and largely functional town, Kayenta is basically a cluster of businesses and mobile homes around the junction of Hwys 160 and 163. Its great draw is being the closest town to Monument Valley, some 20 miles away. It has gas stations, motels, restaurants, a supermarket and an ATM.

The Burger King near the junction has a well-meaning but minimal exhibit on the Navajo Code Talkers. **Roland's Navajoland Tours** (☑928-697-3524) and Sacred Monument Tours offer vehicle, hiking and horseback-riding tours through Monument Valley.

🛏 Sleeping & Eating

A dearth of options sends prices sky-high in summer when demand at the three main motels exceeds capacity. Rates drop by nearly half in the slower seasons.

Basic diners, plus Italian, Mexican and fast-food joints line Hwys 160 and 163.

Hampton Inn   HOTEL $$
(☑ 928-697-3170; www.hamptoninn.com; Hwy 160; r from $169; ❄ 🛜 🏊 🐾) The decor is American Indian, and there's a fitness room and an outdoor pool, perfect for chilling out after a day on the dusty roads. For weekends in summer book well in advance, as the 73 rooms are usually in high demand.

Monument Valley Navajo Tribal Park

When Monument Valley rises into sight from the desert floor, you realize you've always known it. Its brick-red spindles, sheer-walled mesas and grand buttes, stars of countless films, TV commercials and magazine ads, are part of the modern consciousness. And Monument Valley's epic beauty is only heightened by the barren landscape surrounding it: one minute you're in the middle of sand, rocks and infinite sky, then suddenly you're transported to a fantasyland of crimson sandstone towers, thrusting up to 1200ft skyward.

Long before the land became part of the Navajo Reservation, the valley was home to Ancestral Puebloans, who abruptly abandoned the site some 700 years ago. When the Navajo arrived a few centuries ago, they called it 'Valley Between the Rocks.' Today, Monument Valley straddles the Arizona–Utah border and is traversed by Hwy 163.

Unless you're on a tour, you'll need your own wheels to get to Monument Valley.

⊙ Sights

The most famous formations are conveniently visible from the rough 15-mile dirt road looping through **Monument Valley Navajo Tribal Park** (☑ 435-727-5870; www.navajonationparks.org; per 4-person vehicle $20; ⊙ drive 6am-7pm Apr-Sep, 8am-4:30pm Oct-Mar, visitor center 6am-8pm Apr-Sep, 8am-5pm Oct-Mar; 🅿). It's usually possible to drive the loop in your own vehicle, even in standard passenger cars (not RVs), but expect a dusty, bumpy ride. There are multiple overlooks where you can get out and snap away or browse for trinkets and jewelry offered by Navajo

vendors. Most of the formations were named for what they look like: the Mittens, Eagle Rock, Bear and Rabbit, and Elephant Butte. Allow at least 1½ hours for the drive, which starts from the visitor center parking lot at the end of a 4-mile paved road off Hwy 163. There's also a restaurant, gift shop, small museum, tour desk and the View Hotel. National Park passes are not accepted for admission into the park.

☞ Tours

The only way to get off the road and into the backcountry is by taking a Navajo-led tour on foot, on horseback or by vehicle. You'll see rock art, natural arches, and coves such as the otherworldly Ear of the Wind, a bowl-shaped wall with a nearly circular opening at the top. Guides shower you with details about life on the reservation, movie trivia and whatever else comes to mind. Set up in the parking lot at the visitor center, the guides are pretty easygoing, so don't worry about high-pressure sales. Tours leave frequently in summer, less so in winter, with rates from $65 for a 90-minute motorized trip. Outfits in Kayenta and at Goulding's Lodge also offer tours. If you want to set things up in advance, check out the list of guides on the tribal park's website (www. navajonationparks.org). The only hiking trail you are allowed to take without a guide is the Wildcat Trail, a 3.8-mile loop trail around the West Mitten formation. The trailhead is between the View Campground and the visitor center.

Sacred Monument Tours   TOURS
(☑ 435-727-3218; www.monumentvalley.net) Sacred Monument offers vehicle, hiking and horseback-riding tours through Monument Valley. Trail rides are $70/98/125 for one/two/three hours, hikes range from $75 for two to three hours up to $220 for a full day, and jeep tours start at $75 for a 90-minute loop of the Monument Valley circuit and go up to $200 for a full-day tour.

🛏 Sleeping & Eating

Goulding's Camp Park   CAMPGROUND $
(☑ 435-727-3231; www.gouldings.com; Monument Valley, Utah; tent sites $30, RV sites $52-62, cabins $132; ❄ 🛜 🏊) Tucked snugly between red sandstone walls, with a shot of the Mittens from the mouth of the canyon, this is a scenic full-service campground that includes a store, pool (closed in winter) and hot showers. While compact, the cabins have

air-conditioning, wi-fi and bathrooms and can sleep up to six people.

View Campground
CAMPGROUND $

(☑435-727-5802; monumentvalleyview.com/camp ground; Indian Rte 42; tent/RV sites $20/40) This new campground on the Navajo Reservation is located about a quarter-mile southwest of the View Hotel, and enjoys similar stunning perspectives. Restrooms and showers are available, and cabins with bathrooms can also be rented (from $225 per night).

Goulding's Lodge
MOTEL $$

(☑435-727-3231; www.gouldings.com; Monument Valley, Utah; d/ste from $184/199; P※🛇🖵🐾) This historic hotel a few miles west of Monument Valley has 152 modern rooms, most with views of the megaliths in the distance. The style is standard Southwestern, and each room has a flat-screen TV with 200 channels, a refrigerator and air-conditioning. Pets cost $20 per pet per night.

★ View Hotel
HOTEL $$$

(☑435-727-5555; www.monumentvalleyview.com; Indian Rte 42; r/ste from $247/349; ※@🛇) You'll never turn on the TV during the day at this aptly named hotel. Spread over three floors, the 95 Southwestern-themed rooms are pleasant, but nothing compared to the show from the balconies. Those that end in numbers higher than 15 (eg 216) have unobstructed panoramas of the valley below; the best, on the 3rd floor, cost $20 more.

The View restaurant (mains cost $11 to $15) serves three decent meals a day in a dining room with floor-to-ceiling windows and an outdoor patio. Wi-fi only reaches the lobby and some rooms.

Stagecoach Dining Room
AMERICAN $$

(☑435-727-3231; www.gouldings.com; Goulding's Trading Post Rd; mains $12-20; ⊙6:30am-9:30pm, shorter hours in winter) Goulding's restaurant,

Stagecoach Dining Room, is a replica of a film set built for John Ford's 1949 Western *She Wore a Yellow Ribbon*. Get a vitamin kick from the salad bar before tucking into the steaks or Navajo tacos piled high with chile and cheese. At lunchtime it often swarms with coach tourists.

Canyon de Chelly National Monument

Beautiful and spiritual, the remote and variegated Canyon de Chelly feels far removed from time and space. Pronounced 'd-shay' (the name is a corruption of the Navajo word *tsegi*, or 'rock canyon'), it's been inhabited for 5000 years, and shelters prehistoric petroglyphs alongside the 1000-year-old cliff dwellings of Ancestral Puebloans.

Navajos arrived here in the 1700s, using it for farming and as a stronghold and retreat for their raids on other tribes and Spanish settlers; today it's administered for the tribe by the NPS. But if these cliffs could talk, they'd also tell stories of great violence and tragedy. In 1805, Spanish soldiers killed scores of Navajo hiding in what's now called Massacre Cave. In 1864 thousands of Navajos took refuge from the US Army here. Starved out, the survivors were forced to march 300 miles – the Long Walk – to Fort Sumner in New Mexico. Four years later, they returned.

⊙ Sights & Activities

Scenic drives skirting the canyon's northern and southern rim start near the visitor center, past Chinle (the nearest town, which has a gas station, supermarket, bank with ATM, motels and fast-food outlets). Both scenic drives are open year-round and, aside from one hiking trail, they are the only way to see the canyon without joining a guided tour.

TIPS FOR DRIVERS

➡ The main east–west highway across northern Arizona is the 400-mile stretch of I-40, which roughly follows the path of historic Route 66. It runs across the Colorado Plateau, through Flagstaff and south of the Grand Canyon and Navajo Reservation. I-10 enters western Arizona at Blythe and travels about 400 miles to New Mexico via Phoenix and Tucson. South of Phoenix, the I-8 coming east from Yuma joins the I-10.

➡ The sixth-largest state in the Union, Arizona includes some long and lonely stretches of road. On drives such as the I-8 between Yuma and Gila Bend, be aware that cell-phone reception, FM radio, lodging and gas are almost nonexistent.

➡ Lesser roads with speed limits of 55mph or even 65mph can present nasty surprises in the form of unexpected potholes.

> **ⓘ CONDUCTING YOURSELF IN CANYON DE CHELLY**
>
> Today about 40 to 50 large Navajo families still raise animals and grow corn, squash and beans on the land, allowing a glimpse of traditional life.
>
> **Hogans** While visiting, you may see a small structure made of logs, with a door facing east. Called hogans, these are Navajo dwellings. Only enter hogans with a guide.
>
> **Photography** Don't take photographs of people, their homes or property without permission.

If you only have time for one trip, make it the **South Rim Drive**, which runs along the main canyon and has the most dramatic vistas. The 16-mile road passes six viewpoints before dead-ending at the spectacular **Spider Rock Overlook**, with views of the 800ft freestanding two-pronged tower atop of which lives Spider Woman, an important Navajo god.

For the most part, **North Rim Drive** follows a side canyon called **Canyon del Muerto** (the morbid name derives from an ancient American Indian burial ground discovered here), which has four overlooks. At the first, **Antelope House Overlook**, you'll have stunning cliff-top views of a natural rock fortress and cliff dwellings. To see the latter, walk to your right from the walled **Navajo Fortress Viewpoint** to a second walled overlook. With few walls and no railings, this stop may not be suited for small children or pets. The North Rim Drive ends at **Massacre Cave Overlook**, site of an 1805 atrocity by Spanish soldiers, 15 miles from the visitor center. The road continues 13 miles to the town of **Tsaile** (say-*lee*), where **Diné College** has an excellent museum, as well as a library and bookstore with a vast selection of books about the Navajo.

Bring binoculars and water, lock your car and don't leave valuables in sight when leaving it to take the short walks at each scenic point. The lighting for photography on the north rim is best in early morning and on the south rim in late afternoon.

☞ Tours

Entering the canyon is an amazing experience, as walls start at just a few feet but rise dramatically, topping out at about 1000ft.

At many stops, Navajo vendors sell unique jewelry, ceramics and crafts, usually at prices much lower than at the trading posts. Summer tours can get stifling hot and mosquitoes are plentiful, so bring a hat, sunscreen, water and insect repellent. Tour guides offer vehicle, hiking and horseback-riding tours into the canyon. For a list of approved guides, stop by the **visitor center** (☏ 928-674-5500; www.nps.gov/cach; ⊗ 8am-5pm) or check the park's website (www.nps.gov/cach/planyourvisit).

For a vehicle tour, expect to pay around $200 for a three-hour trip for between one and three people.

Hiking

With one exception, you need a guide in order to hike anywhere in the canyon. A backcountry permit (free) is required. Expect to pay a guide about $30 to $40 per hour with a three-hour minimum. Rangers sometimes lead hikes in summer, between Memorial Day and Labor Day.

Otherwise, the steep and stunning **White House Trail** is your only option. Narrow switchbacks drop 550ft down from the White House Overlook on the South Rim Drive, about 6 miles east of the visitor center. It's only 1.25 miles to the photogenic White House Ruin, but coming back up is strenuous, so carry plenty of water and allow up to two hours. In summer, start out early or late in the day to avoid the worst of the heat.

🛏 Sleeping

Spider Rock Campground   CAMPGROUND $
(☏ 928-781-2014, 928-781-2016; www.spiderrockcampground.com; Navajo Hwy 7; tent/RV sites $11/16, hogans $31-47; 🐾) This Navajo-run campground 12 miles from the visitor center on South Rim Drive is surrounded by piñon and juniper trees. No tent? Rent one for $9 or spend the night in a traditional Navajo hogan. Solar-heated showers cost $3, credit cards aren't accepted, and basic drinks and snacks are sold.

Cottonwood Campground   CAMPGROUND $
(☏ 928-674-2106; www.navajonationparks.org; campsite $14; 🐾) Near the visitor center, this Navajo-run campground has 93 primitive sites on a first-come, first-served basis. Water is available from April to October, and there are restrooms but no hookups or showers. Fewer sites are available from November to March. There are grills and a picnic table. Cash only.

Thunderbird Lodge MOTEL **$$**
(📞928-674-5842, 800-679-2473; thunderbird
lodge.com; Rural Rte 7; d/ste $100/110; ❄🐾🛜🏊) This Navajo-owned property is the only hotel actually in Canyon de Chelly. The ranch-style buildings contain 70 comfortable rooms, with wood beams and chunky wood furniture. An inexpensive restaurant serves Navajo and American meals ($5 to $17) and wi-fi is best in the rooms near the lobby.

ℹ Information

En route to the canyon from Chinle, the nearest town, you'll pass the Visitor Center (p193), which has information about guides and tours.

Window Rock

📞928 / POP 2712

The tribal capital of Window Rock sits at the intersection of Hwys 264 and 12, near the New Mexico border. The namesake rock is a nearly circular arch high up on a red sandstone cliff in the northern part of town; at its base is the **Navajo Veterans Memorial Park** (📞928-871-6647; www.navajonationparks.org/htm/veterans.htm; Window Rock Blvd; ⊙8am-7pm) **FREE**. Also worth a quick peek are the nearby **Navajo National Council Chambers** (⊙8am-noon and 1-5pm Mon-Fri), beautifully festooned in murals, where tribal delegates hold legislative sessions. With the interesting Navajo Nation Museum (p194) also found here, the capital is definitely worth a stop if you're in the area, particularly during the **Navajo Nation Fair** (📞928-871-6478; www. navajonationfair.com; ⊙Sep).

⊙ Sights

Navajo Nation Museum MUSEUM
(📞928-871-7941; www.navajonationmuseum.
org; cnr Hwy 264 & Loop Rd; entry by donation;
⊙8am-5pm Mon, 8am-6pm Tue-Fri, 9am-5pm Sat;
🅿♿) The sleek and modern Navajo Nation Museum, dedicated exclusively to the history and culture of the Nation, punches well above its weight. Exhibits range from textiles, silverwork and ceramics to the remains of an ephemeral piece constructed with Ai Weiwei. It's a real hub of the community, run with passion and deep knowledge.

🛏 Sleeping & Eating

The **Quality Inn Navajo Nation Capital**
(📞928-871-4108; www.choicehotels.com; 48 W
Hwy 264; r $89-99; ❄@🛜🏊) offers the only

HUBBELL TRADING POST

Widely respected merchant John Lorenzo Hubbell established this **trading post** (📞928-755-3475; www.nps.gov/hutr; Hwy 264, Mile 446.3; ⊙8am-5pm) **FREE** in 1878 to supply Navajos returning from Fort Sumner with dry goods and groceries. Now run by the NPS, it still sells food, souvenirs and local crafts including kachina dolls, blankets and stunning ceramics, and retains its original fittings right down to the squeaky floorboards. Navajo women often give weaving demonstrations inside the visitor center, which also has informative displays, a play 'store' and period dress-ups for the kids.

Hubbell himself was an avid collector of American Indian textiles, as you'll discover on a tour of his **house** (adult/child $5/free), held at 10am, 11am, 1pm, 2pm and 3pm. Hubbell Trading Post is in the village of Ganado, about 30 miles south of Chinle/Canyon de Chelly and 40 miles north of the I-40.

lodging in town. The in-house restaurant is good for American and Navajo fare, or there are a number of fast-food joints along Hwy 264.

🛍 Shopping

**Navajo Arts &
Crafts Enterprise** ARTS & CRAFTS
(📞928-871-4090; www.gonavajo.com; cnr Hwy 264 & Main St; ⊙9am-8pm Mon-Sat, noon-6pm Sun) For a superb selection of Navajo jewelry and crafts, swing by the Navajo Arts & Crafts Enterprise store in the center of Window Rock. Established in 1941, NACE is wholly Navajo operated and guarantees the authenticity and quality of its products.

ℹ Information

Navajo Nation Tourism Department (📞928-810-8501; www.discovernavajo.com; 100 Taylor Rd, St Michaels; ⊙8am-5pm Mon-Fri) In St Michaels, just west of Window Rock.

HOPI RESERVATION

Scattered across the tops of three rocky, buff-colored mesas and along the valleys below are the villages of the 'Peaceful Ones,' which is what the Hopi call themselves. Their reservation – at the heart of their ancestral territory, though only containing a scant fraction of it – is like a 2532-sq-mile island floating in the Navajo Reservation. To the Hopi, Arizona's oldest and most traditional tribe, this remote terrain is not merely their homeland but also the hub of their spiritual world.

Because of their isolated location, the Hopi have received less outside influence than other tribes and have limited tourist facilities. Aside from ancient Walpi on First Mesa, villages don't hold much intrinsic appeal for visitors. But a tour of the mesas with a knowledgeable guide can open the door to what's truly fascinating about this place: the people, their history and their traditions, which still thrive today.

Sights

First Mesa

Three villages sit atop this mesa and another village, non-traditional Polacca, hugs its base. To explore the mesa-top villages, stop by the First Mesa Consolidated Visitor Center in Polacca to join a tour. Once on the mesa, the first village is **Hano**, which blends imperceptibly into **Sichomovi**. The most dramatic of the three Hopi enclaves is **Walpi**, which dates back to AD 900 and clings like an aerie onto the mesa's narrow end. Sandstone-colored stone houses seem to sprout organically from the cliffs. The last inhabitants, a few older ladies who lived without plumbing or electricity, have left but the homes are still used by families during ceremonies atop the mesa. Arts and crafts sold by local artisans may be available for purchase during your tour.

It's best to call before visiting to confirm timing and availability of tours, which may not run if there are private rituals scheduled on a particular day. First Mesa ceremonial dances are not open to the public. Driving west on Hwy 264, turn right at the stop sign at Mile Marker 390.8 and drive a quarter mile. The visitor center is just left of the post office.

Second Mesa

On Second Mesa, some 10 miles west of First Mesa, the Hopi Cultural Center Restaurant & Inn is the most developed visitor area, providing food and lodging. There's also the small **Hopi Museum** (☏928-734-6650; Hwy 264, Mile 379; adult/child 12yr & under $3/1; ⊙8am-5pm Mon-Fri, 9am-3pm Sat; P), with walls full of historical photographs and simple exhibits that share just enough about the Hopi world to allow you to understand that it's something altogether different from the one you likely inhabit. The diorama of Walpi is also interesting.

Second Mesa has three villages; the oldest, **Shungopavi**, is famous for its Snake dances, when dancers carry live rattlesnakes in their mouths. **Mishongnovi** and **Sipaulovi** sometimes have Social or Butterfly dances open to the public. Call the cultural center to check dates.

Third Mesa

The tribal capital of **Kykotsmovi** sits below Third Mesa with **Batavi**, **Hotevila** and **Old Oraibi** up on top. Old Oraibi was established around AD 1200 and vies with Acoma Pueblo in New Mexico for the title of the USA's oldest continuously inhabited village. To visit Old Oraibi, use a certified guide if you want to explore beyond the galleries and shops on the Hopi Arts Trail.

CONDUCTING YOURSELF ON HOPI LAND

Deeply ingrained in the Hopi way is an ethic of welcoming strangers – they were even nice (for a long time, anyway) to Spanish conquistadors and missionaries. But decades of cultural abuses by visitors, even well-intentioned ones, have led Hopi villages to issue strict guidelines to protect their world. This is not just a matter of cultural survival, it's also about defending what is most deeply sacred to them.

Recordings Each village has its own rules for visitors, which are usually posted along the highways, but generally speaking any form of recording, be it camera, video, audiotape, or even sketching, is strictly forbidden. This is partly for religious reasons but also to prevent commercial exploitation by non-Hopis.

Alcohol/drugs Alcohol and other drug use is also prohibited.

☞ Tours

When visiting Hopi country, the tour is the thing. So little about the place or the culture is obvious, even to the most astute outside eye, that visiting the villages with a knowledgeable local guide is really the only way to get a glimpse inside. There is a list of authorized guides at www. experiencehopi.com. Some guides include a trip to nearby Dawa Park, where thousands of ancient petroglyphs are etched into the rocks. Micah Loma'omvaya of **Hopi Tours** (✆928-205-1634; www.experiencehopi.com), Bertram Tsavadawa of **Ancient Pathways** (✆928-797-8145; www.experiencehopi.com) and Gary Tso of **Left-Handed Hunter Tour Company** (✆928-734-2567, 928-206-7928; www.experiencehopi.com) are also recommended. Prices depend on tour length and group size.

ℹ Information

Make your first stop the **Hopi Cultural Center** (✆928-734-2401; www.hopiculturalcenter.com; Hwy 264, Mile 379; r $115; ⊙restaurant 7am-9pm summer, to 8pm winter) on Second Mesa to pick up information and get oriented.

The **First Mesa Consolidated Visitor Center** (✆928-737-2670; www.experiencehopi.com; Polacca; tour adult/child 17yr & under $20/15; ⊙8-11am & 1-4pm Mon-Sat Jun-Aug, 9-11am & 1-3pm Mon-Sat Sep-May) can arrange tours to Walpi, on First Mesa. For more details about the villages and tourism on the reservation, visit the visitor center website. If you're the type of traveler who likes to barge around discovering things on your own, dial it down a notch here, and please join a tour if you want to explore beyond the highway and the Hopi Arts Trail.

As with the rest of Arizona (but different from the surrounding Navajo Reservation), the Hopi Reservation does not observe daylight saving time from spring to fall. The climate is harsh – ungodly hot in summer and freezing cold in winter – so come prepared either way.

Hopi prefer cash for most transactions. There's an ATM outside the one store in Polacca.

In Polacca there's also a **hospital** (✆928-737-6000; Hwy 264, Mile 388; ⊙24hr emergency). For emergencies and police matters call the **BIA Police** (✆928-738-2228, 928-738-2236).

ℹ Getting There & Away

The Hopi mesas are about 50 miles east of Tuba City and 85 miles west of Window Rock via flat and largely uneventful Hwy 264. Three roads enter the reservation from I-40 in the south. Coming from Flagstaff, the closest approach is by heading east on I-10 to Winslow, then cutting north on Hwy 87 (130 miles total). From Winslow it's 70 miles via Hwy 87, and from Holbrook 80 miles on Hwy 77. Buses operated by Navajo Transit System (p189) pass through from Monday to Thursday between Tuba City and Window Rock.

EASTERN ARIZONA

From Flagstaff east to the New Mexico line, the most dominant scenic feature often seems to be the Burlington Northern-Santa Fe Railway freights that run alongside the interstate. But there are some iconic Route 66 sites along here, and a few spots that will surprise you, just off the road.

Petrified Forest National Park

The 'trees' of **Petrified Forest National Park** (✆928-524-6228; www.nps.gov/pefo; vehicle $20, pedestrians & cyclists $10; ⊙7am-7pm Mar-Sep, shorter hours Oct-Feb) are fossilized logs scattered over a vast area of semi-desert grassland. Up to 6ft in diameter – at least one forms a natural bridge across a ravine – they're strikingly beautiful, with extravagantly patterned cross-sections of wood glinting in ethereal pinks, blues and greens. They're also ancient – at 225 million years old, they're contemporaries of the first dinosaurs.

The trees arrived via major floods, only to be buried beneath silica-rich volcanic ash before they could decompose. Groundwater dissolved the silica, carried it through the logs and crystallized into solid, sparkly quartz mashed up with iron, carbon, manganese and other minerals. Uplift and erosion eventually exposed the logs. Souvenir hunters filched thousands of tons of petrified wood before Teddy Roosevelt made the forest a national monument in 1906 (it became a national park in 1962). Scavenge today and you'll be looking at fines and even jail time.

◉ Sights

Straddling the I-40, Petrified Forest National Park has an entrance at exit 311 off I-40 in the north, and another off Hwy 180 in the south. A 28-mile, paved scenic road links the two. To avoid backtracking, westbound travelers should start in the north, eastbound ones in the south.

Videos describing how the logs were fossilized run regularly at the **Painted Desert Visitor Center** (✆928-524-6228; www.nps.gov/

1 Park Rd, Petrified Forest National Park; ☺8am-5pm) near the north entrance and at the **Rainbow Forest Museum** (✆928-524-6822; www.nps.gov; 6618 Petrified Forest Rd; ☺7am-7pm Mar-Sep, shorter hours Oct-Feb) near the south entrance. Both visitor centers have bookstores, park exhibits and rangers that hand out free maps and informative pamphlets.

The drive has about 15 pullouts with interpretive signs and some short trails. Two trails near the southern entrance provide the best access for close-ups of the petrified logs: the 0.6-mile **Long Logs Trail**, which has the largest concentration, and the 0.4-mile **Giant Logs Trail**, which is entered through the Rainbow Forest Museum and sports the park's largest log.

A highlight in the center section is the 3-mile loop drive (Blue Mesa Scenic Rd) out to **Blue Mesa**, where you'll be treated to 360-degree views of spectacular badlands, log falls and logs balancing atop hills with the leathery texture of elephant skin. The short **Blue Mesa Trail** leads scenically into the badlands. Nearby, at the bottom of a ravine, hundreds of well-preserved petroglyphs are splashed across **Newspaper Rock** like some prehistoric bulletin board. Hiking down is verboten, but free spotting scopes are set up at the overlook.

More petroglyphs, and Ancestral Puebloan ruins, can be found at **Puerco Pueblo** (✆928-524-6228; www.nps.gov; Petrified Forest Rd; entry with Petrified Forest National Park or Federal Interagency Pass; ☺7am-7pm Mar-Sep, shorter hours Oct-Feb), 5 miles north of the Blue Mesa Scenic Rd turnoff, on Petrified Forest Rd.

North of the I-40 lies a Route 66 interpretative marker, where you'll find a map of the whole Mother Road, and an especially spectacular section of the Painted Desert. Nature can really put on a kaleidoscopic show here, especially at sunset: the most mesmerizing views are from **Kachina Point** behind the **Painted Desert Inn** (✆928-524-6228; www.nps.gov; 1 Park Rd; ☺8:30am-4:30pm) FREE.

Kachina Point is also the trailhead for wilderness hiking and camping. There are no developed trails, water sources or food, so come prepared.

Winslow

✆928 / POP 9655 / ELEV 4880FT

Thanks to the lyrics of the Eagles' catchy '70s tune 'Take It Easy,' lonesome little Winslow is now a popular stop on the tourist track.

WORTH A TRIP

METEOR CRATER

Nearly a mile across and 600ft deep, the second-most impressive hole in Arizona was formed by a fiery meteor that screamed into the atmosphere about 50,000 years ago, when giant sloths lived in these parts. **Meteor Crater** (✆800-289-5898, 928-289-5898; www.meteorcrater.com; Meteor Crater Rd; adult/senior/child 6-17yr $18/16/9; ☺7am-7pm Jun–mid-Sep, 8am-5pm mid-Sep–May; P ⌂), 40 miles east of Flagstaff, is an out-of-this-world site for those with a thimbleful of imagination. There are lookout points around the crater's edge (but no hiking to the bottom) and the visitor center is as fun as it is informative.

In the small **Standin' on the Corner Park** (www.standinonthecorner.com; 2nd St & Kinsley Ave) on Route 66 you can pose with a life-size bronze statue of a hitchhiker backed by a charmingly hokey trompe l'oeil mural of that famous girl – my Lord! – in a flatbed Ford. Above, a painted eagle keeps an eye on the action, and sometimes a red antique Ford parks next to the scene. A 2005 fire gutted the building behind the mural, which was miraculously saved.

◉ Sights

Homolovi State Park   STATE PARK
(✆928-289-4106; azstateparks.com; Homolovi State Park Entrance Rd; per vehicle $7, pedestrian & bike $2; ☺visitor center 8am-5pm) This 4000-acre high-grassland park protects the artifacts and structures within this sacred Hopi ancestral homeland. Before the area was converted into a park in 1993, bold thieves used backhoes to remove artifacts. Today, short hikes lead to petroglyphs and partly excavated Hopi and Ancestral Puebloan sites. There's a **campground** (✆520-586-2283; azstateparks.com; Homolovi State Park Entrance Rd; tent & RV sites $15-25) with 53 bookable tent and RV sites. You'll find the park 3 miles northeast of Winslow (exit 257, Hwy 87).

🍴 Sleeping & Eating

La Posada   HISTORIC HOTEL **$$**
(✆928-289-4366; www.laposada.org; 303 E 2nd St; d/deluxe $139/169; ❄🐾🛜) An impressively restored 1930 hacienda designed by star architect *du jour* Mary Jane Colter, this

was the last great railroad hotel built for the Fred Harvey Company along the Santa Fe Railroad. Elaborate tilework, glass-and-tin chandeliers, Navajo rugs and other details accent its palatial Western-style elegance.

★ **Turquoise Room**   SOUTHERN US $$$
(☑ 928-289-2888;   www.theturquoiseroom.net; 305 E 2nd St, La Posada; breakfast $11-12, lunch $10-13, dinner $28-31; ⊙ 7am-4pm & 5-9pm) Even if you're not staying at La Posada, treat yourself to the best meal between Flagstaff and Albuquerque at the hotel's unique in-house restaurant. Dishes have a neo-Southwestern flair, the place mats are handpainted works of art and there's a children's menu as well. The lamb posole (hominy stew), cassoulet of tepary beans and confit duck, and butter-glazed cornbread are just delicious.

❶ Information

Winslow's **Visitor Center** (☑ 928-289-2434; www.winslowarizona.org; 523 W 2nd St; ⊙ 9am-5pm Mon-Fri, to 3pm Sat) is inside the renovated Lorenzo Hubbell Trading Post, founded in 1917.

❶ Getting There & Away

The *Southwest Chief* stops daily (westbound at 7:50pm, eastbound at 5:35am) at La Posada which serves as the (unstaffed) Winslow Amtrak station. Tickets should be pre-bought wherever possible – you may be able to purchase tickets aboard (☑ 800-872-7245 to check), but you will be paying the full, undiscounted fare, in cash (no change).

Holbrook

☑ 928 / POP 5019 / ELEV 5080FT

In the 1880s Holbrook may have been one of the wickedest towns in the Old West ('too tough for women and churches'), but today this collection of rock stores and gas stations is better known as the Route 66 town with the wacky Wigwam Motel. It's also a convenient base for exploring Petrified Forest National Park (p196) and its fossilized wood.

For online tourist information, check out www.holbrookchamber.com.

◉ Sights

**Navajo County
Historical Museum**   MUSEUM
(☑ 928-524-6558; holbrookazmuseum.org; 100 E Arizona St; donations appreciated; ⊙ 8am-5pm) The 1898 county courthouse is home to an eclectic assortment of historical local exhibits as well as Holbrook's chamber of

FORT APACHE

Lying around 85 miles south of Holbrook, on Hwy 77 is **Fort Apache** (☑ information 928-338-4525, museum 928-338-4625; www.wmat.nsn.us; 127 Scout St; adult/senior/child $5/3/free; ⊙ park 7am-sunset, cultural center & museum 8am-5pm Mon-Sat summer, closed Sat winter). A self-guided tour of the park leads to the fort's historic buildings, where an exhibit inside the 1871 officers' quarters highlights Apache scouts and explains why tribal members helped the US Army in the Indian Wars. Admission includes entry to the Kinishba Ruins, a pre-Columbian stone pueblo that once had hundreds of rooms. At the museum, pick up a guide to the ruins, which are at the end of a dirt road 4 miles west of Hwy 73.

The Theodore Roosevelt Boarding School was established here in 1923 and is still in operation.

commerce and visitor center. Each room of the museum highlights a different aspect of Holbrook's history – a creepy highlight is the old county jail, where the windowless cells were still being used as recently as 1976.

⌂ Sleeping & Eating

Wigwam Motel   MOTEL $
(☑ 928-524-3048;   www.galerie-kokopelli.com/ wigwam; 811 W Hopi Dr; r $56-62; ❄) Embrace the kitschy extremes of Route 66 at this 1937 motel, where each room is a self-contained concrete tipi. Each is outfitted with restored 1950s hickory log-pole furniture and retro TVs.

Mesa Italiana   ITALIAN $$
(☑ 928-524-6696; 2318 E Navajo Blvd; mains $12-19; ⊙ 11am-2pm Mon-Fri, 4-9pm daily) Locals vouch for this busy Italian place serving pasta and pizzas. The lunch special – pasta with salad and garlic bread – is just $9.

❶ Getting There & Away

Greyhound stops at the Circle K at 101 Mission Lane, where you can buy tickets. East of Holbrook, Route 66 barrels on as I-40 for 70 miles before entering New Mexico just beyond Lupton. The only attraction to break the monotony of the road is the section cutting through the Painted Desert in Petrified Forest National Park.

WESTERN ARIZONA

The western border of Arizona lies along the Colorado River, which stretches south from the Hoover Dam all the way to Yuma and Mexico. Savvy marketers have dubbed this region the 'West Coast.' The famous **Hoover Dam** is one of a series of mega-dams that regulate the flow of the river after it emerges from the Grand Canyon. In winter, migratory flocks of birds arrive from frigid northern climes seeking out riverside wildlife refuges. At the same time, wingless 'snowbirds' pack dozens of dusty RV parks, especially in Yuma. Although summers are hellishly hot, the cool Colorado brings in scores of water rats and boaters seeking relief from the heat in such places as Lake Havasu and Laughlin.

Bullhead City & Laughlin

📞 928 / POP 45,394 (COMBINED) / ELEV 554FT

Named for a rock that resembled the head of a snoozing bull, Bullhead City began as a construction camp for Davis Dam, built in the 1940s on the site of 19th-century Hardyville. The rock was eventually submerged by Lake Mojave, but the town stuck around and survives today, primarily because of the casinos across the Colorado River in Laughlin, Nevada.

Laughlin definitely has more sizzle than Bullhead City and is known by a number of nicknames: 'Vegas on the cheap,' the 'un-Vegas,' the 'anti-Sin City.' All that's fine by this gambling town, founded in 1964 by gaming impresario Don Laughlin, a former fur-trapper from Minnesota. The image of good, clean fun (no leggy showgirls, no sleazy types touting escort services) is a winner with the blue-haired set and, increasingly, families looking for an inexpensive getaway.

Skip either town in summer when temperatures often soar to a merciless 120°F (almost 50°C).

🏃 Activities

If casinos aren't your thing, check out the hiking and biking trails in the brand-new **Colorado River Heritage Greenway Park & Trails** (www.clarkcountynv.gov; ⏰6am-11pm; 🅿) in Laughlin. You'll find parking and an information kiosk at the Bridge Trailhead, which is on the west side of Casino Dr, just north of Riverside Resort. This recreation area is also known as North Reach.

🛏 Sleeping

Laughlin's big casino hotels are fantastic value, with spacious doubles starting at around $40 midweek and $70 on weekends. Some may charge for wi-fi since they'd rather have you downstairs pulling slots. All are on Casino Dr, which parallels the river.

Golden Nugget   HOTEL $
(📞702-298-7111; www.goldennugget.com/laughlin; 2300 S Casino Dr, Laughlin; d from $72; ✳@🛜❄) This cool and inviting place is the casino where Vegas mogul Steve Wynn cut his teeth back in 1989. The latest owners of this 300-room 'boutique casino' have sunk big bucks into creating an intimate but classy experience, with tropical-themed rooms, a palm-tree-flanked riverfront pool and above-average eateries. Room rates drop to their lowest during the week.

Davis Camp Park   CAMPGROUND $
(📞928-754-7250; www.mcparks.com; 2251 Hwy 68; tent $17, RV site $25-30, vacation home from $80; 🛜❄) If you're traveling with kids and don't want to stay in a Laughlin casino, give serious consideration to this Mojave County Park, which sits on a pretty stretch of the Colorado River not far from the action. You can camp right beside the river or rent a small vacation home. Restrooms, showers, laundry and full hookups are also available.

🍴 Eating & Drinking

All casinos feature multiple restaurants, usually including a buffet, a 24-hour cafe and an upscale steakhouse, along with bars and lounges. Not quite Vegas, Laughlin nonetheless has plenty of places to wet your whistle, either in the casinos themselves or surrounding bars.

Earl's at the Castle   AMERICAN $
(📞928-754-1118; 491 Long Ave, Bullhead City; mains $7.50-9.50; ⏰7am-8pm) Folks are friendly inside this turreted mock-castle in Old Bullhead, where the home cookin's been good since 1970 and the $6.49 breakfast specials are a good deal. Or, for $10, you could go south of the border with *machaca* (Mexican dried beef), eggs and tortillas.

Laughlin Ranch Grill   AMERICAN $$
(📞928-754-1322; www.laughlinranch.com; 1360 William Hardy Dr, Bullhead City; mains $22-27; ⏰10am-9pm Mon-Sat, to 6pm Sun; 🛜) Actually in Bullhead, yet part of the Laughlin

Ranch Golf Club, the Grill aims for mountain-lodge chic, with stone walls, high ceilings, a fireplace and views over the links. Choose from burgers, steaks and pasta or, on Fridays, fish specials.

Hideout   BAR
(www.hideoutlaughlin.com; 2311 S Casino Dr, Laughlin; ⏰24hr; 🐾) The bar is always open at the Hideout, a convenient place to escape the bling and glitz of the casinos. You can also play slots set into the bar (although most people are here to socialise) or catch a game on one of a dozen TV screens. It's on the 2nd floor of Mark's Plaza, across from the Pioneer Hotel & Casino.

ℹ️ Information

Remember, Nevada time is one hour behind Arizona in winter, but in the same time zone in summer (Arizona doesn't observe daylight saving time, apart from the Navajo Reservation).

The **Bullhead Area Chamber of Commerce** (📞928-754-4121; www.bullheadareachamber. com; 1251 Hwy 95; ⏰9am-5pm Mon-Fri) has area info. Pick up copies of the *Entertainer*, a weekly guide to the Laughlin casino scene, here. The **post office** (📞928-758-5711; www. usps.com; 1882 Lakeside Dr, Bullhead City; ⏰8:30am-5pm Mon-Fri, 9am-1pm Sat) is south of Old Bullhead.

Kingman
📞928 / POP 28,912 / ELEV 3300FT

Among Route 66 aficionados, Kingman is known as the main hub of the longest uninterrupted stretch of the historic highway, running from Topock to Seligman. Among its early-20th-century buildings is the former Methodist church at 5th and Spring Sts where Clark Gable and Carole Lombard eloped in 1939. Hometown hero Andy Devine had his Hollywood breakthrough as the perpetually befuddled driver of the eponymous *Stagecoach* in John Ford's Oscar-winning 1939 movie.

Outside interest in Kingman has kept the town vital. Interesting eateries, watering holes and galleries can be found on Beale St, the axis of historic downtown, and a raft of classic motels has been preserved.

Route 66 barrels through town as Andy Devine Ave. It runs parallel to the up-and-coming Beale St. Supermarkets, gas stations and other businesses line up along northbound Stockton Hill Rd, which is also the road to take for Grand Canyon West.

👁 Sights & Activities

👁 In Kingman

Route 66 Museum   MUSEUM
(📞928-753-9889; www.gokingman.com; 120 W Andy Devine Ave; adult/senior/child 12yr & under $4/3/free; ⏰9am-5pm, last entry at 4pm) On the 2nd floor of the 1907 Powerhouse, which also holds the visitor center, this small but engaging museum has an informative historical overview of travel along the Mother Road. Check out the crazy air-conditioner on the 1950 Studebaker Champion! There's also a museum of electric cars here, and your ticket allows entry into the nearby **Mohave Museum of History & Arts** (📞928-753-3195; www. mohavemuseum.org; 400 W Beale St; adult/senior/child 12yr & under $4/3/free; ⏰9am-4:30pm Mon-Fri, 1-4:30pm Sat).

**Hualapai
Mountain Park**   HIKING, MOUNTAIN BIKING
(📞928-681-5700; www.mcparks.com; 6250 Hualapai Mountain Rd; day use per vehicle $7; ⏰7am-7pm) In summer, locals visit this mountain near Kingman for picnics, hiking, mountain biking and wildlife-watching amid cool ponderosa pine and aspen. Also here is the Hualapai Mountain Resort (p201) and the first-come, first-served campground **Hualapai Mountain Park** (📞877-757-0915; tent site/RV site/tipi/cabin $17/30/35/80; 🐾).

👁 On Route 66: Topock to Kingman

Coming from California, Route 66 enters Arizona at Topock, near the 20-mile **Topock Gorge**, a dramatic walled canyon that's one of the prettiest sections of the Colorado River, part of the Havasu National Wildlife Refuge (p206), a significant habitat for birdlife. Companies renting boats for trips through the gorge include **Jerkwater Canoe & Kayak** (📞928-768-7753; www.jerkwatercanoe. com; $46; ⏰launch at 7:30am PCT).

North of here, in **Golden Shores**, you can refuel on gas and grub before embarking on a rugged 20-mile trip to the terrifically crusty, former gold-mining town of **Oatman**, cupped by pinnacles and craggy hills. Beyond Oatman, keep your wits about you as the road twists and turns past tumbleweeds, saguaro cacti and falling rocks as it travels over **Sitgreaves Pass** (3523ft) and corkscrews into the rugged Black Mountains before arriving in Kingman.

☉ On Route 66: Kingman to Williams

Past Kingman, Route 66 arcs north away from the I-40 for 115 dusty miles of original Mother Road through scrubby, lonely landscape. It merges with the I-40 near Seligman, then reappears briefly as Main St in Williams. Gas stations are rare, so make sure you've got enough fuel. The total distance to Williams is 130 miles.

Hackberry General Store   HISTORIC SITE
(☑928-769-2605; www.hackberrygeneralstore. com; 11255 E Route 66, Hackberry; ☉9am-6pm Apr-Oct, 10am-5pm Nov-Mar; ℗) The 1934 Hackberry General Store lures passersby with its eccentrically decorated gas station, vintage cars in faded disrepair and rusted-out ironwork. Located 28 miles northeast of Kingman, it's run by a Route 66 memorialist and is an ideal stop for a cold drink and souvenirs, or information on the route.

✸✦ Festivals & Events

Historic Route 66 Fun Run   SPORTS
(☑928-753-5001; www.azrt66.com; ☉May) This vintage car rally traces the Mother Road from Seligman to Topock on the first weekend in May. Participants get the chance to show off their gleaming toys in Kingman, at the 'Show and Shine.'

Andy Devine Days   CULTURAL
(☑928-757-7919; www.andydevinedaysfestival. com; ☉late Sep) This festival fires up Kingman for one weekend every September, with food stalls, mechanical-bull riding, games, rides, Route 66 art displays, a final-day parade and even a rodeo.

🛏 Sleeping

Kingman has plenty of motels along Route 66/Andy Devine Ave north and south of the I-40. Some are classics of the Mother Road's heyday, and while cheap, retain period fittings and quirky charm.

Hilltop Motel   MOTEL $
(☑928-753-2198; www.hilltopmotelaz.com; 1901 E Andy Devine Ave; r from $44; ✳@🛰🗮🐾) On Route 66, with nice views and a cool neon sign, the Hilltop is a well-preserved vestige of the Mother Road's heyday. Rooms are simple, with period features, and pets are $10 per day.

Hualapai Mountain Resort   LODGE $
(☑928-757-3545; www.hmresort.net; 4525 Hualapai Mountain Rd; r/ste from $79/159; 🐾) This Depression-era Civilian Conservation Corps mess hall is now a mountain retreat of chunky wood furniture, paintings of wild game and a front porch that's made for wildlife-watching among the towering pines. The good on-site restaurant (dinner mains are $13 to $18) serves breakfast, lunch and dinner Wednesday through Sunday. Try to get a table near the window to scan for elk.

🍴 Eating & Drinking

Retro diners and smokin' barbecue joints can be found in Old Kingman, while the more modern sprawl along Stockton Hill Rd holds fast-food chains and other choices. If you need a sundowner, a few neon-washed hangovers intersperse the wine bars, cafes and other more recent arrivals along Beale St.

Mr D'z Route 66 Diner   DINER $
(☑928-718-0066; www.mrdzrt66diner.com; 105 E Andy Devine Ave; mains $8-11; ☉7am-9pm; ℗✳🖐) Put some Bill Haley on the jukebox, slip into a horseshoe booth and be transported back to the happy days of the '50s in this charming little retro diner. The magenta and teal color scheme, smiling staff and walls decked with Americana make for a friendly atmosphere in which to scoff burgers, shakes, sundaes and other diner staples.

Floyd & Co Real Pit BBQ   BARBECUE $
(☑928-757-8227; www.redneckssouthernpitbbq. com; 420 E Beale St; mains $9-13; ☉11am-8pm Tue-Sat; 🖐) The pork, brisket and andouille sausage are smoked to a turn at this popular Beale St barbecue joint – just order your protein, choose your sides, grab a beer, and slide into a booth to contemplate the ephemera on the walls, and the juicy, smoky treat to come. There's also wood-fired pizza on the menu, but why would you?

Beale Street Brews   COFFEE
(☑928-753-1404; www.bealestreetbrews.net; 510 E Beale St; ☉6am-6pm; 🛰) The unpretentious enthusiasm behind this indie coffee shop is very appealing – it has breakfast bagels, a drive-in and a library, with plans for live music, film nights and an alcohol license. Roasted on-site, the coffee's damn good too.

Diana's Cellar Door WINE BAR
(☑928-753-3885; www.the-cellar-door.com; 414 E Beale St; ⊘4-10pm Mon-Wed, 1-10pm Thu, 4pm-midnight Fri & Sat) This downtown wine bar offers about 140 wines by the bottle, 30 by the glass, an international selection of beers and tasty appetizer plates (for under $8). It's a hot little spot that has music in its compact front room from 7pm Tuesday to Saturday.

ℹ️ Information

The Powerhouse Building at 120 W Andy Devine Ave, in the center of Kingman, houses two museums as well as the **Kingman Visitor Center** (☑866-427-7866, 928-753-6106; www.gokingman.com; 120 W Andy Devine Ave; ⊘8am-5pm), with lots of information about Route 66 attractions, and a Hualapai Visitor Center, where you can buy tickets to Skywalk at Grand Canyon West.

Kingman Regional Medical Center (☑928-757-2101; www.azkrmc.com; 3269 Stockton Hill Rd) Has a 24-hour emergency department.

Police (☑928-753-2191, emergency 911; 2730 E Andy Devine Ave)

ℹ️ Getting There & Away

Greyhound (☑928-753-1818; www.greyhound.com; 953 W Beale St) runs several buses daily to Phoenix (from $24, 5½ hours), Las Vegas (from $18, 2¾ hours) and Los Angeles (from $41, 9½ to 11½ hours).

Amtrak (☑800-872-7245; www.amtrak.com) runs the *Southwest Chief*, which stops here once a day, heading both east and west.

Oatman

☑928 / POP 135

Named for Olive Oatman, a westward pioneer captured by Indians and eventually released in the area, this ramshackle hillside town had a brief heyday in the wake of a 1915 gold strike. Since the ore ran dry in 1942, it has reinvented itself as a movie set and unapologetic Wild West tourist trap, complete with staged gunfights (daily at noon, 1:30pm and sometimes 3:30pm) and gift stores named Fast Fanny's Place and the Classy Ass. And speaking of asses, there are plenty of the four-legged kind roaming the streets, begging shamelessly for food. You can buy hay squares in town. Gentle and endearing, these burros are descendents from pack animals left behind by the early miners.

There's a dusty, crusty charm to Oatman, framed by dry, rugged hills and enlivened by events such as the 4th of July egg-fry, where competitors have 15 minutes to cook an edible googy on the reliably scorching sidewalk.

Oatman is best visited as a day trip from Kingman.

🍴 Eating & Drinking

Don't come expecting a late-evening meal, although you're covered for breakfast and lunch.

Olive Oatman Restaurant-Saloon AMERICAN $
(☑928-768-1891; 171 Main St; mains $8-9; ⊘8:30am-5pm) American Indian frybread and Navajo tacos share menu space with more generic American staples such as fried chicken and burgers at this timber-clad restaurant, named for the eponymous Olive. If you're especially hungry at breakfast, try the garbage omelet – everything gets tipped in.

Oatman Hotel BAR
(☑928-768-4408; 181 Main St; ⊘10am-6pm Mon-Fri, 8am-6pm Sat & Sun) This modest two-story adobe hostelry, built as the Durlin hotel in 1902, was where Clark Gable and Carole Lombard spent their 1939 wedding night. Clark apparently returned quite frequently to play cards with the miners in the downstairs saloon, now papered with $1 bills (some $100,000 worth, by the barmaid's estimate). It no longer rents rooms, but there's a dusty museum of ephemera upstairs.

🛍️ Shopping

Cool Springs Station GIFTS & SOUVENIRS
(☑928-768-8366; www.route66coolspringsaz.com; 8275 W Oatman Rd; ⊘9am-5pm) Resurrected in 2004, this unimprovably situated gas station is a Route 66 classic. Built in the 1920s so motorists could refill and recline before tackling the hairpins of the 'gold road' to Oatman, it now has a museum and gift shop. This section of the road, leading into the jaws of the Black Mountains, is name-checked in *The Grapes of Wrath*.

Seligman

☑928 / POP 445 / ELEV 5240FT

Look out for red-and-white Burma Shave signs on the 23 miles of road slicing through rolling hills to Seligman. This tiny town embraces its Route 66 heritage with verve, thanks to the Delgadillo brothers, who for decades were the Mother Road's biggest boosters. Juan passed away in

GRAND CANYON CAVERNS

The **Grand Canyon Caverns** (☑928-422-3223, 855-498-6969; www.grandcanyoncaverns.com; Mile 115, Rte 66; tour adult/child from $16/11; ☺8am-6pm May-Sep, call for off-season hours) lie 25 miles northwest of Seligman. Discovered in 1927 by a woodcutter who literally stumbled across (or into) them, these limestone caves have fascinated visitors ever since. Tours range from the wheelchair-accessible Short Tour (adult/child $16/11, 30 minutes) to the Explorers Tour ($70, 2½ hours), and the new Wild Tour ($90, 2½ hours), which picks up where the Explorer finishes and delves into caverns only recently discovered. Note that children aren't permitted on the Explorers Tour and Wild Tour.

The **Caverns Inn** (☑928-422-3223; gccaverns.com; Mile 115, Rte 66; d/bunkhouse $110/240; ⬆⬆⬆) has basic, well-kept rooms, with wi-fi in the lobby. There's a general store and guest laundry, and breakfast (5am to 9am) is included. The Cavern Suite ($850) is an underground cavern 'room' with two double beds, a sitting area and multicolored lamps. If you ever wanted to live out a post-apocalyptic survivor scenario, here's your chance!

Set over the caverns, the **campground** (☑928-422-4565; gccaverns.com; Mile 115, Rte 66; tent/RV sites $30/40; ⬆) has 51 sites carved out of the juniper forest, plus showers, hookups, a general store, wi-fi in the lobby and a free breakfast from 5am to 9am. Reservations are possible, but not for specific sites.

The **Caverns Restaurant** (☑928-422-3223; gccaverns.com; Mile 115, Rte 66; mains $11-13; ☺11am-8pm Apr-Oct, 12:30-7pm Nov-Mar; ⬆) is nice if you find yourself in need of a feed; it has a small playground and serves simple American fare. The bar opens at 3pm on Fridays and Saturdays and closes at 10pm or later depending on crowd size.

2004, but Angel and his wife Vilma still run Angel & Vilma's Original Route 66 Gift Shop. You can poke around for souvenirs and admire license plates sent in by fans from all over the world.

Angel's madcap brother Juan used to rule prankishly supreme over the Delgadillo's Snow Cap Drive-In, now kept going by his children Cecilia and John.

🛌 Sleeping

Some welcoming indie motels and some classic Route 66 neon greet you driving through Seligman.

Supai Motel   MOTEL $
(☑928-422-4153; www.supaimotelseligman.com; 22450 Rte 66; s/d $72/89; ⬆⬆) For the town's best neon sign and welcoming hosts, look no further than the Supai Motel, a classic courtyard motel offering simple but perfectly fine rooms with refrigerators and microwaves. The Havasu Falls mural is an inspiring way to start the morning.

🍴 Eating & Drinking

Humorous, charismatic and delicious choices can be found on both sides of Route 66. There's only really one bar in Seligman: it's on Route 66, as are a few restaurants also serving alcohol.

**Delgadillo's Snow
Cap Drive-In**   BURGERS $
(☑928-422-3291; 301 Rte 66; mains $5-6.50; ☺10am-6pm Mar-Nov) The Snow Cap is a Route 66 institution. The crazy decor is only the beginning. Wait until you see the menu featuring cheeseburgers with 'dead chicken.' And beware the fake mustard bottle! It's sometimes open at 9am in midsummer.

Westside Lilo's Cafe   CAFE $$
(☑928-422-5456; www.westsidelilos.com; 22855 W Rte 66; breakfast & lunch $8-14, dinner $15-19; ☺6am-9pm; ⬆) Come here for superfriendly service and good American grub, plus German options that reflect Lilo's heritage. And you'll be in trouble the minute you spy the world of pie in the dessert case.

🛍 Shopping

**Angel & Vilma's Original
Route 66 Gift Shop**   GIFTS & SOUVENIRS
(☑928-422-3352; www.route66giftshop.com; 22265 E Rte 66; ☺9am-5pm winter, 8am-6pm rest of the year) Seligman is a town that takes its Route 66 heritage seriously, thanks to the octogenarian Angel ('Angel of Route 66'), his wife Vilma, and his late, lamented brother Juan. Angel and Vilma run this barber and souvenir shop, and though Angel rarely cuts hair anymore, if he's around, he's usually happy to regale you with stories about the Dust Bowl era.

Lake Havasu City

📞 928 / POP 55,553 / ELEV 450-1500FT

This planned city on the banks of artificial Lake Havasu isn't Arizona's most compulsory stop, but it can lay claim to London Bridge. Yes, that would be the original, gracefully arched structure that spanned the Thames from 1831 until 1967, when it was quite literally falling down (as predicted in the old nursery rhyme) and put up for sale. Bought and reassembled by the city's developer, it's now a very popular attraction. Day-trippers come by the busload to walk across it and soak up faux British heritage in the kitschy-quaint 'English Village' at its eastern end.

The lake itself – which can be very pretty – is the other major draw. Formed in 1938 by the construction of Parker Dam, it's much beloved by water rats, especially students on spring break and summer-heat escapees from Phoenix and beyond.

◉ Sights & Activities

Once you've snapped pics of London Bridge, you'll find that most of your options are water-related. Several companies offer boat tours (starting from around $20) from the English Village, at London Bridge's eastern end. Options include one-hour narrated jaunts, half-day and full-day trips, and sunset tours, which can usually be booked on the spot. Several companies also rent jet skis and other watercraft.

London Bridge   BRIDGE
When developer Robert McCulloch needed a gimmick to drum up attention for the planned community of Lake Havasu City, London Bridge came up for sale. Snapped up for just $2.46 million, it was broken into 10,276 slabs and reassembled in the Arizona desert. The first car rolled across in 1971. Listed in the Guinness World Records as the world's largest antique, it's one of Arizona's most incongruous tourist sites, and among its most popular.

London Bridge Beach   BEACH
(1340 McCulloch Blvd; ⊙ sunrise-10:30pm; 🅿) This sandy strip against Bridgewater Channel has eucalypt and palm trees, a sandy beach, playgrounds, ramadas and a fenced dog park with faux fire hydrant in the middle. It also offers a pretty, palm-framed view of the lake and distant peaks. The beach is off W McCulloch Blvd; the nearby **Lake Havasu Marina** (📞 928-855-2159; www.

lakehavasumarina.com; 1100 McCulloch Blvd) has boat ramps but no rentals.

🛏 Sleeping

Rates fluctuate tremendously from summer weekends to winter weekdays. Local budget and national chain hotels line London Bridge Rd.

Windsor Beach Campground   CAMPGROUND $
(📞 928-855-2784, reservations 520-586-2283; www.azstateparks.com; 699 London Bridge Rd, Lake Havasu State Park; campsites $35-40) Sleep just steps from the water at this scenic beach and camping area at Lake Havasu State Park. Amenities include showers, boat-launch facilities, new hookups and the 1.75-mile Mohave Sunset Trail. Day-use is $20 per vehicle Friday through Sunday, and $15 the rest of the week. Sites are available by reservation; there's a minimum stay of two or three days in peak periods.

London Bridge Resort   HOTEL $$
(📞 928-855-0888; www.londonbridgeresort.com; 1477 Queens Bay Rd; r/ste from $234/324; ❄@🛜🏊) Enjoy flat-screen TVs, new mattresses, kitchenettes and rooms with views of London Bridge (of course) at this popular all-suite property, where a replica of a 1762 royal coach greets guests in the lobby. It can feel a little impersonal, but it's a good choice if you want pools, a waterslide, nightclubs, bars and restaurants in one place.

Heat   BOUTIQUE HOTEL $$
(📞 928-854-2833; www.heathotel.com; 1420 N McCulloch Blvd; r/ste from $209/249; ❄🛜) Perhaps the slickest hotel on Arizona's 'West Coast,' Heat offers a majority of rooms with private patios that have views of London Bridge. In the 'inferno' rooms, bathtubs fill from the ceiling. An outdoor cocktail lounge overlooking the bridge and the lake feels almost like the deck of a cruise ship.

🍴 Eating & Drinking

There's no shortage of places to eat in Havasu, with decent pub food and Italian choices leading the pack. Both ends of London Bridge have a couple of decent venues to enjoy a sundowner.

Red Onion   AMERICAN $
(📞 928-505-0302; www.redonionhavasu.com; 2013 N McCulloch Blvd; breakfast & lunch $6.25-12, dinner $10-15; ⊙ 7am-11pm) This diner in Havasu's 'uptown district' is great for breakfast – omelets such as the Sonoran (chorizo, olives, red onion, mushrooms and

Lake Havasu City

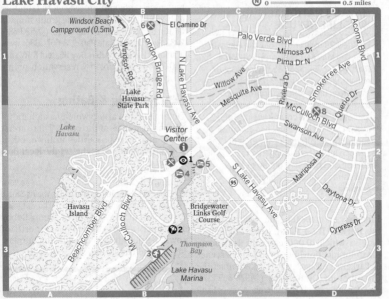

Lake Havasu City

cheddar) deliver a hearty start to your day. Look for salads, sandwiches and burgers at lunch, and service that's friendly, if casual.

Angelina's Italian Kitchen   ITALIAN **$$**
(☏ 928-680-3868; 1530 El Camino Dr; mains $12-28; ☺ 4-10pm) This is Italian American food done the right way: plenty of garlic, plenty of red sauce, and big portions. Seafood (not from the lake, of course) is the star in dishes such as shrimp risotto, and the marsala-braised beef calls out for cooler weather than Lake Havasu normally offers.

Barley Brothers   PUB FOOD **$$**
(☏ 928-505-7837; barleybrothers.com; 1425 N McCulloch Blvd; mains $18-21; ☺ 11am-9pm Sun-Thu, to 10pm Fri & Sat; ☏) It's brews and views at this busy microbrewery overlooking London Bridge, one of the most popular places in town. Steaks, burgers and salads are on the menu, but the place is known for its wood-fired pizzas. There are lots of flat-screen TVs for sports fans, and beer drinkers can choose from six different microbrews. Strangely, there's no outdoor patio.

ℹ Information

Visitor Center (☏ 928-855-5655; www.golake havasu.com; 422 English Village; ☺ 9am-5pm) Has all the need-to-know info.

Parker

☏ 928 / POP 3083 / ELEV 420FT

Hugging a 16-mile stretch of the Colorado River known as the Parker Strip, this tiny town, 35 miles south of Lake Havasu on Hwy 95, is a convenient stop for those wanting to explore the region's unique riparian parks and preserves. All hell breaks loose when the engines of up to 100,00 speed freaks rev up for the colossal **Best in the Desert Parker 425** (www.bitd.com; ☺ late Jan/early Feb) off-road race. If you're here in

HAVASU NATIONAL WILDLIFE REFUGE

Located 29 miles north of Lake Havasu City, the **Havasu National Wildlife Refuge** (☑760-326-3853; www.fws.gov/refuge/havasu) is a major habitat for migratory birds and waterbirds. Look for herons, ducks, geese, blackbirds and other winged creatures (including 25 species of dragonfly) as you raft or canoe through Topock Gorge. Under the surface lurks the endangered razorback sucker, and there are plenty of coves and sandy beaches for picnics and sunning.

June, buy an inner tube and register to join the **Parker Tube Float** (entry $20; ⊘mid-Jun), in which 10,000 entrants float down the Colorado, finishing amid festival scenes at Parker's La Pax County Park. Contact the **Chamber of Commerce** (☑928-669-2174; www.parkeraz.org; 1217 California Ave; ⊘8am-5pm Mon-Fri) for the lowdown on it all.

◉ Sights & Activities

Water-skiing, jet-skiing, fishing, boating and tubing are popular here, and there are plenty of operators along the Parker Strip.

Bill Williams National Wildlife Refuge
NATURE RESERVE

(☑928-667-4144; www.fws.gov/refuge/Bill_Williams_River; 60911 Hwy 95; ⊘visitor center 8am-4pm Mon-Fri, 10am-2pm Sat & Sun) ⚑**FREE** Abutting Cattail Cove, where the Bill Williams River meets Lake Havasu, is this calm wildlife refuge, which helps protect the unique transition zone between the Mojave and Sonoran Desert ecosystems. On a finger of land pointing into the lake, there's a 1.4-mile interpretive trail through a botanic garden of native flora, with shaded benches and access to fishing platforms.

Buckskin Mountain State Park
STATE PARK

(☑928-667-3231; www.azstateparks.com/buckskin; 5476 N Hwy 95; per vehicle $10, pedestrian & cyclist $3; ⊘visitor center 9am-4:30pm Jan-Mar; ⓟ🐾🏊) Tucked along a mountain-flanked bend in the Colorado River about 11 miles north of Parker, this park has a great, family-friendly infrastructure with

a swimming beach, hiking trails, basketball court, cafe and grocery store (summer only). Wi-fi is available at the group ramada at no charge, and **campsites** (☑520-586-2283, River Island State Park 928-667-3386; www.azstateparks.com; 5476 N Hwy 95; tent & RV sites $30-33) are available by reservation online or by phone.

🛏 Sleeping & Eating

Diners rule in Parker, which has a handful of good examples of the genre. There aren't really any great properties in town, but if you must spend the night, try the local Best Western.

Bobby D's Diner
DINER $

(☑928-667-2646; 10230 Harbor Dr; mains $8-10; ⊘8am-3:30pm Sun-Wed, to 8pm Thu-Sat; 🖶) Twist back in time at family-friendly Bobby D's Diner, a '50s-themed place north of town. Settle into a red booth for burgers, shakes and classic oldies.

Yuma

☑928 / POP 94,139 / ELEV 141FT

This sprawling city at the confluence of the Gila and Colorado Rivers celebrated its 100th birthday in 2014. That anniversary coincided with a new emphasis on the city's future, not just its storied past. A revitalized downtown welcomes visitors to Gateway Park and its new plaza as well as a growing trail system that stretches from the park into restored wetlands beside the Colorado. But the past hasn't completely gone away. The infamous territorial prison here, which was nicknamed the Hellhole of the West, still draws tourists to its sun-baked yard. Yuma is also the birthplace of farmworker organizer César Chávez and it's the winter camp of some 80,000 snowbirds craving Yuma's sunny skies, mild temperatures and cheap RV-park living.

To get a better feel for the city and a chance for some exercise, park downtown and walk to the sights (unless it's 100 degrees). From Gateway Park, a stroll upstream along the Colorado River leads to the prison and the east wetlands trails; a short walk downstream leads to the Quartermaster Depot. On Main St, the historic center of a town sadly somewhat hollowed out by suburban sprawl, you'll find restaurants and the inviting **Yuma Art Center** (☑928-373-5202; www.yumaaz.gov; 254 S Main St; ⊘10am-8pm Tue-Sat).

Sights

Yuma Territorial Prison State Historic Park   HISTORIC SITE
(☑928-783-4771; www.azstateparks.com; 1 Prison Hill Rd; adult/child 7-13yr $6/$3; ⊙9am-5pm daily, closed Tue & Wed Jun-Sep) Hunkered on a bluff overlooking the Colorado River, this infamous prison is Yuma's star attraction. Between 1876 and 1909, 3069 convicts were incarcerated here for crimes ranging from murder to 'seduction under the promise of marriage.' The small museum is fascinating, with photos and descriptions of individual inmates and their offenses, and includes a display devoted to the 29 women jailed here. Walking around the yard, behind iron-grille doors and into cells crowded with stacked bunks, you might get retroactively scared straight.

Yuma Quartermaster Depot State Park   HISTORIC SITE
(☑928-783-0071; www.azstateparks.com/yuma-quartermaster; 201 N 4th Ave; adult/child 7-13yr $4/2; ⊙9am-5pm daily, closed Mon Jun–Sep) Decades before the town jail was built, Yuma became a crucial junction in the military supply lines through the West. Its role in getting gear and victuals to the troops is commemorated at the low-key quartermaster depot, set around a manicured green lawn. New exhibits in the Corral House spotlight the Yuma East Wetlands Restoration Project and the Yuma Siphon – a massive 1912 irrigation tunnel running beneath the Colorado River that's still in use today.

Pause-Rest-Worship Church   CHURCH
(S Ave 13E) Around 14 miles north of Yuma, a tiny white-and-blue chapel sits on a patch of farmland on the west side of Hwy 95. A local farmer built the original in 1995 as a memorial to his deceased wife. A freak storm destroyed the structure in 2011, but the community helped rebuild it. The 8ft-by-12ft church seats about 12 and has stained-glass windows. Feeling contemplative? Pull over and step inside.

Sleeping

Yuma has plenty of chain hotels, mostly around exit 2 off the I-8.

Historic Coronado Motor Hotel   MOTEL $$
(☑877-234-5567, 928-783-4453; www.coronadomotorhotel.com; 233 4th Ave; r $134; ❄@🕾☀🐕) The template for motels to come (it was Best Western's first property), the Coronado is a

CASTLE DOME GHOST TOWN
Less celebrated than other mining ghost towns on Arizona's Wild West circuit, this ghost town/outdoor museum nonetheless delivers. The **Castle Dome Museum** (☑928-920-3062; castledomemuseum.org; Castle Dome Mine Rd; adult/child 7-11yr $10/5; ⊙10am-5pm, call for hours Apr 15-Sep) includes more than 50 remaining buildings, testifying to a 19th-century heyday, when it was the epicenter of a silver-mining district with more than 300 working claims.

must for motel-history buffs. Featuring red-tile roofs, bright turquoise doors, two swimming pools and newly upgraded rooms, it's a handsome and historic example of the genre. Some rooms have kitchenettes, there are three laundry rooms, and kids under 13 stay free.

La Fuente Inn & Suites   INN $$
(☑928-329-1814, 800-841-1814; www.lafuenteinn.com; 1513 E 16th St; d from $142; ❄❄🕾☀🐕) At this happy-to-help place, pretty gardens wrap around a modern, Spanish Colonial–style building. The evening social hour is great for mingling with fellow guests over free wine and appetizers. And there's an extensive complimentary breakfast spread in the morning.

Eating & Drinking

Aside from a few charismatic eateries in Yuma's hollowed-out historic heart, it's mainly chain choices in strip malls. You'll also find a small, walkable cluster of bars and lounges on Main St, then sports and cocktail bars in the car-friendly avenues of the city's outer sprawl.

Lutes Casino   AMERICAN $
(☑928-782-2192; www.lutescasino.com; 221 S Main St; mains $7-8; ⊙10am-8pm Mon-Thu, to 9pm Fri & Sat, to 6pm Sun) You won't find any roulette or slots at this charismatic 1920s-era hangout, just a warehouse-sized gathering spot. What's here? Attic-like treasures hanging from the ceiling, movie memorabilia, maybe a dude playing the piano and a true cross-section of the town. Expect diner-style, nuthin' fancy fare. The 'especial' is a burger topped with a sliced hot dog (antacid not included).

ARIZONA YUMA

River City Grill FUSION $$$
(📱 928-782-7988; www.rivercitygrillyuma.com; 600 W 3rd St; lunch $11-13, dinner $25-33; ⊙ 11am-2pm & 5-10pm; 📝) Chic, funky and gourmet, with a shaded outdoor patio in back, the River City Grill does a good take on bouillabaisse, and scores points with vegetarians for delicious mains such as chanterelle risotto. Come here for a snappy weekday lunch or romantic dinner for two.

❶ Information

Visitor Center (📱 800-293-0071, 928-783-0071; www.visityuma.com; 201 N 4th Ave, Yuma Quartermaster Depot State Park; ⊙ 9am-5pm daily Oct-May, closed Mon Jun-Sep) For maps and information.

❶ Getting There & Away

Yuma Airport (📱 928-726-5882; www.yuma airport.com; 2191 E 32nd St) has daily flights to Phoenix.

Greyhound (📱 928-783-4403; 1245 Castle Dome Ave) runs two buses daily to Phoenix (from $20, 3¾ hours).

Amtrak (www.amtrak.com; 281 S Gila St) stops briefly at Yuma station three times weekly with its *Sunset Limited* service between Los Angeles ($83, 5¾ hours) and New Orleans ($317, 41 hours).

SOUTHERN ARIZONA

This is a land of Stetsons and spurs, where cowboy ballads are sung around the campfire under starry, black-velvet skies and thick steaks sizzle on the grill. Anchored by the bustling college town of Tucson, it's a vast region, where long, dusty highways slide past rolling vistas and steep, pointy mountain ranges. Majestic saguaro cacti, the symbol of the region, stretch out as far as the eye can see. Some of the Wild West's most classic tales were begot in small towns like Tombstone and Bisbee, which still attract tourists by the thousands for their Old West vibe. The desert air is hot, sweet and dry by day, cool and crisp at night. And the sunsets? Stupendous.

Tucson

📱 520 / POP 531,641 / ELEV 2643FT

A college town with a long history, Tucson (too-sawn) is attractive, fun-loving and one of the most culturally invigorating places in the Southwest. Set in a flat valley hemmed in by snaggletoothed mountains and swaths of saguaro, Arizona's second-largest city smoothly blends American Indian, Spanish, Mexican and Anglo traditions. Distinct neighborhoods and 19th-century buildings give a rich sense of community and history not found in the more modern, sprawling Phoenix. The eclectic shops toting vintage garb, scores of funky restaurants and dive bars don't let you forget Tucson is a college town at heart, home turf to the 40,000-strong University of Arizona (UA).

Although colorful historic buildings, great bars and restaurants and quirky shops are half of Tucson's charm, the other half lies outside town. Whether it's the beautiful Saguaro National Park, the rugged Santa Catalina Mountains or the world-class Arizona-Sonora Desert Museum, you won't regret exploring beyond the city limits.

Tucson lies mainly to the north and east of I-10 at its intersection with I-19, which runs to the Mexican border at Nogales. Downtown Tucson and the main historic districts are east of I-10, exit 258, at Congress St/Broadway Blvd, a major west–east thoroughfare. Most west–east thoroughfares are called streets, while most north–south thoroughfares are called avenues (with a sprinkling of roads and boulevards). Stone Ave, at its intersection with Congress, forms the zero point for Tucson addresses.

◉ Sights & Activities

Many of Tucson's blockbuster sights, including the Saguaro National Park (p210) and the Arizona-Sonora Desert Museum (p212), are on the city outskirts. The downtown area and 4th Ave near the university are compact to walk, and interesting enough to reward doing so. Opening hours for outdoor attractions may change seasonally, typically opening at an earlier hour during the hot summer.

◉ Downtown

Downtown Tucson has a valid claim to being the oldest urban space in Arizona. Although spates of construction have marred the historical facade, this is still a reasonably walkable city center. SunLink streetcars connect downtown with 4th Ave and the university.

Tucson Museum of Art MUSEUM
(Map p216; 📱 520-624-2333; www.tucsonmuseum ofart.org; 140 N Main Ave; adult $12, senior &

student $10, child 13-17yr $7; ⊘10am-5pm Tue-Sat, noon-5pm Sun) For a small city, Tucson boasts an impressive art museum. There's a respectable collection of American, Latin American and modern art, and the permanent exhibition of pre-Columbian artifacts will awaken your inner Indiana Jones. The special exhibits are varied and interesting, there's a superb gift shop, and the block surrounding the building holds a number of notable historic homes. The museum stays open to 8pm on the first Thursday of the month, when admission is free from 5pm.

Presidio Historic District   AREA
(Map p216; www.nps.gov/nr/travel/amsw/sw7. htm) The Tucson Museum of Art is part of this low-key neighborhood, bounded by W 6th St, W Alameda St, N Stone Ave and Granada Ave, and embracing the site of the original Spanish fort and upmarket 'Snob Hollow.' This is one of the oldest continually inhabited places in North America: the Spanish **Presidio de San Agustín del Tucson** dates back to 1775, but the fort itself was built over a Hohokam site that has been dated to AD 700 to 900.

Barrio Histórico District
(Barrio Viejo)   AREA
(Map p210) This compact neighborhood was an important business district in the late 19th century. Today it's home to funky shops and galleries in brightly painted adobe houses. The barrio is bordered by I-10, Stone Ave and Cushing and 17th Sts.

4th Avenue   STREET
(Map p216; www.fourthavenue.org) Linking historic downtown and the university, lively 4th Ave is a rare breed: a hip, alt-flavored strip with a neighborhood feel and not a single chain store or restaurant (except for Dairy Queen). The stretch between 9th St and University Blvd is lined with buzzing restaurants, coffeehouses, bars, bookstores, galleries, indie boutiques and vintage shops. It has its own traders' association, public wi-fi and events (see the website).

⊙ University of Arizona

Rather than being a collection of public greens, the UA campus seamlessly integrates the desert into its learning space – although there are some soft lawns for the students to lounge around on. There are several excellent museums on campus.

Arizona State Museum   MUSEUM
(Map p210; ✏520-621-6302; www.statemuseum. arizona.edu; 1013 E University Blvd; adult/child 17yr & under $5/free; ⊘10am-5pm Mon-Sat) To learn more about the history and culture of the region's American Indian tribes, visit the Arizona State Museum, the oldest and largest anthropology museum in the Southwest. The exhibit covering the tribes' cultural histories is extensive but easy to navigate, and should appeal to newbies and history buffs alike. These galleries are complemented by much-envied collections of minerals and Navajo textiles.

University of Arizona
Museum of Art   MUSEUM
(Map p210; ✏520-621-7567; www.artmuseum. arizona.edu; 1031 Olive Rd; adult/senior $8/6.50; ⊘9am-4pm Mon-Wed & Fri, 9am-7pm Thu, 9am-5pm Sat, noon-5pm Sun) Founded in its current building in the 1950s, the university's impressive museum showcases 500 years of European and American creativity. The permanent collection features Rodin, Matisse, Picasso and Pollock.

Center for Creative Photography   MUSEUM
(CCP; Map p210; ✏520-621-7968; www.creative photography.org; 1030 N Olive Rd; donations appreciated; ⊘9am-4pm Tue-Fri, 1-4pm Sat) FREE The CCP is known for its ever-changing, high-caliber exhibits. It also administers the archives of Ansel Adams, perhaps the best-regarded landscape photographer in American history, and occasionally displays his works.

Arizona History Museum   MUSEUM
(Map p210; ✏520-628-5774; www.arizona historicalsociety.org; 949 E 2nd St; adult/senior/child 12-16yr $8/6/4; ⊘9am-4pm Mon-Thu, 9am-8pm Fri, 11am-4pm Sat; ▣) For an engaging look at highlights from Arizona's past, spend an hour at this family-friendly museum near the University of Arizona. You can walk though a replica of an old copper mine, learn all about cross-border revolutionary Pancho Villa and see both Geronimo's rifle and Wyatt Earp's pistol.

⊙ East of Downtown

★ **Mini Time Machine**
Museum of Miniatures   MUSEUM
(Map p210; ✏520-881-0606; www.theminitime machine.org; 4455 E Camp Lowell Dr; adult/senior/child 4-17yr $9/8/6; ⊘9am-4pm

Tucson

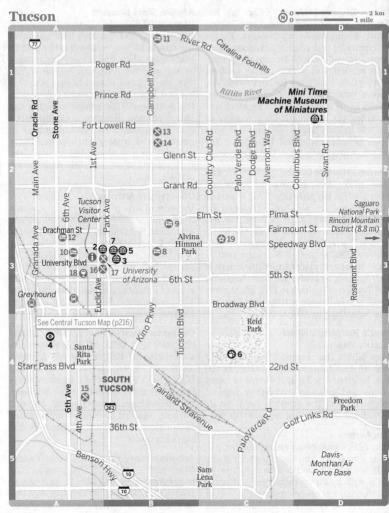

Mini Time Machine Museum of Miniatures

Tucson Visitor Center

University of Arizona

See Central Tucson Map (p216)

SOUTH TUCSON

Tue-Sat, noon-4pm Sun; 🖼) Divided into the Enchanted Realm, Exploring the World and the History Gallery, this delightful museum of miniatures presents dioramas fantastical, historical and plain intriguing. You can also walk over a snow-globe-y Christmas village, peer into tiny homes constructed in the 1700s and 1800s, and search for the little inhabitants of a magical tree. The museum grew from a personal collection in the 1930s. Parents may find themselves having more fun than their kids.

Around Tucson

Several of Tucson's best attractions are about 15 miles west of the University of Arizona. For a scenic, saguaro-dotted drive, follow Speedway Blvd west until it turns into W Gate Pass Rd. As you approach the top of Gates Pass, look for the one-way sign on the right. Follow it into Gates Pass Scenic Overlook (Map p212; W Gates Pass Rd), which offers splendid western perspectives.

★ Saguaro National Park   NATIONAL PARK
(🕿 Rincon 520-733-5153, Tucson 520-733-5158, park information 520-733-5100; www.nps.gov/sagu; 7-day

Tucson

pass per vehicle/bicycle $10/5; ⊘ sunrise-sunset) Saguaros (sah-wah-ros) are icons of the American Southwest, and an entire cactus army of these majestic, ribbed sentinels is protected in this desert playground. Or, more precisely, playgrounds: the park is divided into east and west units, separated by 30 miles and Tucson itself. Both sections – the Rincon Mountain District in the east and Tucson Mountain District in the west – are filled with trails and desert flora; if you only visit one, make it the spectacular western half.

The larger section is the **Rincon Mountain District**, about 15 miles east of downtown. The visitor center (p220) has information on day hikes, horseback riding and backcountry camping. The camping requires a permit ($8 per site per day) and must be obtained by noon on the day of your hike. The meandering 8-mile **Cactus Forest Scenic Loop Drive**, a paved road open to cars and bicycles, provides access to picnic areas, trailheads and viewpoints.

Hikers pressed for time should follow the 1-mile round-trip **Freeman Homestead Trail** to a grove of massive saguaro. For a full-fledged desert adventure, head out on the steep and rocky **Tanque Verde Ridge Trail**, which climbs to the summit of Mica Mountain (8666ft) and back in 20 miles (backcountry camping permit required for overnight use). If you'd rather someone (or something) else did the hard work, family-run **Houston's Horseback Riding** (Map p212; ☎ 520-298-7450; www.tucsonhorseback riding.com; 12801 E Speedway Bvd; per person 2hr tour $60) offers trail rides in the eastern section of the Park.

West of town, the **Tucson Mountain District** has its own Red Hills Visitor Center (p220). The Scenic **Bajada Loop Drive** is a 6-mile graded dirt road through cactus forest that begins 1.5 miles north of the visitor center. Two quick, easy and rewarding hikes are the 0.8-mile **Valley View Overlook** (awesome at sunset) and the half-mile **Signal Hill Trail** to scores of ancient petroglyphs. For a more strenuous trek we recommend the 7-mile **King Canyon Trail**, which starts 2 miles south of the visitor center, near the Arizona-Sonora Desert Museum. The 0.5-mile informative **Desert Discovery Trail**, which is 1 mile northwest of the visitor center, is wheelchair-accessible. Distances for all four hikes are round-trip.

As for the park's namesake cactus, don't refer to the limbs of the saguaro as branches. As park docents will quickly tell you, the mighty saguaro grows arms, not lowly branches – a distinction that makes sense when you consider its human-like features.

Saguaros grow slowly, taking about 15 years to reach a foot in height, 50 years to reach 7ft and almost a century before they begin to take on their typical many-armed appearance. The best time to visit is April, when the cacti begin blossoming with lovely

---

ⓘ TUCSON ATTRACTIONS PASSPORT

For avid explorers, the **Tucson Attractions Passport** ($20) may be a ticket to savings. It's available through www.visittucson.org or at the Tucson Visitor Center (p220) and entitles you to two-for-one tickets and other discounts at major museums, attractions, tours and parks throughout southern Arizona.

Metropolitan Tucson

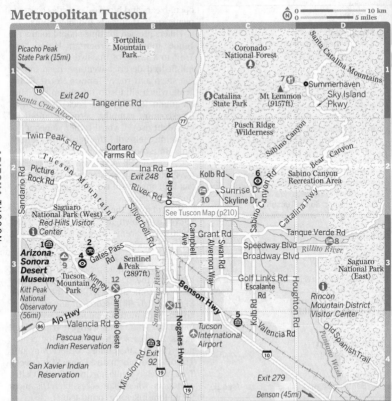

See Tucson Map (p210)

white blooms – Arizona's state flower. By June and July, the flowers give way to ripe red fruit that local American Indians use for food. Their foot soldiers are the spidery ocotillo, the fluffy teddy bear cactus, the green-bean-like pencil cholla and hundreds of other plant species. It is illegal to damage or remove saguaros.

Note that trailers longer than 35ft and vehicles wider than 8ft are not permitted on the park's narrow scenic loop roads.

★ Arizona-Sonora Desert Museum
MUSEUM

(Map p212; ☑ 520-883-2702; www.desertmuseum.org; 2021 N Kinney Rd; adult/senior/child 3-12yr $20.50/18.50/8; ⊙ 8:30am-5pm Oct-Feb, 7:30am-5pm Mar-Sep, to 10pm Sat Jun-Aug) Home to cacti, coyotes and palm-sized hummingbirds, this 98-acre ode to the Sonoran Desert is one-part zoo, one-part botanical garden and one-part museum – a trifecta that'll entertain young and old for easily half a day.

Desert denizens, from precocious coatis to playful prairie dogs, inhabit natural enclosures, the grounds are thick with desert plants, and docents give demonstrations. Strollers and wheelchairs are available, and there's a gift shop, an art gallery, a restaurant and a cafe.

Old Tucson Studios
FILM LOCATION

(Map p212; ☑ 520-883-0100; www.oldtucson.com; 201 S Kinney Rd; adult/child 4-11yr $19/11; ⊙ 10am-5pm daily Feb-Apr, 10am-5pm Fri-Sun May, 10am-5pm Sat & Sun Jun-early Sep; 🅿️👪) Nicknamed 'Hollywood in the Desert,' this old movie set of Tucson in the 1860s was built in 1939 for the filming of *Arizona*. Hundreds of flicks followed, bringing in movie stars from Clint Eastwood to Leonardo DiCaprio. Now a Wild West theme park, it's all about shoot-outs, stagecoach rides, stunt shows and dancing saloon girls. Closed from early September to the end of January, it does open for 'Nightfall' after-dark ghost tours in October.

Metropolitan Tucson

Mission San Xavier del Bac HISTORIC BUILDING
(Map p212; ☑520-294-2624; www.patronato
sanxavier.org; 1950 W San Xavier Rd; donations
appreciated; ⊙museum 8:30am-4:30pm, church
7am-5pm) The dazzling white towers of this
mission rise from the dusty desert floor
8 miles south of Tucson – a mesmerizing
structure that brings an otherworldly glow
to the scrubby landscape surrounding it.
Nicknamed 'White Dove of the Desert,' the
original mission was founded by Jesuit missionary Father Eusebio Kino in 1700, but was
mostly destroyed in the Pima uprising of 1751.

Pima Air & Space Museum MUSEUM
(Map p212; ☑520-574-0462; www.pimaair.org;
6000 E Valencia Rd; adult/senior/child 5-12yr
$16/13/9; ⊙9am-5pm, last entry 3pm; P⛟)
An SR-71 Blackbird spy plane and a massive B-52 bomber are among the stars of
this extraordinary private aircraft museum.
Allow at least two hours to wander through
hangars and around the airfield where more
than 300 'birds' trace the evolution of civil-
ian and military aviation. Take a self-guided
tour using the museum's GPS-guided app, or
shell out an extra $6 for the one-hour tram
tour departing at 10am, 11:30am, 1:30pm
and 3pm from November to May.

◉ **Santa Catalina Mountains**

Straddling the border between the **Coronado National Forest** (Map p212; www.fs.usda.
gov/coronado) and **Catalina State Park** (Map
p212; ☑520-628-5798; azstateparks.com/catalina;
11570 N Oracle Rd; vehicle $7, pedestrian & cyclist
$3; ⊙5am-10pm, visitor center 8am-5pm; P),
the Santa Catalinas northeast of Tucson are
the best-loved and most visited among the
region's mountain ranges. You need a Coronado Recreation Pass ($5/10 per vehicle per
day/week) to park anywhere in the mountain
area. One pass covers Sabino Canyon and Mt
Lemmon. It's available at the USFS **Santa
Catalina Ranger Station** (Map p212; ☑520-
749-8700; www.fs.usda.gov/coronado; 5700 N Sabino Canyon Rd; ⊙8am-4:30pm) at the mouth of
Sabino Canyon, which also has maps, hiking
guides and camping information.

Sabino Canyon (Map p212; ☑520-749-2861;
www.sabinocanyon.com; 5700 N Sabino Canyon Rd;
⊙9am-4:30pm) is a favorite year-round destination for both locals and visitors. For those
that don't fancy hiking, hop-on, hop-off
trams leave from the visitor center every half
an hour, following a nine-stop circuit. The
last stop is only 3.8 miles from the visitor
center, so hikers can listen to the tram driver's narration on the way up then hike back
to the visitor center, either on the road or on
the lofty but exposed **Telephone Line Trail**.
There is no fee, beyond the recreation pass,
if you want to hike into the canyon without
riding the tram. A second shuttle leaves on
each hour to **Bear Canyon**. Parking at Sabino Canyon is $5.

A great way to escape the summer heat
is by following the super-scenic **Sky Island
Parkway** (officially called Catalina Hwy),
which meanders 27 miles from saguaro-
dappled desert to pine-covered forest near
the top of Mt Lemmon (9157ft), passing
through ecosystems as distinct as those
found in Mexico and Canada. Allow for at
least three hours for the round-trip. Of the
vista points, Babad Do'ag, Windy Point and

HISPANIC TUCSON

Founded as a Spanish military outpost
in the 18th century, and close to today's
Mexican border, Tucson is a town with a
rich Hispanic heritage. More than 40% of
the population is Hispanic, Spanish slides
easily off most tongues and high-quality
Mexican restaurants abound.

TUCSON'S WISHING SHRINE

In Barrio Histórico look for **El Tiradito** (Map p216; 356 S Main Ave), a 'wishing shrine' with a tale of passion and murder behind it. Locals say that in the 19th century a young man fell for his wife's mother. Her husband – his father-in-law – killed the young man. The dead lover was never absolved of his sins, and was thus turned away from the conse-crated ground at the nearby Roman Catholic church, so he was buried under the front porch of the house that marks the spot of El Tiradito. Locals took pity on the young man and began offering prayers and burning candles at the site; over time, El Tiradito became a shrine for anyone commemorating a lost loved one. It is reputedly the only Catholic shrine in the country dedicated to a sinner buried in unconsecrated ground.

Aspen are the most rewarding. Get your camera ready for the sweeping views at Windy Point. There is no cost for the drive or for stopping at the vista points, but if you plan to explore the forest you must pay for the aforementioned $5 day-use permit, which can be purchased at the Palisades Visitor Center.

The **Mt Lemmon Ski Valley** (Map p212; 520-576-1321; www.skithelemmon.com; 10300 Ski Run Rd; day lift ticket adult/child $45/25; 10:30am-4:30pm Mon, Thu & Fri, 9am-4:30pm Sat & Sun late Dec-Mar) is the southernmost ski area in the USA. With snow levels rather unpredictable, it's more about the novelty of schussing down the slopes with views of Mexico than having a world-class alpine experience. Rentals, lessons and food are available on the mountain.

Skateboarders have been known to crazily zoom down the highway on their boards. Do not do this.

✯✯ Festivals & Events

Tucson knows how to party and keeps a year-round schedule of events. For details check out www.visittucson.org.

Tucson Gem & Mineral Show   CULTURAL
(520-332-5773; www.tgms.org; Feb) The most famous event on the city's calendar, held on the second full weekend in February, this is the largest gem and mineral show in the world. An estimated 250 retail dealers who trade in minerals, crafts and fossils take over the Tucson Convention Center.

Tucson Folk Festival   MUSIC
(www.tkma.org; May) Going strong since 1985 and held in early May, this music fes-tival brings together more than 120 local, regional and national performers across five stages, and is put on by the Tucson Kitchen Musicians Association.

Fiesta de los Vaqueros   RODE
(Rodeo Week; 520-741-2233; www.tucsonrodec com; 4823 S 6th Ave, Tucson Rodeo Grounds tickets $15-70; last week of Feb) Held fo nearly a century, the Fiesta de los Vaquero brings world-famous cowboys to town an features a spectacular parade with West ern-themed floats and buggies, historica horse-drawn coaches, folk dancers an marching bands.

🛏 Sleeping

Tucson's gamut of lodging options rival Phoenix's for beauty, comfort and location Rates plummet as much as 50% betwee June and September, making what woul otherwise be a five-star mega-splurge a affordable getaway. Chains are abundan along the I-10 and around the airport.

🛏 Downtown

★**Hotel Congress**   HISTORIC HOTEL $
(Map p216; 800-722-8848, 520-622-8848 www.hotelcongress.com; 311 E Congress St d from $109; P ❄ 🛜 🐾) Perhaps Tucson' most famous hotel, this is where infamou bank robber John Dillinger and his gan were captured during their 1934 stay, whe a fire broke out. Built in 1919 and beauti fully restored, this charismatic place feel very modern, despite period furnishing such as rotary phones and wooden radio (but no TVs). There's a popular cafe, ba and club on-site.

🛏 University of Arizona

Quality Inn Flamingo Downtown   MOTEL
(Map p210; 520-770-1910; www.flaming hoteltucson.com; 1300 N Stone Ave; d from $7C ❄ 🛜 🐾 🐾) Recently purchased by the Qual ity Inn chain, the former Flamingo Hote retains some of its Rat Pack vibe, an the fact that Elvis slept here doesn't hur

although the rooms were renumbered and now no one is sure which room he slept in). Rooms come with chic, striped bedding, flat-screen TVs, a good-sized desk and comfy beds. There's a hot breakfast buffet, and pets are $25 per day.

★**Catalina Park Inn**   B&B **$$**
Map p210; ☑ 800-792-4885, 520-792-4541; www.catalinaparkinn.com; 309 E 1st St; r from $145; ☉closed Jun-Aug; ❋@☎❋) Style, hospitality and comfort merge seamlessly at this inviting B&B just west of the University of Arizona. Hosts Mark and Paul have poured their hearts into restoring this 1927 Mediterranean-style villa, and their efforts are on display in each of the six rooms, which vary in style. Don't miss the delicious breakfast – burritos, croissant French toast and more await in the mornings. The East and West Rooms have balcony porches perfect for sipping early morning coffee. The cactus and desert garden has lots of little corners for lazy afternoon cat naps. Small pets are OK in the Cottage Room.

Aloft Tucson   HOTEL **$$**
Map p210; ☑ 520-908-6800; www.starwoodhotels.com; 1900 E Speedway Blvd; d from $145; ❋☎) Tucson is surprisingly light on for stylish hotels. The new Aloft, near the university, isn't an indie property, but it is a slick operation catering to tech-minded, style-conscious travelers. Rooms and common areas pop with bright, spare, yet inviting decor, there's an on-site bar, and 24-hour grab 'n' go food is available beside the lobby.

Metropolitan Tucson

Arizona Inn   RESORT **$$**
Map p210; ☑ 800-933-1093, 520-325-1541; www.arizonainn.com; 2200 E Elm St; d/ste from $229/299; ❋☎❋) High tea in the library,

complete with scones and finger sandwiches, is a highlight here. Croquet might be too, if only we knew the rules. Historic and aristocratic touches such as these provide a definite sense of privilege – and we like it. Mature gardens and old-Arizona grace provide a respite from city life and the 21st century. Rooms are furnished with antiques. Be sure to pop into the country-clubbish Audubon Bar.

Homewood Suites Tucson   HOTEL **$$**
(Map p210; ☑ 520-577-0007; www.windmillinns.com; 4250 N Campbell Ave; r from $131; ❋☎❋❋) Popular with University of Arizona fans during football season, this modern, efficient hotel at St Philip's Plaza is run by the Hilton empire. There's a pool and two fitness rooms, and pets are permitted (with a $75 deposit).

★**Hacienda del Sol**   RANCH **$$$**
(Map p212; ☑ 520-299-1501; www.haciendadelsol.com; 5501 N Hacienda del Sol Rd; d/ste from $209/339; ❋@☎❋) An elite hilltop girls' school built in the 1920s, this relaxing refuge has artist-designed Southwest-style rooms and teems with unique touches like carved ceiling beams and louvered exterior doors to catch the courtyard breeze. The Hacienda del Sol has sheltered Spencer Tracy, Katharine Hepburn, John Wayne and other legends, so you'll be sleeping with history. Its restaurant, the Grill, is fabulous too.

There are horses available for riding the nearby trails (60/90 minutes $40/50), and you can get a rub-down in the in-house spa.

Around Tucson

Gilbert Ray Campground   CAMPGROUND **$**
(Map p212; ☑ 520-724-5000; www.pima.gov; 8451 W McCain Loop Rd; tent/RV sites $10/20; ❋) Camp among the saguaros at this Pima County campground, 13 miles west of

---

TUCSON FOR CHILDREN

Reid Park Zoo (Map p210; ☑ 520-791-3204; reidparkzoo.org; 3400 E Zoo Ct; adult/senior/child 2-14yr $11/8.50/6.50; ☉9am-4pm Oct-May, 8am-3pm Jun-Sep; ⛫) At the compact Reid Park Zoo, a global menagerie, including grizzly bears, jaguars, giant anteaters and pygmy hippos, delights young and old. Cap a visit with a picnic in the surrounding park, which also has playgrounds and a pond with paddleboat rentals.

Tucson Children's Museum (Map p216; ☑ 520-792-9985; www.childrensmuseumtucson.org; 200 S 6th Ave; $8; ☉9am-5pm Tue-Fri, 10am-5pm Sat & Sun; ⛫) Parents sing the praises of the Tucson Children's Museum, which has plenty of engaging, hands-on exhibits – from Dinosaur World to Wee World (as in tiny) and an aquarium. Admission is $3 on the 3rd of each month.

Central Tucson

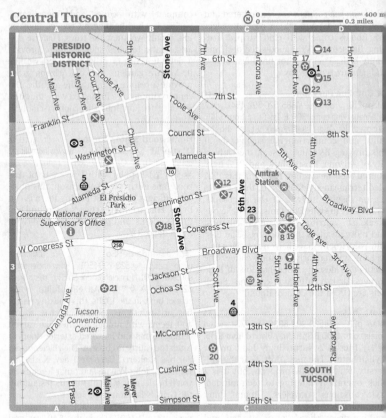

downtown. It has 130 first-come, first-served sites along with water and restrooms, but no showers. There are five tent-only sites but tenters can camp at RV sites. No credit cards. Located near the Arizona-Sonora Desert Museum.

★ **Desert Trails B&B**　　　　　B&B $$
(Map p212; ☑520-885-7295; www.deserttrails. com; 12851 E Speedway Blvd; r/guesthouse from $140/175; ❉🕸☀) Outdoorsy types who want a personable B&B close to Saguaro National Park (Rincon Mountain District) have their answer at Desert Trails on Tucson's eastern fringe. Rooms are comfy with all the latest amenities. John Higgins, an avid backpacker, was a fireman for Saguaro National Park for six years and is glad to share his knowledge about the park's trails. Cut by nearby Wentworth Rd: the Tanque Verde Wash, one of Tucson's noted riparian birding areas, is on your doorstep.

✗ Eating

Tucson's culinary scene delivers a flavor-packed punch, from family-run 'nosherias' to five-star dining rooms. Intricately spiced and authentic Mexican and Southwestern fare is king here, and much of it is freshly prepared from regional ingredients.

★ **Lovin' Spoonfuls**　　　　　VEGAN $
(Map p210; ☑520-325-7766; www.lovinspoon fuls.com; 2990 N Campbell Ave; breakfast $6-9, lunch $5.25-8, dinner $7.25-11.25; ☺9:30am-9pm Mon-Sat, 10am-3pm Sun; ✐) Burgers, country-fried chicken and club sandwiches – the menu reads like one at your typical diner, but there's a big difference: no animal products will ever find their way into this vegan haven. Outstandingly creative choices include the Old Pueblo bean burrito and Buddha's Delight – a gingery stir-fry o cabbage, shiitake and other goodies over brown rice.

Central Tucson

La Cocina SOUTHERN US $
(Map p216; ☑520-622-0351; www.lacocina
tucson.com; 201 N Court Ave; mains $13; ⊙11am-3pm Mon, 11am-10pm Tue-Thu, 11am-2am Fri & Sat, 11am-4pm Sun) The popular La Cocina, within Old Town Artisans in the Presidio district, serves Southwestern fare, Arizona beers and cool live music most nights. It's also opened a pub, the Dusty Monk (open 4pm to 11pm Tuesday to Thursday and 4pm to 2am Friday and Saturday), in the same complex.

Diablo Burger BURGERS $
(Map p216; ☑520-882-2007; www.diablo
burger.com; 312 E Congress St; burgers $10-12; ⊙11am-9pm Sun-Wed, to 10pm Thu-Sat) This satellite of Flagstaff's popular burger joint does a mean patty of open-range, locally sourced beef. Try the Big Daddy Kane, with sharp cheddar, pickles and special sauce. The herby 'Belgian-style' fries are salty, but so good.

Mi Nidito MEXICAN $
(Map p210; ☑520-622-5081; www.minidito.net; 1813 S 4th Ave; mains $9-11; ⊙11am-10:30pm Sun, Wed & Thu, to 2am Fri & Sat) This perennially popular local favorite has seen its share of celebrities: former president Bill Clinton's order (pre–quadruple bypass) at 'My Little Nest' has become the signature president's plate, a heaping mound of Mexican favorites – tacos, tostadas, burritos, enchiladas and more – groaning under melted cheese. Give the *caldo de queso*

(cheese soup) or the *birria* (spicy, shredded beef) a whirl.

Beyond Bread SANDWICHES $
(Map p210; ☑520-332-9965; www.beyondbread.
com; 3026 N Campbell Ave; sandwiches $7-11; ⊙6:30am-8pm Mon-Fri, 7am-8pm Sat, 7am-6pm Sun; ☑) Free chunks of homemade bread are perched temptingly between the door and the front counter at this busy cafe and bakery, which has a handful of locations across town. Their specialties? Daily breads and a mouthwatering array of sandwiches – try Roger's Roast, with beef, lettuce, cheddar and horseradish on toasted pretzel bread. There are veggie sandwiches, soups and salads too.

Wilko PUB FOOD $
(Map p210; ☑520-792-6684; www.barwilko.
com; 943 E University Blvd, at N Park Ave; breakfast $12-13, lunch & dinner $10-13; ⊙11am-10pm Mon-Fri, 8am-10pm Sat & Sun) For a pleasant lunch near the University of Arizona, try this stylish gastropub across the street from campus. Look for salads and pizzas on the menu, plus a few 'tasty misfits.' As for sandwiches, try the jerk chicken with coconut slaw and curry aioli, or the roasted eggplant. At the bar, the beers are microbrewed and the cocktails crafted.

★ **Cafe Poca Cosa** MEXICAN $$
(Map p216; ☑520-622-6400; www.cafepocacosa
tucson.com; 110 E Pennington St; lunch $13-15, dinner $20-24; ⊙11am-9pm Tue-Thu, to 10pm Fri

& Sat) Chef Suzana Davila's award-winning nuevo-Mexican bistro is a must for fans of Mexican food in Tucson. A Spanish-English blackboard menu circulates between tables because dishes change twice daily – it's all freshly prepared, innovative and beautifully presented. The undecided can't go wrong by ordering the 'Plato Poca Cosa' and letting Suzana decide what's best. Great margaritas, too.

Cup Cafe INTERNATIONAL $$
(Map p216; ☎520-798-1618; www.hotelcongress.com/food; 311 E Congress St, Hotel Congress; breakfast $11-12, lunch $12-13, dinner $19-24; ⊗7am-10pm Sun-Thu, to 11pm Fri & Sat; 🛜🖉) Cup Cafe, we like your style: wine-bottle chandeliers, penny-tiled floor and 'Up on Cripple Creek' on the speakers. In the morning (or the afternoon – breakfast is served until 4pm) there's a Creole dish with andouille sausage, eggs, potatoes, buttermilk biscuits and sausage gravy; later, try the fresh tuna nicoise or the lettuce-wrapped chickpea fritters with harissa vinaigrette. The coffee is excellent. The Cup is inside the historic Hotel Congress (p214).

El Charro Café MEXICAN $$
(Map p216; ☎520-622-1922; www.elcharrocafe.com; 311 N Court Ave; lunch $10-12, dinner $16-20; ⊗10am-9pm) This rambling, buzzing hacienda has been making great Mexican food on this site since 1922. It's particularly famous for the *carne seca*, sun-dried lean beef that's been reconstituted, shredded and grilled with green chile and onions. The fabulous margaritas pack a burro-stunning punch, and help while away the time as you wait for your table.

Reilly Craft Pizza & Drink PIZZA $$
(Map p216; ☎520-882-5550; www.reillypizza.com; 101 E Pennington St; mains $14-16; ⊗11am-10pm Mon-Thu, 11am-11pm Fri, noon-11pm Sat, noon-9pm Sun) This gourmet pizza and wine bar has big ideas and mostly manages to deliver on them. Housed in a former funeral parlour (note the chapel-like arches in the airy dining room), it has a good craft-beer selection, and you can chat to the bar staff while they make your cocktail. Book on busy nights.

Tiny's Saloon & Steakhouse AMERICAN $$
(Map p212; ☎520-578-7700; 4900 W Ajo Hwy; mains $12-18; ⊗11am-10pm Mon-Thu, Sat & Sun, to midnight Fri; 🐾) Motorcycles are lined up like horses in front of this well-worn watering hole just west of the city. Inside, once your eyes adjust, slide into a booth, nod at the barflies then order a half-pound steerburger with a cold beer. For a saloon Tiny's is family-friendly during the day. I only accepts cash (although there's an ATM on-site).

Pasco Kitchen & Lounge AMERICAN $$
(Map p210; ☎520-882-8013; www.pascokitchen.com; 820 E University Blvd, Main Gate Sq; mains $13-16; ⊗11am-10pm Sun-Tue, to 11pm Wed & Thu, to midnight Fri & Sat) 🖉 The quinoa farmers market salad with yard bird is superb at this breezy bistro near the University of Arizona. They serve fresh, locally sourced comfort food prepared with panache and a few tasty twists – think grass-fed brisket burgers with Oaxacan cheese, or duck enchiladas with housemade cheese and red sauce. Drop in from 3pm to 6pm daily to sample their great cocktails for just $5.

Hub Restaurant & Ice-Creamery AMERICAN $$
(Map p216; ☎520-207-8201; hubdowntown.com; 266 E Congress St; mains $16-18; ⊗11am-midnight) Exposed bricks, a lofty ceiling, sleek booths and a walk-up ice-cream stand beside the hostess desk – industrial chic takes a Mayberry spin. Upscale comfort food is the name of the game here, from shrimp and grits to chicken potpie, plus a few sandwiches and salads. Even if you're not hungry, you can pop in for a scoop of salted caramel.

Drinking & Nightlife

Congress St in downtown and 4th Ave near the University of Arizona are both busy party strips.

PERROS CALIENTES

Tucson's signature dish is the Sonoran hot dog, a tasty example of what happens when Mexico's cuisine meets America's penchant for excess. It's a bacon-wrapped hot dog layered with tomatillo salsa, pinto beans, shredded cheese, mayo, ketchup, mustard, chopped tomatoes and onions. A dog-slinger so popular it's spawned three more locations in Tucson, **El Guero Canelo** (Map p212; ☎520-295-9005; www.elguerocanelo.com; 5201 S 12th Ave; hot dogs $3-4, mains $7-9; ⊗10am-10pm Sun-Thu, 8:30am-midnight Fri & Sat) is the place to try them.

★ Che's Lounge   BAR
(Map p216; ☑520-623-2088; cheslounge.com;
350 N 4th Ave; ☺noon-2am) This slightly
grungy but hugely popular watering hole
does cheap Pabst Blue Ribbon and features a huge wraparound bar and fantastic
murals by local artist (and bartender) Dono-
van. A popular college hangout, Che's rocks
with live music most Saturday nights and
on the patio on Sunday afternoons (4pm to
7pm) in the summer.

IBT's   GAY
(Map p210; ☑520-882-3053; www.ibtstucson.
com; 616 N 4th Ave; ☺noon-2am) At Tucson's
most sizzling gay fun house, the theme
changes nightly – from drag shows to karaoke – plus the monthly Sunday 'Fun Day,'
with karaoke, DJs and drink specials all
day. Chill on the patio, check out the bods
or sweat it out on the dance floor.

Thunder Canyon Brewery   MICROBREWERY
(Map p216; ☑520-396-3480; www.thunder
canyonbrewery.com; 220 E Broadway Blvd;
☺11am-11pm Sun-Thu, to midnight Fri & Sat) This
cavernous microbrewery, within walking
distance of the Hotel Congress, has more
than 40 beers on tap, serving up its own
creations as well as handcrafted beers from
across the US. There's now a second location at 1234 N Williams St.

Chocolate Iguana   COFFEE
(Map p216; ☑520-798-1211; www.chocolate
iguanaon4th.com; 500 N 4th Ave; ☺7am-6pm
Mon & Tue, 7am-8pm Wed & Thu, 7am-10pm Fri &
Sat, 9am-6pm Sun) Coffee lovers can choose
from numerous brews and a long list of
specialty drinks, while sugar fiends have
their pick of sweets, ice-cream, chocolates
and pastries inside this green-and-purple
cottage. Watching your diet? The delicious
Frozen Explosion is a fat-free mocha, and
the sandwiches ($5 to $6) include healthy
tuna and chicken options.

Surly Wench   BAR
(Map p216; ☑520-882-0009; www.surlywench
pub.com; 424 4th Ave; ☺2pm-2am Mon-Fri,
11am-2am Sat & Sun) This bat cave of a watering hole is generally packed with pierced
pals soaking up cheap drafts, giving the
pinball machine a workout or headbanging
to deafening bands, from punkgrass to alt-
rock, plus a burlesque show the first Friday
of the month. See the website for dates
and times. Burgers, tacos and the like are
available.

☆ Entertainment

The free *Tucson Weekly* (www.tucson
weekly.com) has comprehensive entertainment listings.

Live Music

Rialto Theatre   LIVE MUSIC
(Map p216; ☑520-740-1000; www.rialtotheatre.
com; 318 E Congress St) This gorgeous 1920
vaudeville and movie theater has been
reborn as a top venue for live touring acts.
It features everything from alt-pop to reggae, Latin dance to swing, plus the odd
comedian – basically anyone too big to play
at Club Congress across the street.

Club Congress   LIVE MUSIC
(Map p216; ☑520-622-8848; www.hotelcongress.
com; 311 E Congress St; ☺live music from 7pm,
club nights from 10pm) Skinny jeansters, tou-
sled hipsters, aging folkies, dressed-up
hotties – the crowd at Tucson's most happening club inside the grandly aging Hotel
Congress defines the word eclectic. And
so does the musical lineup, which usually
features the finest local and regional talent, and DJs some nights. And for a no-fuss
drink, there's the Lobby Bar for cocktails, or
the Tap Room, open since 1919.

Flycatcher   LIVE MUSIC
(Map p216; ☑520-207-9251; www.theflycatcher
tucson.com; 340 E 6th St; ☺4pm-2am; ☷) Formerly known as Plush, Flycatcher is a club
to watch when it comes to catching cool
regional bands. Covers are charged only
for bigger acts, and there's a daily happy
hour between 4pm and 8pm.

Cinema & Performing Arts

Loft Cinema   CINEMA
(Map p210; ☑box office 520-795-0844; www.
loftcinema.com; 3233 E Speedway Blvd) For
indie, art-house and foreign movies head
to Loft Cinema, in business since 1972.

Fox Theatre   THEATER
(Map p216; ☑520-547-3040; www.foxtucson
theatre.org; 17 W Congress St; ☺box office
11am-6pm Tue-Fri) It's always worth checking
out what's on at the deco Fox Theatre, a gloriously glittery venue for classic and modern movies, music, theater and dance.

Tucson Music Hall   CLASSICAL MUSIC
(Map p216; ☑520-791-4101; tucsonmusichall.org;
260 S Church Ave) The **Arizona Opera** (☑520-
293-4336; www.azopera.org; tickets from $30) and
Tucson Symphony Orchestra (☑520-792-
9155; www.tucsonsymphony.org) perform here.

Temple of Music & Art THEATER
(Map p216; ☎520-622-2823; www.arizona
theatre.org; 330 S Scott Ave) The **Arizona
Theatre Company** (tickets from $41) stages
shows at this renovated 1920s building.

🛍 Shopping

Tucson's Hispanic heart and undergradu-
ate buzz make it one of the best places to
shop in the state. 4th Ave sprouts indie
boutiques, while Old Town Artisans in the
Presidio district is the place for Mexican
and Southwestern art and crafts.

Old Town Artisans ARTS & CRAFTS
(Map p216; www.oldtownartisans.com; 201 N
Court Ave; ☺10am-5:30pm Mon-Sat, 11am-5pm
Sun Sep-May, to 4pm daily Jun-Aug) Old Town
Artisans in the Presidio Historic District
is a great destination for quality arts and
crafts produced in the Southwest and
Mexico. It's a block-long warren of adobe
apartments filled with galleries and crafts
stores, set around a lush and lovely courtyard (an architectural feature that comes
from Andalucia, in southern Spain, by way
of North Africa).

Bahti Indian Arts ARTS & CRAFTS
(Map p210; ☎520-577-0290; www.bahti.com;
4330 N Campbell Ave, Suite 73, St Philip's Plaza;
☺10am-6pm Mon-Sat, 9am-3pm Sun) Founded
by New Mexican anthropologist and American Indian art collector Tom Bahti in 1952,
this wonderful store carries Zuni fetishes,
Hopi kachinas, Navajo rugs and many
other precious items.

Antigone Books BOOKS
(Map p216; ☎520-792-3715; www.antigonebooks.
com; 411 N 4th Ave; ☺10am-7pm Mon-Thu,
10am-9pm Fri & Sat, 11am-5pm Sun) Great indie
bookstore with a fun, girl-power focus.

ℹ Information

EMERGENCY
Police (☎520-791-4444, emergency 911; 270
S Stone Ave)

MEDIA
Newspapers & Magazines The local mainstream newspapers include the morning *Arizona Daily Star* (tucson.com). The free *Tucson
Weekly* (www.tucsonweekly.com) is chock-full
of great entertainment and restaurant listings.
Tucson Lifestyle (www.tucsonlifestyle.com) is a
glossy monthly mag.
Radio Catch National Public Radio (NPR) on
89.1 FM.

MEDICAL SERVICES
Tucson Medical Center (☎520-327-5461;
www.tmcaz.com/TucsonMedicalCenter; 5301 E
Grant Rd) Has 24-hour emergency services.

POST
Post Office (Map p216; ☎520-903-1958; 141 S
6th Ave; ☺9am-5pm)

TOURIST INFORMATION
General information on Tucson is available from
the **Tucson Visitor Center** (Map p210; ☎800-
638-8350, 520-624-1817; www.visittucson.org;
811 N Euclid Ave; ☺9am-5pm Mon-Fri, to 4pm
Sat & Sun), while specific information on access
and camping in the Coronado National Forest
can be found at the downtown **Coronado National Forest Supervisor's Office** (Map p216;
☎520-388-8300; www.fs.usda.gov/coronado;
300 W Congress St, Federal Bldg; ☺8am-
4:30pm Mon-Fri).

The **Red Hills Visitor Center** (Map p212;
☎520-733-5158; www.nps.gov/sagu; 2700 N
Kinney Rd; ☺9am-5pm) provides information
on the Tucson Mountain District.

Information on and permits for the Saguaro
National Park is at the **Rincon Mountain District Visitor Center** (Map p212; ☎520-733-
5153; www.nps.gov/sagu; 3693 S Old Spanish
Trail; ☺9am-5pm).

ℹ Getting There & Away

Tucson International Airport (Map p212;
☎520-573-8100; www.flytucson.com; 7250 S
Tucson Blvd; 🛜) is 15 miles south of downtown
and served by six airlines, with nonstop flights
to destinations including Atlanta, Denver, Las
Vegas, Los Angeles and San Francisco.

Greyhound (Map p210; ☎520-792-3475;
www.greyhound.com; 471 W Congress St) runs
seven buses to Phoenix (from $10, two hours),
among other destinations.

The *Sunset Limited,* operated by **Amtrak**
(☎800-872-7245, 520-623-4442; www.amtrak.
com; 400 N Toole Ave), comes through on its way
west to Los Angeles (10 hours, three weekly) and
east to New Orleans (36 hours, three weekly).

Adobe Shuttle (☎520-609-0591) runs vans
from Tucson to Kitt Peak National Observatory
(p223), starting at $228 one-way.

ℹ Getting Around

All major car-rental agencies have offices at
the airport. **Arizona Stagecoach** (☎520-
889-1000; www.azstagecoach.com) runs
shared-ride vans into downtown for about $27
per person, about what a taxi with **Yellow Cab**
(☎520-300-0000; www.aaayellowaz.com)
would cost.

The **Ronstadt Transit Center** (Map p216; 215 E Congress St, at 6th Ave) is the main hub for the public buses with **Sun Tran** (Map p216; ✍520-792-9222; www.suntran.com) that serve the entire metro area. Single/day fares are $1.50/4 using the SunGo smart card. The same fares apply on the new streetcar line SunLink.

Tucson to Phoenix

If you just want to quickly travel between Arizona's two biggest cities, Phoenix and Tucson, it's a straight 120-mile shot on a not terribly inspiring stretch of the I-10. However, a couple of rewarding side trips await those with curiosity and a little more time on their hands.

◉ Sights

Picacho Peak State Park   STATE PARK
(✍520-466-3183, camping reservations 877-697-2757; azstateparks.com/picacho; Picacho Peak Rd, off I-10, exit 219; per vehicle $7, pedestrian & cyclist $3, campsites $30; ⊘5am-10pm, visitor center 8am-5pm, park closed late May–mid-Sep) The westernmost battle of the American Civil War was fought near this distinctive peak (3374ft) in 1862: a small band of Confederate Arizona Rangers killed three Union cavalrymen. After the skirmish, Confederate soldiers retreated to Tucson and dispersed, knowing full well that they would soon be greatly outnumbered. The battle is re-enacted every March with lots of pomp, circumstance and period costumes. The pretty state park has a visitor center that acts as a jump-off point for trails onto the mountain.

Biosphere 2   SCIENCE CENTER
(✍520-838-6200; www.b2science.org; 32540 S Biosphere Rd, Oracle; adult/student/child 6-12yr $20/15/13; ⊘9am-4pm) Built to be completely sealed off from Biosphere 1 (the earth), Biosphere 2 is 3 acres of glass domes and pyramids containing six ecosystems: ocean, mangrove, rainforest, savannah, desert and city. In 1991, eight biospherians were sealed inside for a two-year tour of duty, from which they emerged thinner but in fair shape. Tours take in the biospherians' apartments, farm area and kitchen, the 1-million-gallon 'tropical ocean' and the 'technosphere' that made it all possible.

Casa Grande Ruins
National Monument   MONUMENT
(✍520-723-3172; www.nps.gov/cagr; 1100 W Ruins Dr, Coolidge; adult $5, child 15yr & under free; ⊘9am-5pm; Ⓟ) Built around AD 1350, Casa Grande (Big House) is the country's largest Hohokam structure still standing, with 11 rooms spread across four floors and mud walls several feet thick. It's in reasonably good shape, partly because of the metal awning that's been canopying it since 1932. Although you can't walk inside the crumbling structure, you can peer into its rooms. A few strategically placed windows and doors suggest that the structure may have served as an astronomical observatory.

West of Tucson

West of Tucson, Hwy 86 cuts through the Tohono O'odham Indian Reservation, the second-largest in the country. Although this is one of the driest areas in the Sonoran Desert, it's an appealing drive for anyone craving the lonely highway (although you can expect to see a number of green-and-white border-patrol SUVs cruising past). There's a gratifying sense of space out here, as distant clouds dapple saguaro-dressed slopes and the road spools out to the skyline ahead. Gas stations, grocery marts and motels are sparse, so plan ahead and carry plenty of water and other necessities.

Organ Pipe Cactus National Monument

You can't get much further off the grid than **Organ Pipe Cactus National Monument** (✍520-387-6849; www.nps.gov/orpi; Hwy 85; per vehicle $12; ⊘visitor center 8:30am-5pm), a huge, exotic park along the Mexican border. It's a gorgeous, forbidding land that supports an astonishing number of animals and plants, including 28 species of cacti, first and foremost its namesake organ pipe. Giant and columnar cacti, organ pipes are common in Mexico, but very rare north of the border.

The monument is also the only place in the USA to see the senita cactus. Its branches are topped by hairy white tufts, hence the nickname 'old man's beard.' Animals that have adapted to this arid climate include bighorn sheep, coyotes, kangaroo rats, mountain lions and the pig-like javelina. Your best chance of encountering wildlife is in the early morning or evening. Walking around the desert by full moon or flashlight is another good way to catch things on the prowl, but wear boots and watch where you step.

Winter and early spring, when Mexican gold poppies and purple lupine blanket the barren ground, are the most pleasant seasons to visit. Summers are shimmering hot – regularly above 100°F (38°C) – and bring monsoon rains between July and September.

 Activities

Scenic Drives

Two principal scenic drives are open to vehicles and bicycles, both starting near the visitor center. The 21-mile **Ajo Mountain Drive** takes you through a spectacular landscape of steep-sided, jagged cliffs and rock tinged a faintly hellish red. It's a well-maintained but winding and steep gravel road navigable by regular passenger cars (not recommended for RVs over 24ft long). Ranger-led van tours are available from January to March. The other route is the 37-mile **Puerto Blanco Drive**, which has several spectacular viewing points with informaton about the Sonoran Desert.

Hiking

Unless it's too hot, the best way to experience the martian scenery here is on foot. There are several **hiking trails**, ranging from a 200yd paved nature trail to strenuous climbs of more than 4 miles. In winter, free shuttles lead to the trailheads Senita Basin (Tuesday and Friday at 8:30am) and Red Tanks Tinaja (Monday and Thursday at 8:30am), from where hikers traipse back to the campgrounds. Bring a topographical map and a compass whenever hiking cross-country, and know how to use them – a mistake out here can be deadly. Always carry plenty of water, wear a hat and slather yourself in sunscreen.

ℹ️ ILLEGAL ACTIVITY

Rubbing up against the Mexican border, this remote monument is a popular crossing for undocumented immigrants and drug smugglers, and large sections are closed to the public. A steel fence intended to stop illegal off-road car crossings marks its southern boundary. In 2002, 28-year-old ranger Kris Eggle, for whom the visitor center is named, was killed by drug traffickers while on patrol in the park. Call ahead or check the visitor center website for current accessibility.

🛏️ Sleeping & Eating

There are two campgrounds in the Organ Pipe Cactus National Monument: the large **Twin Peaks Campground** (☑520-387-6849, ext 7302; www.nps.gov/orpi; 10 Organ Pipe Dr; tent & RV sites $16) by the visitor center, and the primitive **Alamo Canyon Campground** (☑520-387-6849, ext 7302; www.nps.gov/orpi; campsites $10). Backcountry camping is allowed in nine zones: apply to the visitor center for details and a $5 permit. The closest lodging is in Ajo, about 11 miles north of Why, on Hwy 85. No food is available within the Organ Pipe Cactus National Monument, but there's a cafe in Lukeville, 5 miles south. You'll find a gas station and convenience store in Why, 22 miles north of the visitor center.

ℹ️ Information

Located 22 miles south of Why, the **Kris Eggle Visitor Center** (☑520-387-6849; www.nps.gov/orpi; 10 Organ Pipe Dr; ⊙8am-5pm) has information, drinking water, books, exhibits and ranger-led programs from January to March.

South of Tucson

From Tucson, the I-19 is a straight 60-mile shot south through the Santa Cruz River Valley to Nogales on the Mexican border. A historical trading route since pre-Hispanic times, the highway is unique in the US because distances are posted in kilometers – when it was built there was a strong push to go metric. Speed limits, however, are posted in miles!

Though not terribly scenic, I-19 is a ribbon of superb cultural sights with a bit of shopping thrown in the mix. It makes an excellent day trip from Tucson. If you don't want to backtrack, follow the prettier Hwys 82 and 83 to the I-10 for a 150-mile loop.

Tubac & Tumacácori

☑520 / POP 1191 (TUBAC)

Tubac, about 45 miles south of Tucson, started as a Spanish fort set up in 1752 to stave off Pima attacks. These days, the tiny village depends entirely on tourists dropping money for crafts, gifts, jewelry, souvenirs, pottery and paintings peddled in the majority of its businesses. Compact and lined with prefab, adobe-style buildings, it's attractive but somewhat sterile, barring the interesting Tubac Presidio State Historic Park & Museum.

There are approximately 100 galleries, art studios and crafts stores in town. As

WINDOW TO THE COSMOS

Dark, clear desert skies are the raison d'être for the **Kitt Peak National Observatory** (☑520-318-8726; www.noao.edu/kpno; Hwy 86; tours adult/child $9.75/3.25; ⊙9am-4pm; ☝), the world's largest collection of optical telescopes. Two radio telescopes and 22 optical telescopes sit atop a spectacular 6875ft-high mountaintop, offering stunning views across southern Arizona. The visitor center has exhibits and a gift shop, but no food. Hour-long tours take you inside the building housing the telescopes (alas, you don't get to peer through any of them) and the picnic area draws amateur astronomers at night.

For jaw-dropping views of the cosmos, sign up for the Nightly Observing Program, a four-hour stargazing session starting at sunset and limited to 46 people ($50; no programs from mid-July to the end of August because of monsoon season). This program books up weeks in advance but you can always check for cancellations when visiting. Dress warmly: it gets cold up here! Light dinner included, and note that safety concerns preclude children younger than eight.

Kitt Peak is about 1¼ hours west of Tucson, along Hwy 86; there's no public transportation, but Adobe Shuttle (p220) runs 12-person vans out here from Tucson, starting at $228 one-way.

exhibitions and artists constantly rotate it's hard to recommend any one place over the next, but seeing as Tubac is a small village, you can explore all it has to offer very easily on foot. Just south of Tubac is the fascinating Spanish-era mission of Tumacácori.

☉ Sights

Tubac Presidio State Historic Park & Museum   FORT, STATE PARK
(☑520-398-2252; azstateparks.com; 1 Burruel St; adult/child 7-13yr $5/2; ⊙9am-5pm; ℗) The Presidio was the staging point for de Anza's expedition to California in the 1770s, and today marks the trailhead for a 4.5-mile section of the Juan Bautista de Anza National Historic Trail linking the park and Tumacácori National Historical Park. The foundation of the fort is all that's left at this state park, within walking distance of Tubac's shops and galleries. The attached museum has some interesting exhibits, including Arizona's oldest newspaper-printing press, from 1859.

Tumacácori National Historical Park   MUSEUM
(☑520-398-2341; www.nps.gov/tuma; I-19, exit 29; adult/child 15yr & under $5/2; ⊙9am-5pm; ℗) Three miles south of Tubac, this pink-and-cream edifice shimmers in the desert like a missionary's dream. In 1691 Father Eusebio Kino and his cohorts arrived at the Tumacácori settlement and quickly founded a mission to convert the local American Indians. However, repeated Apache raids and the harsh winter of 1848 drove the community out, leaving the complex to crumble

for decades. For self-guided tours of the hauntingly beautiful ruins (ask for the free booklet) start at the visitor center.

✦ Festivals & Events

The **Tubac Festival of the Arts** is held in early February; **Taste of Tubac** showcases local culinary flair in early April; **Anza Days**, on the third weekend in October, are marked by historical reenactments, including some pretty cool parade-ground maneuvers by faux-Spanish mounted lancers; and in early December the streets light up during **Luminaria Nights**, a Mexican-influenced Christmas tradition. Check the town's website (wwwtubacaz.com) for exact dates.

🛏 Sleeping & Eating

A few pleasant independent inns are nestled among the galleries and cafes. Bistro, cafe, Italian and Mexican food are your main choices.

Tubac Country Inn   B&B $$
(☑520-398-3178; www.tubaccountryinn.com; 13 Burruel St; d/ste from $140/165; ❉☎) The decor at this charming five-room inn is best described as Southwest-lite: Navajo prints, American Indian baskets and chunky wood furniture. Each has a private entrance and a bathtub, and a breakfast basket is delivered to your door in the morning. Children under 12 aren't welcome.

Wisdom's Café   MEXICAN $
(☑520-398-2397; www.wisdomscafe.com; 1931 E Frontage Rd; mains $11-15; ⊙11am-3pm & 5-8pm Mon-Sat) Locally beloved, this institution

WORTH A TRIP

TITAN MISSILE MUSEUM

Twenty-four miles south of Tucson, off I-19 (exit 69) is the popular **Titan Missile Museum** (📞 520-625-7736; www.titanmissilemuseum.org; 1580 Duval Mine Rd, Sahuarita; adult/senior/child 7-12yr $9.50/8.50/6; ⏰ 9:45am-5pm Sun-Fri, 8:45am-5pm Sat, last tour 3:45pm). At this original Titan II missile site, a crew stood ready 24/7 to launch a nuclear warhead within seconds of receiving a presidential order. The Titan II was the first liquid-propelled intercontinental ballistic missile (ICBM) that could be fired from below ground and could reach its target – up to halfway around the world – in 30 minutes or less. Active from 1963 to 1986, this is the only one of 54 Titan II missile sites nationwide to be preserved as a museum.

The 75-minute tours, usually led by retired military types, are both frightening and fascinating. After descending 35ft and walking through several 3-ton blast doors, you enter the control room where you experience a simulated launch before seeing the actual (deactivated, of course) 103ft-tall missile still in its launch duct. The tour is wheelchair-accessible and reservations are essential. Exhibits in the small museum trace the history of the Cold War and related topics.

has been luring 'em in since 1944. The signature 'fruit burros' (fruit-filled crispy tortilla) are famous, but don't overlook standards like enchiladas. Located 2 miles south of Tubac. A sister restaurant, **¡DOS!** (4 Plaza Rd), serving burritos and street tacos, recently opened in the village of Tubac.

🛍 Shopping

Santa Cruz Chili & Spice　　　　　SPICES
(📞 520-398-2591; www.santacruzchili.com; 1868 E Frontage Rd; ⏰ 8am-5pm Mon-Fri, 10am-5pm Sat, to 3pm Sat summer) Warning: if you sample the salsa, you won't be able to resist purchasing a bottle for later consumption. Yep, this spice factory south of Tumacácori National Historical Park has been in business since the 1950s for a reason. And it sells just about every seasoning under the sun. In addition to salsa, go for the homemade chile pastes.

ℹ Information

Tubac Visitor Center (📞 520-398-2252; www.tubacaz.com; 1 Burruel Rd, Tubac Presidio State Historic Park; ⏰ 9am-5pm) This visitor center has maps and information.

Patagonia & the Mountain Empire

Sandwiched between the Santa Rita Mountains and the Patagonia Mountains, just north of the Mexican border, this region is one of the shiniest gems in Arizona. In a valley by the small town of Patagonia are long vistas of lush, windswept upland grassland; dark, knobby forest mountains;

and a crinkle of slow streams. The valleys that furrow across the landscape occupy a special microclimate that is amenable to wine grapes. They also harbor hard-bitten cowboys, artistic refugees and an amazing array of migratory birds.

Patagonia, smaller Sonoita and tiny Elgin, sitting at almost 5000ft above sea level, are cool and breezy. Patagonia and Sonoita were once important railway stops, but since the line closed in 1962 tourism and the arts have been their bread and butter. The beauty of these montane grasslands was not lost on film scouts – *Oklahoma!* and John Wayne's *Red River* were both filmed here.

The main road is Hwy 82, the Patagonia Hwy. Patagonia, with about 800 people, is the local center of activity (relatively speaking). Sonoita isn't much more than an intersection, and Elgin is just the name for a swath of unincorporated land 20 minutes east of Sonoita.

◉ Sights & Activities

Patagonia Lake State Park　　　STATE PARK
(📞 520-287-6965; azstateparks.com/patagonia-lake; 400 Patagonia Lake Rd; vehicle $15-20, pedestrian & cyclist $3; ⏰ park 4am-10pm, visitor center 8:30am-5pm Thu-Mon) A brilliant blue blip dolloped into the mountains, 2.5-mile-long Patagonia Lake was formed by the damming of Sonoita Creek. About 7 miles southwest of Patagonia, the lake is open year-round. At 3750ft above sea level, buffeted by lake and mountain breezes, the air is cool – making this a perfect spot for camping, picnicking, walking, bird-watching, fishing, boating and swimming. The

park's campground makes a fine base for exploring the region. The visitor center is also open 7am to 10pm on Fridays from April through October.

Patagonia-Sonoita

Creek Preserve   NATURE RESERVE

(☑ 520-394-2400; www.nature.org/arizona; 150 Blue Heaven Rd; $6; ⊙ 6:30am-4pm Wed-Sun Apr-Sep, 7:30am-4pm Wed-Sun Oct-Mar) A few gentle trails meander through this enchanting riparian willow forest, beloved by twitchers. Managed by the Nature Conservancy, it shelters seven distinct vegetative ecosystems, four endangered species of native fish and more than 300 species of birds, including rarities from Mexico. For bird-watchers, the peak migratory seasons are April and May, and late August to September. There are guided nature walks on Saturday morning at 9am. Joint admission with the Ramsey Canyon Preserve (p233) is $10.

Paton Center for

Hummingbirds   BIRDWATCHING

(☑ 520-415-6447; tucsonaudubon.org; 477 Pennsylvania Ave; donations appreciated; ⊙ dawn-dusk) Not just a haven for hummingbirds, this center grew from the backyard birding activities of Wally and Marion Paton in the 1970s. Acquired by the Tucson Audubon Society in 2014, it has now recorded sightings of 213 different species and is open to twitchers from dawn to dusk. A chain-link fence surrounds the property, and you'll likely see several cars parked outside.

Wineries

The Sonoita wine region is attracting notice in the viticulture world, and this beautiful, sun-kissed hill country is certainly a pleasant place to get tipsy. A basic map and winery information can be found on the website of the **Sonoita Wine Guild** (sonoitawineguild.com).

Flying Leap Vineyards   WINE

(☑ 520-455-5499; www.flyingleapvineyards.com; 342 Elgin Rd; tasting $10; ⊙ 11am-4pm) In 2013 Flying Leap took over the Canelo Hills Vineyard & Winery, next door to Callaghan Vineyards in Elgin. With small batch wines, an inviting tasting room and a gorgeous view of distant sky islands, this is a delightful place to get to grips with the region's best.

Dos Cabezas Wineworks   WINE

(☑ 520-455-5141; www.doscabezas.com; 3248 Hwy 82; tasting $8-13; ⊙ 10:30am-4:30pm Thu-Sun) This rustically pretty and well-regarded family-run operation is in Sonoita, near the crossroads of Hwys 82 and 83. The fruit comes from two southern Arizonan vineyards.

Callaghan Vineyards   WINE

(☑ 520-455-5322; www.callaghanvineyards.com; 336 Elgin Rd; tasting $10; ⊙ 11am-4pm Thu-Sun) About 20 miles east of Patagonia, Callaghan has traditionally been one of the most highly regarded wineries in the state. To get here, head south on Hwy 83 at the village of Sonoita, then east on Elgin Rd. You get to keep the 21-ounce crystal tasting glass.

🛏 Sleeping

There's a decent range of hotels and motels to choose from, but few really cheap options.

Patagonia Lake State

Park Campground   CAMPGROUND $

(☑ 877-697-2757, 520-287-6965; azstateparks.com/patagonia-lake; 400 Patagonia Lake Rd; campsite $25, with hookups $27-30; ℗) The only cheap accommodations spot in the area. The 105 tent and RV sites and 12 boat-in sites can be booked online or by phone.

Duquesne House   B&B $$

(☑ 520-394-2732; www.theduquesnehouse.com; 357 Duquesne Ave, Patagonia; r $140; @) This photogenic, sky-blue adobe B&B was once a boarding house for miners. Today there are three spacious, eclectically appointed suites with garden areas where you can watch the sun set, listen to the birds chirp, smell the rosemary and generally bliss out. Mondays through Thursdays the B&B offers a 'Bed, No Bread' special – $105 per night with no breakfast.

✗ Eating & Drinking

The region's food scene hasn't quite kept pace with its wines, but there are enough pleasant places to allay hunger, especially in Patagonia and Sonoita.

Velvet Elvis   PIZZA $

(☑ 520-394-2102; www.velvetelvispizza.com; 292 Naugle Ave, Patagonia; mains $8-24; ⊙ 11:30am-8pm; 🐾) Yes, a velvet Elvis does indeed hang on the wall at this gourmet pizza joint in Patagonia. Motorcyclists, foreign visitors and date-night couples – everybody visiting the area – roll in at some point for one of the 14 designer pies, or perhaps rigatoni with spicy sausage. These diet-spoilers will make you feel like Elvis in Vegas: fat and happy.

The Cafe
CAFE $$

(☑520-455-5044; www.cafesonoita.com; 3280 Hwy 82, Sonoita; lunch $10-12, dinner $15-22; ☺11am-3pm Sun-Wed, to 8pm Thu-Sat) This cafe east of the Hwy 82/83 junction is a breezy place to nosh after a day of wine tasting, bird-watching or scenic driving. Salads, sandwiches and burgers are on the menu at lunch, with steak and pasta stepping it up at dinner. The 'black and bleu' salad with steak, blue cheese, baby greens and balsamic is superb.

Wagon Wheel Saloon
BAR

(☑520-394-2433; www.wagonwheelpatagonia. com; 400 Naugle Ave, Patagonia; ☺7am-10pm Sun-Thu, to 1am Fri & Sat) Kick it cowboy-style at the Wagon Wheel, where the bar is big, the ceiling is festooned with wagon wheels and harness and the wildlife is stuffed. It does American breakfast, lunch and dinner too.

❶ Information

The folks in Patagonia's **Regional Visitor Center** (☑520-394-7750, 888-794-0060; www. patagoniaaz.com; 299 McKeown Ave, Patagonia; ☺10am-4pm daily Oct-May, Fri-Sun Jun-Sep) are helpful for birding, camping and wine-touring information. Keep your dial tuned to KPUP 100.5 FM, the awesome local radio station.

❶ Getting There & Away

Patagonia and the Mountain Empire are connected to the rest of the state by Hwys 82 and 83; the closest major town is Nogales, 20 miles to the southwest and straddling the US–Mexico border.

Tombstone

☑520 / POP 1312 / ELEV 4540FT

'Murdered.' 'Shot.' 'Suicide.' 'Killed by Indians.' The epitaphs at Boothill Cemetery tell you everything you need to know about living – and dying – in Tombstone in the late 1800s. How did this godforsaken place come to be? In 1877, prospector Ed Schieffelin braved the dangers of Apache attack in the region and struck it rich. He'd been told the only rock he'd find out here would be his own tombstone, and the name stuck.

Most boomtowns went bust, but Tombstone declared itself 'Too Tough to Die.' Tourism was the new silver and as the Old West became *en vogue*, Tombstone didn't even have to reconstruct its past – by 1962 the entire town was a National Historic Landmark. Yes, it's a tourist trap; but a delightful one and a fun place to find out how the West was truly won.

◉ Sights

Walking around town is free, but you'll pay to visit most attractions.

OK Corral
HISTORIC SITE

(☑520-457-3456; www.ok-corral.com; Allen St, btwn 3rd & 4th Sts; entry $10, without gunfight $6; ☺9am-5pm) Site of the famous gunfight on October 26, 1881, the OK Corral is the heart of both historic and touristic Tombstone. It has models of the gunfighters and other exhibits, including CS Fly's early photography studio and a recreated 'crib,' the kind of room where local prostitutes would service up to 80 guys daily for as little as 25¢ each. Fights are reenacted at 2pm, with additional shows at 11am, noon and 3:30pm on busy days.

Boothill Graveyard
CEMETERY

(☑520-457-3300; www.boothillgiftshop.com; 408 Hwy 80; adult/child 15yr & under $3/free; ☺8am-6pm) **FREE** For a list of the graves – and causes of death – of those buried here, buy the brochure at the entrance. The graves of Billy Clanton and Tom and Frank McLaury, all killed at the shoot-out at the OK Corral, are on Row 2. Some headstones are twistedly poetic: the oft-quoted epitaph for Lester Moore, a Wells Fargo agent, may be the most famous: 'Here lies Lester Moore, Four slugs from a .44, No Les, no More.'

Tombstone Courthouse State Historic Park
MUSEUM

(☑520-457-3311; azstateparks.com/parks/toco; 223 E Toughnut St; adult/child 7-13yr $7/2; ☺9am-5pm) Tombstone's history isn't limited to the shoot-out at the OK Corral, and exhibits at this informative museum spotlight various aspects of the town's colorful past. On the 1st floor, check out town founder Ed Schieffelin's .44 caliber Henry and the local doctor's old-timey bullet-removal kit. Upstairs, you can read about some of the town's most interesting former residents. Seven men were hanged in the courthouse courtyard, and today a couple of nooses dangle ominously from the recreated gallows.

Rose Tree Museum
MUSEUM

(☑520-457-3326; tombstonerosetree.com; 118 S 4th St, at Toughnut St; adult/child 13yr & under $5/free; ☺9am-5pm mid-Feb–mid-May, 1-5pm rest of year) Every spring the world's largest rosebush – planted in 1885 – puts on an intoxicating show in the courtyard of this museum, a beautifully restored Victorian home still owned by the Robertson-Macia family. The inside is brimming with family and town memorabilia, including a 1960 photograph showing the matriarch with Robert Geronimo, son of the Apache chief.

🎉 Festivals & Events

Tombstone events revolve around weekends of Western hoo-ha with shoot-outs (of course!), stagecoach rides, mock hangings and costume contests. The biggest event is **Helldorado Days** (☑520-457-3451; www.tombstonehelldoradodays.com; ⊙3rd weekend in Oct). See the website of the Tombstone Visitor Center for details about other events, which include **Wyatt Earp Days** (☑520-457-3511; www.wyattearpdays.com; ⊙dates vary) and **Vigilante Days** (☑520-457-3434; www.tombstonevigilantes.com; ⊙dates vary).

🛏 Sleeping

Accommodations increase their rates during special events; reservations are recommended at these times.

⭐ **Larian Motel**   MOTEL $
(☑520-457-2272; www.tombstonemotels.com; 410 E Fremont St; r from $79; ❄🐾) This one's a rare breed: a motel with soul, thanks to the personalized attention from the proprietor, cute retro rooms named for historical characters (Doc Holliday, Curly Bill, Wyatt Earp) and a high standard of cleanliness. It's also close to the downtown action. Children aged 12 and under stay free.

Tombstone Bordello B&B   B&B $$
(☑520-457-2394; www.tombstonebordello.com; 107 W Allen St; r/cabin from $99/135; ❄🐾) This fascinating place used to be a house of ill repute, and the names of the rooms – Shady Lady, Fallen Angel, Soiled Dove – embrace its colorful past. The 10-room B&B, built in 1881, was once owned by Big Nose Kate (Doc Holliday's lady friend).

🍴 Eating & Drinking

It's a tourist town, so don't expect any culinary flights of fancy. In keeping with Tombstone's Old West theme, the food here is mostly standard American and Mexican. Most of the saloons have decent grub.

Café Margarita   MEXICAN $
(☑520-457-2277; www.cafe-margarita.com; 131 S 5th St; mains $10-11; ⊙11am-7pm Thu & Sun, to 8pm Fri & Sat) Formerly Nellie Cashman's in the Russ House Hotel, this cantina serves Mexican fare alongside a few Italian dishes. Eat inside or enjoy a prickly-pear margarita on the patio. There's also live music on Friday and Saturday nights.

Crystal Palace Saloon   AMERICAN $$
(☑520-457-3611; www.crystalpalacesaloon.com; 436 E Allen St, at 5th St; mains $15-25; ⊙restaurant 11am-8pm, bar open later) Built in 1879 and thoroughly restored, this lively saloon is a favorite end-of-the-day watering hole for Tombstone's costumed actors. With its long bar, stuffed-elk mount, Old West paintings and cowboy-pleasing menu of burgers and steaks, it feels...Tombstone-y. They say there are bullet holes in the ceiling and blood stains on the floor.

Big Nose Kate's   BAR
(☑520-457-3107; www.bignosekates.info; 417 E Allen St; ⊙10am-midnight) Full of Wild West character, Doc Holliday's girlfriend's bar is a fun place for drinking, featuring great painted glass, historical photographs and live music in the afternoons. Down in the basement is the room of the 'Swamper,' a janitor who purportedly dug a tunnel into the silver mine shaft that ran below the building and helped himself to its riches.

ℹ Information

Tombstone Visitor Center (☑520-457-3929, 888-457-3929; www.tombstonechamber.com; 395 E Allen St, at 4th St; ⊙9am-4pm Mon-Thu, to 5pm Fri-Sun)

Fairbank Visitor Center (Hwy 82, Fairbank; ⊙9:30am-5:30pm Fri-Sun, hours vary) This ghost town's visitor center and small museum is found in the old schoolhouse.

THE LEGENDARY OK CORRAL

Tombstone is the town of the infamous 1881 shoot-out at the OK Corral, when Wyatt Earp, his brothers Virgil and Morgan and their friend Doc Holliday gunned down outlaws Billy Clanton and Tom and Frank McLaury. The fight so caught people's imaginations, it not only made it into the history books but also onto the silver screen – many times. Watch the 1993 flick *Tombstone*, starring Kurt Russell and Val Kilmer, to get you in the mood.

Bisbee

📍 520 / POP 5575 / ELEV 4540FT

Bisbee is wedged between the steep walls of Tombstone Canyon, its roads narrow and twisty, the buildings old and fragile, and there's a monstrous open-pit mine gaping toward the heavens at the east end of town. But take a closer look. Those 19th-century buildings are packed tight with interesting galleries, splendid restaurants and charming hotels. As for the citizens, well, just settle onto a bar stool at a local watering hole and a chatty local will likely share all of the town's gossip before you order your second drink.

Hwy 80 runs through the center of town. Most businesses are found in the Historic District (Old Bisbee), along Main St and near the intersection of Howell and Brewery Aves. Many businesses and restaurants close from Monday to Wednesday, so plan your visit for later in the week.

Bisbee built its fortune on ore found in the surrounding Mule Mountains. Between 1880 and 1975, underground and open-pit mines coughed up copper in sumptuous proportions, generating more than $6 billion worth of metals. Business really took off in 1892 when the Phelps Dodge Corporation, which would soon hold a local monopoly, brought in the railroad. By 1910 the population was 25,000, and with around 50 saloons and bordellos crammed along Brewery Gulch, Bisbee gained a reputation as the liveliest city between El Paso and San Francisco.

FAIRBANK HISTORIC SITE

It's the silence that grabs you on a stroll through **Fairbank** (📞520-457-3062; Hwy 82, just east of San Pedro River; ☉dawn-dusk), 10 miles west of Tombstone. Established in 1881 to serve the New Mexico & Arizona Railroad, Fairbank was a transportation hub for nearby mining towns. The last residents left in the 1970s. There's a visitor center and museum in the restored 1920s schoolhouse (open 9:30am to 4:30pm Friday to Sunday). If it's closed, look for a walking-tour brochure in the kiosk then loop past houses, a stable and an 1882 mercantile building.

As the local copper mines began to fizzle in the 1970s, Bisbee began converting itself into a tourist destination. At the same time hippies, artists and counterculture types migrated here and stayed. The interweaving of the new creative types and the old miners has produced a welcoming bunch of eccentrics clinging to the mountainside. It's now one of the coolest places (weather and attitude) in southern Arizona.

◉ Sights

Lavender Pit   MINE

To see the aftermath of open-pit mining, drive just south of Bisbee on Hwy 80 to the not-so-truthful 'Scenic View' sign. It's pointing toward the Lavender Pit, an immense stair-stepped gash in the ground that produced about 600,000 tons of copper between 1950 and 1974. It's ugly, but it's impressive.

Bisbee Mining &
Historical Museum   MUSEUM
(📞520-432-7071; www.bisbeemuseum.org; 5 Copper Queen Plaza; adult/senior/child 15yr & under $8/7/3; ☉10am-4pm) This two-story museum is affiliated with the Smithsonian Institution, and it shows. Located in the 1897 former headquarters of the Copper Queen Consolidated Mining Company, it does an excellent job tracing the town's past, the changing face of mining and the many uses of copper. You even get to 'drive' a shovel with a dipper larger than most living rooms.

There's a second visitor center attached to the museum, also open 10am to 4pm, but closed for lunch from noon to 1pm.

☞ Tours

Stop by the Bisbee Visitor Center for information about jeep and other tours. Notoriously haunted and eerily atmospheric Bisbee is a great place to take a tour with **Old Bisbee Ghost Tour** (📞520-432-3308; www.oldbisbeeghosttour.com; adult/child 11yr & under from $15/13).

Queen Mine   TOURS
(📞520-432-2071; www.queenminetour.com; 478 Dart Rd, off Hwy 80; adult/child 4-12yr $13/5.50; ♿) Don miners' garb, grab a lantern and ride a mine train 1500ft into one of Bisbee's famous copper mines. The tour, which lasts about an hour, is good fun for kids, but maybe not so much for the claustrophobic (of any age). Call for tour times, which vary, and definitely book ahead.

Bisbee

🛏 Sleeping

Bisbee is refreshingly devoid of chain hotels, with most lodging in historic hotels or B&Bs. Places often fill early on weekends, so come midweek if you don't have a reservation.

★ Shady Dell   CARAVAN PARK **$**
(📞 520-432-3567; www.theshadydell.com; 1 Douglas Rd, Lowell; trailers from $85; ⊙ closed high summer & winter; ❄) This vintage trailer court puts guests up in original '40s or '50s travel trailers, meticulously restored and outfitted with period accoutrements such as vintage radios (playing '50s songs upon arrival) and record players. All have tiny kitchens and swamp coolers, some have toilets, but showers are in the bathhouse. A 1947 Chris Craft yacht and a tiki bus are also available.

School House Inn   B&B **$**
(📞 520-432-2996; www.schoolhouseinnbb.com; 818 Tombstone Canyon; d/ste from $89/129; 🛜) Report to the Principal's Office or get creative in the Art Room. No matter which of the nine darling rooms in this converted 1918 school you choose, you'll be charmed by the detailed decor, the homey comforts, and John (the proprietor). Relax below the 160-year-old live oak in the patio. Rates include a delicious full breakfast.

Letson Loft Hotel   HOTEL **$$**
(📞 520-432-3210; www.letsonlofthotel.com; 26 Main St; r from $150) Urban sophistication meets Victorian quaintness at this sweet eight-room boutique inn in a sensitively restored 1888 building. Original touches

Bisbee

like exposed adobe and brick walls add character to high-ceilinged rooms with flat-screen TVs but no phones. Pastries and coffee are available in the morning, and children under 12 aren't allowed.

Bisbee Grand Hotel   HOTEL **$$**
(📞 520-432-5900; www.bisbeegrandhotel. com; 61 Main St; d/ste from $99/135; ❄🛜) You can sleep inside a covered wagon at this quirky, fun, reputedly haunted two-story hotel from 1906, where the Old West comes to life (or maybe never died). The 13 themed rooms and suites feature Victorian-era decor. Check in at the kick-up-your-heels saloon.

✖ Eating

With options from groaningly lavish diner breakfasts to lighter health-conscious fare, Bisbee is well served for places to eat.

★ Cafe Cornucopia   CAFE $
(📞 520-432-4820; 14 Main St; mains $10-11; 🕙 11am-4pm Mon, Tue, Fri & Sat, 9am-2:30pm Sun) Local art hangs from the exposed brick walls at this small cafe, a welcoming place that feels like home – in a good way. Order homemade soup, quiche, sandwiches and desserts at the counter then settle in for a delicious lunch. Locals chat blithely away, and the green-chile quiche is dependably delicious.

Bisbee Breakfast Club   BREAKFAST $
(📞 520-432-5885; www.bisbeebreakfastclub.com; 75a Erie St, Lowell; breakfast $7-9, lunch $9-10; 🕙 7am-3pm) The breakfasts at this longtime favorite are super-hearty and served with unfussy solicitude. The house-corned beef hash with two eggs, home fries, biscuits and bottomless coffee could set you up for a full day down the mines.

★ Cafe Roka   AMERICAN $$
(📞 520-432-5153; www.caferoka.com; 35 Main St; dinner $20-30; 🕙 5-9pm Thu-Sat, 3-8pm Sun) Past the art-nouveau steel door awaits this sensuously lit grown-up spot with innovative American cuisine that is at once smart and satisfying. The four-course dinners include salad, soup, sorbet and a rotating choice of mains – perhaps lamb albondigas (meatballs) with chimichurri and wild rice. The welcoming central bar is great for solo diners. and reservations are recommended.

Screaming Banshee   PIZZA $$
(📞 520-432-1300; www.screamingbansheepizza. net; 200 Tombstone Canyon Rd; pizzas $14-16; 🕙 4-9pm Tue & Wed, 11am-10pm Thu-Sat, 11am-9pm Sun) The ingredients are fresh, the crust is charred over a wood fire and the end result is tasty. There's a good array of toppings too, from gorgonzola cheese to housemade fennel sausage. The decor is punk rock meets Mardi Gras. It's across from the Iron Man, a 1935 socialist-aesthetic statue of a camp miner in tight flares.

🍷 Drinking & Nightlife

While Brewery Gulch (now Avenue) can't quite muster the 50 saloons and brothels of its heyday, it has more than enough atmospheric and welcoming dives and microbreweries to keep your whistle wet.

St Elmo's   BAR
(📞 520-432-5578; 36 Brewery Ave; 🕙 10am-2am) This charismatic dive bar, established in 1902, claims to be the longest continually run hostelry in Arizona. Today it still attracts a boisterous mix of thirsty locals and tourists, keeping them happy with Pabst Blue Ribbon (and local craft brews), a jukebox, pool table, live music on weekends, and traditions such as silly hat night (Thursdays, hats provided).

Old Bisbee Brewing Company   BREWERY
(📞 520-432-2739; www.oldbisbeebrewingcompany.com; 200 Review Alley; 🕙 noon-10:30pm Sun-Thu, to 11:30pm Fri & Sat) Locally grown hops, Sonoran white wheat and Sonoran mountain limes are just some of the intriguing ingredients that go into the eight lip-smacking barrel-aged brews (plus root beer) served at this simple tap room on Brewery Ave. Grilled bratwurst, vegetarian chili and free popcorn provide the ballast for tasting sessions. The penthouse above can be rented for $105 per night.

🛍 Shopping

You can't walk around in Bisbee without tripping on an art gallery, or an olive-oil or hot-sauce emporium. Items range widely in style and quality; have a wander up Main St to get a feel for what's here.

Va Voom!   VINTAGE
(📞 520-432-1540; 1 OK St; 🕙 11am-5pm Wed-Mon) This eccentric little vintage shop has lots of interesting clothes and ephemera, and carries great T-shirts designed by local artists.

ℹ Information

Bisbee Visitor Center (📞 866-224-7233, 520-432-3554; www.discoverbisbee.com; 478 Dart Rd; 🕙 8am-5pm Mon-Fri, 10am-4pm Sat & Sun) The visitor center is located in the Queen Mine building south of downtown.

Copper Queen Hospital (📞 520-432-5383; www.cqch.org; 101 Cole Ave) Has 24-hour emergency services.

Chiricahua National Monument

A wonderfully rugged yet whimsical wonderland, **Chiricahua National Monument** (📞 520-824-3560; www.nps.gov/chir; 12856 E Rhyolite Creek Rd; 🕙 visitor center

8:30am-4:30pm; P 🏠) FREE is one of Arizona's unique and evocative landscapes. Rain, thunder and wind have chiseled volcanic rocks into fluted pinnacles, natural bridges, gravity-defying balancing boulders and soaring spires reaching skyward like totem poles carved in stone. The remoteness made Chiricahua (pronounced 'cheery-cow-wha') a favorite hiding place of Apache warrior Cochise and his men. Today the same quality attracts birds and wildlife, including bobcats, bears, deer, coatis and javelinas.

Past the entrance, the paved **Bonita Canyon Scenic Drive** climbs 8 miles to Massai Point at 6870ft, passing several scenic pullouts and trailheads along the way. RVs longer than 29ft are not allowed beyond the visitor center, which is about 2 miles along the road.

🏃 Activities

To explore in greater depth, lace up your hiking boots and hit the trails. Eighteen miles of hiking trails range from easy, flat 0.2-mile loops to strenuous 7-mile climbs. If you're short on time, hike the **Echo Canyon Trail** at least half a mile to the Grottoes, an amazing 'cathedral' of giant boulders where you can lie still and enjoy the wind-caressed silence. The most stupendous views are from **Massai Point**, where you'll see thousands of spires positioned on the slopes like some petrified army.

A free hikers' shuttle bus leaves daily from the visitor center at 9am (8:30am from mid-October to April) and goes up to the trailheads at Massai Point or Echo Canyon. Hikers return by hiking downhill. Registration for the shuttle is required at the visitor center.

🛏 Sleeping & Eating

Wilderness camping is not permitted inside the Chiricahua National Monument, but there are two Parks Service–managed campgrounds. All food, utensils and containers must be carried in and out of the Chiricahua National Monument, and be stored in either hard-sided vehicles or bear-proof lockers.

Pinery Canyon Campground CAMPGROUND $
(www.recreation.gov; Forest Rd 42) There is free, dispersed USFS camping offered on a first-come, first-served basis at Pinery Canyon Campground, about 5 miles up Pinery Rd (Forest Rd 42), near the Chiricahua National Monument entrance station.

Bonita Campground CAMPGROUND $
(✆520-824-3560, 877-444-6777; www.recreation. gov; Bonita Canyon Dr; campsites $12; P) Bonita Campground, near the Chiricahua National Monument Visitor Center, has 25 popular, pre-bookable tent and RV sites. There's water, but no hookups or showers.

ℹ Information

Chiricahua National Monument Visitor Center (✆520-824-3560; www.nps.gov; 12856 E Rhyolite Creek Rd; ⊗8:30am-4.30pm) Camping, hiking, birding and general Chiricahua advice.

Benson

✆520 / POP 5105 / ELEV 3576FT

A railway stop since the late 1800s, Benson is now best known as the gateway to the famous **Kartchner Caverns**, among the largest and most spectacular caves in the USA. The town itself is spread out and sleepy.

About 15 miles to the east of Benson, in Dragoon, is the **Amerind Museum & Art Gallery**. The complex is near Texas Canyon in the **Little Dragoon Mountains**, which is known for its clumps of giant and photogenic granite boulders. For a closer look, swing by the historic **Triangle T Guest Ranch**, which got a professional revamp on the reality show *Hotel Impossible*.

👁 Sights

★**Kartchner Caverns State Park** CAVE
(✆information 520-586-4100, reservations 877-697-2757; azstateparks.com/kartchner; 2980 Hwy 90; park entrance per vehicle/bicycle $7/3, tours adult/child $23/13; ⊗park 7am-6pm, visitor center 8am-6pm late Dec-May, shorter hours rest of year; P 🐾) This wonderland of spires, shields, pipes, columns, soda straws and other ethereal formations has been five million years in the making, but miraculously wasn't discovered until 1974. In fact, its very location was kept secret for another 25 years in order to prepare for its opening as Kartchner Caverns State Park. Two tours are available, both about 90 minutes long and equally impressive.

Amerind Museum & Art Gallery MUSEUM
(✆520-586-3666; www.amerind.org; 2100 N Amerind Rd; adult/senior/child 12-18yr $10/9/8; ⊗10am-4pm Tue-Sun; P) The private, nonprofit Amerind Foundation exhibits American Indian artifacts, and history and culture

DON'T MISS

FORT BOWIE

Somewhere between the abandoned stagecoach stop and the sun-bleached cemetery, it hits you: this hike is a little spooky. Why? Because the 1.5-mile trail to Fort Bowie (pronounded 'Boo-ey') is the closest you'll come to time travel in the Southwest. **Fort Bowie National Historic Site** (☑520-847-2500; www.nps.gov/fobo; 3500 Apache Pass Rd, off Hwy 186; ☺trail sunrise-sunset, visitor center 8am-4pm Wed-Sun, call to see if staffed Mon & Tue; ℗☀) was established in 1862 in response to raids by the Chiricahua Apache, and the interpretive trail through this lonely place passes violent skirmish sites. The trailhead is at the parking lot on Apache Pass Rd.

As you walk, you can easily imagine Apache warriors watching your every move from hiding places on the rocky hills that flank the trail. To flip the picture, the trail returns to the parking lot along the ridge of one of those very hills, offering the Apache perspective of the activity below. In the 1880s and 1890s, that activity would have been pioneers and soldiers invading your turf.

The fort itself is mostly in ruins, but black-and-white photos beside various buildings illuminate the 19th-century scene. The location was strategic – close to the regionally important Apache Spring, which sits beside the trail. Inside the visitor center, check out the heliograph, a mirrored device placed on a nearby hilltop to send messages to other heliographs along a series of lofty military outposts.

To get here, follow Hwy 186 south from Willcox and the I-10 for 22 miles to the turnoff. Here, an unpaved but graded road, with mileage signs, runs 8 miles east to the trailhead.

---

from tribes from Alaska to Argentina, from the Ice Age to today. The Western gallery has exceptional works by such renowned artists as Frederic Remington and William Leigh. It's right off I-10 exit 318, in Dragoon.

🛏 Sleeping

Lodging in Benson is mostly about chain motels, which cluster off I-10 exits 302 and 304.

Kartchner Caverns Campground   CAMPGROUND $
(☑520-586-2283; azstateparks.com; 2980 Hwy 90; tent & RV sites $30, cabins $89) The campground within the Kartchner Caverns State Park has 61 tent and RV sites, with hookups, plus four cabins for those without their own shelter. Sites can be reserved between June and October.

Triangle T Guest Ranch   RANCH $$
(☑520-586-7533; www.azretreatcenter.com; 4190 Dragoon Rd; casitas/cabins/bunkhouses $179/249/479; ℗☎) Here you can arrange horseback rides ($45 per hour), enjoy refreshments in the saloon or spend the night in inviting casitas. Campers ($30) and RVers ($50) can set up among the rocks. The saloon is open to the public for lunch and dinner Friday and Saturday, and lunch Sunday, with a Western band on Saturday nights.

🍴 Eating

Mi Casa   MEXICAN $
(☑520-245-0343; 723 W 4th St; mains $11-15; ☺11am-7pm Mon-Fri) This tiny, mustard-yellow hacienda with blue trim serves very good Mexican food. It's pretty much the only place in Benson where you may have to wait for a table.

🛍 Shopping

Singing Wind Bookshop   BOOKS
(☑520-586-2425; 700 W Singing Wind Rd; ☺9am-5pm) If you're a bibliophile and driving near Benson, the Singing Wind Bookshop is a must-visit. One of the Southwest's great indie book stores, this inviting place is run by the wonderful Winnifred 'Winn' Bundy on her ranch, and features events such as cowboy poetry readings. Four miles north of Benson, it can take some finding.

Sierra Vista

☑520 / POP 43,888
Sierra Vista's charms lie largely outside the city's boundaries: precious riparian habitats favored by a rich variety of birds (and their human voyeurs); hiking, horseback riding and biking trails through Coronado National Memorial and the swelling southern uplands; and, nearby, the historic

towns of Tombstone and Bisbee and the Sonoita-Elgin wine country.

◉ Sights

Ramsey Canyon Preserve   NATURE RESERVE
(☑520-378-2785; www.nature.org; 27 E Ramsey Canyon Rd, Coronado National Forest; adult/child $6/free, 1st Sat of month free; ⊘8am-5pm Thu-Mon Mar-Oct, 9am-4pm Thu-Mon Nov-Feb) Up to 15 species of hummingbird flit over the igneous outcrops of this beautiful Nature Conservancy–owned preserve, with especially heavy sightings from April to September. At lower altitudes an incredible diversity of wildlife stalks through Ramsey Canyon: coatis, cougars and javelinas all live here, as does the threatened Chiricahua leopard frog. For $10 you get access to both this and Patagonia-Sonoita Creek Preserve (p225).

San Pedro Riparian National Conservation Area   NATURE RESERVE
(☑520-439-6400; www.blm.gov/arizona; Hwy 90; ⊘visitor center 9:30am-4:30pm) Some 350 bird species (many endangered), more than 80 mammal species and more than 40 species of reptiles and amphibians have been recorded along the 40-mile stretch of the San Pedro River within this 89-sq-mile conservation area. A vital riparian ecosystem, it's also become a corridor for drug smuggling from Mexico – suspicious activity should be reported.

⛏ Sleeping

Aside from a selection of chain motels along Hwy 92 and E Fry Blvd, Sierra Vista boasts some very nice B&Bs oriented toward bird-watching tourists.

★**Casa de San Pedro B&B**   B&B $$
(☑888-257-2050; www.bedandbirds.com; 8033 S Yell Lane; r/ste $190/285; ✳@) A haven for twitchers, this lovely hacienda-style B&B is set among some of Arizona's prime bird-watching territory, and caters knowledgeably to orniphiles, with birding software on the in-house computer and feeders in the grounds. Close to the San Pedro Riparian National Conservation Area, it features 11 comfy rooms with Mexican hardwood furnishings, organized around a lovely courtyard and gardens.

Battiste's B&B   B&B $$
(☑520-803-6908; www.battistebedandbirds.com; 4700 E Robert Smith Lane, Hereford; r $165; 🛜) This B&B is oriented toward bird-watching, and features cozy rooms with colorful Southwestern decor. The owners have counted more than 50 bird species in their backyard and each spring host a pair of nesting elf owls that has become a local attraction. The multiple-night rate drops to $150.

✖ Eating & Drinking

Sierra Vista's size means you'll enjoy more than just multiple Mexican restaurants. E Fry Blvd has Vietnamese and Korean options among the diners and fast-food chains.

❶ Information

Visitor Center (☑800-288-3861, 520-417-6960; visit.sierravistaaz.gov; 3020 E Tacoma St; ⊘8am-5pm Mon-Fri) This helpful center has info on accommodations, birding, hiking, cycling, wineries and other attractions in the area.

New Mexico

Best Places to Eat

➡ Love Apple (p295)

➡ Cafe Pasqual's (p268)

➡ Golden Crown Panaderia (p246)

➡ La Choza (p269)

➡ Buckhorn Saloon (p328)

Best Places to Sleep

➡ La Fonda (p265)

➡ Riverbend Hot Springs (p325)

➡ Inn at Halona (p318)

➡ El Paradero (p265)

➡ Earthship Rentals (p294)

Why Go?

They call this the Land of Enchantment for a reason. Maybe it's the drama of sunlight and shadow playing out across juniper-speckled hills, or the traditional mountain villages of horse pastures and adobe homes. Maybe it's the centuries-old towns on the northern plateaus, overlooked by the magnificent Sangre de Cristos, or the volcanoes, canyons and vast desert plains spread beneath an even vaster sky. The beauty casts a powerful spell. Mud-brick churches filled with sacred art, ancient Indian pueblos, real-life cowboys and legendary outlaws, chile-smothered enchiladas – all add to the pervasive sense of otherness that often makes New Mexico feel like a foreign country.

Maybe the state's all-but-indescribable charm is best expressed in the iconic paintings of Georgia O'Keeffe. The artist herself exclaimed, on her very first visit: 'Well! Well! Well!... This is wonderful! No one told me it was like this.'

But seriously, how could they?

When to Go
Santa Fe

Mid-Aug–mid-Oct New Mexico at its best: gorgeous weather, wild sunflowers, chiles, fiestas.

Dec Ski the Sangres, walk Canyon Rd on Christmas Eve, join in local traditions.

Jun–mid-Aug Prime time for outdoor activities – but beware afternoon storms.

History

Ancestral Puebloan civilization first began to flourish in the 8th century AD, and the impressive structures at Chaco Canyon were begun not long after. By the time Francisco Vasquez de Coronado got here in the 16th century, many Pueblo Indians had migrated to the Rio Grande Valley and were the dominant presence. After Santa Fe was established as the Spanish colonial capital in around 1610, Spanish settlers fanned out across northern New Mexico and Catholic missionaries began their often violent efforts to convert the Puebloans. Following the Pueblo Revolt of 1680, American Indians occupied Santa Fe until 1692, when Don Diego de Vargas recaptured the city.

The US took control of New Mexico in 1846 during the Mexican-American War, and it became a US Territory in 1850. American Indian wars with the Navajo, Apache and Comanche further transformed the region, and the arrival of the railroad in the 1870s prompted an economic boom.

Painters and writers set up art colonies in Santa Fe and Taos in the early 20th century, and New Mexico became the 47th state in 1912. A top-secret scientific community descended on Los Alamos in 1943 and developed the atomic bomb. Some say that four years later, aliens crashed outside of Roswell…

Scenic Routes

One of the best ways to explore New Mexico is to travel its scenic highways. Eight have been selected as National Scenic Byways (www.byways.org), but the state holds plenty of other striking stretches of pavement. Here are a few of its most rewarding roads:

➜ **Billy the Kid Scenic Byway** (www.billybyway.com) This mountain-and-valley loop in southeastern New Mexico swoops past Billy the Kid's stomping grounds, Smokey Bear's gravesite and the orchard-lined Hondo Valley. From Roswell, take Hwy 380 west.

➜ **High Road to Taos** The back road between Santa Fe and Taos passes through sculpted sandstone desert, fresh pine forests and rural villages with adobe churches and horse-filled pastures. The 13,000ft Truchas Peaks soar above. To reach it from Santa Fe, take Hwy 84/285 to Hwy 513.

➜ **NM Hwy 96** From Abiquiú Lake to Cuba, this little road wends through the heart of Georgia O'Keeffe country, beneath the distinct profile of Cerro Pedernal, then past Martian-red buttes and sandstone cliffs striped purple, yellow and ivory.

➜ **NM Hwy 52** Head west from Truth or Consequences into the dramatic foothills of the Black Range, stopping off in the old mining towns of Winston and Chloride. Continue north, emerging onto the sweeping Plains of San Augustin before reaching the bizarre Very Large Array.

ℹ Dangers & Annoyances

Albuquerque sits over 5000ft above sea level, Santa Fe and Taos are at 7000ft and the mountains top 13,000ft – so if you're arriving from sea level, you may feel the altitude. Take it easy for the first day or two, and be sure to drink plenty of water – a good idea, anyway, considering how arid the state is. Combined with altitude, the 300-plus days of sunshine also make this an easy place to get sunburned. And New Mexico leads the nation in lightning-strike deaths per

---

DON'T MISS

NEW MEXICO'S TOP SIGHTS

Steeped in American Indian and Hispanic cultures, soulful **Santa Fe** has world-class art, gourmet restaurants and great local food, adobe architecture and famous festivals. An hour-and-a-half north is **Taos**, art colony and alternative haven, known for its historic Pueblo and world-class ski area. These two towns feel like nowhere else in the USA. Both sit beneath the **Sangre de Cristo Mountains**, laced with hiking, mountain-biking and ski trails. **Chaco Canyon** is remote but contains 1000-year-old ruins of what was once a hub of Ancestral Puebloan civilization.

Among the state's most fantastic natural features are **White Sands National Monument**, a playground where gleaming white dunes ripple, swell and curl through the Tularosa Basin; and **Carlsbad Caverns National Park**, a colossal subterranean fantasyland of stalagmites and stalactites. Most beautiful of all might be the **Ghost Ranch** area, where you can explore the landscape that inspired Georgia O'Keeffe.

New Mexico Highlights

1 Santa Fe (p254) Immersing yourself in art and culture in one of the US's oldest and most unique cities.

2 Taos (p287) Visiting the famous Pueblo, skiing the steeps and getting your mellow on.

3 Chaco Culture National Historical Park (p314) Wondering at the mystery and architectural ingenuity of an ancient civilization.

4 White Sands National Monument (p339) Sliding down the mesmerizing dunes.

5 Carlsbad Caverns National Park (p347) Delving into a vast underground world where time has been suspended.

6 Gila National Forest (p328) Exploring rugged wilderness and soaking in hot springs.

7 Bandelier National Monument (p280) Climbing ladders 140ft high to visit the abandoned Alcove House.

8 Río Grande del Norte National Monument (p297) Hiking or white-water rafting through the mighty Rio Grande Gorge.

9 Lincoln (p341) Walking in the bootprints of Billy the Kid.

10 El Santuario de Chimayó (p283) Getting healed at the 'Lourdes of America.'

capita, so be cautious if hiking in exposed areas during monsoon thunderstorms, which can be downright apocalyptic.

If you're into outdoor adventures, your New Mexico plans may hinge on how wet or dry the year has been. Ski areas may have some of the best or worst conditions in the West depending on snowfall; national forests sometimes close completely during severe summer drought.

As Territorial Governor Lew Wallace put it back in 1880: 'Every calculation based on experience elsewhere fails in New Mexico.' Things here just don't work the way you might expect. That, paired with the *mañana* mindset, may create some baffling moments. Our advice: just roll with it.

❶ Getting There & Around

Most travelers fly into Albuquerque International Sunport (ABQ), but a few flights also land in Santa Fe (SAF).

Amtrak offers passenger train service on the *Southwest Chief*, which runs between Chicago and Los Angeles, stopping in Raton, Las Vegas, Lamy (for Santa Fe), Albuquerque and Gallup. The *Sunset Limited* stops in Deming on its way from Florida to Los Angeles.

A fast and amazingly inexpensive light-rail system, the Rail Runner, connects Albuquerque and Santa Fe. Otherwise, a dwindling network of Greyhound buses links certain New Mexico towns, and northern New Mexico in particular holds some cheap or free regional bus routes. On the whole, though, limited public transportation options and long distances make renting a car the best choice for most visitors.

ALBUQUERQUE

📱 505 / POP 556,500 / ELEV 5312FT

Albuquerque: it's the pink hues of the Sandia Mountains at sunset, the Rio Grande's cottonwood bosque, Route 66 diners and the hometown of Walter White and Jesse Pinkman. It's a bustling desert crossroads and the largest city in the state, yet you can still hear the howls of coyotes when the sun goes down.

Often passed over by travelers on their way to Santa Fe, Albuquerque has plenty of understated appeal beneath its gritty urban facade. Good hiking and mountain-biking trails abound just outside of town, while the city's modern museums explore Pueblo culture, New Mexican art and space. Take the time to let your engine cool as you take a walk among the desert petroglyphs or order up a plate of red chile enchiladas and a local beer.

Central Ave, formerly Route 66, is still Albuquerque's main street, passing from east to west through the state fairground, Nob Hill, the University of New Mexico, downtown and Old Town before crossing the Rio Grande. Street addresses often conclude with a directional designation, such as Wyoming NE, that specifies one of the city's four quadrants: the center point is where Central Ave crosses the railroad tracks, just east of downtown.

◎ Sights

Albuquerque's top sights are largely concentrated in and around Old Town and beside the river, but several interesting attractions – including the Indian Pueblo Cultural Center, Petroglyph National Monument and Sandia Peak Tramway – lie further afield, and are only readily accessible by car.

◎ Old Town

Some of the quaint adobe buildings that line the alleyways of Old Town began life as private residences in 1706, when the first 15 Spanish families called the newly named 'Alburquerque' their home (yes, it originally had an extra 'r', which somehow got lost after the Americans took over). Until the arrival of the railroad in 1880, Old Town Plaza was the hub of daily life. With many museums, galleries and original buildings within walking distance, this is the city's most popular tourist area. As you walk around, keep your mind's eye trained partly on the past. Imagine this area as it began, with a handful of hopeful families grateful to have survived a trek across hundreds of miles of desert wilderness.

★ **New Mexico Museum of Natural History & Science**   MUSEUM
(Map p246; 📱505-841-2800; www.nmnatural history.org; 1801 Mountain Rd NW; adult/child $8/5; ☉9am-5pm Wed-Mon; 🐾) Dinosaur-mad kids are certain to love this huge modern museum, on the northeastern fringes of Old Town. From the T Rex in the main atrium onwards, it's crammed with ferocious ancient beasts. The emphasis throughout is on New Mexico, with dramatic displays on the state's geological origins and details of the impact of climate change; there's also a planetarium and large-format 3D movie theater (both of which have additional admission fees).

★American International
Rattlesnake Museum MUSEUM
(Map p246; ☑505-242-6569; www.rattlesnakes.
com; 202 San Felipe St NW; adult/child $5/3;
☺10am-6pm Mon-Sat, 1-5pm Sun Jun-Aug,
11:30am-5:30pm Mon-Fri, 10am-6pm Sat, 1-5pm
Sun Sep-May) Anyone charmed by snakes and
all things slithery will find this museum fascinating; for ophidiophobes, it's a complete
nightmare, filled with the world's largest
collection of different rattlesnake species.
You'll also find snake-themed beer bottles
and postmarks from every town named 'Rattlesnake' in the US.

★Albuquerque Museum
of Art & History MUSEUM
(Map p246; ☑505-242-4600; www.cabq.gov/
museum; 2000 Mountain Rd NW; adult/child
$4/1; ☺9am-5pm Tue-Sun) With a great Albu-
querque history gallery that's imaginative,
interactive and easy to digest, as well as a
permanent New Mexico art collection that
extends to 20th-century masterpieces from
Taos, this showpiece museum should not be
missed. There's free admission on Saturday
afternoons and Sunday mornings, and free
guided walking tours of Old Town at 11am
(March to mid-December).

While here, grab a bite at the Slate at the
Museum cafe (p247).

San Felipe de Neri Church CHURCH
(Map p246; www.sanfelipedeneri.org; Old Town
Plaza; ☺7am-5:30pm daily, museum 9:30am-5pm
Mon-Sat) Dating in its present incarnation
from 1793, the facade of this adobe church
now provides Old Town's most famous
photo op. Mass is celebrated Monday, Tuesday, Wednesday and Friday at 7am, with
Sunday Mass at 7am, 10:15am and noon.

Turquoise Museum MUSEUM
(Map p246; ☑505-247-8650; www.turquois
emuseum.com; 2107 Central Ave NW; adult/child
$12/10; ☺tours 11am & 1pm Mon-Sat) Reserve
ahead to join owner Joe Dan Lowry on one
of his two daily tours (45 minutes), and get
an enlightening crash course in determining
the value of turquoise – from high quality
to fakes. He's as opinionated as he is knowledgeable, so you're in for an interesting time.

¡Explora! MUSEUM
(Map p246; ☑505-224-8300; www.explora.us;
1701 Mountain Rd NW; adult/child $8/4; ☺10am-
6pm Mon-Sat, noon-6pm Sun; ⊕) From the lofty
high-wire bike to the mind-boggling Light,

CORONADO HISTORIC SITE

About 20 miles north of downtown
Albuquerque, this site (☑505-867-5351;
www.nmmonuments.org; US 550, 1.7 miles
west of I-25 exit 242; adult/child $5/free;
☺8:30am-5pm Wed-Mon) preserves the
ruins of Kuaua Pueblo, which was at its
most active from the 14th to the 16th
centuries. The stars of the show are 14
500-year-old murals, which originally
adorned the walls of a square kiva.
Though the depictions of kachinas (spirit messengers), animals and lighting
bolts are incomplete, the murals offer an
extremely rare glimpse into Ancenstral
Puebloan life. Additional replicas were
created in a kiva on-site (open by tour
only; 10am to 4:30pm).

There's also a **campground** (☑505-
980-8256; off Hwy 550, Bernalillo; tent/
RV sites $14/22) with shade shelters and
showers.

Shadow, Color area, this gung-ho museum
holds a hands-on exhibit for every type of
child (don't miss the elevator). Not traveling
with kids? Check the website to see if you're
around for the 'Adult Night.' Hosted by an
acclaimed local scientist, it's one of the hottest tickets in town.

◉ Albuquerque BioPark

The family-friendly BioPark makes a wonderful escape from the summer heat. A
combo ticket, sold until noon daily, covers
its three main attractions: an aquarium, a
botanic garden and a zoo further south. The
park also includes the open space of Tingley
Beach – in truth, more of a fishing lake than
a beach – to which access is free.

Albuquerque Aquarium AQUARIUM
(Map p241; ☑505-764-6200; www.cabq.gov/
biopark; 2601 Central Ave NW; adult/child 3-12yr
$12.50/4, zoo combo ticket $20/6; ☺9am-5pm,
to 6pm Sat & Sun Jun-Aug) The Albuquerque
Aquarium, a few blocks west of Old Town
and the centerpiece of the northern segment of the Albuquerque BioPark, holds a
285,000-gallon tank where colossal rays and
turtles live side by side with razor-toothed
sharks. Human divers drop in at feeding
time. Tickets include admission to the
Botanic Garden.

NEW MEXICO ALBUQUERQUE

ABQ BioPark Zoo
ZOO

(Map p241; ☑505-768-2000; www.cabq.gov/
biopark; 903 10th St SW; adult/child $12.50/4,
aquarium & garden combo ticket $20/6; ☺9am-
5pm, to 6pm Sat & Sun Jun-Aug) Set on 60 shady
acres beside the Rio Grande, this zoo is home
to more than 250 species and puts on a busy
schedule of events and activities, including daily sea-lion feedings at 10:30am and
3:30pm. Every day except Monday, a half-
hourly miniature train connects the zoo with
the aquarium and botanic gardens 2 miles
northwest (included with the combo ticket).

Botanic Garden
GARDENS

(Map p241; www.cabq.gov/biopark; 2601 Central
Ave NW; adult/child 3-12yr $12.50/4, zoo combo
ticket $20/6; ☺9am-5pm, to 6pm Sat & Sun Jun-
Aug) The twin highlights in this peaceful
park are the two large conservatories of
Mediterranean and desert plants. You'll also
find formal Japanese gardens, an elaborate
model-train layout and a fantasy playground
for kids. The Butterfly Pavilion is open from
May until September, while special events
take place throughout the year. Tickets
include admission to the aquarium.

Downtown

The office-dominated central blocks of Albuquerque's small downtown are busiest during the work week, though a number of bars
and music venues make it one of the more
popular nightlife destinations. The area
around the Alvarado Transportation Center
has a somewhat sketchy vibe.

Nob Hill & UNM Area

A fun and funky place to shop, eat, see art
films or get a haircut at a cigar-wine bar, the
stretch of Central Ave known as Nob Hill
starts at UNM and runs east to about Carl-
isle Blvd. Fashion-lovers can browse colorful
shops for that unique outfit or accessory;
artists will find inspiration and supplies.

University of New Mexico
MUSEUM

(UNM; Map p241; www.unm.edu; Central Ave NE)
There are several museums and galleries
packed into the small but peaceful campus
of UNM, along with abundant public art
and a performing arts center. The **Maxwell
Museum of Anthropology** (Map p241; ☑505-
277-4405; www.unm.edu/~maxwell; 500 University
Blvd NE; ☺9am-4pm Tue-Fri, 10am-4pm Sat)
FREE has a wonderful collection of ancient
Mimbres ceramics while the **Art Museum**

(Map p241; ☑505-277-4001; unmartmuseum.org;
203 Cornell Dr NE; ☺10am-4pm Tue-Fri, to 8pm
Sat) **FREE** often features regional artists.
Visit the UNM Welcome Center (p250) for
information and maps.

Metropolitan Albuquerque

Try joining the locals by walking the
acequias; early risers who value cool temperatures consider the footpaths that border
these long-established irrigation channels a
real gift in summer. Get hold of a decent city
map and find the thin blue lines branching
out in North Valley from the Rio Grande
between Montaño Rd and Paseo del Norte
and around Rio Grande Blvd.

★Indian Pueblo Cultural Center
MUSEUM

(IPCC; Map p241; ☑505-843-7270; www.indian
pueblo.org; 2401 12th St NW; adult/child
$8.40/5.40; ☺9am-5pm) Collectively run
by New Mexico's 19 Pueblos, this cultural
center is an essential stop-off during even
the shortest Albuquerque visit. The museum
downstairs holds fascinating displays on
the Pueblos' collective history and individual artistic traditions, while the galleries
above offer changing temporary exhibitions.
They're arrayed in a crescent around a plaza
that's regularly used for dances and crafts
demonstrations, and as well as the recommended Pueblo Harvest Cafe (p248) there's
also a large gift shop and retail gallery.

National Museum of Nuclear
Science & History
MUSEUM

(☑505-245-2137; www.nuclearmuseum.org;
601 Eubank Blvd SE; adult/child & senior $12/10;
☺9am-5pm; ⓐ) Located at the edge of the
massive Kirtland Air Force Base in Albuquerque's southeast corner, and surrounded
by an outdoor Heritage Park holding dis-
carded missiles and fighter planes, this lively
museum explores the history of nuclear
energy in war and peace, from the Manhattan Project and the Cold War up to today.
Retired military personnel serve as docents.

Petroglyph National
Monument
ARCHAEOLOGICAL SITE

(☑505-899-0205; www.nps.gov/petr; 6001 Unser
Blvd NW; ☺visitor center 8am-5pm) **FREE** The
lava fields preserved in this large desert
park, west of the Rio Grande, are adorned
with more than 23,000 ancient petroglyphs
(1000 BC–AD 1700). Several trails are scattered far and wide: **Boca Negra Canyon**
is the busiest and most accessible (parking

Greater Albuquerque

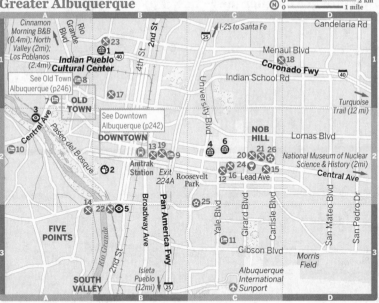

Greater Albuquerque

$1/2 weekday/weekend); **Piedras Marcadas** holds 300 petroglyphs; while **Rinconada Canyon** is a lovely desert walk (2.2 miles round-trip), but with fewer visible petroglyphs.

Sandia Peak Tramway   CABLE CAR
(📞 505-856-7325; www.sandiapeak.com; 30 Tramway Rd NE; adult/youth 13-20yr/child $25/20/15, parking $2; ⏰ 9am-9pm Jun-Aug, 9am-8pm Wed-Mon, from 5pm Tue Sep-May) The United

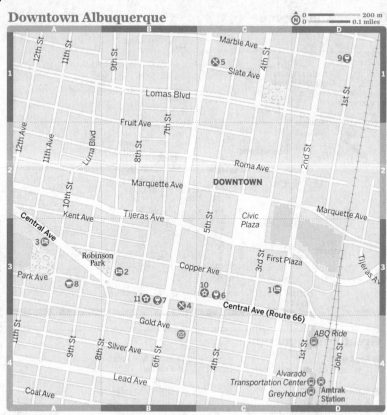

Downtown Albuquerque

States' longest aerial tram climbs 2.7 miles from the desert floor in the northeast corner of the city to the summit of 10,378ft Sandia Crest. The views are spectacular at any time, though sunsets are particularly brilliant. The complex at the top holds gift shops and a **cafeteria** (📞505-243-0605; www.sandiacresthouse.com; Hwy 536; mains $5.50-14; ⏰10am-5pm, weekends only winter), while hiking trails lead off through the woods, and there's also a small **ski area** (📞505-242-9052; www.sandiapeak.com; lift tickets adult/child $55/40; ⏰9am-4pm Fri-Sun mid-Dec–Mar). If you plan on hiking down (or up), a one-way ticket costs $15.

**National Hispanic
Cultural Center**   ARTS CENTER
(Map p241; 📞505-246-2261; www.nhccnm.org; 1701 4th St SW; museum adult/child $6/free; ⏰10am-5pm Tue-Sun) In the historic Barelas

neighborhood, near the river a mile south of downtown, this modern, architecturally imaginative center for Hispanic visual, performing and literary arts holds three galleries used for fine arts exhibitions, performances, salsa classes and fabulous eats at Pop Fizz (p248). Check the website for upcoming events to make the most of it.

Anderson-Abruzzo Albuquerque
International Balloon Museum   MUSEUM
(☎505-768-6020;   www.balloonmuseum.com; 9201 Balloon Museum Dr; adult/child $4/1; ⏰9am-5pm Tue-Sun) Ready to geek out on hot-air balloons? This informative museum covers it all, from the first manned flight in Paris (1783) to Bernoulli's principle (how air pressure creates lift) and an actual Strato-Lab, which reached an altitude of 81,000ft in the 1950s. Take a stab at the balloon simulator here and you'll be ready for the real thing.

South Valley & North Valley   AREA
Both these traditional agricultural areas near the Rio Grande are characterized by open spaces, small ranches, farms, and *acequias* (irrigation ditches paralleled by footpaths). Chickens and horses roam fields between historical adobe and wood-frame houses and newer developments.

Of the two, the larger North Valley is more mixed and upscale, with a reputation as affluent, pastoral, quiet and determined to stay that way. Even though it's just 7 miles north of downtown Albuquerque, it feels a world away.

Corrales   AREA
When Spanish settlers established this village in 1710, Tewa Indians had already been growing crops here for a thousand years. These days, the hills produce surprising quantities of fine wine. Corrales offers splendid strolling through the bosk (riparian woods) and along *acequias*. Drive or walk along the unpaved side roads off Hwy 448 to find rabbits and quail crisscrossing your path among 200-year-old adobes and modern replicas.

Casa Rondeña   WINERY
(☎505-344-5911; www.casarondena.com; 733 Chavez Rd NW; ⏰noon-7pm) This winery in the Los Ranchos area of the North Valley often serves as a wedding venue. At any other time, you can drop in for a $5 wine tasting, and it also offers tours during the area's summer Lavender Festival.

🏃 Activities

Cycling is the ideal way to explore Albuquerque under your own steam. In addition to cycling lanes throughout the city, mountain bikers will dig the foothills trails east of town and the scenic stretch of the Rio Grande in the center. For details of the excellent network of cycling lanes (slated to reach 50 interconnected miles in 2018), see www.bikeabq.org.

★Paseo del Bosque   CYCLING, MOUNTAIN BIKING
(⏰dawn-dusk) A 16-mile multi-use path along the Rio Grande, the Paseo del Bosque is one of Albuquerque's gems. While the paved portion offers easy car-free riding for cyclists, what really makes it special – and beautiful – is the network of trails hidden between the pavement and river. If you rent a mountain bike, you'll have plenty of fun veering through miles of floodplains forest.

La Luz Trail   HIKING
(www.laluztrail.com; FR 444; parking $3) This roughly 8-mile trail (one-way) takes you from the base of the Sandias all the way to the top, rising over 3500ft from the desert floor to pine forests and spectacular views. It's a tough climb and it gets hot, so start early. Take Tramway Blvd (Hwy 556) east from I-25, then turn northeast on FR 333 to the trailhead.

Elena Gallegos
Open Space   HIKING, MOUNTAIN BIKING
(www.cabq.gov; Simms Park Rd; weekday/weekend parking $1/2; ⏰7am-9pm Apr-Oct, closes 7pm Nov-Mar) The western foothills of the Sandias are Albuquerque's outdoor playground, and the high desert landscape here is sublime. As well as several picnic areas, this section holds trailheads for hiking, running and mountain biking; some routes are wheelchair-accessible. Come early, before the sun gets too hot, or late, to enjoy the panoramic views at sunset amid the lonesome howls of coyotes.

Discover Balloons   BALLOONING
(Map p246; ☎505-842-1111; www.discoverballoons.com; 205c San Felipe NW; adult/under 12yr $160/125) Several companies will float you over the city and the Rio Grande, including Discover Balloons. Flights last about an hour, and many are offered early in the morning to catch optimal winds and the sunrise.

✦ Festivals & Events

Friday's *Albuquerque Journal* (www.abq journal.com) includes exhaustive listings of festivals and activities.

★ **International Balloon Fiesta** ⠀⠀BALLOON
(www.balloonfiesta.com; ☉ early Oct) The largest balloon festival in the world. You simply haven't lived until you've seen a three-story-tall Tony the Tiger land in your hotel courtyard, and that's exactly the sort of thing that happens during the festival, which features mass dawn take-offs on each of its nine days, overlapping the first and second weekends in October.

New Mexico Brew Fest ⠀⠀BEER
(www.nmbrewfest.com; ☉ Oct) Celebrate Hoptoberfest with live music and New Mexico's biggest collection of craft brewers in Bernalillo, about 15 minutes' drive north of Albuquerque. You can also get here using the RailRunner. It's usually held during the Balloon Fiesta.

New Mexico State Fair ⠀⠀FAIR
(www.exponm.com; ☉ Sep) New Mexico's biggest jamboree, with live music, games and rides as well as a rodeo and livestock show. Runs for 12 days in September.

Gathering of Nations Powwow ⠀⠀CULTURAL
(www.gatheringofnations.com; ☉ Apr) Dance competitions, displays of American Indian arts and crafts, and the 'Miss Indian World' contest. Held in late April.

🛏 Sleeping

Although Albuquerque holds about 150 hotels – all of which fill during the International Balloon Fiesta and the Gathering of Nations – few are in any way exceptional. If you're looking for character or charm, a B&B makes a better option.

🛏 Old Town

Econo Lodge Old Town ⠀⠀MOTEL $
(Map p241; ☎ 505-243-8475; www.econolodge. com; 2321 Central Ave NW; r $65; P ❄ @ 🛜 🐾) Just 10 minutes' walk west of the plaza, this bright, clean motel makes a great deal for anyone planning to explore the Old Town or the BioPark, with spacious and well-equipped modern rooms, an indoor pool and free hot breakfasts. It also has bikes for rent.

Böttger Mansion ⠀⠀B&B $$
(Map p246; ☎ 505-243-3639; www.bottger.com; 110 San Felipe St NW; r $115-159; P ❄ @ 🛜) The friendly proprietor gives this well-appointed B&B, built in 1912 and one minute's walk from the plaza, an edge over tough competition. Three of its seven themed, antique-furnished rooms have pressed-tin ceilings, one has a Jacuzzi tub, and sumptuous breakfasts are served in a honeysuckle-lined courtyard loved by bird-watchers. Past guests include Elvis, Janis Joplin and Machine Gun Kelly.

Casas de Sueños ⠀⠀B&B $$
(Map p246; ☎ 505-247-4560; www.casasde suenos.com; 310 Rio Grande Blvd SW; r $119-179; P ❄ @ 🛜) Set in luscious gardens a short walk from Old Town, this lovely and peaceful place holds 21 adobe casitas (small

---

ALBUQUERQUE IN...

One Day

Jump-start your belly with a plate of huevos rancheros (fried eggs in a spicy tomato sauce, served atop tortillas) from **Frontier** (p247), before heading to the **Indian Pueblo Cultural Center** (p240) for a heads-up introduction to Pueblo traditions and culture.

Head back into town for lunch, grabbing a bite at **Golden Crown Panaderia** (p246), then wander over to **Old Town** for the afternoon. Walk off lunch admiring the **San Felipe de Neri Church** (p239), browsing the galleries around the plaza and catching up on your snake trivia at the **American International Rattlesnake Museum** (p239) or regional artists at the **Albuquerque Museum of Art & History** (p239). Dine outdoors in **Nob Hill**; Albuquerque's grooviest neighborhood is thick with restaurants.

Two Days

On the second day, bike the **Paseo del Bosque** (p243) or explore **Petroglyph National Monument** (p240) before grabbing a quick lunch at **Pop Fizz** (p248). Reach the top of **Sandia Crest** before sunset, either by tram or by driving, for expansive views of the Rio Grande Valley and some beautiful hikes. When you come back down, linger over delicious food and wine at the **Slate Street Cafe & Wine Loft** (p247).

cottages). All feature handcrafted furniture and original artwork, while some have kitchenettes, fireplaces and/or private hot tubs. Full breakfasts are cooked to order.

Hotel Chaco
HOTEL $$$

(Map p241; ☑ 866-505-7829; www.hotelchaco.com; 2000 Bellamah Ave NW; r from $230; P✳✖🖥🛏🏊) Albuquerque's newest addition takes its inspiration from the ancient site of Chaco Canyon in northwestern New Mexico. Rooms blend modern expectations with traditional motifs, each featuring a Navajo weaving from Toadlena and soothing earth-colored tones. Great views from the rooftop restaurant and bar.

📍 Downtown

Hotel Blue
HOTEL $

(Map p242; ☑ 877-878-4868; www.thehotelblue.com; 717 Central Ave NW; r from $69, ste $129; P✳✖@🖥🛏🏊) Well positioned beside a park on the western edge of downtown, the 134-room Hotel Blue has Tempur-Pedic beds and a free airport shuttle. Bonus points awarded for the good-size pool, the kitchens in the suites and 40in flat-screen TVs.

Route 66 Hostel
HOSTEL $

(Map p242; ☑ 505-247-1813; route66hostel.com; 1012 Central Ave SW; dm $25, r from $30; P@🖥) This pastel-lemon hostel, in a former residence a few blocks west of downtown, holds male and female dorms plus simple private rooms, some of which share bathrooms. The beds are aging, but there's a welcoming atmosphere, with common facilities including a library and a kitchen offering free self-serve breakfasts. Voluntary chores; no check-ins between 1:30pm and 4:30pm.

⭐ Andaluz
BOUTIQUE HOTEL $$

(Map p242; ☑ 505-242-9090; www.hotelandaluz.com; 125 2nd St NW; r from $174; P✳✖@🖥🏊) Albuquerque's finest historic hotel, built in the heart of downtown in 1939, has been comprehensively modernized while retaining period details like its stunning central atrium, where cozy arched nooks hold tables and couches. Rooms feature hypoallergenic bedding and carpets, the **Más Tapas Y Vino** (Map p242; ☑ 505-923-9080; www.hotelandaluz.com; 125 2nd St NW; tapas $6-16, mains $26-36; ☺7am-2pm & 5-9:30pm) restaurant is notable, and there's a rooftop bar. Reserve 30 days in advance for the best rates.

Hotel Parq Central
HOTEL $$

(Map p241; ☑ 888-796-7277; www.hotelparqcentral.com; 806 Central Ave SE; r from $146; P✳✖🖥🏊) This stylish hotel is close to it all, right off I-25 in downtown. With the rooftop Apothecary Lounge providing sunset views and a complimentary shuttle service to nearby destinations, this is a good midrange choice.

📍 Metropolitan Albuquerque

Sandia Peak Inn Motel
MOTEL $

(Map p241; ☑ 505-831-5036; 4614 Central Ave SW; r from $65; P🖥🏊) Old-fashioned, family-run and utterly exemplary Route 66 motel, across the Rio Grande a mile west of Old Town (despite the name, it's nowhere near Sandia Peak), with two floors of decently upgraded rooms plus a small indoor swimming pool and free continental breakfasts.

Sleep Inn Albuquerque
HOTEL $

(Map p241; ☑ 505-244-3325; www.sleepinnalbuquerque.com; 2300 International Ave SE; r from $60; P✳✖@🖥🏊) Of the dozen or so large chain hotels that congregate immediately north of the airport, along Yale Blvd a couple of miles south of Nob Hill, this offers the best bang for your buck, with large, modern, earth-toned rooms, indoor heated pool and free airport shuttles.

Cinnamon Morning B&B
B&B $$

(☑ 800-214-9481; www.cinnamonmorning.com; 2700 Rio Grande Blvd NW; r from $125, casita from $159, guesthouse $249; P✳🖥🏊) This friendly B&B, not far north of Old Town, has three guest rooms in the main house, two casitas with kitchenettes and private patios, and a two-bedroom guesthouse. Lots of Southwest charm and common areas make it a relaxing and homey place to slumber.

⭐ Los Poblanos
B&B $$$

(☑ 505-344-9297; www.lospoblanos.com; 4803 Rio Grande Blvd NW; r $230-450; P✳@🖥🏊) This amazing 20-room B&B, on a 1930s rural ranch that's a National Historic Place, is five minutes' drive north of Old Town. Close to the Rio Grande, it's set amid 25 acres of gardens, lavender fields (blooming mid-June through July) and an organic farm. The gorgeous rooms feature kiva fireplaces, while produce from the farm is served for breakfast.

🍴 Eating

Albuquerque offers plenty of definitive down-home New Mexican grub, plus the region's widest variety of international

Old Town Albuquerque

cuisines. Many traditional eateries are only open from 6am to 2pm (ie no dinner) – if local flavors are a priority, make sure you plan around these hours. More sophisticated dinner options lean more modern American.

✕ Old Town

★ **Golden Crown Panaderia**   BAKERY $
(Map p241; ☎505-243-2424; www.goldencrown.
biz; 1103 Mountain Rd NW; mains $7-20; ☺7am-8pm

Tue-Sat, 10am-8pm Sun) Who doesn't love a friendly neighborhood cafe-bakery? Especially one in a cozy old adobe, with gracious staff, oven-fresh bread and pizza (with green chile or blue-corn crusts), fruity empanadas, smooth espresso coffees and cookies all round? Call ahead to reserve a loaf of quick-selling green chile bread – then eat it hot, out on the patio.

Central Grill & Coffee House   DINER $

(Map p246; ☎505-554-1424; centralgrillcoffeealbuquerque.com; 2056 Central Ave SW; mains $6-9; ☺6:30am-4pm Mon-Sat, to 3pm Sun; P⊞) The best casual eats within walking distance of Old Town, the friendly Central Grill is both reliable and convenient. Expect New Mexican diner fare: pancakes, huevos rancheros, carne adovada burritos and burgers.

Slate at the Museum   CAFE $

(Map p246; ☎505-243-2220; www.slatestreet cafe.com; 2000 Mountain Rd NW; mains $8.50-11.50; ☺10am-3pm Tue-Sun; ☎) Looking for a quick bite in the Old Town? Stop by the Albuquerque Museum of Art for salads, sandwiches, soups and cupcakes from the much-loved downtown bistro.

Antiquity   STEAK $$$

(Map p246; ☎505-247-3545; www.antiquity restaurant.com; 112 Romero St NW; mains $24-35; ☺5-9pm) With just 14 tables in an atmosphere of rustic elegance, Antiquity specializes in steak, seafood and fine wine. The desserts list isn't long, but it doesn't need to be. A favorite of locals and visitors alike.

Downtown

Grove Cafe & Market   MODERN AMERICAN $

(Map p241; ☎505-248-9800; www.thegrove cafemarket.com; 600 Central Ave SE; mains $7-13.50; ☺7am-3pm Tue-Sat, 8am-3pm Sun; ☑) Much more cafe than market, this light, bright EDo (east downtown) bistro is renowned for healthy, all-day organic breakfasts, and does a brisk trade in salads and sandwiches for the office crowd. There's no wi-fi, on principle.

Asian Pear   KOREAN $

(Map p242; ☎505-766-9405; 508 Central Ave SW; mains $6.50-10; ☺10am-4pm Mon-Fri) A delectable no-frills Korean canteen, with housemade BBQ beef and chicken rice bowls as well as bento meals, *sundubu jjigae* (spicy tofu soup) and avocado noodle salad. Most orders come with egg soup, kimchi and fried

turnip cakes on the side. Great downtown pit stop.

Slate Street Cafe & Wine Loft   MODERN AMERICAN $$

(Map p242; ☎505-243-2210; www.slatestreet cafe.com; 515 Slate St; breakfast $7.50-15, lunch $10-15, dinner $11-27; ☺7:30am-3pm Mon-Fri, 9am-2pm Sat & Sun, 5-9pm Tue-Thu, 5-10pm Fri & Sat; ☑) A popular downtown rendezvous, the cafe downstairs is usually packed with people enjoying imaginative comfort food, from green chile mac-and-cheese to herb-crusted pork chops, while the upstairs wine loft serves 25 wines by the glass and offers regular tasting sessions. It's off 6th St NW, just north of Lomas Blvd.

★Artichoke Cafe   MODERN AMERICAN $$$

(Map p241; ☎505-243-0200; www.artichokecafe. com; 424 Central Ave SE; lunch mains $12-19, dinner mains $16-39; ☺11am-2:30pm & 5-9pm Mon-Fri, 5-10pm Sat) Elegant and unpretentious, this popular bistro prepares creative gourmet cuisine with panache and is always high on foodies' lists of Albuquerque's best. It's on the eastern edge of downtown, between the bus station and I-40.

Nob Hill & UNM Area

Frontier   NEW MEXICAN $

(Map p241; ☎505-266-0550; www.frontier restaurant.com; 2400 Central Ave SE; mains $2-8.50; ☺5am-1am; ⊞) This giant cantina that sprawls across several rooms has to be seen to be believed: get in line for enormous buttery cinnamon rolls, smothered enchiladas and some of the best huevos rancheros in town. It may be fast-foody, but the atmosphere and prices are unbeatable.

Annapurna's World Vegetarian Cafe   INDIAN $

(Map p241; ☎505-262-2424; www.chaishoppe. com; 2201 Silver Ave SE; mains $8-12; ☺7am-9pm Mon-Fri, 8am-9pm Sat, 10am-8pm Sun; ☑) This awesome vegetarian and vegan cafe, one block south of Route 66 and part of a small local chain, serves fresh, tasty Indian specialties, including delicately spiced Ayurvedic delights that even carnivores love. It also serves falafel, quesadillas and veggie burgers. Dishes are complemented by authentic chai.

Guava Tree Cafe   LATIN AMERICAN $

(Map p241; ☎505-990-2599; www.guavatree cafe.com; 118 Richmond Dr NE; mains $8.50; ☺11am-4pm Sun-Thu, to 7pm Fri & Sat) Salsa music and Celia Cruz posters give this outpost of Colombian cuisine a healthy shot of pastel-colored soul. Feast on *arepas* (stuffed corn pockets with sweet plantains), hot sandwiches and yucca fries, tropical fruit juice and cafe con leche.

Green Jeans Farmery FOOD HALL $
(Map p241; www.greenjeansfarmery.com; 3600 Cutler Ave NE; ⊙hours vary) Built from converted shipping containers, this hip community hangout features a number of great casual eateries – chef Marie Yniguez from Bocadillos was on *Chopped* in 2017 – as well as a distillery and the Albuquerque outpost of Santa Fe Brewing. It's just off of I-40, northwest of UNM.

Il Vicino Pizzeria ITALIAN $
(Map p241; ☑505-266-7855; www.ilvicino.com; 3403 Central Ave NE; mains $8-11.50; ⊙11am-10pm Sun-Thu, to 11pm Fri & Sat) Line up at the counter to order simple Italian meals such as wood-fired pizza, salads and pasta, but don't forget the real star attraction – spectacular, award-winning microbrewed beer, including Wet Mountain IPA and Slow Down Brown.

Flying Star Cafe AMERICAN $
(Map p241; ☑505-255-6633; www.flyingstarcafe.com; 3416 Central Ave SE; mains $8-13; ⊙7am-10pm Sun-Thu, to 11pm Fri & Sat; 🛜🚗🦽) For visitors, the Nob Hill location of this deservedly popular local chain is the most convenient of outlets throughout Albuquerque and beyond. Locals flock here from early morning onwards, to enjoy an extensive breakfast menu and innovative main courses later on, amid creative, colorful decor. The whole experience is enhanced by the use of organic, free-range and antibiotic-free ingredients.

🍴 Metropolitan Albuquerque

⭐**Pop Fizz** MEXICAN $
(Map p241; ☑505-508-1082; www.pop-fizz.net; 1701 4th St SW, National Hispanic Cultural Center; mains $5-7.50; ⊙11am-8pm; 🛜🦽) These all-natural *paletas* (popsicles) straight-up rock: cool off with flavors such as cucumber chile lime, mango or pineapple habanero – or perhaps you'd rather splurge on a cinnamon-churro ice-cream taco? Not to be outdone by the desserts, the kitchen also whips up all sorts of messy goodness, including carne asada fries, Sonoran dogs and Frito pies.

El Paisa Taqueria MEXICAN $
(Map p241; ☑505-452-8997; 820 Bridge Blvd SW; mains $1.25-4; ⊙7am-11pm) Wedged in among the *chicharronerias* and *tortillerias* across the Rio Grande, unassuming El Paisa will require a bit of deciphering if your taqueria vocab is not up to speed. *Gorditas* (stuffed corn-flour pockets), *tortas* (sandwiches), tacos and burritos are the four main options – fill them with *carnitas* (braised pork), *al pastor* (roasted pork), *asada* (grilled steak) and the like. Cash only.

Eli's Place NEW MEXICAN $
(☑505-345-3935; 6313 4th St NW; mains $8-13; ⊙7am-9pm Mon-Sat, 9am-2pm Sun) Eli's Place is a hallowed Albuquerque dive and you shouldn't be surprised – or worried – if you see a tumbleweed blow through the parking lot as you pull in. Located north of town, it's a simple place with pink tables and daily specials scrawled above the register: think scallop tacos, chipotle bacon cheeseburgers, duck enchiladas and plenty of breakfast favorites.

Pueblo Harvest Cafe AMERICAN INDIAN $$$
(Map p241; ☑505-724-3510; www.indianpueblo.org; 2401 12th St NW; lunch $12-16, dinner $13-28; ⊙7am-9pm Mon-Sat, 7am-4pm Sun; 🚗🦽) A rare chance to sample the *real* local cuisine, with dishes such as blue-corn porridge for breakfast, Tewa tacos for lunch – the Pueblo take on Indian fry bread – and buffalo stew for dinner. On summer weekends it hosts an early-evening Party on the Patio, with horno-oven pizza and live music. Do note that service can be very hit or miss.

🍸 Drinking & Nightlife

Albuquerque's bar scene, which has long focused on downtown and Nob Hill, has been enlivened in recent years by the emergence of a new breed of brewpubs scattered across the city.

⭐**Marble Brewery** BREWERY
(Map p242; ☑505-243-2739; www.marblebrewery.com; 111 Marble Ave NW; ⊙noon-midnight Mon-Sat, to 10:30pm Sun) Popular downtown brewpub, attached to its namesake brewery, with a snug interior for winter nights and a beer garden where local bands play early-evening gigs in summer. Be sure to try its Red Ale.

⭐**Anodyne** BAR
(Map p242; ☑505-244-1820; 409 Central Ave NW; ⊙4pm-1:30am Mon-Sat, 7-11:30pm Sun)

An excellent spot for a game of pool, Anodyne is a huge space with book-lined walls, wood ceilings, plenty of overstuffed chairs, more than 100 bottled beers and great people-watching on Central Ave.

Duel Brewing BREWERY
(Map p242; ☑505-508-3330; duelbrewing.com; 606 Central Ave SW; ⊗ 3-11pm Mon-Thu, noon-midnight Fri & Sat, noon-8pm Sun) Belgian-style tasting flights, pretzels and charcuterie plates bring European cool to downtown ABQ.

Bosque Brewing BREWERY
(Map p241; ☑505-508-5967; www.bosquebrewing.com; 106 Girard Blvd SE; ⊗ 11am-late Mon-Sat, noon-11pm Sun) Minimalist taproom with a horseshoe bar and concrete floors that fills up almost every night of the week thanks to the central Nob Hill location. Six Bosque beers on tap, plus seasonal additions and plenty to nibble on.

Java Joe's CAFE
(Map p242; ☑505-765-1514; www.downtownjavajoes.com; 906 Park Ave SW; ⊗6:30am-3:30pm; ⓐ⓫) Best known these days for its explosive cameo role in *Breaking Bad*, this comfy coffee shop still makes a great stop-off for a java jolt or a bowl of the hottest chile in town.

⭐ Entertainment

For comprehensive listings of Albuquerque's many nightspots and a calendar of upcoming events, pick up the free weekly *Alibi* (www.alibi.com), published every Tuesday. Friday's *Albuquerque Journal* is helpful too.

The UNM Lobos (www.golobos.com) has a full roster of sports teams, but is best known for basketball (men's and women's) and women's volleyball.

Caravan East LIVE MUSIC
(☑505-980-5466; www.caravaneast.com; 7605 Central Ave NE) Put on your cowboy boots and 10-gallon hat and hit the dancefloor to practice your line dancing and two-stepping at this classic Albuquerque music club. Live country and/or Latin bands perform and the ambience is friendly.

Launch Pad LIVE MUSIC
(Map p242; ☑505-764-8887; www.launchpadrocks.com; 618 Central Ave SW) This retro-modern place is the hottest stage for local live music.

PERFORMING ARTS

KiMo Theatre (Map p242; ☑505-768-3544; www.cabq.gov/kimo; 423 Central Ave NW) The gorgeous, historic KiMo Theatre sees performances by big-name national acts, as well as local ballet, theater and cinema.

Popejoy Hall (Map p241; ☑505-925-5858; www.popejoypresents.com; 203 Cornell Dr) On the UNM campus, this is one of the city's main venues for local opera, symphony and theater.

Guild Cinema CINEMA
(Map p241; ☑505-255-1848; www.guildcinema.com; 3405 Central Ave NE; admission $8) The only independently owned, single-screen theater in town programs great indie, avant-garde, Hollywood fringe, political and international features. Stick around for discussions following select films.

Albuquerque Isotopes BASEBALL
(Map p241; www.albuquerquebaseball.com; Ave Cesar Chavez, Isotopes Park, University SE; ⊗ Apr-Aug) First of all: yes, the city's baseball team really was named for the episode of *The Simpsons,* 'Hungry, Hungry Homer,' when America's favorite TV dad tried to keep his beloved Springfield Isotopes from moving to Albuquerque. Thanks to the pop culture nod, the 'topes sell more merchandise than anyone else in the minors. The Rockies' AAA team, it sometimes wins too.

🔒 Shopping

Albuquerque's most interesting shops are in Old Town and Nob Hill.

Santisima ARTS & CRAFTS
(Map p246; ☑505-246-2611; 2nd fl, 328 San Felipe NW; ⊗ approx 11:30am-8:30pm Wed-Mon) Interesting folk-art gallery selling Day of the Dead artifacts and images, some imported from Mexico and some quirky variations by artists including owner Johnny Salas. It's a bit hard to find.

Mariposa Gallery ARTS & CRAFTS
(Map p241; ☑505-268-6828; www.mariposagallery.com; 3500 Central Ave SE; ⊗11am-6pm Mon-Sat, noon-5pm Sun) Beautiful and funky arts, crafts and jewelry, mostly by regional artists.

IMEC   JEWELRY
(International Metalsmith Exhibition Center; Map p241; ☑ 505-265-8352; 101 Amherst SE; ☺ noon-6pm Tue-Sat) Just off Central Ave, IMEC displays and sells intriguing jewelry by local craftspeople.

Silver Sun   JEWELRY
(Map p246; ☑ 505-246-9692; www.silversun albuquerque.com; 116 San Felipe St NW; ☺ 9am-4pm Mon-Fri) A reputable Old Town store specializing in natural American turquoise, as stones as well as finished jewelry.

Palms Trading Post   ARTS & CRAFTS
(Map p246; ☑ 800-748-1656; www.palmstrading. com; 1504 Lomas Blvd NW; ☺ 9am-5:30pm Mon-Fri, 10am-5:30pm Sat) Large gallery where knowledgeable salespeople sell American Indian pottery, jewelry, rugs and crafts.

ℹ Information

EMERGENCY
Police (☑ 505-242-2677; www.apdonline.com; 400 Roma Ave NW)

INTERNET ACCESS
Albuquerque is wired. The Old Town Plaza, Sunport, downtown Civic Plaza, Aquarium and Botanic Garden have free wi-fi, as do Rapid Ride buses.

INTERNET RESOURCES
Albuquerque Journal (www.abqjournal.com) Local news, events and sports.
City of Albuquerque (www.cabq.gov) Public transportation and area attractions.
Gil's Thrilling (And Filling) Blog (www. nmgastronome.com) Local foodie eats his way across ABQ, Santa Fe and the rest of the state.

MEDICAL SERVICES
UNM Hospital (☑ 505-272-2411; 2211 Lomas Blvd NE; ☺ emergency 24hr)
Presbyterian Hospital (☑ 505-841-1234; www. phs.org; 1100 Central Ave SE; ☺ emergency 24hr)

POST
Post Office (Map p242; ☑ 800-275-8777; 201 5th St SW; ☺ 9am-4:30pm Mon-Fri)

TOURIST INFORMATION
Cibola National Forest Office (☑ 505-346-3900; 2113 Osuna Rd NE; ☺ 8am-4:45pm Mon-Fri)
Old Town Information Center (Map p246; ☑ 505-243-3215; www.visitalbuquerque.org; 303 Romero Ave NW; ☺ 10am-5pm Oct-May, to 6pm Jun-Sep)
Sandia Ranger Station (☑ 505-281-3304; 11776 Hwy 337, Tijeras; ☺ 8am-4:30pm Mon-Fri)

UNM Welcome Center (Map p241; ☑ 505-277-1989; 2401 Redondo Dr; ☺ 8am-5pm Mon-Fri)

ℹ Getting There & Away

AIR
New Mexico's largest airport, **Albuquerque International Sunport** (ABQ; Map p241; ☑ 505-244-7700; www.abqsunport.com; 🛜), is 5 miles southeast of downtown and served by multiple airlines. Free shuttles connect the terminal building with the Sunport Car Rental Center at 3400 University Blvd SE, home to all the airport's car-rental facilities.

BUS
The **Alvarado Transportation Center** (Map p242; 100 1st St SW, cnr Central Ave) is home to **Greyhound** (Map p242; ☑ 800-231-2222, 505-243-4435; www.greyhound.com; 320 1st St SW), which serves destinations throughout the state and beyond, though not Santa Fe or Taos.

The **Sandia Shuttle** (☑ 888-775-5696; www. sandiashuttle.com; Santa Fe one-way/round-trip $30/55; ☺ 8:45am-11:45pm) runs from the airport to Santa Fe hourly.

TRAIN
Amtrak's *Southwest Chief* stops at Albuquerque's **Amtrak Station** (☑ 800-872-7245; www. amtrak.com; 320 1st St SW), which is part of the Alvarado Transportation Center. Trains head east to Chicago (from $117, 26 hours) or west to Los Angeles (from $66, 16½ hours), once daily in each direction.

A commuter light rail line, the New Mexico Rail Runner Express (www.nmrailrunner.com), shares the station. It makes several stops in the Albuquerque metropolitan area, but more importantly for visitors it runs all the way north to Santa Fe (one-way $10, 1¾ hours), with eight departures on weekdays and four on weekends.

ℹ Getting Around

TO/FROM THE AIRPORT
The **Sunport Shuttle** (☑ 505-883-4966; www. sunportshuttle.com) runs from the airport to local hotels and other destinations.

BICYCLE
Contact **Parks & Recreation** (☑ 505-768-2680; www.cabq.gov/bike) or visit the website for a free map of the city's elaborate system of bike trails. All ABQ Ride buses are equipped with front-loading bicycle racks.

BUS
ABQ Ride (Map p242; ☑ 505-243-7433; www. cabq.gov/transit; 100 1st St SW; adult/child $1/0.35, day pass $2) is a public bus system

covering most of Albuquerque on weekdays and major tourist spots daily. Maps and schedules are available on the website; most lines run till 6pm. Rapid Ride buses serve the BioPark, Old Town, downtown, Nob Hill and the fairgrounds; bus 66 runs up and down Central Ave.

CAR & MOTORCYCLE

Albuquerque is an easy city to drive around. Streets are wide and there's usually metered or even free parking within blocks from wherever you want to stop.

TAXI

Albuquerque Cab (☑505-883-4888; www. albuquerquecab.com) In general you have to call for a taxi, though they do patrol the Sunport, rail and bus stations.

Albuquerque Area Pueblos

Isleta Pueblo

Isleta Pueblo (www.isletapueblo.com) is best known for its church. Built in 1613, the San Augustin Mission has been in constant use since 1692. A few plaza shops sell local pottery, and there's gambling at the Isleta Casino (☑505-724-3800; www.isleta.com; ⊙8am-4am Mon-Thu, 24hr Fri-Sun). Visitors are welcome to the ceremonial dances on St Augustine's Day (September 4). It's located 16 miles south of Albuquerque at I-25 exit 215.

Sandia Pueblo

About 13 miles north of Albuquerque, Sandia Pueblo (www.sandiapueblo.nsn.us; I-25, exit 234) was established around AD 1300. Thanks to the wealth it has generated from Sandia Casino (☑505-796-7500; www. sandiacasino.com; 30 Rainbow Rd NE; ⊙8am-4am Mon-Thu, 24hr Fri-Sun), it has successfully lobbied to prevent further development of Sandia Crest, which its people have long held sacred. The casino's outdoor amphitheater is one of Albuquerque's major music venues.

ALBUQUERQUE TO SANTA FE

Two alternative routes connect New Mexico's two major cities. It takes just an hour to drive from Albuquerque to Santa Fe along the semi-scenic I-25, or about 90 minutes on the lovelier NM 14, also known as the Turquoise Trail.

KASHA-KATUWE TENT ROCKS NATIONAL MONUMENT

At this surreal **geologic enclave** (Map p276; ☑505-331-6259; Rte 92; per vehicle $5; ⊙7am-7pm mid-Mar–Oct, 8am-5pm Nov–mid-Mar), ash from the ancient Jemez Mountain volcanoes has eroded into tipi-like formations and steep-sided canyons. Two trails lead through the park: the 1.2-mile Cave Loop Trail is short, but only scrapes the surface of this extraordinary terrain. Budget 1½ to two hours, and head instead along the more demanding Canyon Trail, a 3-mile round-trip on which you'll climb through a slot canyon to reach the uplands and enjoy fantastic panoramas. Dogs are not permitted.

It's located between Albuquerque and Santa Fe. To get here, take I-25 exit 259 to Hwy 22, and then follow the road north for 20 miles, passing Cochiti Pueblo and Cochiti Dam.

Along I-25

Potential distractions on the Pueblo lands that lie just off the interstate include the intriguing Kasha-Katuwe National Monument, which offers fantastic hiking, and the Coronado Historic Site (p239).

San Felipe Pueblo

Although the conservative San Felipe Pueblo (I-25, exit 252) does not encourage visitors for most of the year, outsiders are welcome at the spectacular San Felipe Feast Green Corn Dances (May 1), as well as San Pedro Feast Day (June 29).

Kewa Pueblo

Long known as Santo Domingo Pueblo, but more commonly called Kewa Pueblo, this conservative, non-gaming community, poised halfway between Albuquerque and Santa Fe, has traditionally played a prominent role in inter-Pueblo affairs. Several galleries and studios abut the plaza in front of the pretty 1886 Santo Domingo Church, with murals and frescoes by local artists.

The tribe is most famous for heishi (shell bead) jewelry, as well as huge Corn Dances (August 4) and a popular Arts & Crafts Fair in early September.

Turquoise Trail

The Turquoise Trail (www.turquoisetrail.org) was already a major trading route 2000 years ago, when turquoise mined in Cerillos first found its way south to burgeoning civilizations in what's now Mexico. Today, as Hwy 14, it's a National Scenic Byway, lined with quirky communities and other diversions, which makes an attractive back road between Albuquerque and Santa Fe.

Cedar Crest

📞 505 / POP 958 / ELEV 6578FT

The first town you come to on the Turquoise Trail is the little hillside community of Cedar Crest, on the eastern flank of the Sandia Mountains. If you are driving the Sandia Crest Byway, you'll pass the Tinkertown Museum on the way up.

👁 Sights

Tinkertown Museum　　　　　　　MUSEUM
(📞 505-281-5233; www.tinkertown.com; 121 Sandia Crest Rd; adult/child $3.50/1; ⏲ 9am-6pm Apr-Oct; 🚗) A folk-art classic, the Tinkertown Museum stands just up Sandia Crest Rd (NM 165), west of Cedar Crest. Huge, detailed hand-carved dioramas of Western towns, circuses and other scenes come alive with a quarter. Woodcarver and wisdom collector Ross J Ward, who passed away in 2002, built it and surrounded it with antique toys, 'junque' (fancy junk) and suggestions that you eat more mangoes naked.

🛏 Sleeping

Relatively close to Albuquerque, this isn't a bad place to base yourself if you prefer to be closer to the mountains rather than the city. There are a handful of restaurants along the highway.

Turquoise Trail Campground　CAMPGROUND $
(📞 505-281-2005; www.turquoisetrailcampground.com; 22 Calvary Rd; tent/RV sites $19/33, cabins $40-70; 🎧🐾) Camp in a meadow, just off NM 14 near the Tinkertown Museum, with hot showers and cool shade, or rent a simple cabin. This is one of the nicest campsites near Albuquerque, especially if you're in a tent.

Elaine's Bed & Breakfast　　　B&B $$
(📞 505-281-2467; www.elainesbnb.com; 72 Snowline Rd; r $109-159; 🅿🎧) This beautifully decorated lodge, nestled up in the woods with superb views, holds five antique-furnished B&B rooms, each with private bath. The lovely Unicorn room has its own Jacuzzi, while the Sangre de Cristo room has a private balcony, and Elaine herself is a wonderful hostess.

ℹ Getting There & Away

Cedar Crest is located 20 miles east of Albuquerque (about 30 minutes), immediately after you turn north off I-40 onto Hwy 14.

Madrid

📞 505 / POP 204 / ELEV 6020FT

Madrid (pronounced *maa*-drid) was a bustling company coal-mining town in the 1920s and '30s, but after WWII it was all but abandoned. Tie-dyed wanderers bought up cheap lots during the mid-1970s, and their spiritual descendants are still here, having built a thriving arts community. Madrid has become a lot more touristy over the years, but beneath the surface its outlaw heart still beats, and it remains a favorite stop on Harley rallies.

👁 Sights

Madrid Old Coal Town Museum　　MUSEUM
(📞 505-438-3780; www.themineshafttavern.com; 2846 Hwy 14; adult/child $5/3; ⏲ 11am-5pm Apr-Sep) A gleeful and exhaustive celebration of every last detail of mining-town life, holding everything from hospital equipment to old shop fittings, an impressive array of old digging and tunneling equipment and even a steam locomotive.

🛏 Sleeping & Eating

For a one-street town, there are a surprising number of good dining options. Note that tap water here is unpalatable – drink something else.

Java Junction B&B　　　　　　　B&B $$
(📞 505-438-2772; www.java-junction.com; 2855 Hwy 14; ste $129; 🎧) Conveniently located above a cafe where they take their brew very seriously, this friendly B&B consists of just one bright, light kitchenette suite, complete with claw-foot tub and roof terrace.

Hollar Restaurant　　　　　AMERICAN $$
(📞 505-471-4821; thehollar.com; 2849 Hwy 14; mains $11-19; ⏲ 11am-7pm Mon-Wed, to 9pm Thu-Sun) Fried green tomatoes, grits, biscuits and fried chicken, plus all the usual chile-based staples – no wonder this place is so popular.

Throw a great outdoor patio and bar into the mix, along with a decommissioned Santa Fe boxcar, and you've got a winner.

Mama Lisa's Ghost Town Kitchen   CAFE $$
(☎505-471-5769; 2859 Hwy 14; daily specials $9-12; ☉9am-3pm Wed-Sun, hours vary winter) Also known as the No Pity Cafe, this quirky little place offers indoor and outdoor seating, and serves everything from breakfast burritos to gourmet hamburgers and mixed vegetarian plates – not to mention the irresistible red-chile chocolate cake.

☆ Entertainment

Head to the **Mine Shaft Tavern** (☎505-438-3780; www.themineshafttavern.com; 2846 Hwy 14; ☉11:30am-10pm Sun-Thu, to midnight Fri & Sat; ☎) for great craft brews on tap.

Engine House Theatre   THEATER
(☎505-473-0743; www.themineshafttavern.com; 2846 Hwy 14; adult/child $10/4; ☉3pm Sat & Sun May-Oct) Spectacular summer-weekend melodramas in the Mineshaft Tavern's cozy, old-fashioned theater space abound in Wild West desperadoes, scoundrels and vixens. What's more, there's still a steam train right on the stage. Admission includes a six-shooter loaded with marshmallows to unload at the villains.

🔒 Shopping

With dozens of galleries and wacky shops scattered through this one-horse town, it's easy to spend an hour or two browsing.

Weasel and Fitz   ARTS & CRAFTS
(☎505-474-4893; www.weaselandfitz.com; 2878 Hwy 14; ☉10am-6pm Thu-Tue) Quirky sculptures and ornaments made from recycled household items; look especially for the customized vintage plates, featuring portraits transmogrified into animal heads.

Range West   ARTS & CRAFTS
(☎505-474-0925; www.rangewest.com; 2861 Hwy 14; ☉10:30am-5pm, closed Tue & Wed in winter)

NEW MEXICO TURQUOISE TRAIL

NEW MEXICO'S PUEBLOS

New Mexico is home to 19 American Indian Pueblos, concentrated especially in the vicinity of Santa Fe. The word *pueblo* comes from the Spanish for 'village,' and that's exactly what they are – small clusters of adobe houses, which in many cases are still standing right where the conquistadors found them five centuries ago. The American Indian experience here is thus very different from Indian reservations in the rest of the country. While some of today's Pueblos are populated by the descendants of refugees whose homes were destroyed by the Spanish, most Pueblo Indians were not radically displaced and have long and deep ties to their lands.

For a compelling overview of these communities, stop by Albuquerque's **Indian Pueblo Cultural Center** (p240). Operated by the Puebloans themselves, the museum traces the development of Pueblo cultures, including Spanish influence, and features exhibits of the arts and crafts created in each. The website lists a complete schedule of Native dances throughout the state – check here first if you are interested in visiting.

Most Pueblos are not tourist attractions, but simply communities where people live, and offer little for visitors outside of festival weekends. Those that do welcome visitors usually charge admission fees, and either forbid photography or charge additional fees; always check before you take any pictures or videos. One thing you should expect if you visit a Pueblo is conversation – if you are respectful and friendly, it's likely someone will strike up a discussion at some point.

As gambling is only legal in New Mexico on American Indian reservations, many Pueblos run their own casinos, usually well away from the Pueblo proper.

Finally, the Pueblos recommended here are also excellent places to buy crafts direct from the artist; jewelry and ceramics tend to be more unique and better priced than at boutiques in Santa Fe or elsewhere. Our pick of the top three Pueblos for visitors:

Taos Pueblo (p298) The most famous Pueblo in New Mexico, in a gorgeous spot below Pueblo Peak.

Zuni Pueblo (p318) Less touristy than other Pueblos, with creative jewelry and wild scenery; it's 35 miles south of Gallup.

Acoma Pueblo (p321) The dramatic mesa-top Sky City is, along with Taos Pueblo and Arizona's Hopi villages, one of the oldest continually inhabited spots in the US.

Shoplifters be warned: these elegant water fountains, carved from monolithic granite chunks, are not the easiest items in the world to carry.

Seppanen & Daughters
Fine Textiles ARTS & CRAFTS
(☑505-424-7470; www.finetextiles.com; 2879 Hwy 14) Colorful and irresistibly tactile Oaxacan, Navajo and Tibetan rugs.

Cerrillos

☑505 / POP 321 / ELEV 5687FT
A few miles north of Madrid on Hwy 14, Cerrillos still has one foot in the Old West. With unpaved streets threading through an adobe town relatively unchanged since the 1880s, it's home to what may have been the first mine in North America, which started extracting turquoise around AD 100, and reached its peak – under different management – in the 19th century.

⊙ Sights & Activities

Cerrillos Hills State Park PARK
(☑505-474-0196; www.nmparks.com; per vehicle $5; ⊙sunrise-sunset) A mile north of Cerrillos, amid scrubby desert hills pockmarked with historic mining sites, this park holds 5 miles of well-marked hiking and biking trails.

Broken Saddle Riding Co HORSEBACK RIDING
(☑505-424-7774; www.brokensaddle.com; off County Rd 57; rides $65-115; ☀) One- to three-hour horseback rides through juniper-dotted hills and abandoned mines, including a special sunset/moonlight ride. Along the way you'll learn about local history and geology. Children must be eight or older.

SANTA FE

☑505 / POP 69,976 / ELEV 7200FT
Welcome to 'the city different,' a place that makes its own rules without ever forgetting its long and storied past. Walking through its adobe neighborhoods, or around the busy Plaza that remains its core, there's no denying that Santa Fe has a timeless, earthy soul. Indeed, its artistic inclinations are a principal attraction – there are more quality museums and galleries here than you could possibly see in just one visit.

At over 7000ft above sea level, Santa Fe is also the nation's highest state capital. Sitting at the foot of the Sangre de Cristo range, it makes a fantastic base for hiking,

mountain biking, backpacking and skiing. When you come off the trails, you can indulge in chile-smothered local cuisine, buy turquoise and silver directly from American Indian jewelers in the Plaza, visit remarkable churches, or simply wander along the centuries-old, cottonwood-shaded lanes and daydream about one day moving here.

⊙ Sights

For a city of its size, Santa Fe punches way above its weight. Not only is its small downtown core still filled with colonial-era adobe homes and churches, with the region's American Indian heritage apparent everywhere, but they've been joined by an array of world-class museums and art galleries. There's also a separate cluster of wonderful museums on Museum Hill, a short drive southeast.

⊙ Downtown

Downtown Santa Fe still centers on its historic Plaza and the grid of streets that surrounds it. It's easy to while away a full day within these few blocks, punctuating visits to the art and history museums with downtime in the countless cafes, restaurants and shops.

Across the Santa Fe River – dry for much of the year, but lined by verdant footpaths – lie the official buildings of New Mexico's state government. The Guadalupe and Railyard districts, home to lively bars and restaurants, are immediately west, while gallery-lined Canyon Rd stretches away east.

★**The Plaza** PLAZA
(Map p256) For over 400 years, the Plaza has stood at the heart of Santa Fe. Originally it marked the far northern end of the Camino Real from Mexico; later, it was the goal for wagons heading west along the Santa Fe Trail. Today, this grassy square is peopled by tourists wandering from museum to margarita, food vendors, skateboarding kids and street musicians. Beneath the portico of the Palace of the Governors, along its northern side, American Indians sell jewelry and pottery.

★**Palace of the Governors & New**
Mexico History Museum HISTORIC BUILDING
(Map p256; ☑505-476-5100; www.palaceofthe governors.org; 105 W Palace Ave; adult/child $12/free; ⊙10am-5pm, closed Mon Oct-May) The oldest public building in the US, this low-slung adobe complex started out as home to New

Santa Fe

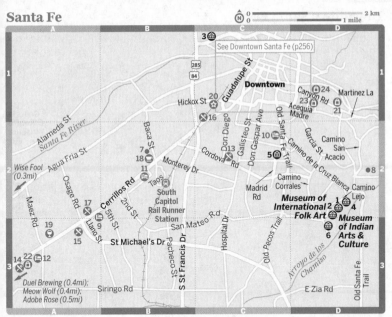

See Downtown Santa Fe (p256)

Santa Fe

Mexico's first Spanish governor in 1610. It was occupied by Pueblo Indians following their revolt in 1680, and after 1846 became the seat of the US Territory's earliest governors. It now holds fascinating displays on Santa Fe's multifaceted past, and some superb Hispanic religious artwork – join a free tour if possible.

★ **Georgia O'Keeffe Museum**   MUSEUM
(Map p256; ☏ 505-946-1000; www.okeeffe museum.org; 217 Johnson St; adult/child \$12/ free; ◎ 10am-5pm Sat-Thu, to 7pm Fri) With 10 beautifully lit galleries in a rambling 20th-century adobe, this museum boasts the world's largest collection of O'Keeffe's work. She's best known for her luminous New

Downtown Santa Fe

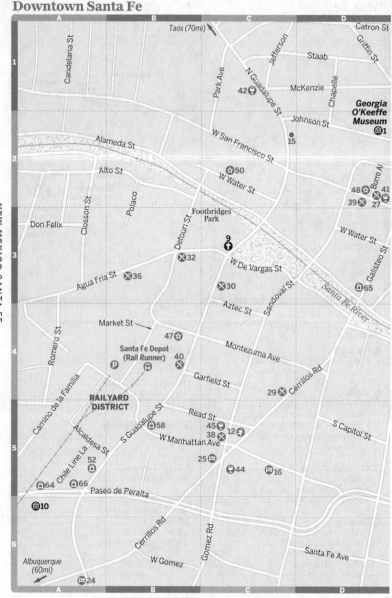

Mexican landscapes, but the changing exhibitions here range through her entire career, from her early years through to her time at Ghost Ranch. Major museums worldwide own her most famous canvases, so you may not see familiar paintings, but you're sure to be bowled over by the thick brushwork and transcendent colors on show.

New Mexico Museum of Art   MUSEUM
(Map p256; ☎505-476-5072; www.nmartmuseum.org; 107 W Palace Ave; adult/child $12/

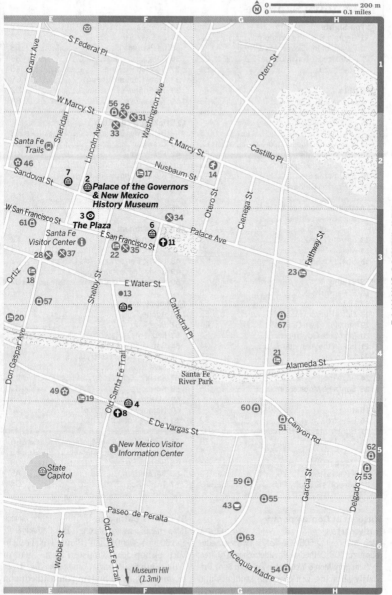

free; ⊙10am-5pm Tue-Sun) Built in 1917 and a prime early example of Santa Fe's Pueblo Revival architecture, the New Mexico Museum of Art has spent a century collecting and displaying works by regional artists. A treasure trove of works by the great names who put New Mexico on the cultural map, from the Taos Society of Artists to Georgia O'Keeffe, it's also a lovely building in which to stroll around, with a cool garden courtyard. Constantly changing temporary exhibitions ensure its continuing relevance.

Downtown Santa Fe

Museum of Contemporary Native Arts MUSEUM
(Map p256; ☎505-922-4242; www.iaia.edu/museum; 108 Cathedral Pl; adult/child $10/free; ☺10am-5pm Mon & Wed-Sat, noon-5pm Sun) Primarily showing work by the students and faculty of the esteemed Institute of American Indian Arts, this museum also has the finest contemporary offerings of American Indian artists from tribes across the US. It's an excellent place to see cutting-edge art and understand its role in modern American Indian culture.

St Francis Cathedral CHURCH
(Map p256; www.cbsfa.org; 131 Cathedral Pl; ☺8:30am-4:30pm) FREE Santa Fe's French-born bishop Jean-Baptiste Lamy – hero of Willa Cather's *Death Comes for the Archbishop* – set about building this cathedral in 1869. Its Romanesque exterior might seem more suited to Europe than the Wild West, but the Hispanic altarpiece inside lends a real New Mexican flavor. A side chapel holds a diminutive Madonna statue that was taken into exile following the Pueblo Revolt, and has been known since the Spaniards' triumphant return in 1692 as *La Conquistadora*.

Loretto Chapel
HISTORIC BUILDING

(Map p256; 505-982-0092; www.lorettochapel.
com; 207 Old Santa Fe Trail; $3; ⊙9am-5pm Mon-
Sat, 10:30am-5pm Sun) Built in 1878 for the
Sisters of Loretto, this tiny Gothic chapel is
famous as the site of St Joseph's Miraculous
Staircase, a spiraling and apparently unsup-
ported wooden staircase added by a mysterious young carpenter who vanished without
giving the astonished nuns his name. The
chapel is no longer consecrated and can be
rented for (nondenominational) weddings.

San Miguel Mission
CHURCH

(Map p256; 401 Old Santa Fe Trail; $1; ⊙10am-4pm
Mon-Sat, Mass 2pm (Latin) & 5pm Sun) Erected
from 1610 onwards, by and for the Tlax-
calan Indians who arrived from Mexico with
Santa Fe's first Spanish settlers, this is considered to be the oldest church in the US.
Much of the original building was destroyed
during the Pueblo Revolt of 1680, so it was
rebuilt with new walls in 1710. Holes in front
of the altar reveal the foundations of an
ancient Pueblo beneath, while the high viga
beams and devotional artwork inside are
well worth a peek.

Santuario de Guadalupe
CHURCH

(Map p256; 100 Guadalupe St; ⊙9am-noon &
1-4pm Mon-Sat, Mass noon Sun) FREE The oldest
shrine in the US to Our Lady of Guadalupe,
the patroness of Mexico, this adobe church
was constructed between 1776 and 1796,
though there have been several additions
and renovations since then. The Spanish
baroque *retablo* (altar painting) inside was
painted in Mexico in 1783, then taken apart
and transported up the Camino Real on
mule back. Other cultural treasures here
include a fine collection of *santos,* wood-
carved portraits of saints.

State Capitol
HISTORIC BUILDING

(Map p256; 505-986-4589; cnr Paseo de Peralta & Old Santa Fe Trail; ⊙7am-6pm Mon-Fri,
plus 9am-5pm Sat in summer) FREE New Mexico's State Capitol, informally known as
the Roundhouse, was laid out in the shape
of the state symbol – also the emblem of
Zia Pueblo – in 1966. Home to the state
legislature, which sits for 60 days in even-
numbered years and just 30 in odd years, it
holds one of the finest (free) art collections
in New Mexico. Visitors must check-in with
the information desk first.

SITE Santa Fe
GALLERY

(Map p256; 505-989-1199; sitesantafe.org;
1606 Paseo de Peralta; adult/child $10/free, Fri
& 10am-noon Sat free; ⊙10am-5pm Thu & Sat,
10am-7pm Fri, noon-5pm Sun) Looming over

NEW MEXICO SANTA FE

SANTA FE FOR CHILDREN

The outdoors are an obvious choice for children of all ages – superb skiing, mountain
biking, hiking and camping options are within a short drive of downtown.

➤ The **Santa Fe Children's Museum** (Map p255; 505-989-8359; www.
santafechildrensmuseum.org; 1050 Old Pecos Trail; adult/child $7.50/5; ⊙9am-5pm Wed-Sun,
to 6:30pm Thu;) features hands-on science and art exhibits for young children, but
adults will enjoy it as well.

➤ The amazing **Museum of International Folk Art** (p260) has a big indoor play area
as well as captivating exhibits.

➤ The combo of mystery narrative and hands-on installations at **Meow Wolf** (p260) will
likely appeal to kids over 10.

➤ Local history is brought to life at the interpretive museum **Rancho de las
Golondrinas** (p260).

➤ Get up close to creepy crawlies at the **Harrell House Bug Museum** (Map p255; 505-
695-8569; harrellhouse.com; 564 N Guadalupe St, DeVargas Center Mall; adult/child $6/4;
⊙10am-6pm Mon-Fri, noon-5pm Sun).

➤ If you're traveling with a budding thespian, check out the backstage tours of the **Santa
Fe Opera** (p270) during opera season. They're interesting and free for anyone under 23.

➤ If you want to get out on your own, **Magical Happenings Babysitting** (505-
982-1570) can have sitters stay with your kids in your hotel room; it's $20 an hour
for one child or $22 an hour for two, with a four-hour minimum and an additional $7
transportation charge. Reserve well in advance.

the Railyard District, the enormous and ever-expanding SITE Santa Fe is a non-profit art gallery dedicated to presenting world-class contemporary art to the local community. Besides radical installation pieces and cutting-edge multimedia exhibitions, it also hosts wine-splashed openings, artist talks, movie screenings and performances of all kinds.

Casa Vieja   HISTORIC BUILDING
(Map p256; 215 E De Vargas St; ⊘9am-6pm) FREE Billing itself as the oldest house in the United States, this two-room adobe building is said to date – in a much altered form – from c 1646. While several Pueblos in the Southwest are certainly much older than the Casa Vieja, it's worth a peek to get a glimpse of the living conditions of early Mexican settlers.

◎ Museum Hill

Four of Santa Fe's finest museums stand together on Museum Hill, 2 miles southwest of the Plaza. This low but beautifully situated mountain-view hillock is not a neighborhood in any sense – all the museums hold superb gift shops, but there's nothing else here, apart from a research library and a good cafe. The Santa Fe Pick-Up runs here from downtown.

★Museum of International Folk Art   MUSEUM
(Map p255; ☑505-827-6344; www.international folkart.org; 706 Camino Lejo; adult/child $12/free; ⊘10am-5pm, closed Mon Nov-Apr) Santa Fe's most unusual and exhilarating museum centers on the world's largest collection of folk art. Its huge main gallery displays whimsical and mind-blowing objects from more than 100 different countries. Tiny human figures go about their business in fully realized village and city scenes, while dolls, masks, toys and garments spill across the walls. Changing exhibitions in other wings explore vernacular art and culture worldwide.

★Museum of Indian Arts & Culture   MUSEUM
(Map p255; ☑505-476-1250; www.indianarts andculture.org; 710 Camino Lejo; adult/child $12/free; ⊘10am-5pm, closed Mon Sep-May) This top-quality museum sets out to trace the origins and history of the various American Indian peoples of the entire Southwest, and explain and illuminate their widely differing cultural traditions. Pueblo, Navajo and Apache interviewees describe the contemporary realities each group now faces, while a truly superb collection of ceramics, modern and ancient, is complemented by stimulating temporary displays.

Wheelwright Museum of the American Indian   MUSEUM
(Map p255; ☑505-982-4636; www.wheelwright. org; 704 Camino Lejo; adult/child $8/free, 1st Sun of month free; ⊘10am-5pm) Mary Cabot established this museum in 1937 to showcase Navajo ceremonial art, and its major strength is Navajo and Zuni jewellery, in particular silverwork. The first gallery hosts temporary exhibits, showcasing American Indian art from across North America. The gift store, known as the Case Trading Post, sells museum-quality rugs, jewelry, kachinas and crafts.

Museum of Spanish Colonial Art   MUSEUM
(Map p255; ☑505-982-2226; www.spanish colonial.org; 750 Camino Lejo; adult/child $8/free; ⊘10am-5pm, closed Mon Oct-Apr) Celebrating the long history of Hispanic culture in New Mexico, this museum places the religious and domestic art of the region in the context of the Spanish colonial experience worldwide. The carved statues and paintings of saints familiar from churches throughout the state are displayed alongside the personal possessions treasured by colonists as reminders of their original homeland.

◎ Metro Santa Fe & Around

★Meow Wolf   MUSEUM
(Map p276; ☑505-395-6369; meowwolf.com; 1352 Rufina Circle; adult/child $18/12; ⊘10am-8pm Sun, Mon, Wed & Thu, to 10pm Fri & Sat) If you've been hankering for a trip to another dimension but have yet to find a portal, the House of Eternal Return by Meow Wolf could be the place for you. The premise here is quite ingenious: visitors get to explore a re-created Victorian house for clues related to the disappearance of a California family, following a narrative that leads deeper into fragmented bits of a multiverse (often via secret passages), all of which are unique, interactive art installations.

Rancho de las Golondrinas   MUSEUM
(Map p276; ☑505-471-2261; www.golondrinas. org; 334 Los Pinos Rd, La Cienega; adult/child $6/free; ⊘10am-4pm Wed-Sun Jun-Sep, tours by

reservation only Apr, May & Oct; 🐾) Built as a fortified residence along the Camino Real, the 'Ranch of the Swallows' is nearly as old as Santa Fe itself. Now it's a 200-acre living museum, reconstructed and populated with historical re-enactors, amid orchards, vineyards and livestock (no pets). Kids will love watching bread being baked in a traditional adobe oven and visiting the blacksmith, the molasses mill and crafts workshops. Assorted themed festivals are held throughout the summer. To find it, follow signs from I-25 exit 276.

Shidoni Foundry GARDENS, GALLERY
(📞 505-988-8001; www.shidoni.com; 1508 Bishop's Lodge Rd, Tesuque; ⊙9am-5pm Mon-Sat; 🐾) **FREE** Five miles north of Santa Fe, the grassy sculpture garden at Shidoni is a great place for a picnic, or for kids to run around the funky artwork. There's also an indoor gallery and a glass-blowing studio. Take a self-guided foundry tour (noon to 1pm Monday to Friday; $5), or come on Saturday to watch 2000°F molten bronze being poured into ceramic shell molds, in the complex, age-old casting technique (call for schedule; $10).

🏃 Activities

Santa Fe's cultural attractions may be second to none, but the locals do not live on art appreciation alone. Before any strenuous activities, remember the elevation: take time to acclimatize, and watch for signs of altitude sickness. Weather changes rapidly and afternoon summer storms are frequent: always bring extra layers and a waterproof shell.

Skiing

Downhill gets most of the attention in these parts, but both the Sangre de Cristo and Jemez mountains have numerous cross-country ski trails.

Ski Santa Fe SKIING
(Map p276; 📞 505-982-4429, snow report 505-983-9155; www.skisantafe.com; lift ticket adult/teen/child $75/60/52; ⊙9am-4pm Dec-Mar) Often overlooked for its more famous cousin outside Taos, the smaller Santa Fe ski area boasts the same dry powder (though not quite as much), with a higher base elevation (10,350ft). It caters to families and expert skiers, who come for the glades, steep bump runs and long groomers a mere 16 miles from town.

Cottam's SPORTS & OUTDOORS
(Map p276; 📞 505-982-0495; www.cottams skishops.com; 740 Hyde Park Rd; adult/child ski-gear rental from $30/22; ⊙7:30am-6pm) Though the ski area rents gear, many people prefer to pick up skis, poles, boots and boards here, on the way to the slopes. It also rents cross-country ski equipment and snowshoes.

Mountain Biking

★ Winsor Trail MOUNTAIN BIKING, HIKING
(Map p276) One of Santa Fe's top trails, the Winsor has two distinct sections: mountain bikers opt for the 13 miles of legendary downhill singletrack that connect the ski area with the town of Tesuque (the hardcore can opt to do this in the reverse direction), while hikers should check out the Upper Winsor, which climbs into gorgeous high country on a 10-mile out-and-back.

Dale Ball Trails MOUNTAIN BIKING, HIKING
(Map p276; www.santafenm.gov/trails_1) Over 20 miles of shared mountain biking and hiking trails, with fabulous desert and mountain views. The 9.7-mile Outer Limits trail is a classic ride here, combining fast singletrack in the north section with the more technical central section. Hikers should check out the 4-mile round-trip trail to Picacho Peak, with a steep but accessible 1250ft elevation gain.

Mellow Velo MOUNTAIN BIKING
(Map p256; 📞 505-995-8356; www.mellowvelo.com; 132 E Marcy St; mountain bikes per day from $40; ⊙10am-6pm Mon-Sat) The kind gentle-folk at this downtown bike shop offer rental and repair, and provide information on regional trails. You can ride to the Dale Ball Trailhead from the shop (3 miles). Pick up trail maps at the store or online.

Rafting

The two rivers worth running in the vicinity of Santa Fe are the **Rio Grande** – for white-water thrills and mellow float trips – and the **Rio Chama** – mellower but better for multiday trips and arguably more scenic. Outfitters offer all sorts of variations on the basic themes, so check which options are available. Once you reserve your trip, you'll know where and what time to meet.

The rafting season generally begins in late April (depending on snowmelt), with the highest water levels in May and June. The rivers mellow out as the summer wears on, and rafting trips generally peter out by early September.

The classic trip for those who want white-water but have little experience or are with children is the **Racecourse** (Class III), on the Rio Grande south of Taos. It's fine for kids over six or seven (depending on the company), and the put-in is closer to Santa Fe. This is also a classic playground for kayakers.

Hardcore boaters head north of Taos to crash through rapids on the renowned **Taos Box** (Class IV), which traverses 16 miles of spectacular wilderness gorge. It's fantastic fun but not for the faint of heart, and commercial companies require rafters to be at least 12 years old. The Taos Box is usually only runnable from May through early July – reserve your trip well in advance.

The Rio Chama has a few Class III rapids, but most of it is fairly flat, making it a great choice for families.

New Wave Rafting Co   RAFTING
(☑800-984-1444;   www.newwaverafting.com; adult/child from $57/51; ⊙mid-Apr–Aug) A variety of half-day, full-day and multiday trips through the Racecourse, Rio Grande, Taos Box and Rio Chama.

Santa Fe Rafting Co   RAFTING
(☑888-988-4914; www.santaferafting.com; per person $65; ⊙mid-Apr–Aug) Runs the Taos Box, the Racecourse, a full-day Rio Grande Gorge trip and mellow float trips.

Kokopelli Rafting Adventures   RAFTING
(☑505-983-3734; www.kokopelliraft.com; adult/child from $60/45; ⊙mid-Apr–Aug) Runs half-day trips on the Rio Grande, and full-day trips through the Taos Box, Racecourse and Rio Chama.

Horseback Riding

No Western fantasy is complete without hopping into a saddle. There's some great riding to be done near Santa Fe itself, as well as further afield, for example with Broken Saddle (p254) in Cerrillos, and at Ghost Ranch (p281) near Abiquiú.

Stables at Bishop's Lodge   HORSEBACK RIDING
(Map p276; ☑505-819-0095; www.bishopslodge stables.com; 1297 Bishop's Lodge Rd; kids ride $30, 1/2hr ride $70/140; ⊙8am-5pm; ⚑) Themed trail rides at the Stables at Bishop's Lodge include 15-minute kids introductory rides,

---

TOP 5 SANTA FE DAY HIKES

There are a ton of trails around Santa Fe. Whether you're looking for all-day adventure or a relaxing amble through a special landscape, you'll find it. Trailheads for all the following hikes are within an hour's drive of the Plaza.

Raven's Ridge Starting along the Upper Winsor Trail from the ski basin parking lot, Raven's Ridge cuts east after the first steep mile of switchbacks to follow the Pecos Wilderness boundary high above the treeline to the top of Lake Peak (12,409ft). A strenuous hike at substantial elevation, it's well worth it if you're acclimatized and in shape. No trail has better views; you can see forever from up here. Loop back by hiking down the ski slopes to complete a round-trip of about 6 miles.

Upper Winsor After its steep first mile from the ski basin, the Upper Winsor Trail mellows out, contouring around forested slopes with a moderate uphill section toward the end. Puerto Nambé (11,050ft), a huge and beautiful meadow in the saddle between Santa Fe Baldy (12,622ft) to the north and Penitente Peak (12,249ft) to the south, is a great place for a picnic. The round-trip is about 10 miles.

Aspen Vista The premier path for immersing yourself in the magical fall foliage, this trail lives up to its name. The first mile or so is super easy, gaining little elevation and following an old dirt road. It gets a little more difficult the further you go; just turn back when you've had enough. The trailhead is at about 10,000ft along the road to the ski basin; it's marked 'Trail No 150.' Mountain bikers love this one too.

La Cieneguilla Petroglyph Site Half a mile along a dirt track from a clearly marked trailhead on Airport Rd, 12 miles southwest of downtown, this trail climbs the low hillside to reach a rocky bluff that's covered with ancient Keresan petroglyphs, including images of the flute player Kokopelli. Allow an hour's hiking time in total.

Tent Rocks There's truly surreal hiking at **Kasha-Katuwe Tent Rocks National Monument** (p251), near Cochiti Pueblo 40 miles southwest of Santa Fe, where short trails meander through a geologic wonderland.

and a sunset ride on Tuesday and Thursday. Although the lodge is under renovation through 2018, the stables will remain open.

Hiking & Backpacking

Some of the best hiking and backpacking in New Mexico is right outside of Santa Fe. The undeveloped **Pecos Wilderness**, in the heart of the **Santa Fe National Forest**, holds almost 1000 miles of trails that lead through spruce and aspen forest, across grassy alpine meadows, and up to several peaks surpassing 12,000ft. The quickest way to get above the treeline is to drive to the ski basin, hop on the Winsor Trail (p261) and trudge up the switchbacks. The most immediately accessible hiking trails are on the Dale Ball Trail System (p261), 3 miles east of downtown.

Randall Davey Audubon Center   OUTDOORS
(Map p276; ☑505-983-4609; nm.audubon.org; 1800 Upper Canyon Rd; ⊘8am-4pm Mon-Sat) Protecting 135 acres along the *acequia* of Santa Fe Canyon near the Dale Ball Trails, this center provides information on the coyotes, bobcats and wildlife of the juniper and piñon forest. The on-site Bear Canyon Trail, a 3-mile round-trip, leads into the steep-sided canyon. Free bird-watching walks take place Saturday at 8:30am.

Fishing

New Mexico's most outstanding fishing holes are better accessed from Taos and the Enchanted Circle, but abundant opportunities out of Santa Fe include Abiquiú and Nambé Lakes. You'll need a license (one/five days $12/24).

High Desert Angler   FISHING
(Map p256; ☑505-988-7688; www.highdesertangler.com; 460 Cerrillos Rd; ⊘8am-6pm Mon-Sat, 11am-4pm Sun) Friendly store a short walk south of downtown, which sells licenses and a large array of gear, and offers fly-fishing lessons plus guided fishing excursions (one/two people from $300/350).

Spas & Wellness

★ Ten Thousand Waves   SPA
(Map p276; ☑505-982-9304; www.tenthousandwaves.com; 3451 Hyde Park Rd; communal tub $24, private tubs per person $35; ⊘9am-10:30pm Wed-Mon, noon-10:30pm Tue Jul-Oct, reduced hours Nov-Jun) This gorgeous Japanese spa offers attractive public and private outdoor soaking tubs, kitted out in a minimalist Zen style

with cold plunges and saunas. Treatments from prenatal, hot stone and Thai massages to herbal wraps start at $117. It's set in the foothills 4 miles northeast of town, and also features an *izakaya* (tapas-style) restaurant and sublime lodging options (p266).

Body   SPA
(Map p255; ☑505-986-0362; www.bodyofsantafe.com; 333 W Cordova Rd; ⊘7:30am-9pm Mon-Fri, 8:30am-9pm Sat, 8:30am-6:30pm Sun) Body offers yoga classes, craniosacral therapy, reflexology treatments and full-body massages. Drop your kids at the supervised play room ($7 per hour) while you de-stress.

La Posada Spa   SPA
(Map p256; ☑505-954-9630; www.laposadadesantafe.com; 330 E Palace Ave; 50min massage from $135; ⊘9am-7pm) Choose from a range of sophisticated therapies at this swanky spot within the La Posada hotel.

🍴 Courses

Liquid Light Glass   ART
(Map p255; ☑505-820-2222; liquidlightglass.com; 926 Baca St No 3; classes from $60; ⊘10am-5pm Mon-Fri, to 4pm Sat) Come here to browse sensuous glass creations in the gallery, or treat yourself to one of the drop-in glass-blowing courses on offer with artists Elodie Holmes and Jannine Cabossel.

Wise Fool   CIRCUS
(☑505-992-2588; www.wisefoolnewmexico.org; 1131 Siler Rd, Suite B; drop-in class $15-25) Ever want to learn the arts of trapeze, juggling, or just plain clowning around? As well as drop-in classes, Wise Fool has multiday intensives for adults and week-long summer day camps for kids.

Santa Fe School of Cooking   COOKING
(Map p256; ☑505-983-4511; www.santafeschoolofcooking.com; 125 N Guadalupe St; 2/3hr class $78/98; ⊘9:30am-5:30pm Mon-Fri, 9:30am-5pm Sat, 10:30am-3:30pm Sun) Sign up for green or red chile workshops to master the basics of Southwestern cuisine, or try your hand at *chile rellenos* (stuffed chile peppers), tamales or more sophisticated flavors such as mustard mango habanero sauce. It also offers several popular restaurant walking tours.

Santa Fe Workshops   PHOTOGRAPHY
(Map p255; ☑505-983-1400; www.santafeworkshops.com; 50 Mt Carmel Rd; from $1150) Develop your inner Ansel Adams awareness at these

legendary workshops, covering all aspects of traditional photography and digital imagery, and lasting from two to five days. Course fees do not include meals and lodging.

Tours

Several companies offer walking and bus tours of Santa Fe and northern New Mexico. Others organize guided trips to the pueblos, as well as air tours and biking, hiking, rafting and horseback-riding trips.

Santa Fe Walkabouts   TOURS
(📞 505-216-9161; www.santafewalkabouts.com; half-day per person around $80) Enthusiastic company offering customized hiking, biking, winter sports and jeep tours all over northern New Mexico. Rates depend on the activity and the size of your party.

A Well-Born Guide/
Have PhD, Will Travel   WALKING
(📞 505-988-8022; www.swguides.com) If the name doesn't lure you in, the tours will. Stefanie Beninato, an informative local historian with a knack for good storytelling, offers lively themed walks around Santa Fe that focus on everything from bars and former brothels to ghosts, architecture and, of course, art, as well as multiday trips around New Mexico.

Seven Directions   TOURS
(📞 877-992-6128; www.sevendirections.net; full-day tour per person around $260) Sightseeing and cultural tours of the city and state, available in French, Italian and Spanish as well as English.

Loretto Line   TOURS
(Map p256; 📞 505-982-0092; www.toursof santafe.com; 207 Old Santa Fe Trail; adult/child $15/12; ⊙ mid-Mar–Oct) Cruise around Santa Fe in an open-sided tram and learn about its history and culture from experienced guides. Six tours are offered per day.

✹ Festivals & Events

The Santa Fe Visitor Center (p273) maintains a calendar of events, musical and theatrical productions and museum shows.

Native Treasures   ART
(📞 505-982-7799; nativetreasures.org; ⊙ May) Three days of top-quality Native art over Memorial Day weekend – participating artists are specially invited by the Museum of Indian Arts & Culture (p260). Expect jewelry, pottery, fine art, textiles and more.

Currents   ART
(currentsnewmedia.org; ⊙ Jun) With an emphasis on video art and technology, this is one of Santa Fe's most cutting-edge events. Expect two weeks of video installations, new media–based performances, animation and the like.

★ International Folk Art Market   CULTURAL
(📞 505-992-7600; www.folkartalliance.org; ⊙ mid-Jul) The world's largest folk art market draws around 150 artists from 50 countries to the Folk Art Museum for a festive weekend of craft shopping and cultural events in July.

★ Spanish Market   CULTURAL
(www.spanishcolonial.org; ⊙ late Jul) Traditional Spanish Colonial arts, from *retablos* and *bultos* (carved wooden religious statues) to handcrafted furniture and metalwork, make this juried show in late July an artistic extravaganza, second only to the Indian Market.

Santa Fe Chamber Music Festival   MUSIC
(📞 505-982-1890; www.santafechambermusic. com; ⊙ Jul & Aug) Santa Fe's *other* major annual cultural event – apart from the opera – fills elegant venues like the Lensic to hear Brahms, Mozart and other masters performed by world-class virtuosos like violinist Pinchas Zukerman and pianist Yuja Wang.

★ Santa Fe Indian Market   CULTURAL
(📞 505-983-5220; www.swaia.org; ⊙ Aug) Over a thousand artists from 100 tribes and Pueblos show work at this world-famous juried show, held the weekend after the third Thursday in August. Around 100,000 visitors converge on the Plaza, at open studios, gallery shows and the Native Cinema Showcase. Come Friday or Saturday to see pieces competing for the top prizes; wait until Sunday before trying to bargain.

A smaller Winter Indian Market is held mid-December at La Fonda (p265).

★ Santa Fe Fiesta &
Burning of Zozobra   CULTURAL
(📞 505-913-1517; www.santafefiesta.org; ⊙ early Sep) This 10-day celebration of the 1692 resettlement of Santa Fe following the 1680 Pueblo Revolt includes concerts, a candlelit procession and the much-loved Pet Parade. Everything kicks off with the unmissable Friday-night torching of Zozobra (burn-zozobra.com) – a 50ft-tall effigy of 'Old Man Gloom' – before some 40,000 people in Fort Marcy Park.

Wine & Chile Fiesta
FOOD & DRINK

(☎ 505-438-8060; www.santafewineandchile.org; ☺ late Sep) A gourmet's fantasy fiesta, with wine tastings and fine cuisine; dinner events sell out early.

Santa Fe Independent Film Festival
FILM

(☎ 505-349-1414; santafeindependent.com; ☺ Oct) Five days of indie cinema in October.

🛏 Sleeping

When it comes to luxury accommodations, Santa Fe has a number of opulent hotels and posh B&Bs, with some unforgettable historic options within a block of the Plaza. Rates steadily diminish the further you go from downtown, with budget and national chain options strung out along Cerrillos Rd toward I-25.

Book well in advance in summer, particularly during the Indian Market and on opera nights, and also in December.

🛏 Downtown Santa Fe

★ El Paradero
B&B $$

(Map p256; ☎ 505-988-1177; www.elparadero.com; 220 W Manhattan Ave; r from $155; P ✳ @ ☎) Each room in this 200-year-old adobe B&B, south of the river, is unique and loaded with character. Two have their own bathrooms across the hall, the rest have en suites; our favorites are rooms 6 and 12. The full breakfasts satisfy, and rates also include afternoon tea. A separate casita holds two kitchenette suites that can be combined into one.

★ Santa Fe Motel & Inn
HOTEL $$

(Map p256; ☎ 505-982-1039; www.santafemotel. com; 510 Cerrillos Rd; r from $149, casitas from $169; P ✳ @ ☎ ☎) Even the motel rooms in this downtown option, close to the Railyard and a real bargain in low season, have the flavor of a Southwestern B&B, with colorful tiles, clay sunbursts and tin mirrors. The courtyard casitas cost a little more and come with kiva fireplaces and little patios. Rates include a full hot breakfast, served outdoors in summer.

Inn on the Alameda
HOTEL $$

(Map p256; ☎ 888-984-2121; www.innonthe alameda.com; 303 E Alameda St; r from $130, casitas from $250; P ✳ @ ☎ ☎ ☎) Handmade furniture, wood-burning fireplaces, luxe linens, elegant breakfasts and afternoon wine-and-cheese receptions bring B&B-style elegance to a pleasantly efficient hotel. Standard

rooms are inexpensive, but it's the casitas and outdoor hot tubs that make it stand out.

Hotel Chimayo
HOTEL $$

(Map p256; ☎ 505-992-5861; www.hotelchimayo. com; 125 Washington Ave; r from $200; P ✳ ☎ ☎) Decor in this welcoming hotel draws on New Mexico's Hispanic traditions, with abundant attractive carvings and wall hangings, while the Low'n'Slow bar is adorned with gleaming hubcaps and images of low riders. Guest rooms have a warm, comfortable feel, and either share or have their own balconies.

Hotel St Francis
HISTORIC HOTEL $$

(Map p256; ☎ 505-983-5700; www.hotel stfrancis.com; 210 Don Gaspar Ave; r from $200; P ✳ @ ☎ ☎) This large hotel, just south of the Plaza, has benefited from recent modernization while retaining enough whitewashed walls, hand-crafted furniture and woolen rugs to evoke the city's mission-era heritage. Gruet has a lovely little tasting room (p270) here, where you can sample its many sparkling wines. Reserve well ahead.

Inn of the Governors
HOTEL $$

(Map p256; ☎ 800-234-4534; www.innofthe governors.com; 101 W Alameda St; r from $209; P ✳ @ ☎ ☎) A sort of upgraded motel, the Inn of the Governors has a hard-to-beat location two blocks from the Plaza. Rooms are elegantly decorated with kiva fireplaces, warm-hued bedspreads and Southwestern-style doors and windows. Parking is free and the outdoor pool is heated year-round.

★ La Fonda
HISTORIC HOTEL $$$

(Map p256; ☎ 800-523-5002; www.lafonda santafe.com; 100 E San Francisco St; r from $259; P ✳ @ ☎ ☎ ☎) Long renowned as the 'Inn at the end of the Santa Fe Trail,' Santa Fe's loveliest historic hotel sprawls through an old adobe just off the Plaza. Retaining its beautiful folk-art windows and murals, it's both classy and cozy, with some wonderful top-floor luxury suites, and superb sunset views from the rooftop **Bell Tower Bar** (Map p256; 100 E San Francisco St; ☺ 3pm-sunset Mon-Thu, 2pm-sunset Fri-Sun May-Oct).

Inn of the Five Graces
BOUTIQUE HOTEL $$$

(Map p256; ☎ 505-992-0957; www.fivegraces. com; 150 E De Vargas St; r $400-875; P ✳ ☎) Much more than just another luxury getaway, this exquisite, one-of-a-kind gem offers an upscale gypsy-style escape. Sumptuous suites are decorated in a lavish Persian-Indian-Asian-fusion theme, with fireplaces, beautifully tiled kitchenettes and a courtyard behind river-rock walls. The Luminaria Villa ($2500 per night) has two master bedrooms, five fireplaces and all the opulence you'd expect for the price.

La Posada de Santa Fe LUXURY HOTEL **$$$**
(Map p256; 505-986-0000; www.laposadade santafe.com; 330 E Palace Ave; r from $250; P✳@🛜♨🐕) This beautiful property, set amid quiet gardens a few blocks east of the Plaza, caters to its guests' every need, with elegantly furnished adobe casitas outfitted with wood-burning fireplaces, as well as smaller rooms in the original Staab House. There's a fabulous spa, while the cigar-friendly Staab House cocktail bar (11:30am to 11pm) is a local favorite.

🛏 Cerrillos Road & Metro Santa Fe

Rancheros de Santa Fe Campground CAMPGROUND **$**
(Map p276; 505-466-3482; www.rancheros.com; 736 Old Las Vegas Hwy; tent/RV sites $26/45, cabins $53; ⏰mid-Mar–Oct; 🛜♨🐕) Eight miles southeast of the Plaza, off I-25 exit 290, Rancheros is really designed for RV camping, though there are simple cabins here too. It's fairly close to the highway, so expect some noise – tent camping is not recommended. Amenities include laundry, showers, a convenience store and evening movies in summer.

Santa Fe International Hostel HOSTEL **$**
(Map p255; 505-988-1153; www.hostelsantafe.com; 1412 Cerrillos Rd; dm $20, r $25-35; P🛜) This not-for-profit hostel, in a disheveled former motel, is in reach of South Capitol Rail Runner station. Three bare-bones rooms hold six-bed dorms, while the rest have private or shared bathrooms. The communal lounge and kitchen make it easy to meet other travelers, and the pantry is stocked with free food. In exchange, short daily chores are required. Wi-fi is $2; cash only.

Silver Saddle Motel MOTEL **$**
(Map p255; 505-471-7663; www.santafesilver saddlemotel.com; 2810 Cerrillos Rd; r from $62; P✳@🛜🐕) This old-fashioned, slightly kitschy Route 66 motel compound offers the best budget value in town. Some rooms have pleasant tiled kitchenettes, while all have shady wooden arcades outside and cowboy-inspired decor inside – get the Kenny Rogers or Wyatt Earp rooms if you can. It's located 3 miles southwest of the Plaza on busy Cerillos Rd.

El Rey Inn HOTEL **$$**
(Map p255; 505-982-1931; www.elreyinn santafe.com; 1862 Cerrillos Rd; r from $139; P✳@🛜♨) This classic courtyard hotel features super Southwestern-themed rooms and suites, scattered through 5 acres of landscaped gardens. Some rooms have kitchenettes, and the sizable heated outdoor pool has a hot tub alongside. The only downside is the location along busy Cerrillos Rd; rooms closest to the street get some traffic noise.

Inn of the Turquoise Bear B&B **$$**
(Map p255; 800-396-4104; www.turquoisebear.com; 342 E Buena Vista St; r $162-340; P✳🛜🐕) Visitors enjoy the quiet now, but this expansive adobe B&B, built by local legend Witter Bynner and partner Robert Hunt, was once home to parties hosting Thornton Wilder, Robert Oppenheimer, Edna St Vincent Millay, Robert Frost and many others. Surrounded by sculpted gardens, its 11 rooms are named for former house guests, and combine authentic ambience with modern amenities.

Sage Inn HOTEL **$$**
(Map p256; 505-982-5952; www.santafe sageinn.com; 725 Cerrillos Rd; r from $129; P✳@♨🐕) While not exactly boutique accommodations, the 155 well-sized rooms here have appealing Southwestern touches, making the Sage Inn a step up from typical chain motels, within reasonable walking distance of downtown (and right next to Whole Foods). Modern and clean, it's a reasonable option for the budget-minded.

★ Ten Thousand Waves RESORT **$$$**
(Map p276; 505-992-5003; www.tenthousand waves.com; 3451 Hyde Park Rd; r $249-299; P✳🛜🐕) This Japanese spa resort, 4 miles northeast of the Plaza, features 13 gorgeous, Zen-inspired freestanding guesthouses. Most come with fireplaces and either a deck or a courtyard, and all are within walking distance of the mountainside hot tubs and massage cabins. Rates include an organic breakfast and morning access to the Kojiro bath before it opens to the public.

Rates drop during the week; reserve well in advance.

Eating

Food is another art form in Santa Fe, and some restaurants are as world-class as the galleries. From spicy, traditional Southwest favorites to cutting-edge cuisine, it's all here. Reservations are always recommended for the more expensive venues, especially during summer and ski season.

The Plaza & Canyon Road

Tia Sophia's
NEW MEXICAN $

(Map p256; 505-983-9880; www.tiasophias.com; 210 W San Francisco St; mains $7-12; ⊙7am-2pm Mon-Sat, 8am-1pm Sun;) Local artists and visiting celebrities outnumber tourists at this long-standing and always packed Santa Fe favorite. Breakfast is the meal of choice, with fantastic burritos and other Southwestern dishes, but lunch is pretty damn tasty too; try the perfectly prepared *chile rellenos,* or the rota of daily specials. The shelf of kids' books helps little ones pass the time.

Burger Stand at Burro Alley
BURGERS $

(Map p256; 505-989-3360; santafeburgersandbeer.com; 207 W San Francisco St; mains $5-15; ⊙11am-11pm;) This hip burger joint and brewery is good for an easy meal in the Old Town – think cheeseburgers with habanero cactus jam, all-beef hot dogs, veggie and vegan options, and shakes and small-batch beer.

Beestro
CAFE $

(Map p256; 505-629-8786; www.thebeestro.com; 101 W Marcy St; mains $8.25-12.50; ⊙9am-4pm Mon-Fri;) Begun by *Apis mellifera* aficionado Greg Menke, the Beestro features a rotating menu of cafe fare (quinoa

tabbouleh, salads, panini) with an emphasis on locally sourced ingredients. Veggie, paleo and gluten-free options. The same owner also runs the neighboring Hive (p272) and **Root Cellar**, the latter open for dinner and on weekends.

La Boca
TAPAS $$

(Map p256; 505-982-3433; www.laboca santafe.com; 72 W Marcy St; tapas $6-16; ⊙11:30am-3pm & 5-10pm) A casual offshoot of the all-but-identical La Boca restaurant in the courtyard off Lincoln Ave, this relaxed central tapas bar offers a changing but consistently tasty selection of Spanish tapas, from spicy garlic shrimp to artichokes with goat cheese, orange zest and mint. Prices are slashed during happy hour.

Rooftop Pizzeria
PIZZA $$

(Map p256; 505-984-0008; rooftoppizzeria.com; 60 E San Francisco St, Suite 301; pizzas $14-20; ⊙11am-10pm) Up on the 3rd floor of the Santa Fe Arcade, the namesake terrace isn't the only attraction at this gourmet pizzeria – think blue-corn crusts that are thin enough to require a fork and knife, wines by the glass and Bosque beer on tap.

★La Plazuela
NEW MEXICAN $$$

(Map p256; 505-982-5511; www.lafonda santafe.com; 100 E San Francisco St, La Fonda de Santa Fe; lunch $11-22, dinner $15-39; ⊙7am-2pm & 5-10pm Mon-Fri, 7am-3pm & 5-10pm Sat & Sun) One of Santa Fe's greatest pleasures is a meal in the Fonda's irresistible

---

LOCAL MAGIC: CHRISTMAS EVE ON CANYON ROAD

On the night before Christmas, Santa Fe is an ethereal spectacle. A thousand adobe buildings glow warm yellow in the lights of the thousands of *farolitos* – real candles nestled in greased brown paper bags – arrayed along its streets, entranceways and even the roofs of its homes and shops.

Walking down gallery-lined Canyon Rd on Christmas Eve is a uniquely Santa Fe experience, and in our book a magical must. There's something overwhelmingly graceful and elegant about the taste of the frosty air, the look of miles of glowing pathways of tiny candles and comradely quiet, the way the night sky meets softly lit windows filled with fine art.

The magic comes partly from the intoxicating sights and scents of the small roadside piñon and cedarwood bonfires that offer guiding light and unforgettable memories. Partly it's a few equestrians prancing on horseback, jingle bells jangling, clickity-clacking along the narrow street, evoking memories of early Santa Feans who led their burros up the 'Road of the Canyon' to gather firewood in mountain forests. Partly it's the shimmering silhouettes of 250-year-old adobes picked out by rows of twinkling *farolitos*.

Dress warmly and arrive early – say, by 6pm – if you want to beat the crowds. As night falls, the streets fill with human revelers and their canine friends, all giddy with the Christmas spirit. Small groups of carolers sing remarkably in tune. Join them, then pop into a gallery for a cup of spiced cider and a quick perusal of post-Leninist Russian art to warm up.

see-and-be-seen central atrium, with its excited bustle, colorful decor and high-class New Mexican food, with contemporary dishes sharing menu space with standards like fajitas and tamales.

★ **Cafe Pasqual's** NEW MEXICAN $$$
(Map p256; ☎505-983-9340; www.pasquals.com; 121 Don Gaspar Ave; breakfast & lunch $14-18.75, dinner $15-39; ⊙8am-3pm & 5:30-10pm; ⊘⊞)
🖋 Whatever time you visit this exuberantly colorful, utterly unpretentious place, the food, most of which has a definite south-of-the-border flavor, is worth every penny of the high prices. The breakfast menu is famous for dishes such as *huevos motuleños*, made with sautéed bananas, feta cheese and more; later on, the meat and fish mains are superb. Reservations taken for dinner only.

La Casa Sena NEW MEXICAN $$$
(Map p256; ☎505-988-9232; www.lacasasena. com; 125 E Palace Ave; lunch $14-22, dinner $15-39; ⊙11am-10pm) Several downtown restaurants have outdoor seating but this is the prettiest, in the flower-filled garden of an old adobe that also has a snug interior. The New Mexican food's good too, with green chile cheeseburgers available all day, and fancier dinner dishes such as pan-seared scallops. Sit in the Cantina section to be serenaded by singing waitstaff from 6pm onwards.

State Capital Kitchen MODERN AMERICAN $$$
(Map p256; ☎505-467-8237; www.statecapital kitchen.com; 500 Sandoval St; mains $29-34, 5-course tasting menu $64; ⊙5-9pm Tue-Thu, to 10:30pm Fri & Sat) Small plates and seasonal cuisine make this gourmet destination something of an anomaly in Santa Fe. You won't find much chile on the menu – instead expect creations along the lines of seared scallops with foie gras, suckling pig wontons or cassoulet with rabbit sausage. Excellent wine list.

Il Piatto ITALIAN $$$
(Map p256; ☎505-984-1091; www.ilpiattosantafe. com; 95 W Marcy St; lunch $11-14, dinner $24-37; ⊙11:30am-4:30pm Wed-Sat, 4:30-10:30pm daily) This classy but welcoming Italian place, on one of the sleepier blocks north of the Plaza, is a good spot for a romantic dinner. The light, zestful flavors are showcased in dishes such as lemon and rosemary roast chicken and squid ink spaghetti with hot peppers.

✖ Guadalupe Street & the Railyard

Cleopatra's Cafe MIDDLE EASTERN $
(Map p256; ☎505-820-7381; www.cleopatra santafe.com; 418 Cerrillos Rd, Design Center; mains $7-17; ⊙11am-8pm Mon-Sat; 🛜⊘) This simple cafe makes up for a slight deficit in ambience with taste and value: big platters of delicious kebabs, hummus, falafel and other Greek and Middle Eastern favorites. It's hidden within the design center.

Raaga INDIAN $$
(Map p256; ☎505-820-6440; www.raagacuisine. com; 544 Agua Fria St; mains $13-20; ⊙4-9pm Mon-Sat; ⊘) Santa Fe's best Indian restaurant prepares delicious curries, biryanis and tandoori specialties with a refreshingly light touch. One flaw: the chai is lame.

Cowgirl BBQ BARBECUE $$
(Map p256; ☎505-982-2565; www.cowgirl santafe.com; 319 S Guadalupe St; mains $10-23; ⊙11:30am-10:30pm Sun-Thu, 11am-11:30pm Fri & Sat; ⊞) With its juicy barbecue, awesome margaritas, outside patio, billiard room and live music – and its exuberant celebration of the women who made the West – this restaurant-bar is a fun place for all ages; there's even a kids' playground out back. Be sure to try the barbecue brisket, say in a quesadilla with red chile.

Tomasita's NEW MEXICAN $$
(Map p256; ☎505-983-5721; www.tomasitas. com; 500 S Guadalupe St; mains $9-20; ⊙11am-9pm Mon-Thu, to 10pm Fri & Sat; ⊞) Sure this raucous, cavernous, Railyard landmark is always packed with tourists, and most likely you'll have to wait, but it's good – even great – for families hauling exuberant kids. Traditional New Mexican dishes here include burritos and enchiladas, and there are huge blue-plate specials.

Joseph's Culinary Pub FRENCH $$$
(Map p256; ☎505-982-1272; www.josephsof santafe.com; 428 Agua Fria St; mains $24-42; ⊙5:30-10pm, closed Mon Nov-Mar) This romantic old adobe, open for dinner only, is best seen as a fine-dining restaurant rather than a pub. Order from the shorter, cheaper bar menu if you'd rather, but it's worth lingering in the warm-hued dining room to savor rich, hybrid French dishes with a modern twist: think campfire cassoulet with housemade sausage or sweet and spicy duck confit.

Metro Santa Fe

★**La Choza** NEW MEXICAN $
(Map p255; ☑505-982-0909; www.lachozasf.
com; 905 Alarid St; lunch $9-13, dinner $10.50-
18; ⊙11:30am-2pm & 5-9pm Mon-Sat; P ⚙)
Blue-corn burritos, a festive interior and
an extensive margarita list make La Choza
a perennial (and colorful) favorite among
Santa Fe's discerning diners. Of the many
New Mexican restaurants in Santa Fe, this
one always seems to be reliably excellent.
As with the Shed, its sister restaurant,
arrive early or reserve.

Los Potrillos MEXICAN $
(Map p255; ☑505-992-0550; 1947 Cerrillos
Rd; mains $10-15; ⊙9am-9pm Thu-Tue) This
upbeat Mexican restaurant with a hefty
menu is another local favorite – choose
between shrimp fajitas, *chiles en nogada*
(stuffed with beef, pecans and raisins), a
mouthwatering variety of tacos and much,
much more.

Clafoutis FRENCH $
(Map p255; ☑505-988-1809; 333 Cordova Rd;
mains $7-12.50; ⊙7am-4pm Mon-Sat) As Oscar
Wilde once quipped, the only way to get rid
of temptation is to give in, and that pretty
much sums up the approach you should
take at this *super bon* French pâtisserie.
Drop by for delectable pastries (*beignets*
on Saturday!) or sit down for breakfast or
lunch, with a tantalizing selection of crepes,
omelettes, quiches and brie sandwiches.

Horseman's Haven NEW MEXICAN $
(Map p276; ☑505-471-5420; 4354 Cerrillos Rd; mains $7.50-12; ⊙8am-8pm Mon-Sat,
8:30am-2pm Sun; ⚙) Hands down, this
diner has the hottest green chile in town –
faint-hearts, order it on the side. Service
is friendly and fast, and the enormous 3D
burrito – a mighty pile incorporating beans,
rice and potatoes – might be the only thing
you need to eat all day.

★**Jambo Cafe** AFRICAN $$
(Map p255; ☑505-473-1269; www.jambocafe.net;
2010 Cerrillos Rd; mains $9-17; ⊙11am-9pm Mon-
Sat) Hidden within a shopping center, this
African-flavored cafe is hard to spot from
the road; once inside, though, it's a lovely
spot, always busy with locals who love its
distinctive goat, chicken and lentil curries,
veggie sandwiches and roti flatbreads, not
to mention the reggae soundtrack.

El Nido STEAK, ITALIAN $$
(☑505-954-1272; www.elnidosantafe.com; 1577
Bishops Lodge Rd; mains $11-27; ⊙4:30-9:30pm)
Helmed by chef Enrique Guerrero, the
culinary action at this beautiful old steakhouse revolves around the open flame, with
a wood-burning grill, rotisserie and pizza
oven taking center stage in the main dining
room. But don't overlook the housemade
pastas either (pappardelle with wild boar
ragu, or Roman favorite *cacio e pepe*) – it's
all simply *perfetto*. Reservations essential.

Take Bishops Lodge Rd or Hwy 285 north
from Santa Fe to exit 168.

Dr Field Goods NEW MEXICAN $$
(Map p255; ☑505-471-0043; drfieldgoods.com;
2860 Cerrillos Rd, Suite A1; mains $13.50-18;
⊙11am-9pm) This locavore deli has a ded-
icated following, and for good reason – it's
a top pick for a casual bite out on Cerillos
Rd. Diners can choose between free-range
buffalo enchiladas, goat tortas with honey
habanero sauce, grilled fish tostadas and
green chile–pulled pork sandwiches, among
other delicacies. A butcher shop and bakery
is a few doors down.

Harry's Roadhouse AMERICAN, NEW MEXICAN $$
(Map p276; ☑505-989-4629; www.harrysroad
housesantafe.com; 96 Old Las Vegas Hwy; lunch
$8.25-14.25, dinner $9.50-23; ⊙7am-9:30pm;
⚙) This casual longtime favorite on the
southern edge of town feels like a rambling
cottage with its various rooms and patio garden – and there's also a full bar. And, seriously, *everything* here is good. Especially
the desserts.

🍷 Drinking & Nightlife

Talk to 10 residents and you'll get 10 different opinions about where to find the best
margarita. You may have to sample the
lot to decide for yourself – get a Margarita
Trail Passport ($3) at participating bars or
the tourist office to help guide your way;
you'll also receive a $1 discount on signa-
ture drinks.

★**Kakawa Chocolate House** CAFE
(Map p256; ☑505-982-0388; kakawachocolates.
com; 1050 Paseo de Peralta; ⊙10am-6pm Mon-
Sat, noon-6pm Sun) Chocolate addicts simply
can't miss this loving ode to the sacred
bean. This isn't your mom's marshmal-
low-laden hot chocolate, though – these
rich elixirs are based on historic recipes and
divided into two categories: European (eg

17th-century France) and Meso-American (Mayan and Aztec). Bonus: it also sells sublime chocolates (prickly pear mescal) and spicy chili caramels.

★**Santa Fe Spirits**　　　　DISTILLERY
(Map p256; ☑505-780-5906; santafespirits. com; 308 Read St; ⊙3-8:30pm Mon-Thu, to 10pm Fri & Sat) The local distillery's $10 tasting flight includes an impressive amount of liquor, including shots of Colkegan single malt, Wheeler's gin and Expedition vodka. Leather chairs and exposed rafters make the in-town tasting room an intimate spot for an aperitif; fans can reserve a spot on the hourly tours of the distillery.

Counter Culture Cafe　　　　CAFE
(Map p255; ☑505-995-1105; 930 Baca St; ⊙8am-9pm Tue-Sat, to 3pm Sun & Mon; ⧖) Hip hangout in the artsy Baca St compound, with loads of good food made from scratch (cinnamon rolls, lemon ricotta pancakes, tom yum soup) in addition to coffee and live music. Cash only.

Duel Brewing　　　　CRAFT BEER
(Map p276; ☑505-474-5301; duelbrewing.com; 1228 Parkway Dr; ⊙noon-10pm Mon-Thu, to midnight Fri & Sat, 1-8pm Sun) An intimate local brewery near Meow Wolf (p260); come here after the art extravaganza for Belgian-style beers and delicious cheese and charcuterie plates.

Santa Fe Brewing　　　　BREWERY
(Map p276; santafebrewing.com; 35 Fire Pl; ⊙11am-10pm Mon-Fri, to 9pm Sat, 2-8pm Sun) New Mexico's oldest brewery is a bit of a haul, 13 miles southwest of town, but fans of Happy Camper IPA and Santa Fe Gold will want to make the trip for a tour (Saturdays at noon) or to sample limited small batches and seasonal brews.

Fire & Hops　　　　PUB
(Map p256; ☑505-954-1635; fireandhopsgastro pub.com; 222 N Guadalupe St; ⊙5-9:30pm Mon-Fri, 2-9:30pm Sat & Sun) From baseball caps and beards to kale-pesto connoisseurs, this gastropub is often overflowing with an eclectic bunch filling up on green chile poutine and pork belly tacos, all washed down with a laudable selection of craft brews. Parking can be problematic; consider a rideshare instead.

Rowley Farmhouse Ales　　　　BAR
(Map p255; ☑505-428-0719; rowleyfarmhouse. com; 1405 Maclovia St; ⊙11:30am-10pm) This

one's for the beer geeks: it specializes primarily in sours – at least one of which is brewed on-site – and saisons (Belgian-style farmhouse ales), but with 20 brews on tap you'll be sure to find something to your liking.

CrowBar　　　　BAR
(Map p256; ☑505-982-0663; 205 W San Francisco St; ⊙10am-2am Tue-Sat, to midnight Sun) A Dia de los Muertos motif and younger crowd makes this one of the hipper choices for a cocktail or three in the Old Town.

New Mexico Hard Cider Taproom　　　　BAR
(Map p256; ☑505-231-0632; www.nmcider.com; 505 Cerrillos Rd; ⊙3-11pm Mon-Thu, noon-11pm Fri-Sun) Apple, pear and specialty ciders pair up with jalapeño popper paninis and greenchile mac and cheese at this kick-back Railyard taproom.

Gruet Tasting Room　　　　WINE BAR
(Map p256; ☑505-989-9463; Hotel St Francis, 210 Don Gaspar Ave; ⊙11am-7pm) The second-largest winery in New Mexico has a lovely bar in the Hotel St Francis (p265), where you can sample five wines for $10. Wines are mostly sparkling and bottles sell at an excellent price.

☆ Entertainment

Performing Arts

Opera, chamber music, performance and visual arts draw patrons from the world's most glittering cities to Santa Fe in July and August. The opera may be the belle of the ball – clad in sparkling denim – but there is plenty going on throughout the year.

★**Santa Fe Opera**　　　　OPERA
(☑505-986-5900; www.santafeopera.org; Hwy 84/285, Tesuque; backstage tours adult/child $10/free; ⊙Jun-Aug, backstage tours 9am Mon-Fri Jun-Aug) Many visitors flock to Santa Fe for the opera alone: the theater is a marvel, with 360-degree views of sandstone wilderness crowned with sunsets and moonrises, while at center stage the world's finest talent performs magnificent masterworks. It's still the Wild West, though; you can even wear jeans. Shuttles run to and from Santa Fe ($24) and Albuquerque ($39); reserve online.

Lensic Performing Arts Center　　　　PERFORMING ARTS
(Map p256; ☑505-988-7050; www.lensic.com; 211 W San Francisco St) A beautifully renovated 1930 movie house, the theater hosts touring

productions and classic films as well as seven different performance groups, including the Aspen Santa Fe Ballet and the Santa Fe Symphony Orchestra & Chorus.

El Flamenco DANCE
(Map p256; ☎505-209-1302; www.entre flamenco.com; 135 W Palace Ave) Run by Spanish codirectors Antonio Granjero and Estefania Ramirez, this top-flight flamenco company was actually founded in Madrid in 1998, before moving full-time to the US in 2010. Spellbinding performances will likely have you ready to sign up for their drop-in classes the next day.

Santa Fe Playhouse THEATER
(Map p256; ☎505-988-4262; www.santafe playhouse.org; 142 E De Vargas St; ⊘Thu-Sun) The state's oldest theater company performs avant-garde and traditional theater and musical comedy, typically with evening programs Thursday to Saturday plus a Sunday matinee.

Adobe Rose THEATER
(Map p276; ☎505-629-8688; adoberosetheatre. org; 1213B Parkway Dr; ⊘Thu-Sun) Santa Fe's Adobe Rose is the main venue for modern theater, usually staging one production every two months.

Live Music
Warehouse 21 LIVE MUSIC
(Map p255; ☎505-989-4423; www.warehouse21. org; 1614 Paseo de Peralta) This youth-oriented arts and activity center in a 3500-sq-ft warehouse by the Railyard occasionally hosts live-music acts.

Vanessie of Santa Fe CABARET
(Map p256; ☎505-982-9966; www.vanessie santafe.com; 427 W Water St) You don't really come to Vanessie for the food, though there's nothing wrong with it. No, the attraction here is the piano bar, featuring blow-dried lounge singers who bring Neil Diamond and Barry Manilow classics to life in their own special way.

🔒 Shopping

Besides the American Indian jewelry sold directly by the artists under the Plaza *portales* (overhanging arches), Santa Fe holds enough shops for you to spend weeks browsing and buying. And don't pass by the museum gift shops without a gander; they often have an excellent selection of quality art, crafts and jewelry for sale.

★Keshi ARTS & CRAFTS
(Map p256; ☎505-989-8728; keshi.com; 227 Don Gaspar Ave; ⊘10am-5pm Mon-Sat, 11am-5pm Sun) If you don't have the opportunity to visit the Zuni Pueblo, you'll at least want to visit this exquisite gallery. Specializing in Zuni fetishes (tiny animal sculptures, each with a special meaning or power), it's generally believed that the animal chooses you – not the other way around. Staff will leave you with plenty of time to commune with individual pieces.

★Blue Rain ART
(Map p256; ☎505-954-9902; www.bluerain gallery.com; 544 S Guadalupe St; ⊘10am-6pm Mon-Sat) This large space in the Railyard district is the top gallery in town representing contemporary American Indian and regional artists. There are generally several shows on at once, encompassing everything from modern pottery and sculpture to powerful landscapes and portraits.

★Santa Fe Farmers Market MARKET
(Map p256; ☎505-983-4098; www.santafefarmers market.com; Paseo de Peralta & Guadalupe St; ⊘7am-1pm Sat year-round, 7am-1pm Tue, 4-8pm Wed May-Nov; 🚻) Local produce, much of it heirloom and organic, is on sale at this spacious indoor-outdoor market, alongside homemade goodies, inexpensive food, natural body products and arts and crafts.

GAME OF SCREENS

Like many a local resident, *Game of Thrones* author George RR Martin felt a definite tinge of regret each time he walked past Santa Fe's much missed **Jean Cocteau Cinema** (Map p256; ☎505-466-5528; www.jeancocteaucinema. com; 418 Montezuma Ave), which closed its doors in 2006. Unlike his neighbors, however, Martin was in a position to do something about it. He bought the place and reopened it in 2013.

The Cocteau is now once more programming art-house and new-release movies, with Martin's reputation helping to draw in writers and performers for special events. Best of all, it's become a tradition for the cinema to hail each new season of *Game of Thrones* with free advance screenings. Costumed fans wait overnight on the sidewalk outside for Q&A sessions with Martin and the various actors.

SANTA FE GALLERY-HOPPING

Originally a Pueblo Indian footpath and later the main street through a Spanish farming community, Santa Fe's most famous art avenue embarked on its current incarnation in the 1920s, when artists led by Los Cinco Pintores (five painters who fell in love with New Mexico's landscape) moved in to take advantage of the cheap rent.

Today Canyon Rd is a top attraction, holding more than a hundred of Santa Fe's 300-plus galleries. The epicenter of the city's vibrant art scene, it offers everything from rare American Indian antiquities to Santa Fe School masterpieces and in-your-face modern work. If gallery-hopping seems a bit overwhelming, don't worry, just wander.

Friday nights are particularly fun: that's when the galleries put on glittering openings, starting around 5pm. Not only are these great social events, but you can also browse while nibbling on cheese, sipping Chardonnay or sparkling cider, and chatting with the artists.

The following is just a sampling of some Canyon Rd (and around) favorites. For more, pick up the handy, free *Collector's Guide* map, or check out www.santafegallery association.org. More contemporary galleries around the Railyard are definitely worth checking out as well.

Adobe Gallery (Map p256; ☑505-955-0550; www.adobegallery.com; 221 Canyon Rd; ⊙10am-5pm Mon-Sat)

Economos/Hampton Galleries (Map p256; ☑505-982-6347; 500 Canyon Rd; ⊙9:30am-4pm, closed Wed & Sun)

Gerald Peters Gallery (Map p256; ☑505-954-5700; www.gpgallery.com; 1005 Paseo de Peralta; ⊙10am-5pm Mon-Sat)

GF Contemporary (Map p255; ☑505-983-3707; www.gfcontemporary.com; 707 Canyon Rd; ⊙10am-5pm Mon-Sat, noon-5pm Sun)

Marc Navarro Gallery (Map p255; ☑505-986-8191; 520 Canyon Rd; ⊙11am-4pm)

Morning Star Gallery (Map p255; ☑505-982-8187; www.morningstargallery.com; 513 Canyon Rd; ⊙9am-5pm Mon-Sat)

Nedra Matteucci Galleries (Map p256; ☑505-982-4631; www.matteucci.com; 1075 Paseo de Peralta; ⊙9am-5pm Mon-Sat)

Milagro Herbs COSMETICS
(Map p256; ☑505-820-6321; www.milagroherbs.com; 419 Orchard Dr; ⊙10am-5:30pm) Created by ethnobotanist Tomas Enos, Milagro Herbs' organic herb-based salves, essential oils, soaps and tinctures have acquired something of a cult following. It's a bit pricey, but the range of products for sale is pretty impressive. You may also run into them at the Farmers Market.

Hive FOOD
(Map p256; ☑505-780-5084; thehivemarket.com; 101 W Marcy St; ⊙10am-9:30pm Tue-Sat, 10am-6pm Sun & Mon) The boutique offshoot of the Beestro (p267), come here for local raw honey and beeswax candles, in addition to jams and sundry arts and crafts.

TAI Modern ARTS & CRAFTS
(Map p256; ☑505-984-1387; www.taimodern.com; 1601 Paseo de Peralta; ⊙10am-5pm Mon-Sat) Featuring fine bamboo crafts by Japanese masters, along with work by Japanese photographers and textile arts from around the world.

Kowboyz CLOTHING
(Map p256; ☑505-984-1256; www.kowboyz.com; 345 W Manhattan Ave; ⊙10am-5:30pm) Secondhand shop selling everything you need to cowboy up. Shirts are a great deal; the amazing selection of boots, however, demands top dollar. Movie costumers in search of authentic Western wear often come here.

Nambé Foundry Outlet HOMEWARES
(Map p256; ☑505-988-5528; www.nambe.com; 924 Paseo de Peralta; ⊙9am-6pm Mon-Sat, 11am-5pm Sun) Large outlet selling jewelry and home and kitchen items made of Nambéware, a silver-like alloy.

Travel Bug BOOKS
(Map p256; ☑505-992-0418; www.mapsofnew mexico.com; 839 Paseo de Peralta; ⊙7:30am-5:30pm

Mon-Sat, 11am-4pm Sun; 🕾) One of the largest selections of travel books and maps you'll ever find; you can even print topo maps on demand, on waterproof paper. Local travelers, authors and photographers give free talks about their adventures on Saturdays at 5pm. There's also a coffee bar with wi-fi.

Seret & Sons   ARTS & CRAFTS
(Map p256; ☑ 505-988-9151; www.seretandsons. com; 224 Galisteo St; ⊙9am-5pm Mon-Fri, 9am-6pm Sat, 9:30am-5pm Sun) Feel like you've stepped into an Asian or Arabian bazaar at this warehouse-like emporium of art and sculpture, overflowing with gorgeous Afghan rugs, Tibetan furniture, giant stone elephants and solid teak doors. Getting such treasures home is easier said than done, but it's fun just to browse too.

Jackalope   ARTS & CRAFTS
(Map p255; ☑ 505-471-8539; www.jackalope. com; 2820 Cerrillos Rd; ⊙9am-6pm) Essential pieces of Southwest decor – albeit largely imported from Mexico – can all be yours at this sprawling shop. Start with a cow skull like the ones Georgia O'Keeffe made famous, snap up a kiva ladder, add some colorful pottery and Navajo pot holders and you'll be set. Don't leave without watching live prairie dogs frolic in their 'village.'

Nambé Foundry Outlet   HOMEWARES
(Map p256; ☑ 505-988-3574; www.nambe.com; 104 W San Francisco St; ⊙9am-6pm Mon-Sat, 10am-5pm Sun) Nambéware, a unique metal alloy that looks like silver without containing silver, lead or pewter, was developed near Nambé, north of Santa Fe, in 1951. Gleaming, elegant bowls, plates and vases, individually sand-cast, are now an essential component of Santa Fe style. There's another, larger outlet facing the start of Canyon Rd.

Nathalie   CLOTHING
(Map p256; ☑ 505-982-1021; www.nathalie santafe.com; 503 Canyon Rd; ⊙10am-5pm Mon-Sat) Come here for exquisite cowboy and cowgirl gear, including gemstone-studded gun holsters, handmade leather, denim couture and lingerie for that saloon girl with a heart of gold. The Spanish Colonial antiques are stunning.

Garcia Street Books   BOOKS
(Map p256; ☑ 505-986-0151; www.garciastreet books.com; 376 Garcia St; ⊙9am-6pm Mon-Sat, to 5pm Sun) Scavengers are rewarded with

excellent bargains as well as the town's best selection of art books, and rarities like the woodblock prints of Willard Clark.

ℹ Information

EMERGENCY
Police (☑ 505-428-3710; 2515 Camino Entrada)

MEDICAL SERVICES
Christus St Vincent Hospital (☑ 505-983-3361; www.stvin.org; 455 St Michaels Dr; ⊙24hr emergency)
Walgreens (☑ 505-982-9811; 1096 S St Francis Dr; ⊙24hr)

POST
Post Office (Map p256; 120 S Federal Pl; ⊙8am-5:30pm Mon-Fri, 9am-4pm Sat)

TOURIST INFORMATION
Santa Fe Visitor Center (Map p256; ☑ 800-777-2489; www.santafe.org; 66 E San Francisco St, Suite 3, Plaza Galeria; ⊙10am-6pm) Several locations in town; most convenient is in the central Plaza Galeria.
New Mexico Visitor Information Center (Map p256; ☑ 505-827-7336; www.newmexico.org; 491 Old Santa Fe Trail; ⊙8am-5pm Mon-Fri, 8am-4pm Sat & Sun) Housed in the historic 1878 Lamy Building, this friendly place offers helpful advice and free coffee.
Public Lands Information Center (Map p276; ☑ 505-954-2002; www.publiclands.org; 301 Dinosaur Trail; ⊙8:30am-4pm Mon-Fri) Staff at this hugely helpful office have maps and information on public lands throughout New Mexico, and can talk you through all the hiking options.

ℹ Getting There & Around

The great majority of visitors reach and explore Santa Fe by car, but the city does have good transport connections with Albuquerque.

AIR
Daily flights to/from Denver, Dallas and Phoenix serve the small **Santa Fe Municipal Airport** (SAF; Map p276; ☑ 505-955-2900; www. santafenm.gov/airport; 121 Aviation Dr), 10 miles southwest of downtown.

BUS
The **Sandia Shuttle Express** (☑ 888-775-5696; www.sandiashuttle.com; $30) connects Santa Fe with the Albuquerque Sunport.

North Central Regional Transit (☑ 505-629-4725; www.ncrtd.org) provides free shuttle bus service from downtown Santa Fe to Española on weekdays, where you can transfer to shuttles to Taos, Los Alamos, Ojo Caliente and other northern destinations. Pick-up/drop-off is by the Santa Fe Trails bus stop on Sheridan St, a block northwest of the Plaza.

On weekends, the **Taos Express** (☑ 866-206-0754; www.taosexpress.com; one way $5; ☺ Sat & Sun) runs north to Taos from the corner of Guadalupe and Montezuma Sts, by the Railyard.

The free **Santa Fe Pick-Up** meets arriving RailRunner trains and loops around downtown until 5:30pm; it also heads out to Museum Hill. **Santa Fe Trails** (Map p256; ☑ 505-955-2001; www.santafenm.gov; one way adult/child $1/free, day pass $2) operates buses from the Downtown Transit Center, with routes M, to Museum Hill, and 2, along Cerrillos Rd, being the most useful for visitors.

The **RTD Mountain Trail** bus serves Ski Santa Fe (passing 10,000 Waves); the fare is $5 each way. Downtown pick-up is at the corner of Sandoval and Water Sts. In summer, bike racks are available on a first-come, first-served basis; the return trip to town is free.

TRAIN
The **Rail Runner** (www.nmrailrunner.com; adult/child $10/5) commuter train offers eight daily connections (four on weekends) with Albuquerque from its terminus in the Railyard and the South Capitol Station, a mile southwest. The trip takes about 1¾ hours. Arriving passengers can make use of the free Santa Fe Trails bus network. **Amtrak** (☑ 800-872-7245; www.amtrak.com) serves Lamy station, 17 miles southeast, with 30-minute bus connections to Santa Fe.

AROUND SANTA FE

Don't get too comfortable in Santa Fe, because there's plenty to explore nearby. Whichever direction you head in, you'll enjoy some of New Mexico's finest scenery, from pine forests to rainbow-colored canyons, mesa lands to mountain views. This area also offers the state's best hot-spring resort, streams made for fly-fishing, endless hiking trails and museums celebrating everything from Pueblo crafts to the building of the atom bomb. Small towns reveal unexpected treasures – from beautiful adobe churches to fabulous local restaurants to studios where artists and artisans create and sell their work.

Northern Pueblos

The eight Northern Pueblos are located north of Santa Fe, mostly in the Rio Grande Valley. They include (from south to north): Tesuque (Map p276; ☑ 505-983-2667), Pojoaque (Map p276; ☑ 505-455-4500; www.pojoaque.org; Hwy

285), Nambé (p283), San Ildefonso (Map p276; ☑ 505-455-2273; www.sanipueblo.org; Hwy 502; per vehicle $10, camera/video/sketching permits $10/20/25; ☺ 8am-5pm), Santa Clara (Map p276; ☑ 505-753-7330), Ohkay Owingeh (Map p276; ☑ 505-852-4400), Picuris (p285) and Taos (p298). Apart from Taos and during village festivals, these communities are not usually tourist destinations; however, there are a few places that are definitely worth a stop. See www.indianpueblo.org for a list of specific feast days and etiquette to observe when visiting.

Tesuque Pueblo

Nine miles north of Santa Fe along Hwy 84/285 is Tesuque Pueblo, whose members played an important role in the Pueblo Revolt of 1680, and later suffered as a result. Today, the reservation encompasses more than 17,000 acres of spectacular landscape, including sections of the Santa Fe National Forest. The San Diego Feast Day (November 12) features dancing, but as a general rule the Pueblo itself does not encourage visitors.

SHOPPING FOR AMERICAN INDIAN ART

Santa Fe's best shopping is beneath the *portales* (overhanging arcades) in front of the **Palace of the Governors** (p254), to which Pueblo Indians travel as far as 200 miles to sell gorgeous handmade jewelry. The tradition started in the 1880s, when Tesuque artisans first greeted arriving trains with all manner of wares. Today up to 1200 members, representing almost every New Mexican tribe, draw lots for the 76 spaces under the vigas each morning. Those lucky enough to procure the desirable spots display bracelets, pendants, fetishes (small carved images) and thick engraved silver wedding bands on bright blankets. Classic turquoise and silver jewelry is the most popular, but you'll find many other regional stones in a rainbow of colors. Most artists are happy to tell you the story behind each piece in his or her open-air gallery – and most are one-of-a-kinds. Not only are the prices better here than in a store but the money goes directly back to the source: the artist. Only attempt to bargain if it's suggested; the vendors may find it insulting.

Pojoaque Pueblo

Although the history of Pojoaque Pueblo predates the Spaniards, a smallpox epidemic in the late 19th century killed most of its inhabitants, and forced the rest to evacuate. No old buildings remain. The few survivors intermarried with other Pueblo people and Hispanics, and a handful returned to the Pueblo in 1932, working to rebuild its traditions, crafts and culture. Their descendants now number about 300 – most of those who live on the Pueblo's land are not American Indian.

The annual Virgin de Guadalupe Procession and Feast Day on December 11 and 12 is celebrated with ceremonial dancing.

☉ Sights

Poeh Cultural Center & Museum   MUSEUM
(Map p276; ☑505-455-5041; www.poehcenter. com; 78 Cities of Gold Rd, Pojoaque; by donation; ☺9am-5pm Mon-Fri, 10am-5pm Sat) Set up by the Pojoaque Pueblo's former governor, artist George Rivera, this center features superb displays on the history and culture of the Pueblo, tracing the story of the Tewa-speaking people from their emergence into this earth. Outside of the museums in Albuquerque and Santa Fe, this is the best place to start if you're interested in visiting the Santa Fe–area Pueblos. A collection of ceramics has recently been repatriated from the Smithsonian Institution. It's located right off Hwy 285.

✕ Eating

El Parasol   NEW MEXICAN $
(☑505-455-7185; www.elparasol.com; 30 Cities of Gold Rd, Pojoaque; mains $3-6; ☺8am-9pm Mon-Sat, 9am-5pm Sun) Although Espagñola's unassuming trailer is still regarded as the best, the Pojoaque outlet is certainly worth a stop. Order at least two chicken-guacamole tacos – handfuls of greasy goodness – or the succulent *carne adovada* (pork in red chile). Look for the colorful beach umbrella off of Hwy 285, just north of the Poeh Cultural Center.

☆ Entertainment

Buffalo Thunder Resort   CASINO
(Map p276; ☑877-455-7775; www.buffalothunder resort.com; 20 Buffalo Thunder Trail) The largest casino in northern New Mexico, the resort here also has a Hilton Hotel, a spa and a golf course. It's 14 miles north of Santa Fe.

OFF THE BEATEN TRACK

PECOS NATIONAL HISTORIC PARK

When the Spanish first reached **Pecos Pueblo** (Map p276; ☑505-757-7241; www.nps.gov/peco; ☺8am-6pm May-Sep, 8:30am-4pm Oct-Apr) **FREE**, they found a five-story, 700-room structure that was a major center for trade between the Pueblo peoples and the Plains Indians to the east. The Spaniards completed a church in 1625, but it was destroyed during the 1680 Pueblo Revolt. A mission church was rebuilt in 1717; today its ruins, alongside remnants of the Pueblo, are the main attraction. It takes around an hour to explore the site thoroughly.

After reaching a peak of 2000 inhabitants, the Pueblo gradually declined, and in 1838 its 17 remaining inhabitants moved to Jemez Pueblo (p279). It's located 30 miles southwest of Santa Fe via I-25 (toward Las Vegas).

San Ildefonso Pueblo

Eight miles west of Pojoaque along Hwy 502, this ancient Pueblo traces its origins back to Bandelier and Mesa Verde. It's best known now as the birthplace of Maria Martinez, who, in 1919, along with her husband, Julian, revived a distinctive traditional black-on-black pottery style. Her work is now world famous and is considered by collectors to be among the finest pottery ever produced.

Several exceptional potters work in the Pueblo, and many different styles are produced, but black-on-black remains San Ildefonso's hallmark. Don't be surprised by irregular studio hours, and if you are considering purchasing a piece, expect to pay at a minimum hundreds of dollars.

Visitors are welcome to Feast Day (January 23) and corn dances, held throughout the summer.

Santa Clara Pueblo

Santa Clara Pueblo itself, just a mile southwest of Española along Hwy 30, springs to life in summer for the Harvest and Blue Corn Dances on Santa Clara Feast Day (August 12) and St Anthony's Feast Day (June 13). During the rest of the year,

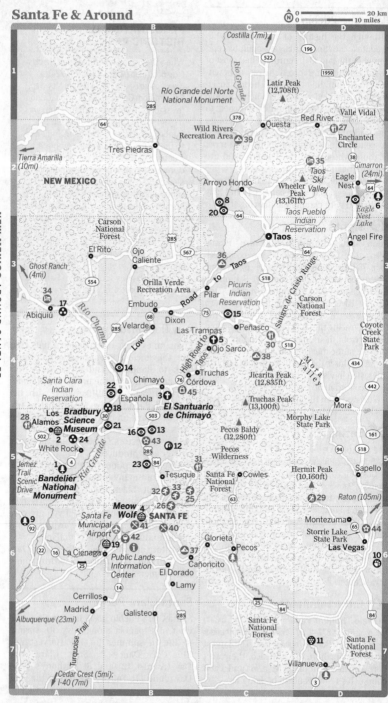

Santa Fe & Around

NEW MEXICO AROUND SANTA FE

various galleries and private homes sell intricately patterned black pottery, but the main reason visitors come here is to see the nearby Puyé Cliff Dwellings.

◎ Sights

Puyé Cliff Dwellings ARCHAEOLOGICAL SITE
(Map p276; www.puyecliffs.com; 300 Hwy 30; adult/child 1hr tour $25/20, 2hr tour $40/35; ⊙hourly tours 9am-6pm Apr-Sep, 9:30am-4pm Oct-Mar) Two separate hour-long tours explore these ancient ruins, 5 miles west of the Santa Clara Pueblo at the entrance to Santa Clara Canyon. Abandoned around 1500, they're similar in style to those at Bandelier National Monument (p280). The most

impressive are sculpted into the cliffside, with the rest freestanding on the mesa-top above. The big appeal is that the Pueblo guides who show you around are directly descended from their original inhabitants, thus providing an actual connection with the vanished past.

Ohkay Owingeh Pueblo

Ohkay Owingeh Pueblo, 5 miles north of Española, was visited in 1598 by Juan de Oñate, who named it San Juan and briefly designated it as the first capital of New Mexico. When it reverted to its original Tewa name in 2005, statues of Popé, who was born here and became the prime instigator of the 1680 Pueblo Revolt, were erected both here in the Pueblo plaza and in Statuary Hall in the US Congress in Washington, DC.

Public events include the Basket Dance (January), Deer Dance (January or February), Corn Dance (June 13), San Juan Feast Day (June 23–24) and a series of Catholic and traditional dances and ceremonies (December 24–26).

The **Native Arts Gallery** (Map p276; ☑505-2369941; 160 Popay Ave, Ohkay Owingeh; ⊙10am-6pm Tue-Sat) stocks a small selection of traditional crafts.

Los Alamos

☑505 / POP 12,019 / ELEV 7320FT

When the top-secret Manhattan Project sprang to life in 1943, it turned the sleepy mesa-top village of Los Alamos into a busy laboratory of secluded brainiacs. Here, in the 'town that didn't exist,' the atomic bomb was developed in almost total secrecy. Humanity can trace some of its greatest achievements and darkest fears directly to this little town. Los Alamos National Laboratory still develops weapons, but it's also at the cutting edge of other scientific discoveries, including mapping the human genome and making mind-boggling supercomputing advances.

Los Alamos remains a place unto itself, where the Lab dominates everything; it has the highest concentration of PhDs per capita in the US, along with the highest per-capita income in New Mexico. In principle, the setting is beautiful, amid the national forest,

CHURCH OF SAN JOSÉ DE GRACIA

Begun in 1760 and constantly defended against Apache raids, the **Church of San José de Gracia** (Map p276; ☑505-351-4360; Hwy 76, Las Trampas; ⊙by appointment, call ahead) in tiny Las Trampas is considered one of the finest surviving 18th-century churches in the USA. Original paintings and carvings remain in excellent condition, and self-flagellation bloodstains from the Los Hermanos Penitentes (a 19th-century secretive religious order with a strong following in the northern mountains of New Mexico) are still visible.

but successive disastrous fires, including the colossal Las Conchas blaze of 2011, have left the surrounding hillsides eerily barren.

◉ Sights & Activities

Outside of town, there's some good rock climbing (with plenty of top-roping), including the **Overlook** and the **Playground** in the basalt cliffs east of Los Alamos.

★ **Bradbury Science Museum** MUSEUM
(Map p276; ☑505-667-4444; www.lanl.gov/museum; 1350 Central Ave; ⊙10am-5pm Tue-Sat, 1-5pm Sun & Mon) FREE You can't actually visit the Los Alamos National Laboratory, where the first atomic bomb was conceived, but the Bradbury Science Museum has compelling displays on the bomb's development and the political context of the time, along with modern research in medical and computer sciences. Two 15-minute films introduce the history of the Manhattan Project and the Lab's current task of maintaining the nuclear stockpile.

Valles Caldera National Preserve NATIONAL PARK
(☑575-829-4100; www.nps.gov/vall; Hwy 4; per vehicle $20; ⊙8am-6pm mid-May–Oct, 9am-5pm Nov–mid-May) Ever wondered what the crater of a dormant supervolcano looks like 1.25 million years after it first blows? At Valles Caldera, the prehistoric explosion was so massive, some 95 cubic miles of pumice, ash and magma was sent into the atmosphere. Home to New Mexico's largest elk herd, the 13.7-mile-wide caldera now consists of volcanic domes and vast meadows that contain miles of hiking and mountain-biking trails in summer and snowshoeing and cross-country skiing trails in winter.

There are no paved roads; a 4WD vehicle is recommended in snow and rain. In summer, 35 free daily permits are available for vehicles.

Los Alamos Historical Museum MUSEUM
(Map p276; ☑505-662-6272; www.losalamoshistory.org; 1050 Bathtub Row; ⊙9:30am-4:30pm Mon-Fri, 11am-4pm Sat & Sun) FREE Housed in a former school building, this interesting museum displays pop-culture artifacts from the atomic age and details the everyday social history of life 'on the hill' during the secret project, as well as other exhibits on area geology and anthropology. Pick up one of the self-guided downtown walking-tour pamphlets.

SCENIC DRIVE: JEMEZ MOUNTAIN TRAIL

West of Los Alamos, Hwy 4 twists and curves through the heart of the Jemez Mountains, on a sublime scenic drive that's made even better by all the places to stop.

The first spot you'll pass is the **Valles Caldera National Preserve** (p278), which is basically what the crater of a dormant supervolcano looks like 1,250,000 years after it first blows. (The explosion was so massive, debris were thrown as far away as Kansas.) Home to New Mexico's largest elk herd, the depression now consists of vast meadows from which hills rise like pine-covered islands. There are miles of hiking and mountain-biking trails in summer and snowshoeing and cross-country skiing trails (groomed and backcountry) in winter. There are no paved roads; a 4WD vehicle is recommended when weather is bad, or if you want to drive through the area in summer, 35 free daily permits are available for vehicles.

The **Las Conchas Trail**, which starts between mile markers 37 and 36, is the next temptation en route. It's a lovely place to hike, following the east fork of the Jemez River for its first 2 miles before climbing out of the canyon.

As you continue along Hwy 4, you can hike into a number of natural hot springs. One of the most accessible is **Spence Hot Springs**, between miles 25 and 24. The temperature's only about 95°F, but it's a gorgeous setting and the inevitable weird naked guy adds authenticity to the experience. For something more rewarding, seek out **San Antonio Hot Springs** – it's a 5-mile hike to the pools, but it's worth it. From Hwy 4, take Hwy 126 and watch for signs for Forest Rd 376 and the trailhead.

The pretty village of Jemez Springs was built around a cluster of hot springs, as was the ruined pueblo at the small **Jemez Historic Site** (📞575-829-3530; www.nmmonuments. org; Hwy 4; adult/child $5/free, joint Coronado ticket $7; ☉8:30am-5pm Wed-Sun). You can experience the waters yourself at the outdoor **Giggling Springs** (📞575-829-9175; www. gigglingsprings.com; 40 Abousleman Loop; per 1/2hr $25/40; ☉11am-5pm Wed-Mon).

Eat at the cavernous **Los Ojos Restaurant & Saloon** (📞575-829-3547; www. losojossaloon.com; Hwy 4; mains $9-13; ☉11am-10pm Mon-Sat, 8am-10pm Sun), usually peopled by some real Wild West characters. If you want to spend the night, try **Cañon del Rio B&B** (📞575-829-4377; www.canondelrio.com; 16445 Hwy 4, Jemez Springs; r $129-139; 🛜📷).

Make sure not to speed through **Jemez Pueblo**, 10 miles south of Jemez Springs. The **Walatowa Visitor Center** (📞575-834-7235; www.jemezpueblo.com; 7413 Hwy 4, Jemez Pueblo; ☉8am-5pm Apr-Oct, 10am-4pm Wed-Sun Nov-Mar) houses a sort-of-interesting museum of Pueblo culture. If you're into wine, take a little detour to **Ponderosa Valley Winery** (www.ponderosawinery.com; 3171 Hwy 290; ☉10am-5pm Tue-Sat, noon-5pm Sun) before emerging onto Hwy 550, between Bernalillo and Cuba. From there, continue on to Albuquerque, back to Santa Fe, or up toward Chaco Canyon and the Four Corners.

Art Center at Fuller Lodge
MUSEUM

(📞505-662-1635; www.fullerlodgeartcenter.com; 2132 Central Ave; ☉10am-4pm Mon-Sat) **FREE** Built in 1928 to serve as the dining hall for the local boys' school, Fuller Lodge, alongside the historical museum, was purchased by the US government for the Manhattan Project. The Art Center mounts mixed-media shows of local and national artists.

Pajarito Mountain
Ski Area
SKIING, MOUNTAIN BIKING

(Map p276; 📞505-662-5725; www.skipajarito. com; lift tickets adult/child $49/34; ☉Dec-early Apr) Ever wanted to ski down the rim of a volcano? This ski area, 7 miles west of downtown, has 40 runs – from easy groomers to challenging bumps – plus a terrain park. In summer, lifts run on weekends ($26) for some serious mountain-biking action, including courses with jump ramps and log rides.

🍴 Eating

Los Alamos is not a place where many tourists choose to spend the night, but a handful of chain motels cater to visiting scientists.

Pyramid Cafe
MEDITERRANEAN $

(Map p276; 📞505-661-1717; www.pyramidcafesf. com; 751 Central Ave; mains $7.50-18; ☉11am-3pm & 4:30-8:30pm Mon-Fri, from noon Sat) Middle Eastern food keeps hungry locals happy here: gyros, falafel and moussaka bring in the crowds – or maybe it's the Turkish coffee.

Blue Window Bistro
AMERICAN $$

(Map p276; 505-662-6305; www.labluewindow bistro.com; 813 Central Ave; lunch $10-12.50, dinner $11.25-28.50; 11am-2:30pm Mon-Fri, 5-8:30pm Mon-Sat) On the north side of the shopping center, this brightly colored cafe is Los Alamos' best dining option. It offers lunchtime gyros and poached salmon, and dinners such as Southwestern chicken and double-cut pork chops.

ⓘ Information

Los Alamos Visitor Center (505-662-8105; www.visitlosalamos.org; 109 Central Park Sq; 9am-5pm Mon-Fri, 9am-4pm Sat, 10am-3pm Sun)

ⓘ Getting There & Around

Los Alamos is 34 miles northwest of Santa Fe on Hwy 502; figure on an hour's drive. To continue west on Hwy 501 into the Jemez Mountains, you will need to pass through a checkpoint. American residents just need to show a driver's license; foreigners should be prepared to show a passport.

One reason Los Alamos makes such a perfect spot for a top-secret base is its extraordinary geography. The town stretches along a series of finger-thin, high-sided mesas, which makes it easy to restrict access to unwanted visitors. It also makes it a baffling place to drive around; follow signs to access the small town center, where Central Ave is the main axis, and don't try to explore further afield. If you do, you will in any case soon come up against security roadblocks.

Bandelier National Monument

The sublime, peach-colored cliffs of Frijoles Canyon, pocked with caves and alcoves that were home to Ancestral Puebloans until the mid-1500s, are the main attraction at **Bandelier National Monument** (Map p276; 505-672-3861; www.nps.gov/band; Hwy 4; per vehicle $20; dawn-dusk;), 12 miles south of Los Alamos and an hour's drive from Santa Fe. A popular day trip, this is one of the most accessible and largest cliff dwellings in New Mexico, and it's rewarding whether you're interested in ancient Southwestern cultures or just want to walk among the pines and watch the light glowing off the canyon walls.

◎ Sights

Tsankawi Ruins
ARCHAEOLOGICAL SITE

(Map p276; Hwy 4;) On the way to the main canyon you'll pass these little-visited ruins, located near the intersection of Hwy 502 and Hwy 4. If you're out for a full day and have the time, definitely stop here. A 1.5-mile loop trail follows an ancient footpath, up ladders to the mesa top to visit the ruins of a 15th-century Pueblo, before winding down the cliff face on the opposite side, passing cave dwellings and petroglyphs.

Unexcavated and undeveloped, the trail feels much more wild than the main canyon, and the landscapes are simply spectacular. There are no roadside signs for the trailhead. As soon as you turn onto Hwy 4, keep your eyes peeled for a gravel parking lot on the left-hand side – it's less than a quarter-mile from the intersection.

⌂ Sleeping

Bandelier has two camping options: car camping at **Juniper Campground** or backcountry camping (free permit required). Backcountry camping is restricted to mesa tops from July to mid-September because of flood danger.

Basic sandwiches are available in the gift shop at the visitor center; it's best if you bring all your own food.

Juniper Campground
CAMPGROUND $

(Map p276; 877-444-6777; www.recreation.gov; campsites $12) Set among the pines near the monument entrance, the park campground holds about 100 campsites, drinking water, toilets, picnic tables and fire grates, but no showers or hookups.

ⓘ Information

Visitor Center (9am-6pm mid-May–mid-Oct, to 5pm rest of year) Has a small museum, self-guided booklets for sale ($1), hiking and backpacking information, and a snack bar. It also runs some great programs, including a once-weekly silent night walk through the main canyon in summer.

ⓘ Getting There & Away

Between May 14 and October 15, visitors cannot drive into the park between 9am and 3pm. Park 8.5 miles north of the Bandelier entrance at the **White Rock Visitor Center** (Hwy 4), and ride a free shuttle bus from there. Factor in additional time to your visit.

Abiquiú

505 / POP 231 / ELEV 6063FT

The tiny adobe village of Abiquiú (rhymes with *barbeque*) is famous thanks to Georgia O'Keeffe, who lived and painted here. With the Rio Chama flowing through farmland, spectacular red rock formations and distant mesas that glow purple in the sunset, the ethereal landscape continues to lure artists.

Abiquiú is on Hwy 84, about 48 miles northwest of Santa Fe and 61 miles west of Taos.

☉ Sights

Georgia O'Keeffe Home HOUSE
(📞505-685-4539; www.okeeffemuseum.org; tours $35-65; ⊙Tue-Sat mid-Mar–mid-Nov) Georgia O'Keeffe died in 1986, at age 98. The Spanish Colonial adobe house she restored is open for guided visits, run by the Georgia O'Keeffe Museum in Santa Fe. Standard tours last one hour, while 'Behind the Scenes' tours are significantly longer. All tend to be booked months in advance, so plan way ahead.

Ghost Ranch HISTORIC SITE
(📞505-685-1000; www.ghostranch.org; US Hwy 84; day pass adult/child $5/3; ♿) From 1934 onwards, before she made her home in Abiquiú, Georgia O'Keeffe lived and worked for extended periods on a dude ranch amid the colorful bluffs 15 miles northwest. Now a retreat center run by the Presbyterian Church, Ghost Ranch welcomes visitors and **overnight guests** (tent & RV sites $25, dm $69, r with/without bath from $119/109; ✳@). Most visitors come here for the hiking trails, the most famous of which is the 3-mile round-trip climb to Chimney Rock.

This distinctive landmark is visible from the highway, but the steep hike up to reach it, which takes around 40 minutes each way, is truly superb. Stupendous views unfold the higher you climb, while Chimney Rock itself, an enormous pillar breaking off from the mesa-top, is breathtaking.

Other activities at Ghost Ranch include guided tours covering themes such as Georgia O'Keeffe or the various movies (such as *City Slickers*) that have been filmed here, as well as horseback riding for riders of all levels ($85). Two small and unremarkable exhibits on local anthropology and paleontology are on display at the ranch museum.

**Monastery of Christ
in the Desert** MONASTERY
(📞505-990-8581; www.christdesert.org; off Hwy 84; ⊙8am-6pm) 🍃**FREE** Day visitors are welcome at this ecosustainable Benedictine monastery, set in a secluded geological wonderland, for a unique spiritual–architectural experience. So long as road conditions comply (check the website), simply follow Forest Service Rd 151, a dirt road that leaves Hwy 84 just north of Ghost Ranch, for 13 beautiful miles.

If you want to get away from it all for an extended time, you can also stay at the monastery (two-night minimum). Rates for the simple rooms ($90), most of which are single and share bathrooms, include vegetarian meals served without conversation, plus contemplative trails and peace and quiet. Requested – not required – chores include minding the gift shop or tending the garden.

The monks also own their own brewery (Abbey Brewing – closed to the public), which produces Belgian-style Monk's Ales. You can find them at some grocery stores in New Mexico, notably Whole Foods.

Poshuouinge Ruins RUINS
(Map p276; Hwy 84) **FREE** The site of a 15th-century 700-room Pueblo, Poshuouinge (Village above the Muddy River) today is little more than prairie dog burrows and earthen mounds indicating the dual-plaza footprint. Nevertheless, amateur archaeologists may enjoy following the half-mile trail up to the overlook. The Forest Service parking lot is 2.4 miles east of Abiquiú, near Family Dollar.

🛏 Sleeping

Most visitors spend the night at Ghost Ranch or visit for the day from Santa Fe or Taos.

Rio Chama Campground CAMPGROUND $
(Forest Service Rd 151; campsites free; ⊙mid-Apr–Oct; ♿) Riverside camping with 11 sites surrounded by brilliant colored cliffs, birds and the silence of the Chama River Canyon Wilderness. It's 1 mile south of the Monastery of Christ in the Desert. There's no drinking water available. First-come, first-served.

Abiquiú Inn HOTEL $$
(Map p276; 📞505-685-4378; www.abiquiuinn. com; US Hwy 84; r from $110, casitas from $120; 🅿📶) This sprawling riverside collection of shaded faux-dobes is peaceful and lovely; some of the spacious rooms have kitchenettes.

🍴 Eating

Dining choices here are few and far between.

Bode's General Store
DELI **$**

(www.bodes.com; US Hwy 84; mains $4-12; ⊙10:30am-3pm Sun-Thu, 5-8pm Fri & Sat; 🛜) Located at the base of Abiquiú along the highway, Bode's (pronounced boh-*dees*) has been here ever since 1919. This is the place to buy everything from artsy postcards and groceries to fishing lures and saddle blankets. Grab a sandwich or tamale at the deli and hang out with the locals. The store itself opens at 6:30am.

Cafe Abiquiú
NEW MEXICAN **$$**

(☑505-685-4378; www.abiquiuinn.com; Abiquiú Inn; lunch $10-14, dinner $21-26; ⊙7am-8pm; 🛜) The restaurant in the main lodge building at the Abiquiú Inn is the nicest place to eat for miles around. You'll find the usual array of New Mexico specialties, though don't expect anything spectacular on the culinary front.

Ojo Caliente

☑505 / POP 816 / ELEV 6983FT

At over 140 years old, Ojo Caliente, 50 miles north of Santa Fe on Hwy 285, is one of the oldest health resorts in the US – and Pueblo Indians were using the hot springs long before that. The resort itself holds soaking pools with various combinations of minerals, as well as a glorious mud bath. Hit the sauna and steam room before indulging in a superpampering spa treatment, a yoga class in a yurt or hiking one of the trails. Admission to the pools is free for resort guests.

🏃 Activities

Hot Springs
HOT SPRINGS

(day pass Mon-Thu $20, Fri-Sun $32; ⊙8am-10pm) Ojo Caliente has 11 unique pools, including unusual mineral springs such as the arsenic pool (good for arthritis), the lithia pool and the iron pool. Other notable features include the meditative soda pool, the ever-popular mud bath and three private pools. If you arrive after 6pm on a weekday, rates drop to $16.

Children under 12 are welcome, but only in the Large Pool between 10am and 6pm.

🛏 Sleeping

The majority of guests stay at the hot springs resort.

Ojo Caliente Mineral Springs Resort & Spa
RESORT **$$**

(☑505-583-2233; www.ojospa.com; 50 Los Baños Rd; r $189, cottages $229, ste $299-399, tent &

RV $40; ❋🛜) In addition to pleasant, if nothing-special, historic hotel rooms, the resort has added some plush, boldly colored suites with kiva fireplaces and private soaking tubs, and New Mexican–style cottages. Rates drop from Monday to Thursday. Note that hot springs access is not included for campers.

Inn at Ojo
B&B **$$**

(☑505-583-9131; www.ojocaliente.com; 11 Los Baños Dr; s/d $110/130; ❋🛜) This friendly small-scale alternative to the resort hotel, on the main approach road a short walk from the springs, offers bright, tastefully decorated rooms above a mercantile store, plus full breakfasts, with gluten-free options available.

🍴 Eating

There are a few eating options along the highway, though most guests eat at the hot springs resort.

Mesa Vista Cafe
MEXICAN **$**

(☑505-583-2245; Hwy 285; lunch $3.10-8.35, dinner $7.50-15; ⊙8am-8pm, shorter hours Nov-Apr) Simple diner on the highway near the resort, serving New Mexican favorites with several veggie options as well as a recommended red chile cheeseburger and the always-intriguing 'spam burger'.

Artesian Restaurant
AMERICAN **$$**

(www.ojospa.com; Hwy 285; lunch $11-16, dinner $16-32; ⊙7:30-11am, 11:30am-2:30pm & 5-9pm; 🛜✍) 🍃 The smart but relaxed dining room at the resort is open for all meals, and prepares organic and local ingredients with aplomb. The wine bar here opens at 3pm.

High Road to Taos

Go on, take the high road. Of the two routes between Santa Fe and Taos, the famous High Road isn't necessarily any prettier than the faster Low Road – beauty is relative here – but it has a special rural mountain feeling that is classic northern New Mexico. The road winds through river valleys, skirts sandstone cliffs and traverses high pine forests, all beneath the gaze of the 13,000ft Truchas Peaks.

Villages en route are filled with old adobe houses with pitched tin roofs. Massive firewood piles rise next to rusting, disassembled pickup trucks in yards surrounded by grassy horse pastures. Many of these towns are home to art studios and traditional handicraft workshops.

The **High Road Art Tour** (www.highroad newmexico.com; ⊙ Sep), held over the last two weekends in September, is a good time to visit. From Chimayo to Truchas to Peñasco plus villages between and beyond, doors open all along the High Road.

Tiny Córdova is best known for its unpainted, austere *santos* (saint) carvings created by local masters such as George Lopez, Jose Delores Lopez and Sabinita Lopez Ortiz – all members of the same artistic family. Stop and see their work at **Sabinita Lopez Ortiz** (Map p276; ☑505-351-4572; County Rd 1317, Córdova; ⊙hours vary) shop, just off County Rd 80.

Nambé Pueblo

Thanks perhaps to its isolated location (or inspirational geology), **Nambé Pueblo** (Map p276; ☑505-455-2036; www.nambepueblo. org) has long been a spiritual center for the Tewa-speaking tribes, a distinction that attracted the cruel attentions of Spanish priests intent on conversion by any means necessary. After the Pueblo Revolt and Reconquista wound down, Spanish settlers annexed much of their land.

Public events include dances at Nambé Falls on July 4, San Francisco de Asis Feast Day (October 4) and the Buffalo Dance (December 24).

Two lovely 20-minute hikes, starting from the Ramada Area 5 miles off Hwy 503, lead to the biggest attraction on Nambé lands, **Nambé Falls** (Map p276; ☑505-455-2304; www.nambepueblo.org; day-use per vehicle $10, camping extra $15; ⊙Apr-Sep).

Chimayó
☑ 505 / POP 3177 / ELEV 6075FT

Even though the High Road to Taos has barely climbed out of the valley, the Hispanic village of Chimayó is generally regarded as the single biggest attraction on the entire route. It's home to a little twin-towered adobe chapel, El Santuario de Chimayó, which is not only extraordinarily pretty, but also ranks as perhaps the most important religious site in New Mexico.

Chimayó is also famous for its arts and crafts, and has a centuries-old tradition of producing superb weaving. Family-run galleries sell magnificent creations.

⊙ Sights

★ **El Santuario de Chimayó**   CHRISTIAN SITE
(Map p276; ☑505-351-9961; www.elsantuario dechimayo.us; ⊙9am-6pm May-Sep, to 5pm Oct-Apr) FREE Often called the Lourdes of America, the chapel was built in 1816, over a spot of earth said to have miraculous healing properties. The faithful come to rub the *tierra bendita* – holy dirt – from a small pit inside the church on whatever hurts; some mix it with water and drink it. The walls of the dirt room are covered with *milagros*,

---

GEORGIA O'KEEFFE

Although classically trained as a painter at art institutes in Chicago and New York, Georgia O'Keeffe was always uncomfortable with traditional European style. For four years after finishing school, she did not paint, and instead taught drawing and did graphic design.

After studying with Arthur Wesley Dow, who shared her distaste for the provincial, O'Keeffe began to develop her own style. She drew abstract shapes with charcoal, representing dreams and visions, and eventually returned to oils and watercolors. These first works caught the eye of her future husband and patron, photographer Alfred Stieglitz, in 1916.

In 1929 O'Keeffe visited Taos' Mabel Dodge Luhan Ranch and returned to paint *The Lawrence Tree*; the tree still presides over the **DH Lawrence Ranch** (p289) in northern New Mexico. O'Keeffe tackled the San Francisco de Asis Church in Ranchos de Taos, painted by so many artists before her, in a way that had never been considered: only a fragment of the mission wall, contrasted against the blue of the sky.

It was no wonder O'Keeffe loved New Mexico's expansive skies, so similar to her paintings' negative spaces. As she spent more time here, landscapes and fields of blue permeated her work. During desert treks, she collected the smooth white bones of animals, subjects she placed against that sky in some of her most identifiable New Mexico pieces.

Telltale scrub marks and bristle impressions reveal how O'Keeffe blended and mixed her vibrant colors on the canvas itself – you'd never know that from photographs, which convey a false, airbrush-like smoothness. You can experience her work firsthand at Santa Fe's **Georgia O'Keeffe Museum** (p255).

small tokens left by those who have been healed.

During Holy Week, around 30,000 pilgrims walk to Chimayó from Santa Fe, Albuquerque and beyond in the largest Catholic pilgrimage in the US, and the church now stands at the center of an ever-growing complex of gift shops, visitor centers and riverside gardens.

🛏 Sleeping & Eating

Several B&Bs in the area cater to pilgrims and travelers.

Casa Escondida   B&B $$
(📞 505-351-4805; www.casaescondida.com; 64 County Rd 100; r from $130; ❄ 🛜 🐾) Set on 6 acres, a mile or so north of Chimayó, this unpretentious and highly recommended B&B features eight beautiful rooms, all en-suite and furnished in Southwestern style. Some have outdoor decks; all share use of a communal covered porch and a hot tub.

Rancho de Chimayó   NEW MEXICAN $
(📞 505-984-2100; www.ranchodechimayo.com; County Rd 98; mains $7-10.75, dinner $10.25-25; ⏱ 11:30am-9pm, closed Mon Nov-Apr) Half a mile north of the Santuario, this bright, spacious garden-set restaurant serves classic New Mexican cuisine, courtesy of the Jaramillo family's famed recipes. Best of all is the basket of warm, fluffy *sopaipillas* (puffed-up pastries) that comes with each dish. The same management offers cozy B&B rooms (from $79) across the street.

🛍 Shopping

★**Centinela Traditional Arts**   ARTS & CRAFTS
(📞 505-351-2180; www.chimayoweavers.com; Hwy 76; ⏱ 9am-6pm Mon-Sat, 10am-5pm Sun) This part studio, part cooperative gallery is run by seventh-generation weaver Irvin Trujillo and his wife Lisa. Irvin's work is displayed at the Smithsonian Institution in Washington, DC and the Museum of Art in Santa Fe. Naturally dyed blankets, vests and pillows are sold, and you're welcome to watch the couple weaving on handlooms.

Oviedo Gallery   ARTS & CRAFTS
(📞 505-351-2280; www.oviedoart.com; Hwy 76; ⏱ 10am-6pm) The Oviedo family has been carving native woods since 1739. Today the Oviedo Gallery is housed in the centuries-old family farm, and also displays and sells a wide range of bronze sculptures, made in the on-site foundry.

Truchas

📍 505 / POP 915 / ELEV 8051FT

Rural New Mexico at its most sincere and picturesque is showcased in Truchas, originally settled by the Spaniards in the 18th century. Robert Redford's *The Milagro Beanfield War* was filmed here (but don't bother with the movie – the book it's based on, by John Nichols, is waaaay better).

To see the village itself, don't follow the main road as it turns left toward Taos, but head straight on uphill toward the Truchas Peaks. Narrow roads, many unpaved, wend between century-old adobes. Fields of grass and alfalfa spread toward the sheer walls and plunging ridges of the mountains. Between the run-down homes, some wonderful galleries double as workshops for local weavers, painters, sculptors and other artists.

🛏 Sleeping

Rancho Arriba   B&B $
(📞 505-689-2374; www.ranchoarriba.com; Hwy 75; r $70-120; @ 🛜) High up at the far end of Truchas village, near the point where trails head off into the Pecos Wilderness, this sprawling old ranch complex offers three B&B rooms in an adobe farmhouse. It has horses and wood stoves, and serves dinner given advance notice.

🛍 Shopping

Ojo Sarco Pottery   ARTS & CRAFTS
(📞 505-557-3254; www.ojosarco.com; County Rd 73; ⏱ 10am-5pm Tue-Sun May-Dec) Turn left 6 miles north of Truchas, onto County Rd 73, then follow signs to find this gallery and check out the fine clay creations of master potters Kathy Riggs and Jake Willson, as well as work by other local artists, from glass-crafters to bell-makers.

High Road Marketplace   ARTS & CRAFTS
(📞 505-689-2689; 1642 Hwy 76; ⏱ 10am-5pm, to 4pm winter) This cooperative art gallery displays a huge range of work by regional artists, from potters and painters to quilters and metalworkers.

Cordovas Handweaving Workshop   ARTS & CRAFTS
(📞 505-689-1124; Hwy 75; ⏱ hours vary) Watch Harry, a friendly fourth-generation weaver, at work, in between browsing his beautiful blankets, placemats and rugs.

Picuris Pueblo

Tucked away inconspicuously below the High Road, just west of the junction of Hwy 76 and Hwy 75, **Picuris Pueblo** (Map p276; ☑575-587-2519; www.picurispueblo.org; photo/video permits $5/10; ⊙8am-5pm Mon-Fri) was once among the largest and most powerful Pueblos in New Mexico. The Picuris built adobe constructions at least seven stories tall and boasted a population approaching 3000. After the Pueblo Revolt and Reconquista, when many retreated to Kansas rather than face De Vargas' wrath, only 500 returned. Call well in advance to arrange a guided tour.

Peñasco

☑575 / POP 1200 / ELEV 7685FT

This scenic village along the Rio Santa Barbara and beneath Jicarita Peak (12,835ft) is the gateway to the less-crowded northern side of the Pecos Wilderness. You'll find trailheads at nearby Santa Barbara Campground. From there, it's possible to access the Skyline Trail, a multiday backpacking loop that traverses above-treeline ridges and can include ascents of Truchas Peak (13,102ft), New Mexico's second-highest, and Jicarita; both are nontechnical walk-ups.

🏃 Activities

Sipapu Ski Resort   SKIING
(Map p276; ☑800-587-2240; www.sipapunm.com; lift tickets adult/13-24yr/child $45/39/29; ⊙mid-Nov–early Apr; ⚑) The snow and terrain at this small, family-oriented ski resort on Hwy 518, 10 miles east of Peñasco toward Mora, can't compare to Taos Ski Valley, but lift tickets are cheap and special deals make it a reasonable place to bring the kids. In summer, Sipapu has one of the country's top-ranked disc (Frisbee) golf courses.

🛏 Sleeping & Eating

The **Santa Barbara Campground** (Map p276; FS Rd 116; RV & tent sites $16; ⊙mid-May–Sep) is the only sleeping option here, and eating options are almost as limited.

Sugar Nymphs Bistro   CAFE $
(☑575-587-0311; www.sugarnymphs.com; 15046 Hwy 75; mains $10-15; ⊙11am-4pm Mon-Thu, to 8pm Fri & Sat, 10:30am-3pm Sun) Alongside the Peñasco Theatre and part of the same operation, this homespun little bistro serves gourmet comfort food using local produce, including a great goat cheese salad and desserts that often sell out.

☆ Entertainment

Peñasco Theatre   THEATER
(☑575-587-2726; www.penascotheatre.org; 15046 Hwy 75) Historic theater that offers myriad programs, concerts, movies and classes throughout the year, including weeklong youth circus camps in summer, thanks to its close connection with Wise Fool, a collective of performance artists who blend clowning, trapeze, puppetry, music and other forms of storytelling.

Low Road to Taos

Don't let the fact that it passes through unpromising Española put you off. This is a spectacular route that follows the Rio Grande Gorge, between towering walls of granite, sculpted volcanic tuff and black basalt. The river tumbles by, carrying white-water rafts downstream, while numerous waterfront pull-offs and picnic spots invite drivers to get out and admire the views.

Ultimately, the Low Road climbs steeply out of the gorge to emerge onto Taos Plateau. The first vista is truly awesome, with both the Sangre de Cristo Mountains straight ahead, and the awesome river canyon on your left, coming suddenly and simultaneously into view.

Embudo

☑505 / POP 354 / ELEV 5880FT

Tiny Embudo, 18 miles north of Española, is no more than a cluster of low-slung homes and ranches on the east side of the highway. A roadside oddity and gourmet trailer provide a reason to stop.

⊙ Sights

Classical Gas   GALLERY
(☑505-852-2995; Hwy 68; ⊙9am-5pm) FREE As you drive through Embudo, your eye will inevitably be caught by the array of ancient gas pumps and Route 66 paraphernalia outside Classical Gas. What's inside is even better: a dazzling array of historic neon signs, put together as a true labor of love by retiree Johnnie Meier.

✗ Eating

Sugar's BBQ
BARBECUE $

(☑ 505-852-0604; 1799 Hwy 68; mains $6-10; ☺ 11am-5pm Thu-Sun) On the east side of the highway a short way south of Classical Gas, this tin-clad trailer has, thanks to its sublimely juicy barbecue, been hailed one of the top 10 roadside joints in America by *Gourmet* magazine. Brisket burritos = genius.

Dixon

☑ 505 / POP 926 / ELEV 6080FT

As you drive through the Rio Grande Gorge, it's well worth taking a slight detour east on Hwy 75, just north of Embudo, to reach this small farming and artist community, a couple of miles off the main road in the gorgeous Rio Embudo Valley. Dixon is famous for its apple orchards, but other crops are grown here too; try to catch the local farmers market on Wednesday afternoon in summer and fall, with food fresh from the fields. Incidentally, ask at the local food co-op, and some kind soul might point you to the waterfalls, up a nearby dirt road.

⊙ Sights

Vivac Winery
WINERY

(☑ 505-579-4441; www.vivacwinery.com; 2075 Hwy 68; tasting $8; ☺ 10am-6pm Mon-Sat, from noon Sun) Right where Hwy 68 meets Hwy 75, this winery is run by the genial Padberg brothers, born and raised in Dixon. The Divino and Diavolo reds are the best – and be sure to sample the handmade chocolates.

La Chiripada Winery
WINERY

(☑ 505-579-4437; www.lachiripada.com; Hwy 75; tasting $10; ☺ 11am-5pm Mon-Sat, from noon Sun) Award-winning vintner, 2.5 miles east of Hwy 68 along Hwy 75, that only uses New Mexican grapes. As well as offering tastings here, it also runs a tasting room in Taos (103 Bent St).

★☆ Festivals & Events

Dixon Studio Tour
CULTURAL

(www.dixonarts.org; ☺ early Nov) New Mexico's original studio tour is still going strong; it's held the first full weekend in November in scenic Dixon, one hour north of Santa Fe.

⊨ Sleeping & Eating

For such a small village, there are plenty of great guesthouses. Book rooms well in advance during November's studio tour.

Zuly's
(☑ 505-579-4001; 234 Hwy 75; mains $6-14; ☺ 7:30am-3pm Tue-Thu, 7:30am-8pm Fri, 9am-8pm Sat) is a great stop when open, otherwise head to the food co-op for groceries, sandwiches and freshly baked pizzas.

Tower Guest House
GUESTHOUSE $

(☑ 505-579-4288; www.vrbo.com/118083; cottage $95; ☻🐾) Located on a garlic farm, this lovely cottage is close to the Rio Embudo. Sleeps three.

La Casita
GUESTHOUSE $

(☑ 505-579-4297; www.vrbo.com/79296; casita $95; ☻🐾) This traditional adobe comes equipped with a kitchen and wood-burning stove. Two-night minimum stay.

Rinconada & Pilar

☑ 505 / ELEV 5905FT

The small community of Rinconada, just north of Dixon on Hwy 68, is home to an appealing little pub as well as a few galleries. Seven miles further north, immediately before Hwy 68 starts its climb toward Taos, tiny Pilar serves as an access point for the southernmost portion of the Río Grande del Norte National Monument. To reach the river and trailheads, branch off the main road onto Hwy 570.

⊨ Sleeping & Eating

Seven campsites are located in the Rio Grande National Monument. Get details at the visitor center in Pilar. There is nowhere to eat in Rinconada or Pilar.

Orilla Verde Recreation Area
CAMPGROUND $

(Map p276; ☑ 575-758-8851; Hwy 570; day-use $3, tent/RV sites $7/15) Seven campgrounds are located along this 6-mile stretch of the Rio Grande, all with picnic tables and toilets. Only four have running water, and of these, only two have RV hookups. Río Bravo Campground is the only campground here with showers. The campgrounds are located on Hwy 570, 1 mile north of the visitor center on Hwy 68.

♟ Drinking & Nightlife

Blue Heron Brewing Co
BREWERY

(☑ 505-579-9188; www.blueheronbrews.com; 2214 Hwy 68; ☺ noon-6pm Sun & Mon, 10am-7pm Wed & Thu, 10am-8pm Fri & Sat) Funky little adobe, formerly a veterinarian's office, where local brewmasters pour handcrafted ales in an arty cafe space – it's a great spot to grab a pint or a growler.

🛍 Shopping

Stephen Kilborn's Studio ARTS & CRAFTS
(📞 575-758-0135; www.stephenkilborn.com; Hwy 68, Pilar; ⊙10am-5pm Mon-Sat, from 11am Sun) The whimsically painted Southwestern-style pottery here puts the 'fun' into functional; sometimes there are great deals on 'factory' seconds.

Rift Gallery ARTS & CRAFTS
(📞505-579-9179; www.saxstonecarving.com; 2249 Hwy 68, Rinconada; ⊙10am-5pm Wed-Sun May-Sep, shorter hours rest of year) Just up the road from the Blue Heron, this gallery showcases the work of sculptor Mark Saxe and Betsy Williams, a potter specializing in the Japanese Karatsu tradition. Each summer they host highly regarded weeklong stone-carving workshops.

TAOS

📞575 / POP 5731 / ELEV 6960FT

A magical spot even by the standards of this Land of Enchantment, Taos remains forever under the spell of the powerful landscape that surrounds it: 12,300ft snowcapped peaks rise behind town, while a sage-speckled plateau unrolls to the west before plunging 800ft straight down into the Rio Grande Gorge. The sky can be a searing sapphire blue or an ominous parade of rumbling thunderheads so big they dwarf the mountains. And then there are the sunsets...

Taos Pueblo, a marvel of adobe architecture, ranks among the oldest continuously inhabited communities in the US, and stands at the root of a long history that also extends from conquistadors to mountain men to artists. The town itself is a relaxed and eccentric place, with classic mud-brick buildings, fabulous museums, quirky cafes and excellent restaurants. Its 5700 residents include bohemians and hippies, alternative-energy aficionados and old-time Hispanic families. It's both rural and worldly, and a little bit otherworldly.

⊙ Sights

The most compelling attraction in the Taos area is unquestionably Taos Pueblo (p298), the largest surviving multistoried Pueblo, built around 1450. Taos itself is surprisingly small – once you've strolled beneath the verandas of the old adobes that surround picturesque **Taos Plaza**, and explored the shops along Bent St to the north and Kit Carson Lane to the east, you've pretty much seen the entire downtown core – but it boasts a phenomenal crop of top-quality museums, galleries and attractions.

★Millicent Rogers Museum MUSEUM
(Map p288; 📞575-758-2462; www.millicent rogers.org; 1504 Millicent Rogers Rd; adult/child $10/2; ⊙10:10am-5pm Apr-Oct, closed Mon Nov-Mar) Rooted in the private collection of model and oil heiress Millicent Rogers, who moved to Taos in 1947, this superb museum, 4 miles northwest of the Plaza, ranges from Hispanic folk art to Navajo weaving, and even modernist jewelry designed by Rogers herself. The principal focus, however, is on American Indian ceramics, and especially the beautiful black-on-black pottery created during the 20th century by Maria Martínez from San Ildefonso Pueblo.

Martínez Hacienda MUSEUM
(Map p288; 📞575-758-1000; www.taoshistoric museums.org; 708 Hacienda Way, off Lower Ranchitos Rd; adult/child $8/4, Blumenschein Museum joint ticket $12; ⊙10am-5pm Mon-Sat, noon-5pm Sun Apr-Oct, closed Wed & Thu rest of the year) Set amid the fields 2 miles southwest of the Plaza, this fortified adobe homestead was built in 1804. It served as a trading post, first for merchants venturing north from Mexico City along the Camino Real, and then west along the Santa Fe Trail. Its 21 rooms, arranged around a double courtyard, are furnished with the few possessions that even a wealthy family of the era would have been able to afford. Cultural events are held here regularly.

Harwood Foundation Museum MUSEUM
(Map p291; 📞575-758-9826; www.harwood museum.org; 238 Ledoux St; adult/child $10/free; ⊙10am-5pm Mon-Sat, noon-5pm Sun Apr-Oct, closed Mon & Tue Nov-Mar) Attractively displayed in a gorgeous and very spacious mid-19th-century adobe compound, the paintings, drawings, prints, sculpture and photographs here are predominantly the work of northern New Mexican artists, both historical and contemporary. Founded in 1923, the Harwood is the second-oldest museum in New Mexico, and is as strong on local Hispanic traditions as it is on Taos' 20th-century school.

Blumenschein Home & Museum MUSEUM
(Map p291; 📞575-758-0505; www.taoshistoric museums.org; 222 Ledoux St; adult/child $8/4, Martínez Hacienda joint ticket $12; ⊙10am-5pm

Taos Area

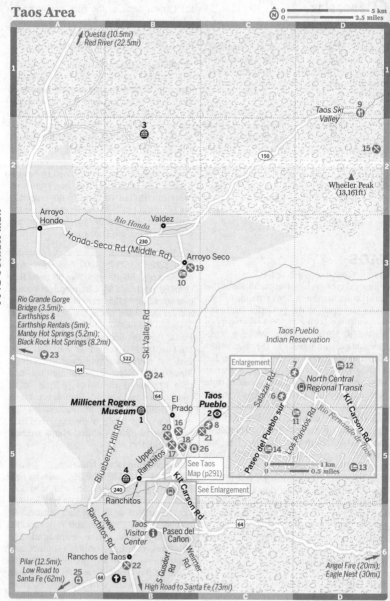

N

0 ____ 5 km
0 ____ 2.5 miles

Questa (10.5mi);
Red River (22.5mi)

Taos Ski
Valley 9

15

Wheeler Peak
(13,161ft)

150

Arroyo
Hondo

Rio Honda   Valdez

Hondo-Seco Rd (Middle Rd)   230   Arroyo Seco
                                     19
                                  10

3

Taos Pueblo
Indian Reservation

Rio Grande Gorge
Bridge (3.5mi);
Earthships &
Earthship Rentals (5mi);
Manby Hot Springs (5.2mi);
Black Rock Hot Springs (8.2mi)

23   64   522   Ski Valley Rd   524

Enlargement

7   12

North Central
Regional Transit

6

Salazar Rd

Millicent Rogers
Museum   1   64   El
Prado   Taos
Pueblo   2

20 16   8
    18 21   11
    17 26

See Taos
Map (p291)

See Enlargement

4   Upper
Ranchitos

Kit Carson Rd

14   Paseo del Pueblo sur   Los Pandos Rd   Rio Fernando de Taos   Kit Carson Rd   13

0 ____ 1 km
0 ____ 0.5 miles

240
Ranchitos

Lower
Ranchitos Rd

Blueberry Hill Rd

Taos
Visitor
Center   Paseo del
Cañon

Kit Carson Rd   64

Pilar (12.5mi);
Low Road to
Santa Fe (62mi)

Ranchos de Taos   22
25   68   5   S Gusdorf Rd   Weimer Rd

High Road to Santa Fe (73mi)

Angel Fire (20mi);
Eagle Nest (30mi)

Mon-Sat, noon-5pm Sun Apr-Oct, closed Wed & Thu rest of year) Wonderfully preserved adobe residence, dating originally from 1797, which provides a vivid glimpse of life in Taos' artistic community during the 1920s. Ernest L Blumenschein, founder member of the Taos Society of Artists, lived here with his wife and daughter, Mary and Helen Greene Blumenschein, both also artists, and every room remains alive with their artworks and personal possessions.

Taos Area

◎ Top Sights
1 Millicent Rogers Museum......................B5
2 Taos Pueblo...C5

◎ Sights
3 DH Lawrence Ranch & Memorial..........B2
4 Martínez Hacienda.................................B5
5 San Francisco de Asís Church..............B6

◎ Activities, Courses & Tours
6 Gearing Up Bicycle Shop......................C4
Rio Grande Stables.........................(see 9)
7 Taos Fly Shop...D4
8 Taos Indian Horse Ranch......................C5
9 Taos Ski Valley......................................D1

◎ Sleeping
10 Abominable Snowmansion..................B3
11 American Artists Gallery House
B&B..D5
Blake..(see 9)
12 El Monte Sagrado................................D4
13 Old Taos Guesthouse...........................D5
Snakedance Condominiums &
Spa...(see 9)

14 Sun God Lodge.......................................C5

◎ Eating
192 at the Blake...............................(see 9)
15 Bavarian...D2
16 El Meze...B5
17 Gutiz...B5
18 Love Apple...B5
Stray Dog Cantina...........................(see 9)
19 Taos Cow...B3
20 Taos Diner..B5
21 Tiwa Kitchen..C5
22 Trading Post Cafe.................................B6

◎ Drinking & Nightlife
Anaconda Bar..................................(see 12)
23 Taos Mesa Brewery.............................A4

◎ Entertainment
24 KTAOS Solar Center............................B4

◎ Shopping
25 Taos Drums...A6
26 Tony Reyna Indian Shop.....................B5

NEW MEXICO TAOS

Taos Art Museum & Fechin Institute
MUSEUM
(Map p291; ☑575-758-2690; www.taosart museum.org; 227 Paseo del Pueblo Norte; adult/ child $10/free; ☉10am-5pm Tue-Sun May-Oct, to 4pm Nov-Apr) Russian artist Nicolai Fechin moved to Taos in 1926, aged 46, and adorned the interior of this adobe home with his own distinctly Russian woodcarvings between 1928 and 1933. Now a museum, it displays Fechin's paintings and sketches along with his private collection and choice works by members of the Taos Society of Artists, and also hosts occasional chamber music performances in summer.

DH Lawrence Ranch & Memorial
HISTORIC BUILDING
(Map p288; ☑575-737-9300; www.dhlawrence taos.org; San Cristobal Rd; ☉10am-2pm Thu & Fri) **FREE** In 1924, Mabel Dodge Luhan gave DH Lawrence's wife, Frieda, this 160-acre ranch, now administered by the University of New Mexico, where the Lawrence-obsessed can pay their respects to the famed author of such classics as *Lady Chatterley's Lover*. Opening hours change according to the weather and the season, so call ahead or check the website before you drive out here. It's located 20 miles north of Taos.

Earthships
ARCHITECTURE
(Map p276; ☑575-613-4409; www.earthship.com; US Hwy 64; self-guided tours $7; ☉9am-5pm Jun-Aug, 10am-4pm Sep-May) 🏴 Numbering 70 Earthships, with capacity for 60 more, Taos' pioneering community was the brainchild of architect Michael Reynolds. Built with recycled materials such as used automobile tires and cans, and buried on three sides, Earthships heat and cool themselves, make their own electricity and catch their own water; dwellers grow their own food. Stay overnight (p294) if possible; the 'tour' is a little disappointing. The visitor center is 1.5 miles west of the Rio Grande Gorge Bridge on US Hwy 64.

San Francisco de Asís Church
CHURCH
(Map p288; ☑575-751-0518; St Francis Plaza, Ranchos de Taos; ☉9am-4pm Mon-Fri) Just off Hwy 68 in Ranchos de Taos, 4 miles south of Taos Plaza, this iconic church was completed in 1815. Famed for the rounded curves and stark angles of its sturdy adobe walls, it was repeatedly memorialized by Georgia O'Keeffe in paint, and Ansel Adams with his camera. Mass is celebrated at 6pm the first Saturday of the month, and usually at 7am, 9am and 11:30am every Sunday.

Rio Grande Gorge Bridge BRIDGE, CANYON
(Map p276) Constructed in 1965, this vertigo-inducing steel bridge carries Hwy 64 across the Rio Grande about 12 miles northwest of Taos. It's the seventh-highest bridge in the US, 565ft above the river and measuring 600ft long. The views from the pedestrian walkway, west over the empty Taos Plateau as well as down the jagged walls of the gorge, will surely make you gulp as you gape. Vendors selling jewelry, sage sticks and other souvenirs congregate on the eastern side.

Kit Carson Home & Museum MUSEUM
(Map p291; ☑ 575-758-4945; www.kitcarsonhome andmuseum.com; 113 Kit Carson Rd; adult/child $7/free; ⊙10am-5pm Mar-Oct, to 4pm Nov-Feb) A short walk east of the Plaza, the little-changed former home of Kit Carson (1809–68) – perhaps the Southwest's most famous mountain man, guide, trapper, soldier and scout – is now a monument to his memory. Only five of its 12 rooms, built in 1825 with 30in adobe walls, are open to visitors. Furnished as Carson might have known them, they hold artifacts including his rifles, telescope, walking cane and saber.

Activities
Hike, bike, raft, ski, fish... The sheer range of outdoor activities in the Taos area is exhaustive. Local outfitters can help you plan and execute your outdoor excursions.

Winter Sports
In winter it's all about skiing. Most of the action takes place at the legendary Taos Ski Valley (p299), located 20 miles northeast of town.

The best cross-country skiing and snow-shoeing is at the Enchanted Forest up by Red River (p301), a 40-mile drive northeast, but there's also a great little area in Carson National Forest at Amole Canyon, 15 miles south of Taos on Hwy 518.

Just north of Amole Canyon along Hwy 518, US Hill – the primo sledding spot in the area – is the most popular place around for kids to get frostbitten and bruised and love every minute of it.

Cottam's Ski & Outdoor SPORTS & OUTDOORS
(Map p291; ☑ 800-322-8267; www.cottams skishops.com; 207a Paseo del Pueblo Sur; adult/child ski rental packages from $30/18; ⊙7am-8pm in season) A reliable place to rent or buy whatever winter gear you need, with another location at the Taos Ski Valley.

Mountain Biking
Where else are you going to find biking this good, this close to the sky? Why bother looking elsewhere when an enormous network of mountain-bike and multi-use trails covers the region of the Carson National Forest between Taos, Angel Fire and Picuris Peak.

The Taos Visitor Center (p298) stocks a surprising amount of information on mountain biking. Standouts include the 9-mile West Rim Trail in the Orilla Verde section of Río Grande del Norte National Monument, which enables strong beginners and intermediate cyclists to enjoy views of the Rio Grande Gorge. Considered one of the nation's best mountain-bike trails, the storied South Boundary Trail is a 28-mile ride for experienced cyclists.

If you really want to challenge yourself, try the 84-mile Enchanted Circle loop. It makes a fine regional road-bike circuit once you've acclimatized to the altitude.

Gearing Up Bicycle Shop CYCLING
(Map p288; ☑ 575-751-0365; www.gearingup bikes.com; 616 Paseo del Pueblo Sur; bikes per day from $45; ⊙10am-6pm Mon-Sat) For mountain-biking info, trail maps, spares and equipment – not to mention bikes – drop in at this friendly central shop, which also rents full-suspension bikes. Helmets ($10) and car racks ($15) are extra.

Hiking & Hot Springs
While there are several day-use trails just outside of Taos, particularly on the south side of Hwy 64 east of town, the best day hiking and backpacking is a little further afield, up in the Wild Rivers area of Río Grande del Norte National Monument, and in the Latir Peak and Pecos wildernesses.

A couple of fabulous hot springs close to the Rio Grand Gorge can be reached by hiking from dirt roads west of Arroyo Hondo, some 9 miles north of Taos. The more readily accessible is Black Rock Hot Springs near the John Dunn Bridge. Manby Hot Springs (aka Stagecoach Hot Springs) is harder to find, but it's a worthy place of pilgrimage – this is where the hot-springs scenes were shot in *Easy Rider*.

Taos

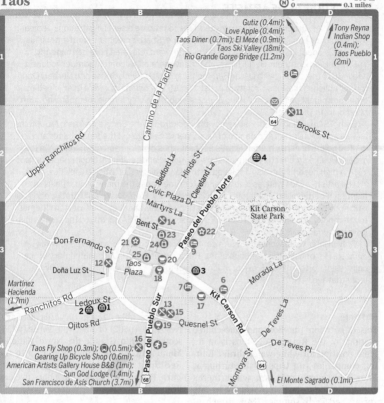

Taos

◎ Sights
1 Blumenschein Home & Museum	B4
2 Harwood Foundation Museum	A4
3 Kit Carson Home & Museum	C3
4 Taos Art Museum & Fechin Institute	C2

◉ Activities, Courses & Tours
5 Cottam's Ski & Outdoor	B4

🛏 Sleeping
6 Casa Benavides Bed & Breakfast	C3
7 Doña Luz Inn	C3
8 El Pueblo Lodge	D1
9 Historic Taos Inn	C3
10 Mabel Dodge Luhan House	D3

✖ Eating
11 Burger Stand at Taos Ale House	D2
Doc Martin's	(see 9)
12 El Gamal	B3
13 La Cueva Cafe	B4
14 Lambert's	B3
15 Raw To Go	B4
16 Taos Diner II	B4

🍷 Drinking & Nightlife
Adobe Bar	(see 9)
17 Caffe Tazza	C3
18 ParCht	B3
19 Taos Mesa Taproom	B4
20 World Cup	B3

✪ Entertainment
21 Alley Cantina	B3
22 Taos Center for the Arts	C3

🛍 Shopping
El Rincón Trading Post	(see 7)
23 Op Cit Books	B3
24 Seconds Ecostore	B3
25 Taos Mountain Outfitters	B3

TAOS SOCIETY OF ARTISTS

In 1893, artist Joseph Henry Sharp visited Taos to prepare a set of illustrations depicting the Pueblo for publication. Smitten with the scene, Sharp spread the word among his colleagues about his 'discovery,' and shortly afterward relocated here permanently.

Ernest Blumenschein, Bert Phillips and many more of his contemporaries followed, and in 1912 they, along with Oscar Berninghaus, Eanger Irving Couse and Herbert Dunton, established the Taos Society of Artists (TSA). The original six were later joined by other prominent painters, including Lucy Harwood, the only female member, and Juan Mirabol from Taos Pueblo.

Early TSA paintings were inspired by the backdrop of the Sangre de Cristo Mountains as well as the buildings and people of Taos Pueblo. Set against the tonal shapes and neutral colors of earth, human figures act as flashes of color seen nowhere else in the desert. Pueblo architecture, with clusters of organic and sculptural block shapes reflecting the high desert light, also appealed to the Taos painters' artistic sensibilities.

The artists' styles were as diverse and experimental as the many philosophies of painting that defined the first half of the 20th century. From Sharp's illustrative and realistic approach and Blumenschein's impressionistic treatment of Southwestern themes to the moody art-deco spirit of Dunton's landscapes, the TSA portrayed the same subjects in myriad ways.

Only in later years would the TSA's contribution to contemporary art be fully recognized. Historically, the paintings of the TSA are seen as a visual documentary of the cultures of northern New Mexico, which had yet to be dramatically influenced by the industrial age.

Rafting

Poised between the Box and Racecourse sections of the Rio Grande, Taos is in an ideal position for white-water thrills. Rafting companies run trips to the turbulent **Taos Box**, north of town, when there's enough water to boat it – usually in late spring and early summer. This stretch of river is not for the easily panicked; the rapids can hit Class V, and the remote feeling of the canyon makes it all that much more intense. From spring to fall, the **Racecourse** – downriver at Pilar – is perpetually popular; it's exciting, but rarely feels death-defying.

Los Rios River Runners RAFTING
(☎575-776-8854; www.losriosriverrunners.com; adult/child half-day from $54/44; ⊙late Apr-Aug) Half-day trips on the Racecourse – in one- and two-person kayaks, as you prefer – full-day trips on the Box (minimum age 12), and multinight expeditions on the scenic Chama. On its 'Native Cultures Feast and Float' you're accompanied by an American Indian guide and have lunch homemade by a local Pueblo family. Rates rise slightly at weekends.

Fishing

The creeks, rivers and lakes around Taos hold enough variety to please experts and beginners alike. Teach the kids at Eagle Nest Lake (p302) or the Orilla Verde (p286) section of Río Grande del Norte National Monument, or take your fly rod up to the **Red River** or down to the **Rio Santa Barbara**. Don't forget to pick up a one-/five-day license for $12/24.

Taos Fly Shop FISHING
(Map p288; ☎575-751-1312; www.taosflyshop.com; 308c Paseo del Pueblo Sur; ⊙9am-5pm) If you're looking for the right flies for the waters around Taos, stop by this helpful shop and find out what's hatching where. It has expert guides (half-/full day from $250/350) and offers fly-fishing instruction.

Tours

Wild Earth Llama Adventures ADVENTURE
(☎800-758-5262; www.llamaadventures.com) Not everyone who loves to hike and camp has the desire to haul a pack around at 11,000ft above sea level. Around Taos, you don't need to – that's what the llamas are for. Wild Earth Llama Adventures runs day hikes and multiday treks in the sweetest spots in the Sangres.

They're experts at getting even young kids out into the backcountry, and their lead guide also happens to be a chef. No, no llama riding, but you'll be too busy doing your 'Julie Andrews in an alpine meadow' impersonation to care.

Day trips (adult/child $125/75) run year-round; multiday trips (adult/child from $425/125 one night) run from March to November.

✨ Festivals & Events

Taos sees numerous athletic and cultural events all year, as well as visual arts workshops; the visitor center (p298) has details. Some of the most memorable and unique are held at Taos Pueblo.

Fiestas de Taos CULTURAL
(www.fiestasdetaos.com; ⊙mid-Jul) New Mexican music and dance fill the streets with parades.

Solar Music Festival MUSIC
(⊙Jun) Big-name acts in town when it's on, though its status has been in flux of late.

🛏 Sleeping

Accommodation options in Taos range from free camping in national forests to gourmet B&Bs in historic adobes. Rates fluctuate week to week, but it's not a place where you can expect to find a decent room in

TAOS TOP 8

Taos Pueblo (p298) Touring the impressive Pueblo and learning about American Indian history.

Taos Ski Valley (p299) Skiing the steeps at New Mexico's top resort.

Millicent Rogers Museum (p287) Admiring one of the finest collections of Southwestern jewelry and art anywhere.

Martínez Hacienda (p287) Getting a flavor of life in a Hispanic frontier town.

Earthship Rentals (p294) Sleeping off the grid in a boutique-chic sustainable dwelling.

Rafting (p292) Running the Taos Box for white-water thrills.

Río Grande del Norte National Monument (p297) Hiking the La Junta Trail down to the confluence of the Rio Grande and Red Rivers – and maybe doing some fly fishing too.

South Boundary Trail (p290) Finding a little slice of heaven on an epic mountain-bike ride.

summer for under $100. June to September and December to February are usually considered high season, with a major spike around Christmas.

Sun God Lodge MOTEL $
(Map p288; ☎575-758-3162; www.sungodlodge. com; 919 Paseo del Pueblo Sur; r from $55; P🐾🤶) The hospitable folks at this well-run two-story motel can fill you in on local history and point you to a restaurant to match your mood. Rooms are clean – if a bit dark – and decorated with low-key Southwestern flair. The highlight is the lush-green courtyard dappled with twinkling lights, a scenic spot for a picnic or enjoying the sunset. It's 1.5 miles south of the Plaza.

★**Mabel Dodge Luhan House** INN $$
(Map p291; ☎505-751-9686; www.mabeldodge luhan.com; 240 Morada Lane; r from $116; P) Every inch of this rambling compound, once home to Mabel Dodge Luhan, the so-called Patroness of Taos, exudes elegant-meets-earthy beauty. Sleep where Georgia O'Keeffe, Willa Cather or Dennis Hopper once laid their heads, or even use a bathroom decorated by DH Lawrence. It also runs arts, crafts, spiritual and creative workshops. Rates include buffet breakfast. Wi-fi in public areas only.

★**Doña Luz Inn** B&B $$
(Map p291; ☎575-758-9000; www.stayintaos.com; 114 Kit Carson Rd; r $119-209; ❄@🤶🐾) Funky and fun, this central B&B is a labor of love by owner Paul Castillo. Rooms are decorated in colorful themes from Spanish colonial to American Indian, with abundant art, murals and artifacts plus adobe fireplaces, kitchenettes and hot tubs. The cozy La Luz room is the best deal in town, and there are also sumptuous larger suites.

★**Historic Taos Inn** HISTORIC HOTEL $$
(Map p291; ☎575-758-2233; www.taosinn.com; 125 Paseo del Pueblo Norte; r from $119; P❄🤶) Lovely and always lively old inn, where the 45 characterful rooms have Southwest trimmings such as heavy-duty wooden furnishings and adobe fireplaces (some functioning, some for show). The famed Adobe Bar (p296) spills into the cozy central atrium, and features live music every night – for a quieter stay, opt for one of the detached separate wings – and there's also a good restaurant (p295).

★**Earthship Rentals**   BOUTIQUE HOTEL **$$**
(Map p276; ☑575-751-0462; www.earthship.com; US Hwy 64; earthship $185-410; 🖥📶) 🅿 How about an off-grid night in a boutique-chic, solar-powered dwelling? Part Gaudí-esque visions, part space-age fantasy, these futuristic structures are built using recycled tires and aluminum cans, not that those components are visible. Set on a beautiful mesa across the river 14 miles northwest, they offer a unique experience, albeit rather different to staying in Taos itself. Drop-ins welcome.

Old Taos Guesthouse   B&B **$$**
(Map p288; ☑575-758-5448; www.oldtaos.com; 1028 Witt Rd; r $149-219; ❄@🖥) Hidden away in a quiet residential neighborhood, this atmospheric treasure has spacious, old-world adobe rooms with undulating walls (just try to find a right angle) and hand-carved wood furnishings and doors; the older rooms are nicest. The shady lawn and gardens beckon, with inviting hammocks and 60-mile sunset views. Seasoned adventurers both, the proprietors can point you toward great excursions.

Casa Benavides Bed & Breakfast   B&B **$$**
(Map p291; ☑575-758-1772; www.taos-casabenavides.com; 137 Kit Carson Rd; r $105-225; ❄@🖥) Spreading through five garden-set buildings a block east of the Plaza, this romantic B&B abounds in fireplaces, patios and balconies. Furniture is mostly antique and handmade, and shares space with artful treasures. A couple of rooms are on the small and dark side, but most are big and bright – check the website. Breakfasts are full and made from scratch.

American Artists Gallery House B&B   B&B **$$**
(Map p288; ☑800-532-2041; www.taosbedandbreakfast.com; 132 Frontier Lane; casitas/r from $115/119; ❄@🖥❄) This quiet garden complex, a mile south of the Plaza, holds tasteful rooms and casitas, all with wood-burning fireplaces. The smallest casita is little more than a shed, albeit a very nice one, while the Jacuzzi suites will blow your mind. George the peacock regularly drops in during the sumptuous breakfasts, while changing art displays come from local galleries.

El Pueblo Lodge   HOTEL **$$**
(Map p291; ☑575-758-8700; www.elpueblolodge.com; 412 Paseo del Pueblo Norte; r from $99; ❄🖥❄❄) Old-fashioned hotel at the northern edge of downtown, where the fake adobe style extends to a spectacular mock-up of nearby Taos Pueblo. Large, clean rooms, some with kitchenettes and/or fireplaces, plus a summer pool, a hot tub, outdoor seating and barbecue grills, and hot breakfast in the morning.

El Monte Sagrado   HOTEL **$$$**
(Map p288; ☑575-758-3502; www.elmontesagrado.com; 317 Kit Carson Rd; r from $209; 🅿❄@🖥❄❄) 🅿 A lush oasis in the high desert, this lavishly decorated ecoresort holds bright, luxurious suites arranged around a flourishing courtyard and whimsically decorated with American Indian, Mexican, Moroccan and Egyptian notes. There's also a full-service on-site spa, plus a good restaurant and the attractive **Anaconda Bar** (Map p288; ☑575-737-9855; 317 Kit Carson Rd, El Monte Sagrado; ⊙2-10pm). Look out for ski deals in winter.

🍴 Eating

Taos rates second only to Santa Fe among New Mexico's culinary hot spots. There are some great options here at both ends of the price spectrum, with plenty of good choices within easy walking distance of the Plaza.

Gutiz   CAFE **$**
(Map p288; ☑575-758-1226; www.gutiztaos.com; 812B Paseo del Pueblo Norte; mains $9-16; ⊙8am-3pm Tue-Sun; ☑) This yummy New Mexican–French-Cajun hybrid makes most everything from scratch, using organic seasonal produce. Breakfast, served until closing, is the focus, with crêpes, *andouille* sausage green chile, brie omelets and croque monsieurs (and madames). Gluten-free choices available.

Taos Diner II   DINER **$**
(Map p291; ☑575-751-1989; 216B Paseo del Pueblo Sur; mains $7.50-11.50; ⊙7am-3pm) Branch of the long-running diner (Map p288; ☑575-758-2374; www.taosdiner.com; 908 Paseo del Pueblo Norte; mains $7.50-11.50; ⊙7:30am-2:30pm; 🅟), on the south side of town.

Burger Stand at Taos Ale House   BURGERS **$**
(Map p291; ☑575-758-5522; www.taosburgersandbeer.com; 401 Paseo del Pueblo Norte; mains $9-14; ⊙11am-11pm) Much like the Santa Fe branch (p267), this hip burger joint is a popular pick for an easy, decent meal – think burgers with bacon, Gouda and chipotle ketchup, all-beef hot dogs, falafel

sandwiches, sweet potato fries and small-batch beer.

La Cueva Cafe
MEXICAN $

(Map p291; 575-758-7001; www.lacuevacafe.com; 135 Paseo del Pueblo Sur; mains $7-14; 10am-9pm Mon-Sat) This little Mexican cafe on downtown's southeastern edge has rapidly established itself as a local classic. Satisfaction is guaranteed, whether you drop in for a morning blast of huevos rancheros, come for dinner to savor the garlic salmon or *cochinita pibil* (shredded citrus-marinated pork, wrapped in a banana leaf), or indulge in a slice of coconut Key lime pie.

Raw To Go
VEGETARIAN $

(Map p291; 575-613-0893; 105b Quesnel St; mains $5-11; 11am-7pm Thu-Sat, 2-7pm Sun;) Expect the unexpected at this pocket-size vegan restaurant; there's no fixed menu, they simply prepare whatever's freshly available on the day. It's all organic and, yes, pretty much all of it is entirely raw. Tasty possibilities include shiitake seaweed soup, bountiful hummus or raw pizza, plus smoothies and homemade kambucha.

El Gamal
MIDDLE EASTERN $

(Map p291; 575-613-0311; www.elgamaltaos.com; 12 Doña Luz St; mains $7-12; 9am-5pm Mon-Wed, 9am-9pm Thu-Sat, 11am-3pm Sun;) Vegetarians rejoice – at this casual Middle Eastern place, there's no meat anywhere. Even if the falafel doesn't quite achieve the stated aim to promote peace through evolving taste buds, it certainly tastes good. There's a kids playroom in the back with tons of toys, plus a pool table and free wi-fi.

El Meze
NEW MEXICAN $$

(Map p288; 575-751-3337; www.elmeze.com; 1017 Paseo del Pueblo Norte; sharing plates $8-14, mains $17-24; 5:30-9:30pm Mon-Sat) Attractive, intimate but often rather hectic restaurant that serves Spanish-style sharing plates such as pork rinds or roasted peppers as well as more substantial mains including duck confit with preserved lemon, pork tamales with green chiles, and a fabulous vegetarian pasta and beans.

Doc Martin's
NEW MEXICAN $$

(Map p291; 575-758-1977; www.taosinn.com; 125 Paseo del Pueblo Norte, Historic Taos Inn; breakfast & lunch $7-15, dinner $15-28; 11am-3pm & 5-9pm Mon-Fri, 7:30am-2:30pm & 5-9pm Sat & Sun) Hang out where Bert Philips (the original Doc Martin's bro-in-law) and Ernest Blumenschein

cooked up the idea of the Taos Society of Artists. Sit by the kiva fireplace, pop a cork on an award-winning wine, dive into the *chile rellenos*, sautéed shrimp with polenta or braised lamb shank, and maybe you'll be inspired to great things as well.

★ Love Apple
NEW MEXICAN $$$

(Map p288; 575-751-0050; www.theloveapple.net; 803 Paseo del Pueblo Norte; mains $17-29; 5-9pm Tue-Sun) A real 'only in New Mexico' find, from the setting in the converted 19th-century adobe Placitas Chapel, to the delicious, locally sourced and largely organic food. Everything – from the local beefburger with red chile and blue cheese, via the tamales with mole sauce, to the wild boar tenderloin – is imbued with regional flavors, and the understated rustic-sacred atmosphere enhances the experience. Reserve; cash only.

★ Lambert's
MODERN AMERICAN $$$

(Map p291; 505-758-1009; www.lambertsoftaos.com; 123 Bent St; lunch $11-14, dinner $23-38; 11:30am-close;) Consistently hailed as the 'Best of Taos,' this charming old adobe just north of the Plaza remains what it's always been – a cozy, romantic local hangout where patrons relax and enjoy sumptuous contemporary cuisine, with mains ranging from lunchtime's barbecue pork sliders to dinner dishes such as chicken mango enchiladas or Colorado rack of lamb.

Trading Post Cafe
ITALIAN $$$

(Map p288; 575-758-5089; www.tradingpostcafe.com; 4179 Hwy 68, Ranchos de Taos; lunch $10.50-17, dinner $16.50-32; 11am-9pm Tue-Sat, 10am-2pm Sun) This longtime favorite strikes a perfect balance of relaxed and refined. Everything on the largely Italian menu, from pasta specials to rosemary chicken, tastes good. Portions tend to be large, so think about splitting a dish – or, if you want to eat cheap but well, get a small salad and small soup. It'll be plenty.

🍷 Drinking & Nightlife

ParCht
WINE BAR

(Map p291; 575-758-1994; parcht.com; 103 E Plaza; 2-9pm Tue-Sat) On the plaza for happy hour? Stop by for a diverse selection of wines from Europe and the West Coast, paired with charcuterie and cheese boards.

Taos Mesa Brewery
BREWERY

(Map p288; 575-753-1900; www.taosmesabrewing.com; 20 ABC Mesa Rd; noon-11pm) This hangar-like space out by the airport has great beers, live music and à la carte tacos, making it a can't-miss après-ski/hike hangout. Indoor seating is limited – but that's to ensure there's space for the funk on Fridays and two-step on Sundays.

Taos Mesa Taproom
BREWERY

(Map p291; ☑ 575-758-1900; 201 Paseo del Pueblo Sur; ⊗noon-11pm) If you don't fancy the 15-minute drive out to the brewery, the in-town taproom will hook you up with the same beers, plus wood-fired pizzas ($13 to $22), hard cider and wine. Parking is limited.

World Cup
COFFEE

(Map p291; ☑ 575-737-5299; 102 Paseo del Pueblo Norte; ⊗7am-6pm) The little World Cup coffeehouse is one of those places that looks too obvious, perfectly poised between the Plaza and the highway, to be any good. Or maybe you don't have that problem? Anyway, if you fancy a quick well-made espresso or succulent pastry, with some good old-fashioned counter-cultural edge, it's actually ideal, albeit short of seating room. Cash only.

Caffe Tazza
CAFE

(Map p291; ☑ 575-758-8706; 122 Kit Carson Rd; ⊗7am-6pm) For a taste of how Taos used to be, back when hippies stalked the earth – or just to enjoy some great coffee – call in at Tazza, which now caters mostly to the crunchy-hipster-tattooed crowd. It's not everyone's cup of tea, but there's plenty of space to kick back, and most evenings see open mics or live music.

Adobe Bar
BAR

(Map p291; ☑ 575-758-2233; Historic Taos Inn, 125 Paseo del Pueblo Norte; ⊗11am-11pm, music 6:30-10pm) There's something about the Adobe Bar. Everyone in Taos seems to turn up at some point each evening, to kick back in the comfy covered atrium, enjoying no-cover live music from bluegrass to jazz, and drinking the famed Cowboy Buddha margaritas. If you decide to stick around, you can always order food from the well-priced bar menu.

☆ Entertainment

KTAOS Solar Center
LIVE MUSIC

(Map p288; ☑ 575-758-5826; www.ktao.com; 9 Ski Valley Rd; ⊗bar 4-9pm Mon-Thu, to 11pm Fri & Sat) Taos' best live-music venue, at the start of Ski Valley Rd, shares its space with much-loved radio station KTAOS 101.9FM. Local and touring acts stop by to rock

the house; when there's no show, watch the DJs in the booth at the 'world's most powerful solar radio station' while hitting happy hour at the bar.

Taos Chamber Music Group
CLASSICAL MUSIC

(www.taoschambermusicgroup.org) As well as classical music from baroque to contemporary, this ensemble also performs folk- and jazz-flavored compositions from all over the world, with concerts at venues throughout New Mexico. You'll find schedules on the website.

Taos Center for the Arts
PERFORMING ARTS

(TCA; Map p291; ☑ 575-758-2052; www.tca taos.org; 133 Paseo del Pueblo Norte) In a remodeled 1890s adobe mansion, the TCA programs local and international performances of everything from chamber music to belly dancing to theatre, as well as readings and movie screenings.

Alley Cantina
LIVE MUSIC

(Map p291; ☑ 575-758-2121; www.alleycantina. com; 121 Teresina Lane; ⊗11:30am-11pm) It figures that the oldest building in Taos is a comfy bar. Built almost four centuries ago by Pueblo Indians, and briefly the office of New Mexico's first US Territorial Governor, it's now a rambling, friendly place with a poolroom, a full pub-grub menu, and live music from zydeco to rock and jazz almost nightly.

🔒 Shopping

Galleries and studios in and around Taos testify to the town's ongoing appeal for artists and craftsworkers. Taos Pueblo is a great place to buy direct from the artists.

Seconds Ecostore
ARTS & CRAFTS

(Map p291; ☑ 575-751-4500; www.seconds ecostore.com; 120 Bent St; ⊗10am-5pm) The pick of several artsy little boutiques in the John Dunn Shops, just north of the Plaza, this quirky store sells all kinds of cool recycled gifts, from solar-powered crickets to purses made from tins and miniature cardboard animal heads.

Op Cit Books
BOOKS

(Map p291; ☑ 575-751-1999; www.opcit.com; 124a Bent St; ⊗10am-6pm) Taos' best bookstore carries a fine stock of regional fiction and nonfiction, plus maps and guides, and the friendly staff are always happy to advise.

RÍO GRANDE DEL NORTE NATIONAL MONUMENT

A vast wedge of northern New Mexico, covering 242,555 acres, was designated in 2013 as Río Grande del Norte National Monument. From its southernmost tip, near Pilar 20 miles south of Taos, it stretches north along the Rio Grande as far as the Colorado state line, and also fans into the roadless wilderness to the west. Administered by the Bureau of Land Management (BLM), it was created to protect vital wildlife habitat, including a corridor used by migratory birds, and to guard against mining and mineral exploitation.

As far as most visitors are concerned, the monument consists of three major components. The first is the **Rio Grande** itself, and in particular the mighty gorge west of Taos, a prime white-water rafting destination. The other two are the Lower and Upper Gorge areas, south and north of Taos. Each offers scenic driving, camping and, above all, superb hiking.

For information on the **Lower Gorge**, call in at the **Rio Grande Gorge Visitor Center** (📞575-751-4899; Hwy 68; ⊘8am-4:30pm May-Oct, 10am-2pm Sep-Apr), where Hwy 68 meets Hwy 570. This popular stretch of river, also known as the **Orilla Verde Recreation Area** (p286), features flat water appreciated by fishers and inner-tubers, as well as waterside picnic tables and seven campgrounds. Six miles along from Hwy 68, Hwy 570 crosses the Rio Grande to reach the **Taos Junction Campground**, and then its surface turns to dirt. You can't drive beside the river all the way to Taos, but hiking trails climb either side of the gorge. We like the 1.3-mile **Slide**, which heads east up a dirt road blocked by a landslide, to give expansive vistas of the Taos Plateau and the Sangre de Cristos. Alternatively, the 9-mile **West Rim Trail** heads all the way north to the Rio Grande Gorge Bridge northwest of Taos. The walking itself is easy, but you'll need a vehicle pick-up at the far end; it also makes a great biking route.

To reach the **Upper Gorge**, drive north of Taos on Hwy 522 for 27 miles, then turn west beyond Questa to follow the spectacular 13-mile Wild Rivers Backcountry Byway, beside one of the most impressive stretches of the Rio Grande Gorge, into the **Wild Rivers Recreation Area** (p301). Several vantage points offer stupendous views – be sure not to miss the Chawalauna Overlook – while a **visitor center** (p301) has details on hiking and camping; five semi-developed tent campgrounds are accessible by car, while hikers can also reach riverside campsites down in the canyon. The **La Junta Trail** plunges 800ft down into the canyon to access the confluence of the Rio Grande and the Red River. It's only 1.3 miles one-way, but the trek back up again is so steep that you'd do better to stay down beside the Rio Grande and hike to the **Little Arsenic Campground**. Climb the gentler (but still demanding) trail to the rim from there to complete a 5-mile loop that takes around three hours.

Taos Drums MUSIC
(Map p288; 📞800-424-3786; www.taosdrums. com; 3956 Hwy 68, Ranchos de Taos; ⊘10am-5pm) Touted as the world's largest selection of American Indian drums, just south of town. All are handmade by masters from Taos Pueblo and covered with real hide. Choose from hand drums, log drums, natural-looking drums or those painted with wildlife or Pueblo motifs.

Taos Mountain Outfitters SPORTS & OUTDOORS
(Map p291; 📞575-758-9292; www.taosmountain outfitters.com; 113 N Plaza; ⊘9am-6pm Mon-Wed, 9am-8pm Thu-Sat, 10am-5pm Sun) Huge store on the Plaza, selling or renting everything you need to get out and play. The helpful staff can supply hiking info and maps.

El Rincón Trading Post VINTAGE
(Map p291; 📞575-758-9188; 114 Kit Carson Rd; ⊘10am-5pm) This shop dates back to the arrival of German trader Ralph Meyers in 1909. Even if you're not looking to buy anything, step into the dusty museum-like backroom devoted to artifacts including Indian crafts, jewelry and Old West memorabilia.

🛈 Information

Holy Cross Hospital (📞575-758-8883; taos hospital.org; 1397 Weimer Rd; ⊘emergency 24hr)

Police (📞575-758-2216; 400 Camino de la Placita)

Post Office (Map p291; 318 Paseo del Pueblo Norte, at Brooks St; ⊘8:30am-5pm Mon-Fri, 8:30am-noon & 12:30-3pm Sat)

Taos Visitor Center (Map p288; ☑575-758-3873; taos.org; 1139 Paseo del Pueblo Sur; ⏱9am-5pm; 🛜) This excellent visitor center stocks information of all kinds on northern New Mexico and doles out free coffee; everything, including the comprehensive *Taos Vacation Guide*, is also available online.

ⓘ Getting There & Around

BUS

Greyhound buses do not serve Taos, but on weekdays, **North Central Regional Transit** (Map p288; ☑866-206-0754; www.ncrtd.org) provides free shuttle service to Española, where you can transfer to Santa Fe and other northern destinations; pick-up/drop-off is at the Taos County offices off Paseo del Pueblo Sur, a mile south of the Plaza.

Taos Express has shuttle service to Santa Fe on Satuday and Sunday (one-way adult/child $5/free), connecting with RailRunner trains to and from Albuquerque.

On weekdays only, the **Chile Line** (www.ncrtd.org) runs north–south along Hwy 68 between the Rancho de Taos post office and Taos Pueblo every 30 minutes. Bus 341 Green also serves the ski valley and Arroyo Seco daily in winter. All buses are wheelchair-accessible and have space for two bikes.

CAR

Half a mile north of town, Paseo del Pueblo Norte forks: to the northeast it becomes Camino del Pueblo and heads toward Taos Pueblo, and to the northwest it becomes Hwy 64. At the next major crossroads 4 miles north of town, Hwy 64 heads west to the Rio Grande Gorge Bridge, Hwy 522 heads northwest to Questa and the Enchanted Circle, and Hwy 150 heads northeast to Arroyo Seco and the Taos Ski Valley.

AROUND TAOS

Taos Pueblo

☑575 / POP 1135 / ELEV 7112FT

New Mexico's most extraordinary – and most beautiful – American Indian site stands 3 miles northeast of Taos Plaza. An absolute must-see for anyone interested in Pueblo Indian life, history and culture, **Taos Pueblo** (Map p288; ☑575-758-1028; www.taospueblo.com; Taos Pueblo Rd; adult/child $16/free; ⏱8am-4:30pm Mon-Sat, 8:30am-4:30pm Sun, closed mid-Feb–mid-Apr) has been continuously inhabited for almost a thousand years, making it a strong contender to be the oldest community in the entire US. It's also the only living American Indian community to be designated both a World Heritage site by Unesco and a National Historic Landmark.

🏃 Activities

Taos Indian Horse Ranch   HORSEBACK RIDING
(Map p288; ☑575-758-3212; 340 Little Deer Horn Rd; 1/2hr easy ride $55/95, 2hr experienced ride $125) This American Indian–owned stables offers guided riding trips through Indian land – experienced riders can go fast. It can also arrange an overnight rafting/riding/camping trip; call for details.

🎊 Festivals & Events

Of all the Pueblos in northern New Mexico, Taos Pueblo has the most events and celebrations open to the public. **San Geronimo Day** (September 29–30) is an important feast day, with dancing and food. The **Christmas Eve** bonfire and procession is also a notable event that's well worth attending.

Taos Pueblo Pow-Wow   CULTURAL
(☑888-285-6344; www.taospueblopowwow.com; adult/child $15/free; ⏱Jul) Plains and Pueblo Indians gather for dances and workshops during the huge Taos Pueblo Pow-Wow in the second week of July, continuing a centuries-old tradition.

🍴 Eating

Tiwa Kitchen   AMERICAN INDIAN $$
(Map p288; ☑575-751-1020; 328 Veterans Hwy; mains $7-15; ⏱8am-4pm Wed-Mon) Pueblo residents and visitors alike flock to one of the few places in the state where you can sit down to a plate of American Indian treats such as *phien-ty* (blue-corn fry bread stuffed with buffalo meat), *twa chull* (grilled buffalo) or a bowl of heirloom green chile grown on Pueblo grounds. Opening hours can be erratic, especially in winter.

🛍 Shopping

Tony Reyna Indian Shop   ARTS & CRAFTS
(Map p288; ☑575-758-3835; Pueblo Rd; ⏱8am-noon & 1-6pm) In business since 1950 and now run by Tony's son Phillip, this simple adobe shop continues to sell a fine assortment of arts and crafts from Taos and neighboring Pueblos.

Arroyo Seco

575 / POP 1310 / ELEV 7634FT

For some unprocessed local flavor, a groovy plaza and a growing art scene, Arroyo Seco is the place to be. It's just 10 minutes north of Taos, halfway to Taos Ski Valley; there's not much to do, but you'll find plenty of ways to do nothing.

Sleeping & Eating

In addition to the hostel, there are three small National Forest campsites (free; May to October) on the road up to Taos Ski Valley; no potable water. There are a few eateries in town.

Abominable Snowmansion HOSTEL $
(Map p288; 575-776-8298; www.snowmansion. com; 476 Hwy 150; dm/tent/tipi $38/45/74, r with/without bath $158/140; P @ 🛜 🐾) Popular and somewhat affordable hostel in the heart of Arroyo Seco, which makes a cozy high-country alternative to paying Taos prices. A big round fireplace in the central lodge warms guests in winter, there's a shared kitchen, and you can choose between clean (if a tad threadbare) private rooms, simple dorms and, in summer, even a tipi and campground.

⭐ **Taos Cow** ICE CREAM $
(Map p288; 575-776-5640; www.taoscow.com; 485 Hwy 150; mains $6-9.25; 7am-7pm, to 6pm in winter; 🛜) The social center of Arroyo Seco makes a great stop-off en route to or from Taos Ski Valley. It's famous above all for its tasty, rich all-natural ice cream, but the espresso coffees, baked goods and deli sandwiches are all good. Cooked breakfasts include green eggs and ham – the green in question being green chile, naturally.

Getting There & Away

Bus 341 Green (free) runs daily between Taos and the ski area, passing Arroyo Seco, in winter.

Taos Ski Valley

Some people move to New Mexico just to ski bum for a couple of years at **Taos Ski Valley** (Map p288; 866-968-7386; www.skitaos. org; lift ticket adult/teen/child $98/81/61; 9am-4pm), and then inevitably end up staying longer than planned. There's just something about the abundant powder, wicked steeps

and laid-back atmosphere that makes this mountain a wintry heaven on earth – that is, if heaven has a 3274ft vertical drop.

Activities

Wheeler Peak HIKING
New Mexico's highest summit, Wheeler Peak (13,161ft), is a popular destination in summer. The Williams Lake Trail offers the shortest route (about 7 miles round-trip), though be prepared for a steep ascent. To get here, head to the Taos Ski Valley, pass the parking lot and continue up Twining Rd for about 2 miles. Park before the Bavarian restaurant.

In winter you can snowshoe up to Williams Lake (4 miles round-trip).

Rio Grande Stables HORSEBACK RIDING
(Map p288; 575-776-5913; www.riogrande stables.net; mid-May–mid-Sep) Based up by the Taos Ski Valley, this recommended company offers rides from one to four hours ($50 to $105), all-day rides and combination horseback/rafting/camping treks they'll customize just for you. Call in advance.

Sleeping

When it comes to Ski Valley lodging, high season typically runs from mid-December through March. From April to November, many lodges are closed, while those that are open offer excellent discounts. Check the Ski Valley website for ski-and-stay deals.

Bull of the Woods Yurt YURT $
(Map p276; 575-758-4761; southwestnordic center.com; yurt Mon-Thu $100, Fri-Sun $145) New Mexico's yurt of choice for backcountry skiers, the Bull of the Woods is in a prime location 2 miles out from the Taos Ski Valley, along the ridge that connects Wheeler Peak with Gold Hill at 10,800ft. Cooking is done on a propane stove (pots and utensils provided) and heating is by wood stove; it sleeps six to 10 people.

The yurt is open year-round, with lower rates outside winter. Unlike many other ski-to huts, you shouldn't need to book a year in advance.

Blake HOTEL $$$
(Map p288; 800-776-1111; www.skitaos.com/ theblake; 116 Sutton Pl; r from $368; 🛜) 🌿
Opened to much fanfare in 2017, the Blake is the new face of the Taos Ski Valley: still quirky and independent, but forward-looking and

environmentally minded. The 80 rooms here are steps from the slopes and range from luxury queens to two-bedroom suites with a gas fireplace and kitchenette.

Snakedance Condominiums & Spa RESORT $$$
(Map p288; ☎800-322-9815; www.snakedancecondos.com; 110 Sutton Pl; apt $275-750; ❄@🛜) This giant complex, which offers varying condo-style digs at the foot of the lifts, is an okay all-round option. It holds a restaurant, a bar, in-room massages and lots of other amenities, including a hot tub, a sauna and in-room kitchens.

Eating

There aren't a ton of options in the base village, but there's enough here that you'll find some variety.

Bavarian GERMAN $$
(Map p288; ☎888-205-8020; 100 Kachina Rd; lunch $13-20, dinner $14-40; ⊙11:30am-8pm) The best dining on the mountain (at the bottom of Lift 4), you can fuel up here on hearty Spätzle (noodles), Wiener Schnitzel, scrumptious Apfelstrudel and big steins of imported beer – and don't miss fondue night on Tuesdays. If you don't have a 4WD for evening access, a complimentary shuttle will pick you up at the base village. Dinner reservations required.

Stray Dog Cantina MEXICAN $$
(Map p288; ☎575-776-2894; straydogtsv.com; 105 Sutton Pl; mains $11-16; ⊙8am-9pm Dec-Apr, 11am-9pm rest of year) Famous for its flame-roasted red and green chile, this Ski Valley institution serves fabulous northern New Mexican cuisine – the breakfast burritos make great fuel-up food – along with fresh margaritas and a big selection of bottled brews. The perfect après-ski or hiking hangout.

192 at the Blake AMERICAN $$$
(Map p288; ☎575-776-5335; www.skitaos.com; 116 Sutton Pl; mains $15-34; ⊙11am-9pm) Nibble on a shared plate of calamari and parsley aioli during après ski or order up a manzo flatbread (carne asada, blue cheese, arugula and caramelized onions) or a grilled bone-in strip steak with truffle fries to refuel after a day on the slopes. A central kiva fireplace and counter seating at the open kitchen keep it casual and cozy.

Getting There & Away

To reach the valley, follow Hwy 64 for 4 miles north of Taos, then head right (northeast) on Hwy 150 toward Arroyo Seco. The 20-mile drive winds along a beautiful mountain stream. In winter, Bus 341 Green (free, one hour) runs several times a day from downtown Taos.

Enchanted Circle

Unplug, sit back, unwind and absorb the beauty. Comprising Hwys 522, 38 and 64, this scenic, looping 83-mile byway is generous with its views – crystalline lakes, pine forests draped with feldspar, alpine highlands rising to Wheeler Peak and rolling steppes carpeted with windswept meadows. You'll understand why they call it the Enchanted Circle as soon as you start driving. To fully experience its sublime natural nuances, though, ride it on a bike. In warm weather, the heady combination of spectacular scenery and challenging altitude entices cyclists from all over the world.

The site www.enchantedcircle.org has information about events along the route. Fill your gas tank in Taos, where it's cheaper, and allow at least a full day to make the journey.

Questa

☎575 / POP 1767 / ELEV 7450FT

Four centuries ago, when Spain held sway in these parts, little Questa, 24 miles north of Taos, was the northernmost settlement in the Americas. Historically a mining town (the nearby molybdenum mine finally closed down in 2014), Questa has recently acquired a new identity as an enclave for artists, subsistence farmers and other organic types who choose to move off the grid.

The curious name comes courtesy of a typo when the modern township was founded in 1842: it was meant to be called 'Cuesta,' Spanish for cliff or large hill, which would fit its looks perfectly.

Just northeast of town, the Latir Peak Wilderness is one of the sweetest spots around, perfect for a rewarding night or two of backpacking, or an intense day hike. Scenic alpine trails that climb high above the treeline include a loop that ascends 12,708ft Latir Peak.

Sleeping & Eating

There are two places renting cabins in Questa and an RV park, but overall you're better off spending the night in Taos. Questa also has limited dining options.

Wild Rivers Recreation Area Campground
CAMPGROUND **$**

(Map p276; day-use $3; campsites $5-7) Five small first-come, first-served campgrounds dot the scenic drive that loops through the sage-speckled recreation area. Potable water and toilets on-site.

Wildcat's Den
DINER **$**

(☑575-586-1119; 2457 Hwy 522; mains $5-9; ⊙11am-5pm Tue-Sat) Burger joint that also serves Mexican-style fast food, featuring its renowned homemade salsa.

❶ Information

Wild Rivers Recreation Area Visitor Center
(☑575-586-1150; Hwy 378; ⊙10am-4pm late May-early Sep) Information on the northern section of the Río Grande del Norte National Monument, including where to camp, fish, mountain bike and hike. The scenic highlight up here is La Junta Point, overlooking the confluence of the Rio Grande and Red River. The center is located 12 miles west of Questa.

Red River

☑575 / POP 482 / ELEV 8650FT

The cusp of the 19th and 20th centuries saw a pretty wild populace of gold miners and mountain men up in Red River, with saloons and brothels lining its muddy thoroughfares. In the early years of the 21st century you'll still encounter mountain men and women, but this time around they're wearing Gore-Tex instead of skins, and looking for a whole different kind of extracurricular activity (for the most part).

Red River now appears as a cluster of cheerfully painted shops and chalets, decked out in German-peasant style with an Old West theme – you'd think it wouldn't work, but it does. The historic buildings and dilapidated mines have been joined by a ski resort, adventure outfitters, ticky-tacky shops galore and, this being New Mexico, art galleries.

Just be warned that the whole place pretty much shuts down during the off-season, from mid-March to mid-May.

🏃 Activities

Take Hwy 578 to the edge of the Wheeler Peak Wilderness (p299) for challenging but oh-so-worth-it hikes. **Horseshoe Lake Trail** leaves the Ditch Cabin Site for a 12-mile

round-trip to the 11,950ft-high lake with good camping and fishing. The trailhead is on FR 58A, off Hwy 578, about 8 miles from Red River.

★ Enchanted Forest
SKIING

(Map p276; ☑575-754-6112; www.enchantedforestxc.com; Hwy 38; adult/teen/child day pass $18/15/9, rentals $16/13/8; ⊙9am-4:30pm Nov-Mar) At New Mexico's premier Nordic ski area, 23 miles of groomed cross-country ski trails and 12 miles of snowshoe trails wend through aspen and fir forests, leading to scenic viewpoints. You can even stay overnight in a **backcountry yurt** ($65 to $100). In summer, hike and mountain bike the trails free of charge.

Don't miss February's **Just Desserts**, when area restaurants set up stands to showcase their sweet stuff.

Red River Ski Area
SKIING

(☑575-754-2223; www.redriverskiarea.com; 400 Pioneer Rd; lift ticket adult/child $73/57) Red River gets most of its tourism in winter, when folks flock to this ski area catering to families and newbies with packages that include lessons and equipment or half-price early-season weekends. Snowboarders and skiers alike should check out the terrain park complete with boxes and rails, specifically designed to lure you east from Angel Fire.

🛏 Sleeping

Many of Red River's 50-plus RV parks, lodges, B&Bs and hotels offer package deals with local outfitters and the ski area, plus healthy discounts on off-season room rates. Attractive USFS campgrounds line the road between Questa and Red River, open from the end of May through September.

Texas Red's Steakhouse
INN **$**

(☑575-754-2922; www.texasredssteakhouse.com; 400 E Main St; r from $84; ❄🛜) Dating from the 1940s, this downtown joint feels historic and quaint but not old. Rooms are small but comfy, and an upstairs lounge holds couches and books. Formerly known as the Lodge at Red River, it now takes its identity from Red River's best beef house, downstairs, which also serves seafood, lamb, chicken and elk.

Copper King Lodge
LODGE **$$**

(☑800-727-6210; www.copperkinglodge.com; 307 E River St; r $86-99, apt $146-206; ❄🛜) Rough-hewn wood, rustic furnishings and a great backyard make these cabin-style

SCENIC DRIVE: VALLE VIDAL LOOP

In the mood for a longer drive through the highlands? Try the 173-mile Valle Vidal Loop, which departs the Enchanted Circle in Questa, heads north past the Wild Rivers Recreation Area on Hwy 522, and rejoins the road more traveled in Eagle Nest via Hwy 64.

The bulk of the route is impassable during winter, and the washboard gravel road of FR 1950 is no picnic at the best of times – bring a spare tire. The northern gate to FR 1950 is closed April 1 to early June for elk calving season, while the southern gate closes January through March to let them winter in peace. Best seen in the morning and evening, the estimated 1500 elk are a major attraction the rest of the year.

From the small town of Costilla, just below the Colorado border, take Hwy 196 east. Before long, the road turns to dirt and heads into a wilderness – where elk, wildcats and bears roam – that's sometimes called 'New Mexico's Yellowstone.'

FR 1950 follows stocked Rio Costilla – a fly-fisher's paradise – and opens on to national forest with unlimited access to multiday backpacking adventures. The road wends through meadows and forest, with outstanding views of granite peaks. Though it's possible to make this drive in a long day trip from Taos, it's much better to stay overnight, either in one of the four developed campgrounds or in the backcountry.

The route becomes blessedly paved again when you make a left onto Hwy 64 for the drive back to Eagle Nest, where you meet the Enchanted Circle once more.

apartments and condos with kitchenettes, stretching beside the river close to the ski lifts (they're ski-in, ski-out in winter), great value. But it's the riverfront hot tub that seals the deal. Rates vary wildly throughout the year.

X Eating

Barbecue, burgers and pizzas keep the hungry skiers and hikers fed. If you prefer line dancing with your barbecue, Red River is a favorite stop on the country-music circuit. Catch live acts on weekends at venues around town.

Shotgun Willie's DINER $
(⏺575-754-6505; www.shotgunwilliescafe.com; 403 W Main St; mains $5-13; ⏱7am-2pm) Locals love this tiny place, serving the ultimate hangover sop-up, artery-clogging breakfast specials of fried eggs, meats and potatoes. The true house specialty is barbecue, served by the pound. Order the brisket combo.

☆ Entertainment

Frye's Old Town Shootout LIVE PERFORMANCE
(⏺575-754-3028; 100 W Main St; ⏱4pm Tue, Thu & Sat Jun-Sep; 🚸) **FREE** In summer, the kids won't want to miss downtown Frye's Old Town Shootout. It celebrates the Second Amendment in all its ten-gallon hat, buckskin-jacket glory, as good guys try to stop the bad guys from robbing a bank and end up in a faux showdown right in the center of town.

ℹ Information

Red River Chamber of Commerce (⏺575-754-3030; www.redriverchamber.org; River St; ⏱8am-5pm) The local chamber of commerce runs a helpful visitor center, and publishes a comprehensive guide with details of the surrounding wilderness.

Eagle Nest

⏺575 / POP 276 / ELEV 8200FT

This windswept high-meadow hamlet is a good place to explore the great outdoors. In winter, it's home to roughly five times as many elk as people; the 1500-strong local herd can frequently be seen browsing on the slopes above the highway.

◉ Sights

Cimarron Canyon State Park STATE PARK
(Map p276; ⏺575-377-6271; www.emnrd.state. nm.us; day-use per vehicle $5) Seven miles east of Eagle Nest on US 64, Cimarron Canyon State Park runs alongside a dramatic 8-mile stretch of the scenic Cimarron River, hued in pine greens and volcanic grays. There are good hiking, fishing and picnic opportunities here, as well as four campgrounds ($10; no hookups).

Eagle Nest Lake State Park LAKE
(Map p276; ⏺575-377-1594; www.nmparks. com; day-use per vehicle $5) The community

of Eagle Nest sits at the edge of a 2400-acre lake that's filled with pike. Motorboat rentals are available at **Eagle Nest Marina** (Map p276; ☎575-377-6941; 28386 Hwy 64; half-day rentals $80; ⊙7am-3:30pm). You can camp here ($10), but it's not as nice as nearby Cimarron Canyon.

🛏 Sleeping

There are two hotels and two campgrounds in Eagle Nest, but few dining options.

Laguna Vista Lodge HISTORIC HOTEL $
(☎575-377-6522; www.lagunavistalodge.com; 51 Therma Dr; r $85-200; ❋☎❋) This in-town lodge doesn't look that promising from outside, but its rooms and cabins are spacious and comfortable – some beside the lake have full kitchens – and it's all part of an Old West complex that includes **Calamity Jane's Restaurant** (mains $8 to $14) and the old-timey Laguna Vista Saloon.

Angel Fire

☎575 / POP 1178 / ELEV 8400FT

Angel Fire may be polarizing, but it remains one of New Mexico's most popular ski resorts. Even if the town itself looks pretty much like time-share condo-land, no one can question the beauty of the surrounding mountains and valleys, and that famous northern New Mexico light.

🏃 Activities

Angel Fire Resort SKIING
(☎800-633-7463; www.angelfireresort.com; Hwy 434; lift ticket adult/teen/child $75/65/55; ⊙Dec-Mar; 🎿) Angel Fire isn't huge (450 acres), but it may be just the right size for beginning skiers and vacationing families. Most trails are green or blue; if you're looking for more of a challenge, there are a few glades and hike-to areas to explore. Additionally, there's a 400ft-long, competition-quality half-pipe, three terrain parks and tubing and sledding hills.

In summer, a bike park with over 60 miles of trails, six ziplines and a disc golf course entertain visitors.

Nordic Center SKIING
(☎575-377-4488; www.angelfireresort.com; 100 Country Club Dr; adult/child day pass $18/10, rentals $18/10; ⊙10am-4pm Fri-Sun) Seven-and-a-half miles of groomed cross-country ski and snowshoeing trails. Rentals and lessons available.

🛏 Sleeping & Eating

Hwy 434, or Mountain View Blvd as it is known in town, is the main drag through Angel Fire and has a couple of places to stay. You'll also find the best selection of restaurants in the Enchanted Circle here.

Elkhorn Lodge LODGE $$
(☎575-377-2811; www.nancyburch.com/elk-horn-lodge; 3377 Hwy 434; r from $200; ❋☎) This central lodge features decks off all rooms, and suites that sleep six and have kitchenettes. Its Campfire Cafe is open for all meals, while the Equestrian Center offers lessons and trail rides.

Lodge at Angel Fire LODGE $$$
(☎800-633-7463; www.angelfireresort.com; 10 Miller Lane; r from $260; ❋☎❋❋) Families will dig the ski resort's ski-chalet-style lodging option, which offers family-oriented packages and organizes children's activities, especially in summer. If you're not traveling with children, it's big enough to not feel like kid central. Three on-site restaurants mean you won't go hungry. Multinight stays are often required.

Om Asian Kitchen ASIAN $
(☎575-322-2015; 3453 Mountain View Blvd; mains $9-16; ⊙11am-8pm) For a change of pace, this friendly spot prepares homemade Asian-esque dishes (pork and shrimp dumplings, kung pao chicken) that don't break the bank.

Elements AMERICAN $$$
(☎575-377-3055; www.angelfireresort.com; 100 Country Club Dr, Angel Fire Resort Country Club; mains $22-36; ⊙5-9pm Tue-Sat) This elegant, opulent mountain-view restaurant is very much Angel Fire's fine-dining option, serving hearty alpine food such as organic elk loin and Vienna-style veal cutlets – vegetarians are advised to seek their pleasures elsewhere.

🍸 Drinking & Nightlife

There are two or three restaurant-bars in town.

Enchanted Circle Brewing BREWERY
(☎505-216-5973; 20 Sage Lane; ⊙11am-9pm) In addition to an array of $3.50 beers during happy hour (4pm to 6pm), the local brewery has teamed up with the Pork Belly Deli to serve good sandwiches and fish tacos to munch on ($8 to $20). Occasional live music on weekend nights.

ℹ Information

Visitor Center (☑ 575-377-6555; www. angelfirefun.com; 3365 Mountain View Blvd; ⊙ 9am-5pm) To call on local expertise and pick up information, be sure to drop in at Angel Fire's visitor center.

ℹ Getting There & Around

Angel Fire is strung out along the northern terminus of Hwy 434, just south of the intersection with Hwy 64. Continue west on Hwy 64 through the Carson National Forest back to Taos.

MORA VALLEY & NORTHEASTERN NEW MEXICO

East of Santa Fe, the lush Sangre de Cristo Mountains give way to high and vast rolling plains. Dusty grasslands stretch to infinity and beyond – or at least to Texas. Cattle and dinosaur prints dot a landscape punctuated by volcanic cones. Ranching is an economic mainstay, and on many stretches of road you'll see more cattle than cars – and quite possibly herds of bison too.

The Santa Fe Trail, along which early traders rolled in wagon trains, ran from Missouri to New Mexico. You can still see the wagon ruts in some places off I-25 between Santa Fe and Raton. For a bit of the Old West without a patina of consumer hype, this is the place.

Raton

☑ 575 / POP 6540 / ELEV 6680FT

Raton may not be a big tourist destination, but this well-preserved town will hold your attention for a short stroll. Founded when the railroad arrived in 1879, it quickly grew into an important railway stop and mining and ranching center. The small historic district along 1st, 2nd and 3rd Sts (between Clark and Rio Grande Aves) harbors over two dozen buildings.

◉ Sights

Folsom Museum   MUSEUM
(☑ 575-278-2122; cnr Hwys 325 & 456; $1.50; ⊙ 10am-5pm Jun-Sep) This whimsical general store holds an eclectic collection of items related to local history (though no actual artifacts from Folsom Man). Not a destination in itself, it's nevertheless a possible detour if you're already at the Capulin Volcano (p305), 8 miles south.

Shuler Theater   THEATER
(www.shulertheater.com; 131 N 2nd St) Still used for performances, this downtown theater dates from 1915, and has an elaborate European rococo interior. The murals gracing its foyer, depicting regional history from 1845 to 1895, were painted in the 1930s by Manville Chapman.

Raton Museum   MUSEUM
(☑ 575-445-8979; www.theratonmuseum.org; 108 S 2nd St; adult/child $5/free; ⊙ 9am-5pm Tue-Sat May-Sep, 10am-4pm Wed-Sat Oct-Apr) Housed in the 1906 Coors Building, the great little Raton Museum features similar displays of fading photos, artifacts from Raton's mining days, and historical accounts of the Santa Fe Trail.

🛏 Sleeping & Eating

Time-warp mom-and-pop motels line 2nd St south of downtown, while the national chain hotels gather on Hwy 64 to the east and west.

Budget Host Melody Lane Motel   MOTEL $
(☑ 575-445-3655; www.budgethostmelodylane. com; 136 Canyon Dr; r from $53; ❄ 🐾) This throwback motel in the north of town is the pick of the locally owned sleeping options, with spacious, clean rooms. Be sure to get a room with a Thermasol steam shower – a mini sauna that works surprisingly well.

Sugarite Canyon State Park   CAMPGROUND $
(☑ 575-445-5607; www.emnrd.state.nm.us; Hwy 526; tent sites $8-10, RV sites $14-18, per vehicle $5; 🐾) The nicest place to stay near Raton, with two campsites set amid the pretty mesas and forests of Sugarite Canyon: Lake Alice and Soda Pocket. Lake Alice is open year-round; Soda Pocket is open May through September. The park is 10 miles northeast of town via Hwy 72 and Hwy 526.

In summer, a number of short hiking trails branch off a half-mile nature trail, while in winter the 7800ft elevation is suitable for cross-country skiing and snowshoeing.

Vermejo Park Ranch   RANCH $$$
(☑ 877-288-7637; www.vermejoparkranch.com; Hwy 555; r incl meals s/d $600/900; @) Maintained by Ted Turner as a luxury fishing and hunting lodge, this beautifully situated ranch sprawls splendidly across 920 sq miles of forests, meadows and mesas 40 miles west of Raton. Guests can take wildlife-watching and photography tours, or ride horses through classic Western terrain. During the autumn, the ranch is open to hunters only.

SCENIC DRIVE: CAPULIN VOLCANO & FOLSOM MAN TERRITORY

A 50-mile loop through the high mountain plains above Raton, Capulin Volcano & Folsom Man Territory isn't just another stretch of pavement – it's a prehistory lesson, complete with extinct volcanoes.

In 1908, local cowboy George McJunkin, a former slave, made one of the most important archaeological discoveries in US history, near the tiny town of Folsom, 40 miles east of Raton. Spotting some strange bones in Wild Horse Arroyo, he realized that these were no ordinary cattle bones. And so he kept them, suspecting correctly that they came from an extinct species of bison. McJunkin mentioned his find to various people, but not until 1926 was the site properly excavated.

Until then, scientists thought that humans had inhabited North America for, at most, 4000 years. With this single find, the facts about the continent's ancient inhabitants had to be completely revised. Subsequent excavations found stone arrowheads in association with extinct bison bones thought to date from 8000 BC. These Paleo-Indians became known as **Folsom Man**. Recent dating techniques suggest that these artifacts are in fact 10,800 years old, among the oldest discovered on the continent, although it's now clear that people have lived in the Americas for even longer.

The area is also renowned for its volcanoes. Rising 1300ft above the surrounding plains, **Capulin Volcano National Monument** (☑575-278-2201; www.nps.gov/cavo; vehicle $7; ☺8am-5pm Jun-Aug, to 4:30pm Sep-May) is the easiest to visit. From the visitor center, a 2-mile road spirals up the mountain to the crater rim. A quarter-mile trail drops into the crater, created by an eruption 60,000 years ago, while a more scenic mile-long trail undulates around the rim, which at its highest point is 8182ft above sea level. Two other trails cross lava flows at the base. The entrance is 3 miles north of Capulin, 30 miles east of Raton on Hwy 87.

✖ Eating & Drinking

Bruno's Pizza & Wings PIZZA $
(☑575-445-9512; www.brunospizzaraton.com; 244 S 1st St; pizzas $9-19; ☺11am-8pm Mon & Wed-Fri, to 9pm Sat & Sun) This friendly spot across from the train station is one of the only eateries of note in Raton. Pizzas run from standard margheritas to more local options, including buffalo wings and green chili toppings. Beer on tap.

Enchanted Grounds CAFE
(☑575-445-2219; 111 Park Ave; ☺7am-4pm Mon-Fri, 8am-2pm Sat; ☎) Downtown Raton is noticeably short on eating options, but you can pick up good coffee and snacks at this small cafe, a lively morning meeting place for locals close to the railroad station.

ⓘ Information

Raton Visitor Center (☑575-445-9551; www.exploreraton.com; 100 Clayton Rd; ☺8am-5pm May-Sep, shorter hours Oct-Apr) Raton's helpful visitor center has statewide information.

ⓘ Getting There & Away

Raton sits at the intersection of I-25 and Hwy 87, 8 miles south of the Colorado border.

Amtrak's *Southwest Chief* stops here, but almost all visitors come in private vehicles. Winter snowstorms may occasionally close Raton Pass, just north of town, potentially stranding drivers heading to or from Colorado.

Clayton

☑575 / POP 2874 / ELEV 5050FT

Sometimes when you're in the mood for a detour to nowhere, there's nowhere to go. That's not true here. Ranches and prairie grasses surround Clayton, a quiet town with a sleepy Western feel, close to the Bravo Dome Field – the world's largest natural deposit of carbon dioxide gas – and the Texas state line.

◉ Sights

Kiowa National Grasslands NATIONAL PARK
(www.fs.fed.us/grasslands) FREE Extending from New Mexico's least-populated county into Texas and Oklahoma, the Kiowa National Grasslands consist of high-plains ranchland – endless, vast and lonely. Farmed throughout the early 20th century, the soil suffered from poor agricultural techniques and essentially blew away during the dust-bowl years of the 1930s. There are two main

parcels: the more popular Mills Canyon, some 75 miles southwest of Clayton, and McNees Crossing, 22 miles northeast of Clayton and once part of the Santa Fe Trail.

Clayton Lake State Park   LAKE
(✆575-374-8808; www.emnrd.state.nm.us; Hwy 370; per vehicle $5) This pretty lake 12 miles northwest of Clayton makes a good spot for swimming and camping (tent/RV sites $10/14), and also holds over 500 dinosaur footprints left by eight different species.

Herzstein Memorial Museum   MUSEUM
(✆575-374-2977; www.herzsteinmuseum.com; 22 S 2nd St; ⊙10am-5pm Tue-Sat May-Aug, to 4pm Sep-Apr) FREE The chief focus here is the biggest event in Clayton's history – the 1901 arrest and hanging of infamous train robber Black Jack Ketchum.

🛏 Sleeping & Eating

Hotel Eklund (✆575-446-1939; www.hotel eklund.com; 15 Main St; r from $90; ❋🛜🐾) is the most atmospheric sleeping choice here. It's also the place for a bite or a sundowner.

Cimarron

✆575 / POP 965 / ELEV 6430FT

Even for this part of the world, Cimarron has a wild past. Right at the far western edge of the plains, just as the mountains begin to swell, it long served as a stop on the Santa Fe Trail, a hangout for gunslingers, train robbers, desperadoes, lawmen and other Wild West figures such as Kit Carson, Buffalo Bill Cody, Annie Oakley, Wyatt Earp, Jesse James and Doc Holliday.

Cimarron's clutch of historic buildings are considerably more peaceful today – until you come upon the Philmont Ranch south of town, that is. The world's largest Scout camp, Philmont has been a rite of passage for Scouts since 1938, introducing over 20,000 teenagers each year to the thrills of 12-day backpacking treks, rattlesnakes in the trail and life without video games.

◉ Sights

St James Hotel   HISTORIC BUILDING
(www.exstjames.com; 617 Collison St) Even if you don't plan to spend the night, be sure to sneak a peek behind the Territorial-style adobe exterior of the old St James Hotel, which started life as a saloon in 1873, and whose venerable walls – sadly, they can't speak – are said to have witnessed the deaths

of 26 men. Not surprisingly, it's said to be so haunted that one room is never rented out.

Philmont Museum   MUSEUM
(✆575-376-1136; www.philmontscoutranch.org; 17 Deer Run Rd; ⊙8am-5:30pm Jun-Aug, shorter hours rest of year) FREE More of a gift shop and bookstore than a museum, there are nonetheless a smattering of Philmont-related artifacts here. Stop by the museum or call ahead to arrange free guided tours of the nearby **Villa Philmonte**, Waite Phillips' 1927 ranch house. In summer, Philmont's Kit Carson Museum – where staff reenact life in 1850s New Mexico – is also worth a visit. It's located 7 miles south of camp.

🛏 Sleeping & Eating

Cimarron has a small selection of mostly mediocre dining options. Head to the St James Hotel for a drink.

Casa del Gavilan   B&B $$
(✆575-376-2246; www.casadelgavilan.com; Hwy 21; r from $116; ◉) Set on 225 acres, surrounded by the Philmont Ranch 6 miles south of Cimarron, this magnificent Pueblo Revival house was built around 1908. The four double rooms are decorated with Southwestern antiques and art and come complete with high ceilings, vigas and thick adobe walls. A two-room guesthouse sleeps up to four people.

St James Hotel   HISTORIC HOTEL $$
(✆575-376-2664; www.exstjames.com; 617 Collison St; r $85-135; ❋🛜) The public spaces here, including a decent midrange restaurant and a bar with a pool table, are pure Victoriana, all dark wood and animal heads. The 12 historic rooms in the main building have a genuine period feel (no TVs); an annex holds 10 modern rooms.

❶ Information

Chamber of Commerce (www.cimarronnm. com; 104 Lincoln St; ⊙hours vary) Not reliably open, though the website is helpful.

Las Vegas

✆505 / POP 13,691 / ELEV 6430FT

The bordellos of America's original sin city, Las Vegas, NM, were dishing out carnal pleasures when that other Vegas was still just a meadow in the wilderness. Established by the Mexican government in 1835 and reappropriated by the United States in

1846, 19th-century Las Vegas was a true-blue boomtown: a place where the Santa Fe Trail and the Santa Fe Railroad passed through, Doc Holliday gambled and opened up a saloon, and Billy the Kid held court with his pal Vicente Silva (leader of the Society of Bandits – New Mexico's toughest gang).

Today, hundreds of historic buildings grace its sleepy downtown, which has repeatedly served Hollywood as a Western backdrop; *Wyatt Earp* and Oscar-winner *No Country for Old Men* are just a couple of the movies filmed here. Las Vegas also acts as gateway to the southeastern corner of the Pecos Wilderness and to Las Vegas National Wildlife Refuge.

Hwy 85, or Grand Ave, which runs north–south parallel to the interstate, is the main thoroughfare; the historic district centers on the Old Town Plaza, a few blocks west.

◉ Sights & Activities

Las Vegas National
Wildlife Refuge   WILDLIFE RESERVE
(Map p276; www.fws.gov; ⊙dawn-dusk) **FREE** Five miles southeast of Las Vegas via Hwys 104 and 281, this 14-sq-mile refuge has marshes, woodlands and grasslands to which upwards of 250 bird species have found their way. Visitors can follow an 8-mile drive or hike one of the nature trails.

Villanueva State Park   PARK
(Map p276; ☑575-421-2957; www.emnrd.state.nm.us; 135 Dodge Rd; per vehicle $5) This pretty state park, about 35 miles south of Las Vegas via I-25 and Hwy 3, lies in a red rock canyon on the Rio Pecos valley. A small visitor center and self-guided trails explain the area's history: this was once a main travel route for American Indians and, in the 1500s, for the Spanish conquistadors. A campground (tent/RV sites $10/18) is open year-round.

Villanueva & San Miguel   HISTORIC SITE
Along Hwy 3, the Spanish colonial villages of Villanueva and San Miguel (which has a fine church, built in 1805) stand amid vineyards belonging to the Madison Winery (Map p276; ☑575-421-8028; Hwy 3; ⊙tastings by appointment), which has a tasting room.

Montezuma Hot Springs   HOT SPRINGS
FREE Just past the town of Montezuma are natural hot springs, where a series of small pools have been built over the years. They're nothing to get too excited about, but if you enjoy a good soak, they're free and easy to access. Bring a swimsuit and towel.

Pecos Wilderness   HIKING
(Map p276; www.fs.fed.us/r3/sfe) Beyond Montezuma, Hwy 65 leads to the eastern edge of the vast Pecos Wilderness. The most popular day hike in this section is a 10-mile round-trip starting at El Porvenir campground (Map p276; Hwy 65; tent & RV sites $8, no hookups; ⊙Apr-Dec), following trail 223 to the flat summit of Hermit Peak (10,160ft), named after an Italian recluse who lived in a cave there in the mid-19th century.

To pick up topo maps and free trail guides, stop into the ranger station (p308).

🛏 Sleeping

The vast majority of sleeping options here are chain motels.

Knight's Inn   MOTEL $
(☑505-425-5994; www.knightsinn.com; 1152 N Grand Ave; r from $49; ❋@🛜🐾) The pick of the many budget motels that line Grand Ave, with clean, large rooms that have been nicely spruced up. Rates include a simple breakfast.

Plaza Hotel   HISTORIC HOTEL $$
(☑505-425-3591; plazahotellvnm.com; 230 Old Town Plaza; r $89-149; ❋@🛜🐾) This historic hotel, opened in 1882, offers affordable rates for its 72 spacious, high-ceilinged rooms. The whole place has an appealing Wild West flavor, and has rightfully brushed shoulders with celebrity in films such as *No Country for Old Men*. Although the floorboards still creak, rooms are plenty comfortable. A convivial bar (p308) and popular restaurant look out over the plaza.

✖ Eating

A handful of good dining options are in town.

MORA VALLEY

Traditional Hispanic ways remain strong in this scenic agricultural valley. The real-life model for Frank Waters' novel *People of the Valley*, it's also one of the poorest nooks in New Mexico, where more than a quarter of families live below the poverty line. The town of Mora is the hub of the valley, with small communities strung out east and west along Hwy 518.

THE RETURN OF THE CASTAÑEDA

Las Vegas was thrilled in 2014 to hear that downtown's landmark Hotel Castañeda is to reopen. Built alongside the railroad station in 1898, as the first in legendary entrepreneur Fred Harvey's chain of Western hotels, the Castañeda only lasted 50 years before closing its doors in 1948.

Now this Mission-Revival gem has been bought – reportedly for a mere $400,000 – by Alan Affeldt, the man responsible for the hugely successful restoration of the extraordinary La Posada hotel in Winslow, Arizona. Set to be refurbished with historic furniture transplanted from the Fonda hotel in Santa Fe, there's lots of potential here – though on our last visit, it still seemed to be a long way off from opening.

World Treasures Traveler's Cafe   CAFE $
(☑505-426-8638; 1814 Plaza St; salads & sandwiches $6-8.50; ☺7am-7pm Mon-Sat; 🛜) With no sign of its presence outside, this plaza coffee-and-sandwich shop is not easy to spot. Once inside, though, it's enormous, housed in a weaving gallery and filled with in-the-know locals enjoying espressos, breakfast waffles and deli sandwiches, plus a book exchange, board games and couches.

El Rialto   MEXICAN $
(☑505-454-0037; 141 Bridge St; mains $10-13; ☺10:30am-8:30pm Tue-Sat) Family-run Mexican restaurant; enter through the swinging saloon doors, and you'll doubtless find local families chowing down on huge, great-value plates of cheese-smothered burritos, tacos and fajitas.

El Fidel   MODERN AMERICAN $$
(☑505-425-6659; 510 Douglas Ave; sandwiches $8-13, pasta $11-14, dinner mains $16-24; ☺11am-3pm & 5-9pm Mon-Fri, 5-9pm Sat, 11am-2pm Sun) Helmed by chef Miguel Velasquez, El Fidel is a remarkable find for such a small town. Stop by for scrumptious sandwiches or salad during lunch, or more elaborate mains at dinner, like the lamb meatballs with walnut-mint pesto and cranberry port au jus. A handful of pasta dishes are served throughout the day.

 Drinking & Entertainment

No casinos, strip clubs or Cirque du Soleil acts here. There are two bars, however.

Borracho's Craft Booze & Brews   BAR
(☑505-615-3561; 139 Bridge St; ☺4pm-close Mon-Sat) The local watering hole features a bit too much corrugated metal, but serves an excellent variety of New Mexico beers, well-mixed cocktails and green-chile-infused vodka.

Byron T's Saloon   BAR
(230 Old Town Plaza, Plaza Hotel; ☺2-9pm) Within the Plaza Hotel and named for its resident ghost, this more upscale saloon occasionally hosts live jazz, blues and country acts.

Fort Union Drive-In   CINEMA
(Map p276; ☑505-425-9934; 3300 7th St; per car $20; ☺Fri-Sun May-Sep) One of New Mexico's few remaining drive-in movie theaters lies just north of town and has great views of the surrounding high desert. Call for showtimes.

ℹ Information

Alta Vista Regional Hospital (☑505-426-3500; www.altavistaregionalhospital.com; 104 Legion Dr; ☺emergency 24hr)
Pecos/Las Vegas Ranger District (☑505-425-3534; 1926 N 7th St; ☺8am-noon & 12.30-4.30pm Mon-Fri)
Police (☑505-425-7504; lasvegaspd.net; 318 Moreno St)
Visitor Center (☑505-425-3707; www.visitlasvegasnm.com; 500 Railroad Ave; ☺9am-5pm)

ℹ Getting There & Away

Las Vegas is located on I-25, 65 miles east of Santa Fe. The Amtrak *Southwest Chief* between Chicago and Los Angeles stops in Las Vegas daily at 12:38pm westbound, 3:03pm eastbound.

CHACO CANYON & NORTHWESTERN NEW MEXICO

New Mexico's wild northwest is home to wide-open, empty spaces. It's still dubbed Indian Country, and for good reason: huge swaths of land fall under the aegis of the Navajo, Zuni, Acoma, Apache and Laguna. This portion of New Mexico showcases remarkable ancient sites alongside modern, solitary American Indian settlements.

And when you've had your fill of culture, you can ride a historic narrow-gauge railroad through the mountains, hike around some trippy badlands or cast for huge trout.

Chama

📍 575 / POP 1016 / ELEV 7875FT

Eight miles south of the Colorado border, little Chama is tucked into a lush valley that's carved into Rocky Mountain foothills. American Indians lived and hunted here for centuries, and Spanish farmers settled the Chama River Valley in the mid-1700s, but it was the arrival of the Denver & Rio Grande Railroad in 1880 that really put Chama on the map. Although the railroad closed, the prettiest part still operates as one of the West's most scenic train trips.

🏃 Activities

★ Cumbres & Toltec Scenic Railway   RAIL
(📞 888-286-2737; www.cumbrestoltec.com; adult/child 2-12yr from $96/50; ⊗ late May–mid-Oct) The longest and highest narrow-gauge steam railroad in the US runs for 64 miles between Chama and Antonito, CO, over the 10,015ft-high Cumbres Pass. A beautiful trip, through mountains, canyons and high desert, it's at its finest in September and October, when the aspens are a-shimmer with golden leaves. Reservations essential, two weeks in advance.

Cumbres Adventure Tours   OUTDOORS
(📞 719-376-2161; www.cumbresadventuretours.com; Hwy 17) All-seasons adventure company, arranging snowmobile trips in winter, and ATV rentals in summer. It's across the border in Colorado, 15 miles north of Chama.

🎉 Festivals & Events

Chama Chile Ski Classic   SPORTS
(www.skichama.com; ⊗ Jan) This fun event includes cross-country ski races, a snowshoe race and even a fat-tire bike race. It's usually held over Martin Luther King Jr weekend in mid-January.

Chama Days   CULTURAL
(⊗ mid-Aug) Features a rodeo, firefighters' water fight and chile cook-off.

🛏 Sleeping & Eating

The best sleeping options here aren't in Chama itself – they're the four backcountry yurts operated by the Southwest Nordic Center (southwestnordiccenter.com), all in the San Juan Mountains on the Colorado side of Cumbres Pass. You'll need to ski in (bring your own gear); stay at just one or organize a full-on yurt-to-yurt trip.

★ Spruce Hole Yurt   YURT $
(📞 575-756-2746; www.yurtsogood.com; Hwy 17, Colorado; 6-person yurt weekday/weekend $115/145; ⊗ Oct-Apr) To experience a bit of wintery mountain magic, ski or snowshoe 2.5 miles to this deluxe backcountry yurt. You'll need all your own gear and food, though beds (sleeps up to six people), kitchen supplies and a wood stove are provided. There's plenty of backcountry skiing (both Nordic and tele) near the yurt. Reserve a year in advance.

Foster Hotel   HISTORIC HOTEL $
(📞 575-756-2296; www.fosters1881.com; 393 S Terrace Ave; r from $58) If you're in search of local culture, look no further. Built in 1881 as a bordello, it's the only building in Chama that survived a massive fire in the 1920s. A few rooms are said to be so haunted they're kept locked shut. The others are a bit rough around the edges; stay for the experience, not for luxury.

Chama Trails Inn   MOTEL $
(📞 575-756-2156; www.chamatrailsinn.com; 2362 Hwy 17; r from $85; ❄ 🐾 🛜) More than just another roadside motel, the 16 character-packed rooms feature abundant Southwest furniture, local artwork and hand-painted tiles. A few rooms are further warmed by gas fireplaces. A communal hot tub and sauna come in handy after hiking.

Elkhorn Lodge & Cafe   CABIN $$
(📞 575-756-2105; www.elkhornlodge.net; Hwy 84; r/cabin from $70/88; ❄ 🐾) On the banks of the Rio Chama, the Elkhorn offers proximity to blue-ribbon fly-fishing spots. Choose a simple but spacious motel room in the main log cabin or a freestanding cabin with kitchenette (great for families).

High Country Restaurant & Saloon   STEAK $$
(📞 575-756-2384; 2289 S Hwy 17; mains $8-28; ⊗ 11am-10pm) The round-the-clock throng of diners tells you this Wild West diner, at the Y-junction south of town, is something out

NEW MEXICO CHAMA

SCENIC DRIVE: CHAMA TO TAOS

This nearly 100-mile route makes a fabulous scenic way to get between Chama and Taos from late May through the first snows in mid-October. The best time for the drive is late September or early October, when the aspens are turning gold.

From Chama, start by taking Hwy 84/64 about 11 miles south to tiny Tierra Amarilla ('yellow earth,' known locally as TA), then head east on scenic Hwy 64. As the road climbs out of the Chama Valley, toward a 10,000ft pass through the Tusas Mountains, you're rewarded by spectacular views of the furrowed cliffs of **Brazos Canyon**.

Before you leave the valley, though, don't miss a visit to **Tierra Wools** (📞575-588-7231; www.handweavers.com; 91 Main St; ⏰9am-6pm Mon-Sat, 11am-4pm Sun May-late Oct, 10am-5pm Mon-Sat late Oct-Apr), a famous century-old co-operative in a rustic, century-old building in Los Ojos, south of Los Brazos, where artisans carry on the Hispanic traditions of hand-spinning, dyeing and weaving. Tierra Wools also offers a two-bedroom **guesthouse** (rooms $75 to $95), and weaving classes in summer.

of the ordinary. Whether you order a simple chile burger, a Mexican staple or one of the pricier daily grilled fish or meat specials, you can bet good money it'll be both substantial and delicious.

❶ Getting There & Away

Chama's old downtown is 1.5 miles north of the so-called Y-junction where Hwy 84/64 turns west toward Farmington and Pagosa Springs, CO, while Hwy 17 heads north toward Antonito, CO.

Jicarilla Apache Reservation

The Apache were relatively late arrivals in the Southwest, migrating in small bands from the north to reach the region around the 14th century, at much the same time as

the related Navajo. Centuries of alternating conflict and cooperation with the Pueblo peoples already living here ensued. Indeed, the name 'Apache' possibly comes from the Zuni word for enemy, apachu.

The current name of the Jicarilla people (pronounced hic-a-*ree*-ya) means 'little basket' in Spanish, reflecting their great skill in basket weaving. Apache crafts generally draw visitors to the 1360-sq-mile reservation.

Tiny **Dulce**, on Hwy 64 in the northern part of the reservation, is the tribal capital. Unlike most reservations, alcohol is available. No permits or fees are needed to drive through, and photography is permitted. The Little Beaver Celebration, which includes a rodeo, powwow and pony race, is held the third weekend of July.

Cuba

🔳 575 / POP 734 / ELEV 6906FT

Attractively overlooked by the Nacimiento Mountains, the village of Cuba is roughly halfway between I-25 to the south and the turnoff for Chaco Canyon. If you like solitude, it's a beautiful spot from which to visit Chaco, though facilities here are minimal. It's also a good spot for hiking; the epic Continental Divide Trail passes just east of town, in the San Pedro Parks Wilderness.

🛌 Sleeping & Eating

There's little in the way of lodging in Cuba outside of a no-frills motel, and not many dining or drinking options.

Sueños Encantados y Casa Vieja   B&B $
(📞505-249-7597; www.suenosencantados.com; San Pablo Rd; r $80-125; 🛜) Set on the grounds of a still-operating 19th-century ranch, this rural B&B conveys the full-on Southwest experience, complete with three rooms in the adobe casa (one with full kitchen). Continental breakfast included; full breakfast is $10 per person. It's located 8 miles south of Cuba, off of County Rd 11.

Frontier Motel   MOTEL $
(📞575-289-3474; 6474 Main St; r from $64; 🅿❄🛜🐾) No frills but not bad; the best feature of the Frontier is that it's within striking distance of Chaco Canyon.

El Bruno's   MEXICAN $$
(📞575-289-9429; www.elbrunos.com; Hwy 550; mains $8-24; ⏰11am-10pm) The best place to

eat for many miles, this riverside restaurant, close to the bridge, serves high-class Mexican specialties from *carne asada* to steak, and has a shaded outdoor patio. The green chile here is tops.

ℹ Information

Cuba Ranger District Office (☑575-289-3264; County Rd 11; ☺8am-4:30pm) Pick up information on local hikes and campgrounds. It's the last building you pass on the left at the southern end of Cuba.

Navajo Dam

Trout are jumpin' and visitors are floatin'. Navajo Lake, which stretches over 30 miles northeast and across into Colorado, was created by damming the San Juan River. At the base of the dam, there's world-class trout fishing. You can fish year-round, but a series of designated zones, each with different regulations, protect the stocks.

🏃 Activities

Simon Canyon Recreation Area HIKING
(County Rd 4280) For a superb short hike, follow County Rd 4280 a mile east of Cottonwood Campground, then walk north into the Simon Canyon Recreation Area. A round-trip hike of 40 minutes leads up onto the rim of this small side canyon, and then to an amazing single-room round tower, somehow built atop a solitary boulder by the Navajo three centuries ago.

Navajo Lake Marina BOATING
(☑505-632-3245; www.navajomarina.com; 1448 Hwy 511; kayaks per hr $12, half-day motorboat rental from $150) Pontoon, speed and houseboats are all available for rental here, as are kayaks and stand up paddleboards. River floating is popular downstream from Navajo Lake. Rent boats here and put in at the Texas Hole parking lot at milepost 12 on Hwy 511. Then lazily float 2.5 miles to Crusher Hole.

Abe's Motel & Fly Shop FISHING
(☑505-632-2194; www.sanjuanriver.com; 1791 Hwy 173; half-/full-day trip from $255/325) This is the best of several outfitters in the tiny community of Navajo Dam who provide equipment, information and guided trips. The more people in your group, the cheaper the trip.

🛏 Sleeping & Eating

Campgrounds and lodges catering to anglers are the primary sleeping options; a handful of burger joints round out the eating choices.

Cottonwood Campground CAMPGROUND $
(☑505-632-2278; www.emnrd.state.nm.us; County Rd 4280; tent/RV sites $8/14) Administered by Navajo Dam State Park, this campground occupies a lovely spot under the cottonwoods on the north side of the San Juan River, 8 miles west of Navajo Lake. It has drinking water and toilets but no showers.

Enchanted Hideaway Lodge LODGE $
(☑505-632-2634; www.enchantedhideawaylodge.com; Hwy 173; ste/house from $70/200; ❅🖥) The Enchanted Hideaway Lodge, 8 miles west of the dam, is a friendly and low-key place to spend a night or two, with several pleasant suites. Fisherfolk on a budget can stay in the good-value Fly Room, while the spacious Stone House can sleep up to eight people.

Soaring Eagle Lodge LODGE $$$
(☑505-632-3721; www.soaringeaglelodge.net; 48 County Rd 4370; r 1-/2-person $270/410; ❅🖥) For anglers especially, this peaceful riverside lodge offers multiday guided fishing tours and half- and full-board options (perfect for those wanting to devote all their waking hours to fishing). Its kitchenette suites are beautifully sited beneath the cliffs; try to get one right on the river. Wi-fi costs extra.

El Pescador NEW MEXICAN $
(☑505-632-2194; www.sanjuanriver.com; 1791 Hwy 173; mains $9-15.50; ☺6:30am-9pm Wed-Sun Mar-Oct) Standard but decent grub – burgers, enchiladas, fish 'n' chips – in Abe's Motel, 6 miles west of the dam. Staff also prepare picnic lunches for fishing trips.

Aztec

☑505 / POP 6578 / ELEV 5623FT
Little Aztec, a sleepy old-fashioned counterpoint to hyperactive Farmington a dozen miles southwest, is best known as the site of the 12th-century Pueblo now preserved at Aztec Ruins National Monument. Its quaint downtown area along Main St holds some interesting century-old architecture.

Halfway between Chaco and Mesa Verde, this is an ideal base for those interested in the Ancestral Puebloan culture and architecture.

◉ Sights

★ Aztec Ruins National Monument
ARCHAEOLOGICAL SITE

(☑ 505-334-6174; www.nps.gov/azru; 84 Ruins Rd; adult/child $5/free; ⊙ 8am-5pm Sep-May, to 6pm Jun-Aug) This prehistoric Pueblo was built around AD 1100, and connected with the larger settlement at Chaco via a road that ran due south. Its central feature, a huge great kiva, has been reconstructed to give an impression of how such places must have looked in use a thousand years ago. Another unique feature are intact original roofs in several rooms. The attached museum is particularly informative; if you can't make it down to Chaco, don't miss this site.

Aztec Museum & Pioneer Village
MUSEUM

(☑ 505-334-9829; www.aztecmuseum.org; 125 N Main Ave; adult/child $5/3; ⊙ 10am-4pm Tue-Sat May-Sep) Small but excellent history museum, with an eclectic collection of historical objects, including telephones, barbershop chairs and a great display of Victorian-era photographs, as well as original and replica early buildings, such as a church, a jail and a bank.

☆ Festivals & Events

Aztec Fiesta Days
FIESTA

(⊙ mid-Jun) The annual Aztec Fiesta Days has arts and crafts, food booths and a bonfire during which 'Old Man Gloom' is burned to celebrate the start of summer.

⌷ Sleeping & Eating

Prices for chain motels in Aztec are slightly higher than in neighboring Farmington, though Aztec is by far the nicer place to stay. It also offers a handful of decent restaurants.

Step Back Inn
HOTEL $

(☑ 505-334-1200; www.stepbackinn.com; 123 W Aztec Blvd; r $98; ❄ 🐾) Much the best place to stay in Aztec, this friendly and unexpectedly smart little motel, on the highway across from Main St and looking more like something you'd expect to find in New England than New Mexico, offers tasteful antique-furnished rooms.

Beer Belly's
BARBECUE $

(☑ 505-333-7154; 1547 W Aztec Blvd; mains $6-10; ⊙ 10:30am-8pm Mon-Sat) This roadside shack just west of town has plenty of chile-smothered everything: smothered burgers, smothered fries, smothered potato skins and delish BBQ to boot. The only problem you'll have is finding a seat.

Wonderful House
CHINESE $$

(☑ 505-334-1832; 115 W Aztec Blvd; mains $11-18; ⊙ 11am-9pm Tue-Sun) The dynamic young staff here, on the main highway next to the Step Back Inn, work hard to live up to its far-from-bashful name, serving up quick-fire platefuls of tasty Chinese food. A recommended stop if you need a break from the same old same.

☆ Entertainment

Historic Aztec Theater
LIVE MUSIC

(☑ 505-427-6748; www.crashmusicaztec.com; 104 N Main St) Great things are afoot in this venerable theater, across from the local museum. It's been brought back to life by a dynamic husband-and-wife duo who run it as a music workshop, and bring in rockabilly, blues and Americana acts to play occasional rip-roaring live gigs. Be sure to check it out if there's a show on.

Farmington

🗹 505 / POP 45,426 / ELEV 5395FT

The region's largest town is a modern oil- and gas-industry center that makes for a convenient, if uninspiring, overnight base. Farmington itself has some nice parkland on the San Juan River, but most visitors are simply passing through en route to Mesa Verde, the Four Corners or the remote and beautiful Chaco Culture National Historical Park.

◉ Sights & Activities

Shiprock
MOUNTAIN

By far the coolest sight around these parts, Shiprock – or *Tsé Bit'a'í* (Rock with Wings) in Navajo – looms eerily over the landscape 40 miles west of Farmington. A 1700ft-high volcanic plug and a lofty landmark for Anglo pioneers, it remains a sacred site to the Navajo. While it's visible from Hwy 64, you'll get better views from Hwy 491 (which, when known as Hwy 666, had a starring role in Oliver Stone's *Natural Born Killers*).

Indian Hwy 13, which almost skirts its base, is another good photo-op area. Note that non-Natives are not allowed within 3 miles of the site.

Salmon Ruins ARCHAEOLOGICAL SITE
(☑505-632-2013; www.salmonruins.com; adult/child $4/1; ⊙8am-5pm Mon-Fri, 9am-5pm Sun May-Oct, from noon Sun Nov-Apr) The ancient Pueblo preserved here was built in the early 1100s by the Chaco people. Abandoned, resettled by refugees from Mesa Verde and again abandoned before 1300, the site also includes the remains of a homestead, petroglyphs, a Navajo hogan and a wick-iup (a rough brushwood shelter). Next to a busy road, the location is not ideal. Follow Hwy 64 11 miles east of Farmington toward Bloomfield.

**Farmington Museum
at Gateway Park** MUSEUM
(☑505-599-1174; www.fmtn.org; 3041 E Main St; suggested donation $3; ⊙8am-5pm Mon-Sat) Farmington's one significant visitor attraction, this large modern museum traces the town's history and growth, with a reconstruction of its first trading post, and also mounts changing art shows. The Energy Wing covers the local gas and oil industry.

★**Bisti/De-Na-Zin
Wilderness Area** HIKING
This undeveloped realm of multicolored hoodoos, sculpted cliffs and balancing rocks is a surreal dream for photographers. Off the beaten track, it's well worth exploring if you're in the area. Follow the well-worn (but unmaintained) path from the parking area for a mile to reach the heart of the formations, then wander as you will, but bring a compass or GPS device.

Overnight camping is allowed – dawn and dusk are the most spectacular times – but you have to haul in all your water.

Farmington's Bureau of Land Management office (p314) has information. Bisti is located 38 miles south of town, off Hwy 371.

★**Festivals & Events**

Northern Navajo Nation Fair CULTURAL
(www.northernnavajonationfair.org; ⊙early Oct) Held in Shiprock and featuring a powwow, traditional dancing and rodeo, this fair is perhaps the most traditional of the large American Indian gatherings. It begins with the Night Way, a complex Navajo healing ceremony, and the Yei Bei Chei chant, which lasts for several days.

Totah Festival CULTURAL
(⊙early Sep) Labor Day weekend, with juried American Indian arts and crafts and a Navajo rug auction.

Riverfest CULTURAL
(⊙late May) Music, arts and crafts, and food.

🛏 **Sleeping & Eating**

You can find every chain hotel imaginable around the intersection of Broadway and Scott Ave. Farmington also has a number of chains and fast-food joints scattered throughout town, as well as a handful of smaller local restaurants.

Silver River Adobe Inn B&B B&B $$
(☑505-325-8219; www.silveradobe.com; 3151 W Main St; r $115-205; ❄🐾) Three miles from downtown, this lovely two-room place offers a peaceful respite among the trees on the San Juan River. Fall asleep to the sound of the river, wake to organic blueberry juice and enjoy a morning walk to the prairie-dog village. There's also an attractive

---

HIKING AZTEC'S GOLDEN ARCHES

The great little *Aztec Arches* brochure, available at Aztec's helpful **visitor center** (☑888-543-4629; www.aztecnm.com; 110 N Ash St; ⊙9am-5pm Tue-Sat; 🛜), provides driving directions to 16 of what it claims are 220 natural sandstone arches hidden away nearby.

Several of the most accessible lie just off Hwy 173, which branches east toward Navajo Dam from US 550, 1 mile north of Aztec. Exactly 5.6 miles along Hwy 173, head south into **Potter Canyon** for half a mile on a dirt road, and park at a little gas well. Three distinct arches loom within a few hundred yards' walk in different directions from here – Pillar Arch directly above the lot, and Outcrop and Alien arches silhouetted to the south and west.

Another group can be found in **Pilares Canyon**, 10.9 miles east of US 550 on Hwy 173. This time you turn left for 0.2 miles, and then left again, driving 0.4 miles to reach Peephole Arch. Be careful if you're in an ordinary vehicle; the road here is very sandy, so it may well be safer to walk from this point to reach Petroglyph, Rooftop and Two Cracks arches.

WORTH A TRIP

FINDING NAVAJO RUGS

Sure, galleries in cities and towns throughout New Mexico sell Navajo rugs, but why not have a little adventure and seek them out close to the homes of the finest weavers? The villages of **Two Grey Hills** and **Toadlena**, tucked into the eastern flank of the Chuska Mountains 35 miles south of Shiprock, are famous as the sources of the finest rugs in Navajo country. Local weavers largely reject commercially produced wool and synthetic dyes, preferring the wool of their own sheep in its natural hues. They card white, brown, grey and black hairs together, blending the colors to the desired effect, then spin and weave the wool – tight – into mesmerizing geometric patterns. Many of these world-class artisans sell their work at the **Toadlena Trading Post** (☑ 888-420-0005; www. toadlenatradingpost.com; ⊕ 9am-6pm Mon-Sat, noon-5pm Sun May-Sep, closed Sun rest of year). Prices range from $125 to $7000 or more. The turn-off is about 4 miles north of Newcomb on Hwy 491. From here it's a beautiful 10-mile drive into the hills to Toadlena.

Another off-the-beaten-path spot to check out American Indian textiles is at the monthly **Crownpoint Navajo Rug Auction** (☑ 505-730-9689; www.crownpointrug auction.com; Crownpoint), where you can talk to and buy from the weavers directly. Check the website for dates and driving directions.

adobe-and-wood guesthouse. Advance reservations required.

Kokopelli's Cave
B&B $$$

(☑ 505-860-3812; kokoscave.com; cave $280; ⊕ closed Dec-Feb) For something truly unique, sleep 70ft underground in this incredible 1650-sq-ft cave dwelling, carved from La Plata River sandstone. Equipped with a kitchen stocked for breakfast, a DVD player and a hot tub, it offers magnificent views over the desert and river, in astonishing isolation. A 3-mile drive on dirt roads and a short hike is required to reach it.

Three Rivers Eatery & Brewhouse
AMERICAN $

(☑ 505-324-2187; www.threeriversbrewery. com; 101 E Main St; mains $9-27, pizza $7.50-13.50; ⊕ 11am-9pm; 🛜👶) Managing to be both trendy *and* kid-friendly, this hip spot spreads through three different buildings along one block, serving pub grub, pizzas and its own microbrews. Try the homemade potato skins or artichoke and spinach dip; burgers are just OK. Spiffy sandwiches (Thai turkey wrap) and soups (broccoli cheddar) are served at lunchtime. Pool tables in the tap room.

🛈 Information

Bureau of Land Management (☑ 505-564-7600; www.blm.gov/nm; 6251 College Blvd; ⊕ 7:45am-4:30pm Mon-Fri) Information on the **Bisti Badlands** (p313) as well as several other sites.

San Juan Regional Medical Center Hospital (☑ 505-609-2000; www.sanjuanregional. com; 801 W Maple St) Has a 24hr emergency department.

Visitors Bureau (☑ 505-326-7602; www. farmingtonnm.org; 3041 E Main St; ⊕ 8am-5pm Mon-Sat) Useful information desk in the Farmington Museum.

🛈 Getting There & Away

Farmington is on Hwy 64, 50 miles south of Durango and 70 miles north of Chaco (bad roads make this at least a 1¾-hour drive).

Great Lakes Airlines (www.flygreatlakes. com) offers daily connections between the **Four Corners Regional Airport** (☑ 505-599-1395; www.fmtn.org/172/Airport), a mile northwest of Farmington, and Denver.

Chaco Culture National Historical Park

At the end of miles of washed-out, potholed dirt roads, in a remote corner of New Mexican desert, are some of the oldest extant ruins in the United States. Begun in the early 9th century, the great houses and colossal kivas here stood at the center of a highly organized and integrated civilization (known today as Ancestral Puebloan or Anasazi) that extended far beyond the immediate area, incorporating some 150 public structures in all. But despite the wealth of archaeological evidence that has been uncovered, Chaco culture, which reached its peak in the 11th century, remains an enigma.

The isolation and extreme climate means that few visitors pass this way (most come for the solstices), but that's all for the better. Desert hikes up sandstone cliffs and to vast 1000-year-old ruins silhouetted against expansive panoramas are perhaps best appreciated with no more than the sound of wind in your ears.

🛏 Sleeping

There is one campground here. Backcountry camping is not permitted, and you'll need to bring your own supplies.

Gallo Campground CAMPGROUND $
(📞877-444-6777; www.recreation.gov; tent & RV sites $15) This lovely but isolated spot is 1 mile east of the visitor center (the only place with water). Reserve ahead or check availability online to ensure you can get a spot.

ℹ Information

Visitor Center (⊙8am-5pm) Pick up self-guided booklets for major sites ($1 each), visit the museum, arrange backcountry hiking permits, and inquire about astronomy programs (April to October) and guided tours of Pueblo Bonito.

ℹ Getting There & Away

The park can only be accessed along rutted dirt roads, which can become impassable after heavy rains or snow. RVs may have trouble even in favorable conditions. It's a minimum 90-minute drive from the closest towns of Farmington, Aztec or Cuba.

Park rangers prefer visitors to enter from the northeast, by turning south onto CR 7900 at mile marker 112.5 on Hwy 550/44, 3 miles south of the Nageezi Trading Post. The first 5-mile stretch from there is paved; you then turn right onto CR 7950, with only 3 miles of the remaining 16 miles to the park entrance being paved. You can also reach the park from the south by following Hwy 9 and then Hwy 57/14 from Cuba or Crownpoint; this road is in even worse shape and not always open.

Always check road conditions before leaving and do not use a GPS for navigation. Bring food and leave with a full tank of gas; neither are available at the park itself.

Gallup

📞505 / POP 22,261 / ELEV 6468FT
The mother town on New Mexico's Mother Road seems stuck in time. Settled in 1881, when the railroad came to town, Gallup had its heyday during the 1950s, and many of its dilapidated old motels, pawnshops and billboards have barely changed since the Eisenhower administration.

Just outside the Navajo Reservation, modern-day Gallup is an interesting mix of Anglos and American Indians. Tourism is limited mostly to Route 66 road-trippers and those in search of American Indian history. Even with visitors, it's not exactly crowded, and at night it turns downright quiet.

Gallup has started to capitalize on its outdoor attractions, and a growing number of mountain bikers come to pedal on the surrounding red mesa tops.

⊙ Sights

Gallup Cultural Center MUSEUM
(📞505-863-4131; 218 E Rte 66; ⊙8am-5pm) FREE This cultural center houses a good little museum of Indian art on the 2nd floor, including excellent collections of kachina dolls both new and old, plus pottery, sand painting and weaving. A 10ft-tall bronze sculpture of a Navajo code-talker honors the sacrifices made by Navajo men in WWII. A tiny theater screens films about Chaco and the Four Corners region.

Historic District AREA
Route 66, the 'main street of America,' runs straight through downtown Gallup's historic district, lined with pretty, renovated light-red sandstone buildings housing kitschy souvenir shops and galleries selling American Indian arts and crafts. A brochure available at the visitor center details around 20 noteworthy structures, built along 1st, 2nd and 3rd Sts between 1895 and 1938.

Rex Museum MUSEUM
(📞505-863-1363; 300 W Rte 66; admission by donation; ⊙9am-5pm Mon-Fri) The small Gallup Historical Museum, in the turn-of-the-19th-century former Rex Hotel, is stuffed with assorted old photos and memorabilia, mostly related to the town's coal-mining past.

🏃 Activities

Gallup has great mountain biking just outside of town, but you'll need your own wheels as there are no rentals here. However, during the summer months the Gallup Cultural Center organizes tours (free) to the High Desert Trail system every Saturday at 9am.

Mentmore Rock Climbing Area CLIMBING
Climbers with gear should check out this sandstone crag, which has plenty of single-pitch bolted sport routes, ranging from 5.8 to 5.12. Anchors are in place for top-roping. Ask for maps and info at the visitor center. Reach the park via Exit 16 off I-40; head north on County Rd 1.

High Desert Trail System MOUNTAIN BIKING
(www.galluptrails.com) Mountain bikers can test their skills 3 miles north of Gallup on Hwy 491, off the Chico/Gamerco Rd. Terrain to suit all skill levels includes plenty of sick slickrock – try the loops off the main trail for the most challenging rides. Pick up maps at the tourist office.

Red Rock Park OUTDOORS
(☏505-722-3839; ⊙park 24hr, museum 8am-4pm Mon-Fri) FREE Gallup is becoming known as the kind of outdoors town where those who wish to can still get lost on the bike trails. Hikers should head 6 miles east to this beautiful park, which holds a little museum and trading post with modern and traditional Indian crafts, a campground and hiking trails.

The 3-mile round-trip Pyramid Rock trail leads past amazing rock formations, with 50-mile views – on clear days – from the 7487ft summit.

✸ Festivals & Events

Gallup Inter-Tribal Indian Ceremonial CULTURAL
(theceremonial.com; ⊙early Aug) Thousands of American Indians and non-Indian tourists throng the streets of Gallup and the huge amphitheater at Red Rock State Park in early August for the Gallup Inter-Tribal Indian Ceremonial. Instigated almost a century ago, it features a professional all-Indian rodeo, beautifully bedecked ceremonial dancers from many tribes and a powwow with competitive dancing.

Navajo Nation Fair CULTURAL
(⊙early Sep) While this huge fair, on the first weekend in September, actually takes place in nearby Window Rock, just across the Arizona state line, it effectively spills over into Gallup, which is in any case a better place to stay.

Red Rock Balloon Rally SPORTS
(www.redrockballoonrally.com; ⊙early Dec) Some 200 colorful hot-air balloons take part in demonstrations and competitions at Red Rock State Park, during the first weekend in December.

Lions Club Rodeo CULTURAL
(www.galluplionsclubrodeo.com; ⊙Jun) The most professional and prestigious of several area rodeos, held in the third week in June.

STRETCH YOUR LEGS: GALLUP MURAL WALK

Outdoor murals all over downtown, portraying local life over the centuries, showcase Gallup's tricultural and distinctly Southwestern soul.

The oldest, like those in the **McKinley County Courthouse** (207 W Hill Ave), were created during the Depression, when President Franklin D Roosevelt's 1930s WPA program set unemployed men to work building and beautifying towns and parks across the country.

Eleven new murals by local artists can be viewed on a 10-block walk. Ranging from abstract to realist, they depict tales of peace and turmoil throughout Gallup's history. Although the murals are large, they don't detract from the overall historic aesthetic; rather, they lend a different look to another small, struggling Western town.

Start at the corner of W Aztec Ave and S 2nd St. The first mural, **Great Gallup** by Paul Newman and Steve Heil, is on the west-facing wall of City Hall and uses assorted media to create a graphic narrative of life in Gallup in panels. Look for locals on horseback in one, and a blue pickup truck, so laboriously detailed it resembles an old photograph, in another. Our other favorite is the last mural on the walk, Irving Bahl's **Gallup Inter-Tribal Indian Ceremonial Mural** on the Ceremonial Building between 2nd and 3rd Sts on Coal Ave, illustrating American Indian traditions and sacred Navajo symbols.

🛏 Sleeping

Chain and independent motels cluster just off I-40 at the edge of Gallup. Only a few of the 1950s motor lodges in town are still open, and most of those are pretty dodgy. Room rates double during Ceremonial week and other big events; book accommodations as far ahead as possible during these times.

Red Rock Park Campground   CAMPGROUND $
(📞 505-722-3839; Churchrock, off Hwy 66; tent/ RV sites $10/20; 🐾) Pop your tent up in this beautiful setting with easy access to tons of hiking trails. Six miles east of town, it has showers, flush toilets, drinking water and a grocery store.

El Rancho   HISTORIC HOTEL $$
(📞 505-863-9311; www.elranchohotel.com; 1000 E Hwy 66; r $98-116, motel r $54-74; 🅿️❄️🛜🐾♨️) Opened in 1937, with a superb lobby resembling a rustic hunting lodge, Gallup's finest historic hotel quickly became known as the 'home of the movie stars.' Big, bright and decorated with eclectic Old West fashions, rooms are named after former guests including Humphrey Bogart and John Wayne. There's also a good restaurant and bar, plus a cheaper, modern motel wing.

🍴 Eating & Drinking

Many restaurants in Gallup do not serve liquor, so choose carefully if you want to have a beer with dinner. You may even get some shopping done: Navajo vendors sell jewelry to diners in many restaurants.

⭐ Silver Stallion Coffee & Bread   BAKERY $
(📞 505-488-2908; 213b W Coal Ave; mains $7-12; ⏰ 6:30am-4pm Tue-Thu, to 8pm Fri & Sat; 🛜🍴) 🌿 The smell of fresh bread permeates this bakery and cafe, by far and away the most urbane spot in Gallup. Pop in for coffee and a pastry in the morning, or sample one of the just-baked pizzas or veggie-friendly sandwiches (on a choice of one of its organic loaves) for lunch. It's hidden in the courtyard off of Coal St.

Bonus: a Navajo silversmith has a workshop in the back room.

Jerry's Cafe   NEW MEXICAN $
(📞 505-722-6775; jerryscafenm.org; 406 W Coal Ave; mains $5-13.75; ⏰ 8am-9pm Mon-Sat) Slide into a booth at this busy old-timer for a generous serving of Gallup atmosphere.

Keep it simple with a bowl of green or red chile, or, if you haven't eaten since yesterday, try Cherelle's Choice – a sopaipilla stuffed with carnitas, jalapeños and guacamole, and smothered with chile, cheese and sour cream.

Genaro's Cafe   NEW MEXICAN $
(📞 505-863-6761; www.genarosrestaurant.com; 600 W Hill Ave; mains $6-15; ⏰ 10:30am-7:30pm Tue-Sat) Smart New Mexican restaurant, three blocks up from Route 66, serving a good range of dishes alongside bowls of posole and chile. If you like it hot, you'll feel right at home here, just like the rest of Gallup – this place can get crowded.

Gallup Coffee   CAFE
(📞 505-410-2505; 203 W Coal Ave; ⏰ 7am-7pm Mon-Fri, 8am-8pm Sat) Local coffee shop with espresso, pour-over and drip.

⭐ Entertainment

Local American Indian people perform social dances at 7pm nightly from June to early September at the McKinley County Courthouse.

El Morro Theatre   THEATER
(📞 505-726-0050; www.elmorrotheatre.com; 207 W Coal Ave) Downtown Gallup's centerpiece is this beautifully restored Spanish Colonial–style theater, which originally opened in 1928. As well as live theater, music and dance, it hosts movies and children's programs.

🛍 Shopping

A large share of Navajo silver jewelry is made in the Gallup area, though quite a bit of it is sold in Santa Fe and elsewhere. Nevertheless, there are a lot of trading posts/pawnshops here, and patient browsing will turn up some interesting pieces.

Gallup Flea Market   MARKET
(340 9th St; ⏰ 9am-5pm Sat) Stop by every Saturday for American Indian arts and crafts and plenty of snacks. Follow 9th St north, from the other side of I-40.

Ellis Tanner Trading Company   ARTS & CRAFTS
(📞 505-863-4434; www.etanner.com; 1980 Hwy 602; ⏰ 8am-7pm Mon-Sat) Just south of town toward Zuni, this long-established store, run by a fourth-generation trader, sells everything from rugs and jewelry to saddles and hardware. Be sure to check out the pawnshop.

ℹ Information

Gallup Visitor Information Center (☑505-722-2228; www.adventuregallup.org; 106 Rte 66; ⊗8:30am-5pm Mon-Fri) Grab a copy of the annual, full-color Gallup visitors guide.

Police (☑505-863-9365; 451 S Boardman Ave)

Post Office (950 W Aztec Ave; ⊗8:30am-5pm Mon-Fri, 10am-1:30pm Sat)

Rehoboth McKinley Christian Hospital (☑505-863-7000; www.rmch.org; 1901 Red Rock Dr; ⊗emergency 24hr)

ℹ Getting There & Away

The downtown train station shares space with the Gallup Cultural Center. **Amtrak's** (☑800-872-7245; www.amtrak.com; 201 E Hwy 66) *Southwest Chief* runs once daily west through Flagstaff, AZ ($30, 2½ hours), and east through Albuquerque ($16, 3½ hours).

Greyhound (☑505-863-9078; www.greyhound.com; 3405 W Hwy 66) buses stop at at Nks Truck Stop, inconveniently located 6 miles west of downtown. Daily buses to major cities throughout the region.

Zuni Pueblo

☑505 / POP 6302 / ELEV 6293FT

The largest Pueblo in New Mexico, Zuni was also the first to be encountered by Coronado's Spanish expedition in 1540. It's now famous for its jewelry and fetishes (small stone animal carvings), and this is perhaps an even better place than Gallup to find some exquisite artistry.

Outside of the trading posts along the main street, you can sign up for a tour of the village at the visitor center, visit the Pueblo museum and even spend the night at the local hotel.

⊙ Sights

A:shiwi A:wan Museum & Heritage Center MUSEUM
(☑505-782-4403; www.ashiwi-museum.org; Ojo Caliente Rd; admission by donation; ⊗9am-5pm Mon-Fri) The Pueblo's museum holds imaginative and informative displays of tribal artifacts and historic photos. It's a worthwhile stop if you're visiting.

✦ Festivals & Events

To participate in any ceremony hosted by the Zuni community, you must attend an orientation; call the visitor center for information.

Shalako RELIGIOUS
(⊗early Dec) The most famous ceremony at Zuni is the all-night Shalako ceremonial dance, held on the first weekend in December and continuing for the next several days.

Zuni Tribal Fair CULTURAL
(⊗late Aug) The Zuni Tribal Fair features a powwow, local food and arts-and-crafts stalls.

🛏 Sleeping & Eating

This is the only place in New Mexico where visitors can stay in the middle of a Pueblo. There are only a handful of eating options here: a pizzeria and a bakery are on the road into the Pueblo, and the Halona Plaza food store has a deli serving lunches.

★ Inn at Halona INN $
(☑505-782-4547; www.halona.com; 23b Pia Mesa Rd; r from $75; ▣🐾) This exceptionally friendly inn, across from the museum behind the Halona Plaza food store, is the only place in New Mexico where visitors can stay in the middle of a Pueblo. Check out which of its eight pleasant and very different rooms, decorated with Zuni arts and crafts, fits your fancy. Breakfast is served in the flagstone courtyard in summer.

🛍 Shopping

Turquoise Village JEWELRY
(☑505-782-5521; www.turquoisevillage.com; 1184 Hwy 53; ⊗9:30am-5pm Mon-Sat) Originally founded to sell turquoise, silver, coral and other raw materials to local artisans, the shop today has arguably the best collection of locally made animal fetishes and jewelry. Prices are very reasonable.

ℹ Information

Zuni Tourism Office (☑505-782-7238; www.zunitourism.com; 1239 Hwy 53; tours $15; ⊗8:30am-5:30pm Mon-Fri, 10:30am-4pm Sat, noon-4pm Sun) When visiting the Zuni Pueblo, first check in at the helpful information center, which offers daily tours of the middle village at 10am, 1pm and 4pm from Monday to Saturday. There are usually one or two artisans working here – a great opportunity to chat and buy crafts direct.

The Our Lady of Guadalupe Mission, featuring impressive kachina murals, is currently closed.

ℹ Getting There & Away

The Pueblo is on Hwy 53, 37 miles south of Gallup.

EL MALPAIS NATIONAL MONUMENT

The rugged **El Malpais National Monument** (www.nps.gov/elma; Hwy 53 & Hwy 117) `FREE` consists of almost 200 sq miles of isolated volcanic terrain. There are numerous trails here, accessible via Hwy 53 or the even prettier Hwy 117, though expect very strenuous, exposed hikes (bring a compass). Pick up permits at the **Information Center** (☑505-783-4774; ⊙8:30am-4:30pm Mar-Sep) on Hwy 53 to explore nearby lava tubes – some of which are ice caves – or learn about possible hikes. The Northwest New Mexico Visitor Center in Grants also has info on El Malpais.

Five major lava flows have been identified; the most recent one is estimated to be between 2000 to 3000 years old. Paleoindians may have witnessed the final eruptions since local Indian legends refer to 'rivers of fire.'

You can camp in the backcountry for free, though you'll need a permit. **Joe Skeen Campground** (Hwy 117) `FREE`, 11 miles south of I-40, is also a possibility, but bring your own water.

This is an isolated area; it's best not to venture out alone.

Grants

☑505 / POP 9253 / ELEV 6460FT

Having boomed first as a railroad stop, and then as a uranium mining town, Grants today seems to be an ever-dwindling strip along Route 66, largely relying on jobs at state prison facilities nearby. Despite the dearth of inspiration in town, there are some great spots to stretch the legs nearby: the enormous swath of El Malpais National Monument to the southwest and the prominent Mt Taylor roughly 20 miles to the northeast.

⊙ Sights & Activities

New Mexico Mining Museum MUSEUM
(☑505-287-4802; 100 N Iron Ave; adult/child $5/3; ⊙9am-4pm Mon-Sat; ⊞) What claims to be the world's only uranium-mining museum also doubles as the local visitor center. Hands-on exhibits are made for kids, who will dig descending the 'mine shaft' into the underground mine – it's a mock-up of course, with a distinct resemblance to a fairground ghost train, but it's fun and informative.

Mt Taylor HIKING
(Hwy 547) Also known as Tsoodził (Turquoise Bead Mountain), this sacred peak marks the traditional southern boundary of Navajo territory. Hikers can summit the 11,301ft extinct volcano via the 5-mile round-trip Gooseberry Springs Trail. To get here, take Hwy 547 to the second Forest Service Rd 193 and follow it to the trailhead – check in with the ranger station for exact directions.

Alternatively, you can drive all the way up to **La Mosca Lookout** at 11,000ft for views.

Take Hwy 547 to Forestry Service Rd 453 (past the trailhead turnoff) and then continue to the Lookout.

🛏 Sleeping & Eating

Sleeping in Grants is restricted to generic chain motels, but campers are in luck: there are two USFS campgrounds near Mt Taylor, in addition to the BLM-run Joe Skeen campground south of town on Hwy 117. Foodwise, Grants is a diner-style town, with a few run-of-the-mill options.

Kendalben BBQ BARBECUE $
(☑505-287-5095; www.bbqgrants.com; 314 Rte 66, Milan; mains $10-30; ⊙10:30am-9pm Mon-Sat) If ribs, chile-rubbed brisket and country music are calling, this is your place. It's about 3 miles west of town on Route 66.

ℹ Information

Northwest New Mexico Visitor Center
(☑505-876-2783; south side of I-40, exit 85; ⊙8am-5pm) Run by the National Park Service, this large modern Pueblo-style building is an invaluable resource for anyone visiting the nearby El Malpais National Monument southwest of Grants. Year-round information and permits are available here.

Cibola National Forest Mount Taylor Ranger Station (☑505-287-8833; www.fs.usda.gov/cibola; 1800 Lobo Canyon Rd; ⊙8am-noon & 12:30-4:30pm Mon-Fri) Stop by for information on hiking and camping in the surrounding national forest.

ℹ Getting There & Away

Grants is slightly more than halfway between Albuquerque (80 miles east) and Gallup (62 miles

SCENIC ROUTE 53

A great alternative way to reach Grants from Gallup is via Scenic Route 53, which runs south of I-40. It takes at least a full day, if not two, to really experience this out-of-this-world landscape of lava tubes and red arches, volcanic craters and ice caves, as well as unique historical attractions and traditional New Mexican towns.

The first place you'll pass through is the small town of Ramah, where the Navajo population still practices sheep raising, weaving and other land-based traditions. The **Stagecoach Cafe** (☏505-783-4288; 3370 Bond St/Hwy 53; mains $6-16; ⊗7am-9pm Mon-Sat) is a worthy place to grab a bite, with friendly service and New Mexican food, and a giant selection of pies. A 20-mile detour off Hwy 53, animal-lovers won't want to miss the **Wild Spirit Wolf Sanctuary** (☏505-775-3032; www.wildspiritwolfsanctuary.org; 378 Candy Kitchen Rd; tours adult/child $10/5, tent/cabin $15/125; ⊗tours 11am, 12:30pm, 2pm & 3:30pm Tue-Sun; ♿). Home to rescued captive-born wolves and wolf-dog mixes, the sanctuary offers four quarter-mile walking tours per day, where you walk with the wolves that roam the large natural-habitat enclosures. If you want to stay overnight, you can choose between primitive camping or a guest cabin; both include all the wolf howling you ever wanted to hear.

Next up is **El Morro National Monument** (☏505-783-4226; www.nps.gov/elmo; Hwy 53; ⊗9am-6pm Jun-Aug, to 5pm Sep-May) FREE, 52 miles southeast of Gallup and home to the extraordinary Inscription Rock. For many centuries, travelers have left their mark on this 200ft outcrop, making it something like a sandstone guestbook, covered with carvings from Pueblo petroglyphs at the top (c 1250) to inscriptions by Spaniard conquistadors and Anglo pioneers. To camp, stay at one of nine basic first-come, first-served sites at the monument (free), or visit **El Morro RV Park & Cabins** (☏505-783-4612; www.elmorro-nm.com; Hwy 53; tent/RV sites $15/30, cabins $84-99; ☏) a mile east of the visitor center with 26 sites and six cabins. The on-site **Ancient Way Cafe** (☏505-783-4612; Hwy 53; mains $6-12; ⊗9am-5pm Sun-Thu, 9am-8pm Fri & Sat; ✈) serves home-cooked American, New Mexican and veggie specialties in a rustic dining room.

For a few more comforts, continue east to find **Cimarron Rose** (☏800-856-5776; www.cimarronrose.com; 689 Oso Ridge Rd; ste $145-210; ☏ ✎, an ecofriendly B&B between miles 56 and 57. There are three Southwestern-style suites (two have kitchens), plus a charming common room. Two goats and a horse fertilize Cimarron's perennial gardens, which provide food and shelter for more than 80 bird species.

The final stop is the vast **El Malpais National Monument** (p319). Pronounced *el-mahl-pie-ees*, meaning 'bad land' in Spanish, it consists of almost 200 sq miles of lava flows bounded by Hwy 53 to the north and Hwy 117 to the east. Stop by the **Information Center** (p319) on Hwy 53 to pick up permits or get the lowdown on possible hikes. Alternatively, pick up the same info at the **Northwest New Mexico Visitor Center** (p319) in Grants.

One interesting but rugged hike, the 7.5-mile (one-way) **Zuni-Acoma Trail** follows part of an ancient Puebloan trade route (as well as the Continental Divide). It leaves from Hwy 53 and crosses four lava flows to end at Hwy 117 (or vice versa). This is best done with two cars.

For further exploration, follow scenic Hwy 117 south from I-40 along sandstone cliffs. Possible hikes here include the recommended **Narrows Trail** (8 miles), with views of La Ventana Natural Arch, and the **Lava Falls Loop** (1 mile), which traverses the now-frozen ripples, fissures, vents and craters of a lava flow.

If you have a high-clearance 4WD, set off along the unpaved County Rd 42, which leaves Hwy 117 about 34 miles south of I-40 and meanders for 40 miles through the BLM country on the west side of El Malpais. It passes several craters, caves and lava tubes (reached by signed trails) and emerges at Hwy 53 near Bandera Crater. Be prepared for poor signage at the many forks en route, so drive during daylight, when you can (hopefully) intuit which turns to make. **Joe Skeen Campground** (p319) has several sites but no water; backcountry camping is also allowed, but free permits are required.

If you go spelunking, the park service requires each person to carry two sources of light and to wear a hard hat. Take a companion wherever you go – this is an isolated area.

west) on I-40. **Greyhound** (☑800-231-2222; www.greyhound.com; 1601 E Santa Fe Ave) buses leave from the Shell station to Albuquerque, Flagstaff and other regional hubs.

Acoma Pueblo

☑505 / POP 4989 / ELEV 6460FT

The modern Acoma Indian reservation consists of three separate communities set in a striking desert landscape, in addition to the Sky City Casino beside the interstate.

The compelling reason to visit Acoma, however, is to see the extraordinary ancient mesa-top Pueblo, 13 miles south of the highway.

◉ Sights

Sky City   INDIAN RESERVATION
(☑800-747-0181; www.acomaskycity.org; Rte 38; tours adult/child $25/17; ⊗hourly tours 8:30am-3:30pm Mar-Oct, 9:30am-2:30pm Sat & Sun Nov-Feb) Journeying to the mesa-top village at Acoma Pueblo, famous as Sky City, is like venturing into another world. There can be few more dramatic locations – it's set atop an isolated outcrop, 367ft above the surrounding plateau and 7000ft above sea level. People have lived here since the 11th century, making Acoma one of the oldest continuously inhabited settlements in North America.

☆☆ Festivals & Events

Festivals and events include the Officer's Feast (February), a harvest dance on San Esteban Day (September 2) and traditional dances at the San Esteban Mission (December 25–28).

🛏 Sleeping & Eating

Sky City Casino   HOTEL $$
(☑888-759-2489; www.skycity.com; I-40, exit 102; r from $107, RV sites from $22; ▓◉▓) Acoma's casino, beside the interstate a dozen miles from Sky City itself, offers 132 motel-style rooms, as well as an RV park. Dining options in the casino include the usual all-you-can-eat buffet.

Y'aak'a Cafe   AMERICAN INDIAN $
(mains $6-9; ⊗9am-3pm) Try the Pueblo Taco, served on fresh fry bread. It's located in the Sky City Cultural Center; grab a bite here before or after your tour.

Laguna Pueblo

Laguna Pueblo, 40 miles west of Albuquerque or 30 miles east of Grants, is New Mexico's youngest Pueblo. Founded in 1699 by a mixed group of settlers fleeing the Spaniards in the aftermath of the Pueblo Revolt, it consists of six small villages, each of which celebrates its own annual feast day, with the largest events on March 19, July 26, August 15 and September 19.

SILVER CITY & SOUTHWESTERN NEW MEXICO

The Rio Grande Valley unfurls from Albuquerque down to the bubbling hot springs of funky Truth or Consequences and on toward Mexico and Texas. En route, it feeds one of New Mexico's agricultural treasures: Hatch, the so-called chile capital of the world. East of the river, the desert is so dry it's been known since Spanish times as the Jornada del Muerto, which literally translates as the 'day-long journey of the dead man.' Pretty appropriate that this area was chosen for the detonation of the first atomic bomb, at what's now Trinity Site.

Away from Las Cruces, the state's second-largest city, residents in these parts are few and far between. To the west, the rugged Gila National Forest is wild with backcountry adventure, while the Mimbres Valley is rich with archaeological treasures.

Socorro

☑575 / POP 8911 / ELEV 4579FT

A quiet layover, Socorro has a good mix of buildings in its downtown, mostly dating from the late 19th century. Its name – *socorro* means 'help' in Spanish – supposedly dates to 1598, when Juan de Oñate's expedition received help from Pilabó Pueblo (now disappeared).

Most visitors are birders drawn to the nearby Bosque del Apache refuge.

◉ Sights

★**Bosque del Apache**
National Wildlife Refuge   WILDLIFE RESERVE
(www.fws.gov/refuge/bosque_del_apache; Hwy 1; per vehicle $5; ⊗dawn-dusk) Renowned among wildlife photographers the world

over, these fields and marshes, 18 miles south of Socorro, are the wintering ground for over 100,000 migratory birds including snow geese, sandhill cranes and bald eagles. The season lasts from late October to March, peaking in December and January. From the visitor center (p324), two 6-mile driving loops circle through the refuge, passing hiking trails and viewing platforms. Bring binoculars (or a telescopic lens), or rent them at the gift shop ($5).

Very Large Array Radio Telescope
OBSERVATORY

(VLA; ☎ 505-835-7000; www.nrao.edu; off Hwy 52; adult/child $6/free; ◷ 8:30am-sunset) In some remote regions of New Mexico, TV reception is little more than a starry-eyed fantasy. About 40 miles west of Socorro, though, 27 huge antenna dishes sprout from the high plains like a couch potato's dream come true. Actually, the 240-ton dishes comprise the National Radio Astronomy Observatory's Very Large Array Radio Telescope. Together, they combine to form a very large eyeball peeking into the outer edges of the universe – which curious travelers can visit on a walking tour.

It would take a 422ft-wide satellite dish to provide the same resolution that this Y-shaped configuration of 82ft-wide antennas offers the observatory. Sure, the giant 'scope may reveal the relativistic electron movement in the heavens and allow geophysicists to wonder at the wobble of the earth on its axis … but what does it tell the rest of us? Well, without them, Jodie Foster never could have flashed forward into our future (or was it her past?) in the movie *Contact*, which was filmed here with a little help from Canyon de Chelly. The radio waves collected by these enormous dishes have increased our understanding of the complex phenomena that make up the surface of the sun. They have given us a gander at the internal heating source deep within the interiors of several planets sharing our orbit. They provide us with just enough information to turn our concepts of time and space inside-out as we extrapolate the existence of varieties of matter that, sans satellites, might only exist in our imaginations as we spin through space on the head of this peculiar little blue-green globe.

San Miguel Mission
CHURCH

(www.sdc.org/~smiguel; 403 San Miguel Rd) FREE The small church built by Socorro's earliest Spanish settlers expanded to become the San Miguel Mission in the 1620s. You'll find it three blocks north of the Plaza. While much altered, the mission still retains its colonial feel, and parts of the walls date back to the original building.

★ Festivals & Events

Festival of the Cranes
CULTURAL

(www.festivalofthecranes.com; ◷ Nov) On the third weekend of November, featuring special tours of Bosque del Apache, wildlife workshops and arts and crafts.

49ers Celebration
CULTURAL

(◷ mid-Oct) All Socorro turns out for the annual 49ers Festival, with parades, dancing and gambling over a long weekend.

THE BLAST HEARD 'ROUND THE WORLD

On just two days a year (the first Saturday in April and October), the public is permitted to tour the Trinity Site, where the first atomic bomb was detonated on July 16, 1945, 50 miles southeast of Socorro. The eerie tour includes the base camp, the McDonald Ranch house where the plutonium core for the bomb was assembled, and ground zero itself. The test was carried out above ground and resulted in a quarter-mile-wide crater and an 8-mile-high cloud mushrooming above the desert. The radiation level of the site is 'only' 10 times greater than the region's background level; a one-hour visit to ground zero will result in an exposure of one-half to one millorentgen (mrem), two to four times the estimated exposure of a typical adult on an average day in the USA. Trinitite, a green, glassy substance resulting from the blast, is still radioactive, still scattered around and still must not be touched. Resist the urge to add it to your road-trip rock collection. This desolate area is overshadowed by 8638ft Oscura Peak (Darkness Peak on state maps). Call the White Sands Missile Range (☎ 575-678-1134) for information.

ONLY IN NEW MEXICO: SCENIC ROUTE 60

Hwy 60 runs west from Socorro to the Arizona border, cutting past the surreal Sawtooth Mountains, across the vast, flat Plains of San Agustin, and through endless juniper hills. A few spots along the way are well worth a detour if you have the time.

Out on the plains, 40 miles west of Socorro, 27 huge antenna dishes (each weighing 230 tons) together comprise a single superpowered telescope – the **Very Large Array Radio Telescope** (p322), run by the National Radio Astronomy Observatory. Four miles south of the highway, they move along railroad tracks, reconfiguring the layout as needed to study the outer limits of the universe. To match this resolution, a regular telescope would have to be 22 miles wide. Not only has the VLA increased our understanding of such celestial phenomena as black holes, space gases and radio emissions, but it's appeared in movies including *Contact*, *Armageddon* and *Independence Day*. They're also unbelievably cool. From the small museum at the visitor center, you can take a self-guided tour.

Further west on Hwy 60, you'll pass through tiny **Pie Town**. Yes, seriously, a town named after pie. And for good reason. They say you can find the best pies in the universe here (which makes you wonder what they've *really* been doing at the VLA). The **Pie-O-Neer Cafe** (☎575-772-2711; www.pie-o-neer.com; Hwy 60; slices from $5; ⊙11:30am-4pm Thu-Sat mid-Mar–Nov) just might prove their case. The pies are dee-lish, the soups and stews it serves are homemade, and you'll be hard pressed to find another host as welcoming as Kathy Knapp – who suggests you call ahead to check someone hasn't eaten all the pie. On the second Saturday of September, Pie Town's **Pie Festival** (www.pietownfestival.com) features baking and eating contests, the coronation of a Pie Queen, Wild West gunfights and horned toad races.

Heading on towards Arizona, out in the high plains around Quemado, gleams the **Lightning Field** (☎505-898-3335; www.diaart.org/sites/main/lightningfield; Quemado; adult/child Jul & Aug $250/100, May, Jun, Sep & Oct $150/100), an art installation created by Walter de Maria in 1977. Four hundred polished steel poles stand in a giant grid; each stainless rod is about 20ft tall, but the precise lengths vary so the tips are all level with each other. During summer monsoons, the poles seem to draw lightning out of hovering thunderheads. The effect is truly electrifying. You can only visit if you stay overnight in the simple on-site cabin, with only six visitors allowed per night. Advance reservations are required.

You can also reach Hwy 60 by heading south along back roads from Zuni Pueblo, Scenic Route 53 and El Malpais.

NEW MEXICO SOCORRO

🛏 Sleeping

California St holds budget motels and a few national chains.

Casa Blanca Bed & Breakfast B&B $
(☎575-835-3027; www.casablancabedandbreak fast.com; 13 Montoya, San Antonio; r $90-110; ⊙Oct-Mar; ☎) This three-room B&B offers basic rooms close to the Bosque del Apache National Wildlife Refuge (p321), 8 miles south of Socorro.

Socorro Old Town B&B B&B $$
(☎575-418-9454; www.socorrobandb.qwestoffice. net; 114 W Baca St; r $125; ※☎) Across from San Miguel Mission in the Old Town neighborhood, and housed in an extensively restored old adobe, this B&B has the feeling of a family home, with easygoing hosts and two clean, comfortable rooms.

🍴 Eating

Socorro's restaurants are uniformly mediocre, though the tiny town of San Antonio, 10 miles south, has two famous burger joints.

Owl Bar Cafe BURGERS $
(☎575-835-9946; 79 Main St, San Antonio; mains $5.15-13; ⊙8am-8pm Mon-Sat) Leave I-25 at Exit 139, 10 miles south of Socorro, to sample the finest green chile cheeseburgers this side of Hatch. The potent mix of greasy beef, soft bun, sticky cheese, tangy chile, lettuce and tomato drips onto the plate in perfect burger fashion.

Socorro Springs Brewing Co ITALIAN **$$**
(☑575-838-0650; www.socorrosprings.com; 1012
N California St; mains $8-20; ☺11am-10pm; 🛜)
Come to this busy pub for clay-oven pizza,
big calzones, decent pasta dishes, lots of
salads and homemade soups. At times, the
selection of brews in the pub section at
the front can be limited, but they're always
smooth and tasty.

Drinking & Nightlife

M Mountain Coffee CAFE
(☑575-838-0809; 110 Manzanares St W; ☺7am-
6pm; 🛜) A casual, comfy-chair coffee shop,
with pastries, bowls of chile and ice cream.

ⓘ Information

**Bosque del Apache National Wildlife Refuge
Visitor Center** (☑575-835-1828; ☺8am-4pm
Sep-May, closed Tue & Wed Jun-Aug)
Socorro Heritage and Visitors Center
(☑575-835-8927; 217 Fisher Ave; ☺9am-5pm
Mon-Fri) The chamber of commerce is helpful.

Truth or Consequences

☑575 / POP 6411 / ELEV 4242FT

Home to New Age devotees, off-the-grid
artists and ecowarriors, Truth or Con-
sequences (T or C) vies for the title of
quirkiest little town in New Mexico. This
high-desert oasis was originally called Hot
Springs, for the cluster of mineral-rich
springs that line the banks of the Rio
Grande hereabouts. It changed its name
to match a popular radio game show in
1950, hoping to increase tourism. The
geothermal energy in the vicinity is sup-
posedly similar to Sedona's, and T or C's
shabby-chic double main drag – split into
two one-way sections downtown, Main St
and Broadway – is filled with crystal shops,
herbalist offices, yoga studios, eclectic art
galleries and off-the-wall boutiques.

⊙ Sights & Activities

It won't take you more than 30 minutes to
get your bearings in tiny T or C by stroll-
ing down Main St and Broadway. Each
day it seems another art gallery or new
herbal-remedy shop opens, and it's fun to
just walk and window-shop.

Elephant Butte Lake State Park LAKE
(☑575-744-5923; www.emnrd.state.nm.us; Hwy
195; vehicle per day $5) Just 5 miles north

of T or C, New Mexico's largest artificial
lake (60 sq miles) is much loved by local
anglers, waterskiers and windsurfers. The
marina (☑575-744-5567; www.marinadelsur.
info; per hour from $60) rents tackle and
boats (for fishing, pontoon and skiing). Try
Fishing Adventures (☑575-740-4710; www.
stripersnewmexico.com) to make sure you take
home your fill of striped bass. There are
tent/RV **campsites** ($8/14) here.

Geronimo Springs Museum MUSEUM
(www.geronimospringsmuseum.com; 211 Main St;
adult/student $6/3; ☺9am-5pm Mon-Sat, noon-
5pm Sun) This engaging mishmash features
a mastodon skull, minerals and artifacts
ranging from Mimbres pottery to beauti-
fully worked cowboy saddles, plus sections
on the Truth or Consequences radio show
and Apache leader Geronimo.

Hot Springs

For centuries people from these parts,
including Geronimo, have bathed in the
area's mineral-laden hot springs. Long said
to have therapeutic properties, the waters
range from 98°F to 115°F (36°C to 46°C).
Since the damming of the Rio Grande
upstream, T or C's springs no longer flow
naturally, but anyone can still tap into the
underlying hot water by digging on their
own property.

Some of T or C's hotels and motels dou-
ble as spas. Guests soak free, and mas-
sages and other treatments are sometimes
available. For sheer open-air enjoyment,
head for the outdoor tubs at River-
bend Hot Springs (☑575-894-7625; www.
riverbendhotsprings.com; 100 Austin St; shared/
private per hour $10/15; ☺8am-10pm). The

EL CAMINO REAL HISTORIC TRAIL

Halfway between Socorro and Truth
or Consequences is this modern
museum (☑575-854-3600; www.
caminorealheritage.org; Hwy 1; adult/child
$5/free; ☺8:30am-5pm Wed-Sun), which
explores the history of the Royal Road.
Panoramic windows overlook the bleak
landscape just outside. To get here,
leave I-25 at exit 115 and turn south
onto Hwy 1. At the time of research,
the monument was closed until further
notice; check online for updates before
making the detour.

swankier **Sierra Grande Lodge & Spa** (☏ 877-288-7637; www.sierragrandelodge.com; 501 McAdoo St; per 30min $30; ⊙ by reservation) holds mineral baths, plus a holistic spa offering massage and aromatherapy.

🎊 Festivals & Events

Truth or Consequences Fiesta ⁣⁣⁣⁣ FIESTA
(annualtorcfiesta.com; ⊙ early May) The T or C Fiesta celebrates the town's 1950 name change with a concert, dance and parade.

🛏 Sleeping & Eating

There are plenty of lodging options here, but you'll need to book ahead to get a room at one of the spa hotels. Don't expect much in the way of eating choices, though the few eateries that are here are a change from the usual New Mexican fare.

⭐ **Riverbend Hot Springs** ⁣⁣⁣⁣ BOUTIQUE HOTEL **$$**
(☏ 575-894-7625; www.riverbendhotsprings.com; 100 Austin St; r $97-218, RV sites $60; ❄ 🛜 🐾) This delightful place, occupying a fantastic perch beside the Rio Grande, is the only T or C hotel to feature outdoor, riverside hot tubs – tiled, decked and totally irresistible. Accommodation, colorfully decorated by local artists, ranges from motel-style rooms to a three-bedroom suite. Guests can use the public pools for free, and private tubs for $10. No children under 12 years.

Blackstone Hotsprings ⁣⁣⁣⁣ BOUTIQUE HOTEL **$$**
(☏ 575-894-0894; www.blackstonehotsprings. com; 410 Austin St; r $85-175; 🅿❄🛜) Blackstone embraces the T or C spirit with an upscale wink, decorating each of its 10 rooms in the style of a classic TV show, from *The Jetsons* to *The Golden Girls* to *I Love Lucy*. Best part? Each room comes with its own oversized tub or waterfall fed from the hot springs. No children under 12.

Passion Pie Cafe ⁣⁣⁣⁣ CAFE **$**
(☏ 575-894-0008; www.deepwaterfarm.com; 406 Main St; breakfast & lunch mains $4.25-9.50; ⊙ 7am-3pm; 🛜) Watch T or C get its morning groove on through the windows of this espresso cafe, and set yourself up with a breakfast waffle; the Elvis (with peanut butter) or the Fat Elvis (with bacon too) should do the job. Later on there are plenty of healthy salads and sandwiches.

Latitude 33 ⁣⁣⁣⁣ ASIAN **$$**
(☏ 575-740-7804; latitude33.sierracountynm.org; 334 S Pershing St; lunch $8-16, dinner $12-28;

CHLORIDE

At the end of the 19th century, tiny Chloride (population 11), in the foothills of the Black Range 40 miles northeast of T or C, was abustle with enough silver miners to support eight saloons. A century later, its historic buildings were on the verge of disintegration, until Don and Dona Edmund began renovating the old **Pioneer Store** (☏ 575-743-2736; www.pioneerstoremuseum.com; by donation; ⊙ 10am-4pm) **FREE** in 1994. Today, this 1880 general store holds a rich collection of miscellany from Chloride's heyday. Immediately behind it, the Edmunds have restored the two-bedroom **Harry Pye Cabin** (☏ 575-743-2736; cabin $125; 🐾) – Chloride's first building – to hold overnight guests.

When Chloride was first founded, everything had to be hauled 60 miles by wagon to get here. It's hardly surprising, therefore, that it's pretty much all still here, including wooden dynamite detonators, farm implements, children's coffins, saddles and explosion-proof telephones used in mines. Landmarks include the Hanging Tree, to which rowdy drunks were tied until they sobered up, the Monte Cristo Saloon (now an artist co-op and gift shop) and a few other buildings in various stages of rehabilitation.

On a typical summer's day, around 10 visitors find their way to Chloride. It's a glorious drive, crossing successive ridges west of the Rio Grande to reach unspoiled little agricultural valleys. Coming from T or C, take I-25 north to exit 83, then Hwy 52 west.

⊙ 11am-8pm Mon-Sat) Relaxed, friendly bistro, tucked away downtown between the two main drags, which serves Asian-inspired dishes at good prices. Think spicy peanut noodles with tofu or green curry chicken.

ⓘ Information

Geronimo Trail Scenic Byway Visitor Center (☏ 575-894-1968; www.geronimotrail.com; 301 S Foch; ⊙ 9am-4:30pm Mon-Sat, to 2:30pm Sun) Also home to the Spaceport America Visitors Center, closed at the time of research.

WORTH A TRIP

SPACEPORT AMERICA: A COSMIC SIDE TRIP

New Mexico has been hurling objects out beyond the stratosphere since 1947, when the first missile was launched from the rolling dunes of White Sands, courtesy of NASA's Werner von Braun. The next big thing? You guessed it – space tourism. In 2006 **Spaceport America** (☑ 844-727-7223; www.spaceportamerica.com; adult/child $45/30), the world's first commercial spaceport, got the green light from state lawmakers, with the hope that private spacecraft would be taking off from the desert 30 miles southeast of Truth or Consequences by 2011.

As intriguing as that sounds, things have unfortunately not gone as planned. As of early 2017, almost no flights by the main tenants, Virgin Galactic and SpaceX, have taken off at all (most suborbital launches have been by UP Aerospace). And since much of the $200-million facility was built using taxpayer dollars – in addition to the state having to cover the costs of an annual operating deficit of $500,000 – New Mexicans have become understandably disenchanted with the project.

It seems the days of 23,000-mile-per-hour privately operated flights into space (per person $250,000) are still a ways off in the future, but fear not space geeks: you can still visit the largely deserted facility on a multi-hour bus tour, and learn about that future as well as take a ride in a G-force machine. Tours should leave from the **visitor center** (p325) in Truth or Consequences, though at the time of research they were, fittingly, temporarily suspended.

Silver City

☑ 575 / POP 10,273 / ELEV 5938FT

Once a rough-and-ready silver hub, Silver City is an endearingly quirky town – you know, the kind of place where a business sign might read, 'dog grooming and metaphysical center.' The streets of its historic downtown hold a lovely mishmash of old brick and cast-iron Victorian and thick-walled red adobe buildings, and the whole place still reeks of the Wild West. Billy the Kid spent some of his childhood here, and a few of his haunts still lurk amid the new coffee shops and art galleries.

A growing number of adventure addicts are coming to Silver City to work and play in its surrounding great outdoors: 15 mountain ranges, four rivers, the cartoonish formations of City of Rocks State Parks and the Gila National Forest are all in the vicinity. Plus, as home to Western New Mexico University, Silver City is infused with a healthy dose of youthful energy.

⊙ Sights & Activities

Western New Mexico University Museum   MUSEUM
(☑ 575-538-6386;   www.wnmu.edu/univ/ museum.shtml; 1000 W College Ave; ⊙ 9am-4:30pm Mon-Fri, 10am-4pm Sat & Sun) **FREE** This excellent museum boasts the world's largest collection of 1000-year-old Mimbres ceramics. Renowned for their vibrant animal motifs – markedly different from the abstract Chaco style – most Mimbres pots were 'terminated' by their owners, by being deliberately punctured with a kill hole. The museum was undergoing renovations through 2017, and is scheduled to reopen in early 2018.

Silver City Museum   MUSEUM
(www.silvercitymuseum.org;   312 W Broadway; suggested donation $3; ⊙ 9am-4:30pm Tue-Fri, 10am-4pm Sat & Sun) Ensconced in an elegant 1881 Victorian house, the local history museum displays a re-created family parlor from the 1890s, as well as collections of Mimbres pottery, photographic archives and temporary exhibits. Climb to its 3rd-floor cupola for panoramic views of downtown.

Pinos Altos   HISTORIC SITE
(www.pinosaltos.org) Established in 1859 as a gold-mining town, Pinos Altos, 7 miles north of Silver City along Hwy 15, is almost a ghost town these days, though its few residents strive to retain its 19th-century flavor. Cruise Main St to see its log-cabin 1866 schoolhouse, an opera house, a reconstructed fort and an 1870s courthouse. The Buckhorn Saloon (p328) is a fabulous spot for dinner or a beer.

Gila Hike and Bike
MOUNTAIN BIKING

(☑575-388-3222; www.gilahikeandbike.com; 103 E College Ave; mountain bikes $30-60 per day; ☉9am-5:30pm Mon-Fri, 9am-5pm Sat, 9am-4pm Sun) Drop into this friendly shop, on downtown's northern edge, to rent a bike or learn about regional single-track routes like the gorgeous trail through the oaks and ponderosas of Signal Peak just above town, with views right to Mexico. It's also the HQ for May's Tour of the Gila race. It also has a few bike racks for vehicles ($10).

⭐ Festivals & Events

Silver City Blues Festival
MUSIC

(www.silvercitybluesfestival.org; ☉May) FREE Held the last full weekend in May, this music fest attracts big-name performers from across the country.

Tour of the Gila
SPORTS

(www.tourofthegila.com; ☉Apr) This five-day bike race culminates with a grueling tour of the mountains.

🛏 Sleeping

Silver City is an affordable place to stay the night, though the choices are limited. There are loads of campgrounds in the nearby Gila Wilderness, as well as a few properties with basic cabins.

City of Rocks State Park
CAMPGROUND $

(☑575-536-2800; www.nmparks.com; Hwy 61; tent/RV sites $10/18) This state park, 33 miles southeast of Silver City via Hwy 180 and Hwy 61, has a 'quirky, cartoonish beauty. More village than 'city,' it's a bit too pocket-sized to count as a hiking destination, but kids will love exploring the pathways between its rounded volcanic towers, and secluded sites with tables and fire pits make it a memorable camping spot.

Palace Hotel
HISTORIC HOTEL $

(☑575-388-1811; www.silvercitypalacehotel.com; 106 W Broadway; r incl breakfast $58-94; ❄🛜) A restored 1882 hotel, the Palace is an atmospheric stopover. All rooms feature old-fashioned Territorial-style decor; they vary from small (with a double bed) to two-room suites (king- or queen-size beds). Expect some historical quirks – water pressure in the showers is very low (ours was unusable) and wi-fi is iffy in some rooms. Breakfast is good, however, and the owners are friendly.

KOA
CAMPGROUND $

(☑800-562-7623; www.campsilvercity.com; 11824 E Hwy 180; tent/RV sites $30/45, cabins from $50; 🛜❄🐕) Five miles east of town, this campground franchise is a clean, child-friendly option with a playground and coin laundry. The 'kamping kabins' are compact but cute and good value, with all the necessities (except bed linens, an extra $7.50 or BYO) packed into the square wooden rooms. Tent campers will find more pleasant locations elsewhere. Reserve in summer.

Murray Hotel
HISTORIC HOTEL $$

(☑575-956-9400; www.murray-hotel.com; 200 W Broadway; r $109-219; ❄🛜) Built in 1938, this downtown hotel is more about art-deco panache than Wild West history; it's a classy spot, with five stories of tastefully retro-furnished rooms. Breakfast included.

🍴 Eating & Drinking

Most of the town's eateries are only open for breakfast and lunch outside of weekends.

Tapas Tree Grill
CAFE $

(☑575-597-8272; www.tapastreegrill.com; 601 N Bullard St; mains $5-10; ☉11am-3pm Wed-Mon, to 7pm Fri; 🍴) Effortlessly mixing banh mi sandwiches and Thai noodle bowls with crêpes, sweet potato empanadas and, of course, burgers, this lunch spot embodies Silver City's quirkiness. Lots of veggie options.

Vicki's Eatery
AMERICAN $

(☑575-388-5430; 315 N Texas St; lunch $7-10, dinner $9.50-16.50; ☉11am-2:30pm Mon-Fri, 7am-2.30pm Sat & Sun, 5-8pm Fri & Sat) Set comfortably – if a little incongruously – in a former Elks Lodge, Vicki's delights with fresh sandwiches, soup and salad, and filet mignon and pasta on weekend nights.

Jalisco Cafe
NEW MEXICAN $

(☑575-388-2060; 103 S Bullard St; mains $7-14; ☉11am-8pm) The most popular place to get your chile fix in Silver City, spanning three dining rooms. The red chile con carne plate is an excellent choice.

Nancy's Silver Cafe
CAFE $

(☑575-388-3480; 514 N Bullard St; mains $6-10; ☉7am-7:30pm Mon-Sat) The preferred hangout of crusty old locals, you can slip into a red vinyl booth here for some straight up, down home, New Mexican grub.

★ 1zero6
GASTRONOMY **$$**

(☎575-313-4418; 1zero6-jake.blogspot.com; 106 N Texas St; mains $19-24; ⊙5-10pm Fri-Sun) When a restaurant is only open three nights a week, you know you'll have to reserve well ahead. Menus change daily and are drawn up in advance according to available ingredients and the chef's whims – expect creations along the lines of pasta *de camarones amarillo* (wild shrimp), pork tenderloin with peaches and guajillo chile or salmon in a pistachio cashew crust.

★ Buckhorn Saloon
STEAK **$$**

(☎575-538-9911; www.buckhornsaloonandopera house.com; 32 Main St, Pinos Altos; mains $11-49; ⊙4-10pm Mon-Sat) Once part opera house, this venerable saloon is Silver City's most atmospheric dining option, offering serious steaks and seafood amid 1860s Wild West decor – try the fresh and tasty buffalo burgers. There's lve music on weekend nights. It's located in Pinos Altos, 7 miles north of Silver City.

SHAKESPEARE IN THE SOUTHWEST

As far as we know, the dusty southwestern corner of New Mexico isn't haunted by spirits speaking in iambic pentameter, but it is where you'll find **Shakespeare** (☎575-542-9034; www. shakespeareghosttown.com; Hwy 494; 90min tours adult/child $4/3), 2.5 miles south of Lordsburg. Among the best-preserved ghost towns in the Old West, it was first established as a stop on the Southern Pacific Mail Line, then grew into a silver-mining boom town.

Plenty of the West's famous outlaws roosted here at one time or another: 'Curly' Bill Brocius, the killer and rustler, called this home; a young Billy the Kid washed dishes at the still-standing Stratford Hotel; and Black Jack Ketchum's gang used to come into town to buy supplies. Shakespeare is open to visitors one weekend each month between June and December, with occasional historical reenactments. Check the website for dates.

Little Toad Creek Brewery
BREWERY

(☎575-956-6144; littletoadcreek.com; 200 N Bullard St; ⊙11am-11pm) The local brewery has seven of its own brews on tap, plus other New Mexico wines and spirits. It's always packed, with a small pub-style food menu.

🔒 Shopping

Lloyd Studios
ARTS & CRAFTS

(☎303-378-0926; www.lloydstudios.com; 306 W Broadway; ⊙10am-6pm Wed-Sat, to 2pm Sun) Candidate for southern New Mexico's most interesting shop. Craftsman William Lloyd fashions art out of antlers and bone, with a special focus on knives and swords. It's unlikely you'll be making any impulse purchases here, but browsing through his gallery and studio is a treat unto itself. Plus there's a whale skull on the wall.

ℹ Information

Gila National Forest Ranger Station (☎575-388-8201; www.fs.fed.us/r3/gila; 3005 E Camino del Bosque; ⊙8am-4pm Mon-Fri)

Gila Regional Medical Center (☎575-538-4000; www.grmc.org; 1313 E 32nd)

Post Office (500 N Hudson St; ⊙8:30am-5pm Mon-Fri, 10am-noon Sat)

Visitor Center (☎575-538-5555; www.silver citytourism.org; 201 N Hudson St; ⊙9am-5pm Mon-Sat, 10am-2pm Sun) This helpful office can provide everything you need to make the most of Silver City.

Gila National Forest

For anyone in search of the isolated and the undiscovered, the Gila (*hee*-la) has it in spades. Its 3.3 million acres cover eight mountain ranges, including the Mogollon, Tularosa, Blue and Black. It was here that legendary conservationist Aldo Leopold spearheaded a movement to establish the world's first designated wilderness area, resulting in the creation of the Gila Wilderness in 1924; in 1980, the adjacent terrain to the east was also designated as wilderness and named after Leopold.

This is some rugged country, just right for black bears, mountain lions and the reintroduced Mexican gray wolves. Trickling creeks are home to four species of endangered fish, including the Gila trout. In other words, it's perfect for hiking, hot springs and a trip to the Mogollon cliff dwellings.

◉ Sights

★ Gila Cliff Dwellings
National Monument ARCHAEOLOGICAL SITE
(☑ 575-536-9461; www.nps.gov/gicl; Hwy 15; adult/child $5/free; ◷ trail 9am-4pm, visitor center to 4:30pm) A relatively small site, these remarkable 13th-century cliff dwellings were only occupied by a small Mogollon group (30 to 80 people) for 20 years. Perfectly situated in six alcoves (some of which are enormous), it is unclear why they were suddenly abandoned, but today the buildings remain relatively intact. It's a long and winding road from Silver City (average time two hours), but pictographs, hot springs, endless hiking opportunities and superb vistas combine to make this a Gila highlight.

Rangers recommend the short hike up to the mesa above Woody's Corral, but there are quite a few other trailheads on the drive up. Behind the visitor's center is the Middle Fork of the Gila River – follow this for about half a mile to reach Lightfeather Hot Springs in the backcountry (you'll get your feet wet, so wear suitable shoes). There are plenty of free **campsites** (www.nps.gov/gicl; Gila Cliff Dwellings National Monument) up here.

Mogollon TOWN
(Hwy 159) Just north of Glenwood, Hwy 159 twists its way off Hwy 180 for a vertiginous 9 miles on the slow-going route to Mogollon, a semi–ghost town (sometimes inaccessible in winter). Once an important mining community, it now holds just a few antique and knickknack shops and, as is typical for middle-of-nowhere New Mexico, one proud little restaurant. This one is called the Purple Onion (p330), and it's as good as you'd hope after making the trip.

Gila Hot Springs HOT SPRINGS
(Hwy 15; day-use $5; ◷ dawn-dusk) Used by American Indians since ancient times, the three pools here are simply lovely. Caretakers regulate the temperatures throughout the day so that they're always about perfect (each pool differs by about one degree), simple sun shades are ideally placed, and the mountainous setting is superb. It's located 3.5 miles before the Gila Cliff Dwellings; turn right onto the dirt road (Access Rd) before the RV Park. There are 12 tent sites available for $6 each. Cash only.

INTO THE HEART OF THE GILA

If you have a high-clearance 4WD and a little extra time, you can follow a scenic road from the Silver City area right through the heart of the Gila. From Hwy 35 north of Mimbres, Forest Rd 150 wends through the forest for 60 miles before emerging onto the sweeping Plains of San Agustin. Another option off Hwy 35 is to drive the rough Forest Rd 151 to the Aldo Leopold Wilderness boundary, then hike a few miles up to the top of McKnight Mountain, the highest summit in the Black Range at 10,165ft.

🏃 Activities

Catwalk Trail HIKING
(off Hwy 174, Glenwood; vehicle $3) On the western side of the forest, 65 miles northwest of Silver City off Hwy 180, this short trail, wheelchair-accessible and great for kids, follows a suspended metal walkway through narrow Whitewater Canyon. You can see the creek rushing beneath your feet. While hardcore hikers may find it disappointingly short, it offers a painless way to experience the Gila.

🛌 Sleeping

The Gila is a huge place, and there are USFS campgrounds scattered throughout much of it, including several on the road up to the cliff dwellings. You'll also find the occasional cabin or guesthouse in small rural towns like Reserve.

Bighorn Campground CAMPGROUND
(☑ 575-539-2481; Hwy 180, Glenwood; ◷ year-round) FREE Six sites in Gila National Forest, a quarter-mile north of Glenwood, with no drinking water or fee. First-come, first-served.

Gila Hot Springs Ranch RANCH $
(☑ 575-536-9551; www.gilahotspringsranch.com; Hwy 15; tent/RV sites $16/20, r from $69; 🛜🏊) This campground across from the Gila Hot Springs has simple rooms with kitchenettes in a giant red barn-like structure, along with an RV park with a spa and showers. If you're in a tent, you might as well sleep at the springs. Horseback rides, guided fishing and wilderness pack trips can be arranged in advance.

Casitas de Gila
GUESTHOUSE $$

(☑ 575-535-4455; www.casitasdegila.com; Casita Flats Rd, near Cliff; casitas $170-225; ☎) For serene forest slumber, rent one of the five stunning adobe-style casitas set on 90 acres of wilderness. Each unit has a fully stocked kitchen, plenty of privacy and one or two bedrooms. Stay a while and rates drop. There are telescopes, an outdoor hot tub and grills to keep you occupied. The guesthouse is about 45 minutes northwest of Silver City.

✖ Eating

Apart from in small towns like Reserve and Glenwood, you'll need to provide your own food here.

Adobe Café & Bakery
BAKERY $

(☑ 575-533-6146; cnr Hwys 180 & 12; mains $9-12; ☺7am-8pm Sun & Mon, to 3pm Wed-Fri) A culinary oasis in the middle of nowhere (aka '7 miles west of Reserve'). Aside from creative renditions of typical diner fare, the Adobe features venison burgers, elk sausage and some good vegetarian options.

Purple Onion
CAFE $

(Main St; mains $5-10; ☺9am-5pm Sat & Sun late May–mid-Oct) One of the few inhabitants of the virtual ghost town of Mogollon, the Purple Onion claims to serve the best burger in New Mexico. We're not sure if it's the best, but given the location it's pretty darn good, as are most of the homemade dishes at this friendly, weekend-only place.

ⓘ Information

In addition to the Gila National Forest offices in Silver City and T or C, Mimbres' **ranger office** (☑ 575-536-2250; Hwy 35, Mimbres; ☺8am-4:30pm Mon-Fri), east of Silver City, is particularly useful.

ⓘ Getting There & Away

The Gila is an enormous tract of land. Silver City, to the south, is a good base for exploring the more accessible areas, including the cliff dwellings – the drive there provides an excellent overview of the region with panoramic views, pull-offs and campsites. Tiny Reserve, on Hwy 12, located at the northwestern flank, is another possible base, with basic lodging and food. Hwy 180 connects Reserve with Silver City and is another scenic stretch. T or C or Hillsboro are more convenient for reaching the eastern slope of the Black Range.

Deming
☑575 / POP 14,609 / ELEV 4337FT

Founded in 1881 as a railway junction, Deming stands in New Mexico's least populous quadrant, surrounded by cotton fields (!) on the northern edge of the Chihuahuan Desert (the water comes from the Mimbres River, underground). Deming is more of a stopover on the interstate rather than an actual destination in itself.

◎ Sights

Deming Luna Mimbres Museum
MUSEUM

(☑ 505-546-2382; www.lunacountyhistorical society.com; 301 S Silver Ave; ☺9am-4pm Mon-Sat) **FREE** One of New Mexico's best regional museums, a sprawling, enormous affair that holds a superb display of Mimbres pottery and a great doll collection, including one rescued from the rubble of Hiroshima. A re-created Victorian street includes the actual contents of many longlost local shops, while another room is devoted to fading snapshots of local families. You can see an actual iron lung and, get this, a braille edition of *Playboy* (maybe someone *was* reading it for the articles).

St Clair Winery
WINERY

(☑ 575-546-1179; www.stclairwinery.com; 1325 De Baca Rd; ☺10am-6pm Mon-Sat, noon-6pm Sun) The tasting room for New Mexico's largest vintner is located beside Hwy 549, 3 miles east of Deming.

Rockhound State Park
PARK

(☑ 575-546-6182; www.nmparks.com; 9880 Stirrup Rd SE; per car $5; ☺7am-dusk) Rockhound State Park, 14 miles southeast of Deming via Hwys 11 and 141, gives visitors the chance to collect all sorts of semiprecious or just plain pretty rocks, including jasper, geodes and thunder eggs. You'll need a shovel and some rockhounding experience to uncover anything special; local experts suggest walking into the Little Florida Mountains for a while before you start searching. The park's Spring Canyon section holds shaded picnic tables and the half-mile Lovers Leap trail.

✯✯ Festivals & Events

Great American Duck Race
CULTURAL

(www.demingduckrace.com; ☺Aug) Deming's biggest annual draw occurs on the fourth weekend in August. Anyone can enter the races to compete for a cash prize. Other wacky events include the Great American Tortilla Toss, Outhouse Races and a Duckling Contest. Entertainment ranges from cowboy poets to musicians, and there's a parade, hot-air balloons and food.

🛏 Sleeping & Eating

You'll find chain hotels around the interstate exits and several Mexican restaurants downtown.

Grand Motor Inn   MOTEL $

(📞 575-546-2632; 1721 E Pine St; r from $50; ✳ 🕸 🛁 🐾) This red-brick motel, on the main road just east of downtown, makes for a decent spot to sleep, with a grassy inner courtyard and a busy restaurant.

Adobe Deli   STEAK $$

(📞 575-546-0361; www.adobedeli.com; 3970 Lewis Flats Rd SE; mains $7-27; ⊙ 11am-5pm & 6-10pm Mon-Sat, 11am-9pm Sun) This amazing, cavernous barn-like structure, on a run-down farm 12 miles east via US 549 (follow Pine St), is filled with stuffed animals from mouflon to marlin and even a mermaid. Food ranges from excellent sandwiches or the specialty onion soup to ribs and giant steaks, while there's often live music, or sports events on a giant TV.

🛍 Shopping

Diaz Farms   FOOD

(📞 575-546-7264; 2485 Silver City Hwy NW; ⊙ 8:30am-5pm) If you're not passing through Hatch, this produce stand is the spot to pick up inexpensive chile ristras, big bags of chile powder (red and green), sacks of whole chiles – why not? – bales of hay. It's north of town on Hwy 180, just past the turnoff to Hatch.

Readers' Cove   BOOKS

(📞 575-544-2512; 200 S Copper St; ⊙ 10am-5pm) If you just finished your book, trade it in at this fantastic used-book store, in a 19th-century adobe house where the shelves are groaning with everything from literature to history to pulp.

ℹ Information

Visitor Center (📞 575-567-1962; www.deming visitorcenter.webs.com; 800 Pine St; ⊙ 9am-5pm Mon-Fri, to noon Sat; 🛜)

ℹ Getting There & Away

Deming is located 60 miles west of Las Cruces and 215 miles east of Tucson on I-10. **Greyhound** (📞 575-546-3881; www.greyhound.com; 420 E Cedar St) runs daily buses along the I-10 corridor.

Las Cruces

📞 575 / POP 101,643 / ELEV 3908FT

Las Cruces and her older and smaller sister city, Mesilla, sit at the edge of a broad basin beneath the fluted Organ Mountains, at the crossroads of two major highways, I-10 and I-25. There's something special about the combination of bright white sunlight, glassy blue skies, flowering cacti, rippling red mountains and desert lowland landscape found here. The city itself, however, is less than a dream town: it's sprawling and beastly hot for much of the year.

An eclectic mix of old and young, Las Cruces is home to New Mexico State University (NMSU), whose 18,000 students infuse it with a healthy dose of youthful liveliness, while at the same time its 350 days of sunshine and numerous golf courses are turning it into a popular retirement destination.

⊙ Sights & Activities

With some 26 granite spires, the Organ Mountains hold some fantastic multipitch climbs. Part of the fun – well, the experience – are some seriously gnarly approaches, however.

★ Organ Mountains-Desert Peaks National Monument   NATIONAL PARK

(📞 575-522-1219; www.organmountains.org; per vehicle $5; ⊙ 8am-5pm) New Mexico's newest national monument consists of several separate components, totaling almost 500,000 acres and all lying within a 50-mile radius of Las Cruces. While much of it is not developed for visitors, the Organ Mountains, which rise up to 9000ft east of the city, are definitely worth exploring. Several trails leave out of the **Dripping Springs Visitor Center**, including the lovely Dripping Springs trail itself, a 3-mile round-trip that passes the century-old remains of a sanatorium and a hotel.

★ Mesilla   AREA

Dating back 150 years and little changed since, Mesilla is a charming old adobe town. Despite the souvenir shops and tourist-oriented restaurants, its beautiful historic Plaza, 4 miles south of Las Cruces, provides a perfect opportunity to lose track of time. The 1855 San Albino Church here offers Mass in English and Spanish. Wander a few blocks in any direction to garner the essence of a mid-19th-century Southwestern border town.

★ **New Mexico Farm &**
Ranch Heritage Museum MUSEUM
(☑ 575-522-4100; www.nmfarmandranchmuseum. org; 4100 Dripping Springs Rd; adult/child $5/3; ⊙ 9am-5pm Mon-Sat, noon-5pm Sun; ⊕) This terrific museum doesn't just display engaging exhibits on the state's agricultural history – it's got livestock too. Enclosures on the working farm alongside hold assorted breeds of cattle, along with horses, donkeys, sheep and goats. The taciturn cowboys who tend the animals proffer little extra information, but they add color, and you can even buy a pony if you have $450 to spare. There are daily milking demonstrations plus weekly displays of blacksmithing, spinning and weaving, and heritage cooking.

New Mexico State University UNIVERSITY
(☑ 575-646-4714; www.nmsu.edu/museums; 775 College Dr) FREE If you're looking to engage the intellect, the university museums are the obvious choice. While small, the exhibits here are well curated. The **Zuhl Museum** (8am to 5pm Monday to Friday), in the visitor center, holds a beautiful collection of polished petrified wood, minerals and fossils. The **University Museum** (noon to 4pm Tuesday to Saturday), in Kent Hall, is also worth a browse, with exhibits on regional culture and history.

White Sands Missile
Test Center Museum MUSEUM
(☑ 575-678-3358; www.wsmr-history.org; ⊙ 8am-4pm Mon-Fri, 10am-3pm Sat) FREE Explore New Mexico's military technology history with a visit to this museum, 25 miles east of Las Cruces along Hwy 70. It represents the heart of the White Sands Missile Range, a major testing site since 1945. There's a missile garden, a real V-2 rocket and a museum with lots of defense-related artifacts. Visitors have to park outside the Test Center gate and check in at the office before walking in.

★ **Festivals & Events**

Fiesta of Our Lady of Guadalupe RELIGIOUS
(⊙ Dec 10-12) Held in the American Indian village of Tortugas, south of Las Cruces, late into the first night, drummers and masked dancers accompany a statue of Mary in a procession. On the following day, participants climb several miles to Tortugas Mountain for Mass; dancing and ceremonies continue into the night in the village.

Southern New Mexico
State Fair & Rodeo CULTURAL
(www.snmstatefairgrounds.net; adult/child $14/10; ⊙ late Sep) Features a livestock show, an auction, a daredevil rodeo and live country music.

International Mariachi Conference MUSIC
(www.lascrucesmariachi.org; ⊙ Oct) Las Cruces celebrates all things mariachi with educational workshops and big-name performances.

🛏 **Sleeping**

Thanks to NMSU, Las Cruces holds a plentiful supply of chain hotels and motels, as well as a scattering of more idiosyncratic options.

★ **Best Western Mission Inn** MOTEL $
(☑ 575-524-8591; www.bwmissioninn.com; 1765 S Main St; r from $71; ❋ 🛜 ⊛) A truly out-of-the-ordinary accommodation option: yes it's a roadside chain motel, but the rooms are beautifully kitted out with attractive tiling, stonework and colorful stenciled designs; they're sizable and comfortable; and the rates are great.

Aguirre Spring Campground CAMPGROUND $
(☑ 575-525-4300; Aguirre Spring Rd; tent & RV sites $7; ⊛) Located on the back (east) side of the Organ Mountains, Aguirre Spring sits at the base of the rocky cliffs; two hiking trails leave from here. It has 59 sites, though it is quite popular – consider reservations on weekends.

★ **Lundeen Inn of the Arts** B&B $$
(☑ 505-526-3326; www.innofthearts.com; 618 S Alameda Blvd, Las Cruces; r/ste $125/155; P ❋ 🛜 ⊛) Each of the 20 guest rooms in this large and very lovely century-old Mexican Territorial–style inn is unique and decorated in the style of a New Mexico artist. Check out the soaring pressed-tin ceilings

in the great room. Owners Linda and Jerry offer the kind of genteel hospitality you seldom find these days.

Hotel Encanto de Las Cruces   HOTEL $$
(☎505-522-4300; www.hotelencanto.com; 705 S Telshor Blvd, Las Cruces; r from $130; ❄️@🐾🛜☷☷) The pick of the city's larger hotels, this Spanish Colonial resort property holds 200 spacious rooms, decorated in warm Southwestern tones, plus a palm-fringed outdoor pool, an exercise room, a restaurant and a lounge with patio.

✖️ Eating

Located in the heart of the world chile capital, both Las Cruces and Mesilla serve up some of the spiciest New Mexican food in the state. Also be on the lookout for pecans in desserts around town – Las Cruces is one of the world's largest pecan producers.

✖️ Las Cruces

Nellie's Cafe   NEW MEXICAN $
(☎575-524-9982; 1226 W Hadley Ave; mains $5-10; ⏲8am-2pm Tue-Sat) Cherished by locals, Nellie's has been serving homemade burritos, *chile rellenos* and tamales for decades now, under the slogan 'Chile with an Attitude.' It's small and humble in decor but big in taste, with deliciously spicy food.

Spirit Winds Coffee Bar   CAFE $
(☎575-521-1222; 2260 S Locust; mains $7-10; ⏲7am-7pm Mon-Fri, 7:30am-7pm Sat, 8am-6pm Sun; 🛜🐾) Join the university crowd for excellent cappuccinos and gourmet tea, plus good sandwiches, salads, soups and pastries. A gift and card shop and occasional live entertainment keep the students, artsy types and business folks coming back.

✖️ Mesilla

⭐Chala's Wood-Fired Grill   NEW MEXICAN $
(☎575-652-4143; 2790 Ave de Mesilla; mains $5-10; ⏲8am-9pm Mon-Sat, to 8pm Sun) With house-smoked carnitas and turkey, house-made bacon and chile-pork sausage, plus *calabacitas* (squash and corn), quinoa salad and organic greens, this place rises well above the standard New Mexican diner fare. Located at the southern end of

WORTH A TRIP

HATCH

The town of Hatch sits at the heart of New Mexico's chile-growing country 40 miles north of Las Cruces, up I-25. New Mexican chiles didn't originate here – most local varieties have centuries-old roots in the northern farming villages around Chimayó and Española – but the soil and irrigation in these parts proved perfect for mass production. Although recent harvests have declined sharply, as imported chile takes over the market, the town still clings to its title as 'Chile Capital of the World.' Even if you miss the annual chile-eating contest during the Labor Day **Chile Festival** (www.hatchchilefest.com; ⏲Sep), just pull off the interstate at Exit 41 and pop into **Sparky's Burgers** (☎575-267-4222; www.sparkysburgers.com; 115 Franklin St; mains $6-11; ⏲10:30am-7pm Thu-Sun) for what might be the best green chile cheeseburger in the state, served with casual pride. If you're looking for some spicy New Mexico souvenirs, virtually every store on the roads into Hatch sells chiles – as ristras, in powdered form, in burlap sacks and even in marmalade.

Mesilla, it's kick-back casual and the price is right.

¡Andele!   NEW MEXICAN $
(☎575-526-9333; www.andelerestaurante.com; 1950 Calle del Norte; mains $5-16.50; ⏲8am-9pm Tue-Sun, to 2:30pm Mon) It's the salsa bar here that everyone raves about, and with good reason. Follow up the homemade chips with *tacos el castor* or smothered enchiladas, or just dig in to a simple bowl of chile. Located at the edge of Mesilla, it also runs **Andele's Dog House**, serving loaded Mexican hot dogs and fries con queso, across the street.

Chope's Bar & Cafe   NEW MEXICAN $
(☎575-233-3420; 16145 S Hwy 28, La Mesa; mains $6-12; ⏲11:30am-1:30pm & 5:30-8pm Mon-Sat) Worth every second of the 15-mile drive south of town, Chope's may not be much to look at, but the hot chile will turn you into an addict within minutes. From *chile rellenos* to burritos, you've seen the

menu before; you just haven't had it this good. The adjacent bar is loads of fun.

La Posta NEW MEXICAN $$
(☑ 575-524-3524; www.laposta-de-mesilla.com; 2410 Calle de San Albino; mains $9-18; ◔11am-9pm) This rambling old adobe was here before Mesilla itself, and became a Butterfield stagecoach stop in the 1850s. Now standing at the corner of the Plaza, it's entered from the next block. With a fabulous atmosphere and almost 100 varieties of tequila, you can almost overlook the ho-hum food.

Double Eagle Restaurant STEAK $$$
(☑ 575-523-6700; www.double-eagle-mesilla. com; 308 Calle de Guadalupe; mains $24-45; ◔11am-10pm Mon-Sat, 11am-9pm Sun) A glorious melange of Wild West opulence, all dark wood and velvet hangings, and featuring a fabulous old bar, this Plaza restaurant is on the National Register of Historic Places. The main dining room offers continental and Southwestern cuisine, especially steaks, while the less formal **Peppers** (mains $7 to $15) occupies the verdant courtyard.

🍸 Drinking & Nightlife

Mesilla has a good brewery plus a handful of atmospheric old saloons – drop by the bars in the Double Eagle or La Posta for a classy margarita.

Spotted Dog Brewery BREWERY
(☑ 575-650-2729; www.spotteddogbrewery.com; 2900 Ave de Mesilla; ◔11:30am-10:30pm Wed & Thu, 11:30am-midnight Fri & Sat, 12:30-8:30pm Sun; 🛜🐾) The local brewery of choice, the Spotted Dog is located rather incongruously next to a gas station at the southern tail of Mesilla. No matter – the seven brews on tap are tops, as are the views of the Organ Mountains from the patio.

Bosque Taproom BREWERY
(☑ 575-571-4626; www.bosquebrewing.com; 901 E University Ave, Bldg 985, Suite 1B; ◔noon-11pm Sun-Thu, to midnight Fri & Sat) The Albuquerque brewery serves up a winning selection of New Mexico's finest, just across from the NMSU campus.

El Patio BAR
(☑ 575-526-9943; 2171 Calle de Parian, Mesilla Plaza; ◔2-11pm Sun-Wed, to 2am Thu-Sat) In an old adobe building, this historic bar has

been rocking Mesilla since the 1930s. It serves tasty cocktails along with live rock and jazz.

☆ Entertainment

Both Mesilla and Las Cruces hold thriving fine-arts and performing-arts communities.

Fountain Theater CINEMA
(☑ 575-524-8287; www.mesillavalleyfilm.org; 2469 Calle de Guadalupe, Mesilla; adult/student $7/6) Home of the nonprofit Mesilla Valley Film Society, this splendid old adobe theater screens foreign and art films.

Center for the Arts THEATER
(☑ 575-646-4515; www.nmsutheatre.com; 1000 E University Ave) The American Southwest Theatre Company performs at the Center for the Arts on the NMSU campus.

Las Cruces Symphony CLASSICAL MUSIC
(☑ 575-646-3709; www.lascrucessymphony.com; 1075 N Horseshoe St) The Las Cruces Symphony performs at the NMSU Music Center Recital Hall.

ℹ️ Information

Las Cruces Visitors Bureau (☑ 575-541-2444; www.lascrucescvb.org; 211 N Water St; ◔8am-5pm Mon-Fri)

Mesilla Visitor Center (☑ 575-524-3262; www. oldmesilla.org; 2231 Ave de Mesilla; ◔9:30am-4:30pm Mon-Sat, 11am-3pm Sun) Inside the town hall, Mesilla's visitor center holds interesting displays on the town's past.

Memorial Medical Center (☑ 575-522-8641; www.mmclc.org; 2450 S Telshor Blvd; ◔emergency 24hr)

Police (☑ 575-526-0795; 217 E Picacho Ave)

Post Office (201 E Las Cruces Ave; ◔8am-6pm Mon-Fri, 8-11:30am Sat)

ℹ️ Getting There & Away

El Paso is a mere 45 miles south of Las Cruces on I-10. The El Paso airport serves major hubs in the American West, in addition to Chicago and Atlanta.

BUS

Greyhound (☑ 575-523-1824; www.greyhound. com; 800 E Thorpe Rd, Chucky's Convenience Store) buses run to all major destinations in the area, including El Paso, Albuquerque and Tucson. The bus stop is about 7 miles north of town.

Las Cruces Shuttle Service (☑ 575-525-1784; www.lascrucesshuttle.com) runs eight to 10 vans daily to the El Paso International Airport ($49 one-way, $33 each additional person), and to Deming, Silver City and other destinations on request.

CARLSBAD CAVERNS & SOUTHEASTERN NEW MEXICO

Two extraordinary natural wonders are tucked away in New Mexico's arid southeast: the mesmerizing White Sands National Monument and the magnificent Carlsbad Caverns National Park. This region also swirls with some of the state's most enduring legends: aliens in Roswell, Billy the Kid in Lincoln, and Smokey Bear in Capitan. Most of the lowlands are covered by hot, rugged Chihuahuan Desert – once submerged under the ocean – but you can always escape to the cooler climes around the popular forest resorts of Cloudcroft or Ruidoso.

Alamogordo

☑ 575 / POP 31,368 / ELEV 4334FT

Despite a dearth of amenities, Alamogordo (Spanish for 'fat cottonwood tree') is the center of an important space and atomic research program. While it's the closest base for visiting White Sands, if you don't mind the extra miles on the odometer, neighboring Cloudcroft is a much more soulful place to lay your head. You can also check out two tiny towns nearby: the art outpost of La Luz and pretty little Tularosa.

◎ Sights

La Luz & Tularosa   AREA
The painters, writers and craftspeople who live in the tiny enclave of La Luz, 4 miles north of Alamogordo, share a passion for creating artwork and living off the land; a wild outpost, it's well worth a browse. Another 10 miles north, the attractive village of Tularosa is dominated by the 1869 St Francis de Paula Church, built in a simple New Mexican style.

New Mexico Museum of Space History   MUSEUM
(☑ 575-437-2840; www.nmspacemuseum.org; 3198 Hwy 2001; adult/child $7/5; ⊙10am-5pm Wed-Sat & Mon, noon-5pm Sun; ⊕) Looming over the northeast corner of town and nicknamed 'the golden cube,' this four-story museum is surrounded by historic missiles, and holds excellent exhibits on space exploration. A Hall of Fame hails pioneers from William Congreve, whose rockets were fired at the Battle of Waterloo, to Neil Armstrong, while other displays cover New Mexico's potential role in commercial space flight. The adjoining **New Horizons Dome Theater** (adult/child $7/5) screens giant-screen movies and has laser **planetarium shows** (adult/child $5/4).

Toy Train Depot   MUSEUM
(☑ 505-437-2855; 1991 N White Sands Blvd; $4; ⊙noon-4:30pm Wed-Sun; ⊕) Railroad buffs and kids flock to this 1898 railway depot, for five rooms of train memorabilia and toy trains, and a 2.5-mile narrow-gauge minitrain you can ride through Alameda Park.

Alamogordo Museum of History   MUSEUM
(☑ 575-434-4438; www.alamogordohistory.com; 1301 N White Sands Blvd; adult/child $3/free; ⊙10am-4pm Mon-Sat) Thoroughly local little museum, focusing on the Mescalero Indians and the mining, railroad and logging industries. Its most cherished holding is a 47-star US flag, ultra-rare because Arizona joined the Union just six weeks after New Mexico.

Alameda Park & Zoo   ZOO
(☑ 575-439-4290; 1321 N White Sands Blvd; adult/3-11yr $2.50/1.50; ⊙9am-5pm; ⊕) Said to be the oldest zoo west of the Mississippi, established in 1898, this small but well-run place features exotics from around the world. Assuming both you and they are in the mood to brave the heat, you may see bears, bald eagles, alligators or the endangered Mexican gray wolf.

🛏 Sleeping

Almost all sleeping options here are chain hotels scattered along White Sands Blvd. There's free dispersed camping off of Hwy 82, east of Alamogordo on the way to Cloudcroft.

THREE RIVERS PETROGLYPH SITE

The remote **Three Rivers Petroglyph National Recreation Area** (☏ 575-525-4300; www.blm.gov/nm/threerivers; County Rd B30, off Hwy 54; per car $5, tent/RV sites $7/18; ☺ 8am-7pm Apr-Oct, to 5pm Nov-Mar) showcases over 21,000 petroglyphs, incised six centuries ago by the Jornada Mogollon people onto the flat surfaces of boulders atop a low ridge at the eastern edge of the Tularosa. The images include birds, animals, masks and human figures, and can be seen on an easy mile hike that leads through mesquite and cacti, with good views of the Sacramento Mountains to the east and White Sands on the western horizon.

There are five camping shelters at the parking lot, along with barbecue grills (free), restrooms, water and two hookups for RVs. Pets are allowed in the campground but not on the trails.

The site is 27 miles north of Alamogordo on Hwy 54, and then 5 miles east on a signed road. If you fancy roughing it for the night, a dirt road continues beyond the petroglyphs for about 9 miles to the White Mountain Wilderness, where you'll find **Three Rivers Campground** (☏ 575-434-7200; www.fs.usda.gov; per vehicle $6).

Super 8
HOTEL $

(☏ 575-434-4205; www.wyndhamhotels.com; 3204 N White Sands Blvd; r incl breakfast from $60; ❄@☎) This pleasant chain is well maintained, with large-format black-and-white landscape photography on the walls and reasonably fast wi-fi.

Oliver Lee Memorial State Park
CAMPGROUND $

(☏ 575-437-8284; www.nmparks.com; 409 Dog Canyon Rd; tent/RV sites $8/14) Spending a night or two in the fully equipped campground in this spring-fed canyon, 12 miles south of Alamogordo, will give you the chance to see ferns and flowers growing in the desert. The 5.5-mile Dog Canyon National Recreational Trail climbs 2000ft over 5.5 miles, for terrific views of the Tularosa Basin.

✖ Eating

Most eateries here are of the fast-food or chain variety.

Rizo's
MEXICAN $

(☏ 575-434-2607; 1480 White Sands Blvd; $8.75-15; ☺ 9am-9pm Tue-Sat, to 6pm Sun; ☎) Service can be a bit brisk at this no-frills place, but it's still one of the town's most reliable eats. In addition to all the usual suspects, you'll find *gorditas* (corn pockets), carne asada fries (topped with about everything) and fresh *agua fresca* and *horchata*.

Pizza Patio & Pub
ITALIAN $

(☏ 575-434-9633; 2203 E 1st St; mains $8.25-12.25; ☺ 11am-7:30pm Mon-Sat; ♣) The something-for-everyone place in Alamogordo, with an outdoor patio and a casual indoor dining room. Pizzas and pastas are OK, salads are big, and pints of beer are on tap.

ℹ Information

Lincoln USFS National Forest Ranger Station (☏ 575-434-7200; www.fs.usda.gov/lincoln; 3463 Las Palomas Rd; ☺ 8am-4:30pm Mon-Fri)

Visitor Center (☏ 575-437-6120; www.alamogordo.com; 1301 N White Sands Blvd; ☺ 8am-5pm Mon-Fri, 9am-4pm Sat, 10am-3pm Sun; ☎)

Gerald Champion Regional Medical Center (☏ 575-439-6100; www.gcrmc.org; 2669 N Scenic Dr; ☺ emergency 24hr)

Police (☏ 575-439-4300; 700 Virginia Ave)

Post Office (930 E 12th St; ☺ 8:30am-5pm Mon-Fri, 9am-noon Sat)

Cloudcroft

☏ 575 / POP 850 / ELEV 8600FT

Nestled almost 20 miles up in the mountains east of Alamogordo, Cloudcroft makes a pleasant escape year-round. In winter there's snow tubing and snowmobiling across powdery meadows. In summer, Cloudcroft offers refreshing respite from the desert heat, plus awesome hiking and biking. The town itself is a quaint place to wander, with some early-19th-century buildings, a low-key mountain vibe and a historic resort hotel, but most visitors are here to play in the surrounding peaks and forests.

⊙ Sights & Activities

Sacramento Peak
Observatory   OBSERVATORY
(📞575-434-7000; nsosp.nso.edu; adult/child $3/
free; ⊙visitor center 9am-5pm, closed Feb) One
of the world's largest solar observatories
is near Sunspot, 20 miles south of Cloudcroft. Though it's primarily for scientists,
tourists can enter the visitor center (note
that tours of the grounds have been suspended indefinitely). The high and beautiful Sunspot Scenic Byway leads to the site,
with the mountains to the east and White
Sands to the west. From Cloudcroft, take
Hwy 130 to Hwy 6563 – and fill your tank
before you set off.

High Altitude   MOUNTAIN BIKING
(📞575-682-1229; 310 Burro Ave; rentals per
day from $30; ⊙10am-5:30pm Mon-Thu, to
6pm Fri & Sat, to 5pm Sun) Trails in the Sacramento Mountains offer great mountain
biking. High Altitude sells outdoor gear,
rents bikes and will point you in the right
direction.

Ski Cloudcroft   SKIING
(📞575-682-2333; www.skicloudcroft.net; 1920
Hwy 82; all-day ski/tube $45/20; ⊙9am-4pm
Dec-Mar) Family-oriented ski resort with
the southernmost run in the US. In winter, grab the lift up and ski, snowboard or
race an inner tube (weekends only) down
the hill.

Lodge Resort Golf Course   GOLF
(📞575-682-2098; www.thelodgeresort.com; 9/18
holes from $28/48; ⊙Apr-Oct) The Lodge Resort
has a beautiful 18-hole golf course that's
among the highest and oldest in the country.

Hiking
Hiking is popular here from April to
November; options range from short hikes
close to town to overnight backpacking
trips. Although trails are often fairly flat, the
9000ft elevation can make for some strenuous hiking if you are not acclimatized. The
most popular day hike is the 2.2-mile **Cloud
Climbing Rail Trail**, which leaves from the
edge of town and ventures out to an amazing old railroad trestle bridge that you may
have glimpsed from Hwy 82 as you drove
up. The **Willie White/Wills Canyon Trails**
loop through open meadows, with a good
chance of seeing elk. The ranger station
(p338) has free trail maps and detailed topo
maps for sale.

✵ Festivals & Events

BAMM Festival   MUSIC
(www.bammfestival.com; ⊙mid-Jun) The outdoor Bad-Ass Mountain Music Festival features regional bands from New Mexico and
Texas over a long weekend in mid-June.

🛌 Sleeping

Cloudcroft is blessed with some heavenly
choices, from one of the state's few hostels to a historic resort. There are several
summer-only USFS campgrounds nearby.

★Cloudcroft Mountain
Park Hostel   HOSTEL $
(📞575-682-0555; www.cloudcrofthostel.com;
1049 Hwy 82; dm $19, r with shared bath $35-60;
🔊📶) Situated on 28 wooded acres, down
the highway 6 miles west of Cloudcroft,
this lurid blue hostel is the best lodging
deal around. Entire families can fit in the
large rooms, which are simple but tidy.
Shared bathrooms are clean, and there's a
fully equipped kitchen with coffee and tea.
The common area is a great place to swap
stories.

★Lodge Resort & Spa   HISTORIC HOTEL $$
(📞800-395-6343; www.thelodgeresort.com; 601
Corona Pl; r $125-235; @🔊📶) Built in 1899
as a getaway for railroad employees, this
historic hilltop lodge is now a full-scale
resort, with a wonderful restaurant, a golf
course, beautiful grounds and a pamper-
ing spa. Period-furnished rooms in the
main Bavarian-style building can be a bit
small but they're cozy, with high beds and
showers, not baths; less-attractive Pavilion
rooms are a few blocks away.

🍴 Eating

There are a handful of good dining options.

Mad Jack's Mountaintop
Barbecue   BARBECUE $
(📞575-682-7577; 105 James Canyon Hwy; mains
$7-16; ⊙11am-5pm Thu-Sun) The devoted
owner here is serious about his Texas style
BBQ – feast on brisket, ribs, pulled pork and
other mouthwatering delicacies such as the
Chile the Kid sandwich.

Rebecca's   AMERICAN $$$
(📞575-682-3131; Lodge Resort, 601 Corona
Pl; lunch $9-15, dinner $22-38; ⊙7-10am,
11:30am-2pm & 5:30-9pm) Up at the Lodge
Resort, Rebecca's is the classiest choice in
Cloudcroft, with rich, meaty dishes such

as chile-crusted rack of lamb to match the opulent Victorian setting. Kick back on the outside deck, have a beer and check out the spectacular views, before you head back into the elegant dining room.

ℹ️ Information

Visit Cloudcroft's online-only **Visitor Center** (📞 575-682-2733; www.cloudcroft.net) or **Sacramento Ranger Station** (📞 575-682-2551; 4 Lost Lodge Rd; ⊙ 8am-4:30pm Mon-Fri) for local info.

Ruidoso

📞 575 / POP 7965 / ELEV 6920FT

Perched on the eastern slopes of Sierra Blanca Peak (11,981ft), Ruidoso is a year-round resort town that's downright bustling in the summer, attracts skiers in winter, has a lively arts scene, and is also home to a renowned racetrack. Neighboring Texans and locals escaping the summer heat of Alamogordo and Roswell are happy campers here (or more precisely, happy cabiners). The lovely Rio Ruidoso, a small creek with good fishing, runs through town.

Hwy 48, the main drag through town, is called Mechem Dr as it approaches Ruidoso from the north, then becomes Sudderth Dr in the small downtown area, and heads east to the Y-intersection with Hwy 70. The community of Alto, 6 miles north on Mechem Dr, holds more accommodations.

◉ Sights & Activities

Ruidoso Downs Racetrack   SPORTS GROUND
(📞 575-378-4431; www.raceruidoso.com; 26225 Hwy 70; grandstand seats free; ⊙ Fri-Mon late May-early Sep) National attention focuses on the Ruidoso Downs racetrack on Labor Day for the world's richest quarter-horse race, the All American Futurity, which has a purse of $2.4 million. The course is also home to the Racehorse Hall of Fame, and the small Billy the Kid Casino.

**Hubbard Museum of
the American West**   MUSEUM
(📞 575-378-4142; www.hubbardmuseum.org; 26301 Hwy 70; adult/child $7/2; ⊙ 9am-5pm Thu-Mon; ♿) This town-run museum focuses on local history, with a wonderful gallery of old photos, and also displays American

Indian kachinas, war bonnets, weapons and pottery. Traces of its original incarnation as the Museum of the Horse linger in various horse-related exhibits – and be sure to check out the fascinating, if completely irrelevant, history of toilets in the restrooms.

Ski Apache   SKIING
(📞 575-464-3600; www.skiapache.com; 1286 Ski Run Rd; lift ticket adult/child $68/48) Unlikely as it sounds, Ski Apache, 18 miles northwest of Ruidoso on the slopes of Sierra Blanca Peak, really is owned by the Apache. Potentially it's the finest ski area south of Albuquerque, a good choice for affordability and fun. Snowfall down here can be sporadic, though – check conditions ahead.

Hiking

Hiking is popular after the snow has melted. Try the 5-mile trail from Ski Apache to Sierra Blanca Peak, an ascent of 2000ft. Take trail 15 from the small parking lot just before the main lot and follow signs west and south along Trails 25 and 78 to Lookout Mountain (11,580ft). An obvious trail continues due south for 1.25 miles to Sierra Blanca Peak. As the mountain is sacred to the Apache, technically you need a permit, though this does not seem to be enforced. The ranger station (p340) has more info on area hikes.

★✦ Festivals & Events

Aspenfest   CULTURAL
(⊙ Oct) Held on the first weekend in October, Aspenfest features a chile cook-off, a classic car show and a street festival.

Oktoberfest   CULTURAL
(www.trekwest.com/oktoberfest;   ⊙ Oct) Bavarian-themed, with German food and beer, along with professional polka dancing and oompah bands. Held the third weekend in October.

**Lincoln County Cowboy
Symposium**   CULTURAL
(www.cowboysymposium.org; ⊙ Oct) Held at Ruidoso Downs on the second weekend in October, with cowboy poetry, chuckwagon cooking and horsebreaking.

**Apache Maiden Puberty
Ceremony**   CULTURAL
(⊙ Jul) Takes over the July 4 weekend, and features a powwow, a rodeo and arts-and-crafts demonstrations.

WHITE SANDS NATIONAL MONUMENT

Undulating through the Tularosa Basin like something out of a dream, these ethereal dunes are a highlight of any trip to New Mexico, and a must on every landscape photographer's itinerary. Try to time a visit to **White Sands** (☑ 575-479-6124; www.nps.gov/whsa; adult/under 16yr $5/free; ☉ 7am-9pm Jun-Aug, to sunset Sep-May) with sunrise or sunset (or both), when the dazzlingly white sea of sand is at its most magical.

From the visitor center drive the 16-mile scenic drive, which loops into the heart of the world's largest gypsum dune field, covering 275 sq miles. Along the way, get out of the car and romp around, or escape the crowds by hiking either the Alkali Flat, a 5-mile (round-trip) backcountry trail through the heart of the dunes, or the simple mile loop nature trail. Don't forget your sunglasses – the sand's as bright as snow.

It's a long, long way to the ocean from here, so don't be surprised to find locals picnicking, playing, sunbathing and generally enjoying the full-on beach experience. Join them by springing for a $15 plastic saucer at the visitor center gift shop, and sledding the back dunes; you can sell it back for $5 at day's end (no rentals to avoid liability). Check the park calendar for sunset strolls and occasional moonlight bicycle rides (adult/child $5/2.50).

Backcountry campsites, with no water or toilet facilities, stand a mile from the scenic drive. Pick up a permit ($3; first-come, first-served) in person at the visitor center at least one hour before sunset. Car campers should ask the rangers for a list of other nearby campsites.

To reach the park, drive Hwy 70 either 50 miles northeast of Las Cruces or 16 miles southwest of Alamogordo – and bear in mind that the road occasionally closes at very short notice for up to three hours, during missile tests.

🛏 Sleeping

Rental cabins are a big deal in Ruidoso. Most have kitchens and grills, and often fireplaces and decks. Some cabins in town are cramped, while newer ones are concentrated in the Upper Canyon. There's also free primitive camping along the forest roads on the way to the ski area; for campsite specifics, ask at the ranger station.

4 Seasons
Real Estate   ACCOMMODATION SERVICES
(☑ 575-257-7577;   www.casasderuidoso.com;
☉ 8am-5pm) Arranges condominium, cabin and lodge rentals.

Sitzmark Chalet   HOTEL $
(☑ 575-257-4140; www.sitzmark-chalet.com; 627 Sudderth Dr; r from $87; ✴ 🛜) This ski-themed chalet offers 17 simple but nice rooms. Picnic tables, grills and an eight-person hot tub are welcome perks.

Bonito Hollow Campground   CAMPGROUND $
(☑ 575-336-4325; www.bonitohollow.com; 221 Hwy 37, Alto; tent/RV sites $20/35, cabin $90; ☉ Mar-Nov; 🛜🐕) Private campground in peaceful wooded surroundings, adjoining Lincoln National Forest. Decent spaces for RVs, though the tent rates only cover two people; it's an additional $10 per person for more. It's 9 miles north of Ruidoso, off Hwy 48.

Upper Canyon Inn   LODGE $$
(☑ 575-257-3005; www.uppercanyoninn.com; 215 Main Rd; r & cabins from $149; ✴ 🛜🐕) Rooms and cabins here range from simple good values to rustic-chic luxury. Bigger doesn't necessarily mean more expensive, so look at a few options. The pricier cabins have some fine interior woodwork and Jacuzzi tubs.

Inn of the Mountain Gods   CASINO HOTEL $$
(☑ 800-545-9011; www.innofthemountaingods.com; 287 Carrizo Canyon Rd; r from $109; ✴ 🛜🐕) This luxury, lakeside casino resort on the Mescalero Apache Reservation offers surprisingly low online rates. Gamblers can feed slots, while guided fishing, paddleboat rentals, a championship golf course and horseback riding are just a concierge call away. Several restaurants, a nightclub and a sports bar are also on-site. It's fun for a night or two.

High Country Lodge   LODGE $$
(☑ 575-336-4321; www.highcountrylodge.net; 859 N Hwy 48, Alto; r from $139; 🛜🐕) This funky

older place near the turn-off for the ski resort welcomes you with three friendly (wooden) bears. It offers a comfortable selection of rustic and basic two-bedroom cabins, each with kitchen, fireplace and porch, plus an indoor pool and hot tub.

Shadow Mountain Lodge LODGE $$
(☑ 575-257-4886; www.smlruidoso.com; 107 Main St; r/cabins from $129/159; ❄️📶🐾) Geared toward couples, the immaculate, romantic rooms in the lodge feature fireplaces, while a wraparound balcony overlooks the landscaped grounds; the hot tub is tucked away in a gazebo. Individual cabins have Jacuzzi tubs and giant TVs.

✖ Eating

Ruidoso has enough restaurants that you'll be able to find some variety here.

★ Cornerstone Bakery CAFE $
(☑ 575-257-1842; www.cornerstonebakerycafe. com; 1712 Sudderth Dr; mains $5.50-11; ⊙ 7am-3pm Mon-Fri, to 4pm Sat & Sun; 🍴) Totally irresistible, hugely popular local bakery and cafe, where everything, from the breads, pastries and espresso to the omelets and croissant sandwiches, is just the way it should be. Stick around long enough and the Cornerstone may become your morning touchstone.

Village Buttery BISTRO $
(☑ 575-257-9251; www.thevillagebuttery.com; 2107 Sudderth Dr; mains $6.75-9; ⊙ 10am-2:30pm Mon-Sat) Go gourmet in Ruidoso: freshly made soups and quiche, tortellini salad and whole-wheat tuna sandwiches, all followed up with just-baked croissants and pie. The catch? (You knew there would be a catch.) It's lunch only.

Michael J's ITALIAN $$
(☑ 575-257-9559; www.michaeljsrestaurant.com; 601 Mechem Dr; mains $14.50-30; ⊙ 5-9pm Tue-Sat) Excellent and very convivial Italian restaurant, cozy and romantic in winter and offering outdoor patio seating in summer. The delicious pasta dishes concentrate on seafood such as clams and shrimp, but it also serves meaty Italian classics using steak and veal.

Casa Blanca NEW MEXICAN $$
(☑ 575-257-2495; 501 Mechem Dr; mains $8-27; ⊙ 11am-9pm Mon-Thu, to 10pm Fri & Sat, to 8pm Sun) Dine on Southwestern cuisine in a renovated Spanish-style house or on the pleasant patio in the summer. It's hard to go wrong with the New Mexican plates, but it's also got big burgers and chicken-fried steak.

🍷 Drinking & Nightlife

There are a few bars and three casinos in town.

Rio Grande Grill & Taproom PUB
(☑ 575-808-8456; www.sierrablancabrewery.com; 441 Mechem Dr; ⊙ 11am-9pm Mon-Sat) The taproom of the Sierra Blanca Brewing Company (based in Moriarty, east of Albuquerque, no relation to the Sherlock Holmes villain), the Rio Grande sometimes feels more like a restaurant than a bar. Don't expect any sawdust on the floor or a raucous night of line dancing, but if you're into craft beer, it's the best pub in town.

Quarters Lounge BAR
(☑ 575-257-9535; 2535 Sudderth Dr; ⊙ 11am-2am Mon-Sat, noon-midnight Sun) The town bar, Quarters has DJs and karaoke nights throughout the week.

☆ Entertainment

Flying J Ranch LIVE MUSIC
(☑ 575-336-4330; www.flyingjranch.com; 1028 Hwy 48; adult/child $27/15; ⊙ from 5:30pm Mon-Sat late May-early Sep, Sat only early Sep–mid-Oct; 🎪) Families with little ones will love this 'Western village,' 1.5 miles north of Alto, as it delivers a full night of entertainment, with gunfights, pony rides and Western music, to go with its cowboy-style chuckwagon dinner.

Spencer Theater for the Performing Arts THEATER
(☑ 575-336-4800; www.spencertheater.com; 108 Spencer Rd, Alto) Larger than you'd expect in small-town New Mexico, and enjoying a stunning mountain setting in Alto, this community theater hosts drama, music and dance performances.

ℹ Information

Visitor Center (☑ 575-257-7395; www.ruidosonow.com; 720 Sudderth Dr; ⊙ 8am-5pm Mon-Fri, 9am-3pm Sat)

Smokey Bear Ranger Station (☑ 575-257-4095; www.fs.usda.gov/lincoln; 901 Mechem Dr; ⊙ 8am-4pm Mon-Fri, plus Sat in summer) Has information about forest service campsites and hiking trails.

ℹ️ Getting There & Away

Ruidoso is 50 miles northeast of Alamogordo and 75 miles west of Roswell. **Greyhound** (☑ 575-257-2660; www.greyhound.com; 344 Sudderth Dr) operates daily service to Alamogordo, Roswell and El Paso, TX.

Lincoln

☑ 575 / POP 50 / ELEV 5702FT

Fans of Western history won't want to miss little Lincoln. Twelve miles east of Capitan along the Billy the Kid National Scenic Byway, this is where the gun battle that turned Billy the Kid into a legend took place.

During Old Lincoln Days, over the first full weekend in August, musicians and mountain folk, doctors and desperadoes wander the streets in period costume, and there are demonstrations of spinning, blacksmithing and other frontier skills. The evening sees the folk pageant, 'The Last Escape of Billy the Kid.'

◉ Sights

Hurd-La Rinconada Gallery   GALLERY
(☑ 800-658-6912; www.wyethartists.com; off Hwy 70, San Patricio; ⊙ 9am-5pm Mon-Sat) San Patricio, a tranquil country village along the Rio Ruidoso, has the kind of golden glow and gentle scenery that's been drawing artists to New Mexico for more than a century. This gallery displays the work of Peter Hurd and his son Michael, plus that of their relatives, the Wyeths.

Lincoln Historic Site   HISTORIC SITE
(☑ 575-653-4082; www.nmmonuments.org/lincoln; adult/child $7/free; ⊙ Apr-Oct) It's hard to believe that in Billy the Kid's era Lincoln was home to a bustling population of nearly 900. Today it is essentially a ghost town, with only about 50 people living here. Those who do, however, are dedicated to preserving its 1880s buildings. Modern influences, such as souvenir stands, are not allowed, and New Mexico has designated the entire town as the Lincoln Historic Site. It's a pretty cool place to get away from this century for a night.

🛏️ Sleeping & Eating

There are no restaurants in Lincoln, though the Wortley Hotel serves meals in summer. The closest year-round dining options are in Capitan, 12 miles west of town.

OFF THE BEATEN TRACK

VALLEY OF FIRES

At the **Valley of Fires Recreation Area** (☑ 575-648-2241; Hwy 380; per vehicle 1/2+ people $3/5), 4 miles west of Carrizozo, you can explore the rocky blackness of a 125-sq-mile lava flow that's 160ft deep in the middle. The paved 0.6-mile nature trail is easy for kids and holds informative signs describing the geology and biology of this volcanic wasteland, or simply hike off-trail, cutting cross-country over the flow. You'll find campsites and shaded picnic tables near the visitor center.

Wortley Hotel   B&B $$
(☑ 575-653-4300; www.wortleyhotel.com; Hwy 380; r $110) A five-room B&B, the Wortley has been a Lincoln fixture since 1874. Watch the world go by from the front-porch rocking chairs, or soak up the history in the period-furnished accommodations.

Hurd Ranch Guest Homes   GUESTHOUSE $$
(☑ 800-658-6912; www.wyethartists.com; 105 La Rinconada, San Patricio; casitas $140-250; 📶🐾) Huge rural property, 14 miles southeast of Lincoln, holding six lovely rental casitas beside an apple orchard, furnished with style, grace and lots of original art, and sleeping up to six people. The on-site gallery shows the work of artist Peter Hurd, his partner Henriette Wyeth and their youngest son Michael Hurd, as well as relatives NC and Andrew Wyeth.

ℹ️ Information

Anderson-Freeman Visitors Center
(⊙ 8:30am-4:30pm) Buy tickets to historic buildings at the Anderson-Freeman Visitors Center, where you'll also find exhibits on Buffalo soldiers, Apaches and the Lincoln County War.

Roswell

☑ 575 / POP 48,611

That Roswell has become a phenomenon in its own right, and a byword for kookiness of all kinds, is entirely due its status as the site of the world's most famous UFO incident – the alleged crash of a real-life flying saucer in the desert nearby, back in July 1947. Whether or not you're a true believer, it's worth coming to Roswell to experience one of America's most enduring and fanatical pop-culture memes. Sure it's about as cheesy as it gets, but conspiracy theorists and *X-Files* fanatics descend from other worlds into Roswell in real seriousness.

The 'Staked Plains' extending east into Texas were long home to roaming buffalo and nomadic American Indian people. Anglo settlers and hunters moved in during the 19th century and wiped out the buffalo, killing some 3.5 million in just two years. The region became desolate and empty; only a few groups of Comanche mixed with other tribes out on the plains, hunting and trying to avoid confinement on reservations. Roswell itself, founded in 1871, served as a stopping place for cowboys driving cattle.

⊙ Sights

★ **International UFO Museum & Research Center** MUSEUM
(📞575-625-9495; www.roswellufomuseum. com; 114 N Main St; adult/child $5/2; ⊙9am-5pm) There's a lot of reading to be done here; display panels are covered with witness statements, newspaper cuttings and extended essays, outlining the 1947 Roswell Incident Timeline and explaining the 'great cover-up.' Serious UFO-logists will lap it up; for skeptics and the merely curious, homemade models and gruesome

mock-ups provide light relief. The library claims to have the world's most comprehensive collection of UFO-related materials; who are we to doubt them?

★ **Roswell Museum & Art Center** MUSEUM
(📞575-624-6744; www.roswellmuseum.org; 100 W 11th St; ⊙9am-5pm Tue-Sat, 1-5pm Sun) FREE Roswell's excellent museum deserves a visit. Seventeen galleries showcase Southwestern artists including Georgia O'Keeffe, Peter Hurd and Henriette Wyeth, along with an eclectic mix of American Indian, Hispanic and Anglo artifacts that illustrate the domestic and spiritual lives of the region's inhabitants. There's also a fascinating display on local rocket pioneer Robert H Goddard, who launched the first successful liquid fuel rocket in 1926. The adjoining Goddard Planetarium was only open for special events at the time of research.

Historical Center for Southeast New Mexico MUSEUM
(📞575-622-8333; www.roswellnmhistory.org; 200 N Lea Ave; admission by donation; ⊙1-4pm) FREE Housed in the 1912 mansion of local rancher James Phelps White, this property is on the National Register of Historic Places, and its interior has been carefully restored to its original early-20th-century decor, with period furnishings, photographs and art.

SMOKEY BEAR'S STOMPING GROUND

You'll see his likeness in state and national forests all over the US. But did you know that Smokey Bear was a real black bear? Once upon a time (back in 1950), a little cub was found clinging to a tree, paws charred from a 17,000-acre forest fire in the Capitan Mountains. What better idea than to name him after the cartoon bear who had been the symbol of fire prevention since 1944? Nursed back to health, Smokey spent his remaining days as a living mascot in the National Zoo in Washington, DC. At **Smokey Bear Historical Park** (📞575-354-2748; 118 W Smokey Bear Blvd; adult/child $2/1; ⊙9am-4:30pm), in the village of Capitan, 12 miles west of Lincoln, you can see his grave and learn about forest fires. Every Fourth of July, the **Smokey Bear Stampede** features a parade, a rodeo, cookouts and other festivities. **Smokey Bear Days**, celebrated the first weekend in May, includes a street dance, wood-carving contest, and craft and antique-car shows.

There's a good little diner next to the park, naturally enough called **Smokey Bear Restaurant** (📞575-354-2257; www.smokeybearrestaurant.com; mains $5-10; ⊙6am-8pm), and serving all Smokey's personal favorites – who knew bears were partial to chicken quesadillas?

Bitter Lake National Wildlife Refuge WILDLIFE RESERVE
(📞575-625-4011; www.fws.gov/refuge/Bitter_ Lake; 4200 E Pine Lodge Rd; ⊙sunrise-sunset Mon-Fri) FREE Wintering water birds gather at this 38-sq-mile refuge, 10 miles northeast of Roswell; many birds remain to nest in the summer. Bring your binoculars for the best views of cranes, geese and other species; hiking and biking trails can get you closer. To reach the refuge, follow signs from either Hwy 380 or Hwy 285/70.

🎇 Festivals & Events

UFO Festival CULTURAL
(www.ufofestivalroswell.com; ⊙Jul) Held on Fourth of July weekend, this celebration of Roswell's 1947 brush with fame attracts visitors from around the planet...and beyond. Interplanetary-travel celebs such as the Duras sisters (Klingon warriors), as well as genuine astronauts, make appearances. Amid enough lectures, films and workshops to make anyone's ears go pointy, don't miss the night parade and alien-costume competitions.

Eastern New Mexico State Fair CULTURAL
(📞575-623-9411; enmsf.com; ⊙Oct) Early October's State Fair sees a rodeo, livestock and agricultural competitions, and chile-eating contests.

🛏 Sleeping

There are plenty of chain hotels at the north end of Main St, as well as independent budget motels west along 2nd St.

Budget Inn MOTEL $
(📞575-623-6050; www.budgetinnroswell.us; 2101 N Main St; r from $49; ❄🐾) Old-fashioned downtown motel that's just about the best value in town, offering basic but clean rooms, with pillow-top mattresses and continental breakfast.

Bottomless Lakes State Park CAMPGROUND $
(📞575-624-6058; www.emnrd.state.nm.us; 545A Bottomless Lakes Rd; tent/RV sites $8/14) The seven lakes at this much-loved park – technically they're sinkholes – provide welcome relief in summer (day-use per vehicle $5). Waterfront campgrounds range from primitive campsites to the developed site at Lea Lake, the only place

Roswell

◉ **Top Sights**
1 International UFO Museum & Research Center B4
2 Roswell Museum & Art Center B3

◉ **Sights**
3 Historical Center for Southeast New Mexico..A4

🛏 **Sleeping**
4 Budget Inn.. B1

🍴 **Eating**
5 Big D's Downtown Dive B4
6 Martin's Capitol Cafe B4
7 Pasta Cafe...B2

🍸 **Drinking & Nightlife**
8 Pecos Flavors Tasting Room.................A4

NEW MEXICO ROSWELL

you're allowed to swim, which has bathrooms and showers. They're 10 miles east of Roswell on Hwy 380, then 5 miles south on Hwy 409.

Heritage Inn · HISTORIC HOTEL $$

(☎575-748-2552; www.artesiaheritageinn.com; 209 W Main St, Artesia; r incl breakfast from $99; ❀@🛜) The nicest place to stay hereabouts is not in Roswell, but in sleepy downtown Artesia, 36 miles south towards Carlsbad. If you're in the mood for slightly upscale digs – bearing in mind you're in southeastern New Mexico – this Victorian-era establishment offers 11 Old West–style rooms. Half have both bath and shower, the rest a shower only.

Eating

Roswell is mostly diner fare, but there are a few other options if you need a change.

Taste of Thai · THAI $

(☎575-622-2412; 1303 W 2nd St; mains $8-13; ⊙11am-9pm Mon-Sat) You can still ask yourself New Mexico's state question here (red or green?), but you'll no doubt appreciate that it applies to curry for a change. The kitchen whips up good standards, from pad Thai to tom yum soup.

Big D's Downtown Dive · AMERICAN $

(☎575-627-0776; 505 N Main St; mains $7-13; ⊙11am-9pm) From the Tomahawk burger (served on fry bread) to the chicken tortilla soup, and the Southwest chicken wontons to the Hard Apple salad, there are enough unique choices on Don Nason's menu to distinguish it from your average diner.

Cowboy Cafe · DINER $

(☎575-622-6363; 1120 E 2nd St; mains $6-15; ⊙6am-2pm) One of the few truly local joints left in town, this is a good option for a breakfast before hitting the UFO museum or the road.

Mama Tucker's · BAKERY $

(☎575-625-1475; 3109 N Main St; ⊙6am-2pm Tue-Sat, 6am-12:30pm Sun) If you're craving something sweet, head a dozen blocks north of downtown and treat yourself to homemade cakes and cookies.

Martin's Capitol Cafe · NEW MEXICAN $

(☎575-624-2111; 110 W 4th St; mains $6-12; ⊙6am-8:30pm Mon-Sat) Roswell holds a fine crop of inexpensive New Mexican restaurants; this one is home-style and dependable, with all the variations on green and red chile you could hope for.

Pasta Cafe · ITALIAN $$

(☎575-624-1111; www.pastacafeitalianbistro. com; 1208 N Main St; lunch $7-13, dinner $11-22; ⊙11am-9:30pm Sun-Thu, to 10:30pm Fri & Sat) One of Roswell's premier date restaurants, this large bistro delivers reliable pizzas and

---

THE TRUTH IS OUT THERE...

It's long now since the heady summer of 1947, when an unidentified flying object fell out of the sky and crash-landed in the desert near Roswell, but the little New Mexican town is still cashing in on the mystery. Those who believe aliens are out there are convinced that the US government has gone to great lengths to cover up the fact that the craft truly was of extraterrestrial origin. They certainly have a compelling case.

In its initial 1947 press release, the government identified the object as a crashed disk. A day later, however, it changed its story: now the disk was really just a weather balloon. The feds then confiscated all the previous releases, cordoned off the area as they collected debris, and posted armed guards to escort curious locals from the site of the 'weather balloon' crash. A local mortician fielded calls from the mortuary office at the government airfield inquiring after small, hermetically sealed coffins for preventing tissue contamination and degeneration.

Now, 70-odd years later, the government remains tight-lipped, and Roswell is the story that will never die. There are frequent eyewitness accounts of flying saucers in the sky, and rumor and misinformation continue to swirl about the original crash, fueling all manner of speculation. In the early 2000s, Roswell even spawned its own TV series about alien-mutant hybrid teenagers trying to survive as humans while keeping their alien powers alive and attempting to get home.

pasta dishes, as well as steak and seafood dishes like the tasty oven-broiled scallops.

Drinking & Nightlife

Pecos Flavors Tasting Room BAR
(☑575-627-6265; pecosflavorswinery.com; 412 W 2nd St; ⊙10am-8pm Mon-Wed & Sat, to 9pm Thu & Fri) Stop by this airy tasting room to sample New Mexican wines by the glass or one of the six local beers on tap. Half-bar, half-boutique, it also has an adjoining **bistro** ($7.25 to $9) that has a hefty selection of sandwiches, including veggie options.

Wellhead BREWERY
(☑575-746-0640; www.thewellheadpub.com; 332 W Main St, Artesia; ⊙11am-9pm Mon-Sat) Modern brewpub restaurant and bar in a 1905 building in downtown Artesia, halfway between Roswell and Carlsbad. As well as decent pub grub, which round here naturally includes green chile stew, it has a fine array of its own beers, including Crude Oil Stout.

ℹ Information

Eastern New Mexico Medical Center (☑575-622-8170; www.enmmc.com; 405 W Country Club Rd; ⊙emergency 24hr)
Police (☑575-624-6770; 128 W 2nd St)
Post Office (415 N Pennsylvania Ave; ⊙8:30am-5pm Mon-Fri, 9am-noon Sat)
Visitors Bureau (☑575-624-6700; www.seeroswell.com; 912 N Main St; ⊙8:30am-5:30pm Mon-Fri, 10am-3pm Sat & Sun; 🛜) Pick up local information and have your picture snapped with an alien at the visitors bureau.

ℹ Getting There & Away

Situated on Hwy 285, Roswell is 75 miles north of Carlsbad and about 200 miles southwest of Albuquerque and Santa Fe. **Greyhound** (☑575-622-2510; www.greyhound.com; 1100 N Virginia Ave) has daily buses to Las Cruces, but no services to Carlsbad.

Carlsbad

☑575 / POP 27,653 / ELEV 3111FT
Previously a remote and sleepy ranching town, Carlsbad received a huge boost in 1923, when Carlsbad Caverns, a 25-mile drive southwest, became a national monument. Now elevated to national park status, the caverns continue to attract some 400,000 visitors each year.

◉ Sights & Activities

Living Desert Zoo &
Gardens State Park ZOO
(☑575-887-5516; www.nmparks.com; 1504 Miehls Dr N, off Hwy 285; adult/child $5/3; ⊙8am-5pm Jun-Aug, 9am-5pm Sep-May, last zoo entry 3:30pm) Northwest of town, this state park is a great place to see and learn about reptiles and roadrunners, wolves and antelopes, along with desert plants such as agave, ocotillo and yucca. A good 1.3-mile trail showcases different habitats of the Chihuahuan Desert.

Carlsbad Museum & Art Center MUSEUM
(☑575-887-0276; 418 W Fox St; ⊙10am-5pm Mon-Sat) **FREE** This museum displays Apache artifacts, pioneer memorabilia from the region, and paintings by artists from the Taos School.

Sitting Bull Falls HIKING
(County Rd 409; per vehicle $5; ⊙8:30am-5pm) An oasis in the desert, Sitting Bull Falls is tucked among the burly canyons of the Guadalupe Mountains, 42 miles southwest of Carlsbad. A spring-fed creek pours 150ft over a limestone cliff, and natural pools below and above the falls are great for swimming – or at least dunking and cooling off. The series of caves behind the waterfalls can only be explored with a ranger.

🛏 Sleeping

Carlsbad holds dozens of chain motels, lined up along Canal St. Rates and room availability are dependent on oil production – when prices are high, hotels fill up with industry workers and you may need to look elsewhere. For primitive dispersed camping, go west on Jones St and just keep going, onto the dirt roads and public lands.

Carlsbad KOA CAMPGROUND $
(☑575-457-2000; www.carlsbadkoa.com; 2 Manthei Rd; tent/RV sites from $28/41; cabins from $60; 🛜🏊🐕) On Hwy 285 about 18 miles north of central Carlsbad, this friendly site offers the choice of air-conditioned 'kamping kabins' or grassy tent sites. There's also a pool, a games room, a grocery store, a laundry, a playground, a dog park and showers. Ask hosts Scott and Susan Bacher about free rides for kids in their retired fire truck.

Carlsbad

Stagecoach Inn MOTEL **$**
(☏ 575-887-1148; stagecoachinncarlsbad.com;
1819 S Canal St; r from $56; ❋🛜🏊) One of
the best values in town, the Stagecoach

has clean rooms, a swimming pool and an
on-site playground for kids.

★**Trinity Hotel** BOUTIQUE HOTEL **$$**
(☏ 575-234-9891; www.thetrinityhotel.com; 201
S Canal St; r $149-209; ❋🛜) Carlsbad's best
hotel is housed in a grand downtown build-
ing that started life as the First National
Bank in 1892. Friendly and family-run, it
has an excellent restaurant. The sitting
room of one suite is inside the old vault;
another still has a bullet hole.

🍴 Eating

Carlsbad is not a huge town, though there
are some good restaurants here. Be aware
that most places close on Sundays.

★**Trinity Restaurant
& Wine Bar** AMERICAN **$$**
(☏ 575-234-9891; www.thetrinityhotel.com;
Trinity Hotel, 201 S Canal St; lunch $8-12, dinner
$14-34; ⏲7am-9pm Mon-Sat; 🅿) This ele-
gant split-level dining room – the ceiling
is so high there's room for a mezzanine
floor – offers Carlsbad's finest dining, with
a menu of steaks, seafood and Italian specialties, and pasta and salad for vegetarians. Carnivores will love the roast pork in
a Cabernet/green chile reduction. Light-
ning-fast lunch service makes it a favorite
rendezvous for downtown employees.

Red Chimney Pit Barbecue BARBECUE **$$**
(☏ 575-885-8744; www.redchimneybbq.com;
817 N Canal St; mains $6.50-16; ⏲11am-2pm &
4:30-8:30pm Tue-Fri, 11am-8:30pm Sat) South-
ern-style, slow-cooked pit barbecue – if
quality meats and tasty sauce aren't your
thing, how about catfish and fried okra?

Lucy's Mexicali Restaurant MEXICAN **$$**
(☏ 575-881-7714; 701 S Canal St; mains $9-18;
⏲11am-9pm Mon-Thu, to 9:30pm Fri & Sat)
Apart from the Mexican menu, Lucy's
serves up tasty margaritas and a good
selection of microbrews – small wonder
it's usually packed with devoted locals and
visitors.

🍸 Drinking & Nightlife

Nightlife is fairly limited.

Lucky Bull Grill PUB
(☏ 575-725-5444; 220 W Fox St; ⏲11am-9pm)
In Carlsbad's old town hall, this is your
spot for a burger and a beer. There's lots of
gooey, salty munchies to complement the

CARLSBAD CAVERNS NATIONAL PARK

While a **cave** (📞 575-785-2232, bat info 505-785-3012; www.nps.gov/cave; Carlsbad Cavern Hwy; adult/child $10/free; ☉ caves 8:30am-5pm late May-early Sep, to 3:30pm early Sep-late May; 🚹) might not sound quite as sexy as redwoods, geysers or the Grand Canyon, there's no question that this one measures up on the NPS' jaw-droppingly ginormous scale: to simply reach the main chamber, you have to either take an elevator that drops the height of the Empire State Building or, more enjoyably, take a spooky 1.25-mile subterranean walk that goes down and down (and down) from the cave mouth into the yawning darkness.

Either way, you'll find yourself in the aptly named Big Room, an underground room 1800ft long (that's the equivalent of 11 American football fields), 255ft high and over 800ft below the surface, where you're free to walk an intricate loop trail (1.25 miles) past a pick of amazing sights, including the world's largest stalagmite and the ever-popular Bottomless Pit. Wear a sweatshirt: the temperature is 56°F year-round.

In addition to the self-guided tour, the park service runs a number of daily guided **tours** (📞 877-444-6777; www.recreation.gov; adult $7-20, child $3.50-10) – advance reservations are essential. They are all excellent and highly informative, providing visitors with access to otherwise closed portions of the cavern, or real spelunking adventures in some of the backcountry caves like Slaughter Canyon. Plus, your guide will inevitably turn out the lights at some point – sitting hundreds of feet below ground in the pitch black is an experience you're likely not to forget.

The cave's other claim to fame is the 400,000-plus Mexican free-tailed bat colony that roosts here from mid-May to mid-October. Wait at the cave mouth at sunset to watch them cyclone out for an all-evening insect feast.

With 30 miles of passages and the largest subterranean chamber in the US, it's hard to get your head around just how big Carlsbad really is. But now consider this: Carlsbad is only one of 120 known caves within the park's borders, and the largest, Lechuguilla, extends for some 136 miles, dropping to a depth of 1600ft. Unfortunately, it's only open to research and exploration teams, with special permission from the park.

If you'd like to explore the Chihuahuan Desert above ground, pick up a permit (free) for a backpacking trip at the **visitor center** (☉ 8am-7pm late May-early Sep, to 5pm rest of year) along with a topo map of the 50-plus miles of hiking trails. November to March is the best time for backpacking – summer temperatures are scorching, while the countless rattlesnakes should be sleeping in winter. The visitor center also has a small cafeteria, where you can have a simple lunch. No food or drinks are permitted in the cave.

---

brews on tap – think chicken fajita nachos, poutine, and chile and bacon smothered chips.

Blue House Bakery & Cafe　　　　CAFE
(📞 575-628-0555; 609 N Canyon St; ☉ 6am-noon Mon-Sat) This sweet Queen Anne house perks the best espresso in southeast New Mexico. Its baked goods are pretty darn good too, as are the breakfast sandwiches. Cheery and family-owned, it also offers an outdoor patio and garden seating.

ℹ Information

Carlsbad Chamber of Commerce (📞 575-887-6516; www.carlsbadchamber.com; 302 S Canal St; ☉ 9am-5pm Mon, 8am-5pm Tue-Fri) Helpful in-town visitor center.

USFS Ranger Station (📞 575-885-4181; 5203 Buena Vista Dr; ☉ 7:30am-4:30pm Mon-Fri) Info on Sitting Bull Falls and hiking and backpacking in Lincoln National Forest.

Carlsbad Medical Center (📞 575-887-4100; www.carlsbadmedicalcenter.com; 2430 W Pierce St; ☉ emergency 24hr)

Police (📞 575-885-2111; 602 W Mermod St)

Post Office (301 N Canyon St; ☉ 8am-5pm Mon-Fri, 10am-1pm Sat)

ℹ Getting There & Away

Carlsbad is some 200 miles east of Las Cruces and 76 miles south of Roswell. The caves are 20 miles southwest of the town; Guadalupe Mountains National Park is 50 miles southwest. **Greyhound** (📞 575-628-0768; www.greyhound.com; 3102 National Parks Hwy) buses depart from Food Jet South, 2 miles south of downtown. Destinations include El Paso, TX, and Las Cruces.

I-40 EAST TO TEXAS

Santa Rosa

📞 575 / POP 2774 / ELEV 4600FT

Settled by Hispanic farmers in the mid-19th century, Santa Rosa's modern claim to fame is, weirdly enough, as the scuba-diving capital of the Southwest. Aside from that and the fact that Route 66 also passes through, there's not much else going on here.

⊙ Sights & Activities

Blue Hole LAKE
(📞 575-472-3763; santarosabluehole.com; 1085 Blue Hole Rd; parking $5; ⊙ 8am-8pm) One of the 10 best dive spots in the US is, surprisingly, right here in li'l ol' Santa Rosa. The hourglass-shaped, 70ft-deep Blue Hole is 138ft in diameter at the surface and has a **dive shop** (open Saturday and Sunday; rentals only) alongside. Fed by a natural spring flowing at 3000 gallons a minute, the water is both very clear and pretty cool (at around 62°F/17°C). Divers should apply for a 10-day certificate ($20).

Puerto de Luna HISTORIC SITE
FREE The tiny village of Puerto de Luna, beside the Pecos River 10 miles south of Santa Rosa, was founded in the 1860s. The drive there is pretty, winding through arroyos surrounded by eroded sandstone mesas on Hwy 91. Once you arrive you'll find an old county courthouse, a village church and a bunch of weathered adobe buildings. It's all quite charming, so long as you're not in a hurry to do something else.

Route 66 Auto Museum MUSEUM
(📞 575-472-1966; www.route66automuseum.com; 2766 Rte 66; $5; ⊙ 7:30am-5:30pm) This museum pays homage to the mother of all roads. Boasting around 35 cars from the 1920s through the 1960s, all in beautiful condition, plus lots of 1950s memorabilia, it's a fun place; enjoy a milkshake at the '50s-style snack shack. If you're in the market for a beautifully restored old Chevy, friendly owner 'Bozo' also deals in antique cars.

🛏 Sleeping & Eating

Chain hotels cluster around the I-40 exits. The main street holds several family-owned diners and roadside cafes, abounding in Route 66 allure.

Joseph's Bar & Grill DINER $
(📞 575-472-3361; josephsbarandgrill.com; 1775 Historic Rte 66; mains $9-12; ⊙ 8am-10pm) Route 66 nostalgia lines the walls of this popular place, family-run since 1956. The bountiful Mexican and American menu ranges from Santa Fe enchiladas with blue-corn tortillas to catfish, burgers and steaks. Joseph's also mixes some serious margaritas.

Silver Moon DINER $
(📞 505-472-3162; 3701 Historic Route 66; mains $9-14; ⊙ 9am-10pm) This trademark Route 66 eatery first opened its doors in 1959, and serves homemade *chile rellenos* and other tasty diner grub dressed up with a New Mexican twist. It's popular with travelers following Route 66's old roadhouse trail, as well as locals who come for a morning coffee and a plate of bacon and eggs.

Tucumcari

📞 575 / POP 5152 / ELEV 4100FT

The largest I-40 town between Albuquerque and Amarillo, Tucumcari is a ranching and farming community sited between the mesas and the plains that's also home to one of the best-preserved sections of Route 66. Not surprisingly, it still caters to travelers, with inexpensive motels, several classic pre-interstate buildings and souvenir shops.

⊙ Sights & Activities

Drive the kids down Tucumcari's main street at night, when dozens of old neon signs cast a blazing glow. Relics of Tucumcari's Route 66 heyday, the bright, flashing signs were installed by business owners in the hope of luring tired travelers to stop for the night.

Mesalands Dinosaur Museum MUSEUM
(📞 575-461-3466; www.mesalands.edu/community/dinosaur-museum; 222 E Laughlin St; adult/child $6.50/4; ⊙ 10am-6pm Tue-Sat Mar-Aug, noon-5pm Tue-Sat Sep-Feb; 🐾) This engaging museum showcases all manner of prehistoric beasts, from ferocious 40ft

crocodiles to battling saber-tooth cats and the T-Rex-like Torvosaurus. Dinosaur bones are cast in bronze, which not only shows fine detail, but also makes them works of art. There are plenty of hands-on exhibits for kids; one ancient monster is even fitted with a saddle for photo opportunities.

Tucumcari Historical Museum MUSEUM
(☑575-461-4201; 416 S Adams St; adult/child $5/1; ☺9am-3pm Tue-Sat) Downtown museum of local history that's eclectic to say the least, with everything from a stuffed eagle and a Japanese flag to an entire firehouse and a fighter plane stranded in the yard. Several rooms feature reconstructions of early Western interiors, such as a sheriff's office, a classroom and a hospital room.

Art Murals WALKING
Buildings on and around Route 66 in downtown Tucumcari are adorned with large murals depicting local historical highlights. The life work of artists Doug and Sharon Quarles, they can be appreciated on a mural walk that makes a great way to stretch your legs and experience Tucumcari's Route 66 legacy. Grab a map from the visitor center and get walking.

🛏 Sleeping

While the usual chain motels cluster around the I-40 exits, Tucumcari also boasts some cool old independent motels along historic Route 66.

★ **Blue Swallow Motel** MOTEL $
(☑575-461-9849; www.blueswallowmotel.com; 815 E Tucumcari Blvd; r from $75; ❅🐾) Spend the night in this beautifully restored Route 66 motel listed on the State and National Registers of Historic Places, and feel the decades melt away. The place has a great lobby, friendly owners and vintage, uniquely decorated rooms with little chairs out on the forecourt, plus a James Dean mural, and a classic neon sign boasting '100% refrigerated air conditioning.'

Historic Route 66 Motel MOTEL $
(☑575-461-1212; www.tucumcarimotel.com; 1620 E Rte 66; r from $42; ❅🐾) When it comes to budget digs, you can't beat this recently renovated motel, with giant plate-glass doors and mesa views; look for the light

NEW MEXICO TUCUMCARI

THE LEGEND OF BILLY THE KID

Even the most basic information about Billy the Kid tends to cast a shadow larger than the outlaw himself. Here's what we know, or don't. Most historians agree that he was born sometime in 1859, most likely in New York City (or Indiana or Missouri). He may be buried in Old Fort Sumner, where his skull may have been stolen and possibly recovered) – that is, unless he colluded with his presumed assassin, Sheriff Pat Garrett, and lived to a ripe old age…somewhere.

The Kid didn't start out as a murderer. His first known childhood crimes included stealing laundry and fencing butter. In the mid-1870s, about the time the teenage Billy arrived in New Mexico, the 400 residents of Lincoln shopped at 'Murphy's,' the only general store in the region. In 1877, though, Englishman John Tunstall arrived and built a competing general store.

Within a year, Tunstall was dead, allegedly shot by Murphy and his boys. The entire region erupted in what became known as the Lincoln County War. Tunstall's most famous follower was a wild teenager named Henry McCarty, alias William Bonney, aka Billy the Kid, who was on the run from his previous home in Silver City. Over the next several months the Kid and his gang gunned down any members of the Murphy faction they could find. Repeatedly captured or cornered, the Kid managed brazen and lucky escapes before finally being shot by Sheriff Pat Garrett near Fort Sumner in 1881, where he lies in a grave in a barren yard. Maybe.

Near the end of his term as governor in 2010, Bill Richardson considered granting the Kid a posthumous pardon, based on historical evidence that he'd been promised one by territorial governor Lew Wallace if he'd give testimony about the murder of Lincoln County Sherriff William Brady in 1878. The Kid testified but, rather than being pardoned, was sentenced to death. After much deliberation, and partly due to protests raised by descendants of Pat Garrett and Lew Wallace, the pardon was declined.

plane outside. The 25 rooms are cheap, clean and heads and shoulders above the usual motel stay, with comfy beds and quality pillows. Small dogs are welcome, and it even has an espresso bar.

Eating

There are a handful of diners and BBQ joints scattered throughout town, though few are open for dinner, and there's little in the way of nightlife.

Kix on 66 DINER **$**
(☑ 575-461-1966; www.kixon66.com; 1102 E Tucumcari Blvd; mains $5-10; ⊗ 6am-2pm; ☎) Very popular morning hangout serving breakfast in all shapes and sizes, from huevos rancheros to biscuits and gravy, plus espresso coffees, doughnuts and lunch sandwiches.

ⓘ Information

Visitor Center (☑ 575-461-1694; www.tucumcarinm.com; 404 W Rte 66; ⊗ 8:30am-5pm Mon-Fri) Useful tourist information from the chamber of commerce.

Fort Sumner

☑ 575 / POP 975 / ELEV 4032FT

Anyone who has read up on Western history will know Fort Sumner: this is the place where General Carleton exiled the Navajo and Apache in an attempt to 'civilize' them – with catastrophic results – and is also the site of Billy the Kid's last showdown with Sheriff Pat Garrett. If you're not into history, however, keep on driving.

◉ Sights

★ **Bosque Redondo**
Memorial at Fort Sumner MUSEUM
(☑ 575-355-2573; www.bosqueredondomemorial.com; 3647 Billy the Kid Rd; ⊗ 8:30am-4:30pm Wed-Mon) FREE The convoluted name sums up

the tragic history of this bleak, windswept spot, beside the Pecos River 6 miles southeast of town. Fort Sumner was built in 1862 to guard the Bosque Redondo Reservation, a prison to some 9000 Navajos forced from their homeland on the Long Walk, plus 500 captured Mescalero Apaches. Over 2000 Navajos died before an 1868 treaty authorized their return home. A powerful exhibit tells the whole story; the fort itself was, fittingly, washed away in a flood.

Billy the Kid Museum MUSEUM
(www.billythekidmuseumfortsumner.com; 1601 E Sumner Ave; adult/child $5/3; ⊗ 8:30am-5pm, closed Sun Oct–mid-May) Home to a private collection of more than 60,000 items, this main-street museum is a veritable shrine to the famous outlaw – don't miss the photo of the Kid enjoying a game of croquet (really!). American Indian artifacts and items from Wild West frontier life fill several rooms, and there's also a shed filled with classic 1950s cars.

✯ Festivals & Events

Old Fort Days CULTURAL
(⊗ Jun) Held on the second weekend in June, this festival features a rodeo, goat roping, shootouts and athletic events.

🛏 Sleeping

Super 8 MOTEL **$**
(☑ 575-355-7888; www.super8.com; 1559 E Sumner Ave; r from $72; ✳ ☎ 🐾) All but next door to the Billy the Kid Museum, this chain motel is the best accommodation option in Fort Sumner.

ⓘ Information

Chamber of Commerce (☑ 575-355-7705; fortsumnerchamber.com; 707 N 4th St; ⊗ 9am-4pm Mon-Fri)

Utah

Best Places to Eat

➡ Red Iguana (p436)
➡ Hell's Backbone Grill (p393)
➡ Sego Restaurant (p420)
➡ Crumb Brothers Artisan Bakery (p445)
➡ Riverhorse on Main (p460)

Best Places to Sleep

➡ Sundance Resort Lodging (p466)
➡ Torrey Schoolhouse B&B (p390)
➡ Valley of the Gods B&B (p361)
➡ Under the Eaves Inn (p412)

Why Go?

Welcome to nature's most perfect playground. From red-rock mesas to skinny slot canyons, powder-bound slopes and slick rock trails, Utah's diverse terrain will stun you. The biking, hiking and skiing are world-class. And with more than 65% of the state lands public, including 13 national parks and monuments, the access is simply superb.

Southern Utah is defined by red-rock cliffs, sorbet-colored spindles and seemingly endless sandstone desert. The pine-forested and snow-covered peaks of the Wasatch Mountains dominate northern Utah. Interspersed are old pioneer remnants, ancient rock art and ruins, and traces of dinosaurs.

Mormon-influenced rural towns can be quiet and conservative, but the rugged beauty has attracted outdoorsy progressives as well. Salt Lake City (SLC) and Park City, especially, have vibrant nightlife and progressive dining scenes. So pull on your boots and stock up on water: Utah's wild and scenic hinterlands await.

When to Go
Salt Lake City

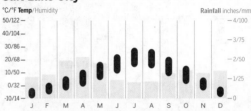

Apr–May Mild weather makes spring an excellent time to hike, especially in southern Utah.

Oct Colorful foliage comes out, but a welcome touch of warmth lingers.

Jan–Mar Powder hounds gear up for the slopes near Salt Lake City and Park City mountain resorts.

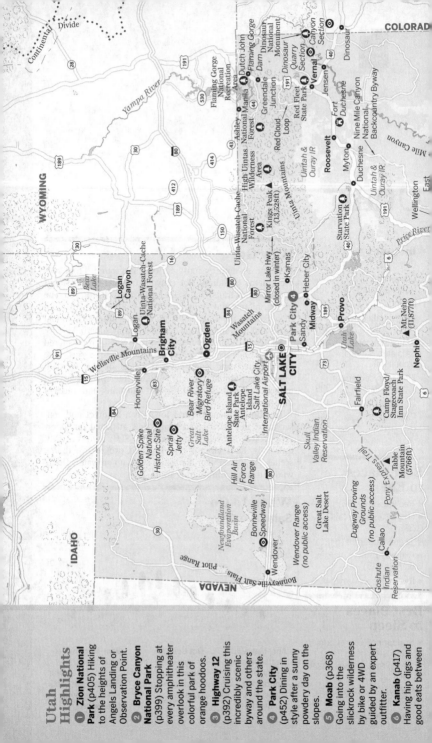

Utah Highlights

1 Zion National Park (p405) Hiking to the heights of Angels Landing or Observation Point.

2 Bryce Canyon National Park (p399) Stopping at every amphitheater overlook in this colorful park of orange hoodoos.

3 Highway 12 (p392) Cruising this incredibly scenic byway and others around the state.

4 Park City (p452) Dining in style after a sunny powdery day on the slopes.

5 Moab (p368) Going into the slickrock wilderness by bike or 4WD guided by an expert outfitter.

6 Kanab (p417) Having hip digs and good eats between

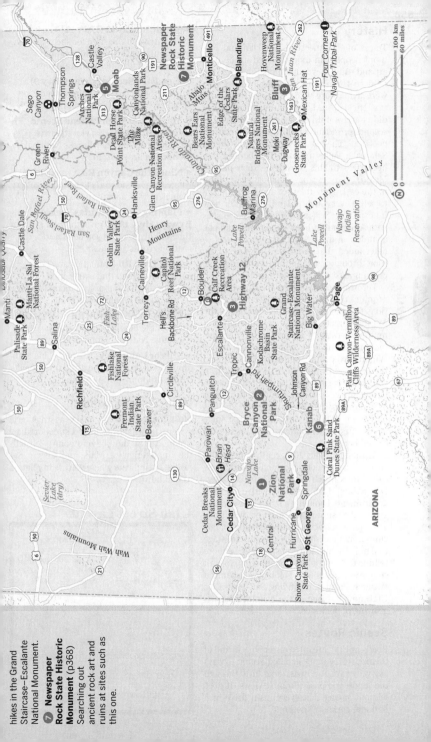

hikes in the Grand Staircase–Escalante National Monument.

7 Newspaper Rock State Historic Monument (p368) Searching out ancient rock art and ruins at sites such as this one.

History

Traces of the Ancestral Puebloan and Fremont people can today be seen in the rock art and ruins they left behind. But it was the modern Ute, Paiute and Navajo tribes who were living here when European explorers first trickled in. Larger numbers of settlers didn't arrive until after Brigham Young, the second president of the Mormon church, declared 'This is the place!' upon seeing Salt Lake Valley in 1847. The faithful pioneers fled to this territory – then part of Mexico – to escape religious persecution in the east. They then set about attempting to settle every inch of land, no matter how inhospitable, which resulted in skirmishes with American Indians – and more than one abandoned ghost town. (One group was so determined that it lowered its wagons by rope through a hole in the rock to continue on an impassable mountain trail.)

For nearly 50 years after the United States acquired the land, the Utah Territory's petitions for statehood were rejected due to the Mormon practice of polygamy (the taking of multiple wives). Tensions and prosecutions mounted until 1890, when Mormon leader Wilford Woodruff officially discontinued the practice. In 1896 Utah became the 45th state. About the same time, Utah's remote backcountry served as the perfect hideout for notorious Old West 'bad men,' such as native son Butch Cassidy, and the last spike of the first intercontinental railroad was driven here.

Throughout the 20th century the influence of the modern Mormon church, now called the Church of Jesus Christ of Latter-Day Saints (LDS), was pervasive in state government. Though it's still a conservative state, LDS supremacy may be waning – less than 60% of today's population claims church membership (the lowest percentage to date). The urban/rural split may be more telling for future politics: roughly 75% of state residents now live along the urbanized Wasatch Front surrounding Salt Lake City. Utah now has one of the country's fastest-growing populations.

Scenic Routes

Roads in Utah are often attractions in and of themselves. State-designated Scenic Byways (www.byways.org) twist and turn through the landscape past stunning views. It goes without saying that every main drive in a national park is a knockout.

➡ **Scenic Byway 12 (Hwy 12)** The best overall drive in the state for sheer variety: from sculpted slickrock to vivid red canyons and forested mountain tops.

➡ **Zion Park Scenic Byway (Hwy 9)** Runs through red-rock country and Zion National Park, between I-15 and Hwy 89.

➡ **Markagunt High Plateau Scenic Byway (Hwy 14)** High elevation vistas, pine forests and Cedar Breaks National Monument are en route.

➡ **Nine Mile Canyon Rd** A rough and rugged back road leads to a virtual gallery of ancient rock art and ruins.

➡ **Flaming Gorge–Uintas Scenic Byway (Hwy 191)** Travel through geologic time on this road: as you head north, the roadside rocks get older.

➡ **Burr Trail Rd** Dramatic paved backcountry road that skirts cliffs, canyons, buttes, mesas and monoliths on its way to the Waterpocket Fold.

➡ **Cottonwood Canyon Rd** A 4WD trek through the heart of Grand Staircase–Escalante National Monument.

➡ **Mirror Lake Hwy (Rte 150)** This high-alpine road cruises beneath 12,000ft peaks before dropping into Wyoming.

Utah Street Layout

Most towns in Utah follow a street grid system, in which numbered streets radiate from a central hub (or zero point) – usually the intersection of Main and Center Sts. Addresses indicate where you are in relation to that hub.

Utah Street Layout

MOAB & SOUTHEASTERN UTAH

Experience the earth's beauty at its most elemental in this rocky-and-rugged desert corner of the Colorado Plateau. Beyond the few pine-clad mountains, there's little vegetation to hide the impressive handiwork of time, water and wind: the thousands of red-rock spans in Arches National Park, the sheer-walled river gorges from Canyonlands to Lake Powell, and the stunning buttes and mesas of Monument Valley. The town of Moab is the best base for adventure, with as much four-wheeling, white-knuckle rafting, outfitter-guided fun as you can handle. Or you can lose the crowd while looking for Ancestral Puebloan rock art and dwellings in miles of isolated and undeveloped lands.

Note that many regional restaurants and shops – and even some motels – close or have variable hours after the May to late-October high season.

Bluff

📋 435 / POP 320

Tiny-tot Bluff isn't much more than a spot in the road. But a few great motels and a handful of restaurants, surrounded by stunning red rock, make it a cool little base for exploring the far southeastern corner of the state. From here you can easily reach Moki Dugway (30 miles), Hovenweep National Monument (40 miles), Monument Valley (47 miles) and Natural Bridges National Monument (61 miles) – just to mention a few area sights –as well as explore the surrounding Bureau of Land Management (BLM) wilderness.

There's no visitor center here at the crossroads of Hwys 191 N and 163. You can log onto www.bluff-utah.org, but local business owners and staff are your best resource. To preserve the night sky, Bluff has few streetlights.

◉ Sights & Activities

The BLM field office (p361) in Monticello has information about the public lands surrounding Bluff. Local motel Recapture Lodge (p357) also sells topographic maps for hiking; a public trail leads down from the lodging to the San Juan River.

Sand Island Petroglyphs ARCHAEOLOGICAL SITE
(www.blm.gov; Sand Island Rd, off Hwy 163; ⊙24hr) FREE On BLM land 3 miles west of Bluff, these freely accessible petroglyphs were

DON'T MISS

OFF-ROAD ADVENTURES

Sure, some of Utah's rugged beauty can be seen roadside. But one of the great things about the state is how much of it is set aside for public use. You'll gain a whole new perspective on, and appreciation of, the terrain if you delve deeper. Not-to-be-missed outdoor adventures are available for all skill levels, and outfitters are there to help. Challenge yourself by rappelling into the narrow canyons around Zion National Park (p405) or mountain biking on the steep and sinister **Slickrock Trail** (p365) in Moab. Or take it easy on your body (though not your vehicle) by going off-pavement along one of the state's many 4WD roads. Whether you're rafting on the **Colorado River** or skiing fresh powder in the **Wasatch Mountains**, you'll see the state in a whole new way.

created between 800 and 2500 years ago. The nearby campground boat launch is the starting point for San Juan River adventures.

Hovenweep National Monument PARK
(www.nps.gov/hove; Hwy 262; tent & RV sites $10; ⊙ park dusk-dawn, visitor center 8am-6pm Jun-Sep, 9am-5pm Oct-May) FREE Meaning 'deserted valley' in Ute language, Hovenweep is a remote area of former Ancestral Puebloan settlements straddling the Colorado–Utah border and once home to a large population before drought forced people out in the 1200s. There are six sets of unique tower ruins, but only the impressive ruins in the Square Tower area are readily accessible. It's under one hour from Bluff, accessed by several routes.

★ Far Out Expeditions HIKING
(📋 435-672-2294; www.faroutexpeditions.com; day tours $295) Interested in remote ruins and rock art? Vaughn Hadenfeldt, a longtime canyon expert, leads popular single- and multiday hikes into the desert surrounds.

Wild Rivers Expeditions RAFTING
(📋 800-422-7654; www.riversandruins.com; half-day trip adult/child $89/69) Float through the San Juan River canyons with this history- and geology-minded outfitter; you'll also get to stop and see petroglyphs. Trips meet at the Bluff Adventure Center.

Southeastern Utah

N 0 _____ 30 km
0 _____ 15 miles

Price (38mi)

Uintah & Ouray IR

Grand Junction
(CO) (23mi)

191

Price River

6

50

6

Sego
Canyon

Cisco

Green River
State Park

Green River

70

70

Thompson
Springs

128

Salina (85mi)

50

70

191

Arches
National
Park

Castle
Valley

128

La Sal Mountains

141

San Rafael Swell

San Rafael Reef

24

San Rafael River

Green River

313

279

Moab

La Sal
Mountain
Loop Rd

San Rafael Desert

Dead Horse Point
State Park

Potash Rd

Manti-La Sal
National
Forest

90

Goblin
Valley
State Park

Canyonlands
National Park
(Horseshoe
Canyon)

Island in
the Sky

Anticline
Overlook

Hole 'n
the Rock

24 Hanksville

Canyonlands
National
Park

La Sal
Junction

46

La Sal

Capitol Reef
National Park (36mi)

95

Hans Flat
Ranger Station

The
Maze

Needles
Overlook

191

Burr
Point

Glen Canyon
National
Recreation Area

The
Needles

Henry
Mountains
(11,500ft)

211

Bears Ears
National
Monument

Newspaper Rock
Recreation Area

276

Abajo Mtns

101

Monticello

491

Hite Marina

95

Manti-La Sal
National
Forest

Abajo Peak
(11,360ft)

Montezuma
Canyon Rd

Mesa Verde
National Park
(45mi)

Ticaboo

Natural Bridges
National
Monument

Edge of the
Cedars
State Park

Blanding

Lake
Powell

Mule Canyon
Ruins

Butler Wash Ruins

Hovenweep
National
Monument

Ferry

Bullfrog Marina

275

95

191

Hall's Crossing
Marina

276

261

Grand Gulch
Primitive Area

Cedar Mesa

Comb Wash Rd

Comb Ridge

262

Hatch
Trading Post

San Juan River

Moki
Dugway

Muley Point
Overlook

Valley of
the Gods

162

Bluff

Montezuma
Creek

Goosenecks
State Park

163

Mexican Hat

Sand Island
Petroglyphs

191

Aneth

162

Oljato

Monument Valley

Goulding's
Lodge

Navajo
Indian
Reservation

Four Corners
Navajo Tribal Park

41

ARIZONA

Monument Valley
Navajo Tribal Park

160

UTAH BLUFF

Buckhorn Llama ADVENTURE
(☑435-672-2466; www.llamapack.com; guided trip per day $250) Llama-supported multiday pack trips into hard-to-reach wilderness.

🛏 Sleeping

There are a few cozy lodging options in town. For camping, head out to the parks.

★**Recapture Lodge** MOTEL $
(☑435-672-2281; www.recapturelodge.com; Hwy 191; d $98; 🏵@🛜🏊) This locally owned rustic motel makes the best base for area adventures. Super-knowledgeable staff help out with trip planning and present educational slide shows in season. There's a hot tub and shady pool, and the property has 3.5 miles of walking trails.

Hovenweep NPS
Campground CAMPGROUND $
(tent & RV sites $10) This campground is about a mile from the ranger station and is open year-round on a first-come, first-served basis. The 31 sites rarely fill, but are busiest in summer. There are toilets and picnic facilities. Spring water is available when weather permits, usually from April to October only.

Sand Island Campground CAMPGROUND $
(☑435-587-1500; www.blm.gov; Sand Island Rd; tent & RV sites $10; ⏷May-Oct) The San Juan River location helps cool things off at these 27 first-come, first-served sites. Pit toilets and drinking water only; no hookups, no showers.

Desert Rose Inn & Cabins MOTEL $$
(☑435-672-2303, 888-475-7673; www.desertrose inn.com; 701 W Main St; r $130-179, cabins $179-289; ➾🏵@🛜🏊) Wraparound porches and log construction add warmth to this big motel at the edge of town, with quilt-covered pine beds in extra-large rooms and cabins. Showers are surprisingly weak considering the price point. There's also an on-site restaurant and swimming pool.

La Posada Pintada B&B $$
(☑435-459-2274; www.laposadapintada.com; 239 N 7th E; r $100-125; 🏵🛜) With cool, airy spaces and whimsical touches of Mexican decor, this family-run inn makes for a comfortable stop. Its six rooms are ample; some feature jet tubs and balconies, and all have minifridges and coffeemakers. Breakfast is served on the back patio.

🍴 Eating

For a tiny town, Bluff has good dining options (though mostly closed in winter). A few restaurants serve beer and wine.

★**Comb Ridge Bistro** CAFE $
(☑435-485-5555; combridgebistro.com; 680 S Hwy 191; breakfast mains $5-7, dinner mains $10-17; ⏷8am-3pm & 5-9pm Tue-Sun; 🛜🍴) An adobe gallery and cafe with standout single-pour coffee, blue-corn pancakes and sandwiches loaded with peppers and eggs. Dinner includes pasture-raised beef in the form of homemade meatloaf or whiskey burgers, organic salads and good vegetarian options.

Cottonwood Steakhouse STEAK $$
(☑435-672-2282; www.cottonwoodsteakhouse. com; Hwy 191, cnr Main & 4th East Sts; mains $18-27; ⏷5:30-9:30pm Mar-Nov) Salad, steak and beans are big on the menu at this Wild West venue with an outdoor grill (closed in windy conditions). For small appetites, it's worth splitting a plate.

Twin Rocks Cafe
& Trading Post AMERICAN INDIAN $$
(913 E Navajo Twins Dr; mains $6-21; ⏷7am-9pm; 🍴) Locals flock here for fry bread (deep-fried dough) as a breakfast sandwich, a Navajo taco at lunch or accompanying stew with dinner. Has good service and vegetarian options. Beer is also served.

ℹ Information

Hovenweep National Monument Ranger Station (☑970-562-4282; www.nps.gov/hove; McElmo Rte; ⏷8am-6pm Apr-Sep, to 5pm Oct-Mar; 🚻)

HIKING HOVENWEEP NATIONAL MONUMENT

Three easy-to-moderate loop **hiking trails** (none longer than 2 miles) leave from near the ranger station and pass a number of buildings in the Square Tower area. The trails give both distant and close-up views of the ancient sites whose fragile, unstable walls are easily damaged – please stay on the trail and don't climb on the sites. Visitors are reminded that all wildlife is protected – including rattlesnakes – but you are more likely to see the iridescent collared lizard scampering near the trail. Brochures are available for self-guided tours and also describe plant life along the trails.

NATURAL BRIDGES NATIONAL MONUMENT

Forty miles west of Blanding via Hwy 95, this **monument** (www.nps.gov/nabr; Hwy 275; 7-day pass per vehicle $10, tent & RV sites $10; ☺ 24hr, visitor center 8am-6pm May-Sep, 9am-5pm Oct-Apr) became Utah's first National Park Service (NPS) land in 1908. The highlight is a dark-stained, white-sandstone canyon containing three easily accessible natural bridges. The oldest, the **Owachomo Bridge**, spans 180ft but is only 9ft thick. The flat 9-mile Scenic Drive loop is ideal for biking.

Kachina Bridge is the youngest and spans 204ft. The 268ft span of **Sipapu Bridge** makes the top five of any 'largest in the US' list (the other four are in Utah, too). All three bridges are visible from the Scenic Drive loop road with easy-access overlooks.

Most visitors never venture below the canyon rim, but they should. Descents may be a little steep, but distances are short; the longest is just over half a mile one-way. Enthusiastic hikers can take a longer trail that joins all three bridges (8 miles). Don't skip the 0.3-mile trail to the **Horsecollar Ruin** cliff dwelling overlook. The elevation here is 6500ft; trails are open all year, but steeper sections may be closed after heavy rains or snow.

The 12 first-come, first-served sites at the **campground** (☎ 435-692-1234; www.nps.gov/nabr; Hwy 275; campsites $10), almost half a mile past the visitor center, are fairly sheltered among scraggly trees and red sand. The stars are a real attraction here – this has been designated an International Dark Sky Park and is one of the darkest in the country. There are pit toilets and grills, but water is available only at the visitor center; no hookups. The campground fills on summer afternoons, after which you are directed to camp in a designated area along Hwy 275. No backcountry camping is allowed. Towed trailers are not suitable for the loop drive.

The nearest services are in Blanding. If you continue west on Hwy 95 from Natural Bridges, and follow Hwy 276, the services of Lake Powell's Bullfrog Marina (p383) are 140 miles away.

Mexican Hat

☎ 435 / POP 31 / ELEV 4244FT

The settlement of Mexican Hat is named after a sombrero-shaped rock off Hwy 163. The town is little more than a handful of simple, somewhat uninspired lodgings, a couple of places to eat and a store or two on the north bank of the San Juan River. The south bank marks the edge of the Navajo Reservation. Monument Valley is 20 miles to the south; Bluff is 27 miles to the east.

◉ Sights

Goosenecks State Park   STATE PARK
(stateparks.utah.gov; vehicle $5, campsite $10) If instead of heading south to Mexican Hat you turn north on Hwy 261, you'll come to a 4-mile paved road that turns west to Goosenecks State Park. The attraction here is the mesmerizing view of the San Juan River. The serpentine path, carved by years of running water, is dramatically evident from above. You can see how the river snaked back on its course, leaving gooseneck-shaped spits of land untouched. There are pit toilets, picnic tables and free campsites.

🍽 Sleeping & Eating

There's a couple of lodgings, but head to Bluff or Blanding for more options. You'll also find a few restaurants and a store here.

San Juan Inn   MOTEL $
(☎ 800-447-2022, 435-683-2220; www.sanjuaninn.net; Hwy 163; r from $84, apt $265, yurt from $90; ❄ 🛜) The cliffside San Juan Inn perches high above the river. These basic motel rooms are the nicest in town, with quilted comforters and flat-screen TVs. There's also a **trading post** (☺ 7am-9pm) and restaurant on-site. Yurt accommodations are in round tents decked out with air-conditioning, wi-fi and views.

Goulding's Lodge   MOTEL $$
(☎ 435-727-3231; www.gouldings.com; Hwy 163; r from $130, tent/RV sites $25/36; ❄ 🏊) For years this was the only area hotel, luring tourists with million-dollar views of the colossal red buttes. The full-service property still has a lot to offer, including a restaurant, museum, indoor heated swimming pool, gas station and campground. Pets require an extra fee.

Old Bridge Grille DINER **$**
(☑435-683-2322; www.sanjuaninn.net; Hwy 163; mains $7-15; ☺7am-11pm) This year-round grill has greasy-spoon cooking and some whopping Navajo tacos (fry bread with chili and taco fixings), plus the only full liquor license for at least 50 miles.

Blanding

☑435 / POP 3600

En route between Bluff (22 miles) and Moab (75 miles) is this aptly named agricultural and mining center. Not much to look at, it's worth checking out for its two specialized museums and the nearby outdoors, though it's slim pickings for hotels and restaurants (which do not serve alcohol).

◉ Sights

★ **Dinosaur Museum** MUSEUM
(☑435-678-3454; www.dinosaur-museum.org; 754 S 200 W; adult/child $3.50/2; ☺9am-5pm Mon-Sat mid-Apr–mid-Oct) Despite being born of owners Steven and Sylvia Czerkas' personal collection, the Dinosaur Museum is ambitious; the goal is to cover the complete history of the world's dinosaurs. Mummified remains and fossil replicas go a long way toward this goal, but most interesting is the collection of dinosaur-movie-related memorabilia.

 **LOCAL PASSPORTS**

Southeastern Utah national parks sell a **Southeast Utah Parks Pass** (per vehicle $50) that's good for a year's entry to Arches and Canyonlands National Parks, plus Hovenweep and Natural Bridges National Monuments. **National Park Service Passes** (www.nps.gov/findapark/passes.htm; per vehicle adult/senior $80/10), available online and at parks, allow year-long access to all federal recreation lands in Utah and beyond – and are a great way to support the Southwest's amazing parks.

Edge of the Cedars
State Park Museum MUSEUM
(☑435-678-2238; www.stateparks.utah.gov; 660 W 400 N; adult/child $5/3; ☺9am-5pm Mon-Sat, 10am-4pm Sun) More a museum than a park, with ancient American Indian artifacts and the best pottery collection in the Southwest. Informative displays provide a good overview of area cultures. Outside you can climb down into a preserved ceremonial kiva built by the Ancestral Puebloans c 1100. The encroaching subdivision makes you wonder what other sites remain hidden under neighboring houses.

UTAH BLANDING

SCENIC DRIVE: MOKI DUGWAY

Ready for a ride? Eleven miles north of **Goosenecks** (p358), **Moki Dugway** is a roughly paved, hairpin-turn-filled section of Hwy 261 that ascends 1100ft in just 3 miles (you descend traveling south). This roller-coaster ride offers another route to Lake Powell. Wide pullouts allow a few overviews, but hairpin turns lack good visibility.

Miners dug out the extreme switchbacks in the 1950s to transport uranium ore.

Past the northern end of the Dugway, take the first western-traveling road to **Muley Point Overlook**. This sweeping cliff-edge viewpoint looks south to Monument Valley and other stunning landmarks in Arizona. Pay attention, as the unsigned turnoff is easy to miss.

Follow Hwy 261 further north to the wild and twisting canyons of Cedar Mesa and Grand Gulch Primitive Area, both hugely popular with backcountry hikers. The BLM-administered area also contains hundreds of Ancestral Puebloan sites, many of which have been vandalized by pot hunters. (It bears repeating that all prehistoric sites are protected by law, and authorities are cracking down on offenders.) Some hikes require permits.

The 4-mile, one-way Kane Gulch (600ft elevation change) leads to the **Junction Ruin** cliff dwelling. To hike in most canyons you need a $2 day-use permit ($8 overnight). In season (March to June 15, September and October) some walk-in permits are available at the helpful **Kane Gulch Ranger Station** (p384), but the number is strictly limited, so make advance reservations by calling the Monticello **field office** (p361). Off-season, self-serve permits are available at trailheads. Know that this is difficult country with primitive trails; the nearest water is 10 miles away at **Natural Bridges National Monument** (p358).

The Dugway is not for anyone who's sensitive to heights (or for vehicles over 28ft long).

MONUMENT VALLEY

From Mexican Hat, Hwy 163 winds south-west and enters the Navajo Reservation and – after 22 miles – Monument Valley, on the Arizona state line. Though you'll recognize it instantly from TV commercials and Hollywood movies (it was where Forrest Gump stopped his cross-country run), nothing compares with seeing the sheer chocolate-red buttes and colossal mesas for real. To get close, you must visit Arizona's **Monument Valley Navajo Tribal Park** (p191).

Sleeping & Eating

Abajo Haven Guest Ranch LODGE $
(435-979-3126; www.abajohaven.com; 5440 N Cedar Edge Lane; cabins $89) Outdoor adventure in the Abajo Mountains. Stay in a nicely rustic cabin (king and two twin beds each), have an old-fashioned cook-out and go on a guided hike to ancient sites 1½ hours from your cabin.

Stone Lizard Lodge MOTEL $$
(435-678-3323; www.stonelizardlodging.com; 88 W Center St; r $104-109, ste $155-249;) More than a motel, with spacious rooms sporting Southwestern themes, homemade cinnamon rolls for breakfast and a huge back garden with strawberries for the picking. The suites feel like a welcoming home. Wander into the office to borrow a book from the great regional library.

Pop's Burritos MEXICAN $
(435-678-2413; 148 S Main St; mains $6; 6am-10pm Mon-Sat) An egg-and-potato burrito smothered in green chili can put you on your way with a happy belly. While we'd like to see more of a kick, as fast-food options go, this one is a winner.

Shopping

Blue Mountain Artisans ARTS & CRAFTS
(www.bluemountainartisans.com; 215 E Center St; 11am-6pm Wed-Sat) A wonderful artists' co-op with pottery, paintings and photography.

Information

Blanding Visitor Center (435-678-3662; www.blandingutah.org; cnr Hwy 191 N & 200 E; 8am-7pm Mon-Sat) The Blanding Visitor Center puts out a guide that covers the whole region from Bluff to Natural Bridges. If you're here, the small pioneer artifact collection is worth a look.

Monticello

435 / POP 2000

Monticello (mon-ti-sell-o) sits up in the foothills of the Abajo (or Blue) Mountains, and is a bit cooler than other towns in the region. As the seat of San Juan County, it's the place to get information about the far southeast corner of Utah. Here you're midway between Moab (54 miles) and Bluff (47 miles); both have better places to stay but this is the closest town to the Canyonlands' Needles District (p366).

Just west of town, **Manti–La Sal National Forest** (www.fs.fed.us/r4/mantilasal; off N Creek Rd; 24hr) FREE has an alpine environment that's a novelty in the arid canyonlands.

Sights

Bears Ears National Monument PARK
(www.fs.fed.us/visit/bears-ears-national-monument) Designated as a National Monument in December 2016 as one of President Barack Obama's last acts, Bears Ears covers a large 1.35-million-acre swath of southeastern Utah. It's co-managed by the BLM and Forest Service. The area protects important sites of cultural significance to American Indian peoples, with ancient rock art, dwellings, ceremonial sites and granaries in a landscape of mesas and desert canyons.

Canyon Country Discovery Center MUSEUM
(435-587-2156; www.fourcornersschool.org; 1117 N Main St; adult/child $9/6; 10am-6pm Mon-Fri, to 9pm Sat) As part of the Four Corners School of Outdoor Education, this learning exhibit center also offers field trips, workshops, professional development training, citizen science projects, and classes on the on-site campus and off.

Sleeping & Eating

There are a few motels and lodges here, but a greater selection up the road in Moab. The same applies to restaurants.

Inn at the Canyons HOTEL $$
(435-587-2458; www.monticellocanyonlandsinn.com; 533 N Main St; r from $109;) Popular modernized motel rooms on the main drag with hot tub and swimming pool.

VALLEY OF THE GODS

Up and over, through and around: the 17-mile unpaved road (County Rd 242) that leads through **Valley of the Gods** (www.blm.gov) is like a do-it-yourself roller coaster amid some mind-blowing scenery. In other states, this incredible butte-filled valley would be a national park, but such are the riches of Utah that here it is merely a BLM-administered area. Locals call it 'mini–Monument Valley.'

The field office in Monticello puts out a BLM pamphlet, available online, identifying a few of the sandstone monoliths and pinnacles, including **Seven Sailors**, **Lady on a Tub** and **Rooster Butte**.

Free, dispersed camping among the rock giants is a dramatic – if shadeless – prospect. In such an isolated, uninhabited place, the night sky is incredible. Or splurge for a secluded refuge at **Valley of the Gods B&B** (☑970-749-1164; valleyofthegodsbandb.com; off Hwy 261; s/d $145/175, cabins $195) 🐾 a 1930s homestead with giant beam-and-post ceilings, stone showers and off-the-grid charm. Homemade breakfasts are monumental and the owners are happy to share hiking and travel tips. It's 6.5 miles north of Hwy 163. Water is trucked in, biofuels are used and solar power is harnessed out of necessity (leave your hair dryer at home).

A high-clearance vehicle is advised for driving the Valley of the Gods. A rental car can make it on a very dry day, but don't go without a 4WD if it has rained recently. Allow an hour for the 17-mile loop connecting Hwys 261 and 163. The nearest services are in Mexican Hat, 7 miles southwest of the Hwy 163 turnoff.

Canyonlands Lodge at Blue Mountain   CABIN **$$$**
(☑435-220-1050; www.canyonlandslodge.com; Hwy 191; cabins from $395; ❋🐾) A giant log lodge adjacent to the national forest 10 miles south of Monticello.

Peace Tree Juice Cafe   CAFE **$**
(516 N Main St; mains $8-20; ⊙7:30am-4pm daily, plus 5-9pm May-Sep; 🐾) A great place for full breakfasts, organic espresso, smoothies or a healthy lunch wrap.

ⓘ Information

BLM Monticello Field Office (☑435-587-1510; 435 N Main St; ⊙7:45am-noon & 1-4:30pm Mon-Fri) The place to inquire about backcountry hiking and to buy BLM topo maps. If you like to get way, way off the beaten path on multiday hikes, ask about the brilliantly empty Dark Canyon Primitive Area.

Southeast Utah Welcome Center (☑435-587-3401; visitmonticello.org; 216 S Main St; ⊙9am-6pm) The multiagency visitor center has extensive information on all public lands in southeastern Utah and complimentary coffee.

ⓘ Getting There & Away

Transportation is via private vehicle. From Monticello there's a shortcut to Canyonlands National Park's Needles District (22 miles instead of the main route's 34 miles). Take County Rd 101 (Abajo Dr) west to Harts Draw Rd (closed in winter); after 17 scenic miles you join Hwy 211 near Newspaper Rock State Historic Monument (p368). Befitting the region's religious character, Hwy 666, which goes to Colorado, was officially renamed Hwy 491 in 2003.

Canyonlands National Park

A 527-sq-mile vision of ancient earth, **Canyonlands National Park** (www.nps.gov/cany; per vehicle 7 days $25, tent & RV sites without hookups $15-20; ⊙24hr) is Utah's largest national park. Vast serpentine canyons tipped with white cliffs loom high over the Colorado and Green Rivers, their waters 1000ft below the rim rock. Skyward-jutting needles and spires, deep craters, blue-hued mesas and majestic buttes dot the landscape.

The Colorado and Green Rivers form a Y dividing the park into three separate districts, inaccessible to one another from within the park. Cradled atop the Y is the most developed and visited district, **Island in the Sky** (30 miles, 45 minutes from Moab). Its viewpoints look down into the incredible canyons of the other sections.

The thin hoodoos, sculpted sandstone and epic 4WD trails of the **Needles District** are 75 miles and 90 minutes south of Moab. Drivers need serious skill to

Canyonlands National Park

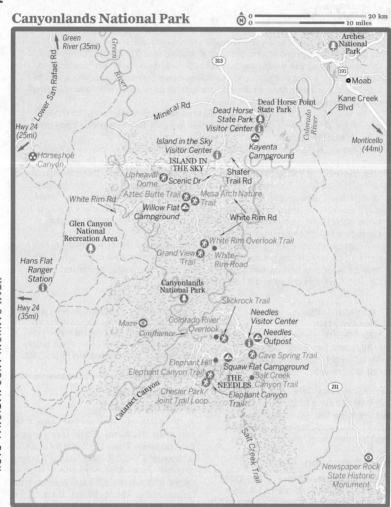

N 0 ___ 20 km
0 ___ 10 miles

Green
River (35mi)

Arches
National
Park

313

191

Moab

Lower San Rafael Rd

Green River

Mineral Rd

Dead Horse Point
State Park

Dead Horse
State Park
Visitor Center

Kane Creek
Blvd

Hwy 24
(25mi)

Horseshoe
Canyon

Island in the Sky
Visitor Center

Kayenta
Campground

Colorado River

Monticello
(44mi)

ISLAND IN
THE SKY

Upheaval
Dome

Scenic Dr

Shafer
Trail Rd

White Rim Rd

Aztec Butte Trail

Mesa Arch Nature
Trail

Willow Flat
Campground

White Rim Rd

Glen Canyon
National
Recreation Area

White Rim Overlook Trail

Hans Flat
Ranger
Station

Grand View
Trail

White
Rim Road

Canyonlands
National Park

Hwy 24
(35mi)

Slickrock Trail

Needles
Visitor Center

Maze

Colorado River
Overlook

Confluence

Needles
Outpost

Cave Spring Trail

Elephant Hill

Squaw Flat Campground

Elephant Canyon Trail

Salt Creek

Cataract Canyon

Chesler Park/
Joint Trail Loop

THE
NEEDLES

Canyon Trail

Elephant Canyon
Trail

211

Salt Creek Trail

Newspaper Rock
State Historic
Monument

traverse the 4WD-only roads of the **Maze** (130 miles, 3½ hours from Moab), the most inaccessible section.

Fees & Permits

In addition to the park entrance fee, permits are required for overnight backpacking, mountain biking, 4WD trips and river trips. Designated camp areas abut most trails; open-zone camping is permitted in some places. Horses are allowed on all 4WD trails. Permits are valid for 14 days and are issued at the visitor center or ranger station where your trip begins. Reservations are available by fax or mail from

the NPS Backcountry Permits Office (p367) up to two weeks ahead. A few space-available permits may be available same-day, but advanced reservations are essential for spring and fall trips. Costs are as follows:

Backpackers $30 per group of seven

General mountain bike or 4WD day-use $30 for up to three vehicles

Needles Area 4WD day-use $10 per vehicle

River trips $30 reservation plus $20 per person fee

Regulations

Canyonlands follows most of the national park hiking and backcountry use regulations. A few rules to note:

➡ No all-terrain vehicles (ATVs) allowed. Other 4WD vehicles, mountain bikes and street-legal motorbikes are permitted on dirt roads.

➡ Backcountry campfires are allowed only along river corridors; use a fire pan, burn only driftwood or downed tamarisk, and pack out unburned debris.

➡ Free or clean-aid rock climbing is allowed, except at archaeological sites or on most named features marked on US Geological Survey (USGS) maps. Check with rangers.

➡ New regulations require bear-proof food canisters and human waste removal in some backcountry areas; check with the park for details.

Island in the Sky

You'll comprehend space in new ways atop the appropriately named Island in the Sky (www.nps.gov/cany; vehicle/cyclist $25/10). This 6000ft-high flat-topped mesa drops precipitously on all sides, providing some of the longest, most enthralling vistas of any park in southern Utah. The 11,500ft Henry Mountains bookend panoramic views in the west, and the 12,700ft La Sal Mountains are to the east. Here you can stand beneath a sparkling blue sky and watch thunderheads inundating far-off regions while you contemplate applying more sunscreen. The island sits atop a sandstone bench called the White Rim, which indeed forms a white border 1200ft below the red mesa top and 1500ft above the river canyon bottom. An impressive 4WD road descends from the overlook level.

The complimentary video at the visitor center provides great insight into the nature of the park. Remember to keep your park entry receipt – admission to Island in the Sky includes entry to Needles, too.

Overlooks and trails line each road. Most trails at least partially follow cairns over slickrock. Bring lots of water and watch for cliff edges!

⊙ Sights & Activities

Ask rangers about longer hikes off the mesa that are strenuous, steep and require

WORTH A TRIP

BUTLER WASH & MULE CANYON RUINS

The drive along Hwy 95 between Blanding and Natural Bridges National Monument (p358) provides an excellent opportunity to see isolated Ancestral Puebloan ruins. No need to be a back-country trekker here: it's only a half-mile hike to **Butler Wash Ruins** (14 miles west of Blanding), a 20-room cliff dwelling. Scramble over the slickrock boulders (follow the cairns) and you're rewarded with an overlook of the sacred kivas, habitation and storage rooms that were used c 1300.

Though not as well preserved, the base of the tower, kiva and 12-room **Mule Canyon Ruins** (20 miles west of Blanding) are more easily accessed. Follow the signs to the parking lot just steps from the masonry remains. The pottery found here links the population (c 1000 to 1150) to the Mesa Verde group in southern Colorado; Butler Wash relates to the Kayenta group of northern Arizona. Both are on freely accessible, BLM-administered land.

advance planning. There's one major, hard-to-follow backpacking route: the Syncline Loop (8.3 miles, five to seven hours).

★ **White Rim Road**   MOUNTAIN BIKING, DRIVING
Blazed by uranium prospectors in the 1950s, primitive White Rim Rd encircling Island in the Sky is the top choice for 4WD and mountain-biking trips. This 70-mile route is accessed near the visitor center via steeply descending Shafer Trail Rd. It generally takes two to three days in a vehicle or three to four days by bike. Since the route lacks any water sources, cyclists should team up with a 4WD support vehicle or travel with a Moab outfitter. Permits are required and rangers do patrol. *A Naturalist's Guide to the White Rim Trail*, by David Williams and Damian Fagon, is a good resource.

Hiking
Several easy trails pack a lot of punch.

Grand View Trail   HIKING
At the end of the Island in the Sky road, this trail follows a 2-mile round-trip course at rim's edge. Even if you don't hike, **Grand View Point Overlook** is a must-see.

MESA VERDE NATIONAL PARK, COLORADO

More than 700 years after its inhabitants disappeared, Mesa Verde (☎970 529 4465; www.nps.gov/meve; 7-day car/motorcycle pass Jun-Aug $20/10, Sep-May $15/7; P📷🚻🍽) ✏ retains an air of mystery. No one knows for sure why the Ancestral Puebloans left their elaborate cliff dwellings in the 1300s. Anthropologists love it here: Mesa Verde is unique among American national parks in its focus on maintaining this civilization's cultural relics rather than its natural treasures. It's a wonderland for adventurers of all sizes, who can clamber up ladders to carved-out dwellings, see rock art and delve into the mysteries of ancient America.

Mesa Verde National Park occupies 81 sq miles of the northernmost portion of the mesa. Ancestral Puebloan sites are found throughout the park's canyons and mesas, perched on a high plateau south of Cortez and Mancos.

The National Parks Service (NPS) strictly enforces the Antiquities Act, which prohibits the removal or destruction of any antiquities and prohibits public access to many of the 4000 known Ancestral Puebloan sites.

The park entrance is off US 160, midway between Cortez and Mancos. From the entrance, it's about 21 miles to park headquarters, Chapin Mesa Museum and Spruce Tree House. Along the way are Morefield Campground (4 miles) and the panoramic viewpoint at Park Point (8 miles) and the Far View Lodge – about 11 miles. Towed vehicles are not allowed beyond Morefield Campground.

Chapin Mesa

There is no other place in Mesa Verde where so many remnants of Ancestral Puebloan settlements are clustered so closely together, providing an opportunity to see and compare examples of all phases of construction – from pothouses to Pueblo villages to the elaborate multiroom cities tucked into cliff recesses. Pamphlets describing the most excavated sites are available at either the visitor center (☎970-529-5034, 800-305-6053; www.nps.gov/meve; ⊙8am-7pm Jun–early Sep, to 5pm early Sep–mid-Oct, closed mid-Oct–May; 📶🚻) or Chapin Mesa Museum.

On the upper portion of Chapin Mesa are the Far View Sites, which make up perhaps the most densely settled area in Mesa Verde after 1100. The large-walled Pueblo sites at Far View House enclose a central kiva and planned room layout that was originally two stories high. To the north is a small row of rooms and an attached circular tower that probably once extended just above the adjacent 'pygmy forest' of piñon pine and juniper trees. This tower is one of 57 in Mesa Verde that may once have served as watchtowers, religious structures or astronomical observatories for agricultural schedules.

South from park headquarters, the 6-mile Mesa Top Rd circuit connects 10 excavated mesa-top sites, three accessible cliff dwellings and many vantages of inaccessible cliff dwellings from the mesa rim. It's open 8am to sunset.

Cliff Palace & Mesa Top Loops

This is the most visited part of the park. Access to the major Ancestral Puebloan sites is only by ranger-led tour, and tickets must be pre-purchased at the visitor center.

Wetherill Mesa

The less-frequented western portion of Mesa Verde offers a comprehensive display of Ancestral Pueblo relics. The Badger House Community consists of a short trail connecting four excavated surface sites depicting various phases of Ancestral Puebloan development.

Upheaval Dome   HIKING

A half-mile spur leads to an overlook of a geological wonder that was possibly the result of a meteorite strike 60 million years ago. Experts can take Syncline Loop, the difficult 8.3-mile hike around the dome, with a spur trail (3 miles round-trip) into its core area – it's considered the park's most challenging trail.

Aztec Butte Trail   HIKING

Near the Y in the main road, this moderate 2-mile round-trip climbs slickrock to stellar views and an ancient granary ruin.

White Rim Overlook Trail   HIKING
A mile before Grand View Point, this is a good spot for a picnic and a 1.8-mile round-trip hike.

Mesa Arch Nature Trail   HIKING
Hike this half-mile loop at sunrise, when the arch, dramatically hung over the very edge of the rim, glows a fiery red.

Scenic Driving Tour
From the visitor center the road leads past numerous overlooks and trailheads, ending after 12 miles at **Grand View Point** – one of the Southwest's most sweeping views, rivaled only by the Grand Canyon and nearby Dead Horse Point State Park. Halfway there, a paved spur leads (past **Aztec Butte**) northwest 5 miles to **Upheaval Dome** trailhead. The visitor center has driving tour information.

🛏 Sleeping
Backcountry camping in the Island is mostly open-zone (not in prescribed areas), but is still permit-limited. Nearby Dead Horse Point State Park (p367) also has camping; food, fuel and lodging are available in Moab.

Willow Flat Campground   CAMPGROUND $
(www.nps.gov/cany/planyourvisit/islandinthesky. htm; Island in the Sky; tent & RV sites $15; ☺ year-round) Seven miles from the Island in the Sky Visitor Center (p367), the first-come, first-served, 12-site Willow Flat Campground has vault toilets but no water, and no hookups. Bring firewood and don't expect shade. Arrive early to claim a site during spring or fall.

Needles District
Named for the spires of orange-and-white sandstone jutting skyward from the desert floor, the otherworldly terrain of the **Needles District** (www.nps.gov/cany; vehicle/cyclist $25/10) is so different from Island in the Sky that it's hard to believe they're both in the same national park. The Needles receives only half as many visitors as the Island since it's more remote – though only 90 minutes from Moab – and there are fewer roadside attractions (but most are well worth the hike). The payoff is huge: peaceful solitude and the opportunity to participate in, not just observe, the vastness of canyon country. Morning light is best for viewing the rock spires. Needles

INDIAN CREEK
When driving into the Needles District, look up about 16.5 miles along Hwy 211. Even if you don't rock climb, it's fascinating to watch the experts scaling the narrow cliffside fissures near Indian Creek. There's a small parking lot from where you can cross the freely accessible Nature Conservancy and BLM grazing land.

Visitor Center lies 2.5 miles inside the park boundaries and provides drinking water. Hold on to your receipt; admission includes entry to Island in the Sky.

◎ Sights & Activities
Needles has a couple of short trails (none are wheelchair-accessible), but getting off the beaten path is this section's premier attraction. Many challenging day-hikes connect in a series of loops, some requiring route-finding skills, while 50 miles of 4WD and mountain-biking roads (permit required) crisscross the park. Know what you're doing, though, or risk damaging your vehicle and endangering yourself. Towing fees run from $1000 to $2000 (yes, really). If you're renting a 4WD vehicle, check the insurance policy; you might not be covered here.

★ Chesler Park/Joint Trail Loop   HIKING
Get among the namesake 'needles' formations. An awesome 11-mile route loops across desert grasslands, past towering red-and-white-striped pinnacles and between deep, narrow slot canyons, some only 2ft across. Elevation changes are mild, but the distance makes it an advanced day hike.

Elephant Canyon Trail   HIKING
For gorgeous scenery, the Elephant Canyon Trail (11-mile loop) to **Druid Arch** is hard to beat. The *National Geographic Trails Illustrated* Canyonlands map should suffice, but if you're inclined to wander, pick up a 7½-minute quadrangle USGS map at the Needles Visitor Center.

Slickrock Trail   HIKING
Scamper across slickrock to fabulous views of the canyon; on the return route, you face the district's needles and spires in the distance (2.4-mile loop, moderate).

Cave Spring Trail
HIKING

Especially popular with kids, the Cave Spring Trail (0.6-mile loop, easy to moderate) leads up ladders and over slickrock to an abandoned cowboy camp. The handprint pictographs on the last cave's walls are haunting.

Elephant Hill
MOUNTAIN BIKING, DRIVING

This 32-mile round-trip is the most well-known and technically challenging route in the state, with steep grades and tight turns (smell the burning brakes and clutches). If you've always wanted to rock climb on wheels, you've found the right trail. Don't try this as your first 4WD or mountain-bike adventure.

Colorado River Overlook
MOUNTAIN BIKING, DRIVING

The route to the Colorado River Overlook is easy in a vehicle and moderately easy on a mountain bike. Park and walk the final, steep 1.5-mile descent to the overlook.

Salt Creek Canyon Trail
MOUNTAIN BIKING, DRIVING

Following the district's main drainage, archaeology junkies love the rock art along this 27-mile loop; moderately easy for vehicles and moderate for bikes.

Scenic Driving Tour

Though not much of a drive-by park, the paved road continues almost 7 miles from the visitor center to **Big Spring Canyon Overlook**. Parking areas along the way access several short trails to sights, including arches, **Pothole Point**, Ancestral Puebloan ruins and petroglyphs. Use the park map you receive on entry to navigate.

🛏 Sleeping & Eating

Backcountry camping, in prescribed areas only, is quite popular, so it's hard to secure an overnight permit without advance reservation. Monticello (34 miles) and Moab (75 miles) are the nearest full-service towns.

Squaw Flat Campground
CAMPGROUND $

(www.nps.gov/cany; Needles; tent & RV sites $15; ⊘year-round) This first-come, first-served, 26-site campground 3 miles west of the Needles Visitor Center fills up every day from spring to fall. It has flush toilets and running water, but no showers and no hookups. Opt for side A, where many sites (12 and 14, for example) are shaded by juniper trees and cliffs. Maximum allowable RV length is 28ft.

Needles Outpost
CAMPGROUND $

(☏435-979-4007; Hwy 211; tent & RV sites $20; ⊘Apr-Nov) If Squaw Flat is full, the dusty private campground at Needles Outpost is an alternative. Shower facilities are $3 for campers, $7 for noncampers. An on-site store sells limited camping supplies, gasoline and propane. The lunch counter and grill (open 8:30am to 4:30pm) serves sandwiches and burgers.

Maze

A 30-sq-mile jumble of high-walled canyons, the Maze is a rare preserve of true wilderness for hardy backcountry veterans. The colorful canyons are rugged, deep and sometimes completely inaccessible. Many of them look alike and it's easy to get turned around – hence the district's name. (Think topographic maps and GPS.) Rocky roads absolutely necessitate reliable, high-clearance 4WD vehicles. Plan on spending at least three days, though a week is ideal.

If you're at all inexperienced with four-wheel driving, stay away. Be prepared to repair your jeep and, at times, the road. There may not be enough money on the planet to get you towed out of here. Most wreckers won't even try.

Predeparture, always contact the Hans Flat Ranger Station for conditions and advice. The station is 136 miles (3½ hours) from Moab, and has a few books and maps, but no other services. Take Hwy 191 south, I-70 west, and then Hwy 24 south. Hans Flat is 16 miles south of Horseshoe Canyon. The few roads into the district are poor and often closed with rain or snow; bring tire chains from October to April.

Horseshoe Canyon

Way far west of Island in the Sky, Horseshoe Canyon shelters one of the most impressive collections of millennia-old rock art in the Southwest. The centerpiece is the **Great Gallery** and its haunting Barrier Canyon-style pictographs from between 2000 BC and AD 500. The heroic, bigger-than-life-size figures are magnificent. Artifacts recovered here date back as far as 9000 BC.

That said, it's not easy to get to. The gallery lies at the end of a 6.5-mile round-trip hiking trail descending 750ft from a dirt road. Plan on six hours. Rangers lead hikes here on Saturday and Sunday from April through October; contact the Hans Flat Ranger Station for times. You can camp on BLM land at the trailhead, though it's really a parking lot. There is a single vault toilet, but no water.

From Moab the trip is about 120 miles (2¾ hours). Take Hwy 191 north to I-70 west, then Hwy 24 south. About 25 miles south of I-70, past the turnoff for Goblin Valley State Park, turn east and follow the gravel road 30 miles. Hanksville is 45 miles (1½ hours).

ℹ️ Information

There are several information centers. **Island in the Sky** (📞 435-259-4712; www.nps.gov/cany; Hwy 313; ⏱ 8am-6pm Mar-Oct, 9am-4:30pm Nov-Feb) and the **Needles District** (📞 435-259-4711; Hwy 211; ⏱ 8am-6pm Mar-Oct, 9am-4:30pm Nov-Feb) have visitor centers. Many of the official park brochures are available online, while the Indian Creek website (www.friendsofindiancreek.org) has information on Moab-area climbing and conservation. The information center in Moab (p379) also covers the park.

Canyonlands NPS Headquarters (📞 435-719-2313; www.nps.gov/cany; 2282 SW Resource Blvd, Moab; ⏱ 8am-4:30pm Mon-Fri)

Hans Flat Ranger Station (📞 435-259-2652; www.nps.gov/cany; Hans Flat Rd, Hwy 24; ⏱ 8am-4:30pm)

NPS Backcountry Permits Office (📞 reservations 435-259-4351; canypermits.nps.gov/index.cfm; 2282 SW Resource Blvd, Moab; permits $10-30; ⏱ 8:30am-noon Mon-Fri)

ℹ️ Getting There & Around

The easiest way to tour Canyonlands is by car. Traveling between districts takes two to six hours, so plan to visit no more than one per day.

Overlooks are easy enough to reach. To explore further you'll need to contend with difficult dirt roads, great distances and limited water resources. Speed limits vary but are generally between 25mph and 40mph.

Outfitters in Moab have hiker shuttles and guide rafting, hiking, biking and 4WD tours in the park.

Dead Horse Point State Park

The views at Dead Horse Point (www.stateparks.utah.gov; Hwy 313; park day use per vehicle $15, tent & RV sites $35; ⏱ park 6am-10pm, visitor center 8am-6pm Mar-Oct, 9am-4pm Nov-Feb) pack a wallop, extending 2000ft down to the winding Colorado River, up to La Sal Mountains' 12,700ft peaks and out 100 miles across Canyonlands' mesmerizing staircase landscape. (You might remember it from the final scene of *Thelma & Louise*,

where they drove off into the abyss.) If you thrive on rare, epic views, you're gonna love Dead Horse.

Around the turn of the 20th century, cowboys used the mesa top as a sort of natural corral by driving wild horses onto it and blocking the ridge. The story goes that one season ranch hands forgot to release the horses they didn't cull, and the stranded equines supposedly died with a great view of the Colorado River.

🛏️ Sleeping & Eating

Visitors should bring their own provisions. For restaurants and groceries, head to nearby Moab.

Kayenta Campground CAMPGROUND $
(📞 800-322-3770; www.stateparks.utah.gov; sites $30, yurts $90) South of the visitor center, this 21-site campground provides limited water and a dump station, but no hookups. Reservations are accepted from March to October, but you can often secure same-day sites by arriving early. Fill RVs with water in Moab. Three yurts offer rad views of the surrounding wilderness.

ℹ️ Information

Dead Horse State Park Visitor Center (stateparks.utah.gov/parks/dead-horse; ⏱ 8am-6pm mid-Mar–mid-Oct, 9am-5pm mid-Oct–mid-Mar) This excellent visitor center has exhibits, on-demand videos, books and maps, along with ranger-led walks and talks in summer.

---

127 HOURS: BETWEEN A ROCK AND A HARD PLACE

What started out as a day's adventure turned into a harrowing ordeal for one outdoorsman exploring some spectacular slots near **Canyonlands National Park** (p361) in the spring of 2003. Canyoneering southeast of the remote **Horseshoe Canyon** (p366) section in Bluejohn Canyon, Aron Ralston became trapped when a crashing boulder pinned his hand and wrist. The story of how he cut himself out of the situation – literally, as he cut off his own arm with a pocketknife – was first turned into a compelling book, and then the 2010 Oscar-nominated movie *127 Hours*. The film showcases both the amazing beauty of Utah's canyonlands and the brutal reality of its risks.

ℹ️ Getting There & Away

Drive Hwy 313 south from Hwy 191, 30 miles northwest of Moab, following the road as it turns left into the park (if you go straight you'll reach Island in the Sky; p363). Toward the end of the drive, the road traverses a narrow ridge just 90ft across. Access is via private vehicle only.

Moab

📞 435 / POP 5100

Doling out hot tubs and pub grub after a dusty day on the trail, Moab is southern Utah's adventure base camp. Mobs arrive to play in Utah's recreation capital. From the hiker to the four-wheeler, the cult of recreation borders on fetishism.

Starting in the 1950s, miners in search of 'radioactive gold' – uranium – blazed the network of back roads that laid the groundwork for this 4WD mecca. Neither mining nor the hundreds of Hollywood films shot here have influenced the character of Moab as much as the influx of fat-tire, mountain-bike enthusiasts.

The town becomes overrun from March through October. The impact of all those feet, bikes and 4WDs on the fragile desert is a serious concern. People here love the land, even if they don't always agree about how to protect it. If the traffic irritates you, just remember – you can disappear into the vast desert in no time.

⊙ Sights

Between breakfast and dinner there's not much going on in Moab; most people get out of town for activities.

Moab Giants   AMUSEMENT PARK
(📞435-355-0288; www.moabgiants.com; SR 313, 112 W; adult/child from $16/12; ⊙9am-5pm; 🚼) This new paleo-amusement park features giant life-size replica dinosaurs, walking trails, 3D videos that might even bring you to a fourth dimension in some sections, information on dino tracks and more. It might be garish for some, but with a $10 million initial investment, it will certainly be entertaining.

Museum of Moab   MUSEUM
(www.moabmuseum.org; 118 E Center St; adult/child $5/free; ⊙10am-6pm Mon-Sat Apr-Oct, noon-5pm Mon-Sat Nov-Mar) Regional exhibits feature everything from paleontology and geology to uranium mining and American Indian art.

DON'T MISS

NEWSPAPER ROCK

This tiny **Newspaper Rock State Historic Monument** FREE showcases a single large sandstone rock panel packed with more than 300 petroglyphs attributed to Ute and Ancestral Puebloan groups during a 2000-year period. The many red rock figures etched out of a black 'desert varnish' surface make for great photos. It's located 50 miles south of Moab, east of Canyonlands National Park on Hwy 211.

🏃 Activities

The visitor center (p379) has a collection of free brochures highlighting rock art, movie locations, driving tours, and 4WD and hiking trails near town. Moab abounds in outfitters for mountain biking, white-water rafting, hiking, and backcountry ATV and jeep tours. Many operators will help you plan multisport or multiday adventures. The visitor center has a complete list of all outfitters.

Aquatics & Fitness Center   SWIMMING
(📞435-259-8226; 374 Park Ave; adult/child $9/7, showers only $5; ⊙5:30am-7:45pm Mon-Fri, 9am-7:45pm Sat, 11am-5pm Sun) A new top-notch facility with an indoor pool and huge outdoor pools for the community.

Mountain Biking

Moab's mountain biking is world-famous. Challenging trails ascend steep slickrock and wind through woods and up 4WD roads. People come from everywhere to ride the famous **Slickrock Trail** (Sand Flats Recreation Area; www.discovermoab.com/sandflats.htm; car/cyclist $5/2) and other challenging routes. If you're a die-hard, ask about trips to the Maze (p366). Bike shop websites and www.discovermoab.com/biking.htm are good trail resources, or pick up *Above & Beyond Slickrock*, by Todd Campbell, and *Rider Mel's Mountain Bike Guide to Moab.*

Follow BLM guidelines, avoid all off-trail riding and pack everything out (including cigarette butts). Spring and fall are the busiest seasons. In summer you'd better start by 7am; otherwise, the heat is searing.

New bikers would do well to hire a guide. For rentals, reserve road or full-suspension bikes in advance.

★**Rim Cyclery**   MOUNTAIN BIKING
(📞435-259-5333; www.rimcyclery.com; 94 W 100 N; ⊙8am-6pm) Moab's longest-running

family-owned bike shop not only does rentals and repairs, it also has a museum of mountain-bike technology, and rents cross-country skis in the winter.

★ **Whole Enchilada**   MOUNTAIN BIKING
Accessed from the top of Geyser Pass at 10,600ft, this masterpiece combines the Burro Pass, Hazard County, Jimmy Keen, UPS, LPS and Porcupine Rim Trails, offering everything from high-mountain descents to slickrock. It's a full-day affair for advanced riders with 7000ft of vertical drop and 26.5 miles of trails.

Chile Pepper Bike Shop   MOUNTAIN BIKING
(☑ 435-259-4688, 888-677-4688; www.chilebikes. com; 702 S Main St; ⊙8am-6pm) This shop rents bikes; checking bikes out at 4:30pm with returns the next day at 1pm means you could potentially get two rides in. It also repairs bikes, dishes out local trail beta and has plenty of maps.

Poison Spider Bicycles   MOUNTAIN BIKING
(☑ 435-259-7882, 800-635-1792; www.poisonspider bicycles.com; 497 N Main St; ⊙8am-7pm) Friendly staff are always busy helping wheel jockeys map out their routes. Well-maintained road and suspension rigs for rent.

Rim Tours   CYCLING
(☑ 435-259-5223; www.rimtours.com; 1233 S Hwy 191; ⊙9am-5pm) Well-organized and well-supported bike trips cover territory all across southern Utah. Trips range from half-day to four-day supported tours, including rental of sparkling Santa Cruz full-suspension 29ers. Day trips depart at 7am; reserve ahead.

Western Spirit Cycling Adventures   TOURS
(☑ 435-259-8732, 800-845-2453; www.western spirit.com; 478 Mill Creek Dr; ⊙9am-5pm) Canyonlands' White Rim, Bryce to Zion and nationwide multiday tours.

Moab Cyclery   MOUNTAIN BIKING
(☑ 435-259-7423, 800-451-1133; www.moabcyclery. com; 391 S Main St; ⊙8am-6pm) Good half-, full-, multiday and multisport tours. A high performance bike shop offering rentals and sales; biker shuttles available.

White-Water Rafting

Whatever your interest, be it bashing through rapids or gentle floats for studying canyon geology, rafting may prove the highlight of your vacation. Rafting season runs from April to September; jet-boating season lasts longer. Water levels crest in May and June.

Most local rafting is on the Colorado River, northeast of town, including the Class III to IV rapids of **Westwater Canyon**, near Colorado; the wildlife-rich 7-mile Class I float from **Dewey Bridge to Hittle Bottom** (no permit required); and the Class I to II **Moab Daily**, the most popular stretch near town (no permit required; expect a short stretch of Class III rapids).

Rafters also launch north of Moab to get to the legendary Class V rapids of **Cataract Canyon** (NPS permit required). This Colorado River canyon south of town and the Confluence is one of North America's most intense stretches of white water. If you book anything less than a five-day outfitter trip to get here, know that some of the time downstream will be spent in a powered boat. Advanced do-it-yourself rafters wanting to

TOP MOAB MOUNTAIN-BIKING TRAILS

Slickrock Trail (p368) Moab's legendary trail will kick your ass. The 12.7-mile round-trip, half-day route is for experts only (as is the practice loop).

White Rim Road (p363) Canyonlands National Park's 70-mile, three- to four-day journey around a canyon mesa top is epic.

Bar-M Loop (p380) Bring the kids on this easy, 8-mile loop skirting the boundary of Arches, with great views and short slickrock stretches.

Gemini Bridges A moderate, full-day downhill ride past spectacular rock formations, this 13.5-mile one-way trail follows dirt, sand and slickrock.

Klondike Bluffs Trail Intermediates can learn to ride slickrock on this 15.6-mile round-trip trail, past dinosaur tracks to Arches National Park.

Moonlight Meadow Trail Beat the heat by ascending La Sal Mountains to 10,600ft on this moderate 10-mile loop among aspens and pines (take it easy: you *will* get winded).

Park to Park Trail A new paved-road bike path travels one-way from Moab into Arches National Park (30 miles), or you can turn off and follow the Hwy 313 bike lane to the end of Canyonlands' Island in the Sky park (35 miles).

Moab

UTAH MOAB

Tag-A-Long Expeditions (0.1mi);
Moab Desert Adventures (0.1mi);
Poison Spider Bicycles (0.1mi);
Holiday Inn Express (1.3mi)

Swanny
City Park

Main St

300 North

200 North

Walnut La

100 North

Williams Way

100 West

Center St

Moab Information Center

Canyonlands
Natural History Association

Main St

100 South

200 South

300 South

Milt's (0.2mi);
Western Spirit Cycling
Adventures (0.4mi)

Grand Ave

Kane Creek Blvd

Huntridge Dr

Aspen Ave

Uranium Ave

Canyonlands Campground (100yds);
Chile Pepper Bike Shop (0.2mi);
Moab Brewery (0.2mi); Paradox Pizza (0.2mi);
BLM Office (0.3mi);
Rim Tours (1mi); Lazy Lizard Hostel (1.2mi);
Canyonlands Field Institute (1.3mi)

Main St

Slickrock Cinemas 3
(0.1mi)

100 East

200 East

300 East

Milt Creek

Moab

run it will have to book a jet-boat shuttle or flight return.

North of Moab is a Class I float along the **Green River** that's ideal for canoes. From there you can follow John Wesley Powell's 1869 route. (Note that additional outfitters operate out of the town of Green River itself.)

Visitors can choose from full-day float trips, white-water trips, multiday excursions and jet-boat trips. Day trips are often available on short notice, but overnight trips should be booked well ahead. Know the boat you want: an oar rig is a rubber raft that a guide rows; a paddleboat is steered by the guide and paddled by passengers; motor rigs are large boats driven by a guide (such as jet boats).

Do-it-yourselfers can rent canoes, inflatable kayaks or rafts with required personal flotation devices and accessories. Rentals are discounted for multiday jaunts.

Without permits, you'll be restricted to mellow stretches of the Colorado and Green Rivers; if you want to run Westwater Canyon or enter Canyonlands on either river, you'll need a permit. Contact the BLM (p379) or NPS (p367), respectively. Reserve equipment, permits and shuttles way in advance.

Sheri Griffith Expeditions RAFTING
(☑800-332-2439; www.griffithexp.com; 2231 S Hwy 191; ⊙8am-6pm) Operating since 1971, this rafting specialist has a great selection of river trips on the Colorado, Green and San Juan Rivers – from family floats to Cataract Canyon rapids, and from a couple of hours to a couple of weeks.

OARS TOURS
(☑435-259-5919, 800-346-6277; www.oars.com; 2540 S Hwy 191; ⊙8am-7pm) Has a permit for Canyonlands National Park and guides single- or multiday combination hiking and rafting tours.

Navtec Expeditions ADVENTURE
(☑435-259-7983; www.navtec.com; 321 N Main St; ⊙7am-6pm) Comprehensive rafting excursions, including Cataract Canyon, combo hiking and 4WD trips.

Adrift Adventures ADVENTURE
(☑435-259-8594, 800-874-4483; www.adrift.net; 378 N Main St) Rafting, jet-boat rides, sportboat rides, 4WD land excursions and multisport packages, plus Arches National Park bus tours.

Canyon Voyages Adventure Co ADVENTURE
(☑800-733-6007; www.canyonvoyages.com; 211 N Main St) In addition to half- to five-day mild white-water and kayaking trips, Canyon organizes multisport excursions that include options like hiking, biking, paddle boarding and canyoneering. Kayak, canoe and outdoor equipment rental available.

Hiking

Don't limit yourself to the national parks – there's great hiking on surrounding public lands as well.

★ **Canyonlands Field Institute**   TOURS
(☑ 435-259-7750; www.cfimoab.org; 1320 S Hwy 191; ⊗ May-Oct) This nonprofit operation uses proceeds from guided tours to create youth outdoor-education programs and train local guides. It offers occasional workshops and seminars throughout the summer. Top tours include the Rock Art Tour (8am Friday to Sunday), the geology-focused Arches Sunset Tour (4pm Friday to Sunday) and customized river trips.

Deep Desert Expeditions   HIKING
(☑ 435-260-1696; www.deepdesert.com; 2-hiker half-day from $250; ⊗ 8am-7pm) Archaeological hikes, photo treks, multiday guided backpacking and catered camping in all seasons.

Fisher Towers Trail   HIKING
The Fisher Towers Trail takes you past these towering sandstone monoliths, the tallest of which rises 900ft. The west-facing monoliths get quite hot in the afternoon, so wait for sunset, when rays bathe the rock in color and cast long shadows. (Bring a flashlight; many lingering hikers have ended up stuck on the trail in the dark.)

Corona Arch Trail   HIKING
To take in petroglyphs and two spectacular, rarely visited rock arches, hike the moderately easy Corona Arch Trail, the trailhead for which lies 6 miles up Potash Rd (Hwy 279). Follow cairns along the slickrock to **Bowtie** and **Corona Arches**. You may recognize Corona from a well-known photograph in which an airplane is flying through it – this is one big arch!

Grandstaff Trail   HIKING
(Hwy 128) This moderately easy trail includes a 2.5-mile walk (five miles round-trip) along a stream. Scoot down a shaded side canyon to find petroglyphs, then continue to the 243ft-wide **Morning Glory Natural Bridge**, at a box canyon. Plan on three to four hours. The trailhead is 3 miles north of Moab.

Hidden Valley Trail   HIKING
For a moderate-to-difficult rim hike above Moab, try the Hidden Valley Trail, which meanders through a pristine hanging valley in the Behind the Rocks Wilderness Study Area. The trailhead is on BLM land at the end of Angel Rock Rd. Plan on taking four to six hours.

La Sal Mountains   HIKING
(www.fs.usda.gov; La Sal Mountain Loop) To escape summer's heat, head up Hwy 128 to the Manti–La Sal National Forest lands, in the mountains east of Moab, and hike through white-barked aspens and ponderosa pines.

Moonflower Canyon   HIKING
If you're short on time, take the easy 1-mile round-trip hike along Moonflower Canyon, a shaded stroll on mostly level ground that ends at a sandstone bowl beneath hanging gardens. A perennial stream makes this hike a cooler, less dusty alternative. The trailhead lies 1.2 miles from town along Kane Creek Rd. Look for petroglyphs at the parking area.

Four-Wheel Driving

The area's primitive backroads are coveted by 4WD enthusiasts. You can rent or take group 4WD tours, or 'land safaris,' in multipassenger-modified, six- to eight-person humvee-like vehicles. Note that rafting companies may have combination land/river trips.

Off-road utility vehicles like Rhinos and Mules (seating two to four), or four-wheelers (straddled like a bicycle) are available for rent. Personal 4WD vehicles and ATVs require an off-highway vehicle (OHV) permit, available at the visitor center. Outfitter hours shorten between November through February.

The Moab Information Center (p379) has good free route info, as well as *Moab Utah Backroads & 4WD Trails* by Charles Wells, and other books for sale. Canyonlands National Park (p361) also has some epic 4WD tracks.

If you go four-wheeling, stay on established routes. The desert looks barren, but it's a fragile landscape of complex ecosystems. Biological soil crusts can take up to a century to regenerate after even one tire track (really).

Hell's Revenge   SCENIC DRIVE
(www.discovermoab.com/sandflats.htm; Sand Flats Rd, Sand Flats Recreation Area) The best-known 4WD road in Moab is in the BLM-administered area east of town, which follows an 8.2-mile route up and down shockingly steep slickrock. For experienced drivers only. Be sure to stick to the motorized vehicle trails.

Dan Mick's Jeep Tours   DRIVING
(☑ 435-259-4567; www.danmick.com; 3-person tours from $300) Private Jeep tours and guided drive-your-own-4WD trips with good ol' boy Dan Mick. A highly regarded local operation.

SEGO CANYON

It's rare to see the rock art of three different ancient cultures on display all in one canyon, but that's precisely what you can do at Sego. On the south-facing wall, the Barrier Culture pictographs are the oldest (at least 2000 years old); the wide-eyed anthropomorphic creatures take on a haunted, ghost-like appearance to modern eyes. The Fremont petroglyphs were carved about 1000 years ago. Many of the line-art figures are wearing chunky ornamentation and headdresses (or is it antennae?). The third panel is from the 19th-century American Indian Ute tribe; look for the horses and buffalo.

The canyon itself is 4 miles north of I-70 at Thompson Springs (41 miles north of Moab, 26 miles east of Green River). If you drive half a mile further north up the canyon, you come to a little ghost town. The few buildings here were deserted when a mining camp was abandoned in the 1950s.

Coyote Land Tours
DRIVING
(☎ 435-260-3056; www.coyotelandtours.com; adult/child $59/39) Popular daily tours in a bright-yellow Mercedes-Benz Unimog off-road vehicle (seats 12); call ahead. Your bad-ass driver, John Marshall, is certified as an Emergency Medical Technician, off-road driver and US Marshal desert tracker.

Moab Adventure Center
ADVENTURE
(☎ 435-259-7019, 866-904-1163; www.moab adventurecenter.com; 225 S Main St) The open-air, canopy-topped land safaris offered here are popular. This megacenter also arranges, alone or in combination, rafting trips, Jeep rental, horseback riding, rock climbing, guided hikes, scenic flights and even Arches National Park bus tours.

High Point Hummer & ATV Tours
ADVENTURE
(☎ 435-259-2972, 877-486-6833; www.highpoint hummer.com; 281 N Main St) Take a two- to four-hour thrill ride up the slickrock on a group Hummer tour; follow a guide as you drive yourself on a four-wheeler or utility vehicle tour; or rent an ATV yourself.

Rock Climbing & Canyoneering
Climb up cliffsides, rappel into rivers and hike through slot canyons with local outfitters, who have the inside scoop on the area's lesser-known gems.

Windgate Adventures
ADVENTURE SPORTS
(☎ 435-260-9802; www.windgateadventures.com; half-day canyoneering $160; ⏱ 7:30am-6pm) Private guide Eric Odenthal leads guided climbing, canyoneering, rappelling and photo trips.

Moab Desert Adventures
OUTDOORS
(☎ 804-814-3872; www.moabdesertadventures. com; 415 N Main St; ⏱ 7am-7pm) Top-notch climbing tours scale area towers and walls; the 140ft arch rappel is especially exciting. Canyoneering trips are also available.

Desert Highlights
ADVENTURE
(☎ 800-747-1342, 435-259-4433; www.desert highlights.com; 50 E Center St; canyoneering from $120) Canyoneering and pack raft trips here are big on personal attention. Offers trips to some worthy, little-known destinations.

Moab Cliffs & Canyons
ADVENTURE SPORTS
(☎ 877-641-5271, 435-259-3317; www.cliffsand canyons.com; 253 N Main St) Canyoneering, climbing and scenic hiking trips.

Wall Street
CLIMBING
(Potash Rd) Rock climbers in town gravitate toward Wall Street; it's Moab's El Capitan, so it gets crowded.

Air Adventures

Redtail Aviation
SCENIC FLIGHTS
(☎ 435-259-7421; flyredtail.com; 94 Aviation Way, Suite F; aerial tour $189; ⏱ 8am-5pm) Fly high above Arches, Canyonlands, Lake Powell, San Rafael Swell, Monument Valley and more.

Canyonlands Ballooning
BALLOONING
(☎ 435-655-1389, 877-478-3544; www.canyonlands ballooning.com; 4hr per person $322) Soar over canyon country and Manti–La Sal Mountains. Discounts are available in low season. The meeting place is 6.5 miles north of the entrance to Arches National Park on Hwy 191.

Skydive Moab
ADVENTURE SPORTS
(☎ 435-259-5867; www.skydivemoab.com; tandem 1st jump $225) Skydiving and base-jumping with stunning desert views.

Skiing & Snowshoeing
It's a local secret that La Sal Mountains, which lord over Moab off Hwy 128, receive tons of powder, just perfect for cross-country skiing – and there's a hut-to-hut ski system.

Other Activities

Red Cliffs Lodge
HORSEBACK RIDING
(☎ 435-259-2002, 866-812-2002; www.redcliffs lodge.com; Mile 14, Hwy 128) In Castle Valley, 15 miles north of town, Red Cliffs Lodge

UTAH MOAB

WORTH A TRIP

COLORADO RIVER SCENIC BYWAY (HWY 128)

This curvy 31-mile drive follows the winding Colorado River through gorgeous red-rock country of mesas, rock walls, alfalfa fields and sagebrush. Extend the trip with the La Sal Mountain Loop Rd.

Drive north on Main St/Hwy 191 and turn right (east) onto Hwy 128. The road winds through red-rock canyons along the Colorado River's serpentine course, which is why it is known in the area as 'the river road.' Arches National Park lies on the north side of the river for the first 15 miles.

Six miles from Hwy 191 you'll reach Big Bend Recreation Site, where you can picnic by the river; climbers will enjoy the low-key bouldering here.

Eleven miles further on, you'll pass the La Sal Mountain Loop Rd turnoff and Castleton Tower, a narrow 400ft spire that rises above Castle Valley, and is one of the area's most iconic rock climbs. Across from Castleton, the Nuns and Priests Pinnacles shoot up in a graceful line.

At mile marker 21, the Fisher Towers rise almost as high as the Eiffel Tower (at 900ft; Titan is the tallest).

Ten miles ahead, you'll reach the Dewey Bridge site. Built in 1916, it was among the first spans across the Colorado. The bridge was destroyed by accidental fire in 2008 and its future is currently in limbo due to the high cost of reconstruction. Park near the site to watch rafters running downriver.

When ready, return to Moab or double back to the La Sal Mountain Loop Rd. I-70 lies 13 miles north.

provides horseback trail rides (March to November), offered mornings and evenings. If you book a multisport rafting trip that includes horseback riding, you'll still be coming here.

Moab Photo Tours TOURS
(☑ 435-260-2639; www.moabphototours.com) Area photo workshops and tours by local photographers.

Matheson Wetlands Preserve BIRDWATCHING
(☑ 435-259-4629; www.nature.org; 934 W Kane Creek Blvd; ☉ dawn-dusk) FREE The Nature Conservancy oversees the 890-acre preserve just west of town. You can spot over 200 species of bird in this wetlands area. Also expect chances of seeing beaver, muskrat and river otter.

✻ Festivals & Events

Moab loves a party, and throws them regularly. For a full calendar, consult www.discovermoab.com.

Moonshadows in Moab SPORTS
(☑ 435-259-2698; www.moonshadowsinmoab.com; ☉ Jul) Biking by July moonlight. The fully-supported ride takes place between Dead Horse Point (p367) and Canyonlands' Island in the Sky (p363).

Moab Music Festival MUSIC
(☑ 435-259-7003; www.moabmusicfest.org; ☉ Sep) World-class classical musicians converge on the landscape of the Utah Canyonlands region.

Summer Concert Series MUSIC
(www.discovermoab.com/calendar.htm; Swanny Park; ☉ 5:30-9pm Fri) FREE A new concert series that coincides with the Farmers Market (p378). For concert details, inquire at the Moab Information Center (p379).

Skinny Tire Festival SPORTS
(www.skinnytirefestival.com; ☉ early Mar) Road cycling festival with four rides in super scenic locations around Moab, including the parks.

🛏 Sleeping

Though there's a huge number of motels, they are often booked out. Reserve as far ahead as possible. For a full lodging list, see www.discovermoab.com. Prices drop by as much as 50% outside March to October.

Moab Utah Lodging ACCOMMODATION SERVICES
(www.moabutahlodging.com) Local listings.

Kokopelli Lodge MOTEL $
(☑ 435-259-7615; www.kokopellilodge.com; 72 S 100 E; r $79-149; ❄ 🖥 🖨) Retro styling meets with desert chic at this great-value budget motel. Amenities include a hot tub, a BBQ grill and secure bike storage.

Lazy Lizard Hostel
HOSTEL **$**

(📞 435-259-6057; www.lazylizardhostel.com; 1213 S Hwy 191; dm/s/d $12/32/36, cabins $37-58; 🅿 ✳ @ 🛜) This hippie hangout is popular with European travelers and the non-car set. Located behind A-1 storage, it has frayed couches, worn bunks, a small kitchen and a peaced-out patio. The little cabins out back are the way to go.

★ Cali Cochitta
B&B **$$**

(📞 435-259-4961, 888-429-8112; www.moabdream inn.com; 110 S 200 E; cottages $155-190; ✳ 🛜) Charming and central, these adjoining brick cottages offer snug rooms fitted with smart decor. A long wooden table on the patio makes a welcome setting for communal breakfasts. You can also take advantage of the porch chairs, hammock or backyard hot tub in the Zen garden.

Red Moon Lodge
B&B **$$**

(📞 512-565-7612; www.redmoonlodge.com; 2950 Old City Park Rd; d $159; ⊘ Feb-Oct; 🛜) 🖉 Tucked alongside a creek bed with tall cottonwoods, this round house is Moab's most sustainable stay. There's organic breakfasts, solar power and sustainable xeriscaping. Fanning out on a stone patio, rooms feature firm beds, attractive woven rugs and solid furniture. There are no phones or TV. Instead imbibe the Zen spirit, explore the grounds and stretch out on the yoga platform.

3 Dogs and a Moose
B&B **$$**

(📞 435-260-1692; www.3dogsandamoosecottages. com; 171 W Center St; cottages $135-305; ✳ 🛜 ⚲) Lovely and low-key, these four downtown cottages make an ideal base camp for groups and families who want a little socializing in situ. The style is French country meets playful modern. Even better, you can pick your own tomatoes in the landscaped yard, where there are also hammocks, a bike wash, a grill and a hot tub.

Pack Creek Ranch
LODGE **$$**

(📞 888-879-6622; www.packcreekranch.com; off La Sal Mountain Loop; cabins $175-235; 🛜 ⚲) This hidden Shangri-la's log cabins are tucked beneath mature cottonwoods and willow trees in the La Sal Mountains, 2000ft above Moab. Most feature fireplaces; all have kitchens and gas grills (bring groceries). No TV or phones. Edward Abbey is among the artists and writers who came here for inspiration. Amenities include horseback riding and an indoor hot tub and sauna.

Gonzo Inn
MOTEL **$$**

(📞 435-259-2515, 800-791-4044; www.gonzoinn. com; 100 W 200 S; r $189, ste $235-275; ✳ @ 🛜 ⚲ ⚲) Less an inn than a chain-style motel spruced up with retro-'70s steel accents and sleek cement showers, the Gonzo Inn is friendly, and we love the location off the main drag. No fear and loathing here, it caters well to cyclists, with a bicycle wash and repair station as well as a laundry. Rooms have refrigerators and coffee makers.

Castle Valley Inn
B&B **$$**

(📞 435-259-6012; www.castlevalleyinn.com; 424 Amber Lane, off La Sal Mountain Loop; r & cabins $135-235; ✳) For tranquility, it's hard to beat this top option off La Sal Mountain Loop Rd, 15 miles north of Moab. With cozy quilts and handmade aspen furniture, rooms (in the main house or new bungalows) sit amid apple, plum and apricot orchards. Bungalows offer full kitchen and grill; there's also an outdoor hot tub. Ideal for cycling Castle Valley.

Big Horn Lodge
MOTEL **$$**

(📞 435-259-6171; www.moabbighorn.com; 550 S Main St; r from $129; ⊖ ✳ 🛜 ⚲) With a kitschy Southwestern-style facade and cozy interiors paneled with knotty pine, this two-story motel is a strong bet. Service is taken seriously and there are loads of extras (including a heated swimming pool inches from the road, refrigerators and coffee makers).

★ Sunflower Hill Inn
INN **$$$**

(📞 435-259-2974; www.sunflowerhill.com; 185 N 300 E; r $208-293; ✳ 🛜 ⚲) Wow! This is one of the best bets in town. A top-shelf B&B, Sunflower Hill offers 12 rooms in a quaint country setting. Grab a room in the cozier cedar-sided early-20th-century home over the annex rooms. All rooms come with quilt-piled beds and antiques – some even have jetted tubs.

Sorrel River Ranch
LODGE **$$$**

(📞 877-317-8244; www.sorrelriver.com; Mile 17, Hwy 128; r from $529; ✳ @ ⚲) Southeast Utah's only full-service luxury resort and gourmet restaurant was originally an 1803 homestead. The lodge and log cabins sit on 240 lush acres, with riding areas and alfalfa fields along the Colorado River. Details strive for rustic perfection, with bedroom fireplaces, handmade log beds, copper-top tables and Jacuzzi tubs.

Amenities include an on-site spa (open to the public), fitness facility, salon and hot tub, kitchenettes and horseback riding. Families welcome. Has a two-night minimum stay.

Best Western Plus Canyonlands Inn
MOTEL $$$

(📞435-259-2300; www.canyonlandsinn.com; 16 S Main St; r from $278; ❄📶🏊) A comfortable choice at the central crossroads of downtown, this independently owned hotel features ginormous rooms, fitness center, laundry, playground and outdoor pool. It's a little removed from Main St, but you still get a hint of noise.

Red Cliffs Lodge
LODGE $$$

(📞435-259-5050; www.redcliffslodge.com; Mile 14, Hwy 128; ste/cabin $240/340; ❄📶🏊🐕) Dude ranch meets deluxe motel. These comfortable rooms feature vaulted knotty-pine ceilings, kitchenettes with dining tables, and private (though cramped) patios, some overlooking the Colorado River. Larger rooms are ideal for families. Also offers horseback riding and a hot tub, an on-site movie museum for Western buffs and wine tasting. Pets are allowed and horse boarding is available.

Camping

Up the Creek Campground
CAMPGROUND $

(📞435-260-1888; www.moabupthecreek.com; 210 E 300 S; tent sites 1/2 people $25/32; ⊙Mar-Oct) There's something about this shady, tent-only grove with flower beds, lush lawns and recycling that fosters a sense of community. The 20 sites are within walking distance of downtown. Showers are included, but are also available to nonguests for $6; no fires.

Goose Island Campground
CAMPGROUND $

(www.blm.gov; Hwy 128; campsites $15) Ten no-reservation riverside BLM campgrounds lie along a 28-mile stretch of Hwy 128 that parallels the Colorado River northwest of town. The 19-site Goose Island, just 1.4 miles from Moab, is the closest. Pit toilets, no water.

ℹ️ SHOWERING ESSENTIALS

Area BLM, national and state park campgrounds do not have showers. You can wash up at several in-town campgrounds, at the **Moab Arts & Recreation Center** (📞435-259-6272; www.moabrecreation.com; 111 E 100 N; ♿) and at biking outfitter **Poison Spider Bicycles** (p369), for a fee (around $6).

Canyonlands Campground
CAMPGROUND $

(📞435-259-6848; www.canyonlandsrv.com; 555 S Main St; tent sites $36-40, RV sites with hookups $55, camping cabins $81; ⊙year-round; ❄📶🏊) Old-growth-tree-shaded sites, right in town but still quiet. Includes showers, laundry, store, small pool and playground. Rates are slightly higher for events and holidays.

🍴 Eating

There's no shortage of places to fuel up in Moab, from backpacker coffeehouses to gourmet dining rooms. Pick up the *Moab Menu Guide* (www.moabmenuguide.com) at area lodgings. Some restaurants close or operate on variable days, from December through March.

⭐ Milt's
BURGERS $

(📞435-259-7424; 356 Mill Creek Dr; mains $4-9; ⊙11am-8pm Mon-Sat) Meet greasy goodness. A triathlete couple bought this classic 1954 burger stand and smartly changed nothing. Heaven is one of their honest burgers made from grass-fed wagyu beef, jammed with pickles, fresh lettuce, a side of fresh-cut fries and creamy butterscotch milkshake. Be patient: the line can get long. It's near the Slickrock Trail (p368).

EklectiCafé
AMERICAN $

(352 N Main St; breakfast & sandwiches $5-10; ⊙7am-2:30pm Mon-Sat, to 1pm Sun; 📶🐕) Soy-ginger-seaweed scrambled eggs anyone? This wonderfully quirky cafe lives up to its eclectic name with its food choice and decor. Come for organic coffee, curried wraps and vegetarian salads. Dinner served some weekend evenings.

Jailhouse Café
BREAKFAST $

(101 N Main St; breakfast $11-14; ⊙7am-noon Mar-Oct) The eggs Benedict here is hard to beat but the line goes deep on weekends. Wholegrain waffles and ginger pancakes are other temptations. In a former jailhouse, with patio seating.

Fiesta Mexicana
MEXICAN $

(📞435-259-4366; 202 S Main St; mains $8-17; ⊙11am-10pm) With dark pleather booths, fishbowl margaritas and some competent delivery of the usual suspects, this regional chain restaurant is not a bad choice. Our favorites are the chicken mole enchiladas and *carne asada*, grilled skirt steak served with plenty of onion and guacamole. The service couldn't be friendlier.

Crystal's Cakes and Cones ICE CREAM $
(☑435-259-9393; www.crystalscakesandcones.
com; 26 Center St; ice cream $2-5; ⊘noon-9pm)
For a little piece of Americana, queue up at
this popular ice creamery. Though the ice
cream isn't locally made, local teenagers
serve ever-growing lines with a smile.

Twisted Sistas CAFE $$
(☑435-355-0088; 11 E 100 N; lunch $11-13, mains
$16-30; ⊘noon-3pm & 5-9pm Fri-Tue, 5-9pm Thu;
⊅) For a calm alternative to the breweries,
this low-lit cafe delivers warm ambience,
attentive service and tasty food inspired by
global flavors. For lighter fare, try the tapas,
such as stuffed piquillo peppers and lollipop
chicken. There's also a full bar. Check out the
rooftop patio.

Sabaku Sushi SUSHI $$
(☑435-259-4455; www.sabakusushi.com; 90 E
Center St; rolls $6-11, mains $13-19; ⊘5pm-mid-
night Tue-Sun) The ocean is about a million
miles away, but with overnight delivery from
Hawaii, you still get a creative selection of
fresh rolls, catches of the day and a few Utah
originals at this small hole-in-the-wall sushi
joint. Go for happy hour (5pm to 6pm on
Wednesdays and Thursdays) for discounts
on rolls.

Stick with the status quo with traditional
sashimi and *nigiri* offerings or get adventurous with the lip-smacking Elk Tataki and
Devil's Garden Roll (topped with a pineap-
ple habanero sauce).

Arches Thai THAI $$
(☑435-355-0533; 60 N 100 W; mains $8-21;
⊘11am-9pm Wed-Mon; ⊅) This large, new dining room is geared up to serve, with a pleasant, ample space and good-value lunches
that come with soup and crab wontons.
With options for tofu, seafood or organic
chicken in typical curries and noodle dishes.
Also serves Vietnamese pho.

Cowboy Grill AMERICAN $$
(☑435-259-2002; redcliffslodge.com; Hwy 128,
Mile 14, Red Cliffs Lodge; breakfast & lunch $10-16,
dinner mains $14-32; ⊘6:30-10am, 11:30am-2pm
& 5-10pm) Incredible sunset Colorado River
views are to be had from the patio or from
behind the huge picture windows here. Oh,
and the hearty, all-American meat and seafood dishes are also quite good.

Paradox Pizza PIZZA $$
(☑435-259-9999; 729 S Main St; pizzas $14-23;
⊘shop 11am-10pm, delivery 4-10pm) You may
want to order your scrumptious locally
sourced and organically oriented pizzas
to go; the dining area is kinda small and
generic. There are also salads and huge portions of tiramisu.

Eddie McStiff's AMERICAN $$
(www.eddiemcstiffs.com; 59 S Main St; mains $10-20;
⊘11:30am-midnight, to 1am Fri & Sat; ☎) Though
it's as much taproom-bar as restaurant, the
burgers and pizzas (gluten-free available)
are almost as popular as the beer here. Salad
topped with grilled salmon hits the right note
after too many burgers on the road. Occasional live music brightens the night.

Singha Thai THAI $$
(☑435-259-0039; 92 E Center St; mains $14-18;
⊘11am-3pm & 5-9:30pm Mon-Sat, 5-9:30pm Sun;
⊅) Ethnic food is as rare as rain in these
parts, so locals pile into this authentic Thai
cafe for curries and organic basil chicken.
Service is sleepy and the ambience generic,
but if you're hot for spice, it delivers.

★ Desert Bistro SOUTHERN US $$$
(☑435-259-0756; www.desertbistro.com; 36 S 100
W; mains $20-60; ⊘5:30-11pm Wed-Sun) Stylized
preparations of game and fresh, flown-in
seafood are the specialty at this welcoming
white-tablecloth restaurant inside an old
house. Think smoked elk in a huckleberry
glaze, pepper-seared scallops and jicama
salad with crisp pears. Everything is made
onsite, from freshly baked bread to delicious
pastries. Great wine list, too.

Jeffrey's Steakhouse STEAK $$$
(☑435-259-3588; www.jeffreyssteakhouse.com;
218 N 100 W; mains $18-42; ⊘5-10pm) In a his-
toric sandstone house, Jeffrey's is serious
about beef, which comes grain-fed, wagyu-
style and only sometimes in generous cuts.
If the night is too good to end, head upstairs
to the upscale Ghost Bar (p378). Reservations advised.

Sorrel River Grill MODERN AMERICAN $$$
(☑435-259-4642; Hwy 128, Mile 17, Sorrel River
Ranch; breakfast $10-16, lunch $12-18, dinner $30-
50; ⊘7am-3pm & 5-10pm Mar-Oct, 8-10am &
5:30-7:30pm Nov-Feb) For romance, it's hard
to beat the wraparound verandah overlooking red-rock canyons outside Moab. Dine
on heirloom tomato soup, wedge salad and
chili-rubbed pork tenderloin served with
buttery polenta. The New American menu
changes seasonally, but expect seared steaks,

succulent rack of lamb and the freshest seafood flown in.

Self-Catering

Moab Farmers Market MARKET $
(www.moabfarmersmarket.com; 400 N 100 W;
☺5-8pm Fri May-Oct) Local farms vend their
summer produce in Swanny City Park, with
free concerts.

Moonflower Market HEALTH FOOD $
(☑435-259-5712; www.moonflower.coop; 39 E
100 N; ☺8am-8pm; ☑) Nonprofit health-food
store with great picnic supplies, including
takeout sandwiches, and loads of community info.

🍷 Drinking & Nightlife

Utah isn't known for its nightlife, though
Moab is a lively place to drink a beer and
trade tales of trail adventures. The two local
brewpub restaurants are good places to drink
and they offer food.

Ghost Bar BAR
(☑435-259-3588; 218 N 100 W; ☺7-11pm) A loungey, dime-sized jazz nook serving wine and
a full list of cocktails; upstairs at Jeffrey's
Steakhouse (p377).

Wake & Bake CAFE
(☑435-259-2420; 59 S Main St, McStiff's Plaza;
☺7am-7pm; ☎) Great vibe at this groovy cafe
next to a bookstore; ice cream and sandwiches available.

Woody's Tavern BAR
(☑435-259-3550; www.worldfamouswoodystavern.
com; 221 S Main St; ☺11am-midnight) Full bar
with pool tables and a great outdoor patio;
live music Friday and Saturday in season.

Moab Brewery BREWERY
(☑435-259-6333; www.themoabbrewery.com; 686
S Main St; ☺11:30am-11pm; ☎) Choose from
a list of nine microbrews made in the vats
just behind the bar area. The vast and varied
menu is more impressive than the food itself.
Be aware that service isn't a strong suit.

☆ Entertainment

Canyonlands by Night & Day THEATER
(☑435-259-5261, 800-394-9978; www.canyon
landsbynight.com; 1861 N Hwy 191; adult/child
$69/59; ☺Apr-Oct; ♣) Start with dinner riverside, then take an after-dark boat ride on
the Colorado, with an old-fashioned light
show complete with historical narration. It
also offers day tours and magic shows.

Slickrock Cinemas 3 CINEMA
(☑435-259-4441; 580 Kane Creek Blvd) First-run
movies.

🛍 Shopping

Every few feet along downtown's Main St,
there's a shop selling T-shirts and American
Indian–esque knickknacks, but there are
some good galleries among the mix.

Every second Saturday in spring and fall
there's an evening artwalk that includes
artists' receptions; contact the Moab Arts
Council (www.moabartscouncil.org) for
more information.

Gear Heads Outdoor Store SPORTS & OUTDOORS
(☑888-740-4327, 435-259-4327; www.gearhead
outfitters.com; 471 S Main St; ☺8:30am-6pm)
Stock up on all the outdoor gear you need,
including climbing ropes, route guides,
books and water-jug refills. The knowledgeable staff are quite helpful.

Back of Beyond Books BOOKS
(☑435-259-5154; www.backofbeyondbooks.com;
83 N Main St; ☺9am-6pm; ☎) Excellent indie
bookstore with extensive regional and natural history selection and topographic maps.

ℹ Information

EMERGENCY
Cell phones work in town, but not in canyons or
the parks.
Grand County Emergency Coordinator
(☑435-259-8115) Search and rescue.
Police (☑911; 217 E Center St)

INTERNET ACCESS
Grand County Public Library (www.
moablibrary.org; 257 E Center St; ☺9am-8pm
Mon-Fri, to 5pm Sat; ☎) Easy 15-minute free
internet; register for longer access.

MEDICAL SERVICES
Moab Regional Hospital (☑435-719-3500;
mrhmoab.org; 450 W Williams Way) A major
regional facility with level IV trauma care.

ℹ WATER REFILLING STATIONS

In addition to the water stations at area
national park visitor centers, you can
refill your jugs for free at Gear Heads
Outdoor Store. Alternatively, go to the
natural, outdoor tap at **Matrimony
Springs** (Hwy 128).

Moab Happenings (www.moabhappenings.
com) is a free publication also available online
with events listings.

BLM Office (☑ 435-259-2100; www.blm.gov/
ut/st/en/fo/moab.html; 82 E Dogwood Ave;
⊙7:45am-4:30pm Mon-Fri) While most people
head to the visitor center, you can get pamphlets and ask about basic camping and BLM
use issues here.

Canyonlands Natural History Association
(☑ 435-259-6003, 800-840-8978; www.cnha.
org; 3031 S Hwy 191; ⊙8am-7pm) Sells area-
interest books and maps online, and at national
park visitor centers.

Moab Information Center (www.
discovermoab.com; 25 E Center St; ⊙8am-
7pm; 🛜) Excellent source of information on
area parks, trails, activities, camping and
weather. Extensive bookstore and knowledgeable staff. Walk-in only.

National Park Service Passes (p359) Park
service passes can be purchased at any park
entry station or at the information center in
Moab.

ℹ Getting There & Around

Moab is 235 miles southeast of Salt Lake City,
150 miles northeast of Capitol Reef National
Park, and 115 miles southwest of Grand Junction, CO.

    Canyonlands Airport (CNY; www.
moabairport.com; off Hwy 191), 16 miles north of
town, receives flights from Salt Lake City. Major
car-rental agencies, such as **Enterprise** (☑ 435-
259-8505; N Hwy 191, Mile 148; ⊙8am-5pm
Mon-Fri, to 2pm Sat), have representatives at
the airport.

    Boutique Air (☑ 855-268-8478; www.
boutiqueair.com) flies to Salt Lake City and
Denver.

    There are also limited bus and shuttle van ser-
vices, including **Elevated Transit** (☑ 888-353-
8283; www.elevatedtransit.com; Moab to Salt
Lake City airport $70) and **Moab Luxury Coach**
(☑ 435-940-4212; www.moabluxurycoach.com;
3320 E Fairway Loop) to get you to Salt Lake
City, Grand Junction, Colorado and regional
destinations.

    A private vehicle is pretty much a requirement
to get around Moab and the parks.

    Vehicle traffic is heavy in high season. There
are a number of bike paths in and around town;
the Moab Information Center can offer a map
guide.

    Coyote Shuttle (☑ 435-259-8656; www.
coyoteshuttle.com) and **Roadrunner Shuttle**
(☑ 435-259-9402; www.roadrunnershuttle.
com) travel on-demand to Canyonlands Airport
and do hiker-biker and river shuttles.

Arches National Park

Giant sweeping arcs of sandstone frame
snowy peaks and desert landscapes at
Arches National Park, 5 miles north of
Moab. Explore the highest density of rock
arches anywhere on earth: more than 2500
in a 116-sq-mile area. You'll lose all perspective on size at some, such as the thin and
graceful Landscape Arch – among the largest in the world – which stretches more than
290ft across. The smallest is only 3ft across.
An easy drive makes the spectacular arches
accessible to all. Fiery Furnace (p380) is a
not-to-be-missed area of the park, though a
guided tour is required to reach it.

⊙ Sights & Activities

The **park** (☑ 435-719-2299; www.nps.gov/arch;
Hwy 191; 7-day pass per vehicle $25; ⊙24hr, visitor
center 7:30am-6:30pm Mar-Oct, 9am-4pm Nov-
Feb) has many short hikes; the most popular
stops lie closest to the visitor center (p381).
There are also some fairly easy hikes here.
Many quick walks lead to named formations,
such as **Sand Dune Arch** (0.4-mile round-
trip) and **Broken Arch** (1-mile round-trip).

Delicate Arch   HIKING
You've seen this arch before: it's the unofficial state symbol, stamping nearly every
Utah tourist brochure. The best way to experience it is from beneath. Park near **Wolfe
Ranch**, a well-preserved 1908 pioneer cabin.
From there a footbridge crosses **Salt Wash**
(near American Indian rock art) and marks
the beginning of the moderate-to-strenuous,
3-mile round-trip trail to the arch itself.

Devils Garden Trail   HIKING
At the paved road's end, 19 miles from the
visitor center (p381), Devils Garden trailhead
marks the beginning of a 2- to 7.7-mile round-
trip hike that passes eight arches. Most people only go 1.3 miles to **Landscape Arch**, a
gravity-defying, 290ft-long behemoth. Further along, the trail gets less crowded, growing rougher and steeper toward **Double O
Arch** and **Dark Angel Spire**.

Windows Trail   HIKING
Tight on time? Do part or all of this easy
1-mile round-trip, which brings you up to
North Window, where you can look out to
the canyon beyond. Continue on to **South
Window** and the castle-like **Turret Arch**.
Don't forget to see **Double Arch**, just across
the parking lot.

Arches National Park

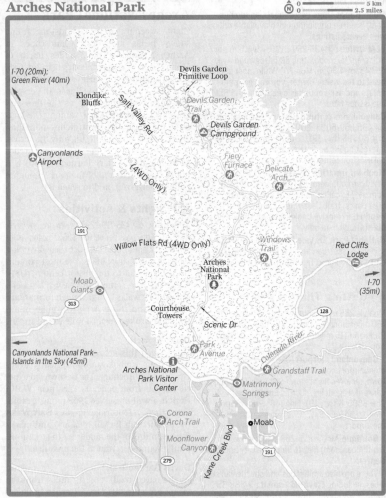

Fiery Furnace HIKING
(www.nps.gov/arch/planyourvisit/fiery-furnace.
htm; permits adult/child $6/3; ☉ Mar-Oct)
This narrow sandstone labyrinth with no
marked trails provides an extra level of
adventure for visitors. Due to the extreme
nature of hiking here, permits (available
at the Arches visitor center) are required.
Otherwise, paid ranger-led walking tours
are offered from April through September.
These tours run 2½ to three hours and are
generally offered twice daily (morning and
afternoon).

Bar-M Loop MOUNTAIN BIKING
Bring the kids on this easy, 8-mile loop skirting the boundary of Arches, with great views
and short slickrock stretches. Connect from
here to the more advanced Moab Brands
trails.

Scenic Driving Tour

The park's one main road snakes up ancient
Navajo sandstone, past many trailheads
and incredible formations, such as Park
Avenue, a mile-long trail past a giant fin of
rock reminiscent of a New York skyline, and
Balanced Rock, a 3577-ton boulder sitting

atop a spindly pedestal, like a fist shooting out of the earth. Don't miss the two small spur roads that veer off to the west (43 miles round-trip in total). Use the park map received on entry to navigate.

Rock Climbing

Rock climbing is allowed only on unnamed features. Routes require advanced techniques. No permits are necessary, but ask rangers about current regulations and route closures. For guided canyoneering into the Fiery Furnace, contact an outfitter in Moab.

🛏 Sleeping

There's stiff competition for camping in the park but there are plenty of campgrounds throughout the region and lodging galore in Moab. Moab is also the place to stock up on food – none is available in the park.

Devils Garden Campground CAMPGROUND $
(📞877-444-6777; www.recreation.gov; tent & RV sites $25) Surrounded by red rock and scrubby piñons, the park's only campground is 19 miles from the visitor center. From March to October, sites are available by reservation. Book months ahead.

ℹ Information

Crowds are often unavoidable, and parking areas overflow on weekends, spring to fall. In summer arrive by 9am, when crowds are sparse and temperatures bearable, or visit after 7pm and enjoy a moonlight stroll. July highs average 100°F (38°C); carry at least 1 gallon of water per person if hiking. Two rugged back roads lead into semi-solitude, but 4WD is recommended – ask at the visitor center.

Arches canyoneering and climbing permits are available online (archespermits.nps.gov) or through the **Arches National Park Visitor Center** (www.nps.gov/arch; 7-day pass per vehicle/motorcycle/bike $25/15/10; ⊗9am-4pm). While there, watch the informative video, check ranger-led activity schedules and pick up your Fiery Furnace tickets. **The Grand County Emergency Coordinator** (📞435-259-8115) carries out search and rescue operations.

ℹ Getting There & Around

Several outfitters in Moab run motorized park tours. **Moab Adventure Center** (p373) and **Adrift Adventures** (p371). **Tag-A-Long Expeditions** (📞800-453-3292; www.tagalong.com; 452 N Main St; ⊗7am-4pm) has scenic-drive van tours; it also ventures into the backcountry.

Green River

📍435 / POP 929

Hugging the interstate, Green River offers more utility than charm, but its cheap motels and uncrowded restaurants can be a relief if you're coming from Moab. It's also a useful base for boating the Green River or exploring parts of the San Rafael Swell.

The Colorado and Green Rivers were first explored in 1869 and 1871 by the legendary one-armed Civil War veteran, geologist and ethnologist John Wesley Powell. The town was settled in 1878, and now mainly relies on the limited tourism for income. Moab is 53 miles southeast.

If you're passing through on the third weekend in September, be sure to attend the Melon Days festival – this is, after all, the 'world's watermelon capital.'

◎ Sights

Outside of town there's an unpredictable geyser, and fossil track sites; ask at the visitor center (p383) for directions.

Green River State Park PARK
(www.stateparks.utah.gov; Green River Blvd; per car $5; ⊗6am-10pm Mar-Oct, 8am-5pm Nov-Feb) Shady Green River State Park has picnic tables, a boat launch and a nine-hole golf course, but no trails.

John Wesley Powell River History Museum MUSEUM
(📞435-564-3427; www.jwprhm.com; 885 E Main St; adult/child $6/2; ⊗9am-7pm Mon-Sat, noon-5pm Sun Apr-Oct, 9am-5pm Nov-Mar) Learn about John Wesley Powell's amazing travels at this comprehensive museum, with a 20-minute film based on his diaries. It has good exhibits on the Fremont Indians, geology and local history.

🏃 Activities

White-water rafting trips are the most popular, but the Green River is flat between the town and the confluence of the Colorado River, making it good for floats and do-it-yourself canoeing. The current, however, is deceptively strong – swim only with a life jacket.

★**Little Wild Horse Canyon** HIKING
This canyon 7 miles west of Goblin Valley is suitable for beginners, offering plenty of serpentine twists that can be combined with a return via Bell Canyon on an 8.2-mile circuit.

WORTH A TRIP

GOBLIN VALLEY STATE PARK

A Salvador Dalí–esque melted-rock fantasy, a valley of giant stone mushrooms, an otherworldly alien landscape or the results of a cosmological acid trip? No matter what you think the stadium-like valley of stunted hoodoos resembles, one thing's for sure – the 3654-acre **Goblin Valley State Park** (☏435-275-4584; www.stateparks.utah.gov/parks/goblin-valley; Goblin Valley Rd, off Hwy 24; per car $13; ⊙park 6am-10pm, visitor center 8am-5pm) is just plain fun.

A few trails lead down from the overlooks to the valley floor, but after that there's no path to follow. You can climb down, around and even over the evocative 'goblins' (2ft- to 20ft-tall formations). Kids and photographers especially love it.

Its 19-site **campground** (☏800-322-3770; utahstateparks.reserveamerica.com; tent & RV sites $25, yurt $80) books up on most weekends. West of the park off Goblin Valley Rd is BLM land, with good, free dispersed camping, but no services (stay on designated roads).

Twenty miles further south on Hwy 24 is Hanksville (population 350, elevation 4300ft); if you don't need gas, there's little reason to stop. It's better to stay in Green River, Torrey or at Lake Powell, depending on where you're headed. The BLM Field Office has maps and information for surrounding lands, particularly the Henry Mountains. Before continuing south, fill up your car and carry your own food and water. There are no more services until you get to Bullfrog Marina (70 miles) or Mexican Hat (130 miles).

It's 1½ hours west of Green River via I-70 and Hwy 24.

Holiday River Expeditions RAFTING
(☏800-624-6323, 435-564-3273; www.holiday expeditions.com; 10 Holiday River St; day trip $190) Offers multiday rafting tours on the Green and Yampa Rivers and day trips through Westwater on the Green; themed trips (naturalist, women-only, mountain biking etc) are available.

🛏 Sleeping

Midrange chain motels are surprisingly well represented along Business 70 (Main St).

Green River State Park CAMPGROUND $
(☏800-322-3770; utahstateparks.reserveamerica. com; tent/RV sites $21/30, cabins $60) Though the 42 green and shady campsites and few cabins in this riverfront park are open year-round, the restrooms are closed December through February. Water, showers and boat launch on site; no hookups.

Robbers Roost Motel MOTEL $
(☏435-564-3452; www.rrmotel.com; 325 W Main St; r from $58; ❄🐾🌐) A steal, with super-clean rooms and accommodating staff. Small-and-simple budget rooms are well cared for.

River Terrace Inn MOTEL $$
(☏435-564-3401, 877-564-3401; www.river-terrace.com; 1880 E Main St; r $116-120; ❄🌐🏊) Ask for a riverfront room, with a terrace overlooking the water. Rooms are well-kept and the swimming pool is a godsend on hot days.

🍴 Eating & Drinking

Green River restaurants are unremarkable but you can stock up at the grocery store and buy fresh watermelon from roadside stands in summer. Stop by Ray's Tavern for some very local nightlife.

Green River Coffee Co CAFE $
(☏435-817-6343; 115 W Main St; breakfast & lunch sandwiches $5-8; ⊙8am-2pm; 🛜) As the sign says, 'We're open when we're here.' Drop in and discuss politics with the local coffee circle, grab a sandwich on thick-sliced wheat bread peppered with veggies, or catch up on your used-book reading at this super-relaxed coffeehouse.

Melon Vine Food Store MARKET $
(☏435-564-3228; 76 S Broadway; ⊙8am-7pm Mon-Sat) Grocery store; deli sandwiches available.

Ray's Tavern BURGERS $$
(☏435-564-3511; 25 S Broadway; dishes $8-27; ⊙11am-9:30pm) Residents and rafters alike flock to this regionally famous local beer joint for the best hamburgers and fresh-cut French fries around. The steaks aren't bad, either. Pass the time reading the displayed T-shirts donated by river runners from around the world, or have a game of pool with a Utah microbrew in hand.

ℹ️ Information

Since it's near the Colorado border, there are helpful park and regional information centers here. Stop in before you continue on.

Emery County Visitor Center (☑435-564-3600, 888-564-3600; www.emerycounty.com/travel; 885 E Main St; ⊙8am-8pm Mar-Oct, 8am-4pm Tue-Sun Nov-Feb) Attached to the local museum, pick up info and river guidebooks and maps here.

ℹ️ Getting There & Away

Green River is 182 miles southeast of Salt Lake City and 53 miles northwest of Moab. It is the only town of note along I-70 between Salina, UT (108 miles west), and Grand Junction, CO (102 miles east) – so fuel up.

Green River is the only stop in southeastern Utah on the daily **Amtrak** (☑800-872-7245; www.amtrak.com; 250 S Broadway) *California Zephyr* train run. Next stop east is Denver, CO (10¾ hours).

As it sits on the I-70, Green River has better bus connections than most towns.

Moab Luxury Coach (☑435-940-4212; 525 E Main St, Rodeway Inn) operates a scheduled van service to and from Salt Lake City (3½ hours) and Moab (one hour).

Greyhound (☑435-564-3421, 800-231-2222; www.greyhound.com; 525 E Main St, Rodeway Inn; 🛜) buses go to Grand Junction, CO ($28, one hour and 40 minutes) with wi-fi on board.

Glen Canyon National Recreation Area & Lake Powell

In the 1960s the construction of a massive dam flooded Glen Canyon, forming Lake Powell, a recreational playground. Almost 50 years later this is still an environmental hot-button topic, but generations of Western families have grown up boating here. Water laps against stunning, multihued cliffs that rise hundreds of feet; narrow channels and tributary canyons twist off in every direction.

Lake Powell stretches for more than 185 miles, surrounded by millions of acres of desert incorporated into the Glen Canyon National Recreation Area. Most of the watery way lies within Utah. However, Glen Canyon Dam itself, the main Glen Canyon National Recreation Area visitor center, the largest and most developed marina (Wahweap) and the biggest lakeside town (Page) are all in Arizona.

⊙ Sights

Grand Gulch Primitive Area   PARK
(www.blm.gov) Popular with backcountry hikers, this BLM-administered area also contains hundreds of Ancestral Puebloan sites, many of which have been vandalized by pot hunters. (It bears repeating that all prehistoric sites are protected by law, and authorities are cracking down on offenders.) Some hikes require permits due to their fragility and popularity. With little to no trail signage and some tough terrain, it's best for experienced hikers.

Rainbow Bridge National Monument   PARK
(☑928-608-6200, tours 928-645-2433; www.nps.gov/rabr) Rainbow Bridge is the largest natural bridge in the world, at 290ft high and 275ft wide. A sacred Navajo site, it resembles the graceful arc of a rainbow. Most visitors arrive by boat (www.lakepowell.com), with a 2-mile round-trip hike. The natural monument is located on the south shore of Lake Powell, about 50 miles by water from Wahweap Marina in Arizona.

Halls Crossing   MARINA
(☑435-684-7000) Connects to Bullfrog Marina by 30-minute ferry. On Lake Powell's east shore, 238 miles from Page.

🏃 Activities

Bullfrog Marina   BOATING
(☑435-684-3000; www.lakepowell.com; Hwy 276; 3-day houseboat rentals from $1896; ⊙9am-4pm Mar-Oct; 🛝) Rents out boats – 19ft runabouts and personal watercraft by the day, but houseboats are its big business. You can rent a 46ft boat that sleeps 12 for a minimum of three days; weekly rates are cheaper. There are also luxury options. Invest in the waterproof Lake Powell Photomap so you can pilot your craft to some great canyon hikes.

🛏️ Sleeping & Eating

There are campgrounds and a few lodges. Demand is high in peak season. There are a few restaurants but bringing your own provisions is necessary to fill in the gaps, particularly if you are houseboating.

Lone Rock Beach   CAMPGROUND $
(Utah Hwy 89; sites $20; 🛝) A strikingly beautiful natural setting on the edge of Lake Powell is the home of this sprawling first-come, first-served campground. It's a popular spot with families and college revelers alike in high season – escape to the dunes or the far

edges of the lot if you're looking for quiet. It's just north of the state line, 2 miles south of Big Water.

Halls Crossing Campground CAMPGROUND $
(☑ 435-684-7008; www.lakepowell.com/rv-camping/halls-crossing-rv-campground; tent & RV sites $47; ☺ Mar-Oct; 🐾) Offers 21 pull-through spaces (with hookups) and 41 campsites with showers, grills and restrooms. Pets must be on a leash.

Ticaboo Lodge MOTEL $
(☑ 435-788-2110; www.ticaboo.com; Hwy 276; r $89; ☺ May-Sep; 🛜🏊) Inland 12 miles or so from Bullfrog Marina (p383), Ticaboo Lodge is a fine money-saving sleeping alternative with a three-meal-a-day restaurant and bar attached. The big, interior-access motel rooms all have two queen beds and are quite tidy.

Defiance House Lodge HOTEL $$
(☑ 435-684-3000; www.lakepowell.com; Hwy 276; r $145-169; ☺ Mar-Oct; ❄🛜) Modern, attractive rooms and killer views characterize this hotel sitting pretty in Glen Canyon National Recreation Area's Bullfrog Marina (p383). It has modern amenities and an in-house restaurant.

Anasazi Restaurant AMERICAN $$
(Hwy 276; breakfast $8-12, mains $10-28; ☺ 7am-10pm Mar-Oct) Anasazi serves pretty standard all-American fare (think meatloaf, tacos, sandwiches and pizza), but it does try to use local produce and sustainable practices.

ℹ Information

Find information at the **Kane Gulch Ranger Station** (Hwy 261; day/overnight permit $2/8; ☺ 8am-noon Mar–mid-Nov) or **Big Water Visitor Center** (☑ 435-675-3200; 100 Upper Revolution Way, Big Water; ☺ 9am-5:30pm Apr-Oct, 8am-4:30pm Tue-Sat Nov-Mar) near Lake Powell.

The **Bullfrog Visitor Center** (☑ 435-684-7423; ☺ 9am-5pm May-Aug) offers great general information.

ℹ Getting There & Around

Access is via private vehicle. To continue driving south on Hwy 276, take the **ferry** (☑ 435-893-4747; www.lakepowell.com; pedestrian/cyclist/car $10/15/25; ☺ closed Dec-Feb) to Halls Crossing. Be aware that the marinas and ferry service can close when there are low water levels.

Dangling Rope Smallest marina, accessible only by boat. Forty lake-miles from Page.

Halls Crossing (p383) Connects to Bullfrog Marina by 30-minute ferry. On Lake Powell's east shore, 238 miles from Page.

Hite May be closed due to low water levels. At Lake Powell's north end, 148 lake-miles from Page.

ZION & SOUTHWESTERN UTAH

Wonder at the deep-crimson canyons of Zion National Park; hike among the delicate pink-and-orange minarets at Bryce Canyon; drive past the swirling gray-white-and-purple mounds of Capitol Reef. Southwestern Utah is so spectacular that the vast majority of the territory has been preserved as national park or forest, state park or BLM wilderness. Rugged and remote Grand Staircase–Escalante National Monument (GSENM) is larger than Rhode Island and Delaware put together. The whole area is ripe for outdoor exploration, with narrow slot canyons to shoulder through, pink sand dunes to scale and wave-like sandstone formations to seek out.

Note that getting to some of the most noteworthy sites can be quite an uphill hike, and elevation changes in the region – mountainous highs to desert lows – pose a weather challenge. But any effort you make usually more than pays off with a stunning view of our eroding and ever-changing earth.

Capitol Reef National Park

American Indians once called this colorful landscape (☑ ext 4111 435-425-3791; www.nps.gov/care; cnr Hwy 24 & Scenic Dr; admission free, 7-day scenic drive per vehicle $10, tent & RV sites $20; ☺ 24hr, visitor center & scenic drive 8am-6pm Apr-Oct, to 4:30pm Nov-Mar) of tilted buttes, jumbled rocks and sedimentary canyons the Land of the Sleeping Rainbow. The park's centerpiece is Waterpocket Fold, a 100-mile-long monocline (a buckle in the earth's crust) that blocked explorers' westward migration as a reef blocks a ship's passage. Known also for its enormous domes – one of which echoes Washington, DC's Capitol Dome – Capitol Reef harbors fantastic hiking trails, rugged 4WD roads and 1000-year-old Fremont petroglyph panels. At the park's heart grow the shady orchards of Fruita (p387), a Mormon settlement dating back to the 1870s. Most services, including Torrey, 11 miles west.

Southwestern Utah

50 km
25 miles

N

Burr Point

Hanksville

Henry Mountains

Capitol Reef National Park

Notom-Bullfrog Rd

Burr Trail Rd

Circle Cliffs

Burr Trail Switchbacks

Ticaboo

276

95

24

Bullfrog Marina
Hell's Crossing
Bullfrog Marina

Lake Powell

Glen Canyon National Recreation Area

Navajo Mtn (10,388ft)

Hole-in-the-Rock

Navajo Indian Reservation

Torrey
Teasdale
Bicknell
Loa
72
24

Aquarius Plateau

Boulder Mountain (3449ft)

Anasazi State Park
Boulder
Calf Creek Recreation Area

Escalante River

Dry Fork

Hole-in-the-Rock Rd

Escalante
Natural Bridge

Devils Garden

Smoky Mountain Rd

Colorado River

Lake Powell

Page

Otter Creek Reservoir

Dixie National Forest

Hell's Backbone Rd

Upper Calf Creek Falls

Escalante Petrified Forest State Park

Escalante River Canyon

Grosvenor Arch

Grand Staircase-Escalante National Monument

Alstrom Point

Big Water

Piute State Park
Piute Reservoir

62

Circleville

Dixie National Forest

Canyon City
Tropic

Cannonville
Kodachrome Basin State Park

Paria River

Cottonwood Canyon Rd

Lower Hackberry

Paria Contact Station

89

62

Red Canyon

Bryce Canyon National Park

Pahreah (Ghost Town)

Grosvenor Arch

Paria Canyon-Vermilion Cliffs Wilderness Area

Beaver
153

89

12

143

Panguitch

Panguitch Lake

Skutumpah Rd

White Cliffs

Vermilion Cliffs

Buckskin Gulch

The Wave
Wire Pass

15

22

Minersville

130

Parowan

Brian Head

Cedar Breaks National Monument

Pink Cliffs

Johnson Canyon Rd

Kanab

89 89A

Milford
21

Hatch

Navajo Lake
Duck Creek Village

Glendale

Mt Carmel
Orderville
Mt Carmel Junction

14

143

148

(closed in winter)

Zion National Park

Coral Pink Sand Dune State Park

Kalbab-Palute Indian Reservation

Cedar City

56

Mt Carmel
Springdale
Rockville

9

59

Hildale
Colorado City

389

Kaibab-Paiute Indian Reservation

Escalante Desert

Indian Peak Range

Enterprise Reservoir

Modena
56

Pine Valley Mountain Wilderness

Silver Reef (ghost town)

Leeds
Virgin

Hurricane
Washington

9

Central
Veyo

18

Snow Canyon State Park

Mountain Meadows Massacre Monument

St George
Santa Clara
Ivins

15

Paiute Shivwits IR

Las Vegas (95mi)

Nevada

Arizona

Capitol Reef National Park

UTAH CAPITOL REEF NATIONAL PARK

N
0   20 km
0   10 miles

Cathedral Valley

Caineville Wash Rd

Hartnet Rd

Waterpocket Fold

6
10

Cathedral Valley Loop

Caineville

Fremont River

24

Torrey

2
1
3
8
7
Visitor Center
5

Scenic Dr

4

Pleasant Cr

Capitol Reef National Park

Notom-Bullfrog Rd

Dixie National Forest

Henry Mountains

12

11

Bitter Creek Divide (5650ft)

9

Burr Trail Rd

Boulder

Boulder Mail

Upper Muley Twist Canyon Trailhead

Lower Muley Twist Canyon Trailhead

Deer Creek

The Gulch

Calf Creek

Waterpocket Fold

Bryce Canyon National Park (40mi)

Escalante River

Hole-in-the-Rock Rd

Grand Staircase–Escalante National Monument

Glen Canyon National Recreation Area

Capitol Reef National Park

The narrow park runs north–south following the Waterpocket Fold. A little over 100 miles southwest of Green River, Hwy 24 traverses the park. Capitol Reef's central region is the Fruita Historic District. To the far north lies Cathedral Valley, the least-visited section; toward the south you can cross over into Grand Staircase–Escalante National Monument (p394) on the Burr Trail Rd.

◎ Sights & Activities

There's no fee to enter or traverse the park in general, but the Scenic Dr has an admission fee. For backcountry hikes, ask for pamphlets at the visitor center or check online. Ranger Rick Stinchfield's *Capitol Reef National Park: The Complete Hiking and Touring Guide* is also a great reference.

Fruita Historic District HISTORIC SITE
(☑ fruit hotline 435-425-3791) Fruita (*froo*-tuh) is a cool, green oasis, where shade-giving cottonwoods and fruit-bearing trees line the Fremont River's banks. The first Mormon homesteaders arrived here in 1880; Fruita's final resident left in 1969. Among the historic buildings, the NPS maintains 2700 cherry, apricot, peach, pear and apple trees planted by early settlers. Visit between June and October to pluck ripe fruit from the trees, for free, from any unlocked orchard. For availability, ask rangers or call the fruit hotline.

Pick only mature fruit; leave the rest to ripen. Near the orchards is a wonderful picnic area, with roaming deer and birds in the trees – a desert rarity. Across the road from the blacksmith shop (just a shed with period equipment) is the **Ripple Rock Nature Center** (⊙ 1-5pm Wed-Sun late May–mid-Aug; ⚐) **FREE**, a family-oriented learning center. The **Gifford Homestead** (⊙ 8am-5pm Mar-Oct) is an old homestead museum where you can also buy ice cream, Scottish scones or salsas and preserves made from the orchard fruit. Don't skip purchasing one of its famous pies – up to 13 dozen are sold daily (and they usually run out!).

Panorama Point &
Gooseneck Overlook VIEWPOINT
Two miles west of the visitor center off Hwy 24, a short, unpaved road heads to Panorama Point and Gooseneck Overlook. The dizzying 800ft-high viewpoints above serpentine Sulphur Creek are worth a stop. Afternoon light is best for photography.

Capitol Reef Scenic Drive SCENIC DRIVE
(7-day pass per vehicle/person $5/3) This rolling, mostly paved drive along the **Waterpocket Fold** is a geology diorama come to life, with arches, hoodoos, canyon narrows and other unique features easily within view, plus day-hiking opportunities, too. The best of the route is its last 2 miles between the narrow sandstone walls of Capitol Gorge. It'll knock your socks off.

Pay admission at the visitor center or self-service kiosk. The 9.3-mile road starts at the Scenic Dr fee station, just south of Fruita Campground. Pick up a self-guided driving-tour brochure or audio CD; online visit www.nps.gov/care/planyourvisit/scenicdrive.htm. To continue south past Pleasant Creek, a 4WD vehicle is advised.

Fremont River Guides FISHING
(☑ 435-491-0242; www.flyfishingsouthernutah.com; PO Box 186, Bicknell; half-/full-day trips from $225/350) Go fishing on the Fremont River or Boulder Mountain.

Cathedral Valley
Loop MOUNTAIN BIKING, SCENIC DRIVE
(Caineville Wash Rd) Long-distance mountain bikers and 4WDers love this 58-mile route through Cathedral Valley, starting 18.6 miles east of the visitor center. The bumpy, roughshod backcountry road explores the remote northern area of the park and its alien desert landscapes, pierced by giant

UTAH CAPITOL REEF NATIONAL PARK

sandstone monoliths eroded into fantastic shapes. Before starting, check conditions at the visitor center and purchase an interpretive route guide.

Grand Wash Trail   HIKING
Along Scenic Dr, a good dirt road leads to Grand Wash Trail (2.25 miles, easy), a flat hike between canyon walls that, at one point, tower 80 stories high but are only 15ft apart. You can follow an offshoot of level slickrock to the cool Cassidy Arch (2 miles) or continue further to link with other trails.

Notom-Bullfrog Rd   SCENIC DRIVE
This is a rough, rough road that heads south from Hwy 24 (5 miles east of the visitor center) paralleling Waterpocket Fold. Thirty-two miles south, you can turn west toward Hwy 12 and Burr Trail Rd in Grand Staircase–Escalante National Monument. Along the way, Strike Valley Overlook has one of the best comprehensive views of the Waterpocket Fold itself.

Capitol Gorge Trail   HIKING
At the end of Scenic Dr is Capitol Gorge Trail (1 mile, easy), which leads past petroglyphs. Spur trails lead to Pioneer Register, where names carved in the rock date back to 1871, and giant water pockets known as the Tanks. Look for the spur to the Golden Throne formation off Capitol Gorge Trail (another mile).

Hickman Bridge Trail   HIKING
This popular walk (1 mile, moderate) includes a canyon stretch, a stunning natural bridge and wildflowers in spring. Mornings are coolest; it starts about 2 miles east of the visitor center off Hwy 24.

🛌 Sleeping & Eating
The nearest motel lodgings are in Torrey.

The park has one large campground and several small ones. Free primitive camping is possible year-round at Cathedral Valley Campground (☎435-425-3791; www.nps.gov/care; cnr Hartnet & Cathedral Rds; ⊗year-round), at the end of River Ford Rd, and at Cedar Mesa Campground (☎435-425-3791; www.nps.gov/care; ⊗year-round), about 23 miles south along Notom-Bullfrog Rd.

Visitors can get a slice of pie or ice cream at the general store in the park; otherwise head east toward Torrey for multiple dining options.

Fruita Campground   CAMPGROUND $
(www.nps.gov/care; Scenic Dr; sites $20) This terrific 71-site campground sits under mature cottonwood trees alongside the Fremont River, surrounded by orchards. First-come, first-served sites have access to water, but no showers. Spring through fall, sites fill up early.

Duke's Slickrock   AMERICAN $
(☎435-542-3235; www.dukesslickrock.com; 275 E Hwy 24, Hanksville; mains $10-18; ⊗7am-10pm) If you're entering Capitol Reef from the east, take a lunch break at the friendliest cowboy grill this side of the swell. The food is straightforward and filling, the service is great, and there's a tipi tent site out back.

ℹ Information
➡ Occasional summer thunderstorms pose a serious risk of flash flooding. Always check weather with rangers at the visitor center.

➡ Bugs bite in May and June.

➡ Summer temperatures can exceed 100°F (38°C) at the visitor center (5400ft), but it's cooler than Moab. If it's too hot, ascend to Torrey (10°F/6°C cooler) or Boulder Mountain (30°F/17°C cooler).

➡ Remember that Capitol Reef has little shade. Drink at least one quart of water for every two hours of hiking and wear a hat.

Visitor Center (☎435-425-3791; www.nps.gov/care; cnr Hwy 24 & Scenic Dr; ⊗8am-6pm Jun-Aug, 8am-4:30pm Sep-May) Inquire about ranger-led programs, watch the short film, then ooh and aah over the 64-sq-ft park relief map, carved with dental instruments. The bookstore sells several interpretive trail and driving tour maps as well as area-interest books and guides.

Torrey
📍435 / POP 362

With shy pioneer charm and quiet streets backed by red-rock cliffs, Torrey is a relaxing stop. A former logging and ranching center, its mainstay now is outdoor tourism. Capitol Reef National Park (p384) is only 11 miles east, Grand Staircase–Escalante National Monument (p394) is 40 miles south and national forests surround the town. Summer brings a whiff of countercultural sophistication and great dining – but from November to February the town shuts down.

SCENIC DRIVE: BURR TRAIL RD

Burr Trail Rd, the region's most immediately gratifying and dramatic backcountry drive, is a comprehensive introduction to southern Utah's geology. You pass cliffs, canyons, buttes, mesas and monoliths – in colors from sandy-white to deep coral red. Sweeping curves and steep up-and-downs add to the attraction. Just past the **Deer Creek trailhead** look for the towering vertical red-rock slabs of **Long Canyon**.

Stop at the crest for views of the sheer Circle Cliffs, which hang like curtains above the undulating valley floor. Still snowcapped in summer, the Henry Mountains rise above 11,000ft on the horizon.

After 30 paved miles (1½ hours), the road becomes loose gravel as it reaches **Capitol Reef National Park** (p384) and the giant, angled buttes of hundred-mile-long **Waterpocket Fold**. The dramatic **Burr Trail Switchbacks** follow an original wagon route through this monocline. Be sure to see the switchbacks before returning to Boulder. Another option is to turn onto Notom-Bullfrog Rd and continue north to Hwy 24 (32 miles) near Torrey, or south to Glen Canyon and Lake Powell (35 miles). Note that this part of the route is rough, and not generally suited to 2WDs.

◉ Sights & Activities

Capitol Reef is the major area attraction, but there are other freely accessible public lands nearby.

Fishlake National Forest   PARK
(www.fs.usda.gov/fishlake) More than 300 miles of trails cover this mountainous forest; 4WD roads lead north of town around **Thousand Lake Mountain** (11,306ft). Hwy 72, 16 miles west of town in Loa, is a paved route through the same area. **Fish Lake**, a giant trout fishery, is 21 miles northwest of Loa, off Hwy 25. Check with the Fremont River/Loa Ranger District Office (p391) for info.

☞ Tours & Outfitters

Guides and outfitters cover the surrounding area well (Capitol Reef National Park (p384), national forest lands, Grand Staircase–Escalante National Monument (p394) and beyond).

★ Hondoo Rivers & Trails   ADVENTURE
(☑ 435-425-3519; www.hondoo.com; 90 E Main St; ☺ 8am-8pm) One of southern Utah's longest-operating backcountry guides, Hondoo specializes in horseback riding, but also offers 4X4 tours, shuttles and guided hiking trips. Half-day trips (by horse, 4X4 or foot) cost $120; full-day trips with lunch cost $150.

Capitol Reef Backcountry Outfitters   ADVENTURE
(☑ 435-425-2010; www.backcountryoutfitters.com; 875 E Hwy, junction Hwys 12 & 24) In addition to 4WD and hiking packages, Backcountry

Outfitters also rents bicycles and ATVs. Shuttles and guided bike, ATV and horseback rides are available, too.

Thousand Lakes RV Park   DRIVING
(☑ 435-425-3500, 800-355-8995; www.thousandlakesrvpark.com; 1110 W Hwy 24; Jeeps per day from $130) Rents 4WD Jeeps.

Boulder Mountain Adventures & Alpine Angler's Flyshop   FISHING
(☑ 435-425-3660; www.alpineadventuresutah.com; 310 W Main St; day trip fly-fishing $225) Guided fishing trips and multiday excursions that include both horseback riding and fishing.

☆☆ Festivals & Events

Bicknell International Film Festival   FILM
(www.thebiff.org; ☺ Jul) If you're here on the third weekend in July, don't miss the Bicknell International Film Festival, just a couple miles up Hwy 24 in Bicknell. This wacky B-movie spoof on Sundance includes films, parties, a swap meet and the 'fastest parade in America.'

⌂ Sleeping

Torrey has pleasant and varied accommodation options from basic motels to B&Bs. Camping is available in Capitol Reef National Park (p384) and in Dixie (p392) and Fishlake National Forests.

Singletree Campground   CAMPGROUND $
(☑ 877-444-6777; www.recreation.gov; Hwy 12; sites $12-26) The Fishlake National Forest runs this basic 13-site tent and RV campground at an elevation of 8600ft on forested

Boulder Mountain, 12 miles south of Torrey along Hwy 12. There's drinking water, vault toilets and an RV dump station.

Sunglow Campground
CAMPGROUND $

(☑877-444-6777; www.recreation.gov; Forest Rd 143, Bicknell; campsites $30) Often windy, this USFS campground tucked back amid red-rock cliffs has reservable tent and RV sites. It offers drinking water, picnic tables and flush toilets. Look for the turnoff from Hwy 24, just east of Bicknell.

Cowboy Homestead Cabins
CABIN $

(☑888-854-5871; www.cowboyhomesteadcabins. com; Hwy 12; cabins $89-99; ☎🐾) Rustic, pine-paneled roadside cabins with kitch-enettes, 3 miles south of Torrey. The cabins have a sofa sleeper and can sleep a family.

Austin's Chuckwagon Motel
MOTEL $

(☑435-425-3335; www.austinschuckwagonmotel. com; 12 W Main St; r $67-107, cabins $163; ☯Mar-Oct; ✳☎🏊🐾) Rustic wood buildings ring the pool and shady grounds here at the town center. Good-value-for-money motel rooms have sturdy, basic furnishings; cabins also have kitchens. The on-site general store, deli and laundromat are a bonus.

★Lodge at Red River Ranch
INN $$

(☑435-425-3322; www.redriverranch.com; 2900 W Hwy 24, Teasdale; r $179-250; @☎) In the grand tradition of Western ranches, the great room here has a three-story open-beam ceiling, timber walls and Navajo rugs. Details are flawless – from the country quilts on high-thread-count sheets to the cowboy memorabilia in the fine-dining room. Wander its 2000-plus acres, or enjoy the star-filled sky from the outdoor hot tub. No room TVs. Just west of Torrey.

★Torrey Schoolhouse B&B
B&B $$

(☑435-633-4643; www.torreyschoolhouse.com; 150 N Center St; r $120-160; ☯Apr-Oct; ✳☎) Ty Markham has done an exquisite job of bringing this rambling 1914 schoolhouse back to life as a B&B. Antiques and country elegance contrast with the fascinating black-and-white photos of classes starting from a century back. After a full gourmet breakfast you might need to laze in the garden a while before hiking.

Broken Spur Inn & Steakhouse
MOTEL $$

(☑435-425-3775; www.brokenspurinn.com; 955 E Hwy 24; r $110-125; P✳☎🏊🐾) Spacious hill-top motel rooms are set back from Torrey's

MESA FARM MARKET

Stop in Caineville at **Mesa Farm Market** (☑435-456-9146; www.mesa farmmarket.com; Hwy 24, Caineville; ☯7am-7pm Mar-Oct; ☑) 🌾 for straight-from-the-garden organic salads, juices, goat cheese and freshly baked artisan bread from an outdoor stone-hearth oven.

busy highway junction. Soak sore muscles in the glass-enclosed heated swimming pool or Jacuzzi. Has a pet fee.

Muley Twist Inn B&B
B&B $$

(☑800-530-1038, 435-425-3640; www.muleytwist inn.com; 249 W 125 S, Teasdale; r $99-150; ☯Apr-Oct; ✳☎) Set against a towering red-sandstone dome, this big wooden farmhouse with a wraparound verandah looks small. It isn't. Casual rooms at the down-to-earth inn are spacious and bright. In Teasdale, just west of Torrey.

Capitol Reef Resort
MOTEL $$

(☑435-425-3761; www.capitolreefresort.com; 2600 E Hwy 24; r $139-179, cabins & tipis from $249; P✳☎🏊) One of the closest resorts to the Capitol Reef National Park (p384), this large motel complex flirts with modern cowboy style. Tipis and Conestoga wagons offer something different (if only in theory); they're quite luxuriant. It feels somewhat corporate, but the views from the back rooms onto the red rocks are gorgeous and the outdoor heated pool has its obvious appeal.

Skyridge Inn
B&B $$

(☑435-425-3222, 877-824-1508; www.skyridgeinn. com; 950 E Hwy 24; r $125-175; ✳☎) Sitting on 75 acres, with romantic country style and gorgeous views of red rock from the porch, this farmhouse provides a relaxing retreat 1 mile east of Torrey.

🍴 Eating & Drinking

Torrey has a small selection of restaurants. The nearest **supermarket** (☑435-836-2841; www.royalsfoodtown.com; 135 S Main St, Loa; ☯7am-8pm Mon-Sat, 7am-7pm winter) is 16 miles west, in Loa.

Slacker's Burger Joint
BURGERS $

(☑435-425-3710; 165 E Main St; burgers $6-8; ☯11am-8pm Mon-Thu, to 9pm Fri & Sat) Order an old-fashioned burger (beef, chicken, pastrami or veggie), hand-cut fries (the sweet-potato version is delish) and thick milkshake (in a rainbow of cool flavors like cherry cordial), then enjoy – inside, or out at the picnic tables.

Rim Rock Patio PIZZA $
(www.therimrock.net; 2523 E Hwy 24; mains $8-12; ⊙ noon-11pm May-Oct) The best place in Torrey to drink beer also serves up good pizzas, salads, sandwiches and ice cream. Families and friends play darts or disc golf, listen to live bands and hang out.

**Austin's Chuckwagon
General Store** MARKET $
(12 W Main St; ⊙ 7am-10pm Apr-Oct) Sells camping supplies, groceries, beer and deli sandwiches to go. There's an ATM, showers and laundromat too.

Rim Rock Restaurant AMERICAN $$
(☑ 435-425-3398; www.therimrock.net; 2523 E Hwy 24; mains $15-33; ⊙ 5-9:30pm Mar-Dec) Grilled steaks, pasta and fish come with a million-dollar view of red-rock cliffs. Arrive before sunset for the best show. There's also a full bar.

Capitol Reef Cafe AMERICAN $$
(☑ 435-425-3271; www.capitolreefinn.com; 360 W Main St; breakfast & lunch $6-12, dinner mains $10-22; ⊙ 7am-9pm Apr-Oct) Whenever possible, this cozy cafe uses local and organic ingredients in its vegetable-heavy dishes. Area trout and locally made pies are a hit.

★ Cafe Diablo TEX-MEX $$$
(☑ 435-425-3070; www.cafediablo.net; 599 W Main St; lunch $10-14, dinner mains $22-40; ⊙ 11:30am-10pm mid-Apr-Oct; ☑) One of southern Utah's best, with outstanding, highly stylized Southwestern cooking, including vegetarian dishes that burst with flavor. Think stuffed poblano peppers with quinoa and red chili mole (a sauce of complex spices), Mayan tamales and ribs with pomegranate-chipotle glaze. Book ahead: you don't want to miss this one.

Robber's Roost Books & Beverages CAFE
(www.robbersroostbooks.com; 185 W Main St; snacks $3-6; ⊙ 8am-4pm Mon-Sat, 1-4pm Sun May-Oct; ☜) Linger over a latte and a scone on comfy couches by the fire at this peaceful cafe-bookstore with bohemian bonhomie. Sells local-interest books and maps.

☆ Entertainment

Support the local arts scene by attending an **Entrada Institute** (www.entradainstitute.org; ⊙ Sat Jun-Aug) event, such as an author reading or evening of cowboy music and poetry, at Robber's Roost Books & Beverages.

❶ Information

Fremont River/Loa Ranger District Office
(☑ 435-836-2811; www.fs.fed.us/r4/fishlake; 138 S Main St, Loa; ⊙ 9am-5pm Mon-Fri) Information about area park lands, including Dixie National Forest.

Teasdale Ranger Station (☑ 435-425-3702; 138 E Main St, Teasdale; ⊙ 9am-5pm Mon-Fri) Information about area parks.

Wayne County Travel Council (☑ 800-858-7951, 435-425-3365; www.capitolreef.org; Hwy 24; ⊙ noon-7pm Mon-Sat Apr-Oct) Friendly source of area-wide information.

Sevier Valley Hospital (☑ 435-893-4100; 1000 N Main St, Richfield) Medical services.

❶ Getting There & Away

Rural and remote, Torrey has no public transportation. Activity outfitters can provide hiker shuttles to Capitol Reef National Park.

Boulder

☑ 435 / POP 222

A tiny slice of heaven and a great base to explore the surrounding desert wilderness. Until 1940, this isolated outpost received its mail by mule – it's still so remote that the federal government classifies it as a 'frontier community.' Its diverse population includes artists, ecologists, farmers and cowboys. Though only 32 miles south of Torrey on Hwy 12, you have to traverse 11,317ft-high Boulder Mountain to get here. Note that pretty much all services shut down November through March.

◉ Sights & Activities

Hikes in the northern area of Grand Staircase–Escalante National Monument are near here, but the national forest and BLM lands in the area are also good for hiking and backcountry driving. Burr Trail Rd is the most scenic drive, but Hell's Backbone has its thrills, too.

Anasazi State Park Museum MUSEUM
(www.stateparks.utah.gov; Main St/Hwy 12; $5; ⊙ 8am-6pm Mar-Oct, 9am-5pm Nov-Feb) This petite museum protects the Coomb's Site,

DON'T MISS

HIGHWAY 12 SCENIC BYWAY

Arguably Utah's most diverse and stunning route, **Hwy 12 Scenic Byway** (www.scenicbyway12.com) winds through rugged canyon land on a 124-mile journey west of Bryce Canyon to near Capitol Reef. The section between Escalante and Torrey traverses a moonscape of sculpted slickrock, crosses narrow ridge backs and climbs over an 11,000ft-tall mountain.

Pretty much everything between Torrey and Panguitch is on or near Hwy 12. Highlights include foodie-oriented eateries in tiny-tot Boulder; Lower Calf Creek Falls Recreation Area for a picnic; a hike in Grand Staircase–Escalante National Monument; and an incredible drive through arches and Technicolor red rock in Red Canyon. Take time to stop at the many viewpoints and pullouts, especially at Mile 70, where the Aquarius Plateau lords over giant mesas, towering domes, deep canyons and undulating slickrock, all unfurling in an explosion of color.

excavated in the 1950s and inhabited from AD 1130 to 1175. The minimal ruins aren't as evocative as some in southeastern Utah, but it's well worth seeing the re-created six-room pueblo and excellent exhibits about the Ancestral Puebloan peoples. Get backcountry road updates and backcountry permits at a seasonal information desk staffed by rangers.

Box–Death Hollow Wilderness Area PARK (www.blm.gov) This ruggedly beautiful wilderness area surrounds Hell's Backbone Rd. The 16-mile backpack **Boulder Mail Trail** follows the mule route the post used to take.

Dixie National Forest PARK (www.fs.usda.gov/dixie) North of Boulder, the Escalante District of this 2 million-sq-acre forest has trails and campgrounds, including a few up on Boulder Mountain.

☞ Tours & Outfitters

Earth Tours HIKING (☑ 435-691-1241; www.earth-tours.com; day tours from $150; 🎒) Choose from half- and full-day area hikes and 4WD trips into the backcountry in and around Bryce, Escalante, Boulder Mountain and Capitol Reef. Keith will pick you up at your hotel in Torrey or Boulder.

Escalante Canyon Outfitters HIKING (ECO; ☑ 435-691-3037, 888-326-4453; www.ecohike.com; ⊙ Mar–Nov) Started by cofounder of the Southern Utah Wilderness Alliance, Grant Johnson, ECO has well-regarded multiday treks with a canyonland or archaeological-site focus.

Hell's Backbone Ranch & Trails HORSEBACK RIDING (☑ 435-335-7581; www.bouldermountaintrails.com; off Hell's Backbone Rd; 2hr ride $60) Head across the slickrock plateau into Box–Death Hollow Wilderness Area or up the forested mountain on two-hour to full-day area horseback rides. Or perhaps you'd prefer a multiday camping trip or cattle drive?

🛏 Sleeping

The few lodgings here suit a wide range of tastes. Trolling for a campsite in high season can be tough – don't leave it till the last minute.

Boulder Mountain Guest Ranch LODGE $ (☑ 435-335-7480; www.bouldermountainguestranch.com; off Hell's Backbone Rd; r $80-115, cabins $115-125, tipi $55; ⊙ mid-May–Oct; ✳🐾) This giant log lodge is in a peaceful 160-acre wilderness with trails, a waterfall and outfitter-led hikes and activities. Think rustic, with a happy hippie vibe. Bunk and queen rooms enjoy a communal atmosphere; out-cabins are more private. The dining room has chef-cooked meals at breakfast and dinners use garden produce.

★ Boulder Mountain Lodge LODGE $$ (☑ 435-335-7460; www.boulder-utah.com; 20 N Hwy 12; r $140-175, ste $325, apt $230; ✳@🐾🏊) Watch the birds flit by on the adjacent 15-acre wildlife sanctuary and stroll through the organic garden – Boulder Mountain Lodge has a strong eco-aesthetic. It's an ideal place for day-hikers who want to return to high-thread-count sheets, plush terry robes, spa treatments and an outdoor hot tub. The on-site Hell's Backbone Grill is a southern Utah must-eat.

Kiva Koffeehouse
Cottage Rooms   COTTAGE **$$**
(☑435-826-4550;   www.kivakoffeehouse.com/
kottage.htm; Hwy 12, Mile 73; r $190; ☺Apr-Oct;
🛜) Two cushy hideaway rooms at the Kiva
Koffeehouse with whirlpool tubs and fire-
places – and the same stellar views.

✖ Eating
Boulder has some of the finest eats of south-
ern Utah, and a small market for self-catering.

★Burr Trail Grill
& Outpost   MODERN AMERICAN **$**
(☑435-335-7511; cnr Hwy 12 & Burr Trail Rd; dishes
$8-18; ☺grill 11:30am-9:30pm, outpost 8:30am-6pm
Mar-Oct; 🛜) The organic vegetable tarts and
eclectic burgers sold here (plus scrumptious
homemade cookies and cakes) almost rival
the more famous restaurant, Hell's Backbone
Grill, next door. We like the homey vibe. It's
worth browsing the Outpost art gallery, gift
shop and coffeehouse.

Kiva Koffeehouse   CAFE **$**
(☑435-826-4550; www.kivakoffeehouse.com; Hwy
12, Mile 73; dishes $4-12; ☺8:30am-4:30pm Wed-
Mon Apr-Oct) Just past the Aquarius Plateau,
you reach this singular coffeehouse, whose
round structure was built directly into the
cliffside. Floor-to-ceiling glass windows, sep-
arated by giant timber beams, overlook the
expansive canyons beyond. Serves barista
coffee and yummy baked goods.

★Hell's Backbone Grill   MODERN AMERICAN **$$**
(☑435-335-7464; www.hellsbackbonegrill.com; 20
N Hwy 12, Boulder Mountain Lodge; breakfast $10-
12, lunch $9-17, dinner $17-36; ☺7:30-11:30am &
5-9:30pm Mar-Nov; ☑) 🌿 Earthy preparations
of Southwestern dishes include gorgeous
salads made from organic garden produce
and braised beef in rich preparations. While
this restaurant, a pioneer in sustainable eating and mindfulness, has garnered regional
fame, not all dishes are winners – the tofu
is a dud. Breakfasts remain satisfying, and
there are lunchboxes for hikers. Dinner reservations are a must.

ℹ Information
The tiny town has no visitor center, but info is
available online at www.boulderutah.com.
Boulder Interagency Desk (☑435-335-7382;
Hwy 12, Anasazi State Park Museum; ☺9am-
5pm mid-Mar–mid-Nov) BLM and other public-
land trail and camping information.

Escalante
☑435 / POP 800
Your gateway to the north side of the Grand
Staircase–Escalante National Monument
(GSENM), Escalante is a mix of ranchers,
old-timers, artists and post-monument-
creation outdoors-lovers. The town itself
doesn't exude character, but a friendly
selection of lodgings and restaurants make
it a decent base camp. Numerous outfitters
make this their base for hiking excursions,
and you could, too. At the head of several
park back roads, it's not far from the most
popular GSENM hikes.

⊙ Sights & Activities
The GSENM provides most of the attraction
for the area; hikes off Hwy 12 and Hole-in-
the-Rock Rd are within 12 to 30 miles' drive.

Escalante Petrified Forest State Park   PARK
(www.stateparks.utah.gov; $8; ☺8am-10pm day-
use) Two miles west of town, the centerpiece
of this state park is a 130-acre lake. Hike
uphill about a mile on an interpretive route
to see pieces of colorful petrified wood,
millions of years old. Follow another short
interpretive trail for further examples. The
sites at the campground (p394) are reservable; showers available.

☞ Tours & Outfitters
Excursions of Escalante   ADVENTURE
(☑800-839-7567; www.excursionsofescalante.com;
125 E Main St; all-day canyoneering $175; ☺8am-
6pm) For area canyoneering and climbing
trips, Excursions is the best; it does hiker
shuttles and guided photo hikes, too. Has an
on-site cafe.

Escape Goats   ADVENTURE
(☑435-826-4652; www.escapegoats.us; day hike
$150) Take an evening tour or day hike to
dinosaur tracks, slot canyons and ancient
sites. There's also fully catered backpacking trips (three days $750) including gear.
Recommended.

Escalante Outfitters   ADVENTURE
(☑435-826-4266;   www.escalanteoutfitters.com;
310 W Main St; natural history tours $45; ☺7am-
9pm) A traveler's oasis, this store sells area
books, topographic maps, camping and hiking gear, and is attached to a cafe. Reputable guided hikes, fly-fishing, natural-history
tours and mountain-bike rentals available.

Rising DT Trails
HORSEBACK RIDING

(☑ 435-616-3045; www.escalantehorsetours.com) Dave Trainor offers recommended rides through GSENM.

🛏 Sleeping

Escalante is replete with toy-sized motels and cozy B&Bs.

Escalante Petrified Forest State Park Campground
CAMPGROUND $

(☑ 800-322-3770; utahstateparks.reserveamerica. com; sites $25; 🐕🐾) This 22-site, reservable campground has water, picnic tables, fire pits and restrooms with wonderfully hot showers. It's 2 miles northwest of town along Hwy 12. RV sites with hookups.

Circle D Motel
MOTEL $

(☑ 435-826-4297; www.escalantecircledmotel.com; 475 W Main St; r $75-99, cottage $125; 🌀🛜🐾) We love the little library of guidebooks and hiking information in the rooms. The friendly proprietor goes out of his way to accommodate guests at this partially updated, older motel. Room microwaves and minifridges are standard.

Escalante Grand Staircase B&B
B&B $$

(☑ 435-826-4890; www.escalantebnb.com; 280 W Main St; d $142; 🌀🛜) A wonderful find, with eight spacious rooms sporting individual entrances, skylights and porches. Rooms feature landscape murals with Western motifs. Tom, the host, provides vast quantities of coffee and extensive trail information, with helpful binders containing photos and directions.

🍴 Eating

For its size, Escalante has an OK selection of eateries and markets.

Escalante Mercantile Natural Grocery
MARKET $

(☑ 435-826-4114; 210 W Main St; ☺ 9am-7pm Mon-Sat, 10am-5pm Sun) A well-stocked natural grocer, better with dry goods than produce.

Griffin Grocery
MARKET $

(☑ 435-826-4226; 59 W Main St; ☺ 8am-7pm Mon-Sat) The only full-selection grocery in town.

Esca-Latte Cafe & Pizza
PIZZA $

(310 W Main St; breakfast $3-6, pizza $12-26; ☺ 8am-9pm Mar-Oct; 🛜) Espresso drinks and decent quick bites. There's granola and quiche at breakfast, and tasty homemade pizza and beer. Hikers will want to pack one of the monster cinnamon buns.

Circle D Eatery
AMERICAN $$

(☑ 435-826-4125; www.escalantecircledeatery.com; 475 W Main St; mains $11-25; ☺ 7am-9:30pm, limited hours Nov-Feb) Has attentive service and satisfying burgers using local beef on fresh jalapeño buns, served with shoestring fries. Smoked meats are a specialty, but there are also pastas, salads and hearty breakfasts.

ℹ Information

Escalante Interagency Visitor Center
(☑ 435-826-5499; www.ut.blm.gov/ monument; 775 W Main St; ☺ 8am-4:30pm daily Apr-Sep, Mon-Fri Oct-Mar) *The* source for information about area public lands; jointly operated by the BLM, the USFS and NPS. Ask here about trails, road conditions and camping.

Kazan Memorial Clinic (☑ 435-826-4374; 65 W Main St; ☺ 9am-5pm Mon, Wed & Fri) Limited medical care; the closest hospital is in Panguitch.

Post Office (☑ 435-826-4314; 230 W Main St; ☺ 7:15am-3:45pm Mon-Fri, 8:30am-noon Sat)

ℹ Getting There & Away

Escalante is 28 miles south of Boulder, roughly halfway between Capitol Reef (76 miles) and Bryce Canyon (50 miles).

Visitors need to arrive in their own car. If you're planning on exploring the backcountry, rent a 4WD from somewhere like **High Adventure Rentals** (☑ 435-616-4640; www. highadventurerentals.com).

Grand Staircase–Escalante National Monument

Nearly twice the size of Rhode Island, the 1.9-million-acre **Grand Staircase–Escalante National Monument** (GSENM; ☑ 435-826-5499; www.blm.gov; ☺ 24hr) FREE is the largest park in the Southwest with some of the least visited – yet most spectacular – scenery. Its name refers to the 150-mile-long geological strata that begins at the bottom of the Grand Canyon and rises, in stair steps, 3500ft to Bryce Canyon and Escalante River Canyon. The striped layers of rock reveal 260 million years of history.

Established amid some local controversy by President Bill Clinton in 1996, the monument is unique in that it allows some uses that would be banned in a national park (such as hunting and grazing, by permit). Tourist infrastructure is minimal and limited to towns on the park's edges. Hwy 12

UTAH GRAND STAIRCASE–ESCALANTE NATIONAL MONUMENT

skirts the northern boundaries between Boulder, Escalante and Tropic. Hwy 89 arcs east of Kanab into the monument's southwestern reaches.

The park encompasses three major geological areas. The Grand Staircase is in the westernmost region, south of Bryce Canyon and west of Cottonwood Canyon Rd. The Kaiparowits Plateau runs north–south in the center of the monument, east of Cottonwood Canyon Rd and west of Smoky Mountain Rd. Canyons of the Escalante lies at the easternmost sections, east of Hole-in-the-Rock Rd and south of the Burr Trail, adjacent to Glen Canyon National Recreation Area.

◉ Sights & Activities

The BLM puts out handy one-page summaries of the most-used day trails. GSENM is also filled with hard-core backcountry treks. Ask rangers about **Coyote Gulch**, off Hole-in-the-Rock Rd; **Escalante River Canyon**; **Boulder Mail Trail**; and the **Gulch**, off the Burr Trail. Falcon Guide's *Hiking Grand Staircase–Escalante* is the most thorough park-hiking handbook, but we like the more opinionated *Hiking From Here to Wow: Utah Canyon Country*, with great details and color photographs. The waterproof Trails Illustrated/ National Geographic map *No 710 Canyons of the Escalante* is good, but to hike the

---

SOUTHERN UTAH'S BEST SCENIC DRIVES

People come from around the world to drive in southern Utah, and Hwy 12 and Burr Trail may be the biggest draws. But from paved desert highways for RV-cruisers to rugged backcountry trails for Jeepsters, there are drives for every taste.

Comb Wash Rd (near Bluff) Straddling Comb Ridge, Comb Wash Rd (or CR 235) is a dirt track that runs for about 20 miles between Hwys 163 and 95 (parallel to Hwy 191) west of Blanding and Bluff. Views are fantastic – bring binoculars – and the ridge contains numerous ancient cliff dwellings. High-clearance 4WD vehicles recommended; in wet weather, this road is impassable.

Colorado River Byway (near Moab) Hwy 128 follows the river northeast to Cisco, 44 miles away just off I-70. Highlights are Castle Rock, the 900ft-tall Fisher Towers, the 1916 Dewey Bridge (one of the first across the Colorado) and sightings of white-water rafters.

La Sal Mountain Loop Rd (near Moab) This road heads south into the Manti–La Sal forest from 15 miles north of Moab, ascending switchbacks (long RVs not recommended) into the refreshingly cool forest, with fantastic views. Connects with Hwy 191, 8 miles south of Moab. The 67-mile (three- to four-hour) paved loop closes in winter.

Loop-the-Fold (near Torrey) This 100-mile loop links several top drives; roughly half is on dirt roads generally accessible to 2WD passenger vehicles. Pick up a driving guide ($2) at the Capitol Reef National Park visitor center. West of the park are the rocky valleys of Hwy 12. It only gets better after turning east along Burr Trail Rd to Strike Valley Overlook. Then take the rough Notom-Bullfrog Rd north to finish the loop at Hwy 24.

Caineville Wash Rd (near Torrey) Just east of Capitol Reef National Park, turn north off Hwy 24 to otherworldly monoliths like Temple of the Sun and Temple of the Moon on Caineville Wash Rd. Continue on into the northern part of the park and Glass Mountain, a 20ft mound of fused selenite. Two-wheel drive is usually fine for the first 15.5 miles. With a 4WD you can make this a 58-mile Cathedral Valley loop along Hartnet Rd, which fords the Fremont River just before rejoining Hwy 24.

Hell's Backbone Rd (near Boulder) The gravel-strewn 48 miles from Hwy 12 along Hell's Backbone Rd to Torrey is far from a shortcut. You'll twist, you'll turn, you'll ascend and descend hills, but the highlight is a single-lane bridge atop an impossibly narrow ridge called Hell's Backbone.

Hwy 14 (near Cedar City) This paved scenic route leads 42 miles over the Markagunt Plateau, ending in Long Valley Junction at Hwy 89. The road rises to 10,000ft, with splendid views of Zion National Park to the south. Make sure you detour at Cedar Breaks National Monument.

backcountry you'll need USGS 7½-minute quadrangle maps. Pick these up at any visitor center.

Boulder Outdoor Survival School
OUTDOORS

(☎800-335-7404; www.boss-inc.com) Learn how to survive in this forbidding wilderness. The school operates seven-day and longer courses in GSENM with subjects including primitive living and hunter-gathering.

Lower Calf Creek
HIKING

(Hwy 12, Mile 75; $5; ☉day-use dawn-dusk) The most popular and accessible GSENM hike lies halfway between Torrey and Boulder. This sandy, 6-mile round-trip track skirts a year-round running creek through a spectacular canyon before arriving at a 126ft waterfall – a joy on a hot day. Pick up the interpretive brochure to help spot ancient granary ruins and pioneer relics.

Upper Calf Creek Falls Trail
HIKING

(Hwy 12, btwn Mile 81 & 82) A short (2.2-mile round-trip) but steep and strenuous trail leads down slickrock and through a desert moonscape to two sets of pools and waterfalls, which appear like a mirage at hike's end.

Escalante Natural Bridge Trail
HIKING

(Hwy 12) Be ready to get your feet wet. You'll crisscross a stream seven times before reaching a 130ft-high, 100ft-long natural bridge and arch beyond (4.4 miles round-trip). The trail is 15 miles east of Escalante.

Devils Garden
HIKING

(Hole-in-the-Rock Rd, Mile 12; 🌲) Easy hikes are scarce in GSENM – the closest thing is a foray into Devils Garden, where rock fists, orbs, spires and fingers rise 40ft above the desert floor. A short walk from the car leads to giant sandstone swirls and slabs. From there you have to either walk in the sand or over, among and under the sandstone – like you're in a giant natural playground.

Hole-in-the-Rock Road
SCENIC DRIVE

(off Hwy 12) The history is often wilder than the scenery along much of this 57-mile, dusty washboard road, but it does have several sights and trailheads. From 1879 to 1880, more than 200 pioneering Mormons followed this route settling southeastern Utah. When the road is dry, cars can travel until the last, extremely rugged 7 miles, apt only for 4WD vehicles.

Skutumpah & Johnson Canyon Roads
SCENIC DRIVE

The most westerly route through the monument, the unpaved Skutumpah Rd (scoot-em-paw) heads southwest from Cottonwood Canyon Rd near Kodachrome Basin State Park (p398) to later intersect with Johnson Canyon Rd. First views are of Bryce Canyon's Pink Cliffs. A great little slot-canyon hike, accessible to young and old, is 6.5 miles south of the turnoff at Willis Creek.

Johnson Canyon
SCENIC DRIVE

Heading into GSENM, the paved scenic drive into Johnson Canyon is popular. Movies have been filmed here, and 6 miles along you can see in the distance the Western set where the longtime TV classic *Bonanza* was filmed (on private land). Turn north off Hwy 89, 9 miles east of Kanab.

☞ Tours & Outfitters

Outfitters and guide services that operate in GSENM are based in Boulder, Escalante, Torrey and Kanab.

🛏 Sleeping & Eating

There are two developed campgrounds in the northern part of the monument and free dispersed camping. Pick up the required permit at a visitor center.

Biting insects are a problem in spring and early summer. Watch for scorpions and rattlesnakes.

Most eating is done in Escalante, Boulder or Kanab, or at your own campsite in the monument.

Remember: water sources must be treated or boiled, and campfires are permitted only in certain areas (use a stove instead).

Calf Creek Campground
CAMPGROUND $

(www.blm.gov/ut; Hwy 12; tent & RV sites $15) Beside a year-round creek, this campground is surrounded by red-rock canyons (hot in summer) and has 14 incredibly popular, nonreservable sites. Drinking water is available; there are no hookups. It's near the trailhead to Lower Calf Creek, 15 miles east of Escalante.

Deer Creek Campground
CAMPGROUND $

(www.blm.gov/ut; Burr Trail Rd; tent sites $10; ☉mid-May–mid-Sep) This campground, 6 miles southeast of Boulder, has few sites and no water, but does have pit toilets. It sits beside a year-round creek beneath tall trees.

ⓘ Information

Food, gas, lodging and other services are available in Boulder, Escalante, Torrey and Kanab.

The park headquarters is in Kanab (p421).

For more information about the Monument, consult the Escalante Interagency Visitor Center (p394).

ⓘ Getting There & Around

There is no public transportation to the park. Much of it is remote. Make sure that you have sufficient gas, food and water in case of an emergency.

High-clearance 4WD vehicles allow you the most access, since many roads are unpaved and only occasionally bladed. (Most off-the-lot SUVs and light trucks are *not* high-clearance vehicles.) Heed all warnings about road conditions. Remember to buy gasoline whenever you see it.

Some outfitters in towns around the park have hiker shuttles or 4WD rentals. However, if you plan to do a lot of back road exploring, rent a car. Those arriving via Las Vegas will find it the cheapest rental base in the region.

Highway 89

Few linger here, but the tiny old towns along the way have some restaurant and lodging gems hidden within (beware seasonal closings).

Independent motels and a few eateries line Hwy 89 in Hatch, 25 miles southwest of Bryce Canyon and 15 miles south of Panguitch.

Further south, 50 miles from Bryce and 26 miles to Zion, Glendale is a historic little Mormon town founded in 1871. Today it's an access point for GSENM. From Hwy 89, turn onto 300 North at the faded sign for GSENM; from there it turns into Glendale Bench Rd, which leads to scenic Skutumpah & Johnson Canyon Rds.

At the turnoff for Hwy 9, Mt Carmel Junction has art galleries, two gas stations (one with a sandwich counter) and lodgings about 15 slow-and-scenic miles from the east entrance of Zion, and 18 miles north of Kanab.

⊙ Sights

★ **Maynard Dixon**
Living History Museum MUSEUM
(www.thunderbirdfoundation.com; 2200 S State St, Mt Carmel; self-guided/docent tour $10/20; ⊙10am-5pm Mar-Nov) In Mt Carmel, the *Architectural Digest*–noted Maynard Dixon

Living History Museum is where renowned Western painter Maynard Dixon (1875–1946) lived and worked in the 1930s and '40s. Docent-led tours are by appointment only. Look for the house at Mile 84 on Hwy 89 (called State St in town), about 6 miles south of Glendale; it's easy to miss.

Thunderbird Foundation
for the Arts ARTS CENTER
(☑435-648-2653; www.thunderbirdfoundation.com; 2200 S State St, Mt Carmel; ⊙10am-5pm Mar-Nov) Runs exhibits and artist retreats in adjacent spaces.

🛏 Sleeping

There are a few roadside motels, a B&B and Cottonwood Meadow Lodge, one of Utah's most stunning lodges, along this stretch of road.

Hatch Station Motel MOTEL $
(☑435-735-4015; 177 S Main St, Hatch; r $72; ⊙mid-Mar–late Oct; ❄🐾) Bargain rooms roadside.

★**Cottonwood Meadow Lodge** LODGE **$$**
(☏435-676-8950; www.brycecanyoncabins.com; Hwy 89, Mile 123; cabins & houses $165-295; ☽mid-Apr–Oct; ☏) Dubbed 'cowboy-licious' by a wizened ranch hand, this lodge delivers open-range dreams. Recycled from a Mormon saw town, the private ranch, 2 miles south of Hwy 12, near Panguitch, occupies acres of tawny grass and tumbling sagebrush. Cabins range from a rustic-chic bunkhouse with wooden plank floors to stylish farmhouses with gleaming kitchens, blazing hearths and porch rockers.

A trout pond stocked with browns and rainbows is in easy reach; otherwise there are miles of roads and open space for country walkers and mountain bikers. Lest they help themselves to the grass-raised beef on-site, pets are not allowed.

Arrowhead Country Inn & Cabins B&B **$$**
(☏435-648-2569, 888-821-1670; www.arrowhead bb.com; 2155 S State St; r $99-139, cabins $139-289; ▧☏▧☏) The quilt-covered four-poster beds sure are comfy. The east fork of the Virgin River meanders behind the inn and a trail leads from here to the base of the white cliffs. It's located 2.5 miles north of Mt Carmel Junction and Hwy 9. Two cabins are pet-friendly.

Historic Smith Hotel B&B **$$**
(☏435-648-2156, 800-528-3558; www.historic smithhotel.com; 295 N Main St, Glendale; r $109-119; ▧☏▧) More comfortable than a favorite old sweater; don't let the small rooms turn you off. The proprietors are a great help in planning your day and the big breakfast tables are the place to meet other intrepid travelers from around the globe. Great back decks, a hot tub and garden, too.

✖ Eating

Hatch has the best selection of eateries along this stretch of Hwy 89.

★**Café Adobe** AMERICAN **$**
(☏435-735-4020; 16 N Main St, Hatch; mains $10-18; ☽8am-8pm Mar–mid-Nov) It's worth the 15-mile trek from Panguitch south to Hatch to sample this spot's gourmet hamburgers, creative sandwiches and decadent pies. Don't pass up the homemade tortilla chips and chunky salsa. Locals from the whole region congregate here.

Galaxy Diner DINER **$**
(☏435-735-4017; 177 N Main St, Hatch; mains $5-8; ☽6:30am-2pm mid-Mar–late Oct) Get your butterscotch malts and three-egg omelets at this button-cute 1950s diner and ice cream parlor, next to a Harley-Davidson shop.

Forscher German Bakery BAKERY **$**
(☏435-648-3040; www.forscherbakery.com; 110 E State St, Orderville; mains $4-12; ☽8am-6pm) Break your driving fast with fresh pastries, sandwiches on the bakery's signature sourdough and flatbread pizza. This modern German bakery in nondescript Orderville puts you right back into the mood for sightseeing. Head's up: the founder is actually Dutch.

Hatch Station Dining Car AMERICAN **$$**
(☏435-735-4015; 177 S Main St, Hatch; mains $9-24; ☽noon-8pm mid-Mar–late Oct) Serves the best prime rib around, in knickknacky surrounds. Next door, there's a convenience store selling used cowboy boots (perfect if you lack the patience to break 'em in).

Kodachrome Basin State Park

Petrified geysers and dozens of red, pink and white sandstone chimneys – some nearly 170ft tall – resemble everything from a sphinx to a snowmobile at **Kodachrome Basin State Park** (☏435-679-8562; www.stateparks.utah.gov; off Cottonwood Canyon Rd; per vehicle $8; ☽day-use 6am-10pm). The park lies off Hwy 12, 9 miles south of Cannonville and 26 miles southeast of Bryce Canyon National Park. Visit in the morning or afternoon, when shadows play on the red rock.

◉ Sights & Activities

Most sights are along hiking and mountain-biking trails. The moderately easy, 3-mile round-trip **Panorama Trail** gives the best overview. Be sure to take the side trails to **Indian Cave**, where you can check out the handprints on the wall (from 'cowboys' or 'Indians'?), and **Secret Passage**, a short hike through a narrow slot canyon. **Angel Palace Trail** (1-mile loop, moderate) has great desert views from on high.

Red Canyon Trail Rides (p402), based near Bryce, offers horseback rides.

⛏ Sleeping & Eating

There are several on-site campgrounds, though it may be hard to get a spot. Bring your own provisions; a small **camp store**

(⊗8am-6:30pm Sun-Thu, to 8pm Fri & Sat Apr-Oct) can fill in the gaps, but don't count on it.

Bryce View Campground CAMPGROUND $
(☑435-679-8562; www.reserveamerica.com; tent/ RV site $19/28; ⊗Mar-Nov) New in 2015, comprising 11 reservable sites with fire rings, vault toilet and water tap.

Basin Campground CAMPGROUND $
(☑800-322-3770; www.reserveamerica.com; sites $16) The 26 well-spaced sites at this park service campground get some shade from juniper trees. Good hot showers, too.

Zion & Bryce Canyon National Parks

If you think you've seen every possible hue of sandstone, the rising or setting sun over Utah's national parks will show you otherwise.

👉 Tours

Road Scholar TOURS
(☑800-454-5768; www.roadscholar.org) This nonprofit organization offers learning trips, including bus, walking and hiking tours, and group-oriented outdoor activities.

Backroads, Inc TOURS
(☑510-527-1555, 800-462-2848; www.backroads. com) Offers walking, hiking, cycling and multisport trips for all ages (including families with children) at Zion, Bryce Canyon and the Grand Canyon's North Rim.

Southern Utah Scenic Tours DRIVING
(☑435-867-8690, 435-867-8690; www. utahscenictours.com) Offers Grand Circle tours of the Southwest and southern Utah backroads trips (including the Grand Canyon's North Rim and Monument Valley) by bus, van or SUV, departing from Las Vegas.

Adventure Bus BUS
(☑888-737-5263, 909-633-7225; www. adventurebus.com) Offers sleep-aboard bus tours of southern Utah's national parks and the Grand Canyon, departing from Salt Lake City. For all ages.

Green Tortoise BUS
(☑800-867-8647; www.greentortoise.com) Youth-oriented backpacker trips utilize converted sleeping-bunk buses to visit southern Utah's national parks, departing from Las Vegas.

🛏 Sleeping

National Recreation Reservation Service ACCOMMODATION SERVICES
(☑877-444-6777, 518-885-3639; www.recreation. gov) For camping reservations in national parks, national forests and other federal recreation lands (eg BLM), contact the National Recreation Reservation Service. Adds a fee for reservation.

Reserve America ACCOMMODATION SERVICES
(☑800-322-3770, 518-885-3639; www.reserve america.com; reservation fee $9) For Utah state park campgrounds, contact Reserve America.

Bryce Canyon National Park

The sorbet-colored, sandcastle-like spires and hoodoos of **Bryce Canyon National Park** (☑435-834-5322; www.nps.gov/brca; Hwy 63; 7-day pass per vehicle $30; ⊗24hr, visitor center 8am-8pm May-Sep, to 4:30pm Oct-Apr) pop up like Dr Seuss creations. Though southern Utah's smallest national park, Bryce packs the most immediate visual punch: at sunset an orange wash sets the otherworldly rock formations ablaze. Steep trails descend the rim into 1000ft amphitheaters of pastel daggers, through a maze of fragrant juniper and undulating high-mountain desert. The location, 77 miles east of Zion and 39 miles west of Escalante, makes this a must-stop on any southern Utah park itinerary.

The narrow, 56-mile-long park is an extension of the sloping Paunsaugunt Plateau, which rises from 7894ft at the visitor center (p404) to 9115ft at **Rainbow Point**, the plateau's southernmost tip. High altitude means cooler temperatures here than at other Utah parks. From May to September, combat the congestion by using the shuttle. Weatherwise, June and September are ideal; in July and August expect thunderstorms and mosquitoes.

⊙ Sights & Activities

During summer and early fall, rangers lead canyon-rim walks, hoodoo hikes, geology lectures, campfire programs and kids' ecology walks. If you're here when skies are clear and the moon's full, don't miss the two-hour **Moonlight Hike** among the hoodoos. Register same-day at the visitor center (p404), but do so early.

Rim Road Scenic Drive SCENIC DRIVE
The lookout views along the park's 18-mile-long main road are amazing; navigate

Bryce Canyon National Park

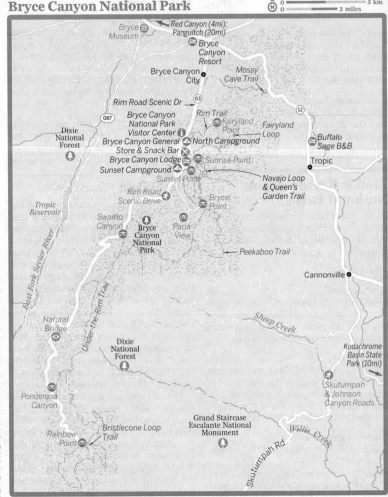

using the park brochure you receive at the entrance. **Bryce Amphitheater** – where hoodoos stand like melting sandcastles in shades of coral, magenta, ocher and white, set against a deep-green pine forest – stretches from **Sunrise Point** to Bryce Point.

For full effect, be sure to walk all the way out to the end of any of the viewpoints; a shaft of sunlight suddenly breaking through clouds as you watch can transform the scene from grand to breathtaking.

Note that the scenic overlooks lie on the road's east side. You can avoid left turns on the very busy road by driving all the way

south to Rainbow Point, then turning around and working your way back, stopping at the pullouts on your right. From late May to early September, a free shuttle (p404) goes as far as Bryce Amphitheater, the most congested area. You can hop off and back on at viewpoints. The free Rainbow Point bus tour hits the highlights daily at 9am and 1pm; inquire at the visitor center (p404).

Bryce Museum   MUSEUM
(www.brycewildlifeadventure.com; 1945 W Hwy 12; $8; ⊘9am-7pm Apr–mid-Nov) Displays dioramas of more than 800 animals from

around the world, as well as live fallow deer, American Indian artifacts, and butterfly and giant-bug exhibits. It also rents bicycles and ATVs and is a good location to start the nearby bike path. Call ahead to see if kid-size bikes are available. You can also rent a bike rack for your car.

Paria View   VIEWPOINT
Three miles north of **Swamp Canyon**, signs point to the Paria View viewpoint, which lies 2 miles off the main road. This is *the* place to come for sunsets. Most of the hoodoo amphitheaters at Bryce face east, making them particularly beautiful at sunrise, but not sunset. The amphitheater here, small by comparison but beautiful nonetheless, faces west toward the Paria River watershed.

Natural Bridge   LANDMARK
Natural Bridge is an extremely popular stop, and with good reason: a stunning span of eroded, red-hued limestone juts from the edge of the overlook. Though called a bridge, it's technically an arch. A bridge forms when running water, such as a stream, causes the erosion. In this case, freezing and thawing of water inside cracks and crevices, combined with gravity, shattered rock to create the window. Even if you're tight on time, squeeze this stop onto your agenda.

Ponderosa Canyon   VIEWPOINT
Ponderosa Canyon offers long vistas over giant ponderosa pines and a small amphitheater of hoodoos and burnt-orange cliffs, which are especially breathtaking in morning light. If you're feeling ambitious, descend a stretch of the moderately strenuous **Agua Canyon Connecting Trail**, a lightly traveled, steep trail that drops past woods into a brilliant amphitheater of hoodoos before joining the **Under-the-Rim Trail** after 1.6 miles.

Hiking
The views from the overlooks are amazing, but the best thing about Bryce is that you can also experience the weirdly eroding hoodoos up close. For solitude during peak season, explore trails on the canyon floor. Descents and ascents can be long and steep, and the altitude makes them extra strenuous. Take your time: most trails skirt exposed drop-offs.

Rim Trail   HIKING
The easiest hike, this 0.5- to 5.5-mile-long (one-way) trail outlines **Bryce Amphitheater**

from Fairyland Point to Bryce Point. Several sections are paved and wheelchair accessible, the most level being the half-mile between **Sunrise** and **Sunset Points**. In the summer, you could easily take the shuttle to any one point and return from another instead of backtracking to a car.

Navajo Loop   HIKING
This 1.4-mile trail descends 521ft from Sunset Point and passes through the famous narrow canyon called **Wall St**. Combine part of the Navajo with the Queen's Garden Trail for an easier ascent. Once you hike the 320ft to Sunrise Point, follow the Rim Trail back to your car (2.9-mile round-trip).

Many moderate trails descend below the rim, but this is one of the most popular.

Queen's Garden Trail   HIKING
(🚸) Good for kids, the easiest trail into the canyon makes a gentle descent over sloping erosional fins. The moderate 1.8-mile out-and-back hike passes elegant hoodoo formations but stops short of the canyon floor.

Views of the amphitheater as you descend are superb – a maze of colorful rock spires extends to Bryce Point, and deep-green pines dot the canyon floor beneath undulating slopes seemingly tie-dyed pink, orange and white. As you drop below the rim, watch for the stark and primitive bristlecone pines, which at Bryce are about 1600 years old (specimens in California are 5000 years old). These ancient trees' dense needles cluster like foxtails on the ends of the branches.

After a series of switchbacks, turn right and follow signs to Queen's Garden. The short spur from the main trail passes through a tunnel and emerges among exceptionally beautiful hoodoo castles in striking whites and oranges amid rich-green pines. After looping around a high wall and passing through two more tunnels, bear right and follow signs to **Queen Victoria**. The trail's namesake monarch peers down from a white-capped rock, perched atop her throne, lording over her kingdom.

The trail is accessed from Sunrise Point, where you follow signs to the trailhead off the Rim Trail. On your return hike, you can follow the same route back to the rim or link up with the Navajo Loop via the Queen's Garden Connecting Trail, which drops to the canyon floor.

UTAH ZION & BRYCE CANYON NATIONAL PARKS

Fairyland Loop
HIKING

With a trailhead at **Fairyland Point** north of the visitor center, this 8-mile round-trip makes for a good half-day hike (four to five hours). The tall hoodoos and bridges unfold best if you go in a clockwise direction. On the trail there's a 700ft elevation change, plus many additional ups and downs.

Bristlecone Loop
HIKING

The 1-mile Bristlecone Loop, at road's end near Rainbow Point, is an easy walk past 1600-year-old bristlecone pines, with 100-mile vistas.

Mossy Cave Trail
HIKING

Outside main park boundaries (east of the entrance), off Hwy 12 at Mile 17, take the easy half-mile one-way walk to the year-round waterfall off Mossy Cave Trail – a summertime treat and frozen winter spectacle.

Peekaboo Trail
HIKING

The fairly level 7-mile-long Peekaboo Trail, which leaves from Bryce Point, allows dogs and horses. Not recommended in high summer – it doesn't always smell the best.

Backcountry Hikes
HIKING

(permits $5-15) Only 1% of all visitors venture onto the backcountry hikes. You won't walk among many hoodoo formations here, but you will pass through forest and meadows with distant views of rock formations. And oh, the quiet.

The 23-mile **Under-the-Rim Trail**, south of Bryce Amphitheater, can be broken into several athletic day hikes. The 11-mile stretch between Bryce Point and Swamp Canyon is one of the hardest and best. Get backcountry permits and trail info from rangers at the visitor center.

☞ Tours & Outfitters

Ruby's Inn Activities
ADVENTURE

(☏435-834-5341, 866-866-6616; www.rubysinn.com; 1000 S Hwy 63; half-day ride $90) Just outside the park, Ruby's offers guided horseback rides, ATV tours and mountain-bike rental – not to mention the rodeo performances, helicopter rides and snowmobiling. Inquire at the inn.

Bryce Wildlife Adventures
ADVENTURE

(☏435-834-5555; www.brycewildlifeadventure.com; 1945 W Hwy 12, Bryce Museum; bicycle per hr $12, 3hr ATV ride $105; ⊙9am-7pm Apr-Oct) ATV and mountain-bike rentals, near public land trails outside the park.

Canyon Trail Rides
HORSEBACK RIDING

(☏435-679-8665; www.canyonrides.com; Hwy 63, Bryce Canyon Lodge; 2hr/half-day tour $65/90) The national park's only licensed outfitter operates out of the park lodge. You can take a short, two-hour trip to the canyon floor or giddy-up for a half day through the dramatic hoodoos on Peekaboo Trail.

Red Canyon Trail Rides
HORSEBACK RIDING

(☏800-892-7923, 435-834-5441; www.redcanyontrailrides.com; Hwy 12, Bryce Canyon Pines; 2hr ride $60; ⊙Mar-Nov) Ride for as little as a half-hour or as long as a whole day on private and public lands outside the park, including Red Canyon (p415).

Western Spirit Cycling
CYCLING

(☏435-259-8732, 800-845-2453; www.westernspirit.com; 6-day trip $1395) Cycling adventures from Bryce to Zion.

Backroads Bicycle Adventures
CYCLING

(☏800-462-2848; www.backroads.com; 6-day trip from $2500) A world-wide bike touring company with trips that cycle through the park.

Rim Tours
CYCLING

(☏800-626-7335, 435-259-5223; www.rimtours.com; half-day from $90) Offers guided mountain-bike trips to Utah's canyon country.

⭐ Festivals & Events

Astronomy Festival
LIGHT SHOW

(www.nps.gov/brca/planyourvisit/astrofest.htm; ⊙mid-Jun) Bryce Canyon's annual four-day Astronomy Festival celebrates the exceptional viewing of the night skies at Bryce. It features talks, walks and stargazing with experts, the park's Astronomy Rangers and the Salt Lake Astronomical Society. A rocket-building workshop appeals to kids.

Bryce Canyon Rim Run
SPORTS

(www.rubysinn.com/bryce-canyon-rim-run; ⊙Aug) Held in August, the run follows a 6-mile course partially along the Bryce Canyon rim outside the park.

🛏 Sleeping

The park has one lodge and two campgrounds. Most travelers stay just north of the park in Bryce Canyon City, near the Hwy 12/63 junction, or 11 miles east in Tropic. Other lodgings are available along Hwy 12, and 24 miles west in Panguitch. Red Canyon (p415) and Kodachrome Basin State Park (p398) also have campgrounds.

⚑ Inside the Park

Trailers are allowed only as far as Sunset Campground, 3 miles south of the entrance. Purchase backcountry camping permits at the visitor center.

North Campground   CAMPGROUND $
(☑ 877-444-6777; www.recreation.gov; Bryce Canyon Rd; tent/RV sites $20/30) Near the visitor center, this trail-side campground is enormous, with 101 sites with campfire rings. A short walk from the campground takes you to showers, a coin laundry and a general store. A fee-for-use sanitary dump station ($5) is available in summer months at the south end. RV reservations are available six months out.

It's divided into four loops. In summer Loops A and B are for RVs over 20ft only and provide many pull-through spots. Loops C and D accommodate vehicles less than 20ft. Loops A and B sit up high amid tall trees, while Loop C is closest to the canyon rim (sites 59 through 61 have canyon views, though little privacy). Loop D sits on a hill amid small to medium-size trees.

Sunset Campground   CAMPGROUND $
(☑ 877-444-6777; www.recreation.gov; Bryce Canyon Rd; tent/RV site $20/30; ☉ Apr-Sep) Just south of Sunset Point, this 102-site campground offers more shade than North Campground but has few amenities beyond flush toilets. Inquire about availability at the visitor center, and secure your site early. Twenty tent sites can be reserved up to six months ahead.

Loop A allows RVs, though it has few pull-through spots (generators are allowed 8am to 8pm). Loops B and C are reserved for vehicles under 20ft. Loop B offers less shade, while Loop C's sites vary widely in quality; for shade and privacy, try for sites on the outer ring.

Bryce Canyon Lodge   LODGE $$
(☑ 877-386-4383, 435-834-8700; www.brycecanyonforever.com; Hwy 63; r & cabins $208-270; ☉ Apr-Oct; @ 🖥) Built in the 1920s, the main park lodge exudes rustic mountain charm, with a large stone fireplace and exposed roof timbers. Most rooms are in two-story wooden satellite buildings with private balconies. The walls prove thin if the neighbors are noisy. In the perfect woodsy setting, the retro-cool Western cabins have gas fireplaces and creaky porches. No TVs.

Wi-fi operates in parts of the main lodge.

⚑ Outside the Park

A full list of area motels is available at www.brycecanyoncountry.com.

Ruby's RV Park & Campground   CAMPGROUND $
(☑ 866-878-9373, 435-834-5301; www.rubysinn.com; 1000 S Hwy 63; tent sites $30, tipis $40, RV sites with partial/full hookups $42/48, cabins $64; ☉ Apr-Oct; 🖥🖥) This crowded campground, 3 miles north of the Bryce visitor center, has amenities, including flush toilets, showers, drinking water, a coin laundry, electrical hookups, a dump station, restaurant, general store and hot tub. Both double-bunk cabins and tipis use shared bathroom facilities. Bring your own sleeping bag. Though over-the-top commercial, it's nonetheless convenient. Online reservations and walk-ins accepted.

Best Western Plus Bryce Canyon Grand Hotel   HOTEL $$
(☑ 435-834-5700, 866-866-6634; www.brycecanyongrand.com; 30 N 100 E, Bryce Canyon City; d/ste $210/310; ☉ Apr-Oct; 🖥@🖥🖥) This Best Western hotel is the best digs in this strip, with stylish, ample rooms featuring flat-screen TVs and a breakfast bar that spoils you for choice. Amenities include an outdoor swimming pool, fitness center and coin laundry.

Best Western Ruby's Inn   HOTEL $$
(☑ 435-834-5341, 866-866-6616; www.rubysinn.com; 1000 S Hwy 63; r $145-160, ste $220; 🖥@🖥🖥) A gargantuan motel complex with ample facilities, 1 mile before the park entrance. Standard rooms feature two beds, either queen or king size, coffeemakers and hair dryers. The sprawling property includes a grocery store with camping supplies, gas stations, a post office, coin laundry, pool and hot tub, showers, currency exchange, internet and a liquor store (a rarity around here).

The tour desk can book helicopter tours and horseback riding. Ruby's also rents bicycles and ATVs. In summer there's a nightly rodeo (except Sunday); it's best to make reservations in high season.

Bryce Canyon Resort   MOTEL $$
(☑ 800-834-0043, 435-834-5351; www.brycecanyonresort.com; cnr Hwys 12 & 63; r $145-189, cabins $215; 🖥🖥🖥🖥) Four miles from the park, this is a great alternative. Remodeled rooms include newer furnishings and extra amenities, while economy rooms are standard.

Some units have kitchenettes. Cottages have kitchenettes and sleep up to six. Pets are extra. There's also a heated outdoor swimming pool, small campground and restaurant.

Bryce View Lodge
MOTEL **$$**

(📞 888-279-2304, 435-834-5180; www.bryce viewlodge.com; d $120; ☺ Apr-Oct; ☻ @ 🖙 🖘) Geared to budget travelers, these 130 standard rooms are decent, though smaller than Ruby's Inn and with fewer amenities. Guests enjoy free access to all the facilities across the street at Ruby's, including the pool and hot tub.

✗ Eating

Nobody comes to Bryce for the cuisine. Expect so-so Western fare like grilled pork chops and chicken-fried steaks. If you're vegetarian, BYOV or subsist on salad and fries.

Inside the Park

Bryce Canyon General Store & Snack Bar
MARKET **$**

(Bryce Canyon Rd; dishes $3-9; ☺ noon-10pm) In addition to foodstuff and sundries, the general store near Sunrise Point (p400) sells hot dogs, cold drinks, packaged sandwiches, chili, soup and pizza.

★ Bryce Canyon Lodge Restaurant
AMERICAN **$$$**

(📞 435-834-5361; Bryce Canyon Rd; breakfast & lunch $10-20, dinner $10-35; ☺ 7am-10pm Apr-Oct) 🍃 While service may lag, meals deliver, with excellent regional cuisine, ranging from fresh green salads to bison burgers, braised portobellos and steak. All food is made on-site and the certified green menu offers only sustainable seafood. The wine list is decent and, best of all, the low-lit room is forgiving if you come covered in trail dust.

Outside the Park

Bryce Canyon Pines Restaurant
AMERICAN **$$**

(📞 435-834-5441; Hwy 12; breakfast & lunch $5-14, dinner mains $12-24; ☺ 6:30am-9:30pm Apr-Oct) This supercute diner is classic Utah, with waitstaff that dote, Naugahyde booths and even a crackling fire on cold days. Expect hearty plates of meat and potatoes, perfect BLTs and meal-size soups. While mains feel run-of-the-mill, locals come for towering wedges of homemade pie, such as the banana blueberry creme.

Ebenezer's Barn & Grill
BARBECUE **$$$**

(📞 800-468-8660; ebenezersbarnandgrill.com; 1000 S Hwy 63; dinner show $32-38; ☺ 7pm mid-May–Sep) A kitschy but good-natured evening of country-and-western music with a big BBQ dinner (drinks not included). Options include salmon, steak, pulled pork or chicken served with beans and cornbread. Since it's wildly popular, reservations are necessary. It's run by Ruby's Inn and located across the street.

ⓘ Information

Some services are just north of the park boundaries on Hwy 63.

The NPS newspaper, *Hoodoo*, lists hikes, activities and ranger-led programs.

Bryce Canyon National Park Visitor Center (📞 435-834-5322; www.nps.gov/brca; Hwy 63; ☺ 8am-8pm May-Sep, 8am-6pm Oct & Apr, 8am-4:30pm Nov-Mar; 🖘) Check here for weather, hiking and road conditions and campground availability. Exhibits show plant, animal life and geologic displays and there's an excellent 20-minute orientation video. The park headquarters are here, as are first aid, phones and wi-fi in the lobby. Families can pick up 'Junior Ranger Activity Guides'. Located adjacent to the entrance station.

Bryce Canyon Natural History Association (📞 435-834-4600; www.brycecanyon.org) A nonprofit that aids the park service with educational, scientific and interpretive activities. The association operates the bookstore, and staff answer questions in the visitor center. Its excellent online shop sells books, maps, videos, music and trip-planning packets tailored to individual traveler's needs.

ⓘ Getting There & Around

It's best to have your own vehicle. Some overland bus tours visit Bryce Canyon National Park.

The nearest town is Tropic, 11 miles northeast on Hwy 12.

A private vehicle is the only transportation option from fall through spring. In summer, the voluntary **shuttle** (☺ 8am-8pm late May-Sep) keeps you from getting stuck without a parking spot. (Note: the park's visitor center parking lot fills up, too.) Leave your car at the Ruby's Inn or Ruby's Campground stops, and ride the bus into the park. The shuttle goes as far as Bryce Point; buses come roughly every 15 minutes, 8am to 8pm. A round-trip without exiting takes 50 minutes. Tune in to 1610AM on your radio as you approach Bryce to learn about current shuttle operations. The *Hoodoo* newspaper shows routes.

No trailers are permitted south of Sunset Point. If you're towing, leave your load at your campsite or in the trailer turnaround lot at the visitor center.

East Zion

Most travelers blaze through this quieter side of the park, but it's worth a closer look. For families, East Zion makes an ideal base camp with ranch activities and room to roam without park crowds. Eighteen miles north of Kanab, the turnoff for Hwy 9 leads about 15 miles to the east entrance of Zion National Park.

🏃 Activities

Nippletop   HIKING
Hiking up Nippletop (6715ft) is a great way to experience Zion's east-side wilderness. The hike is relatively short (3 miles round-trip) and only ascends about 1500ft – steep, but not too steep. The summit is class 3 (exposed but nontechnical), so you should only attempt this if you have climbing or mountaineering experience.

Shelf Canyon   HIKING
This is a fun little scramble to a secret canyon just east of the main tunnel. Short and sweet, it involves lots of low-grade bouldering and is definitely not for casual hikers. As you follow the canyon further back it gets increasingly narrow, eventually ending in a cave-like formation filled with narrow ledges that you can clamber up.

🛏 Sleeping & Eating

There's camping and several guest ranches. Eat at the ranches or rent a cabin equipped with kitchen.

Zion Ponderosa Ranch Resort   RANCH $$
(📞 800-293-5444; www.zionponderosa.com; Twin Knolls Rd; luxury tent $119, RV site $55, cabin $139-199; 🛜🏊) Families love this activity-rich ranch on 4000 acres on Zion's eastern side. Guests can hike, bike, canyoneer, climb, swim, play sports, ride four-wheelers and horses, and eat three meals a day right here (packages available). Wi-fi-enabled camping sites and cabins (linens included) are served by huge showers/bathrooms.

Zion Mountain Ranch   CABIN $$$
(📞 866-648-2555, 435-688-1039, campground 435-648-3302; www.zmr.com; Hwy 9; cabins $181-714, 1hr horseback ride $45; ❄@) Six different cabin types and a variety of larger lodges

are available at this luxury ranch. Buffalo roam, though it is a bit closer to the highway than might be expected. Activities, including horseback riding (available to nonguests) and fly-fishing, can be arranged through the resort. It's about 3 miles from Zion's east entrance.

Cordwood Restaurant   AMERICAN $$$
(Hwy 9; mains $16-45; ⏱7am-10pm Apr-Oct; 🔊) 🍴 This rustic farm-to-table restaurant offers the only gourmet dining in East Zion plus beer and wine. Think organic salads, Montana bison burgers and cheeseboards with local honeycombs. Pick up a jar of picked vegetables. The kids will love playing with chickens out back and colts and baby goats in springtime.

Zion National Park

Get ready for an overdose of awesome. The soaring red-and-white cliffs of Zion Canyon (p407), one of southern Utah's most dramatic natural wonders, rise high over the Virgin River. Hiking downriver through the Narrows (p406) or peering beyond Angels Landing (p412) after a 1400ft ascent is indeed amazing. But, for all its awe-inspiring majesty, the **park** (www.nps.gov/zion; Hwy 9; 7-day pass per vehicle $30; ⏱24hr, visitor center 8am-7:30pm Jun-Aug, closes earlier Sep-May) also holds more delicate beauties: weeping rocks, tiny grottoes, hanging gardens and meadows of mesa-top wildflowers. Lush vegetation and low elevation give these magnificent rock formations a different feel from the barren parks in the east.

Most of the park's 4.3 million annual visitors enter along Zion Canyon floor. Even the most challenging hikes become congested between May and September (shuttle required). Yet, there are other options. Up-country, on the mesa tops (7000ft), it's easy to escape the crowds – and the heat. And the Kolob Canyons section, 40 miles northwest by car, sees one-tenth of the visitors year-round.

ℹ Fees & Permits

Note that you have to pay the park entry fee to drive through the park on Hwy 9, whether you plan to stop or not. Keep your receipt: it's good for both the main and Kolob Canyons sections.

Online permit reservations ($5 reservation fee) are available for many trips, up until 5pm the preceding day. For busy routes there may be a lottery. Twenty-five percent of available permits remain reserved for walk-in visitors the day before or day of a trip. Trying to get a next-day walk-in permit on a busy weekend is like trying to get tickets to a rock concert; lines form at the **Backcountry Desk** (p410) by 6am or earlier.

◉ Sights & Activities

The park occupies 147,000 acres. Driving in from east Zion, Hwy 9 undulates past yellow sandstone before getting to tighter turns and redder rock after the Zion–Mt Carmel Tunnel. Zion Canyon – with most of the trailheads and activities – lies off Hwy 9 near the south entrance, and the town of Springdale. No roads within the park directly connect this main section with the Kolob Canyons section in the northwest. Unless you hike, you'll have to drive the 40 miles (an hour) between the two, via Hwy 9, Rte 17 and I-15.

Zion Lodge   HISTORIC BUILDING
(☑ lodge 435-772-7700; www.zionlodge.com; Zion Canyon Scenic Dr) Whether you plan to stay at the Zion Lodge or not, a visit to this historic lodge, smack in the middle of Zion Canyon, is a must. Although the architecture itself pales in comparison to some of its counterparts in other national parks, its location is incomparable. Stunning red-rock cliffs surround you on all sides, and views of Lady Mountain, Heaps Canyon and the Virgin River are simply stunning. Evening nature programs and talks are also hosted on the grounds.

Zion Nature Center   NATURE CENTER
(☑ 435-772-3256; South Campground, off Hwy 9; ⊙ 1-6pm late May-Aug; ⊕) FREE During the summer, many children's programs are held at the Zion Nature Center, just past the South Campground (p409). There is a variety of interactive exhibits here.

Zion Canyon Scenic Drive   SCENIC DRIVE
The premier drive in the park leads between towering cliffs of an incredible red-rock canyon and accesses all the major front-country trailheads. A shuttle bus ride is required April through October. If you've time for only one activity, this is it. Your first stop should be the **Human History Museum** (⊙ 9am-7pm late May-early Sep, 10am-5pm Mar-late May & early Sep-Nov) FREE, a great introduction to the park. There are shuttle stops, and turnouts, at viewpoints like **Court of the Patriarchs**, at Zion Lodge and the end point, the Temple of Sinawava.

Highway 9   SCENIC DRIVE
East of the main park entrance, Hwy 9 rises in a series of six tight switchbacks before the 1.1-mile Zion–Mt Carmel Tunnel, an engineering marvel constructed in the late 1920s. It then leads quickly into dramatically different terrain – a landscape of etched multicolor slickrock, culminating at the mountainous **Checkerboard Mesa**.

Kolob Terrace Road Drive   SCENIC DRIVE
The less-visited, higher-elevation alternative to Zion Canyon Scenic Drive. Sweeping vistas of cliffs, mountains and finger canyons dominate this stunning, 5-mile red-rock route, rich with overlooks. The scenic road, off I-15, lies 40 miles from the main visitor center.

Mountain Bike Buddies   CYCLING
(☑ 800-860-6460; www.mountainbikebuddies.com; shuttle per day $60) By reservation, arranges do-it-yourself bike tours that include pickup, bike rental and shuttle to and from trailheads around St George and Zion.

Canyon Trail Rides   HORSEBACK RIDING
(☑ 435-679-8665, 435-772-3810; www.canyonrides.com; 1hr/half-day trips $45/90; ⊙ Mar-Nov) Zion's official horseback-riding concessionaire operates across from Zion Lodge (p409). Ride on the Sand Bench Trail along the Virgin River. Minimum age of seven/10 for the 1hr/half-day trips.

Hiking

Zion has everything from short day hikes for families to multiday backpacking trips. Trails can be slippery; ask rangers about weather conditions before you depart.

There are hundreds of miles of backcountry (overnight) hiking trails with wilderness camping and enough quiet to hear the whoosh of soaring ravens overhead. If you hike the entirety of Zion, north to south, it's a four-day traverse of 50-plus miles. All backcountry hiking and camping requires a permit.

Flash floods occur year-round, particularly in July and August. Check weather and water conditions with rangers before hiking in river canyons. If you hear thunder, if water rises suddenly or goes muddy, or if you feel sudden wind accompanied by a roar, immediately seek higher ground. Climbing a few feet can save your life; if you can't, get behind a rock fin. There's no outrunning a flash flood.

★**The Narrows**   HIKING
The most famous backcountry route is the unforgettable Narrows, a 16-mile journey into skinny canyons along the Virgin River's north

fork (June through October). Plan on getting wet: at least 50% of the hike is in the river.

The trip takes 12 hours; split it into two days, spending the night at one of the designated campsites you reserved or finish the hike in time to catch the last park shuttle. The trail ends among the throngs of day hikers on **Riverside Walk** (♿) at the north end of Zion Canyon. A trailhead shuttle is necessary for this and other one-way trips.

Zion Canyon HIKING
Spring to fall, the mandatory shuttle stops at all major trailheads along Zion Canyon Scenic Dr, allowing one-way hikes. In low season you can park at these stops, but you'll have to hike back to your car. Hikes rate from easy to strenuous; the most notable are the Narrows, Observation Point Trail and Canyon Overlook Trail.

Of the easy-to-moderate trails, the paved, mile-long Riverside Walk at the end of the road is a good place to start. When the trail ends, you can continue along in the Virgin River for 5 miles to **Big Springs**; this is the bottom portion of the Narrows – a difficult backpacking trip. Yes, you'll be hiking in the water (June through October), so be prepared.

A steep, but paved, half-mile trail leads to the lower of the **Emerald Pools**. Here water tumbles from above a steep overhang, creating a desert varnish that resembles rock art. It's worth your while to hike a mile further up the gravel to the more secluded Upper Pool. Note: you will have to scramble up (and back down) some stair-like rocks. The quarter-mile-long **Weeping Rock Trail** climbs 100ft to hanging gardens.

Hidden Canyon Trail has sheer drop-offs and an 850ft elevation change in just over a mile before you reach the narrow, shady canyon. Think of it as an easier test of your fear of heights.

The most work (2150ft elevation change) is rewarded with the best views – at the top of Observation Point Trail (4 miles). From here you look down on Angels Landing – heck, the whole park really. A backcountry shortcut leads here with much less legwork – the **East Mesa Trail**.

The paved **Pa'rus Trail** parallels the scenic drive from Watchman Campground (p412) to the main park junction (about 2 miles). It's the only trail that allows bicycles and dogs.

The only marked trail along Hwy 9 in east Zion is **Canyon Overlook Trail**, a

EAST ZION

East Zion has several little-traveled, up-country hikes that provide an entirely different perspective on the park, leading off from Zion Ponderosa Ranch Resort (p405). **Cable Mountain** and **Deertrap Mountain**, to name two, have incredible views.

It feels deliciously like cheating to wander through open stands of tall ponderosa pines and then descend 500ft to **Observation Point** instead of hiking 2500ft uphill from the Zion Canyon floor; **East Mesa Trail** (6.4 miles round-trip, moderate difficulty) does just that. It's less legwork because it's a hearty drive. Getting to the trailhead requires a 4WD for the last few miles, but Zion Ponderosa Ranch Resort and outfitters in Springdale can provide hiker shuttles. Ask rangers for details.

Note that at 6500ft, these trails may be closed due to snow from November through March.

moderately easy half-mile walk, yielding thrilling views 1000ft down into Zion Canyon. But you can also stop at Hwy 9 pullouts where there are some interesting narrow canyon hikes and slickrock scrabbles. In summer, locals park at one turnout, climb down, cross under the road and follow a wash to the river for a cool dip...happy searching! Just be aware of your surroundings, and stay in the wash or on the rock to avoid damaging the desert ecology.

Kolob Terrace Road HIKING
Fourteen miles west of Springdale, Kolob Terrace Rd takes off north from Hwy 9, weaving in and out of BLM and national park highlands. (The road is closed due to snow from at least November to March.) **Wildcat Canyon Trailhead** lies about 28 miles north, after a hairpin turn.

Kolob Canyon HIKING
In the northwestern section of the park, the easiest trail is at the end of the road: **Timber Creek Trail** (0.5 miles) follows a 100ft ascent to a small peak with great views. The main hike is the 2.7-mile-long **Taylor Creek Trail**, which passes pioneer ruins and crisscrosses the creek.

UTAH ZION & BRYCE CANYON NATIONAL PARKS

Zion National Park

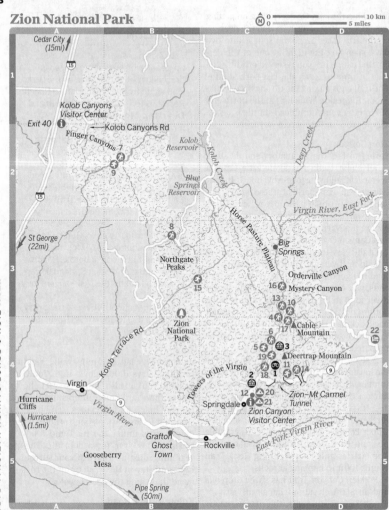

Climbing & Canyoneering

If there's one sport that makes Zion special, it's canyoneering. Rappelling over the lip of a sandstone bowl, swimming icy pools, tracing a slot canyon's curves...canyoneering is beautiful, dangerous and sublime all at once. Zion's slot canyons are the park's most sought-after backcountry experience; reserve far in advance.

Zion Canyon also has some of the most famous big-wall rock climbs in America. However, there's not much for beginners or those who like bolted routes. Permits are required for all canyoneering and climbing.

Get information at the Backcountry Desk (p410) at the Zion Canyon Visitor Center (p415), which also has route descriptions written by climbers.

Guided trips are prohibited in the park. Outfitters in Springdale hold courses outside Zion, after which students can try out their newfound skills in the park.

Subway   OUTDOORS

This incredibly popular canyoneering route (9.5 miles, 1850ft elevation change) has four or five rappels of 20ft or less, and the namesake, tube-looking slickrock formation.

Zion National Park

Start at the Wildcat Canyon Trailhead off Kolob Terrace Rd. Hiker shuttle required.

Pine Creek Canyon   OUTDOORS
A popular canyoneering route with moderate challenges and rappels of 50ft to 100ft, Pine Creek has easy access from near the Canyon Overlook Trail in East Zion. A backcountry permit and wetsuit are required.

👉 Tours & Outfitters

Zion Canyon Field Institute   TOURS
(☑ 435-772-3264, 800-635-3959; www.zionpark. org; programs $45-85) Explore Zion by moonlight, take a wildflower photography class, investigate Kolob Canyon's (p407) geology or help clean up the Narrows (p406). All courses and tours include some hiking.

Ride Along with a Ranger   DRIVING
(www.nps.gov/zion; Zion Canyon Visitor Center; ☻May-Oct) **FREE** The entertaining, ranger-led Zion Canyon shuttle tour (90 minutes)

makes stops not on the regular route. It's a great nonhiking alternative for those with limited mobility. Reserve up to three days in advance at the visitor center (p415).

Red Rock Shuttle & Tours   DRIVING
(☑ 435-635-9104;   www.redrockshuttle.com)
Offers private van tours of Zion ($100 per person for six hours).

🛏 Sleeping

Both of the park's large, established campgrounds are near the Zion Canyon Visitor Center (p415) in Springdale. For wilderness camping at designated areas along the West Rim, La Verkin Creek, Hop Valley and the Narrows you'll need a permit. More lodging and camping is available in Springdale.

South Campground   CAMPGROUND $
(☑ 435-772-3256; Hwy 9; tent & RV sites $20; ☻year-round; 🐾) The South Campground sits north of the visitor center (p415) beside the busy Pa'rus Trail (p407). The 127 campsites are entirely first-come, first-served, so show up before 9am for the best chances of finding an open site. The campground has no electrical hookups for RVs; generator use is allowed from 8am to 10am and 6pm to 8pm. There's a dump station, however.
  Pets are allowed in RVs only.

★ Zion Lodge   LODGE $$
(☑ 435-772-7700, 888-297-2757; www.zionlodge. com; Zion Canyon Scenic Dr; cabins/r $227/217; ✳@📶) We love the stunning surrounding red-rock cliffs and the location in the middle of Zion Canyon (along with the red permit that allows you to drive to the lodge in shuttle season). But be warned: today's reconstructed lodge is not as grand as other national-park lodges (the 1920s original burned down in 1966). Nevertheless, you'll need to reserve months ahead.

🍴 Eating

Zion Lodge has the only in-park dining; otherwise head to Springdale, just outside the park.

Castle Dome Café   CAFE $
(Zion Canyon Scenic Dr, Zion Lodge; mains $5-12; ☻6:30am-5pm Mar-Oct) This counter-service cafe serves sandwiches, pizza, salads, Asian-ish rice bowls and ice cream. A beer garden serving local suds is located on the patio from May through mid-October.

UTAH ZION & BRYCE CANYON NATIONAL PARKS

Red Rock Grill

AMERICAN $$

(☑ 435-772-7760; Zion Canyon Scenic Dr, Zion Lodge; breakfast & sandwiches $6-15, dinner $16-30; ⏱ 6:30-10am, 11:30am-2:30pm & 5-9pm Mar-Oct, hours vary Nov-Feb) Settle into your replica log chair or relax on the big deck with magnificent canyon views. Though the dinner menu touts its sustainable-cuisine stance for dishes like roast pork loin and flatiron steak, the results are hit-or-miss. Dinner reservations recommended. Full bar.

❶ Information

Visitor center hours vary slightly month to month.

Backcountry Desk (☑ 435-772-0170; www. nps.gov/zion; ⏱ 7am-7:30pm late May-early Sep, reduced hours rest of year) Issues required permits for backcountry camping, canyoneering and rock climbing. Located at the **Zion Canyon Visitor Center** (p415) in Springdale.

Backcountry Permits (☑ 435-772-0170; www. nps.gov) Permits are required for all overnight trips (including camping and rock climbs with bivouacs), all through-hikes of the Virgin River (including the Narrows top hike) and any canyoneering hikes requiring ropes for descent. Use limits are in effect on some routes to protect the environment.

National Park Rangers Emergency (☑ 435-772-3322) Call for emergencies.

Kolob Canyons Visitor Center (☑ 435-586-0895; www.nps.gov/zion; Kolob Canyons Rd; ⏱ 8am-7:30pm late May-Sep, to 5pm rest of year) Small visitor center in the Kolob Canyons section of the park.

❶ Getting There & Around

In Springdale, shuttle companies specialize in transporting hikers to and from trailheads. Outfitters that offer hiker shuttles (two-person minimum, reservation required) to backcountry and canyoneering trailheads include **Zion Adventure Company** (☑ 435-772-1001; www.zionadventures.com) and **Zion Rock & Mountain Guides** (☑ 435-772-3303; www. zionrockguides.com).

BUS

There is no public transportation to the park, though some overland bus tours stop here. The **St George Express** (☑ 435-652-1100; www. stgeorgeexpress.com; round-trip to St George $100) provides private transportation to St George and Las Vegas, NV.

CAR & MOTORCYCLE

Arriving from the east on Hwy 9, you have to pass through the free Zion–Mt Carmel Tunnel.

If your RV or trailer is 7ft 10in wide or 11ft 4in high or larger, it must be escorted through, since vehicles this big need both lanes. Motorists requiring an escort pay $15 over the entrance fee, good for two trips.

Between April and October, rangers are stationed at the tunnel from 8am to 8pm daily; at other times, ask at the entrance stations. Vehicles prohibited at all times include those more than 13ft 1in tall or more than 40ft long.

PARK SHUTTLE

How you get around Zion depends on the season. From mid-March through early November passenger vehicles are not allowed on **Zion Canyon Scenic Drive** (p406). The park operates two free, linked shuttle loops.

The **Zion Park Shuttle** makes nine stops along the canyon, from the main visitor center to the Temple of Sinawava (a 45-minute round-trip).

The **Springdale Shuttle** makes six regular stops and three flag stops along Hwy 9 between the park's south entrance and the Majestic View Lodge in Springdale, the hotel furthest from the park. You can ride the Springdale Shuttle to **Zion Canyon Giant Screen Theatre** (p414) and walk across a footbridge into the park. The visitor center and the first Zion shuttle stop lie on the other side of the kiosk.

The propane-burning park shuttle buses are wheelchair-accessible, can accommodate large backpacks and carry up to two bicycles or one baby stroller. Schedules change, but generally shuttles operate from at least 6:45am to 10pm, every 15 minutes on average.

Springdale

☑ 435 / POP 550 / ELEV 3898FT

When the cottonwoods are budding against the red cliffs, Springdale is the perfect little park town, though more frequently, it's a bottleneck of traffic entering Zion National Park (p405). The main drag – well, the only drag – features eclectic cafes, galleries and restaurants touting local produce and organic ingredients. Many residents were drawn here for the surroundings, but you will occasionally run into a lifelong local who thinks they're 'just rocks.'

❍ Sights & Activities

Hiking trails in Zion are the area's biggest attraction. There are also some awesome, single-track, slickrock mountain-bike trails as good as Moab's. Ask local outfitters about Gooseberry Mesa, Hurricane Cliffs and Rockville Bench.

Springdale River Park PARK
Local park with river access.

Zion Cycles MOUNTAIN BIKING
([✉] 435-772-0400; www.zioncycles.com; 868
Zion Park Blvd; half-/full-day rentals from $30/40,
car racks from $15; ⊘9am-7pm Feb-Nov) Next
to Zion Mountain School, this is the most
helpful bike shop in town, with lots of info
on local trails and tandem, road and mountain-bike rentals. No tours.

Red Desert Adventures ADVENTURE SPORTS
([✉] 435-668-2888; www.reddesertadventure.com;
canyoneering day from $195) A small company
with experienced area guides; provides
private guided hiking, biking, climbing
and canyoneering. Prices drop with more
participants.

Zion Guru ADVENTURE SPORTS
([✉] 435-632-0432; www.utahcanyonoutdoors.com;
792 Zion Park Blvd; half-day canyoneering from
$150; ⊘9am-7pm) Guests rave about this
holistic outfitter offering wellness programs
as well as adventures in canyoneering,
climbing and hiking, photography tours and
park shuttles. Rental gear for canyoneering
is in top condition.

Tubing

The Virgin River is swift, rocky and only
about knee-deep: more of a bumpy adventure ride than a leisurely float, but tubing
(outside the park only) is popular in the
summer. Note that from June to August,
the water warms to only 55°F to 65°F (13°C
to 18°C). Zion Canyon Campground (p412)
and some other riverside lodgings have good
water-play access.

🗗 Tours & Outfitters

Outfitters lead hiking, biking, climbing,
rappelling and multisport trips on the every-
bit-as-beautiful BLM lands near the park.
We highly recommend canyoneering as a
quintessential area experience.

Outfitters are also one-stop shops for
adventure needs: they sell ropes and maps,
have classes, provide advice and suit you
up with rental gear (harnesses, helmets,
canyoneering shoes, dry suits, fleece layers,
waterproof packs and more). The hiker shuttles and gear rental are especially handy for
one-way slot-canyon routes and Narrows
(p406) hikes.

Rates are generally quoted per person,
usually with a two-person minimum, and go
down with more participants.

Zion Outback Safaris ADVENTURE
([✉] 866-946-6494; www.zionjeeptours.com; 3hr
Jeep tour $88) Backroad 4WD tours in a
12-seat modified truck. Prices are the same
for children and adults.

Zion Rock & Mountain Guides ADVENTURE
([✉] 435-772-3303; www.zionrockguides.com; 1458
Zion Park Blvd; canyoneering day $195; ⊘8am-
8pm Mar-Oct, hours vary Nov-Feb) More down-to-
business than other outfitters, and especially
good for sporty types. Guides have a good
reputation, though the in-store service is
very hit-or-miss.

Zion Mountain School ADVENTURE
([✉] 435-633-1783; www.guidesinzion.com; 868
Zion Park Blvd; canyoneering day course from $190;
⊘8am-8pm Mar-Oct, hours vary Nov-Feb) Local
outfitter located behind the Zion Noodle
Company, offering gear rental, courses and
guided trips. It also has public showers ($5).

Zion Adventure Company ADVENTURE
([✉] 435-772-1001; www.zionadventures.com; 36
Lion Blvd; canyoneering day from $177; ⊘8am-
8pm Mar-Oct, 9am-noon & 4-7pm Nov-Feb) The
main outfitter in town and certainly the
most organized. The focus is on renting
gear for the Narrows (p406), but it also
offers a good selection of canyoneering and
climbing trips and courses. Solo travelers
looking to bring the price down for guided
trips by hooking up with others should
try here first. Canyoneering and camping
equipment for sale.

Bike Zion MOUNTAIN BIKING
([✉] 435-772-0320; www.bikingzion.com; 1458 Zion
Park Blvd, Zion Rock & Mountain Guides; half-/full-
day rental $25/35, car racks from $15; ⊘8am-8pm)
Zion Rock's on-site sister cycle shop; has a
variety of rentals and does tours. We never
saw anyone in the store, so it's best if you
call ahead.

Zion Outfitters ADVENTURE SPORTS
([✉] 435-772-5090; zionoutfitter.com; 95 Zion Park
Blvd; day bike/tube rentals $35/20; ⊘7:30am-
8pm Mar-Oct, hours vary Nov-Feb) Ideally located
at the park entrance, this is the smallest of
the outdoor stores. Handy for cruiser bikes,
tube rentals and other gear. It also has public showers ($5).

🎋 Festivals & Events

Springdale has many celebrations; contact
the Zion Canyon Visitors Bureau (p415) for
specifics.

St Patrick's Day
PARADE

The St Patrick's Day (March 17) parade and celebration includes a green Jell-O sculpture competition.

Zion Canyon Music Festival
MUSIC

(www.zioncanyonmusicfestival.com) One weekend in late September is filled with folk and other music.

🛏 Sleeping

The lower the address number on Zion Park Blvd, the closer to the park entrance; all lodgings are near shuttle stops. Look for slightly less expensive B&Bs around Zion (in Rockville, for example). Note that rates plummet in the off-season.

Zion Park Motel
MOTEL $

(☑ 435-772-3251; www.zionparkmotel.com; 865 Zion Park Blvd; r from $97; ❀🕈🗺) It's a wonder what a coat of paint can do for old wood-paneled rooms. Microwaves and mini-refrigerators are the main perks at this family-owned and supremely central budget option.

Zion Canyon Campground & RV Resort
CAMPGROUND $

(☑ 435-772-3237; www.zioncamp.com; 479 Zion Park Blvd; tent/RV sites with hookups $39/49; @🕈🗺🐾) Water and tubing access at this 200-site campground are just across the Virgin River from the national park. Attached to the Quality Inn (☑ 435-772-3237, 877-424-6423; www.zioncamp.com; 479 Zion Park Blvd; r from $136; @🕈🗺) motel; shared amenities include heated pool, laundry, camp store, playground and restaurant. It's mainly for RVs, though it can be a handy backup for tent campers if you can't get a spot in the park.

Not all sites have shade. Pets in RVs only.

Watchman Campground
CAMPGROUND $

(☑ reservations 877-444-6777; www.recreation. gov; Hwy 9, Zion National Park; tent sites $20, RV sites with hookups $30; ⊙ year-round; 🐾) Towering cottonwoods provide fairly good shade for the 184 well-spaced sites at Watchman (95 have electricity), located south of the visitor center (p415). Sites are by reservation (six months in advance) and you should book a minimum several months ahead, otherwise it's unlikely you'll get a spot. Fire grates, drinking water, RV hookups and flush toilets; no showers.

Sites along the river cost $4 extra. Pets are allowed in RVs only.

> **DON'T MISS**
>
> ## ANGELS LANDING TRAIL
>
> 'How far did you get?' is the question asked every morning at coffee shops all over Springdale, as hikers compare notes on Angels Landing. This strenuous four-hour, 5-mile (round-trip) hike is not just a physical challenge, but a mental one for those with a fear of heights. Start at the trailhead across the road from the Grotto picnic area.

★ Under the Eaves Inn
B&B $$

(☑ 435-772-3457; www.undertheeaves.com; 980 Zion Park Blvd; r $109-189; ❀🕈) From colorful tractor reflectors to angel art, the owners' collections enliven every corner of this quaint 1930s bungalow. The fireplace suite is huge; other character-filled rooms are snug. Hang out in the arts-and-crafts living room or on Adirondack chairs and swings in the gorgeous gardens. The best room is the upstairs suite with clawfoot tub. Local restaurant coupon for breakfast.

★ Red Rock Inn
B&B $$

(☑ 435-772-3139; www.redrockinn.com; 998 Zion Park Blvd; cottages $199-259; ❀🕈) Five romantic country-contemporary cottages spill down the desert hillside, backed by incredible red rock. Enjoy the full hot breakfast (egg dish and pastries) that appears at the door either on the hilltop terrace or your private patio. One suite features an outdoor hot tub.

Driftwood Lodge
HOTEL $$

(☑ 888-801-8811, 435-772-3262; www.driftwood lodge.net; 1515 Zion Park Blvd; r $169-269; ❀🕈🗺🐾) Rich textures and dark leathers mold the upscale style of thoroughly remodeled rooms at this eco-minded lodging. Some of the contemporary suites have pastoral sunset views of field, river and mountain beyond. With an expansive pool on the grounds. Breakfast included.

Novel House Inn
B&B $$

(☑ 435-772-3650, 800-711-8400; www.novel house.com; 73 Paradise Rd; r $159-275; ❀) Incredible detail has gone into each of the author-themed rooms: Rudyard Kipling has animal prints and mosquito netting, and a pillow in the Victorian Dickens room reads 'Bah humbug.' Breakfast coupons; hot tub.

Flanigan's Inn
HOTEL $$
(☑ 800-765-7787, 435-772-3244; www.flanigans.com; 428 Zion Park Blvd; r from $179, ste from $289; ❄ 🛜 ⌘) Rejuvenate your spirit by indulging in a seaweed and mineral mud wrap, walking the hilltop meditation labyrinth and sinking into your king-size bed in front of a crackling fire. Suites are deliciously plush with vaulted ceilings, bold color schemes and tasteful art; most sleep up to six. Standard rooms vary, so check out a few first. There are also two villas.

Canyon Vista Lodge
LODGE $$
(☑ 435-772-3801; www.canyonvistabandb.com; 897 Zion Park Blvd; ste $169-209; ❄ 🛜) All the homey comfort of a B&B, coupled with the privacy of a hotel. Individual entrances lead out from Southwestern or Old World–esque rooms onto a wooden porch or a sprawling patio and lawn with river access. Breakfast coupons; hot tub on-site.

Zion Canyon Bed & Breakfast
B&B $$
(☑ 435-772-9466; www.zioncanyonbnb.com; 101 Kokopelli Circle; r $159-199; ❄ 🛜) Deep canyon colors echo the scenery and over-the-top Southwestern styling. Everywhere you turn there's another gorgeous red-rock view framed perfectly in an oversized window. Full gourmet breakfasts and mini-spa.

Harvest House
B&B $$
(☑ 435-772-3880; www.harvesthouse.net; 29 Canyon View Dr; r $140-170; ❄ 🛜) Modern B&B alternative with full breakfast.

★ Desert Pearl Inn
HOTEL $$$
(☑ 888-828-0898, 435-772-8888; www.desertpearl.com; 707 Zion Park Blvd; r from $239; ❄ @ 🛜 ⌘) How naturally stylish: twig sculptures decorate the walls and molded metal headboards resemble art. Opt for a spacious riverside king suite to get a waterfront patio. The most sophisticated design in town and popular with hip Angelenos. Breakfast included.

Cliffrose Lodge
HOTEL $$$
(☑ 435-772-3234, 800-243-8824; www.cliffroselodge.com; 281 Zion Park Blvd; r $319-399; ❄ 🛜 ⌘) Kick back in a lounge chair or take a picnic lunch to enjoy on the five gorgeous acres of lawn and flower gardens leading down to the river. High-thread-count linens and pillow-top mattresses are among the upscale touches. Suites sleep up to six and feature full kitchens. This is a good high-end choice for families.

✖ Eating
Springdale has plenty of cheerful options geared at the high visitor population. Few are outstanding. Most restaurants open for dinner serve beer and wine. Note that many places in town limit hours variably – or close entirely – off-season.

Sol Foods Downtown Supermarket
MARKET $
(☑ 435-772-3100; 995 Zion Park Blvd; ⊙ 7am-11pm Apr-Oct, 9am-8pm Nov-Mar) Springdale's grocery store has a decent selection, with plenty of variety, organic items and camping-friendly meals. There's also a salad bar and deli with $6 sandwiches. Groceries are pricey, however.

Zion Deli
DELI $
(☑ 435-772-3843; 866 Zion Park Blvd; sandwiches $8; ⊙ 9am-8:30pm) Sharing a space with a souvenir shop, this one-counter wonder turns out good sandwiches (including boxed lunches for the park), breakfasts, chocolates and ice cream, all to go.

MeMe's Cafe
EUROPEAN $
(☑ 435-772-0114; www.memescafezion.com; 975 Zion Park Blvd; mains $10-14; ⊙ 7am-9pm) For a coffee and sweet crepes, make MeMe's Cafe your first stop of the day. It also serves paninis, quiches and salads, and, for dinner, beef brisket and pulled pork.

Oscar's Cafe
SOUTHERN US $$
(www.cafeoscars.com; 948 Zion Park Blvd; mains $12-18, breakfast $6-12; ⊙ 8am-9pm) From green-chili-laden omelets to pork *verde* burritos (with a green salsa), expect big servings of Southwestern spice. There's also smoky ribs, garlic burgers and beer on tap. The Mexican-tiled patio with twinkly lights (and heaters) is a favorite hangout in the evening. The breakfast is quite popular, which might mean a late start in the park.

Whiptail Grill
SOUTHERN US $$
(☑ 435-772-0283; www.whiptailgrillzion.com; 445 Zion Park Blvd; mains $11-17; ⊙ noon-9pm Mar-Nov; 🛜 🍴) The old gas-station building isn't much to look at, but deep shade and fresh tastes abound: think gorgeous *chiles rellenos* and *carne asada* tacos grilled to perfection. Desserts are rich with a kick. Outdoor patio tables fill up quick.

Café Soleil
CAFE $$
(☑ 435-772-0505; cafesoleilzionpark.com; 205 Zion Park Blvd; mains $9-13; ⊙ 7am-7pm; 🛜 🍴) The food is every bit as good as the free-trade

coffee. Try the Mediterranean hummus wrap or giant vegetable frittata; pizza and salads too. It's a good spot to grab sandwiches for hiking. Breakfast served till noon.

Spotted Dog   AMERICAN $$
(☑ 435-772-0700; www.flanigans.com; 428 Zion Park Blvd; breakfast $8, mains $13-24; ⊙ 7-11am & 5-9pm Mar-Nov) One of the more inventive top-end dining choices in Springdale, the Spotted Dog has a seasonal menu with a focus on regional specialties. Expect delicacies like Cedar Mountain lamb shank, wild game meatloaf and Rocky Mountain trout. Spacious dining areas plus two outdoor patios.

Flying Monkey   PIZZA $$
(☑ 435-772-3333; www.pizzainzion.com; 975 Zion Park Blvd; pizzas $12-16, mains $12-30; ⊙ 8am-9:30pm) Wood-fired goodness at great prices, though service is slow. Expect interesting ingredients like fennel and yellow squash on your roast veggie pizza or Italian sausage with the prosciutto on your oven-baked sandwich. Also serves breakfast.

Bit & Spur Restaurant
& Saloon   SOUTHERN US $$
(www.bitandspur.com; 1212 Zion Park Blvd; mains $13-28; ⊙ 5-11pm daily Mar-Oct, 5-10pm Thu-Sat Nov-Feb; ☎) Sweet-potato tamales and chili-rubbed rib-eyes are two of the classics at this local institution. Inside, the walls are wild with local art; outside on the deck, it's all about the red-rock sunset. Full bar.

Thai Sapa   ASIAN $$
(☑ 435-772-0510; www.thaisapazion.com; 145 Zion Park Blvd; mains $10-18; ⊙ 11am-9:30pm) This mix of Thai, Chinese and Indian cuisine is your only Asian-cuisine option in town.

★ King's Landing   AMERICAN $$$
(☑ 435-772-7422; www.klbzion.com; 1515 Zion Park Blvd, Driftwood Lodge; mains $16-38; ⊙ 5-9pm) 🍴 With a lauded Las Vegas chef and his pastry chef wife at the helm, this hotel-restaurant surpasses expectations. Bison fettuccine with truffle oil, charred octopus and verdant greens entice. Locals love its intimacy. There are also good burgers, vegetarian fare that does not bore and beautiful desserts. Reserve ahead.

🍷 Drinking & Entertainment

Springdale is not big on nightlife, but there is a sports bar (☑ 435-772-3700; 1149 Zion Park Blvd; ⊙ noon-10pm) and brewery (with early closing hours).

★ Deep Creek Coffee Co   CAFE
(932 Zion Park Blvd; ⊙ 6am-4pm; ☎) The town's best coffee, with espresso drinks and fresh pastries daily.

Zion Canyon Brew Pub   BREWERY
(www.zionbrewery.com; 95 Zion Park Blvd; ⊙ noon-9pm; ☎) The local brewery has a killer location, with an outdoor patio that cozies up to the Virgin River and the park entrance. Nine varieties of suds are on tap, from Red Altar to Delusion Ale. It does have a full food menu, but all you really need are the pretzel sticks and you're good to go.

Zion Canyon Giant Screen Theatre   CINEMA
(☑ 435-772-2400;   www.zioncanyontheatre.com; 145 Zion Park Blvd; admission varies) Catch the 40-minute *Zion Canyon: Treasure of the Gods* on a six-story screen – it's light on substance but long on beauty. Also look for local outdoors documentaries and one Hollywood flick at 7pm.

🛍 Shopping

Eclectic boutiques and souvenir shops are scattered the length of Zion Park Blvd. Beyond the gorgeous nature photography, look for the three-dimensional oil paintings of Anna Weiler Brown and the colorful multimedia works of Deb Durban, both locals. Hours vary off-season.

Worthington Gallery   ART
(☑ 435-772-3446;   worthingtongallery.com;   789 Zion Park Blvd; ⊙ 10am-8pm) Represents 20 different potters from across the Southwest.

LaFave Gallery   ART
(☑ 435-772-0464;   secure.lafavegallery.com; 1214 Zion Park Blvd; ⊙ 11am-6pm) Large collection of ceramics, jewelry, sculpture and paintings, but pride of place here goes to the work of local photographer David Pettit. Also sells signed prints.

Redrock Jewelry   JEWELRY
(☑ 435-772-3836; 998 Zion Park Blvd; ⊙ 10am-6pm Mar-Oct, off-season hours vary) Gorgeous, locally crafted jewelry.

Farmers Market   FOOD
(www.zionharvest.org; 1212 Zion Park Blvd; ⊙ 9am-noon Sat May–mid-Oct) Don't miss the farmers market in the Bit & Spur parking lot on Saturday mornings.

David J West Gallery   ART
(☑ 435-772-3510;   www.davidjwest.com;   801 Zion Park Blvd; ⊙ 10am-9pm Tue-Sun Mar-Oct, to 8pm

Nov-Feb) Iconic local-landscape photography; sells some photo gear.

ℹ Information

For information, go online to www.zionpark.com and www.zionnationalpark.

Zion Canyon Visitor Center (☑ 435-772-3256; www.nps.gov/zion; Hwy 9, Zion National Park; ⊙8am-7:30pm late May-early Sep, 8am-5pm rest of year) Several rangers are on hand to answer questions at the main visitor center; ask to see the picture binder of hikes to know what you're getting into. Find out about ranger-led activities here.

Springdale Visitor Center (☑ 435-429-1555; www.zionnationalpark.com; 1101 Zion Park Blvd; ⊙7am-10pm) If nothing else is open, this private visitor center owned by the Hampton Inn can be helpful with local information, although it's a bit of a smoke screen for a gift shop. There are maps and area books available.

Zion Canyon Visitors Bureau (☑ 888-518-7070; www.zionpark.com; ⊙9am-5pm Mon-Fri) Offers comprehensive accommodations listings of family-friendly motels and hotels, as well as boutique inns and B&Bs.

Zion Wilderness Desk (☑ 435-772-0170; www.nps.gov/zion; Zion Canyon Visitor Center; ⊙7am-7:30pm late May-Sep, 8am-4:30pm rest of year) Provides backcountry trail and camping information and permits. Some permits available online.

Zion Canyon Medical Clinic (☑ 435-772-3226; 120 Lion Blvd; ⊙9am-5pm Tue-Sat Mar-Oct, shorter hours Nov-Feb) Walk-in urgent-care clinic.

Post Office (☑ 435-772-3950; 625 Zion Park Blvd; ⊙7:30am-1pm & 1:30-3pm Mon-Fri, 10am-1pm Sat)

ℹ Getting There & Around

There's no public transportation to the town; come with your own wheels. From mid-March through early November the free Springdale Shuttle runs every 15 minutes between 7am and 8pm, with stops in town and Zion National Park.

Red Canyon

Impressive, deep-ocher-red monoliths rise up roadside as you drive along Hwy 12, 10 miles west of the Hwy 63/Bryce Canyon turnoff. The aptly named **Red Canyon** (☑ 435-676-2676; www.fs.usda.gov/recarea/dixie; Scenic Byway 12, Dixie National Forest; ⊙park 24hr, visitor center 9am-6pm Jun-Aug, 10am-4pm May & Sep) FREE provides super-easy access to these eerie, intensely colored formations. In fact, you have to cross under two

blasted-rock arches to continue on the highway. A network of trails leads hikers, bikers and horseback riders deeper into these national-forest-service lands. Check out the excellent geologic displays and pick up trail maps at the visitor center (p416).

🕴 Activities

Several moderately easy hiking trails begin near the visitor center. There are also excellent mountain-biking trails in the area. Outfitters near Bryce Canyon National Park (p399) rent mountain bikes and offer horseback rides through Red Canyon.

Thunder Mountain Trail   MOUNTAIN BIKING
(🖼) The best trail in the region, the Thunder Mountain loop has 5 paved miles ideal for families; the other 7.8 miles are strenuous and involve sand and switchbacks (start the ride toward Bryce to ride uphill on the pavement and downhill on the dirt). Be aware that horses share the trail.

Red Canyon Trails   HIKING
Several moderately easy hiking trails begin near the visitor center: the 0.7-mile (30-minute) **Arches Trail** passes 15 arches as it winds through a canyon; and the 0.5-mile (30-minute) **Pink Ledges Trail** passes red-rock formations. For a harder hike, try the 2.8-mile (two to four hours) **Golden Wall Trail**; you can extend it to a 5-mile round-trip by adding **Buckhorn Trail**.

Red Canyon Bicycle Trail   CYCLING
(🖼) This newish bike path runs 8.6 miles along Hwy 12 from Thunder Mountain trailhead to East Fork Rd. It's paved and perfect for families. There are plans to eventually extend the path all the way to Bryce.

Scenic Rim Trail Rides   HORSEBACK RIDING
(☑ 800-679-5859, 435-679-8761; www.brycecanyonhorseback.com; 1000 S Hwy 63, Ruby's Inn; 4hr ride $95) Guided horseback rides to Thunder Mountain and other Red Canyon locations. Based at Best Western Ruby's Inn.

🛏 Sleeping

Look to Panguitch and Hatch for dining and further sleeping options.

Red Canyon Campground   CAMPGROUND $
(☑ 435-676-2676; www.fs.usda.gov; Scenic Byway 12; tent & RV sites $20; ⊙mid-May–Sep) Surrounded by limestone formations and ponderosa pines, the 37 no-reservation sites here are quite scenic. Quiet-use trails (no

ATVs) lead off from here, making this a good alternative to Bryce Canyon National Park (p399) camping. There are showers and a dump station, but no hookups. It's 10 miles west of the Hwy 12/63 junction.

Red Canyon Village CAMPGROUND $
(📞 435-676-2243; www.redcanyonvillage.com; cnr Hwys 12 & 89; sites $39, cabins $50-125; ☉ Apr-Sep) If you can't secure a site at the Red Canyon Campground, try this park, which also operates a small store. Options include tent sites, RV hookups and cabins. Cabins are micro-size, without private bathrooms.

ⓘ Information

Visitor Center (📞 435-676-2676; Hwy 12; ☉ 9am-6pm Jun-Aug, 10am-4pm May & Sep) Check out the excellent geologic displays and pick up trail maps at the visitor center.

Panguitch

📞 435 / POP 1500

Founded in 1864, historically Panguitch was a profitable pioneer ranching and lumber community. Since the 1920s inception of the national park, the town has had a can't-live-with-or-without-it relationship with Bryce Canyon (p399), 24 miles east. Lodging long ago became the number-one industry, as it's also used as an overnight stop halfway between Las Vegas (234 miles) and Salt Lake City (245 miles).

Other than some interesting turn-of-the-20th-century brick homes and buildings, it has few attractions. Main St has an antique store or two, but mostly people fill up with food and fuel, rest up and move on. In a pinch you could use it as a base for seeing Bryce, Zion and Cedar Breaks.

Panguitch is the seat of Garfield County and hosts numerous festivals.

✦ Festivals & Events

Quilt Walk Festival ART
(www.quiltwalk.org; ☉ mid-Jun) The popular Quilt Walk Festival honors pioneer history and also features historic home tours, theater shows, tractor parades and a chocolate fair.

Garfield County Fair STREET CARNIVAL
(☉ late Aug) One of the most anticipated events of the year, this 75-year tradition hosts live bands and features parades, classic car shows, barbecues, livestock sales and rodeos for an entire week.

Panguitch Valley Balloon Rally FAIR
(Chariots in the Sky; www.panguitchvalleyballoon rally.com; ☉ late Jun) A huge hot-air balloon festival featuring music and family activities.

🛏 Sleeping

Cute B&Bs and old-fashioned motels are the order of the day in Panguitch.

Purple Sage MOTEL $
(📞 435-676-2659, 800-241-6889; www.purplesage motel.biz; 132 E Center St; r $69-120; ☉ Mar-Oct; ❄ 🕸 🐾) Comfy, as motels go, this tidy spot slips in sweet extras such as pillow-top mattresses, new furnishings and coffeemakers. Staff are helpfully chatty. Pets may be allowed; check first in person.

Panguitch House B&B $
(📞 435-899-0190, 435-676-2574; www.panguitch housebandb.com; 259 E Center St; r $89; ❄ 🕸) The nicely simple, new B&B rooms in this renovated red-brick home are an excellent alternative to a motel. The price is more than right and the friendly hosts provide a big breakfast and advice on area adventures.

Panguitch KOA CAMPGROUND $
(📞 435-676-2225, 800-562-1625; koa.com/camp grounds/panguitch; 555 S Main St; tent/RV site $25/39; 🕸 🏊 ❄) Offers complete facilities, including a swimming pool. Showers cost $5 for nonguests.

Color Country Motel MOTEL $
(📞 435-676-2386, 800-225-6518; www.colorcoun trymotel.com; 526 N Main St; r from $65; 🏊) An economical, standard motel with perks – a pool and outdoor hot tub.

★ Red Brick Inn B&B $$
(📞 435-690-1048; www.redbrickinn.com; 161 N 100 W; d $130, ste $220-250; ☉ Apr-Oct; ❄ 🕸) Warm California native Peggy runs this 1919 charmer that once served as the town hospital. Rooms are cozy and comfortable, breakfasts are elaborate and outstanding and stories abound. Chill out swinging in a garden hammock or pedaling a loan bike. Ask in advance about pets.

Grandma's Cottage RENTAL HOUSE $$
(📞 435-690-9495; www.grandmascottages.com; 90 N 100 W; 2-6-person rentals $100-180; ☉ Mar-Nov; ❄) Excellent for groups and families, these renovated cottages and homes around central Panguitch have been lovingly put together by a semiretired couple. Except for the studio cottage, the decor is nothing like grandma's.

Think savvy and stylish. Themes vary – there's a 1960s hideout, a country cottage and a historic brick home, all with gorgeous touches and cable TV. Some accommodations have cooking facilities and washer/dryer.

Marianna Inn Motel MOTEL $$
(☑ 435-676-8844, 800-598-9190; www.marianna inn.com; r $90-130; ❀ ❁ ❀) Rooms in the dollhouse-like motel with the large, shaded swing deck are standard. But the newest additions – deluxe log-style rooms – are worth splurging on. BBQ grill available for guests.

✖ Eating

The selection of restaurants is a little slim. Remember that eateries in Hatch are also close by.

Henrie's Drive-in BURGERS $
(154 N Main St; burgers $5-8; ⊙ 11am-10pm Mar-Oct) Craving a deliciously greasy burger and fries? Look no further and don't forget the strawberry milkshake.

Cowboy's Smokehouse BBQ BARBECUE $$
(☑ 435-676-8030; 95 N Main St; breakfast & lunch $5-12, dinner $15-32; ⊙ 4-8pm Tue & Wed, 4-9pm Thu-Sat) Sweet staff serve steaks and brisket with housemade sauce, but the food quality can be erratic. Portions are generous.

ℹ Information

Garfield County Tourism Office
(☑ 800-444-6689, 435-676-1160; www. brycecanyoncountry.com; 55 S Main St; ⊙ 9am-5pm) Provides regional travel and event information.

Powell Ranger Station (☑ 435-676-9300; www.fs.fed.us/dxnf; 225 E Center St; ⊙ 8am-4:30pm Mon-Fri) **Dixie National Forest** (p392) camping and hiking info.

Garfield Memorial Hospital (☑ 435-676-8811; 224 N 400 E; ⊙ 24hr) A small hospital with trauma care services.

Garfield County Sheriff's Office (☑ 435-676-2678; 375 N 700 W)

Post Office (☑ 435-676-8853; 65 N 100 W; ⊙ 8:30am-5pm Mon-Fri, 9:30am-noon Sat)

Kanab

☑ 435 / POP 4500

Vast expanses of rugged desert surround the remote outpost of Kanab. Look familiar? Hundreds of Western movies were shot here. Founded by Mormon pioneers in 1874, Kanab was put on the map by John Wayne and other gun-slingin' celebs in the 1940s and '50s. Just about every resident had something to do with the movies from the 1930s to the '70s. You can still see a couple

---

ON BUTCH CASSIDY'S TRAIL

Nearly every town in southern Utah claims a connection to Butch Cassidy (1866–1908?), the Old West's most famous bank and train robber. As part of the Wild Bunch, Cassidy (né Robert LeRoy Parker) pulled 19 heists from 1896 to 1901. Accounts usually describe him with a breathless romanticism, likening him to a kind of Robin Hood. Bring up the subject in these parts and you'll likely be surprised at how many folks' grandfathers had encounters with him. The robber may even have attended a dance in the old **Torrey Schoolhouse**, now a B&B. And many a dilapidated shack or a canyon, just over yonder, served as his hideout. The most credible claim for the location of the famous Robbers' Roost hideout is in the **Henry Mountains**.

In the wee town of **Circleville**, located 28 miles north of Panguitch, stands the honest-to-goodness boyhood home of the gun-slingin' bandit. The cabin is partially renovated but uninhabited, 2 miles south of town on the west side of Hwy 89. When reporters arrived after the release of the film *Butch Cassidy and the Sundance Kid* (1969), they met the outlaw's youngest sister, who claimed that Butch did in fact not die in South America in 1908, but returned for a visit after that. Writers have been digging for the truth to no avail ever since. You can see where they filmed Robert Redford's famous bicycle scene at the **Grafton ghost town**, outside Rockville.

Local lore holds that Cassidy didn't steal much in Utah because this is where his bread was buttered. Whatever the reason, the Wild Bunch's only big heist in the state was in April, 1897, when the gang stole more than $8000 from Pleasant Valley Coal Company in Castle Gate, 4 miles north of Helper on Hwy 191. The little **Western Mining & Railroad Museum** (☑ 435-472-3009; wmrrm.com; 296 S Main St, Helper; adult/child $2/1; ⊙ 10am-5pm Mon-Sat May-Aug, 11am-4pm Tue-Sat Sep-Apr), 8 miles north of Price, has exhibits on the outlaws, including photos, in the basement. For more, check out *The Outlaw Trail*, written by Charles Kelly.

of movie sets in the area and hear old-timers talk about their roles.

Kanab sits at a major crossroads: GSENM is 20 miles away, Zion 40 miles, Bryce Canyon 80 miles, Grand Canyon's North Rim 81 miles and Lake Powell 74 miles. It makes a good base for exploring the southern side of GSENM and Paria Canyon–Vermilion Cliffs formations such as the Wave (p421). **Coral Pink Sand Dunes State Park** is a big rompin' playground to the northwest.

◉ Sights & Activities

The Kane County Office of Tourism (p421) has an exhibit of area-made movie posters and knowledge about sites.

★ Best Friends Animal Sanctuary   WILDLIFE RESERVE

(✆ 435-644-2001; www.bestfriends.org; Hwy 89, Angel Canyon; ⊙ 9:30am-5:30pm; ⊕) FREE Kanab's most famous attraction is outside of town. Surrounded by more than 33,000 mostly private acres of red-rock desert 5.5 miles north of Kanab, Best Friends is the largest no-kill animal rescue center in the country. The center shows films and gives facility tours four times a day; call ahead for times and reservations. The 1½-hour tours let you meet some of the more than 1700 horses, pigs, dogs, cats, birds and other critters on-site.

Volunteers come from around the country to work here. Spending the night in one of eight one-bedroom cottages with kitchenettes ($140) or in a one-room cabin ($92) and volunteering for at least a half-day allows visitors to borrow a dog, cat or pot-bellied pig for the night. (Cottages should be booked well in advance.) It also has RV sites ($45) with hookups.

The sanctuary is located in Angel Canyon (Kanab Canyon to locals), where scores of movies and TV shows were filmed during Kanab's Hollywood heyday. The cliff ridge about the sanctuary is where the Lone Ranger reared and shouted 'Hi-yo Silver!' at the end of every episode.

Kanab Heritage Museum   MUSEUM

(✆ 435-644-3966; www.kanabheritagemuseum.com; 13 S 100 E; admission by donation; ⊙ 10am-5pm Mon-Fri May 1-Sep 30) For a glimpse into the region's popular history, this small museum is worth a stop. While the few pieces of historical memorabilia aren't particularly riveting, it's fun to browse the 30-plus spiral-bound notebooks filled with movie newspapers, magazine articles, written histories and photographs.

Parry Lodge   HISTORIC SITE

(www.parrylodge.com; 89 E Center St; ⊙ movies 8pm Sat Jun-Aug) FREE Built in the 1930s, this hotel was movie central. Stars stayed here and owner Whit Parry provided horses, cattle and catering for the sets. There are nostalgic photos, and old Westerns play in a barn (✆ 888-289-1722; 89 E Center St) FREE out back on summer Saturday nights.

Little Hollywood   FILM LOCATION

(297 W Center St; ⊙ 7:30am-11pm Apr-Oct, 10am-5pm Nov-Mar) FREE Wander through a bunkhouse, saloon and other buildings used in Western movies filmed locally, including *The Outlaw Josey Wales,* and learn some tricks of the trade (such as low doorways to make movie stars seem taller). This classic roadside attraction sells all the Western duds and doodads you could care to round up.

Squaw Trail   HIKING

Accessed just north of Jacob Hamblin Park at the end of 100 East, this short but steep 800ft scramble leads to spectacular views of Kanab and the surrounding desert wilderness. It's about a mile to the city overview; you can continue another 0.5 miles to the top, with 360-degree views, or retrace your steps.

This hike is best in spring or fall, when the summer heat has faded and the cottonwoods turn brilliant yellow. Park next to the baseball fields and look for signs. An information kiosk at the trailhead gives directions for linking to trails to the east and west to create a series of loops for up to 6 miles.

Allen's Outfitters   HORSEBACK RIDING

(✆ 435-689-1660; half-/full-day trail ride $100/130, 2hr trail ride $70) Offers one-hour, two-hour, half-day, full-day and custom-designed overnight or multiday horseback rides through the woods and to overlooks. Children must be at least five years old. Reservations are not required for short rides – just stop by the corrals just south of Jacob Lake Lodge.

⌲ Tours

★ Dreamland Safari   TOURS

(www.dreamlandtours.net; slot canyon tour $90) Hikes with naturalist tour guides to gorgeous backcountry sites and slot canyons reached by 4WD. It also offers nature photography and multiday backpacking trips.

Seldom Seen Adventures ADVENTURE

(📞888-418-9908; www.seldomseenadventures.net; 89 W Center St; day hike $129) Family oriented, personalized tours of the national parks, Grand Staircase–Escalante National Monument and wilderness areas, with canyoneering, 4WD tours, super fat-tire biking and hiking. Also offers transfers.

Paria Outpost ADVENTURE

(📞928-691-1047; www.paria.com; Hwy 89, Mile 21; tour $175) Friendly, flexible and knowledgeable. Offers guided horseback rides in Grand Staircase–Escalante National Monument, as well as 4WD tours and guided hikes.

Windows of the West
Hummer Tours ADVENTURE

(📞888-687-3006; www.wowhummertours.com; 2hr tour $99) Personalizable backcountry excursions (two hours to full-day) to slot canyons, petroglyphs and spectacular red-rock country.

🎆 Festivals & Events

Kaibab Paiute Tribal
Heritage Days CULTURAL

(🕐Aug) Tribes of Southern Paiute celebrate with dancing, songs, competition, Native American food and crafts and children's activities. All events are open to the public.

Western Legends Roundup FILM

(📞800-733-5263; www.westernlegendsroundup.com; 🕐late Aug) The town lives for the annual Western Legends Roundup in late August. There are concerts, gunfights, cowboy poetry, dances, quilt shows, a film festival and more. Take a bus tour to all the film sites, or sign up for a Dutch-oven cooking lesson.

🛏 Sleeping

Kanab has a great selection of B&Bs and lodgings. For a full listing see www.visitsouthernutah.com.

Hitch'n Post Campground CAMPGROUND $

(📞435-644-2142, 800-458-3516; www.hitchnpostrvpark.com; 196 E 300 S; tent/RV sites with hookups $18/29, camping cabins $32-36; 🛰🐾) Friendly 17-site campground near the town center; has laundry and showers.

⭐**Canyons Lodge** MOTEL $$

(📞435-644-3069, 800-644-5094; www.canyonslodge.com; 236 N 300 W; r $169-179; 🆒@🛰🐾🐾) 🅿 A renovated motel with an art-house Western feel. There's a warm welcome, free cruiser bikes and good traveler

assistance. In summer, guests enjoy twice-weekly live music and wine and cheese by the fire pit. Rooms feature original artwork and whimsical touches. Recycles soaps and containers.

Savage Point B&B B&B $$

(📞435-644-2799; www.savagepointbedbreakfast.com; 53 S 200 E; ste $125; 🛰🐾) Bunk at a cozy home filled with winsome pets and hosts. Laurel and Russell, a guide and ranger, are helpful with hiking tips. Guests have their own separate entrance. There's a Finnish sauna and cold pool in the garden area, pick-your-own fruit and fresh farm eggs for breakfast.

Flagstone MOTEL $$

(📞435-644-2020; 223 W Center St; r $129-139; 🆒🛰) A fully refurbished upscale motel. All rooms have full kitchens and accessories to enjoy a cup of coffee. Forget your idea of dusty old motels: there are king beds, flat-screen TVs and sleek style here.

Purple Sage Inn B&B $$

(📞435-644-5377, 877-644-5377; www.purplesageinn.com; r $135-165; 🆒🛰) A former Mormon polygamist's home, this later became a hotel, where Western author Zane Grey stayed. Now it's a B&B with exquisite antique details. Zane's namesake room – with its quilt-covered wood bed, sitting room and balcony access – is our favorite.

Quail Park Lodge MOTEL $$

(📞435-215-1447; www.quailparklodge.com; 125 N 300 W; r/ste $149/159; 🆒@🛰🐾🐾) With Schwinn cruiser bicycles and a postage-stamp-size pool, retro pervades all 13 rooms at this refurbished 1963 motel with surprisingly plush rooms. Mod cons include free phone calls, microwaves, mini-refrigerators and complimentary gourmet coffee.

Canyons Boutique Hotel BOUTIQUE HOTEL $$

(📞435-644-8660; www.canyonshotel.com; 190 N 300 W; r $189-199; 🆒🛰🐾) From the architecture to appointments, this inn is a modern-day remake of period Victoriana. Ethan Allen furnishings, gas fireplaces and jetted tubs grace every room, but it all looks a little stiff in these parts. Look for the new on-site restaurant.

Parry Lodge MOTEL $$

(📞888-289-1722, 435-644-2601; www.parrylodge.com; 89 E Center St; r $119-149; 🆒🛰🐾🐾) The aura of bygone Westerns is the best feature of this rambling old classic motel. Some rooms bear the names of movie stars who stayed here, like Gregory Peck or Lana Turner. If quality is your concern, opt for the L-shaped double queen room, nicely refurbished in cottage decor.

🍴 Eating

An oasis in a food desert, Kanab's dining scene offers impressive creativity for such a tiny town.

★ Kanab Creek Bakery · BAKERY $

(kanabcreekbakery.com; 238 W Center St; mains $6-16; ⊙6:30am-2pm Tue-Sun) For fancy-pants pastries and gourmet breakfasts, this is your first (and only) stop. Croissants, *boules* (tiny pieces of chocolate-coated cake truffle), baguettes and rye bread are baked daily. Try the *shakshuka* (a cast-iron skillet of eggs in a rich pepper sauce). For lunch there's roast chicken and paella baked in the wood-fired oven.

Escobar's · MEXICAN $

(373 E 300 S; mains $7-12; ⊙11am-9:30pm Sun-Fri) Sometimes it feels like all of Kanab is stuffed into this busy, family run restaurant with swift service and XL portions. Start with the complimentary homemade chips and salsa and move on to a green chili burrito and a chilled mug of beer.

Peekaboo Kitchen · CAFE $

(📞435-689-1959; peekabookitchen.com; 233 W Center St; mains $10-15; ⊙7am-10pm; 🖉) A godsend to green diets, this new cafe goes big on vegetarian and vegan dishes, salads and beet chips. The artisan pizzas are pretty good too. Breakfast options include lattes, eggs Benedict served in artichokes and pumpkin flapjacks. If you are bone tired, it can also deliver.

Fusion House · ASIAN $

(📞435-644-8868; www.fusionhousekanab.com; 18 E Center St; mains $11-16; ⊙10:30am-9pm Mon-Sat, noon-9pm Sun; 🐟🖉) Casual Asian fusion – think Japanese-style pork katsu curry, coconut shrimp, udon noodle soups, and fried rice with spinach and pine nuts – served in a diner-like setting on Kanab's main drag. With vegan options.

Luo's Cafe · CHINESE $

(📞435-644-5592; www.luoscafechinese.com; 365 S 100 E; mains $6-18; ⊙11am-10pm Mon-Sat; 🖉) For a change. Surprisingly good Chinese food; great vegetable selection.

★ Sego Restaurant · MODERN AMERICAN $$

(📞435-644-5680; 190 N 300 W, Canyons Boutique Hotel; mains $14-23; ⊙5-9pm Tue-Sat) If Kanab is aspiring to be the next Sedona, this boutique hotel-restaurant will fast track things. Gorgeous eats range from foraged mushrooms with goat cheese to noodles with red-crab curry and a decadent flourless torte for dessert. There are also craft cocktails and local beers. Hours may be expanding. Reserve ahead: there are few tables.

Houston's Trail's End Restaurant · AMERICAN $$

(📞435-644-2488; www.houstons.net; 32 E Center St; breakfast $5-15, mains $9-25; ⊙7am-10pm) Join the locals for chicken-fried steak and razzleberry pie – you know the food must be good if they'll frequent a place where the waiters wear cowboy boots and toy six-shooters. No alcohol.

Rocking V Cafe · AMERICAN $$$

(📞435-644-8001; www.rockingvcafe.com; 97 W Center St; lunch $8-18, dinner $18-48; ⊙11:30am-10pm; 🖉) Fresh ingredients star in dishes like hand-cut buffalo tenderloin and chargrilled zucchini with curried quinoa. Local artwork decorating the 1892 brick storefront is as creative as the food. Off-season hours vary.

☆ Entertainment

Crescent Moon Theater · THEATER

(📞435-644-2350; www.crescentmoontheater.com; 150 S 100 E; ⊙May-Sep) Cowboy poetry, bluegrass music and comedic plays are just some of what is staged here. Monday is Western-movie night.

🛍 Shopping

Western clothing and bric-a-brac are sold, along with American Indian knickknacks, at shops all along Center St.

Willow Canyon Outdoor Co · SPORTS & OUTDOORS

(📞435-644-8884; www.willowcanyon.com; 263 S 100 E; ⊙7:30am-8pm, off-season hours vary) It's easy to spend hours sipping espresso and perusing the eclectic books here. Before you leave, outfit yourself with field guides, camping gear, USGS maps, hiking clothes and gas for your camp stove.

ℹ Information

As the biggest town around the GSENM, Kanab has several grocery stores, ATMs, banks and services.

UTAH KANAB

Kane County Office of Tourism (☎435-644-5033, 800-733-5263; www.visitsouthernutah.com; 78 S 100 E; ☺8:30am-6pm Mon-Fri, to 4pm Sat) The main source for area information; great old Western movie posters and artifacts on display.

BLM Kanab Field Office (☎435-644-4600; 318 N 100 E; ☺8am-4pm Mon-Fri)

GSENM Visitor Center (☎435-644-1300; www.ut.blm.gov/monument; 745 E Hwy 89; ☺8am-4:30pm) Provides road, trail and weather updates for the **Grand Staircase–Escalante National Monument** (p394).

Kane County Hospital (☎435-644-5811; 355 N Main St; ☺24hr) The closest medical facility to GSENM.

Post Office (39 S Main St; ☺9am-4pm Mon-Fri, to 2pm Sat)

Police Station (☎435-644-5807; 140 E 100 S)

Paria Canyon–Vermilion Cliffs Wilderness Area

With miles of weathered, swirling slickrock and slot-canyon systems that can be hiked for days without seeing a soul, it's no wonder that this wilderness area is such a popular destination for hearty trekkers, canyoneers and photographers. Day-hike permits cost $5 to $7 and several are very tough to get. Remember that summer is scorching; spring and fall are best – and busiest. Beware of flash floods.

Trailheads lie along House Rock Valley Rd (4.7 miles west of the contact station); it's a dirt road that may require 4WD. Inquire with rangers.

◉ Sights & Activities

Toadstools   LANDMARK

This wander gives passersby a taste of the harsh Utah desert and cool rocks. The thin sand trail meanders through the scrub-brush, desert boulders and hoodoos about 1 mile to the first toadstool, a sandstone rock in the form of, you guessed it, a toadstool. Slanting, late-afternoon light is best for catching the shape and depth of the eerie features. The unmarked trailhead sits at a small parking area 1.4 miles east of the Paria Contact Station.

Hiking

Day hikers fight like dogs to get a North Coyote Buttes permit. This trail-less expanse of slickrock includes one of the Southwest's most famous formations – the **Wave** (www.az.blm.gov/paria; permit $7). The nearly magical

sight of the slickrock that appears to be seething and swirling in waves is well worth the 6-mile, four- to five-hour round-trip hike. Go online to request advance permits four months ahead; otherwise you can hope for one of the handful of next-day walk-in permits available. Line up for the lottery by 7am in spring and fall at the GSENM Visitor Center in Kanab.

As an alternative, take the 3.4-mile round-trip hike starting at **Wire Pass** (day permit $6) trailhead, a popular slot-canyon day hike with self-service trailhead permits. The pass dead-ends where Buckskin Gulch narrows into some thrillingly slight slots. Another option is to start at the Buckskin Gulch trailhead and hike 3 miles one-way to its narrow section.

South Coyote Buttes   HIKING

(permit $7) An alternative to North Coyote Buttes if you want to see related slickrock formations is to get a next-day permit for South Coyote Buttes. The permit is in much less demand (and not reservable online), but a 4WD is absolutely required for the deep-sand access roads. Ask rangers for directions.

Buckskin Gulch to White House   HIKING

(day permit $6) This 16-mile backpack starts at the Buckskin Gulch trailhead and ends at White House trailhead. Those overnighting must obtain a backcountry permit online in advance.

⟟ Sleeping & Eating

There are campsites and a few lodges. In the backcountry, use of human-waste carry-out bags is encouraged; the **Paria Contact Station** (☎435-644-1200; www.blm.gov; Hwy 89, Mile 21; ☺8:30am-4pm Mar 15-Nov 15) provides them for free. Bring your own provisions to the park. Water can also be refilled at the contact station.

White House Campground   CAMPGROUND $

(www.blm.gov; Hwy 89, Paria Contact Station; tent sites $5) This primitive campground along the Paria River is frequently used as the endpoint of a Buckskin Gulch trip or the beginning of a Paria Canyon trip. The five walk-in sites have pit toilets, but no water and few trees. It's 2 miles down a dirt road behind the contact station, at the White House trailhead.

Stateline Campground   CAMPGROUND

(House Rock Valley Rd) **FREE** On the Utah/Arizona state line, this attractive, small campground is the most central for Wire Pass or North Coyote Buttes. It's first-come,

CEDAR BREAKS NATIONAL MONUMENT

Sculpted cliffs and towering hoodoos glow like neon tie-dye in a wildly eroded natural amphitheater encompassed by **Cedar Breaks National Monument** (☑435-586-9451, 435-586-0787; www.nps.gov/cebr; Hwy 148; 7-day pass per person $6; ☉late May–mid-Oct). The majestic kaleidoscope of magenta, salmon, plum, rust and ocher rises to a height of 10,450ft atop the Markagunt Plateau. The compact park lies 22 miles east and north of Cedar City, off Hwy 14. There are no cedar trees here, by the way: early pioneers mistook the evergreen junipers for cedars.

This altitude gets more than a little snow, and the monument's one road, Hwy 148, is closed from sometime in November through to at least May. Summer temperatures range from only 40°F to 70°F (4°C to 21°C); brief storms drop rain, hail and even powdery white snow. In season, rangers hold geology talks and star parties at the small **visitor center** (☑435-586-9451; Hwy 148; ☉8am-6pm Jun–mid-Oct).

No established trails descend into the breaks, but the park has five viewpoints off Hwy 148 and there are rim trails. **Ramparts Trail** – one of southern Utah's most magnificent trails – leaves from the visitor center. The elevation change on the 3-mile round-trip is only 400ft, but it can be tiring because of the overall high elevation. Alpine Pond Trail is a lovely, though less dramatic, 4-mile loop.

The first-come, first-served **Point Supreme Campground** (p423) has water and restrooms, but no showers; its 28 sites rarely fill.

first-served, with picnic tables, fire pits and pit toilets. It's 1 mile south of the Wire Pass trailhead, 9.3 miles south of Hwy 89. The clay road can be impassable when wet.

ℹ Information

In-season info and permits are picked up at **Paria Contact Station** (p421), 44 miles east of Kanab. Rangers at the **BLM Kanab Field Office** (p421) are in charge of permits from November 16 through March 14.

Cedar City

☑435 / POP 28,860 / ELEV 5850FT

This sleepy college town comes to life every summer when the Shakespeare festival takes over. Associated events, plays and tours continue into fall. Year-round you can make one of the many B&Bs a quiet home base for exploring the Kolob Canyons section of Zion National Park or Cedar Breaks National Monument. At roughly 6000ft, cooler temperatures prevail here than in Springdale (60 miles away) or St George (55 miles); there's even occasional snow in May.

◉ Sights & Activities

**Frontier Homestead
State Park Museum** MUSEUM
(frontierhomestead.org; 635 N Main St; $4; ☉9am-5pm Mon-Sat; 🚼) Kids love the cabins and

the brightly painted 19th-century buggies, as well as the garden full of old farm equipment to run through. Living history demos take place June through August.

Cedar Cycle CYCLING
(☑435-586-5210; cedarcycle.com; 38 E 200 S; road/mountain-bike rental per day $35/39; ☉9am-5:30pm Mon-Fri, 10am-2pm Sat) After you rent a bike, the knowledgeable staff here can point you to local trails.

✷ Festivals & Events

Cedar City is known for its year-round festivities. For a full schedule, see www.cedarcity.org.

Utah Shakespeare Festival THEATER
(☑435-586-7878; www.bard.org; 351 W Center St, Southern Utah University; tickets from $20; ☉late Jun-Oct) Southern Utah University puts on three of the bard's plays and three contemporary dramas each summer season in Cedar City. Productions are well regarded, but don't miss the extras, all free: 'greenshows' with Elizabethan minstrels, literary seminars discussing the plays and costume classes. Backstage and scene-changing tours cost extra.

From mid-September into late October three more plays are presented – one Shakespearean, one dramatic and one musical.

The venues are the open-air **Adams Shakespearean Theatre**, an 819-seat reproduction of London's Globe Theater; the modern 769-seat **Randall L Jones Theatre**, where backstage tours are held; the outdoor **Beverley Taylor Sorenson Center for the Arts**, new in 2016, and the less noteworthy **Auditorium Theatre** used for matinees and rainy days. Make reservations at least a few weeks in advance. At 10am on the day of the show, obscured-view gallery seats for the Adams performance go on sale at the walk-up **ticket office** (cnr College Ave & S 300 W; ☉10am-7pm late Jun–Aug & mid-Sep–Oct).

Note that children under six are not allowed at performances, but childcare ($20) is available.

Neil Simon Festival   THEATER
(www.simonfest.org; ☉mid-Jul–mid-Aug) American plays staged midsummer.

🛏 Sleeping

Weekends during the Shakespearean Festival may cost more than the high season (March through October). A proliferation of good B&Bs is a boon for couples.

Point Supreme Campground   CAMPGROUND $
(www.nps.gov/ceb; tent & RV sites without hookups $20; ☉Jun-Sep; 🐾) Cedar Breaks' Point Supreme Campground has water and restrooms. Ten of the 25 sites can be reserved.

Abbey Inn   MOTEL $
(☎435-586-6522; www.abbeyinncedar.com; 940 W 200 N; d $89-106; 🅿❄🐾📶🏊) Though it's marooned on a busy road with chain businesses, this remodeled brick motel features new furniture, white linens and a cool colonial style. Rooms have hair dryers, flat-screen TVs, microwaves and refrigerators. There's a full buffet breakfast, swimming pool and spa.

Big Yellow Inn   B&B $$
(☎435-586-0960; www.bigyellowinn.com; 234 S 300 W; r $99-199; ❄@📶) This purpose-built Georgian Revival inn has room to roam, with a dining room, a library, a den and many porches. Upstairs rooms are elegantly ornate with period decor. Downstairs, the ground-floor walk-out rooms are simpler and a bit more 'country.' The owners also oversee several adjunct B&B properties and vacation rentals around town.

PAROWAN GAP

People have been passing this way for millennia, and the **Parowan Gap** (www.blm.gov) petroglyphs prove it. Look closely as you continue walking along the road to find panels additional to those signed. Archaeoastronomers believe that the gap in the rocks opposite the petroglyphs may have been used as part of an ancient, astronomically based calendar. Cedar City's tourism office has colorful interpretive brochures explaining site details.

Iron Gate Inn   B&B $$
(☎800-808-4599, 435-867-0603; www.theirongateinn.com; 100 N 200 W; r $129-159; ❄@📶) With an on-site winery, this distinct 1897 Second Empire Victorian house features large, modern-luxury guest rooms, rambling porches and a big yard. Enjoy your breakfast on the large shady patio.

Anniversary House   B&B $$
(☎800-778-5109, 435-865-1266; www.theanniversaryhouse.com; 133 S 100 W; r $99-144; ❄📶🐾) Remarkably comfortable rooms, a great-to-talk-to-host and thoughtful extras make this one of our faves. Savor freshly baked cake and complimentary beverages in the mission-style dining room or lounge around in the landscaped backyard with hot tub and grill. Outdoor kennel available.

🍴 Eating & Drinking

Dining options are pretty good for the region, with more trendy and stylish choices starting to emerge. Restaurant hours are usually extended variably during Shakespeare weekends.

★Centro   PIZZA $
(☎435-867-8123; 50 W Center St; pizzas $10-15; ☉11am-10pm Mon-Sat) Serving wood-fired Neapolitan pizza and heaping bowls of fresh salad in a sleek atmosphere, Centro is a hub for hedonist appetites. Touches like hand-crushed tomato sauce and homemade fennel sausage up the ante. Though the wine list is basic, there's a good selection of brews. Good service.

Sonny Boy's BBQ   BARBECUE $
(☎435-867-8010; sonnyboysbbq.com; 126 N Main St; mains $6-15; ☉11am-9pm Mon-Thu, to 10pm Fri

OFF THE BEATEN TRACK

FREMONT INDIAN STATE PARK

Sixty miles northwest of Cedar City, off I-70, **Fremont Indian State Park & Museum** (435-527-4631; stateparks. utah.gov; 3820 W Clear Creek Canyon Rd; per vehicle $6; ☺9am-6pm, museum closed Sun) is a great introduction to one of Utah's other ancient peoples. Fremont Indians inhabited more northerly areas than the well-known ancient group known as the Anasazi, or Ancestral Puebloans. Indications are that the Fremont were fairly sedentary agriculturalists who tended to settle in small groups. Though much is still up for debate, many sites were probably plowed under on ground settled by Mormon pioneers (farmers do tend to like the same areas).

The park contains one of the largest collections of Fremont Indian rock art in the state – more than 500 panels on 14 interpretive trails. There's also a reconstructed kiva you can climb down into. Be sure to watch the visitor center film and pick up an interpretive brochure for the trails. To learn more, *Traces of Fremont* by Steven Simms is an excellent resource. Other Fremont sites include those in **Dinosaur National Monument** (www.nps.gov/dino; off Hwy 40, Vernal; 7-day pass per vehicle $20; ☺24hr), Nine Mile Canyon (p471) and Sego Canyon.

& Sat) Don't be fooled by the cookie-cutter shopping plaza setting. There's a huge meat smoker outside, rolls of paper towels on the tables and sticky barbecue on the menu. It's filled with international visitors looking for a slice of Americana and locals with their king cab pickups.

Rusty's Ranch House STEAK $$
(435-586-3839; rustysranchhouse.com; 2275 E Hwy 14; mains $13-26; ☺5-10pm Mon-Sat) Three miles east of town on Hwy 14, this steakhouse certainly has the nicest location in Cedar City. Expect moose and bison heads on the wall and all the steak, ribs and buffalo wings you can eat.

Grind Coffeehouse CAFE
(435-867-5333; 19 N Main St; ☺7am-7pm Mon-Sat; 🛜) Hang out with the locals and have a barista-made brew, a great hot sandwich or a big salad. Sometimes there's music on the menu.

🛍 Shopping

Groovacious Records MUSIC
(435-867-9800; 195 W 650 S #2; ☺11am-6:30pm Mon-Sat) The local music store (with awesome vinyl) hosts concerts and other events.

ℹ Information

Cedar City & Brian Head Tourism & Convention Bureau (800-354-4849, 435-586-5124; www.scenicsouthernutah.com; 581 N Main St; ☺8:30am-5pm Mon-Sat; 🛜) Area-wide info and free internet use. A tiny Daughters of Utah Pioneers Museum (581 North Main St; ☺1-4pm Tue & Fri) is located here.

Cedar City Ranger Station (435-865-3200; www.fs.usda.gov/dixie; 1789 N Wedgewood Lane; ☺8am-5pm Mon-Fri) Provides Dixie National Forest (p392) information and can advise on USFS campsites.

Valley View Medical Center (435-868-5000; www.intermountainhealthcare.org; 1303 N Main St; ☺24hr)

Police (435-586-2956; 10 N Main St)

Post Office (435-586-6701; 333 N Main St)

ℹ Getting There & Away

The **Cedar City Regional Airport** (435-867-9408; www.cedarcity.org/airport.html; Aviation Way, off Hwy 56) has flights to Salt Lake City from Monday through Saturday. There's some long-distance bus service available through **Greyhound** (800-231-2222; www.greyhound. com; 1495 W 200 N) but long intermediary stops can make travel times arduous. Your best bet is to arrange for private transportation in and around Cedar City.

Brian Head

The highest town in Utah, Brian Head towers over Cedar City, 35 miles southwest. 'Town' is a bit of an overstatement: this is basically a big resort. From Thanksgiving through April, snow bunnies come to test the closest slopes to Las Vegas (200 miles). Snowmobiling in winter and mountain biking in summer are also popular. Check the ski resort website for lodging and skiing packages – two nights in Vegas and two nights in Brian Head can be quite reasonable.

🏃 Activities

A resort highlight is the kickin' six-lane snow-tubing area (with surface lift), and

SCENIC DRIVE: HWY 14

As scenic drives go, Hwy 14 is awesome. It leads 42 miles over the Markagunt Plateau, cresting at 10,000ft for stunning vistas of Zion National Park and Arizona. The surrounding area is part of Dixie National Forest. For information, contact Cedar City Ranger Station. Though Hwy 14 remains open all winter, snow tires or chains are required between November and April.

Hiking and biking trails past the Cedar Breaks National Monument turnoff on Hwy 14 have tremendous views, particularly at sunset. They include the short (less than a mile one-way) Cascade Falls and Bristlecone Pine Trail and the 32-mile Virgin River Rim Trail. A signed turnoff 24.5 miles from Cedar City leads to jumbled lava beds.

Boating and fishing are the activities of choice at Navajo Lake, 25 miles east of Cedar City. You can rent canoes ($25) or motorboats ($80 to $175 per day) or stay over in a historic 1920s cabin at Navajo Lake Lodge. The rustic lodgings include bedding, but no refrigerators.

Five miles further east, Duck Creek Visitor Center provides information for nearby trails and fishing in the adjacent pond and stream. Here at 8400ft, the 87 pine-shaded sites at Duck Creek Campground are blissfully cool in summer. The ever-expanding log-cabin town Duck Creek Village has more services, including a couple of restaurants, realty offices, cabin-rental outfits, a laundromat and an internet cafe. The village area is big with off-road enthusiasts – ATVs in summer and snowmobiles in winter.

About 7 miles east of Duck Creek, a signed, passable dirt road leads the 10 miles to Strawberry Point, an incredibly scenic overview of red-rock formations and forest lands.

Summer Chairlift   MOUNTAIN BIKING, HIKING
(☉ 9:30am-4:30pm Fri-Sun Jul-Sep) During July and August the elevation keeps temperatures deliciously cool. Ride the summer chairlift up to 11,000ft for an alpine hike or mountain biking. The visitor center puts out a list of area trails.

Brian Head Resort   SKIING
(☑ 435-677-2035; www.brianhead.com; Hwy 143; 1-day lift ticket adult/child $59/43) Advanced skiers might grow impatient with the short trails (except on a powder day), but there's lots here to love for beginners, intermediates and free-riders. Lines are usually short and it's the only resort in Utah within sight of the red-rock desert. The lowdown: 1320ft vertical drop, base elevation 9600ft, 640 acres and seven high-speed triple lifts.

🛏 Sleeping & Eating

In addition to several lodges, a long list of condo rentals is available on the visitor center website. The hotels have on-site restaurants and there's typical resort fare on the mountain.

Grand Lodge   HOTEL $$
(☑ 888-282-3327, 435-677-4242; www.grandlodge brianhead.com; 314 Hunter Ridge Rd; r $159-179; @ 🛜 ≋) For our mountain-lodging buck, what could be better than warming by an outdoor fireplace or dining under giant timber-frame trusses like those at the Grand Lodge?

Cedar Breaks Lodge & Spa   LODGE $$
(☑ 877-505-6343, 435-677-3000; www.cedar breakslodge.com; 223 Hunter Ridge Rd; apt from $169; @ 🛜 ≋) Villa apartments at Cedar Breaks Lodge & Spa sleep four to eight and have kitchens – great for families. There's also a day spa and restaurant.

🛍 Shopping

Georg's Ski & Bike Shop   SPORTS & OUTDOORS
(☑ 435-677-2013; www.georgsskishop.com; 612 UT-143; ☉ 9am-5pm) Georg's Ski & Bike Shop, by the bridge, sells and rents clothing, mountain bikes, cross-country skis and sleds.

ℹ Information

Brian Head Visitor Center (☑ 435-677-2810; www.visitbrianhead.org; 56 N Hwy 148; ☉ 8am-4:30pm Mon-Fri; 🛜) The tiny Brian Head Visitor Center leaves pamphlets out after hours.

there's a mini-terrain park for snowboarders. Forty-two miles of cross-country trails surround Brian Head, including semi-groomed trails to Cedar Breaks National Monument.

UTAH BRIAN HEAD

St George

📞 435 / POP 77,000

Nicknamed 'Dixie' for its warm weather and southern location, St George has long been attracting winter residents and retirees. (Brigham Young, second president of the Mormon church, was one of the first snowbirds in the one-time farming community here.) An interesting-if-small historic downtown core, area state parks and a dinosaur-tracks museum hold some attraction. But for travelers, the abundant and affordable lodging are what make this an oft-used stop between Las Vegas and Salt Lake City – or en route to Zion National Park after a late-night flight.

◉ Sights

Pick up a free, full-color, historic-building walking tour brochure at the visitor center (p429). The intersection of Temple and Main Sts is at the heart of the old town center.

Children's Museum MUSEUM
(www.sgchildrensmuseum.org; 86 S Main St; suggested donation adult/child $4/3; ⊙10am-6pm Tue-Sat; 🖐) St George has plenty of 'No' signs: no touching this, no climbing that, no sitting here and definitely no skateboarding anywhere. So if the kids are starting to get a little antsy, let them loose here, where they can touch, climb and play to their hearts' delight. It's best suited for ages two to 10.

Dinosaur Discovery Site MUSEUM
(www.utahdinosaurs.org; 2180 E Riverside Dr; adult/child under 12yr $6/3; ⊙10am-6pm Mon-Sat, shorter hours Oct-Feb) St George's oldest residents aren't retirees from Idaho, but Jurassic-era dinosaurs. Entry gets you an interpretive tour of the huge collection of tracks, beginning with a video. The casts were first unearthed by a farm plow in 2000 and rare paleontology discoveries, such as dinosaur swim tracks, continue to be made.

Brigham Young Winter Home MUSEUM
(📞435-673-2517; 67 W 200 N; ⊙10am-6:30pm) FREE A tour of the Mormon leader's seasonal home and headquarters illuminates a lot about early town and experimental-farming history.

Mormon Temple RELIGIOUS SITE
(440 S 300 E; ⊙visitor center 9am-9pm) The 1877 Mormon Temple, Utah's first, has a visitor center.

🏃 Activities

Trails crisscross St George. Eventually they'll be connected and the trail along the Virgin River will extend to Zion National Park (p405); get a map at the visitor center. Mountain-bike rental costs $30 to $45 per day. And don't forget that Snow Canyon State Park is nearby.

Green Valley Trail MOUNTAIN BIKING
(off Sunbrook Rd) Also called Bearclaw Poppy, this 6-mile trail offers first-rate, playground-like mountain biking on slickrock.

Arts to Zion TOURS
(www.artstozion.org) Check the website for information about self-touring artist studios throughout St George.

Golf
A handful of local golf courses are open to the public (many more are private). Reserve up to two weeks in advance at www.sgcity.org/golf.

👉 Tours & Outfitters

Desert Rat Outdoor Store OUTDOORS
(📞435-628-7277; www.thedesertrat.net; 468 West St George Blvd; ⊙9am-6pm Mon-Sat) This outdoor store will outfit you for any activity and provide area advice. Also sells all the gear you might need.

Paragon Adventures ADVENTURE SPORTS
(📞435-673-1709; www.paragonadventure.com) The offerings from this popular outfitter include road or mountain-bike tours, rock climbing, small-group canyoneering, interpretive hikes and popular zipline adventures.

Red Rock Bicycle Company MOUNTAIN BIKING
(📞435-674-3185; www.redrockbicycle.com; 446 W 100 S; mountain bikes per 24hr $50, car racks from $15; ⊙9am-7pm Mon-Sat, 11am-5pm Sun) Rentals and servicing available.

🎉 Festivals & Events

A full festival list is available at www.stgeorge chamber.com.

Dixie Roundup SPORTS
(📞435-628-8282; ⊙mid-Sep) A mid-September weekend full of Western fun, including a parade and rodeo.

🛏 Sleeping

Around Easter time, St George becomes Utah's spring-break capital.

Chalet Motel
MOTEL **$**

(☑ 435-628-6272; www.chaletmotelstgeorge.com; 664 E St George Blvd; s/d $69/79; [P][❄][🎧]) With a friendly Southern welcome, this impeccable motel stands out among the vast competition. Singles have kitchenettes and all units have updated bathrooms.

Dixie Palm Motel
MOTEL **$**

(☑ 866-651-3997, 435-673-3531; www.dixiepalms motel.com; 185 E St George Blvd; r from $79; [❄][🎧][🏊]) It may not look like much outside, but regular maintenance and TLC put the Dixie Palm at the head of the low-budget pack. The 15 rooms have mini-refrigerators and microwaves; a handful have full kitchens.

★ Seven Wives Inn
B&B **$$**

(☑ 435-628-3737, 800-600-3737; www.sevenwives inn.com; 217 N 100 W; r $120-199; [❄][@][🎧][🏊]) Two 1800s homes and a cottage feature lovely bedrooms and suites surrounded by well-tended gardens and a small pool. The name comes from settlers' times, when one of the owners harbored fugitive polygamists (including one with seven wives) in the 1880s. The cottage is pet-friendly.

Inn at Entrada
RESORT **$$**

(☑ 435-634-7100; www.innatentrada.com; 2588 West Sinagua Trail; ste from $149, casitas $349; [P][❄][🎧][🏊]) Nestled in red rock and xeriscaped for low-water consumption, this private country club has luxury adobe cottages with hot tubs, gas fireplaces and ample amenities. It's primarily a golfing destination, and also has an on-site restaurant and spa. There's a $20 resort fee. It's located 6 miles north of town off Snow Canyon Pkwy.

Red Mountain Resort & Spa
RESORT **$$$**

(☑ 435-673-4905, 877-246-4453; www.redmoun tainresort.com; 1275 E Red Mountain Circle; retreats per person from $220; [❄][@][🎧][🏊][🐾]) A Zen-chic sensibility pervades this low-profile yoga-centric adobe resort, right down to the silk pillows that echo the copper color of surrounding cliffs. Full meals, guided hikes, spa services and yoga classes are generally included depending on the accommodation package. There's an additional $25 resort fee. It's located 7 miles northwest of town off Snow Canyon Pkwy.

Green Valley Spa
RESORT **$$$**

(☑ 435-628-8060, 800-237-1068; www.greenvalley spa.com; 1871 W Canyon View Dr; r from $229; [@][🏊]) Luxury spa and sports resort: 4000-sq-ft golf center, 14 tennis courts and six swimming pools. Hiking and weight-loss programs feature prominently. It's located 5 miles southwest of town.

✕ Eating & Drinking

There's atmospheric dining downtown. All the big chain restaurants and megamarts you'd expect line up along I-15. Many restaurants close on Sunday.

SNOW CANYON STATE PARK: ST GEORGE'S PLAYGROUND

Red and white swirls of sandstone flow like lava, and actual lava lies broken like sheets of smashed marble in this small, accessible park. **Snow Canyon** (☑ 435-628-2255; stateparks.utah.gov; 1002 Snow Canyon Dr, Ivins; per vehicle $6; ⊘ day-use 6am-10pm; [♿]) is a 7400-acre sampler of southwest Utah's famous land features, 11 miles northwest of St George. Easy trails, perfect for kids, lead to tiny slot canyons, cinder cones, lava tubes and fields of undulating slickrock. Summers are blazing hot: visit in early morning or come in spring or fall.

The park was named after prominent Utah pioneers Lorenzo and Erastus Snow, not frozen precipitation, but for the record it does very occasionally snow here. Check the website for free park events like hikes and talks.

Hiking trails loop off the main road. **Jenny's Canyon Trail** is an easy 1-mile round-trip to a short slot canyon. Wind through a cottonwood-filled field and past ancient lava flows to a 200ft arch on **Johnson Canyon Trail** (2-mile round-trip). A 1000ft stretch of sand dunes serves as a playground for the kiddies, old and young, near a picnic area.

Cycling is popular on the main road through the park, a 17-mile loop from St George (where you can rent bikes). There's also great **rock climbing** in the park, particularly for beginners, with over 150 bolted and sport routes, plus top roping.

Apart from during the unrelenting summer, the 35-site **campground** (☑ 800-322-3770; utahstateparks.reserveamerica.com; tent/RV sites with partial hookups $20/25; [🐾]) is great, and so scenic. You can reserve one of the 30 pre-bookable sites (14 with electrical and water hookups) up to four months in advance. Showers and dump station available.

HILDALE-COLORADO CITY

Just 42 miles southeast of St George on Hwy 9, straddling the Utah–Arizona border, sit the twin towns of Hildale (population 2921) and Colorado City (population 4830). Though the official Mormon church eschewed plural marriage in 1890, there are still those who believe it is a divinely decreed practice.

The majority of the residents here belong to the polygamy-practicing Fundamentalist Church of Jesus Christ of Latter-Day Saints (FLDS). The spotlight focused on this religious community when leader Warren Jeffs was convicted of being an accomplice to rape here in 2007. After that, many of the FLDS faithful, including Jeffs, moved to a fenced compound in Texas. There he was convicted of child sexual assault for 'spiritual marriages' resulting in the pregnancies of underage girls, and sentenced to life in a Texas prison in 2011.

Other than residents' old-fashioned clothing and a proliferation of really large houses (for multiple wives and their many children), these look like any other American towns. We recommend you respect the residents' privacy. However, if you walk into a Wal-Mart in Washington or Hurricane and see several varying-age females shopping together wearing pastel-colored, prairie-style dresses and lengthy braids or elaborate up-dos, it's a pretty safe guess that they are sister wives. Other, less conspicuous sects are active in the state as well.

★ **Riggatti's Wood Fired Pizza**　　PIZZA $
(☑ 435-674-9922; www.riggattis.com; 73 N Main St; pizzas $8-14; ⊙ 11am-9pm Mon-Sat) With a fanatical local following, this tiny pizzeria is a boon for travelers searching for thin-crust pizzas with bubbling mozzarella and pesto. Grab one of the very few counter seats and save room for hot cinnamon sticks.

Bombay Cafe　　INDIAN $
(☑ 435-673-8888; bombaycafesg.com; 57 N 700 E; mains $8-12; ⊙ 11am-2:30pm & 5-9pm Mon-Sat) This tiny hole-in-the-wall is run by Pakistani batik artist Shazad Sheikh and his wife, Rabia. You'll find chicken tikka masala, daal chana, naan and other classic dishes alongside a small collection of handmade saris and scarves for sale.

Thomas Judd's General Store　　ICE CREAM $
(76 Tabernacle St; ice cream from $3; ⊙ 9:30am-5:30pm Mon-Sat) Stop for a sweet scoop of ice cream or piece of nostalgic candy.

Bear Paw Cafe　　CAFE $
(☑ 435-634-0126; 75 N Main St; mains $7-10; ⊙ 7am-3pm; ﹙ﾟ﹚) This homey cafe is St George's most popular breakfast spot, with patrons waiting curbside even in the low season. Try a half-order if your appetite isn't mammoth. There's an extensive kids' menu.

★ **Xetava Gardens Cafe**　　AMERICAN $$
(☑ 435-656-0165; www.xetavagardenscafe.com; 815 Coyote Gulch Ct; breakfast $7-12, lunch & dinner $12-19; ⊙ 9am-5pm Sun-Thu, 9am-9pm Fri & Sat; ☑) We'd drive much further than 8 miles for the organic, locavore fare served here in a stunning red-rock setting. Expect small plates (mahi cake), salads, ciabatta sandwiches, gyros and burgers.

Anasazi Steakhouse　　STEAK $$
(☑ 435-674-0095; www.anasazisteakhouse.com; 1234 W Sunset Blvd; mains $12-30; ⊙ 5-9:30pm) Grill your steak (or shrimp or portabello mushroom...) yourself on a hot volcanic rock.

★ **Painted Pony**　　MODERN AMERICAN $$$
(☑ 435-634-1700; www.painted-pony.com; 2 W St George Blvd, Ancestor Sq; lunch $10-12, dinner mains $25-36; ⊙ 11:30am-10pm Mon-Sat, 4-10pm Sun) Think gourmet comfort food and great salads. At dinner you might choose a juniper-brined pork chop; at lunch, meatloaf with a port-wine reduction and rosemary mashed potatoes.

George's　　PUB
(☑ 435-216-7311; georgescornerrestaurant.com; 2 W St George Blvd; ⊙ 7am-midnight; ☎) This central pub anchors historic Ancestor Sq. Local beers on tap and a reliable, if unexciting, menu; weekend brunch is popular.

☆ Entertainment

St George gets pretty quiet after dark. For any area music or events, check listings in the free monthly newspaper the *Independent* (www.suindependent.com).

OC Tanner Amphitheater THEATER
(☑435-652-7994; www.octannershows.com; 300
Lion Blvd; ⊙mid-May–Aug) Outdoor amphitheater surrounded by red rock; stages classical, bluegrass, country and other concerts
and performances.

St George Musical Theater THEATER
(☑435-628-8755; sgmusicaltheater.com; 37 S 100
W) Puts on musicals year-round in different
locations.

❶ Information

Additional information is available at www.
utahsdixie.com and www.sgcity.org.

Chamber of Commerce (☑435-628-1658;
www.stgeorgechamber.com; 97 E St George
Blvd; ⊙9am-5pm Mon-Fri) The visitor center
caters to relocating retirees, and has loads of
city info.

Dixie Regional Medical Center (☑435-251-
1000; www.intermountainhealthcare.org; 1380
E Medical Center Dr; ⊙24hr)

St George Field Office (☑435-688-3200;
345 E Riverside Dr; ⊙7:45am-5pm Mon-Fri,
10am-3pm Sat) Get interagency information on
surrounding public lands: USFS, BLM and state
parks. Topographic maps and guides available.
Staff can also suggest where to camp for free
on BLM land.

Utah Welcome Center (☑435-673-4542;
travel.utah.gov; 1835 S Convention Center Dr,
Dixie Convention Center; ⊙8:30am-5:30pm)
Statewide information 2 miles south of St
George. There's a wildlife museum (think taxi-
dermy) on-site with the same hours.

❶ Getting There & Away

AIR

Taxis and all the big-chain car-rental companies
are represented at the St George Municipal
Airport. Note that Las Vegas McCarran International Airport, 120 miles south, often has better
flight and car-rental deals than Utah airports.

Delta (☑800-221-1212; www.delta.com)
connects Salt Lake City and St George several
times daily.

United Express (☑800-864-8331; www.
united.com) has four weekly flights to and from
Los Angeles, CA.

BUS

There's Greyhound bus service to Salt Lake City
and Las Vegas, NV.

St George Express (☑435-652-1100; www.
stgeorgeexpress.com; one-way Las Vegas $39)
is a shuttle service to Las Vegas, NV (two hours)
and Zion National Park (p405). Provides door-
to-door service.

Tropic
☑435 / POP 520 / ELEV 6309FT

Founded in 1891 by Mormon pioneers, the
tiny town of Tropic is a satellite to Bryce
Canyon National Park (p399), located 10
miles east on Hwy 12. The farming community got its start with the creation of Tropic
Ditch, which diverted water from Bryce Canyon to irrigate fields.

☞ Tours

★Mecham Outfitters HORSEBACK RIDING
(☑435-679-8823; www.mechamoutfitters.com;
half-day ride $75) Longtime locally run outfit-
ter leading highly recommended half- and
full-day horse rides, including through slot
canyons, in nearby Dixie National Forest
(p392) and on Grand Staircase–Escalante
National Monument (p394) lands.

⌨ Sleeping

Tropic serves Bryce Canyon National Park
(p399). It has a selection of motels, camping,
cabins and B&B lodgings.

Pine Lake Campground CAMPGROUND $
(☑Escalante Ranger District 435-826-5400, group
reservations 877-444-6777; www.recreation.gov;
sites $15; ⊙Jun-Sep) In a pretty pine forest
near a reservoir, 11 miles north of the Hwy
12/63 junction then 6 miles east on unpaved
Clay Creek. Powerboats aren't allowed, but
expect ATVs. Only groups may reserve.
There's no trash collection and amenities are
limited to vault toilets and drinking water.

★Buffalo Sage B&B B&B $$
(☑435-679-8443; www.buffalosage.com; 980 N
Hwy 12; d $120; ⊙May-Sep; ✿☎) Up on a bluff
west of town, three exterior-access rooms
lead out to an expansive, upper-level deck
or ground-level patio with great views. The
owner's background in art is evident in the
decor. Do note that the communal living
area is shared by cats and a dog. The full
breakfast accommodates vegetarians.

Bryce Country Cabins CABIN $$
(☑435-679-8643, 888-679-8643; www.bryce
countrycabins.com; 320 N Main St; cabins
$125; ⊙Feb-Oct; ✿☎) Friendly and fam-
ily run, these well-designed pine cabins
are centered around an outdoor fire pit,
perfect for stargazing around a bonfire.
The only drawback is they're right on the
main street. Deluxe cabins have cozy furniture and vaulted ceilings. Perks include

TVs, coffeemakers, small porches and charm – it's among the best simple accommodations near Bryce.

Stone Canyon Inn INN $$$
(☑866-489-4680, 435-679-8611; www.stonecan yoninn.com; 1220 Stone Canyon Lane; cabins $235-360; ❄☎) In a Wild West setting of scrub hills backed by Technicolor sunsets, this stately stone-and-wood lodging offers adventure out the back door – stroll or bike to your heart's content. Cabins are spacious and luxuriously private, though trumped by the charm of the main house, where a restaurant was recently added. There's a Finnish sauna. It's 1.3 miles from Main St.

✖ Eating

Restaurant offerings are few, but there's fast food, American dining and a gourmet option.

Clarke's Grocery MARKET $
(121 N Main St; sandwiches $5-8; ☉7:30am-8pm Mon-Sat, 2-8pm Sun) Tropic's only grocery store has a deli sandwich counter and homemade baked goods.

Pizza Place AMERICAN $
(☑435-679-8888; 21 N Main St; mains $8-15; ☉11am-9pm) Think wood-fired flatbread piled high with fresh ingredients. When locals eat out, they come to this family-owned joint with the pulse of Tropic. Hours vary seasonally.

Stone Hearth Grille AMERICAN $$$
(☑435-679-8923; www.stonehearthgrille.com; 1380 W Stone Canyon Lane; mains $22-38; ☉5-10pm) In a lovely rural setting staring out at the bluffs, this upscale lodge restaurant serves rib-eye steaks, quinoa-stuffed peppers and satisfying green salads alongside a decent wine list. It's the best dinner option in the area. The deck seating offers a heavy dose of romance.

❶ Information

Cannonville Visitor Center (☑435-826-5640; 10 Center St, Cannonville; ☉8am-4:30pm Apr-Oct) Five miles east of Tropic.

SALT LAKE REGION

The vast Salt Lake Valley is the spot Brigham Young claimed when he announced 'This is the place!' to his pioneering followers in 1847. Today almost 80% of the state's population, nearly 2 million people, live along the eastern edge of the Wasatch Mountains from Ogden to Provo. Salt Lake City (SLC) sits smack in the middle of this concentration; banked against the foothills, its sprawl is often well-camouflaged.

To the north and west lie the Great Salt Lake and 100 miles of salt flats stretching into Nevada.

Salt Lake City

☑801, 385 / POP 1,153,340

Sparkling Salt Lake, with its bluebird skies and powder-dusted mountains, is Utah's capital city. The only Utah city with an international airport, it still manages to emanate a small-town feel. Downtown is easy to get around and fairly quiet come evening. It's hard to grasp that 1.2 million people live in the metro area. While it's the Mormon equivalent of Vatican City, and the LDS owns a lot of land, less than half the population are church members. The university and excellent outdoor access have attracted a wide range of residents. A liberal spirit permeates the coffeehouses and yoga classes, where elaborate tattoos are the norm. Foodies find much to love among the multitude of international and organic dining options. And when the trail beckons, it's a scant 45 minutes from the Wasatch Mountains' brilliant hiking and skiing. Friendly people, great food and outdoor adventure – what could be better?

❂ Sights

Mormon Church–related sights cluster mostly near the town center point for SLC addresses: the intersection of Main and South Temple Sts. (Streets are so wide – 132ft – because they were originally built so that four oxen pulling a wagon could turn around.) The downtown hub underwent a renaissance with the development of City Creek. To the east, the University-Foothills District has most of the museums and kid-friendly attractions.

◉ Temple Square & Around

Temple Square PLAZA
(Map p438; www.visittemplesquare.com; cnr S Temple & N State Sts; ☉grounds 24hr, visitor centers 9am-9pm) **FREE** The city's most famous sight occupies a 10-acre block surrounded by 15ft-high walls. LDS docents give free, 30-minute tours continually,

Greater Salt Lake City

leaving from the visitor centers at the two entrances on South and North Temple Sts. Sisters, brothers and elders are stationed every 20ft or so to answer questions. (Don't worry, no one is going to try to convert you – unless you express interest.) In addition to the noteworthy sights, there are administrative buildings and two theater venues.

Salt Lake Temple
RELIGIOUS SITE

(Map p438; Temple Sq) Lording over Temple Sq is the impressive 210ft-tall Salt Lake Temple. Atop the tallest spire stands a statue of the angel Moroni, who appeared to LDS founder Joseph Smith. Rumor has it that when the place was renovated, cleaners found old bullet marks in one of the gold-plated surfaces. The temple and ceremonies are private, open only to LDS members in good standing.

Tabernacle
CHRISTIAN SITE

(Map p438; www.mormontabernaclechoir.org; Temple Sq; ☺9am-9pm) **FREE** The domed, 1867 auditorium – with a massive 11,000-pipe organ – has incredible acoustics. A pin dropped in the front can be heard in the back, almost 200ft away. Free daily organ recitals are held at noon Monday through Saturday, and at 2pm Sunday.

Family History Library
LIBRARY

(Map p438; familysearch.org/locations/saltlakecity-library; 35 N West Temple St; ☺8am-5pm Mon, to 9pm Tue-Fri, 9am-5pm Sat) **FREE** Thousands of people come to Salt Lake City every year to research their family history here, the largest genealogical resource on earth. Because the LDS believes you must pray on your ancestors' behalf to help them along their celestial path, it has acquired a mind-boggling amount of genealogical information to help identify relatives. Volunteers scour the globe microfilming records in the tiniest of villages and then make them freely available here, as well as through libraries across the country.

Beehive House HISTORIC SITE

(Map p438; ☑ 801-240-2671; www.visittemple square.com; 67 E South Temple St; ☺ 9:30am-8:30pm Mon-Sat) FREE Brigham Young lived with one of his wives and families in the Beehive House during much of his tenure as governor and church president in Utah. The required tours vary; some offer historic house details over religious education, depending on the LDS docent.

The attached 1855 Lion House, which was home to a number of Young's other wives, has a self-service restaurant in the basement. Feel free to look around the dining rooms during mealtimes.

Museum of Church History & Art MUSEUM

(Map p438; www.churchhistorymuseum.org; 45 N West Temple St; ☺ 9am-9pm Mon-Fri, 10am-7pm Sat & Sun) FREE Adjoining Temple Sq, this museum has impressive exhibits of pioneer history and fine art.

◉ Greater Downtown

Clark Planetarium MUSEUM

(Map p438; ☑ 385-468-7827; www.clark planetarium.org; 110 S 400 W; adult/child $9/7; ☺ 10am-10pm Sun-Thu, to 11pm Fri & Sat) You'll be seeing stars at Clark Planetarium, home to the latest and greatest 3D sky shows and Utah's only IMAX theater. There are free science exhibits, too. The planetarium is on the edge of the Gateway (Map p438; www. shopthegateway.com; 200 S to 50 N, 400 W to 500 W; ☺ 10am-9pm Mon-Sat, noon-6pm Sun), a combination indoor-outdoor shopping complex anchored by the old railway depot.

Wheeler Historic Farm FARM

(Map p431; ☑ 385-468-1755; www.wheelerfarm. com; 6351 S 900 E, South Cottonwood Regional Park; hay ride $3, house tour adult/child $4/2; ☺ daylight hours; 🖫) FREE Kids can help farmhands milk cows, churn butter and feed animals at this historic 1886 farm. There's also blacksmithing, quilting and hay rides in summer.

Discovery Gateway MUSEUM

(Map p438; www.discoverygateway.org; 444 W 100 S; $8.50; ☺ 10am-6pm Mon-Thu, to 7pm Fri & Sat, noon-6pm Sun; 🖫) This enthusiastic, hands-on children's museum is possibly the best city attraction for families. The mock

network-news desk in the media zone looks particularly cool for budding journos.

Utah State Capitol HISTORIC BUILDING

(Map p438; www.utahstatecapitol.utah.gov; 350 N State St; ☺ 7am-8pm Mon-Fri, 8am-6pm Sat & Sun, visitor center 8:30am-5pm Mon-Fri) FREE The grand, 1916 State Capitol is set among 500 cherry trees on a hill north of Temple Sq. Inside, colorful Works Progress Administration (WPA) murals of pioneers, trappers and missionaries adorn part of the building's dome. Free guided tours (hourly, 9am to 5pm Monday to Friday) start at the 1st-floor visitor center; self-guided tours are available from the visitor center.

Pioneer Memorial Museum MUSEUM

(Map p438; www.dupinternational.org; 300 N Main St; ☺ 9am-5pm Mon-Sat, to 8pm Wed) FREE You'll find relics from the early days at Daughters of Utah Pioneers (DUP) museums throughout Utah, but the Pioneer Memorial Museum is by far the biggest. The vast, four-story treasure trove is like Utah's attic, with a taxidermied two-headed lamb and human-hair artwork in addition to more predictable artifacts.

Gilgal Garden GARDENS

(Map p438; www.gilgalgarden.org; 749 E 500 S; ☺ 8am-8pm Apr-Sep, 9am-5pm Oct-Mar) FREE Talk about obscure: Gilgal Garden is a quirky little green space hidden in a residential neighborhood. Most notably, this tiny sculpture garden contains a giant stone sphinx wearing Mormon founder Joseph Smith's face.

◉ University-Foothills District

★ Natural History Museum of Utah MUSEUM

(Map p434; nhmu.utah.edu; 301 Wakara Way; adult/child 3-12yr $15/10; ☺ 10am-5pm Thu-Tue, to 9pm Wed) Rio Tinto Center's stunning architecture forms a multistory indoor 'canyon' that showcases exhibits to great effect. Walk up through the layers as you explore both indigenous peoples' cultures and natural history. Past Worlds paleontological displays are the most impressive – an incredible perspective from beneath, next to and above a vast collection of dinosaur fossils offers the full breadth of prehistory.

Red Butte Garden GARDENS

(Map p434; www.redbuttegarden.org; 300 Wakara Way; adult/child $12/7; ☺ 9am-9pm May-Aug)

Both landscaped and natural gardens cover a lovely 150 acres, with access to trails in the Wasatch foothills. Check online to see who's playing at the popular, outdoor summer concert series also held here. Daylight hours in low season.

This is the Place Heritage Park HISTORIC SITE
(Map p434; www.thisistheplace.org; 2601 E Sunnyside Ave; adult/child $13/9; ☺9am-5pm Mon-Sat, 10am-5pm Sun; 🖰) Dedicated to the 1847 arrival of the Mormons, this heritage park covers 450 acres. The centerpiece is a living-history village where, June through August, costumed docents depict mid-19th-century life. Admission includes a tourist-train ride and activities. The rest of the year, access is limited to varying degrees at varyingly reduced prices; you'll at least be able to wander around the exterior of the 41 buildings. Some are replicas, but some are originals, such as Brigham Young's farmhouse.

Utah Museum of Fine Arts MUSEUM
(Map p434; ☎801-581-7332; umfa.utah.edu; 410 Campus Center Dr; adult/child $9/7; ☺10am-5pm Tue, Thu & Fri, to 8pm Wed, 11am-5pm Sat & Sun) Soaring galleries showcase permanent collections of tribal, Western and modern art.

◎ South Salt Lake

Thanksgiving Point AMUSEMENT PARK
(☎801-768-2300; www.thanksgivingpoint.org; 3003 N Thanksgiving Way, Lehi; all-attraction pass adult/child $25/20, museum adult/child $15/12; ☺10am-8pm Mon-Sat; 🖰) Fifty-five acres of gardens, a petting farm, golf course, giant movie theater, dining and shopping: what doesn't the Thanksgiving Point infotainment complex have? The on-site Museum of Ancient Life is the highest-tech and kid-friendliest dinosaur museum in the state. Take exit 287 off I-15; Lehi is 28 miles south of downtown SLC.

★Museum of Ancient Life MUSEUM
(☎801-768-2300; www.thanksgivingpoint.org; 3003 N Thanksgiving Way, Lehi; museum only adult/child $15/12; ☺10am-8pm Mon-Sat; 🖰) A family friendly museum at Thanksgiving Point. Prehistoric life is on display with exhibits on dinosaurs and aquatic life, lots of interactive exhibits that teach about fossils found all over the world, and a 3D theater. Little ones

can dig for their own bones, dress up a dinosaur, play in a watery Silurian reef ....

🏃 Activities

The best of SLC's outdoor activities are 30 to 50 miles away in the Wasatch Mountains, but gear is available in town. You can rent bicycles, camping and ski equipment galore.

Wasatch Touring ADVENTURE SPORTS
(Map p438; ☎801-359-9361; www.wasatchtouring.com; 702 E 100 S) Rents bikes, kayaks, climbing shoes and ski equipment.

SLC Bicycle Co CYCLING
(Map p438; www.slcbike.com; 247 S 500 E; rentals from $25; ☺10am-6pm Mon-Fri, to 5pm Sat) A competent bike shop that rents road bikes and tandems. There are also group rides organized on Wednesdays and Saturdays.

Splore RAFTING
(Map p431; ☎801-484-4128; www.splore.org; 4029 Main St; ☺9am-5pm Mon-Fri) If traveling with someone with a physical or mental disability, book a raft trip with this operator.

Church Fork Trail HIKING
(Mill Creek Canyon Rd, off Wasatch Blvd) Looking for the nearest workout with big views? Hike the 6-mile round-trip, pet-friendly trail up to Grandeur Peak (8299ft). Mill Creek Canyon is 13.5 miles southwest of downtown.

☞ Tours & Outfitters

Utah Mountain Adventures ADVENTURE
(☎801-550-3986; www.utahmountainadventures.com; cnr 2070 E & 3900 S, #B) Offering everything from backcountry skiing to avalanche education, rock and ice climbing and mountaineering, this reputable outfitter can help you explore the Wasatch safely and with maximum enjoyment. A franchise of Exum Mountain Guides.

Utah Heritage Foundation WALKING
(☎801-533-0858; www.utahheritagefoundation.com; tours per person $10) Gives tours of SLC's historic landmarks and distributes free self-guided walking-tour brochures.

REI OUTDOORS
(Map p431; ☎801-486-2100; www.rei.com; 3285 E 3300 S; ☺10am-9pm Mon-Fri, 9am-7pm Sat, 11am-7pm Sun) Rents and sells camping equipment, climbing shoes, kayaks and most winter-sports gear. It also stocks a

South Salt Lake

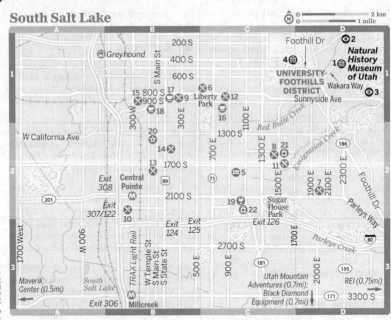

great selection of maps and activity guides, and has an interagency public-lands help desk (p442) inside.

Festivals & Events

Utah Arts Festival CULTURAL
(www.uaf.org; ☉ Jun) Concerts, exhibitions and craft workshops over three days; late June.

Days of '47 CULTURAL
(www.daysof47.com; ☉ Jul) A pioneer parade, rodeo and re-enacted encampment are all part of the July-long festival celebrating the city's first settlers.

Utah Pride Festival CULTURAL
(www.utahpridecenter.org; ☉ Jun) Gay pride festival in June, with outdoor concerts, a parade and a 5km run.

Sleeping

Downtown chain properties cluster around S 200 West near 500 South and 600 South; there are more in Mid-Valley (off I-215) and near the airport. At high-end hotels rates are lowest on weekends. Parking downtown is often not included. Look for camping and alternative lodging in the Wasatch Mountains.

Wildflowers B&B B&B $
(Map p434; ☏ 385-419-2301; wildflowersbb.com; 936 E 1700 S; r $90-125) Quaint to the core, this old-fashioned B&B revels in stained glass and period furnishings. Cheaper than most B&Bs in town, it's probably worth it for the breakfast alone. It sits in a characterful neighborhood of Salt Lake with plenty of shops and restaurants.

Avenues Hostel HOSTEL $
(Map p438; ☏ 801-539-8888, 801-359-3855; www.saltlakehostel.com; 107 F St; dm $40, r $60-80, apt $120; ❄@🕾) A well-worn hostel with nice oddball staff and decent guest kitchens. Women have it best, with their own wing and TV lounge. It's a mix of international travelers and long-term residents, but a convenient location.

★ Engen Hus B&B $$
(Map p431; ☏ 801-450-6703; engenhusutah.com; 2275 E 6200 S; r $125-140; 🕾) Ideally positioned for mountain jaunts, this lovely home features four rooms with handmade quilts on log beds and flat-screen TVs. Hosts are knowledgeable about local hiking. The cozy quotient is high, with board games, a hot-tub deck and DIY laundry. Dig the buffet breakfast with the likes of caramel

South Salt Lake

French toast. Has a room that's accessible to travelers in wheelchairs.

★ **Inn on the Hill**   INN **$$**
(Map p438; ☑801-328-1466; www.inn-on-the-hill.com; 225 N State St; r $155-240; P☀@🛜) Exquisite woodwork and Maxfield Parrish Tiffany glass adorn this sprawling, 1906 Renaissance Revival mansion-turned-inn. Guest rooms are classically comfortable, not stuffy, with Jacuzzi tubs and some fireplaces and balconies. Great shared spaces include patios, a billiard room, a library and a dining room where chef-cooked breakfasts are served.

The location is high above Temple Sq; expect great views and an uphill hike back from town.

Hotel RL   HOTEL **$$**
(Map p438; ☑801-521-7373; www.redlion.com/salt-lake; 161 W 600 S; r from $239; P☀@🛜🏊)

Sleek comfort in a remodeled Red Lion hotel with almost 400 rooms, which feature black-and-white wall murals and flatscreen TVs. There's a classic diner attached, a modern-woodsy design lounge, 24-hour gym and outdoor pool and Jacuzzi. As big box hotels go, this one delivers.

Anniversary Inn   B&B **$$**
(Map p438; ☑801-363-4950, 800-324-4152; www.anniversaryinn.com; 678 E South Temple St; ste $168-190; P☀@🛜) Sleep among the tree trunks of an enchanted forest or inside an Egyptian pyramid: these 3D themed suites are nothing if not over the top. The quiet location is near a few good restaurants, and not far from Temple Sq.

Peery Hotel   HOTEL **$$**
(Map p438; ☑800-331-0073, 801-521-4300; www.peeryhotel.com; 110 W 300 S; r $95-199; P☀@🛜) Egyptian-cotton robes and sheets, carved dark-wood furnishings, individually decorated rooms – prepare to be charmed by the 1910 Peery. Small but impeccable bathrooms have pedestal sinks and aromatherapy bath products. This throwback hotel stands smack in the center of the Broadway Ave entertainment district – walking distance to restaurants, bars and theaters. Parking is extra.

Hotel Monaco   BOUTIQUE HOTEL **$$**
(Map p438; ☑801-595-0000; www.monaco-saltlakecity.com; 15 W 200 S; r $229-279; P☀@🛜🐾) Subdued with a dollop of funk, rich colors and plush prints create a whimsical vibe at this boutique chain. Here, pampered-guest pets receive special treatment, and the front desk will loan you a goldfish if you need company. Evening wine receptions are free, as are cruiser bicycles; parking is extra.

Beija Flor   B&B **$$**
(Map p431; ☑801-580-3283; www.beijaflorbnb.com; 2293 E 6200 S; r $100-130; 🛜) Catering to international travelers, this Brazilian–American-run log B&B has comfortable rooms, a huge patio garden and a family living room built around a huge stone fireplace. It also does Utah fishing tours.

Haxton Manor   B&B **$$**
(Map p438; ☑801-363-4646; www.haxtonmanor.com; 943 E South Temple St; r $119-199; P🛜) A stately 1905 home with a beehive fireplace and seven English-style guest rooms. The four-poster beds and jetted tubs are a nice

SCENIC DRIVE: PONY EXPRESS TRAIL

Follow more than 130 miles of the original route that horse-and-rider mail delivery took on the **Pony Express Trail Backcountry Byway** (www.byways. org), from Fairfield to Callao. You'll drive through wide-open desert rangeland with stations, many in ruins, placed throughout. The trail begins at one of the former stops, in **Camp Floyd/ Stagecoach Inn State Park** (www. byways.org), 25 miles southwest of I-15 along Hwy 73. Most of the road is maintained gravel or dirt and is passable to ordinary cars in good weather. In winter, snow may close the route; watch for flash floods in summer.

touch. It's run by an on-site manager, not a home owner.

Ellerbeck Mansion B&B B&B $$$
(Map p438; ☑ 801-355-2500, 800-966-8364; www. ellerbeckbedandbreakfast.com; 140 North B St; r $207-317) Rambling red-brick mansion with homey, eclectic decor. Walking distance to downtown.

🍴 Eating

What SLC lacks in nightlife it certainly makes up for in dining. Many ethnic and organically minded restaurants are located within the downtown core. Dining enclaves dot the atmospheric neighborhoods 9th and 9th and 15th and 15th as well as the canyons. Food trucks are also popular: look for the Asian-inspired Chow Truck, which gets local raves.

★ **Tosh's Ramen** RAMEN $
(Map p434; ☑ 801-466-7000; 1465 State St; mains $9-11; ⊙ 11:30am-3pm & 5-9pm Tue-Sat) Ecstasy by the steaming oversized bowl, Tosh's ramen comes with silken broth and crunchy sprouts, topped with a poached egg if you like it that way. It couldn't get more authentic. Try to carve out some room for an order of spicy wings. Everyone is drawn to this happy place in a nondescript strip mall, so go early.

★ **Red Iguana** MEXICAN $
(Map p431; www.rediguana.com; 736 W North Temple St; mains $10-18; ⊙ 11am-10pm Mon-Thu,

to 11pm Fri, 10am-11pm Sat, 10am-9pm Sun) Mexico at its most authentic, aromatic and delicious – no wonder the line is usually snaking out the door at this family-run restaurant. Ask for samples of the mole to decide on one of seven chili- and chocolate-based sauces. The incredibly tender *cochinita pibil* (shredded roast pork) tastes like it's been roasting for days.

Rye Diner & Drinks MODERN AMERICAN $
(Map p438; ☑ 801-364-4655; www.ryeslc.com; 239 S 500 E; dinner mains $6-17; ⊙ 9am-2pm Mon-Fri, 9am-3pm Sat & Sun, 6-11pm Fri & Sat; 🍴) Call it a modern diner, with a spare look and locally sourced supplies. For an outing with friends it's satisfying and cheap enough. Think fried chicken and waffles, quinoa with maple syrup or poke bowls. There's a slew of craft cocktails and live LCD viewing of the small concert house next door.

Caputo's Deli DELI $
(Map p434; ☑ 801-486-6615; 1516 S 1500 E; mains $5-15; ⊙ 7am-8pm Mon-Sat) Stock up on gorgeous cheeses, marinated peppers, fresh sandwiches and pastries at this deli counter and gourmet store.

Bagel Project BAKERY $
(Map p434; ☑ 801-906-0698; bagelproject.com; 779 S 500 E; snacks $4-8; ⊙ 6:30am-2pm Mon-Fri, 7:30am-2pm Sat & Sun) Top-notch bagels are made with old-world care by the owners straight outta Jersey. Chewy, simple, satisfying. It also sells *bialys* (Polish rolls with caramelized onions), gourmet coffee and sandwiches.

From Scratch AMERICAN $
(Map p438; ☑ 801-961-9000; fromscratchslc. com; 62 Gallivan Ave; mains $12-15; ⊙ 11:30am-3pm & 5-9:30pm Mon-Thu, 11:30am-3pm & 5-10:30pm Fri & Sat) A casual eatery focusing on fresh and fast, with bubbly-crust wood-fired pizzas taking center stage. The burger with caramelized onions served on a soft brioche bun is a close second. There are also soups, salads and bomber-sized beers.

Vertical Diner VEGAN $
(Map p434; ☑ 801-484-8378; verticaldiner.com; 234 W 900 S; mains $8-16; ⊙ 10am-10pm Mon-Fri, 9am-10pm Sat & Sun; 🍴) If you are not vegan, you might prefer seeking out authentic international eats as opposed to these watered-down versions, but that's not to say

Vertical does not have its fans. The oversized tiramisu could rock your world.

Les Madelines FRENCH $
(Map p438; ☑801-355-2294; lesmadelines.com; 216 E 500 S; mains $3-11; ⊗8am-4pm Tue-Sat) French cafe serving artful sandwiches overflowing with greens, lavender lemonade and soft pull-apart monkey bread. There are good breakfasts too.

Pho Tay Ho VIETNAMESE $
(Map p434; ☑801-466-3650; www.photayho. com; 1766 S Main St; mains $6-11; ⊗11am-3:30pm & 5-8:30pm Tue-Sat, to 7:30pm Sun) For steaming bowls of pho garnished with basil, mint and bean sprouts, along with a salty lemonade, it's hard to beat this no-frills, bargain restaurant with three generations of women working together.

Chanon THAI $
(Map p434; ☑801-532-1177; www.chanonthai. com; 278 E 900 S; lunch mains $7-9, dinner $9-13; ⊗11:30am-3pm Wed-Fri, 5-9pm Wed-Sun; ✐) Endorsed by frequenters of Southeast Asia, Chanon specializes in spicy, authentic food with plenty of vegetarian offerings. Look for daily specials, like fresh mango with sticky rice.

Ruth's Diner DINER $
(Map p431; www.ruthsdiner.com; 4160 Emigration Canyon Rd; mains $6-16; ⊗8am-10pm) Once a rail-car diner, Ruth's has expanded into a sprawling institution. We love the canyon surrounds – and the eggs Benedict. Summer concerts sometimes accompany dinner.

Downtown Farmers Market MARKET $
(Map p438; www.slcfarmersmarket.org; Pioneer Park, cnr 300 S & 300 W; ⊗8am-2pm Sat mid-Jun–late Oct, 4pm-dusk Tue Aug-Sep) Regionally grown produce, ready-to-eat baked goodies and local crafts.

Blue Plate Diner DINER $
(Map p434; www.theblueplatediner.com; 2041 S 2100 E; mains $6-16; ⊗7am-9pm) A hip, retro diner that gets serious about bacon. With a soda fountain, colorful patio and postcards from around the country as decoration.

Del Mar al Lago PERUVIAN $$
(Map p434; ☑801-467-2890; 310 Bugatti Ave S; mains $16-24; ⊗11am-4pm & 6-9pm Mon-Thu, 11am-10pm Fri & Sat) Get ready for a treat. The Peruvian patrons tell you it's authentic. Chef Wilmer from Trujillo cooks up the country's best dishes, including ceviche (fish marinated in lime), yucca fries and *causas* (seasoned mashed potato) with jalapeño aioli.

Takashi JAPANESE $$
(Map p438; ☑801-519-9595; 18 W Market St; rolls $10-18, mains $10-19; ⊗11:30am-2pm & 5:30-10pm Mon-Sat) Who wouldn't be tempted by 'sex on rice'? The best of a number of surprisingly good sushi restaurants here in landlocked Salt Lake, and often packed. Even LA restaurant snobs rave about the innovative rolls at this ever-so-chic establishment.

Mazza MIDDLE EASTERN $$
(Map p434; www.mazzacafe.com; 1515 S 1500 E; sandwiches $8-10, dinner $15-25; ⊗11am-9pm Mon-Thu, to 10pm Fri & Sat; ✐) In an inviting space with warm tones and copper highlights, this local favorite consistently delivers well-known fare like kebabs, shawarma and hummus plus wonderful regional specialties, many from Lebanon. We love what they do with lamb and eggplant.

★**Avenues Bistro on Third** BISTRO $$$
(Map p438; ☑801-831-5409; avenuesbistroon third.com; 564 E 3rd Ave; mains $16-37; ⊗11am-10pm Wed-Fri, 9am-3pm & 5pm-close Sat & Sun) ✐ An intimate, food-first experience. Enter the tiny house in the Avenues to a handful of tables around an open grill. The owner is seating guests and chatting with neighbors. The fare: fresh greens with Utah trout, trumpet mushrooms brushed in honey lavender and homemade fig newtons all melt in your mouth.

Copper Onion INTERNATIONAL $$$
(Map p438; ☑801-355-3282; www.thecopper onion.com; 111 E Broadway Ave; brunch & small

---

SALT LAKE CONNECT

Visit Salt Lake (Map p438; ☑801-534-4900; www.visitsaltlake.com; 90 S West Temple St, Salt Palace Convention Center; ⊗9am-6pm Mon-Fri, to 5pm Sat & Sun) sells one- to three-day discounted attraction passes called Salt Lake Connect Passes, online and at its visitor center. But unless you plan to visit every child-friendly attraction in the town – and some outside of town – it probably isn't worth your while.

UTAH SALT LAKE CITY

Downtown Salt Lake City

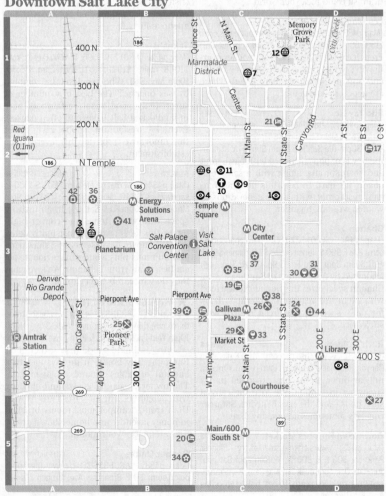

plates $7-15, dinner mains $22-29; ⏰11am-3pm & 5-10pm) Locals keep the Copper Onion bustling at every seating... And for good reason: small plates like wagyu stroganoff and pasta carbonara call out to be shared. Save room for the citrus and chèvre cheesecake. A design-driven rustic decor provides a convivial place to enjoy it all.

Its casual extension Copper Commons, located next door, is equally popular.

Pago   AMERICAN $$$
(Map p434; ☎801-532-0777; www.pagoslc. com; 878 S 900 E; mains $20-39; ⏰11am-3pm

Mon-Fri, 10am-2:30pm Sat & Sun, 5-10pm Mon-Sun) 🍃 Earthy and interesting, with seasonal eclectic mains like Moroccan fried chicken with frisée or truffle burgers. Dine at the few sidewalk tables and you'll feel like part of the chummy neighborhood. Supports local farms. Dinner reservations recommended.

🍷 Drinking & Nightlife

Pubs and bars that also serve food are mainstays of SLC's nightlife, and no one minds if you mainly drink and nibble. A

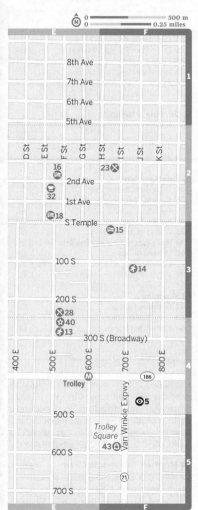

UTAH SALT LAKE CITY

meet friends and make friends, but it gets pretty loud.

★ Jack Mormon Coffee Co — CAFE

(Map p438; www.jackmormoncoffee.com; 82 E St; ⊙10am-6pm Mon-Sat) Utah's finest roaster also serves mean espresso drinks. When the temps rise, locals binge on a Jack Frost.

Publik — COFFEE

(Map p434; ☑385-229-4205; publikcoffee.com; 931 E 900 S; ⊙7am-6pm Mon-Fri, 8am-6pm Sat & Sun) Grow a beard and don your beanie and flannels to join Salt Lake's coolest sipping nitro cold brew at this warehouse-cum-cafe. Publik is a small-batch roaster; it also serves some mean avocado toast.

Bar X — COCKTAIL BAR

(Map p438; 155 E 200 S; ⊙4pm-2am Mon-Fri, 6pm-2am Sat, 7pm-2am Sun) So low-lit and funky, it's hard to believe you're down the street from Temple Sq. Cozy up to the crowded bar with a Moscow Mule and listen to Motown or funk (or the guy at the next table saying to his date, 'Your voice is pretty').

Epic Brewing Company — CAFE

(Map p434; www.epicbrewing.com; 825 S State St; ⊙11am-9pm Mon-Thu, 10am-11pm Fri & Sat, 11am-7pm Sun) Utah's first full-strength beer brewery. You have to have at least something small to eat (Utah law), but then they pour small tastes (40¢ to $1) or full glasses of their 30 ales, IPAs, lagers and stouts.

The Sour Apple Saison and Brainless Belgian-style ale are two of our favorites. When the weather is bad, seating is limited to a small tasting counter.

The Rest — COCKTAIL BAR

(Map p438; ☑801-532-4452; 331 Main St; ⊙5pm-1am Tue-Sat) This low-lit novelty is worth the stumbling around it might take to find it if you are looking for something different. Go downstairs from Bodega, a convenience store/tavern to get to the cool speakeasy part. Strong honey-lavender and lime-cucumber concoctions go down easy with an order of billowy beignets. By reservation only.

Uinta Brewing Co — BREWERY

(Map p431; ☑801-467-0909; www.uinta brewing.com/brewhouse-pub; 1722 Fremont Dr; ⊙11am-8pm Mon-Thu, to 9pm Sat & Sun) Riding the wave of rustic cool, this warehouse houses a pretty good brewpub with organic

complete schedule of local bar music is available in the *City Weekly* (www.city weekly.net).

★ Beer Bar — PUB

(Map p438; www.beerbarslc.com; 161 E 200 S; ⊙11am-2am Mon-Sat, 10am-2am Sun) With shared wooden tables and over 140 beers and 13 sausage styles, Beer Bar is a little slice of Bavaria in Salt Lake City. The crowd is diverse and far more casual than at Bar X next door (a linked venue). A great place to

Downtown Salt Lake City

and gluten-free beer options. The session ale with peach notes goes down nicely with an order of wings.

Wasatch Brew Pub MICROBREWERY
(Map p434; ☑ 801-783-1127; www.wasatchbeers.com; 2110 Highland Dr; ⊙ 10am-midnight Sun-Thu, to 1am Fri & Sat) Excellent microbrews and appetizers at the Sugarhouse, a shopping-center structure (in the neighborhood of the same name) that screams warehouse-chic. It's convenient for locals, but a distance from downtown.

☆ Entertainment

We wouldn't say the nightlife here is all that hot; major dance clubs change frequently and few are open more than a couple of nights a week. See the *City Weekly* (www.cityweekly.net) for listings. Classical entertainment options, especially around Temple Sq, are plentiful.

Music, Theater & Cinema

There are concerts on Temple Sq, at the **Library** (Map p438; www.slcpl.org; 210 E 400 S; ⊙ 9am-9pm Mon-Thu, to 6pm Fri & Sat, 1-5pm Sun)

and in Red Butte Garden (p432) in the summertime. The Salt Lake City Arts Council provides a complete cultural events calendar on its website (www.slcgov.com/calendars). Most tickets can be reserved through **ArtTix** (☑ 801-355-2787, 888-451-2787; artsaltlake.org).

★ **Mormon Tabernacle Choir** LIVE MUSIC
(☑ 801-570-0080, 801-240-4150; www.mormon tabernaclechoir.org) Hearing the world-renowned Mormon Tabernacle Choir is a must-do on any SLC bucket list. A live choir broadcast goes out every Sunday at 9:30am. September through November, and January through May, attend in person at the Tabernacle (p431). Free public rehearsals are held here from 8pm to 9pm Thursday.

From June to August and in December – to accommodate larger crowds – choir broadcasts and rehearsals are held at the 21,000-seat LDS Conference Center. Performance times stay the same, except that an extra organ recital takes place at 2pm, Monday through Saturday.

Eccles Theatre
THEATER

(Map p438; ☑ 385-468-1010; www.eccles.theater saltlakecity.com; 131 Main St) Opened in 2016, this gorgeous building has two theaters (one seating 2500 people), showing Broadway shows, concerts and other entertainment.

Brewvies Cinema Pub
CINEMA

(Map p438; ☑ 801-355-5500; www.brewvies.com; 677 S 200 W) Join locals quaffing craft beer and downing pub grub while watching new releases and indie films. There's billiards too. It's an SLC institution.

Urban Lounge
CONCERT VENUE

(Map p438; ☑ 801-746-0557; www.theurban loungeslc.com; 241 S 500 E; cover free-$15; ☺ 9pm-2am) A late-night music venue and cocktail lounge with small indie acts and international artists; some free shows.

Gallivan Center
CONCERT VENUE

(Map p438; www.thegallivancenter.com; 200 S, btwn State & Main Sts) Bring a picnic to the outdoor concert and movie series at the Gallivan Center, an amphitheater in a garden. Performances run in summer.

Depot
CONCERT VENUE

(Map p438; ☑ 801-355-5522; www.smithstix.com; 400 W South Temple St) Primary concert venue for rock acts.

Capitol Theater
THEATER

(Map p438; artssaltlake.org; 50 W 200 S) This historic theater is the primary venue of the Salt Lake City Arts Council, with theater, dance, opera and symphonies.

Rose Wagner Performing Arts Center
THEATER

(Map p438; artsaltlake.org; 138 W 300 S) Many of SLC Arts Council's dramatic and musical theater performances are staged here.

Sports

Utah Jazz
BASKETBALL

(Map p438; ☑ 801-325-2500; www.nba.com/jazz; 301 W South Temple St) Utah Jazz, the men's professional basketball team, plays at the **Vivint Smart Home Arena** (Map p438; www. vivintarena.com; 301 W South Temple St), where concerts are also held.

Real Salt Lake
SOCCER

(☑ 844-732-5849; www.rsl.com; 9256 State St, Rio Tinto Stadium; ☺ Mar-Oct) Salt Lake's winning Major League Soccer team (*ree*-al) has a loyal local following and matches are fun to take in at the **Rio Tinto Stadium** (☑ 801-727-2700; 9256 State St, Sandy).

Utah Grizzlies
ICE HOCKEY

(Map p431; ☑ 801-988-8000; www.utahgrizzlies. com; 3200 S Decker Lake Dr, West Valley City) The International Hockey League's Utah Grizzlies plays at the **Maverik Center** (Map p431; ☑ tickets 800-745-3000; www.maverikcenter.com; 3200 S Decker Lake Dr, West Valley City), which hosted most of the men's ice hockey competitions during the 2002 Winter Olympics.

Salt Lake Bees
BASEBALL

(Map p434; ☑ tickets 801-325-2337; www.slbees. com) The AAA minor-league affiliate of the Anaheim Angels plays at **Smith's Ballpark** (Map p434; ☑ 801-350-6900; 77 W 1300 S).

🔒 Shopping

An interesting array of boutiques, antiques and cafes line up along Broadway Ave (300 South), between 100 and 300 East. Drawing on Utah pioneer heritage, SLC has quite a few crafty shops and galleries scattered around; a few can be found on the 300 block of W Pierpont Ave. Many participate in the one-day Craft Salt Lake expo in August.

Unhinged
FASHION & ACCESSORIES

(Map p434; ☑ 801-467-6588; unhingedslc.com; 2165 S Highland Dr; ☺ 10am-9pm Mon-Sat, noon-5pm Sun) Locally made and up-cycled products are the focus of this boutique, a designer yard sale if ever there was one. Stocks men's and women's clothing, oddball gifts and accessories.

Utah Artist Hands
ARTS & CRAFTS

(Map p438; www.utahands.com; 163 E Broadway; ☺ noon-6pm Mon-Fri, to 5pm Sat) Local artists' work, all made in-state, runs the gamut from fine art and photography to scarves and pottery.

Sam Weller Books
BOOKS

(Map p438; ☑ 801-328-2586; www.wellerbook works.com; 607 Trolley Sq; ☺ 11am-8pm Mon-Thu, 10am-9pm Fri & Sat, noon-5pm Sun) The city's biggest and best independent bookstore also has a praiseworthy local rare-book selection at its downtown location.

15th Street Gallery
ART

(Map p434; ☑ 801-468-1515; 15thstreetgallery.com; 1519 S 1500 E; ☺ 10am-6pm Mon-Fri, to 5pm Sat) A tasteful modern gallery showing local art, with original jewelry that won't break the bank.

Black Diamond Equipment
SPORTS & OUTDOORS
(Map p431; blackdiamondequipment.com; 2092 E 3900 S; ☉10am-7pm Mon-Sat, 11am-5pm Sun) Retail store for leading manufacturer of climbing and ski gear that headquarters here in SLC.

ℹ Information

EMERGENCY
Local Police (☎801-799-3000; 315 E 200 S)

INTERNET ACCESS
Main Library (www.slcpl.org; 210 E 400 S; ☉9am-9pm Mon-Thu, 9am-6pm Fri & Sat, 1-5pm Sun; 🛜) Free wireless and internet access.

MEDICAL SERVICES
University Hospital (☎801-581-2121; 50 N Medical Dr) For emergencies, 24/7.

Salt Lake Regional Medical Center (☎801-350-4111; www.saltlakeregional.com; 1050 E South Temple St; ☉24hr emergency)

MONEY
Note that it can be difficult to change foreign currency in Utah outside SLC.

Wells Fargo (☎801-238-5060; www.wellsfargo.com; 79 S Main St; ☉9am-5pm Mon-Fri, to 2pm Sat)

POST
Post Office (Map p438; ☎801-532-5501; www.usps.com; 230 W 200 S; ☉8am-5:30pm Mon-Fri, 9am-2pm Sat)

TOURIST INFORMATION
Bike SLC (www.bikeslc.com) Invaluable map resources showing the best cycling routes in Salt Lake City and around, put out by the city.

Downtown SLC (www.downtownslc.org) Arts, entertainment and business information about the downtown core.

Public Lands Information Center (Map p431; ☎801-466-6411; www.publiclands.org; 3285 E 3300 S, REI Store; ☉10:30am-5:30pm Mon-Fri, 9am-1pm Sat) Recreation information for nearby public lands (state parks, BLM, USFS), including the Wasatch-Cache National Forest.

Visit Salt Lake (p437) Publishes a free visitor-guide booklet; large gift shop on-site at the visitor center.

WEBSITES
City Weekly (www.cityweekly.net) Free alternative weekly with good restaurant and entertainment listings; twice annually it publishes the free *City Guide*.

Deseret News (www.desnews.com) Conservative, church-owned paper reflecting the views of LDS.

Salt Lake Magazine (www.saltlakemagazine.com) Lifestyle and food magazine for Salt Lake City, with some statewide coverage.

Salt Lake Tribune (www.sltrib.com) Utah's largest-circulation daily paper.

ℹ Getting There & Away
Springdale and Zion National Park are 308 miles to the south; Moab and Arches National Park are 234 miles south and east.

AIR
Five miles northwest of downtown, **Salt Lake City International Airport** (SLC; Map p431; ☎801-575-2400; www.slcairport.com; 776 N Terminal Dr; 🛜) has mostly domestic flights, though you can fly direct to Canada and Mexico.

Delta (☎800-221-1212; www.delta.com) is the main SLC carrier.

BUS
Greyhound (Map p434; ☎800-231-2222; www.greyhound.com; 300 S 600 W; 🛜) has buses to nationwide destinations.

TRAIN
Amtrak (☎800-872-7245; www.amtrak.com) stops here between California and Denver, CO.

LGBTQI+ SLC

Many from the LGBTQI+ community here feel that the state is inevitably headed in a more progressive direction. That said, it is a very conservative state. Salt Lake City has Utah's only gay scene, however limited. Pick up the free *Q Salt Lake* (www.qsaltlake.com) for listings. **Utah Pride Festival** (p434), held over one weekend in June, is a big party and parade. The town's closest thing to a gay-ish neighborhood is 9th and 9th (900 South and 900 East), where **Coffee Garden** (Map p434; 895 E 900 S; ☉6am-11pm Sun-Thu, to midnight Fri & Sat; 🛜) is the neighborhood cafe. The Utah Pride Center has the largest LGBT library in the state, housed at the University of Utah Marriott Library.

The **Union Pacific Rail Depot** (340 S 600 W) is serviced daily by Amtrak trains.

ℹ Getting Around

Two major interstates cross at SLC: I-15 runs north–south, I-80 east–west. I-215 loops the city. The area around Temple Sq is easily walkable, and free public transportation covers much of the downtown core, but to go beyond you will need your own vehicle.

TO/FROM THE AIRPORT

Express Shuttle (☑ 801-596-1600; www.xpressshuttleutah.com; to downtown $17) Shared van service to/from the airport.

Utah Transit Authority (UTA; www.rideuta.com; one-way $2.50; 🛜) With light-rail service to the international airport and downtown area. Bus 550 travels downtown from the parking structure between terminals 1 and 2.

Yellow Cab (☑ 801-521-2100) Private taxi to Park City and area destinations.

BICYCLE

GREENbike (www.greenbikeslc.org; 24hr pass $7) Salt Lake City's bike-share program has B-cycle stations all over downtown for rider convenience. Use your credit card at a kiosk to rent.

CAR & MOTORCYCLE

National rental agencies have SLC airport offices.

Rugged Rental (☑ 801-977-9111, 800-977-9111; www.ruggedrental.com; 2740 W California Ave; ⊙8am-6pm Mon-Sat) Rents 4WDs, SUVs and passenger cars. Rates are often better here than at the major companies.

PUBLIC TRANSPORTATION

Trax, UTA's light-rail system, runs from Central Station (600 W 250 S) west to the University of Utah and south past Sandy. The center of downtown SLC is a free-fare zone. During ski season, UTA buses serve Park City ($4.50 one way).

Antelope Island State Park

The Great Salt Lake is the largest body of water west of the Great Lakes, but it's hard to say just exactly how big it is. The best place to experience the lake (and see the birds) is at **Antelope Island State Park** (☑ 801-773-2941; stateparks.utah.gov; Antelope Dr; day-use per vehicle $10, tent & RV sites without hookups $15; ⊙7am-10pm Jul-Sep, to 7pm Oct-Jun). White-sand beaches, birds and buffalo attract people to the pretty, 15-mile-long park.

The largest island in the Great Salt Lake is home to a 500-strong herd of American bison, or buffalo. The fall roundup, for veterinary exams, is a thrilling spectacle. Also making their year-round home here are burrowing owls and raptors, as well as namesake antelope, bighorn sheep and deer.

Nineteen miles of hiking trails provide many opportunities to view wildlife; however, some trails are closed during mating and birthing seasons. In addition to an 8-mile driving loop, there's a white, sandy beach to the south on Bridger Bay with basic facilities and showers.

◉ Sights

Fielding Garr Ranch   HISTORIC SITE
(⊙9am-5pm) A dirt-road spur leads 11 miles to the Fielding Garr Ranch. Take a look around what was a working farm from 1848 until 1981, back when Antelope Island State Park was created. Check the park website for ranger tours or cowboy poetry gatherings on-site.

🛏 Sleeping & Eating

There are campground accommodations in the park.

Bridger Bay Campground   CAMPGROUND $
(☑ reservations 800-322-3770; utahstateparks.reserveamerica.com; tent & RV sites $15) The 18-site Bridger Bay Campground has shelters for shade, water and pit toilets, but no hookups.

Buffalo Island Grill   AMERICAN $
(☑ 801-897-3452; Bridger Bay Beach; mains $7-10; ⊙11am-8pm May-Sep) Burgers, onion rings and chicken sandwiches on paper plates will quell your hunger.

ℹ Information

Visitor Center (park entry per vehicle $10; ⊙9am-6pm) Inquire about the many ranger-led activities, watch an introductory video and pick up a map at the visitor center.

Brigham City

☑ 435 / POP 18,500 / ELEV 4436FT

Brigham City is pretty small, with a few natural attractions, and one famous restaurant. The stretch of Hwy 89 south of town is known as the 'Golden Spike Fruitway' – from July through September it's crowded with fruit stands vending the abundant

WORTH A TRIP

THE REMOTE NORTHWEST

On May 10, 1869, the westward Union Pacific Railroad and eastward Central Pacific Railroad met at Promontory Summit. With the completion of the transcontinental railroad, the face of the American West changed forever. **Golden Spike National Historic Site** (www.nps.gov/gosp; per vehicle $7; ⏰ 9am-5pm), 32 miles northwest of Brigham City on Hwy 83, has an interesting museum and films, auto tours and several interpretive trails. Steam-engine demonstrations take place June through August. Aside from Golden Spike National Historic Site, few people visit Utah's desolate northwest corner. But while you're here …

At the end of a dirt road (4WD recommended but not required) 15 miles southwest of the Golden Spike visitor center, there's a wonderfully unique outdoor art installation, the **Spiral Jetty** (p444). Created by Robert Smithson in 1970, it's a 1500ft coil of rock and earth spinning out into the water. It's a little hard to find – get directions from the visitor center.

local harvest. One week in September Brigham City celebrates 'Peach Days.'

◉ Sights & Activities

★ **Spiral Jetty**   LANDMARK
(www.spiraljetty.org) Created by Robert Smithson in 1970, this beyond-cool art installation is a 1500ft coil of rock and earth spinning out into the water. It's a little hard to find; get directions from Box Elder County Tourism.

Bear River Migratory Bird Refuge   WILDLIFE RESERVE
(www.fws.gov/refuge/bear_river_migratory_bird_refuge; W Forest St; ⏰ dawn-dusk) FREE This bird refuge engulfs almost 74,000 acres of marshland on the northeastern shores of the Great Salt Lake. The best time for bird-watchers is during fall (September to November) and spring (March to May) migrations. Birds banded here have been recovered as far away as Siberia and Colombia.

The refuge's Wildlife Education Center is 16 miles west. Cruising along the 12-mile,

barely elevated touring road to it feels like you're driving on water.

Crystal Hot Springs   HOT SPRINGS
(☑ 435-279-8104; www.crystalhotsprings.net; 8215 N Hwy 38; pool adult/child $7/5, slides $10; ⏰ 10am-10pm Mon-Sat, to 8pm Sun) Get into hot water year-round at this location, 10 miles north of Brigham City in Honeyville. Adults float in different-temperature soaking pools while kids zip down the water slides (open shorter hours than the pools November through February).

Wildlife Education Center   BIRDWATCHING
(☑ 435-734-6426; 2155 W Forest St; ⏰ 10am-5pm Mon-Fri, to 4pm Sat) FREE At the Bear River Migratory Bird Refuge, this educational center plays replicated migratory calls year-round. Free bird-watching tours leave from here twice daily; reserve ahead. The center is just after the I-15 intersection.

🛏 Sleeping & Eating

Brigham City is an easy day trip from Salt Lake City, and there are a few motels.

Crystal Hot Springs Campground   CAMPGROUND $
(www.crystalhotsprings.net; tent/RV sites with hookup $20/30) Small campground serving Crystal Hot Springs.

Days Inn   HOTEL $
(☑ 435-723-3500, 888-440-2021; www.daysinn.com; 1033 S 1600 W; r $75-115; 🛜🐾) Among the better motels in town.

Maddox Ranch House   STEAK $$
(☑ 800-544-5474; www.maddoxfinefood.com; 1900 S Hwy 89; mains $17-28, lunch from $10; ⏰ 11am-9pm Tue-Thu, to 9:30pm Fri & Sat) People travel for hours for these thick beef or bison steaks cut from locally raised livestock. It all started in the ranch out back in 1949. Don't expect anything fancy – this is a family-owned place, serving families. Pay extra for shrimp on your complimentary seafood cocktail appetizer and be sure to try the raspberry butter on the homemade bread.

Reservations are not accepted. Even if you go early, you can expect to wait.

ℹ Information

BLM (☑ 801-977-4300; www.blm.gov) Online resource for area public lands.

Box Elder County Tourism (☑ 877-390-2326; www.boxelder.org; 1 S Main St; ⊙ 8am-5pm Mon-Fri) Information on area attractions.

Logan

☑ 435 / POP 48,900 / ELEV 4350FT

With university charm and pretty rural surroundings, Logan is a quintessential old-fashioned community with strong Mormon roots. It's situated 80 miles north of Salt Lake City in bucolic Cache Valley, which offers year-round outdoor activities. Logan Canyon offers hiking and biking galore.

⊙ Sights

American West Heritage Center   NOTABLE BUILDING
(www.awhc.org; 4025 S Hwy 89; ⊙ 9am-5pm; ⊛) A 19th-century frontier community comes to life with hands-on, living-history activities at a Shoshone Nation camp and a pioneer settlement at the American West Heritage Center, south of Logan. The center hosts the popular weeklong **Festival of the American West** in July, a must for frontier buffs and great for families. Visitors can stop by for self-guided tours.

🛏 Sleeping & Eating

As a university town, Logan has a range of good lodging options. There are a couple of B&Bs around town, and midrange chain motels are well represented on Hwy 89.

Logan offers the hippest eats in northern Utah. Enjoy its full-octane coffee and artisan pizza and baked goods.

Beaver Creek Lodge   LODGE $$
(☑ 435-753-1076, 800-946-4485; www.beavercreeklodge.com; Mile 487, Hwy 89; r $149) Beaver Creek Lodge in Logan Canyon offers horseback riding and snowmobiling packages. No room phones but there are flatscreen TVs and in-room refrigerators.

★**Crumb Brothers Artisan Bakery**   BAKERY $
(☑ 435-753-0875; www.crumbbrothers.com; 291 S 300 W; mains $6-9; ⊙ 7am-6pm Wed-Sat, 9am-3pm Sun) For baked goods that border on ecstasy, Crumb Brothers Artisan Bakery delivers. It also bakes gorgeous, crusty organic breads on-site. If you're in town on Sunday, stop in for some serious brunch.

OFF THE BEATEN TRACK

LOGAN CANYON SCENIC BYWAY

Pick up a free interpretive trail guide at the Cache Valley Visitor Bureau (p445) in Logan before driving the 40-mile riverside drive through **Logan Canyon Scenic Byway** (www.logancanyon.com; Hwy 89, btwn Logan & Garden City). Wind your way up through the Bear River Mountains, past Beaver Mountain, before descending to the 20-mile-long Bear Lake, a summer water-sports playground. Along the way there are numerous signposted hiking and biking trails.

It's beautiful year-round, but July wildflowers and October foliage are particularly brilliant. There are campgrounds in the Uinta-Wasatch-Cache National Forest (p464).

Jack's Wood Fired Oven   PIZZA $
(☑ 435-754-7523; jackswoodfiredoven.blogspot.com; 256 N Main St; pizzas $10-16; ⊙ 11:30am-9pm, to 10pm Fri-Sun) In the evening, upscale Jack's fills with Utah hipsters drinking Uinta Brewing Co drafts with exotic thin-crust pizzas that might include house-pickled jalapeños or prosciutto and chipotle peaches. Gluten-free options available.

ℹ Information

Cache Valley Visitor Bureau (☑ 435-755-1890, 800-882-4433; www.explorelogan.com; 199 N Main St; ⊙ 9am-5pm Mon-Fri) Pick up information about the myriad outdoor options and a free interpretive booklet here.

WASATCH MOUNTAINS

Giant saw-toothed peaks on the eastern edge of Utah's urban centers, these forested slopes provide a popular haven. The Wasatch Mountain Range is nature's playground year-round, but in winter a fabulous low-density, low-moisture snowfall – 300in to 500in yearly – blankets the terrain. Perfect snow and thousands of acres of high-altitude slopes helped earn Utah the honor of hosting the 2002 Winter Olympics. Skiing in the Wasatch range is some of the best in North America.

Wasatch Mountains

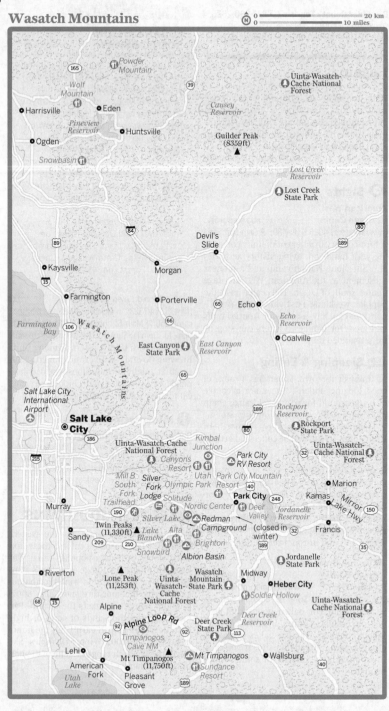

Resort towns cluster near the peaks; Park City, on the eastern slopes, is the most well known and quasi-cosmopolitan. Salt Lake City resorts, on the western side, are easiest for townies to reach. Ogden is the sleeper hit and Sundance is known as much for its film festival as its ski trails. Most areas lie within an hour of the international airport: leave New York or Los Angeles in the morning to be skiing by noon.

ℹ Information

Ski Utah (www.skiutah.com) puts out excellent annual winter vacation guides – in paper and online.

The **Utah Avalanche Center** (www.utahavalanchecenter.org) is an essential resource for skiers, especially those going into the backcountry.

SKI SEASON

➤ Ski season runs mid-November to mid-April – only **Snowbird** (p448) stays open much past Easter. However, snow varies: in a record winter deep powder can hang around until June.

➤ Saturday is busiest; Sunday ticket sales drop by a third because LDS members are in church.

➤ Summer season is from late June until early September.

HOURS

Day lifts usually run from 9am to 4pm.

PRICES

Children's prices are good for ages six to 12; kids under six usually ski for free. All resorts rent out equipment in the form of mountain-bike, ski or snowboard packages. You can save a few bucks by renting off-mountain, but if there's a problem with the equipment, you're stuck. Ski schools are available at all resorts.

CONDITIONS

Most resorts have jumped into the digital age and have powder reports, blogs and weather-condition updates you can view on their websites or sign up to receive via email.
Logan Ranger District Office (☎ 435-755-3620; 1500 East Hwy 89; ⊗ 8:30am-4:30pm) Check here for conditions on Logan Canyon Scenic Byway (p445).

DANGERS & ANNOYANCES

Backcountry enthusiasts: heed avalanche warnings! Take a course at a resort, carry proper equipment and check conditions. Drink plenty of fluids, too: dehydrated muscles injure easily.

ℹ Getting There & Around

Buses and shuttles from Salt Lake City and between resorts are widely available, so you don't need to rent a car to reach most resorts.

Salt Lake City Ski Resorts

Although they are closer to Salt Lake City than Park City, these resorts are no less worthy of your attention. Because of Great Salt Lake–affected snow patterns, these resorts receive almost twice as much snow as Park City. The four resorts east of Salt Lake City sit 30 to 45 miles from the downtown core at the end of two canyons. In summer, access the numerous hiking and biking trails that lead off from both canyons.

Follow Hwy 190 up to family-oriented Solitude (p450) and skier fave Brighton (p451) in Big Cottonwood Canyon. In summer you can continue over the mountain to Heber City and Park City. To the south, Little Cottonwood Canyon is home to the seriously challenging terrain at Snowbird (p448) and the all-round ski-purist special, Alta (p449).

🏃 Activities

Ski Utah Interconnect
Adventure Tour SKIING
(☎ 801-534-1907; www.skiutah.com/interconnect; pass $395; ⊗ mid-Dec–mid-Apr) Ski six resorts in one day by linking them via backcountry terrain with expert guides. Best for those who already have backcountry ski experience and a good level of fitness. The price tag includes lunch, lift tickets and all transportation.

ℹ Information

For lodging/skiing package deals, see www.visitsaltlake.com or contact resorts directly.
Cottonwood Canyons Foundation
(☎ 801-947-8263, 801-466-6411; www.cottonwoodcanyons.org) USFS ranger-led programs available at Alta (p449), Brighton (p451) and Snowbird (p448).
Ski City Super Pass (www.visitsaltlakecity.com/ski/superpass; 3-day pass adult/child $246/114) A deal to ski all the Salt Lake resorts: it covers Alta, Brighton, Snowbird and Solitude (p450), with three- to 10-day packages available. No blackout days and free transportation on UTA ski buses.

ⓘ Getting There & Around

There are **UTA** (☎ 801-743-3882; www.rideuta. com; intercanyon $2.25, ski shuttle $4.50) buses from Salt Lake City, plus private shuttles, such as **Canyon Transportation** (☎ 801-255-1841, 800-255-1841; www.canyontransport. com; adult/child one-way $39/25) and **Alta Shuttle** (☎ 801-274-0225, 866-274-0225; www. altashuttle.com; one-way $38), and rental car options.

ⓘ Getting Around

Six ski-service park-and-ride lots are available around town; the most convenient is **Holladay Park & Ride Lot** (6200 S Wasatch Blvd, Salt Lake City). Buses also run between resorts in the same valley. The UTA runs a ski bus to all the resorts, and there are also shared shuttle services.

Snowbird

If you can see it, you can ski it at **Snowbird** (☎ 800-232-9542; www.snowbird.com; Hwy 210, Little Cottonwood Canyon; day lift-ticket adult/ child $116/55), the industrial-strength resort with extreme steeps, long groomers, wide-open bowls (one of them an incredible 500 acres across) and a kick-ass terrain park. The challenging slopes are particularly popular with speed demons and testoster-one-driven snowboarders.

The lowdown: 3240ft vertical drop, base elevation 7760ft; 2500 acres, 27% beginner, 38% intermediate, 35% advanced; four high-speed quads, six double lifts, one tramway. The only conveyor-pull tunnel in the US links the need-for-speed **Peruvian Gulf** area and intermediate terrain in **Mineral Basin**. Wednesday, Friday and Saturday, one lift remains open until 8:30pm for night skiing.

Snowbird has the longest season of the four Salt Lake City resorts, with skiing usually possible mid-November to mid-May.

🏃 Activities

The combined **Alta-Snowbird Pass** (adult/ child $128/84) permits skiers (not boarders)

> ### ⓘ SKI FOR FREE
>
> After 3pm you can ski for free on the Sunnyside lift at Alta. The program is set up to get beginners – or those for whom it's been a while – onto the slopes.

access to both areas, for a total of 4700 skiable acres. Inquire at the resort about snowmobiling, backcountry tours and snowshoeing in winter.

In summer, the Peruvian lift and tunnel offer access to **Mineral Basin** hiking and wildflowers. Pick up basic trail maps at the resort.

White Pine Lake Trail HIKING
At 10,000ft, this is a good though strenuous trail just over 3 miles one-way. Watch rocky slopes around the lake for the unique pika – a small, short-eared, tailless lago-morph (the order of mammals that includes rabbits).

Cecret Lake Trail HIKING
At the end of the canyon road, Cecret Lake Trail is an easy 1-mile loop with spectacular wildflowers in July and August.

Aerial Tram CABLE CAR
(tram only adult/child $20/17; ☺ 9am-4pm Dec-May, 11am-8pm Jun-Aug, 11am-5pm Sep-Nov) The 125-passenger aerial tram ascends 2900ft in only 10 minutes; die-hards do 'tram laps,' racing back down the mountain to reascend in the same car they just rode up on. If you like to ski like a teenager, you'll flip out when you see this mountain.

🛏 Sleeping

Snowbird has five kinds of accommodations, including hotels and condos, all booked through the resort's central phone number and website (www.snowbird.com/ lodging); packages including lift tickets are available. In summer, prices drop precipitously.

Cliff Lodge HOTEL $$$
(☎ 801-933-2222; www.snowbird.com/lodging/ theclifflodge; r $450-620; ⊚ 🤶 ⌘) The splashy black-glass-and-concrete 500-room Cliff Lodge is like a cruise ship in the mountains, with every possible destination-resort amenity – from flat-screen TVs to a recently remodeled, luxurious full-service spa. Request a 'spa level' room to have unlimited access to the rooftop pool. Otherwise check out the dramatic 10th-story glass-walled bar and settle for the level-three swimming pool with ski-run views.

Right at the heart of the resort's Snowbird Center pedestrian village, this lodge always bustles.

Inn at Snowbird
HOTEL $$$

([☑]801-933-2222; www.snowbird.com/lodging/the-inn; r $315-500; [❄][✉]) Snowbird's most homey and inviting property has a simple, almost residential feel. Studio rooms have kitchens and wood-burning fireplaces. Bring groceries and save a bundle.

✗ Eating

Snowbird resort has 15 eating outlets, including standards like a coffee shop, pizza place, steakhouse and après-ski bars.

Creekside Café & Grill
CAFE $

([☑]801-933-2477; Gadzoom Lift Base; breakfast & sandwiches $7-13; ◷9am-2:30pm Dec-Apr) This 3000-sq-ft deck is a great place to grab a sandwich slopeside.

General Gritts
MARKET $

(Snowbird Center; ◷11am-6pm) A grocery store with deli sandwiches and liquor sales.

Steak Pit
AMERICAN $$$

([☑]801-933-2260; www.snowbird.com/dining/steak-pit; 9385 S Snowbird Center Dr; mains $19-60; ◷6-9pm) If you like your steak hand-cut and served with smoked sea salt and twice-baked potatoes, this on-mountain restaurant calls your name. With cozy leather booths, decent seafood options and an extensive wine list.

Alta

Dyed-in-the-wool skiers make a pilgrimage to **Alta** ([☑]801-359-1078, 888-782-9258; www.alta.com; Little Cottonwood Canyon; day lift-pass adult/child $96/50), at the top of the valley. No snowboarders are allowed here, which keeps the snow cover from deteriorating, especially on groomers. Locals have grown up with Alta, a resort filled not with see-and-be-seen types, but rather the see-and-say-hello crowd. Wide-open powder fields, gullies, chutes and glades, such as **East Greeley**, **Devil's Castle** and **High Rustler**, have helped make Alta famous. Warning: you may never want to ski anywhere else.

The lowdown: 2020ft vertical drop, base elevation 8530ft; 2200 skiable acres, 25% beginner, 40% intermediate, 35% advanced; three high-speed chairs, four fixed-grip chairs. You can ski from the Sunnyside lift for free after 3pm; it's great for families with little ones who tire easily (lifts close at 4:30pm).

For more general information, see www.discoveralta.com.

◉ Sights & Activities

The **Alta-Snowbird Pass** (adult/child $128/84) permits access to both areas for a stunning 4700 acres of skiing. Expert powder hounds should ask about off-piste snow-cat skiing in Grizzly Gulch.

No lifts run in summer, but there are 10 miles of local trails.

Albion Basin
NATURAL FEATURE

(www.fs.fed.us/wildflowers/regions/intermoun tain/AlbionBasin) From July to August, Albion Basin is abloom with wildflowers. July, when an annual wildflower festival is held, is usually peak season.

🛏 Sleeping

The lodging options at Alta are like the ski area: simple and just as it's been for decades. Every place here has ski-in, ski-out access and a hot tub. Winter rates include breakfast and dinner and require a four-night minimum stay.

Albion Basin Campground
CAMPGROUND $

([☑]800-322-3770; www.recreation.gov; Little Cottonwood Canyon Rd; campsites $19-57; ◷Jul-Sep) Sleep surrounded by July and August wildflowers at this campground. The 19 sites sit at 9500ft among meadows and pine trees, 11 miles up the canyon. Drinking water, no showers; no dogs allowed.

Snowpine Lodge
HOTEL $$

([☑]801-742-2000; www.thesnowpine.com; male dm $161, r with private/shared bath $425/255) Granite-block-built Snowpine Lodge, Alta's most basic, is the die-hard skier's first choice. An eight-room expansion overlooks Eagle's Nest and Albion Basin.

Rustler Lodge
HOTEL $$$

([☑]888-532-2582, 801-742-2200; www.rustler lodge.com; r $636-979; [@][❄][✉]) After extensive renovations, you can bask in all the creature comforts of a city hotel at Rustler Lodge. Take an early morning stretch class before you hit the slopes and refresh in the euca-lyptus sauna afterwards. All rates include breakfast and dinner.

Alta Lodge
LODGE $$$

([☑]801-742-3500, 800-707-2852; www.altalodge.com; dm $161, d with private/shared bath $329/236; [@][❄][✉]) A mid-century modernist lodge frequented by Ivy Leaguers playing back-gammon in the cozy attic bar (open to nonguests). Expect to make friends at family-style dinners in this simply comfortable Alta classic. No TVs.

🍴 Eating

Resort fare is decent, with a range of offerings from burgers to fancy elk dinners. Lodge restaurants and snack bars are seasonal (December through March) and open to the public.

Alf's
BURGERS $

(☑ 801-799-2295; Cecret Lift Base; sandwiches $8-15; ⊙ 9:30am-4pm) Mid-mountain, this casual spot serves burgers surrounded by antique skis on the walls.

Collin's Grill
AMERICAN $$

(Watson's Shelter, Wildcat Base; mains $13-22; ⊙ 11am-2:30pm Dec-Apr) Mid-mountain try Collin's Grill for homemade artisanal soups and breads (make reservations), natural meats that are regionally sourced and crab cakes dribbling in lobster cream sauce.

Shallow Shaft Restaurant
AMERICAN $$$

(☑ 801-742-2177; 10199 E Hwy 210, Alta Town; mains $26-42; ⊙ 5-10pm Dec-Apr, 6-9pm Thu-Sat Jul-early Sep) Chef Curtis Kraus uses locally produced ingredients whenever possible on his seasonally changing menu. In winter, pine nuts and quince flavor seafood and meats such as double-cut pork chops; in summer it may be fresh salsa.

Solitude

Though less undiscovered than it once was, you can feel sometimes as if you've got the mountain to yourself at Solitude (☑ 801-534-1400; www.skisolitude.com; 12000 Big Cottonwood Canyon Rd; day lift-ticket adult/child $83/53). It's still something of a local secret, so there's room to learn plus lots of speedy, roller-coaster-like corduroy to look forward to once you've gotten your ski legs. The lowdown: 2047ft vertical drop, base elevation 7988ft; 1200 acres, 20% beginner, 50% intermediate, 30% advanced; eight lifts. Three new quads have been added in recent years.

If you're an expert, you'll dig the 400 acres of lift-assist cliff bands, gullies, over-the-head powder drifts and super-steeps at off-piste Honeycomb Canyon. Everything here, including the expert grooming, is first-class.

🏃 Activities & Tours

Ice Skating Rink
SKATING

(Village; ⊙ 3-8pm Jan-Mar) FREE In the ski village surrounded by fire pits, this is a lovely way to spend an evening. It's only open to overnight guests.

Solitude Nordic Center
SKIING

(skisolitude.com/winter-activities/nordic-skiing-nordic-center; day pass adult/child $18/free; ⊙ 8:30am-4:40pm Dec-Mar & Jun-Aug) North of the resort's base, with 12 miles of groomed classic and skating lanes and 6 miles of snowshoeing tracks through enchanting forests of aspen and pine.

Sunrise Lift
MOUNTAIN BIKING, HIKING

(day pass $20; ⊙ Wed-Sun Jun-Aug) June through August, the Sunrise lift opens for chair-assist mountain biking and hiking.

Wasatch Powderbird Guides
ADVENTURE

(☑ 801-742-2800; www.powderbird.com; per day from $1540) Offers helicopter skiing and scenic flights.

Summer Activities

In summer, the Nordic Center becomes a visitor center and the boardwalk encircling Silver Lake becomes the easiest child and mobility-impaired nature trail around. Ask about guided owl-watching walks. No swimming, no dogs allowed (this is Salt Lake City's watershed). You can also rent mountain bikes and motorized mountain scooters, and play disc (Frisbee) golf at the resort.

Many hiking trails leave from various trailheads outside the resorts along Hwy 190; look for trailhead signs. One of the most attractive hikes is the 2-mile round-trip Lake Blanche Trail, beginning at the Mill B South Fork trailhead, about 5 miles into the canyon.

🛏 Sleeping

Most of the 'village' lodgings at Solitude are atmospheric, alpine-esque condos. Central reservations (☑ 800-748-4754; www.skisolitude.com) often has packages that cut room rates by as much as half.

Silver Fork Lodge
LODGE $$

(☑ 801-533-9977, 888-649-9551; www.silverfork lodge.com; 11332 E Big Cottonwood Canyon Rd;

r from $165, breakfast & sandwiches $10-13, dinner $11-34; ☺8am-9pm Sun-Thu, to 9:30pm Fri & Sat) A great alternative to resort eating and drinking is this classic mountain roadhouse. In summer sit outside and watch hummingbirds buzz across gorgeous alpine scenery. Western furnishings outfit the twin, queen and bunk-bed rooms; floors creak a little. In winter, warm up in the hot tub. Free shuttle to Brighton and Solitude resorts.

Creekside Lodge APARTMENT $$$
(☎800-748-4754; www.skisolitude.com; apt $446-790; ☏☒) Of the four full-kitchen condo-lodge properties at Solitude, the wood-and-stone Creekside Lodge is closest to the slopes; rooms have wood-burning fireplaces and balconies. All accommodations share Club Solitude's heated outdoor pool, sauna, fitness room, games room and movie theater. Summer rates are significantly lower.

Inn at Solitude HOTEL $$$
(☎800-748-4754; www.skisolitude.com; 12000 Big Cottonwood Canyon Rd, Brighton; r $269-359; @☏☒) The alpine-esque Inn at Solitude is the only hotel-style lodging; there's an on-site spa and hot tub. All accommodations share Club Solitude's heated outdoor pool, sauna, fitness room, games room and movie theater.

✕ Eating & Drinking

There are on-mountain options and hotel restaurants.

Honeycomb Grill AMERICAN $$
(12000 E Big Cottonwood Canyon Rd; mains $9-27; ☺11am-9pm) Dishing up warming bowls of elk chili, poutine and wood-fired breads, this casual on-mountain restaurant will either fuel your afternoon powder quest or send you straight to a nap.

★ Yurt AMERICAN $$$
(☎801-536-5709; skisolitude.com/village-dining/the-yurt; 12000 Big Cottonwood Canyon Rd; dinner per person $130; ☺5:30pm Tue-Sun Dec-Mar, 6:30pm Wed-Sun Jul-Sep) For an adventurous treat, hike or snowshoe a mile into the woods for a sumptuous, but unpretentious, five-course dinner in a bona fide canvas yurt. Bring your own wine and reserve way ahead. (Note: there's another yurt

ⓘ ALL-ACTIVITIES PASS

An **all-activities pass** (Activity Center; adult/child $39/24; ☺11am-8pm mid-Jun–Aug) includes numerous diversions: take a tramway up to Hidden Peak, ride the luge-like Alpine Slide, zipline down 1000ft, climb a rock wall or trampoline bungee jump. Full-suspension mountain bikes can be rented for three hours ($35). Horseback riding, backcountry 4WD and ATV tours are available, too.

dinner at the Canyons in Park City, but this is the original and the best.)

Departs from the Powderhorn Adventure Center.

Silver Fork Lodge Dining Room AMERICAN $$$
(☎801-533-9977; 11332 E Big Cottonwood Canyon Rd, Brighton; dinner mains $18-38; ☺8am-9pm) Creative comfort food is served in the rustic dining room, which feels like a cozy log cabin with its crackling fireplace.

Wasatch Mountain Table AMERICAN $$$
(☎801-536-5765; www.skisolitude.com/wasatch-mountain-table; per person $85; ☺5:30pm Jun-Aug, dates vary) In summer, check out Wasatch Mountain Table, a farm-to-table option that brings fine dining outdoors alongside Wasatch Creek.

Thirsty Squirrel BAR
(Village; ☺2-10pm Mon-Thu, noon-10pm Fri-Sun Dec-Mar) You can sip suds at the Thirsty Squirrel, but the Big Cottonwood Canyon's best après-ski and bar scene is at Brighton.

Brighton

Slackers, truants and bad-ass boarders rule at **Brighton** (☎801-532-4731, 800-873-5512; www.brightonresort.com; Big Cottonwood Canyon Rd; day lift-ticket adult/child $79/free; ☖). But don't be intimidated: the low-key resort where many Salt Lake residents first learned to ski remains a good first-timers' spot, especially if you want to snowboard. Thick stands of pines line sweeping groomed trails and wide boulevards, and from the top, the views are gorgeous. The whole place is a throwback: come for the ski-shack appeal coupled with high-tech slope improvements and modernized lodge.

The lowdown: 1745ft vertical drop, base elevation 8755ft; 1050 acres, 21% beginner, 40% intermediate, 39% advanced; six chair lifts. One hundred percent of Brighton's terrain is accessible by high-speed quads. There's a half-pipe and terrain park and a liberal open-boundary policy on non avalanche-prone days.

No lifts operate during summer months, but locals still hike the alpine meadows and picnic by area lakes. Lands near the top of Big Cottonwood Canyon are part of the Uinta-Wasatch-Cache National Forest (p464).

🏃 Activities

The park has some of the area's best night skiing (200 acres, 22 runs), open until 9pm Monday to Saturday. A magic-carpet slope lift means beginners can just step on and go, or you can leave the kiddies behind at the day-care center.

🛏 Sleeping & Eating

Lodging options are fewer than at nearby resorts. **Millicent Chalet** (8183 S Brighton Loop Rd; ⊙ vary depending on season) is the modern day-lodge base, with various self-service food options.

Redman Campground CAMPGROUND $
(www.recreation.gov; Solitude Service Rd; tent/RV sites $23/69; ⊙ late Jun-Sep) Camp near the top of Big Cottonwood Canyon, 13 miles in, at this 44-site campground. Trails lead off to lakes from the creekside ground at 8500ft. No swimming, no dogs allowed: this is Salt Lake City's watershed. Water is available, but no showers.

Brighton Lodge HOTEL $$
(🖀 801-532-4731, 800-873-5512; www.brighton resort.com; dm $129, r $149-209) The 20 bare-bones-basic rooms here go quick; they're within spitting distance of the lifts. No room TVs, but there are more than 200 movies you can watch in the common room, or just sit by the fireplace after you've hot-tubbed it. Room prices are crazy low in summer.

Brighton Store & Cafe CAFE $
(🖀 435-649-9156; 11491 Big Cottonwood Canyon Rd; breakfast & sandwiches $6-12; ⊙ 8:30am-4:30pm) This homey convenience store serves year-round.

Molly Green's PUB FOOD $$
(12601 E Big Cottonwood Canyon; pizza $10-24, mains $8-29; ⊙ 11am-10pm Mon-Sat, 10am-10pm Sun Dec-Mar) For après-ski drinks and pub grub, you gotta go to the A-frame right on the hill. Molly Green's has a roaring fire, a gregarious old-school vibe and great slopeside views. There's also a funky red bus snack bar in the parking lot.

Park City

🖀 435 / POP 8000 / ELEV 6900FT
With a dusting of snow, the century-old buildings on main street create a snow globe scene come to life. A one-time silver boom-and-bust town, pretty Park City is now lined with condos and mansions in the valleys. Utah's premier ski village boasts fabulous restaurants and cultural offerings. It recently annexed the adjacent Canyons Resort to become the largest ski resort in North America.

Park City first shot to international fame when it hosted the downhill, jumping and sledding events at the 2002 Winter Olympics. Today it's the permanent home base for the US Ski Team. There's usually snow through mid-April.

Come summer, more residents than visitors gear up for hiking and mountain biking among the nearby peaks. June to August, temperatures average in the 70s; nights are chilly. Spring and fall can be wet and boring; resort services, limited in summer compared with winter, shut down entirely between seasons.

◎ Sights & Activities

Skiing is the big area attraction, but there are activities enough to keep you more than busy in both summer and winter. Most are based out of the three resorts: Canyons, Park City Mountain and Deer Valley.

★ Utah Olympic Park AMUSEMENT PARK
(🖀 435-658-4200; www.utaholympiclegacy. com; 3419 Olympic Pkwy; museum free, activity day pass adult/child $70/45; ⊙ 10am-6pm, tours 11am-4pm) Visit the site of the 2002 Olympic ski jumping, bobsledding, skeleton, Nordic combined and luge events, which continues to host national competitions. There are 10m, 20m, 40m, 64m, 90m and 120m Nordic ski-jumping hills as well as a bob-sled-luge run. The US Ski Team practices

here year-round – in summer, the freestyle jumpers land in a bubble-filled jetted pool, and the Nordic jumpers on a hillside covered in plastic. Call for a schedule; it's free to observe.

The engaging and interactive Alf Engen Ski Museum, also on-site, traces local skiing history and details the 2002 Olympic events. Experts offer 45-minute **guided tours** on the hour.

Not content to just watch the action? No problem. Reserve ahead and adults can take a 70mph to 80mph **bobsled ride** with up to an incredible 4 to 5Gs of centrifugal force. The summer **Quicksilver Alpine Slide** is suitable for drivers over eight years old and riders who are three to seven. Clip on a harness and ride the 50mph **Extreme Zip Line** or the shorter **Ultra Zip Line**. Saturdays in summer there's a **Freestyle Show** that takes off at 1pm. Inquire about bobsled, skeleton, free-jump and freestyle lessons year-round.

★**Park City Museum**   MUSEUM
(www.parkcityhistory.org; 528 Main St; adult/child $10/4; ☺10am-7pm Mon-Sat, noon-6pm Sun) A well-staged interactive museum touches on the highlights of the town's history as a mining boomtown, hippie hangout and premier ski resort. There are fascinating exhibits on the world's first underground ski lift, a real dungeon in the basement and a 3D map of mining tunnels under the mountain.

Alf Engen Ski Museum   MUSEUM
(☎435-658-4240; 3419 Olympic Pkwy; ☺10am-6pm) **FREE** Interactive exhibits tell the history of skiing in the West. There's also a **virtual-reality ski theater** and **2002 Olympic Winter Games Museum**. It's at the Utah Olympic Park.

Skiing, Snowboarding & Sledding

All three resorts and in-town sports shops have equipment rental and ski lessons. Activity pick-up service is available from most resorts. Reservations are always a must.

Park City Mountain Resort   SNOW SPORTS, ADVENTURE SPORTS
(☎435-649-8111; www.parkcitymountainresort.com; 1310 Lowell Ave; lift ticket adult/child $134/86; 🖝) From boarder dudes to parents with tots, everyone skis Park City Mountain

Resort, host of the Olympic snowboarding and giant slalom events. The awesome terrain couldn't be more family friendly – or more accessible, rising as it does right over downtown.

The lowdown: 3100ft vertical drop, base elevation 6900ft; 3300 acres, 17% beginner, 52% intermediate, 31% advanced; seven high-speed lifts, eight fixed-grip chairs, one magic carpet. Park City's skiable area covers nine peaks, ranging from groomers and wide-open bowls (750 acres of them!) to cotton-mouth-inducing super steeps and the nation's only superpipe. Experts: make a beeline to **Mt Jupiter**; the best open trees are in the **Black Forest**. For untracked powder, take the Eagle lift up to **Vista**. Test your aerial technique on an Olympic-worthy boarding and freestyle course at three amazing terrain parks.

Kids' trails are marked with snow-bug statues near the magic-carpet lift and the resort will hook teens up with area locals who provide the lay of the land. Check out the online activity planner at www.mymountainplanner.com. To avoid crowds, stay out late: **night skiing** lasts until 9pm. In winter, there's open-air **ice skating** at the Resort Center.

Though the resort has no affiliated hotels, it does offer package lodging/skiing deals with nearby properties, and restaurants and après-ski are on-site. The fact that **Town Lift** takes you right from Main St up to the village area makes all downtown accommodations accessible.

In summer, the Town Lift serves hiking and mountain biking. The alpine pass is priced by height: those over 54in pay the adult fare for access to the alpine slide ($34), lifts and base-area activities. There's also a super-long zipline ride (2300ft, 550ft high) and an adventure zone with climbing wall, spiderweb climb, boulder climb and slide.

Deer Valley   SNOW SPORTS, ADVENTURE SPORTS
(☎435-649-1000, snowmobiling 435-645-7669; www.deervalley.com; Deer Valley Dr; day lift ticket adult/child $128/80, round-trip gondola ride $17; ☺snowmobiling 9am-5pm) Want to be pampered? Deer Valley, a resort of superlatives, has thought of everything – from tissue boxes at the base of slopes to ski valets. Slalom, mogul and freestyle-aerial competitions in the 2002 Olympics were held here, but the resort is just as famous for

Park City

N

0   200 m
0   0.1 miles

Windy Ridge Cafe (0.8mi);
White Pine Touring (0.8mi);
Good Karma (1.1mi)

Squatters
Roadhouse Grill (1mi);
Utah Olympic
Park (8mi)

13

Silver Creek

9th St

19

Main St

The Shop
(0.25mi);
Chateau Apres
Lodge (0.4mi)

Deer Valley Dr

7

8th St

Town Lift

Park Ave

18

17

Old Town Guest
House (0.2mi);
Park City Mountain
Resort (0.8mi)

3

16

Heber Ave

22

9

Main Street
Visitor Center

6th St

21

J&G Grill (1mi);
St Regis Deer Valley (1.1mi);
Deer Valley (1.1mi)

4

Deer Valley Dr

Swede Al

14

11

Park City
Museum

Park Ave

1

6

Park City
Transit Center

5th St

Woodside Ave

10

P

Marsac Ave

P

2

4th St

Visitor
Information
Center

12

Main St

Swede Al

20

Main Street
Mall

8

3rd St

Park Ave

Norfolk Ave

2nd St

5

15

Ontario Canyon

Park City

its superb dining, white-glove service and uncrowded slopes as meticulously groomed as the gardens of Versailles.

Note that there's no snowboarding allowed. Resort-owned **snowmobiling** takes place 5 miles down the road on Garff Ranch; reserve ahead with the resort.

The lowdown: 3000ft vertical drop, base elevation 6570ft; 2026 acres, 27% beginner, 41% intermediate, 32% advanced; one high-speed gondola, 11 high-speed quads, nine fixed-grip chairs. Every trail follows the fall line perfectly, which means you'll never skate a single cat-track. **Lady Morgan** has 200 acres of new terrain (65 acres of which is gladed), well separated from the Jordanelle Gondola area. Only a prescribed number of daily lift tickets are sold, so powder hounds can find hundreds of acres of untracked glades and steeps, days after a storm.

In summer, Deer Valley has more than 50 miles of **hiking** and **mountain-biking** trails served by its three operating lifts (scenic chairlift all-day adult/child $42/33). You can also purchase just one lift ride to get a head start on hiking. **Horseback riding** and free guided hikes are available by request.

Wasatch Powderbird SKIING
(☑ 801-742-2800, 800-974-4354; www.powder bird.com; full-day tours from $1260) Advanced skiers can arrange area heli-skiing packages that include six to seven runs.

Canyons Village at Park City SNOW SPORTS, ADVENTURE SPORTS
(☑ 435-649-5400; www.thecanyons.com; 4000 Canyons Resort Dr; lift ticket adult/child $134/86) Bolstered by tens of millions of dollars in improvements, and now merged with Park City Resorts, Canyons seeks novelty with the first North American 'bubble' lift (an enclosed, climate-controlled lift), expanded services, 300 new acres of advanced trails and an increased snow-making capability. The resort currently sprawls across nine aspen-covered peaks 4 miles outside of town, near the freeway.

The lowdown: 3190ft vertical drop, base elevation 6800ft; 4000 acres, 10% beginner, 44% intermediate, 46% advanced; 19 lifts, including a gondola. Varied terrain on 176 trails means there's something for all levels, with wide groomers for beginners and intermediates, three terrain parks and lots of freshies on a powder day. Experts: head to **Ninety-Nine 90**. There's a liberal open-boundary policy (heed avalanche warnings) as well as six natural half-pipes, one of them a whopping mile long, perfect for boarding.

Cross-country skiing and **sleigh rides**, for pleasure or to dinner, are also available. You can even ride or drive a state-of-the-art Snow Cat groomer. Sightseers can take the recently relocated **gondola** (round-trip $20) up not only for the views, but for Belgian waffles or lunch in the **Red Pine** area.

Summertime activities abound. A scenic ride on the **gondola** (day pass adult/junior $24/21) is great for sightseers, but hiking

SCENIC DRIVE: MIRROR LAKE HWY

This alpine route, also known as Hwy 150, begins about 12 miles east of Park City in **Kamas** and climbs to elevations of more than 10,000ft as it covers the 65 miles into Wyoming. The highway provides breathtaking mountain vistas, passing by scores of lakes, campgrounds and trailheads in the Uinta-Wasatch-Cache National Forest (p464). Note that sections may be closed to traffic well into spring due to heavy snowfall; check online first.

trails also lead off from here. Mountain bikers pay slightly more for lift service (adult/junior $30/26). **Gravity Bike Park** has varied trails accessed by the High Meadow Lift. Other activities include a zipline, disc golf, miniature golf, lake pedal-boats and hot-air balloon rides.

On weekends in summer and winter live-music concerts rock the base area.

Gorgoza Park   SNOW SPORTS
(☑ shuttle 435-645-9388; www.gorgoza.com; 3863 West Kilby Rd, at I-80; tubing per 2hr adult/child $28/17; ⊙ 1-8pm Mon-Fri, noon-8pm Sat & Sun mid-Dec–Mar; 🅟) Lift-served snow tubing takes place at Park City Mountain's Gorgoza Park, 8 miles north of town, off I-80. Plunge down three beginner or four advanced lanes; for kids under 12 there's a **miniature snowmobile track**, and even littler ones will enjoy the **Fort Frosty play area** (free with tubing ticket) with carousel. The Park City Mountain Resort–wide shuttle will take you out there directly if you reserve.

White Pine Touring Nordic Center   SKIING
(☑ 435-649-8710; www.whitepinetouring.com; cnr Park Ave & Thaynes Canyon Dr; day pass adult/child $18/8; ⊙ 9am-6pm) In town, the Nordic Center grooms a 12-mile cross-country course (rental available) with 2-, 3- and 6-mile loops of classic and skating lanes. Skate skiing lessons available.

Other Snow Sports

All Seasons Adventures   SNOW SPORTS
(☑ 435-649-9619; www.allseasonsadventures.com; 2hr snowshoe tour $79, singletrack mountain biking $95) Dog sledding, sleigh rides, cross-country skiing, snowshoe tours, as well as summer activities, such as guided kayaking, hiking, mountain biking, horseback riding, ATV riding and geocaching scavenger races around the area. Rates are per person.

Rocky Mountain Recreation of Utah   SNOW SPORTS, OUTDOORS
(☑ 435-645-7256; www.rockymtnrec.com; Weber Canyon Rd, Stillman Ranch; sleigh ride $55, 1hr snowmobile tour $109, 1hr horseback ride $66) Snowmobile tours, horse-drawn sleigh rides (to dinner or just around) and dog sledding. Also offers horseback rides, wagon rides with dinner ($84) and guided pack and fly-fishing trips.

Hiking

You'll feel on top of the world in the peaks over Park City, where over 300 miles of trails crisscross the mountains. Pick up a summer trail map at the visitor information center (p461).

Mountain Vista Touring   ADVENTURE SPORTS
(☑ 435-640-2979; www.parkcityhiking.com; hiking from $75) An adventure outfitter doing yoga, SUP, hiking, biking and trail running. Guided trips include hot springs dips in a geothermal crater and moonlight hikes.

Mountain Biking

Park City's big secret is its amazing mountain biking. The visitor information center (p461) has trail maps and you can rent bikes from sports shops in town and at all the resorts; some even have lift-assist riding.

Mid-Mountain Trail   MOUNTAIN BIKING
One of the best for mountain biking is this 20-mile singletrack trail (at 8000ft) connecting Silver Lake Lodge at Deer Valley (p453) to Pinecrest in the north. You can also start at Park City Mountain (p453), bike the steep **Spiro Trail** up to Mid-Mountain, then return on roads for a 22-mile loop.

Historic Union Pacific Rail Trail   MOUNTAIN BIKING
(stateparks.utah.gov) This 28-mile multiuse trail that's also a state park is perfect for mountain biking. Pick it up at Bonanza Dr just south of Kearns Blvd.

White Pine Touring   ADVENTURE SPORTS
(☑ 435-649-8710; www.whitepinetouring.com; 1790 Bonanza Dr; 3hr cycling tour $125) Offers bike rentals and guided biking tours. Free

guided rides are offered every Tuesday for women and for all on Thursdays, with a BBQ included each last week of the month. In winter, guided cross-country ski trips ($175, three hours) take you 20 minutes away from Park City and can include yurt camping accommodations.

Spas & Massage

When you've overdone it on the slopes, a spa treatment may be just what the doctor ordered. Deer Valley (p453) and the Canyons (p455) both have swanky spas.

The Shop   YOGA
(www.parkcityyoga.com; 1167 Woodside Ave; by donation, $7 minimum) Stretch out the kinks with an Anusara yoga class at this amazing warehouse space. Walk-ins welcome.

Aura Spa   SPA
(435-658-2872; www.auraspaforthespirit.com; 405 Main St; 1hr from $90) Schedule energy-balancing chakra work after your rubdown at in-town Aura Spa.

✦✦ Festivals & Events

Sundance Film Festival   FILM
(888-285-7790; www.sundance.org/festival; late Jan) Independent films and their makers, and movie stars and their fans, fill the town to bursting for 10 days in late January. Passes, ticket packages and the few individual tickets sell out well in advance – plan ahead.

🛏 Sleeping

Mid-December through mid-April is winter high season, with minimum stays required; rates rise during Christmas, New Year's and the Sundance Film Festival. Off-season rates

drop 50% or more. For better nightlife, stay in the old town. A complete list of condos, hotels and resorts in Park City is at www.visitparkcity.com.

Resort websites offer attractive accommodations and lift ticket packages. For budget options, consider staying down in Salt Lake City or Heber Valley.

Chateau Apres Lodge   HOSTEL $
(435-649-9372; www.chateauapres.com; 1299 Norfolk Ave; dm $50, r $140-165;) The only budget-oriented accommodations in town is this basic, 1963 lodge – with a 1st-floor dorm – near the town ski lift. Reserve ahead, as it's very popular with groups and seniors.

Park City RV Resort   CAMPGROUND $
(435-649-8935; www.parkcityrvresort.com; 2200 Rasmussen Rd; tent sites $21, RV sites with hookups $30-45;) Amenities galore (games room, playground, laundry, hot tub, fishing pond, kids' climbing wall ...), 6 miles north of town at I-80.

★ Old Town Guest House   B&B $$
(435-649-2642; www.oldtownguesthouse.com; 1011 Empire Ave; r $169-229;) Grab the flannel robe, pick a paperback off the shelf and snuggle under a quilt on your lodge-pole bed or kick back on the large deck at this comfy in-town B&B. The host will gladly give you the lowdown on the great outdoors, guided ski tours, mountain biking and the rest.

Newpark Resort   HOTEL $$
(435-649-3600; www.newparkresort.com; 1476 Newpark Blvd; r from $188;) A stylish new hotel tucked into the shopping

UTAH PARK CITY

GETTING INTO SUNDANCE FESTIVAL

This 10-day festival in late January takes over both Park City and Sundance Resort completely. Films screen not just there but at venues in Salt Lake City and Ogden as well. Accommodation rates soar across the Wasatch front, yet rooms are snapped up months in advance – passes ($450 to $3500), ticket packages and individual tickets (from $20) are similarly difficult to get.

First you need to reserve a time slot to purchase online at www.sundance.org/festival starting in December (sign up for text-message announcements). You then call during your appointed hour to reserve, but there are no guarantees (note that seats may be a little easier to secure during week two, as week one is generally for the industry). Any remaining tickets are sold a few days ahead online and at the main **Park City Box Office** (435-658-3456; 136 Heber Ave, Gateway Center; 8am-7pm mid-Jan–late Jan). If you don't succeed, do like the locals and go skiing – the slopes are remarkably empty during this period.

plaza. Extra points for heated floors and elevated beds with down duvets. Rooms have wood details, flat-screen TVs and coffeemakers; some include kitchens. There's a pool and hot tub, but breakfast isn't part of the package.

Goldener Hirsch HOTEL $$

(☎435-649-7770; www.goldenerhirschinn.com; 7570 Royal St, Deer Valley; r $155-300; 🖥) You can tell the Goldener was fashioned after a lodge in Salzburg by the hand-painted Austrian furniture, feather-light duvets and European stone fireplaces. 'Stay & Ski Deer Valley' packages available. A favorite.

Treasure Mountain Inn HOTEL $$

(☎435-655-4501; www.treasuremountaininn.com; 255 Main St; r $158-206, ste from $275; ❄🖥) 🏄 Park City's first member of the Green Hotel Association utilizes wind energy and serves organic food in its breakfast restaurant. Some of the upscale condos – decorated in earthy tones – have fireplaces, and all have kitchens.

Park City Peaks HOTEL $$

(☎435-649-5000; www.parkcitypeaks.com; 2121 Park Ave; d/ste $219/319; ❄@🖥🏊) Comfortable, contemporary rooms include access to a heated outdoor pool, hot tub, restaurant and bar. Great deals off-season. December through April, breakfast is included.

Holiday Inn Express HOTEL $$

(☎435-658-1600; www.holidayinnexpress.com; 1501 W Ute Blvd; r $150-173; 🖥🏊) Save money by staying outside the downtown area, near Kimball Junction stores and restaurants.

★ Torchlight Inn B&B $$$

(☎435-612-0345; www.torchlightinn.com; 253 Deer Valley Dr; r from $328; P❄🖥) Right off the traffic circle, this new six-room inn charms with elegant and inviting contemporary spaces, gas fireplaces and flat-screen TVs. There's also a rooftop hot tub, Jeep rentals on-site and two friendly bulldogs to keep you company. Has friendly, helpful service, family suites and wheelchair access (including an elevator).

★ Washington School House BOUTIQUE HOTEL $$$

(☎435-649-3800; www.washingtonschoolhouse.com; 543 Park Ave; r $405; ❄🖥🏊) Architect Trip Bennett oversaw the restoration that turned an 1898 limestone schoolhouse on a hill into a luxurious boutique hotel with 12 suites. How did the children ever concentrate when they could gaze out at the mountains through 9ft-tall windows instead?

Montage HOTEL $$$

(☎888-604-1301; www.montagehotels.com/deervalley; 9100 Marsac Ave, Empire Pass, Deer Valley; r from $515; P❄@🖥🏊❄) Among the top area resorts, Montage wows with personalized service and extras like a kids' activity center, bowling and a gorgeous spa with trainers and yoga that fills a whole floor. Après-ski finds guests, side by side in black tie and robes, enjoying mulled wine and s'mores or braving the heated alpine pool. Rooms go for understated elegance.

St Regis Deer Valley HOTEL $$$

(☎435-940-5700; www.stregisdeervalley.com; 2300 Deer Valley Dr E; r from $446; ❄@🖥🏊) You have to ride a private funicular just to get up to the St Regis, so whether you're lounging by the outdoor fire pits, dining on the terrace or peering from your balcony, the views are sublime. The studied, elegant rusticity here is the height of Deer Valley's luxury lodging. Forget lessons – where else can you ski with an Olympian?

Hyatt Centric Park City HOTEL $$$

(☎435-940-1234; www.escalalodge.hyatt.com; 3551 North Escala Ct; r $209-269, ste from $409; ❄🖥🏊❄) Finished in 2011, the upscale lodge rooms are all meant to have a residential feel. Indeed, suites have full kitchens and a personal grocery shopping service is available throughout. From here you're not more than a few ski strides away from the Canyons (p455) resort lifts.

Waldorf Astoria HOTEL $$$

(☎435-647-5500; www.waldorfastoriaparkcity.com; 2100 Frostwood Dr; r from $319; @🖥🏊) Top luxury property at the Canyons (p455).

Sky Lodge HOTEL $$$

(☎435-658-2500; www.skyparkcity.com; 201 Heber Ave; ste $675; ❄@🖥🏊) The urban-loft-like architecture containing the chic Sky Lodge suites both complements and contrasts the three historic buildings that house the property's restaurants. You can't be more stylish, or more central, if you stay here.

✕ Eating

Park City is well known for exceptional upscale eating – a reasonably priced meal is harder to find. The ski resorts have numerous eating options in season. Dinner reservations are required at all top-tier places in winter. From April through November restaurants reduce opening hours variably, and may take extended breaks, especially in May.

★ Vessel Kitchen   CAFE $
(🗷 435-200-8864; www.vesselkitchen.com; 1784 Uinta Way; mains $7-13; ☺8am-9pm; 🖈🐾) Locals in the know head to this gourmet cafeteria in the shopping plaza for fast, value eats. With kombucha on tap, avocado toast and lovely winter salads and stews, there's something for everyone. Even kids. Breakfasts shine with skillets of *shak-shuka* (poached eggs in tomato sauce) and sweet-potato hash.

Java Cow Coffee & Ice Cream   CAFE $
(🗷 435-647-7711; 402 Main St; dishes $4-12; ☺7am-10pm; 🐾) Enjoy a scoop of site-made ice cream like Mooana (with organic banana chunks) along with your Ibis coffee at this always lively cafe. Sandwiches and crepes, too.

Vinto   ITALIAN $
(🗷 435-615-9990; www.vinto.com; 900 Main St, Summit Watch Plaza; dishes $8-17; ☺11am-10pm Mon-Sat, 4-9pm Sun) Minimalist surrounds are suitably stylish for Main St. But the wood-fired pizzas and light, fresh Italian dishes surprisingly won't break your bank. Has gluten-free options.

Maxwell's   PIZZA $
(🗷 435-647-0304; www.maxwellsece.com; 1456 Newpark Blvd; pizza slices $3.50, dishes $10-17; ☺11am-1am) Eat with the locals at the pizza, pasta and beer joint tucked in a back corner of the stylish outdoor Redstone Mall, north of town. Huge, crispy-crusted 'Fat Boy' pizzas never linger long on the tables. Gluten-free options available.

Bodega on Main   TAPAS $$
(🗷 435-649-6979; www.bodegaonmainparkcity. com; 710 Main St; mains $10-38; ☺5:30-10pm) Don't underestimate the seduction of a deep pour of tempranillo paired with cheese-stuffed peppers and lamb lollipops. Small bites are the thing in this new eatery emanating rustic cool. Located in an interior plaza.

Wasatch Brew Pub   PUB FOOD $$
(🗷 435-649-0900; www.wasatchbeers.com; 250 Main St; lunch & sandwiches $10-15, dinner $10-30; ☺11am-10pm Mon-Fri, 10am-10pm Sat & Sun) Very friendly brewpub with quality eats like meatloaf, seared ahi salad and calamari fried in Hefeweizen, served alongside thirst-quenching Polygamy Porter. If you are feeling frisky, go for the jalapeño cream ale: each batch is made with 150lb of the peppers. It's at the top of Main St.

Good Karma   INDIAN, FUSION $$
(www.goodkarmarestaurants.com; 1782 Prospector Ave; breakfast $8-13, mains $12-25; ☺7am-10pm; 🖈) 🍽 Whenever possible, local and organic ingredients are used in the Indo-Persian meals at Good Karma. Start the day with Punjabi eggs and dine on curries and grilled meats. You'll recognize the place by the Tibetan prayer flags flapping out front.

Squatters Roadhouse Grill   PUB FOOD $$
(🗷 435-649-9868; www.squatters.com; 1900 Park Ave; burgers $10-15, mains $10-23; ☺8am-10pm Sun-Thu, to 11pm Fri & Sat; 🖈) A favorite local hangout and the best of the town brewpubs, as far as food goes. We love the Asiago, cheddar and Havarti mac-and-cheese. Breakfast is served until 2pm daily.

Silver Star Cafe   AMERICAN $$
(🗷 435-655-3456; www.thesilverstarcafe.com; 1825 Three Kings Dr; breakfast & small plates $9-14, dinner mains $19-32; ☺8am-9pm) We can't decide if it's the creative, hearty Western dishes or the perfect, out-of-the-way mountain-base location that hooked us. Either way, we love kicking back on the sunny patio après-ski or enjoying the weekend singer-songwriter showcases. Try the cauliflower poutine or buttermilk fried chicken with braised greens.

Windy Ridge Cafe   AMERICAN $$
(🗷 435-647-0880; www.windyridgefoods.com; 1250 Iron Horse Dr; lunch $10-15, dinner $13-27;

UTAH PARK CITY

DISCOUNT DINING

In the spring and summer, look for half-off main-dish coupons in the *Park Record* newspaper. *Park City Magazine* puts out a full menu guide.

11am-3pm & 5-9pm) Escape the Main St mayhem at this out-of-the-way American cafe. There's a long list of salads to choose from, also available as sides, and comfort food like herb-roasted chicken and baked meatloaf.

Eating Establishment AMERICAN $$
(435-649-8284; 317 Main St; breakfast & sandwiches $9-15, dinner $16-20; 8am-10pm) Local institution; service can be hit-or-miss.

★ Riverhorse on Main AMERICAN $$$
(435-649-3536; www.riverhorseparkcity.com; 540 Main St; dinner mains $38-60; 5-10pm Mon-Thu, to 11pm Fri & Sat, 11am-2:30pm & 5-10pm Sun;) A fine mix of the earthy and exotic, with cucumber quinoa salad, polenta fries and macadamia-crusted halibut. There's a separate menu for vegetarians. A wall-sized window and the sleek modern design creates a stylish atmosphere. Reserve ahead: this is a longtime, award-winning restaurant.

★ J&G Grill AMERICAN $$$
(435-940-5760; www.jggrilldeercrest.com; 2300 Deer Valley Drive E, Deer Valley Resort; lunch mains $17-31, dinner mains $33-65; 7am-9pm) A favorite of locals, who love the tempura onion rings and seared scallops with sweet chili sauce. The bold flavors of meat and fish star here at one of celebrity chef Jean-Georges Vongerichten's collaborative projects. The mid-mountain St Regis (p458) setting is spectacular.

Handle AMERICAN $$$
(435-602-1155; handleparkcity.com; 136 Heber Ave; mains $10-48; 5pm-late) Riding the wave of rustic chic, this American small-plate eatery does nicely. Try a craft cocktail and soak up the ambience in semicircular booths or along the marble bar. Oysters with grilled lemon, hot-wings-style cauliflower and fish in rich Romanesco sauce are some of the hits. Sources locally.

The Farm AMERICAN $$$
(435-615-8080; Canyons Village, Red Pine Gondola; lunch mains $18-21, dinner mains $30-48; 11:30am-10pm) From the window boxes of fresh herbs and a menu stacked with Niman Ranch natural beef and organic greens, this is farm-to-table. Braised baby eggplant with harissa spice, oxtail soup and watercress salad offer something original slope-side, finally. Has good cocktails and a kids' menu.

Viking Yurt NORWEGIAN $$$
(435-615-9878; www.vikingyurt.com; parking 345 Lowell Ave; per person 6-course meal & transport $130; by reservation 11am & 6pm) More of an experience than a meal – it isn't every day that a sleigh whisks you to dinner on the mountaintop serenaded by a baby grand. A candlelit dinner includes glogg, hearty Norwegian fare and a cheese course. If you have any allergies, do advise ahead. Dress warm for the ride.

Shabu FUSION $$$
(435-645-7253; www.shabuparkcity.com; 442 Main St; small plates & rolls $11-22, mains $18-45; 11am-2:30pm & 5-11pm Thu-Tue) Hip, inventive Asian small plates, including addictive firecracker shrimp, warming ramen and namesake *shabu shabu* (a hot pot of flavorful broth with meat or veggies). For bigger appetites, go for the miso-glazed black cod or *moo shu* duck in cherry pad thai sauce.

Zoom AMERICAN $$$
(435-649-9108; 660 Main St; lunch mains $10-24, dinner mains $24-55; 11:30am-2:30pm & 5-10pm) Earning due acclaim, with an emphasis on regional dishes like seared Utah trout and artisan greens with pear and brie, this atmospheric, Robert Redford–owned restaurant occupies a rehabbed train depot. A perennial Utah-state restaurant award winner.

Wahso ASIAN $$$
(435-615-0300; www.wahso.com; 577 Main St; mains $30-56; 5:30-10pm Wed-Sun, closed mid-Apr–mid-Jun) Park City's cognoscenti flock to this modern pan-Asian phenomenon, where fine-dining dishes may include lamb vindaloo or Malaysian snapper. The sake martinis pack the right kind of punch. Expect to see and be seen.

🍸 Drinking & Nightlife

Main St is where it's at. In winter there's action nightly; weekends are most lively off-season. For listings, see www.thisweek inparkcity.com. Several restaurants, such as Squatters Roadhouse Grill and Wasatch Brew Pub, also have good bars.

★ High West Distillery BAR
(435-649-8300; www.highwest.com; 703 Park Ave; 11am-9pm Sun-Thu, to 10pm Fri & Sat, tours 3pm & 4pm) This former livery and Model A-era garage is now home to Park City's most happenin' nightspot. The ski-in distillery

was founded by a biochemist whose home-made rye whiskey fuels a spicy lemonade bound to kill the strongest colds.

Old Town Cellars WINE BAR
(📞 435-649-3759; 890 Main St; ⏰ 2-10pm Mon-Thu, to 11pm Fri & Sat) This tiny wine bar achieves what many splashy haunts don't around here: intimacy. Locally owned with great service. Meat and cheese boards with blended wines are presented by staff in the know.

Spur BAR
(📞 435-615-1618; www.thespurbarandgrill.com; 350 Main St; ⏰ 10am-1am) What an upscale Western bar should be: rustic walls, leather couches, roaring fire. Good grub, too. Live music on weekends in summer or daily in ski season.

Campos Coffee COFFEE
(📞 435-731-8377; 1345 Lowell Ave; ⏰ 7:30am-5pm) Strong Australian coffee comes to PC, with the added benefit of Vegemite toast.

Atticus CAFE
(📞 435-214-7241; www.atticustea.com; 738 Main St; ⏰ 7am-7pm) Park City's best espresso bar also serves tea lattes. Its soup and sandwiches are probably the best-value grub in town, plus there are gluten-free options. Also a bookstore, with a little seating.

Park City Brewery BREWERY
(📞 435-200-8906; www.parkcitybrewery.com; 2720 Rasmussen Rd; ⏰ 3-7pm Tue-Fri, 11am-7pm Sat & Sun) The anti–Park City: a bare-bones warehouse serving pitchers of suds with popcorn. There's live trivia on Wednesday evenings.

☆ Entertainment

Symphony, chamber music, bluegrass, jazz and other musical events happen throughout summer and winter; pick up the free *This Week in Park City* (www.parkcityweek.com).

Eccles Center ARTS CENTER
(📞 435-655-3114; www.ecclescenter.org; 1750 Kearns Blvd) Hosts theater, dance, live music and talks organized by the Park City Institute. Check the website for events.

Escape Room Park City ARTS CENTER
(📞 435-604-0556; www.escaperoomparkcity.com; 136 Heber Ave, #207; per person $40) An entertainment center where participants are put in a locked room to solve a mystery

spun around a collapsed silver mine. Very Park City.

🛍 Shopping

The quality of stores along Main St has improved in recent years. In addition to souvenirs, you'll find outdoor clothing brands and upscale galleries. The Park City Gallery Association (www.parkcitygalleryassociation.com) is a good online resource for local galleries.

Tanger Outlet MALL
(📞 435-645-7078; www.tangeroutlet.com; 6699 N Landmark Dr N100, Kimball Junction; ⏰ 9am-9pm Mon-Sat, 10am-7pm Sun) Dozens of outlets and other outdoor mall shops at the junction with I-80 (exit 145).

ℹ Information

TOURIST INFORMATION

Visitor Information Center (📞 435-658-9616; www.visitparkcity.com; 1794 Olympic Pkwy; ⏰ 9am-6pm; 🖥) Vast visitor center with a coffee bar, a terrace and incredible views of the mountains at Olympic Park. Visitor guides available online.

Main Street Visitor Center (📞 435-649-7457; 528 Main St; ⏰ 10am-7pm Mon-Sat, noon-6pm Sun) Small desk with tourist information and discount ski passes for sale.

INTERNET ACCESS

Park City Library (📞 435-615-5600; parkcitylibrary.org; 1255 Park Ave; ⏰ 10am-9pm Mon-Thu, 10am-6pm Fri & Sat, 1-5pm Sun) Free internet access.

MEDIA

➤ **Magazines** *Park City Magazine* (www.parkcitymagazine.com) is a glossy magazine with some events listings.

➤ **Newspapers** The community newspaper *Park Record* (www.parkrecord.com) has been in circulation for more than 130 years.

MEDICAL SERVICES

Park City Clinic (📞 435-649-7640; intermountainhealthcare.org/locations/park-city-clinic; 1665 Bonanza Dr) Urgent care and 24-hour emergency room.

POST

Post Office (📞 435-615-9651; 450 Main St; ⏰ 9am-5:30pm Mon-Fri, 9am-1pm Sat)

ℹ Getting There & Away

Downtown Park City is 5 miles south of I-80 exit 145, 32 miles east of Salt Lake City and 40 miles from Salt Lake City International Airport (p442).

Hwy 190 (closed October through March) crosses over Guardsman Pass between Big Cottonwood Canyon and Park City. In addition to public buses, a number of van services go to the airport and other mountain destinations:

All Resort Express (☑ 435-649-3999; www. allresort.com; one-way $39)

Canyon Transportation (☑ 800-255-1841; www.canyontransport.com; shared van $39)

Park City Transportation (☑ 435-649-8567; www.parkcitytransportation.com; shared van $39)

Powder for the People (☑ 435-649-6648)

Utah Transit Authority (www.rideuta.com; one-way $4.50)

❶ Getting Around

Traffic can slow you down, especially on weekends; bypass Main St by driving on Park Ave. Parking can also be challenging and meter regulations are strictly enforced. Free lots are available in Swede Alley; those by 4th and 5th Sts are especially convenient.

The excellent **public transit system** (www. parkcity.org; 558 Swede Alley; ⏰ 8am-11pm winter) covers most of Park City, including the three ski resorts, and makes it easy not to need a car to get around.

Ogden

☑ 435 / POP 84,250

During Ogden's heyday, historic 25th St was lined with brothels and raucous saloons; today the restored buildings house restaurants, galleries, bakeries and bars. The old town is atmospheric, but the main attraction here is 20 miles east in the Wasatch Mountains of Ogden Valley. Since skiing here is more than an hour's drive from Salt Lake City, most metro area residents head to Park City or the SLC resorts, leaving Snowbasin and Powder Mountain luxuriously empty. The villages of Huntsville and Eden, halfway between town and mountains, are nearest to the resorts.

◉ Sights & Activities

Ogden Eccles Dinosaur Park   MUSEUM
(☑ 801-393-3466; www.dinosaurpark.org; 1544 E Park Blvd; adult/child $7/6; ⏰ 10am-8pm Mon-Sat, to 6pm Sun, closed Sun Nov-Mar; 🔆) Prepare for your children to squeal as a couple of animatronic dinosaurs roar to life inside the museum at Ogden Eccles Dinosaur Park. Outside, it's like a giant playground where you can run around, under and over life-size plaster-of-Paris dinosaurs.

Union Station   MUSEUM
(www.theunionstation.org; 2501 Wall Ave; adult/child $6/4; ⏰ 10am-5pm Mon-Sat) This old train station houses three small museums dedicated to antique autos, natural history and firearms.

Powder Mountain   SNOW SPORTS
(☑ 801-745-3772; www.powdermountain.com; Rte 158, Eden; day lift-ticket adult/child $79/44, snow cat ride $25) Backcountry enthusiasts groove on Powder Mountain. They've had banner years of late, and its over-7000 skiable acres mean there's plenty of elbow room. Half of the area is lift-served by four chairs (one high-speed) and three rope tows. There are two terrain parks and night skiing till 10pm. Best of all, two weeks after a storm, you'll still find powder.

Snow cat rides access 3000 acres of exclusive bowls, glades and chutes for a day of gliding on powder. Inquire about backcountry guided tours and snow-kiting lessons. The rest of the lowdown: 3005ft vertical drop; base elevation 6895ft; 25% beginner, 40% intermediate, 35% advanced.

Snowbasin   SNOW SPORTS
(☑ 801-620-1100, 888-437-5488; www.snowbasin. com; 3925 E Snowbasin Rd, Huntsville; day lift-ticket adult/child $99/55; ⏰ gondola 9am-6pm Sat & Sun) Snowbasin hosted the 2002 Olympic downhill, and it continues to be a competitive venue today. Terrain varies from gentle slow-skiing zones to wide-open groomers and boulevards, jaw-dropping steeps to gulp-and-go chutes. There are also four terrain parks and a dedicated snow tubing lift and hill. It grooms 26 miles of cross-country skiing, both classic and skating; ask about yurt camping.

The lowdown: 3000ft vertical drop, base elevation 6400ft; 3000 acres, 20% beginner, 50% intermediate, 30% expert; one tram, two gondolas, two high-speed quads, four fixed-grip chairs. The lift system is one of the most advanced in the Southwest, but for now Snowbasin remains a hidden gem with fantastic skiing, top-flight service and nary a lift line. The exposed-timber-and-glass Summit Day Lodge (accessible to non-skiers) has a massive four-sided fireplace and a deck overlooking daredevil steeps, in addition to good restaurants.

In summer, the gondola takes you up to Needles restaurant and hiking and mountain-biking trails (with gondola assist); bike rentals available. Check online for the Sunday afternoon outdoor concert series line-up.

iFly ADVENTURE SPORTS
(📞 801-528-5348; www.iflyutah.com; 2261 Kiesel Ave; per flight $55; ⏰ 11am-9pm Mon-Sat) Take off on an indoor skydiving adventure at iFly; reservations required.

Nordic Valley SNOW SPORTS
(📞 801-745-3511; nordicvalley.com; 3567 Nordic Valley Way, Eden; day lift-ticket adult/child $45/30; ⏰ 9am-8pm; 🚠) The old-fashioned mom-and-pop mountain. At only 1600 skiable acres and with a 1604ft vertical drop, who'd think Nordic Valley would garner superlatives? But since all five lifts are lit until 9pm, it has some of the largest night-skiing terrain in Utah, and the magic-carpet lifts provide good access for kids. Runs comprise 25% beginner, 50% intermediate and 25% advanced.

🛏 Sleeping

Cradled by mountains, Ogden Valley is the preferred place to stay. If you choose to stay in town, you'll have more eating and drinking options.

🛏 Ogden Town

Of the standard chain motels near I-15, the Comfort Inn is among the newest.

Ben Lomond Historic Suite Hotel HOTEL $$
(📞 801-627-1900, 877-627-1900; www.benlomond suites.com; 2510 Washington Blvd; r $105-210; ❄@🛜🏊) Traditional rooms in this 1927 Italian Revival–style downtown hotel could use an update, but you can't beat the local history connection.

Hampton Inn & Suites HOTEL $$
(📞 801-394-9400, 800-426-7866; www.hampton innogden.com; 2401 Washington Blvd; r from $189; ❄@🛜) Contemporary rooms; short walk to restaurants.

🛏 Ogden Valley

⭐**Snowberry Inn** B&B $$
(📞 801-745-2634, 888-746-2634; www.snowberry inn.com; 1315 N Hwy 158, Eden; r $109-129; ❄) This family-owned log-cabin B&B couldn't be cozier, with wood stoves, an outdoor hot tub (winter only) and games room with pool table. There are no room TVs. Ski packages available.

Atomic Chalet B&B B&B $$
(📞 801-425-2813; www.atomicchalet.com; 1st St, Huntsville; r $115-150; 🛜) Down-to-earth and comfy, this cedar-shake cottage makes an excellent home away from home. After a day spent skiing or hiking, relax in the hot tub, watch a film from the DVD collection or play a game of billiards.

Alaskan Inn INN $$
(📞 801-621-8600; www.alaskaninn.com; 435 Ogden Canyon Rd, Ogden; cabin & ste $119-194; ❄🛜) Luxury Western-themed suites with in-room Jacuzzi and cabins in the picturesque canyon, just outside Ogden Valley. Wi-fi only reaches some rooms, so ask ahead.

There are no accommodations owned by the ski resorts, but all three have condo partners that offer ski packages; check their websites. The town of Eden is closest to Powder and Wolf Mountains; Huntsville is closest to Snowbasin. For a full lodging list, see www.ovba.org.

🍴 Eating & Drinking

Look for restaurants in Ogden town on historic 25th St between Union Station and Grant Ave.

There's a handful of bars centered around 25th St.

🍴 Ogden Town

Grounds for Coffee CAFE $
(www.groundsforcoffee.com; 126 25th St; dishes $2-8; ⏰ 6:30am-8pm Mon-Thu, to 10pm Fri & Sat, 8am-6pm Sun; 🛜🅿) This local coffeehouse offers the usual espresso drinks, plus baked goods and some sandwiches in an artsy, 1800s storefront setting.

Roosters 25th Street Brewing Co PUB FOOD $$
(📞 801-627-6171; www.roostersbrewingco.com; 253 25th St; brunch & sandwiches $8-10, mains $9-24; ⏰ 11am-10pm Mon-Thu, 11am-11pm Fri & Sat, to 9pm Sun) Once a house of ill repute, this great old town building is now an upscale gastro brewpub serving Polygamy Porter as a house draft. There are also gluten-free options. It has a sister restaurant in Union Station (p462), at the end of the street.

Brewski's BAR
(📞 801-394-1713; brewskisonline.net; 244 25th St; ⏰ 10am-1am Mon-Sat, to midnight Sun) With more than 20 beers on tap, darts, a pool table and live-music weekends.

Ogden Valley

★ **Shooting Star Saloon** PUB FOOD $
(☎ 801-745-2002; 7350 E 200 S, Huntsville; burgers $5-8; ⊙ noon-9pm Wed-Sat, to 8pm Sun) Open since 1879, tiny Shooting Star is Utah's oldest continuously operating saloon. Seek this place out: the cheeseburgers – and cheap beer – are justifiably famous, though none so much as the 'starburger,' featuring a Polish knockwurst on top. For small appetites, there's a miniburger. Cash only.

Eats of Eden ITALIAN $$
(☎ 801-745-8618; www.eatsofedenutah.com; 2529 N Hwy 162, Eden; mains $10-20; ⊙ 11:30am-9pm Tue-Sat) Bring your après-ski appetite to this rustic wood-finished restaurant for buffalo burgers, pizza and pasta. In the summer there's seating on the small patio facing the valley.

Carlos & Harley's TEX-MEX $$
(☎ 801-745-8226; 5510 E 2200 N, Eden; mains $8-20; ⊙ 11am-9pm) A lively, kitschy Mexican cantina serving margaritas and Tex-Mex inside the old Eden General Store.

Gray Cliff Lodge Restaurant AMERICAN $$$
(www.graycliffodge.com; 508 Ogden Canyon, Ogden; brunch $16.50, dinner $18-41; ⊙ 5-10pm Tue-Sat, 10am-10pm Sun) An old-fashioned resort restaurant, with classics like whole trout, fried chicken and homemade pie. It's an institution in Ogden Canyon.

☆ Entertainment

Motor-Vu Drive-In THEATER
(www.motorvu.com; 5368 S 1050 W; adult/child $8/3.50; ⊙ dusk Fri-Sun Mar-Nov) The kids will love piling in the car to catch a flick at this old-time drive-in movie theater. There's a swap-meet here on Saturday at 8am.

ⓘ Information

For the online lowdown on valley activities, eateries and lodging, see www.ovba.org.

Ogden Visitors Bureau (☎ 800-255-8824, 866-867-8824; www.visitogden.com; 2438 Washington Blvd; ⊙ 9am-5pm Mon-Fri)

Outdoor Information Center (☎ 801-625-5306; www.fs.fed.us; 324 25th St; ⊙ 9am-5pm Mon-Fri year-round, plus 9am-5pm Sat Jun-Sep)

ⓘ Getting There & Away

Greyhound (☎ 801-394-5573, 800-231-2222; www.greyhound.com; 2393 Wall Ave; to Salt Lake City $10) has bus service to Ogden town, but you really need a car to get around anywhere in the valley.

Heber City & Midway

Twenty miles south of Park City, Heber City (population 12,260) and its vast valley make an alternative base for exploring the surrounding mountains. A popular steam-powered railway runs from here. A scant 3 miles east, Midway (population 4020) is modeled after an alpine town, with hand-painted buildings set against the slopes. Here you'll find activity-laden resorts – great for families – and a thermal crater you can swim in. Resort activities are open to all, and cross-country skiing is available close to both towns.

⊙ Sights & Activities

Much of the forested mountains east of the towns have hiking, biking, cross-country skiing, ATV and snowmobile trails that are part of the **Uinta-Wasatch-Cache National Forest** (www.fs.usda.gov/uwcnf).

Timpanogos Cave National Monument CAVE
(☎ 801-756-5238; www.nps.gov/tica; off Hwy 92; tour adult/child $8/4; ⊙ 7am-5:30pm Jun-Aug, 8am-5pm Sep & Oct) Three beautiful caves in Timpanogos Cave National Monument are accessible on ranger-led tours.

★ **Homestead Crater** SWIMMING
(☎ 435-654-1102; www.homesteadresort.com; 700 N Homestead Dr, Homestead Resort, Midway; $16; ⊙ noon-8pm Mon-Thu, 10am-8pm Fri & Sat, 10am-6pm Sun) Swim in a 65ft-deep geothermal pool (90°F, or 32°C, year-round) beneath the 50ft-high walls of a limestone cone open to the sky. There's even snorkel gear to rent. It's way cool. Reservations required.

Soldier Hollow ADVENTURE SPORTS
(☎ 435-654-2002; www.soldierhollow.com; off Hwy 113; Nordic pass adult/child $10/5, snow tubing adult/child $24/22; ⊙ 9am-4:30pm, snow tubing noon-8pm Mon-Sat, noon-4pm Sun) A must-ski for Nordic ski aficionados. Soldier Hollow, 2 miles south of Midway, was the Nordic course used in the 2002 Olympics; its 19 miles of stride-skiing and skating lanes are also open to snowshoeing. For nonskiers, there's a 1201ft-long **snow-tubing hill**; book in advance on weekends,

since ticket sales are capped. Snow season is December through March.

From May through October, the resort's gorgeous 36-hole golf course, mountain biking trails and horseback riding are popular. Equipment rentals are available.

Heber Valley Historic Railroad RAIL
(📞 435-654-5601; www.hebervalleyrr.org; 450 S 600 W, Heber City; adult/child from $20/15) The 1904 Heber Valley Historic Railroad chugs along on scenic trips through the steep-walled Provo Canyon, as well as taking numerous themed trips.

🛏 Sleeping

The standard chain gang of motels are available on Main St in Heber City.

Swiss Alps Inn MOTEL $
(📞 435-654-0722; www.swissalpsinn.com; 167 S Main St, Heber City; r from $68; 📶🐾) This independent motel has huge rooms with hand-painted doors. Guests get a free milkshake from the associated restaurant next door.

Mt Timpanogos Campground CAMPGROUND $
(📞 877-444-6777; www.reserveamerica.com; tent & RV sites $21; ⏱ May-Oct) On the north side of Provo Canyon, take the paved, 16-mile Alpine Loop Rd (Hwy 92), an incredibly scenic, twisting road past 11,750ft Mt Timpanogos. At 6800ft, stay overnight at the Mt Timpanogos Campground; it has pit toilets, and water. A trailhead leads from here into the surrounding wilderness area filled with fir trees.

Homestead Resort RESORT $$
(📞 435-654-1102; www.homesteadresort.com; 700 N Homestead Dr, Midway; r $129-179; 📶🐾) Most destination family resorts of this caliber faded into obscurity a generation ago. A collection of homey buildings and cottages gathers around the resort's village green. Activities include 18-hole golf, cycling, horseback riding, hot-spring swimming, spa treatments, volleyball, shuffle board and croquet. The restaurants are good, too; some of the packages include meals.

Blue Boar Inn INN $$
(📞 435-654-1400; www.theblueboarinn.com; 1235 Warm Springs Rd, Midway; r $175-295; 📶) It's as if an ornate Bavarian inn had been teleported to Utah – everything from the hand-painted exterior to the ornately carved wooden furniture screams Teutonic.

🍴 Eating

There's a good range of dining options, thanks to this area's popularity in winter and summer.

Tarahumara MEXICAN $
(📞 435-654-3465; 380 E Main St, Midway; mains $8-15; ⏱ 11am-9pm Sun-Wed, to 10pm Thu-Sat) Locals dig the salsa bar and salad buffet that shore up classic northern Mexican cuisine. *Carne asada* (rib eye) and smothered enchiladas are done up quite tastily. Service can be wanting.

Snake Creek Grill AMERICAN $$
(📞 435-654-2133; www.snakecreekgrill.com; 650 W 100 S/Hwy 113, Heber City; mains $14-26; ⏱ 5:30-9:30pm Wed-Sat, to 8:30pm Sun) One of northern Utah's best restaurants looks like a saloon from an old Western. The all-American Southwest-style menu features gorgeous salads, blue-cornmeal-crusted trout and sticky, addictive ribs. Located halfway between downtown Heber City and Midway.

Blue Boar Inn INTERNATIONAL $$$
(📞 435-654-1400; www.theblueboarinn.com; 1235 Warm Springs Rd, Midway; breakfast & sandwiches $12-18, dinner $30-39; ⏱ 7am-10pm) A frequent winner of Utah's 'Best in State' award for its fine European-style cuisine. The inn's dining room (open to nonguests) is worth the reservation you need to make.

ℹ Information

Most of the services are in Heber City.
Heber Ranger Station (📞 435-654-0470; 2460 S Hwy 40, Heber City; ⏱ 8am-4pm Mon-Fri)
Heber Valley Chamber of Commerce (📞 435-654-3666; www.hebervalleycc.org; 475 N Main St, Heber City; ⏱ 8am-5pm)

ℹ Getting There & Away

Most visitors arrive via private vehicle. Highway 190 continues over Guardsman Pass (closed in winter) to Big Cottonwood Canyon and Salt Lake City.

Some **Greyhound** (📞 801-394-5573, 800-231-2222; www.greyhound.com; to Salt Lake City from $10) routes make a roadside stop in Heber City.

UTAH HEBER CITY & MIDWAY

Sundance Resort

Art and nature blend seamlessly at Sundance, a magical resort-cum-artist-colony founded by actor Robert Redford, where bedraggled urbanites connect with the land and rediscover their creative spirits. Participate in snow sports, ride horseback, fly-fish, write, do yoga, indulge in spa treatments, climb or hike Mt Timpanogos, nosh at several wonderful eateries and then spend the night in rustic luxury. Day-trippers should ask for trail maps and activity guides at the general store (p467).

Mt Timpanogos, the second-highest peak in the Wasatch, lords over the mountain resort, which is family and newbie-friendly. The 500-skiable-acre hill is primarily an amenity for the resort, but experienced snow riders will groove on the super-steeps. Sundance hosts numerous cultural events year-round, from its namesake film festival (p457) and screenwriting and directing labs to writers' workshops and music seminars. In summer there are outdoor films, plays, author readings and great music series at the amphitheater.

Activities

Sundance Mountain Resort SNOW SPORTS
(📞 reservations 801-223-4849; 8841 Alpine Loop Scenic Byway; day lift-ticket adult/child $70/43) Robert Redford's ski resort could not be more idyllic. There are four chairlifts and a beginner area. Most terrain is intermediate and advanced, climbing 2150ft up the northeast slope of Mt Timpanogos. It hosts the independent Sundance Film Festival (p457) and the nonprofit Sundance Institute.

Nordic Center SKIING
(🕐 9am-5pm Dec-early Apr) Has 16 miles of groomed classic and skating lanes on all-natural snow. You can also snowshoe 6 miles of trails past frozen waterfalls (ask about nighttime owl-watching walks). The woods are a veritable fairyland.

Mountain Biking MOUNTAIN BIKING
(full-day lifts/trails only $24/5; 🕐 10am-6:30pm) May through September, there's lift-assist hiking and mountain biking at Sundance, with mountain bike rentals available.

Art Studio ART
(🕐 10am-5pm) A creative center where you can throw pottery, learn photography and make jewelry.

🛏 Sleeping

Make no mistake: staying over at the resort means splurging to various degrees. At festival times availability is scarce.

Sundance Resort Lodging RESORT $$$
(📞 800-892-1600, 801-225-4107; www.sundance resort.com; 9521 Alpine Loop Rd, Provo; r $315-540, houses from $1100; 🐾) Lucky enough to be staying over? Rough-hewn cottage rooms are secluded, tucked among the trees on the grounds – the perfect place to honeymoon or write your next novel. The decor differs throughout, but all rooms have pine walls and ever-so-comfy furnishings, plus quilts, paperback books and board games; some have kitchens. Two- to four-bedroom houses are also available.

All rates include ski passes in winter and lift passes in summer (two per room).

Eating & Drinking

There are eating options for every budget here, but if you like high-end dining you're in for a treat.

★**Foundry Grill** AMERICAN $$
(📞 866-932-2295; breakfast & sandwiches $14-24, dinner $14-44; 🕐 7-11am, 11:30am-4pm & 5-9pm Mon-Sat, 9am-2pm & 5-9pm Sun) Sundance's Foundry Grill offers pizzas with artisan greens, Utah steelhead trout and rib-eye steaks. It strikes a good balance between home-cooked favorites spruced up (truffled mac and cheese), classic Western fare (tender lamb shank, anyone?) and fine dining.

★**Tree Room** AMERICAN $$$
(📞 866-627-8313; mains $28-48; 🕐 5-9pm Tue-Thu, to 10pm Fri & Sat) Sundance's top-flight restaurant, Tree Room, is a study in rustic-mountain chic – with a big tree trunk in the middle of the room. Here the modern American menu items are as artfully presented as the chichi clientele. From spiced-right Moroccan chicken to fragrant scallops in coconut chowder, you'd be hard-pressed to find a better meal this side of San Francisco.

Owl Bar BAR
(🕐 3-11pm Mon-Thu, to 1am Fri, noon-1am Sat, to 11pm Sun) Built of cast-off barn wood, the centerpiece of the Owl Bar is a century-old bar where the real Butch Cassidy once drank. The place looks like a Wild West roadhouse, but it's full of art freaks, mountain hipsters and local cowboys imbibing

by a roaring fireplace. On Friday and Saturday there's often live music.

🛍 Shopping

General Store ARTS & CRAFTS
(www.sundancecatalog.com; ⊙9am-9pm) Sells stylish high-end artisan handicrafts, home furnishings and jewelry (catalog available).

ⓘ Getting There & Away

The resort is 13 miles northeast of Provo. During ski season, bus 880 stops here, leaving from Provo central station. The usual access is via private vehicle.

Provo

✈ 435 / POP 116,300
The third-largest city in Utah, Provo is a conservative Mormon town. (It's also known as 'Happy Valley,' as more antidepressants are prescribed here than in any other part of Utah.) Remember Donny & Marie Osmond, the saccharine 1970s sibling singing sensation? This is their hometown. Unless you're a big fan, the most compelling reason to visit is to see **Brigham Young University** (BYU; www.byu. edu; Campus Dr) on a day trip from Salt Lake City, 45 miles north. University Ave, Provo's main thoroughfare, intersects Center St in the small old downtown core. Note that the whole place pretty much shuts down on Sunday.

⊙ Sights & Activities

Museum of Art MUSEUM
(☑801-378-2787; ⊙10am-6pm Tue, Wed & Fri, to 9pm Mon & Thu, noon-5pm Sat) FREE Brigham Young University's what's-this-doing-here Museum of Art is one of the biggest in the Southwest, with a concentration on American art.

Fifth Water Hot Spring Trail HIKING
Hike to three scenic waterfalls and worthwhile hot springs on Fifth Water Creek, a tributary to the Diamond Fork River, east of Spanish Fork. The easy trail is 4.5 miles round-trip. To get there, take the Three Forks trailhead in Diamond Fork Canyon, 10 miles in from the Spanish Fork Trail Rd off Hwy 6 E. It's 9 miles south of Provo.

Mt Nebo Scenic Byway SCENIC DRIVE
From Provo, this scenic drive loops through Uinta-Wasatch-Cache National

---

WORTH A TRIP

MT TIMPANOGOS

An incredibly scenic journey, the 16-mile **Alpine Loop Rd** (Hwy 92) makes the journey past **Mt Timpanogos** (11,750ft). At 6800ft, stay overnight at the **Mt Timpanogos Campground** (p465), which has pit toilets and water but no hookups. A trailhead leads from here into the surrounding fir-tree-filled wilderness. The paved loop is accessed via the north side of Provo Canyon.

Spectacular, star-like helictite formations are on view at three mid-mountain caverns in **Timpanogos Cave National Monument** (p464). Book ahead or get there early for a 90-minute ranger-led tour – they fill up. To get to the caves, it's an uphill hike (that must be done within an hour before your tour time). Hwy 92 is closed December through March.

Forest (p464) between Nephi and Payson. Reaching over 9000ft, there are breathtaking views of Utah valley, the Wasatch Mountains and 11,928ft Mt Nebo, the tallest mountain in the Wasatch Range. The 38-mile route takes under two hours, but you'll want to stop.

To get there, head south from Provo on Hwy 15 to Nephi if you want to return to Provo at the end of the drive, since Payson is closer to the city.

Peaks Ice Arena ICE SKATING
(☑801-377-8777; www.peaksarena.com; 100 N Seven Peaks Blvd; ⊙Mon-Sat) Ice skate where the Olympic hockey teams faced off in 2002. Free-skate hours vary.

🍴 Sleeping & Eating

There are chain hotels and B&Bs, though Provo is close enough to Salt Lake City that you can easily make it in a day. The historic downtown area has numerous little ethnic restaurants, many around the intersection of Center St and University Ave.

Hines Mansion B&B B&B $$
(☑801-374-8400, 800-428-5636; www.hines mansion.com; 383 W 100 S; r $145-225; @☎) Antiques are used sparingly in this 1895 mansion-turned-B&B. The 'Library' guest room has a 'secret passage' door to the bathroom.

Guru's
CAFE $

(www.guruscafe.com; 45 E Center St; mains $6-15; ⊗8am-9pm Mon & Tue, to 10pm Wed-Sat; 🖉) Spanning several restaurant spaces, this casual Provo staple does tasty rice bowls, big salads and bakery goods. Popular with both moms and students.

★Communal
CAFE $$

(📞801-373-8000; communalrestaurant.com; 102 N University Ave; mains $10-30; ⊗11:30am-2pm & 5-10pm Tue-Fri, 5-10pm Sat, 9am-2pm Sun; 🖉) 🍴 Hipster central, the Sunday brunch at Communal is as packed as the Mormon temple and you'll soon find out why: the brûléed grapefruit, Texas toast with arugula and fried egg, and habanero-glazed shrimp and grits are all stellar choices. Try the Mexican hot chocolate. There's also wine and local beer.

Black Sheep
SOUTHERN US $$

(📞801-607-2485; www.blacksheepcafe.com; 19 N University Ave; lunch $11-14, dinner $13-22; ⊗11:30am-9pm Mon-Fri, noon-10pm Sat; 🖉) Black Sheep earns accolades for cafe food done with Southwestern and American Indian flair. Offerings include cactus pear salads or green and red chile posole with fry bread. Don't skip the Mexican-style street corn that's been grilled and sprinkled with spices.

ℹ Information

Hinckley Alumni & Visitor Center (📞801-422-4678; cnr W Campus & N Campus Drs; ⊗8am-6pm Mon-Sat) The Brigham Young University campus is enormous and known for its squeaky-clean student dress codes. Drive 450 East north toward the visitor center for tours (arrange in advance).

Utah Valley Visitors Bureau (📞801-851-2100; www.utahvalley.org; 111 S University Ave; ⊗8:30am-5pm Mon-Fri, 9am-3pm Sat) Get information inside the beautiful courthouse.

ℹ Getting There & Away

There's convenient public transportation with **UTA** (📞801-743-3882, 888-743-3882; www.rideuta.com; Central Station; to Salt Lake City $6.10) to Salt Lake City and Sundance Resort (p466).

NORTHEASTERN UTAH

A remote and rural area, Northeastern Utah is high-wilderness terrain (much of which is more than a mile above sea level) that has traditionally attracted farmers and miners. Rising oil prices spurred oil and gas development in the rocky valleys, which in turn has led to increased services in towns like Vernal. Most travelers come to see Dinosaur National Monument, but you'll also find other dino dig sites and museums, as well as Fremont Indian rock art and ruins in the area. Up near the Wyoming border, the Uinta Mountains and Flaming Gorge attract trout fishers and wildlife-lovers alike.

Vernal
📞 435 / POP 10,400

A big pink allosaurus welcomes you to the capital of self-dubbed 'Dinoland' – Vernal is the closest town to Dinosaur National Monument (20 miles east). For amateur paleontologists, it's boomtown. The rafting is worthwhile too, particularly on a crackling-hot day.

Great drives through public lands and parks abound. Ten miles northeast of Vernal on Hwy 191, check out hundreds of fossilized dinosaur tracks at Red Fleet State Park. Eleven miles northwest, the 200ft of McConkie Ranch Petroglyphs are well worth checking out. Visit both as part of the 74-mile Red Cloud Loop. To do this loop, continue on Hwy 191 for 21 miles north of Vernal, then take off west on Red Cloud Scenic Backway. The road starts out tame, then rises sharply up to 10,000ft in twists and turns. The one-and-a-half-lane road has steep drop-offs and dramatic pine scenery amid the eastern Uinta peaks.

For more rock art and ruins, do the Nine Mile Canyon Drive, including the gorgeous road to Flaming Gorge 35 miles north.

◉ Sights & Activities

McConkie Ranch Petroglyphs
ARCHAEOLOGICAL SITE

(Dry Fork Canyon Rd; by donation; ⊗dawn-dusk) Worth the drive, the McConkie Ranch Petroglyphs sit 10 miles northeast of town. The 800-year-old Fremont Indian petroglyphs require some rock scrambling to see. Generous ranch owners built a little self-serve info shack with posted messages and a map. Being on private land has really helped; these alien-looking anthropomorphs are in much better shape than the many that have been desecrated by vandals on public lands. Follow 3000 West to the north out of Vernal.

Utah Field House of Natural History State Park Museum
MUSEUM

(☑435-789-3799; statesparks.utah.gov; 496 E Main St; ⊙9am-7pm Apr-Aug, to 5pm low season; ♿) **FREE** The informative film at the Utah Field House of Natural History is the best all-round introduction to Utah's dinosaurs. Interactive exhibits, video clips and, of course, giant fossils are wonderfully relevant to the area. As soon as the growing institution fills up its new 22,000-sq-ft space, this museum will be tops in the state. Some kids we know think it is already. Ask about volunteering for museum-curator-led digs.

High Uintas Wilderness Area
PARK

(www.fs.usda.gov/main/uwcnf) The Uinta Mountains are unusual in that they run east–west, unlike all other major mountain ranges in the lower 48. Several peaks rise to more than 13,000ft, including Kings (13,528ft), which is the highest point in the Southwest. The central summits lie within the High Uintas Wilderness Area, part of Ashley National Forest, which provides 800 sq miles of hiking and horseback-riding opportunities.

Red Fleet State Park
PARK

(☑435-789-4432; statesparks.utah.gov; day-use $7, tent/RV sites $15/25; ⊙6am-10pm Apr-Oct, 8am-5pm Nov & Dec) Twelve miles northeast of Vernal, Red Fleet State Park offers boating, camping and an easy hike to a series of fossilized dinosaur tracks (best visited when the reservoir isn't full). Campsites are a mix of reservable and first-come, first-served.

Starvation State Park
PARK

(statesparks.utah.gov; Hwy 40, Duchesne; day-use $7; ⊙6am-10pm Jun-Aug, 8am-5pm Sep-May) The name comes from the theft of buried provisions, left either by trappers or American Indians. In different versions of the story, each group blamed the other, though in all likelihood bears were to blame for the ensuing hunger at Starvation State Park. Subsequent homesteaders tried surviving on the Strawberry River, but with a short growing season and frozen ground they had no better luck. Today the park contains a 3500-acre reservoir as well as plenty of picnickers.

Dinosaur River Expeditions
RAFTING

(☑800-345-7238; www.dinosaurriverexpeditions. com; 550 E Main St; day trip adult/child $90/70)

The Green and Yampa Rivers are the main waterways in the area; both have some rapids and more genteel floats. River trips (May through September) run from day trips to five-day expeditions.

Don Hatch River Expeditions
RAFTING

(☑435-789-4316, 800-342-8243; www.donhatch rivertrips.com; 221 N 400 E; 1-day tour adult/ child $105/85) Don Hatch River Expeditions, now partnered with OARS, runs a variety of one- to five-day trips locally and throughout the region.

🍽 Sleeping & Eating

Chain hotels and motels are plentiful, but not always great value. Beyond the inevitable fast food, a few restaurants and brewpubs add variety.

Landmark Inn & Suites
MOTEL $

(☑435-781-1800, 888-738-1800; www.landmark-inn.com; 301 E 100 S; r from $90; ☎) Contemporary comforts like deluxe mattresses and flat-screen TVs come standard in the upscale motel rooms here.

Lower Beach Campground
CAMPGROUND $

(☑800-322-3770; utahstateparks.reserveamerica. com; tent & RV sites with hookups $18-28; ⊙Jun-Sep) There's primitive camping and the 60-site Lower Beach Campground in Starvation State Park, with showers and a sandy beach. Don't forget to bring food.

Holiday Inn Express & Suites
HOTEL $$

(☑800-315-2621, 435-789-4654; www.holidayinn. com/vernal; 1515 W Hwy 40; r $119-176; ❄☎☀) One of the nicest chain hotels in town, the HI Express has loads of amenities (fitness center, business center, laundry, morning

---

ON THE BONE TRAIL: DINOSAUR DIAMOND

Open year-round, **Dinosaur Diamond** (utah.com/scenic-drive/dinosaur-diamond) is a 45-mile national scenic byway connecting active quarries where paleontologists are unearthing dinosaur fossils. The route includes **Dinosaur National Monument**, the **Utah Field House of Natural History** (p469), the **College of Eastern Utah Prehistoric Museum** (p472) and **Cleveland-Lloyd Dinosaur Quarry** (p471).

SCENIC DRIVE: FLAMING GORGE-UINTAS SCENIC BYWAY

Heading north from Vernal, 80 miles into the northeastern Uintas Mountains, Flaming Gorge-Uintas Scenic Byway (Hwy 191) is a drive and a geology lesson all in one. As you climb up switchbacks to 8100ft, the up-tilted sedimentary layers you see represent one billion years of history. Interpretive signs explain what different colors and rock compositions indicate about the prehistoric climate in which they were laid down. It's a great route for fall color and wildlife-watching, too.

newspapers and turn-down service). Kids' laughter often fills the indoor pool and whirlpool.

Don Pedro's Family Mexican Restaurant
MEXICAN $

(☑ 435-789-3402; klcyads.com/don-pedros; 3340 N Vernal Ave; dishes $8-15; ⊙ 11am-2pm & 5-10pm) You won't write home about it, but Don Pedro's is a step up from the fast-food scene, with filling burritos and chilled margs that do the trick after a hot day in the sun.

Vernal Brewing Company
PUB FOOD $$

(☑ 435-781-2337; www.vernalbrewingco.com; 55 S 500 E; mains $11-20; ⊙ 11:30am-9pm Mon-Sat) This craft brewery has come to dinosaur town and it's a home run. There are five house brews on tap, including a peach-infused wheat ale. Dine on gooey mac and cheese, green salad topped with grilled salmon or a red-blooded American burger.

ⓘ Information

Quarry Visitor Center (⊙ 8am-6pm mid-May–late Sep, 9am-5pm late Sep–mid-May)

Dinosaurland Tourist Board (Vernal Chamber of Commerce; ☑ 800-477-5558; www.dinoland.com; 134 W Main St; ⊙ 9am-5pm Mon-Fri) Provides information on the entire region; pick up driving-tour brochures for area rock art and dino tracks here.

Vernal Ranger Station (☑ 435-789-1181; 355 N Vernal Ave; ⊙ 8am-5pm Mon-Fri) The Vernal Ranger Station has details on camping and hiking in Ashley National Forest, to the north.

ⓘ Getting There & Away

Vernal is 145 miles west of Park City and 112 miles north of Price. Visitors should come with their own vehicle, preferably a 4WD if you want to explore the surrounding backcountry.

Flaming Gorge National Recreation Area

Flaming Gorge (www.fs.usda.gov/ashley) provides 375 miles of shoreline around a reservoir on the Utah–Wyoming state line. As with many artificial lakes, fishing and boating are prime attractions. Various records for giant lake trout and kokanee salmon have been set here. Keep an eye out for common wildlife such as moose, elk, pronghorn antelope and mule deer; you may also see bighorn sheep, black bears and mountain lions. Information is available from www.flaminggorgecountry.com.

⚡ Activities

Trout Creek Flies
FISHING

(☑ 435-885-3355; www.troutcreekflies.com; 1155 Little Hole Rd, Dutch John; half-day fishing $375; ⊙ 7am-7pm) The best fishing in the Flaming Gorge National Recreation Area is found with a guide. Aim to fly-fish late June to early July, before the river is flooded with fun floaters. Trout Creek also rents rafts and runs a floater shuttle. For details, see its Facebook page.

Cedar Springs Marina
BOATING

(☑ 435-889-3795; www.cedarspringsmarina.com; off Hwy 191, Dutch John; daily fishing/ski boat rental $240/360; ⊙ Apr-Oct) Rent a fishing, pontoon or ski boat or get active with a kayak or paddleboat. It's located 2 miles east of Flaming Gorge Dam.

🛏 Sleeping

Choose between resorts, a B&B, campgrounds and lodges with activities. Resorts have decent restaurants, and convenience stores in Dutch John have deli counters.

Nine Mile Bunk & Breakfast
RANCH $

(☑ 435-637-2572; 9mileranch.com; r $70-85, cabin $50-80, campsite $15) Offers big ranch-house rooms on spacious grounds (with themes like Elvis or Hawaii). You can also stay in an old log pioneer cabin or pitch a tent at the shady campground (showers extra). The rustic accommodations are run by a 'retired' ranching couple who are the nicest folks you'd ever want to meet. They run canyon tours too.

Canyon Rim Campground   CAMPGROUND $
(☑ 877-444-6777; www.recreation.gov; Red Canyon Rd, off Hwy 44; tent & RV sites $20) The ponderosa pine forest location, at 7000ft-plus elevation and with excellent clifftop views, makes Canyon Rim, in Flaming Gorge National Recreation Area, a top choice. Water; no showers or hookups. Keep an eye out for bighorn sheep.

Red Canyon Lodge   CABIN $$
(☑ 435-889-3759; www.redcanyonlodge.com; 790 Red Canyon Rd, Dutch John; 2-/4-person cabin from $155/165; 🛜 🐾) Rustic and luxury log cabins on groomed grounds with activities like fishing, rowing, rafting and horseback riding. Alpine cabins are smaller but cozy; the higher-priced Ponderosa cabins are deluxe, with kitchenettes and wood stoves. There are no TVs or phones. Wi-fi is available in the restaurant.

ℹ Information

USFS Flaming Gorge Headquarters (☑ 435-784-3445; www.fs.usda.gov/ashley; 25 W Hwy 43, Manila; park day-use $5; ⏰ 8am-5pm Mon-Fri) Provides information about hiking and camping in summer, cross-country skiing and snowmobiling in winter.
Flaming Gorge Dam Visitor Center (☑ 435-885-3135; Hwy 191; ⏰ 9am-5pm May-Sep) With information on this recreation area on the Utah–Wyoming line.

Price & San Rafael Swell

Though a true Utah backwater, Price can serve as a base for exploring enticing backcountry dinosaur and ancient rock-art sites in the scenic San Rafael Swell and beyond. It's en route from Green River (65 miles) to Vernal (112 miles).

These southern lands between Hwys 10 and 6/24 are the canyons, arches and cliffs of the San Rafael Swell. Look for the purples, grays and greens that indicate ancient seabeds, in addition to the oxygenated oranges and reds of this anticline. The area is all BLM land, where free dispersed camping and some four-wheel driving is allowed. Sights include a 1200ft canyon drop at Wedge Overlook, Barrier Canyon–style pictographs at Buckhorn Wash and a suspension footbridge. Ask for a basic map at the

town visitor center (p472) or the quarry site. For more details, go online to www.emerycounty.com/travel.

◉ Sights & Activities

Cleveland-Lloyd Dinosaur Quarry   ARCHAEOLOGICAL SITE
(☑ 435-636-3600; www.blm.gov; off Hwy 10; adult/child $5/2; ⏰ 10am-5pm Thu-Sat, noon-5pm Sun late Mar-Oct) Thirty miles south of Price you can visit an actual dinosaur dig site producing over 12,000 bones. A dozen species of dinosaur were buried here 150 million years ago, but the large concentration of meat-eating allosaurs has helped scientists around the world draw new conclusions. Excavations are intermittent but ongoing; check out the visitor center's excellent exhibits. Several hikes lead off from there, too. Take Rte 10 south to the Elmo/Cleveland turnoff and follow signs on the dirt road.

SCENIC DRIVE: NINE MILE CANYON

Abundant rock art is the attraction on the **Nine Mile Canyon National Backcountry Byway**, billed as the 'longest art gallery in the world.' You can also spot Fremont granaries and structures along the canyon walls (bring binoculars). Many of the petroglyphs are easy to miss; some are on private property. Pick up a free guide at area restaurants, or at the Carbon County Office Of Tourism and Visitor Center (p472) or the Utah Welcome Center outside Dinosaur National Monument (p428). Allow at least three to five hours for the 70-mile unpaved ride from Wellington (on Hwy 6) to Myton (on Hwy 40). Get gas before you go: there are no services.

About 23 miles northeast along Nine Mile Canyon Byway from the Hwy 6/191 turnoff, you can stay at the simple **Nine Mile Bunk & Breakfast** (p470), with two big ranch-house rooms on spacious grounds; plus you can stay in an old pioneer cabin or pitch a tent on-site. The rustic accommodations are run by a 'retired' ranching couple who are the nicest folks you'd ever want to meet. They run canyon tours too.

College of Eastern Utah
Prehistoric Museum   MUSEUM
(☑435-613-5060; www.usueastern.edu/museum; 155 East Main St; adult/child $6/3; ⊙9am-5pm Mon-Sat) In the same building as the Castle Country Travel Desk, you can see real fossils, not replicas, at the College of Eastern Utah Prehistoric Museum. Look for the Utah raptor, first identified in this part of the world. All the bones on display were discovered within two hours of the museum, and the university sponsors many active digs.

Range Creek Wildlife
Management Area   ARCHAEOLOGICAL SITE
(☑435-636-0260;   www.wildlife.utah.gov/ range_creek) For more than six decades, the Wilcox Ranch protected the ancient archaeological sites in what is now Range Creek Wildlife Management Area, east of East Carbon (25 miles southeast of Price). Since the family turned the property over to the government, the public has been allowed limited 4WD road access with permits. The best way to explore is with a full-day 4WD tour.

The Utah digital library puts out a handy brochure with directions, available online at digitallibrary.utah.gov.

Tavaputs Ranch   TOURS
(☑435-637-1236; www.tavaputsranch.com; State Hwy 6 N; per person incl meals & activities $200, 4WD tour $150; ⊙mid-Jun–Sep) A Western lodge with more knotty pine than you can take in. Included in the lodging price are three meals, backcountry hikes, scenic drives and wildlife tours on the 15,000-acre spread; horseback riding and the 4WD tour of the ruins at Range Creek are extra.

🛏 Sleeping & Eating

Free camping is allowed off established roads on the San Rafael Swell BLM lands. The motels off Hwy 6/191 and on Main St aren't exactly exciting, but they are plentiful.

If the wonderful brewery is closed, look for other eateries along Main St.

San Rafael Swell Bed & Breakfast   B&B $$
(☑435-381-5689;www.sanrafaelbedandbreakfast. com; 15 E 100 N, Castle Dale; r incl breakfast $85-140; ❄🐾) In Castle Dale, San Rafael Swell Bed & Breakfast offers a personal touch with imaginative themed rooms that transport you to Asia, Hawaii and an English garden. Less expensive rooms share a bathroom.

Grogg's Pinnacle
Brewing Company   BREWERY
(☑435-637-2924;   www.groggspinnaclebrewing. com; 1653 N Carbonville, Helper; mains $9-20; ⊙11am-10pm, to 8pm Sun) The place to be and the best place around for grub is Grogg's Pinnacle Brewing Company, with friendly staff, tasty casual-American fare and microbrews on tap. (Though barely 3 miles north of Price, it's technically in Helper.)

ℹ Information

Carbon County Office Of Tourism and Visitor Center (☑435-636-3701; www.castlecountry. com; 751 E 100 N, Price; ⊙9am-5pm Mon-Sat) The incredibly knowledgeable staff here can tell you all the secret rock-art sites and help you plan out your regional route.

BLM Price Field Office (☑435-636-3600; www.blm.gov; 125 S 600 W, Price; ⊙9am-4:30pm Mon-Fri) Has information about hiking, camping and recreation in the San Rafael Swell.

Understand Southwest USA

Southwest USA Today

Today, the defining issue of the Southwest is its stewardship. Public lands account for 59% of the region. Yet the Southwest is the fastest growing region in the nation, and has been for several decades. Academics estimate that the population stands to double between 2000 and 2050. With the current panorama, natural resources have never been more important. Pressures on the region include not only growth but how increasing demands will interact with climate change and land use.

Best on Film

Stagecoach (1939) Monument Valley may be the true star of this John Ford Western drama.

Butch Cassidy & the Sundance Kid (1969) Follows the adventures of two real-life outlaws who hid out in Utah.

Thelma & Louise (1991) Two gal pals run from the law and into stunning Southwest scenery.

The Hangover (2009) It's a bachelor party gone wrong – or right – in Las Vegas.

127 Hours (2010) Aron Ralston's harrowing experience in Utah's red-rock country.

Best in Print

The Grapes of Wrath (John Steinbeck; 1939) Dust Bowl migrants follow Route 66 west to California.

Desert Solitaire (Edward Abbey; 1968) Essays about the Southwest and industrial tourism by a no-holds-barred eco-curmudgeon.

Bean Trees (Barbara Kingsolver; 1988) Thoughtful look at motherhood and cross-cultural adoption in Tucson.

House of Rain (Craig Childs; 2007) Traces a vanished civilization across the Southwest.

The Emerald Mile (Kevin Fedarko, 2013) An epic Colorado River adventure through the Grand Canyon.

This Land Is Your Land

In 2016, one of Barack Obama's last acts as president was to establish Bears Ears National Monument, protecting a swath of 1.35 million acres of land in southern Utah around existing national parks and monuments. The area, to be co-managed by indigenous tribes in the region, is coveted for its sheer quantity of ancient rock carvings. It also includes intact cliff dwellings and stunning red-rock wilderness. In a region where tourism is central to the economy, its conservation equals a forward-thinking investment.

Not everyone agrees. The state, under the leadership of Governor Gary Herbert, would prefer to revoke the designation and introduce more oil and gas development leases on public lands. Under the Trump administration, the monument is particularly vulnerable, as the administration seeks to dismantle the legacy of the previous one. Leases are already in the works on the doorstep of national parks, near both Chaco Canyon in Arizona and Zion in Utah.

In a pointed letter, Patagonia founder Yvon Chouinard condemned the government's preference for industry profit on public lands, reminding naysayers that the outdoor recreation industry contributes $12 billion annually to the state. Patagonia's subsequent boycott of Salt Lake City's huge Outdoor Retailer Show brought the rest of the outdoor industry with them. Within days, the convention pulled out of Utah.

In Nevada, rancher Cliven Bundy grabbed the spotlight in 2014 when federal officials tried to impound 900 head of his cattle after Bundy's alleged failure to pay federal grazing fees and fines. But when Bureau of Land Management officials arrived to collect the animals, Bundy supporters met them armed with semi-automatic weapons. The BLM backed down, but Bundy still faces federal charges related to the standoff.

Who-has-rights-to-what has become a national hot-button topic. The issue extends into US society as increasingly intolerant policies toward immigration take hold nationwide. At the beginning of the Trump administration, surprise deportations of undocumented immigrants and the promise of a 1954-mile wall along the Mexican border (at an estimated cost of $21 billion to taxpayers) signaled difficult times to come for a region largely bolstered by immigrant labor and a fluid Latino identity.

The Climes They Are a-Changin'

Climate change is having an especially harsh impact on the Southwest, which was already the hottest and driest region in the US. Drought conditions have been persistent for the last 14 years. According to the Environmental Protection Agency, temperatures have increased by almost 2°F in the last century. The future is looking parched.

The Southwest has been hit hard by forest fires in recent years, with numerous blazes costing lives, homes and volumes of public land at an enormous cost to the government.

But fire isn't the region's only natural foe. A decades-long drought left reservoirs along the Colorado River at less than half their capacity. The lifeblood of the whole basin, not just wildlife, the Colorado River supplies drinking water for 36 million people and water for more than 10% of the nation's crops.

The good news? An above-average snow pack in 2017 should – at least temporarily – raise water levels in Lake Powell. At the other extreme, in 2013 severe flooding in Colorado affected a 4500-sq-mile area across the state's Front Range, killing eight people and incurring property damage estimated at about $2 billion.

On the Sunny Side

It's not all bad news. The Southwest's economic landscape has some bright spots. After the purchase and use of recreational marijuana became legal in Colorado in 2014, it has since contributed $2.4 billion to the state economy, bolstering education, infrastructure and social programs. In 2017, Nevada legalized recreational pot and New Mexico could follow suit.

In Las Vegas, online retailer Zappos revitalized downtown Las Vegas by moving its headquarters there and creating a haven for start-ups. While results haven't fully materialized, the bet is still on.

Ecofriendly initiatives continue. Solar initiatives in this sunny region abound. Bike-share programs and expanded bike lanes in Denver, Salt Lake, and even the Grand Canyon, are bringing back pedal power. Cities such as Denver, Salt Lake and Phoenix have made huge investments in light rail to bolster a car-free culture.

POPULATION: **14.8 MILLION**

STATE UNEMPLOYMENT RATES (DECEMBER 2016): **ARIZONA 4.8%, NEW MEXICO 6.2%, NEVADA 5.1%, UTAH 3.1%**

US UNEMPLOYMENT RATE (DECEMBER 2016): **4.9%**

· ·

if the Southwest were 100 people

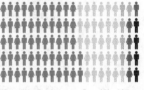

57 would be Caucasian
29 would be Hispanic or Latino
5 would be Native American
5 would be African American
4 would be Asian

· ·

belief systems
(% of population)

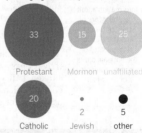

33 Protestant
15 Mormon
25 unaffiliated
20 Catholic
2 Jewish
5 other

· ·

population per sq mile

the Southwest   USA   California

= 30 people

History

Landscape and water have shaped the Southwest. Prehistoric settlers carved out irrigation systems for farming, building communities in the process. Prospectors and pioneers followed, lured by the promise of mineral riches, ranch land, religious freedom, unfettered adventure and self-determination. Civilization resulted. The wild was tamed with churches, government and enormous dams. In the 20th and 21st centuries the Southwest proved amenable to big-sky science projects, becoming home to rocket and atomic-bomb test sites, world-class observatories and a very modern spaceport.

The First Americans

Archaeologists believe that the region's first inhabitants were hunters – descendants of those hardy souls who crossed the Bering Strait into North America 25,000 years ago. The population grew and wild game became extinct, forcing hunters to augment their diets with berries, seeds, roots and fruits. After 3000 BC, contact with farmers in present central Mexico led to the beginnings of agriculture in the Southwest. Primitive corn was grown, and by 500 BC beans and squash were also cultivated. Between 300 BC and AD 100, distinct groups began to settle in villages in the Southwest.

Those Who Came Before, by Robert H and Florence C Lister, is an excellent source of information about the prehistory of the Southwest and the archaeological sites of the national parks and monuments of this area.

The Hohokam, Mogollan & Ancestral Puebloans

By about AD 100, three dominant cultures were emerging in the Southwest: the Hohokam of the desert, the Mogollon of the central mountains and valleys, and the Ancestral Puebloans. Archaeologists originally called the Ancestral Puebloans the Anasazi, which comes from a Navajo term meaning 'ancient enemy' and has fallen out of favor.

The Hohokam lived in the deserts of Arizona from 300 BC to AD 1400, adapting to desert life by creating an incredible river-fed irrigation system. They also developed low earthen pyramids and sunken ball courts with sloped earthen walls. These oval-shaped courts, which varied in size, may have been used for organized games as well as for markets and community gatherings.

TIMELINE	AD 100	1300s	1598
	The region's dominant indigenous cultures emerge. The Hohokam settle in the desert, the Mogollon in the mountains and valleys and Ancestral Puebloans build cliff dwellings around the Four Corners.	The Ancestral Puebloans living in Mesa Verde, CO, abandon a sophisticated city of cliff dwellings.	A large force of Spanish explorers, led by Don Juan de Oñate, stops near present-day El Paso, TX, and claims the land to the north of New Mexico for Spain.

The Mogollon people settled near the Mexican border from 200 BC to AD 1400. They lived in small communities, often elevated on isolated mesas or ridge tops, and built pit dwellings, which were simple structures of wood, shrubs and mud erected over small depressions in the ground. Although the Mogollon farmed, they depended more on hunting and foraging for food. Growing villages featured the kiva – a circular, underground chamber used for ceremonies and other communal purposes.

Around the 13th or 14th century, the Mogollon were likely being peacefully assimilated by the Ancestral Puebloan groups from the north. One indication of this is the beautiful black-on-white Mimbres pottery with its distinctive animal and human figures executed in a geometric style reminiscent of Puebloan ware. (The Mimbres were Mogollons who lived in a remote valley area in southwestern New Mexico between 1100 and 1150 AD.) The Gila Cliff Dwellings in New Mexico are a late-Mogollon site with Puebloan features.

The Ancestral Puebloans inhabited the Colorado Plateau – also called the Four Corners area – which comprises parts of northeastern Arizona, northwestern New Mexico, southwestern Colorado and southeastern Utah. This culture left the Southwest's richest archaeological sites and ancient settlements, some of which are still inhabited.

Today, descendants of the Ancestral Puebloans live in Pueblo Indian communities along New Mexico's Rio Grande, and in the Acoma, Zuni and Laguna Pueblos in northwest New Mexico. The oldest links with the Ancestral Puebloans are found among the Hopi tribe of northern Arizona. The mesa-top village of Old Oraibi has been inhabited since the 1100s, making it the oldest continuously inhabited settlement in North America.

By about 1400, the Hohokam had abandoned their villages. There are many theories on this tribe's disappearance, but the most likely explanation involves a combination of factors, including drought, overhunting, conflict among groups and disease. The Mogollon people were more or less incorporated into the Ancestral Puebloans, who had also all but disappeared from their ancestral cliff dwellings at Mesa Verde in southwestern Colorado by the 1400s – their mass exodus began in the 1300s.

New in 2017, Utah's Bears Ears National Monument protects more than 100,000 cultural and archeological sites dating back to 11,000 BC. Managed in conjunction with the Navajo Nation, Ute Mountain and Ute Tribes, Hopi, Uintah and others, the park could also provide a needed boost to their economies.

The Spanish Era

Francisco Vásquez de Coronado led the first major expedition into North America in 1540. It included 300 soldiers, hundreds of American Indian guides and herds of livestock. It also marked the first major violence between Spanish explorers and the native people.

1609	1680	1846–48	1847
Santa Fe, America's oldest capital city, is founded. The Palace of Governors is the only remaining 17th-century structure; the rest of Santa Fe was destroyed by a 1914 fire.	During the Pueblo Revolt, northern New Mexico Pueblos drive out the Spanish after the latter's bloody campaign to destroy Puebloan kivas and ceremonial objects.	The battle for the West is waged with the Mexican-American War. The Treaty of Guadalupe Hidalgo ends the fighting, and the US annexes most of Arizona and New Mexico.	Mormons fleeing religious persecution arrive in Salt Lake City by wagon train; over the next 20 years more than 70,000 Mormons will escape to Utah via the Mormon Pioneer Trail.

The expedition's goal was the fabled, immensely rich Seven Cities of Cibola. For two years they traveled through what is now Arizona, New Mexico and as far east as Kansas, but instead of gold and precious gems, the expedition found adobe pueblos, which they violently commandeered. During the Spaniards' first few years in northern New Mexico, they tried to subdue the Pueblos, resulting in much bloodshed.

The fighting started in Acoma Pueblo, in today's New Mexico, when a Spanish contingent of 30 men led by one of the nephews of conquistador Juan de Oñate demanded tax payment in the form of food. The Acoma Indians responded by killing him and about half of his force. Oñate retaliated with greater severity. Relations with the American Indians, poor harvests, harsh weather and accusations of Oñate's cruelty led to many desertions among the colonizers. By 1608 Oñate had been recalled to Mexico. A new governor, Pedro de Peralta, was sent north to found a new capital in 1609. Santa Fe remains the capital of New Mexico today, the oldest capital in what is now the USA.

Almost two centuries later, in an attempt to link Santa Fe with the newly established port of San Francisco and to avoid American Indian raids, small groups of explorers pressed into what is now Utah but were turned back by the rugged and arid terrain. The 1776 Dominguez-Escalante expedition was the first to survey Utah, but no attempt was made to settle there until the arrival of the Mormons in the 19th century.

In addition to armed conflict, Europeans introduced smallpox, measles and typhus, to which the American Indian people had no resistance. Pueblo populations were decimated by these diseases, shattering cultures and trade routes and proving a destructive force that far outstripped combat.

The Indian Wars

For decades, US forces pushed west across the continent, killing or forcibly moving whole tribes of American Indians who were in their way. The most widely known incident in the Southwest is the forceful relocation of many Navajo in 1864. US forces, led by Kit Carson, destroyed Navajo fields, orchards and houses, and forced the people into surrendering or withdrawing into remote parts of Canyon de Chelly in modern-day Arizona.

Eventually starvation forced them out. About 9000 Navajo were rounded up and marched 400 miles east to a camp at Bosque Redondo, near Fort Sumner, NM. Hundreds of American Indians died from sickness, starvation or gunshot wounds along the way. The Navajo call this 'The Long Walk.'

In Search of the Old Ones by David Roberts explores the culture of the Ancestral Puebloans and examines the reasons why they may have left their villages. It's a good resource for off-the-beaten-path hiking too.

Cliff Dwellings

Mesa Verde National Park, CO

Bandelier National Monument, NM

Gila Cliff Dwellings National Monument, NM

Montezuma Castle National Monument, AZ

Walnut Canyon National Monument, AZ

Navajo National Monument, AZ

1849	1862	1864	1869
A regular stagecoach service starts along the Santa Fe Trail. The 900-mile trail will serve as the country's main transportation route until the arrival of the railroad 60 years later.	Confederate rangers defeat Union cavalry forces at Picacho Peak in Arizona during the Civil War. It is the war's westernmost battle.	Kit Carson captures 9000 Navajo and forces them to walk 400 miles to a camp near Fort Sumner. Hundreds of American Indians die along 'The Long Walk.'	One-armed Civil War veteran John Wesley Powell leads the first Colorado River descent, a grueling 1000-mile expedition through the Grand Canyon's rapids that kills half of his men.

PETROGLYPHS WRITTEN ON THE LAND

Petroglyphs can be found etched into desert-varnished boulders across the Southwest. This rock art is simple yet mysterious and always leaves us wondering: who did this, and why? What were they trying to say?

Dating from at least 4000 BC to as late as the 19th century, rock art in the Southwest has been attributed to every known ancestral and modern people. In fact, one way archaeologists track the spread of ancestral cultures is by studying their distinctive rock-art styles, which tend to be either abstract or representational and anthropomorphic. Representational rock art is almost always more recent, while abstract designs appear in all ages.

We can only speculate about what it means. This symbolic writing becomes obscure the moment the cultural context for the symbols is lost. Archaeologists believe much of the art was the work of shamans or elders communicating with the divine. Some of the earliest abstract designs may have been created in trance states.

Certain figures and motifs seem to reflect a heavenly pantheon, while other rock art may tell stories – real or mythica – of successful hunts or battles. Some etchings may have served as simple agricultural calendars, marking the start of harvest season, for example, by the way a shadow falls across a picture.

Other images may have marked tribal territory, and some may have been nothing more than idle doodling. But no matter what the meaning, each rock-art site – whether a petroglyph (inscribed or pecked into the stone) or pictograph (painted figure) – is irreplaceable, whether as a valuable part of the human archaeological record or the continuing religious traditions and cultural patrimony of contemporary tribes.

Preserve rock-art sites for future generations by observing these rules of etiquette:

➡ Do not disturb or remove any artifacts or features of the site.

➡ Do not trace, repaint, remove graffiti or otherwise touch or apply any materials to the rock art.

➡ Stay back at least 10ft from all rock-art panels, using binoculars or a zoom lens for better views.

The last serious conflicts took place between US troops and the Apache. Raiding was the essential path to manhood for the Apache. As US forces and settlers moved into Apache land, they became obvious targets. Raids continued under the leadership of Mangas Coloradas, Cochise, Victorio and, finally, Geronimo, who surrendered in 1886 after being promised that he and the Apache would be imprisoned for two years and then allowed to return to their homeland. As with many promises of the time, this too was broken.

1881	1919	1931	1938
In 1881, Wyatt Earp, along with his brothers Virgil and Morgan, and Doc Holliday, kill Billy Clanton and the McLaury brothers during the OK Corral shoot-out in Tombstone, AZ.	The Grand Canyon becomes the USA's 15th national park. Only 44,173 people visit the park that year, compared to six million in 2016.	Nevada legalizes gambling and drops the divorce residency requirement to six weeks; this, along with legalized prostitution and championship boxing, carries the state through the Great Depression.	Route 66 becomes the first cross-country highway to be completely paved, including more than 750 miles across Arizona and New Mexico.

Even after the wars were over, American Indians continued to be treated like second-class citizens for many decades. Non–Native Americans used legal loopholes and technicalities to take over reservation land. Many children were removed from reservations and shipped off to boarding schools where they were taught in English and punished for speaking their own languages or behaving 'like Indians' – this practice continued into the 1930s.

The cry 'Geronimo!' became popular for skydivers after a training group of US Army paratroopers in 1940 saw the movie *Geronimo* (1939). Afterward they began shouting the great warrior's name for courage during their jumps.

Anasazi, a Navajo word meaning 'ancient enemy,' is a term to which many modern Pueblo Indians object; it's no longer used.

The Westward Push

In 1803 the Louisiana Purchase resulted in the USA acquiring a huge tract of land (from Louisiana to the Rocky Mountains) from the French, doubling the size of the country. The Spanish colonies of the Southwest now abutted US territory and the two countries maintained an uneasy peace.

When Mexico became independent from Spain in 1821, the newly independent Mexicans welcomed US traders and a major trade route was established. This was the infamous Santa Fe Trail between Missouri and Santa Fe, a trail traversed by thousands of people until the railway arrived about 60 years later.

In the 1830s and 1840s, with growing nationalist fervor and dreams of continental expansion, many Americans came to believe it was 'manifest destiny' that all the land should be theirs. In 1836 a group of Texans fomented a revolution against Mexico. Their loss at the Alamo that year was a pivotal event, and 'Remember the Alamo!' became a rallying cry for Texans.

Ten years later the US annexed the Texas Republic and, when Mexico resisted, the US waged war for it and California, in 1846. Having suffered from American Indian raids in its sparsely populated north, Mexico was ill-equipped to defend itself from US attacks. The Mexican-American War led to the eventual loss of much of Mexico's northern territory.

In 1848 Mexico was soundly defeated, and the land north of the Gila River was claimed by the state and ceded into the New Mexico Territory. The US soon realized that the best route from the Mississippi River to the burgeoning territory of California lay south of the Gila River, passing through the Mexican town of Tucson. In 1854, pursuant to the $10 million Gadsden Purchase, the US bought this remaining strip of land, which included Tucson south to Tumacacori, AZ, and the Mesilla Valley, NM.

1943	1945	1946	1947
High in the northern New Mexican desert, Los Alamos is chosen as the headquarters of the Manhattan Project, the code name for the research and development of the atomic bomb.	The first atomic bomb is detonated in a desolate desert area in southern New Mexico that is now part of the White Sands Missile Range.	The opening of the glitzy Flamingo casino in Vegas kicks off a building spree. Sin City reaches its first golden peak in the '50s.	An unidentified object falls in the desert near Roswell. The government first calls it a crashed disk, but the next day calls it a weather balloon and closes off the area.

Nineteenth-century Southwest history is strongly linked to transportation development. During early territorial days, movement of goods and people from the East to the Southwest was very slow. Horses, mule trains and stagecoaches represented state-of-the-art transportation. In addition to the Santa Fe Trail, major routes included the Old Spanish Trail, which ran from Santa Fe into central Utah and across Nevada to Los Angeles, CA. Regular stagecoach services along the Santa Fe Trail began in 1849; the Mormon Trail reached Salt Lake City in 1847.

The arrival of more people and resources via the railroad led to further land exploration and the frequent discovery of mineral deposits. The Civil War distracted most of the country between 1861 and 1865 as Union and Confederate forces clashed bloodily in the East. After the war, in the 1870s and 1880s, many mining towns cropped up across the Southwest. Some are now ghost towns, while others such as Tombstone, AZ, and Silver City, NM, remain active.

The West was officially tamed in 1912, when New Mexico and Arizona became, respectively, the 47th and 48th states in the Union.

The Wild West

Romanticized tales of gunslingers, cattle rustlers, outlaws and train robbers fuel Wild West legends. Good and bad guys were designations in flux – a tough outlaw in one state became a popular sheriff in another. Gunfights were more frequently the result of mundane political struggles in emerging towns than storied blood feuds. New mining towns mushroomed overnight, playing host to rowdy saloons and bordellos where miners would come to brawl, drink, gamble and be fleeced.

Legendary figures Billy the Kid and Sheriff Pat Garrett, both involved in the infamous Lincoln County War, were active in the late 1870s. Billy the Kid reputedly shot and killed more than 20 men in a brief career as a gunslinger – he himself was shot and killed by Garrett at the tender age of 21. In 1881, Wyatt Earp, along with his brothers Virgil and Morgan, and Doc Holliday, shot dead Billy Clanton and the McLaury brothers in a blazing gunfight at the OK Corral in Tombstone, AZ – the showdown took less than a minute. Both sides accused the other of cattle rustling, but the real story will never be known.

Butch Cassidy and the Sundance Kid once roamed much of Utah. Cassidy, a Mormon, robbed banks and trains with his Wild Bunch during the 1890s but never killed anyone.

For fascinating behind-the-scenes stories about Wild West legends, along with their photographs, pick up a copy of the monthly magazine *True West* (www.truewestmagazine.com) during your trip or check out the website to see who's in the spotlight.

1957	1963	1973	1996
Los Alamos opens its doors to ordinary people for the first time. The city was first exposed to the public after the atomic bomb was dropped on Japan.	The controversial Glen Canyon Dam is finished and Lake Powell begins, eventually covering Ancestral Puebloan sites and rock formations but creating 1960 miles of shoreline and a boater fantasyland.	The debut of the MGM Grand in 1973 signals the dawn of the era of corporate-owned megaresorts and sparks a building bonanza along the Strip that's still going on today.	President Bill Clinton establishes Utah's Grand Staircase–Escalante National Monument, which is unique in allowing some activities (such as hunting and grazing by permit) usually banned in national parks.

Depression, War & the Boom Years

Who Made the Bomb?

The Making of the History of the Atom Bomb by Rebecca Press Schwartz (2008) argues that presenting the atomic bomb as the genius project of Los Alamos physicists (and not the broader military) was a wildly successful PR move to get past the stigma of chemical weapons and find approval.

While the 1930s saw much of the USA in a major depression, the Southwest remained relatively prosperous.

Las Vegas came on to the scene after the completion of a railroad linking Salt Lake City and Los Angeles in 1902. It grew during the despair of the '30s and reached its first golden peak (the second came at the turn of the century) during the fabulous '50s, when mob money ran the city and all that glittered really was gold.

During the Depression, the region benefited from a number of federal employment projects, and WWII rejuvenated a demand for metals mined in the Southwest. In addition, production facilities were located in New Mexico and Arizona to protect those states from the vulnerability of attack. Migrating defense workers precipitated population booms and urbanization, which was mirrored elsewhere in the Southwest.

The struggle for an adequate supply of water for the growing desert population marked the early years of the 20th century, resulting in federally funded dam projects such as the 1936 Hoover Dam and, in 1963, Arizona's Glen Canyon Dam and Lake Powell. Water supply continues to be a key challenge to life in this region, with dwindling snow packs and ongoing drought conditions exacerbating the issue.

The Atomic Age

In 1943, Los Alamos, then a boys' school perched on a 7400ft mesa, was chosen as the top-secret headquarters of the Manhattan Project, the code name for the research and development of the atomic bomb. The 772-acre site, accessed by two dirt roads, had no gas or oil lines and only one wire service, and it was surrounded by forest.

The late environmentalist and essayist Edward Abbey wrote that the canyon country of the Colorado Plateau once had a living heart – Glen Canyon, now drowned beneath Lake Powell.

Isolation and security marked every aspect of life on 'the hill.' Scientists, their spouses, army members providing security, locals serving as domestic help and manual laborers lived together in a makeshift community. They were surrounded by guards and barbed wire and unknown even to nearby Santa Fe; the residents' postal address was simply 'Box 1663, Santa Fe.'

Not only was resident movement restricted and mail censored, there was no outside contact by radio or telephone. Perhaps even more unsettling, most employee-residents had no idea why they were living in Los Alamos. Knowledge was on a 'need to know' basis; everyone knew only as much as their job required.

In just under two years, Los Alamos scientists successfully detonated the first atomic bomb at New Mexico's Trinity site, now White Sands Missile Range.

2002	2004	2006	2010
Salt Lake City hosts the Winter Olympics and becomes the most populated place to ever hold the winter Games, as well as the first place women competed in bobsled racing.	Sin City is back! Las Vegas enters its second golden heyday, hosting 37.5 million visitors, starting work on its latest megaresort and becoming the number-one party destination.	Warren Jeffs, leader of the Fundamentalist Church of Jesus Christ of the Latter-Day Saints (FLDS) is charged with aggravated assaults of two underage girls. He is serving a life-plus-20-years sentence.	Arizona passes controversial legislation requiring police officers to request identification from anyone they suspect of being in the US illegally. Immigration-rights activists call for a boycott of the state.

After the US detonated two atomic bombs in Japan, the secret city of Los Alamos was exposed to the public and its residents finally understood why they were there. The city continued to be clothed in secrecy, however, until 1957 when restrictions on visiting were lifted. Today, the lab is still the town's backbone, and a tourist industry embraces the town's atomic history by selling T-shirts featuring exploding bombs and bottles of La Bomba wine.

Some of the original scientists disagreed with the use of the bomb in warfare and signed a petition against it – beginning the love/hate relationship with nuclear development still in evidence in the Southwest today. Controversies continue over the locations of nuclear power plants as well as the transportation and disposal of nuclear waste, notably at Yucca Mountain, 90 miles from Las Vegas.

Everett Ruess, a 20-year-old artist and vagabond, explored southern Utah and the Four Corners region in the early 1930s. He disappeared under mysterious circumstances outside of Escalante in November 1934. Read his evocative letters in the book *Everett Ruess: A Vagabond for Beauty*.

2011	2012	2014	2016
Jared Loughner is charged with shooting Arizona Congresswoman Gabrielle Giffords outside a Tucson grocery store. Giffords suffers a critical brain injury, six others are killed.	New Mexico and Arizona celebrate 100 years of statehood with special events and commemorative stamps. Arizona was the last territory in the Lower 48 to earn statehood.	On January 1, the legal sale of recreational marijuana begins in Colorado, followed by Nevada in 2017.	Before leaving office, President Barack Obama creates Bears Ears National Monument in Utah, although its status remained precarious with the incoming Republican administration.

The Way of Life

Rugged individuality is the cultural idiom of the Southwest. But the reality? It's a bit more complex. The major identities of the region, centered on a trio of tribes – Anglo, Hispanic and American Indian – are as vast and varied as the land that has shaped them. Whether their personal religion involves aliens, art, nuclear fission, slot machines, peyote or Joseph Smith, there's plenty of room for you in this beautiful, barely tamed chunk of America.

People of the Southwest

Early Settlers

Although the region's culture as a whole is united by the psychology, mythology and spirituality of its harsh, arid desert landscape, the people here are a sundry assortment of characters not so easily branded. The Southwest has long drawn stout-hearted pioneers pursuing slightly different agendas from those of the average American.

Mormons arrived in the mid-1800s seeking religious freedom. Cattle barons staked their claims with barbed wire and remote ranches, luring cowboys in the process. Old mining towns were founded by fierce individualists – prospectors, mining-company executives, gamblers, storekeepers and madams.

When the mining industry went bust in the 20th century, boomtowns became ghost towns for a while, before a new generation of idealistic entrepreneurs transformed them into New Age art enclaves and Old West tourist towns. Scientists flocked to the empty spaces to develop and test atomic bombs and soaring rockets.

Residents Today

More than 100,000 images documenting the history and people of the Colorado Plateau are viewable online as part of the Colorado Plateau Archives, a collection established by the Cline Library at Northern Arizona University (http://library.nau.edu/speccoll).

Today, these places attract folks similar to the original white pioneers – solitary, focused and self-reliant. Artists are drawn to the Southwest's clear light, cheap housing and wide, open spaces. Collectors, in turn, follow artists and gentrify towns such as Santa Fe and Taos in New Mexico, Prescott in Arizona and Durango in Colorado. Near Truth or Consequences, NM, global entrepreneur Richard Branson of Virgin Galactic is fine-tuning a commercial spacecraft that will launch paying customers into space from the scrubby desert.

Not all new arrivals are Type A personalities. Mainstream outcasts still come to the Southwest to 'turn on, tune in and drop out.' For years, these disparate individuals managed to get along with little strife. In recent years, however, state and local governments – and vocal citizens – have clashed with federal agencies and policies, most noticeably in Arizona and Nevada.

In Arizona, the state's efforts to stop illegal immigration have destroyed the kumbaya vibe and garnered national headlines. These efforts include Arizona's controversial SB 1070 – a law that requires police officers to ask for ID from anyone they suspect of being in the country illegally – and a simultaneous surge in federal border-patrol agents and checkpoints.

WHAT'S IN A NAME?

Though the stereotypes that too often accompany racial labels are largely ignored in the Southwest, it's still a challenge for publishers to figure out the most accurate (and politically correct) term for various ethnic groups. Here's the rundown on our terminology:

American Indian After introducing themselves to one very confused Christopher Columbus, the original Americans were labeled 'Indians.' The name stuck, and 500 years later, folks from Mumbai are still trying to explain that, no, they don't speak a word of Tewa. 'Native American' is also widely used, and the two terms are often considered interchangable. However, the best term to use is always each tribe's specific name, though this can also get complicated. The name 'Navajo,' for instance, was bestowed by the Spanish; in Athabascan, Navajo refer to themselves as Diné. What to do? Simply try your best, and if corrected, respect each person's preference.

Anglo Though 'Caucasian' is the preferred moniker (even if their ancestors hailed from nowhere near the Caucuses) and 'white' is the broadest and most useful word for European Americans, in this region the label for non-Iberian Europeans is 'Anglo' ('of England'). Even English speakers of Norwegian-Polish ancestry are Anglo around here, so get used to it.

Hispanic It's common (but sometimes considered offensive) to hyphenate: 'Mexican-American,' 'Venezuelan-American,' etc. Obviously, it's easier, if less precise, to use 'Latino' to describe people hailing from the Spanish-speaking Americas. Then add to that list 'Chicano,' 'Raza' and 'Hispano,' a de-anglicized term currently gaining popularity, and everyone's confused. But, because this region was part of Spain for 225 years and Mexico for only 25, and many folks can trace an unbroken ancestry back to Spain, 'Hispanic' ('of Spain') is the term used throughout this state, sprinkled with 'Spanish' and all the rest.

The anti-immigration rhetoric isn't common in day-to-day conversation, but heightened press coverage of the most vitriolic comments, coupled with the checkpoints and ever-present border patrol vehicles, do cast a pall over the otherwise sunny landscape.

Regional Identity

For the most part, other regions of the Southwest have retained the live-and-let-live philosophy, and residents of the Southwest are more easygoing than their counterparts on the East and West Coasts. They tend to be friendlier too. Even at glitzy restaurants in the biggest cities (with the exception of Las Vegas), you'll see more jeans and cowboy boots than haute couture.

Chat with a local at a low-key pub in Arizona, and they'll likely tell you they're from somewhere else. They moved out here for the scenery, unpolluted air and slower pace of life. Folks in this region consider themselves environmentally friendly. Living a healthy lifestyle is important, and many residents like to hike, mountain bike, ski and ride the rapids. They might have money, but you won't necessarily know it. It's sort of a faux pas to flaunt your wealth.

Las Vegas is a different story. But a place where you can go from Paris to Egypt in less than 10 minutes can't possibly play by the rules. This is a town that's hot and knows it. The blockbuster comedy *The Hangover* stoked its image as party central. The identity here is also a little different – there's an energy to Sin City not found elsewhere in the region. People from Vegas don't say they're from the Southwest, or even from Nevada. They say they're from Las Vegas, dammit.

If Vegas is all about flaunting one's youthful beauty, then Arizona may just be its polar opposite. In the last decade, Arizona has done a great job at competing with Florida for the retiree-paradise

In *Finders Keepers* (2010) journalist and naturalist Craig Childs examines the ethics of collecting prehistoric artifacts – whether for study or for sale – discovered in the Southwest.

award – the warm weather, dry air, abundant sunshine, and lots and lots of space draw more seniors each year. You'll see villages of RV parks surrounding Phoenix and Tucson, and early-bird specials are the plat du jour at many restaurants.

Arizona and New Mexico have large American Indian and Hispanic populations, and these residents take pride in maintaining their cultural identities through preserved traditions and oral-history lessons.

Lifestyle

In a region of such diversity and size, it's impossible to describe the 'typical' Southwestern home or family. What lifestyle commonalities, after all, can be seen in the New Age mystics of Sedona, the businesspeople, lounge singers and casino workers of Las Vegas and the Mormon faithful of Salt Lake City? Part of touring the Southwest is comparing and contrasting all these different identities.

POLYGAMY & THE MORMON CHURCH

Throughout its history, Utah has been a predominately Mormon state; more than 60% of the current population has church affiliation. But as late church president Gordon Hinckley was fond of saying, the Church of Jesus Christ of Latter-Day Saints (or LDS, as the modern Mormon faith is known) has nothing to do with those practicing polygamy today.

Members of the LDS believe the Bible is the Word of God and that the *Book of Mormon* is 'another testament of Jesus Christ,' as revealed to LDS church founder Joseph Smith. It was in the 1820s that the angel Moroni is said to have led Smith to the golden plates containing the story of a family's exodus from Jerusalem in 600 BC, and their subsequent lives, prophesies, trials, wars and visitations by Jesus Christ in the new world (Central America). Throughout his life he is said to have received revelations from God, including the 1843 visitation that revealed the righteous path of plural marriage to the prophet. Polygamy was formally established as church doctrine in 1852 by the second president, Brigham Young.

For all the impact plural marriage has had, it seems odd that the practice was officially endorsed for less than 40 years. By the 1880s US federal laws had made polygamy a crime. With the threatened seizure of church assets looming, president Wilford Woodruff received spiritual guidance and abdicated polygamy in 1890.

Today the church has more than 15 million members and a missionary outreach that spans the globe. But what happened to polygamy? Well, fundamentalist sects broke off to form their own churches almost immediately; they continue to practice today. The official Mormon church disavows any relationship to these fundamentalists, and shows every evidence of being embarrassed by the past.

The number of people estimated to be still practicing or recognizing polygamy are about 38,000, mostly in Utah and surrounding areas. Some you'd never recognize; they're just large families. Others belong to isolated, cultlike groups such as the FLDS in Hildale-Colorado City on the Utah-Arizona border, which have distinct styles of dress and hair. Some of these sects have become notorious for crimes committed by some of their members.

Though polygamy itself is illegal, prosecution is rare. Without a confession or videotaped evidence, the case is hard to prove. Men typically marry only their first wife legally (subsequent wives are considered single mothers by the state, and are therefore entitled to more welfare). The larger Utah populace is deeply ambivalent about polygamy. Tens – maybe hundreds – of thousands of them wouldn't exist but for the historic practice, including me. My great-great-great grandmother, Lucy Bigelow, was a wife of Brigham Young.

Utah's heavily Mormon population stresses traditional family values; drinking, smoking and premarital sex are frowned upon. You won't see much fast fashion or hear much cursing here.

Family and religion are also core values for American Indian and Hispanic people throughout the region. For the Hopi, tribal dances are such sacred events they are mostly closed to outsiders. And although many American Indian and Hispanic people are now living and working in urban areas, large family gatherings and traditional customs are still important facets of daily life.

Because of its favorable weather and boundless possibilities for outdoor adventures, much of the Southwest is popular with transplants from the East and West coasts. In cities such as Santa Fe, Telluride, Las Vegas, Tucson and Flagstaff, you'll find a blend of students, artists, wealthy retirees, celebrity wannabes and adventure junkies.

In urban centers throughout the region (with the exception of Utah) many people consider themselves 'spiritual' rather than religious, and forgo church for Sunday brunch. Women work the same hours as men, and many children attend daycare.

With the exception of Mormon Utah, attitudes toward gays and lesbians in the Southwest are generally open, especially in major cities such as Las Vegas, Santa Fe and Phoenix.

Sports

Professional sports teams are based in Phoenix and Salt Lake City. The Arizona Diamondbacks of Phoenix play major league baseball from April through September; the only Southwestern major-league football team, the Arizona Cardinals, play from September through December.

Basketball is more competitive; you can watch hoops with Salt Lake City's Utah Jazz or the Phoenix Suns, both men's teams that play November through April. The women's pro basketball team, Phoenix Mercury, plays June through August.

Because pro tickets are hard to get, you'll have a better shot with college sports. Albuquerque teams across the board are quite popular. The University of Arizona Wildcats consistently place among the best basketball teams in the nation.

Several major-league baseball teams (such as the Chicago White Sox) migrate from the cold, wintry north from late February through March for training seasons in warmer Arizona. They play in what is aptly referred to as the Cactus League.

The Phoenix Suns protested Arizona's new immigration law in 2010 by changing the team's name on their jerseys to 'Los Suns' (that's Spanglish) for one game.

American Indian Southwest

Jeff Campbell

The Southwest is sometimes called 'Indian Country,' but this nickname fails to capture the diversity throughout this region. From the Apache to the Zuni, each tribe maintains distinctions of law, language, religion, history and custom. Members within a tribe are linked by common heritage, but follow broadly diverse paths as they navigate the legacy of their ancestors and outside cultures. These differences turn the Southwest's seemingly borderless, painted desert into a kaleidoscopic league of nations.

The People

The cultural traditions and fundamental belief systems of the Southwest's tribes reflect their age-old relationship to the land, the water, the sky and the creatures that inhabit those elements. This relationship is reflected in their crafts, their dances and their architecture.

Culturally, tribes grapple with dilemmas about how to prosper in contemporary America while protecting their traditions from erosion and their lands from further exploitation, and how to lift their people from poverty while maintaining their sense of identity and the sacred.

The People by Stephen Trimble, published in 1993, is as comprehensive and intimate a portrait of Southwest native peoples as you'd hope to find, bursting with American Indian voices and beautiful photos.

Apache

The Southwest has four major Apache reservations: New Mexico's Jicarilla Apache reservation and Mescalero Apache reservation, and Arizona's San Carlos Apache reservation and Fort Apache reservation, home to the White Mountain Apache Tribe.

Apache tribes descend from Athabascans who migrated from Canada around 1400. These nomadic hunter-gatherers became warlike raiders, particularly of Pueblo tribes and European settlements, and fiercely resisted their relocation to reservations.

The most famous Apache is Geronimo, a Chiricahua Apache who resisted the American takeover of Indian lands until he was finally subdued by the US Army aided by White Mountain Apache scouts.

Havasupai

N Scott Momaday's Pulitzer Prize–winning *House Made of Dawn* (1968), about a Pueblo youth, launched a wave of American Indian literature.

The Havasupai reservation abuts Arizona's Grand Canyon National Park beneath the Canyon's south rim. The tribe's one village, Supai, is reached by an 8-mile hike or a mule or helicopter ride from road's end at Hualapai Hilltop.

Havasupai (hah-vah-*soo*-pie) means 'people of the blue-green water,' and tribal life has always been dominated by the Havasu Creek tributary of the Colorado River. Reliable water meant the ability to irrigate fields, which led to a season-based village lifestyle.

The deep Havasu Canyon also protected them from others; this extremely peaceful people basically avoided Western contact until the 1800s. Today, the tribe relies on tourism, and Havasu Canyon's

Native American Pueblos & Reservations

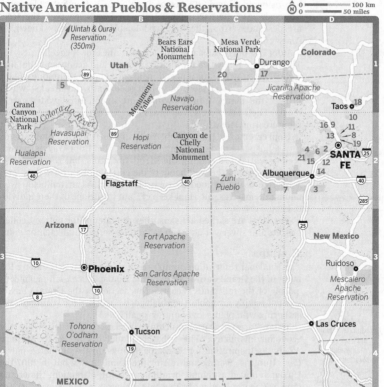

Native American Pueblos & Reservations

◉ Sights

1 Acoma Pueblo	C2
2 Cochiti Pueblo	D2
3 Isleta Pueblo	D2
4 Jemez Pueblo	D2
5 Kaibab-Paiute Reservation	A1
6 Kewa (Santo Domingo) Pueblo	D2
7 Laguna Pueblo	D2
8 Nambé Pueblo	D2
9 Ohkay Owingeh (San Juan) Pueblo	D2
10 Picuris Pueblo	D2
11 Pojoaque Pueblo	D2
12 San Felipe Pueblo	D2
13 San Ildefonso Pueblo	D2
14 Sandia Pueblo	D2
15 Santa Ana Pueblo	D2
16 Santa Clara Pueblo	D2
17 Southern Ute Reservation	C1
18 Taos Pueblo	D1
19 Tesuque Pueblo	D2
20 Ute Mountain Reservation	C1
21 Zia Pueblo	D2

gorgeous waterfalls draw a steady stream of visitors. The tribe is related to the Hualapai.

Hopi

The Hopi reservation occupies more than 1.5 million acres in the middle of the Navajo reservation. Most Hopi live in 12 villages at the base and on top of three mesas jutting from the main Black Mesa. The village of Moenkopi is to the west. Old Oraibi, on Third Mesa, is considered (along with Acoma Pueblo) the continent's oldest continuously inhabited settlement. Like all Pueblo peoples, the Hopi are descended from the Ancestral Puebloans (formerly known as Anasazi).

Hopi (*ho*-pee) translates as 'peaceful ones' or 'peaceful person.' The Hopi are renowned for their traditional and deeply spiritual lifestyle. They practice an unusual, near-miraculous technique of 'dry farming'; they don't plow, but plant seeds in 'wind breaks', which protect the plants from blowing sand, and natural water catchments. Their main crop has always been corn, a resource central to their creation story.

Hopi ceremonial life is complex and intensely private, and extends into all aspects of daily living. Following the 'Hopi Way' is considered essential to bringing the life-giving rains, but the Hopi also believe it fosters the well-being of the entire human race. Each person's role is determined by their clan, which is matrilineal. Even among themselves, the Hopi keep certain traditions of their individual clans private.

The Hopi are skilled artisans; they are famous for pottery, coiled baskets and silverwork, as well as for their ceremonial kachina dolls.

Hualapai

The Hualapai reservation occupies around a million acres along 108 miles of the Grand Canyon's south rim. Hualapai (*wah*-lah-pie) means 'people of the tall pines'; because this section of the Grand Canyon was not readily farmable, the Hualapai were originally seminomadic, gathering wild plants and hunting small game.

Today, forestry, cattle ranching, farming and tourism are the economic mainstays. The tribal headquarters in Peach Springs, AZ, is the inspiration for 'Radiator Springs' in the animated movie *Cars*. Hunting, fishing and rafting are prime draws, but in 2007 the Hualapai added a unique, headline-grabbing attraction: the Grand Canyon's Skywalk glass bridge that juts over a side canyon 4000ft (1220m) below your feet.

Navajo

The Navajo reservation, more formally known as the Navajo Nation, is by far the largest and most populous in the US, covering more than 17 million acres (more than 27,000 sq miles) in Arizona and parts of New Mexico and Utah. Using a Tewa word, the Spanish dubbed them 'Navajos' to distinguish them from their kin the Apache, but Navajo (*nah*-vuh-ho) call themselves the Diné (dee-*nay;* 'the people') and their land Dinétah.

Nationwide, there are about 300,000 Navajo, making it the USA's second-largest tribe (after the Cherokee). The Navajo's Athabascan tongue is the most spoken American Indian language, with 170,000 speakers, despite its notorious complexity. In the Pacific Theater during WWII, Navajo 'code talkers' sent and received military messages in Navajo; Japan never broke the code, and the code talkers were considered essential to US victory.

Like the Apache, the Navajo were feared nomads and warriors who both traded with and raided the Pueblos, and who fought settlers and the US military. They also borrowed generously from other traditions: they acquired sheep and horses from the Spanish, learned pottery and weaving from the Pueblos and picked up silversmithing from Mexico. Today, the Navajo are renowned for their woven rugs, pottery and inlaid silver jewelry. Their intricate sandpainting is used in healing ceremonies.

For decades, traditional Navajo and Hopi have successfully thwarted US industry efforts to strip-mine sacred Big Mountain, but the fight continues. Black Mesa Indigenous Support (https://supportblackmesa.org) tells their story.

HOPI KACHINAS

In the Hopi religion, maintaining balance and harmony between the spirit world and our 'fourth world' is crucial, and the spirit messengers called kachinas (also spelled katsinas) play a central role. These supernatural beings are spirits of deities, animals and even deceased clan members, and they can bring rain, influence the weather, help in daily tasks and punish violators of tribal laws. They are said to live atop Southwest mountains; on the winter solstice they travel to the Hopi Pueblos, where they reside until the summer solstice.

In a series of kachina ceremonies and festivals, masked dancers impersonate the kachinas; during these rituals, it is believed the dancers are inhabited by and become the kachinas. There are hundreds of kachina spirits: some are kindly, some fearsome and dangerous, and the elaborate, fantastical costumes dancers wear evoke the mystery and religious awe of these beings. In the 1990s, to keep these sacred ceremonies from becoming trivialized as tourist spectacles, the Hopi closed most to the public.

Kachina dolls (*tithu* in Hopi) are brightly painted, carved wooden figures traditionally given to young Hopi girls during certain kachina festivals. The religious icons become treasured family heirlooms. The Hopi now carve some as art meant for the general public.

The reservation has significant mineral reserves – Black Mesa, for instance, contains the USA's largest coal deposit, perhaps 21 billion tons – and modern-day mining of coal, oil, gas and uranium has been an important, and controversial, economic resource. Mining has depleted the region's aquifer, contaminated water supplies (leading, some claim, to high cancer rates), and affected sacred places.

Tribal headquarters are in Window Rock, AZ. The reservation's numerous cultural and natural attractions include Monument Valley, Canyon de Chelly National Monument, Navajo National Monument and Antelope Canyon.

Pueblo

There are 19 Pueblo reservations in New Mexico. Four of them lead west from Albuquerque – Isleta, Laguna, Acoma and Zuni – and 15 Pueblos fill the Rio Grande Valley between Albuquerque and Taos: Sandia, San Felipe, Santa Ana, Zia, Jemez, Kewa (or Santo Domingo), Cochiti, San Ildefonso, Pojoaque, Nambé, Tesuque, Santa Clara, Ohkay Owingeh (or San Juan), Picuris and Taos. For information about each of the pueblos, see www.indianpueblo.org.

These tribes are as different as they are alike. Nevertheless, the word 'pueblo' (Spanish for 'village') is a convenient shorthand. All are believed to be descended from the Ancestral Puebloans and to have inherited their architectural style and their agrarian, village-based life – often atop mesas.

Pueblos are unique among Native Americans. These adobe structures can have up to five levels, connected by ladders, and are built with varying combinations of mud bricks, stones, logs and plaster. In the central plaza of each pueblo is a kiva, an underground ceremonial chamber that connects to the spirit world.

With a legacy of missionary activity, pueblos tend to have Catholic churches, and many Pueblo Indians now hold both Christian and native religious beliefs. This unmerged, unconflicted duality is a hallmark of much of Puebloan modern life.

Paiute

The Kaibab-Paiute reservation is on the Arizona-Utah border. The Kaibab (*cay*-bob) are a band of Southern Paiute (*pie*-oot) renowned

The Indian Arts and Crafts Board (www.doi.gov/iacb) publishes a directory of American Indian–owned businesses, listed by state, and also punishes deceptive merchants.

LEGAL STATUS

Although Arizona's major tribes are 'sovereign nations' and have significant powers to run their reservations as they like, their authority – and its limitations – is granted by Congress. While they can make many of their own laws, plenty of federal laws apply on reservations, too. The tribes don't legally own their reservations – it's public land held in trust by the federal government, which has a responsibility to administer it in a way that's beneficial for the tribes. Enter the Bureau of Indian Affairs.

While Native Americans living on reservations have officially been American citizens since 1924, can vote in state and national elections, and serve heroically in the armed forces, they are not covered by the Bill of Rights. Instead, there's the Indian Civil Rights Act of 1968, which does grant reservation dwellers many of the same protections found in the Constitution, but not all. This is not an entirely bad thing. In some ways, it allows tribal governments to do things that federal and state government can't, which helps them create a system more attuned to their culture.

for basketmaking who migrated to the Colorado Plateau around 1100. These peaceful hunter-gatherers moved frequently across the arid, remote region for seasonal agricultural needs and animal migrations.

The tribe's lifestyle changed drastically in the 1850s when Mormons began settling the region, taking over the land for their farms and livestock. The Kaibab-Paiute reservation, located on the Arizona Strip west of Fredonia, is next to a vitally important regional spring, one that was also important to the Mormons. Today, near the spring, their reservation includes a public campground and Pipe Spring National Monument. Here the Kaibab-Paiute worked with the National Park Service to create rich displays about American Indian life.

Bears Ears Inter-Tribal Coalition (http://bearsearscoalition.org) is a historic consortium of five sovereign tribal nations united to conserve the cultural patrimony of Bears National Monument in Utah, created in December, 2016.

Ute

Along with the Navajo and Apache tribes, Utes helped drive the Ancestral Puebloans from the region in the 1200s. By the time of European contact, seven Ute tribes occupied most of present-day Colorado and Utah (named for the Utes). In the 16th century, Utes eagerly adopted the horse and became nomadic buffalo hunters and livestock raiders.

There are three main Ute reservations. With more than 4.5 million acres, the Uintah and Ouray reservation in northeastern Utah is the second largest in the US. Ranching and oil and gas mining are the tribe's main industries. The Ute Mountain Utes (who call themselves the Weeminuche) lead half-day and full-day tours to petroglyph sites and cliff dwellings in Ute Mountain Tribal Park; their reservation abuts Mesa Verde National Park in southwestern Colorado. The Southern Ute Reservation relies in part on a casino for income.

Tohono O'odham

The Tohono O'odham reservation is the largest of four reservations that make up the Tohono O'odham Nation in the Sonoran Desert in southern Arizona. Tohono O'odham (to-ho-no oh-oh-dum) means 'desert people.' The tribe was originally seminomadic, moving between the desert and the mountains seasonally. They were famous for their calendar sticks, which were carved to mark important dates and events, and they remain well known for their baskets and pottery. Today, the tribe runs three casinos and the Mission San Xavier del Bac in southern Arizona.

The Arts

American Indian art nearly always contains ceremonial purpose and religious significance; the patterns and symbols are woven with spiritual meaning that provides an intimate window into the heart of Southwest people. By purchasing arts from American Indian people, visitors have a direct, positive impact on tribal economies, which depend in part on tourist dollars. The **Indian Arts and Crafts Board** (www.doi.gov/iacb) promotes economic development in American Indian groups via the expansion of the arts and crafts market.

Pottery & Basketry

Pretty much every Southwest tribe has pottery and/or basketry traditions. Originally, each tribe and even individual families maintained distinct styles, but modern potters and basketmakers readily mix, borrow and reinterpret classic designs and methods.

Pueblo pottery is perhaps most acclaimed of all. Typically, local clay determines the color, so that Zia pottery is red, Acoma white, Hopi yellow, Cochiti black and so on. Santa Clara is famous for its carved relief designs, and San Ildefonso for its black-on-black style, which was revived by world-famous potter Maria Martinez. The Navajo and Ute Mountain Utes also produce well-regarded pottery.

Pottery is nearly synonymous with village life, while more portable baskets were often preferred by nomadic peoples. Among the tribes who stand out for their exquisite basketry are the Jicarilla Apache (whose name means basketmaker), the Kaibab-Paiute, the Hualapai and the Tohono O'odham. Hopi coiled baskets, with their vivid patterns and kachina iconography, are also notable.

Navajo Weaving

According to Navajo legend, Spider Woman taught humans how to weave, and she seems embodied today in the iconic sight of Navajo women patiently shuttling handspun wool on weblike looms, creating the Navajo's legendary rugs (originally blankets), so tight they held water. Preparation of the wool and sometimes the dyes is still done by hand, and finishing a rug takes months (occasionally years).

Authentic Navajo rugs are expensive, and justifiably so, ranging from hundreds to thousands of dollars. They are not average souvenirs but artworks that will last a lifetime, whether displayed on the wall or the floor. Take time to research, even a little, so you recognize when quality matches price.

Silver & Turquoise Jewelry

Jewelry using stones and shells has always been a native tradition; silverwork did not arrive until the 1800s, along with Anglo and Mexican contact. In particular, Navajo, Hopi and Zuni became renowned for combining these materials with inlaid-turquoise silver jewelry. In addition to turquoise, jewelry often features lapis, onyx, coral, carnelian and shells.

Authentic jewelry is often stamped or marked by the artisan, and items may come with an Indian Arts and Crafts Board certificate; always ask. Price may also be an indicator: a high tab doesn't guarantee authenticity, but an absurdly low one probably signals trickery. A crash course can be had at the August Santa Fe Indian Market.

The Hopi Arts Trail (www.hopiartstrail.com) spotlights artists and galleries on the Hopi reservation. The website has descriptions of participating galleries, with directions, phone numbers and the type of art sold.

To learn about Navajo rugs, visit www.gonavajo.com. To see traditional weaving demonstrations, visit the Hubbell Trading Post in Ganado, AZ.

Etiquette

When visiting a reservation, ask about and follow any specific rules. Almost all tribes ban alcohol, and some ban pets and restrict cameras. All require permits for camping, fishing and other activities. Tribal rules may be posted at the reservation entrance, or visit the tribal office or the reservation's website.

The other thing is attitude and manner. When you visit a reservation, you are visiting a unique culture with perhaps unfamiliar customs. Be courteous, respectful and open-minded, and don't expect locals to share every detail of their lives.

Ask first, document later Some tribes restrict cameras and sketching entirely; others may charge a fee, or restrict them at ceremonies or in certain areas. If you want to photograph a person or their property, ask permission; a tip may or may not be expected.

Pueblos are not museums At Pueblos, the incredible adobe structures are homes. Public buildings will be signed; if a building isn't signed, assume it's private. Don't climb around. Kivas are nearly always off-limits.

Ceremonies are not performances Treat ceremonies like church services: watch silently and respectfully, without talking, clapping or taking pictures, and wear modest clothing. Powwows are more informal, but remember: unless they're billed as theater, ceremonies and dances are for the tribe, not you.

Privacy and communication Many American Indians are happy to describe their tribe's general religious beliefs, but this is not always the case, and details about rituals and ceremonies are often considered private. Always ask before discussing religion and respect each person's boundaries. Also, American Indian people consider it polite to listen without comment; silent listening, given and received, is another sign of respect.

To donate to a cause, consider Black Mesa Weavers for Life and Land (www.blackmesaweavers.org), which helps traditional Diné sheep raisers and artisans in Navajoland market handmade weavings, yarn, and crafts.

Southwest Cuisine

Whoever advised 'moderation in all things' has clearly never enjoyed a Sonoran dog in Tucson. Same goes for a messy plate of *huevo rancheros* at a small-town Arizona diner. Or a loaded green-chile cheeseburger in New Mexico. Food in the Southwest is a tricultural celebration not suited for the gastronomically timid, or anyone on a diet. One or two dainty bites? Not likely. But admit it, isn't food part of the reason you're here?

Cultural Influences

Three ethnic groups – American Indian, Hispanic and cattle-country Anglo – influence Southwestern food culture. Traditional American Indian crops are the foundation of Southwestern cuisine, providing the main ingredients: corn, beans, squash, and, of course, chiles. Spain and Mexico controlled territories from Texas to California well into the 19th century, and after the United States took over, most inhabitants – and their cooking styles – simply stayed put. The American miners, cowboys and pioneers who subsequently streamed into the new territories also contributed to the Southwest style of cooking. Much of the Southwest is cattle country, and whether you are in Phoenix, Silver City or Las Vegas you can expect a good steak.

Staples & Specialities

Huevos rancheros is the quintessential Southwestern breakfast; eggs prepared to order are served on top of two fried corn tortillas, loaded with beans and potatoes, sprinkled with cheese and served swimming in chile. Breakfast burritos are built by stuffing a flour tortilla with eggs, bacon or chorizo, cheese, chile and sometimes beans.

A Southwestern lunch or dinner will often start with a big bowl of corn chips and salsa. Almost everything comes with beans, rice and your choice of warm flour or corn tortillas, topped with chile, cheese and sometimes sour cream. Blue-corn tortillas are one colorful New Mexican contribution to the art of cooking. Guacamole is also a staple, and better restaurants will mix the avocado, lime, cilantro (coriander), tomato and onion creation right at your table.

You can't visit New Mexico without ordering a Frito pie – a messy concoction of corn chips, beef chile, cheese and sour cream. You can find it in some diners and it's always served at city festivals.

Mexican & New Mexican Food

In Arizona, Mexican fare is of the Sonoran type, with specialties such as *carne seca* (dried beef). Meals are usually served with refried beans, rice, and flour or corn tortillas; chiles are relatively mild. Tucsonans refer to their city as the 'Mexican food capital of the universe,' a claim which, unsurprisingly, is hotly contested by a few other places. Colorado restaurants serve Mexican food, but they don't insist on any accolades for it.

New Mexico's food is different from, but reminiscent of, Mexican food, and a reflection of the region's hardscrabble rural roots. Pinto beans are served whole instead of refried; posole (a corn stew) may replace rice. Chiles aren't used so much as a condiment (like salsa) but more as an essential ingredient in almost every dish. *Carne adovada* (marinated pork chunks) is a specialty. *Calabacitas* is another staple dish in New Mexico, and probably the best way to get your daily vegetable intake. It consists of sautéed squash (or zucchini), corn and green chile, and is often topped with cheese. Like a bowl of green or red chile, every cook will have their own version of this popular classic.

If a restaurant references red or green chile or chile sauces on the menu, it probably serves New Mexican–style dishes. Expect the chile to smother everything – even burritos. The town of Hatch in particular is known for its chiles.

Mexican food is often hot and spicy, but it doesn't have to be. If you don't like spicy food, go easy on the salsa.

American Indian Food

Modern American Indian cuisine bears little resemblance to that eaten before the Spanish conquest, but it is distinct from Southwestern cuisine. Navajo and Indian tacos – fried bread usually topped with beans, meat, tomatoes, chile and lettuce – are readily available. Chewy *horno* bread is baked in the beehive-shaped outdoor adobe ovens *(hornos)* using remnant heat from a fire built inside the oven, then cleared out before cooking.

Most other American Indian cooking is game-based and usually involves squash and locally harvested ingredients such as berries and piñon nuts. Though becoming better known, it can be difficult to find, especially outside of New Mexico and Arizona. Your best bets are festival food stands, powwows, rodeos, Pueblo feast days, casino restaurants or people's homes at the different Pueblos.

For American Indian fare, try Albuquerque's Indian Pueblo Cultural Center (p240), Tiwa Kitchen (p298) near Taos Pueblo, the restaurant at the View Hotel (p192) in Monument Valley, the Hopi Cultural Center Restaurant (p196) on the Hopi Reservation and Kai (p128) at Wild Horse Pass Resort in Chandler, AZ.

Steak & Potatoes

Home, home on the range, where the ranches and the steakhouses reign. Have a hankerin' for a juicy slab of beef with a salad, baked potato and beans? Look no further than the Southwest, where there's a steakhouse for every type of traveler. The steak-and-potato fixation filters down to more humble eateries as wel – burgers and fries are ubiquitous in all states. In Utah, the large Mormon population influences culinary options – good, old-fashioned American food such as chicken, steak, potatoes, vegetables, homemade pies and ice cream prevail.

Fruit & Vegetables

Beyond the chile pepper, Southwestern food is characterized by its use of posole, *sopaipillas* (deep-fried puff pastry) and blue corn. Posole, Spanish for hominy, is dried or frozen kernels of corn processed in a lime solution to remove the hulls. It can be served plain as a side dish, but is best as a spicy stew. Blue-corn tortillas have a heartier flavor than the more common yellow-corn tortillas. Pinto beans, served either whole or refried, are a basic element of most New Mexican dishes.

Beans, long the staple protein of New Mexicans, come in many colors, shapes and preparations. They are usually stewed with onions, chiles and spices and served somewhat intact or refried to a creamy consistency. Avocados are a delightful staple, made into

Eat Your Words

carne seca – beef that is sun-dried before cooking

fry bread – deep-fried, doughy American Indian bread

sopaipilla – deep-fried puff pastry with honey

calabacitas – squash, corn and chile side dish

mole – spicy chocolate-flavored chile sauce

zesty guacamole. 'Guac' recipes are as closely guarded and vaunted by cooks as their bean recipes.

Modern Cuisine

An eclectic mix of Mexican and Continental (especially French) traditions began to flourish in the late 1970s and continues to grow. Try innovative combinations such as chiles stuffed with lobster or barbecued duck tacos. Generally speaking, cities such as Phoenix, Tucson, Santa Fe and Albuquerque have the most contemporary Southwestern restaurants.

And while Vegas is not known for its Southwestern flavors, it is indisputably the culinary capital of the region. Celebrity chefs are in every resort, and whatever indulgence you're up for – chocolate fountains, caviar by the pool, fusion sushi – you can bet it's here.

Beer, Wine & Margaritas

Craft Beer & Microbreweries

Microbrewery and craft-beer production has skyrocketed in the US. There are some 4200 microbreweries and brewpubs across the country and craft-beer sales accounted for 12.8% of the domestic market in 2015. The term microbrew is used broadly these days, and tends to include beer produced by large, well-established brands such as Sam Adams and Sierra Nevada. According to the Brewers Association, however, a true craft brewery must produce no more than six million barrels annually. It must also be independently owned and made with traditional ingredients.

These smaller craft breweries are popping up everywhere across the Southwest, from small towns to urban centers. They are a popular gathering spot for an after-work drink, and often a good meal. New breweries are always opening in Flagstaff, AZ, and you can find them easily by following the Flagstaff-Grand Canyon Ale Trail (www.flagstaffaletrail.com). Durango, CO, is another regional hub for microbreweries, such as Ska Brewery.

Popular regional beers are often sold in local grocery and liquor stores. Note that many microbrews are considered 'big beers' – meaning they have a high alcohol content.

Order chile powder and dried pods and check out authentic New Mexican recipes at http://diazfarms.com.

Wine & Wineries

There are three things a good wine grape needs: lousy soil, lots of sunshine and dedicated caretakers, all of which can be found in New Mexico and Arizona. For a full rundown of New Mexico's 40-plus producers, visit the New Mexico Wine Growers Association (www.nmwine.com). Gruet Winery, which specializes in sparkling wines, has a lovely tasting room in Santa Fe.

In Arizona, the best-known wine region is in the southern part of the state near Patagonia. The Verde Valley between Phoenix and Flagstaff is close on Patagonia's heels in terms of quality and publicity. The Arizona Wine Growers Association (http://arizonawine.org) lists the state's wine producers.

Margaritas

Margaritas are the alcoholic drink of choice and synonymous with the Southwest, especially in heavily Hispanic New Mexico and Arizona. Margaritas vary in taste depending on the quality of the ingredients used, but all are made from tequila, a citrus liquor (Grand Marnier, Triple Sec or Cointreau) and either freshly squeezed lime or premixed Sweet & Sour.

Our perfect margarita includes freshly squeezed lime (say no to the ultrasugary and high-carb packaged mix), a high-end tequila (skip the gold and go straight to silver or pure agave – we like Patron or Herrendura Silver) and Grand Marnier liquor (better than sickly sweet Triple Sec). Ask the bartender to add a splash of orange juice if your drink is too bitter or strong.

Margaritas are either served frozen, on the rocks (over ice) or straight up. Most people order them with salt. Traditional margaritas are lime flavored, but these days the popular drink comes in a rainbow of flavors – best ordered frozen. Prickly-pear margaritas, made with syrup from prickly-pear cacti, are typically bright pink and easily found in Arizona.

Coffee Shops

For something nonalcoholic, you'll find delicious espresso shops in the bigger cities and sophisticated small towns; however, in rural Arizona or Nevada you're likely to get nothing better than stale, weak diner coffee. Santa Fe, Phoenix, Durango, Truth or Consequences, Flagstaff and Tucson all have excellent coffee shops with comfortable couches for reading or studying. Basically, if the Southwestern town has a college, it will have a good coffee shop.

Vegetarians & Vegans

Most metro-area eateries offer at least one veggie dish, although few are devoted solely to meatless menus. These days, fortunately, almost every larger town has a natural-food grocer. You may go wanting in smaller hinterland towns, however, where beef still rules. In that case, your best bet is to assemble a picnic from the local grocery store.

'Veggie-heads' will be happiest in New Mexico and Arizona, where they go nuts (or more specifically, go piñon). Thanks to the area's long-standing appeal to hippie types, vegetarians and vegans will have no problem finding something delicious on most menus, even at drive-throughs and tiny dives. One potential pitfall? Traditional Southwestern cuisine uses lard in beans, tamales, *sopaipillas* (deep-fried puff pastry) and flour (but not corn) tortillas, among other things. Be sure to ask – often, even the most authentic places have a pot of pintos simmering for vegetarians.

Best Vegetarian Eateries

Green (Phoenix, AZ)

Lovin' Spoonfuls (Tucson, AZ)

Macy's (Flagstaff, AZ)

Annapurna's World Vegetarian Cafe (Albuquerque, NM)

Veggie Delight (Las Vegas, NV)

Sage's Cafe (Salt Lake City, UT)

Geology & the Land

David Lukas

From blistering deserts to snowcapped mountains and every climate zone in between, the Southwest's ecological diversity astounds. The drive into the Santa Catalina Mountains outside Tucson joins searing desert to snow-blanketed fir forests within 30 miles. It's the ecological equivalent of going from southern Arizona to Canada. These contrasts, often in close proximity, make the Southwest a fascinating place to explore. Geologic diversity is also highly photogenic: think redrock buttes, delicate arches, twisted hoodoos and crumbling spires.

The Land

Geologic History

It may be hard to imagine now, but the Southwest was once inundated by a succession of seas. There is geological evidence today of deep bays, shallow mud flats and coastal dunes. During this time North America was a young continent on the move, evolving slowly and migrating northward from the southern hemisphere over millions of years.

Extremely ancient rocks (among the oldest on the planet) exposed in the deep heart of the Grand Canyon show that the region was under water two billion years ago, and younger layers of rocks in southern Utah reveal that this region was continuously or periodically under water until about 60 million years ago.

At the end of the Paleozoic era (about 245 million years ago), a collision of continents into a massive landmass known as Pangaea deformed the Earth's crust and produced pressures that uplifted an ancestral Rocky Mountains. Though this early mountain range lay to the east, it formed rivers and sediment deposits that began to shape the Southwest. In fact, erosion leveled the range by 240 million years ago, with much of the sediment draining westward into what we now call Utah. Around the same time, a shallow tropical sea teeming with life, including a barrier reef that would later be sculpted into Carlsbad Caverns, covered much of southern New Mexico.

For long periods of time (between episodes of being underwater), much of the Southwest may have looked like northern Egypt today: floodplains and deltas surrounded by expanses of desert. A rising chain of island mountains to the west apparently blocked the supply of wet storms, creating a desert and sand dunes that piled up thousands of feet high. Now preserved as sandstone, these dunes can be seen today in the famous Navajo sandstone cliffs of Zion National Park.

Mountains & Basins

This sequence of oceans and sand ended around 60 million years ago as North America underwent a dramatic separation from Europe, sliding westward over a piece of the Earth's crust known as the East

Pacific plate and leaving behind an ever-widening gulf that became the Atlantic Ocean. This East Pacific plate collided with, and pushed down, the North American plate.

This collision, named the Laramide orogeny, resulted in the birth of the modern Rocky Mountains and uplifted an old basin into a highland known today as the Colorado Plateau. Fragments of the East Pacific plate also attached themselves to the leading edge of the North American plate, transforming the Southwest from a coastal area to an interior region increasingly detached from the ocean.

In contrast to the compression and collision that characterized earlier events, the Earth's crust began stretching in an east–west direction about 30 million years ago. The thinner, stretched crust of New Mexico and Texas cracked along zones of weakness called faults, resulting in a rift valley where New Mexico's Rio Grande now flows. These same forces created the stepped plateaus of northern Arizona and southern Utah.

Increased pulling in the Earth's crust between 15 and eight million years ago created a much larger region of north–south cracks in western Utah, Arizona and Nevada known as the Basin and Range province. Here, parallel cracks formed hundreds of miles of valleys and mountain ranges that fill the entire region between the Sierra Nevada and the Rocky Mountains.

During the Pleistocene glacial period, large bodies of water accumulated throughout the Southwest. Utah's Great Salt Lake is the most famous remnant of these mighty Ice Age lakes. Basins with now completely dry, salt-crusted lakebeds are especially conspicuous on a drive across Nevada.

For the past several million years the dominant force in the Southwest has probably been erosion. Not only do torrential rainstorms readily tear through soft sedimentary rocks, but the rise of the Rocky Mountains also generates large powerful rivers that wind throughout the Southwest, carving mighty canyons in their wake. Nearly all the contemporary features in the Southwest, from arches to hoodoos, are the result of weathering and erosion.

For an insight into how indigenous peoples used this landscape, read *Wild Plants and Native Peoples of the Four Corners*, by William Dunmire and Gail Tierney, published in 1997.

Geographic Makeup

The Colorado Plateau is an impressive and nearly impenetrable 130,000-sq-mile tableland lurking in the corner where Colorado, Utah, Arizona and New Mexico join. Formed in an ancient basin as a remarkably coherent body of neatly layered sedimentary rocks, the plateau has remained relatively unchanged even as the lands around it were compressed, stretched and deformed by powerful forces.

The most powerful indicators of the plateau's long-term stability are the distinct and unique layers of sedimentary rock stacked on top of each other, with the oldest dating back two billion years. In fact, the science of stratigraphy – the reading of Earth history through its rock layers – stemmed from work at the Grand Canyon, where an astonishing set of layers has been laid bare by the Colorado River cutting across them. Throughout the Southwest, and on the Colorado Plateau in particular, layers of sedimentary rock detail a rich history of ancient oceans, coastal mudflats and arid dunes.

All other geographic features of the Southwest seem to radiate out from the plateau. To the east, running in a north–south line from Canada to Mexico, are the Rocky Mountains, the source of the mighty Colorado River, which gathers on the mountains' high slopes and cascades across the Southwest to its mouth in the Gulf of California. East of the Rocky Mountains, the eastern third of New

Mexico grades into the Llano Estacado – a local version of the vast grasslands of the Great Plains.

In Utah, a line of mountains known collectively as the Wasatch Line bisects the state nearly in half, with the eastern half on the Colorado Plateau, and the western half in the Basin and Range province. Northern Arizona is highlighted by a spectacular set of cliffs called the Mogollon Rim that runs several hundred miles to form a boundary between the Colorado Plateau to the north and the highland region of central Arizona. The mountains of central Arizona decrease in elevation as you travel into the deserts of southern Arizona.

Four deserts – the Sonoran, Mojave, Chihuahuan and Great Basin – stretch across the Southwest. Each is home to an array of well-adapted reptiles, mammals and plants. Look closely to discover everything from fleet-footed lizards to jewel-like wildflowers.

As Southwest author Edward Abbey wrote in *Desert Solitaire: A Season in the Wilderness,* 'The desert is a vast world, an oceanic world, as deep in its way and complex and various as the sea.' The Southwest's four distinct desert zones are superimposed on an astonishing complex of hidden canyons and towering mountains.

The often-used term 'slickrock' refers to the fossilized surfaces of ancient sand dunes. Pioneers named it slickrock because their metal-shoed horses and iron-wheeled wagons would slip on the surface.

Landscape Features

Red Rocks

The Southwest is jam-packed with one of the world's greatest concentrations of remarkable rock formations. One reason for this is that the region's many sedimentary layers are so soft that rain and erosion readily carve them into fantastic shapes. But not any old rain. It has to be hard rain that is fairly sporadic because frequent rain would wash the formations away. Between rains, long arid spells keep the eroding landmarks intact.

The range of colors on rocky landscapes in the Southwest derive from the unique mineral composition of each rock type, but most visitors to the parks are content to stand on the rim of Grand Canyon or Bryce Canyon and see the play of light on the orange and red rocks.

This combination of color and soft rock is best seen in badlands, where the rock crumbles so easily you can actually hear the hillsides sloughing away. The result is an otherworldly landscape of rounded knolls, spires and folds painted in outrageous colors. Excellent examples can be found in Arizona's Painted Desert of Petrified Forest National Park, at Utah's Capitol Reef National Park or in the Bisti Badlands south of Farmington, New Mexico.

Arches National Park has more than 2000 sandstone arches. The opening in a rock has to measure at least 3ft in order for the formation to qualify as an arch.

More-elegantly sculptured and durable versions are called hoodoos. These towering, narrow pillars of rock can be found throughout the Southwest, but are magnificently showcased at Utah's Bryce Canyon National Park. Although formed in soft rock, these precarious spires differ from badlands because parallel joints in the rock create deeply divided ridges that weather into rows of pillars.

Under special circumstances, sandstone may form fins and arches. Utah's Arches National Park has a remarkable concentration of these features, thought to have resulted from a massive salt deposit that was laid down by a sea 300 million years ago. Squeezed by the pressure of overlying layers, this salt body apparently domed up then collapsed, creating a matrix of rock cracked along parallel lines. Erosion along deep vertical cracks left behind fins and narrow walls of sandstone that sometimes partially collapse to create freestanding arches.

GEOLOGY & THE LAND THE LAND

Streams cutting through resistant sandstone layers form natural bridges, which are similar in appearance to arches. Three examples of natural bridges can be found in Utah's Natural Bridges National Monument. These formations are the result of meandering streams that double back on themselves to cut at both sides of a rock barrier. At an early stage of development these streams could be called goosenecks as they loop across the landscape. A famous example can be found at the Goosenecks State Park in Utah.

Edward Abbey shares his desert philosophy and insights in his 1968 classic *Desert Solitaire: A Season in the Wilderness*, a must-read for desert enthusiasts and conservationists.

Sandstone Effects

Many of the Southwest's characteristic features are sculpted in sandstone. Laid down in distinct horizontal layers, like a stack of pancakes, these rocks erode into unique formations, such as flat-topped mesas. Surrounded by sheer cliffs, mesas represent a fairly advanced stage of erosion in which all of the original landscape has been stripped away except for a few scattered outposts that tower over everything else. The eerie skyline at Monument Valley on the Arizona–Utah border is a classic example.

Where sandstone layers remain fairly intact, it's possible to see details of the ancient dunes that created the sandstone. As sand dunes were blown across the landscape millions of years ago they formed fine layers of cross-bedding that can still be seen in the rocks at Zion National Park. Wind-blown ripple marks and tracks of animals that once walked the dunes are also preserved. Modern sand dunes include the spectacular dunes at White Sands National Monument in New Mexico, where shimmering white gypsum crystals thickly blanket 275 sq miles.

Looking beneath the surface, the 85-plus caves at Carlsbad Caverns National Park in southern New Mexico are chiseled deep into a massive 240-million-year-old limestone formation that was part of a 400-mile-long reef similar to the modern Great Barrier Reef of Australia.

Geology of the Grand Canyon

Arizona's Grand Canyon is the best-known geologic feature in the Southwest and for good reason: not only does its immensity dwarf the imagination, but it also records two billion years of geologic history – a huge amount of time considering the Earth is just 4.6 billion years old.

The Canyon itself, however, is young – a mere five to six million years old. Carved out by the powerful Colorado River as the land

CRYPTOBIOTIC CRUSTS: WATCH YOUR STEP!

Cryptobiotic crusts, also known as biological soil crusts, are living crusts that cover and protect desert soils, literally gluing sand particles together so they don't blow away.

Cyanobacteria, one of the Earth's oldest life forms, start the process by extending mucous-covered filaments into dry soil. Over time these filaments and the sand particles adhering to them form a thin crust that is colonized by algae, lichen, fungi and mosses.

This crust plays a significant role in desert food chains, and also stores rainwater and reduces erosion. Unfortunately, the thin crust is easily fragmented under heavy-soled boots and tires. Once broken, the crust takes 50 to 250 years to repair itself. In its absence, winds and rains erode desert soils, and much of the water that would nourish desert plants is lost.

Many sites in Utah, in particular, have cryptobiotic crusts. Protect these crusts by staying on established trails.

bulged upward, the 277-mile-long canyon reflects the differing hardness of the 10-plus layers of rocks in its walls. Shales crumble easily and form slopes, while resistant limestones and sandstones form distinctive cliffs.

The layers making up the bulk of the canyon walls were laid during the Paleozoic era, 570 to 245 million years ago. These formations perch atop a group of one- to two-billion-year-old rocks lying at the bottom of the inner gorge of the canyon. Between these two distinct sets of rock is the Great Unconformity, a several-hundred-million-year gap in the geologic record where erosion erased 12,000ft of rock and left a huge mystery.

Wildlife

The Southwest's landscape may seem desolate but this doesn't mean it lacks wildlife – on the contrary. However, the plants and animals of North America's deserts are a subtle group and it takes patience to see them. Many visitors will drive through without noticing any at all. While a number of species are widespread, others have adapted to the particular requirements of their local environment and live nowhere else in the world. Deep canyons and waterless wastes limit travel and dispersal opportunities for animals and plants as well as for humans, and all life has to hunker down and plan carefully to survive.

Animals

Reptiles & Amphibians

While most people expect to see snakes and lizards in a desert, it's less obvious that frogs and toads find a comfortable home here as well. But on a spring evening, many of the canyons of the Southwest reverberate with the calls of canyon tree frogs or red-spotted toads. With the rising sun, these are replaced by several dozen species of lizards and snakes that roam among rocks and shrubs.

Blue-bellied fence lizards are particularly abundant in the region's parks, but visitors can always hope to encounter a rarity such as the strange and venomous 'Gila monster' lizard. Equally fascinating, if you're willing to hang around and watch for a while (but never touch or bother), are the Southwest's many colorful rattlesnakes. Quick to anger and able to deliver a painful or toxic bite, rattlesnakes are placid and retiring if left alone.

Birds

More than 400 species of birds can be found in the Southwest, bringing color, energy and song to every season. There are blue grosbeaks, yellow warblers and scarlet cardinals. There are massive golden eagles and tiny vibrating calliope hummingbirds. In fact, there are so many interesting birds that it's the foremost reason many people travel to the Southwest. Springtime is particularly rewarding, as songbirds arrive from their southern wintering grounds and begin singing from every nook and cranny.

One recent arrival at the Grand Canyon tops everyone's list of must-see wildlife. With a 9ft wingspan, the California condor looks more like a prehistoric pterodactyl than any bird you've ever seen. Pushed to the brink of extinction, these unusual birds are staging a minor comeback at the Grand Canyon. After several decades in which no condors lived in the wild, a few wild pairs are now nesting on the canyon rim.

An estimated nine million free-tailed bats once roosted in Carlsbad Caverns. Though reduced in recent years, the evening flight is still one of the premier wildlife spectacles in North America.

Fall provides another birdwatching highlight when sandhill cranes and snow geese travel in long skeins down the Rio Grande Valley to winter at the Bosque del Apache National Wildlife Refuge in New Mexico. The Great Salt Lake is one of North America's premier sites for migrating birds, including millions of ducks and grebes stopping each fall to feed before continuing south.

Mammals

The Southwest's most charismatic wildlife species were largely exterminated by the early 1900s. A combination of factors has contributed to their decline over the decades, including loss of habitat, overhunting and oil and gas development. First to go was the grizzly bear. After that, herds of buffalo, howling wolves and the tropical jaguars that crossed the border out of Mexico also disappeared from the region. Prairie dogs (actually small rodents) vanished with hardly a trace, even though they once numbered in the billions.

Like the California condor, however, some species are being reintroduced. A small group of Utah prairie dogs were successfully released in Bryce Canyon National Park in 1974. Mexican wolves were released into the wilds of eastern Arizona in 1998 amid public controversy.

Mule deer still roam as widely as ever, and coyote are seen and heard nearly everywhere. Small numbers of elk, pronghorn antelope and bighorn sheep dwell in their favorite habitats (forests for elk, open grasslands for pronghorns and rocky cliffs for bighorns), but it takes a lot of luck or some sharp eyes to spot them. Even fewer people will observe a mountain lion, one of the wildest and most elusive animals in North America.

Plants

Although the Southwest is largely a desert region, the presence of many large mountain ranges creates a remarkable diversity of niches for plants. One way to understand the plants of this region is to understand life zones and the ways each plant thrives in its favored zone.

At the lowest elevations, generally below 4000ft, high temperatures and lack of water create a desert zone where drought-tolerant plants such as cacti, sagebrush and agave survive. Many of these species have greatly reduced leaves to reduce water loss, or they hold water (cacti, for example) to survive long hot spells.

At mid elevations, from 4000ft to 7000ft, conditions cool a bit and more moisture is available for woody shrubs and small trees. In much of Nevada, Utah, northern Arizona and New Mexico, piñon pines and junipers blanket vast areas of low mountain slopes and hills. Both trees are short and stout to help conserve water.

Nearly pure stands of stately, fragrant ponderosa pine are the dominant tree at 7000ft on many of the West's mountain ranges. In fact, this single tree best defines the Western landscape and many animals rely on it for food and shelter; timber companies also consider it their most profitable tree.

High mountain, or boreal, forests composed of spruce, fir, quaking aspen and a few other conifers are found on the highest peaks in the Southwest. This is a land of cool, moist forests and lush meadows with brilliant wildflower displays.

There are more than 100 species of cacti in the Southwest. The iconic saguaro can grow up to 50ft tall, and a fully hydrated giant saguaro can store more than a ton of water.

Many of the Southwest's most common flowers can be found in *Canyon Country Wildflowers*, by Damian Fagan (1998). Chapters are arranged by the color of the flowers, including white, yellow and blue.

WHAT'S THE BLM?

The Bureau of Land Management (BLM; www.blm.gov) is a Department of Energy agency that oversees more than 245 million surface acres of public land, much of it in the West. It manages its resources for a variety of uses, from energy production to cattle grazing to recreational oversight. What does that mean for you? All kinds of outdoor fun.

BLM lands feature both developed camping and dispersed camping. Generally, when it comes to dispersed camping on BLM land, you can camp where you want as long as your campsite is at least 900ft from a water source used by wildlife or livestock. You cannot camp in one spot for more than 14 days. Don't leave campfires unattended and be sure to pack out what you pack in, which means that all of your personal belongings and trash, including food scraps, should be taken with you when you leave.

Some regions may have more specific rules. Check state camping requirements on the BLM website. For developed campground information you can also visit www. recreation.gov.

Environmental Issues

Forest Fires

Sustained droughts in the Southwest are contributing to forest fires of unprecedented size. Scientists posit three connected factors. The first is climate change, which may be contributing to the extended Western drought. Dry conditions are exacerbated when snow packs are low because there is less melting runoff for streams. Also, with higher temperatures, the evaporation of existing water sources happens more quickly.

Another factor may be increased development, which leads more people to forest lands. Finally, the long-running forestry practice of fire suppression may have allowed the build-up of more underbrush, which can ignite and fuel the fire.

The worst wildfire in recent history was Yarnell Hill in Central Arizona, which killed 19 firefighters who were part of the elite Granite Mountain Hotshots, in June 2013. As recently as 2016, large summer wildfires burned across Western states, including 31 simultaneous fires in Arizona and New Mexico.

As wildfires become more frequent, finding funds to fight them becomes an ever-greater challenge, putting lives, homes and wilderness at risk.

Drought, Dams & Water Loss

A study published in 2017 by *Science Advances* says that if carbon emissions continue unchecked, there's a 99% chance of a mega-drought worse than anything seen in the past 2000 years.

The most vulnerable to these changes are American Indians, according to the EPA. Dry wells and reduced drinking supplies are already a reality facing Navajo communities. There's danger of crop and livestock loss as well.

Need visual proof of water loss? Look at Lake Mead behind the Hoover Dam. The 'bath-tub ring' – where the adjacent canyon walls have been bleached by minerals in the water – grows taller ever year as the water level drops.

The construction of dams and human-made water features throughout the Southwest has radically altered the delicate balance of water that sustained life for countless millennia. Dams, for

Visit www. publiclands. org for a one-stop summary of recreational opportunities on government-owned land in the Southwest. The site also has maps, a book index, links to relevant agencies and updates on current conditions.

example, halt the flow of warm waters and force them to drop their rich loads of life-giving nutrients. These sediments once rebuilt floodplains, nourished myriad aquatic and riparian food chains, and sustained the life of ancient endemic fish now on the edge of extinction. In place of rich annual floods, dams now release cold waters in steady flows that favor the introduced fish and weedy plants that have overtaken the West's rivers.

In other areas, the steady draining of aquifers to provide drinking water for cows and sprawling cities is shrinking the water table and drying up unique desert springs and wetlands that countless animals once depended on during the dry season. Cows further destroy the fragile desert crust with their heavy hooves, and also graze on native grasses and herbs that are soon replaced by introduced weeds. Development is increasingly having the largest impact, as uniquely adapted habitats are bulldozed to make room for more houses.

The region's stately pine and fir forests have largely become thickets of scrawny little trees. The cutting of trees and building of roads in these environments can further dry the soil and make it harder for young trees and native flowers to thrive. Injuries to an ecosystem in an arid environment take a very long time to heal.

Nuclear Power & Waste

Ongoing environmental controversies include the location of nuclear power plants and the transport and disposal of nuclear waste, most notably at Yucca Mountain 90 miles from Las Vegas. The defunct facility would take a decade and $30 billion dollars in funding to revive, though President Trump indicated during his campaign that he would consider reinstating the project.

A radiation leak contaminated 22 workers at the Waste Isolation Pilot Plant near Carlsbad, NM, in 2014. The probable cause of the leak? A chemical reaction between organic kitty litter – used to pack 57 barrels of nuclear waste – and nitrate salts in the waste.

Arts & Architecture

Art has always been a major part of Southwest culture and one of the most compelling ways for its people to express their heritage and ideologies. From ancient cultures to settlers, current American Indian cultures and recent immigrants, the rich history and cultural texture of the Southwest is a fertile source of inspiration for artists, filmmakers, writers, photographers and musicians.

Literature

From the classic Western novels of Zane Grey, Louis L'Amour and Larry McMurtry to contemporary writers such as ecosavvy Barbara Kingsolver and American Indian Louise Erdrich, authors imbue their work with the scenery and sensibility of the Southwest. Drawing from the mystical reality that is so infused in Latin literature, Southwestern style can sometimes be fantastical and absurdist, yet poignantly astute.

DH Lawrence moved to Taos in the 1920s for health reasons, and went on to write the essay 'Indians and Englishmen' and the novel *St Mawr*. Through his association with artists such as Georgia O'Keeffe, he found some of the freedoms from puritanical society that he'd long sought.

Tony Hillerman, an enormously popular author from Albuquerque, wrote *Skinwalkers, People of Darkness, Skeleton Man* and *The Sinister Pig*. His award-winning mystery novels take place on the Navajo, Hopi and Zuni reservations.

Hunter S Thompson, who committed suicide in 2005, wrote *Fear and Loathing in Las Vegas,* set in the temple of American excess in the desert; it's the ultimate road-trip novel, in every sense of the word.

Edward Abbey, a curmudgeonly ecowarrior who loved the Southwest, created the thought-provoking and seminal works *Desert Solitaire* and *The Journey Home: Some Words in Defense of the American West*. His classic *Monkey Wrench Gang* is a fictional and comical account of real people who plan to blow up Glen Canyon Dam before it floods Glen Canyon.

John Nichols wrote *The Milagro Beanfield War,* part of his New Mexico trilogy. It's a tale of a Western town's struggle to take back its fate from the Anglo land barons and developers. Robert Redford's movie of the novel was filmed in Truchas, NM.

Barbara Kingsolver lived for a decade in Tucson before publishing *The Bean Trees* in 1988. Echoing her own life, it's about a young woman from rural Kentucky who moves to Tucson. Her 1990 novel, *Animal Dreams,* gives wonderful insights into the lives of people from a small Hispanic village near the Arizona–New Mexico border and from an Indian Pueblo.

Pam Houston's collection *Cowboys Are My Weakness* is filled with funny, sometimes sad, stories about love in the great outdoors.

> **Top Art & Culture Destinations**
>
> Phoenix, AZ
>
> Santa Fe, NM
>
> Taos, NM
>
> Indian Pueblo Cultural Center, NM
>
> Salt Lake City, UT

> The National Cowboy Poetry Gathering – the bronco of cowboy poetry events – is held in January in Elko, NV. Ropers and wranglers have waxed lyrical here for more than 30 years (www.western folklife.org).

Film & TV

Hollywood is enjoying a renaissance in the Southwest, with New Mexico as the star player. Former governor Bill Richardson (2002–10) wooed Hollywood producers and their production teams to the state with a 25% tax rebate on production expenditures. His efforts helped inject more than $3 billion into the economy.

On television, the critically acclaimed American TV series *Breaking Bad* (2008–13) was set and filmed in and around Albuquerque. Its spin-off, *Better Call Saul*, was also shot in Albuquerque. Arizona drug-war movie *Sicario* (2015) was directed by Denis Villeneuve and starred Emily Blunt, Benicio del Toro and Josh Brolin.

Joel and Ethan Coen shot the 2007 Oscar winner *No Country for Old Men* almost entirely around Las Vegas, NM (doubling for 1980s west Texas). The Coen brothers returned in 2010 to film their remake of *True Grit*, basing their production headquarters in Santa Fe and shooting on several New Mexico ranches.

Las Vegas, NV, had a starring role in 2009's blockbuster comedy *The Hangover*, an R-rated buddy film that earned more than $467 million worldwide. Visitors regularly line up to try to catch a glimpse of Chumlee and other cast members in *Pawn Stars*, a History Channel reality show set in Gold & Silver Pawn in Las Vegas.

A few places have doubled as film and TV sets so often that they have come to define the American West. In addition to Utah's Monument Valley, popular destinations include Moab, for *Thelma and Louise* (1991), Dead Horse Point State Park, also in Utah, for *Mission Impossible: 2* (2000), Lake Powell, AZ, for *Planet of the Apes* (1968) and Tombstone for the eponymous *Tombstone* (1993). Scenes in *127 Hours* (2010), about Aron Ralston's harrowing experience trapped in Blue John Canyon in Utah's Canyonlands National Park, were shot in and around the canyon.

The region also specializes in specific location shots. Snippets of *Casablanca* (1942) were actually filmed in Flagstaff's Hotel Monte Vista, *Butch Cassidy and the Sundance Kid* (1969) was shot at the Utah ghost town of Grafton and *City Slickers* (1991) was set at Ghost Ranch in Abiquiú, NM.

In Albuquerque, *Breaking Bad* fans can visit Twisters (4257 Isleta Blvd), which doubles as Gus Fring's Los Pollos Hermanos. Rebel Donut (www.rebeldonut.com; 400 Gold Ave) sells a Blue Sky doughnut with blue sugar crystals – a nod to Walter White's Blue Meth.

Music

The larger cities of the Southwest are the best options for classical music. Choose from Phoenix's Symphony Hall, which houses the Arizona Opera and the Phoenix Symphony Orchestra, the famed Santa Fe Opera, the New Mexico Symphony Orchestra in Albuquerque, and the Arizona Opera Company in Tucson and Phoenix.

Nearly every major town attracts country, bluegrass and rock groups. A notable major venue is Flagstaff's Museum Club (p157), with a lively roster of talent. Surprisingly, Provo, UT, has a thriving indie-rock scene, which offers a stark contrast to the Osmond-family image that Utah often conjures.

Las Vegas is a mecca for entertainers of every stripe; headliners include popular icons such as Celine Dion and Ricky Martin, but for a little gritty goodness head to **The Joint** (Map p64; ☑702-693-5222; www.hardrockhotel.com; Hard Rock; most tickets $40-200; ☑108) at Hard Rock Hotel & Casino.

Try to catch a mariachi ensemble (typically dressed in tight, ornately sequined costumes) at southern New Mexico's International Mariachi Conference (www.lascrucesmariachi.org).

EARTHSHIP ARCHITECTURE

The eye-catching Earthships, located about 2 miles west of the Rio Grande outside Taos, NM, is the world's premier sustainable, self-sufficient community. Its environmentally friendly architectural form, pioneered in northern New Mexico, consists of auto tires packed with earth, stacked with rebar and turned into livable dwellings (http://earthship. org). The community looks like Mos Eisley Spaceport from *Star Wars*.

The brainchild of architect Mike Reynolds, Earthships are a form of biotecture (biology plus architecture: buildings based on biological systems of resource use and conservation) that maximizes available resources so you'll never have to be on the grid again.

Walls made of old tires are laid out for appropriate passive solar use, packed with tamped earth, and then buried on three sides for maximum insulation. The structures are outfitted with photovoltaic cells and an elaborate gray-water system that collects rain and snow, which filters through several cycles that begin in the kitchen and end in the garden.

Though the Southwest is their home, Earthships have landed in Japan, Bolivia, Scotland, Mexico and beyond, and are often organized into communities.

Architecture

Not surprisingly, architecture has three major cultural regional influences in the Southwest. First and foremost are the ruins of the Ancestral Puebloans – most majestically their cliff communities – and Taos Pueblo. These traditional designs and examples are echoed in the Pueblo Revival style of Santa Fe's New Mexico Museum of Art and are speckled across the city and the region today.

The most traditional structures are adobe – mud mixed with straw, formed into bricks, mortared with mud and smoothed with another layer of mud. This style dominates many New Mexico cityscapes and landscapes.

The mission-style architecture of the 17th and 18th centuries is visible in religious and municipal buildings such as Santa Fe's State Capitol. It is characterized by red-tile roofs, ironwork and stucco walls. The domed roof and intricate designs of Arizona's Mission San Xavier del Bac embody the Spanish Colonial style.

The third influence was 1800s Anglo settlers, who brought many new building techniques and developed Territorial-style architecture, which often included porches, wood-trimmed doorways and other Victorian influences.

Master architect Frank Lloyd Wright was also a presence in the Southwest, most specifically at Taliesin West in Scottsdale, AZ. More recently, architectural monuments along Route 66 include kitschy motels lit by neon signs that have forever transformed the concept of an American road trip.

Painting, Sculpture & Visual Arts

The region's most famous artist is Georgia O'Keeffe (1887–1986), whose Southwestern landscapes are seen in museums throughout the world. The minimalist paintings of Agnes Martin (1912–2004) began to be suffused with light after she moved to New Mexico. Also highly regarded is Navajo artist RC Gorman (1932–2005), known for sculptures and paintings of Navajo women. Gorman lived in Taos for many years.

Both Taos and Santa Fe, NM, have large and active artist communities considered seminal to the development of Southwestern art. Santa Fe is a particularly good stop for those looking to browse and buy art and native crafts. More than 100 galleries and boutiques line the city's Canyon Rd, and American Indian vendors sell high-quality jewelry and crafts beside the plaza.

The vast landscapes of the region have long lent themselves to large-format black-and-white photographs such as those by Ansel Adams, whose archives are housed at the Center for Creative Photography (p209) at the University of Arizona.

For something different, pop into art galleries and museums in Las Vegas, specifically the Bellagio, which partners with museums and foundations around the world for knock-out exhibitions, and the new City Center, which hosts art by internationally renowned artists such as Jenny Holzer, Maya Lin and Claes Oldenburg.

Acoma Pueblo's 40,000-sq-ft Sky City Cultural Center and Haak'u Museum showcases vibrant tribal culture ongoing since the 12th century.

Dance & Theater

American Indians have a long tradition of performing sacred dances throughout the year. Ceremonial or ritual religious dances are spiritual, reverential community occasions, and many are closed to the public. When these ceremonies are open to the public, some tribes (such as the Zuni) require visitors to attend an orientation; always contact the tribes to confirm arrangements.

Social dances are typically cultural, as opposed to religious, events. They are much more relaxed and often open to the public. They occur during powwows, festivals, rodeos and other times, both on and off the reservation. Intertribal dance competitions (the lively 'powwow trail') are quite popular; the dancing may tell a story or be just for fun, to celebrate a tribe or clan gathering. The public may even be invited to join the dance.

American Indians also perform dances strictly for the public as theater or art. Though these may lack community flavor, they are authentic and wonderful.

Classical dance options include Ballet West in Salt Lake City and Ballet Arizona in Phoenix. Dance and theater productions are flashy and elaborate in Las Vegas, where they have always been a staple of the city's entertainment platform. In Utah, Park City's George S and Dolores Doré Eccles Center for the Performing Arts hosts varied events.

Folk Art & Kitsch

The Southwest is a repository for kitsch and folk art. In addition to the predictable American Indian knockoffs and beaded everything (perhaps made anywhere but there), you'll find invariable UFO humor in Roswell and unexpected atomic-age souvenirs at Los Alamos, both in New Mexico. Pick up an Atomic City T-shirt, emblazoned with a red and yellow exploding bomb, or a bottle of La Bomba wine. If you need a shot glass, Route 66 has you covered.

More serious cultural artifacts fill the Museum of International Folk Art (p260) in Santa Fe.

Jewelry & Crafts

Hispanic and American Indian aesthetic influences are evident in the region's pottery, paintings, weavings, jewelry, sculpture, woodcarving and leatherworking. Excellent examples of Southwestern American Indian art are displayed in many museums, most notably in Phoenix's Heard Museum (p115) and Santa Fe's Museum of Contemporary Native Arts (p258). Contemporary and traditional American Indian art is readily available in hundreds of galleries.

Survival Guide

Directory A–Z

Accommodations

Definitely book accommodations in advance during summer, the winter holidays and spring break.

Apartment & House Rentals Often good-value and unique properties, with kitchens and good wi-fi connections.

B&Bs These family-run homes generally offer value and personality.

Camping From RVs to the backcountry, the Southwest is a camper's dream destination. You should always reserve months ahead where possible – particularly for national parks and if you're in an RV.

Hotels Great range of choices in urban centers, not so much in rural areas.

Motels Chain motels line the roadsides everywhere, catering to a range of budgets and comfort levels.

Apartment & House Rentals

➡ House and condo rentals are prevalent in this region and are sometimes a good way to meet locals.

➡ Lodging can range from single rooms in someone's house and one-bedroom condos at a ski resort to adobe casitas and entire ranch houses.

➡ Rates are flexible, and can be as little as $25 a night or as much as several hundred dollars, depending on what you are renting.

➡ Access to a kitchen is almost always included.

➡ In addition to the usual online rental agencies, you can also check visitor bureaus for links to local rental agencies – this is particularly common in ski towns.

B&Bs & Inns

B&Bs are a good choice for travelers looking for more personal attention and a friendly home base for regional exploration, but they may not work as well for longer stays, especially if you want to cook your own meals.

PRACTICALITIES

Emergency & Important Numbers

If you need any kind of emergency assistance, call ☑911. Some rural phones might not have this service, in which case dial ☑0 for the operator and ask for emergency assistance.

Country code ☑1

International access code ☑011

Emergency ☑911

National sexual assault hotline ☑800-656-4673

Statewide road conditions ☑511

Smoking

➡ Arizona, Colorado, New Mexico and Utah ban smoking in enclosed work spaces, including restaurants and bars. Nevada's statewide ban permits smoking in bars, casinos and designated restaurant smoking rooms.

Etiquette

➡ **Greetings** Southwesterners tend to be very courteous, even when greeting strangers in small towns or at the parks; try to reciprocate.

➡ **Tipping** Respect tipping norms.

➡ **Photography** Avoid photographing individuals, including American Indian people, without consent.

➡ In smaller towns, simple guesthouses may charge $80 to $130 a night for rooms with a shared bathroom, breakfast included.

➡ Fancier B&Bs have more charming features, such as kiva fireplaces, courtyards or lounge areas. They typically charge $125 to $195 per night with a private bathroom, although could cost more than $250 per night.

➡ Most B&Bs have fewer than 10 rooms, and many don't allow pets or young children.

➡ Many B&Bs require a two-night stay on weekends.

Camping & Holiday Parks

DISPERSED CAMPING

Free dispersed camping (independent camping at nonestablished sites) is permitted in many backcountry areas including national forests and Bureau of Land Management (BLM) lands, and less often in national and state parks.

Dispersed camping can be particularly helpful in the summer when every motel within 50 miles of the Grand Canyon is full. Try Kaibab National Forest beside the southern and northern boundaries of the national park. Stake your spot among the ponderosas, taking care not to camp within a quarter-mile of any watering hole or within a mile of any developed campgrounds or administrative or recreational sites. Drop in at the closest BLM or ranger office for information on the best dispersed camping sites.

CAMPGROUNDS & CAMPSITES

➡ Developed campgrounds can be divided into two categories: more basic, but often more beautiful, national forest and state park campgrounds, and private campgrounds that

usually have more amenities (showers, pool, wi-fi) but are less private; the latter are geared more toward RVs.

➡ The more developed areas (especially national parks) usually require reservations months in advance. To reserve a campsite on federal lands, book through Recreation.gov.

➡ Some state parks and federal lands have first-come, first-served campsites – show up early in the morning and stake out a spot.

➡ Basic campgrounds usually have toilets, water spouts, fire pits and picnic tables.

➡ Some desert sites don't have access to drinking water. It is always a good idea to have a few gallons of water in your vehicle when you're out on the road.

➡ Some camping areas are open year-round, while others are open only from May through to the first snowfall – check in advance

if you're planning to slumber outdoors in winter.

➡ Basic tenting usually costs $10 to $25 a night.

➡ More developed campgrounds are geared to RV travel and cost $25 to $45 a night.

Guest Ranches

Guest ranches can serve as entire vacations, with active schedules of horseback riding, cattle roundups, rodeo lessons, cookouts or other Western activities.

When planning, be aware that ranches in the desert lowlands may close in summer, while those in the mountains may close in winter or convert into skiing centers.

The website of the **Arizona Dude Ranch Association** (www.azdra.com) has a helpful dude-ranch comparison chart for the Grand Canyon State.

Hostels

Hostels are not as plentiful or as nice as in other parts of the world, though you will

SLEEPING PRICE RANGES

The following price ranges are based on standard double occupancy in high season. Unless otherwise noted, breakfast is not included, bathrooms are private and lodging is open year-round. Rates generally don't include taxes, which vary considerably between towns and states.

$ less than $100

$$ $100–$250

$$$ more than $250

Most places are nonsmoking, although some national chains and local budget motels may offer smoking rooms.

find a few dorm beds here and there.

➡ Most hostels in the Southwest are run independently and are not part of **Hostelling International USA** (📞240-650-2100; www. hiusa.org). They often have private or single rooms, sometimes with their own bathrooms. Kitchen, laundry, noticeboard and TV facilities are typically available.

➡ Expect to pay anywhere from $20 to $45 for a dorm bed.

Hotels
➡ There are a huge range of hotels in Southwestern cities, from luxury hot spring resorts to affordable boutique options. Prices vary tremendously from season to season.

➡ Rates don't include state and local occupancy taxes, which can be as high as 13% combined.

➡ During high season and special events, prices may rise, but you never know when a convention may take over several hundred rooms and make beds hard to find.

Lodges
➡ Normally situated within national parks, historic lodges are rustic looking but are usually quite comfy inside. Basic rooms and cabins generally start at $100 but increase as the view and decor improves.

➡ Lodges often represent the only noncamping option inside a park, and so many are fully booked months in advance.

➡ If you need a room at the last minute, call as you might be lucky and hit on a cancellation.

Motels
Chain motels are prevalent throughout the US. In smaller towns, they will often be your

only option. The most basic motels have at-the-door parking, with exterior room doors. These are convenient, though some folks, especially single women, may prefer the nicer places with safer interior corridors.

Prices advertised by motels are called rack rates and are not written in stone. You may find rates as low as $40, but expect most to fall into the $60 to $150 range; that price range is your best bet if you are expecting a certain basic level of quality, safety and cleanliness. Children are often allowed to stay free with their parents. Note that wi-fi speed in many motels is generally poor to unusable.

Discount Cards

From printable internet coupons to coupons found in tourist magazines, there are price reductions aplenty. For lodging, pick up one of the coupon books stacked outside highway visitor centers. These typically offer some of the cheapest rates out there.

Senior Cards
Travelers aged 50 and older can receive rate cuts and benefits at many places. Inquire about discounts at hotels, museums and restaurants before you make your reservation.

US citizens aged 62 and older are eligible for the Senior Pass ($10), which allows lifetime entry into all national parks and discounts on some services (Golden Age Passports are still valid).

A good resource for travel bargains is the American Association of Retired Persons (www.aarp.org), an advocacy group for Americans aged 50 years and older.

Electricity

Type A
120V/60Hz

Type B
120V/60Hz

Food & Drink

The Southwest has a fine range of eating options (p495), most of which require same-day reservations at most, or no reservations at all. Exceptions include top-end restaurants, particularly in Las Vegas, which should be booked up to several weeks ahead.

Restaurants Mexican, pizzerias, farm-to-table, Asian – in urban areas you'll find just about every cuisine you can imagine.

Diners Particularly popular, down-home diners mix breakfasts and burgers with typically Southwest fare, like chile-smothered enchiladas. Often only open for breakfast and lunch.

Cafes & Brewpubs Good for reliable comfort food, but occasionally you'll find a place that goes above and beyond.

Health

When it comes to health care, the US has some of the finest in the world. The problem? Unless you have good insurance, it can be prohibitively expensive. It's essential to purchase travel health insurance if your regular policy doesn't cover you when you're abroad. At a minimum you need coverage for medical emergencies and treatment, including hospital stays and an emergency flight home if necessary.

There is good hospital and emergency care in populated areas but remote areas in and around some national parks may be far from services. For this reason, accident evacuation insurance is an important add-on.

Environmental Hazards

ALTITUDE SICKNESS

Visitors from lower elevations undergo rather dramatic physiological changes as they adapt to high altitudes. Symptoms, which tend to manifest during the first day after reaching altitude, may include headache, fatigue, loss of appetite, nausea, sleeplessness, increased urination and hyperventilation due to overexertion. Symptoms normally resolve within 24 to 48 hours.

The rule of thumb is not to ascend until the symptoms resolve. More severe cases may display extreme disorientation, ataxia (loss of coordination and balance), breathing problems (especially a persistent cough) and vomiting. People afflicted should descend immediately and get to a hospital.

To avoid discomfort, drink plenty of water and take it easy – at 7000ft, a pleasant walk around Santa Fe can wear you out faster than a steep hike at sea level.

DEHYDRATION

Visitors to the desert may not realize how much water they're losing, as sweat evaporates almost immediately and increased urination (to help the blood process oxygen more efficiently) can go unnoticed.

Drink more water than usual – think a gallon (about 4L) a day if you're active. Parents can carry fruit and fruit juices to help keep kids hydrated. Severe dehydration can easily cause disorientation and confusion, and even day hikers have become lost and then died because they ignored their thirst. Bring plenty of water, even on short hikes, and drink it!

HEAT EXHAUSTION & HEATSTROKE

Dehydration or salt deficiency can cause heat exhaustion. Take time to acclimatize to high temperatures and make sure you get enough liquids. Salt deficiency is characterized by fatigue, lethargy, headaches, giddiness and muscle cramps. Salt tablets may help.

Vomiting or diarrhea can also deplete your liquid and salt levels.

Anhydrotic heat exhaustion, caused by the inability to sweat, is quite rare. Unlike other forms of heat exhaustion, it may strike people who have been in a hot climate for some time, rather than newcomers. Always use water bottles on long trips. One gallon of water per person per day is recommended if hiking.

Long, continuous exposure to high temperatures can lead to the sometimes-fatal condition heatstroke, which occurs when the body's heat-regulating mechanism breaks down and the body temperature rises to dangerous levels. Hospitalization is essential for extreme cases, but meanwhile get out of the sun, remove clothing, cover the body with a wet sheet or towel and fan continually.

TAP WATER

Tap water is safe for drinking unless otherwise recommended.

Vaccinations

Check www.cdc.gov for updated recommendations. Currently, vaccines for these diseases are required for US immigration:

➡ Mumps

➡ Measles

➡ Rubella

➡ Polio

➡ Tetanus and diphtheria

➡ Pertussis

➡ Haemophilus influenzae type B (Hib)

➡ Hepatitis A

→ Hepatitis B

→ Rotavirus

→ Meningococcal disease

→ Varicella

→ Pneumococcal disease

→ Seasonal influenza

Insurance

If your health insurance does not cover you for medical expenses abroad, consider supplemental insurance. Find out in advance if your insurance plan will make payments directly to providers or reimburse you later for overseas health expenditures.

Consult your homeowner's (or renter's) insurance policy before leaving home to confirm whether or not you are insured for theft of items in your car while traveling. You might need liability insurance if driving a rental car, in case of a collision.

Worldwide travel insurance is available at www.lonelyplanet.com/bookings. You can buy, extend and claim online anytime – even if you're already on the road.

International Visitors

US entry requirements continue to change. All travelers should double-check current visa and passport regulations well before coming to the USA.

Visas

Generally not required for stays of up to 90 days for countries in the Visa Waiver Program (VWP). Electronic System for Travel Authorization (ESTA) required (apply online in advance).

Entering the Country

Getting into the US can be complicated and the entry requirements continue to evolve. Plan ahead. For up-to-date information about visas and immigration, start with the **US State Department** (☏ main switchboard 202-647-4000; www.travel.state.gov).

→ Apart from most Canadian citizens and those entering under the VWP, all foreign visitors to the US need a visa. Pursuant to VWP requirements, citizens of certain countries may enter the US for stays of 90 days or fewer without a US visa. This list is subject to continual reexamination and bureaucratic rejigging. Check travel.state.gov/content/visas/english/visit/visa-waiver-program.html to see which countries are included under the waiver and for a summary of current VWP requirements.

→ If you are a citizen of a VWP country you do not need a visa only if you have a passport that meets current US standards and you get approval from the ESTA in advance. Register online with the Department of Homeland Security at esta.cbp.dhs.gov at least 72 hours before arrival. The fee is $14. Canadians are currently exempt from ESTA.

→ Visitors from VWP countries must still present at the port of entry all the same evidence as for a nonimmigrant visa application. They must demonstrate that their trip is for 90 days or fewer and that they have a round-trip or onward ticket, adequate funds to cover the trip and binding obligations abroad.

→ Every foreign visitor entering the USA from abroad needs a passport. In most cases, your passport must be valid for at least another six months after you are due to leave the USA. If your passport doesn't meet current US standards you'll be turned back at the border.

Internet Access

→ Public libraries in most cities and towns offer free internet access, either at computer terminals or through a wireless connection, usually for 15 minutes to an hour (a few may charge a small fee). In some cases you may need to obtain a guest pass or register.

→ If you can bring your laptop do so, as most places that serve coffee also offer free wi-fi as long as you order a drink. Several national companies – McDonald's, Panera Bread, Barnes & Noble – provide free wi-fi.

→ Computers with internet access can be found in small business centers in many chain hotels.

→ Airports and campgrounds often offer laptop owners the chance to get online for free or a small fee.

→ You may be charged for wi-fi use in nice hotels and resorts.

→ Check www.wififreespot.com for a list of free wi-fi hot spots nationwide.

Legal Matters

→ If you are arrested for a serious offense in the US, you are allowed to remain silent, entitled to have an attorney present during any interrogation and are presumed innocent until proven guilty.

→ You have the right to an attorney from the very first moment you are arrested. If you can't afford one, the state must provide one for free.

→ All persons who are arrested are legally allowed to make one phone call. If you don't have a lawyer or family member to help you, call your embassy or consulate.

➡ If you are stopped by the police for everyday matters, there is no system of paying fines on the spot. The officer should explain to you how the fine can be paid, and many matters can be handled by mail or online.

LGBTI+ Travelers

The most visible gay communities are in major cities. Utah and southern Arizona are typically not as free-wheeling as San Francisco. Gay travelers should be careful in predominantly rural areas – simply holding hands could provoke aggressive responses.

The most active gay community in the Southwest is in Phoenix. Santa Fe and Albuquerque have active gay communities, and Las Vegas has an active gay scene. Conservative Utah has little

gay life outside Salt Lake City. The following are useful resources:

Damron (www.damron.com) Publishes classic gay travel guides.

Gay Yellow Network (www.glyp.com) Has listings for numerous US cities including Phoenix and Las Vegas.

Lambda Legal Defense Fund (☑in Los Angeles 213-382-7600; www.lambdalegal.org) The website lists legal protections for LGBT people and their families by state.

National Gay & Lesbian Task Force (☑Washington, DC 202-393-5177; www.thetaskforce.org) The website of this national activist group covers news and politics.

OutTraveler (www.outtraveler.com) News, tips and in-depth stories about gay travel for destinations around the world.

Purple Roofs (www.purpleroofs.com) Lists gay-owned and gay-friendly B&Bs and hotels.

Money

ATMs widely available in cities and towns, but less prevalent on American Indian land. Credit cards accepted in most hotels and restaurants.

Most locals do not carry large amounts of cash for everyday transactions, and rely instead on credit cards, ATMs and debit cards. Small businesses may refuse to accept bills larger than $50.

ATMs & Cash

➡ ATMs are great for quick cash influxes and can negate the need for traveler's checks entirely. Watch out for ATM surcharges as they may charge $3 to $5 per withdrawal. Some ATMs in Vegas may charge more.

➡ The Cirrus and Plus systems both have extensive ATM networks that will give cash advances on major credit cards and allow cash withdrawals with affiliated ATM cards.

➡ Look for ATMs outside banks and in large grocery stores, shopping centers, convenience stores and gas stations.

➡ To avoid possible account-draining scams at self-serve gas stations, consider paying with cash instead of using your debit card at the pump.

Credit Cards

Major credit cards are widely accepted throughout the Southwest, including at car-rental agencies and most hotels, restaurants, gas stations, grocery stores and tour operators. It's highly recommended that you carry at least one card.

Currency Exchange

➡ Banks are usually the best places to exchange currency. Most large city banks offer currency exchange, but banks in rural areas do not.

THE SOUTHWEST WITH PETS

When it comes to pet-friendly travel destinations, the Southwest is one of the best. More and more hotels accept pets these days, although some charge extra per night, others make you leave a deposit and still others have weight restrictions – less than 35lb is usually the standard.

Some hotels have additional pet fees, or limited rooms that accept pets – call in advance to check their policies. One of the most unique pet-friendly options in the Southwest is in Santa Fe: head to the swank **Ten Thousand Waves** (Map p276; ☑505-992-5003; www.tenthousandwaves.com; 3451 Hyde Park Rd; r $249-299; P☂).

At national parks, check first before you let your pet off the leash – many forests and park lands have restrictions on dogs. If you're planning a long day in the car, vets recommend stopping at least every two hours to let your dog pee, stretch their legs and have a long drink of water. If your dog gets nervous or nauseated in the car, it is safe and effective to give them Benadryl (or a generic equivalent) to calm them down. The vet-recommended dosage is 1mg per pound. For information on pet care, consult www.humanesociety.org.

When stopping to eat during a downtown stroll, don't immediately tie your dog up outside the restaurant. Ask first about local laws.

→ Currency-exchange counters at the airports and in tourist centers typically have the worst rates; ask about fees and surcharges first.

Australia	A$1	$0.78
Canada	C$1	$0.80
Europe	€1	$1.18
Japan	¥100	$0.90
Mexico	10 pesos	$0.53
New Zealand	NZ$1	$0.71
UK	£1	$1.33

For current exchange rates see www.xe.com.

National & State Parks

National Parks

Before visiting any national park, check out its website using the search tool on the National Park Service (NPS) home page (www.nps.gov). On the Grand Canyon's website (www.nps.gov/grca), you can download the seasonal newspaper, *The Guide*, for the latest information on prices, hours and ranger talks. There is a separate edition for both the North and South Rims.

→ At the entrance of a national or state park, be ready to hand over cash (credit cards may not always be accepted). Costs range from nothing at all to $30 per vehicle for a seven-day pass.

→ If you're visiting several parks in the Southwest, you may save money by purchasing the America the Beautiful annual pass ($80). It admits all passengers in a vehicle (or four adults for per-person fee areas) to all national parks and federal recreational lands for one year. With the pass, children under 16 are admitted free.

→ US citizens and permanent residents aged 62 and older are eligible for a lifetime Senior Pass.

→ US citizens and permanent residents with a permanent disability may qualify for a free Access Pass.

→ Check park websites for notices about Fee-Free Days, when no admission is charged.

State Parks

Some state parks in Arizona operate on a five-day schedule, closed Tuesdays and Wednesdays. Before visiting an Arizona state park, check its website to confirm opening times.

Opening Hours

Opening hours vary throughout the year. Many attractions open longer in high season. We've provided high-season hours.

Banks 8:30am to 4:30pm Monday to Thursday, to 5:30pm Friday; some open 9am to 12:30pm Saturday

Bars 5pm to midnight, to 2am Friday and Saturday

Restaurants breakfast 7am to 10:30am Monday to Friday, brunch 9am to 2pm Saturday and Sunday, lunch 11:30am to 2:30pm Monday to Friday, dinner 5pm to 9:30pm, later Friday and Saturday

Stores 10am to 6pm Monday to Saturday, noon to 5pm Sunday

Photography

Print film can be found in drugstores and at specialty camera shops. Digital-camera memory cards are available at chain retailers such as Best Buy and Target.

Some American Indian reservations prohibit photography and video recording completely; when it's allowed you may be required to purchase a permit. Always ask permission to photograph someone close-up; anyone who agrees may expect a small tip.

Lonely Planet's *Guide to Travel Photography* is full of helpful tips for photography while on the road.

Post

→ The US Postal Service provides great service for the price. For 1st-class mail sent and delivered within the US, postage rates are 49¢ for letters up to 1oz (21¢ for each additional ounce) and 34¢ for standard-size postcards.

→ If you have the correct postage, drop your mail into any blue mailbox. To send a package weighing 13oz or more, go to a post office.

→ International airmail rates are $1.15 for a 1oz letter or postcard.

→ Call private shippers such as United Parcel Service (UPS) and Federal Express to send more important or larger items.

Public Holidays

New Year's Day January 1

Martin Luther King Jr Day 3rd Monday of January

Presidents Day 3rd Monday of February

Easter March or April

Memorial Day Last Monday of May

Independence Day July 4

Labor Day 1st Monday of September

Columbus Day 2nd Monday of October

Veterans Day November 11

Thanksgiving 4th Thursday of November

Christmas Day December 25

Safe Travel

Southwestern cities generally have less violent crime than larger US cities but it is present. Take precautions:

→ Avoid open areas, canyon rims or hilltops during lightning storms.

→ Avoid riverbeds and canyons when storm clouds gather; flash floods are deadly.

→ When camping in bear country, place your food inside a food box (one is often provided by the campground).

→ Step carefully on hot summer afternoons and evenings, when rattlesnakes like to bask on the trail.

→ Scorpions lurk under rocks and woodpiles; use caution.

Driving Advice

Take these precautions when driving:

→ Pull off to the side of the road in dust storms and wait it out. They don't usually last long.

→ Watch for livestock on highways and on American Indian reservations and areas marked 'Open Rangelands.'

→ Lock car doors and don't leave any valuables visible, especially at trailhead parking lots.

Telephone

→ Always dial 1 before toll-free (800, 888 etc) and domestic long-distance numbers.

→ Some toll-free numbers may only work within the region or from the US mainland. But you'll only know if it works by making the call.

→ All phone numbers in the US consist of a three-digit area code followed by a seven-digit local number.

→ All five Southwestern states require you to dial the full 10-digit number for all phone calls because each state has more than one area code. You will not be charged for long-distance fees when dialing locally.

→ When calling a cell phone anywhere in the USA you need to always dial the 10-digit number; however, you do not need to dial the country code (1) when calling from within the United States.

→ Pay phones aren't as readily found now that cell phones are more prevalent. But keep your eyes peeled and you'll find them. If you don't have change, you can use a calling card.

→ To make international calls direct, dial 011 + country code + area code + number. An exception is to Canada, where you dial 1 + area code + number. International rates apply for Canada.

→ For international operator assistance, dial 0. The operator can provide specific rate information and tell you which time periods are the cheapest for calling.

→ If you're calling the Southwest from abroad, the international country code for the US is 1. All calls to the Southwest are then followed by the area code and the seven-digit local number.

Mobile Phones

Cell-phone reception can be nonexistent in remote or mountainous areas and map apps can lead you astray. Some models of unlocked mobile phones with a US chip or foreign phones with an international plan should work in areas with coverage.

Phonecards

Private prepaid phonecards are available from convenience stores, supermarkets and pharmacies. AT&T sells a reliable phone card that is widely available in the US.

Toilets

Public toilets are common in parks and town centers; otherwise, service stations, restaurants and hotels have bathrooms for guest use.

Tourist Information

American Southwest (www.americansouthwest.net) Covers parks and natural landscapes.

Best Friends Animal Society (www.bestfriends.org) Has a wealth of general info. If you're volunteering at the Kanab, UT, center – working with adoptable dogs, rational horse training etc – you may be able to bring one of the dogs to your hotel, and many hotels approve.

Bureau of Land Management (BLM; www.blm.gov) Oversees public lands with recreational uses for the public.

Carson National Forest (p44) A 1.5-million-acre mountain recreation area in northern New Mexico.

Family Travel Files (www.thefamilytravelfiles.com) Ready-made vacation ideas, destination profiles and travel tips.

TIPPING

Airport & Hotel Porters Tip $2 per bag, minimum $5 per cart.

Bartenders Tip 10% to 15% per round, minimum per drink $1.

Housekeeping Tip $2 to $4 per night, left under card provided.

Restaurant Servers Tip 15% to 20%, unless gratuity is included in the bill.

Taxi Drivers Tip 10% to 15%, rounded up to the next dollar.

Valet Parking Tip minimum $2 when keys handed back.

'KILLER' BEES

Africanized 'killer' bees have made it to southern Arizona. Chances are you won't run into any killer-bee colonies, but here are a few things to know:

➡ Bees are attracted to dark colors, so hike in something light.

➡ Forget the perfume, and if a bee starts 'bumping' you, it could be its way of warning you that you're getting too close to the hive.

➡ If you do attract the angry attention of a colony, RUN! Cover your face and head with your clothing, your hands, or whatever you can, and keep running.

➡ Don't flail or swat, as this will only agitate them.

➡ They should stop following you before you make it half a mile. If you can't get that far, take shelter in a building or a car or under a blanket.

➡ Don't go into the water – the swarm will hover above and wait for you to come up for air.

➡ If you do get stung by lots of bees, get medical help. To remove the stingers, scrape them away, don't pull, which will inject more venom.

Grand Canyon Association (www.grandcanyon.org) Has an extensive online bookstore for the park.

Kids.gov (www.kids.gov) Eclectic, enormous national resource where you can download songs and activities, and learn a bit about each state's history.

Woodall's (www.woodalls.com) RV website with information on campgrounds and forum for the RV community.

Travelers with Disabilities

Travel within the Southwest is getting better for people with disabilities, but it's still not easy. Public buildings are required to be wheelchair accessible and to have appropriate rest-room facilities. Public transportation services must be made accessible to all and telephone companies have to provide relay operators for the hearing impaired. Many banks provide ATM instructions in braille, curb ramps are common, many busy intersections have audible crossing signals, and most chain hotels have suites for guests with disabilities. Still, it's best to call ahead to check.

➡ Disabled US residents and permanent residents may be eligible for the lifetime Access Pass, a free pass to national parks and more than 2000 recreation areas managed by the federal government. Visit store.usgs.gov/pass/access.html.

➡ Accessing Arizona (www.accessingarizona.com) has information about wheelchair-accessible activities in Arizona. It's slightly out-of-date but still useful.

➡ For reviews about the accessibility of hotels, restaurants and entertainment venues in metropolitan Phoenix, check out www.brettapproved.com.

➡ **Arizona Raft Adventures** (☎800-786-7238, 928-526-8200; www.azraft.com; 6-day Upper Canyon hybrid/paddle trips $2097/2197, 10-day Full Canyon motor trips $3160) ✔ can accommodate disabled travelers on rafting trips through the Grand Canyon.

➡ The Utah tourism office has a list of programs and resources for disabled travelers in Utah at travel.utah.gov/publications/onesheets/Accessible_Utah_web.pdf.

➡ **Wheelchair Getaways** (☎Arizona & Las Vegas 888-824-7413, Colorado 800-238-6920, New Mexico 800-408-2626, main office 800-642-2042; www.wheelchairgetaways.com) rents accessible vans in cities across the Southwest including Phoenix, Tucson, Albuquerque, Las Vegas and Boulder City.

➡ Download Lonely Planet's free Accessible Travel guide from lptravel.to/AccessibleTravel.

➡ **Society for Accessible Travel & Hospitality** (SATH; ☎212-447-7284; www.sath.org) is a useful global resource for information on traveling with a disability.

Transportation

GETTING THERE & AWAY

Most travelers to the Southwest arrive by air and car, with bus running a distant third place. The train service is little used but available. Major regional transportation hubs include Las Vegas, Phoenix, Albuquerque and Salt Lake City.

Flights, tours and rail tickets can be booked online at www.lonelyplanet.com/bookings.

Air

Unless you live in or near the Southwest, flying in and renting a car is the most time-efficient option. Most domestic visitors fly into Phoenix, Las Vegas or Albuquerque. International visitors, however, usually first touch down in Los Angeles, New York, Miami, Denver or Dallas/Fort Worth before catching an onward flight to any number of destinations.

Airports & Airlines

International visitors might consider flying into Los Angeles and driving. **Los Angeles Airport** (LAX; www.lawa.org/welcomeLAX.aspx; 1 World Way) is an easy day's drive from western Arizona or southwestern Utah, via Las Vegas. Other good options include **Denver International Airport** (DEN; ☎303-342-2000; www.

flydenver.com; ☎) and **Tucson International Airport** (TUS; ☎520-573-8100; www.tucsonairport.org; ☎).

Airlines with frequent access to the region include **United Express** (☎800-864-8331; www.united.com), **Southwest Airlines** (☎800-435-9792; www.southwest.com) and **Great Lakes** (☎307-433-2899; www.greatlakesav.com).

DEPARTURE TAX

Departure tax is included in the price of a ticket.

Land

Border Crossings

From Yuma, AZ, you can cross into Baja California and Mexico. Nogales, AZ, is also a prime border town. The biggest gateway from New Mexico to reach Ciudad Juárez is El Paso, TX. In New Mexico, visitors cross on foot from Columbus to Palomas, where there is little more than a souvenir shop.

Don't forget your passport if you are crossing the border.

INSPECTION STATIONS

When entering California, agricultural inspection stations at the Arizona–California border may ask you to surrender fruit in an attempt to stop the spread of pests associated with produce.

Bus

➡ **Greyhound** (☎800-231-2222; www.greyhound.com) is the main carrier to and within the Southwest, operating buses several times a day along major highways between large towns.

➡ To save money on bus travel, plan seven days in advance, buy tickets online, travel on weekdays, and travel with a companion. Search the internet for special deals. Students, military personnel, seniors and children under 12 receive discounts.

➡ Bus tours go from US hub cities outside and within the region. **Green Tortoise** (☎800-867-8647; www.greentortoise.com) is a fun-loving tour company popular with younger travelers. Serving a broader age range, **Adventure Bus** (☎888-737-5263, 909-633-7225; www.adventurebus.com) specializes in travel to the Grand Canyon and the Moab area but also offers an Arizona Desert Explorer trip, a New Mexico Magic trip, and an Arizona and New Mexico combo option.

Car & Motorcycle

Getting to the Southwest from other regions of the US is easy. Be aware that the distances between towns can be big, so fill up on gasoline at every opportunity. In rural areas repair services may be limited; it's best to contract AAA services or similar for emergency service, towing and repairs.

It is not worth the hassle of driving overland from Mexico unless you are on a long-distance trip with your own vehicle. The website www.dmv.org has information about crossing the US–Mexico border by car. To enter the US via Mexico driving you will need the following:

➡ passport

➡ vehicle title

➡ Mexican Vehicle Import Permit

➡ receipts for associated fees

➡ Mexican tourist permit 'FMT'

➡ appropriate visa to enter the US.

Train

➡ Three **Amtrak** (☏800-872-7245; www.amtrak.com) trains cut a swath through the Southwest, but they are not connected to one another. Use them to reach the region but not for touring.

➡ The *Southwest Chief* runs daily between Chicago and Los Angeles, via Kansas City. Significant stations include Albuquerque, NM, and Flagstaff and Williams, AZ. On-board guides provide commentary through national parks and American Indian regions.

➡ The *California Zephyr* runs daily between Chicago and San Francisco (Emeryville) via Denver, with stops in Salt Lake City and Reno, NV.

➡ The *Sunset Limited* runs thrice weekly from Los Angeles to New Orleans and stops in Tucson, AZ.

➡ Book tickets in advance and look for deals. Children, seniors and military personnel receive good discounts.

➡ Amtrak's USA Rail Pass offers coach class travel for 15, 30 and 45 days, with

travel limited to eight, 12 or 18 one-way segments. Changing trains or buses completes one segment. In other words, every time you step off the train to either visit a city or to get on another Amtrak train or vehicle, you use up one of your allotted segments. Plan carefully.

➡ It's not unusual for Amtrak trains, especially on longer routes, to run late.

GETTING AROUND

Air

Because distances between places in the Southwest are so great, regional airports are located in a number of smaller towns such as Yuma and Flagstaff, AZ, and Carlsbad and Taos, NM. These airports primarily serve residents and business people, and flying between these places is quite expensive and impractical.

Bicycle

Cycling is a cheap, convenient, healthy, environmentally sound and fun way to travel. In the Southwest – because of altitude, distance and heat – it's also a good workout. Cyclists are generally treated courteously by motorists.

➡ Carry at least a gallon of water and refill bottles at every opportunity. Dehydration is a major problem in the arid Southwest.

➡ Airlines accept bicycles as checked luggage, but since each airline has specific requirements, it's best to contact them for details.

➡ Bicycle rentals are readily available. Expect to spend $25 to $50 a day for a beach cruiser or basic mountain bike.

➡ Moab is generally considered the mountain-biking capital of the Southwest. The countryside around Sedona is also great for biking.

➡ Cyclists are permitted on some interstates in all five Southwestern states, but they may not be allowed if there is a nearby alternative route or frontage road. Cycling on interstates is typically not allowed in urban areas.

➡ In New Mexico and in certain counties in Nevada and Arizona (including Flagstaff and Tucson), helmets are required by law for those under 18. There are no requirements in Colorado and Utah, but they should be worn to reduce the risk of head injury.

➡ Consider your environmental impact. Know your environment and regulations before you ride. Bikes are restricted from entering wilderness areas and some designated trails but may be used in Bureau of Land Management (BLM) singletrack trails and National Park Service (NPS) sites, state parks, national and state forests.

Bus

➡ **Greyhound** (☏800-231-2222; www.greyhound.com) only stops at smaller towns that happen to be along the way, in which case the bus terminal is likely to be a grocery-store parking lot or something similar. To see if Greyhound serves a town, look for the blue and red Greyhound symbol.

➡ The best schedules often involve overnight routes; the best fares often require seven days' advance notice.

➡ Since bus terminals are often in the more dangerous areas of town, stay alert and be discreet with valuable personal property.

➡ Greyhound no longer offers service to Santa Fe, NM. Your best bet is to ride to Albuquerque, NM, then hop onto the adjacent *Rail Runner* train, which takes 90 minutes to get to Santa Fe.

➡ To visit the national parks you will need to rent a car, as public transportation is mostly nonexistent.

Car & Motorcycle

Once you reach the Southwest, traveling by car is the best way to get around and allows you to reach rural areas not served by public transportation. If you do not relish long drives, you can take buses and trains between a limited number of major destinations and then rent a car. But that's both time-consuming and more expensive than driving yourself and stopping along the way. State laws relating to driving are subject to frequent change, especially those relating to cell-phone use while driving.

The interstate system is thriving in the Southwest, but smaller state roads and fine scenic byways offer unparalleled opportunities for exploration.

➡ I-10 runs east–west through southern Arizona.

➡ I-40 runs east–west through Arizona and central New Mexico.

➡ I-70 runs east–west through central Utah.

➡ I-80 runs east–west through northern Utah.

➡ I-15 links Las Vegas to Salt Lake City.

➡ I-25 runs through central New Mexico to Denver, CO.

➡ Route 66 roughly follows the modern-day I-40 through Arizona and New Mexico.

On scenic drives in the Southwest, don't be surprised if you glance in your rearview mirror and see a pack of motorcycles roaring up behind you. Arizona's backroads are popular with motorcycle riders, and Harleys and other bikes are often lined up like horses in front of watering holes on lonely highways.

Long-distance motorcycle driving can be dangerous because of the fatigue factor. Use caution during long hauls.

Automobile Associations

The **American Automobile Association** (AAA; ☎800-874-7532, towing, roadside assistance 800-222-4357; www.aaa.com) provides members with maps and other information. Members also get discounts on car rentals, air tickets and some hotels and sightseeing attractions, as well as emergency road service and towing. AAA has reciprocal agreements with automobile associations in other countries. Be sure to bring your membership card from your home country.

Emergency breakdown services are available 24 hours.

Driver's Licenses

➡ Foreign visitors can legally drive a car in the USA for up to 12 months using their home country's driver's license.

➡ An IDP (International Driving Permit) will have more credibility with US traffic police, especially if your normal license doesn't have a photo or isn't in English. Your home country's automobile association can issue an IDP, valid for one year. Always carry your license together with the IDP.

➡ To ride a motorcycle in the US, you need either a valid US state motorcycle license or an IDP endorsed for motorcycles.

Fuel

Gas stations are common and many are open 24 hours. Small-town stations may be open only from 7am to 8pm or 9pm.

At most stations, you must pay before you pump. The more modern pumps have credit/debit card terminals built into them, so you can pay right at the pump. At more expensive, 'full service' stations, an attendant will pump your gas for you; no tip is expected.

Insurance

➡ Liability insurance covers people and property that you might hit.

➡ For damage to a rental vehicle, a collision damage waiver (CDW) is available for about $27 to $29 per day. If

BUSES AROUND THE SOUTHWEST

FROM	TO	FARE ($)*	DURATION (HR)
Albuquerque, NM	Salt Lake City, UT	85	20
Las Vegas, NV	Phoenix, AZ	36	8½-9
Phoenix, AZ	Tucson, AZ	18	2
Tucson, AZ	Albuquerque, NM	70	12½-17¼

*One-way prices

you have collision coverage on your vehicle at home, it might cover damage to rental cars; inquire before departing.

➜ Some credit cards offer reimbursement coverage for collision damages when you use the card to rent a car; check before departing. There may be exceptions for rentals of more than 15 days or for exotic models, jeeps, vans and 4WD vehicles. Check your policy.

➜ Many rental agencies stipulate that damage a car suffers while being driven on unpaved roads is not covered by the insurance they offer. Check with the agent when you make your reservation.

Motor Home (RV)

Most hub cities have the option for motor home or RV rentals. If you are not looking to drive the rough back roads it can be a good way to access the Southwest. Rental agencies include **Adventure Touring RV Rentals** (☏877-778-9569; www.adventuretouring.com),

Adventure on Wheels (☏800-943-3579; wheels9. com) and **Cruise America** (☏800-671-8042; www. cruiseamerica.com).

Rental

➜ Rental cars are readily available at all airports and many downtown city locations.

➜ With advance reservations for a small car, the daily rate with unlimited mileage is about $30 to $60.

➜ Larger companies don't require a credit-card

CROSSING THE MEXICAN BORDER

Travel Advisories

The issue of crime-related violence in Mexico has been front and center in the international press for several years. Nogales, AZ, for example, is safe for travelers, but Nogales, Mexico, was a major locus for the drug trade and its associated violence. Ciudad Juárez, located to the south of Las Cruces, NM, and El Paso, TX, has one of the highest murder rates in Mexico. At time of research the US State Department had issued travel advisories for the city and Copper Canyon. Specific details about safety in these regions can be found at https://travel.state.gov/content/passports/en/alertswarnings/mexico-travel-warning.html.

As such, we cannot safely recommend crossing the border for an extended period to these cities and other areas under an advisory until the security situation changes. Day trips are OK, but anything past that may be risky.

The US State Department (https://travel.state.gov/) recommends that travelers visit its website before traveling to Mexico. Here you can check for travel updates and warnings and confirm the latest border crossing requirements. Before leaving, US citizens can sign up for the Smart Traveler Enrollment Program (https://step.state.gov/step/) to receive email updates prior to departure.

Western Hemisphere Travel Initiative Requirements

Border-crossing requirements are subject to change. Travelers should double-check regulations before arriving at the border. US and Canadian citizens entering the US from Mexico at airports of entry must present a valid passport.

To enter by land or sea, US citizens must present a Western Hemisphere Travel Initiative (WHTI)-compliant document such as a valid passport, US passport card, Trusted Traveler Program card (NEXUS, SENTRI, Global Entry or FAST), or an Enhanced Driver's License. Canadian citizens entering the US by sea or land must present a valid passport issued by the Government of Canada; a Trusted Traveler Program card (NEXUS, FAST or SENTRI); or an Enhanced Driver's License.

US and Canadian citizens under age 16 can also enter using only proof of citizenship, such as a birth certificate or Naturalization Certificate. Visit www.cbp.gov/travel/us-citizens/western-hemisphere-travel-initiative for current rules.

Driving in Mexico

Driving across the border is a serious hassle. At the border, or at the checkpoint 13 miles south of it, you need to pick up a free Mexican tourist card. US or other nations' auto insurance is not valid in Mexico, and we strongly suggest you buy Mexican insurance on the US side of the border. Rates depend on coverage and your car's age, model and value.

deposit, which means you can cancel without a penalty if you find a better rate.

→ Midsize cars are often only a tad more expensive.

→ Deals abound and the business is competitive so it pays to shop around. Aggregator sites such as www.kayak.com can provide a good cross-section of options. You can often snag great last-minute deals via the internet; rental reservations made in conjunction with an airplane ticket often yield better rates.

→ Most companies require that you have a major credit card, are at least 25 years old and have a valid driver's license. Some national agencies may rent to drivers between the ages of 21 and 25 but may charge a daily fee.

→ If you decide to fly into one city and out of another, you may incur drop-off charges. Check the amount before finalizing your plans. Dropping off the car in another state may raise the rate.

→ To rent a Harley-Davidson or Honda motorcycle to cruise Arizona's scenic highways, try Funtime Rentals in Phoenix.

→ Most hub cities have the option for motor home or RV rentals. If you are not looking to drive the rough back roads it can be a good way to access the Southwest.

Road Conditions & Hazards

Be extra defensive while driving in the Southwest. Everything from dust storms to snow to roaming live-stock can make conditions dangerous. Near Flagstaff, watch for elk at sunset on I-17. The animals like to soak up warmth from the blacktop (or so we've heard).

You don't want to hit an elk, which can weigh between 500lb and 900lb.

Distances are great in the Southwest and there are long stretches of road without gas stations. Running out of gas on a hot and desolate stretch of highway is no fun, so pay attention to signs that caution 'Next Gas 98 Miles.'

For updates on road conditions within a state, call ☑511. From outside a state, try one of the following:

Arizona (☑888-411-7623; www.az511.com)

Nevada (☑877-687-6237; www.nvroads.com)

New Mexico (☑800-432-4269; m.nmroads.com)

Southern Colorado (☑303-639-1111; www.cotrip.org)

Utah (☑866-511-8824; www.commuterlink.utah.gov)

Road Rules

→ Driving laws are slightly different in each state, but all require the use of safety belts.

→ In every state, children under five years of age must be placed in a child safety seat secured by proper restraints.

→ The maximum speed limit on rural interstates in Arizona, Colorado, Nevada and New Mexico is 75mph, and can get as high as 80mph in Utah. That drops to 65mph in urban areas in Southwestern states but obey all traffic signs that require a lower speed. On undivided highways, the speed-limit range is based on local population and other factors.

→ Bans on cell-phone use and texting while driving are becoming more common. Currently, you cannot talk on a hand-held device in Nevada and parts of New Mexico. In Utah and

Colorado cell-phone use for drivers under the age of 18 is prohibited. Texting while driving is banned in Colorado, Utah, Nevada and New Mexico. These laws are becoming stricter and are subject to change.

Motor Home (RV)

→ Rentals range from ultra-efficient VW campers to plush land yachts.

→ After the size of the vehicle, consider the impact of gas prices, gas mileage, additional mileage costs, insurance and refundable deposits; these can add up quickly. It pays to shop around and read the fine print.

→ Base rate for a four-person vehicle can be anywhere from $420 to $1800 weekly in the summer, plus 34¢ for each additional mile not included in your package. Get out a good map and a calculator to determine if it's practical.

→ Before heading out, consult www.rvtravel.com for tips galore.

→ Purchase a campground guide from Woodall's (www.woodalls.com), which also has a great all-round website, or check koa.com. KOA also publishes a free annual campground directory listing its US and Canadian campgrounds.

Train

Several train lines provide services using historic steam trains. Although they are mainly for sightseeing, the Williams to Grand Canyon run is a destination in itself. More scenic train rides are located in Clarkdale, AZ, Chama, NM, Santa Fe, NM, and Durango, CO.

Behind the Scenes

SEND US YOUR FEEDBACK

We love to hear from travelers – your comments keep us on our toes and help make our books better. Our well-traveled team reads every word on what you loved or loathed about this book. Although we cannot reply individually to your submissions, we always guarantee that your feedback goes straight to the appropriate authors, in time for the next edition. Each person who sends us information is thanked in the next edition – the most useful submissions are rewarded with a selection of digital PDF chapters.

Visit **lonelyplanet.com/contact** to submit your updates and suggestions or to ask for help. Our award-winning website also features inspirational travel stories, news and discussions.

Note: We may edit, reproduce and incorporate your comments in Lonely Planet products such as guidebooks, websites and digital products, so let us know if you don't want your comments reproduced or your name acknowledged. For a copy of our privacy policy visit lonelyplanet.com/privacy.

OUR READERS

Many thanks to the travelers who used the last edition and wrote to us with helpful hints, useful advice and interesting anecdotes:

Michael Dales, Gwen Holt, Robert Pelchat, Maaike Pypekamp, Ine Reijnen

WRITER THANKS

HUGH MCNAUGHTAN

My sincere thanks to everyone who helped me through an epic research trip through Arizona – Tas and my girls, editor Alex, the ever-helpful support crew at LP, and the kind people of the Grand Canyon State. And Matt for the mescal.

CAROLYN MCCARTHY

My many thanks go out to the Utah tourism office and friends Drew and Zinnia, Francisco Kjolseth and Meg and Dave. Thanks also to my co-writers, especially Chris Pitts. Utah worked its magic once more. It is a privilege to go back year after year.

CHRISTOPHER PITTS

Thanks to the inordinately kind people of New Mexico, in particular Michael Benanav in Dixon, John Feins and Cynthia Delgado in Santa Fe, and all the rangers at the national parks – especially the guy who led the incredible Carlsbad Cave tour – keep up the great work! At the writing desk, thanks to co-authors Carolyn McCarthy, Benedict Walker and Hugh McNaughtan for suggestions, and Alex Howard for keeping the whole project on track.

HELENA SMITH

Many thanks to everyone who offered warm hospitality in Lake Tahoe, most especially Naomi Terry for keeping us company, and Anna and her family for hospitality and local expertise. King was a great road-trip buddy, and so was Art Terry, who drove and DJ'd me round California, and made every exploration a joy.

BENEDICT WALKER

A huge thank you to Alex Howard from LP for granting me this amazing opportunity and sticking by me until I got 'er done. I dedicate this update to Mr and Mrs Bruce and Cheryl Cowie, my self-adopted Canadian parents and the original high rollers of my world. Thanks to Mum for giving Nanna's prayer-chair a workout; to Kirk, Alex and friends for showing me their Vegas; to Justin and the burners in Reno; my birthday buddy Nicole in Carson City; and my favorite American, Brad, for speaking my language and keeping me sane. You all rock.

ACKNOWLEDGEMENTS

Climate map data adapted from Peel MC, Finlayson BL & McMahon TA (2007) 'Updated World Map of the Köppen-Geiger Climate Classification', *Hydrology and Earth System Sciences*, 11, 1633–44.

Cover photograph: The Wave, Paria Canyon-Vermilion Cliffs Wilderness, Peter Unger/Getty

THIS BOOK

This 8th edition of *Southwest USA* was curated by Hugh McNaughtan and researched and written by Hugh, Carolyn McCarthy, Christopher Pitts and Benedict Walker with contributions by Jeff Campbell, Jennifer Denniston, David Lukas and Helena Smith. The previous edition was written by Amy C Balfour, Carolyn McCarthy and Greg Ward.

This guidebook was produced by the following:

Destination Editors
Evan Godt, Alexander Howard

Product Editors Hannah Cartmel, Rachel Rawling

Senior Cartographer
Alison Lyall

Book Designer Lauren Egan

Assisting Editors Michelle Bennett, Nigel Chin, Andrea Dobbin, Helen Koehne, Anne Mulvaney

Assisting Cartographer
Hunor Csutoros

Cover Researcher
Naomi Parker

Thanks to Kate Chapman, Paul Harding, Liz Heynes, Mel Mansur, Anne Mason, Kate Mathews, Susan Paterson, Gabrielle Stefanos, Tony Wheeler

Index

N

NOTES

Map Legend

Sights

- Beach
- Bird Sanctuary
- Buddhist
- Castle/Palace
- Christian
- Confucian
- Hindu
- Islamic
- Jain
- Jewish
- Monument
- Museum/Gallery/Historic Building
- Ruin
- Shinto
- Sikh
- Taoist
- Winery/Vineyard
- Zoo/Wildlife Sanctuary
- Other Sight

Activities, Courses & Tours

- Bodysurfing
- Diving
- Canoeing/Kayaking
- Course/Tour
- Sento Hot Baths/Onsen
- Skiing
- Snorkeling
- Surfing
- Swimming/Pool
- Walking
- Windsurfing
- Other Activity

Sleeping

- Sleeping
- Camping

Eating

- Eating

Drinking & Nightlife

- Drinking & Nightlife
- Cafe

Entertainment

- Entertainment

Shopping

- Shopping

Information

- Bank
- Embassy/Consulate
- Hospital/Medical
- Internet
- Police
- Post Office
- Telephone
- Toilet
- Tourist Information
- Other Information

Geographic

- Beach
- Gate
- Hut/Shelter
- Lighthouse
- Lookout
- Mountain/Volcano
- Oasis
- Park
- Pass
- Picnic Area
- Waterfall

Population

- Capital (National)
- Capital (State/Province)
- City/Large Town
- Town/Village

Transport

- Airport
- BART station
- Border crossing
- Boston T station
- Bus
- Cable car/Funicular
- Cycling
- Ferry
- Metro/Muni station
- Monorail
- Parking
- Petrol station
- Subway/SkyTrain station
- Taxi
- Train station/Railway
- Tram
- Underground station
- Other Transport

Note: Not all symbols displayed above appear on the maps in this book

Routes

- Tollway
- Freeway
- Primary
- Secondary
- Tertiary
- Lane
- Unsealed road
- Road under construction
- Plaza/Mall
- Steps
- Tunnel
- Pedestrian overpass
- Walking Tour
- Walking Tour detour
- Path/Walking Trail

Boundaries

- International
- State/Province
- Disputed
- Regional/Suburb
- Marine Park
- Cliff
- Wall

Hydrography

- River, Creek
- Intermittent River
- Canal
- Water
- Dry/Salt/Intermittent Lake
- Reef

Areas

- Airport/Runway
- Beach/Desert
- Cemetery (Christian)
- Cemetery (Other)
- Glacier
- Mudflat
- Park/Forest
- Sight (Building)
- Sportsground
- Swamp/Mangrove